The Principles of Computer Hardware

The Principles of Computer Hardware

Alan Clements

School of Computing and Mathematics,
University of Teesside

Third Edition

OXFORD
UNIVERSITY PRESS

OXFORD

UNIVERSITY PRESS

Great Clarendon Street, Oxford OX2 6DP

Oxford University Press is a department of the University of Oxford.
It furthers the University's objective of excellence in research, scholarship,
and education by publishing worldwide in

Oxford New York

Athens Auckland Bangkok Bogota Buenos Aires Cape Town
Chennai Dar es Salaam Delhi Florence Hong Kong Istanbul Karachi
Kolkata Kuala Lumpur Madrid Melbourne Mexico City Mumbai Nairobi
Paris São Paulo Shanghai Taipei Tokyo Toronto Warsaw

with associated companies in   Berlin   Ibadan

Oxford is a registered trade mark of Oxford University Press
in the UK and in certain other countries

Published in the United States
by Oxford University Press Inc., New York

First published 1985
Second edition 1991
Third edition 2000, reprinted (with corrections) 2000, 2001, 2002

A catalogue record for this book is available from the British Library

Library of Congress Cataloging in Publication Data
(Data available)

ISBN 0 19 856454 6 (hbk.)
ISBN 0 19 856453 8 (pbk.)

Typeset by Newgen Imaging Systems (P) Ltd., Chennai, India
Printed in U.K. by Bath Press Ltd., Bath, Avon

Preface

The Principles of Computer Hardware is intended for students taking a first-level introductory course in electronics, computer science, or information technology. The approach is one of *breadth before depth*, and we cover a wide range of topics under the general umbrella of computer hardware. Writing a book is easy, at least in comparison with finding a name for it. I named this book after the module I wrote it for.

I have written *The Principles of Computer Hardware* to achieve two goals. The first is to teach students the basic concepts on which the stored-program digital computer is founded. These include the representation and manipulation of information in binary form, the structure or *architecture* of a computer, the flow of information within a computer, and the exchange of information between its various peripherals. That is, we answer the question 'How does a computer work and how is it organized?' The second goal is to provide students with a firm foundation for further study later in their course. In particular, the elementary treatment of gates and Boolean algebra provides a basis for a second-level course in digital design, and the introduction to the CPU and assembly language programming provides a basis for further courses on computer architecture/organization or microprocessor systems design.

The faculty of each university selects its own set of topics for inclusion in an introductory course on computer architecture and digital systems. Some courses emphasize digital design and Boolean algebra. Some emphasize computer architecture (the assembly language programmer's view of a computer), and some emphasize the other elements of a computer (memory, peripherals, and computer communications). I have decided to include a wide range of topics in order to suit as many courses as possible. Although covering a large number of subject areas means that we can't treat individual topics in great depth, the whole point of this book is to bring together all the hardware aspects of a computer system.

A prior knowledge of computer science is not required for entry to many courses in universities, and this book is therefore written for those with no previous knowledge of computer science. The only background information needed by the reader is an understanding of elementary algebra. Because students following a course in computer science or computer technology will also be studying programming in a high-level language, no attempt is made to teach programming in a high-level language, and we assume that the reader is familiar with the concepts underlying a high-level language.

When writing this book, I set myself three objectives. By adopting an informal style, I hope to increase the enthusiasm of the otherwise faint-hearted programmer who may be put off by the formal approach of other, more traditional, books. I have also tried to give students an insight into computer hardware by explaining why things are as they are, instead of presenting them with information as a piece of dogma to be learned and accepted without question. I have included several subjects that would seem out of place in an elementary first-level course. Such topics (e.g. advanced computer arithmetic, timing diagrams, reliability, RISC architectures) have been included to show how the computer hardware of the real world often differs from that of the first-level course in which only the basics are taught. I've also broadened the range of topics normally found in first-level courses in computer hardware and provided sections introducing operating systems and local area networks, as these two topics are so intimately related to the hardware of the computer. Finally, I have discovered that stating a formula or a theory is not enough— many students like to see an actual application of the formula. Wherever possible I have provided examples.

Like most introductory books on computer architecture, I have chosen a specific microprocessor as a model. The ideal computer architecture is both powerful (rich in features) and yet easy to understand without exposing the student to a steep learning curve. Some microprocessors have very complicated architectures that confront students with too much fine detail early in their course. I have chosen Motorola's 68000 microprocessor because it is easy to understand and incorporates many of the most important features of a high-performance architecture. I would emphasize that this book isn't designed to provide a practical course in assembly language programming on the 68000. It is intended only to illustrate the operation of a central processing unit by means of a typical assembly language. We also take a look at a rather different microprocessor, the ARM, that embodies many of the principles of the RISC (reduced instruction set computer).

Although primarily aimed at first- and second-year university students (that is, freshmen and sophomores), this book should appeal to those in British universities taking BTEC courses in computing, or Part I of the BCS examination, and to the layperson who just wants to find out how computers work.

Teesside
1999

By the way, you will see the words *computer*, CPU, *processor*, *microprocessor*, and *microcomputer* in this and other texts. The part of a computer that actually executes a program is called a CPU (central processing unit) or more simply a *processor*. A *microprocessor* is a CPU fabricated on a single chip of silicon. A computer that is constructed around a *microprocessor* can be called a *microcomputer*. To a certain extent, these terms are frequently used interchangeably.

A.C.

Reading guide

We've already said that this book provides a traditional introductory course in computer architecture plus additional material to broaden its scope and fill in some of the gaps left in such courses. Because students following an introductory course might find it difficult to distinguish between foreground and background material, the following guide might help to indicate the more fundamental components of the course.

Chapter 2   The vast majority of Chapter 2 deals with essential topics such as gates, Boolean algebra, and Karnaugh maps. Therefore this chapter is essential reading.

Chapter 3   In this chapter we demonstrate how to design the sequential circuits required to construct a computer. We first introduce the *bistable* (flip-flop) used to construct *sequential circuits*, which requires a quantum jump in understanding over earlier sections on gates and similar logic elements. Introductory texts on computer organization often cover only the basic idea of the flip-flop and its application as a storage element in registers and counters. Students are expected to be able to design moderately complex circuits built from gates, but are expected only to appreciate the role of sequential circuits.

Chapter 4   This chapter deals with the way in which numbers are represented inside a computer and the way in which they are manipulated in simple arithmetic operations. Apart from some of the coding theory and details of multiplication and division, almost all of this chapter is essential reading. Section 4.8 on floating point arithmetic goes into more detail than some other texts because a few students have difficulty in understanding how floating point numbers are represented and manipulated. The final part of Chapter 4 introduces multiplication and division and describes how these operations are actually carried out inside computers. Multiplication and division can be omitted if the student is not interested in how these operations are implemented.

Chapter 5   This is the heart of the book and is concerned with the structure and operation of the computer itself. The section dealing with the operation of the computer's control unit that decodes and executes instructions may be omitted on a first reading. The control unit is normally encountered in a second- or third-level course, but has been included here for the purpose of completeness and to provide an insight into how the computer actually turns a binary-coded instruction into a sequence of events that carry out the instruction.

Chapter 6   Having introduced the architecture of a CPU we include an overview of assembly language programming and the design of simple 68000 assembly language programs. This chapter relies heavily on the 68000 cross-assembler and simulator provided with the book. You can use this software to investigate the behavior of the 68000 on a PC. Readers interested only in the structure of the CPU may omit this chapter.

Chapter 7   The previous two chapters have concentrated on a popular CISC (complex instruction set computer). In this chapter we look at the trend in computer architecture towards greater simplicity and introduce the RISC or *reduced instruction set computer* architecture, which achieves a high level of performance by overlapping the various stages in the execution of an instruction. We look at the ARM family of processors and introduce the software package that enables you to write programs for an ARM and to run them on a PC.

Chapter 8   This chapter deals with input/output techniques and peripherals such as printers and CRT terminals that enable the computer to communicate with the external world. We are interested in two aspects of an interface: the way in which information is transferred between a computer and peripherals, and the peripherals themselves. We also take a look at some of the interface chips that facilitate the connection of the computer to its peripherals. The final part of this chapter describes some of the peripherals that you would find in a typical PC (keyboard, display, printer, and mouse). We also look at some of the more unusual peripherals that, for example, can measure how fast a body is rotating. Input/output techniques are essential reading and should not be left out, although the details of the serial and parallel interfaces may be omitted.

Chapter 9 Information isn't stored in a computer in just one type of storage device. It's stored in DRAM, on disk, on CD-ROM, and on tape. This chapter examines the operating principles and characteristics of some of the storage devices found in a computer. There's a lot of detail in this chapter. Some readers may wish to omit the design of memory systems (for example, address decoding and interfacing) and just concentrate on the reasons why computers have so many different types of memory.

Chapter 10 Some topics in computer architecture can be placed under more than one heading. In this chapter we deal with hardware topics that are closely related to the computer's operating system. The two most important elements of a computer's hardware that concern the operating system are *multiprogramming* and *memory management*. These topics are intimately connected with interrupt handling and data storage techniques and serve as practical examples of the use of the hardware described in Chapters 8 and 9. We also look at one of the more sophisticated memory topics: the use of cache memory to enhance a computer's performance. Those who require a basic introduction to computer hardware may omit this chapter, although it best illustrates how hardware and software come together in the operating system.

Chapter 11 The techniques used to link computers to create computer networks are not normally covered by first-level texts on computer architecture. However, the growth of both local area networks and the Internet have propelled computer communications to the forefront of computing. For this reason we would expect students to read this chapter even if some of it falls outside the scope of their syllabus.

Chapter 12 The final chapter looks at several of the more advanced topics that we omitted from earlier chapters. The first topic concerns the electrical behavior of practical gates—real gates consume power and delay signals and we have to take account of these effects. The second topic deals with the reliability of systems—the designer needs to be able to predict how reliable his or her system is likely to be. Moreover, the designer sometimes needs to enhance the reliability of a system when it is used in an important application. The final topic concerns the way in which analog signals are converted into digital form and vice versa. We also demonstrate how a computer can process digital signals to perform control functions and signal processing.

The history of this book

Like people, books are born. *The Principles of Computer Hardware* was conceived in December 1980. At the end of their first semester our freshmen were given tests to monitor their progress. The results of the test in my course called 'The principles of computer hardware' were rather poor, so I decided to do something about it. I thought that detailed lecture notes written in a style accessible to the students would be the most effective solution.

Because I'd volunteered to give a short course on computer communications to the staff of the Computer Centre during the Christmas holiday, I didn't have enough free time to produce the notes. By accident I found that the week immediately before Christmas was the cheapest time of the year for package holidays. So I went to one of the Canary Islands for a week, sat down by the pool surrounded by folders full of reference material and a bottle of Southern Comfort, and wrote the core of this book—number bases, gates, Boolean algebra, and binary arithmetic. Shortly afterwards I added the section on the structure of the CPU.

These notes produced the desired improvement in the end-of-year exam results and were well received by the students. In the next academic year my notes were transferred from paper to a mainframe computer and edited to include new material and to clean up the existing text.

I decided to convert the notes into a book. The conversion process involved adding topics, not covered by our syllabus, to produce a more rounded text. While editing my notes, I discovered what might best be called the *inkblot effect*. Text stored in a computer tends to expand in all directions because it's so easy to add new material at any point; for example, you might write a section on disk drives. When you next edit the section on disks, you can add more depth or breadth.

The final form of this book took what today might be called a 'breadth before depth' approach. That is, I covered a large number of topics rather than treating fewer topics in greater depth. It was my intention to give students taking our introductory hardware/architecture course a reasonably complete picture of the computer *system*.

The first edition of *The Principles of Computer Hardware* proved successful, and I was asked to write a second edition, which was published in 1990. The major change between the first and second editions was the adoption of the 68000 microprocessors as a vehicle to teach computer architecture. I have retained this processor in the current edition. Although members of the Intel family have become the standard processors in the personal computer world, Motorola's 68K family of microprocessors is much better suited to teaching computer architecture. In short, the 68K supports most of the features that computer scientists wish to teach students, and just as importantly, the 68000 is much easier to understand. Moreover, the 68K family and its derivatives are widely used in embedded systems.

By the mid-1990s the second edition was showing its age. The basic computer science and the underlying principles were still fine, but the details of actual hardware had changed dramatically over a very short time. The most spectacular progress was in the capacity of hard disks—by the late 1990s disk capacity was increasing by 60 percent per year.

This third edition still uses the 68000 to teach computer architecture. However, we've now included a 68000 cross-assembler and simulator that allows students to create and run 68000 programs on any PC. We also provide coverage of another interesting microprocessor architecture: the ARM processor. The manufacturers of this processor, Advanced RISC Machines, have kindly allowed OUP to include some of their development software on the CD that is provided with this book. Readers will also be able to write ARM programs and run them on a PC.

When I used the second edition to teach logic design to my students, they either had to design circuits on paper or to build relatively simple circuits using *logic trainers*—boxes with power supplies and connectors that allow you to wire a handful of simple chips together. Dave Barker, one of my former students has constructed a logic simulator program called Digital Works that runs under Windows on a PC. Digital Works allows you to place logic elements anywhere within a window and to wire the gates together. Inputs to the gates can be provided manually (via the mouse) or from clocks and sequence generators. You can observe the outputs of the gates on synthesized LEDs or as a waveform or table. Moreover, Digital Works permits you to encapsulate a circuit in a macro and then use this macro in other circuits. In other words, you can take gates and build simple circuits, and take the simple circuits and build complex circuits, and so on.

Acknowledgements

Few books are entirely the result of one person's unaided efforts and this is no exception. I would like to thank all those who wrote the books about computers on which my own understanding is founded. Some of these writers conveyed the sheer fascination of computer architecture that was to change the direction of my own academic career. It really is amazing how a large number of gates (a circuit element whose operation is so simple as to be trivial) can be arranged in such a way as to perform all the feats we associate computers with today.

I am grateful for all the comments and feedback I've received from my wife, colleagues, students, and reviewers over the years. Their feedback has helped me to improve the text and eliminate some of the errors that I'd missed in editing. More importantly, their help and enthusiasm has made the whole project worthwhile.

Although I owe a debt of gratitude to a lot of people, I would like to mention four people who have had a considerable impact. Alan Knowles of Manchester University read drafts of both the second and third editions with a precision well beyond that of the average reviewer. Paul Lambert, one of my colleagues at The University of Teesside, wrote the 68000 cross-assembler and simulator that I use in my teaching and which is so important to Chapter 6 when we deal with assembly language.

Dave Barker, one of my former students and an excellent programmer, wrote the logic simulator called Digital Works that accompanies this book. I would particularly like to thank Dave for providing a tool that enables students to construct circuits and test them without having to solder wires together.

One of the major changes to this edition is the addition of the chapter on the ARM processor. I would like to thank Steve Furber of Manchester University (one of the ARM's designers) for encouraging me to use this very interesting device.

To Len Northan in memoriam
To Stephen Seidman

Contents

Chapter 1

Introduction to computer hardware

To begin with I feel we ought to define the terms *hardware* and *software*. Of course I could give a deeply philosophical definition, but perhaps an empirical one is more helpful. If any part of a computer system clatters on the floor when dropped, it's hardware. If it doesn't, it's software. This is a good working definition, but it's incomplete because it implies that hardware and software are entirely unrelated entities. As we will discover in later chapters, software and hardware are often intimately related. Moreover, the operation of much of today's hardware is controlled by firmware (software embedded in the structure of the hardware).

The hardware of a computer includes all the physical components that make up the computer system. These components range from the central processing unit to the memory and input/output devices. The programs that control the operation of the computer are called the *software*. When a program is inside a computer its physical existence lies in the state of electronic switches within the computer, or the magnetization of tiny particles on magnetic tape or disk. That is, we can't point to a program in a computer any more than we can point to a thought in the brain.

Two terms closely related to hardware are *architecture* and *organization*. A computer's architecture is an abstract view of the computer and describes what it can do. Essentially, a computer's architecture is the assembly language programmer's view of the machine. You could say that architecture has a similar meaning to *functional specification*. The architecture is an abstraction of the computer. A computer's *organization* describes how the architecture is implemented; that is, it defines the hardware used to implement the architecture. Let's look at a simple example that distinguishes between architecture and organization. A computer with a 32-bit architecture performs operations on numbers that are 32 bits wide. You could build two versions of this computer. One is a high-performance device that adds two 32-bit numbers in a single operation. The other is a low-cost processor that gets a 32-bit number by bringing two 16-bit numbers from memory one after the other. Both computers end up with the same result, but one takes longer to get there. They have the same architecture but different organizations.

Although hardware and software are different entities, it's interesting to note that there is often a trade-off between them. Some operations can be carried out either by a special-purpose hardware system or by means of a program stored in the memory of a general-purpose computer. The fastest way to execute a given task is to build a circuit dedicated exclusively to the task. Writing a program to perform the same task on an existing computer may be much cheaper, but the task will take longer, as the computer's hardware wasn't optimized to suit the task.

Developments in computer technology in the late 1990s further blurred the distinction between hardware and software. Digital circuits are composed of gates that are wired together. From the mid-1980s onward manufacturers were producing large arrays of gates that could be interconnected electronically to create a particular circuit. As technology progressed it became possible to reconfigure the connections between gates while the circuit was operating. That is, the circuit could modify itself—paving the way for computers that are able to evolve.

Why do we teach computer hardware?

We can watch a television program without understanding how a cathode ray tube operates, or fly in a Jumbo jet without ever knowing the meaning of thermodynamics. Why then should the lives of computer scientists and programmers be made miserable by forcing them to learn what goes on inside a computer?

There are several reasons for teaching a course on computer hardware, the most important of which are:

1. Programming itself involves implicit hardware operations. As an example, consider inputting or outputting data.

Whenever programmers send data to a computer or receive data from it, they are using hardware devices about which they must have some prior knowledge. Sometimes this involves an understanding of the format of the data. Suppose that data is to be presented on a video display. It is clearly sensible to break the data up into segments or pages ending at some logical point and display the data a page at a time. This is better than ending a screen in the middle of a sentence and then expecting the viewer to remember the first half of the sentence.

2. Some operations in high-level languages require an understanding of topics that are best learned in a course on computer architecture. Typical examples are Boolean operations in bit-mapped graphics and pointers in C.

3. Hardware defines the limitations of the computer. Any computer user must be aware of its restrictions. There's no point in buying a computer to allow 80 students simultaneous access to 80 terminals if the computer operating at maximum capacity can service only 40 terminals. Similarly, an on-board navigation computer in an aircraft must be capable of operating at a sufficiently high speed to compute a course correction before the aircraft has strayed too far off track.

4. Programming can't always be divorced from hardware. Although one computer programmer writing packages in COBOL to calculate wages in an office is far removed from the finer details of hardware, another programmer might be involved with interfacing a computer to a system. For example, consider a microprocessor used to control the temperature of a chemical reaction in an oil refinery. This system converts the temperature inside a vessel into a voltage, transforms the voltage into a digital or numerical value, reads it into the computer, processes this number, outputs another number to a device that converts it into a voltage, and finally uses this voltage to control a heater. Such a wide range of activities requires the expertise of both the electrical engineer and the programmer. If the job is to be done at all well, they must be able to communicate with each other. Sometimes, they may even be the same person—a programmer well versed in electrical engineering or vice versa.

5. It is aesthetically pleasing to understand hardware. The examples provided at the start of this section are not entirely appropriate. The passenger in an aircraft is not interested in the workings of a jet engine, but the pilot is. A detailed knowledge of the engines is not vital to his or her job, but understanding them gives the pilot a measure of satisfaction. Similarly, programmers who understand precisely what happens after their jobs have been submitted to the computer also have more personal satisfaction than their counterparts who regard the internal operation of a computer as a type of black magic.

An overview of the book

It's very difficult to know just what should be included in an introductory course on computer architecture, organization, and hardware—or what should be excluded from it. Any topic can always be expanded to an arbitrary extent. For example, if we begin with gates and Boolean algebra, do we go on to actual semiconductor devices and then to semiconductor physics? In this book, we have attempted to include those topics relevant to points (1) to (5) above, at an introductory level. However, some of my material may surprise those familiar with conventional introductory texts. I have included a somewhat wider range of material because the area of influence encompassed by the digital computer has expanded greatly in recent years. I have also gone out of my way to highlight the divergence between theory and practice; for example, when including a conventional introduction to gates and Boolean algebra I have also made it clear that the designer is concerned with other (economic) considerations as well as logic design. The major subject areas dealt with in this book are:

Computer arithmetic   Our system of arithmetic using the base ten has evolved over thousands of years. The computer carries out its internal operations on numbers represented in the base two. This anomaly isn't due to some magic power inherent in binary arithmetic but simply because it would be uneconomic to design a computer to operate in denary (base ten) arithmetic. At this point I must make a comment. Time and time again, I read in the popular press that the behavior of digital computers and their characteristics are due to the fact that they operate on bits using binary arithmetic whereas we humans operate on digits using decimal arithmetic. That idea is nonsense. Since there is a simple relationship between binary and decimal numbers, the fact that computers represent information in binary form is a mere detail of engineering. It's the architecture and organization of a computer that makes it behave in such a different way to the brain.

Basic logic elements and Boolean algebra   The technology we have today determines what a computer can do. We introduce the basic logic elements, or *gates*, from which a computer is made and show how these can be put together to create more complex units, such as arithmetic units. The behavior of these gates determines both the way in which the computer carries out arithmetic operations and the way in which the functional parts of a computer interact to execute a program. We need to understand gates in order to appreciate why the computer has developed in the way it has. The operation of circuits containing gates can be described in terms of a formal notation called *Boolean algebra*. An introduction to Boolean algebra is provided because it enables designers to build circuits with the least number of gates.

As well as gates, computers require devices called *flip-flops* that can store a single binary digit. The flip-flop is the basic component of many memory units. We provide an introduction to flip-flops and their application to *sequential circuits* such as counters, timers, and sequencers.

Computer organization This topic is concerned with how a computer is arranged in terms of its building blocks (i.e. the logic and sequential circuits made from gates and flip-flops). We introduce the architecture of a simple hypothetical computer and show how it can be organized in terms of functional units. That is, we show how the computer goes about reading an instruction from memory, decoding it, and then executing it.

Assembly language The primitive instructions that directly control the operation of a computer are called *machine code* instructions and are composed of sequences of binary values stored in memory. As programming in machine code is exceedingly tedious, an aid to machine code programming called *assembly language* has been devised. Assembly language is shorthand permitting the programmer to write machine code instructions in a simple abbreviated form of plain language. High-level languages (C, Pascal, BASIC, Java) are sometimes translated into a series of assembly language instructions by a compiler as an intermediate step on the way to pure machine code. This intermediate step serves as a debugging tool for programmers who wish to examine the operation of the compiler and the output it produces.

Programmers writing in assembly language require a detailed knowledge of the architecture of the machine they are using, unlike the corresponding programmers operating in high-level languages. At this point I must say that we introduce assembly language to explain the operation of the central processing unit. Apart from certain special exceptions, all programs should be written in a high-level language whenever possible.

Input/output It's no good having a computer unless it can take in new information (programs and data), and output the results of its calculations. In this section we show how information is actually moved into and out of the computer. The operation of three basic input/output devices is described: the keyboard, the display, and the printer.

At the end of this book we also examine the way in which analog signals can be converted into digital form, processed digitally by a computer, and then converted back into analog form. Until the mid-1990s it was uneconomical to process rapidly changing analog signals (e.g. speech, music, video) digitally. The advent of high-speed low-cost digital systems has opened up a new field of computing called *digital signal processing* (DSP). We provide a short introduction to DSP.

Memory devices A computer needs memory to hold its programs, data, and any other information it may require at some point in the future. In this section we look at the immediate access store and the secondary store (sometimes called backing store). An immediate access store provides a computer with the data it requires in approximately the same time it takes the computer to execute one of its machine-level operations. The secondary store is very much slower and it takes thousands of times longer to access data from a secondary store than from an immediate access store. However, secondary storage is used because it is immensely cheaper than immediate access store and is also non-volatile (i.e. the data isn't lost when you switch the computer off). The most popular form of secondary store is the disk drive, which relies on magnetizing a moving magnetic material to store data. Optical storage technology in the form of the CD-ROM and DVD became popular in the 1990s because it combines the relatively fast access time of the disk with the large capacity and low cost of the tape drive.

Operating systems and the computer An operating system coordinates all the functional parts of the computer and provides an interface for the user. We can't cover the operating system here because it would require a book in its own right. However, because the operating system is intimately bound up with the computer's hardware, we do cover two of its aspects—*multiprogramming* and *memory management*. Multiprogramming is the ability of a computer to appear to run two or more programs simultaneously. Memory management permits several programs to operate as though each alone occupied the computer's memory, and enables a computer with a small, high-speed random access memory, and a large, low-speed serial access memory (i.e. hard disk), to appear as if it had a single large, high-speed random access memory.

Computer communications Computers are *networked* when they are connected together. Networking computers has many advantages, not least of which is the ability to share expensive peripherals such as printers and scanners. Today we have two types of network—the local area network (LAN) that interconnects computers within a building, and the wide area network that interconnects computers over much greater distances (e.g. the Internet). Consequently, we have devoted a section to showing how computers communicate with each other. Three aspects of computer communications are examined. The first is the *protocols* or rules that govern the way in which information is exchanged between systems in an orderly fashion. The second is the way in which digital information in a computer is encoded in a form suitable for transmission over a serial channel, the various types of channel, the characteristics of the physical channel, and how data is reconstituted at the receiver. The third provides a brief overview of both local area and wide area networks.

1.1 The digital computer

Before beginning the discussion of computer hardware proper, we need to say what a computer is (and is not), and to define a few terms. If ever an award were to be given to those guilty of misinformation in the field of computer science, it would go to the creators of HAL in *2001*, of R2D2 in *Star Wars*, of K9 in *Doctor Who*, and of Data in *Star Trek: The Next Generation*. These, and other similar fictional machines,

have generated the popular myth that a computer is a reasonably close approximation to a human brain and is a repository for all knowledge so that, somewhere in its memory banks, it contains an infinite accumulation of data. To be fair, computer technology is progressing at such a rate that the goal of an apparently intelligent machine is no longer a science fiction writer's dream.

The reality of most of today's computers is a little more mundane. A computer is a machine that takes in information from the outside world, processes it according to some pre-determined set of operations, and delivers the processed information. This definition of a computer is remarkably unhelpful, because it attempts to define the word *computer* in terms of the equally complex words *information*, *operation*, and *process*. Perhaps a better approach is to provide examples of what computers do by looking at the role of computers in data processing, numerical computation (popularly called *number crunching*), workstations, automatic control systems, and electronic systems.

1.1.1 The computer as a data processor

Figure 1.1 represents the conventional idea of the computer designed to deal with the payroll of a large factory. We are going to call the whole thing a computer, in contrast with

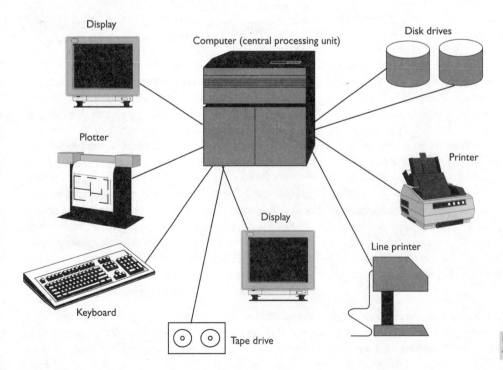

Fig. 1.1 The computer as a data processor.

those who would say that the CPU (central processing unit) is the computer and all the other devices are peripherals. Somewhere inside the computer's immediate access memory is a program, a collection of primitive machine-code operations whose purpose is to calculate an employee's pay based on the number of hours worked, the basic rate of pay, and the overtime rate. Of course, this program would also deal with tax and any other deductions.

The function of the printer in a data processing system is largely self-explanatory. It is an electromechanical device that prints letters and numbers on a piece of paper and can directly produce the pay-slips. Because the computer's immediate access memory is relatively expensive, only enough is provided to hold the program and the data it is currently processing. The mass of information on the employees is normally held in secondary store as a disk file. Whenever the CPU requires information about a particular employee, the appropriate data is taken from the disk (or, more accurately, copied) and placed in the immediate access store. The time taken to perform this operation is a small fraction of a second, but is many times slower than reading from the immediate access store. However, the cost of storing information on disk is very low indeed and this compensates for its relative slowness.

The tape transport provides a form of store that is much cheaper than the disk (tape is sometimes called *tertiary* storage). In some installations the data on the disks is copied onto tape periodically and the tapes stored in the basement for security reasons. Every so often (more often in some installations than others) the system is said to *crash*, and everything grinds to a halt. When this happens the last tape dump can be reloaded and the system assumes the state it was in a short time before the crash. Incidentally, the term 'crash' had the original meaning of a failure resulting from a read/write head in a disk drive crashing into the rotating surface of a disk and physically damaging the magnetic coating on its surface. In practice, 'crash' has come to mean any system failure.

The terminals (i.e. keyboard and display) allow operators to enter data directly into the system. This information could be the number of hours an employee has worked in the current week. The terminal can also be used to ask specific questions, such as 'How much tax did Mr. XYZ pay in November?' To be a little more precise, the keyboard doesn't actually ask questions, but it allows the programmer to execute a program containing the relevant question. The keyboard can be used to modify the program itself so that new facilities may be added as the system grows. Computers found in data processing are often characterized by their large secondary stores and their extensive use of printers and terminals.

1.1.2 The computer as a numeric processor

In the previous example of a computer as a data processor, the computer devotes much of its time to the manipulation of data in the form of symbols representing information about the employees of a firm. In such applications of the computer, the amount of time spent performing arithmetic (as understood by a mathematician) on numbers is quite small compared with data processing operations.

Numeric processing, or *number crunching*, refers to computer applications involving a very large volume of mathematical operations—sometimes billions of operations per job. Most of the applications of numeric processing are best described as *scientific*. For example, consider the application of computers to the modeling of the processes governing the weather. The atmosphere is a continuous, three-dimensional medium composed of molecules of different gases. The scientist can't easily deal with a continuous medium, but can make the problem more tractable by considering the atmosphere to be composed of a very large number of cubes. Each of these cubes is considered to have a uniform temperature, density, and pressure. That is, the gas making up a cube shows no variation whatsoever in its physical properties. Variations exist only between adjacent cubes. A cube has six faces and the scientist can create a model of how the cube interacts with each of its six immediate neighbors.

The scientist may start by assuming that all cubes are identical (there is no initial interaction between cubes), and then consider what happens when a source of energy, the Sun, is applied to the model. The effect of each cube on its neighbor is calculated, and the whole process is repeated cyclically (iteration). In order to get accurate results, the size of the cubes should be small, otherwise the assumption that the properties of the air in the cube are uniform will not be valid. Moreover, the number of iterations needed to get the results to converge to a steady state value is often very large. Consequently, this type of problem often requires very long runs on immensely powerful computers, or *supercomputers* as they are sometimes called. The pressure to solve complex scientific problems has been one of the major driving forces behind the development of computer architecture.

Numeric processing also pops up in some *real-time* applications of computers. Here, the term *real-time* indicates that the results of a computation are required within a given time. Consider the application of computers to air traffic control. A rotating radar antenna sends out a radio signal that is echoed back from a target. Since radio waves travel at a fixed speed (the speed of light), radar can be used to measure the bearing and distance (*range*) of each aircraft. At time t, target

i at position $P_{i,t}$ returns an echo giving its range $r_{i,t}$ and bearing $b_{i,t}$. Unfortunately, because of the nature of radar receivers, a random error is added to the value of each echo from a target.

The computer obtains the data from the radar receiver for n targets, updated p times every minute. From this raw data, which is corrupted by noise, the computer must compute the position of each aircraft and its track, and warn the air traffic controller of any possible conflicts. All this requires considerable high-speed numerical computation.

Computers used in numeric processing applications are frequently characterized by powerful and very expensive CPUs, very high-speed memories and relatively modest quantities of input/output devices and secondary storage. The first two generations of microprocessors could not be used in most numeric applications. During the 1980s special-purpose numeric processors were designed to augment the power of microprocessors. These were called *numeric coprocessors* and were designed to handle some of the numeric tasks that are not well suited to conventional microprocessors. Today, most powerful microprocessors have special-purpose arithmetic coprocessors on the same chip as the rest of the computer. However, the microprocessor has not yet replaced the supercomputer. Some supercomputers are constructed from large arrays of microprocessors operating in parallel.

1.1.3 The personal computer and workstation

The 1980s witnessed two significant changes in computing—the introduction of the personal computer and the workstation. Although primitive personal computers have been around since the mid-1970s, the IBM PC, Apple Macintosh, Atari ST and the Commodore Amiga transformed the personal computer from an enthusiast's toy into a useful tool.

Personal computers bring computing power to people in offices and in their own homes. Commercial software such as word processors, databases, and spreadsheets has revolutionized the office environment, just as computer-aided design (CAD) packages have revolutionized the industrial design environment. Today's engineer can design a circuit and simulate its behavior using one software package and then create a layout for a printed circuit board (PCB) with another package. Indeed, the output from the PCB design package may be suitable for feeding directly into the machine that actually makes the PCBs.

We are witnessing the growth of an industry that permits an individual to design and produce systems that once required a whole team of people. Even more impressively, a single engineer can now do in one or two days things that took the design team weeks or even months to do.

Probably the most important application of the personal computer is in word processing. For the first time ordinary people are able to write letters, articles, and books that can be edited and printed. Today's personal computers have immensely sophisticated word processing packages that create a professional-looking result and even include spelling and grammar checkers to remove embarrassing mistakes. When powerful personal computers are coupled to laser printers, anyone can use desktop publishing packages capable of creating manuscripts that were once the province of the professional publisher.

Although everyone is familiar with the personal computer, the concept of the *workstation* is less widely understood. I can't find a suitable formal definition for the workstation, so I'm going to provide my own definition. *Workstation: a personal computer that was bought for you by your boss and which you could never afford on your salary.* In other words, the workstation is a super personal computer or a personal minicomputer.

Workstations are produced by manufacturers such as Apollo, Sun, HP, Digital, Silicon Graphics, and Xerox. Workstations share many of the characteristics of personal computers and are used by engineers or designers to do the type of things described above. Where they differ from the personal computer is in their performance. Workstations are very powerful indeed and use state-of-the-art microprocessors and very large memories. A workstation often has a very high-performance graphics display system and a large monitor (19 or 21 inches).

Apart from its sheer performance, a workstation's most significant feature is its graphics facilities. Personal computers are now very powerful and have large secondary storage facilities, but they often lack state-of-the-art graphics facilities. The workstation provides the graphics facilities required by the designer using CAD packages. For example, the mechanical engineer needs CAD packages to display objects in three dimensions, to rotate these objects to show how they appear from any particular viewpoint, and to shade (or render) them. If objects are to be represented in anything like a reasonable detail, the display system must have a resolution of at least 1024×1024 or more points (i.e. pixels). Perhaps we could define a PC as 'Yesterday's workstation with a smaller screen'. Sadly, the drop in price of microprocessors, memory, and hard disks has not been closely matched by display devices (either CRTs or liquid crystal displays).

By the late 1990s the state-of-the-art PC had a clock speed of 500 MHz, 128 Mbyte of random access memory, an 11 Gbyte hard disk, and a display system with support for 3D graphics. The distinction between 'workstation' and 'personal computer' had become almost meaningless.

1.1.4 The computer in automatic control

The majority of computers are found neither in data processing nor in numeric processing activities. The advent of the microprocessor and low-cost computing has put the computer at the heart of many automatic control systems. When used as a control element, the computer is normally *embedded* in a larger system and is invisible to the observer. By invisible we mean that the operator (or the general public) may not be aware of the existence of the computer. Consider a computer installed in a pump in a gas station to count and check the cash it receives and then deliver a measured amount of fuel. The user doesn't care whether the pump is controlled by the latest microprocessor or by a clockwork mechanism, as long as it functions correctly.

A good example of a computer in automatic control is an aircraft's automatic landing system, illustrated in Fig. 1.2. In this example, the aircraft's *position* (height, distance from touchdown, and distance off the runway centerline) and *speed* are determined by various radio techniques in conjunction with a ground-based instrument-landing system. Information about the aircraft's position is fed to the three computers that, individually, determine the error in the aircraft's course. The error is the difference between the aircraft's measured position and the position it should be in. The output from the computer is the signals required to move the aircraft's control surfaces (ailerons, elevator, and rudder) and, if necessary, adjust the engine thrust. In this case the computer's program is held in immediate access memory of a variety called read-only memory (ROM) that can be read from but not written to. Once the program to land the aircraft has been developed, it requires only occasional modification.

The automatic landing system requires three computers, each working on the same calculation with the same inputs. The outputs of the computers are fed to a majority logic circuit called a voting network. If all three inputs to the majority logic circuit are the same, its output is identical to its inputs. If one computer fails, the circuit selects its output to be the same as that produced by the two good computers. This arrangement is called *triple modular redundancy* and makes the system highly reliable.

Another example of the computer as a complex automatic controller can be found in the automobile. Car manufacturers want to increase the efficiency and performance of the internal combustion engine, while at the same time reducing the emission of harmful combustion products. Figure 1.3 illustrates the structure of a computerized fuel injection system that improves the performance of an engine. The temperature

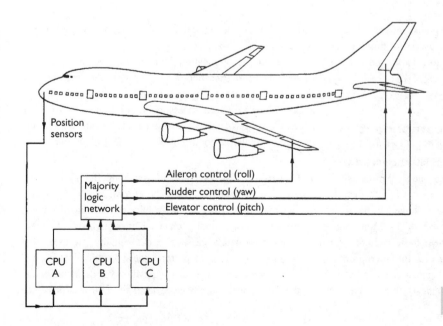

Fig. 1.2 The computer as a control element in a flight control system.

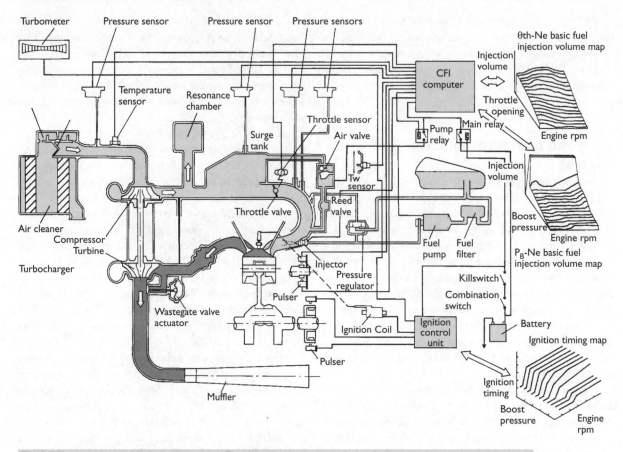

Fig. 1.3 The computerized fuel injection system. This diagram demonstrates the sophistication of a computerized system.

and pressure of the air, the angle of the crankshaft, and several other variables have to be measured thousands of times a second. These input parameters are used to calculate how much fuel should be injected into each cylinder.

1.1.5 The computer as a component

When the microprocessor first appeared in the 1970s, one of its many impacts on society was to generate friction between departments of electrical engineering and departments of computer science in universities. Members of both departments thought that the microprocessor belonged to them. A computer scientist saw the microprocessor as little more than a low-cost minicomputer with rather basic facilities. An electronic engineer, on the other hand, saw the microprocessor as just another component, albeit a sophisticated and complex. one. Even today many (if not most) microprocessor

applications do indeed fall into the category of the microprocessor as a component.

Consider the application of a microprocessor to a hi-fi cassette deck. At first thought, a microprocessor may seem a little out of place in a system devoted to the processing of analog signals. Microprocessors aren't generally used to process analog signals in conventional cassette decks, but they do facilitate the control of the cassette deck in four ways:

1. **Controlling the mechanical parts of the system** In low-cost cassette recorders the record, playback, pause, and rewind controls are large buttons that directly move the various cogs and mechanical linkages inside the unit. High-performance cassette decks employ electronically activated solenoids to perform these functions. By using a microprocessor to read the position of the switches on the front panel, an advanced level of control is possible.

For example, if the user presses fast rewind while the deck is in the fast forward mode, the microprocessor can slow, stop, and put the tape in rewind mode, all in an orderly manner. If this operation were performed manually, without a pause to let the tape slow down, the tape would at best be stretched and at worst would snap. Here computer power is being used to perform a relatively trivial operation that adds value to the system.

2. **The control of a tape counter** In very simple cassette decks the tape position indicator is a mechanical revolution counter, displaying typically from 000 to 999 as the tape moves. By using a microprocessor to perform this function, new facilities can be added to the tape deck. For example, you can ask the cassette deck to rewind from its current position to a given point on the tape and to replay the previous section. As there's a simple relationship between the tape counter value and the length of the tape, it is possible to indicate either the time elapsed since the beginning of the tape, or the time to go before the end of the tape.

3. **The setting up of the bias and equalization systems** Analog recording systems have two parameters associated with them: *bias* and *equalization*. Cassette decks have a switch that selects one of three pairs of values of bias and equalization corresponding to the three basic types of tape (ferro, chrome, and metal). On some of the more advanced decks a microprocessor records a series of tones at the beginning of the tape and then adjusts the values of bias and equalization to the optimum for that particular tape.

4. **Signal processing in a digital tape deck** Microprocessor technology couldn't be applied economically to the processing of analog signals (i.e. speech and music) until the mid-1980s. Today, the compact disc (CD) and the digital audio tape (DAT) store sound digitally. Sound can be converted to digital form, recorded on tape digitally, played back digitally, and then reconverted into analog form ready to feed into an amplifier and loudspeaker system. Special microprocessors that process signals in digital form have been developed to cope with these new recording systems.

The *glass cockpit* provides another example of the computer as a circuit element. Until the mid-1980s, the flight instrumentation of all large commercial aircraft was almost entirely electromechanical and relied more on the skills of the watchmaker than the electronic engineer. Today the mechanical

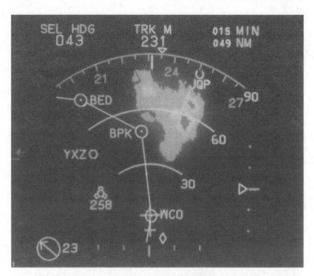

Fig. 1.4 Computer-controlled displays in the glass cockpit. This figure illustrates the primary navigation display (or horizontal situation indicator) that the pilot uses to determine the direction in which the aircraft is traveling (in this case 231°—approximately south-west). In addition to the heading, the display indicates the position and density of cloud and the location of radio beacons. The three arcs indicate range from the aircraft (30, 60, 90 nautical miles).

devices that display height, speed, engine performance, and the attitude of the aircraft are being replaced by electronic displays controlled by microcomputers. Most of the displays are based on the cathode ray tube—hence the expression '*glass cockpit*'. Electronic displays are not only easier to read and more reliable than their mechanical counterparts, but they provide only the information required by the flight crew at any instant.

Figure 1.4 illustrates an aircraft display that combines a radar image of clouds together with navigational information. In this example the pilot can see that the aircraft is routed from radio beacon WCO to BKP to BED and will miss the area of storm activity. Interestingly enough, this type of indicator has been accused of *deskilling* pilots, since they no longer have to create their own mental image of the position of their aircraft with respect to the world from much cruder instruments.

In the 1970s the USA planned a military navigation system based on satellite technology called GPS (*global positioning system*) that became fully operational in the 1990s. The civilian use of this military technology turned out to be one of the most important and unexpected growth areas in the late 1990s. GPS provides another interesting application of the computer as a component in an electronic system. The principles governing GPS are very simple. A satellite contains a very accurate atomic clock and it broadcasts both the time and its position.

Suppose you pick up the radio signal from one of these so-called Navstar satellites, decode it, and compare the reported time with your watch. You may notice that the time from the satellite is, say, one fifteenth of a second out. That doesn't mean that the US military has wasted its tax dollars on faulty atomic clocks, but that the signal has been traveling through space for 1/15 s before it reaches you. Since the speed of light is 300 000 km/s, you know that the satellite must be 20 000 km away. Every point that is 20 000 km from the satellite falls on the surface of a sphere whose center is the satellite.

If you perform the same operation with a second satellite, you know that you are on the surface of another sphere. These two spheres must intersect. Three-dimensional geometry tells us that the points at which two spheres merge is a ring. If you receive signals from three satellites, the three spheres intersect at just two points. One of these points is normally located under the surface of the Earth and can be disregarded. You can therefore work out your exact position on the surface of the Earth. This scheme relies on you having access to the exact time (i.e. your own atomic clock). However, by receiving signals from a fourth satellite you can calculate the time as well as your position.

Several manufacturers produce small low-cost GPS receivers that receive signals from the Navstar satellites (there are 24 of them), decode the timing signals and the ephemeris (i.e. satellite position), and calculate the position in terms of latitude and longitude. By embedding a microprocessor in the system, you can process the position data in any way you want. For example, by comparing successive positions you can work out your speed and direction. If you enter the coordinates of a place you wish to go to, the processor can continually give you a bearing to head, a distance to your destination, and an estimated time of arrival.

By adding a liquid-crystal display and a map stored in a read-only memory to a GPS receiver, you can make a hand-held device that shows where you are with respect to towns, roads, and rivers. By 1997 you could buy a device for about $400 that showed exactly where you were on the surface of the Earth to an accuracy of a few meters.

The GPS/microprocessor/display system is a major growth area because it can be used in so many applications. Apart from its obvious applications to sailing and aviation, GPS can be included in automobiles (the road maps are stored on CD-ROMs). GPS can even be integrated into expensive systems that don't move. If the system moves (because it has been stolen), the GPS detects the new position and reports it to the police.

1.2 Mainframe, mini, and micro

One of the many ways of categorizing computers is to slot them into three pigeonholes labeled mainframe computer, minicomputer, and microcomputer. In the beginning there was only the *mainframe* computer. Yesterday's mainframe computer was a physically large and fabulously expensive machine complete with a priesthood of programmers, operators, and maintenance engineers. Such a colossus was found only in large organizations and often employed as a general-purpose machine for scientific, industrial, or data processing applications. In industry, mainframes were used to design products and simulate their behavior as well as to deal with such mundane operations as payroll calculations. Perhaps one of the most notable features of a mainframe was its wide range of peripherals—video displays, printers, plotters, communications network controllers, and disk and tape drives. Today's mainframe computers are still used by large scientific organizations and often achieve their high levels of performance by using many processors all operating in parallel on different parts of a task.

Computer power was required by more than those in large industries. Scientists in small laboratories wanted to speed up their analysis of scientific data. Engineers wanted to control dams by measuring the flow of water upstream and hence predict the future level of the water. Owners of small companies wanted to keep track of their stock levels, the addresses of their clients, their tax returns, their invoices, and a whole host of data relating to their businesses. Academics wanted to teach computer programming to classes. In all these cases the mainframe would have proved prohibitively expensive. Computer manufacturers provided a solution to such problems in the form of the *minicomputer*, a cut-down mainframe. The 1970s was the era of the minicomputer (the most famous of which was DEC's PDP-11). Minicomputers often had multi-user operating systems that allowed several people to use the computer at the same time. Today, the term *minicomputer* has largely been replaced by the term *workstation* (although workstations are often operated by a single user).

The microprocessor is nothing more than a central processing unit on a single chip of silicon. Its importance is a consequence of its staggeringly low cost and minute size. Alone, a microprocessor can do nothing. In conjunction with memory, a power supply, and the necessary peripherals it can be said to form a *microcomputer*. By the 1990s the term *microcomputer* had largely been replaced by the term *personal computer*. Several minicomputer manufacturers designed microprocessors that were functionally equivalent to the CPUs in their own minicomputers.

Characteristics of computers

There's no precise definition of a mainframe, minicomputer, or microcomputer, so we shall list some of the attributes that may be used to characterize them. In one sense we can say that a minicomputer (workstation) occupies the middle ground of computing, and we can characterize mainframe computers as occupying the high ground and microcomputers as occupying the low ground.

Cost   The minicomputer (or workstation) is much cheaper than the mainframe. Equally the microcomputer is cheaper than a minicomputer. It's difficult to talk about actual computer costs because both performance and cost change almost daily. Perhaps we might talk about price ratios, where mainframe : workstation : PC is of the order of 100 : 5 : 1.

Physical size   The mainframe takes up a largish chunk of real estate—once it took up a whole floor of a building. The size of a minicomputer varies between that of the average wardrobe and a typical desktop personal computer. The average microcomputer (i.e. PC) sits quite happily on the office desk and most of its cabinet is filled with empty space. Apart from peripherals such as the keyboard and display, it's perfectly possible to fit most of a PC in the space occupied by a small paperback book. The *laptop computer* is a microcomputer that has been miniaturized to fit in a typical briefcase. Laptop computers cost between 50 and 100 percent more than desktop computers of the same capability. The cost increase is partially due to the cost of the liquid-crystal display (which is more expensive than a CRT), and partially due to the fact that people are willing to pay a premium for portability.

Peripherals   A single mainframe almost certainly has a wide spectrum of users (especially in a university or research establishment), each with their own particular requirements. Such a diverse range of users demands a wide range of peripherals: disks to store user programs and data, displays and printers, telecommunications equipment to link the computer to installations in other towns and even countries, and graphics equipment capable of producing complex diagrams, etc. The minicomputer is frequently dedicated to a single task (say controlling and evaluating an experiment) and often has few peripherals: perhaps a single disk drive, a couple of displays, and a printer. The drop in the cost of peripherals for personal computers now means that many home users of the computer have more peripherals than a minicomputer in a university a few years ago.

Performance   A computer's *performance* is an expression of its computing power. Because performance is determined by many factors (clock speed, CPU design, memory size and speed, cache memory, etc.) it is difficult to determine performance. Performance can be measured by executing a certain set of instructions a given number of times and then recording the time taken—this is called a *benchmark*. Mainframe computers have very high levels of performance and can execute hundreds of millions or more instructions a second.

A workstation may have only a fraction of the computational power of the latest mainframe (this is not true of some of the most powerful workstations). We say *latest* because the advance in computer technology is so rapid that today's low-cost workstation is often far more powerful than yesterday's mainframe. One of the reasons for the minicomputer's lower computational power is that it frequently uses smaller word lengths than mainframes. The word length of a computer is the number of bits (ones and zeros) in its basic unit of information storage and manipulation. The effects of word lengths on computer performance are dealt with later, but here it's sufficient to state that one effect of a short word length is to increase the number of arithmetic operations needed to perform a particular calculation to a given level of precision.

Technology   It is reasonable to say that today's high-performance mainframe computers are built with the most sophisticated available technology—they use technology that was either in the research laboratory yesterday or was far too expensive to apply to commercial ventures.

Minicomputers and workstations often use technology that has been tried and tested in mainframes and has reached the stage at which it can be miniaturized and produced on a much larger scale. Microcomputers use technology that has been developed for very large-scale low-cost production.

1.3 The stored program computer—an overview

Before discussing the *stored program computer*, consider first the human being. It's natural to compare today's wonder, the computer, with the human, just as the Victorians did with their technology. They coined expressions like, 'He has a screw loose', or 'He has run out of steam', in their endeavor to

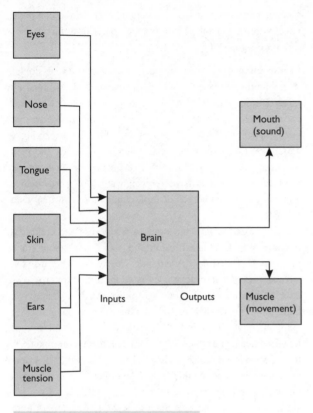

Fig. 1.5 The organization of a human being.

describe humans in terms of their mechanical technology. There have been times when the computer has been compared with the human brain and periods when the computer has been contrasted with it. It was once common to call the computer a high-speed moron—a remark made by those who didn't understand the nature of the digital computer.

Figure 1.5 shows how a human can be viewed as a system with inputs, a processing device, and outputs. The inputs are sight (eyes), smell (nose), taste (tongue), touch (skin), sound (ear), and position (muscle tension). The brain processes information from these sensors and stores new information. The storage aspect of the brain is important because it modifies the brain's operation by a process we call *learning*. Because the brain learns from all new stimuli, it doesn't always exhibit the same response to a given stimulus. Once a child has been burned by a flame the child reacts differently the next time it encounters fire.

The brain's ability to both store and process information is shared by the digital computer. However, most current computers can't mimic the operation of the brain, and simplistic

comparisons between the computer and the brain are often misleading at best and mischievous at worst. A branch of computer science is devoted to the study of computers that do indeed share some of the brain's properties and attempt to mimic the human brain. These computers are called *neural nets*. We do not cover neural nets in this text.

The output from the brain is used to generate speech or to control the muscles needed to move the body.

Figure 1.6 shows how a computer can be compared with a human. A computer can have all the inputs a human has and inputs for things we can't detect. By means of photoelectric devices and radio receivers, a computer can sense ultraviolet light, infrared, X-rays, and radio waves. The computer's output is also more versatile than that of humans. Computers can produce mechanical movement (by means of motors), generate light (TV displays), sound (loudspeakers), or even heat (by passing a current through a resistor).

The computer's counterpart of the brain is its *central processing unit* plus its storage unit (memory). Like the brain, the computer processes its various inputs and produces an output.

We don't intend to write a treatise on the differences between the brain and the computer, but it is necessary to make a comment here to avoid some of the misconceptions about digital computers. It is probable that the processing and memory functions of the brain are closely interrelated, whereas in the computer they are normally distinct. Some scientists believe that a major breakthrough in computing will come only when computer architecture takes on more of the features of the brain. In particular, the digital computer is serially organized and performs a single instruction at a time, whereas the brain has a highly parallel organization and is able to carry out many activities at the same time.

Somewhere in every computer's memory is a block of information that we call a *program*. The word 'program' has the same meaning as it does in the expressions *program of studies* or *program of music*. A computer program is a collection of statements or instructions defining the actions to be carried out by the computer sequentially. The classic analogy with a computer program is a recipe in a cookery book. The recipe is a sequence of commands that must be obeyed one by one and in the correct order. Our analogy between the computer program and the recipe is particularly appropriate because the cookery instructions involve operations on ingredients, just as the computer carries out operations on data stored in memory.

Figure 1.7 describes the digital computer, which can be divided into two parts: a *central processing unit* (or CPU) and a *memory* system. The CPU reads the program from memory

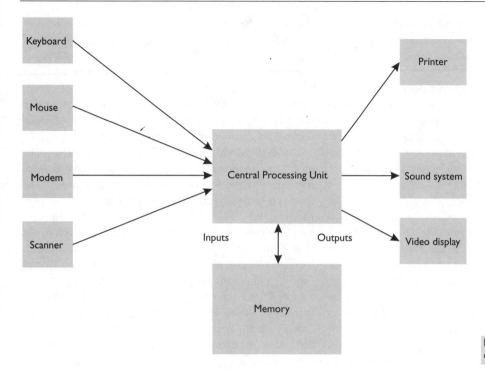

Fig. 1.6 The organization of a computer.

and *executes* the operations specified by the program. The word *execute* means carry out; for example, the instruction *add A to B* causes the addition of a quantity called *A* to a quantity called *B* to be carried out. The actual nature of these instructions does not matter here. What is important is that the most complex actions carried out by a computer can be broken down into a number of more primitive operations. But then again, the most sublime thoughts of Einstein or Beethoven can be reduced to a large number of impulses transmitted across the synapses of the cells in their brains.

The memory system stores two types of information: the program and the data acted on or created by the program.

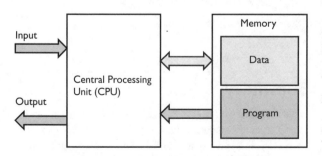

Fig. 1.7 Structure of the general-purpose digital computer.

It isn't necessary to store both the program and data in the *same* memory. However, for various reasons, most computers do store programs and data in a single memory system. Such computers are called *von Neumann machines* in honor of one of the pioneers of the computer—John von Neumann. Although this book is concerned with von Neumann machines, there are other ways of constructing computational devices; for example, the *neural network* operates in a totally different way from a conventional computer and has more in common with the human brain than the von Neumann machine.

A computer is little more than a black box that moves *information* from one point to another and processes the information as it goes along. When we say *information* we mean the data and the instructions held inside the computer. Figure 1.7 shows two *information-carrying* paths connecting the CPU to its memory. The lower path, with the single arrowhead from the memory to the CPU (heavily shaded in Fig. 1.7), indicates the route taken by the computer's *program*. The CPU reads the sequence of commands that make up a program one by one from its memory.

The upper path (lightly shaded in Fig. 1.7), with arrows at *both* its ends, transfers data between the CPU and memory. The program controls the flow of information along the data path. This data path is *bidirectional*, because data can flow in two directions. During a *write cycle* data generated by the program flows from the CPU to the memory, where it is stored for later use. During a *read cycle* the CPU requests the retrieval of a data item from memory, which is transferred from the memory to the CPU.

Suppose the instruction $x = y + z$ is stored in memory. The CPU must first fetch the instruction from memory and bring it to the CPU. Once the CPU has analyzed or *decoded* the instruction it has to get the values of 'x' and 'y' from memory. The actual values of x and y are read from the memory and sent to the CPU. The CPU adds these values and sends the result, z, back to memory for storage. By the way, the type of computer we are going to discuss later can't do anything as sophisticated as $x = y + z$. A real computer has to get y, get z and add it to y, and put the result in z.

Figure 1.8 demonstrates how the instructions making up a program and data coexist in the same memory. In this case the memory has eight locations, numbered from 0 to 7. Memory is normally regarded as an array of storage locations (boxes or pigeonholes). Each of these boxes has a unique location or *address* containing data. For example, in the simple memory of Fig. 1.8 address 5 contains the number 7. One great difference between computers and people is that we number m items from 1 to m, whereas the computer numbers them from 0 to $m - 1$. This is because the computer regards 0 (zero) as a valid identifier. Unfortunately, people often confuse 0 the identifier with 0 meaning *nothing*.

Information in a computer's memory is accessed by providing the memory with the address (i.e. location) of the desired data. Only one memory location is addressed at a time. If we wish to search through memory for a particular item (because we don't know its address), we have to read the items one at a time until we find the desired item. However, it appears that the human memory works in a very different way. Information is accessed from our memories by applying a *key* to all locations within the memory (brain). This key is related to the data being accessed (in some way) and is not related to its location within the brain. Any memory locations containing information that associates with the key respond to the access. In other words, the brain carries out a parallel search of its memory for the information it requires.

Accessing many memory locations in parallel permits more than one location to respond to the access and is therefore very efficient. Suppose someone says 'chip' to you. The word *chip* is the key that is fed to all parts of your memory for matching. Your brain might produce responses of: *chip (silicon)*, *chip (potato)*, *chip (on shoulder)* and *chip (gambling)*.

The program in Fig. 1.8 occupies consecutive memory locations 0–3, and the data locations 4–6. The first instruction, *get [4]*, means fetch the contents of memory location number 4 from the memory. We employ square brackets to denote the contents of the address they enclose, so that in this case $[4] = 2$. The next instruction, at address 1, is *add it to [5]*, and means add the number brought by the previous instruction to the contents of location 5. Thus, the computer adds 2 and 7 to get 9. The third instruction, *put result in [6]*, tells the computer to put the result (i.e. 9) in location 6. This it does, and the 1 that was in location 6 before this instruction was obeyed is replaced by 9. The final instruction in location 3 tells the computer to stop.

We can summarize the operation of a digital computer by means of a little piece of *pseudocode* (pseudocode is a method of writing down an algorithm in a language that is a cross between a computer language, such as Pascal or Java, and plain English). We shall meet pseudocode again.

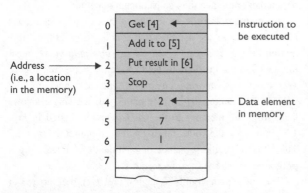

Fig. 1.8 The program and data in memory.
Note: Throughout this book square brackets denote 'the contents of' so that in this figure, [4] is read as 'the contents of memory location number 4' and is equal to 2.

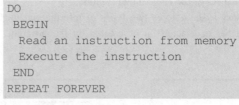

```
DO
  BEGIN
    Read an instruction from memory
    Execute the instruction
  END
REPEAT FOREVER
```

Summary

In this chapter we have considered how the computer can be looked at as a component or, more traditionally, as part of a large system. Besides acting in the obvious role as a *computer system*, computers are now built into a wide range of everyday items, from toys to automobile ignition systems. In particular, we have introduced some of the topics that make up a first-level course in computer architecture or computer organization.

We have introduced the notion of the von Neumann computer, which stores instructions and data in the *same* memory. The von Neumann computer reads instructions from memory, one by one, and then executes them in turn.

As we progress through this book, we are going to examine how the computer is organized and how it is able to step through instructions in memory and execute them. We will also show how the computer communicates with the world outside the CPU and its memory.

Problems

Unlike the problems at the end of other chapters, these problems are more philosophical and require further background reading if they are to be answered well.

1. List 10 applications of microprocessors you can think of and classify them into the groups we described (e.g. computer as a component). Your examples should cover as wide a range of applications as possible.

2. Do you think that a *digital* computer could ever be capable of feelings, free will, original thought, and self-awareness in a similar fashion to humans? If not, why not?

3. Some of the current high-performance civil aircraft, such as the A320 AirBus, have *fly-by-wire* control systems. In a conventional aircraft, the pilot moves a yoke that provides control inputs that are fed to the flying control surfaces and engines by mechanical linkages or by hydraulic means. In the A320 the pilot moves the type of joystick normally associated with computer games. The pilot's commands from the joystick (called a *sidestick*) are fed to a computer and the computer interprets them and carries them out in the fashion it determines is most appropriate. For example, if the pilot tries to increase the speed to a level at which the airframe might be overstressed, the computer will refuse to obey the command. Some pilots and some members of the public are unhappy about this arrangement. Are their fears rational?

4. The computer has often been referred to as a *high-speed moron*. Is this statement fair?

5. Computers use binary arithmetic (i.e. all numbers are composed of 1s and 0s) to carry out their operations. Humans normally use decimal arithmetic (0–9) and have symbolic means of representing information (e.g. the Latin alphabet or the Chinese characters). Does this imply a fundamental difference between people and computers?

6. Shortly after the introduction of the computer, someone said that two computers could undertake all the computing in the world. At that time the best computers were no more powerful than today's pocket calculators. The commentator assumed that computers would be used to solve a fe scientific problems and little else. As the cost and size of computers has been reduced, the role of computers has increased. Is there a limit to the applications of computers? Do you anticipate any radically new applications of computers?

7. A microprocessor manufacturer, at the release of its new super chip, was asked the question, 'What can your microprocessor do?' The manufacturer said it was now possible to put it in washing machines so that the user could tell the machine what to do verbally, rather than by adjusting the settings manually. At the same time we live in a world in which many of its inhabitants go short of the very basic necessities of life: water, food, shelter, and elementary health care. Does the computer make a positive contribution to the future well-being of the world's inhabitants? Is the answer the same if we ask about the computer's short-term effects or its long-term effects?

8. The workstation makes it possible to design and to test (by simulation) everything from other computers to large mechanical structures. Coupled with computer communications networks and computer-aided manufacturing, it could be argued that many people in technologically advanced societies will be able to work entirely from home. Indeed, all their shopping and banking activities can be also be performed from home. Do you think that this step will be advantageous or disadvantageous? What will be the effects on society of a population that can, largely, work from home?

9. In a von Neumann machine, programs and data share the same memory. The operation 'get [4]' reads the contents of memory location number 4, and you can then operate on the number you've just read from this location. However, the contents of this location may not be a number. It may be an *instruction* itself. Consequently, a program in a von Neumann machine can modify itself. Can you think of any implications that this statement has for computing?

10. When discussing the performance of computers we introduced the *benchmark*, a synthetic program whose execution time provides a figure of merit for the performance of a computer. If you glance at any popular computer

magazine, you'll find computers compared in terms of benchmarks. Furthermore, there are several different benchmarks. A computer that performs better than others when executing one benchmark might not do so well when executing a different benchmark. What are the flaws in benchmarks as a test of performance and why do you think that some benchmarks favor one computer more than another?

Chapter 2

Gates, circuits, and combinational logic

We begin our study of the digital computer by investigating the basic elements from which it is constructed—*gates* and *flip-flops*, which are also known as *combinational* and *sequential* logic elements, respectively. A combinational logic element is a circuit whose output depends only on its current inputs, whereas the output from a sequential element depends on its past history (i.e. a sequential element is able to remember its previous inputs). We describe only combinational logic in this chapter and devote the next chapter to sequential logic.

Before we introduce the gate, we highlight the difference between digital and analog systems and explain why computers are constructed from digital logic circuits. After describing the properties of several basic gates we demonstrate how a few gates can be connected together to carry out useful functions in the same way that bricks can be put together to build a house or a school.

Not very long ago, students often had little opportunity to investigate the behavior of gates because there were few laboratory facilities for building other than relatively trivial circuits. This edition of *The Principles of Computer Hardware* includes a Windows-based simulator called *Digital Works* that lets you construct complex circuits and then examine their behavior on a PC.

The behavior of digital circuits can be described in terms of a formal notation called *Boolean algebra*. We include an introduction to Boolean algebra because it allows you to analyze circuits containing gates and sometimes enables circuits to be constructed in a simpler form. Boolean algebra leads on to *Karnaugh maps*, a graphical technique for the simplification and manipulation of Boolean equations.

The final part of this chapter introduces a special type of logic device, the *tri-state* gate, that allows you to connect lots of separate digital circuits together by means of a common highway called a *bus*. A digital computer is composed of nothing more than digital circuits, buses, and sequential logic elements (i.e. the storage devices described in the next chapter).

2.1 Analog and digital systems

Before we can appreciate the meaning and implications of digital systems, it's necessary to look at the nature of analog systems. The term *analog* is derived from the noun *analogy* and means a quantity that is related to, or resembles, or corresponds to, another quantity. For example, the length of a column of mercury in a thermometer is an analog of the temperature because the length of the mercury is proportional to the temperature. Analog electronic circuits represent physical quantities in terms of voltages or currents.

The most significant feature of an analog system is that an analog variable can have any value between its maximum and minimum limits. For example, if a variable X is represented by a voltage in the range $-10\,\text{V}$ to $+10\,\text{V}$, X may assume any one of an infinite number of values within this range. In other words, we can say that X is *continuous* in value and can change its value by an arbitrarily small amount. If a graph of X is plotted as a function of time, we find that X is also a continuous function of time (see Fig. 2.1); that is, X doesn't jump instantaneously from one value to another. In Fig. 2.1, a fragment of the graph of X is magnified to reveal fluctuations that you can't see on the main graph. No matter how much you magnify this graph, the line will remain continuous and unbroken.

The design of analog circuits (e.g. audio amplifiers, cassette tape decks, and televisions) is a most demanding process, because analog signals must be processed without

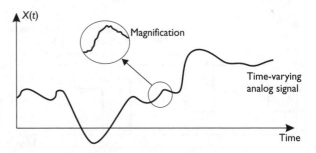

Fig. 2.1 Characteristics of an analog variable.

changing their shape. Changing the shape of an analog signal results in its degradation or *distortion*.

Information inside a computer is represented in *digital* form. A digital variable is *discrete* in both value and in time, as Fig. 2.2 demonstrates. In Fig. 2.2 the digital variable Y must take one of four possible values. Moreover, Y changes from one discrete value to another *instantaneously*. In practice, no physical (i.e. real) variable can change instantaneously and a real signal must pass through intermediate values as it changes from one discrete state to another. We will return to this topic in later chapters when we introduce the *timing diagram*.

All variables and constants in a digital system must take a value chosen from a set of values called an *alphabet*. In decimal arithmetic the alphabet is composed of the symbols 0, 1, 2, ..., 9, and in Morse code the alphabet is composed of the four symbols dot, dash, short space, and long space. Other digital systems are Braille, semaphore, and the days of the week.

A major advantage of representing information in digital form is that digital systems are resistant to error. A digital symbol can be distorted, but as long as the level of distortion is not sufficient for the symbol to be confused with a different symbol, the original symbol can always be recognized and reconstituted. For example, if you write the letter K by hand, most readers will be able to recognize it as a K unless it is so badly formed that it looks like another letter, such as an R or C.

Digital computers use an alphabet composed of two symbols called 0 and 1 (sometimes called *false and true*, or low and high, or off and on). A digital system with two symbols is called a *binary* system. The physical representation of these symbols can be made as unlike each other as possible to give the maximum discrimination between the two digital values. Computers once stored binary information on paper tape—a hole represented one binary value and no-hole represented the other. When reading paper tape the computer has only to distinguish between a hole and no-hole. Suppose we decided to replace this binary computer by a decimal computer.

Imagine that paper tape were to be used to store the ten digits 0–9. A number on the tape would consist of no-hole or a hole in one of nine sizes (ten symbols in all). How does this computer distinguish between a size six hole and a size five or a size seven hole? Such a system would require extremely precise electronics.

A single binary digit is known as a *bit* (BInary digiT) and is the smallest unit of information possible; that is, a bit can't be subdivided into smaller units. Ideally, if a computer runs off, say, 3 V, a low level would be represented by 0.0 V and a high level by 3.0 V.

The next four paragraphs show how 0s and 1s are handled by real logic elements and may be skipped if you are not interested in the details. We're going to describe LS TTL logic—a family of logic elements that run off 5 V. This family is now being replaced by devices that run off a lower voltage and have better characteristics. However, we use LS TTL here because it is still in common use and is widely covered in other literature—we examine the characteristics of a more modern logic family in Chapter 12.

In a system using a 5 V power supply you might think that the state of a bit is represented by exactly 0 V or 5 V. Unfortunately, we can't construct such precise electronic devices cheaply. We can, however, construct devices that use two *ranges* of voltage to represent the binary values 0 and 1. For example, LS TTL logic represents a 0 state by a signal in the range 0–0.4 V, and a 1 state by a signal in the range 2.8–5 V.

Figure 2.3 illustrates the two ranges of voltage used by an LS TTL logic element to represent 0 and 1 states. Digital component manufacturers make several promises to users. First, they guarantee that the output of a gate in a logical

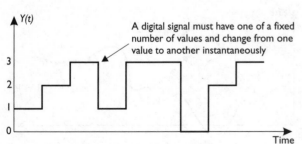

Fig. 2.2 Characteristics of an ideal digital variable.

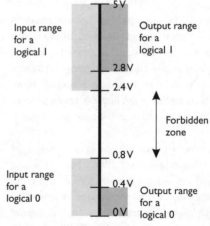

Fig. 2.3 Two states of a typical LS TTL logic element.

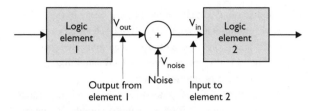

Fig. 2.4 Connecting two gates together.

0 state will be in the range 0–0.4 V, and that the output of a gate in a logical 1 state will be in the range 2.8–5.0 V (see Fig. 2.3). Similarly, they guarantee that the input circuit of a gate will recognize a voltage in the range 0–0.8 V as a logical 0 and a voltage in the range 2.4–5.0 V as a logical 1.

Figure 2.4 shows two gates wired together so that the output of gate 1 becomes the input of gate 2. The signal at the output of gate 1 is written V_{out} and the input to gate 2 is written V_{in}. An *adder* (represented by the circle with a '+') is placed between the two gates so that the input voltage to the second gate is given by $V_{in} = V_{out} + V_{noise}$; that is, a voltage called V_{noise} is added to the output from gate 1. In a real circuit there is, of course, no such adder. The adder in Fig. 2.4 is fictitious and demonstrates how the output voltage may be modified by the addition of noise or interference. All electronic circuits are subject to such interference; for example, the effect of noise on a weak TV signal is to create *snow* on the screen.

If you look at Fig. 2.3 again, you will see that the range of *input* signals that are recognized as representing a 1 state (i.e. 2.4–5 V) is greater than the range of output signals produced by a gate in a 1 state (i.e. 2.8–5 V). By making the input range greater than the output range, the designer compensates for the effect of noise or unwanted signals. Suppose a noise spike of −0.2 V is added to a logical 1 output of 2.8 V to give a total input signal of 2.6 V. This signal, when presented to the input circuit of a gate, is greater than 2.4 V, and is still guaranteed to be recognized as a logical 1. The difference between the input and output ranges for a given logic value is known as the gate's *guaranteed noise immunity*. A further discussion of the electrical characteristics of logic elements is given in Chapter 12.

Before we begin to look at gates themselves, we need to clear up a few points concerning binary digital values and the way in which notation is used to describe digital values.

Notes on logic values

1. Every logic input or output must assume one of two discrete states. There is no such thing as a valid intermediate state (a state that is neither 1 nor 0).

2. Each logic input or output can exist in only one state at any one time.

3. Each logic state has an inverse or *complement* that is the opposite of its current state. The complement of a true or one state is a false or zero state, and vice versa.

4. A logic value can be a *constant* or a *variable*. If it is a constant it always remains in that state. If it is a variable, it may be switched between the states 0 and 1. A Boolean constant is frequently called a *literal*.

5. A variable is often named by the action it causes to take place. The following logical variables are all self-evident: START, STOP, RESET, COUNT, and ADD. It is clearly reasonable to select meaningful names for logical variables, just as it is in high-level programming languages.

6. The signal level (i.e. high or low) that causes a variable to carry out the function suggested by its name is *arbitrary*. If a high voltage causes the action, the variable is called *active-high*. If a low voltage causes the action, the variable is called *active-low*. Thus, if an active-high signal is labeled START, a high level (i.e. START = 1) will initiate the action. If the signal is active-low and labeled $\overline{\text{START}}$, a low level will trigger the action.

7. By convention, a system of logic that treats a low level as a 0 or false state and a high level as a 1 or true state is called *positive logic*. Most of this chapter uses positive logic.

8. It soon becomes tedious stating over and over again that a particular signal is set to a high level or to a low level to perform a certain action. The term *asserted* is used to indicate that a signal is placed in the level that causes its activity to take place. For example, if we say that START is asserted, we mean that it is placed in a high state to cause the action determined by START. Similarly, if we say that $\overline{\text{LOAD}}$ is asserted, we mean that it is placed in a low state to trigger the action.

2.2 Fundamental gates

One of the most remarkable facts about the digital computer is that all its circuits consist of nothing more than the interconnection of primitive elements called *gates*. The three fundamental types of gate are the AND, OR, and NOT gate. We also describe two other gates called NAND and NOR gates that are derived from the fundamental gates. Later we shall see that all other gates, and therefore all digital circuits, may be designed from the appropriate interconnection of NAND (or NOR) gates alone. In other words, the most complex digital computer can be reduced to a mass of NAND gates. This statement doesn't devalue the computer any more than saying that the human brain is just a lot of neurones joined in a particularly complex way devalues the brain.

We don't use gates to build computers because we like them or because Boolean algebra (i.e. the mathematics used to describe the properties of gates) is great fun. We use gates because they provide us with a way of mass producing cheap and reliable digital computers.

What is a gate?

The word *gate* conveys the idea of a two-state device—*open or shut*. A gate may be thought of as a black box with one or more input terminals and an output terminal. The gate processes the digital signals at its input terminals to produce a digital signal at its output terminal. The particular type of the gate determines the actual processing involved. The output C of a gate with two input terminals A and B can be expressed in conventional algebra as $C = F(A, B)$, where A, B, and C are two-valued variables and F is a logical function.

It's important to stress that the output of a gate is a function only of its inputs. When we introduce the *sequential* circuit, we will discover that the sequential circuit's output depends on its *previous output* as well as its *current inputs*. We can demonstrate the concept of a gate by means of an example from the analog world. Consider the algebraic expression $y = F(x) = 2x^2 + x + 1$. If we think of x as the input to a black box and y its output, the block diagram of Fig. 2.5 demonstrates how y is generated by a sequence of operations on x. The operations performed on the input are those of addition, multiplication, and squaring. Variable x enters the 'squarer' and comes out as x^2. The output from the squarer enters a multiplier (along with the constant 2) and comes out

as $2x^2$, and so on. By applying all the operations in Fig. 2.5 to input x, we end up with output $2x^2 + x + 1$. The boxes carrying out these operations are entirely analogous to gates in the digital world—except that gates don't do anything as complicated as addition or multiplication.

Before dealing with the gates themselves and their interconnections to form digital (or *switching*) circuits, it's necessary to mention a few basic conventions. Because we write from left to right, many (but not all) logic circuits are also read from left to right; that is, information flows from left to right, with the inputs of gates on the left and the outputs on the right.

Because a circuit often contains many signal paths, some of these paths may have to cross over each other when the diagram is drawn on two-dimensional paper. We need a means of distinguishing between wires that join and wires that simply cross each other (rather like highways that merge and highways that fly over each other). The standard procedure is to regard two lines that simply cross as not being connected, as Fig. 2.6 illustrates. The connection of two lines is denoted by a *dot* at their intersection.

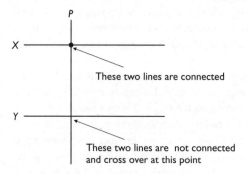

Fig. 2.6 Circuit conventions.

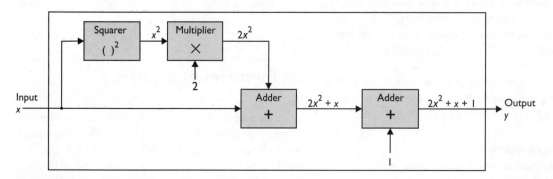

Fig. 2.5 The analog processor.

The voltage at any point along a line (i.e. conductor) is constant, and therefore the logical state is also constant everywhere on the line. If one end of a conductor is in a logical state X, then every point along the line is in the same logic state. If this line is connected to the input of several gates, then the input to each gate is also in a logical state X. In Fig. 2.6, the values of X and P must be the same because the two lines are connected.

A corollary of the statement that the same logic state exists everywhere on a conductor is that a line must not be connected to the output of more than one circuit—otherwise the state of the line will be undefined if the outputs differ. At the end of this chapter we will introduce gates with special *tri-state* outputs that can be connected together without causing havoc.

The AND gate

The AND gate is a circuit with two or more inputs and a single output. The output of an AND gate is true if and only if each of its inputs is also in a true state. Conversely, if one or more of the inputs to the AND gate is false, the output will also be false. Figure 2.7 provides the circuit symbol for both a 2-input AND gate and a 3-input AND gate. Note that the *shape* of the gate indicates its AND function (this will become clearer when we introduce the OR gate).

The classic way of visualizing an AND gate is in terms of an electric circuit or a highway, as illustrated in Fig. 2.8. Electric current (or traffic) flows along the circuit (road) only if switches (bridges) A and B are closed. The logical symbol for the AND operator is a dot, so that A AND B can be written A·B. As in normal algebra, the dot is often omitted and A·B can be written AB. The logical AND operator behaves like the multiplier operator in conventional algebra; for example, the expression $(A+B)\cdot(C+D)=A\cdot C+A\cdot D+B\cdot C+B\cdot D$ in both Boolean and conventional algebra.

A useful way of describing the relationship between the inputs of a gate and its output is the *truth table*. In a truth table the value of each output is tabulated for every possible combination of the inputs. Because the inputs are two-valued (i.e. binary with states 0 and 1), a circuit with n inputs has 2^n lines in its truth table. The order in which the 2^n possible inputs are taken is not important, but by convention the order

corresponds to the natural binary sequence (we discuss binary numbers in Chapter 4). Table 2.1 describes the natural binary sequences for values of n from 1 to 4.

Table 2.2 illustrates the truth table for a two-input AND gate, although there's no reason why we can't have any number of inputs to an AND gate. Some real gates have three or four inputs and some have 10 or more inputs. However, it doesn't matter how many inputs an AND gate has. Only one line in the truth table will contain a 1 entry, because all inputs must be true for the output to be true.

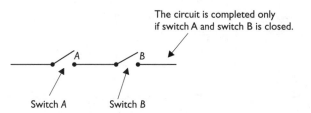

The circuit is completed only if switch A and switch B is closed.

Fig. 2.8 The representation of an AND gate.

$n=1$	$n=2$	$n=3$	$n=4$
0	00	000	0000
1	01	001	0001
—	10	010	0010
	11	011	0011
	—	100	0100
		101	0101
		110	0110
		111	0111
		—	1000
			1001
			1010
			1011
			1100
			1101
			1110
			1111

Table 2.1 The 2^n possible values of an n-bit variable for $n=1$ to 4.

Inputs A	B	Output F = A·B
0	0	0
0	1	0
1	0	0
1	1	1

False because one or more inputs is false

True because both inputs are true

Table 2.2 Truth table for the AND gate.

(a) Two-input AND gate   A, B → C = A·B

(b) Three-input AND gate   A, B, C → D = A·B·C

Fig. 2.7 The AND gate.

When we introduce computer arithmetic, computer architecture, and assembly language programming, we will see that computers don't operate on bits in isolation. Computers process entire groups of bits at a time. These groups are called *words* and are typically 8, 16, 32, or 64 bits wide. The AND operation, when applied to words, is called a *logical* operation to distinguish it from an arithmetic operation such as addition, subtraction, or multiplication. When two words take part in a logical operation such as an AND, the operation takes place between the individual *pairs* of bits; for example, bit a_i of word A is ANDed with bit b_i of word B to produce bit c_i of word C. Consider the effect of ANDing the following two 8-bit words: A $= 11011100$ and B $= 01100101$.

```
1  1  0  1  1  1  0  0  ←—— word A
0  1  1  0  0  1  0  1  ←—— word B
0  1  0  0  0  1  0  0  ←—— C = A·B
```

In this example the result C $=$ A·B is given by 01000100. Why should anyone want to AND together two words? If you AND bit x with 1, the result is x (because Table 2.2 demonstrates that $1 \cdot 0 = 0$ and $1 \cdot 1 = 1$). If you AND bit x with 0 the result is 0 (because the output of an AND gate is true only if both inputs are true). Consequently, a logical AND is used to *mask* certain bits in a word by forcing them to zero. For example, if we wish to clear the leftmost four bits of an 8-bit word to zero, ANDing the word with 00001111 will do the trick. The following example demonstrates the effect of an AND operation with a 00001111 mask.

```
1  1  0  1  1  0  1  1  ←—— source word
0  0  0  0  1  1  1  1  ←—— mask
0  0  0  0  1  0  1  1  ←—— result
```

The OR gate

The output of an OR gate is true if any one (or more than one) of its inputs is true. Notice the difference between AND and OR operations. The output of an AND is true only if all inputs are true whereas the output of an OR is true if at least one input is true. The circuit symbols for a 2-input and a 3-input OR gate are given in Fig. 2.9. The logical symbol for an OR operation is a plus sign, so that the logical operation A OR B is written as A$+$B. The logical OR operator is the same as the conventional addition symbol because the OR operator behaves like the addition operator in algebra (the reasons for this will become clear when we introduce Boolean algebra). Table 2.3 provides the truth table for a two-input OR gate.

The behavior of an OR gate can be represented by the switching circuit of Fig. 2.10. A path exists from input to output if either of the two switches is closed.

Note that the use of the term *OR* here is rather different from the English usage of *or*. The Boolean OR means (either A or B) or (both A and B), whereas the English usage often means A or B but not (A and B). For example, consider the contrasting use of the word *or* in the two phrases: 'Would you like tea or coffee?' and 'Reduced fees are charged to members who are registered students or under 25'. We shall see that the more common English use of the word *or* corresponds to the Boolean function known as the EXCLUSIVE OR, an important function that is frequently abbreviated to EOR or XOR.

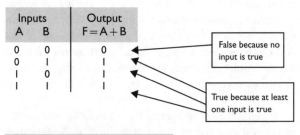

(a) Two-input OR gate

(b) Three-input OR gate

Fig. 2.9 The OR gate.

Inputs		Output
A	B	F = A+B
0	0	0
0	1	1
1	0	1
1	1	1

False because no input is true

True because at least one input is true

Table 2.3 Truth table for the OR gate.

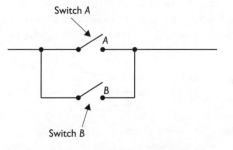

Fig. 2.10 The representation of an OR gate.

A computer can also perform a logical OR on words, as the following example illustrates.

```
1 0 0 1 1 1 0 0 ⟵ word A
0 0 1 0 0 1 0 1 ⟵ word B
1 0 1 1 1 1 0 1 ⟵ C = A + B
```

The logical OR operation is used to set one or more bits in a word to a logical 1. The term *set* means make a logical one, just as *clear* means reset to a logical zero. For example, the least-significant bit of a word is set by ORing it with $00\ldots01$. By applying both AND and OR operations to a word we can selectively clear or set its bits. Suppose we have an 8-bit binary word and we wish to clear bits 6 and 7 and set bits 4 and 5. If the bits of the word are d_0 to d_7, we can write:

d_7	d_6	d_5	d_4	d_3	d_2	d_1	d_0	
0	0	1	1	1	1	1	1	Source word / AND mask
0	0	d_5	d_4	d_3	d_2	d_1	d_0	First result
0	0	1	1	0	0	0	0	OR mask
0	0	1	1	d_3	d_2	d_1	d_0	Final result

The NOT gate

The NOT gate is also called an *inverter* or a *complementer*, and is a two-terminal device with a single input and a single output. If the input of an inverter is X, its output is NOT X, which is written $\overline{X}$ or X*. Figure 2.11 illustrates the symbol for an inverter and Table 2.4 provides its truth table. Some teachers vocalize $\overline{X}$ as 'not X' and others as 'X not'. The inverter is the simplest of gates because the output is the opposite of the input. If the input is 1 the output is 0, and vice versa. By the way, the triangle in Fig. 2.11 doesn't represent an inverter. The small circle at the output of the inverter indicates the inversion operation. We shall see that this circle indicates logical inversion wherever it appears in a circuit.

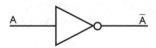

Fig. 2.11 The NOT gate or inverter.

Input	Output
A	F = $\overline{A}$
0	1
1	0

Table 2.4 Truth table for the inverter.

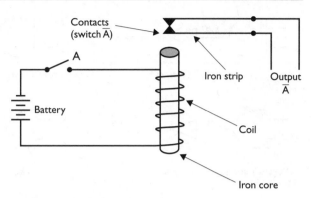

Fig. 2.12 The operation of a relay.

We can visualize the operation of the NOT gate in terms of the *relay* illustrated in Fig. 2.12. A relay is an electromechanical switch (i.e. a device that is partially electronic and partially mechanical). The relay in Fig. 2.12 consists of an iron core around which a coil of wire is wrapped. When a current flows through a coil, it generates a magnetic field that causes the iron core to act as a magnet. Situated close to the iron core is a pair of contacts, the lower of which is mounted on a springy strip of iron. If switch A is open, no current flows through the coil and the iron core remains unmagnetized. The relay's contacts are normally closed so that they form a switch that is closed when switch A is open.

If switch A is closed, a current flows through the coil to generate a magnetic field that magnetizes the iron core. The contact on the iron strip is pulled toward the core, opening the contacts and breaking the circuit. In other words, closing switch A opens the relay's switch and vice versa. The system in Fig. 2.12 behaves like a NOT gate. The relay is used by a computer to control external devices and is described further when we deal with input and output devices.

Like both the AND and OR operations, the NOT function can also be applied to words:

```
1 1 0 1 1 1 0 0 ⟵ word A
0 0 1 0 0 0 1 1 ⟵ B = Ā
```

The NAND and NOR gates

The two most widely used gates in real circuits are the NAND and NOR gates. These aren't fundamental gates because the NAND gate is derived from an AND gate followed by an inverter (Not AND) and the NOR gate is derived from an OR gate followed by an inverter (Not OR), respectively. The circuit symbols for the NAND and NOR gates are given in Fig. 2.13. The little circle at the output of a NAND gate

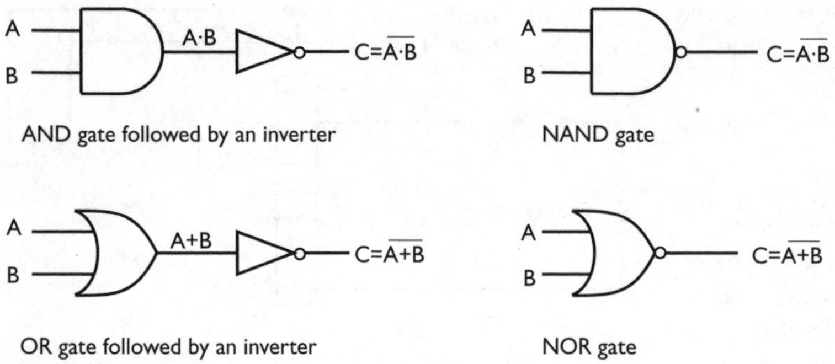

$$C = \overline{A \cdot B} \qquad \text{AND gate followed by an inverter}$$

$$C = \overline{A \cdot B} \qquad \text{NAND gate}$$

$$C = \overline{A + B} \qquad \text{OR gate followed by an inverter}$$

$$C = \overline{A + B} \qquad \text{NOR gate}$$

Fig. 2.13 Circuit symbols for the NAND and NOR gates.

represents the symbol for inversion or complementation. It is this circle that converts the AND gate to a NAND gate and an OR gate to a NOR gate. Later, when we introduce the concept of mixed logic, we will discover that this circle can be applied to the inputs of gates as well as to their outputs.

Table 2.5 gives the truth table for the NAND and the NOR gates. As you can see, the output columns in the NAND and NOR tables are just the complements of the outputs in the corresponding AND and OR tables.

We can get a better feeling for the effect that different gates have on two inputs, A and B, by putting all the gates together in a single table (Table 2.6). We have also included the EXCLUSIVE OR (i.e. EOR) and its complement the EXCLUSIVE NOR (i.e. EXNOR) in Table 2.6 for reference. The EOR gate is derived from AND, OR, and NOT gates and is described in more detail later in this chapter. It should be noted here that $\overline{A} \cdot \overline{B}$ is not the same as $\overline{A \cdot B}$, just as $\overline{A} + \overline{B}$ is not the same as $\overline{A + B}$.

2.2.1 Gates as transmission elements

One of the problems encountered by those teaching digital logic is that students say, 'That's very nice, but what's the point of it all?' It's not immediately apparent what gates do until you have constructed complete circuits containing several gates. However, we can provide more of an insight into what gates do by treating them as *transmission elements* that control the flow of information within a computer.

We are going to take three two-input gates (i.e. AND, OR, EOR) and see what happens when we apply a variable to one input and a control signal to the other input. Figure 2.14 illustrates three pairs of gates. Each pair demonstrates the situation in which the control input C is set to a logical 0 and a logical 1 state. The other input is a variable X and we wish to determine the effect the gate has on the transmission of X through it.

Figures 2.14(a) and (b) demonstrate the behavior of an AND gate. When C = 0, an AND gate is disabled and its output is forced into a logical zero state. When C = 1, the AND gate is enabled and its X input is transmitted to the output unchanged. We can think of an AND gate as a simple switch that allows or inhibits the passage of a logical signal. Similarly, in Figs. 2.14(c) and (d) an OR gate is enabled by C = 0 and disabled by C = 1. However, when the OR gate is disabled, its output is forced into a logical one state.

The EOR gate in Figs. 2.14(e) and (f) is a more interesting device. When its control input is 0, it transmits the other input

NAND				NOR		
A	B	$C=\overline{A \cdot B}$		A	B	$C=\overline{A+B}$
0	0	1		0	0	1
0	1	1		0	1	0
1	0	1		1	0	0
1	1	0		1	1	0

Table 2.5 Truth table for the NAND and NOR gates.

Inputs		Output					
A	B	AND A·B	OR A+B	NAND $\overline{A \cdot B}$	NOR $\overline{A+B}$	EOR $A \oplus B$	EXNOR $\overline{A \oplus B}$
0	0	0	0	1	1	0	1
0	1	0	1	1	0	1	0
1	0	0	1	1	0	1	0
1	1	1	1	0	0	0	1

Table 2.6 Truth table for six gates.

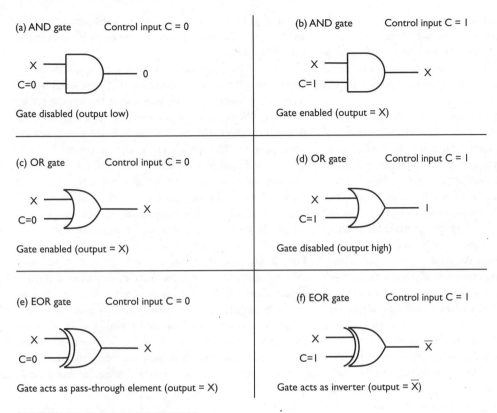

(a) AND gate   Control input C = 0

X
C=0   0

Gate disabled (output low)

(b) AND gate   Control input C = 1

X
C=1   X

Gate enabled (output = X)

(c) OR gate   Control input C = 0

X
C=0   X

Gate enabled (output = X)

(d) OR gate   Control input C = 1

X
C=1   1

Gate disabled (output high)

(e) EOR gate   Control input C = 0

X
C=0   X

Gate acts as pass-through element (output = X)

(f) EOR gate   Control input C = 1

X
C=1 $\overline{X}$

Gate acts as inverter (output = $\overline{X}$)

Fig. 2.14 Gates as transmission elements.

unchanged. But when C = 1, it transmits the complement of X. The EOR gate can best be regarded as a *programmable inverter*. Later we shall make good use of this property of an EOR gate.

The reason we've introduced the concept of a gate as a transmission element is that digital computers can be viewed as a complex network through which information flows and this information is operated on by gates as it flows round the system.

2.2.2 Positive, negative, and mixed logic

At this point we are going to introduce the concepts of *positive logic*, *negative logic*, and *mixed logic*. Some readers may find that this section interrupts their progress toward a better understanding of the gate and may therefore skip ahead to the next section.

Up to now we have blurred the distinction between two essentially unconnected concepts. The first concept is the relationship between low/high voltages in a digital circuit, 0 and 1 logical levels, and true/false logic values. The second concept is the logic function; for example, AND, OR, and NOT. So far, we have used *positive logic*, in which a

high-level signal represents a logical one state and this state is called true.

Table 2.7 provides three views of the AND function. The leftmost column provides the logical truth table in which the output is true only if all inputs are true (we have used T and F to avoid reference to signal levels). The middle column describes the AND function in positive logic form in which the output is true (i.e. 1) only if all inputs are true (i.e. 1).

The right-hand column in Table 2.7 uses *negative logic*, in which 0 is true and 1 is false. The output A·B is true (i.e. 0) only when both inputs are true (i.e. 0).

Logical form			Positive logic			Negative logic		
A	B	A·B	A	B	A·B	A	B	A·B
F	F	F	0	0	0	1	1	1
F	T	F	0	1	0	1	0	1
T	F	F	1	0	0	0	1	1
T	T	T	1	1	1	0	0	0

Table 2.7 Truth table for AND gate in positive and negative logic forms.

As far as digital circuits are concerned, there's no fundamental difference between logical 1s and 0s and it's as sensible to choose a logical 0 level as the true state as it is to choose a logical 1 state. Indeed, many of the signals in real digital systems are active-low, which means that their activity is carried out by a low-level signal.

Suppose we regard the low level as true and use negative logic. Table 2.7 shows that we have an AND gate whose output is low if and only if each input is low. It should also be apparent that an AND gate in negative logic functions as an OR gate in positive logic. Similarly, a negative logic OR gate functions as an AND gate in positive logic. In other words, the *same* gate is an AND gate in negative logic and an OR gate in positive logic. Figure 2.15 demonstrates the relationship between positive and negative logic gates.

For years engineers used the symbol for a positive logic AND gate in circuits using active-low signals, with the result that the reader was confused and could only understand the circuit by mentally transforming the positive logic gate into its negative logic equivalent. In mixed logic both positive logic and negative logic gates are used together in the same circuit. The choice of whether to use positive or negative logic is determined only by the desire to improve the clarity of a diagram or explanation.

Why do we have to worry about positive and negative logic? If we stuck to positive logic, life would be much simpler. True, but life is never that simple. Many real electronic systems are activated by low-level signals and that makes it sensible to adopt negative logic conventions. Let's look at an example. Consider a circuit that is activated by a low-level

signal only when input A is a low level and input B is a low level. Figure 2.16 demonstrates the circuit required to implement this function.

In Fig. 2.16(a) we employ positive logic and draw an OR gate because the output of an OR gate is 0 only when both its inputs are 0. There's nothing wrong with this circuit, but it's confusing. When you see a gate with an 'OR shape' you think of an OR function. However, in this case, the gate is actually performing an AND operation on low-level signals.

What we need is a means of preserving the AND shape and indicating we are using negative logic signals. Figure 2.16(b) does just that. By placing inverter circles at the AND gate's inputs and output we immediately see that the output of the gate is low if and only if both of its inputs are low.

There is no physical difference between the circuits of Figs. 2.16(a) and (b). They are both ways of representing the same thing. However, the meaning of circuit 2.16(b) is clearer. Consider another example of mixed logic in which we use both negative and positive logic concepts. Suppose a circuit is activated by a low-level signal if input A is low and input B high, or input D is high, or input C is low. Figure 2.17 shows how we might draw such a circuit.

For most of this book we will continue to use positive logic.

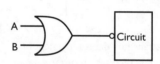

(a) Positive logic system
The circuit is activated when
A is low and B is low

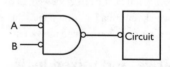

(b) Negative logic system
The circuit is activated when
A is low and B is low

Fig. 2.16 Mixed logic.

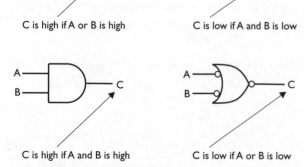

C is high if A or B is high

C is low if A and B is low

C is high if A and B is high

C is low if A or B is low

Fig. 2.15 Positive and negative logic.

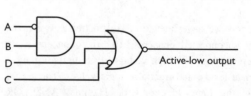

Active-low output

Fig. 2.17 Using mixed logic.

2.3 Applications of gates

We now look at four simple circuits, each of which is built from a few basic gates. It's my intention to demonstrate that a few gates can be connected together in such a way as to create a circuit whose function and importance may readily be appreciated by the reader. Following this informal introduction to circuits we introduce *Digital Works*, a Windows-based program that lets you construct and simulate circuits containing gates on a PC. We then return to gates and provide a more formal section on the analysis of logic circuits by means of Boolean algebra.

Circuits are constructed by connecting gates together. The output from one gate can be connected (i.e. wired) to the input of one or more other gates. However, two outputs cannot be connected together.

Example 1 Consider the circuit of Fig. 2.18, which uses three 2-input AND gates labeled G1, G2, and G3 and a 3-input OR gate labeled G4. This circuit has three inputs A, B, and C, and an output F. What does it do?

We can tackle this problem in several ways. One approach is to create a truth table that tabulates the output F for all the

Inputs			Intermediate values			Output
A	B	C	$P = A \cdot B$	$Q = B \cdot C$	$R = A \cdot C$	$F = P + Q + R$
0	0	0	0	0	0	0
0	0	1	0	0	0	0
0	1	0	0	0	0	0
0	1	1	0	1	0	1
1	0	0	0	0	0	0
1	0	1	0	0	1	1
1	1	0	1	0	0	1
1	1	1	1	1	1	1

Table 2.8 Truth table for Fig. 2.18.

eight possible combinations of the three inputs A, B, and C. Table 2.8 corresponds to the circuit of Fig. 2.18 and includes columns for the outputs of the three AND gates as well as the output of the OR gate, F.

The three intermediate signals P, Q, and R are defined by $P = A \cdot B$, $Q = B \cdot C$, and $R = A \cdot C$. Figure 2.18 tells us that we can write down the output function, F, as the logical OR of the three intermediate signals P, Q, and R; that is, $F = P + Q + R$.

We can substitute the expressions for P, Q, and R to get $F = A \cdot B + B \cdot C + A \cdot C$. This is a *Boolean equation*, but it doesn't help us a lot at this point. However, by visually inspecting the truth table for F we can see that the output is true if two or more of the inputs A, B, and C are true. That is, this circuit implements a *majority logic* function whose output takes the same value as the majority of inputs. We have already seen how such a circuit is used in an automatic landing system in an aircraft by choosing the output from three independent computers to be the best (i.e. majority) of three inputs. Using just four basic gates, we've constructed a circuit that does something useful.

Example 2 As in the previous example, the circuit of Fig. 2.19 has three inputs, one output, and three intermediate values (we've also included a mixed logic version of this circuit on the right-hand side of Fig. 2.19). By inspecting the

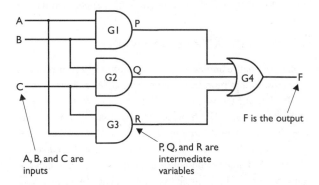

A, B, and C are inputs

P, Q, and R are intermediate variables

F is the output

Fig. 2.18 The use of gates—Example 1.

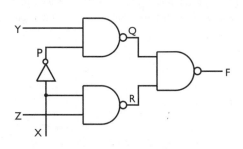

Fig. 2.19 The use of gates—Example 2.

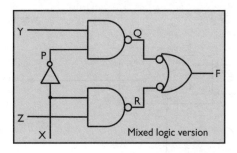

Mixed logic version

truth table for this circuit (Table 2.9) we can see that when the input X is 0, the output, F, is equal to Y. Similarly, when X is 1, the output is equal to Z. The circuit of Fig. 2.19 behaves like an electronic switch, connecting the output to one of two inputs, Y or Z, depending on the state of a control input X.

The circuit of Fig. 2.19 is called a *two-input multiplexer* and can be represented by the arrangement of Fig. 2.20. Because the word *multiplexer* appears so often in electronics, it is frequently abbreviated to MUX.

We are now going to derive an expression for F in terms of inputs X, Y, and Z in two different ways. From the circuit diagram of Fig. 2.19 we can derive an equation for F by writing the output of each gate in terms of its inputs.

$$F = \overline{Q \cdot R}$$

$$Q = \overline{Y \cdot P}$$

$$P = \overline{X}$$

Therefore $Q = \overline{Y \cdot \overline{X}}$ by substituting for P

$$R = \overline{X \cdot Z}$$

Therefore $F = \overline{\overline{Y \cdot \overline{X}} \cdot \overline{X \cdot Z}}$

When we introduce Boolean algebra we will see how this type of expression can be simplified. Another way of obtaining a Boolean expression is to use the truth table. Each time a logical one appears in the output column, we can write down

Inputs			Intermediate values			Output
X	Y	Z	$P = \overline{X}$	$Q = \overline{P \cdot Y}$	$R = \overline{X \cdot Z}$	$F = \overline{Q \cdot R}$
0	0	0	1	1	1	0
0	0	1	1	1	1	0
0	1	0	1	0	1	1
0	1	1	1	0	1	1
1	0	0	0	1	1	0
1	0	1	0	1	0	1
1	1	0	0	1	1	0
1	1	1	0	1	0	1

Table 2.9 Truth table for Fig. 2.19.

the set of inputs that cause the output to be true. In Table 2.9 the output is true when:

(1) X = 0, Y = 1, Z = 0 $(\overline{X} \cdot Y \cdot \overline{Z})$

(2) X = 0, Y = 1, Z = 1 $(\overline{X} \cdot Y \cdot Z)$

(3) X = 1, Y = 0, Z = 1 $(X \cdot \overline{Y} \cdot Z)$

(4) X = 1, Y = 1, Z = 1 $(X \cdot Y \cdot Z)$

There are four possible combinations of inputs that make the output true. Therefore, the output can be expressed as the logical sum of the four cases (1)–(4) above; that is,

$$F = \overline{X} \cdot Y \cdot \overline{Z} + \overline{X} \cdot Y \cdot Z + X \cdot \overline{Y} \cdot Z + X \cdot Y \cdot Z$$

This function is true if any of the conditions (1)–(4) are true. A function represented in this way is called a *sum-of-products* (S-of-P) expression because it is the logical OR (i.e. sum) of a group of terms each composed of several variables ANDed together (i.e. products). A sum-of-products expression represents one of the two standard ways of writing down a Boolean expression.

An alternative way of writing a Boolean equation is called a *product-of-sums* (P-of-S) expression and consists of several terms ANDed together. The terms are made up of variables ORed together. A typical product-of-sums expression has the form

$$F = (A + \overline{B} + C) \cdot (\overline{A} + B + C) \cdot (\overline{A} + \overline{B} + \overline{C})$$

Later we shall examine ways of converting sum-of-products expressions into product-of sums expressions and vice versa.

Each of the terms (1)–(4) in Example 2 is called a *minterm*. A minterm is an AND (product) term that includes each of the variables in either its true or complemented form. For example, in the case above $\overline{X} \cdot Y \cdot \overline{Z}$ is a minterm, but if we had had the term $\overline{X} \cdot Y$ that would not be a minterm, since $\overline{X} \cdot Y$ includes only two of the three variables. When an equation is expressed as a sum of minterms, it is said to be in its *canonical* form. Canonical is just a fancy word that means standard.

As the output of the circuit in Fig. 2.19 must be the same whether it is derived from the truth table or from the logic

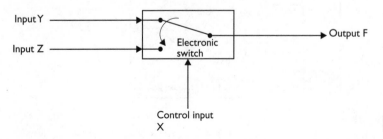

Input Y

Input Z

Electronic switch

Output F

Control input
X

Fig. 2.20 The logical representation of Fig. 2.19.

diagram, the two equations we have derived for F must be equivalent, with the result that

$$\overline{\overline{Y \cdot \overline{X} \cdot X \cdot Z}} = \overline{X} \cdot Y \cdot \overline{Z} + \overline{X} \cdot Y \cdot Z + X \cdot \overline{Y} \cdot Z + X \cdot Y \cdot Z$$

This equation demonstrates that a given Boolean function can be expressed in more than one way.

The multiplexer of Fig. 2.19 may seem a very long way from computers and programming. However, multiplexers are found somewhere in every computer because computers operate by modifying the flow of data within a system. A multiplexer allows one of two data streams to flow through a switch that is electronically controlled. Let's look at a highly simplified example. The power of a digital computer (or a human brain) lies in its ability to make decisions. Decision taking in a computer corresponds to the *conditional branch*; for example

```
IF Day=Weekday
   THEN update stock
   ELSE print stock list
```

We can't go into the details of how such a construct is implemented here (we do that in Chapter 5). What we would like to do is to demonstrate that something as simple as a multiplexer can implement something as sophisticated as a conditional branch. Consider the system of Fig. 2.21. Two numbers P and Q are fed to a comparator, where they are compared. If they are the same, the output of the comparator is 1 (otherwise it's 0). The same output is used as the control input to a multiplexer that selects between two values X and Y. In practice, such a system would be rather more complex (because P, Q, X, and Y are all multi-bit values), but the basic principles are the same.

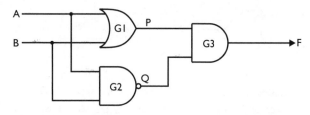

Fig. 2.22 The use of gates—Example 3.

Inputs		Intermediate values		Output
A	B	$P = A + B$	$Q = \overline{A \cdot B}$	$F = P \cdot Q$
0	0	0	1	0
0	1	1	1	1
1	0	1	1	1
1	1	1	0	0

Table 2.10 Truth table for the circuit of Fig. 2.22 (Example 3).

Example 3 Figure 2.22 describes a simple circuit with three gates: an OR gate, an AND gate, and a NAND gate. This circuit has two inputs, two intermediate values, and one output. Table 2.10 provides its truth table.

The circuit of Fig. 2.22 represents one of the most important circuits in digital electronics, the *exclusive or* (also called EOR or XOR). The exclusive or corresponds to the normal English use of the word *or* (i.e. one or the other but not both). The output of an EOR gate is true if one of the inputs is true but not if both inputs are true.

An EOR circuit always has two inputs (remember that AND and OR gates can have any number of inputs). Because the EOR function is so widely used, the EOR gate has its own

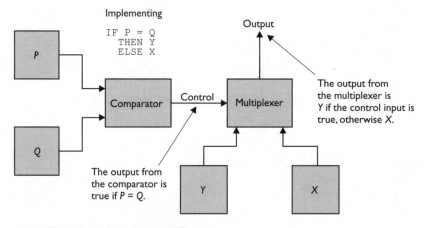

Fig. 2.21 Application of the multiplexer.

Fig. 2.23 Circuit symbol for an EOR gate.

special circuit symbol (Fig. 2.23) and the EOR operator its own special logical symbol '⊕'; for example, we can write

$$F = A \text{ EOR } B = A \oplus B$$

The EOR is not a fundamental gate because it is constructed from basic gates.

Because the EOR gate is so important, we will discuss it a little further. Table 2.10 demonstrates that F is true when $A = 0$ and $B = 1$, or when $A = 1$ and $B = 0$. Consequently, the output $F = \overline{A} \cdot B + A \cdot \overline{B}$. From the circuit in Fig. 2.22 we can write

$$F = P \cdot Q$$
$$P = A + B$$
$$Q = \overline{A \cdot B}$$

Therefore $F = (A + B) \overline{A \cdot B}$

As these two equations (i.e. $F = \overline{A} \cdot B + A \cdot \overline{B}$ and $F = (A + B) \cdot \overline{A \cdot B}$) must be equivalent, we can therefore also build an EOR function in the manner depicted in Fig. 2.24.

It's perfectly possible to build an EOR with four NAND gates (Fig. 2.25). We leave it as an exercise for the reader to verify that Fig. 2.25 does indeed represent an EOR gate. To demonstrate that two different circuits have the same function, all you need do is to construct a truth table for each circuit.

If the outputs are the same for each and every possible input, the circuits are equivalent.

The EOR is a remarkably versatile logic element that pops up in many places in digital electronics. The output of an EOR is true if its inputs are *different*, and false if they are the *same*. As we've already stated, unlike the AND, OR, NAND, and NOR gates the EOR gate can have only two inputs. The EOR gate's ability to detect whether its inputs are the same allows us to build an equality tester that indicates whether or not two words are identical (Fig. 2.26).

In Fig. 2.26 two *m*-bit words (Word 1 and Word 2) are fed to a bank of *m* EOR gates. Bit *i* from Word 1 is compared with bit *i* from Word 2 in the *i*th EOR gate. If these two bits are the same, the output of this EOR gate is zero.

If the two words in Fig. 2.26 are equal, the outputs of all EORs are zero and we need to detect this condition in order to declare that Word 1 and Word 2 are identical. An AND gate will give a 1 output when all its inputs are 1. However, in this case, we have to detect the situation in which all inputs are 0. We can therefore connect all *m* outputs from the *m* EOR gates to an *m*-input NOR gate (because the output of a NOR gate is 1 if all inputs are 0).

If you look at Fig. 2.26 you can see that the outputs from the EOR gates aren't connected to a NOR gate but to an *m*-input AND gate with inverting inputs. The little bubbles at the AND gate's inputs indicate inversion and are equivalent to NOT gates. When all inputs to the AND gate are 0, the inverters will invert these to all 1s and the output of the AND gate will go to a 1 (exactly what we want). In mixed logic we can regard an AND gate with active-low inputs and an active-high output as a NOR gate.

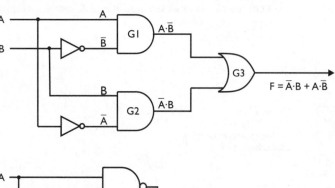

Fig 2.24 An alternative circuit for an EOR gate.

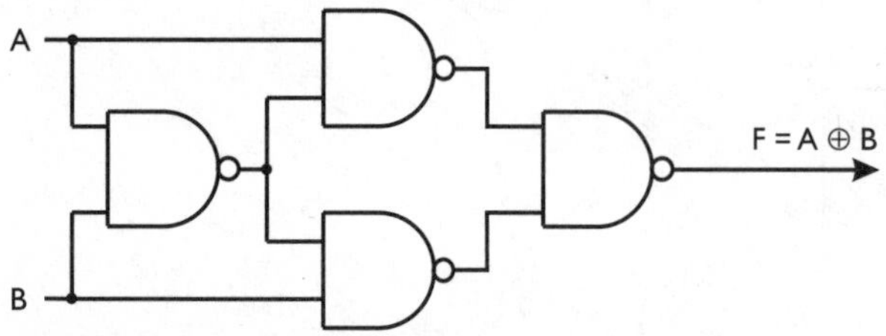

Fig. 2.25 An EOR circuit constructed with NAND gates only.

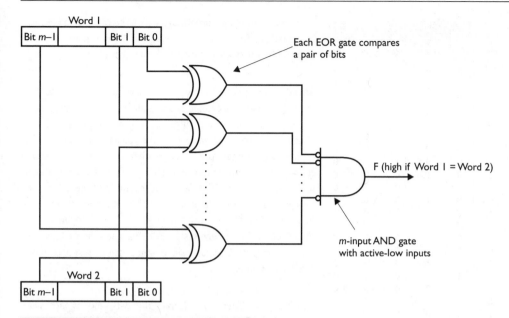

Fig. 2.26 The application of EOR gates in an equality tester.

Remember that we required an equality detector (i.e. comparator) in Fig. 2.21 (Example 2) to control a multiplexer. We've just built one.

Example 4 The final example of important circuits constructed from a few gates is the prioritizer whose circuit is given in Fig. 2.27. As this is a rather more complex circuit than the previous three examples, we'll explain what it does first. A prioritizer deals with competing requests for attention and grants service to just one of those requesting attention. The prioritizer is a device with n inputs and n outputs. Each of the inputs is assigned a priority from 0 to $n-1$ (assume that the highest priority is input $n-1$ and the lowest is 0). If two or more inputs are asserted simultaneously, only the output corresponding to the input with the highest priority is asserted. Computers use this type of circuit to deal with simultaneous requests for service from several peripherals (e.g. disk drives, the keyboard, the mouse, and the modem).

Consider the 5-input prioritizer circuit in Fig. 2.27. The prioritizer's five inputs x_0 to x_4 are connected to the outputs of five devices that can make a request for attention (input x_4 has the highest priority). That is, device i can put a logical 1 on input x_i to request attention at priority level i. If several inputs are set to 1 at the same time, the prioritizer sets only one of its outputs to 1; all the other outputs remain at 0. For example, if the input is $x_4, x_3, x_2, x_1, x_0 = 00110$, the output $y_4, y_3, y_2, y_1,$

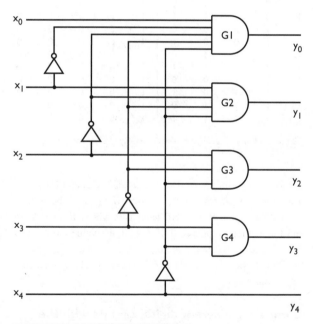

Fig. 2.27 Example 4—the priority circuit.

$y_0 = 00100$, because the highest level of input is x_2. Table 2.11 provides a truth table for this prioritizer.

If you examine the circuit of Fig. 2.27, you can see that output y_4 is equal to input x_4 because there is a direct connection. If x_4 is 0, then y_4 is 0; and if x_4 is 1 then y_4 is 1. The value of x_4 is

Inputs					Outputs				
x_4	x_3	x_2	x_1	x_0	y_4	y_3	y_2	y_1	y_0
0	0	0	0	0	0	0	0	0	0
0	0	0	0	1	0	0	0	0	1
0	0	0	1	0	0	0	0	1	0
0	0	0	1	1	0	0	0	1	0
0	0	1	0	0	0	0	1	0	0
0	0	1	0	1	0	0	1	0	0
0	0	1	1	0	0	0	1	0	0
0	0	1	1	1	0	0	1	0	0
0	1	0	0	0	0	1	0	0	0
0	1	0	0	1	0	1	0	0	0
0	1	0	1	0	0	1	0	0	0
0	1	0	1	1	0	1	0	0	0
0	1	1	0	0	0	1	0	0	0
0	1	1	0	1	0	1	0	0	0
0	1	1	1	0	0	1	0	0	0
0	1	1	1	1	0	1	0	0	0
1	0	0	0	0	1	0	0	0	0
1	0	0	0	1	1	0	0	0	0
1	0	0	1	0	1	0	0	0	0
1	0	0	1	1	1	0	0	0	0
1	0	1	0	0	1	0	0	0	0
1	0	1	0	1	1	0	0	0	0
1	0	1	1	0	1	0	0	0	0
1	0	1	1	1	1	0	0	0	0
1	1	0	0	0	1	0	0	0	0
1	1	0	0	1	1	0	0	0	0
1	1	0	1	0	1	0	0	0	0
1	1	0	1	1	1	0	0	0	0
1	1	1	0	0	1	0	0	0	0
1	1	1	0	1	1	0	0	0	0
1	1	1	1	0	1	0	0	0	0
1	1	1	1	1	1	0	0	0	0

Table 2.11 Truth table for the circuit of Fig. 2.27 (Example 4).

fed to the input of the AND gates G4, G3, G2, and G1 in the lower priority stages via an inverter. If x_4 is 1, the logical level at the inputs of the AND gates is 0, which disables them and forces their outputs to 0. If x_4 is 0, the value fed back to the AND gates is 1 and therefore they are not disabled by x_4. Similarly, when x_3 is 1, gates G3, G2, and G1 are disabled, and so on.

Comparing different digital circuits with the same function

It should now be apparent that not only can a given function be represented by more than one Boolean expression, but that different combinations of gates may be used to implement the function. This isn't the place to go into great depth on the detailed design of logic circuits, but it is interesting to see how the designer might go about selecting one particular implementation in preference to another.

Some of the basic criteria by which circuits are judged are listed below. In general, the design of logic circuits is often affected by other factors than those described here.

Speed The speed of a circuit (i.e. how long it takes the output to respond to a change at an input) is approximately governed by the maximum number of gates through which a change of state must propagate (i.e. pass). The output of a typical gate might take 5 ns to change following a logic change at its input ($5\,\text{ns} = 5 \times 10^{-9}\,\text{s}$). Figures 2.22 and 2.24 both implement an EOR function. In Fig. 2.22 there are only two gates in series, whereas in Fig. 2.24 there are three gates in series. Therefore the implementation of an EOR function in Fig. 2.22 is 50 percent faster. All real gates don't have the same propagation delay, since some gates respond more rapidly than others.

Number of interconnections It costs money to wire gates together. Even if a printed circuit is used, somebody has to design it, and the more interconnections used the more expensive it will be. Equally, increasing the number of interconnections in a circuit also increases the probability of failure due to a faulty connection. One parameter of circuit design that takes account of the number of interconnections is the total number of inputs to gates. In Fig. 2.22 there are six inputs, whereas in Fig. 2.24 there are eight inputs.

Number of packages Simple gates of the types we're describing here are normally available in 14 pin packages (two pins of which are needed for the power supply). As it costs virtually nothing to add extra gates to the silicon chip, only the number of pins (i.e. external connections to the chip) limits the total number of gates in a physical package. Thus, an inverter requires two pins, so that six inverters are provided on the chip. Similarly, a two-input AND/NAND/OR/NOR gate needs three pins, so four of these gates are put on the chip. Because each of these circuits uses three different types of gate, both circuits require three 14 pin integrated circuits. Even so, the circuit of Fig. 2.22 is better than that of Fig. 2.24 because there are more unused gates left in the ICs, freeing them for use by other parts of the computer system. Note that the circuit of Fig. 2.25 uses only one package because all gates are the same type.

You should appreciate that this is an introductory text and what we have said is appropriate only to logic circuits constructed from basic logic elements. Computer-aided design techniques are used to handle more complex systems with hundreds of gates. Indeed, complex circuits are largely constructed from programmable digital elements.

2.4 Introduction to Digital Works

We now introduce a Windows-based logic simulator called *Digital Works* that enables you to construct a logic circuit from simple gates (AND, OR, NOT, NAND, NOR, EOR, XNOR) and to analyze the circuit's behavior. Digital Works also supports the tri-state logic gate that enables you to construct systems with buses. In the next chapter we will discover that Digital Works simulates both simple 1-bit storage elements called flip-flops and larger memory components such as ROM and RAM.

After installing Digital Works on your system, you can run it to get the initial screen shown in Fig. 2.28. We have annotated six of the most important icons on the toolbars.

A circuit is constructed by using the mouse to place gates on the screen or *workspace*, and a 'wiring tool' to connect the gates together. The input to your circuit may come from a clock generator (a continuous series of alternating 1s and 0s), a sequence generator (a user-defined sequence of 1s and 0s), or a manual input (from a switch that you can push by means of the mouse). You can observe the output of a gate by connecting it to a light called an LED. You can also send the output of the LED to a window that displays either a waveform or a sequence of binary digits.

Digital Works has been designed to be consistent with the Windows philosophy and has a help function that provides further information about its facilities and commands. The **File** command in the top toolbar provides the options you would expect (e.g. Load, Save, Save As).

2.4.1 Creating a circuit

We are going to design and test an EOR circuit that has the logic function $\overline{A}\cdot B + A\cdot\overline{B}$. This function can be implemented

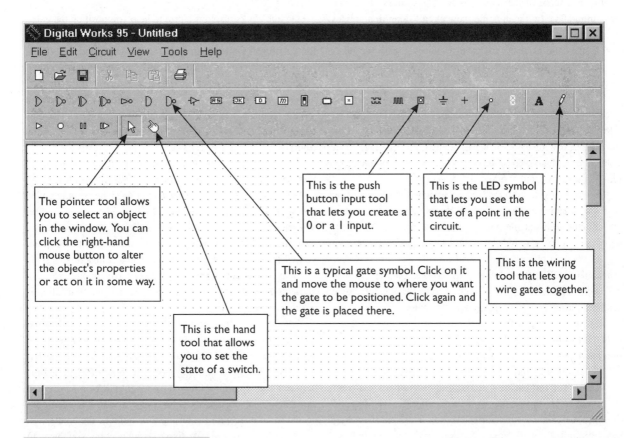

Fig. 2.28 Digital Works—the initial screen.

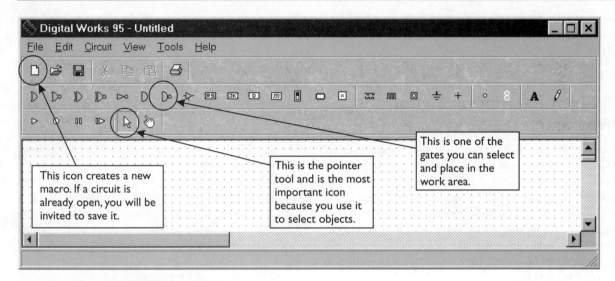

Fig. 2.29 Beginning a session with Digital Works.

with two inverters, two AND gates, and an OR gate. Figure 2.29 shows three of the icons we are going to use to create this circuit. The first icon is the 'new circuit' icon that creates a fresh circuit (which Digital Works calls a *macro*). The second icon is the *pointer tool* used to select a gate (or other element) from the toolbars. The third icon is a gate that can be planted in the work area.

Let's start by planting some gates on the work area (we know that the EOR circuit requires two AND gates, an OR gate, and two inverters). First click on the pointer tool on the bottom row of icons. If it hasn't already been selected, it will become depressed when you select it. The pointer tool remains selected until another tool is selected.

You select a gate from the list on the second row of icons by first left clicking on the gate with the pointer tool and then left clicking at a suitable point in the workspace, as Fig. 2.30 demonstrates. If you hold the control key down when placing a gate, you can place multiple copies of the gate in the workspace. The OR gate is shown in broken outline because we've just placed it (i.e. it is currently 'selected'). Once a gate has been placed, you can select it with the mouse by clicking the left button and drag it wherever you want. You can click the right button to modify the gate's attributes (e.g. the number of inputs).

You can tidy up the circuit by moving the gates within the work area. You left click a gate and drag it to where you want it. Figure 2.31 shows the work area after we've dragged the gates to create a symmetrical layout. You can even drag gates around the work area after they have been wired up, and reposition wires by left clicking and dragging any *node*

(a node is a point on a wire that consists of multiple sections or links).

Digital Works displays a grid to help you position the gates. The grid can be turned on or off, and the spacing of the grid lines changed. Objects can be made to snap to the grid. These functions are accessed via the **View** command in the top line.

Before continuing, we need to save the circuit. Figure 2.32 demonstrates how we use the conventional **File** function in the toolbar to save a circuit. We have called this circuit **OUP_EOR1**, and Digital Works inserts the extension **.dwm**.

The next step is to wire up the gates to create a circuit. First select the *wiring tool* from the toolbar by left clicking on it (Fig. 2.33). Then position the cursor over the point at which you wish to connect a wire and left click. The cursor changes to *wire* when it's over a point that can legally be connected to. Left click to attach a wire and move the cursor to the point you wish to connect. Left click to create a connection. Instead of making a direct connection between two points, you can click on the workspace to create a node (i.e. the connection is a series of straight lines).

You can make the wiring look neat by clicking on intermediate points to create a signal path made up of a series of straight-line segments. If you select the pointer tool and left click on a wire, you can drag any of its nodes (i.e. the points between segments on a line). If you right click on a wire you can delete it or change its color. Once a wire has been connected to another wire (or an input or output), the connection point can't be moved. To move a connection you have to delete the wire and connect a new one.

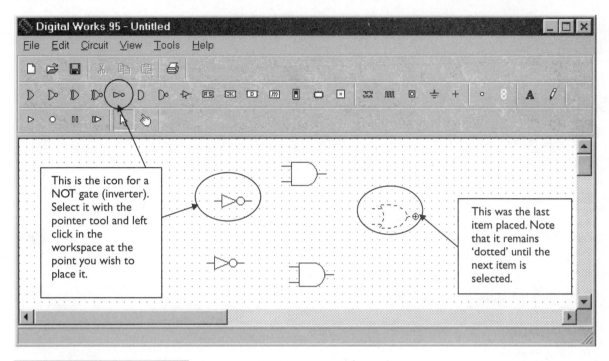

Fig. 2.30 Placing gates in the work area.

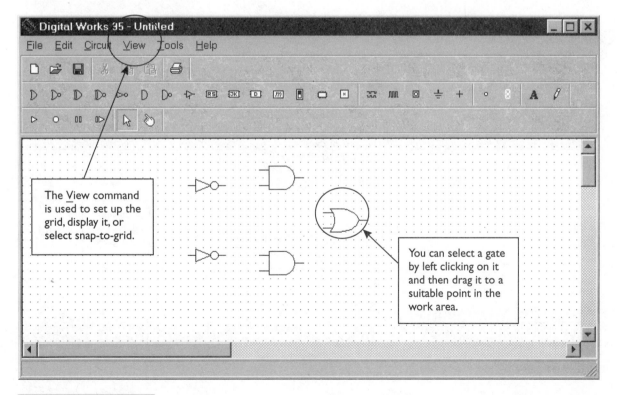

Fig. 2.31 Tidying up the circuit.

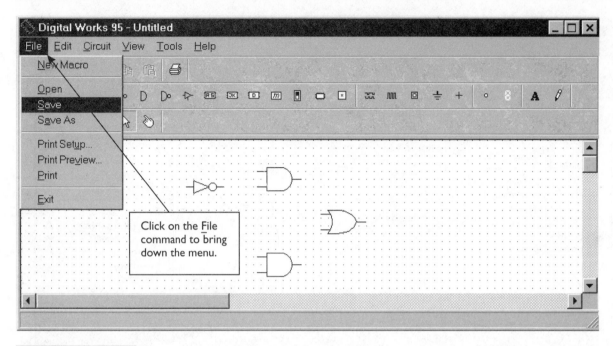

Fig. 2.32 Saving the circuit.

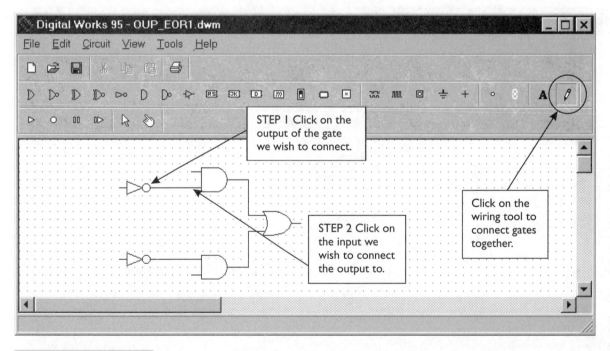

Fig. 2.33 Wiring gates together.

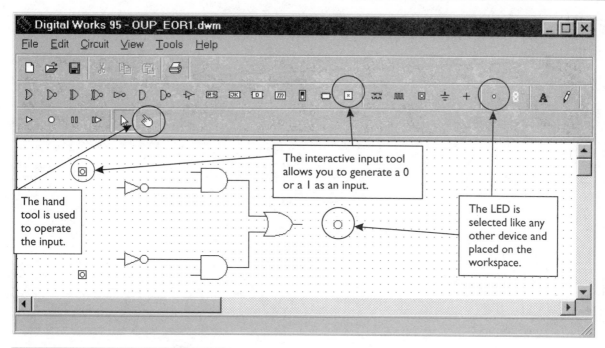

Fig. 2.34 Adding inputs and outputs to the circuit.

Digital Works permits a wire to be connected only between two legal connections. In Fig. 2.33 the inputs to the two inverters and the circuit's outputs aren't connected anywhere. This is because each wire must be connected between two points—it can't just be left hanging. In order to wire up the inputs and output we need points we can connect the wire to. In this case we are going to use the interactive input device to provide an input signal from a push button and the LED to show the state of the output.

In Fig. 2.34 we have added two interactive inputs and an LED to the circuit. When we run the simulator, we can set the states of the inputs to provide a 0 or a 1 and we can observe the state of the output on the LED.

We can now wire up the inputs and the output and complete the rest of the wiring, as shown in Fig. 2.35. At this stage we could run the circuit if we wanted. However, we will use the text tool (indicated by the letter **A** on the middle toolbar) to give the circuit a title. Click on the **A** and then click on the place at which you wish to add the text to open the text window. This brings down a text box. Enter the text and click **OK** to place it on the screen.

We also wish to label the circuit's inputs and outputs. Although you can use the text tool to add text at any point, input and output devices (e.g. clocks, switches, LEDs) can be given names. We will use this latter technique

because the names attached to input and output devices are automatically used to label the timing diagrams we will introduce later.

Figure 2.36 shows the circuit with annotation. The label 'EOR circuit' has been added by the text tool, and inputs A and B have been labeled by right clicking on the input devices. In Fig. 2.36 we have right clicked on the LED to bring down a menu and then selected **Text** to invoke the text box (not shown). You enter the name of the output (in this case Sum) into the text box and click ok. This label is then appended to the LED on the screen. You can change the location of the label by right clicking on its name, selecting **Text Style** from the menu and then selecting the required position (**L**eft, **R**ight, **T**op, **B**ottom).

2.4.2 Running a simulation

We are now ready to begin simulation. The bottom row of icons is concerned with running the simulation. The leftmost icon (ringed in Fig. 2.37) is left clicked to begin the simulation. The next step is to change the state of the *interactive input* devices. If you click on the hand tool icon, the cursor changes to a *hand* when positioned anywhere over the work area.

By putting the hand cursor over one of the input devices, you can left click the mouse to change the status of the input

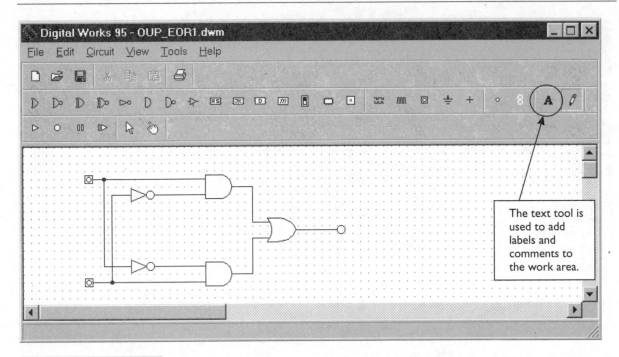

Fig. 2.35 Completing the circuit.

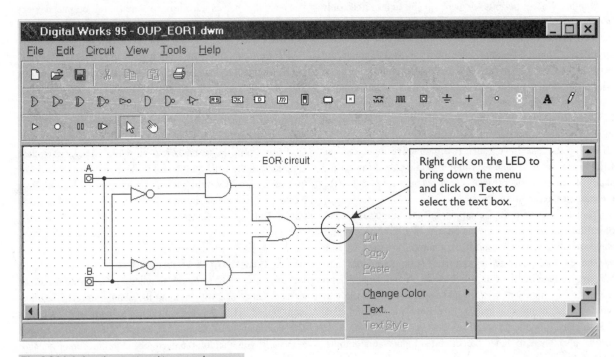

Fig. 2.36 Labeling the circuit and inputs and outputs.

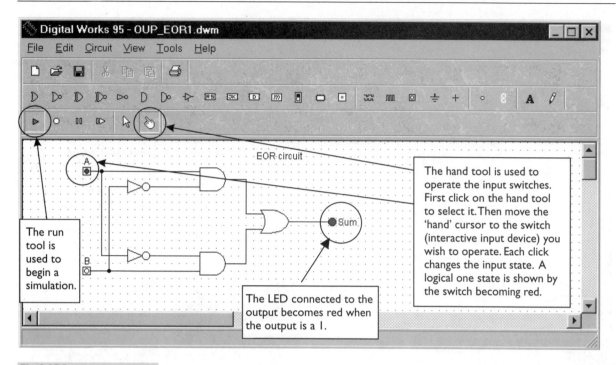

Fig. 2.37 Running the simulator.

(i.e. input 0 or input 1). When the input device is supplying a 1, it becomes red. Figure 2.37 shows the situation input A = 1, B = 0, and the Sum = 1 (the output LED becomes red when it is connected to a 1 state). You can change the states of the input devices to generate all the possible input values 0,0, 0,1, 1,0, and 1,1 to verify that the circuit is an EOR (the output LED should display the sequence 0,1,1, 0).

Just observing the outputs of the LEDs is not always enough to get a picture of the circuit's behavior. We need a record of the states of the inputs and outputs. Digital Works provides a **Logic History** function that records and displays inputs and outputs during a simulator run. Any input or output device can be added to **Logic History**. If you select 'input A' with the pointer tool and then right click, you get a pull-down menu from which you can activate the **Add to Logic History** function to record the value of input A. When this function is selected (denoted by a tick on the menu), all input is copied to a buffer (i.e. store). As we have two inputs, A and B, we will have to assign them to the **Logic History** function independently.

To record the output of the LED, you carry out the same procedure you did with the two inputs A and B (i.e. right click on the LED and select **Add to Logic History**); see Fig. 2.38.

In order to use the **Logic History** function, you have to activate it from the **Tools** function on the toolbar. Selecting **Tools** pulls down a menu, from which you have to select the

Logic History window. Figure 2.39 shows the **Logic History** window after a simulation run. Note that the inputs and outputs have the labels you gave them (i.e. A, B, and Sum).

We now need to say something about the way the simulator operates. The simulator uses an internal clock, and a record of the state of inputs and outputs is taken at each clock pulse. Figure 2.40 shows how you can change the clock speed from the toolbar by pulling down the **Circuit** menu and selecting **Clock Speed**.

We're not interested in clocks at this stage because we are looking at a circuit that doesn't have a clock. However, because the signals are read and recorded at each clock pulse, the entire simulation is over in a second or so. Blink and you miss it.

We need to stop the clock to perform a 'manual' simulation. The **Logic History** window contains a copy of the *run*, *stop*, *pause*, and *single-step* icons to allow you to step through the simulation. Figure 2.41 provides further details of the **Logic History** window. The waveform in Fig. 2.41 was created by putting the simulator in the pause mode and executing a single cycle at a time by clicking on the single-step button. Between each cycle we have used the hand tool to change the inputs to the EOR gate. Note that we can use the hand tool both to change the state of the inputs and to single step (you don't have to use the pointer tool to perform a single step).

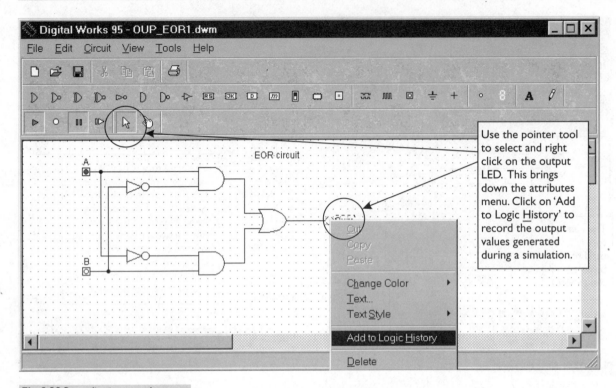

Fig. 2.38 Recording inputs and outputs.

The logic history can be displayed either as a waveform, as in Fig. 2.41, or as a binary sequence, as in Fig. 2.42, by clicking on the display mode icon in the **Logic History** window. You can also select the number of states to be displayed in this window.

2.4.3 The clock and sequence generator

Inputting data into a digital circuit by using the hand tool to manipulate push buttons and switches is suitable for simple circuits, but not for more complex systems. Digital Works provides two means of generating signals automatically. One is a simple *clock generator* that produces a constant stream of alternating 1s and 0s, and the other is a *sequence generator* that produces a user-defined stream of 1s and 0s. The sequence generator is controlled by Digital Works' own clock, and a new 1 or 0 is output at each clock pulse. Figure 2.43 shows the icons for the clock and pulse generators and demonstrates how they appear when placed in the work area.

Figure 2.44 demonstrates how you can define a sequence of pulses you wish to apply to one of the inputs of a circuit

(in this example, a single AND gate). One of the inputs to the AND gate comes from the clock generator and the other from the sequence generator. We've added LEDs to the gate's inputs and output to make it easy to observe the state of all signals.

Let's go through the operations required to place and set up a sequence generator (called a bit generator by Digital Works). First left click on the sequencer icon on the toolbar and then move the cursor to the point at which you wish to locate this device in the workspace. Then right click both to place it in the workspace and to bring down the menu that controls the bit generator. From the pull-down menu, select **Edit Sequence** and the window shown in Fig. 2.44 appears. You can enter a sequence either from the computer's keyboard or by using the mouse on the simulated keyboard in the **Edit Sequence** window. You can enter the sequence in either binary or hexadecimal form (see Chapter 4 for a discussion of hexadecimal numbers).

We can run the simple circuit by clicking on the run icon. When the system runs you will see the LEDs turn on and off. The speed of the clock pulses can be altered by clicking on **Circuit** in the toolbar to pull down a menu that allows you to set the clock speed.

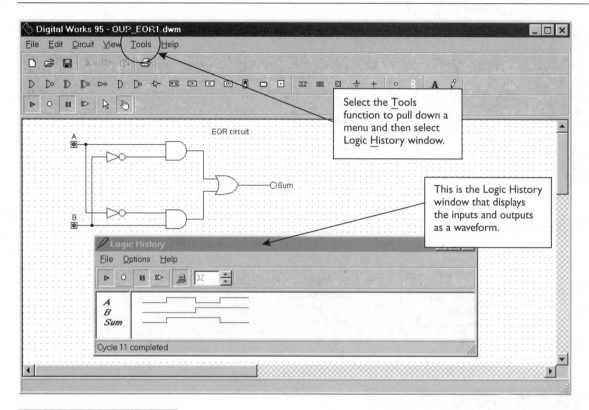

Fig. 2.39 The Logic History window.

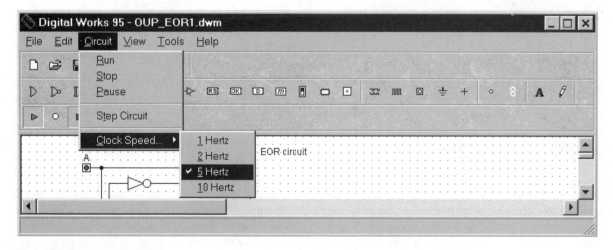

Fig. 2.40 Changing the clock rate.

2.4.4 Using Digital Works to create embedded circuits

Up to now, we have used Digital Works to create simple circuits composed from fundamental gates. You could create an entire microprocessor in this manner, but it would rapidly become too complex to use in any meaningful way. Digital Works allows you to convert a simple circuit into a logic element itself. The new logic element can be used as a

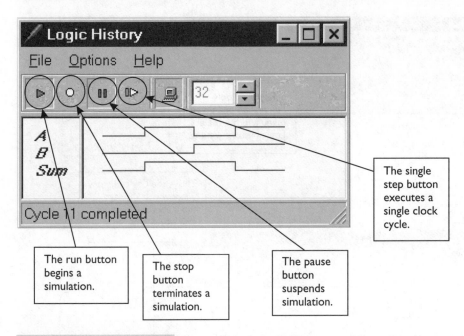

The single step button executes a single clock cycle.

The run button begins a simulation.

The stop button terminates a simulation.

The pause button suspends simulation.

Fig. 2.41 Controlling the simulation.

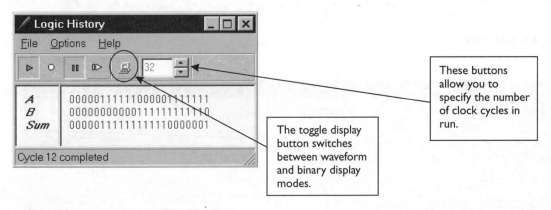

These buttons allow you to specify the number of clock cycles in run.

The toggle display button switches between waveform and binary display modes.

Fig. 2.42 Viewing the simulation as binary sequence.

building block in the construction of more complex circuits. These complex circuits can be converted into new logic elements, and so on. Turning circuits into reusable black boxes is analogous to the use of subroutines in a high-level language.

Let's take the simple two-input multiplexer described in Fig. 2.45 and convert it into a black box with four terminals: two inputs A and B, a control input C whose state selects one of the inputs, and an output. When we constructed this circuit with Digital Works, we used the *macro tag* icon to place macro tags at the circuit's inputs and outputs. A macro tag can be wired up to the rest of the circuit exactly like an input or

output device. You left click on the macro tag icon to select it and then move the cursor to the place on the workspace you wish to insert the macro tag (i.e. the input or output port). Then you wire the macro tag to the appropriate input or output point of the circuit. Note that you can't apply a macro tag to the input or output of a gate directly—you have to connect it to an input or output by a wire.

You can also place a macro tag anywhere within the workspace by right clicking the mouse when using the wiring tool. Right clicking terminates the wiring process, inserts a macro tag, and activates a pull-down menu.

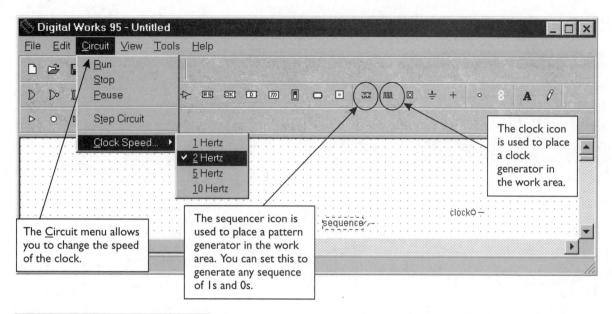

The clock icon is used to place a clock generator in the work area.

The Circuit menu allows you to change the speed of the clock.

The sequencer icon is used to place a pattern generator in the work area. You can set this to generate any sequence of 1s and 0s.

Fig. 2.43 The clock generator and sequencer.

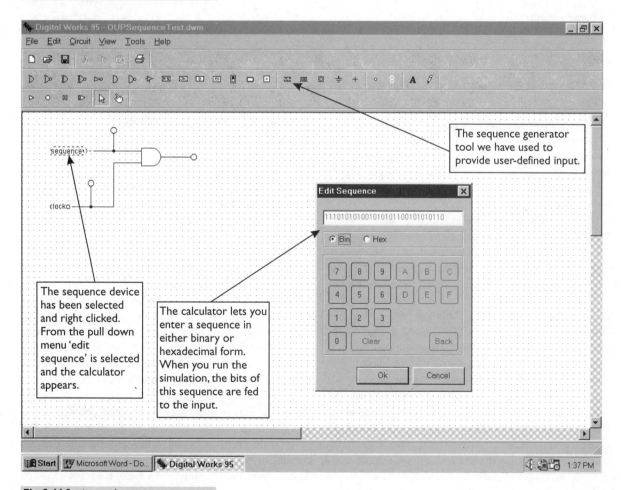

The sequence generator tool we have used to provide user-defined input.

The sequence device has been selected and right clicked. From the pull down menu 'edit sequence' is selected and the calculator appears.

The calculator lets you enter a sequence in either binary or hexadecimal form. When you run the simulation, the bits of this sequence are fed to the input.

Fig. 2.44 Setting up the sequence generator.

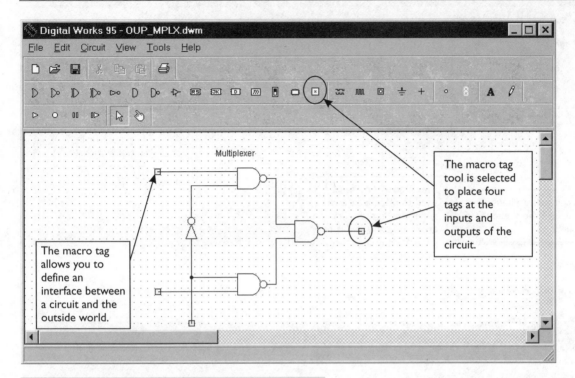

Fig. 2.45 Converting the two-input multiplexer circuit into a black box.

We are going to take the circuit of Fig. 2.45 and convert it into a black box with four terminals (i.e. the macro tags). This new circuit is just a new means of representing the old circuit—it is not a different entity. Indeed, this circuit doesn't have a different file name and is saved in the same file as the original circuit.

The first step is to create the macro (i.e. black box) itself. This is a slightly involved and repetitive process because you have to repeat the procedure once for each of the macro tags. Place the cursor over one of the macro tags in Fig. 2.46 and right click to pull down the menu. Select **Template Editor** from the menu with a leftclick. A new window called **Template Editor** appears (Fig. 2.46). You create a black box representation of the circuit in this window. Digital Works allows you to draw a new symbol to represent the circuit (in Fig. 2.46 we've used a special shape for the multiplexer).

Figure 2.46 shows the **Template Editor** window. We have used the simple *polyline* drawing tool provided by Digital Works to create a suitable shape for the representation of the multiplexer. You just click on this tool in the **Template Editor** window and draw the circuit by clicking in the workspace at the points you wish to draw a line. You exit the drawing mode by double clicking. You can also add text to the drawing by using the text tool. Figure 2.46 shows the shape

we've drawn for the multiplexer and the label we've given it. To add a label or text to the circuit, select the text tool and click on the point at which you wish to insert the text. This action will pull down the **Edit Text** box.

The next step is to add pins to the black box in the **Template Editor** window and associate them with the macro tags in the original circuit of Fig. 2.45. Once this has been done, you can use the black box representation of the multiplexer in other circuits. The pins you have added to the black box are the connections to the circuit at the macro tags.

Click on the pin icon in the **Template Editor** and then left click in the workspace at the point you wish to locate this pin—see Fig. 2.47. You then right click on this new pin and select **Associate with Tag**. This operation associates the pin you have just placed with a macro tag in the circuit diagram. Each new pin placed on the circuit in the **Template Editor** window is automatically numbered in sequence.

We add additional pins to the black box by closing the **Template Editor**, going back to the circuit, clicking on one of the unassigned pins and selecting **Associate with Tag** again. Remember that Digital Works automatically numbers the pins in the circuit diagram as you associate them with tags. We can finish the process by using the text tool to add labels to the four pins—Fig. 2.48. We have now created a new

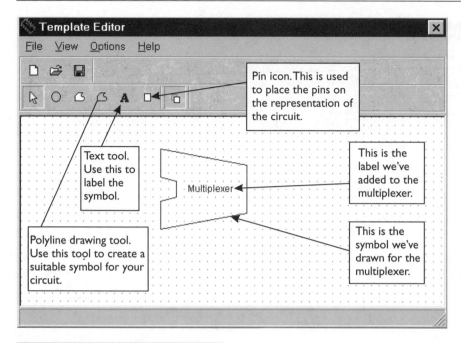

Fig. 2.46 Drawing a symbol for the new circuit.

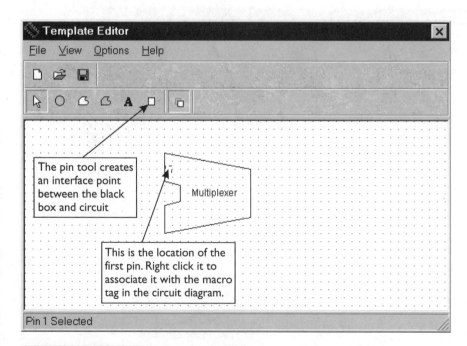

Fig. 2.47 Creating an interface point in the black box.

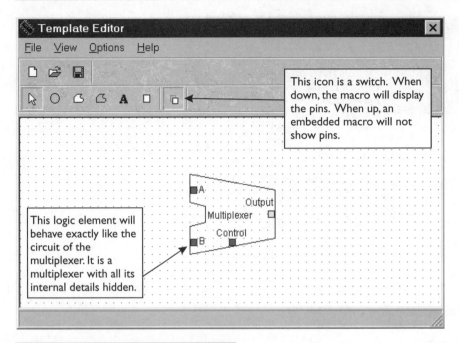

Fig. 2.48 The completed black box representation.

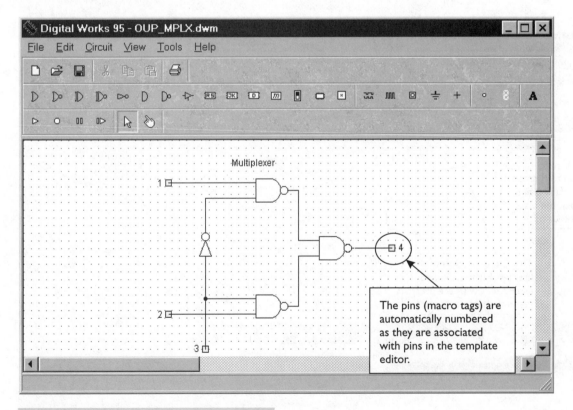

Fig. 2.49 The original circuit with the macro tags numbered.

element that behaves exactly like the circuit from which it was constructed, and which can itself be used as a circuit element.

Figure 2.49 shows the original or expanded version of the circuit. Note how the pins have been numbered automatically.

To summarize, you create a black box representation of a circuit by carrying out the following sequence of operations:

- In Digital Works add and connect (i.e. wire up) a macro tag to your circuit

- Right click the macro tag to enter the template editor

- Use the template editor to add a pin to the circuit representation

- In the template editor, select this pin and right click to associate it with the macro tag in the circuit diagram

- Close the template editor

- Repeat these operations, once for each macro tag

When you exit Digital Works, saving your circuit also saves its black box representation. You can regard these two circuits as being bound together—with one representing a shorthand version of the other. Note that the template editor also has a save function. Using this save function simply saves the drawing you've created but not the pins, the circuit or its logic.

2.4.5 Using a macro

Having created a black box circuit (i.e. a macro), we can now use it as a building block just like any other logic element. We will start a new circuit in Digital Works and begin with an empty work area. The macro for a 2-input multiplexer we have just created and saved is used like other circuit elements. You click on the embed macro icon (see Fig. 2.50) and move the pointer to the location in the workspace where you wish to place the macro. Then you left click and select the appropriate macro from the pull-down menu that appears.

The macro is automatically placed at the point you clicked on and can be used exactly like a circuit element placed from one of the circuit icons. Remember that the macro is the same as the circuit—the only difference is its on-screen representation.

In Fig. 2.50 we have placed two of the multiplexers in the workspace prior to wiring them together. Figure 2.51 demonstrates how we can wire these two macros together, add a gate, and provide inputs and LED displays.

2.4.6 Modifying a circuit

Suppose you build a circuit that contains one or more macros (e.g. Fig. 2.51) and wish to modify it. A circuit can be modified in the usual way by opening its file in Digital Works and

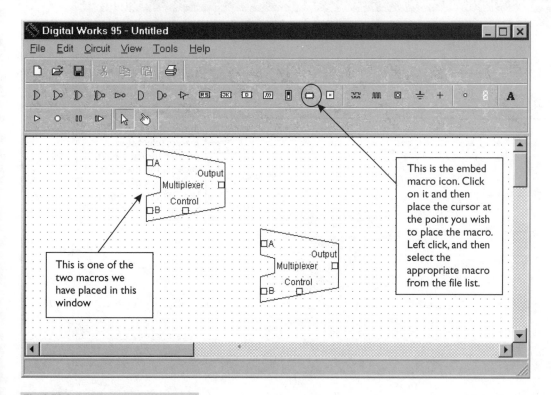

Fig. 2.50 Embedding a macro in a circuit.

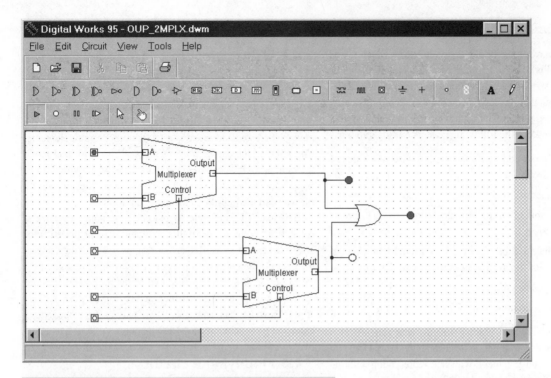

Fig. 2.51 Embedding two macros, wiring them, and creating a new macro.

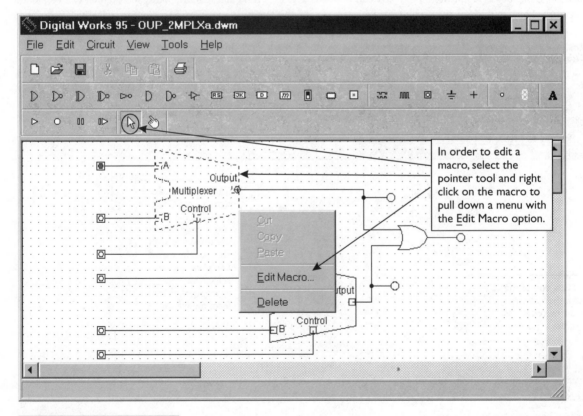

In order to edit a macro, select the pointer tool and right click on the macro to pull down a menu with the Edit Macro option.

Fig. 2.52 Editing a macro in a circuit.

making any necessary changes. Digital Works even allows you to edit (i.e. modify) a circuit while it's running.

In order to modify a macro itself, you have to return to the macro's expanded form (i.e. the circuit that the macro represents). A macro is expanded by right clicking on the macro's symbol and selecting the **Edit Macro** function from the pull-down menu that appears. Figure 2.52 shows the system of Fig. 2.50 in which the macro representation of the multiplexer in the upper left-hand side of the workspace has been right clicked on.

Selecting the **Edit Macro** function converts the black box macro representation into the original circuit, as Fig. 2.53 demonstrates. You can now edit this circuit in the normal way. When editing has been completed, you select the **Close Macro** icon that appears on the lowest toolbar. Closing this window returns to the normal circuit view, which contains the macro that has now been changed.

There are two macros in the circuit diagram of Fig. 2.52. If we edit one of them, what happens to the other and what happens to the original circuit? Digital Works employs object embedding rather than object linking. When a macro is embedded in a circuit, a copy of the macro is embedded in the circuit. If you modify a macro only that copy is changed. The original macro is not altered. Moreover, if you have embedded several copies of a macro in a circuit, only the macro that you edit is changed.

Figure 2.54 demonstrates the effect of editing the macro version of a two-input multiplexer. Figure 2.54(a) shows the modified expanded macro. An OR gate has been wired to the A and B inputs on pins 1 and 2, and a macro tag added to the output of the OR gate. By clicking on the macro tag, the **Template Editor** window is invoked. You can add a pin and assign it to the macro tag. When you exit the template editor and close the macro, the final circuit of Fig. 2.54(b) appears (we have added an LED to the output of the new macro).

2.5 An introduction to Boolean algebra

We've already seen that you can describe circuits containing gates in terms of variables and functions (i.e. AND, OR, and

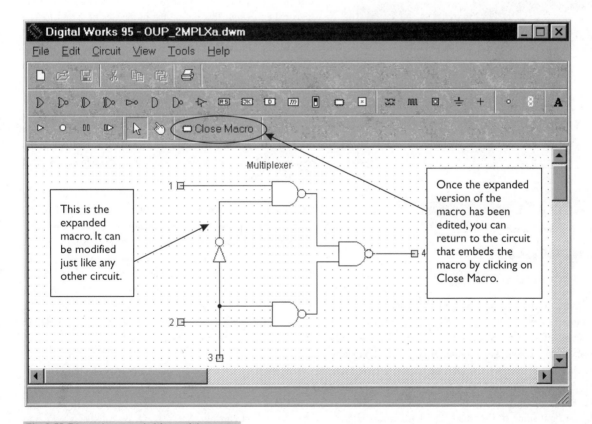

Fig. 2.53 Editing the expanded form of the macro.

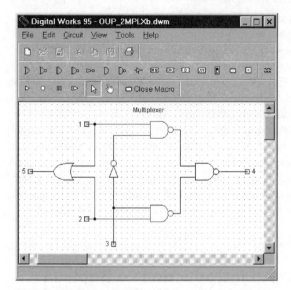

(a) The modified macro

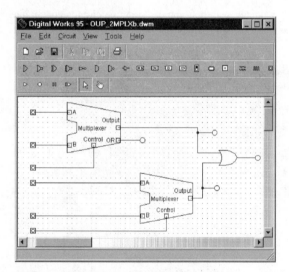

(b) The circuit with the modified macro

Fig. 2.54 Example of editing a macro.

NOT). Consider an AND gate with input variables A and B, and an output C. We can write the *Boolean equation* C = A·B that uses variables A, B, and C, and an operator (i.e. the AND function). In this section we introduce Boolean algebra, show how equations are manipulated, and demonstrate how logic circuits can be constructed with only one type of gate. Students requiring only a very basic knowledge of Boolean algebra can omit some of the fine detail that appears later in this section.

George Boole was an English mathematician (1815–64) who developed a mathematical analysis of logic and published it in his book *An Investigation of the Laws of Thought* in 1854. Boole's algebra of logic would probably have remained a tool of the philosopher, had it not been for the development of electronics in the 20th century.

In 1938 Claude Shannon published a paper entitled *A symbolic analysis of relays and switching circuits* that applied Boolean algebra to switching circuits using relays. Such circuits were widely used in telephone exchanges and later in digital computers. Today, Boolean algebra is used to design digital circuits and to analyze their behavior.

Digital design is concerned with the conversion of ideas or specifications into actual hardware, and Boolean algebra is a tool that facilitates this process. In particular, Boolean algebra permits an idea to be expressed in a mathematical form and the resulting expression to be simplified and then translated into the real hardware of gates and other logic elements.

Let's begin with a formal definition just in case this book falls into the hands of a mathematician. Boolean algebra (or any other algebra) consists of a set of elements E, a set of functions F that operate on members of E, and a set of basic laws called *axioms* that define the properties of E and F. The set of elements making up a Boolean algebra are variables and literals (i.e. constants) that have fixed values of 0 or 1. A Boolean algebra with n variables has a set of 2^n possible permutations of these variables.

Only three functions or operations are permitted in Boolean algebra. The first two are the logical OR represented by a plus (e.g. A + B) and the logical AND represented by a dot (e.g. A·B). Some texts use a ∪ (cup) or a ∨ to denote the logical OR operator, and a ∩ (cap) or a ∧ to denote a logical AND operator.

The use of the plus and dot symbols is rather confusing because the same symbols are used for addition and multiplication in everyday life. One reason that these particular symbols have been chosen is that they behave (subject to the postulates of Boolean algebra) rather like conventional addition and multiplication. Another possible reason Boole chose + and · to represent the logical OR and AND functions is that Boole's background was in probability theory. The chance of throwing a 1 *or* a 2 with two throws of a single die is 1/6 + 1/6, whereas the chance of throwing a 1 *and* a 2 is $1/6 \times 1/6$.

The third operation permitted in Boolean algebra is that of negation or complementation and is denoted by a bar over a literal or a variable. The complement of 0 (i.e. $\overline{0}$) is 1, and vice versa. The equation $X + Y \cdot \overline{Z} = A$ is read as 'X or Y and not Z equals A'. The priority of an AND operator is higher than that of an OR operator, so that the expression means $A = X + (Y \cdot Z)$ and not $A = (X + Y)\overline{Z}$. Some texts use an asterisk to denote negation and some use a stroke. Thus, we can write NOT(X) as $\overline{X}$ or X* or /X.

The arithmetic operations of *subtraction* and *division* do not exist in Boolean algebra. For example, the Boolean expression $X + Y = X + Z$ cannot be rearranged in the form

$$(X + Y) - X = (X + Z) - X$$

which would lead to $Y = Z$. If you don't believe this, then consider the case $X = 1$, $Y = 1$, and $Z = 0$. The left-hand side of the equation yields $X + Y = 1 + 1 = 1$, and the right-hand side yields $X + Z = 1 + 0 = 1$. That is, the equation is valid even though Y is not equal to Z.

2.5.1 Axioms and theorems of Boolean algebra

An *axiom* or *postulate* is a fundamental rule that has to be taken for granted (i.e. the axioms of Boolean algebra define the framework of Boolean algebra from which everything else can be derived). The first axiom is called the *closure property*, which states that Boolean operations on Boolean variables or constants always yield Boolean results. If variables A and B belong to a set of Boolean elements, the operations $A \cdot B$, $A + B$, and NOT A and NOT B also belong to the set of Boolean elements.

Boolean variables obey the same commutative, distributive, and associative laws as the variables of conventional algebra. We take these laws for granted when we do everyday arithmetic; for example, the commutative law states that $6 \times 3 = 3 \times 6$. Table 2.12 describes the commutative, distributive, and associative laws of Boolean algebra.

We approach Boolean algebra by first looking at the action of NOT, OR, and AND operations on constants. The effect of these three operations is best illustrated by means of the truth

table given in Table 2.13. These rules may be extended to any number of variables.

We can extend Table 2.13, which defines the relationship between the Boolean operators and the literals (i.e. constants) 0 and 1, to the relationship between a Boolean operator, a variable, and a literal (see Table 2.14).

We can prove the validity of the equations in Table 2.14 by substituting all the possible values for X (i.e. 0 or 1). For example, consider the axiom $0 \cdot X = 0$. If $X = 1$ we have $0 \cdot 1 = 0$ which is correct because *by definition* the output of an AND gate is true if and only if all its inputs are true. Similarly, if $X = 0$ we have $0 \cdot 0 = 0$, which is also correct. Therefore, the expression $0 \cdot X = 0$ is correct for all possible values of X. A proof in which we test a theorem by examining all possibilities is called *proof by perfect induction*.

The axioms of Boolean algebra could be used to simplify equations, but it would be too tedious to keep going back to

NOT	AND	OR
$\overline{0} = 1$	$0 \cdot 0 = 0$	$0 + 0 = 0$
$\overline{1} = 0$	$0 \cdot 1 = 0$	$0 + 1 = 1$
	$1 \cdot 0 = 0$	$1 + 0 = 1$
	$1 \cdot 1 = 1$	$1 + 1 = 1$

Table 2.13 Basic axioms of Boolean algebra.

AND	OR	NOT
$0 \cdot X = 0$	$0 + X = X$	$\overline{\overline{X}} = X$
$1 \cdot X = X$	$1 + X = 1$	
$X \cdot X = X$	$X + X = X$	
$X \cdot \overline{X} = 0$	$X + \overline{X} = 1$	

Table 2.14 Boolean operations on a constant and a variable.

$A + B = B + A$ $A \cdot B = B \cdot A$	The AND and OR operators are **commutative** so that the order of the variables in a sum or product group does not matter.
$A \cdot (B \cdot C) = (A \cdot B) \cdot C$ $A + (B + C) = (A + B) + C$	The AND and OR operators are **associative** so that the order in which sub-expressions are evaluated does not matter.
$A \cdot (B + C) = A \cdot B + A \cdot C$ $A + B \cdot C = (A + B)(A + C)$	The AND operator behaves like multiplication and the OR operator like addition. The first **distributive** property states that in an expression containing both AND and OR operators the AND operator takes precedence over the OR. The second distributive law, $A + B \cdot C = (A + B)(A + C)$, is not valid in conventional algebra.

Table 2.12 Commutative, distributive, and associative laws of Boolean algebra.

first principles. Instead, we can apply the axioms of Boolean algebra to derive some *theorems* to help in the simplification of expressions. Once we have proved a theorem by using the basic axioms, we can apply the theorem to equations.

Theorem 1	$X + X \cdot Y = X$	
Proof	$X + X \cdot Y = X \cdot 1 + X \cdot Y$	Using $1 \cdot X = X$ and commutativity
	$= X(1 + Y)$	Using distributivity
	$= X(1)$	Because $1 + Y = 1$
	$= X$	
Theorem 2	$X + \overline{X} \cdot Y = X + Y$	
Proof	$X + \overline{X} \cdot Y = (X + X \cdot Y) + \overline{X} \cdot Y$	By Theorem 1 $X = X + X \cdot Y$
	$= X + X \cdot Y + \overline{X} \cdot Y$	
	$= X + Y(X + \overline{X})$	Remember that $\overline{X} + X = 1$
	$= X + Y(1)$	
	$= X + Y$	
Theorem 3	$X \cdot Y + \overline{X} \cdot Z + Y \cdot Z = X \cdot Y + \overline{X} \cdot Z$	
Proof	$X \cdot Y + \overline{X} \cdot Z + Y \cdot Z = X \cdot Y + \overline{X} \cdot Z + Y \cdot Z(X + \overline{X})$	Remember that $(\overline{X} + X) = 1$
	$= X \cdot Y + \overline{X} \cdot Z + X \cdot Y \cdot Z + \overline{X} \cdot Y \cdot Z$	Multiply bracketed terms
	$= X \cdot Y(1 + Z) + \overline{X} \cdot Z(1 + Y)$	Apply distributive rule
	$= X \cdot Y(1) + \overline{X} \cdot Z(1)$	$(1 + Y) = 1$
	$= X \cdot Y + \overline{X} \cdot Z$	

We can also prove Theorem 3 by the method of perfect induction. To do this, we set up a truth table and demonstrate that the theorem holds for all possible values of X, Y, and Z (Table 2.15). Because the columns labeled $X \cdot Y + \overline{X} \cdot Z$ and $X \cdot Y + \overline{X} \cdot Z + Y \cdot Z$ in Table 2.15 are identical for all possible inputs, these two expressions must be equivalent.

Inputs								
X	Y	Z	$\overline{X}$	$X \cdot Y$	$\overline{X} \cdot Z$	$Y \cdot Z$	$X \cdot Y + \overline{X} \cdot Z$	$X \cdot Y + \overline{X} \cdot Z + Y \cdot Z$
0	0	0	1	0	0	0	0	0
0	0	1	1	0	1	0	1	1
0	1	0	1	0	0	0	0	0
0	1	1	1	0	1	1	1	1
1	0	0	0	0	0	0	0	0
1	0	1	0	0	0	0	0	0
1	1	0	0	1	0	0	1	1
1	1	1	0	1	0	1	1	1

← same →

Table 2.15 Proof of Theorem 3 by perfect induction.

Theorem 4 $X(X+Y)=X$

Proof $X(X+Y)=X\cdot X+X\cdot Y$ Multiply by X

$\qquad\qquad\quad =X+X\cdot Y$ Because $X\cdot X=X$

$\qquad\qquad\quad =X$ By Theorem 1

Theorem 5 $X(\overline{X}+Y)=X\cdot Y$

Proof $X(\overline{X}+Y)=X\cdot\overline{X}+X\cdot Y$

$\qquad\qquad\quad =0+X\cdot Y$ Because $X\cdot\overline{X}=0$

$\qquad\qquad\quad =X\cdot Y$

Theorem 6 $(X+Y)(X+\overline{Y})=X$

Proof $(X+Y)(X+\overline{Y})=X\cdot X+X\cdot\overline{Y}+X\cdot Y+\overline{Y}\cdot Y$

$\qquad\qquad\qquad\quad =X+X\cdot\overline{Y}+X\cdot Y$ Because $X\cdot X=X$, $Y\cdot\overline{Y}=0$

$\qquad\qquad\qquad\quad =X(1+\overline{Y}+Y)$

$\qquad\qquad\qquad\quad =X$

Theorem 7 $(X+Y)(\overline{X}+Z)=X\cdot Z+\overline{X}\cdot Y$

Proof $(X+Y)(\overline{X}+Z)=\overline{X}\cdot X+X\cdot Z+\overline{X}\cdot Y+Y\cdot Z$ Multiply brackets

$\qquad\qquad\qquad\quad =X\cdot Z+\overline{X}\cdot Y+Y\cdot Z$ Because $X\cdot\overline{X}=0$

$\qquad\qquad\qquad\quad =X\cdot Z+\overline{X}\cdot Y$ By Theorem 3

Theorem 8 $(X+Y)(\overline{X}+Z)(Y+Z)=(X+Y)(\overline{X}+Z)$

Proof $(X+Y)(\overline{X}+Z)(Y+Z)=(X\cdot Z+\overline{X}\cdot Y)(Y+Z)$ By Theorem 7

$\qquad\qquad\qquad\qquad\quad =X\cdot Y\cdot Z+X\cdot Z\cdot Z+\overline{X}\cdot Y\cdot Y$
$\qquad\qquad\qquad\qquad\quad\ \ +\overline{X}\cdot Y\cdot Z$

$\qquad\qquad\qquad\qquad\quad =X\cdot Y\cdot Z+X\cdot Z+\overline{X}\cdot Y+\overline{X}\cdot Y\cdot Z$ Because $Y\cdot Y=Y$

$\qquad\qquad\qquad\qquad\quad =X\cdot Z(Y+1)+\overline{X}\cdot Y(1+Z)$

$\qquad\qquad\qquad\qquad\quad =X\cdot Z+\overline{X}\cdot Y$

$\qquad\qquad\qquad\qquad\quad =(X+Y)(\overline{X}+Z)$ By Theorem 7

We provide an alternative proof for Theorem 8 when we
look at de Morgan's theorem later in this chapter.

Theorem 9 $\overline{X\cdot Y\cdot Z}=\overline{X}+\overline{Y}+\overline{Z}$

Proof   To prove that $\overline{X\cdot Y\cdot Z}=\overline{X}+\overline{Y}+\overline{Z}$, we assume that the
expression is true and test its consequences.
If $\overline{X}+\overline{Y}+\overline{Z}$ is the complement of $X\cdot Y\cdot Z$, then from
the basic axioms of Boolean algebra, we have
$(\overline{X}+\overline{Y}+\overline{Z})\cdot(X\cdot Y\cdot Z)=0$ and $(\overline{X}+\overline{Y}+\overline{Z})+(X\cdot Y\cdot Z)=1$

Subproof 1 $(\overline{X}+\overline{Y}+\overline{Z})\cdot X\cdot Y\cdot Z=\overline{X}\cdot X\cdot Y\cdot Z+\overline{Y}\cdot X\cdot Y\cdot Z+\overline{Z}\cdot X\cdot Y\cdot Z$

$\qquad\qquad\qquad\qquad\qquad\quad =\overline{X}\cdot X(Y\cdot Z)+\overline{Y}\cdot Y(X\cdot Z)+\overline{Z}\cdot Z(X\cdot Y)$

$\qquad\qquad\qquad\qquad\qquad\quad =0$

Subproof 2

$$\begin{aligned}(\overline{X}+\overline{Y}+\overline{Z})+X{\cdot}Y{\cdot}Z &= Y{\cdot}Z{\cdot}(X)+\overline{X}+\overline{Y}+\overline{Z} \qquad \text{Re-arrange equation}\\ &= Y{\cdot}Z+\overline{X}+\overline{Y}+\overline{Z} \qquad\qquad \text{Use } A{\cdot}B+\overline{B}=A+\overline{B}\\ &= (\overline{Y}+Y{\cdot}Z)+\overline{X}+\overline{Z} \qquad\quad \text{Re-arrange equation}\\ &= \overline{Y}+Z+\overline{Z}+\overline{X}\\ &= \overline{Y}+1+\overline{X}=1 \qquad\qquad\quad \text{Use } Z+\overline{Z}=1\end{aligned}$$

As we have demonstrated that
$(\overline{X}+\overline{Y}+\overline{Z}){\cdot}X{\cdot}Y{\cdot}Z=0$ and that
$(\overline{X}+\overline{Y}+\overline{Z})+X{\cdot}Y{\cdot}Z=1$, it follows that $\overline{X}+\overline{Y}+\overline{Z}$ is
the complement of $X{\cdot}Y{\cdot}Z$.

Theorem 10 $\overline{X+Y+Z}=\overline{X}{\cdot}\overline{Y}{\cdot}\overline{Z}$

Proof   One possible way of proving Theorem 10 is to use
the method we used to prove Theorem 9. For the
sake of variety, we will prove Theorem 10
by perfect induction (see Table 2.16).

X	Y	Z	X+Y+Z	$\overline{X+Y+Z}$	$\overline{X}$	$\overline{Y}$	$\overline{Z}$	$\overline{X}{\cdot}\overline{Y}{\cdot}\overline{Z}$
0	0	0	0	1	1	1	1	1
0	0	1	1	0	1	1	0	0
0	1	0	1	0	1	0	1	0
0	1	1	1	0	1	0	0	0
1	0	0	1	0	0	1	1	0
1	0	1	1	0	0	1	0	0
1	1	0	1	0	0	0	1	0
1	1	1	1	0	0	0	0	0

← same →

Table 2.16 Proof of Theorem 10 by perfect induction.

Theorems 9 and 10 are collectively called *de Morgan's theorem*. This theorem can be stated as 'an entire function is complemented by replacing AND operators by OR operators, replacing OR operators by AND operators, and complementing variables and literals'. We make extensive use of de Morgan's theorem later.

An important rule in Boolean algebra is called the *principle of duality*. Any expression that is true is also true if AND is replaced by OR (and vice versa) and 1 replaced by 0 (and vice versa). Consider the following examples of duals.

Expression	Dual	
$X=X+X$	$X=X{\cdot}X$	(replace $+$ by $\cdot$)
$1=X+1$	$0=X{\cdot}0$	(replace $+$ by $\cdot$ and replace 1 by 0)

$X=X(X+Y)\qquad X=X+X{\cdot}Y \qquad$ (replace $\cdot$ by $+$ and replace $+$ by $\cdot$)

As you can see, the dual of each expression is also true.

Observations

When novices first encounter Boolean algebra, it is not uncommon for them to *invent* new theorems that are incorrect (because they superficially look like existing theorems). We include the following observations because they represent the most frequently encountered misconceptions.

Observation 1 $\overline{X{\cdot}Y}+X{\cdot}Y$ is not equal to 1
$\overline{X{\cdot}Y}+X{\cdot}Y$ cannot be simplified

Observation 2 $\overline{X}{\cdot}Y+X{\cdot}\overline{Y}$ is not equal to 1
$\overline{X}{\cdot}Y+X{\cdot}\overline{Y}$ cannot be simplified

Observation 3 $\overline{X \cdot Y}$ is not equal to $\overline{X} \cdot \overline{Y}$

Observation 4 $\overline{X + Y}$ is not equal to $\overline{X} + \overline{Y}$

Observation 5   If a theorem is true for a variable P, it's true for another variable Q. For example, if $P + P \cdot Z = P$, then $Q + Q \cdot Z = Q$. Obvious, isn't it? But students often have trouble dealing with situations in which P is replaced not by Q but by $\overline{P}$. In this case, if we have a theorem $X + X \cdot Y = X$, then it is also true that $\overline{X} + \overline{X} \cdot Y = \overline{X}$. All we have done is to replace X by $\overline{X}$.

Observation 6   If a theorem is true for a variable P, it is true for a compound variable $Q = P$. For example, if $P = X + Y \cdot Z$ then by using $P \cdot \overline{P} = 0$, we have $(X + Y \cdot Z) \cdot \overline{X + Y \cdot Z} = 0$ or $(X + Y \cdot Z)\,(\overline{X \cdot Y \cdot Z}) = 0$.

Observation 7   Table 2.17 provides a truth table for all possible functions of two variables A and B. These two variables have $2^2 = 4$ possible different combinations. We can associate a different function with each of these $4^2 = 16$ values to create all possible functions of two

variables. In other words there are only 16 possible types of 2-input gate, and Table 2.17 describes them all Some of the functions correspond to functions we've already met.

Examples of the use of Boolean algebra in simplifying equations

Having presented the basic rules of Boolean algebra, the next step is to show how it's used to simplify Boolean expressions. Such equations are often derived from the description of a particular logic circuit. By simplifying these equations you can sometimes produce a cheaper version of the logic circuit. However, the following equations are generally random functions chosen to demonstrate the rules of Boolean algebra.

(a) $X + \overline{Y} + \overline{X} \cdot Y + (X + \overline{Y}) \cdot \overline{X} \cdot Y$

(b) $\overline{X} \cdot Y \cdot \overline{Z} + \overline{X} \cdot Y \cdot Z + X \cdot \overline{Y} \cdot Z + X \cdot Y \cdot Z$

(c) $\overline{\overline{X} \cdot Y \cdot \overline{X} \cdot \overline{Z}}$

(d) $(X + \overline{Y})(\overline{X} + Z)(Y + \overline{Z})$

(e) $(W + X + Y \cdot Z)(\overline{W} + X)(\overline{X} + Y)$

(f) $W \cdot X \cdot \overline{Z} + \overline{X} \cdot Y \cdot Z + W \cdot X \cdot \overline{Y} + X \cdot Y \cdot Z + \overline{W} \cdot Y \cdot Z$

(g) $\overline{W} \cdot X \cdot Z + W \cdot Z + X \cdot Y \cdot \overline{Z} + \overline{W} \cdot X \cdot Y$

(h) $(X + Y + Z)(\overline{X} + Y + Z)(\overline{X} + Y + \overline{Z})$

Inputs		Functions															
A	B	F_0	F_1	F_2	F_3	F_4	F_5	F_6	F_7	F_8	F_9	F_{10}	F_{11}	F_{12}	F_{13}	F_{14}	F_{15}
0	0	0	1	0	1	0	1	0	1	0	1	0	1	0	1	0	1
0	1	0	0	1	1	0	0	1	1	0	0	1	1	0	0	1	1
1	0	0	0	0	0	1	1	1	1	0	0	0	0	1	1	1	1
1	1	0	0	0	0	0	0	0	0	1	1	1	1	1	1	1	1

Function	Expression	Name
F_0	0	
F_1	$\overline{A + B}$	NOR
F_2	$\overline{A} \cdot B$	
F_3	$\overline{A}$	NOT
F_4	$A \cdot \overline{B}$	
F_5	$\overline{B}$	NOT
F_6	$A \oplus B$	EOR
F_7	$\overline{A \cdot B}$	NAND
F_8	$A \cdot B$	AND
F_9	$\overline{A \oplus B}$	ENOR
F_{10}	B	
F_{11}	$\overline{A} \cdot B + \overline{A} \cdot \overline{B} + A \cdot B = \overline{A \cdot \overline{B}} = \overline{A} + B$	
F_{12}	A	
F_{13}	$A \cdot \overline{B} + A \cdot \overline{B} + A \cdot B = \overline{\overline{A} \cdot B} = A + \overline{B}$	
F_{14}	$A + B$	OR
F_{15}	1	

Table 2.17 All possible functions of two variables.

Solutions

When I simplify Boolean expressions, I try to keep the order of the variables alphabetical, making it easier to pick out logical groupings.

(a) $X+\overline{Y}+\overline{X}\cdot Y+(X+\overline{Y})\cdot\overline{X}\cdot Y=X+\overline{Y}+\overline{X}\cdot Y+X\cdot\overline{X}\cdot Y+\overline{X}\cdot\overline{Y}\cdot Y$

$\qquad\qquad\qquad\qquad\qquad=X+\overline{Y}+\overline{X}\cdot Y \qquad\qquad\qquad$ As $\overline{A}\cdot A=0$

$\qquad\qquad\qquad\qquad\qquad=X+Y+\overline{Y} \qquad\qquad\qquad\quad$ As $A+\overline{A}\cdot B=A+B$

$\qquad\qquad\qquad\qquad\qquad=1 \qquad\qquad\qquad\qquad\qquad\quad$ As $A+\overline{A}=1$

Note: When a Boolean expression can be reduced to the constant (literal) 1, the expression is always true and is independent of the variables.

(b) $\overline{X}\cdot Y\cdot\overline{Z}+\overline{X}\cdot Y\cdot Z+X\cdot\overline{Y}\cdot Z+X\cdot Y\cdot Z=\overline{X}\cdot Y\cdot(\overline{Z}+Z)+X\cdot Z\cdot(\overline{Y}+Y)$

$\qquad\qquad\qquad\qquad\qquad\qquad\qquad=\overline{X}\cdot Y\cdot(1)+X\cdot Z\cdot(1)$

$\qquad\qquad\qquad\qquad\qquad\qquad\qquad=\overline{X}\cdot Y+X\cdot Z$

(c) $\overline{\overline{\overline{X}\cdot Y}\cdot\overline{X\cdot Z}}=\overline{\overline{\overline{X}\cdot Y}}+\overline{\overline{X\cdot Z}} \qquad\qquad\qquad$ By Theorem 9

$\qquad\qquad\quad=\overline{X}\cdot Y+X\cdot Z \qquad\qquad\qquad\qquad$ As $\overline{\overline{F}}=F$

Note: Both expressions in examples (b) and (c) simplify to $\overline{X}\cdot Y+X\cdot Z$, demonstrating that these two expressions are equivalent. These equations are those of the multiplexer with (b) derived from the truth table (Table 2.9) and (c) from the circuit diagram of Fig. 2.19.

(d) $(X+\overline{Y})(\overline{X}+Z)(Y+\overline{Z})=(X\cdot\overline{X}+X\cdot Z+\overline{X}\cdot\overline{Y}+\overline{Y}\cdot Z)(Y+\overline{Z})$

$\qquad\qquad\qquad\qquad\qquad=(X\cdot Z+\overline{X}\cdot\overline{Y}+\overline{Y}\cdot Z)\cdot(Y+\overline{Z}) \qquad$ As $\overline{X}\cdot X=0$

$\qquad\qquad\qquad\qquad\qquad=(X\cdot Z+\overline{X}\cdot\overline{Y})(Y+\overline{Z}) \qquad\qquad\quad$ By Theorem 3

$\qquad\qquad\qquad\qquad\qquad=X\cdot Y\cdot Z+X\cdot\overline{Z}\cdot Z+\overline{X}\cdot\overline{Y}\cdot Y+\overline{X}\cdot\overline{Y}\cdot\overline{Z}$

$\qquad\qquad\qquad\qquad\qquad=X\cdot Y\cdot Z+\overline{X}\cdot\overline{Y}\cdot\overline{Z}$

(e) $(W+X+Y\cdot Z)(\overline{W}+X)(\overline{X}+Y)=(W\cdot\overline{W}+\overline{W}\cdot X+\overline{W}\cdot Y\cdot Z+W\cdot X+X\cdot X+X\cdot Y\cdot Z)(\overline{X}+Y)$

$\qquad\qquad\qquad\qquad\qquad\qquad=(\overline{W}\cdot X+\overline{W}\cdot Y\cdot Z+W\cdot X+X+X\cdot Y\cdot Z)(\overline{X}+Y)$

$\qquad\qquad\qquad\qquad\qquad\qquad=(X+\overline{W}\cdot Y\cdot Z)(\overline{X}+Y)$

$\qquad\qquad\qquad\qquad\qquad\qquad=X\cdot\overline{X}+X\cdot Y+\overline{W}\cdot\overline{X}\cdot Y\cdot Z+\overline{W}\cdot Y\cdot Y\cdot Z$

$\qquad\qquad\qquad\qquad\qquad\qquad=X\cdot Y+\overline{W}\cdot\overline{X}\cdot Y\cdot Z+\overline{W}\cdot Y\cdot Z$

$\qquad\qquad\qquad\qquad\qquad\qquad=X\cdot Y+\overline{W}\cdot Y\cdot Z(\overline{X}+1)$

$\qquad\qquad\qquad\qquad\qquad\qquad=X\cdot Y+\overline{W}\cdot Y\cdot Z$

Note: This procedure could have been shortened if we had noticed that $(\overline{W}+X)(\overline{X}+Y)$ was of the form $(A+B)\cdot(\overline{A}+C)=A\cdot C+\overline{A}\cdot B$ from Theorem 7. Continuing along these lines we get:

$(W+X+YZ)(\overline{W}+X)(\overline{X}+Y)=(W+X+YZ)(XY+\overline{W}\ \overline{X})$

$\qquad\qquad\qquad\qquad\qquad\qquad=WXY+W\overline{W}\ \overline{X}+XXY+\overline{W}\ \overline{X}X+XYYZ+\overline{W}\ \overline{X}YZ$

$\qquad\qquad\qquad\qquad\qquad\qquad=WXY+XY+XYZ+\overline{W}\ \overline{X}YZ$

$\qquad\qquad\qquad\qquad\qquad\qquad=XY(W+1+Z)+\overline{W}\ \overline{X}YZ \qquad\qquad$ As $W+1+Z=1$

$\qquad\qquad\qquad\qquad\qquad\qquad=XY+\overline{W}\ \overline{X}YZ$

$\qquad\qquad\qquad\qquad\qquad\qquad=XY+\overline{W}YZ \qquad\qquad\qquad\qquad\qquad$ By Theorem 2

(f) $WX\overline{Z}+\overline{X}YZ+WX\overline{Y}+XYZ+\overline{W}YZ=WX\overline{Z}+YZ(\overline{X}+X+\overline{W})+WX\overline{Y}$

$\qquad\qquad\qquad\qquad\qquad\qquad\qquad\qquad=WX\overline{Z}+YZ+WX\overline{Y}$

$\qquad\qquad\qquad\qquad\qquad\qquad\qquad\qquad=WX(\overline{Y}+\overline{Z})+YZ$

Note that $YZ=\overline{\overline{Y}+\overline{Z}}$ so we can write

$\qquad\qquad\qquad\qquad\qquad\qquad=W\cdot X(\overline{Y}+\overline{Z})+\overline{\overline{Y}+\overline{Z}}$

$\qquad\qquad\qquad\qquad\qquad\qquad=WX+YZ \qquad\qquad\qquad\qquad\qquad$ Because $A+\overline{A}\cdot B=A+B$

(g) $\overline{W}XZ + WZ + XY\overline{Z} + \overline{W}XY = Z(\overline{W}X + W) + XY\overline{Z} + \overline{W}XY$
$= Z(X + W) + XY\overline{Z} + \overline{W}XY$
$= XZ + WZ + XY\overline{Z} + \overline{W}XY$
$= X(Z + Y\overline{Z}) + WZ + \overline{W}XY$
$= X(Z + Y) + WZ + \overline{W}XY$
$= XZ + XY + WZ + \overline{W}XY$
$= XZ + XY(1 + \overline{W}) + WZ$
$= XZ + XY + WZ$

(h) $(X + Y + Z)(\overline{X} + Y + Z)(\overline{X} + Y + \overline{Z}) = (Y + Z)(\overline{X} + Y + \overline{Z})$ As $(A + B)(A + \overline{B}) = A$
$= Z(\overline{X} + Y) + Y\cdot\overline{Z}$ As $(A + B)(\overline{A} + C) = A\cdot C + \overline{A}\cdot B$
$= \overline{X}\cdot Z + Y\cdot Z + Y\cdot\overline{Z}$
$= \overline{X}\cdot Z + Y(Z + \overline{Z})$
$= \overline{X}\cdot Z + Y$

These examples illustrate the 'art' of manipulating Boolean expressions. It is difficult to be sure we have reached an optimal solution. Later we study Karnaugh maps, which provide an approach which gives us confidence that we've reached an optimal solution.

The design of a 2-bit multiplier

So far all the applications of Boolean algebra have been textbook examples without any real significance other than to provide a test-bed for the rules of Boolean algebra. The following example illustrates how Boolean algebra is applied to a practical problem.

A designer wishes to produce a 2-bit by 2-bit binary multiplier. The two 2-bit inputs are X_1, X_0 and Y_1, Y_0 and the 4-bit product at the output terminals is Z_3, Z_2, Z_1, Z_0. We have not yet introduced binary arithmetic (see Chapter 4), but nothing difficult is involved here. We begin by considering the block diagram of the system (Fig. 2.55) and constructing its truth table.

The multiplier has four inputs, X_1, X_0, Y_1, Y_0 (indicating a 16-line truth table) and four outputs. Table 2.18 provides a truth table for the binary multiplier. Each four-bit input represents the product of two 2-bit numbers so that, for example, an input of $X_1, X_0, Y_1, Y_0 = 1110$ represents the product

11×10 or 3×2. The corresponding output is a four-bit product, which, in this case, is 6 or 0110 in binary form.

From Table 2.15, we can derive expressions for the four outputs, Z_0 to Z_3. Whenever a truth table has m output

$X \times Y = Z$	Inputs				Output			
	X		Y		Z			
	X_1	X_0	Y_1	Y_0	Z_3	Z_2	Z_1	Z_0
$0 \times 0 = 0$	0	0	0	0	0	0	0	0
$0 \times 1 = 0$	0	0	0	1	0	0	0	0
$0 \times 2 = 0$	0	0	1	0	0	0	0	0
$0 \times 3 = 0$	0	0	1	1	0	0	0	0
$1 \times 0 = 0$	0	1	0	0	0	0	0	0
$1 \times 1 = 1$	0	1	0	1	0	0	0	1
$1 \times 2 = 2$	0	1	1	0	0	0	1	0
$1 \times 3 = 3$	0	1	1	1	0	0	1	1
$2 \times 0 = 0$	1	0	0	0	0	0	0	0
$2 \times 1 = 2$	1	0	0	1	0	0	1	0
$2 \times 2 = 4$	1	0	1	0	0	1	0	0
$2 \times 3 = 6$	1	0	1	1	0	1	1	0
$3 \times 0 = 0$	1	1	0	0	0	0	0	0
$3 \times 1 = 3$	1	1	0	1	0	0	1	1
$3 \times 2 = 6$	1	1	1	0	0	1	1	0
$3 \times 3 = 9$	1	1	1	1	1	0	0	1

Table 2.18 Truth table for a 2-bit by 2-bit multiplier.

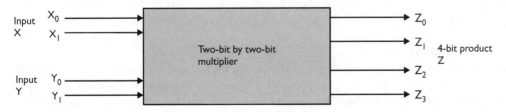

Input X X_0 — X_1 — Two-bit by two-bit multiplier — Z_0, Z_1, Z_2, Z_3 4-bit product Z

Input Y Y_0 — Y_1 —

Fig. 2.55 A 2-bit multiplier.

columns, a set of m Boolean equations must be derived. One equation is associated with each of the m columns. To derive an expression for Z_0, the four minterms in the Z_0 column are ORed logically.

$$
\begin{aligned}
Z_0 &= \overline{X}_1 \cdot X_0 \cdot \overline{Y}_1 \cdot Y_0 + \overline{X}_1 \cdot X_0 \cdot Y_1 \cdot Y_0 + X_1 \cdot X_0 \cdot \overline{Y}_1 \cdot Y_0 + X_1 \cdot X_0 \cdot Y_1 \cdot Y_0 \\
&= \overline{X}_1 \cdot X_0 \cdot Y_0 (\overline{Y}_1 + Y_1) + X_1 \cdot X_0 \cdot Y_0 (\overline{Y}_1 + Y_1) \\
&= \overline{X}_1 \cdot X_0 \cdot Y_0 + X_1 \cdot X_0 \cdot Y_0 \\
&= X_0 \cdot Y_0 (\overline{X}_1 + X_1) \\
&= X_0 \cdot Y_0
\end{aligned}
$$

$$
\begin{aligned}
Z_1 &= \overline{X}_1 \cdot X_0 \cdot Y_1 \cdot \overline{Y}_0 + \overline{X}_1 \cdot X_0 \cdot Y_1 \cdot Y_0 + X_1 \cdot \overline{X}_0 \cdot \overline{Y}_1 \cdot Y_0 + X_1 \cdot \overline{X}_0 \cdot Y_1 \cdot Y_0 + X_1 \cdot X_0 \cdot \overline{Y}_1 \cdot Y_0 + X_1 \cdot X_0 \cdot Y_1 \cdot \overline{Y}_0 \\
&= \overline{X}_1 \cdot X_0 \cdot Y_1 (\overline{Y}_0 + Y_0) + X_1 \cdot \overline{X}_0 \cdot Y_0 (\overline{Y}_1 + Y_1) + X_1 \cdot X_0 \cdot \overline{Y}_1 \cdot Y_0 + X_1 \cdot X_0 \cdot Y_1 \cdot \overline{Y}_0 \\
&= \overline{X}_1 \cdot X_0 \cdot Y_1 + X_1 \cdot \overline{X}_0 \cdot Y_0 + X_1 \cdot X_0 \cdot \overline{Y}_1 \cdot Y_0 + X_1 \cdot X_0 \cdot Y_1 \cdot \overline{Y}_0 \\
&= X_0 \cdot Y_1 (\overline{X}_1 + X_1 \cdot \overline{Y}_0) + X_1 \cdot Y_0 (\overline{X}_0 + X_0 \cdot \overline{Y}_1) \\
&= X_0 \cdot Y_1 (\overline{X}_1 + \overline{Y}_0) + X_1 \cdot Y_0 (\overline{X}_0 + \overline{Y}_1) \\
&= \overline{X}_1 \cdot X_0 \cdot Y_1 + X_0 \cdot Y_1 \cdot \overline{Y}_0 + X_1 \cdot \overline{X}_0 \cdot Y_0 + X_1 \cdot \overline{Y}_1 \cdot Y_0
\end{aligned}
$$

$$
\begin{aligned}
Z_2 &= X_1 \cdot \overline{X}_0 \cdot Y_1 \cdot \overline{Y}_0 + X_1 \cdot \overline{X}_0 \cdot Y_1 \cdot Y_0 + X_1 \cdot X_0 \cdot Y_1 \cdot \overline{Y}_0 \\
&= X_1 \cdot \overline{X}_0 \cdot Y_1 (\overline{Y}_0 + Y_0) + X_1 \cdot X_0 \cdot Y_1 \cdot \overline{Y}_0 \\
&= X_1 \cdot \overline{X}_0 \cdot Y_1 + X_1 \cdot X_0 \cdot Y_1 \cdot \overline{Y}_0 \\
&= X_1 \cdot Y_1 (\overline{X}_0 + X_0 \cdot \overline{Y}_0) \\
&= X_1 \cdot Y_1 (\overline{X}_0 + \overline{Y}_0) \\
&= X_1 \cdot \overline{X}_0 \cdot Y_1 + X_1 \cdot Y_1 \cdot \overline{Y}_0
\end{aligned}
$$

$$
Z_3 = X_1 \cdot X_0 \cdot Y_1 \cdot Y_0
$$

We have now obtained four simplified sum of products expressions for Z_0 to Z_3; that is,

$$
\begin{aligned}
Z_0 &= X_0 \cdot Y_0 \\
Z_1 &= \overline{X}_1 \cdot X_0 \cdot Y_1 + X_0 \cdot Y_1 \cdot \overline{Y}_0 + X_1 \cdot \overline{X}_0 \cdot Y_0 + X_1 \cdot \overline{Y}_1 \cdot Y_0 \\
Z_2 &= X_1 \cdot \overline{X}_0 \cdot Y_1 + X_1 \cdot Y_1 \cdot \overline{Y}_0 \\
Z_3 &= X_1 \cdot X_0 \cdot Y_1 \cdot Y_0
\end{aligned}
$$

It's interesting to note that each of the above expressions is *symmetric* in X and Y. This is to be expected—if the problem itself is symmetric in X and Y (i.e. $3 \times 1 = 1 \times 3$), then the result should also demonstrate this symmetry. There are many ways of realizing the expressions for Z_0 to Z_3. The circuit of Fig. 2.56 illustrates one possible way.

2.5.2 De Morgan's theorem

Theorems 9 and 10 provide the designer with a powerful tool because they enable an AND function to be implemented by an OR gate and inverter. Similarly, these theorems enable an OR gate to be implemented by an AND gate and inverter. We first demonstrate how de Morgan's theorem is applied to Boolean expressions and then show how circuits can be converted to NAND-only or NOR-only forms. You may wonder why anyone should wish to implement circuits in NAND (or NOR) logic only. There are several reasons for this, but, in general, NAND gates operate at a higher speed than AND gates and NAND gates can be built with fewer components (at the chip level). Later we shall examine in more detail how a circuit can be designed entirely with NAND gates only.

To apply de Morgan's theorem to a function the ANDs are changed into ORs, ORs into ANDs, and variables (and literals) are complemented. The following examples illustrate the application of de Morgan's theorem.

1. $F = \overline{\overline{X \cdot Y} + \overline{X \cdot Z}}$ We wish to apply de Morgan's theorem to the right-hand side

$= \overline{\overline{X \cdot Y}} \cdot \overline{\overline{X \cdot Z}}$ The $+$ becomes $\cdot$, and variables '$X \cdot Y$' and '$X \cdot Z$' are complemented

$= (\overline{X} + \overline{Y})(\overline{X} + \overline{Z})$ Variables $\overline{X \cdot Y}$ and $\overline{X \cdot Z}$ are themselves complemented

As you can see, the first step is to replace the OR by an AND operator. The compound variables $X \cdot Y$ and $X \cdot Z$ are complemented to get $\overline{X \cdot Y}$ and $\overline{X \cdot Z}$. The process is continued by applying de Morgan to the two complemented groups (i.e. $\overline{X \cdot Y}$ becomes $\overline{X} + \overline{Y}$ and $\overline{X \cdot Z}$ becomes $\overline{X} + \overline{Z}$).

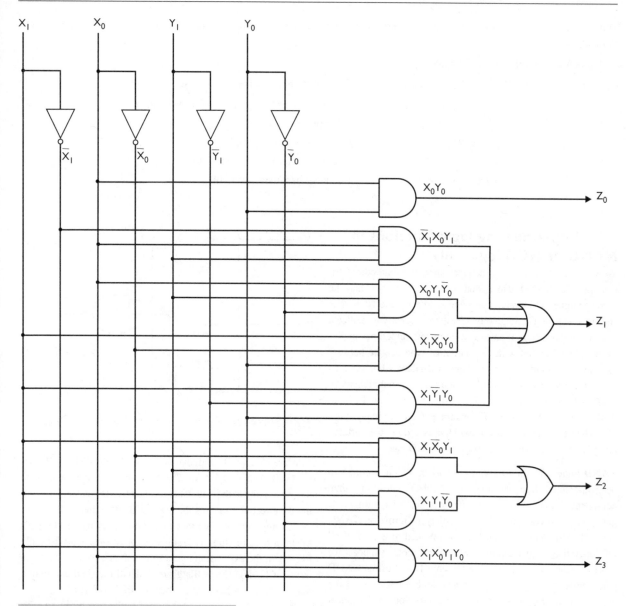

Fig. 2.56 A possible circuit for the 2-bit multiplier.

2. $F = \overline{\overline{A \cdot B} + C \cdot D + \overline{A \cdot D}}$

    $= \overline{A \cdot B} \cdot \overline{C \cdot D} \cdot \overline{A \cdot D}$ Replace $+$ by $\cdot$ and complement the product terms

    $= (\overline{A} + \overline{B})(\overline{C} + \overline{D})(\overline{A} + \overline{D})$ Expand the complemented product terms

3. $F = \overline{A \cdot B(C + E \cdot D)}$ This is a product

    $= \overline{A} + \overline{B} + \overline{C + E \cdot D}$ Replace $\cdot$ by $+$ and complement variables

    $= \overline{A} + \overline{B} + \overline{C} \cdot \overline{E \cdot D}$ Evaluate the complemented expression (change $+$ to $\cdot$)

    $= \overline{A} + \overline{B} + \overline{C} \cdot (\overline{E} + \overline{D})$ Final step, evaluate $\overline{E \cdot D}$

This example demonstrates how you have to keep applying de Morgan's theorem until there are no complemented terms left to evaluate.

4. A proof of Theorem 8 by de Morgan's theorem

$(X+Y) \cdot (\overline{X}+Z) \cdot (Y+Z) = \overline{\overline{(X+Y) \cdot (\overline{X}+Z) \cdot (Y+Z)}}$ Complement twice because $X = \overline{\overline{X}}$.

$= \overline{\overline{X+Y} + \overline{\overline{X}+Z} + \overline{Y+Z}}$ Remove inner bar by applying de Morgan

$= \overline{\overline{\overline{X} \cdot \overline{Y}} + X \cdot \overline{Z} + \overline{Y} \cdot \overline{Z}}$ Complement the 2-variable groups

$= \overline{\overline{X} \cdot \overline{Y} + X \cdot \overline{Z}}$ Use Theorem 3 to simplify

$= \overline{\overline{X} \cdot \overline{Y}} \cdot \overline{X \cdot \overline{Z}}$ Remove outer bar, change $+$ to $\cdot$

$= (X+Y)(\overline{X}+Z)$ Remove bars over 2-variable groups

2.5.3 Implementing logic functions in NAND or NOR logic only

We've already stated that some gates are better than others; for example, the NAND gate is both faster and cheaper than the corresponding AND gate. The same is true for the NOR gate and the OR gate. Consequently, it's often necessary to realize a circuit using one type of gate only. Engineers sometimes implement a digital circuit with one particular type of gate because there is not a uniform range of gates available. For obvious economic reasons manufacturers don't sell a comprehensive range of gates (e.g. 2-input AND, 3-input AND, ..., 10-input AND, 2-input OR, ... etc.). For example, there are many types of NAND gate, from the quad two-input NAND to the thirteen-input NAND, but there are few types of AND gates.

NAND logic   We first look at the way in which circuits can be constructed from nothing but NAND gates and then demonstrate that we can also fabricate circuits with NOR gates only. To construct a circuit solely in terms of NAND gates, de Morgan's theorem must be invoked to get rid of all OR operators in the expression. For example, suppose we wish to generate the expression $F = A + B + C$ using NAND gates only. We begin by applying a double negation to the expression, as this does not alter the expression's value but it does give us the opportunity to apply de Morgan's theorem.

$F = A + B + C$ The original expression using OR logic

$F = \overline{\overline{F}} = \overline{\overline{A+B+C}}$ Double negation has no effect on the value of a function

$F = \overline{\overline{A} \cdot \overline{B} \cdot \overline{C}}$ Apply de Morgan's theorem

We have now converted the OR function into a NAND function. The three NOT functions that generate $\overline{A}$, $\overline{B}$, and $\overline{C}$ can be implemented in terms of NOT gates or by means of two-input NAND gates with their inputs connected together.

Figure 2.57 shows how the function $F = A + B + C$ can be implemented in NAND logic only. If the inputs of a NAND

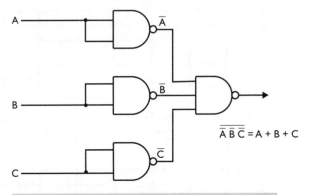

Fig. 2.57 Implementing $F = A + B + C$ with NAND logic only.

gate are A and B, and the output is C, then $C = \overline{A \cdot B}$. But if $A = B$ then $C = \overline{A \cdot A}$ or $C = \overline{A}$. You can better understand this by looking at the truth table for the NAND gate, and imagining the effect of removing the lines A, B = 0, 1 and A, B = 1, 0.

It's important to note that we are not applying de Morgan's theorem here to simplify Boolean expressions. We wish only to convert the expression into a form suitable for realization in terms of NAND (or NOR) gates. Indeed, the final expression may be much more complex than its original form.

By applying the same techniques to the two-bit by two-bit multiplier we designed earlier we can convert the expressions for the four outputs into NAND-only logic.

$Z_0 = X_0 Y_0 = \overline{\overline{X_0 Y_0}}$ (i.e. NAND gate follwed by NOT gate = AND gate)

$Z_1 = \overline{X_1} X_0 Y_1 + X_0 Y_1 \overline{Y_0} + X_1 \overline{X_0} Y_0 + X_1 \overline{Y_1} Y_0$

$= \overline{X_1} X_1 Y_0 + X_0 Y_1 \overline{Y_0} + X_1 \overline{X_0} Y_0 + X_1 \overline{Y_1} Y_0$

$= \overline{\overline{\overline{X_1} X_0 Y_1} \cdot \overline{X_0 Y_1 \overline{Y_0}} \cdot \overline{X_1 \overline{X_0} Y_0} \cdot \overline{X_1 \overline{Y_1} Y_0}}$

$Z_2 = X_1 \overline{X_0} Y_1 + X_1 Y_1 \overline{Y_0}$

$= \overline{\overline{X_1 \overline{X_0} Y_1 + X_1 Y_1 \overline{Y_0}}}$

$= \overline{\overline{X_1 \overline{X_0} Y_1} \cdot \overline{X_1 Y_1 \overline{Y_0}}}$

$Z_3 = X_1 X_0 Y_1 Y_0$

$\quad = \overline{\overline{X_1 X_0 Y_1 Y_0}}$

Figure 2.58 shows the implementation of the multiplier in terms of NAND logic only. Note that this circuit performs exactly the same function as the circuit of Fig. 2.56.

NOR logic The procedures we've just used may equally be applied to the implementation of circuits using NOR gates only. By way of illustration, the value of Z_3 in the 2-bit multiplier can be converted to NOR logic form in the following way:

$Z_3 = X_1 \cdot X_0 \cdot Y_1 \cdot Y_0$

$\quad = \overline{\overline{X_1 \cdot X_0 \cdot Y_1 \cdot Y_0}}$

$\quad = \overline{\overline{X_1} + \overline{X_0} + \overline{Y_1} + \overline{Y_0}}$

Note that negation may be implemented by an inverter or by a NOR gate with its inputs connected together.

As a final example of NAND logic consider Fig. 2.59. A Boolean expression can be expressed in sum-of-products form as $A \cdot B + C \cdot D$. This expression can be converted to NAND logic as

$$\overline{\overline{A \cdot B} \cdot \overline{C \cdot D}}$$

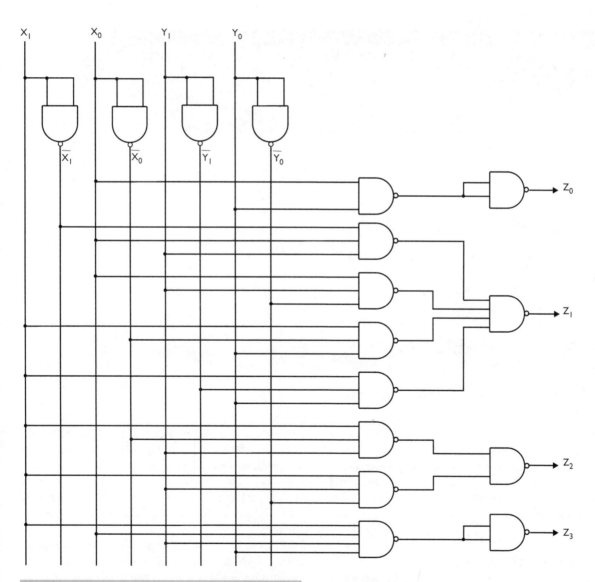

Fig. 2.58 Implementing the multiplier circuit in NAND logic only.

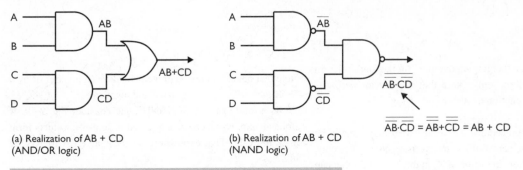

(a) Realization of AB + CD
(AND/OR logic)

(b) Realization of AB + CD
(NAND logic)

$$\overline{\overline{AB}\cdot\overline{CD}} = \overline{\overline{AB}+\overline{CD}} = AB + CD$$

Fig. 2.59 Implementing the function $A\cdot B + C\cdot D$ in AND/OR and NAND logic.

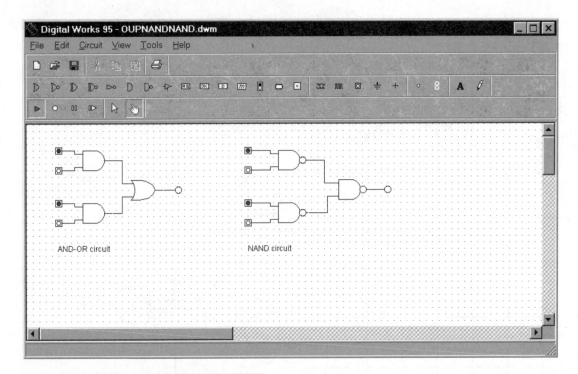

Fig. 2.60 Using Digital Works to investigate two circuits.

Note how the three-gate circuit in Fig. 2.59(a) can be converted into the three-gate NAND circuit of Fig. 2.59(b). Figure 2.60 shows the construction of the two versions of AB + CD in Digital Works. We have provided an LED at each output and manually selectable inputs to enable you to investigate the circuits.

2.5.4 Karnaugh maps

The *Karnaugh map*, or more simply the *K-map*, is a graphical technique for the representation and simplification of a Boolean expression. Although the Karnaugh map can simplify Boolean equations with five or six variables, we will use it to solve problems with only three or four variables. Other techniques, such as the *Quine–McCluskey* method, can be applied to the simplification of Boolean expressions in more than six variables. However, these techniques are beyond the scope of this book.

When you use algebraic techniques to simplify a Boolean expression you sometimes reach a point at which you can't proceed, because you're unable to find further simplifications. It's not easy to determine whether the equation is indeed in its simplest form or whether you just can't see the next step. Karnaugh maps show unambiguously when a Boolean expression has been reduced to its most simple form.

The Karnaugh map is just a two-dimensional form of the truth table, drawn in such a way that the simplification of a Boolean expression can immediately be seen from the location of 1s on the map. A system with n variables has 2^n lines in its truth table and 2^n squares on its Karnaugh map. Each square on the Karnaugh map is associated with a line (i.e. minterm) in the truth table. Figure 2.61 shows Karnaugh maps for one to four variables.

As you can see from Fig. 2.61, each line in a truth table is mapped onto a Karnaugh map; for example, in four variables each logical combination from $A·B·C·D$ to $\overline{A}·\overline{B}·\overline{C}·\overline{D}$ has a unique location. However, the key to the Karnaugh map is the *layout* of the squares. Adjacent squares differ by only one variable. By *adjacent* we mean horizontally and vertically adjacent, but not diagonally adjacent. For example, if

you look at the three-variable map of Fig. 2.61(c) you will see that the leftmost two terms on the top line are $\overline{A}·\overline{B}·\overline{C}$ and $\overline{A}·B·\overline{C}$. The only difference between these terms is $\overline{B}$ and B.

Figure 2.62 demonstrates the structure of a four-variable Karnaugh map with variables A, B, C, and D. This map has been repeated four times and, in each case, the region in which the selected variable is true has been shaded. The unshaded portion of each map represents the region in which the chosen variable is false.

We will soon see that you need to develop three skills to use a Karnaugh map. The first is to plot terms on the map (i.e. transfer a truth table or a Boolean expression onto the map). The second skill is the ability to group the 1s you've plotted on the map. The third skill is to read the groups of 1s on the map and express each group as a product term.

We now use a simple three-variable map to demonstrate how a truth table is mapped onto a Karnaugh map. One- and

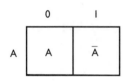

(a) One-variable Karnaugh map

(b) Two-variable Karnaugh map

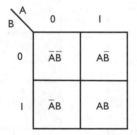

(c) Three-variable Karnaugh map

(d) Four-variable Karnaugh map

Fig. 2.61 The Karnaugh map.

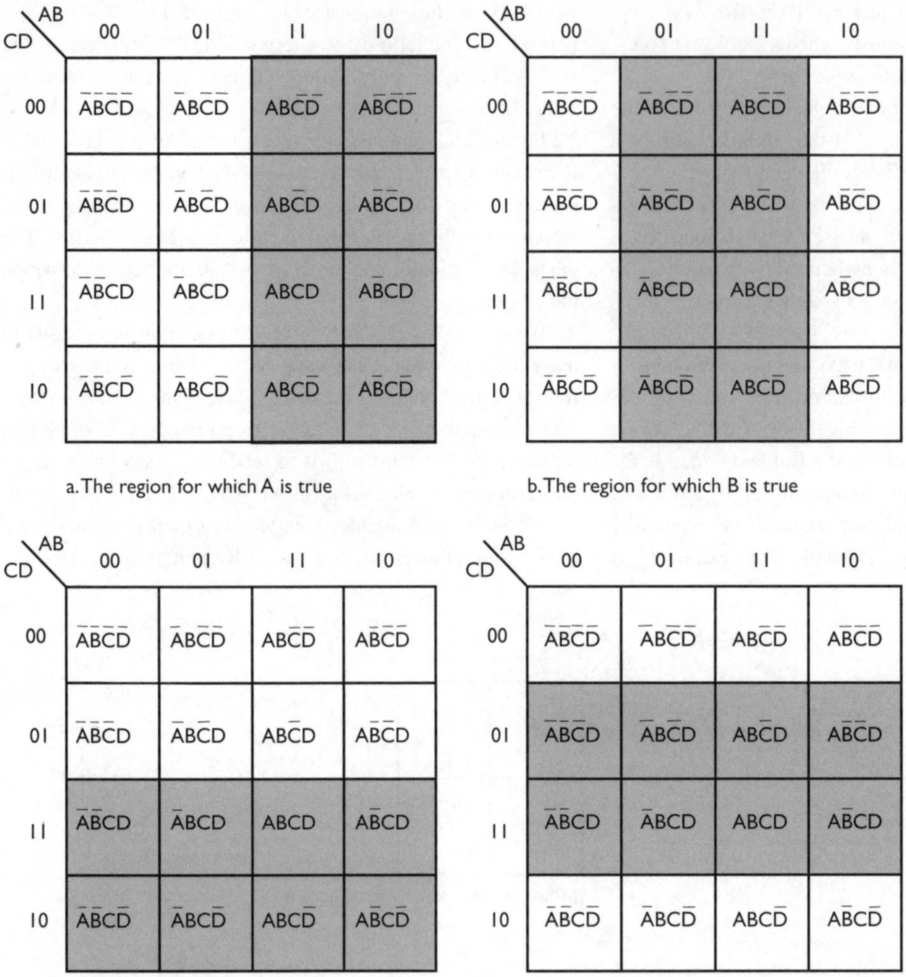

a. The region for which A is true (columns 11 and 10 shaded)

CD \ AB	00	01	11	10
00	$\overline{A}\,\overline{B}\,\overline{C}\,\overline{D}$	$\overline{A}\,B\,\overline{C}\,\overline{D}$	$A\,B\,\overline{C}\,\overline{D}$	$A\,\overline{B}\,\overline{C}\,\overline{D}$
01	$\overline{A}\,\overline{B}\,\overline{C}\,D$	$\overline{A}\,B\,\overline{C}\,D$	$A\,B\,\overline{C}\,D$	$A\,\overline{B}\,\overline{C}\,D$
11	$\overline{A}\,\overline{B}\,C\,D$	$\overline{A}\,B\,C\,D$	$A\,B\,C\,D$	$A\,\overline{B}\,C\,D$
10	$\overline{A}\,\overline{B}\,C\,\overline{D}$	$\overline{A}\,B\,C\,\overline{D}$	$A\,B\,C\,\overline{D}$	$A\,\overline{B}\,C\,\overline{D}$

b. The region for which B is true (columns 01 and 11 shaded)

CD \ AB	00	01	11	10
00	$\overline{A}\,\overline{B}\,\overline{C}\,\overline{D}$	$\overline{A}\,B\,\overline{C}\,\overline{D}$	$A\,B\,\overline{C}\,\overline{D}$	$A\,\overline{B}\,\overline{C}\,\overline{D}$
01	$\overline{A}\,\overline{B}\,\overline{C}\,D$	$\overline{A}\,B\,\overline{C}\,D$	$A\,B\,\overline{C}\,D$	$A\,\overline{B}\,\overline{C}\,D$
11	$\overline{A}\,\overline{B}\,C\,D$	$\overline{A}\,B\,C\,D$	$A\,B\,C\,D$	$A\,\overline{B}\,C\,D$
10	$\overline{A}\,\overline{B}\,C\,\overline{D}$	$\overline{A}\,B\,C\,\overline{D}$	$A\,B\,C\,\overline{D}$	$A\,\overline{B}\,C\,\overline{D}$

c. The region for which C is true (rows 11 and 10 shaded)

CD \ AB	00	01	11	10
00	$\overline{A}\,\overline{B}\,\overline{C}\,\overline{D}$	$\overline{A}\,B\,\overline{C}\,\overline{D}$	$A\,B\,\overline{C}\,\overline{D}$	$A\,\overline{B}\,\overline{C}\,\overline{D}$
01	$\overline{A}\,\overline{B}\,\overline{C}\,D$	$\overline{A}\,B\,\overline{C}\,D$	$A\,B\,\overline{C}\,D$	$A\,\overline{B}\,\overline{C}\,D$
11	$\overline{A}\,\overline{B}\,C\,D$	$\overline{A}\,B\,C\,D$	$A\,B\,C\,D$	$A\,\overline{B}\,C\,D$
10	$\overline{A}\,\overline{B}\,C\,\overline{D}$	$\overline{A}\,B\,C\,\overline{D}$	$A\,B\,C\,\overline{D}$	$A\,\overline{B}\,C\,\overline{D}$

d. The region for which D is true (rows 01 and 11 shaded)

CD \ AB	00	01	11	10
00	$\overline{A}\,\overline{B}\,\overline{C}\,\overline{D}$	$\overline{A}\,B\,\overline{C}\,\overline{D}$	$A\,B\,\overline{C}\,\overline{D}$	$A\,\overline{B}\,\overline{C}\,\overline{D}$
01	$\overline{A}\,\overline{B}\,\overline{C}\,D$	$\overline{A}\,B\,\overline{C}\,D$	$A\,B\,\overline{C}\,D$	$A\,\overline{B}\,\overline{C}\,D$
11	$\overline{A}\,\overline{B}\,C\,D$	$\overline{A}\,B\,C\,D$	$A\,B\,C\,D$	$A\,\overline{B}\,C\,D$
10	$\overline{A}\,\overline{B}\,C\,\overline{D}$	$\overline{A}\,B\,C\,\overline{D}$	$A\,B\,C\,\overline{D}$	$A\,\overline{B}\,C\,\overline{D}$

Fig. 2.62 Regions of a Karnaugh map.

two-variable maps represent trivial cases and aren't considered further. Figure 2.63 shows the truth table for a three-variable function and the corresponding Karnaugh map. Each of the three 1s in the truth table is mapped onto its appropriate square on the Karnaugh map.

A three-variable Karnaugh map has four vertical columns, one for each of the four possible values of two out of the three variables. For example, if the three variables are A, B, and C, the four columns represent all the possible combinations of A and B. Thus, the first (leftmost) column is labeled 00 and represents the region for which A = 0, B = 0. The next column is labeled 01, and represents the region for which A = 0, B = 1. The next column is labeled 11 (not 10), and represents the region for which A = 1, B = 1. Remember that adjacent columns differ by only one variable at a time. The fourth column, 10, represents the region for which A = 1, B = 0. In fact, a Karnaugh map is made up of all possible 2^n *minterms* for a system with *n* variables.

The three-variable Karnaugh map in Fig. 2.63 has two horizontal rows, the upper row corresponding to C = 0 and the lower to C = 1. Any square on this Karnaugh map represents a unique combination of the three variables, from $A \cdot B \cdot C$ to $\overline{A} \cdot \overline{B} \cdot \overline{C}$

Figure 2.63 demonstrates how a function of three variables, $F = \overline{A} \cdot \overline{B} \cdot \overline{C} + \overline{A} \cdot B \cdot \overline{C} + A \cdot \overline{B} \cdot C$ is plotted on a Karnaugh map. If it isn't clear how the entries in the table are plotted on

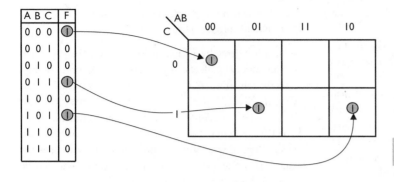

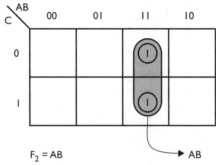

Fig. 2.63 Relationship between a Karnaugh map and truth table.

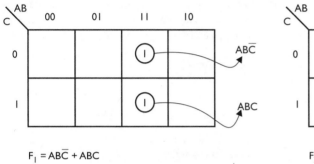

Fig. 2.64 Plotting two functions on Karnaugh maps.

the Karnaugh map, examine Fig. 2.63 and work out which cell on the map is associated with each line in the table. A square containing a logical 1 is said to be covered by a 1.

At this point it's worth noting that no two 1s plotted on the Karnaugh map of Fig. 2.63 are adjacent to each other, and that the function $F = \overline{A}\cdot\overline{B}\cdot\overline{C} + \overline{A}\cdot B\cdot C + A\cdot\overline{B}\cdot C$ cannot be simplified. To keep the Karnaugh maps as clear and uncluttered as possible, squares that do not contain a 1 are left unmarked even though they must, of course, contain a 0.

Consider Fig. 2.64, in which the function $F_1 = A\cdot B\cdot\overline{C} + A\cdot B\cdot C$ is plotted on the left-hand map. The two minterms in this function are $A\cdot B\cdot\overline{C}$ and $A\cdot B\cdot C$ and occupy the cells for which $A = 1, B = 1, C = 0$, and $A = 1, B = 1, C = 1$, respectively. If you still have difficulty plotting minterms, just think of them as coordinates of squares; for example, $A\cdot B\cdot\overline{C}$ has the coordinates 1,1, 0 and corresponds to the square ABC = 110.

In the Karnaugh map for F_1 two separate adjacent squares are covered. Now look at the Karnaugh map for $F_2 = A\cdot B$ at the right-hand side of Fig. 2.64. In this case a *group* of two squares is covered, corresponding to the column $A = 1, B = 1$. As the function for F_2 does not involve the variable C, a 1 is entered in the squares for which $A = B = 1$ and $C = 0$, and $A = B = 1$ and $C = 1$; that is, a 1 is entered for all values of C

for which AB = 11. When plotting a product term like A·B on the Karnaugh map, all you have to do is to locate the region for which AB = 11.

It is immediately obvious that both Karnaugh maps in Fig. 2.64 are identical, so that $F_1 = F_2$ and $A\cdot B\cdot\overline{C} + A\cdot B\cdot C = A\cdot B$. From the rules of Boolean algebra $A\cdot B\cdot C + A\cdot B\cdot\overline{C} = A\cdot B\cdot(C + \overline{C}) = A\cdot B(1) = A\cdot B$. It should be apparent that two adjacent squares in a Karnaugh map can be grouped together to form a single simpler term. It is this property that the Karnaugh map exploits to simplify expressions.

Simplifying sum-of-product expressions with a Karnaugh map

The first step in simplifying a Boolean expression by means of a Karnaugh map is to plot all the 1s (i.e. minterms) in the function's truth table on the Karnaugh map. The next step is to combine adjacent 1s into groups of one, two, four, eight, or sixteen. The groups of minterms should be as large as possible—a single group of four minterms yields a simpler expression than two groups of two minterms. The final stage in simplifying an expression is reached when each of the groups of minterms (i.e. the product terms) are ORed together to form the simplified sum-of-products expression. This process is best demonstrated by means of examples. In what follows, a four-variable map is chosen to illustrate the examples.

Transferring a truth table to a Karnaugh map is easy because each 1 in the truth table is placed in a unique square on the map. We now have to demonstrate how the product terms of a general Boolean expression are plotted on the map. Figures 2.65–2.70 present six functions plotted on Karnaugh maps. In these diagrams various *sum-of-products* expressions have been plotted directly from the equations themselves, rather than from the minterms of the truth table. The following notes should help in understanding these diagrams.

1. For a four-variable Karnaugh map:

   one-variable product term covers 8 squares
   two-variable product terms cover 4 squares

three-variable product terms cover 2 squares
four-variable product terms cover 1 squares

2. A square covered by a 1 may belong to more than one term in the sum-of-products expression. For example, in Fig. 2.66 the minterm $\overline{A}\cdot\overline{B}\cdot C\cdot D$ belongs to two groups, $\overline{A}\cdot\overline{B}$ and $C\cdot D$. If a 1 on the Karnaugh map appears in two groups, it is equivalent to adding the corresponding minterm to the overall expression for the function plotted on the map *twice*. Repeating a term in a Boolean expression does not alter the value of the expression, because one of the axioms of Boolean algebra is $X + X = X$.

3. The Karnaugh map is not a square or a rectangle as it appears in these diagrams. A Karnaugh map is a *torus* or *doughnut* shape. That is, the top edge is adjacent to the

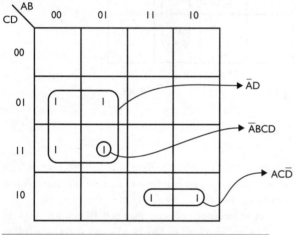

The two-variable term $\overline{A}\cdot D$ covers 4 squares (the region A = 0 and D = 1). Note that the term $\overline{A}\cdot B\cdot C\cdot D$ covers one square and is part of the same group as $\overline{A}\cdot D$.

Fig. 2.65 Plotting $F = \overline{A}D + AC\overline{D} + \overline{A}BCD$ on a Karnaugh map.

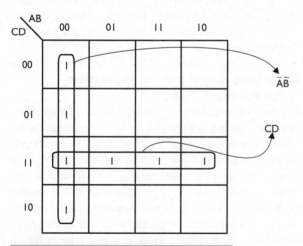

The two-variable term $\overline{A}\cdot\overline{B}$ covers 4 squares (the region A = 0 and B = 0). The two-variable term $C\cdot D$ covers 4 squares (the region C = 1 and D = 1). The term $\overline{A}\cdot\overline{B}\cdot C\cdot D$ is common to both groups.

Fig. 2.66 Plotting $F = \overline{A}\,\overline{B} + CD$ on a Karnaugh map.

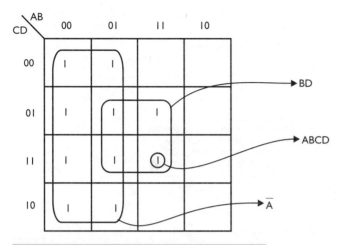

The one-variable term $\overline{A}$ covers 4 squares (the region A = 0).

Fig. 2.67 Plotting $F = \overline{A} + BD + ABCD$ on a Karnaugh map.

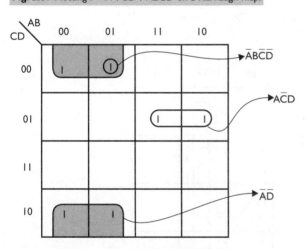

The four-variable term $\overline{A} \cdot \overline{D}$ covers 4 squares (the region A = 0, D = 0). Note that two squares are at the top (A = 0, C = 0, D = 0) and two are at the bottom (A = 0, C = 1, D = 0).

Fig. 2.68 Plotting $F = \overline{A}\,\overline{D} + A\overline{C}D + \overline{A}BC\overline{D}$ on a Karnaugh map.

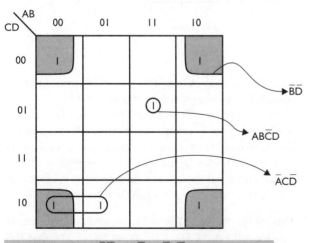

The four-variable term $\overline{B} \cdot \overline{D}$ covers 4 squares (the region B = 0, D = 0). In this case the adjacent squares are the corner squares. If you examines any pair of horizontally or vertically adjacent corners, you will find that they differ in one variable only.

Fig. 2.69 Plotting $F = \overline{B}\,\overline{D} + AB\overline{C}D + \overline{A}C\overline{D}$ on a Karnaugh map.

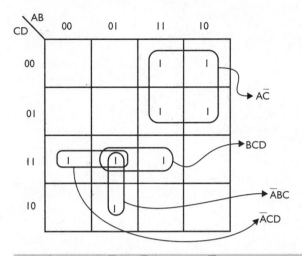

Three two-variable groups overlap. In this example, the square (i.e., minterm) $\overline{A}\cdot B\cdot C\cdot D$ belongs to groups $B\cdot C\cdot D$, $\overline{A}\cdot B\cdot C$, and $\overline{A}\cdot C\cdot D$.

Fig. 2.70 Plotting $F = \overline{A}CD + \overline{A}BC + BCD + A\overline{C}$ on a Karnaugh map.

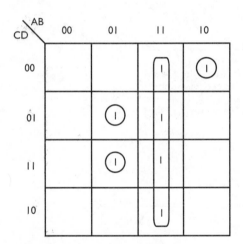 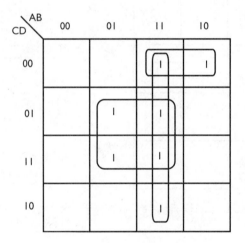

Fig. 2.71 Karnaugh map for Example 1.

bottom edge and the left-hand edge is adjacent to the right-hand edge. For example, in Fig. 2.68 the term $\overline{A}\cdot\overline{D}$ covers the two minterms $\overline{A}\cdot\overline{B}\cdot\overline{C}\cdot\overline{D}$ and $\overline{A}\cdot B\cdot\overline{C}\cdot\overline{D}$ at the top, and the two minterms $\overline{A}\cdot\overline{B}\cdot C\cdot\overline{D}$ and $\overline{A}\cdot B\cdot C\cdot\overline{D}$ at the bottom of the map. Similarly, in Fig. 2.69 the term $\overline{B}\cdot\overline{D}$ covers all four corners of the map. Whenever a group of terms extends across the edge of a Karnaugh map, we have shaded it to emphasize the wrap-around nature of the map.

4. In order either to read a product term from the map or to plot a product term on the map, it is necessary to ask the question, what minterms (squares) are covered by this term?

Consider the term $\overline{A}\cdot D$ in Fig. 2.65. This term covers all squares for which $A = 0$ and $D = 1$ (a group of 4).

Having shown how terms are plotted on the Karnaugh map, the next step is to apply the map to the simplification of the expressions. Once again, we demonstrate this process by means of examples. In each case, the original function is plotted on the left-hand side of the figure and the regrouped ones (i.e. minterms) are plotted on the right-hand side.

Example 1   Figure 2.71 gives a Karnaugh map for the expression $F = A\cdot B + \overline{A}\cdot B\cdot\overline{C}\cdot D + \overline{A}\cdot B\cdot C\cdot D + A\cdot\overline{B}\cdot\overline{C}\cdot D$. The simplified function is $F = A\cdot B + B\cdot D + A\cdot\overline{C}\cdot D$.

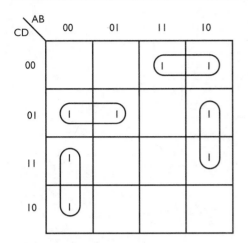
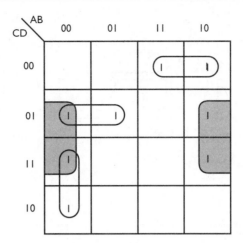

Fig. 2.72 Karnaugh map for Example 2.

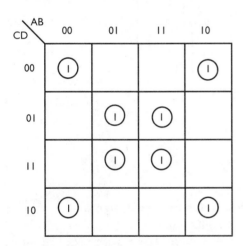
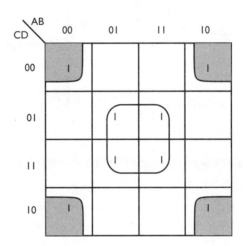

Fig. 2.73 Karnaugh map for Example 3.

Example 2 $F = A \cdot \overline{C} \cdot \overline{D} + \overline{A} \cdot \overline{B} \cdot C + \overline{A} \cdot \overline{C} \cdot D + A \cdot \overline{B} \cdot D$ (Fig. 2.72). In this case there is only one regrouping possible. The simplified function is $F = \overline{B} \cdot D + A \cdot \overline{C} \cdot \overline{D} + \overline{A} \cdot \overline{C} \cdot D + \overline{A} \cdot \overline{B} \cdot C$.

Example 3 $F = \overline{A} \cdot \overline{B} \cdot \overline{C} \cdot \overline{D} + A \cdot \overline{B} \cdot \overline{C} \cdot \overline{D} + \overline{A} \cdot B \cdot \overline{C} \cdot D + A \cdot B \cdot \overline{C} \cdot D + \overline{A} \cdot B \cdot C \cdot D + A \cdot B \cdot C \cdot D + \overline{A} \cdot \overline{B} \cdot C \cdot \overline{D} + A \cdot \overline{B} \cdot C \cdot \overline{D}$ (Fig. 2.73). This function can be simplified to two product terms with the result that $F = \overline{B} \cdot \overline{D} + B \cdot D$.

Example 4 $F = \overline{A} \cdot B \cdot \overline{C} + \overline{A} \cdot \overline{B} \cdot C + \overline{A} \cdot B \cdot \overline{C} + A \cdot B \cdot \overline{C} + A \cdot B \cdot C$ (Fig. 2.74). In this case we can see that it is possible to group the minterms together in two ways, both of which are equally valid; that is, there are two equally correct simplifications of this expression. We can write either $F = \overline{A} \cdot \overline{B} + \overline{A} \cdot \overline{C} + A \cdot B$ or $F = \overline{A} \cdot \overline{B} + B \cdot \overline{C} + A \cdot B$.

Applications of Karnaugh maps

Apart from the use of Karnaugh maps in the simplification of Boolean expressions, Karnaugh maps can be used to convert *sum-of-products* expressions to the corresponding *product-of-sums* form. The first step in this process involves the generation of the complement of the sum-of-products expression.

Example 5 The example provided by the Karnaugh map in Fig. 2.75 demonstrates how we can use the Karnaugh map to obtain the complement of a sum-of-products expression. Consider the expression $F = \overline{C} \cdot \overline{D} + \overline{A} \cdot \overline{B} + A \cdot \overline{B} + C \cdot \overline{D}$ (left-hand side of Fig. 2.75). If the squares on a Karnaugh map covered by 1s represent the function F, then the remaining squares covered by 0s must represent $\overline{F}$, the complement of F.

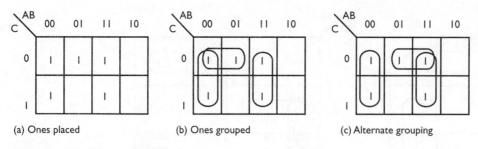

(a) Ones placed   (b) Ones grouped   (c) Alternate grouping

Fig. 2.74 Karnaugh map for Example 4.

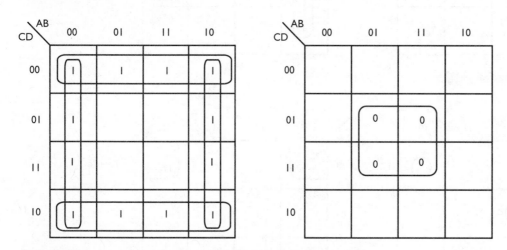

Fig. 2.75 Example 5—using a Karnaugh map to obtain the complement of a function.

In the right-hand side of Fig. 2.75, we have plotted the complement of this function. The group of four 0s corresponds to the expression $\overline{F} = B \cdot D$

Example 6 We are now going to use a Karnaugh map to convert of sum-of-products expression into a product-of-sums expression. In Example 5, we used the Karnaugh map to get the complement of a function in a product-of-sums form. If we then complement the complement, we get the function but in a sum-of-products form (because de Morgan's theorem allows us to step between SoP and PoS forms). Let's convert $F = A \cdot B \cdot C + \overline{C} \cdot D + \overline{A} \cdot B \cdot D$ into product of sums form (Fig. 2.76).

The complement of F is defined by the zeros on the map and may be read from the right-hand map as

$$\overline{F} = \overline{C} \cdot \overline{D} + \overline{B} \cdot C + \overline{A} \cdot \overline{D}$$
$$F = \overline{\overline{C} \cdot \overline{D} + \overline{B} \cdot C + \overline{A} \cdot \overline{D}}$$
$$= (C + D)(B + \overline{C})(A + D)$$

We now have an expression for F in product-of-sums form.

Using the Karnaugh map to design a circuit with NAND logic

Now that we've demonstrated how Karnaugh maps are used to simplify and transform Boolean expressions, we're going to apply the Karnaugh map to the design of a simple logic circuit using NAND logic only.

A fire detection system protects a room against fire by means of four sensors. These sensors comprise a flame detector, a smoke detector, and two high-temperature detectors located at the opposite ends of the room. Because such sensors are prone to errors (i.e. false alarms or the failure to register a fire), the fire alarm is triggered only when two or more of the sensors indicate the presence of a fire simultaneously. The output of a sensor is a logical 1 if a fire is detected, otherwise a logical 0.

The output of the fire alarm circuit is a logical 1 whenever two or more of its inputs are a logical one. Table 2.19 gives the truth table for the fire detector circuit. The inputs from the four sensors are labeled A, B, C, and D. Because it is necessary only to detect two or more logical 1s on any of the lines,

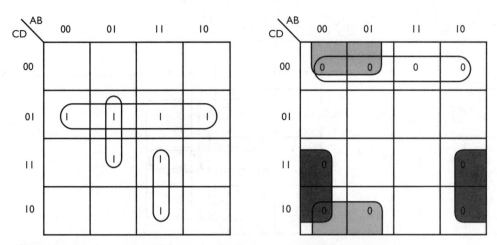

Fig. 2.76 Example—using a Karnaugh map to convert an expression from SoP to PoS form.

Inputs				Output
A	B	C	D	F
0	0	0	0	0
0	0	0	1	0
0	0	1	0	0
0	0	1	1	1
0	1	0	0	0
0	1	0	1	1
0	1	1	0	1
0	1	1	1	1
1	0	0	0	0
1	0	0	1	1
1	0	1	0	1
1	0	1	1	1
1	1	0	0	1
1	1	0	1	1
1	1	1	0	1
1	1	1	1	1

Table 2.19 Truth table for a fire detector.

the actual order of A, B, C, and D columns doesn't matter. The circuit is to be constructed from two-input and three-input NAND gates only.

The output of the circuit, F, can be written down directly from Table 2.19 by ORing the 11 minterms to get the expression

$$F = \overline{A} \cdot \overline{B} \cdot C \cdot D + \overline{A} \cdot B \cdot \overline{C} \cdot D + \overline{A} \cdot B \cdot C \cdot \overline{D} + \overline{A} \cdot B \cdot C \cdot D$$
$$+ A \cdot \overline{B} \cdot \overline{C} \cdot D + A \cdot \overline{B} \cdot C \cdot \overline{D} + A \cdot \overline{B} \cdot C \cdot D + A \cdot B \cdot \overline{C} \cdot \overline{D}$$
$$+ A \cdot B \cdot \overline{C} \cdot D + A \cdot B \cdot C \cdot \overline{D} + A \cdot B \cdot C \cdot D$$

Plotting these 11 minterms terms on a Karnaugh map we get Fig. 2.77(a). The next step is to group these terms together into six groups of four minterms (Fig. 2.77(b)). Note that the minterm A·B·C·D belongs to all six groups.

Therefore, the simplified sum-of-products form of F is given by

$$F = A \cdot B + A \cdot C + A \cdot D + B \cdot C + B \cdot D + C \cdot D$$

This expression is (as you might expect) the sum of all possible two-variable combinations.

In order to convert the expression into NAND logic only form, we have to eliminate the five logical OR operators. We do that by complementing F twice and then using de Morgan's theorem.

$$F = \overline{\overline{F}} = \overline{\overline{A \cdot B + A \cdot C + A \cdot D + B \cdot C + B \cdot D + C \cdot D}}$$
$$= \overline{\overline{A \cdot B} \cdot \overline{A \cdot C} \cdot \overline{A \cdot D} \cdot \overline{B \cdot C} \cdot \overline{B \cdot D} \cdot \overline{C \cdot D}}$$

Although we have realized the expression in NAND logic as required, it calls for a six-input NAND gate. If the expression for F is examined, it can be seen that six terms are NANDed together, which is the same as ANDing them and then inverting the result. Because of the associative property of Boolean variables, we can write $X(Y \cdot Z) = (X \cdot Y)Z$, and hence extending this to our equation we get

$$F = \overline{\overline{A \cdot B} \cdot \overline{A \cdot C} \cdot \overline{A \cdot D} \cdot \overline{B \cdot C} \cdot \overline{B \cdot D} \cdot \overline{C \cdot D}}$$

Figure 2.78 shows how this expression can be implemented in terms of two- and three-input NAND gates.

We could have attacked this problem in a slightly different way. If the Karnaugh map for F is examined it's apparent that most squares are covered by 1s. The remaining squares, covered by 0s, give F, the complement of the function, in a moderately simple form (Fig. 2.79). We can write down F from this Karnaugh map as

$$\overline{F} = \overline{A} \cdot \overline{B} \cdot \overline{D} + \overline{A} \cdot \overline{B} \cdot \overline{C} + \overline{A} \cdot \overline{C} \cdot \overline{D} + \overline{B} \cdot \overline{C} \cdot \overline{D}$$

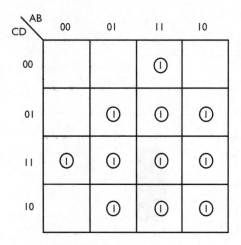

(a) Location of the 1s

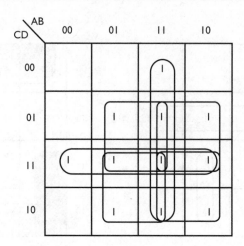

(b) After grouping the 1s

Fig. 2.77 Karnaugh map corresponding to Table 2.19.

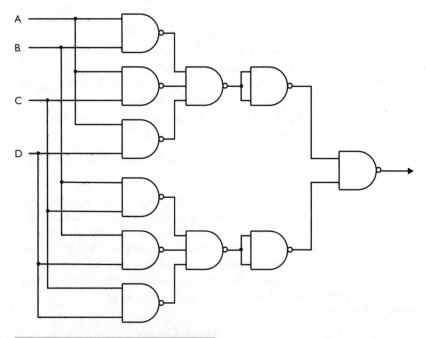

Fig. 2.78 NAND-only circuit for fire detector.

and

$$F = \overline{A} \cdot \overline{B} \cdot D + \overline{A} \cdot B \cdot C + A \cdot \overline{C} \cdot D + B \cdot C \cdot D$$
$$= \overline{\overline{A} \cdot \overline{B} \cdot D} \cdot \overline{\overline{A} \cdot B \cdot C} \cdot \overline{A \cdot \overline{C} \cdot D} \cdot \overline{B \cdot C \cdot D}$$

We leave it as an exercise to the reader to work out whether this expression can be realized with as few gates as the expression we derived directly from the Karnaugh map for F.

Karnaugh maps and don't care conditions

We now demonstrate how Karnaugh maps can be applied to a class of problems in which the truth table isn't fully specified; that is, for certain input conditions the output is undefined. In all the logic design problems we have encountered so far, a specific output value has been associated with each of the possible input values. Occasionally, a system exists in which a

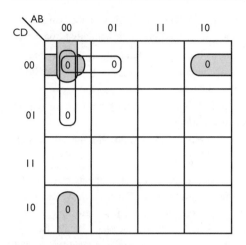

Fig. 2.79 Karnaugh map for $\overline{F}$.

certain combination of inputs can't happen (or, if it does, we don't care what the output is). In such cases, the output may be defined as either true or false. After all, if a particular input is impossible, the corresponding output is meaningless. Or is it?

Consider the Karnaugh map of Fig. 2.80 for $F = \overline{A} \cdot B \cdot D + A \cdot B \cdot C \cdot D$. Now suppose that the input conditions $A \cdot B \cdot \overline{C} \cdot D$ and $A \cdot \overline{B} \cdot \overline{C} \cdot D$ cannot occur. We have marked these two inputs on the map with an X. The value of X is undefined (if the input can't occur then the value of the output is undefined).

If input can't occur and the output is undefined, we can cover that square with a 0 or a 1. In Fig. 2.80(b) we have effectively made one of the Xs a 1 and one of the Xs a 0. Now, we can write the output function as $F = B \cdot D$, which is simpler than the function in Fig. 2.80(a).

A don't care condition is set to a 0 or a 1 in order to simplify the solution. However, there is an important exception. Although an impossible input can't occur in normal circumstances, it could under fault conditions (e.g. an input circuit fails). No designer would assign an output to an impossible input condition that might lead to a dangerous situation.

However, the ultimate aim is to cover all the 1s in the map and to incorporate them in the smallest number of large groups.

The following example demonstrates the concept of *impossible* input conditions. An air conditioning system has two temperature control inputs. One input, C, from a cold-sensing thermostat, is true if the temperature is below 15 °C and false otherwise. The other input, H, from a hot-sensing thermostat, is true if the temperature is above 22 °C and false otherwise. Table 2.20 lists the four possible logical conditions for the two inputs.

The input condition $C = 1$, $H = 1$ in Table 2.20 has no real meaning, because it's impossible to be too hot and too cold simultaneously. Such an input condition could arise only if at least one of the thermostats failed. Consider now the example of an air conditioning unit with four inputs and four outputs. Table 2.21 defines the meaning of the inputs to the controller.

The controller has four outputs: P, Q, R, and S. When $P = 1$ a heater is switched on, and when $Q = 1$ a cooler is

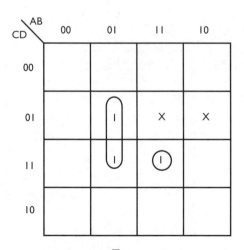

(a) The function $F = \overline{A}BD + ABCD$

Note that the inputs $AB\overline{C}D$ and $\overline{A}\overline{B}\overline{C}D$ cannot occur

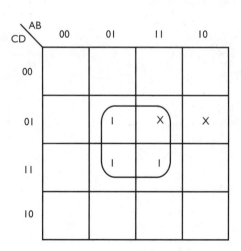

(b) The function $F = BD$

Minterm $AB\overline{C}D$ is included to simplify the expression

Fig. 2.80 The effect of don't care conditions.

Inputs		Meaning
C	H	
0	0	Temperature OK
0	I	Too hot
I	0	Too cold
I	I	Impossible condition

Table 2.20 Truth table for a pair of temperature sensors.

switched on. Similarly, a humidifier is switched on by $R = 1$, and a dehumidifier by $S = 1$. In each case a logical 0 switches off the appropriate device. The relationship between the inputs and outputs is as follows.

- If the temperature and humidity are both within limits, switch off the heater and the cooler. The humidifier and dehumidifier are both switched off unless stated otherwise.
- If the humidity is within limits, switch on the heater if the temperature is too low or switch on the cooler if the temperature is too high.

- If the temperature is within limits, switch on the heater if the humidity is too low or the cooler if the humidity is too high.
- If the humidity is high and the temperature low, switch on the heater. If the humidity is low and the temperature high, switch on the cooler.
- If both the temperature and humidity are high switch on the cooler and dehumidifier.
- If both the temperature and humidity are too low switch on the heater and humidifier.

The relationship between the inputs and outputs can now be expressed in terms of a truth table (Table 2.22). We can draw Karnaugh maps for P to S, plotting a 0 for a zero state, a 1 for a one state, and an X for an impossible state. Remember that an X on the Karnaugh map corresponds to a state that cannot exist and therefore its value is known as a *don't care* condition.

Figure 2.81 provides a Karnaugh map corresponding to output P (i.e. the heater). We have marked all the don't care conditions with an X. We could replace the Xs by 1s or 0s. However, by forcing some of the don't care outputs to be a 1, we can convert a group of 1s into a larger group.

Input	Name	Meaning when input = 0	Meaning when input = I
H	Hot	Temperature < upper limit	Temperature > upper limit
C	Cold	Temperature > lower limit	Temperature < lower limit
W	Wet	Humidity < upper limit	Humidity > upper limit
D	Dry	Humidity > lower limit	Humidity < lower limit

Table 2.21 Truth table for a climate controller.

Inputs				Outputs	Condition			
H	C	W	D		P	Q	R	S
					heater	cooler	humidifier	dehumidifier
0	0	0	0	OK	0	0	0	0
0	0	0	I	Dry	I	0	0	0
0	0	I	0	Wet	0	I	0	0
0	0	I	I	Impossible	X	X	X	X
0	I	0	0	Cold	I	0	0	0
0	I	0	I	Cold and dry	I	0	I	0
0	I	I	0	Cold and wet	I	0	0	0
0	I	I	I	Impossible	X	X	X	X
I	0	0	0	Hot	0	I	0	0
I	0	0	I	Hot and dry	0	I	0	0
I	0	I	0	Hot and wet	0	I	0	I
I	0	I	I	Impossible	X	X	X	X
I	I	0	0	Impossible	X	X	X	X
I	I	0	I	Impossible	X	X	X	X
I	I	I	0	Impossible	X	X	X	X
I	I	I	I	Impossible	X	X	X	X

Table 2.22 Truth table for a climate controller.

HC \ WD	00	01	11	10
00		1	X	
01	1	1	X	
11	X	X	X	X
10		1	X	

Fig. 2.81 Karnaugh map for P (the heater).

The Karnaugh map of Fig. 2.82(a) corresponds to output P. We have included six of the don't care conditions within the groupings to get $P = C + H \cdot D$.

Figure 2.82 provides Karnaugh maps for outputs P, Q, R, and S. In each case we have chosen the don't care conditions to simplify the output function. You should appreciate that by taking this approach we have designed a circuit that sets the output 1 for some don't care inputs and 0 for other don't care inputs. You cannot avoid this. The output of any digital circuit must always be in a 0 or a 1 state. As we said at the beginning of this chapter, there is no such state as an indeterminate state. It is up to the designer to choose what outputs are to be assigned to don't care inputs.

2.6 Special-purpose logic elements

So far, we've looked at the primitive logic elements from which all digital systems can be constructed. As technology

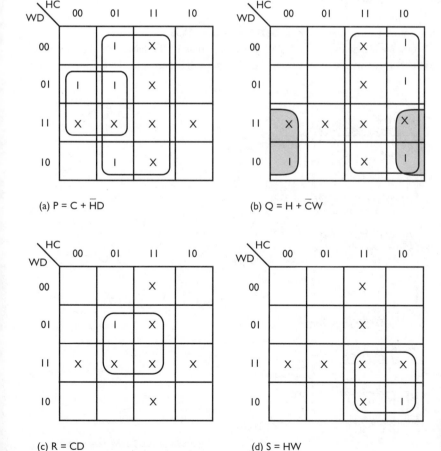

(a) $P = C + \overline{H}D$

(b) $Q = H + \overline{C}W$

(c) $R = CD$

(d) $S = HW$

Fig. 2.82 Karnaugh maps for outputs P, Q, and R.

has progressed, more and more components have been fabricated on single chips of silicon to produce increasingly complex circuits. Today, you can buy chips with hundreds of thousands of gates that can be interconnected electronically (i.e. the chip provides a digital system whose structure can be modified electronically). Indeed, by combining microprocessor technology, electronically programmable arrays of gates, and artificial intelligence, we can now construct self-modifying (self-adaptive) digital systems.

Let's briefly review the development of digital circuits. The first digital circuits contained a few basic NAND, NOR, AND gates, etc., and were called *small-scale integration* (SSI). As technology progressed it became possible to put tens of gates on a chip, and manufacturers connected gates together to create logic functions such as a four-bit adder, a multiplexer, and a decoder (these functions are described later). Such circuits are called *medium-scale integration* (MSI).

By the 1970s entire systems began to appear on a single silicon chip, of which the microprocessor is the most spectacular example. The technology used to make such complex systems is called *large-scale integration* (LSI). In the late 1980s LSI gave way to *very large-scale integration* (VLSI), which allowed designers to fabricate millions of transistors on a chip. Initially, VLSI technology was applied to the design of memories rather than microprocessors. Memory systems are

much easier to design because they have a regular structure (i.e. a simple memory cell is replicated millions of times).

A major change in digital technology occurred in the mid-1990s. From the 1970s to the 1990s, digital logic had (largely) used a power supply of $+5$ V. As the number of gates per chip approached the low millions, the problem of *heat management* created a limit to complexity. It was obvious that more and more transistors couldn't be added to a chip without limit because the power they required would destroy the chip. Radiators and fans were used to keep chips cool. Improvements in silicon technology in the 1990s provided digital logic elements that could operate at 3 V or less and, therefore, create less heat. A further impetus to the development of low-power systems was provided by the growth of the laptop computer market.

We now look at the characteristics of some of the simple digital circuits that are still widely available—even though VLSI systems dominate the digital world, designers often have to use simple gates to interface these complex chips to each other.

2.6.1 Small-scale ICs

Figure 2.83 illustrates some of the basic SSI gates available in 14-pin *dual-in-line*, DIL, packages. Dual-in-line simply

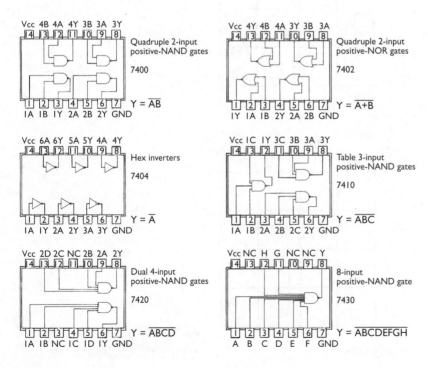

Fig. 2.83 Typical SSI logic elements.

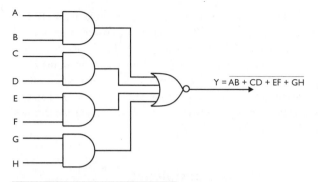

$$Y = \overline{AB + CD + EF + GH}$$

Fig. 2.84 The AND-OR-INVERT gate.

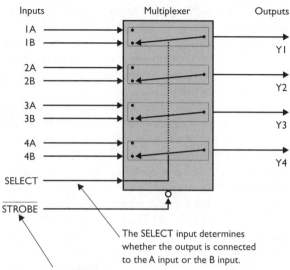

The SELECT input determines whether the output is connected to the A input or the B input.

The $\overline{\text{STROBE}}$ input enables the multiplexer. When $\overline{\text{STROBE}} = 1$ all Y outputs are set to zero. When $\overline{\text{STROBE}} = 1$ the outputs are either the A or B inputs.

Fig. 2.85 The 74157 quad two-input multiplexer.

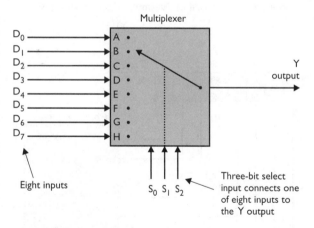

Fig. 2.86 The 1-of-8 multiplexer.

means that there are two parallel rows of pins (i.e. contacts) forming the interface between the chip and the outside world. The rows are 0.3 inches apart and the pins are spaced by 0.1 inch. Two pins are used for the power supply ($\text{Vcc} = +5.0\,\text{V}$, and ground $= 0\,\text{V}$). These devices are often called *74-series* logic elements because the part number of each chip begins with 74; for example, a 7400 chip contains four NAND gates.

In each example in Fig. 2.83 as many gates of a given type as possible are put in the package. For all practical purposes, only the number of pins to the DIL package limits the number of gates in an SSI circuit.

Figure 2.84 illustrates a typical simple logic building block constructed from basic gates called an AND-OR-INVERT gate. This SSI circuit can be used to implement more complex logic functions. The 7454 generates the function $F = \overline{A \cdot B + C \cdot D + E \cdot F + G \cdot H}$, the inverse of a sum-of-products expression. We can apply de Morgan's theorem and rewrite the expression $F = (\overline{A} + \overline{B}) \cdot (\overline{C} + \overline{D}) \cdot (\overline{E} + \overline{F}) \cdot (\overline{G} + \overline{H})$. If a Boolean equation can be expressed in the form above, it can be generated by a single chip rather than the two or more chips needed if basic gates were used. When more than about 10 to 20 gates are put on a single chip to achieve a logical function such as a *multiplexer*, the circuit is called an MSI (medium-scale integration) chip.

2.6.2 The multiplexer

A particularly common function arising regularly in digital design is the *multiplexer* that we met earlier in this chapter. Figure 2.85 shows the 74157, a quad two-input multiplexer which is available in a 16-pin MSI circuit. The prefix *quad* simply means that there are four multiplexers in one package.

Each of the four Y outputs is connected to the corresponding A input pin when $\text{SELECT} = 0$, and to the B input when $\text{SELECT} = 1$. The multiplexer's $\overline{\text{STROBE}}$ input forces all Y

outputs into logical 0 states whenever $\overline{\text{STROBE}} = 1$. We have already described one use of the multiplexer in Section 2.3 when we looked at some simple circuits.

Figure 2.86 illustrates the structure of a 1-of-8 data multiplexer, which has 8 data inputs, $D_0, D_1, D_2, ..., D_7$, an output Y, and three data select inputs, S_0, S_1, S_2. When $S_0, S_1, S_2 = 0$, 0, 0 the output is $Y = D_0$, and when $S_0, S_1, S_2 = 1, 0, 0$ the output $Y = D_1$, etc. That is, if the binary value at the data select input is i, the output is given by $Y = D_i$.

A practical version of the 1-of-8 multiplexer is the 74LS151, which is similar to that of Fig. 2.86 except that it also has an output that is the complement of Y (i.e. $W = \overline{Y}$) and an active-low $\overline{\text{STROBE}}$ input.

A typical application of the 1-of-8 multiplexer is in the selection of one out of eight logical conditions within a digital system. Figure 2.87 demonstrates how the 1-of-8 multiplexer might be used in conjunction with a computer's *flag* register to select one of eight logical conditions. We cover registers in the next chapter—all we need know at this point is that a register is a storage unit that holds the value of one or more bits.

The flag register in Fig. 2.87 stores the value of up to eight so-called *flags* or marker bits. When a computer performs an operation (such as addition or subtraction) it sets a zero flag if the result was zero, a negative flag if the result was negative, and so on. These flags define the *state* of the computer. In Fig. 2.87 the eight flag bits are connected to the eight inputs of the multiplexer. The 3-bit code on S_0 to S_2 determines which flag bit is routed to the multiplexer's Y output. This code might be derived from the instruction that the computer is currently executing. That is, the bits of the instruction can be used to select a particular flag (via the multiplexer) and the state of this flag bit used to determine what happens next.

Suppose a computer instruction has the form IF $x = 0$ THEN do something. The computer compares x with 0, which sets the zero flag if x is equal to zero. The bits that encode this instruction provide the code on S_0 to S_2 that routes the Z flag to the Y output. Finally, the computer uses the value of the Y output to 'do something' or not to 'do something'. Later we shall see how alternative courses of action are implemented by a computer.

2.6.3 The demultiplexer

The inverse function of the multiplexer is the demultiplexer that converts a binary code on n inputs into an asserted level on one of 2^n outputs. The demultiplexer circuit of Fig. 2.88 has three inputs A, B, and C, and eight outputs Y_0 to Y_7. The three inverters generate the complements of the inputs A, B, and C. Each of the eight AND gates is connected to three of the six lines A, $\overline{A}$, B, $\overline{B}$, C, $\overline{C}$ (each of the three variables must appear in either its true or complemented forms).

The output of the first gate, Y_0, is $\overline{A} \cdot \overline{B} \cdot \overline{C}$, and is 1 if all inputs to the AND gates are 1 (i.e. $\overline{A} = 1$, $\overline{B} = 1$, $\overline{C} = 1$). Therefore, Y_0 is 1 when $A = 0$, $B = 0$, $C = 0$. If you examine the other AND gates, you will see that each gate is enabled by one of the eight possible combinations of A, B, C.

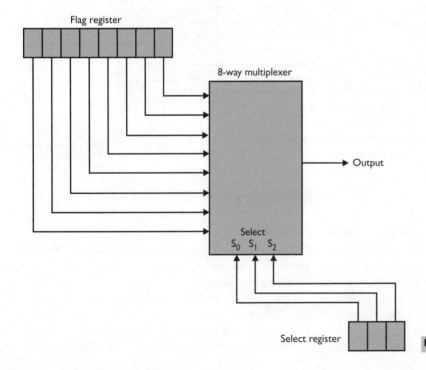

Fig. 2.87 Using the 1-of-8 multiplexer.

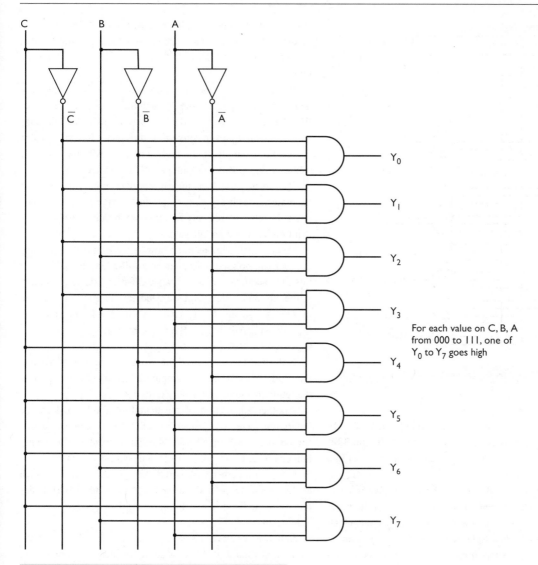

Fig. 2.88 The demultiplexer (three-line to eight-line decoder).

For each value on C, B, A
from 000 to 111, one of
Y_0 to Y_7 goes high

This circuit is called a *3-line to 8-line demultiplexer*, because it converts a 3-bit binary value, A, B, C, into one of $2^3 = 8$ outputs. Table 2.23 provides a truth table for this circuit, which is also called a *decoder* because it can take, for example, the bits that define a computer instruction and decode it into individual actions as Fig. 2.89 demonstrates.

Let's look at an actual demultiplexer, the 74138 3-line to 8-line demultiplexer (Fig. 2.90). The 74138's eight outputs, $\overline{Y}_0$ to $\overline{Y}_7$, are active-low and remain in a 1 state unless the corresponding input is selected. The device has three enable inputs, $\overline{E1}$, $\overline{E2}$, E3, which must be 0, 0, 1 respectively, for the

Inputs			Outputs							
A	B	C	Y_0	Y_1	Y_2	Y_3	Y_4	Y_5	Y_6	Y_7
0	0	0	1	0	0	0	0	0	0	0
0	0	1	0	1	0	0	0	0	0	0
0	1	0	0	0	1	0	0	0	0	0
0	1	1	0	0	0	1	0	0	0	0
1	0	0	0	0	0	0	1	0	0	0
1	0	1	0	0	0	0	0	1	0	0
1	1	0	0	0	0	0	0	0	1	0
1	1	1	0	0	0	0	0	0	0	1

Table 2.23 Truth table for a three-line demultiplexer.

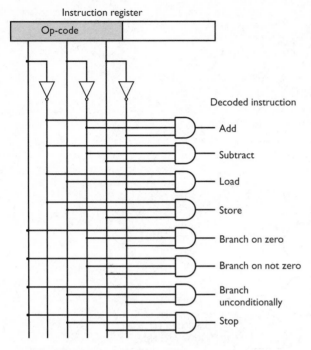

Instruction register

Op-code

Decoded instruction

Add

Subtract

Load

Store

Branch on zero

Branch on not zero

Branch unconditionally

Stop

Fig. 2.89 Application of a demultiplexer as an instruction decoder.

chip to be selected. When the chip is selected, one (and only one) of the eight outputs is forced into a 0 state by the 3-bit code at the select inputs, A, B, C. Remember that the 74138's outputs are *active-low*.

One application of this circuit is as a *device selector* (i.e. it is used to activate one of several devices in the same way you push a button to select a floor in an elevator). Suppose that a system has eight devices and only one can be active (in use) at any instant. If each device is enabled by a 0

at its input, the binary code applied to the 74138's C, B, A inputs will determine which device is selected (assuming that the 74138 is enabled by 0, 0, 1 at its $\overline{E1}$, $\overline{E2}$, E3 enable inputs).

We can look at the demultiplexer in another way. The demultiplexer generates the 2^n minterms of an n-bit function. Why? Because a three-variable function has eight minterms and the demultiplexer converts a three-bit code into 1 of 8 values. For example, if you present a 74138 with the code 101 (representing $C \cdot \overline{B} \cdot A$), output Y_5 will be asserted.

By ORing together the appropriate minterms we can generate an arbitrary sum of products expression in n variables. In other words, any function can be implemented by a demultiplexer and an OR gate.

Figure 2.91 demonstrates how a three-line to eight-line decoder can be used to implement a full-adder that adds three bits to generate a sum and a carry. Chapter 4 discusses binary arithmetic and adders—all we need say here is that the sum of bits A, B, and C_{in} is given by the Boolean expression $\overline{C_{in}} \cdot \overline{A} \cdot B + \overline{C_{in}} \cdot A \cdot \overline{B} + C_{in} \cdot \overline{A} \cdot \overline{B} + C_{in} \cdot A \cdot B$ and the carry by $\overline{C_{in}} \cdot B \cdot A + C_{in} \cdot \overline{B} \cdot A + C_{in} \cdot \overline{A} \cdot B + C_{in} \cdot A \cdot B$.

Note that the outputs of the 74LS138 are active-low and therefore it is necessary to employ a NAND gate to generate the required sum-of-products expression.

Another application of the demultiplexer is in decoding binary characters. Consider the ISO/ASCII character code (to be described in Chapter 4) that represents the alpha-numeric characters (A–Z, 0–9 and symbols such as !, @, #, $, %, ...) together with certain non-printing symbols such as the back space and carriage return. The ASCII codes for some of these non-printing control codes are given in Table 2.24.

Suppose we have a system that receives an ASCII code from a keyboard and we wish to decode its function in

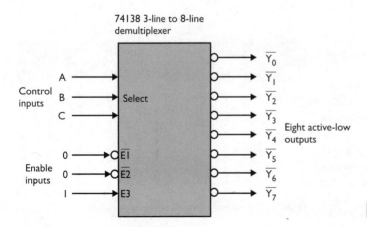

74138 3-line to 8-line demultiplexer

A

Control inputs B

C

Select

0 — $\overline{E1}$

Enable inputs 0 — $\overline{E2}$

1 — E3

$\overline{Y_0}$
$\overline{Y_1}$
$\overline{Y_2}$
$\overline{Y_3}$
$\overline{Y_4}$
$\overline{Y_5}$
$\overline{Y_6}$
$\overline{Y_7}$

Eight active-low outputs

Fig. 2.90 The 74138 three-line to eight-line decoder.

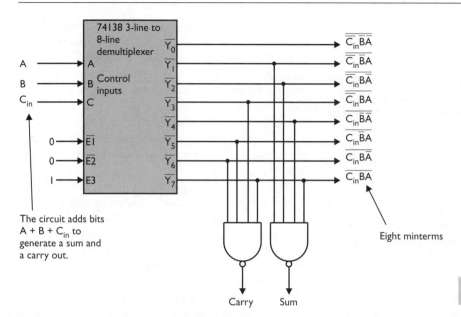

The circuit adds bits A + B + C_{in} to generate a sum and a carry out.

Eight minterms

Fig. 2.91 Generating a logic function with a demultiplexer.

Mnemonic	Name	Value
BS	Back space	00001000
LF	Line feed	00001010
CR	Carriage return	00001101
HT	Horizontal tabulate	00001001
VT	Vertical tabulate	00001011

Table 2.24 ASCII control characters.

hardware. By examining the control codes above, it can be seen that all the codes of interest start with 00001. We can use the most-significant five bits to enable a 74LS138 three-line to eight-line decoder. The decoder would then decode the

three least-significant bits of the word $00001d_2d_1d_0$ to distinguish between the control codes. Figure 2.92 demonstrates how this is achieved. Each output from the decoder can be fed to a circuit to perform the appropriate action (e.g. carriage return).

Medium-scale logic devices like the 74138 make it easy to design circuits with just a handful of chips. However, many circuits are now constructed from special-purpose user programmable logic elements. Indeed, today's very low-cost single-chip microprocessors sometimes make it feasible to program the microprocessor to carry out the required logic function. These microprocessors are called *microcontrollers* to distinguish them from their more powerful relatives in PCs and workstations.

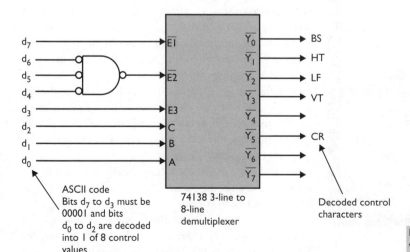

ASCII code
Bits d_7 to d_3 must be 00001 and bits d_0 to d_2 are decoded into 1 of 8 control values

74138 3-line to 8-line demultiplexer

Decoded control characters

Fig. 2.92 Decoding ASCII control characters with a demultiplexer.

2.7 Tri-state logic

The logic elements we introduced at the beginning of this chapter are used to create functional units in which one or more logical outputs are generated from several inputs. A computer is composed of the interconnection of such functional units together with the storage elements (registers) to be described in Chapter 3. We now examine a special type of gate that enables the various functional units of a computer to be interconnected. This new gate can be any of the gates we've already described—it's not the gate's logical function that's different, it's the behavior of its output. A logic element with a *tri-state* output has the special property that the output can be in a 0 state, a 1 state, or an *unconnected* state (hence the term *tri*-state). Before we can explain the operation of tri-state gates, we have to introduce the reason for their existence—the *bus*.

2.7.1 Buses

A computer is like a city. Just as *roads* link homes, shops, and factories, *buses* link logical units and storage devices. Figure 2.93 shows a digital system composed of five functional units, A, B, C, D, and E. These units are linked together by means of two data highways (or buses), P and Q, permitting data to be moved from one unit to another. Data can flow onto the bus from a device connected to it and off the bus to any other device. Buses may be unidirectional (i.e. data always flows the same way) or bi-directional (i.e. data can flow in two directions—but not simultaneously).

Buses are not strictly necessary; it's possible to provide direct connections between those parts of a digital system that exchange information. Equally, public highways are not necessary; each home could have a private path to all other homes, factories, shops, and services with which it needs to communicate. In both these cases the sheer number of interconnections is uneconomic unless there are very few functional units (or homes).

A bus is normally represented diagrammatically by a single thick line or a wide shaded line, as in Fig. 2.93. An actual bus is composed of several individual wires (i.e. electrical connections). Modern computer buses have 100 or more lines, because a bus has to carry data, addresses, control signals, and even the power supply. Indeed the nature of a bus can be an important factor in the choice of a computer (consider the PC with its ISA, and PCI buses).

Figure 2.94 demonstrates how a bus is arranged. Logical units A and B are connected to an m-bit data bus and are able to transmit data to the bus or receive data from it. We are not concerned with the nature of the processes A and B here, but simply wish to show how they communicate with each other via the bus. For clarity, the connections to only one line of the bus are shown. Similar arrangements exist for bits d_1 to d_{m-1}.

Suppose unit A wishes to send data to unit B. The system in unit A puts data on the bus via gate A_{out} and B receives the data from the bus via gate B_{in}. These two gates look like inverters, but they aren't because they don't have *bubbles* at their output. Such a gate is called a *buffer* and just copies the signal at its input terminal to its output terminal (i.e. the gate doesn't change the state of the data passing through it). We will soon see why a gate whose logical operation is 'output = input' is needed.

Such an arrangement is, in fact, unworkable, and a glance at Fig. 2.95 will show why. In Fig. 2.95(a) the outputs of two AND gates are connected together. Figure 2.95(b) shows the same circuit as Fig. 2.95(a) except that we've included the internal organization of the two gates. Essentially, a gate's output circuit consists of two electronic switches that can connect the output to the $+5\,V$ power supply or to the $0\,V$ (i.e. ground) power supply. These switches are transistors that are either conducting or non-conducting. Because only one switch is closed at a time, the output of a gate is always connected either to $+5\,V$ or to ground.

In Fig. 2.95(b) the output from gate G1 is in a logical 1 state and is pulled up towards $+5\,V$ by a switch inside the gate. Similarly, the output from G2 is a logical 0 state and is

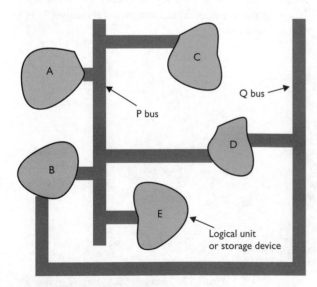

Fig. 2.93 Functional units and buses.

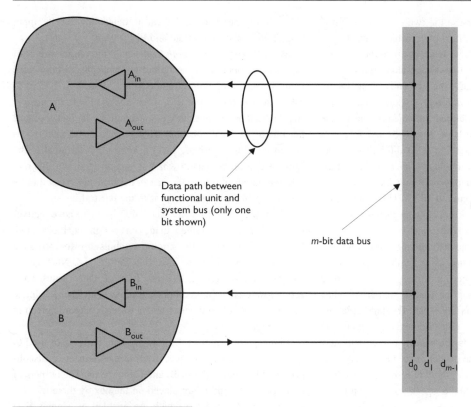

Fig. 2.94 Connecting systems to the bus.

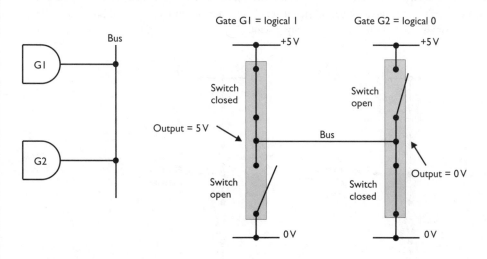

(a) Logical arrangement
Two outputs connected together

(b) Physical arrangement
Two outputs connected together

Fig. 2.95 Connecting two outputs together.

pulled down towards 0 V. Because the two outputs are wired together and yet their states differ, two problems exist. The first is philosophical. The logical level at all points along a conductor is constant, because the voltage along the conductor is constant. However, because the two ends of the bus in Fig. 2.95(b) are connected to *different* voltages, the logical level on the conductor is undefined and breaks one of the rules of Boolean algebra. We have already stated that in a Boolean system there is no such thing as a valid indeterminate state lying between a logical 1 and a logical 0. Secondly, and more practically, a direct physical path exists between the +5 V power supply and ground (0 V). This path represents a *short circuit*, and the current flowing through the two output circuits could even destroy the gates.

The *tri-state gate* resolves the difficulty of connecting outputs together. Tri-state logic is not, as its name might suggest, an extension of Boolean algebra into ternary or three-valued logic. It is a method of resolving the conflict that arises when two outputs are connected as in Fig. 2.95. Tri-state logic disconnects from the bus all those gates not actively engaged in transmitting data. In other words, a lot of tri-state outputs may be wired to a bus, but only one of them may be actively connected to the bus internally. We shouldn't speak of tri-state logic or tri-state gates, we should speak of (conventional) gates with *tri-state outputs*.

Figure 2.96 illustrates the operation of a gate with a tri-state output. In fact, any type of gate can have a tri-state output. All tri-state gates have a special ENABLE input. When ENABLE = 1, the gate behaves normally and its output is either a logical 1 or a logical 0 depending on its input (Fig. 2.96(a) shows a 0 state and Fig. 2.96(b) a 1 state).

When ENABLE = 0, *both* switches in the output circuit of the gate are open, and the output is physically disconnected from the gate's internal circuitry (Fig. 2.96(c)). If I were to ask what state the output is in when ENABLE = 0, the answer should be that the question is meaningless. In fact, because the output of an un-enabled tri-state gate is normally connected to a bus, the logic level at the output terminal is the same as that on the bus to which it is connected. For this reason, the output of a tri-state gate in its third state is said to be *floating*. It floats up and down with the bus traffic.

Most practical tri-state gates do, in fact, have active-low enable inputs rather than active-high enable inputs. Figure 2.97 provides the circuit symbols for four tri-state buffers, two of which are inverting buffers (i.e. NOT gates) and two non-inverting buffers. Two of these gates have active-low enable inputs and two active-high enable inputs. The truth table of an inverter with a tri-state output is given in Table 2.25.

Figure 2.98 demonstrates how tri-state buffers are used to implement a bused structure. The buffers connect or disconnect the three networks A, B, and C to the bus. The outputs of networks A, B, and C are placed on the bus by three tri-state buffers Ao, Bo, and Co which are enabled by signals E_{Ao}, E_{Bo}, and E_{Co}, respectively. If any network wishes to put data on to the bus it must set its enable signal (e.g. E_{Bo}) to a 1. It is vital that no more than one of E_{Ao}, E_{Bo}, and E_{Co} be at a 1 level at any instant.

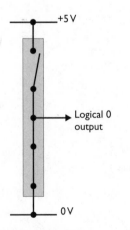

(a) Lower switch closed.
Output connected to ground

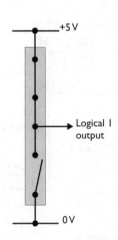

(b) Upper switch closed.
Output connected to +5 V

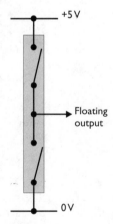

(c) Both switches open.
Output disconnected

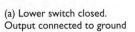

Fig. 2.96 The operation of the tri-state output.

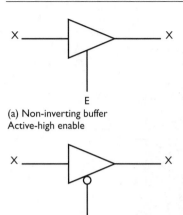

(a) Non-inverting buffer
Active-high enable

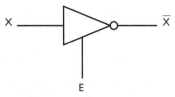

(b) Inverting buffer
Active-high enable

(c) Non-inverting buffer
Active-low enable

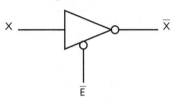

(d) Inverting buffer
Active-low enable

Fig. 2.97 Logic symbol for the tri-state buffer.

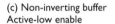

ENABLE	A	Output	
0	0	X	Output floating
0	I	X	Output floating
I	0	0	Output same as input
I	I	I	Output same as input

Table 2.25 Truth table for the non-inverting tri-state buffer with an active-high enable input.

Each of the networks receives data from the bus via its own input buffers (Ai, Bi, and Ci). If a network wishes to receive data, it enables its input buffer by asserting one of E_{Ai}, E_{Bi}, or E_{Ci}, as appropriate. For example, if network C wishes to transmit data to network A, all that is necessary is for E_{Co} and E_{Ai} to be set to a logical 1 simultaneously. All other enable signals remain in a logical 0 state for the duration of the information transfer.

Note that the input buffers (Ai, Bi, Ci) are not always necessary. If the data flowing from the bus into a network goes only into the input of one or more gates, a buffer is not needed. If, however, the input data is placed on an internal bus (local to the network) on which other gates may put their output, the buffer is necessary to avoid conflict between the various other outputs that may drive the local bus.

The bus in Fig. 2.98 is bidirectional; that is, data can flow onto the bus or off the bus. The pairs of buffers are arranged back-to-back (e.g. Ai and Ao) so that one buffer reads data from the bus and the other puts data on the bus—but not at the same time.

In the description of the bused system in Fig. 2.98 the names of the gates and their control signals have been carefully chosen. Ao stands for A_{out}, and Ai for A_{in}. This labels the gate and the *direction* in which it transfers data with respect to the network it is serving. Similarly, E_{Ao} stands for *enable gate A out*, and E_{Ai} for *enable gate A in*. By choosing consistent and meaningful names, the reading of circuit diagrams and their associated text is made easier.

Further details of a bused system will be elaborated on in Chapter 3, and Chapter 5 on the structure of the CPU makes extensive use of buses in its description of how the CPU actually carries out basic computer operations.

Digital Works supports tri-state buffers. The device palette provides a simple non-inverting tri-state buffer with an active-high enable input. Figure 2.99 shows a system with a single bus to which three tri-state buffers are connected. One end of the bus is connected to an LED to show the state of the bus.

Digital Works requires you to connect a wire between two points so we've added a macro tag to the bottom of the bus to provide an anchor point (we don't use the macro tag for its normal purpose in this example).

The input of each tri-state gate in Fig. 2.99 is connected to the interactive input tool, which can be set to a 0 or a 1 by the hand tool. Similarly, the enable input of each gate is connected to an interactive input tool.

By clicking on the run icon and then using the hand tool to set the input and enable switches, we can investigate the operation of the tri-state buffer. In Fig. 2.99 inputs 1 and 3 are set to 1 and only buffer 3 is enabled. Consequently, the output of buffer 3 is placed on the bus and the bus LED is illuminated.

We have stated that you shouldn't enable two or more of the tri-state gates at the same time. If you did, that would create bus contention as two devices attempted to put data on the bus simultaneously. In Fig. 2.100 we have done just that and

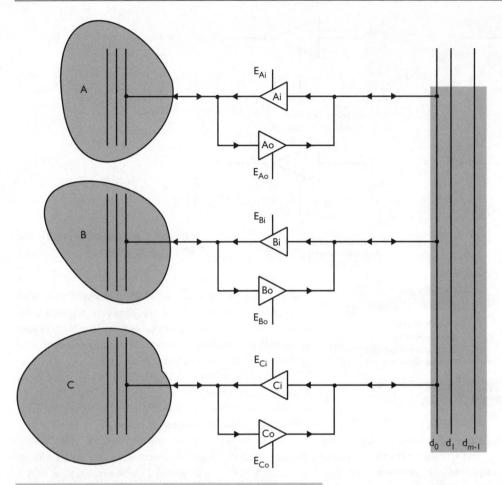

Fig. 2.98 Interconnecting logic elements with a bus and tri-state buffers.

used the hand tool to enable buffer 2 as well as buffer 3. As you can see, the simulation has stopped (the run button is in the off state) and an error message has been generated at the buffer we've attempted to enable.

2.8 Programmable logic

In this short section we introduce some of the single-chip *programmable logic elements* that can be configured by the user to perform any function they require. We begin by explaining how digital electronics has changed over the past two decades.

Few fields of human endeavor (if any) have developed as rapidly as digital electronics. Curiously enough, even those at the forefront of this technology were often caught unawares by its success. There are two reasons for this unprecedented

progress. The first is that semiconductor manufacturing technology has steadily improved because our understanding of both engineering and semiconductor physics has grown. The second is that each improvement in performance and reduction in the cost of chips creates a new demand. For example, the analog integrated circuit made the first generation of personal audio products possible (i.e. the personal radio and tape cassette player). The success of these products and the potential for growth and products led to the development of better and more compact technology (e.g. the portable CD player). In turn this led to the development of better batteries and the extension to the portable phone, the personal organizer, the laptop computer, and so on.

Economic considerations in designing digital systems vary widely with the application. For example, an engineer designing an on-board computer in a satellite is concerned largely with optimizing three parameters: weight, reliability, and

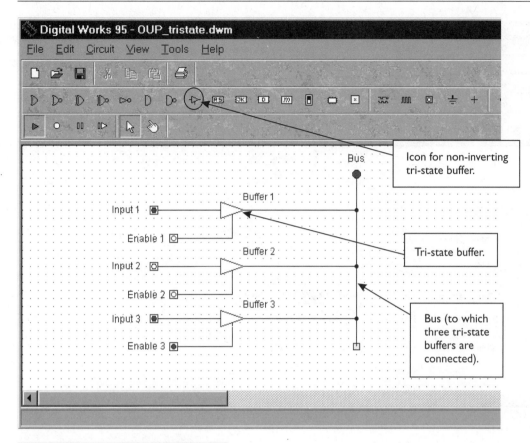

Fig. 2.99 Using tri-state buffers in Digital Works.

power consumption. The designer of washing machine controllers may be concerned almost entirely with minimizing the cost of the circuit, because a small saving multiplied by a large number of units amounts to a considerable quantity of money. In particular, the cost of assembly, packaging, and testing has caused designers to attempt to minimize the component count in any digital system. If you bought, for example, a printer in the 1970s you would find it full of circuit boards covered with hundreds of integrated circuits. Today you might find a tiny circuit board with just a couple of immensely powerful special-purpose chips in a box largely full of empty space.

In the earlier days of logic design, systems were constructed with lots of basic logic elements; for example, the two-input OR gate, the five-input NAND gate, and so on. The introduction of medium-scale integration by the major semiconductor manufacturers generated a range of basic building blocks, from multiplexers to digital multiplier circuits, and allowed the economic design of more complex systems. We

now introduce the next step in the history of digital systems—*programmable logic* that can be configured by the user.

2.8.1 The read-only memory as a logic element

Semiconductor manufacturers find it easier to design regular circuits with repeated circuit elements than special-purpose highly complex systems. A typical regular circuit is the *read-only memory* or ROM. We deal with memory in a later chapter. All we need say here is that a ROM is a device with n address input lines specifying 2^n unique locations within it. Each location, when accessed, produces an m-bit value on its m output lines. It is called *read-only* because the output corresponding to a given input cannot be modified (i.e. written into) by the user. A ROM is specified by its *number of locations $\times$ width of each location*; for example, a 16×4 ROM has 16 locations each containing 4 bits.

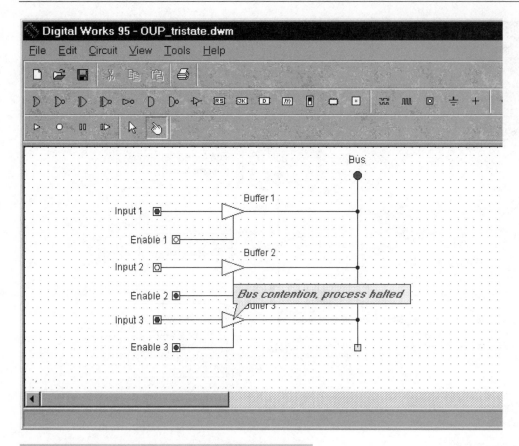

Fig. 2.100 Attempting to enable two tri-state drivers simultaneously.

An alternative approach to the design of digital systems with basic gates or MSI elements is to use ROMs to implement the required function as a *look-up table*. Earlier in this chapter we designed a 4-bit multiplier using both AND, OR, NOT gates and NAND-only gates. Figure 2.101 shows how a 16×4 ROM implements this multiplier circuit. The binary code, X_1, X_0, Y_1, Y_0, at the four address inputs selects one of the 16 possible locations, each containing a 4-bit word corresponding to the desired result. The manufacturer or user of the ROM writes the appropriate output into each of these 16 locations; for example, the location 1011, corresponding to 10×11 (i.e. 2×3), has 0110 (i.e. 6) written into it.

The ROM directly implements not the circuit but the truth table. The value of the output is stored for each of the possible inputs. The ROM look-up table doesn't even require Boolean algebra to simplify the sum-of-products expression derived from the truth table. Not only does a ROM look-up table save a large number of logic elements, but the ROMs themselves can be readily replaced to permit the logic functions to be modified (to correct errors or to add improved facilities). Unfortunately, the ROM look-up table is limited to about 20 inputs and eight outputs (i.e. $2^{20} \times 8 = 8$ Mbit). The ROM can be programmed during its manufacture or a PROM (*programmable* ROM) can be programmed by means of a special device.

2.8.2 Programmable logic families

The problem with the ROM is that it requires a very large number of bits to implement moderately complex digital circuits. Semiconductor manufacturers have created much simpler logic elements than ROMs containing a regular structure of AND and OR gates that can be interconnected by the user to generate the required logical function.

Figure 2.102 provides a simplified picture of how programmable logic devices operate. The three inputs on the left-hand side of the diagram are connected to six vertical lines (three lines for the inputs and three for their complements).

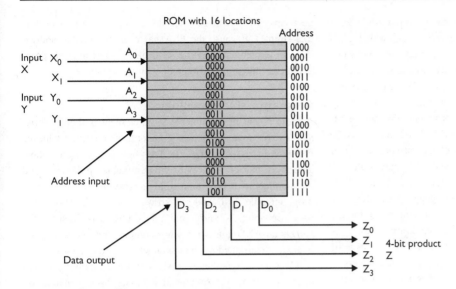

Fig. 2.101 Using a ROM to implement a multiplier.

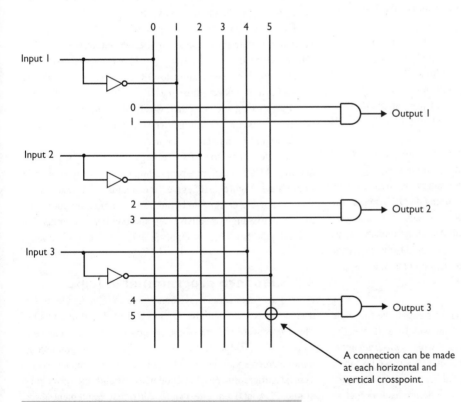

Fig. 2.102 Conceptual structure of a programmable logic device.

On the right of the diagram are three two-input AND gates whose inputs run horizontally. The key to programmable logic is the *fusible link* between each horizontal and vertical conductor.

Links between gates are broken by passing a sufficiently large current through the link to melt it. By leaving a link intact or by blowing it, the outputs of the AND gates can be determined by the designer. A real programmable device has many more input variables than in Fig. 2.102 and the AND gates might have an input for each of the variables and their complements. The digital designer selects the appropriate programmable device from a manufacturer's catalog and adapts the Boolean equations to fit the type of gates on the chip. The engineer then plugs the chip into a special programming machine that interconnects the gates in the desired way.

Programmable logic elements enable complex systems to be designed and implemented without requiring large numbers of chips. Without the present generation of programmable logic elements, many of the low-cost microcomputers would be much more bulky, consume more power, and cost considerably more.

Today's designers have a large number of programmable logic elements at their disposal; for example, the PAL (programmable array logic), the PLA (programmable logic array), and the PROM (programmable read-only memory). The PROM and the PAL are special cases of the PLA. Figure 2.103 illustrates the structure of these logic elements, each of which contains an AND gate array and an OR gate array. The difference between the various types of programmable logic element depends on whether one or both of the AND and OR arrays are programmable.

A programmable logic array contains both programmable AND and OR arrays. Many applications do not require such a versatile logic element and the programmable logic element with its fixed AND array and programmable OR array, or the programmable array logic with its fixed OR array and programmable AND array, are more suitable. Programmable logic elements are generally available in 20- or 24-pin packages, have 16 or more inputs/outputs, and contain tens of gates.

Programmable logic array

The *programmable logic array*, PLA, was one of the first field programmable logic elements to become widely available. The PLA has an AND–OR gate structure with a *programmable* array of AND gates whose inputs may be variables, their complements, or don't care states. The OR gates are also programmable, which means that you can define each output as the sum of any of the product terms. A typical PLA has 48 AND gates (i.e. 48 *product terms*) for 16 input variables, compared with the 65 536 required by a 16-input PROM. Figure 2.104 provides a simple example of a PLA that has

been programmed to generate three outputs (no real PLA is this simple). Because the PLA has a programmable address decoder implemented by the AND gates, you can cr ate product terms containing between one and *n* variables.

Programmable array logic

A more recent programmable logic element is the *programmable array logic*, PAL, which is not to be confused with the PLA we discussed earlier. The PAL falls between the simple gate array that contains only programmable AND gates and the more complex programmed logic array. The PLA has both programmable AND and OR arrays, whereas the PAL has a programmable AND array but a *fixed* OR array. In short, the PAL is an AND gate array whose outputs are ORed together in a way determined by the manufacturer of the device.

Consider a hypothetical PAL with three inputs x_0–x_2 and three outputs y_0–y_2. Assume that inputs x_0–x_2 generate six product terms P_0–P_5. These product terms are, of course, *user programmable* and may include an input variable in a true, complement, or don't care form. In other words, you can generate any six product terms you want.

The six product terms are applied to three two-input OR gates to generate the outputs y_0–y_2. Each output is the logical OR of two product terms. Thus, $y_0 = P_0 + P_1$, $y_1 = P_2 + P_3$, and $y_2 = P_4 + P_5$. We have chosen to OR three *pairs* of products. We could have chosen three *triplets* so that $y_0 = P_1 + P_2 + P_3$, $y_1 = P_4 + P_5 + P_6$, etc. In other words, the way in which the product terms are ORed together is a function of the device and is not programmable by the user.

Most designers don't require large numbers of sum terms and the PAL's absence of a programmable OR array is of little importance. Figure 2.105 gives the details of a few simple PALs. They are designated by number of inputs, output polarity (i.e. active-high or active-low), and number of outputs; for example, the 14L4 has 14 inputs and four active-low outputs.

2.8.3 Modern programmable logic

Over the years, logic systems have evolved. Once the designer was stuck with basic gates and MSI building blocks. The 1980s were the era of the programmable logic element, with PROMs, PALs, PLAs, and so on. Today's programmable logic elements are constructed on a much grander scale. Typical programmable logic devices extend the principles of the PLA and employ *macro cells* that implement more complex building blocks containing storage elements as well as AND, OR, and EOR gates.

A more recent innovation in programmable logic is the *electrically programmable and erasable logic element* that can

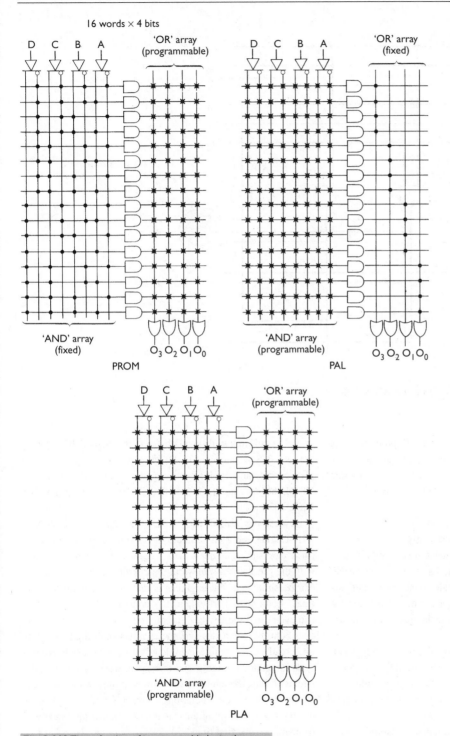

Fig. 2.103 Three families of programmable logic elements.

Inputs

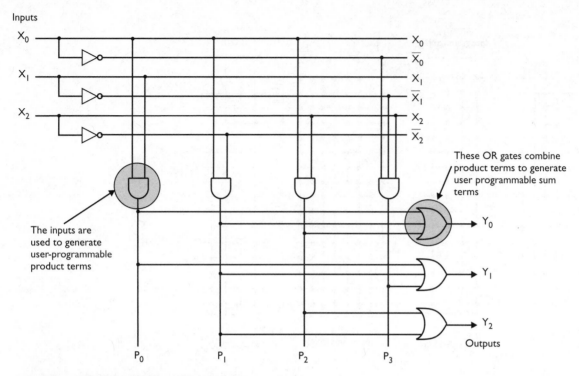

These OR gates combine product terms to generate user programmable sum terms

The inputs are used to generate user-programmable product terms

Fig. 2.104 Example of a circuit built with a programmable logic array.

be programmed, erased, and reprogrammed. Reprogrammable logic elements represent a considerable saving at the design stage. Moreover, they can be used to construct systems that can be reconfigured by downloading data from disk.

Design techniques for modern logic

There's little point in developing massively complex programmable logic elements if they can't easily be used. Although the Boolean algebra and logic construction methods we've described earlier in this chapter are perfectly good for simple circuits, more efficient design techniques and tools are needed for complex circuits.

Device manufacturers have developed logic languages that run on PCs and make it possible to configure these programmable logic elements. You can express the required functions in Boolean form and the software will generate the data necessary to program the device.

Just as high-level languages have replaced assembly language in computer programming, circuit designers use high-level design languages. One such language is called VHDL (VHSIC hardware description language, where VHSIC = very high-speed integrated circuit) which permits you to specify a

digital circuit in a high-level abstract language. VHDL started out as a US Department of Defense project to specify complex circuits and evolved into a general-purpose design tool. VHDL became an IEEE standard in 1987 with the number IEEE 1076.

A designer armed with VHDL can specify a circuit in VHDL code and then simulate the circuit's behavior on a PC (or a workstation under Unix). The simulator can even cope with the problems of delays in the circuit. Because the device can be simulated, the engineer is reasonably certain that the final circuit will work when it is constructed. This software can even drive the devices that program these logic elements.

About three decades ago, the engineer built digital circuits on 'breadboards' with hundreds of small-scale and medium-scale integrated circuits—and then spent weeks debugging the circuit. Today, the engineer can express complex logical operations in a high-level notation, design a circuit, simulate its behavior, and then program a real device knowing that it will (probably) work first time.

The following fragment of VHDL code is taken from *VHDL of Programmable Logic* by Kevin Skahill (Addison-Wesley, 1996) and demonstrates how a quad four-bit multiplexer can be specified. This device has four four-bit inputs

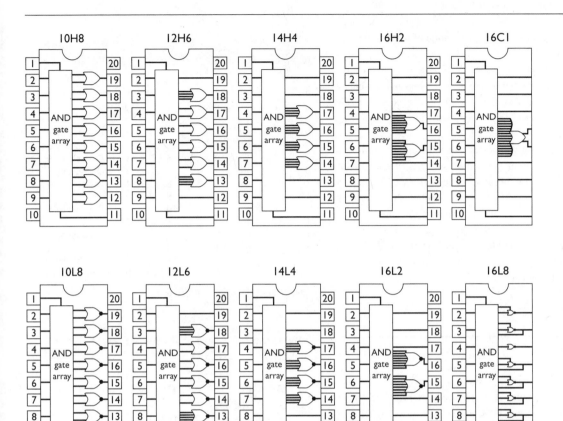

Fig. 2.105 Typical PALs.

a to *d* and a four-bit output *x*. A two-bit input *s* determines which of the four inputs is connected to the output.

```
library ieee;
use ieee.std_logic_1164.all;
entity mux is port(

  a,b,c,d: in std_logic_vector(3 downto 0) ;
  s:       in std_logic_vector(1 downto 0) ;
  x:       out std_logic_vector (3 downto 0));
end mux;

architecture archmux of mux is
begin
with s select
    x<=a when "00",
       b when "01",
       c when "10",
       d when others;
end archmux;
```

Readers who have programmed in almost any high-level language would probably be able to follow this fragment of VHDL. It consists of a declaration block that defines the inputs and outputs and a process block that defines what the circuit is to do.

Summary

In this chapter we have looked at the basic set of elements used to create any digital system—the AND, OR, and NOT gates. We have demonstrated how simple functions can be generated from gates by first converting a problem in words into a truth table and then using either graphical or algebraic methods to convert the truth table into a logical expression and finally into a circuit made up of gates. At the end of this chapter we briefly mentioned the new families of programmable logic elements and their design tools that have revolutionized the creation of today's complex digital systems.

We have introduced Digital Works, a design tool that enables you to create digital circuits and observe their behavior. We also introduced the tri-state buffer, a device that enables you to connect logic subsystems to each other via a common data highway called a bus.

In the next chapter we look at sequential circuits built from flip-flops. As the term *sequential* suggests, these circuits involve the time factor, because the logical state of a sequential device is determined by its current inputs and its past history (or behavior). Sequential circuits form the basis of counters and data storage devices. Once we have covered sequential circuits, we will have covered all the basic building blocks necessary to design a digital system of any complexity (e.g. the digital computer).

Inputs				Number	F	
A	B	C	D			
0	0	0	0	0	0	
0	0	0	1	1	0	
0	0	1	0	2	0	
0	0	1	1	3	0	
0	1	0	0	4	1	Divisible by 4
0	1	0	1	5	1	Divisible by 5
0	1	1	0	6	1	Divisible by 6
0	1	1	1	7	1	Divisible by 7
1	0	0	0	8	1	Divisible by 4
1	0	0	1	9	0	
1	0	1	0	10	1	Divisible by 5
1	0	1	1	11	0	
1	1	0	0	12	1	Divisible by 6
1	1	0	1	13	0	
1	1	1	0	14	1	Divisible by 7
1	1	1	1	15	0	False by definition

Table 2.26 Truth table for Problem 1.

Examples

Problem 1

A circuit has four inputs, A, B, C, D, representing the 16 natural binary integers from 0000 to 1111 (i.e. 0 to 15). Input A is the most-significant bit and D the least-significant bit. The output of the circuit, F, is true if the input is divisible by a multiple of 4, 5, 6, or 7, with the exception of 15, in which case the output is false. Zero is not divisible by 4, 5, 6, or 7.

(a) Draw a truth table to represent the algorithm.
(b) From the truth table obtain a simplified sum-of-products expression for F by means of Boolean algebraic techniques.
(c) Draw a Karnaugh map and hence obtain a simplified sum-of-products expression for F.
(d) Express F in product-of-sums form.
(e) Design a logic circuit to implement F using NAND gates only.

Solution 1

(a) The truth table for this problem is given in Table 2.26.
(b) We can obtain a sum-of-products expression for F from Table 2.26 by writing down the sum of the minterms (i.e. the lines with a 1).

$$F = \overline{A} \cdot B \cdot \overline{C} \cdot \overline{D} + \overline{A} \cdot B \cdot \overline{C} \cdot D + \overline{A} \cdot B \cdot C \cdot \overline{D} + \overline{A} \cdot B \cdot C \cdot D$$
$$+ A \cdot \overline{B} \cdot \overline{C} \cdot \overline{D} + A \cdot \overline{B} \cdot C \cdot \overline{D} + A \cdot B \cdot \overline{C} \cdot \overline{D} + A \cdot B \cdot C \cdot \overline{D}$$

By means of Boolean algebra the expression can be simplified to

$$F = \overline{A} \cdot B \cdot \overline{C}(\overline{D} + D) + \overline{A} \cdot B \cdot C(\overline{D} + D) + A \cdot \overline{B} \cdot \overline{D}(\overline{C} + C)$$
$$+ A \cdot B \cdot \overline{D}(\overline{C} + C)$$
$$= \overline{A} \cdot B \cdot \overline{C} + \overline{A} \cdot B \cdot C + A \cdot \overline{B} \cdot \overline{D} + A \cdot B \cdot \overline{D}$$
$$= \overline{A} \cdot B(\overline{C} + C) + A \cdot \overline{D}(\overline{B} + B)$$
$$= \overline{A} \cdot B + A \cdot \overline{D}$$

(c) Figure 2.106 gives the Karnaugh map for F. The squares covered by 1's can be formed into two groups of four (see Fig. 2.107). This gives $F = \overline{A} \cdot B + A \cdot \overline{D}$ which is (reassuringly) the same as the result obtained in part (b) above.

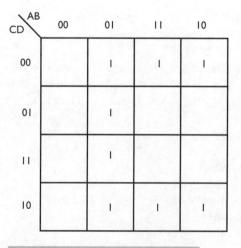

Fig. 2.106 Karnaugh map for F (Problem 1).

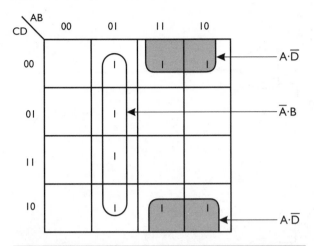

Fig. 2.107 Karnaugh map for F after regrouping the minterms (Problem 1).

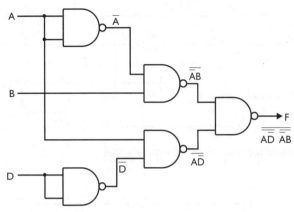

Fig. 2.108 NAND-only circuit for Problem 1.

(d) To obtain a product-of-sums expression, it is necessary to generate the complement of F in a sum-of-products form, and then complement it as follows:

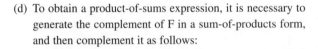

$$F = \overline{A}\cdot B + A\cdot \overline{D}$$
$$\overline{F} = \overline{\overline{A}\cdot B + A\cdot \overline{D}} \qquad \text{Get the complement of F}$$
$$= (A + \overline{B})(\overline{A} + D) \qquad \text{Complement of F in product-of-sums form}$$
$$= A\cdot \overline{A} + A\cdot D + \overline{A}\cdot \overline{B} + \overline{B}\cdot D \qquad \text{Multiply out sum terms}$$
$$= A\cdot D + \overline{A}\cdot \overline{B} + \overline{B}\cdot D \qquad \text{Complement of F in sum-of-products form}$$
$$= A\cdot D + \overline{A}\cdot \overline{B} \qquad \text{Complement in simplified sum-of-products form}$$
$$F = \overline{A\cdot D + \overline{A}\cdot \overline{B}} \qquad \text{Complement the complement to get F}$$
$$= (\overline{A} + \overline{D})(A + B) \qquad \text{Function in required product-of-sums form}$$

Note that the complement of F in sum-of-products form could have been obtained directly from the Karnaugh map of F by considering the squares covered by zeros.

(e) To convert the expression $F = \overline{A}\cdot B + A\cdot \overline{D}$ into NAND logic form, the '+' must be eliminated.

$$F = \overline{\overline{F}} = \overline{\overline{\overline{A}\cdot B + A\cdot \overline{D}}} = \overline{\overline{\overline{A}\cdot B} + \overline{A\cdot \overline{D}}}$$

The inverse functions $\overline{A}$ and $\overline{B}$ can be generated by two-input NAND gates with their inputs connected together. Figure 2.108 implements F in NAND logic only.

Problem 2

(a) Using AND, OR, and NOT gates only, design circuit diagrams to generate P and Q from inputs X, Y, and Z, where $P = (X + \overline{Y})(Y \oplus Z)$ and $Q = \overline{Y}\cdot Z + X\cdot Y\cdot \overline{Z}$. Do not simplify, or otherwise modify, these expressions.

(b) By means of a truth table establish a relationship between P and Q.

(c) Compare the circuit diagrams of P and Q in terms of speed (propagation delay) and cost of implementation.

Solution 2

(a) The circuit diagram for $P = (X + \overline{Y})(Y \oplus Z)$ is given by Fig. 2.109, and the circuit diagram for $Q = \overline{Y}\cdot Z + X\cdot Y\cdot \overline{Z}$ by Fig. 2.110.

(b) The truth table for functions P and Q is given in Table 2.27. From the truth table it can be seen that P = Q.

(c) We can compare the two circuits in terms of speed and cost.

Propagation delay The maximum delay in the circuit for P is four gates in series in the Y path (i.e. NOT gate, AND gate, OR gate, AND gate). The maximum delay in the circuit for Q is three gates in series in both Y and Z paths (i.e. NOT gate, AND gate, OR gate). Therefore the circuit for Q is 33 percent faster than that for P.

Cost Total number of gates needed to implement P = 7. Total number of gates needed to implement Q = 5. Total inputs in the circuit for P = 12. Total inputs in the circuit for Q = 9. Clearly, the circuit for Q is better than that for P both in terms of the number of gates and the number of inputs to the gates.

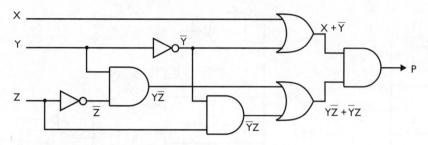

Fig. 2.109 Circuit diagram for P for Problem 2.

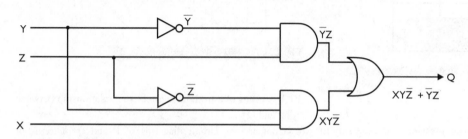

Fig. 2.110 Circuit diagram for Q for Problem 2.

X	Y	Z	$X+\bar{Y}$	$Y\oplus Z$	$P=(X+\bar{Y})(Y\oplus Z)$	$\bar{Y}\cdot Z$	$X\cdot Y\cdot\bar{Z}$	$Q=\bar{Y}\cdot Z+X\cdot Y\cdot\bar{Z}$
0	0	0	1	0	0	0	0	0
0	0	1	1	1	1	1	0	1
0	1	0	0	1	0	0	0	0
0	1	1	0	0	0	0	0	0
1	0	0	1	0	0	0	0	0
1	0	1	1	1	1	1	0	1
1	1	0	1	1	1	0	1	1
1	1	1	1	0	0	0	0	0

Table 2.27 Truth table for Problem 2.

Problem 3

(a) Show that the exclusive or, EOR, operator is *associative*, so that

$$A\oplus(B\oplus C)=(A\oplus B)\oplus C$$

(b) Demonstrate that any logic function can be implemented in terms of EOR and AND gates only.

Solution 3

(a) $A\oplus(B\oplus C)=A\oplus(B\cdot\bar{C}+\bar{B}\cdot C)$

$\qquad = A\overline{(B\cdot\bar{C}+\bar{B}\cdot C)}+\bar{A}(B\cdot\bar{C}+\bar{B}\cdot C)$

$\qquad = A(\bar{B}+C)(B+\bar{C})+\bar{A}\cdot\bar{B}\cdot\bar{C}+\bar{A}\cdot B\cdot C$

$\qquad = A\cdot(\bar{B}\cdot\bar{C}+B\cdot C)+\bar{A}\cdot B\cdot\bar{C}+\bar{A}\cdot\bar{B}\cdot C$

$\qquad = A\cdot\bar{B}\cdot\bar{C}+A\cdot B\cdot C+\bar{A}\cdot B\cdot\bar{C}+\bar{A}\cdot\bar{B}\cdot C$

$(A\oplus B)\oplus C=(A\cdot\bar{B}+\bar{A}\cdot B)\oplus C$

$\qquad = (A\cdot\bar{B}+\bar{A}\cdot B)\bar{C}+\overline{(A\cdot\bar{B}+\bar{A}\cdot B)}C$

$\qquad = A\cdot\bar{B}\cdot\bar{C}+\bar{A}\cdot B\cdot\bar{C}+\overline{(A\cdot\bar{B}+\bar{A}\cdot B)}\cdot C$

$\qquad = A\cdot\bar{B}\cdot\bar{C}+\bar{A}\cdot B\cdot\bar{C}+\bar{A}\cdot\bar{B}\cdot C+A\cdot B\cdot C$

Both of these expressions are equal and therefore the operator $\oplus$ is associative.

(b) Consider $F=A\oplus B$.

$$F=A\cdot\bar{B}+\bar{A}\cdot B$$

If $A=0$ then $F=B$ because $0\cdot\bar{B}+1\cdot B=B$.

If $A=1$ then $F=\bar{B}$.

In other words, if one input to an EOR gate is connected to a logical one, the other input appears at the output in a *complemented* form. Therefore, the EOR gate can act as an inverter. If an EOR gate connected as an inverter is applied to the output of an AND gate, the AND gate is transformed into a NAND gate. Because all logic functions can be generated by NAND gates only, it follows that all logic functions can be generated by AND gates and EOR gates acting as inverters.

Problem 4

Design a BCD-to-7-segment decoder (BCD means binary-coded decimal). The decoder has a 4-bit natural binary BCD input represented by D, C, B, A, where A is the least-significant bit. Assume that the BCD input can never be greater than 9 (Chapter 4 describes BCD codes). The seven-segment decoder illustrated by Fig. 2.111 has seven outputs (a to g) that are used to illuminate any combination of bars a to g of a

7-segment display; for example, if the code for 2 (i.e. 0010) is sent to the decoder, segments a, b, d, e, and g are illuminated to form a '2'.

Solution 4

The truth table for this problem is given in Table 2.28. This table has four inputs and seven outputs (one for each of the segments).

We can now solve the equation for segments a to g. By using Karnaugh maps the don't care conditions can be catered for.

Figure 2.112 gives the Karnaugh map for segment a. From the Karnaugh map we can write down the expression for $a = D + B + C \cdot A + \overline{C} \cdot \overline{A}$.

An alternative approach is to obtain a by considering the zeros on the map to get the complement of a. From

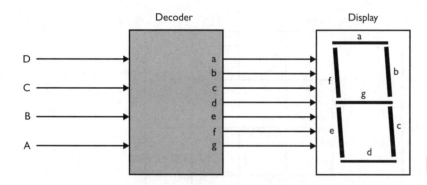

Fig. 2.111 The 7-segment display.

Inputs				Character	Outputs						
D	C	B	A		a	b	c	d	e	f	g
0	0	0	0	0	I	I	I	I	I	I	0
0	0	0	I	1	0	I	I	0	0	0	0
0	0	I	0	2	I	I	0	I	I	0	I
0	0	I	I	3	I	I	I	I	0	0	I
0	I	0	0	4	0	I	I	0	0	I	I
0	I	0	I	5	I	0	I	I	0	I	I
0	I	I	0	6	I	0	I	I	I	I	I
0	I	I	I	7	I	I	I	0	0	0	0
I	0	0	0	8	I	I	I	I	I	I	I
I	0	0	I	9	I	I	I	0	0	I	I
I	0	I	0	Forbidden code	X	X	X	X	X	X	X
I	0	I	I	Forbidden code	X	X	X	X	X	X	X
I	I	0	0	Forbidden code	X	X	X	X	X	X	X
I	I	0	I	Forbidden code	X	X	X	X	X	X	X
I	I	I	0	Forbidden code	X	X	X	X	X	X	X
I	I	I	I	Forbidden code	X	X	X	X	X	X	X

Table 2.28 Truth table for a 7-segment display.

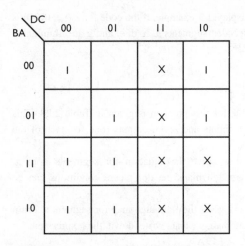

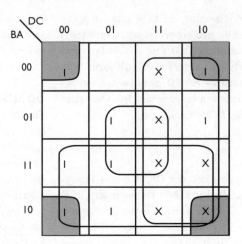

Fig 2.112 Karnaugh map for segment a (Problem 4).

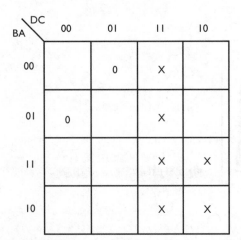

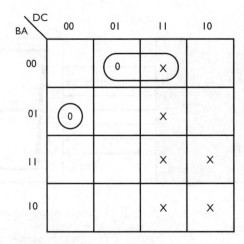

Fig. 2.113 Karnaugh map for the complement of segment a (Problem 4).

the Karnaugh map in Fig. 2.113 we can write $a = \overline{\overline{D} \cdot \overline{C} \cdot \overline{B} \cdot A + C \cdot \overline{B} \cdot \overline{A}}$. Therefore,

$$a = \overline{\overline{D} \cdot \overline{C} \cdot \overline{B} \cdot A + C \cdot \overline{B} \cdot \overline{A}} = (D + C + B + \overline{A})(\overline{C} + B + A)$$
$$= D \cdot \overline{C} + D \cdot B + D \cdot A + C \cdot \overline{C} + C \cdot B + C \cdot A + \overline{C} \cdot B + B \cdot B + B \cdot A + \overline{C} \cdot \overline{A} + B \cdot \overline{A} + \overline{A} \cdot A$$
$$= D \cdot \overline{C} + D \cdot B + D \cdot A + C \cdot B + C \cdot A + \overline{C} \cdot B + B + B \cdot A + \overline{C} \cdot \overline{A} + B \cdot \overline{A}$$
$$= D \cdot \overline{C} + D \cdot A + C \cdot A + B + \overline{C} \cdot \overline{A}$$
$$= D \cdot \overline{C} + C \cdot A + B + \overline{C} \cdot \overline{A}$$

This expression offers no improvement over the first realization of a.

Figure 2.114 provides the Karnaugh map for segment b, which (after simplification) gives $b = \overline{C} + \overline{B} \cdot \overline{A} + B \cdot A$. We can

proceed as we did for segment a and see what happens if we use $\overline{b}$. Plotting zeros on the Karnaugh map for $\overline{b}$ (Fig. 2.115)

we get $\overline{b} = C \cdot \overline{B} \cdot A + C \cdot B \cdot \overline{A}$. Therefore,

$$b = \overline{C \cdot \overline{B} \cdot A + C \cdot B \cdot \overline{A}}$$
$$= (\overline{C} + B + \overline{A})(\overline{C} + \overline{B} + A) = \overline{C} + B \cdot A + \overline{B} \cdot \overline{A}$$

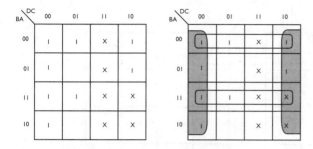

Fig. 2.114 Karnaugh map for segment b (Problem 4).

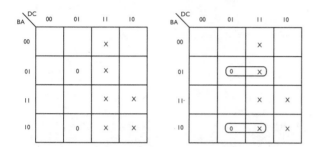

Fig. 2.115 Karnaugh map for the complement of segment b (Problem 4).

Inputs				A>B	A<B	A=B
A	B	C	D			
A_1	A_0	B_1	Z_0	X	Y	Z
0	0	0	0	0	0	1
0	0	0	1	0	1	0
0	0	1	0	0	1	0
0	0	1	1	0	1	0
0	1	0	0	1	0	0
0	1	0	1	0	0	1
0	1	1	0	0	1	0
0	1	1	1	0	1	0
1	0	0	0	1	0	0
1	0	0	1	1	0	0
1	0	1	0	0	0	1
1	0	1	1	0	1	0
1	1	0	0	1	0	0
1	1	0	1	1	0	0
1	1	1	0	1	0	0
1	1	1	1	0	0	1

Table 2.29 Truth table for the comparator (Problem 5).

This expression yields the same result as that obtained directly by considering the ones on the Karnaugh map. The equations for the remaining five segments can be considered in a similar way.

Problem 5

A logic circuit has two 2-bit natural binary inputs A and B. A is given by A_1, A_0, where A_1 is the most-significant bit. Similarly, B is given by B_1, B_0, where B_1 is the most-significant bit. The circuit has three outputs, X, Y, and Z. This circuit compares A with B and determines whether A is greater or less than B, or is the same as B. The relationship between inputs A and B and outputs X, Y, Z is as follows:

Condition	X	Y	Z
A>B	1	0	0
A<B	0	1	0
A=B	0	0	1

Design a circuit to implement this function.

Solution 5

The truth table for this problem (Table 2.29) is obtained by treating the A and B inputs as 2-bit numbers (i.e. $0, 0 = 0$,

$0, 1 = 1$, $1, 0 = 2$, and $1, 1 = 3$) and then comparing the A and B inputs.

We can use a Karnaugh map to derive expressions for outputs X, Y, and Z, as Fig. 2.116 demonstrates. We have used this example to demonstrate *symmetry* in Boolean systems. Notice the relationship between the column corresponding to the X output (A>B) and the Y output (A<B). These outputs are complements for all cases except when A=B. You would expect this symmetry from the very nature of the problem.

From Fig. 2.116 we can write down expressions for X, Y, and Z as

$$X = A_1 \cdot \overline{B}_1 + A_1 \cdot A_0 \cdot \overline{B}_0 + A_0 \cdot \overline{B}_1 \cdot \overline{B}_0$$
$$Y = \overline{A}_1 \cdot B_1 + \overline{A}_1 \cdot \overline{A}_0 \cdot B_0 + \overline{A}_0 \cdot B_1 \cdot B_0$$
$$Z = \overline{A}_1 \cdot \overline{A}_0 \cdot \overline{B}_1 \cdot \overline{B}_0 + \overline{A}_1 \cdot A_0 \cdot \overline{B}_1 \cdot B_0 + A_1 \cdot A_0 \cdot B_1 \cdot B_0 + A_1 \cdot \overline{A}_0 \cdot B_1 \cdot \overline{B}_0$$

Figure 2.117 gives a circuit for the comparator constructed from AND, OR, and NOT gates. Note that we have provided circuits for X and Y (although you might derive one from the other by means of an inverter).

Problem 6

A logic circuit has two four inputs D, C, B, A that represent two pairs of bits (D, C) and (B, A). Bits B, A are subtracted from bits D, C to give a result F_1, F_0 and an *n*-bit that indicates a negative result. Table 2.30 provides a truth table for this problem. Construct three Karnaugh maps for the outputs and use them to obtain simplified sum-of-product expressions.

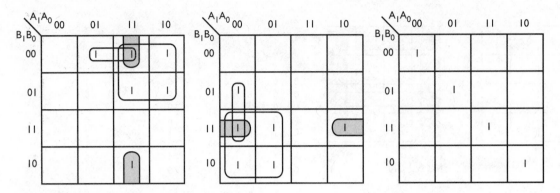

Fig. 2.116 Karnaugh map for a comparator (Problem 5).

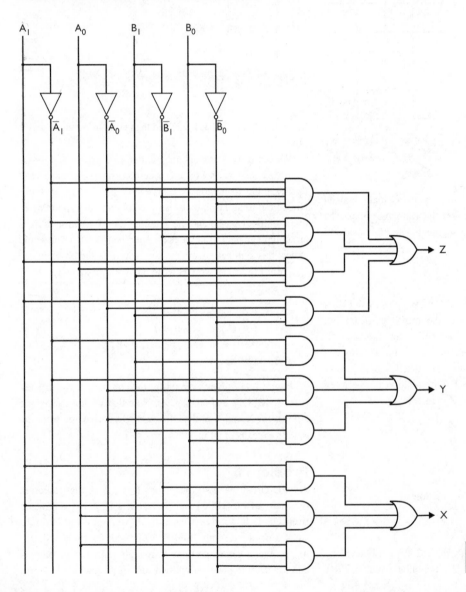

Fig. 2.117 Circuit for a comparator (Problem 5).

Inputs				Number	Outputs		
D	C	B	A		n	F_1	F_0
0	0	0	0	$0-0=0$	0	0	0
0	0	0	1	$0-1=-1$	1	0	1
0	0	1	0	$0-2=-2$	1	1	0
0	0	1	1	$0-3=-3$	1	1	1
0	1	0	0	$1-0=1$	0	0	1
0	1	0	1	$1-1=0$	0	0	0
0	1	1	0	$1-2=-1$	1	0	1
0	1	1	1	$1-3=-2$	1	1	0
1	0	0	0	$2-0=2$	0	1	0
1	0	0	1	$2-1=1$	0	0	1
1	0	1	0	$2-2=0$	0	0	0
1	0	1	1	$2-3=-1$	1	0	1
1	1	0	0	$3-0=3$	0	1	1
1	1	0	1	$3-1=2$	0	1	0
1	1	1	0	$3-2=1$	0	0	1
1	1	1	1	$3-3=0$	0	0	0

Table 2.30 Truth table for Problem 6.

Solution 6

By the three Karnaugh maps corresponding to outputs n, F_1, and F_0 in the truth table. The 1s have been regrouped under each truth table to provide the minimum number of large groups.

We can write down expressions for n, F_1, and F_0 from Fig. 2.118 as

$$n = \overline{D}\cdot B + \overline{C}\cdot B\cdot A + \overline{D}\cdot \overline{C}\cdot A$$
$$F_1 = \overline{D}\cdot \overline{C}\cdot B + D\cdot C\cdot \overline{B} + D\cdot \overline{B}\cdot \overline{A} + \overline{D}\cdot B\cdot A$$
$$F_0 = \overline{C}\cdot A + C\cdot \overline{A}$$

Problems

1. Explain the meaning of the terms

    (a) sum of products

    (b) product of sums

    (c) minterm

    (d) truth table

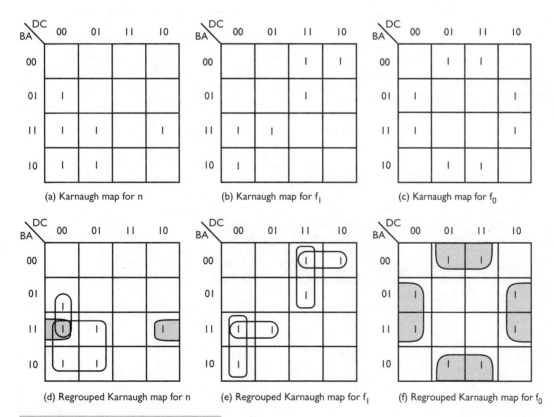

(a) Karnaugh map for n

(b) Karnaugh map for f_1

(c) Karnaugh map for f_0

(d) Regrouped Karnaugh map for n

(e) Regrouped Karnaugh map for f_1

(f) Regrouped Karnaugh map for f_0

Fig. 2.118 The Karnaugh maps for Problem 6.

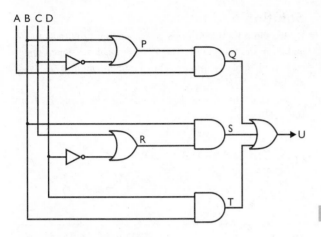

Fig. 2.119 Circuit for Problem 2.

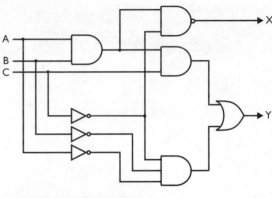

Fig. 2.120 Circuit for Problem 5.

(e) literal
(f) constant
(g) variable

2. Tabulate the values of the variables, P, Q, R, S, T, U in the circuit of Fig. 2.119, for all possible input variables A, B, C, D. The truth table for this problem should be expressed in the form of Table 2.31.

3. For the circuit of Fig. 2.119 in Problem 2 obtain a Boolean expression for the output, U, in terms of the inputs A, B, C, D. You should obtain an expression for the output U by considering the logic function of each gate.

4. For the truth table of Problem 2 (Table 2.31) obtain a sum of minterms expression for U and use Boolean algebra to obtain a simplified sum of products expression for U.

5. Use a truth table to obtain the relationship between outputs X and Y, and the input variables A, B, C for the circuit in

Fig. 2.120. From the truth table write down Boolean expressions for X and Y. Derive expressions for X and Y by considering the Boolean equations of the gates.

Demonstrate that the two results (i.e. those derived from the truth table and those derived from the Boolean equations) are equivalent by substituting literals (000, 001, etc.) for A, B, and C in the Boolean equations.

6. Draw logic diagrams using AND, OR, NOT gates only, to implement the following Boolean expressions. In each case draw the diagrams directly from the equations and do not attempt to simplify the expressions.

(a) $F = \overline{A} \cdot B + A \cdot \overline{B}$
(b) $F = (A + B + C)(A \cdot B + A \cdot C)$
(c) $F = (A + \overline{C})(A + B \cdot \overline{D})$
(d) $F = \overline{A} + \overline{C} \cdot A + B \cdot \overline{D}$
(e) $F = (A \cdot \overline{B} + \overline{A} \cdot B + A \cdot \overline{C})(\overline{A} \cdot \overline{B} + \overline{A} \cdot \overline{B} + A \cdot \overline{C})$

Inputs				Output					
A	B	C	D	$P = B + \overline{C}$	$Q = P \cdot A$	$R = C + \overline{D}$	$S = B \cdot R$	$T = B \cdot D$	$U = Q + S + T$
0	0	0	0	I	0	I	0	0	0
0	0	0	I	.	.	.	.	.	.
0	0	I	0	.	.	.	.	.	.
0	0	I	I	.	.	.	.	.	.
0	I	0	0	.	.	.	.	.	.
0	I	0	I	.	.	.	.	.	.
...									
...									
I	I	I	I	I	I	I	I	I	I

Table 2.31 Truth table for Problem 2.

7. Plot the following functions on a Karnaugh map.

   (a) $F = A \cdot B \cdot C + \overline{A} \cdot \overline{B} \cdot \overline{C}$

   (b) $F = \overline{A} \cdot \overline{B} \cdot C + A \cdot \overline{B} \cdot \overline{C} + \overline{A} \cdot B \cdot C$

   (c) $F = \overline{A} + A \cdot B + A \cdot C + A \cdot B \cdot C$

   (d) $F = A + B \cdot \overline{A} \cdot C + D$

   (e) $F = A \cdot B \cdot C \cdot D + A \cdot B \cdot \overline{C} \cdot D + B \cdot D$

8. How would you plot the following expressions on a Karnaugh map?

   (a) $(\overline{A} + B + C)(\overline{D} + \overline{B})(\overline{A} + C)$

   (b) $(A \cdot \overline{B} + A \cdot B + \overline{A} \cdot C)(\overline{A} \cdot D + A \cdot \overline{B} + A \cdot C)$

9. Simplify the following expressions by means of Boolean algebra. That is, do not use Karnaugh maps.

   (a) $A \cdot \overline{B} \cdot \overline{C} + \overline{A} \cdot \overline{B} \cdot \overline{C} + A \cdot B \cdot \overline{C} + \overline{A} \cdot \overline{B} \cdot C$

   (b) $A \cdot B \cdot C + \overline{A} \cdot B \cdot C + A \cdot \overline{B} \cdot \overline{C} + A \cdot \overline{B} \cdot C + \overline{A} \cdot B \cdot \overline{C} + \overline{A} \cdot \overline{B} \cdot \overline{C}$

   (c) $A \cdot B \cdot C + A \cdot \overline{B} \cdot \overline{C} + \overline{A} \cdot \overline{B} \cdot C + A \cdot B \cdot \overline{C} + A \cdot \overline{B} \cdot C + A \cdot B \cdot \overline{C} + \overline{A} \cdot B \cdot \overline{C} + \overline{A} \cdot B \cdot C$

10. Simplify the following expressions.

    (a) $(A + B + C)(\overline{A} + B + \overline{C})$

    (b) $(A \cdot \overline{B} + \overline{A} \cdot B + \overline{A} \cdot C)(A \cdot \overline{B} + A \cdot \overline{B} + A \cdot C)$

    (c) $A + \overline{B} + (A + C \cdot D)(A + \overline{B} \cdot C)$

    (d) $A \cdot \overline{B} + B \cdot \overline{C} + A \cdot \overline{B} \cdot \overline{C} + A \cdot B \cdot \overline{C} \cdot D$

    (e) $(\overline{A} + B)(A + \overline{B} + \overline{C})(A + B + \overline{C})(\overline{A} + \overline{B} + C)$

11. Use de Morgan's theorem to complement the following expressions. Do not simplify the expressions either before or after you complement them.

    (a) $\overline{B} \cdot \overline{C} + B \cdot C$

    (b) $B \cdot C \cdot D + \overline{B} \cdot \overline{C}$

    (c) $B(C + D) + \overline{B} \cdot \overline{C}$

    (d) $A \cdot B(\overline{C} \cdot D + C \cdot D)$

    (e) $A \cdot B(A \cdot \overline{D} + \overline{C} \cdot D)$

    (f) $B \cdot C + \overline{B} \cdot \overline{C}(A \cdot D + \overline{A} \cdot D)$

12. Convert the following expressions to sum-of-products form.

    (a) $(A + B)(\overline{B} + C)(\overline{A} + C)$

    (b) $(C + D)(A \cdot \overline{B} + A \cdot C)(\overline{A} \cdot \overline{C} + B)$

    (c) $(A + B + C)(A + C \cdot D)(D + F)$

13. Simplify

    (a) $A \oplus B \oplus C$

    (b) $A \cdot \overline{B}(C \oplus A)$

14. Convert the following expressions to product-of-sums form.

    (a) $A \cdot B + \overline{A} \cdot \overline{B} + B \cdot C$

    (b) $\overline{A} \cdot \overline{B} + B \cdot C + \overline{B} \cdot \overline{C} \cdot D$

   (c) $A \cdot B + \overline{A} \cdot C + B \cdot \overline{C}$

   (d) $A \cdot \overline{B} \cdot \overline{C} + \overline{A} \cdot \overline{B} \cdot \overline{C} + \overline{A} \cdot B \cdot \overline{C} + \overline{A} \cdot \overline{B} \cdot C$

15. A circuit has four inputs, P, Q, R, S, representing the natural binary numbers $0000 = 0$, to $1111 = 15$. P is the most significant bit. The circuit has one output, X, which is true if the number represented by the input is divisible by three. (Regard zero as being indivisible by three.) Design a truth table for this circuit, and hence obtain an expression for X in terms of P, Q, R, and S. Give the circuit diagram of an arrangement of AND, OR, and NOT gates to implement this circuit. Design a second circuit to implement this function using NAND gates only.

16. A device accepts natural binary numbers in the range 0000 to 1111 that represent 0 to 15. The output of the circuit is true if the input to the circuit represents a prime number and is false otherwise. Design a circuit using AND, OR, and NOT gates to carry out this function. A prime number is an integer that is greater than 1 and is divisible only by itself and 1. Zero and one are not prime numbers.

17. Demonstrate how you would use a 4-line to 16-line demultiplexer to implement the system in Problem 16.

18. A logic circuit accepts a natural binary number DCBA in the range 0 to 15 (the least significant bit is bit A). The output is the square of the input; for example, if $DCBA = 0101_2 = 5_{10}$, the output is $00010101_2 = 25_{10}$. Design a circuit to implement this function.

19. A logic circuit has three inputs C, B, A, where A is the least significant bit. The circuit has three outputs R, Q, and P. For any binary code applied to the input terminals (A, B, C) the output is given by the input plus 1; for example, if C, B, A = 0, 1, 1, the output R, Q, P is 1, 0, 0. Note that $111 + 1 = 000$ (i.e. there is no carry out). Design a circuit to implement this system.

20. A 4-bit binary number is applied to a circuit on four lines D, C, B, and A. The circuit has a single output, F, which is true if the number is in the range 3 to 12, inclusive. Draw a truth table for this problem, and obtain a simplified expression for F in terms of the inputs. Implement the circuit:

    (a) in terms of NAND gates only

    (b) in terms of NOR gates only

21. A circuit has four inputs D, C, B, A encoded in 8421 natural binary form. The inputs in the range $0000_2 = 0$ to $1011_2 = 11$ represent the months of the year from January (0) to December (11). Inputs in the range 1100 to 1111

(i.e. 12 to 15) cannot occur. The output of the circuit is a logical one if the month represented by the input has 31 days. Otherwise the output is false. The output for inputs in the range 1100 to 1111 is undefined.

(a) Draw a truth table to represent the problem and use it to construct a Karnaugh map.

(b) Use the Karnaugh map to obtain a simplified expression for the function.

(c) Construct a circuit to implement the function using AND, OR, and NOT gates.

(d) Construct a circuit to implement the function using NAND gates only.

(e) Construct a circuit to implement the function using NOR gates only.

22. A multiplexer has eight inputs Y_0 to Y_7 and a single output Z. A further three inputs A, B, C (A = least significant bit) determine which output the single input X is connected to. For example, if A, B, C = 110, the output $Y_6 = X$ and all other outputs are low. Design a circuit to implement this function.

23. What is tri-state logic and why is it used in digital systems?

24. Use Digital Works to construct a circuit that realizes the expression

$$\overline{A} \cdot B \cdot C + \overline{A} \cdot \overline{B} \cdot C + \overline{A} \cdot \overline{B} \cdot \overline{C} + A \cdot B \cdot C$$

Simplify the above expression and use Digital Works to construct a new circuit. Demonstrate that the two circuits are equivalent (by comparing their outputs for all inputs).

25. Suppose you wish to transmit up to 16 digital signals between two points separated by some distance and you have only five lines. However, you don't have to transmit all 16 values at once; they can be sent one at a time.

How would you solve this problem? *Hint:* Think about the nature of the multiplexer and demultiplexer.

26. Use Digital Works to construct the system of Problem 25 and demonstrate that your system works.

Chapter 3

Sequential logic

We now introduce a new type of circuit that is constructed from *sequential* logic elements—memory devices that remember their previous inputs. Up to this point the logic circuits we've encountered were all built with *combinational elements*. The principal characteristic of a combinational circuit is that its output is a function of its inputs *only*; that is, given a knowledge of the circuit's inputs and its Boolean function, we can always calculate the state of its outputs. In this chapter we introduce the *sequential circuit*, whose output depends not only on its current inputs, but also on its *previous* inputs. Even if we know a sequential circuit's Boolean equations, we can't determine its output state without a knowledge of its past history (i.e. its previous internal states). The basic building blocks of sequential circuits are the *flip-flop*, *bistable*, and *latch*, just as the basic building block of the combinational circuit is the gate.

It's not our intention to deal with sequential circuits at anything other than an introductory level, as their full treatment forms an entire branch of digital engineering. Sequential circuits can't be omitted from introductory texts on computer hardware because they are needed to implement registers, counters, and shifters, all of which are fundamental to the operation of the central processing unit.

Figure 3.1 describes the conceptual organization of a sequential circuit. An input is applied to a combinational circuit using AND, OR, and NOT gates to generate an output. The output is fed to a memory circuit that holds the value of the output. The information held in this memory is called the *internal state* of the circuit.

Figure 3.1 demonstrates that the sequential circuit's previous output together with its current input is used to generate

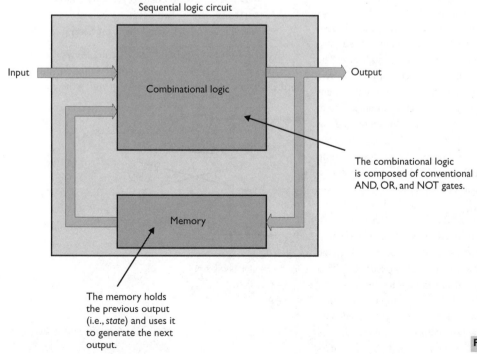

Sequential logic circuit

Input

Combinational logic

Output

The combinational logic
is composed of conventional
AND, OR, and NOT gates.

Memory

The memory holds
the previous output
(i.e., *state*) and uses it
to generate the next
output.

Fig. 3.1 The sequential circuit.

the *next* output. This statement contains a very important implicit concept, the idea of a *next state*. Sequential circuits have a clock input that triggers the transition from the *current* state to the *next* state. The *counter* is a good example of a sequential machine because it stores the current count that is updated to become the next count. We ourselves are state machines because our future behavior depends on our past inputs—if you burn yourself getting something out of the oven, you approach the oven with more care next time.

We begin our discussion of sequential circuits with the *bistable* or *flip-flop*. A bistable is so called because its output can remain in one of two stable states indefinitely, even if the input changes. That is, for a particular input, the bistable's output may be high or low, the actual value depending on the previous inputs. Such a circuit remembers what has happened to it in the past and is therefore a form of memory element. A more detailed discussion of memory elements is given in Chapter 8. A bistable is the smallest possible memory cell and stores only a single bit of information. The term *flip-flop*, which is synonymous with bistable, gives the impression of the circuit going *flip* into one state and then *flop* into its complement. Once upon a time bistables were constructed from electromagnetic relays that really did make a flip-flop sound as they jumped from one state into another.

The term *latch* is also used to describe certain types of flip-flop. A latch is a flip-flop that is unclocked (i.e. its operation isn't synchronized with a timing signal called a *clock*). The RS flip-flop that we describe first can also be called a latch.

Sequential systems can be divided into two classes: *synchronous* and *asynchronous*. Synchronous systems use a master clock to update the state of all flip-flops periodically. The speed of a synchronous system is determined by its slowest device and all signals must have settled to steady state values by the time the system is clocked. In an asynchronous system a change in an input signal triggers a change in another circuit and this change ripples through the system (an asynchronous system is rather like a line of closely spaced dominoes on edge—when one falls it knocks its neighbor over and so on). Reliable asynchronous systems are harder to design than synchronous systems, although they are faster and consume less power. We will return to some of these topics later.

We can approach flip-flops in two ways. One is to demonstrate what they do by defining their characteristics as an abstract model and then show how they are constructed. That is, we say this is a flip-flop and this is how it behaves—now let's see what it can do. The other way of approaching flip-flops is to demonstrate how they can be implemented with just two gates and then show how their special properties are put to work. We intend to follow the latter path. Some readers

may prefer to skip ahead to the summary of flip-flops at the end of this section and then return when they have a global picture of the flip-flop.

3.1 The RS flip-flop

We begin our discussion of the flip-flop with the simplest member of the family, the RS flip-flop. Figure 3.2 illustrates one of the most complex logic circuits in this book. What differentiates this circuit from the combinational circuits of Chapter 2 is that the gates are *cross-coupled* and the output of a gate is fed back to its input. Although Fig. 3.2 uses no more than two 2-input NOR gates, its operation is not immediately apparent.

The circuit has two inputs, A and B, and two outputs, X and Y. A truth table for the NOR gate is provided alongside Fig. 3.2 for reference. From the Boolean equations governing the NOR gates we can readily write down expressions for outputs X and Y in terms of inputs A and B.

(1) $X = \overline{A + Y}$

(2) $Y = \overline{B + X}$

If we substitute the value for Y from equation (2) in equation (1), we get:

$$
\begin{aligned}
(3) \quad X &= \overline{A + \overline{B + X}} \\
&= \overline{A} \cdot \overline{\overline{B + X}} && \text{By de Morgan's theorem} \\
&= \overline{A} \cdot (B + X) && \text{Two negations cancel} \\
&= \overline{A} \cdot B + \overline{A} \cdot X && \text{Expand the expression}
\end{aligned}
$$

Because Boolean algebra doesn't define the operations of division or subtraction we can't simplify this equation any further and are left with an expression in which the *output* is a

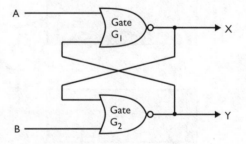

Truth table for NOR gate

P	Q	$\overline{P+Q}$
0	0	1
0	1	0
1	0	0
1	1	0

Fig. 3.2 Two cross-coupled NOR gates.

function of the *output*; that is, the value of X depends on X. Equation (3) is correct but its meaning isn't obvious. We have to look for another way of analyzing the behavior of cross-coupled gates. Perhaps a better approach to understanding this circuit is to assume a value for output X and for the inputs A and B and then see where it leads us.

Analyzing a sequential circuit by assuming initial conditions

Figure 3.3(a) shows the cross-coupled NOR gate circuit with the initial condition X = 1 and A = B = 0. Figure 3.3(b) shows the same circuit redrawn to emphasize the way in which data flows between the gates. As the inputs to gate G_2 are X = 1, B = 0, its output, $Y = \overline{X + B}$, must be 0. The inputs to gate G_1 are Y = 0 and A = 0, so that its output, X, is $\overline{Y + A}$ which is 1. Now note that this situation is self-consistent. The output of gate G_1 is X = 1, which is fed back to the input of gate G_1 to keep X in a logical 1 state. That is, the output actually maintains itself. It should now be a little clearer why equation (3) has X on *both* sides (i.e. $X = \overline{A} \cdot B + \overline{A} \cdot X$).

Had we assumed the initial state of X to be 0 and inputs A = B = 0, we could have proceeded as follows. The inputs to G_2 are X = 0, B = 0 and therefore its output is $Y = \overline{X + B} = \overline{0 + 0} = 1$. The inputs to G_1 are Y = 1 and A = 0, and its output is $X = \overline{Y + A} = \overline{1 + 0} = 0$. Once more we can see that the circuit is self-consistent. The output can remain indefinitely in either a 0 or a 1 state for the inputs A = B = 0.

The next step in the analysis of the circuit's behavior is to consider what happens if we change inputs A and B. Assume that the X output is initially in a logical 1 state. If input B to gate G_2 goes high while input A remains low, the output of gate G_2 (i.e. Y) is unaffected, because the output of a NOR gate is low if either of its inputs is high. As X is already high, the state of B has no effect on the state of Y.

If now input A goes high while B remains low, the output, X, of gate G_1 must fall to a logical 0 state. The inputs to gate G_2 are now both in logical 0 states, and its output Y rises to a logical 1. However, because Y is fed back to the input of gate G_1, the output X is maintained at a logical 0 even if A returns to a 0 state.

The effect of setting A to a 1 causes output X to flip over from a 1 to a 0, and to *remain* in that state when A returns to a 0. We call an RS flip-flop a *latch* because of its ability to capture a signal. Table 3.1 provides a truth table for the circuit of Fig. 3.2. Two tables are presented—one appropriate to the circuit we have described and one with its inputs and outputs relabeled.

Table 3.1(a) corresponds exactly to the two NOR gate circuit of Fig. 3.2, and Table 3.1(b) to the idealized form of this circuit that's called an *RS flip-flop*. There are two differences between Tables 3.1(a) and 3.1(b). Table 3.1(b) uses the conventional labeling of an RS flip-flop with inputs R and S and an output Q. The other difference is in the entry for the case in which A = B = 1, and R = S = 1. The effect of these differences will be dealt with later.

We have already stated that the circuit of Fig. 3.2 defines its output in terms of itself (i.e. $X = \overline{A} \cdot B + \overline{A} \cdot X$). The truth table gets round this problem by creating a new variable, X^+ (or Q^+), where X^+ is the *new* output generated by the *old* output X and the current inputs A and B. The equation can be rewritten as $X^+ = \overline{A} \cdot B + \overline{A} \cdot X$. The input and output columns of the truth table are now not only separated in space (e.g. input on the left and output on the right) but also in *time*. The *current* output X is combined with inputs A and B to generate a *new* output X^+. The value of X that produced X^+ no longer exists and belongs only to the past.

Labels R and S in Table 3.1(b) correspond to *reset* and *set*, respectively. The word 'reset' means 'make 0' (*clear* has the same meaning) and 'set' means 'make 1'. The output of all

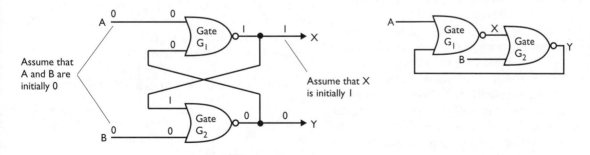

(a) Analyzing the circuit by assuming initial conditions

(b) An alternative view of the circuit

Fig. 3.3 Analyzing the behavior of cross-coupled NOR gates.

(a) Truth table for Fig. 3.2

Inputs			Output
A	B	X	X⁺
0	0	0	0
0	0	I	I
0	I	0	I
0	I	I	I
I	0	0	0
I	0	I	0
I	I	0	0
I	I	I	0
	↑	↑	
	Old X	New X	

(b) Truth table for relabeled Fig. 3.2

Inputs			Output
R	S	Q	Q⁺
0	0	0	0
0	0	I	I
0	I	0	I
0	I	I	I
I	0	0	0
I	0	I	0
I	I	0	?
I	I	I	?
		↑	↑
		Old Q	New Q

The truth table is interpreted as follows. The output of the circuit is currently X (or Q), and the new inputs to be applied to the input terminals are A, B (or R, S). When these new inputs are applied to the circuit, its output is given by X⁺ (or Q⁺). For example, if the current output X is I, and the new values of A and B are A = I, B = 0, then the new output, X⁺, will be 0. This value of X⁺ then becomes the next value of X when new inputs A and B are applied to the circuit.

Table 3.1 Truth table for the circuit in Fig. 3.2.

flip-flops is called Q by a historical convention. Examining the truth table reveals that whenever R = 1, the output Q is reset to 0. Similarly, when S = 1 the output is set to 1. When R and S are both 0, the output does not change; that is, $Q^+ = Q$.

If both R and S are simultaneously 1, the output is conceptually undefined (hence the question marks in truth table 3.1(b)), because the output can't be set and reset at the same time. In the case of the RS flip-flop implemented by two NOR gates, the output X does, in fact, go low when A = B = 1. In practice, the user of an RS flip-flop should avoid the condition R = S = 1. This statement is, perhaps, a little too harsh. It is possible to assert both the R and S inputs to an RS flip-flop simultaneously—if you know exactly how the flip-flop will behave under these circumstances.

The two NOR-gate flip-flop of Fig. 3.2 has two outputs X and Y. An examination of the circuit for all inputs except A = B = 1 reveals that X and Y are complements. Because of the symmetric nature of flip-flops, almost all flip-flops have two outputs, Q and its complement $\overline{Q}$. However, the complement of Q may not always be available to the user of the flip-flop since many commercial devices leave $\overline{Q}$ buried on the chip and not brought out to a pin. Figure 3.4 gives the circuit representation of an RS flip-flop.

We can draw the truth table of the RS or any other flip-flop in two ways. Up to now we've presented truth tables with *two* output lines for each possible input, one line for Q = 0 and one

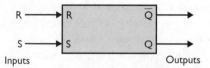

Fig. 3.4 Circuit representation of the RS flip-flop as a black box.

Inputs		Output	Description
R	S	Q⁺	
0	0	Q	No change
0	I	I	Set output to I
I	0	0	Reset output to 0
I	I	X	Forbidden

Table 3.2 An alternative truth table for the RS flip-flop.

for Q = 1. An alternative approach is to employ the algebraic value of Q and is illustrated by Table 3.2.

When R = S = 0 the new output, Q⁺, is simply the old output Q. In other words, the output doesn't change state and remains in its previous state as long as R and S are both 0. The inputs R = S = 1 result in the output Q⁺ = X. The symbol X is used in truth tables to indicate an *indeterminate* or *undefined* condition. In Chapter 2 we used the same symbol to indicate a *don't care* condition. An indeterminate condition is one whose outcome can't be calculated, whereas a don't care condition is one whose outcome does not matter to the designer.

Characteristic equation of an RS flip-flop

We have already demonstrated that you can derive an equation for a flip-flop by analyzing its circuit. Such an equation is called the flip-flop's *characteristic equation*. Instead of using an actual circuit, we can derive a characteristic equation from the flip-flop's truth table. Figure 3.5 plots Table 3.1(b) on a Karnaugh map. We have indicated the condition R = S = 1 by X because it is a forbidden condition.

From this truth table we can write $Q^+ = S + Q \cdot \overline{R}$.

Note that this equation is slightly different from the one we derived earlier because it treats R = S = 1 as a don't care condition.

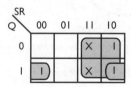

Fig. 3.5 Karnaugh map for the characteristic equation of an RS flip-flop.

3.1.1 Building an RS flip-flop from NAND gates

We can construct an RS flip-flop from two cross-coupled NAND gates just as easily as from two NOR gates. Figure 3.6 illustrates a two-NAND gate flip-flop whose truth table is given in Table 3.3.

The only significant difference between the NOR gate flip-flop of Fig. 3.2 and the NAND gate flip-flop of Fig. 3.6 is that the inputs to the NAND gate flip-flop are active-low. If we were to place inverters at the R and S inputs to the NAND gate flip-flop, it would then be logically equivalent to the NOR gate flip-flop of Fig. 3.2.

The '*no change*' input to the NAND gate flip-flop is R, S = 1, 1; the output is cleared by forcing R = 0 and set by forcing S = 0; the forbidden input state is R, S = 0, 0. Suppose that we did set the inputs of a NAND-gate RS flip-flop to 0, 0 and then released the inputs to 1, 1 to enter the no change state. What would happen? The answer is that we can't predict the final outcome. Initially, when both inputs are 0s, *both* outputs of the RS flip-flop must be 1s (because the output of a NAND gate is a 1 if either of its inputs are a 0). The real problem arises when the inputs change state from 0, 0 to 1, 1. Due to tiny imperfections, either one or the other input would go high before its neighbor and cause the flip-flop to be set or reset.

Real applications of RS flip-flops may employ either two NAND or two NOR gates, depending only on which gates provide the simpler solution. In practice, the majority of RS flip-flops are often constructed from NAND gates because most circuits use active-low signals. We began our discussion of RS flip-flops with the NOR gate circuit (unlike other texts that introduce first the more common NAND gate flip-flop) because we have discovered that many students find it hard to come to terms with negative logic (i.e. logic in which the low state is the active state).

3.1.2 Applications of the RS flip-flop

An important application of RS flip-flops is in the recording of short-lived events. If the Q output of a flip-flop is in a zero state, a logical 1 pulse at its S input (assuming the R input is 0) will cause Q to be set to a 1, and to remain at a 1, until the R input resets Q. The effect of a pulse at the S input followed by a pulse at the R input of an RS flip-flop is illustrated in Fig. 3.7.

Consider the following application of RS flip-flops to an indicator circuit. If an aircraft is flown outside its performance envelope no immediate damage may be apparent, but its structure might be permanently weakened. To keep things simple, we will consider three possible events that are considered harmful and might endanger the aircraft:

1. Exceeding the maximum permissible speed V_{ne}.
2. Extending the flaps above the flap-limiting speed V_{fl}. That is, the flaps must not be lowered if the aircraft is going faster than V_{fl}.
3. Exceeding the maximum acceleration (g-force) G_{max}.

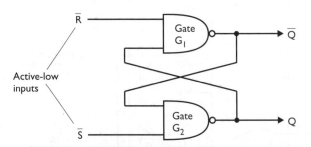

Fig. 3.6 RS flip-flop constructed from two cross-coupled NAND gates.

Inputs		Output	Description
R	S	Q+	
0	0	X	Forbidden
0	1	1	Reset output to 0
1	0	0	Set output to 1
1	1	Q	No change

Table 3.3 Truth table for an RS flip-flop constructed from NAND gates.

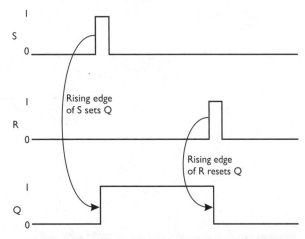

Fig. 3.7 Timing diagram of the effect of pulses on an RS flip-flop's inputs.

If any of the above parameters are exceeded (even for only an instant), a lasting record of the event must be made.

Figure 3.8 shows the arrangement of warning lights used to indicate that one of these conditions has been violated. Transducers that convert acceleration or velocity into a voltage measure the acceleration and speed of the aircraft. The voltages from the transducers are compared with the three threshold values (V_{ne}, V_{fl}, G_{max}) in comparators, whose outputs are true if the threshold is exceeded, otherwise false. In order to detect the extension of flaps above the flap-limiting speed, the output of the comparator is ANDed with a signal from the flap actuator circuit that is true when the flaps are down.

The three signals from the comparators are fed, via OR gates, to the S inputs of three RS flip-flops. Initially, on switching on the system, the flip-flops are automatically reset by applying a logical 1 pulse to all R inputs simultaneously. If at any time one of the S inputs becomes true, the output of that flip-flop is set to a logical 1 and triggers an alarm. All outputs are ORed together to illuminate a master warning light. A master alarm signal makes it unnecessary for the pilot to have to scan all the warning lights periodically. An additional feature of the circuit is a test facility. When the warning test button is pushed, all warning lights should be illuminated and remain so until the reset button is pressed. A test facility verifies the correct operation of the flip-flops and the warning lights.

A pulse-train generator

Another simple application of the RS flip-flop is illustrated by the pulse-train generator of Fig. 3.9, that generates a sequence of N pulses each time it is triggered by a positive transition at its START input. The value of N is user-supplied and is fed to the circuit by three switches to select the values of C_c, C_b, C_a. This circuit uses the counter that we will meet later in this chapter.

The key to this circuit is the RS flip-flop, G_6, used to start and stop the pulse generator. Assume that initially the R and S inputs to the flip-flop are $R = 0$ and $S = 0$ and that its output Q is a logical 0. Since one of the inputs to AND gate G_1 is low, the pulse train output is also low.

When a logical 1 pulse is applied to the flip-flop's START input, its Q output rises to a logical 1 and enables AND gate G_1. A train of clock pulses at the second input of G_1 now appears at the output of the AND gate. This *gated* pulse train is applied to the input of a counter (to be described later) that

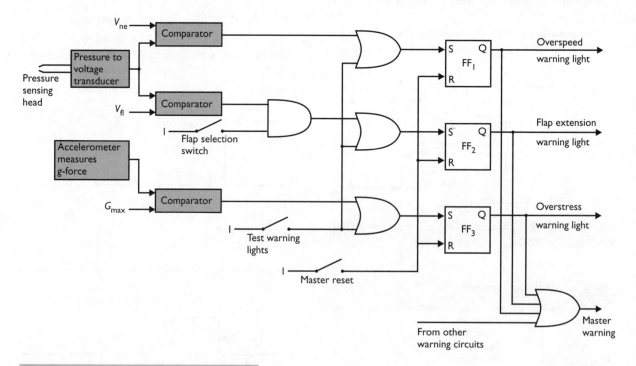

Fig. 3.8 Application of RS flip-flops in a warning system.

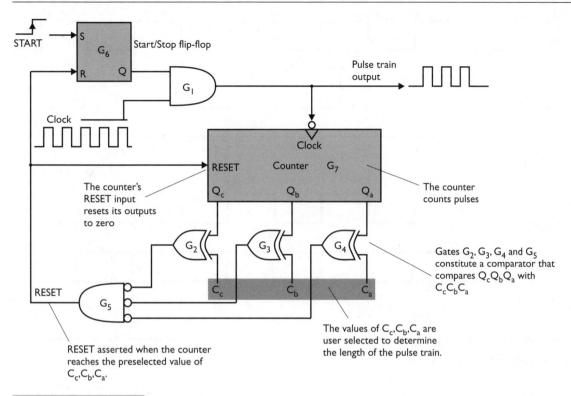

Fig. 3.9 Pulse train generator.

counts pulses and generates a 3-bit output on Q_a, Q_b, Q_c, corresponding to the number of pulses counted in the range 0 to 7. The outputs of the counter are fed to an *equality detector* composed of three EOR gates G_2 to G_4 plus NOR gate G_5. A second input to the equality detector is the user-supplied count value C_a, C_b, C_c. The outputs of the EOR gates are combined in NOR gate G_5 (notice that it is drawn in negative logic form to emphasize that the output is 1 if all its inputs are 0).

Figure 3.10 gives a timing diagram for the pulse generator. Initially the counter is held in a reset state ($Q_a = Q_b = Q_c = 0$). When the counter is clocked, its output is incremented by one on the falling edge of each clock pulse. The counter counts upward from zero and the equality detector compares the current count on Q_a, Q_b, Q_c, output with the user-supplied inputs C_a, C_b, C_c. When the output of the counter is equal to the user-supplied input, the output of gate G_5 goes high and resets both the counter and the RS flip-flop. Resetting the counter forces the counter output to 0. Resetting the RS flip-flop disables AND gate G_1 and no further clock pulses appear at the output of G_1. In this application of the RS flip-flop, its S input is triggered to start an action and its R input is triggered to terminate the action.

3.1.3 The clocked RS flip-flop

The RS flip-flop of Fig. 3.2 responds immediately to signals applied to its inputs according to its truth table. There are, however, situations when we want the RS flip-flop to ignore its inputs until a suitable time. The circuit of Fig. 3.11 demonstrates how this is accomplished by turning the RS flip-flop into a *clocked* RS flip-flop.

A normal, unmodified, RS flip-flop lies in the inner box in Fig. 3.11. Its inputs, R′ and S′, are derived from the external inputs R and S by ANDing them with a clock input C—some texts call these two AND gates '*steering gates*'. As long as C = 0, the inputs to the RS flip-flop, R′ and S′, are forced to remain at 0, no matter what is happening to the external R and S inputs. The output of the RS flip-flop remains constant as long as these R′ and S′ inputs are both 0.

Whenever C = 1, the external R and S inputs to the circuit are transferred to the flip-flop so that R′ = R and S′ = S, and the flip-flop responds accordingly. The clock input may be thought of as an *inhibitor*, restraining the flip-flop from acting until the right time. Figure 3.12 demonstrates how we can conveniently build a clocked RS flip-flop from NAND gates.

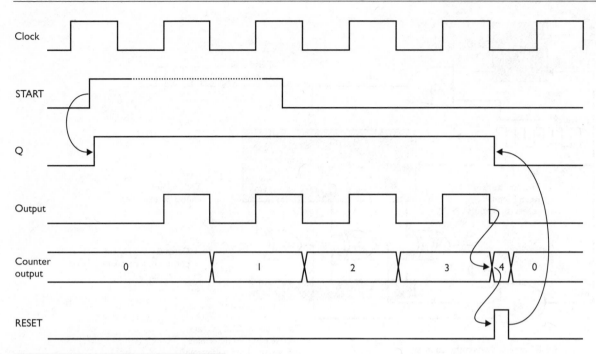

Fig. 3.10 Timing diagram of pulse train generator.

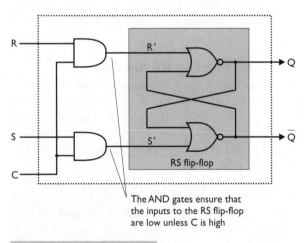

The AND gates ensure that the inputs to the RS flip-flop are low unless C is high

Fig. 3.11 The clocked RS flip-flop.

The subject of clocked flip-flops is dealt with in more detail later in this section.

3.2 The D flip-flop

Like the RS flip-flop, the D flip-flop has two inputs, one called D and the other C. The D input is often referred to as

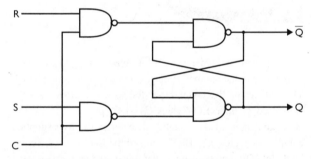

Fig. 3.12 Building a clocked RS flip-flop with NAND gates.

the *data* input and C as the *clock* input. The D flip-flop is, by its nature, a clocked flip-flop and we will call the act of pulsing the C input high and then low *clocking* the D flip-flop.

Whenever a D flip-flop is clocked, the value at its D input is transferred to its Q output and the output then remains constant until the next time it is clocked. Some people call the D flip-flop a *staticizer* because it records the state of the D input and holds it constant until it's once more clocked. Others call it a *delay* element because, if the D input changes state at time *T* but the flip-flop is clocked *t* seconds later, the output Q doesn't change state until *t* seconds after the input. I think of the D flip-flop as a census taker. When it is clocked it takes a census of the input and remembers it until the next census is taken. The truth table for a D flip-flop is given in Table 3.4.

The circuit of a D flip-flop is provided in Fig. 3.13 and consists of an RS flip-flop plus a few gates. The two AND gates turn the RS flip-flop into a clocked RS flip-flop. As long as the C input to the AND gates is low, the R and S inputs are clamped at 0 and Q cannot change.

When C goes high, the S input is connected to D and the R input to $\overline{D}$. Therefore, (R, S) must either be (0, 1) if D = 1, or (1, 0) if D = 0. Consequently, D = 1 sets the RS flip-flop, and D = 0 clears it.

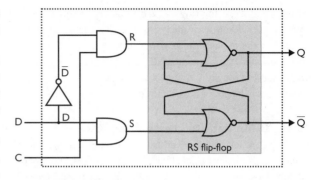

Fig. 3.13 Circuit of a D flip-flop.

Practical sequential logic elements

Just as some of the semiconductor manufacturers have provided a range of combinational logic elements in single packages, they have done the same with sequential logic elements. Indeed, there are far more special-purpose sequential logic elements than combinational logic elements. Practical flip-flops are more complex than those presented hitherto in this chapter. Real circuits have to cater for real-world problems. We have already said that the output of a flip-flop is a function of its current inputs and its previous output. What happens when a flip-flop is first switched on? The answer is quite simple. The Q output takes on a random state, assuming no input is being applied that will force Q into a 0 or 1 state.

Random states may be fine at the gaming tables in Las Vegas; they're less helpful when the control systems of a nuclear reactor are first energized. For this reason, many flip-flops are provided with special control inputs that are used to place them in a known state. Figure 3.14 illustrates the 74LS74, a dual positive-edge triggered D flip-flop that has two active-low control inputs called *preset* and *clear* (abbreviated $\overline{PRE}$ and $\overline{CLR}$). In normal operation both $\overline{PRE}$ and $\overline{CLR}$ remain in logical 1 states. If $\overline{PRE} = 0$ the Q output is set to a logical 1, and if $\overline{CLR} = 0$ the Q output is cleared to a logical

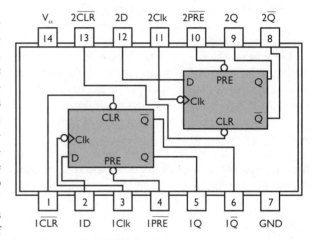

Fig. 3.14 The 74LS74 D flip-flop.

0. As in the case of the RS flip-flop, the condition $\overline{PRE} = \overline{CLR} = 0$ should not be allowed to occur.

These preset and clear inputs are *unconditional* in the sense that they override all activity at the other inputs of this flip-flop. For example, asserting $\overline{PRE}$ sets Q to 1 irrespective

Full form					Algebraic form		
Inputs			Output		Inputs		Output
C	D	Q	Q⁺		C	D	Q⁺
0	0	0	0	$Q^+ \leftarrow Q$ No change	0	0	Q
0	0	1	1	$Q^+ \leftarrow Q$ No change	0	1	Q
0	1	0	0	$Q^+ \leftarrow Q$ No change	1	0	0
0	1	1	1	$Q^+ \leftarrow Q$ No change	1	1	1
1	0	0	0	$Q^+ \leftarrow D$			
1	0	1	0	$Q^+ \leftarrow D$			
1	1	0	1	$Q^+ \leftarrow D$			
1	1	1	1	$Q^+ \leftarrow D$			

Table 3.4 Truth table for a D flip-flop.

of the state of the flip-flop's C and D inputs. When a digital system is made up from many flip-flops that must be set or cleared at the application of power, their $\overline{\text{PRE}}$ or $\overline{\text{CLR}}$ lines are connected to a common $\overline{\text{RESET}}$ line and this line is momentarily brought to a logical zero level by a single pulse shortly after the power is switched on.

Using D flip-flops to create a register

In Chapter 5 we shall discover that a computer is composed of little more than combinational logic elements, buses, and groups of flip-flops called *registers* that transmit data to and receive data from buses. A typical example of the application of D flip-flops is provided by Fig. 3.15, in which an *m*-bit wide data bus transfers data from one part of a digital system to another. Data on the bus is constantly changing as different devices use it to transmit their data from one register to another.

The D inputs of a group of *m* D flip-flops are connected to the *m* lines of the bus. The clock inputs of all flip-flops are connected together, allowing them to be clocked simultaneously. As long as $C = 0$, the flip-flops ignore data on the bus and their Q outputs remain unchanged. Suppose some device wishes to transfer its data to the flip-flops. It first puts its data on the bus and then the flip-flops are clocked, latching the data into them. When the clock has returned to zero, the data remains frozen in the flip-flops.

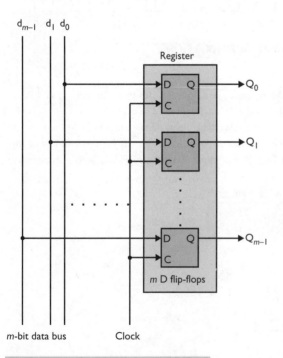

Fig. 3.15 Using D flip-flops to create a register.

Using Digital Works to create a register

We are now going to use Digital Works to create a simple bused system using D flip-flops. Although Digital Works implements both RS and D flip-flops, we'll construct a D flip-flop from basic gates. Figure 3.16 shows a single 1-bit cell in a register (we can construct an *m*-bit register by using *m* identical elements in parallel).

If you examine Fig. 3.16 you will find that the flip-flop is more complex than the simple D flip-flop of Fig. 3.13. We have added a tri-state gate to the Q output to allow the flip-flop to drive a bus or to be disconnected from the bus. Furthermore, we've added an input multiplexer to allow the D input to be connected to one of two sources, A and B. The inputs and output of Fig. 3.16 are

- A input
- B input
- A/B select input
- Clock input
- Enable output
- Q output

In Fig. 3.17 we've used Digital Work's macro facility to convert the circuit in Fig. 3.16 into a black-box macro that can be used as a circuit element to build more complex systems.

Figure 3.18 provides a test bed for three of the *register slices*. We have provided one bit of three registers and three buses (input bus A, input bus B, and output bus C). Each register slice is connected to all three buses. We've added input devices to all the control inputs to enable us to experiment with this circuit.

The system in Fig. 3.18 can't do a lot, but what it can do is very important. Because we've added input devices to buses A and B, we can force our own data on bus A and B. We can select whether each register slice gets its input from bus A or bus B by setting the value of the *Input select* input to 1 (bus A) or 0 (bus B). Data is clocked into any of the register slices by clocking it (i.e. setting its clock input to 1 to capture the data and then setting the clock input to 0 to latch and retain the data). Finally, data from any of the three register slices can be put on bus C by asserting the appropriate output.

This circuit is important because it forms the heart of a typical computer. All we need to create an ALU (arithmetic and logic unit) are the circuits that take data from bus C, process it and copy the result to the A or B bus.

A typical register chip

You can obtain a single package containing several flip-flops connected together to implement a register. Figure 3.19

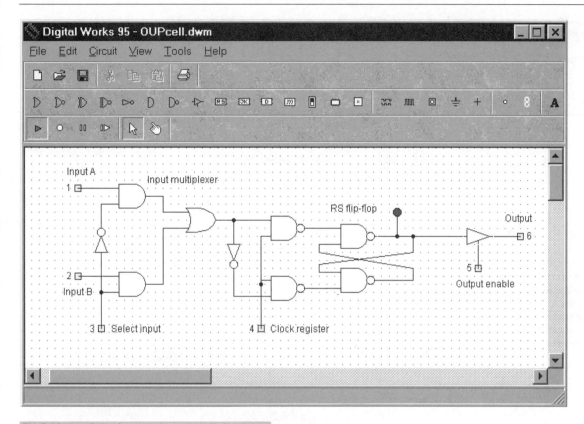

Fig. 3.16 Using D flip-flops to create one cell of a register.

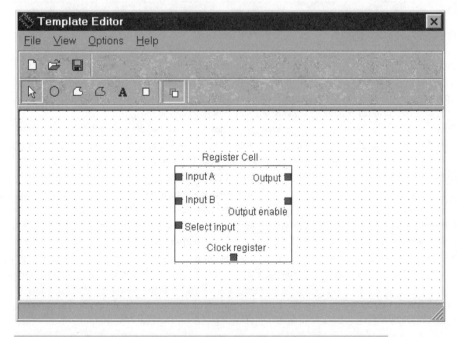

Fig. 3.17 Converting the circuit of Fig. 3.16 into a macro (i.e. black box representation).

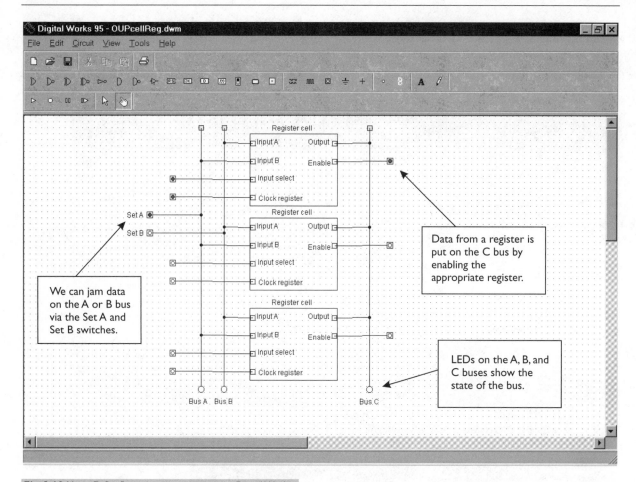

Fig. 3.18 Using D flip-flops to create a register in Digital Works.

illustrates the 74LS373, an octal register composed of D flip-flops that is available in a 20-pin package with eight inputs, eight outputs, two power supply pins, and two control inputs. The clock input, G, is a level-sensitive clock, that, when high, causes the value at D_i to be transferred to Q_i. All eight clock inputs are connected together internally so that the G input clocks each flip-flop simultaneously.

The 74LS373's other control input is active-low $\overline{OE}$ (output enable), which is used to control the output of all flip-flops. When $\overline{OE} = 0$, the flip-flop behaves exactly as we would expect. When $\overline{OE} = 1$, the eight Q outputs are internally disconnected from the output pins of the device; that is, the 74LS373 has tri-state outputs and $\overline{OE}$ is used to turn off the chip's output circuits when it is not driving a bus.

Figure 3.20 demonstrates how the 74LS373 octal register might be used in a digital system. Four 74LS373 octal registers are connected to a common data bus. Each register is arranged

so that *both* its outputs and its inputs are connected to the same bus. Consequently, each register can transmit data onto the bus or receive data from the bus.

Each register has tri-state outputs controlled by an output enable pin, $\overline{OE}$. When $\overline{OE}$ is asserted low, the corresponding register drives the bus. The registers are clocked by an active-high clock input labeled G.

IC5a is a 2-line to 4-line decoder (i.e. this is a demultiplexer of the type we described in Chapter 2). When this device is enabled, the 2-bit binary *source code* at the input of IC5a causes one of its output lines, $\overline{Y}_0$ to $\overline{Y}_3$, to go low. These outputs are connected to the respective $\overline{OE}$ inputs of the four registers. Each of the four possible source codes enables one of the registers. For example, if the source code at the input to IC5a is 01, the output of register 1 is enabled and the contents of register 1 are placed on the bus. The outputs of all other registers remain internally disconnected from the bus.

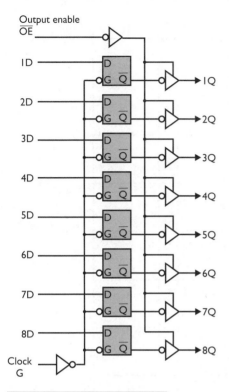

Fig. 3.19 The 74LS373 octal register.

3.3 Clocked flip-flops

Before we introduce the JK flip-flop we look more closely at the idea of *clocking* sequential circuits. Clocked circuits allow logic elements to respond to their inputs only when the inputs are valid. Some writers use the term *trigger* rather than clock, because 'triggering a flip-flop' gives the impression of causing an event to take place at a discrete instant. We begin by examining the effect of delays on the passage of signals through systems.

Figure 3.21 demonstrates the effect of circuit delays on a system with two inputs A and B that are acted upon by *processes* A, B, and C to produce an output. The nature of the processes is not important because we're interested only in the way in which they delay signals passing through them. Imagine that at time $t = 0$, the inputs to processes A and B become valid (i.e. these are the correct inputs to be operated on by the processes). Assume that process A in Fig. 3.21 introduces a two-unit delay and process B a one-unit delay.

Although the output from process B becomes valid at $t = 1$, it's not until $t = 2$ that the output of process A has become valid. The outputs of processes A and B are fed to process C that has a two-unit delay. Clearly, the desired output from C due to inputs A and B is not valid until at least four time units after $t = 0$. The output from process C changes at least once before it settles down to its final value. (Why? Because of the different delays through processes A and B.) This poses a problem. How does an observer at the output of process C know when to act upon the data from C?

What we need is some means of capturing data only when we know that it's valid—see Fig. 3.22. If a D flip-flop is placed at the output of process C and is clocked four units of time after $t = 0$, the desired data will be latched into the flip-flop and held constant until the next clock pulse. Clocked systems hold digital information constant in flip-flops while the information is operated on by groups of logic elements, analogous to the processes of Fig. 3.21. Between clock pulses, the outputs of the flip-flops are processed by the logic elements and the new data values are presented to the inputs of flip-flops.

After a suitable time delay (longer than the time taken for the slowest process to be completed), the flip-flops are clocked. The outputs of the processes are held constant until the next time the flip-flops are clocked. A clocked system is often called *synchronous*, as all processes are started simultaneously on each new clock pulse. An *asynchronous* system is one in which the end of one process signals (i.e. triggers) the start of the next. Obviously, an asynchronous system must be faster

The 74LS139 contains two complete 2-line to 4-line decoders in a single 16-pin package. The second half of this package acts as a destination decoder. Each of the four outputs from IC5b is connected to one of the clock inputs, G, of the four registers. Since the clock inputs are active-high and the outputs of the decoder are active-low, it's necessary to invert these outputs. Four inverters, IC6, perform this function.

When IC5b is enabled, one of its outputs is asserted and the corresponding register clocked. Clocking a register latches data from the data bus.

Suppose the contents of register 1 are to be copied into register 3. The source code at IC5a is set to 01 and the destination code at IC5b is set to 11. This puts the data from register 1 on the bus and latches the data into register 3. We can easily relate the example of Fig. 3.20 to the digital computer. One of the most fundamental operations in computing is the assignment which can be represented in a high-level language as A = B and in a low-level languages as MOVE A, B. The action MOVE A, B (i.e. transfer the contents of A to B) is implemented by specifying A as the source and B as the destination.

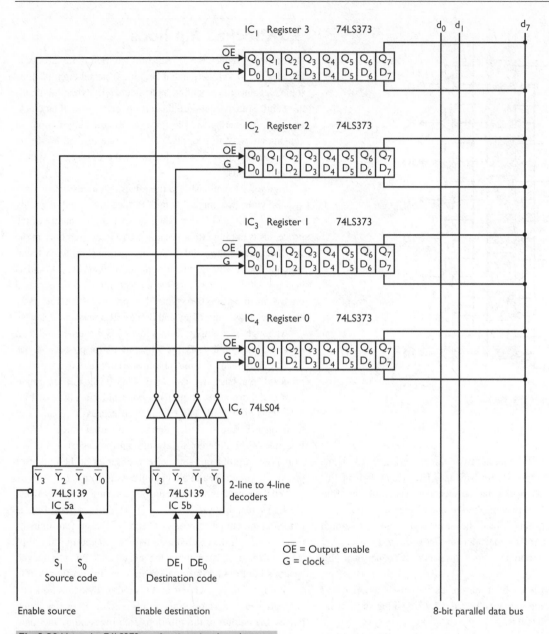

Fig. 3.20 Using the 74LS373 octal register in a bused system.

than the corresponding synchronous system. Asynchronous systems are more complex and difficult to design than synchronous systems and popular wisdom says that they are best avoided because they are inherently less reliable than synchronous circuits. However, the 1990s did see a renewed interest in asynchronous systems because of their speed and lower power consumption.

Now consider the effect of placing D flip-flops at the outputs of processes A, B, and C in the system of Fig. 3.23. Before continuing, we need to make a few observations about this *timing diagram*. Figure 3.23 shows the logical state of several points in a system as a function of time. The diagram is read from left to right (the direction of time flow). Signals are represented by parallel lines to demonstrate that the signal

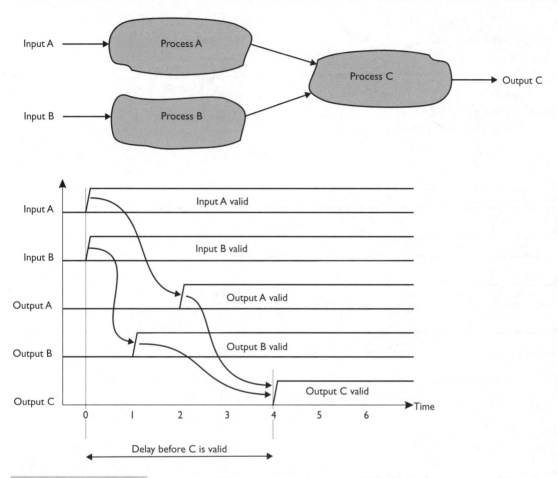

Fig. 3.21 Processes and delays.

values may be 1s or 0s (we don't care). What matters is the time at which signals change. Changes are shown by the parallel lines crossing over. Lines with arrowheads are drawn between points to demonstrate cause and effect; for example, the line from 'Input A' to 'Output A' shows that a change in 'Input A' leads to a change in 'Output A'.

In this example we assume that each of the processes introduces a single unit of delay and the flip-flops are clocked simultaneously every unit of time. Figure 3.23 gives the timing diagram for this system. Note how a new input can be accepted every unit of time, rather than every two units of time as you might expect. The secret of our increase in throughput is called *pipelining* because we are operating on different data at different stages in the pipeline. For example, when process A and process B are operating on data i, process C is operating on data $i-1$ and the latched output from process C corresponds to data $i-2$.

When we introduce the RISC processor in Chapter 7, we will discover that pipelining is a technique used to speed up the operation of a computer by overlapping consecutive operations.

Ways of clocking flip-flops

A clocked flip-flop can capture a digital value and hold it constant. There are, however, three ways of clocking a flip-flop:

1. Whenever the clock is asserted (i.e. a level-sensitive flip-flop)

2. Whenever the clock is changing state (i.e. an edge-sensitive flip-flop)

3. Capture data on one edge of the clock and transfer it to the output on the following edge (i.e. a master–slave flip-flop)

A *level-sensitive* clock triggers a flip-flop whenever the clock is in a particular logical state (some flip-flops are clocked by a logical 1 and some by a logical 0). The clocked RS flip-flop

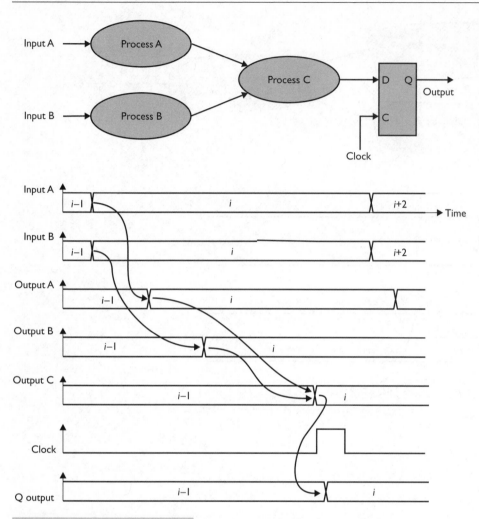

Fig. 3.22 Latching the output of a system.

of Fig. 3.11 is level-sensitive because the RS flip-flop responds to its R and S inputs whenever the clock input is high. Unfortunately, a level-sensitive clock is unsuitable for certain applications. Consider the system of Fig. 3.24, in which the output of a D flip-flop is fed through a logic network and then back to its D input. If we call the output of the flip-flop the current Q, then the current Q is fed through the logic network to generate a new input D. When the flip-flop is clocked, the value of D is transferred to the output to generate Q^+.

Unfortunately, if the clock is level sensitive, the new Q^+ can rush through the logic network, change D and hence the output. This chain of events will continue in an oscillatory fashion with the 'dog chasing its tail'. To avoid such unstable or unpredictable behavior, we need an infinitesimally short clock pulse to capture the output and hold it constant. As such

a pulse short pulse can't easily be created, the *edge-sensitive* clock has been introduced to solve the feedback problem. Level-sensitive clocked D flip-flops are often perfectly satisfactory in applications such as registers connected to data buses, because the duration of the clock is usually small compared with the time for which the data is valid.

3.3.1 Edge-triggered flip-flops

An edge-triggered flip-flop is clocked not by the level or *state* of the clock (i.e. high or low), but by the *transition* of the clock signal from zero to one or one to zero. The former case is called a positive or rising-edge sensitive clock, and the latter is called a negative or falling-edge sensitive clock. As the rising (or falling) edge of most pulses has a duration of

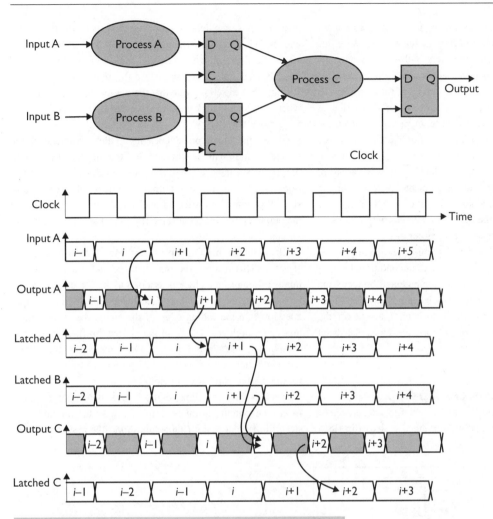

Fig. 3.23 Latching the input and output of processes to implement pipelining.

less than 2 ns, an edge-triggered clock can be regarded as a level-sensitive clock triggered by a pulse of an infinitesimally short duration. A nanosecond (ns) is a thousand millionth (10^{-9}) of a second. For this reason, the problem described by Fig. 3.24 ceases to exist because there's insufficient time for the new output to race back to the input within the duration of a single rising edge.

There are circumstances when edge-triggered flip-flops are unsatisfactory because of a phenomenon called clock *skew*. If, in a digital system, several edge-triggered flip-flops are clocked by the same edge of a pulse, the exact times at which the individual flip-flops are clocked vary. Variation in the arrival time of pulses at each clock input is called *clock skew* and is caused by the different paths by which clock pulses reach each flip-flop. Electrical impulses move through circuits

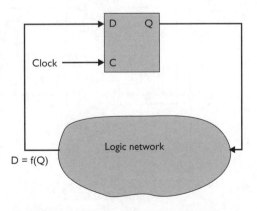

Fig. 3.24 Feedback and the level-sensitive clock.

121

at somewhat less than the speed of light, which is 30 cm per nanosecond. Unless each flip-flop is located at the same distance from the source of the clock pulse and unless any additional delays in each path due to other logic elements are identical, the clock pulse will arrive at the flip-flops at different instants. Moreover, the delay a signal experiences going through a gate changes with temperature and even the age of the gate. Suppose that the output of flip-flop A is connected to the input of flip-flop B and they are clocked together. Ideally, at the moment of clocking, the old output of A is clocked into B. If, by bad design or bad luck, flip-flop A is triggered a few nanoseconds before flip-flop B, B sees the new output from A, not the old (i.e. previous) output—it's as if A were clocked by a separate and earlier clock.

Figure 3.25 gives the circuit diagram of an actual positive edge-triggered D flip-flop that also has unconditional preset and clear inputs. Edge-triggering is implemented by using the active transition of the clock to clock latches 1 and 2 and then feeding the output of latch 2 back to latch 1 to cut off the clock in the NAND gate. That is, once the clock has been detected, the clock input path is removed.

3.3.2 The master–slave flip-flop

The master–slave (MS) flip-flop has the external appearance of a single flip-flop, but internally is arranged as two flip-flops operating in series. One of these flip-flops is called the *master* and the other the *slave*. The term 'slave' is used because the slave flip-flop follows what the *master* does. Figure 3.26 describes a simple RS master–slave flip-flop composed of two RS flip-flops in series. Note that the master flip-flop is enabled when the clock is high and the slave flip-flop is enabled when the clock is low.

When the clock pulse goes high, the input data at the R and S terminals is copied into the master flip-flop in Fig. 3.26 that behaves according to the rules for an RS flip-flop. At this point, the output terminals of the master–slave flip-flop aren't affected and don't change state because the output comes from the slave flip-flop that is in a hold state because its clock is low.

Because the master flip-flop of Fig. 3.26 uses a level-sensitive RS flip-flop, the master responds to data at its RS inputs as long as the clock is asserted high. The data at the RS inputs is latched by the master at the instant the clock input goes low. On the falling edge of the clock, the slave's clock input goes high and data from the master flip-flop's outputs is copied into the slave flip-flop. Only now may the output terminals change state. Figure 3.27 provides a timing diagram for the master–slave RS flip-flop.

Master–slave flip-flops totally isolate their input terminals from their output terminals simply because the output of the slave flip-flop does not change until *after* the input conditions

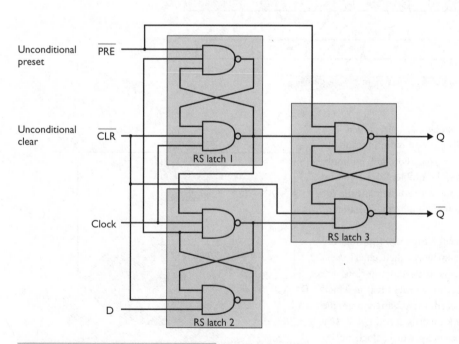

Fig. 3.25 Circuit of an edge-triggered flip-flop.

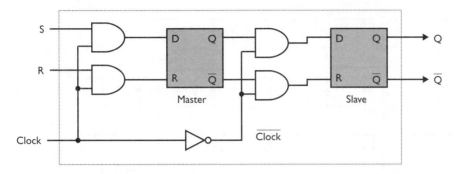

Fig. 3.26 The master–slave RS flip-flop.

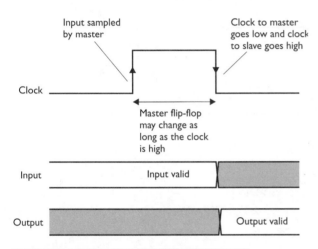

Fig. 3.27 Timing diagram of a master–slave RS flip-flop.

have been sampled and latched internally in the master. Conceptually, the master–slave flip-flop behaves like an air-lock in a submarine or spacecraft. An airlock exists to transfer people between regions of different pressure (air-to-vacuum or air-to-water) without ever permitting a direct path between the two pressure regions. A flip-flop is analogous to an airlock because its output must not be fed directly back to its input. To operate an airlock in a submarine, divers in the water open the airlock, enter and close the door behind them. The divers are now isolated from both the water outside and the air inside. When the divers open the door into the submarine, they step inside and close the airlock door behind them.

In order to demonstrate how the different types of clocked flip-flop behave, Fig. 3.28 presents the output waveforms for a four clocked D flip-flop when presented with the same input.

3.4 The JK flip-flop

The JK flip-flop can be configured, or programmed, to operate in one of two modes. All JK flip-flops are clocked and the majority of them operate on the master–slave principle. The truth table for a JK flip-flop is given in Table 3.5, and Fig. 3.29 gives its logic symbol. Note that a bubble at the clock input to a flip-flop indicates that the flip-flop changes state on the *falling* edge of a clock pulse.

Table 3.5 demonstrates that for all values of J and K, except $J = K = 1$, the JK flip-flop behaves exactly like an RS flip-flop with J acting as the set input and K acting as the reset input. When J and K are both true, the output of the JK flip-flop *toggles*, or changes state, each time the flip-flop is clocked. That is, if Q was a 0 it becomes a 1 and vice versa. It is this property that puts the JK flip-flop at the heart of many counter circuits, the operation of which is dealt with in the next section.

We can derive the characteristic equation for a JK flip-flop by plotting Table 3.5 on a Karnaugh map (Fig. 3.30). This gives $Q^+ = J \cdot \overline{Q} + \overline{K} \cdot Q$.

Figure 3.31 demonstrates how a JK flip-flop can be constructed from NAND gates and Fig. 3.32 describes a master–slave JK flip-flop.

3.5 Summary of flip-flop types

To understand flip-flops, it is necessary to appreciate that, unlike combinational circuits, flip-flops have internal states as well as external inputs. That is, the output of a flip-flop depends on its *internal state*, which, in turn, depends on the previous inputs of the flip-flop. Flip-flops are therefore *memory elements*. The most common forms of flip-flop are the D flip-flop, the RS flip-flop and the JK flip-flop. Each flip-flop has two outputs, Q and its complement $\overline{Q}$, although the

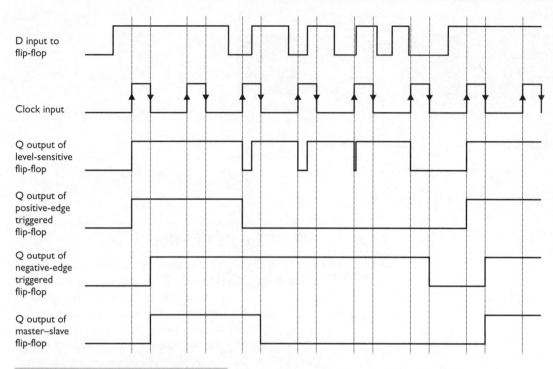

D input to
flip-flop

Clock input

Q output of
level-sensitive
flip-flop

Q output of
positive-edge
triggered
flip-flop

Q output of
negative-edge
triggered
flip-flop

Q output of
master–slave
flip-flop

Fig. 3.28 Comparison of flip-flop clocking modes.

Full form					Algebraic form			
Inputs		Output			Inputs		Output	
J	K	Q	Q⁺		J	K	Q⁺	
0	0	0	0	No change	0	0	Q	No change
0	0	I	I	No change	0	I	0	Clear
0	I	0	0	Reset Q	I	0	I	Set
0	I	I	0	Reset Q	I	I	$\overline{Q}$	Toggle
I	0	0	I	Set Q				
I	0	I	I	Set Q				
I	I	0	I	$Q^+ \leftarrow \overline{Q}$				
I	I	I	0	$Q^+ \leftarrow \overline{Q}$				

Table 3.5 Truth table for a JK flip-flop.

complementary output is not always connected to a pin in an integrated circuit. Most flip-flops are clocked and have a clock input that is used to trigger the flip-flop. Flip-flops often have unconditional preset and clear inputs that can be used to set or clear the output, respectively. The term 'unconditional' simply means that these inputs override any clock input.

The D flip-flop

The D flip-flop is the easiest flip-flop to understand. D flip-flops have two inputs, a D (data) input and a C (clock) input. The output of a D flip-flop remains in its previous state until

its C input is clocked. When its C input is clocked, the Q output becomes equal to D *until the next time it is clocked.*

The RS flip-flop

An RS flip-flop has two inputs, R (reset) and S (set). As long as both R and S are 0, the Q output of the RS flip-flop is constant and remains in its previous state. When R = 1 and S = 0, the Q output is forced to 0 (and remains at zero when R returns to 0). When S = 1 and R = 0, the Q output is forced to 1 (and remains at one when S returns to 0). The input conditions R = S = 1 produce an indeterminate state and should

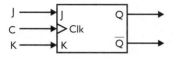

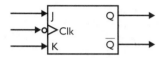

(a) Positive-edge triggered
JK flip-flop

(b) Negative-edge triggered
JK flip-flop

Fig. 3.29 Representation of the JK flip-flop.

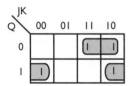

Fig. 3.30 Deriving the characteristic equation of a JK flip-flop.

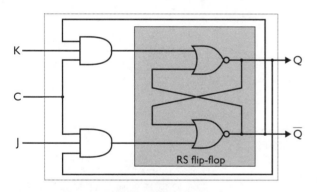

Fig. 3.31 Construction of a basic JK flip-flop.

be avoided by the user of the RS flip-flop. Clocked RS flip-flops behave as we have described, except that their R and S inputs are treated as zero until the flip-flop is clocked. When the RS flip-flop is clocked, its Q output behaves as we have just described.

The JK flip-flop

The JK flip-flop always has three inputs, J, K, and a clock input C. As long as a JK flip-flop is not clocked, its output remains in the previous state. When a JK flip-flop is clocked, it behaves like an RS flip-flop (where J = S, K = R) for all input conditions except J = K = 1. If J = K = 0, the output does not change state. If K = 1 and J = 0, the Q output is reset to zero. If J = 1 and K = 0, the Q output is set to 1. If both J and K are 1, the output changes state (or *toggles*) each time it is clocked.

3.6 Applications of sequential elements

Just as the logic gate is combined with other gates to form combinational circuits such as adders and multiplexers, flip-flops can be combined together to create a class of circuits called sequential circuits. Here, we are concerned with two particular types of sequential circuit: the *shift register* that moves a group of bits left or right, and the *counter* that steps through a sequence of values.

3.6.1 Shift register

We have already seen that *m* D-type flip-flops can create a register that stores an *m*-bit word; for example, Fig. 3.15. By slightly modifying the circuit of the register we can build a *shift register* whose bits can be moved one place right every time the register is clocked. For example, the binary pattern

	01110101	
becomes	00111010	after the shift register is clocked once
and	00011101	after it is clocked twice
and	00001110	after it is clocked three times, etc.

Note that after the first shift, a 0 has been shifted in from the left-hand end and the 1 at the right-hand end has been lost. We used the expression *binary pattern* because, as we shall see later, the byte 01110101 can represent many things. However, when the pattern represents a binary number, shifting it one place right has the effect of dividing the number by two (just as shifting a decimal number one place right divides it by ten). Similarly, shifting a number one place *left* multiplies it by 2. Later we will see that special care has to be taken when shifting signed two's complement binary numbers right (the sign-bit has to be dealt with).

Figure 3.33 demonstrates how a shift register is constructed from D flip-flops. The Q output of each flip-flop is connected to the D input of the flip-flop on its right. All clock inputs are connected together so that each flip-flop is clocked simultaneously. When the *i*th stage is clocked, its output, Q_i, takes on the value from the stage on its left, that is $Q_i \leftarrow Q_{i+1}$. Data presented at the input of the left-hand flip-flop, D_{in}, is shifted into the $(m-1)$th stage at each clock pulse. Figure 3.33

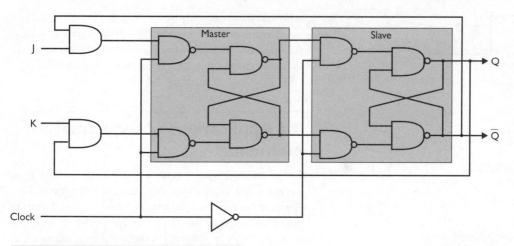

Fig. 3.32 Circuit diagram of a master–slave JK flip-flop.

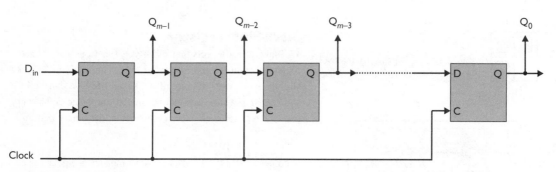

Fig. 3.33 The shift register.

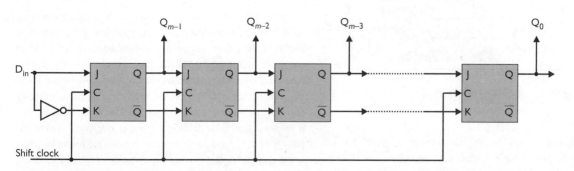

Fig. 3.34 Shift register composed of JK flip-flops.

describes a *right*-shift register—we will look at registers that shift the data sequence left shortly.

It should be obvious that the flip-flops in a shift register must either be edge-triggered or master–slave flip-flops, otherwise if a level-sensitive flip-flop were used, the value at the input to the left-hand stage would ripple through all stages

as soon as the clock went high. We can construct a shift register from JK flip-flops just as easily as from RS flip-flops, as Fig. 3.34 demonstrates. We leave it as an exercise to the reader to work out how this arrangement operates.

Figure 3.35 shows a five-stage shift register that contains the initial value 01101. At each clock pulse the bits are shifted

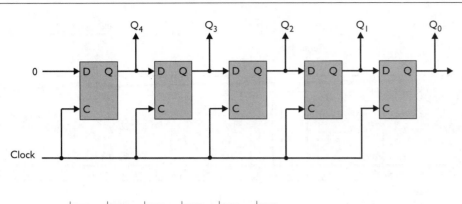

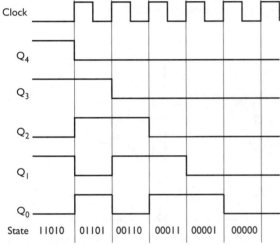

Fig. 3.35 Example of a 5-stage shift-right register.

right and a 0 enters the most-significant bit stage. This figure also provides a timing diagram for each of the five Q outputs. The output of the right-hand stage, Q_0, consists of a series of five sequential pulses, corresponding to the five bits of the word in the shift register (i.e. 11010).

A shift register is often used to convert a parallel word of m bits into a serial word of m consecutive bits. Such a circuit is called a *parallel to serial converter*. If the output of an m-bit parallel to serial converter is connected to the D_{in} input of an m-bit shift register, after m clock pulses the information in the parallel to serial converter has been transferred to the second (right-hand) shift register. Such a shift register is called a *serial to parallel converter* and Fig. 3.36 describes a simplified version. In practice, a means of loading parallel data into the parallel to serial converter is necessary (see Fig. 3.37). Note that there is almost no difference between a parallel to serial converter and a serial to parallel converter.

Many serial data transmission systems (see Chapter 11) operate on this principle.

The only flaw in our shift register (when operating as a parallel to serial converter) is the lack of any facilities for loading it with m bits of data at one go, rather than by shifting in m bits through D_{in}. Figure 3.37 shows a right-shift register with a parallel load capacity. A two-input multiplexer, composed of two AND gates, an OR gate, and an inverter, switches a flip-flop's D input between the output of the previous stage to the left (*shift* mode) and the load input (*load* mode). The control inputs of all multiplexers are connected together to provide the mode control, labeled load/$\overline{\text{shift}}$. When we label a variable name1/name2, we mean that when the variable is high it carries out action *name1* and when it is low it carries out action *name2*. If load/$\overline{\text{shift}} = 0$ the operation performed is a shift and if load/$\overline{\text{shift}} = 1$ the operation performed is a load.

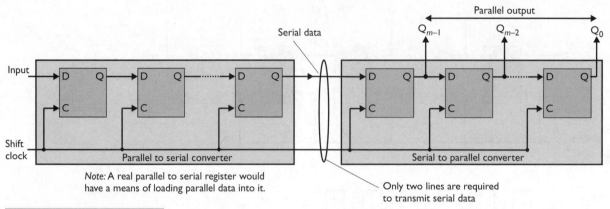

Fig. 3.36 Serial to parallel converter.

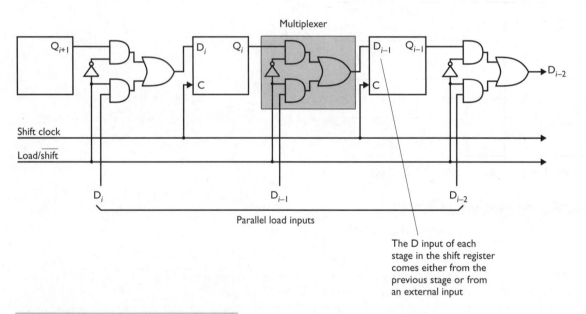

Fig. 3.37 Shift register with a parallel load capability.

Constructing a left-shift register with JK flip-flops

Although we have considered the right-shift register, a left-shift register is equally easy to design. The input of the ith stage, D_i, is connected to the output of the $(i-1)$th stage so that, at each clock pulse, $Q_i \leftarrow D$. In terms of the previous example:

$$
\begin{array}{lll}
 & 01110101 & \\
\text{becomes} & 11101010 & \text{after 1 shift left} \\
\text{and} & 11010100 & \text{after 2 shifts left}
\end{array}
$$

The structure of a left-shift register composed of JK flip-flops is described in Figure 3.38.

When we introduce the instruction set of a typical computer we'll see that there are several types of shift (logical, arithmetic, circular). These operations all shift bits left or right—the only difference between them concerns what happens to the bit shifted in. So far we've described the *logical* shift, where a 0 is shifted in and the bit shifted out at the other end is lost. In an *arithmetic* shift the sign of a two's complement number is preserved when it is shifted right (this will become clear when we introduce the representation of negative

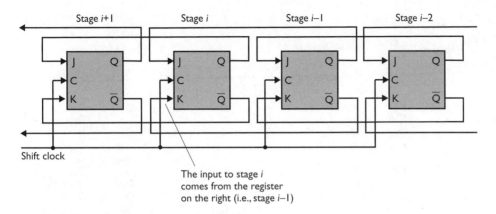

Stage i+1   Stage i   Stage i−1   Stage i−2

Shift clock

The input to stage *i* comes from the register on the right (i.e., stage *i*−1)

Fig. 3.38 The left-shift register.

numbers in the next chapter). In a *circular* shift the bit shifted out of one end becomes the bit shifted in at the other end. Table 3.6 describes what happens when the 8-bit value 11010111 undergoes three types of shift.

A typical shift register

Figure 3.39 gives the internal structure of a 74LS95 parallel-access bi-directional shift register chip. You access the shift register through its pins and cannot make connections to the

Shift type	Shift left	Shift right
Original bit pattern before shift	11010111	11010111
Logical shift	10101110	01101011
Arithmetic shift	10101110	11101011
Circular shift	10101111	11101011

Table 3.6 The effect of logical, arithmetic, and circular shifts.

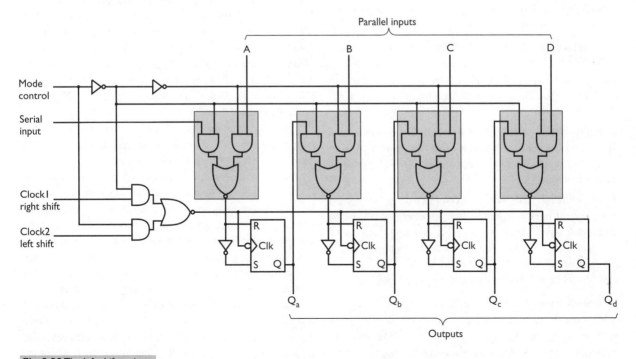

Fig. 3.39 The left-shift register.

Inputs								Outputs			
Mode control	Clocks		Serial	Parallel inputs							
	2 (L)	I (R)		A	B	C	D	Q_a	Q_b	Q_c	Q_d
I	I	x	x	x	x	x	x	Q_{a0}	Q_{b0}	Q_{c0}	Q_{d0}
I	↓	x	x	A	B	C	D	A	B	C	D
I	↓	x	x	Q_b	Q_c	Q_d	D	Q_{bn}	Q_{cn}	Q_{dn}	D
0	0	I	x	x	x	x	x	Q_{a0}	Q_{b0}	Q_{c0}	Q_{d0}
0	x	↓	I	x	x	x	x	I	Q_{an}	Q_{bn}	Q_{cn}
0	x	↓	0	x	x	x	x	0	Q_{an}	Q_{bn}	Q_{cn}
↑	0	0	x	x	x	x	x	Q_{a0}	Q_{b0}	Q_{c0}	Q_{d0}
↓	0	0	x	x	x	x	x	Q_{a0}	Q_{b0}	Q_{c0}	Q_{d0}
↓	0	I	x	x	x	x	x	Q_{a0}	Q_{b0}	Q_{c0}	Q_{d0}
↑	I	0	x	x	x	x	x	Q_{a0}	Q_{b0}	Q_{c0}	Q_{d0}
↑	I	I	x	x	x	x	x	Q_{a0}	Q_{b0}	Q_{c0}	Q_{d0}

Notes 1. Left shift operations assume that Q_b is connected to A, Q_c to B, and Q_d to C
2. x = don't care
3. ↓ and ↑ indicate high-to-low and low-to-high transitions, respectively
4. Q_{a0} indicates the level at Q_a before the indicated inputs were established
5. Q_{an} indicates the level of Q_a before the ↓ transition of the clock

Table 3.7 Function table for a 74LS95 shift register.

internal parts of its circuit. Indeed, its actual internal implementation may differ from the published circuit. As long as it behaves like its published circuit, the precise implementation of its logic function does not matter to the end user. The 74LS95 is a versatile shift register and has the following functions.

1. Parallel load   The four bits of data to be loaded into the shift register are applied to its parallel inputs, the mode control input is set to a logical one, and a clock pulse applied to the clock 2 input. The data is loaded on the falling edge of the clock 2 pulse.

2. Right-shift   A shift right is accomplished by setting the mode control input to a logical zero and applying a pulse to the clock 1 input. The shift takes place on the falling edge of the clock pulse.

3. Left-shift   A shift left is accomplished by setting the mode control input to a logical one, and applying a pulse to the clock 2 input. The shift takes place on the falling edge of the clock pulse. A left-shift requires that the output of each flip-flop be connected to the parallel input of the previous flip-flop, and serial data entered at the D input.

Table 3.7 provides a function table for this shift register (taken from the manufacturer's literature). This table describes the behavior of the shift register for all combinations of its inputs. Note that the table includes don't care values of inputs and the effects of input *transitions* (indicated by ↑ and ↓).

3.6.2 Asynchronous counters

A counter is a sequential circuit with a clock input and m outputs. Each time the counter is clocked, one or more of the outputs change state. These outputs form a sequence with N unique values. After the Nth value has been observed at the counter's output terminals, the next clock pulse causes the counter to assume the same output as it had at the start of the sequence; that is, the sequence is *cyclic*. For example, a counter may display the sequence 01234501234501 …, or the sequence 9731097310973 … .

A counter composed of m flip-flops can generate an arbitrary sequence with a length of not greater than 2^m cycles before the sequence begins to repeat itself.

One of the tools frequently employed to illustrate the operation of sequential circuits is the *state diagram*. Any system with internal memory and external inputs such as the flip-flop can be said to be in a state that is a function of its internal and external inputs. A state diagram shows some (or all) of the possible states of a given system. A labeled circle represents each of the states and the states are linked by unidirectional lines showing the paths by which one state becomes another state.

Figure 3.40 gives the state diagram of a JK flip-flop that has just two states, S_0 and S_1. S_0 represents the state $Q = 0$ and S_1 represents the state $Q = 1$. The transitions between states S_0 and S_1 are determined by the values of the JK inputs at the time the flip-flop is clocked. In Fig. 3.40 we have labeled the

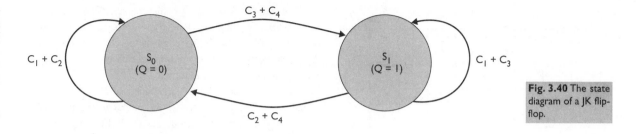

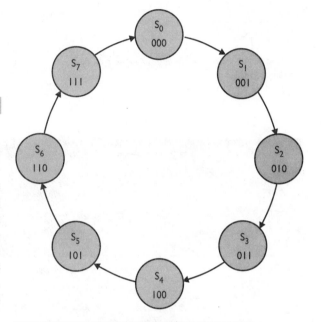

Fig. 3.40 The state diagram of a JK flip-flop.

J	K	Condition
0	0	C_1
0	1	C_2
1	0	C_3
1	1	C_4

Table 3.8 Relationship between JK inputs and conditions C_1 to C_4.

flip-flop's input states C_1 to C_4. Table 3.8 defines the four possible input conditions, C_1, C_2, C_3, and C_4, in terms of J and K.

From Fig. 3.40 it can be seen that conditions C_3 or C_4 cause a transition from state S_0 to state S_1. Similarly, conditions C_2 or C_4 cause a transition from state S_1 to state S_0. Condition C_4 causes a change of state from S_0 to S_1 and also from S_1 to S_0. This is, of course, the condition $J = K = 1$ which causes the JK flip-flop to toggle its output. Some conditions cause a state to change to *itself*; that is, there is no overall change. Thus, conditions C_1 or C_2, when applied to the system in state S_0, have the effect of leaving the system in state S_0.

The binary up-counter

The state diagram of a 3-bit binary up-counter is given in Fig. 3.41 (an up-counter counts upward 1, 2, 3, …, in contrast with a down-counter, which counts downward …, 3, 2, 1). In this state diagram there is only a single path from each state to its next higher neighbor. As the system is clocked, it cycles through the states S_0 to S_7 representing the natural binary numbers 0 to 7. The actual design of counters in general can be quite involved, although the basic principle is to ask 'What input conditions are required by the flip-flops to cause them to change from state S_i to state S_{i+1}?'

The design of an asynchronous natural binary up-counter is rather simpler than the design of a counter for an arbitrary sequence. Figure 3.42 gives the circuit diagram of a 3-bit binary counter composed of JK flip-flops and Fig. 3.43 provides its timing diagram. The J and K inputs to each flip-flop are connected to constant logical 1 levels. Consequently, whenever a flip-flop is clocked its output changes state. The flip-flops are arranged so that the Q output of one stage triggers the

Fig. 3.41 The state diagram of a binary 3-bit up-counter.

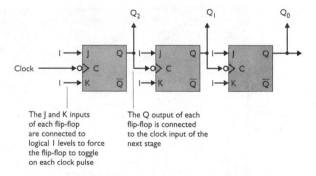

The J and K inputs of each flip-flop are connected to logical I levels to force the flip-flop to toggle on each clock pulse

The Q output of each flip-flop is connected to the clock input of the next stage

Fig. 3.42 Circuit of an asynchronous binary up-counter.

clock input of the next higher stage (i.e. the output Q_i of stage i triggers the clock input of stage $i+1$). The flip-flops in Fig. 3.42 are master–slave clocked, and the outputs change on the negative edge of the clock pulse.

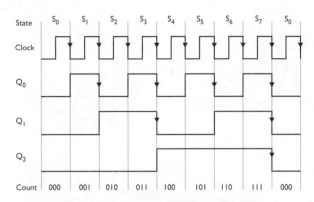

Fig. 3.43 Timing diagram of an asynchronous 3-bit binary up-counter.

Consider the first stage of this counter. When the clock input makes a complete cycle (0 to 1 to 0), the Q output changes state on the falling edge of the clock. It takes two clock cycles to make the Q output execute one cycle; that is, the flip-flop divides the input by 2.

The asynchronous binary up-counter of Fig. 3.42 is also called a *ripple counter* because the output of the first stage triggers the input of the second stage and the output of the second stage triggers the input of the third stage, and so on. Consequently, a change of state at the output of the first stage ripples through the counter until it clocks the final stage. The propagation delay through each stage of the counter determines its maximum speed of operation. The timing diagram of Fig. 3.43 isn't exact because it doesn't show the ripple effect—when one stage changes state, there's a short delay before stages to its right change state.

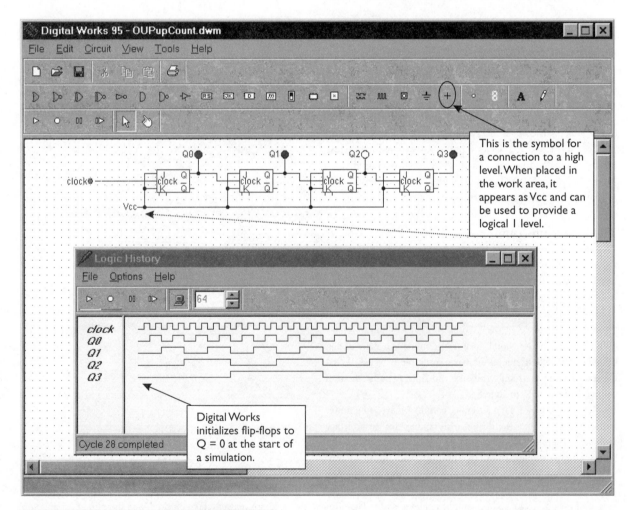

Fig. 3.44 Using Digital Works to create a binary up-counter.

Figure 3.44 demonstrates the construction of a four-stage binary up-counter in Digital Works. We have wired all J and K inputs together and connected them to V_{cc} (the positive power supply, which provides a logical 1 to cause the JK flip-flops to toggle when clocked). We have labeled each of the Q outputs and used the **Logic History** function to capture the output waveform. Digital Works clears all flip-flops at the start of each run. However, the flip-flops have two unlabeled set and clear inputs that can be used to preset outputs to 1 or 0, respectively (these are not used in this application).

The binary down-counter

We can also create a binary down-counter that counts backwards from 7 to 0. Figure 3.45 demonstrates the effect of connecting the $\overline{Q}$ output of each stage in a ripple counter to the clock input of the next stage. You can also create a binary down-counter by using JK flip-flops that are clocked on the positive or rising edge of the clock pulse by connecting Q_i to Clk_{i+1}.

A typical counter

Figure 3.46 illustrates a typical counter, the 74177 4-bit *presettable* binary counter. When we call a counter (or any other digital circuit) presettable, we mean that it can be loaded or initialized with predetermined data. In other words, we can determine its internal state by loading if from an external source. The pin-out of the 74177 is given in Fig. 3.47 together with its internal arrangement. The circuit of Fig. 3.46 uses a *T flip-flop*. The T stands for *toggle*, because its output changes state every time it is clocked. The T flip-flop is functionally equivalent to a JK flip-flop with $J = K = 1$.

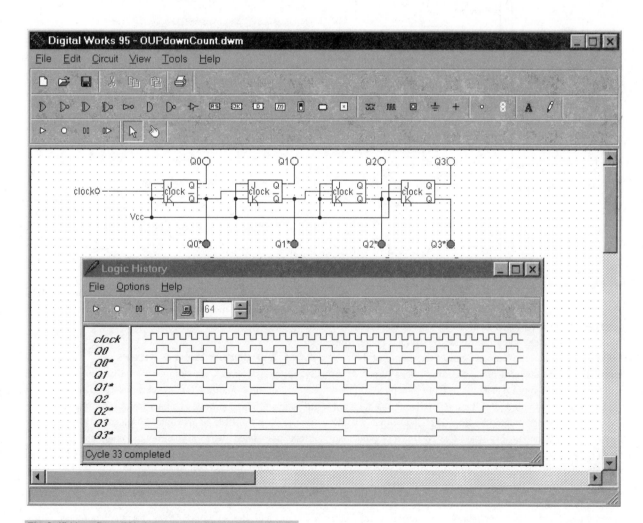

Fig. 3.45 Using Digital Works to create a binary down-counter.

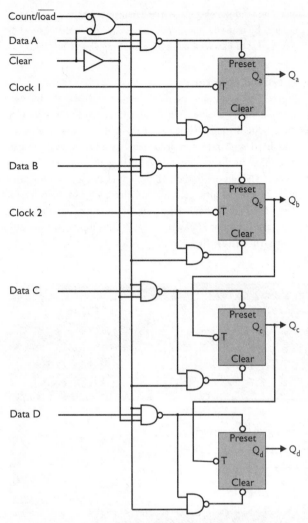

Fig. 3.46 Circuit of the 74177 presettable 4-bit binary counter.

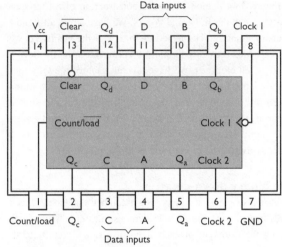

Fig. 3.47 Pinout of the 74177 counter.

The counter is arranged as a divide-by-two stage followed by a divide-by-eight stage. To divide by 16 (i.e. count from 0000 to 1111) it's necessary to connect the output of the first stage (Q_a) to the clock of the succeeding stages (clock 2) by connecting pin 5 to pin 6. The count input is applied to clock 1 and on each falling edge of the clock pulse the contents of the counter are incremented by one. The $\overline{\text{Clear}}$ input sets the value of each Q output to 0 when $\overline{\text{Clear}} = 0$. The Count/load input permits normal counting when high, and allows four bits to be loaded into the counter when low. This facility is used to preset the counter so that it counts up from i (rather than 0), where i is the value loaded into it.

Counters find many applications in digital computers. Anticipating Chapter 5, we will find that at the heart of all

computers is a program counter or instruction counter that, at any instant, contains the address or location of the next instruction to be executed. After each instruction has been executed, the counter is incremented. The program counter is so called, not because it counts programs, but because it has the circuit, or function, of a counter.

The pulse generator revisited

When we introduced the RS flip-flop we used it to start and stop a simple pulse generator that created a train of n pulses. Figure 3.48 shows a pulse generator in Digital Works. This system is essentially the same as that in Fig. 3.9, except that we've built the counter using JK flip-flops and we've added LEDs to examine the signals produced when the system runs. Note also that the RS flip-flop can be set only when the flip-flop is in the reset mode.

3.6.3 Synchronous counters

Synchronous counters are composed of flip-flops that are all clocked at the same time (i.e. synchronously). The outputs of *all* stages of a synchronous counter become valid at the same time (to a reasonable approximation) and the ripple-through effect associated with asynchronous counters is entirely absent. Synchronous counters can be easily designed to count through any arbitrary sequence just as well as the natural sequence 0, 1, 2, 3, ...

We design a synchronous counter by means of a state diagram and the *excitation table* for the appropriate flip-flop (either RS or JK). An excitation table is nothing more than

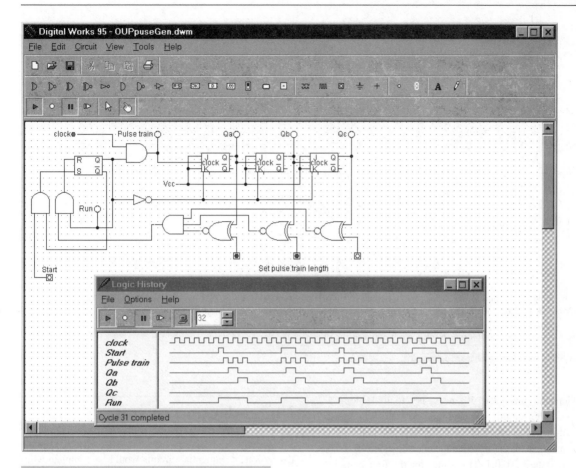

Fig. 3.48 Using Digital Works to design a pulse generator.

a version of a flip-flop's truth table arranged to display the input states required to force a given output transition. Table 3.9 illustrates the excitation table of a JK flip-flop. Suppose we wish to force the Q output of a JK flip-flop to make the transition from 0 to 1 the next time it is clocked. Table 3.9 tells us that the J, K input should be 1, d (where d = don't care).

Why is the K input a don't care condition when we want a $0 \rightarrow 1$ transition? If we set J = 1 and K = 0, the flip-flop is set when it's clocked and Q^+ becomes 1. If, however, we set J = 1 and K = 1, the flip-flop is toggled when it's clocked and the output Q = 0 is toggled to Q = 1. Clearly, the state of the K input doesn't matter when we wish to set Q^+ to 1 given that Q = 0 and J = 1. It should now be clear why all the transitions in the JK's excitation table have a don't care input—a given state can be reached from more than one starting point.

The next step in designing a synchronous counter is to construct a truth table for the system to determine the JK inputs required to force a transition to the required next state for each of the possible states in the table. It is much easier to explain this step by example rather than by algorithm.

Suppose we wish to design a synchronous counter to count through the natural sequence 0, 1, 2, 3, 4, 5, 6, 7, 8, 9, 0, ... (such a counter is called a *binary-coded decimal* or modulo-10 counter). As there are ten states, we require four JK flip-flops because $2^3 < 10 < 2^4$. Table 3.10 provides a truth table for this counter.

Inputs		Transition
J	K	$Q \rightarrow Q^+$
0	d	$0 \rightarrow 0$
1	d	$0 \rightarrow 1$
d	1	$1 \rightarrow 0$
d	0	$1 \rightarrow 1$

Table 3.9 Excitation table of a JK flip-flop.

Count	Output				Next state				J, K inputs required to force transition							
	Q_d	Q_c	Q_b	Q_a	Q_d	Q_c	Q_b	Q_a	J_d	K_d	J_c	K_c	J_b	K_b	J_a	K_a
0	0	0	0	0	0	0	0	1	0	d	0	d	0	d	1	d
1	0	0	0	1	0	0	1	0	0	d	0	d	1	d	d	1
2	0	0	1	0	0	0	1	1	0	d	0	d	d	0	1	d
3	0	0	1	1	0	1	0	0	0	d	1	d	d	1	d	1
4	0	1	0	0	0	1	0	1	0	d	0	0	0	d	1	d
5	0	1	0	1	0	1	1	0	0	d	d	0	1	d	d	1
6	0	1	1	0	0	1	1	1	0	d	d	0	d	0	1	d
7	0	1	1	1	1	0	0	0	1	d	d	1	d	1	d	1
8	1	0	0	0	1	0	0	1	d	0	0	d	0	d	1	d
9	1	0	0	1	0	0	0	0	d	1	0	d	0	d	d	1
10	1	0	1	0	x	x	x	x	x	x	x	x	x	x	x	x
11	1	0	1	1	x	x	x	x	x	x	x	x	x	x	x	x
12	1	1	0	0	x	x	x	x	x	x	x	x	x	x	x	x
13	1	1	0	1	x	x	x	x	x	x	x	x	x	x	x	x
14	1	1	1	0	x	x	x	x	x	x	x	x	x	x	x	x
15	1	1	1	1	x	x	x	x	x	x	x	x	x	x	x	x

The 'd's in the table correspond to *don't care* conditions due to the excitation table of the JK flip-flop. The 'x's correspond to don't care conditions due to unused states; for example, the counter never enters states 1010 to 1111. There is, of course, no fundamental difference between x and d. We've chosen different symbols in order to distinguish between the origins of the don't care states.

Table 3.10 Truth table for a synchronous counter.

To understand Table 3.10 it's necessary to look along a line and to say, 'Given this state and the next state, what must the inputs of the flip-flops be to force the transition to the next state?' For example, in the first line the current state is 0,0,0,0 and the next state is 0,0,0,1. The values for the four pairs of J, K inputs are obtained from the excitation table in Table 3.9. Three of these outputs cause the transition $0 \rightarrow 0$ and one causes the transition $0 \rightarrow 1$. Therefore, the three pairs of J, K inputs required are 0, d (for the 0 to 0 transitions) and the other J, K input is 1, d for the 0 to 1 transition.

From the truth table of the synchronous counter we can write down eight Karnaugh maps for the Js and Ks. Figure 3.49 gives the Karnaugh maps for this counter. These maps can be simplified to give

$$J_d = Q_c \cdot Q_b \cdot Q_a \qquad K_d = Q_a$$
$$J_c = Q_b \cdot Q_a \qquad K_c = Q_b \cdot Q_a$$
$$J_b = \overline{Q_d} \cdot Q_a \qquad K_b = Q_a$$
$$J_a = 1 \qquad K_a = 1$$

We can now write down the circuit diagram of the synchronous counter (Fig. 3.50). Remember that d denotes a don't care condition and indicates that the variable marked by a d may be a 0 or a 1 state. The same technique can be employed to construct a counter that will step through any arbitrary sequence. We will revisit this technique when we look at state machines.

3.7 Introduction to state machines

No discussion of sequential circuits would be complete without at least a mention of state machines. The state machine offers the designer a formal way of specifying, designing, testing, and analyzing sequential systems. Since the detailed study of state machines is beyond the scope of this introductory text, we shall simply introduce some of the basic concepts here.

It would be nearly impossible to find a text on state machines without encountering the general state machines called Mealy machines and Moore machines (after G. H. Mealy and E. Moore). Figure 3.51 illustrates the structure of a Mealy state machine and Fig. 3.52 the structure of a Moore state machine. Both machines have a combinational network that operates on the machine's inputs and on its internal states to produce a new internal state. The output of the Mealy machine is a function of the current inputs and the internal state of the machine, whereas the output of a Moore machine is a function of the internal state of the machine only.

Example of a state machine

As we have already said, the state machine approach to the design of sequential circuits is by no means trivial. Here, we will design a simple state machine by means of an example.

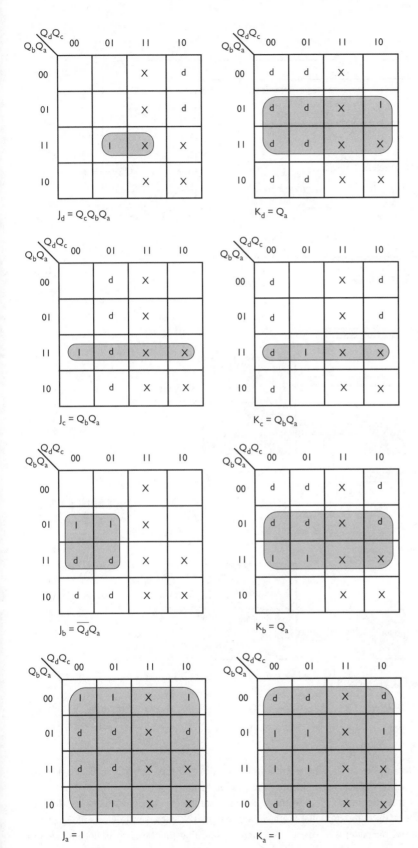

Fig. 3.49 Karnaugh maps for a synchronous counter.

$J_d = Q_c Q_b Q_a$

$K_d = Q_a$

$J_c = Q_b Q_a$

$K_c = Q_b Q_a$

$J_b = \overline{Q_d} Q_a$

$K_b = Q_a$

$J_a = 1$

$K_a = 1$

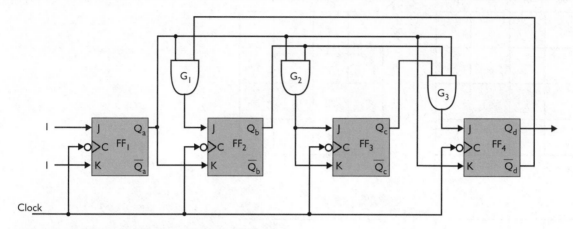

Fig. 3.50 Circuit diagram for a 4-bit synchronous BCD counter.

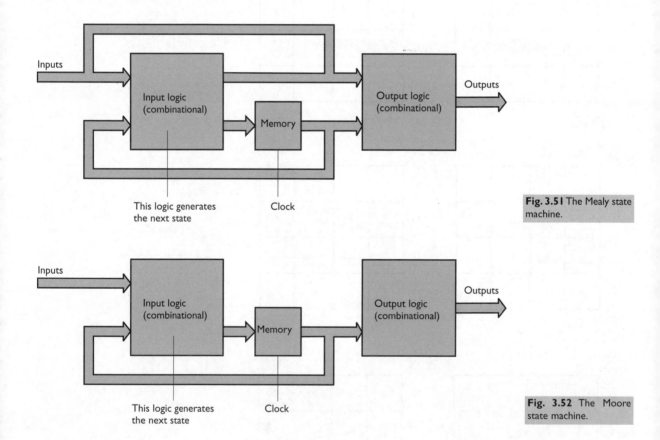

Fig. 3.51 The Mealy state machine.

Fig. 3.52 The Moore state machine.

Suppose we require a sequence detector that has a serial input X and an output Y. If a certain sequence of bits appears at the input of the detector, the output goes true. Sequence detectors are widely used in digital systems to split a stream of bits into units or frames by providing special bit patterns between adjacent frames and then using a sequence detector to identify the start of a frame.

In the following example we design a sequence detector that produces a true output Y whenever it detects the sequence 010 at its X input. Note that this detector is not intended to detect overlapped sequences; for example, the input 010100 is treated as 010 100 and the system detects 010 only once.

Figure 3.53 shows a black box state machine that detects the sequence 010 in a bit stream. We have provided input and output sequences to demonstrate the machine's action.

For example, if the input sequence is

000110011010110001011

the output sequence will be

000000000000100000010

(the output generates a 1 in the state following the detection of the pattern).

We solve the problem by constructing a state diagram as illustrated in Fig. 3.54. Each circle represents a particular state of the system and transitions between states are determined by the current input to the system at the next clock pulse.

A state is marked name/value, where *name* is the label we use to describe the state (e.g. states A, B, C, D in Fig. 3.54) and *value* is the output corresponding to that state. The transition between states is labeled *a/b*, where *a* is the input condition and *b* the output value after the next clock. For example, the transition from state A to state B is labeled 0/0 and indicates that if the system is in state A and the input is 0, the next clock pulse will force the system into state B and set the output to 0.

Figure 3.55 provides a partial state diagram for this sequence detector with details of the actions that take place during state transitions. State A is the initial state in Fig. 3.55. Suppose we receive an input while in state A. If input X is a 0 we may be on our way to detecting the sequence 010, and therefore we move to state B along the line marked 0/0 (the output is 0 because we have not detected the required sequence yet). If the input is 1, we return to state A because we have not even begun to detect the start of the sequence.

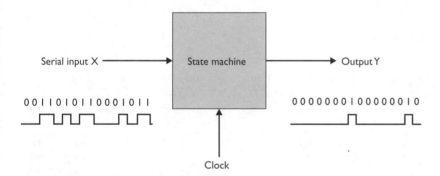

Fig. 3.53 State machine to detect the sequence 010.

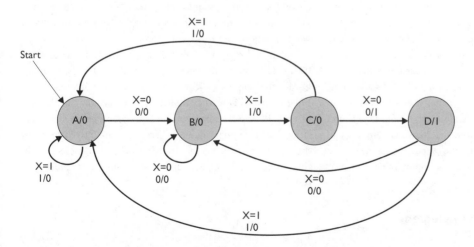

Fig. 3.54 State diagram for a 010 sequence detector (X is the current input).

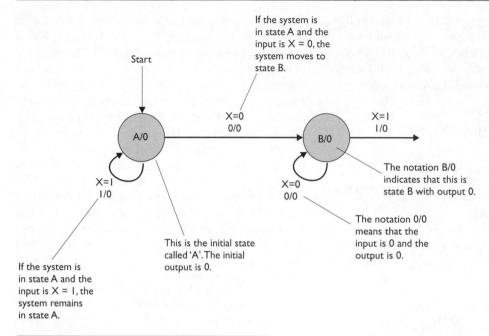

Start

If the system is
in state A and the
input is X = 0, the
system moves to
state B.

X=0
0/0

X=1
1/0

A/0

B/0

The notation B/0
indicates that this is
state B with output 0.

X=1
1/0

X=0
0/0

The notation 0/0
means that the
input is 0 and the
output is 0.

This is the initial state
called 'A'. The initial
output is 0.

If the system is
in state A and the
input is X = 1, the
system remains
in state A.

Fig. 3.55 Details of the state counter diagram of Fig. 3.53.

Current state	Output	Next state	
		X=0	X=1
A	0	B	A
B	0	B	C
C	0	D	A
D	1	B	A

Table 3.11 State table for 010 sequence detector.

Current state	Q_1	Q_2	Output	Next state	
				X=0	X=1
A	0	0	0	0,1	0,0
B	0	1	0	0,1	1,0
C	1	0	0	1,1	0,0
D	1	1	1	0,1	0,0

Table 3.12 Modified state table for a sequence detector.

From state B there are two possible transitions. If we detect a 0 we remain in state B because we are still at the start of the desired sequence. If we detect a 1, we move on to state C (we have now detected 01). From state C a further 1 input takes us right back to state A (because we have received 011). However, if we detect a 0 we move to state D and set the output to 1 to indicate that the sequence has been detected. From state D we move back to state A if the next input is a 1, and back to state B if it is a 0. From the state diagram we can construct a state table that defines the output and the next state corresponding to each current state and input. Table 3.11 provides a state table for Fig. 3.54.

Constructing a circuit to implement the state table

The next step is to go about constructing the circuit itself. If a system can exist in one of several *states*, what then defines the

current state? In a sequential system flip-flops are used to hold state information—in this example there are four states, which implies at least two flip-flops.

Table 3.12 expands Table 3.11 to provide numeric states 0,0 to 1,1 to represent states A to D (i.e. Q_1, Q_2, where Q_1 and Q_2 are the outputs of flip-flops that hold the internal state). Finally, we can construct Table 3.13 to determine the JK input of each JK flip-flop that will force the appropriate state transition, given the next input x. Table 3.13 is derived by using the excitation table of the JK flip-flop (see Table 3.9). The final step is to create a circuit diagram form Table 3.13 (i.e. Fig. 3.56).

$$J_1 = Q_1 + Q_2 \cdot X$$
$$J_2 = \overline{X}$$
$$K_1 = Q_2 + X$$
$$K_2 = X$$

Current state			Next state		Output			
Q_1	Q_2	X	Q_1	Q_2	J_1	K_1	J_2	K_2
0	0	0	0	1	0	d	1	d
0	0	1	0	0	0	d	0	d
0	1	0	0	1	0	d	d	0
0	1	1	1	0	1	d	d	1
1	0	0	1	1	d	0	1	d
1	0	1	0	0	d	1	0	d
1	1	0	0	1	d	1	d	0
1	1	1	0	0	d	1	d	1

Table 3.13 Determining the JK outputs of the sequence detector.

Figure 3.57 demonstrates the construction of the sequence detector in Digital Works. We've added LEDs to show the state of the flip-flop outputs and control signals and have provided an example of a run. Note the output pulse after the sequence 010. We used the programmable sequence generator to provide a binary pattern for the test.

Summary

In this chapter we've looked at the flip-flop that provides data storage facilities in a computer and which can be used to create counters and shift registers as well as more general forms of state machine. We have introduced the RS, D, and JK flip-flops. All these flip-flops can capture data and the JK flip-flop is able to operate in a *toggle* mode in which its output changes state each time it is clocked. Any of these flip-flops can be converted into the other two flip-flops by the addition of a few gates.

We have also introduced the idea of clocking or triggering flip-flops. A flip-flop can be triggered by a clock at a given level or by the change-in-state of a clock. The master–slave flip-flop latches data at its input when the clock is high (or low) and transfers data to the output (slave) when the clock changes state.

Sequential machines fall into two categories. Asynchronous sequential machines don't have a master clock and the output from one flip-flop triggers the flip-flop it's connected to. In a synchronous sequential machine all the flip-flops are triggered at the same time by means of a common master clock. Synchronous machines are more reliable.

Examples

Problem 1

Design an 8-bit shift register to perform the following operations.

(a) Load each stage from an 8-bit data bus   (parallel load)
(b) Logical shift left   (0 in, MSB lost)
(c) Logical shift right   (0 in, LSB lost)
(d) Arithmetic shift left   (same as logical shift left)
(e) Arithmetic shift right   (MSB replicated, LSB lost)
(f) Circular shift left   (MSB moves to LSB position)
(g) Circular shift right   (LSB moves to MSB position)

The circuit is composed of eight master–slave JK flip-flops and has a clock input that causes operations (a) to (g) above to be carried out on its falling edge. The circuit has five control inputs:

R   When R = 1 shift right, when R = 0 shift left.
S   When S = 1 perform a shift operation, when S = 0 a parallel load.
L   When L = 1 perform a logical shift (if S = 1).
A   When A = 1 perform an arithmetic shift (if S = 1).
C   When C = 1 perform a circular shift (if S = 1).

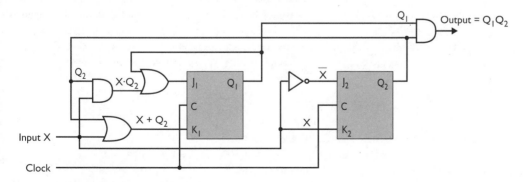

Fig. 3.56 Circuit to detect the sequence 010.

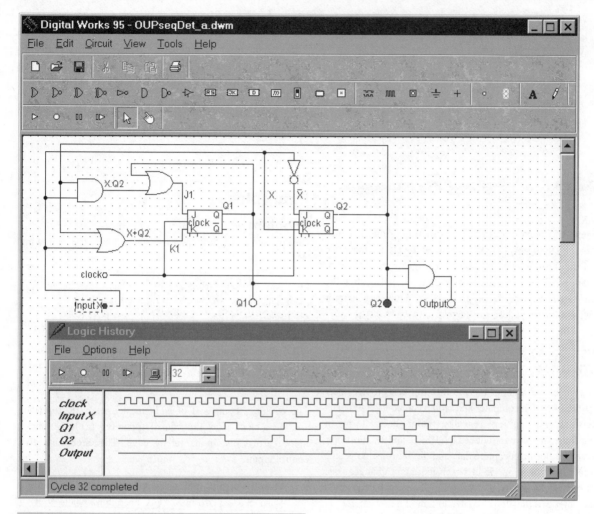

Fig. 3.57 Using Digital Works to implement the sequence detector.

Note that illegal combinations of L, A, and C cannot occur because only one type of shift can be performed at a time. Therefore, more than one of L, A, and C, will never be true simultaneously.

For all eight stages of the shift register obtain algebraic expressions for J and K in terms of control inputs R, S, L, A, C, and the outputs of the flip-flops.

Solution I

Figure 3.58 illustrates five stages of the shift register. These are the end stages Q_7 and Q_0, the most significant and least significant bit stages, respectively. A non-end stage, Q_i, together with its left-hand neighbor Q_{i+1} and its right-hand neighbor Q_{i-1} must also be considered.

All stages except 0 and 7 perform the same functions: parallel load, shift right, and shift left. As the JK flip-flops always load data from one source or another, only the inputs J = 1, K = 0, or J = 0, K = 1 have to be considered. Consequently, $J = \overline{K}$, and we need only derive expressions for J, as the corresponding values for K can be obtained from an inverter.

Stage i

Parallel load	$J_i = D_i$	$S = 0$
Shift right	$J_i = Q_{i+1}$	$S = 1, R = 1$
Shift left	$J_i = Q_{i-1}$	$S = 1, R = 0$

Therefore, $J_i = \overline{S} \cdot D_i + S(R \cdot Q_{i+1} + \overline{R} \cdot Q_{i-1})$

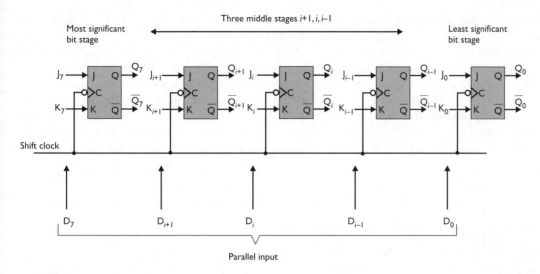

Fig. 3.58 End and middle stages of a shift register.

Stage 0 (LSB)

Parallel load	$J_0 = D_0$	$S = 0$
Shift right logical	$J_0 = Q_1$	$S = 1, R = 1, L = 1$
arithmetic	$J_0 = Q_1$	$S = 1, R = 1, A = 1$
circular	$J_0 = Q_1$	$S = 1, R = 1, C = 1$
Shift left logical	$J_0 = 0$	$S = 1, R = 0, L = 1$
arithmetic	$J_0 = 0$	$S = 1, R = 0, A = 1$
circular	$J_0 = Q_7$	$S = 1, R = 0, C = 1$

Therefore, $J_0 = \overline{S} \cdot D_0 + S(R \cdot L \cdot Q_1 + R \cdot A \cdot Q_1 + R \cdot C \cdot Q_1 + \overline{R} \cdot L \cdot 0 + \overline{R} \cdot A \cdot 0 + \overline{R} \cdot C \cdot Q_7)$

$\qquad = \overline{S} \cdot D_0 + S(R \cdot L \cdot Q_1 + R \cdot A \cdot Q_1 + R \cdot C \cdot Q_1 + \overline{R} \cdot C \cdot Q_7)$

$\qquad = \overline{S} \cdot D_0 + S(R \cdot Q_1 (L + A + C) + \overline{R} \cdot C \cdot Q_7) \qquad$ *Note*: $L + A + C = 1$

$\qquad = \overline{S} \cdot D_0 + S(R \cdot Q_1 + \overline{R} \cdot C \cdot Q_7)$

Stage 7 (MSB)

Parallel load	$J_7 = D_7$	$S = 0$
Shift right logical	$J_7 = 0$	$S = 1, R = 1, L = 1$
arithmetic	$J_7 = Q_7$	$S = 1, R = 1, A = 1$
circular	$J_7 = Q_0$	$S = 1, R = 1, C = 1$
Shift left logical	$J_7 = Q_6$	$S = 1, R = 0, L = 1$
arithmetic	$J_7 = Q_6$	$S = 1, R = 0, A = 1$
circular	$J_7 = Q_6$	$S = 1, R = 0, C = 1$

Therefore, $J_7 = \overline{S} \cdot D_7 + S(R \cdot L \cdot 0 + R \cdot A \cdot Q_7 + R \cdot C \cdot Q_0 + \overline{R} \cdot L \cdot Q_6 + \overline{R} \cdot A \cdot Q_6 + \overline{R} \cdot C \cdot Q_6)$

$\qquad = \overline{S} \cdot D_7 + S(R \cdot A \cdot Q_7 + R \cdot C \cdot Q_0 + \overline{R} \cdot Q_6 (L + A + C))$

$\qquad = \overline{S} \cdot D_7 + S(R(A \cdot Q_7 + C \cdot Q_0) + \overline{R} \cdot Q_6)$

Problem 2

Design a 4-bit asynchronous ripple-through decade counter to count from 0 to 9 cyclically. Use JK master–slave flip-flops with an unconditional active-low clear input. Provide a timing diagram to illustrate the operation of the circuit.

Solution 2

A decade (i.e. decimal) counter can be derived from a binary counter by resetting the counter to zero at the appropriate point. A four-stage binary counter counts from 0000 to 1111 (i.e. 0 to 15). To create a decade counter the state ten (1010) must be detected and used to reset the flip-flops. Figure 3.59 provides a possible circuit.

The binary counter counts normally from 0 to 9. On the tenth count $Q_3 = 1$, and $Q_1 = 1$. This condition is detected by the NAND gate whose output goes low, resetting the flip-flops. The count of ten exists momentarily as Fig. 3.60 demonstrates. We could have detected the state ten with $Q_3, Q_2, Q_1, Q_0 = 1010$. However, that would have required a 4-input gate and is not strictly necessary. Although $Q_3 = 1$ and

$Q_1 = 1$ corresponds to counts 10, 11, 14, and 15, the counter never gets beyond 10.

Note that the reset pulse must be long enough to reset all flip-flops to zero. If the reset pulse were too short and, say, Q_1 was reset before Q_3, the output might be reset to 1000. The counting sequence would now be: 0, 1, 2, 3, 4, 5, 6, 7, 8, 9, (10), 8, 9, 8, 9, …. However, such a problem is unlikely to occur in this case, since the reset pulse is not removed until at least the output of one flip-flop and the NAND gate has

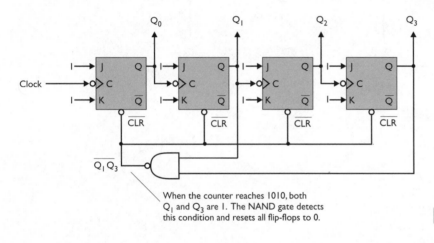

When the counter reaches 1010, both Q_1 and Q_3 are 1. The NAND gate detects this condition and resets all flip-flops to 0.

Fig. 3.59 Circuit of a decimal counter.

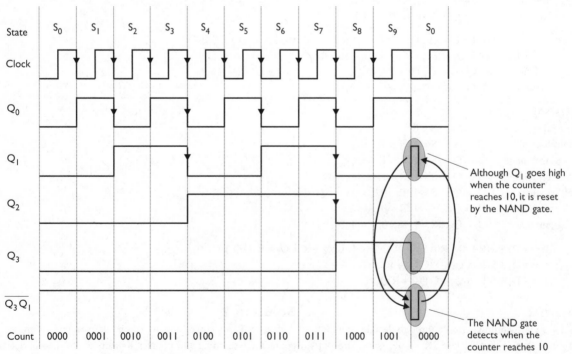

Although Q_1 goes high when the counter reaches 10, it is reset by the NAND gate.

The NAND gate detects when the counter reaches 10

Fig. 3.60 Timing diagram of a decimal counter.

changed state. The combined duration of flip-flop reset time plus a gate delay will normally provide sufficient time to ensure that all flip-flops are reset.

It is possible to imagine situations in which the circuit would not function correctly. Suppose that the minimum reset pulse required to guarantee the reset of a flip-flop were 50 ns. Suppose also that the minimum time between the application of a reset pulse and the transition $Q \leftarrow 0$ were 10 ns, and that the propagation delay of a NAND gate were 10 ns. It would indeed be possible for the above error to occur. This example demonstrates the dangers of designing asynchronous circuits!

Problems

1. What is a sequential circuit and in what way does it differ from a combinational circuit?

2. Explain why it is necessary to employ *clocked* flip-flops in sequential circuits (as opposed to unclocked flip-flops).

3. The behavior of an RS flip-flop is not clearly defined when R = 1 and S = 1. Design an RS flip-flop that does not suffer from this restriction.

4. For the waveforms in Fig. 3.61 draw the Q and $\overline{Q}$ outputs of an RS flip-flop constructed from two NOR gates (as in Fig. 3.2).

5. What are the three basic flip-flop clocking modes and why is it necessary to provide so many clocking modes?

6. For the input and clock signals of Fig. 3.62, provide a timing diagram for the Q output of a D flip-flop. Assume that the flip-flop is:

   (a) Level-sensitive
   (b) Positive-edge triggered
   (c) Negative-edge triggered
   (d) A master–slave flip-flop

7. Assuming that the initial state of the circuit of Fig. 3.63 is given by C = 1, D = 1, P = 1, and Q = 0, complete the table. This question should be attempted by calculating the

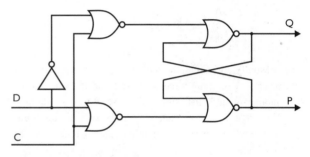

Fig. 3.63 Circuit for Problem 7.

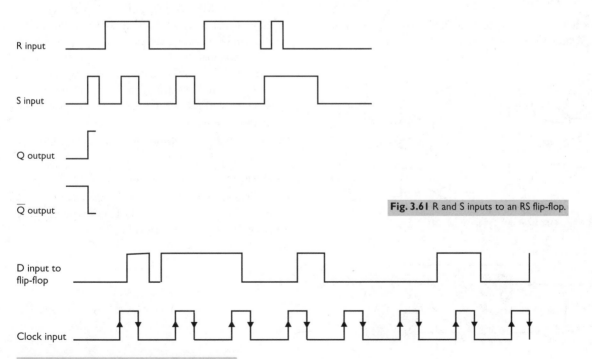

Fig. 3.61 R and S inputs to an RS flip-flop.

Fig. 3.62 Timing diagram of a clock and data signal.

effect of the new C and D on the inputs to both cross-coupled pairs of NOR gates and therefore on the outputs P and Q. As P and Q are also inputs to the NOR gates, the change in P and Q should be taken into account when calculating the effect of the next inputs C and D. Remember that the output of a NOR is 1 if both its inputs are 0, and is 0 otherwise.

C	D	P	Q
1	1	1	0
1	0		
0	0		
1	1		
0	1		
1	1		
0	1		
0	0		
1	0		

Modify the circuit to provide a new input S which, when 1, will at any time set P to 1 and Q to 0. Provide another input R that will similarly set P to 0 and Q to 1. Note that R and S cannot both be a 1 at the same time, and therefore the condition R = S = 1 need not be considered.

8. What additional logic is required to convert a JK flip-flop into a D flip-flop?

9. Demonstrate that the flip-flops in Fig. 3.64 are equivalent. Are they exactly equivalent?

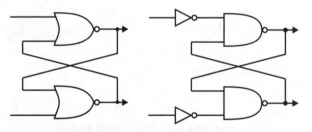

Fig. 3.64 Circuit for Problem 9.

10. Many flip-flops have unconditional *preset* and *clear* inputs. What do these inputs do and why are they needed in sequential circuits?

11. A T flip-flop has a single clock input and outputs Q and $\overline{Q}$. Its Q output toggles (changes state) each time it is clocked. The T flip-flop behaves exactly like a JK flip-flop with its J and K inputs connected permanently to a logical one. Design a T flip-flop using a D flip-flop.

12. Why haven't D and RS flip-flops been replaced by the JK flip-flop, since the JK flip-flop can, apparently, do everything a D flip-flop or an RS flip-flop can do?

13. What is a *shift register* and why is it so important in digital systems?

14. Design a shift register that has two inputs: a clock input and a shift input. Whenever this register receives a pulse at its shift input, it shifts its contents *two* places right.

15. Analyze the operation of the circuit of Fig. 3.65 by constructing a timing diagram (assume that Q_0 and Q_1 are initially 0). Construct the circuit using Digital Works and observe its behavior. This is an important circuit—can you suggest why?

16. Analyze the operation of the circuit of Fig. 3.66 by constructing a timing diagram (assume any initial value for Q_0 to Q_3). Construct the circuit using Digital Works and observe its behavior. This type of circuit is an important circuit in digital systems because it can be used to generate a pseudo-random sequence; that is, the sequence of bits at its Q_0 output look (to an observer) as if they constitute a random series of 1s and 0s. Longer series of random numbers are generated by increasing the number of stages in the shift register. The input is the exclusive OR of two or more outputs.

17. Use Digital Works to construct the circuit of Fig. 3.67 and then investigate its behavior.

18. Investigate the behavior of the circuit in Fig. 3.68.

19. Explain the meaning of the terms *asynchronous* and *synchronous* in the context of sequential logic systems. What is the significance of these terms?

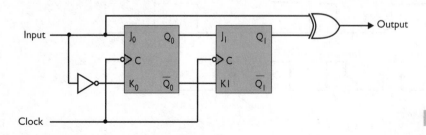

Fig. 3.65 Circuit diagram for Problem 15.

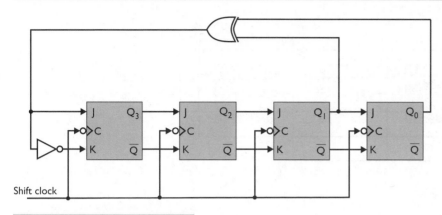

Fig. 3.66 Circuit diagram for Problem 16.

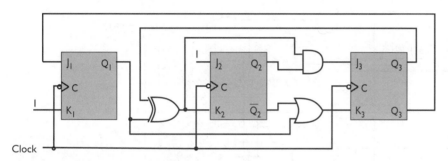

Fig. 3.67 Circuit diagram for Problem 17.

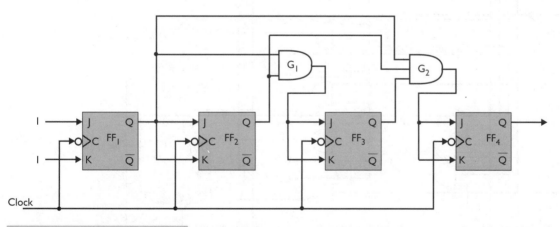

Fig. 3.68 Circuit diagram for Problem 18.

20. Design an asynchronous base 13 counter that counts through the natural binary sequence from 0 (0000) to 12 (1100) and then returns to zero on the next count.

21. Design a synchronous binary duodecimal (i.e. base 12) counter that counts through the natural binary sequence from

0 (0000) to 11 (1011) and then returns to zero on the next count. The counter is to be built from four JK flip-flops.

22. Design a synchronous modulo 9 counter using:
    (a) JK flip-flops
    (b) RS flip-flops (with a master–slave clock)

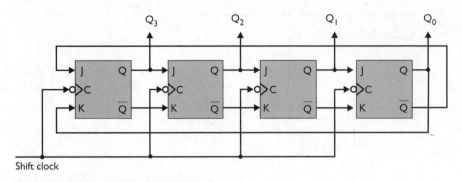

Fig. 3.69 Circuit diagram of a Johnson counter.

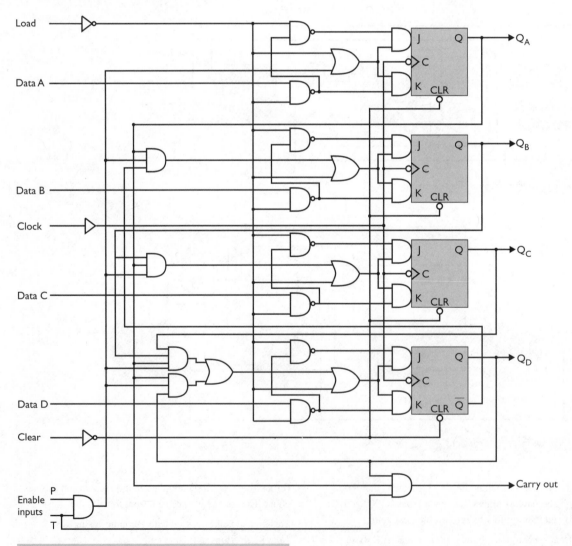

Fig. 3.70 Organization of a 74162 synchronous decade counter.

23. Design a *programmable* modulo 10/modulo 12 synchronous counter using JK flip-flops. The counter has a control input, TEN/TWELVE, which when high causes the counter to count modulo 10. When low, TEN/$\overline{\text{TWELVE}}$ causes the counter to count modulo 12.

24. How would you determine the maximum rate at which a synchronous counter could be clocked?

25. The circuit in Fig. 3.69 represents a *Johnson counter*. This is also called a *twisted ring* counter because feedback from the last (rightmost) stage is fed back to the first stage by crossing over the Q and $\overline{\text{Q}}$ connections. Investigate the operation of this circuit.

26. Design a simple digital time of day clock that can display the time from $00:00:00$ to $23:59:59$. Assume that you have a clock pulse input derived from the public electricity supply of 50 Hz (Europe) or 60 Hz (USA).

27. Figure 3.70 gives the internal organization of a 74162 synchronous decade (i.e. modulo 10) counter. Investigate its operation. Explain the function of the various control inputs. Note that the flip-flops are master–slave JKs with asynchronous (i.e. unconditional) clear inputs.

28. Design a modulo 8 counter with a clock and a control input UP. When UP = 1, the counter counts 0, 1, 2, …, 7. When UP = 0, the counter counts down 7, 6, 5, …, 0. This circuit is a programmable up/down counter.

29. Design a counter using JK flip-flops to count through the following sequence:

Q_2	Q_1	Q_0	
0	0	1	
0	1	0	
0	1	1	
1	1	0	
1	1	1	
0	0	1	sequence repeats

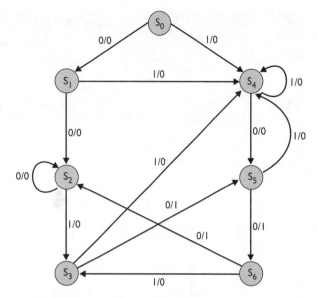

Fig. 3.72 State diagram of a sequence processor.

30. Investigate the action of the circuit in Fig. 3.71 when it is presented with the input sequence 111000001011111, where the first bit is the rightmost bit. Assume that all flip-flops are reset to Q = 0 before the first bit is received.

31. Design a state machine to implement the state diagram defined in Fig. 3.72.

32. Figure 3.73 provides a screenshot of a session using Digital Works. Examine the behavior of the circuit both by constructing it and by analyzing it.

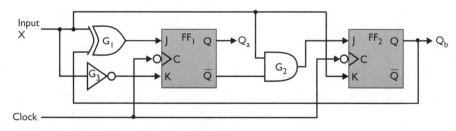

Fig. 3.71 Circuit diagram of a sequence processor.

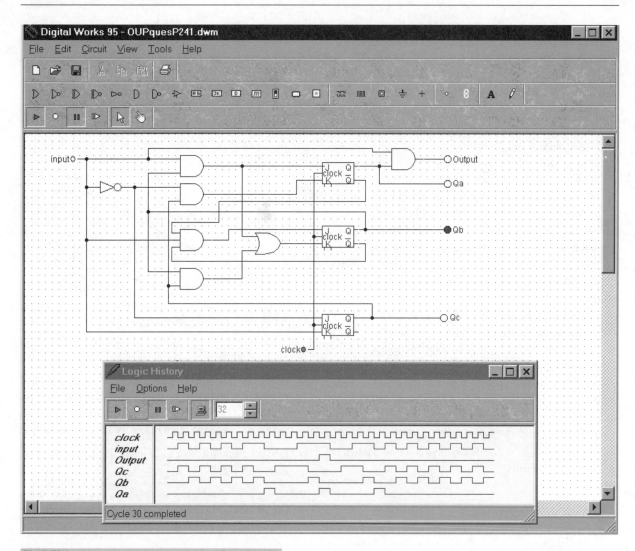

Fig. 3.73 A sequential circuit constructed with Digital Works.

Chapter 4

....

Computer arithmetic

Because of the ease with which binary logic elements can be manufactured and because of their remarkably low price, it was inevitable that the binary number system was chosen to represent numerical data within a digital computer. This chapter examines how numbers are represented in digital form, how they are converted from one *base* to another, and how they are manipulated within the computer. We begin with an examination of binary codes in general and demonstrate how patterns of ones and zeros can represent a range of different quantities.

The main theme of this chapter is the class of binary codes used to represent numbers in digital computers. We look at how numbers are converted from our familiar decimal (or *denary*) form to binary form and vice versa. Binary arithmetic is useless without the hardware needed to implement it, so we examine some of the circuits of adders and subtractors. Later, we take a break from numeric data and introduce error-detecting codes that enable the computer to determine whether data has been corrupted (i.e. inadvertently modified). Other topics included here are ways in which we represent and handle *negative* as well as positive numbers and how we perform simple arithmetic operations in assembly language. We look at the way in which the computer deals with very large and very small numbers by means of a system called *floating point* arithmetic. Finally, we describe how computers carry out multiplication and division—operations that are much more complex than addition or subtraction.

4.1 Bits, bytes, words, and characters

The smallest quantity of information that can be stored and manipulated inside a computer is the *bit*, which can take the values 0 or 1. Digital computers store information in their memories in the form of groups of bits called *words*. The number of bits per word varies from computer to computer. Note that a computer with a 4-bit word is not less accurate

than a computer with a 64-bit word. The difference is one of performance and economics. Computers with small words are cheaper to construct than computers with long words. If a computer has a 4-bit word and you want to manipulate a 64-bit entity, you have to do it in $64/4 = 16$ chunks. Typical word lengths of computers both old and new are:

Cray-1 supercomputer	64 bits
ICL 1900 series mainframe	24 bits
UNIVAC 1100 mainframe	36 bits
PDP-11 minicomputer	16 bits
VAX minicomputer	32 bits
8085, Z80, 6802, 6809 microprocessors	8 bits
8086 microprocessor	16 bits
Third-generation Intel and Motorola microprocessors	32 bits
Fourth-generation microprocessors	64 bits
Special-purpose graphics processors	128 bits
Some microcontrollers	4 bits

A group of eight bits has come to be known as a *byte*. Today's microprocessors and minicomputers are byte-oriented, with word lengths that are integer multiples of 8 bits (i.e. their data elements and addresses are 8, 16, 32, or 64 bits). A word is spoken of as being 2, 4, or 8 bytes long, because its bits can be formed into 2, 4, or 8 groups of eight bits, respectively. By the way, some early computers grouped bits into *sixes* and called them bytes. One of the irritations of computer science is its flexible jargon, where the same term has different meanings in different contexts. For example, some computer manufacturers employ the term *word* to mean a 16-bit value (as opposed to a byte, which is an 8-bit value), and *longword* to mean a 32-bit value. Other manufacturers use the term *word* to refer to a 32-bit value and *halfword* to refer to a 16-bit value. Throughout this text we will use *word* to mean the basic unit of information operated on by a computer, except when we are describing the 68000 microprocessor in the next chapter.

An n-bit word can be arranged into 2^n unique bit patterns, as Table 4.1 demonstrates for $n = 1, 2, 3,$ and 4. So, what do the n bits of a word represent? The simple and correct answer

Bits n	Bit patterns 2^n	Values
1	2	0, 1
2	4	00, 01, 10, 11
3	8	000, 001, 010, 011, 100, 101, 110, 111
4	16	0000, 0001, 0010, 0011, 0100, 0101, 0110, 0111, 1000, 1001, 1010, 1011, 1100, 1101, 1110, 1111

Table 4.1 The relationship between the number of bits in a word and the number of patterns.

is *nothing*, because there is no intrinsic meaning associated with a pattern of 1s and 0s. The meaning of a particular pattern of bits is the meaning given to it by the programmer. As Humpty Dumpty said to Alice: '[A word] means just what I choose it to mean—neither more nor less.'

The following are some of the entities that a word may represent.

An instruction An *instruction* or operation to be performed by the CPU is represented by a single word in computers with 32-bit or longer words. The relationship between the bit pattern of the instruction and what it does is arbitrary and is determined by the designer of the computer. A particular sequence of bits that means add A to B on one computer might have an entirely different meaning on another computer. Computers with short word lengths require two or more consecutive words to make up an instruction, although some 8-bit machines have single byte instructions.

A numeric quantity A word, either alone or as part of a sequence of words, may represent a numerical quantity. Numbers can be represented in one of many formats: BCD integer, unsigned binary integer, signed binary integer, BCD floating point, binary floating point, complex integer, complex floating point, double precision integer, etc. The meaning of these terms and the way in which the computer carries out its operations in the number system represented by the term is examined later. Once again we stress that the byte 10001001 may represent the value -119 in one system, 137 in another system, and 89 in yet another system. We can think of a more human analogy. What is *GIFT*? To a Bulgarian it might be their login password; to an American it might be something to look forward to on their birthday; to a German it is something to avoid, as it means *poison*. Only the *context* in which GIFT is used determines its meaning.

A character There are many applications of computers in which text is input, processed, and the results printed. The most obvious and spectacular example is the word processor. Programs themselves are frequently submitted to the computer in text form. The *alphanumeric* characters (A to Z, a to z,

0 to 9) and the symbols *, -, +, !, ?, etc. are assigned binary patterns so that they can be stored and manipulated within the computer. Although you can devise many different ways of representing characters, one particular code is now in widespread use throughout the computer industry called the ISO 7-bit character code.

This code is also known as *ASCII code* (American Standard Code for Information Interchange), and represents a character by seven bits, allowing a maximum of $2^7 = 128$ different characters. Of these 128 characters, 96 are the normal printing characters (including both upper and lower cases). The remaining 32 characters are non-printing characters that carry out special functions such as carriage return, backspace, and line feed. Table 4.2 defines the relationship between the bits of the ASCII code and the character they represent.

To convert an ASCII character into its 7-bit binary code, you read the upper-order three bits of the code from the column in which the character falls, and the lower-order four bits of code from the row. Table 4.2 numbers the rows and columns in both binary and hexadecimal forms (we'll introduce hexadecimal numbers shortly); for example, the ASCII representation of the letter 'Z' is given by $5A_{16}$ or 1011010_2. Since most computers use 8-bit bytes, the ASCII code for 'Z' would be 01011010 (some systems might not set the most-significant bit to zero as we've done—but that doesn't matter here). If you wish to print the letter 'Z' on a printer, you send the ASCII code for Z, 01011010, to the printer.

The ASCII codes for the decimal digits 0, 1, 2, 3, 4, 5, 6, 7, 8, and 9, are 30_{16}, 31_{16}, 32_{16}, 33_{16}, 34_{16}, 35_{16}, 36_{16}, 37_{16}, 38_{16}, and 39_{16}, respectively. For example, the *symbol* for the number 4 is represented by the ASCII code 00110100_2, whereas the *binary value* for 4 is represented by 00000100_2. When you hit the key '4' on a keyboard, the computer receives the input 00110100 and *not* 00000100. Whenever you read input from a keyboard or send output to a display, you have to convert between the *codes* for the numbers and the *values* of the numbers. In high-level languages this translation takes place automatically.

The two left-hand columns of Table 4.2, representing ASCII codes 0000000 to 0011111, do not contain letters,

	0 000	1 001	2 010	3 011	4 100	5 101	6 110	7 111
0 0000	NULL	DCL	SP	0	@	P	'	p
1 0001	SOH	DCI	!	1	A	Q	a	q
2 0010	STX	DC2	'	2	B	R	b	r
3 0011	ETX	DC3	#	3	C	S	c	s
4 0100	EOT	DC4	$	4	D	T	d	t
5 0101	ENQ	NAK	%	5	E	U	e	u
6 0110	ACK	SYN	&	6	F	V	f	v
7 0111	BEL	ETB	'	7	G	W	g	w
8 1000	BS	CAN	(	8	H	X	h	x
9 1001	HT	EM	)	9	I	Y	i	y
A 1010	LF	SUB	*	:	J	Z	j	z
B 1011	VT	ESC	]	;	K	[	k	}
C 1100	FF	FS	,	<	L	\	l	|
D 1101	CR	GS	-	\	M	]	m	}
E 1110	SO	RS	.	>	N	^	n	~
F 1111	SI	US	/	?	O	_	o	DEL

Table 4.2 The ASCII code.

numbers, or symbols. These columns are non-printing codes that are used either to control printers and display devices or to control data transmission links. Data link control characters such as ACK (acknowledge) and SYN (synchronous idle) are associated with communications systems that mix the text being transmitted with the special codes required to regulate the flow of the information.

The popular 7-bit ASCII code provides 128 characters and has been extended to the 8-bit ISO 8859−1 Latin code (the extension to ASCII includes accented characters such as Å, ö, and é). However, this code is not suited to many of the world's languages. A 16-bit code, called *Unicode*, has been designed to represent the characters of most of the world's written languages (a large slice is taken up by the thousands of characters in Chinese and Japanese). The first 256 characters of Unicode map onto the ASCII character set, making ASCII to Unicode conversion very easy. The programming language Java has adopted Unicode as the standard means of character representation.

A picture element   One of the many entities that have to be digitally encoded is the picture or graphical display. Pictures vary widely in their complexity and there are a correspondingly large number of ways of representing pictorial information. For example, pictures can be parametrized and stored as a set of instructions that can be used to recreate the image (i.e. the picture is specified in terms of lines, arcs, and polygons and their positions within the picture). When the picture is to be displayed or printed, it is recreated from its parameters.

A simple way of storing pictorial information is to employ symbols that can be put together to make a picture. Such an approach is popular with the low-cost microprocessor systems associated with computer games, where the symbols are called *sprites*.

More complex and detailed pictures cannot readily be parametrized or reduced to a few fairly crude symbols. Often, the only way such a picture can be stored is as a *bit-map*. Any picture can be transformed into a rectangular array of pixels or picture elements. By analogy with the bit, a pixel is the smallest unit of information of which a picture is composed. Unlike a bit, the pixel can have attributes such as color. Consider an A4 size picture (approximately 210 mm by 297 mm). If we wish to store a reasonably high-definition A4 picture, we must use approximately 12 pixels/mm in both the horizontal and vertical axes. That is, 1 square millimeter is made up of $12 \times 12 = 144$ pixels, and therefore the entire picture is composed of $210 \times 296 \times 144 = 8\,951\,040$ pixels which represents over 1 Mbyte of storage if the picture is monochrome. If the picture were in color and each pixel could have one of 256 different colors, the total storage requirement would be over 8 Mbyte. These parameters explain why high-quality computer graphics requires such expensive equipment. Typical high-quality color video displays have a resolution of 1024×1024 (i.e. 2^{20} pixels) per frame. There are, however, techniques for compressing the amount of storage required by a picture. Such techniques operate by locating areas of a constant color and intensity and storing the shape and location of the area and its color.

4.2 Number bases

Before we introduce numbers in the context of computers, we really need to say what we mean by *numbers*. The numbers we use to count things (i.e. 1, 2, 3, 4, ...) are called *natural numbers* and are *integers* (whole numbers). Natural numbers are so called because they don't depend on our mathematics (there are three stars in Orion's belt whether or not there are humans on the Earth to count them). The way in which we count is defined by the *number system*, which uses 10 special *symbols* to represent numbers.

Not all numbers are natural. For example, we have invented *negative* numbers to handle certain concepts. We have *real* numbers that describe non-integer values, including fractions. Real numbers themselves are divided into *rational* and *irrational* numbers. A rational number can be expressed as a *fraction* (e.g. 7/12), whereas an irrational number can't be expressed as one integer divided by another. Paradoxically, we can draw a line that has a finite length but we can't write down the length as a real number. If a square measures one inch by one inch, its diagonal is $\sqrt{2}$ inches long. You can draw the diagonal, but the value of $\sqrt{2}$ in our number system cannot be expressed by a finite number of digits.

We have introduced these basic concepts because they have implications for the way in which computers process numeric information.

Our modern number system, which includes a symbol to represent zero, was introduced into Europe from the Hindu–Arabic world in about 1400. This system represents decimal numbers by means of *positional notation*. By *positional* we mean that the value or *weight* of a digit depends on its location within a number. In our system, when each digit moves one place left it is multiplied by 10 (the base or radix). Thus, the 9 in 95 is worth 10 times the 9 in 59. Similarly, a digit is divided by 10 when moved one place right (e.g. consider 0.90 and 0.09).

If the concept of *positional notation* seems obvious and not worthy of mention, consider the Romans. They conquered most of the known world, invented Latin grammar, and yet their mathematics was terribly cumbersome. Because the Roman world did not use a positional system to represent number, each new large number had to have its own special symbol. Their number system was one of *give and take* so that if X = 10 and I = 1, then XI = 11 (i.e. 10 + 1) and IX = 9 (i.e. 10 − 1). The decimal number 1970 is represented in Roman numerals by MCMLXX (i.e. 1000 + (1000 − 100) + 50 + 10 + 10). The Romans did not have a symbol for zero.

The number *base* lies at the heart of both conventional and computer arithmetic. Humans use base 10 and computers use base 2. However, we sometimes use other bases even in our everyday lives. For example, we get base 60 from the Babylonians (60 seconds = 1 minute and 60 minutes = 1 hour). We can express the time 1:2:3 (1 hour 2 minutes 3 seconds) as $1 \times 60 \times 60 + 2 \times 60 + 3$ seconds. Similarly, we occasionally use the base 12 (12 = 1 dozen, $12 \times 12 = 1$ gross).

We are now going to examine how a number is represented in a general base using positional notation. We write integer N that is made up of n digits in the form

$$a_{n-1}\, a_{n-2} \ldots a_1\, a_0$$

The a_is that make up the number are called *digits* and can take one of b values (where b is the base in which the number is expressed). If this sounds complex, consider the decimal number 821686, where the six digits are $a_0 = 6$, $a_1 = 8$, $a_2 = 6$, $a_3 = 1$, $a_4 = 2$, and $a_5 = 8$, and these digits are taken from a set of 10 symbols (0 to 9).

The same notation can be used to express real values by using a *radix point* (e.g. decimal point in base 10 arithmetic or binary point in binary arithmetic) to separate the integer and fractional parts of the number. In this case we have used m digits to the right of the radix point.

$$a_{n-1}a_{n-2} \ldots a_1 a_0 \cdot a_{-1} a_{-2} \ldots a_{-m}$$

The value of this number expressed in positional notation in the base b is written is defined as

$$N = a_{n-1}b^{n-1} + \cdots + a_1 b^1 + a_0 b^0 + a_{-1} b^{-1}$$
$$+ a_{-2} b^{-2} + \cdots + a_{-m} b^{-m}$$
$$= \sum_{i=-m}^{n-1} a_i b^i$$

In other words, the value of a number is equal to the sum of its digits, each of which is multiplied by a *weight* according to its position in the number. Let's look at some examples of how this formula works. The decimal number 1982 is equal to $1 \times 10^3 + 9 \times 10^2 + 8 \times 10^1 + 2 \times 10^0$ (i.e. one thousand + nine hundreds + eight tens + two). Similarly, 12.34 is equal to $1 \times 10^1 + 2 \times 10^0 + 3 \times 10^{-1} + 4 \times 10^{-2}$. The value of the binary number 10110.11 is given by $1 \times 2^4 + 0 \times 2^3 + 1 \times 2^2 + 1 \times 2^1 + 0 \times 2^0 + 1 \times 2^{-1} + 1 \times 2^{-2}$, or, in decimal, $16 + 4 + 2 + 0.5 + 0.25 = 22.75$. Remember that the value of r^0 is 1 (i.e. any number to the power zero is 1).

In base seven arithmetic, the number 123 is equal to the decimal number $1 \times 7^2 + 2 \times 7^1 + 3 \times 7^0 = 49 + 14 + 3 = 66$. Because we are talking about different bases in this chapter, we will sometimes use a *subscript* to indicate the base; for example, $123_7 = 66_{10}$.

Decimal	$b = 10$	$a = \{0,1,2,3,4,5,6,7,8,9\}$	
Binary	$b = 2$	$a = \{0,1\}$	
Octal	$b = 8$	$a = \{0,1,2,3,4,5,6,7\}$	
Hexadecimal	$b = 16$	$a = \{0,1,2,3,4,5,6,7,8,9,A,B,C,D,E,F\}$	

Table 4.3 Four number bases.

Bit	Value	Component	Action
7	0	Heater 1	off
6	1	Heater 2	on
5	0	Heater 3	off
4	1	Valve 1	on
3	0	Valve 2	off
2	0	Valve 3	off
1	1	Pump 1	on
0	1	Pump 2	on

Table 4.4 Decoding the binary sequence 01010011.

To be more precise, we should make it clear that we're talking about *natural positional numbers*. The natural numbers have positional *weights* of 1, 10, 100, 1000, ... (decimal) or 1, 2, 4, 8, 16, 32, ... (binary). When we talk about the *weight* of a number we mean the value by which it is multiplied by virtue of its position in the number. It's perfectly possible to have weightings that are not successive powers of an integer; for example, we can choose a binary weighting of 2, 4, 4, 2, which means that the number 1010 is interpreted as $1 \times 2 + 0 \times 4 + 1 \times 4 + 0 \times 2 = 6$.

We are interested in four bases: decimal, binary, octal, and hexadecimal (the term *hexadecimal* is often abbreviated to *hex*). We should stress that the *octal* base is little used today and has almost entirely been replaced by the hexadecimal base. Table 4.3 shows the digits used by each of these bases. Because the hexadecimal base has 16 digits, we have had to use the letters A to F to indicate values between 10 and 15.

People normally work in decimal and computers in binary. It is not unreasonable to assume that we use base 10 because we have ten fingers and thumbs. We shall see later that the purpose of the octal and hexadecimal systems is as an aid to human memory. It is almost impossible to remember long strings of binary digits. By converting them to the octal or hexadecimal bases (a very easy task) the shorter octal or hexadecimal numbers can be more readily committed to memory. Furthermore, as hexadecimal numbers are more compact than binary numbers (1 hexadecimal digit = 4 binary digits), they are used in computer texts and *core-dumps*. The latter term refers to a printout of part of the computer's memory, an operation normally performed as a diagnostic aid when all else has failed. For example, the 8-bit binary number 10001001 is equivalent to the hexadecimal number 89. Clearly, 89 is more easy to remember than 10001001.

There are occasions where binary numbers offer people advantages over other forms of representation. Suppose a computer-controlled chemical plant has three heaters, three valves, and two pumps, which are designated H1, H2, H3, V1, V2, V3, P1, P2, respectively. An 8-bit word from the computer is fed to an interface unit that converts the binary ones and zeros into electrical signals to switch on (logical one) or switch off (logical zero) the corresponding device. For example, the binary word 01010011 has the effect described in Table 4.4 when presented to the control unit.

By inspecting the binary value of the control word, the status of all devices is immediately apparent. If the output had been represented in decimal (83), hexadecimal (53), or octal (123), the relationship between the number and its intended action would not have been so obvious.

How many bits does it require to represent a decimal number?

If we are going to represent decimal numbers in binary form, we need to know how many binary digits are required to express, say, an n-digit decimal number; for example, how many bits does it take to represent numbers up to 90 000 000? The following explanation requires an understanding of *logarithms*. If your arithmetic is rusty, just accept that you need about 3.3 bits for every decimal digit.

Suppose we require m bits to represent the largest n-digit decimal number, which is, of course, 99 ... 999 or $10^n - 1$. We require the largest binary number in m bits (i.e. 11 ... 111 or $2^m - 1$) to be equal to or greater than the largest decimal number in n bits (i.e. 99 ... 999). That is,

$$10^n - 1 \leqslant 2^m - 1$$

That is, $10^n \leqslant 2^m$.

Taking logarithms to base 10 we get

$\log_{10} 10^n \leqslant \log_{10} 2^m$ *Note*: $\log_{10} 10^n = n \log_{10} 10$, and

$n \log_{10} 10 \leqslant m \log_{10} 2$ $\log_{10} 10 = 1$

$n \leqslant m \log_{10} 2$

$m \geqslant 3.322n$

In other words, it takes approximately $3.3n$ bits to represent an n-bit decimal number. For example, if we wish to represent decimal numbers up to 1 000 000 in binary, we must use at least 6×3.3 bits, which indicates a 20-bit word length.

If there's one point that we would like to emphasize here, it's that the rules of arithmetic are the same in base x as they are in base y. In other words, all the rules we learned for base 10 arithmetic can be applied to base 2, base 16, or even base 5 arithmetic. For example, the base 5 numbers 123_5 and 221_5

represent, in decimal, $1 \times 5^2 + 2 \times 5^1 + 3 \times 5^0 = 38_{10}$, and $2 \times 5^2 + 2 \times 5^1 + 1 \times 5^0 = 61_{10}$, respectively. Let's add both pairs of numbers together using the conventional rules of arithmetic in base 5 and base 10.

Base 5	Base 10
123	38
+221	+61
344	99

If we add 123_5 to 221_5 we get 344_5, which is equal to the decimal number $3 \times 5^2 + 4 \times 5^1 + 4 \times 5^0 = 99_{10}$. Adding the decimal numbers 38_{10} and 61_{10} also gives us 99_{10}. Now that we've looked at the structure of binary and decimal numbers, the next step is to consider how we convert a number in one base into its equivalent value in another base.

4.3 Number base conversion

It's sometimes necessary to convert numbers from one base to another by means of a pencil-and-paper method. This statement is particularly true when working with microprocessors at the assembly language or machine code level. In general, computer users need not concern themselves with conversion between number bases, as the computer will have software to convert a decimal input into the computer's own internal binary representation of the input. Once the computer has done its job, it converts the binary results into decimal form before printing them.

A knowledge of the effect of number bases on arithmetic operations is sometimes quite vital, as, for example, even the simplest of decimal fractions (say $1/10 = 0.1$) has no exact binary equivalent. That is, a rational number expressed in a finite number of digits in one base may require an infinite number of digits in another base. Suppose the computer were asked to add the decimal value 0.1_{10} to itself and stop when the result reaches 1. The computer may never stop, because the decimal value 0.1_{10} cannot be exactly represented by a binary number, with the result that the sum of 10 binary representations of 0.1 is never exactly 1. The sum may be 1.0000000000001 or 0.99999999999, which is almost as good as 1, but it is not the same as 1, and a test for equality with 1 will always fail.

4.3.1 Conversion of integers

In this section we are going to demonstrate how integers are converted from one base to another.

Decimal to binary To convert a decimal integer to binary, divide the number successively by 2, and after each division record the remainder, which is either 1 or 0. The process is terminated only when the result of the division is 0 remainder 1. In all the following conversions R represents the remainder after a division.

For example, 123_{10} becomes

$$
\begin{array}{lll}
123 \div 2 = 61 & R = 1 & \\
61 \div 2 = 30 & R = 1 & \\
30 \div 2 = 15 & R = 0 & \\
15 \div 2 = 7 & R = 1 & \\
7 \div 2 = 3 & R = 1 & \\
3 \div 2 = 1 & R = 1 & \\
1 \div 2 = 0 & R = 1 & \text{Most-significant bit}
\end{array}
$$

The result is read from the most-significant bit (the last remainder) upwards to give $123_{10} = 1111011_2$.

Decimal to octal The process is as above except that division by 8 is used. In this case, the remainder is a number in the range 0 to 7. As before, the process of conversion ends when the final result is 0 remainder R (where $0 \leqslant R < 8$).

For example, 4629 becomes

$$
\begin{array}{ll}
4629 \div 8 = 578 & R = 5 \\
578 \div 8 = 72 & R = 2 \\
72 \div 8 = 9 & R = 0 \\
9 \div 8 = 1 & R = 1 \\
1 \div 8 = 0 & R = 1
\end{array}
$$

Therefore, $4629_{10} = 11025_8$.

Decimal to hexadecimal Decimal numbers are converted from decimal into hexadecimal form in exactly the same way that decimal numbers are converted into binary form. However, in this case the remainder lies in the decimal range 0 to 15, corresponding to the hexadecimal range 0 to F.

For example, 53241_{10} becomes

$$
\begin{array}{ll}
53241 \div 16 = 3327 & R = 9 \\
3327 \div 16 = 207 & R = 15_{10} = F_{16} \\
207 \div 16 = 12 & R = 15_{10} = F_{16} \\
12 \div 16 = 0 & R = 12_{10} = C_{16}
\end{array}
$$

Therefore, $53241_{10} = CFF9_{16}$.

Binary to decimal It is possible to convert a binary number to decimal by adding together the requisite powers of two. This technique is suitable for relatively small binary numbers up to about seven or eight bits.

For example, 1010111_2 is represented by

```
64  32  16   8   4   2   1    64
 1   0   1   0   1   1   1 = 16
                             4
                             2
                           + 1
                           ────
                            87
```

A more methodical technique is based on a recursive algorithm as follows. Take the leftmost non-zero bit, double it, and add it to the bit on its right. Now take this result, double it, and add it to the next bit on the right. Continue in this way until the least-significant bit has been added in. The recursive procedure may be expressed mathematically as:

$$(a_0 + 2(a_1 + 2(a_2 + \dots)))$$

where the least-significant bit of the binary number is a_0.

For example, 1010111_2 becomes

```
1     0     1     0     1     1     1
└→ 2
   2
   └→ 4
      5
      └→ 10
         10
         └→ 20
            21
            └→ 42
               43
               └→ 86
                  87
```

Therefore, $1010111_2 = 87_{10}$.

Octal to decimal   Remember that we said that any rule that applies to base x also applies to base y. If we convert binary numbers to decimal by continually adding $2a_i$ to a_{i-1}, then we convert from octal to decimal by continually adding $8a_i$ to a_{i-1}. An octal number is expressed in decimal form as

$$(a_0 + 8(a_1 + 8(a_2 + \dots)))$$

We take the leftmost digit, multiply it by eight, and add it to the digit on its right. We then multiply this subtotal by eight and add it to the next digit on its right. The process ends when the leftmost digit has been added to the subtotal.

For example, 6437_8 becomes

```
6     4     3     7
└→ 48
   52
   └→ 416
      419
      └→ 3352
         3359
```

Therefore, $6437_8 = 3359_{10}$.

Hexadecimal to decimal   The method is identical to the procedures for binary and octal except that 16 is used as a multiplier.

For example, $1AC_{16}$ becomes

```
1     A     C
└→ 16
   26
   └→ 416
      428
```

Therefore, $1AC_{16} = 428_{10}$.

Conversions between binary, octal, and hexadecimal

In much of this book, binary numbers are represented in *hexadecimal* form. Although some older texts favor the octal format, this base is ill-fitted to the representation of 8- or 16-bit binary values. Octal numbers were more popular when people used 12-, 24-, or 36-bit computers. We shall use hexadecimal representations of binary numbers simply because of the ease with which conversions may be made between binary and hexadecimal numbers.

Binary to octal   Form the bits into groups of three starting at the binary point and moving leftwards. Replace each group of three bits with the corresponding octal digit (0 to 7).

For example, the bits of 11001011101_2 can be regrouped as follows and the groups replaced by octal digits.

```
11   001   011   101
 3     1     3     5
```

Therefore, $11001011101_2 = 3135_8$. Note how the binary number has been condensed to a more manageable size.

Binary to hexadecimal   The binary number is formed into groups of four bits starting at the binary point. Each group is replaced by a hexadecimal digit from 0 to 9, A, B, C, D, E, F.

For example, 11001011101 becomes

```
110   0101   1101
 6     5      D
```

Therefore, $11001011101_2 = 65D_{16}$.

Octal to binary Converting an octal number into its binary equivalent requires the reverse procedure of converting from binary to octal. Each octal digit is simply replaced by its 3-bit binary equivalent. It is important to remember that, for example, 3 must be replaced by 011 and not by 11. For example, 41357_8 becomes

```
 4    1    3    5    7
100  001  011  101  111
```

Therefore, $41357_8 = 100001011101111_2$.

Hexadecimal to binary Each hexadecimal digit is replaced by its 4-bit binary equivalent. For example, $AB4C_{16}$ becomes

```
  A     B     4     C
1010  1011  0100  1100
```

Therefore, $AB4C_{16} = 1010101101001100_2$.

Conversion between hexadecimal and octal values is best performed via binary (e.g. hexadecimal to binary to octal). For example, to convert the hexadecimal number 12BC to octal form we perform the following actions:

$12BC_{16} = 1\ 0010\ 1011\ 1100_2$ (form groups of four bits from the right)

$1001010111100_2 = 1\ 001\ 010\ 111\ 100_2$ (after regrouping)

$1\ 001\ 010\ 111\ 100_2 = 11274_8$ (convert 3-bit groups to octal digits)

4.3.2 Conversion of fractions

The conversion of fractions from one base to another is carried out in a similar way to the conversion of integers, although it's rather more tedious to manipulate fractions manually. Fortunately, it's rare to have to perform actual pencil and paper conversion of fractions outside the classroom. One way of effectively abolishing fractions is to treat all fractions as integers scaled by an appropriate factor. For example, the binary fraction 0.10101 is equal to the binary integer 10101 divided by 2^5 (i.e. 32), so that, for example, 0.10101 is the same as $10101/2^5 = 21/32 = 0.65625$.

Converting binary fractions to decimal fractions
The algorithm for converting binary fractions to their decimal equivalent is based on the fact that a bit in one column is worth half the value of a bit in the column on its left. Starting at the rightmost non-zero bit, take that bit and halve it. Now add the result to the next bit on its left. Halve this result and add it to the next bit on the left. Continue until the binary point is reached.

For example, consider the conversion of 0.01101_2 into decimal form.

```
0.      0      1      1      0      1
                           1/2 ←┘
                           1/2
                    1/4 ←┘
                    5/4
             5/8 ←┘
             13/8
       13/16 ←┘
       13/16
13/32←┘
```

Therefore, $0.01101_2 = 13/32$.

Converting decimal fractions to binary fractions
The decimal fraction is multiplied by two and the integer part noted. The integer, which will be either 1 or 0, is then stripped from the number to leave a fractional part. The new fraction is multiplied by 2 and the integer part noted. We continue in this way until the process ends or a sufficient degree of precision has been achieved. The binary fraction is formed by reading the integer parts from the top to the bottom as illustrated below.

For example, 0.6875_{10} becomes

```
0.6875 × 2 → 1.3750
0.3750 × 2 → 0.7500
0.7500 × 2 → 1.5000
0.5000 × 2 → 1.0000
0.0000 × 2 ends the process
```

Therefore, $0.6875_{10} = 0.1011_2$.

Now consider 0.1_{10}:

```
0.1000 × 2 → 0.2000
0.2000 × 2 → 0.4000
0.4000 × 2 → 0.8000
0.8000 × 2 → 1.6000
0.6000 × 2 → 1.2000
0.2000 × 2 → 0.4000
0.4000 × 2 → 0.8000
0.8000 × 2 → 1.6000
0.6000 × 2 → 1.2000
0.2000 × 2 → 0.4000
0.4000 × 2 → 0.8000
```

etc.

Therefore, $0.1_{10} = 0.00011001100\ldots\ldots_2$ etc. As we pointed out before, 0.1_{10} cannot be expressed exactly in binary form (with a finite number of digits).

Converting between octal/hexadecimal fractions and decimal fractions

We can convert between octal or hexadecimal fractions and decimal fractions using the same algorithms we used for binary conversions. All we have to change is the base (i.e. 2 to 8 or 2 to 16). Consider the following example.

Convert 0.12_{10} into its octal equivalent.

$0.12 \times 8 \rightarrow \mathbf{0}.96$
$0.96 \times 8 \rightarrow \mathbf{7}.68$
$0.68 \times 8 \rightarrow \mathbf{5}.44$
$0.44 \times 8 \rightarrow \mathbf{3}.52$
$0.52 \times 8 \rightarrow \mathbf{4}.16$
$0.16 \times 8 \rightarrow \mathbf{1}.28$

etc.

Therefore, $0.12_{10} = 0.075341_8$.

Similarly, consider the conversion of 0.123_{16} into a decimal fraction.

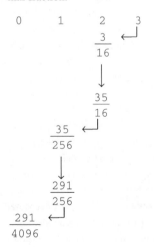

Binary to octal/hexadecimal fraction conversion and vice versa

The conversion of binary fractions to octal or hexadecimal bases is as easy as the corresponding integer conversions. The only point worth mentioning is that when binary digits are split into groups of three (octal) or four (hex), we start grouping bits at the binary point and move to the right. Any group of digits remaining on the right containing fewer than three (four) bits must be made up to three (four) bits by the addition of zeros to the right of the least-significant bit. The following examples illustrate this point.

Binary to octal	0.10101100_2	$\rightarrow 0.101\ 011\ 00(0)$	$\rightarrow 0.530_8$
Binary to octal	0.10101111_2	$\rightarrow 0.101\ 011\ 11(0)$	$\rightarrow 0.536_8$
Binary to hexadecimal	0.10101100_2	$\rightarrow 0.1010\ 1100_2$	$\rightarrow 0.AC_{16}$
Binary to hexadecimal	0.101011001_2	$\rightarrow 0.1010\ 1100\ 1(000)$	$\rightarrow 0.AC8_{16}$
Octal to binary	0.456_8	$\rightarrow 0.100\ 101\ 110$	$\rightarrow 0.100101110_2$
Hexadecimal to binary	$0.ABC_{16}$	$\rightarrow 0.1010\ 1011\ 1100$	$\rightarrow 0.101010111100_2$

Numbers containing an integer part and a fraction part (e.g. 110101.11010 in base 2 or 123.8125 in decimal) are converted from one base to another in two stages. The integer part is converted and then the fractional part (using any appropriate conversion technique).

4.4 Special-purpose codes

Throughout this book a group of binary digits generally represents one of three things: a numerical quantity, an instruction, or a character. However, many different codes exist in the world of computing and digital systems, each of which is best suited to the particular job for which it was designed.

4.4.1 BCD codes

A common alternative to natural binary arithmetic is called BCD or *Binary-Coded Decimal*. In theory BCD is a case of having your cake and eating it. We have already stated that computer designers use two-state logic elements on purely economic grounds. This, in turn, leads to the world of binary arithmetic and the consequent problems of converting between binary and decimal representations of numeric quantities. Binary-coded decimal numbers accept the inevitability of two-state logic by coding the individual decimal digits into groups of four bits. Table 4.5 shows how the 10 digits, 0 to 9, are represented in BCD, and how a decimal number is converted to a BCD form.

BCD arithmetic is identical to decimal arithmetic and differs only in the way the 10 digits are represented. The following example demonstrates how a BCD addition is carried out.

Decimal	BCD
2634	0010 0110 0011 0100
3825	0011 1000 0010 0101
6459	0110 0100 0101 1001

Binary code	BCD value
0000	0
0001	1
0010	2
0011	3
0100	4
0101	5
0110	6
0111	7
1000	8
1001	9
1010	Forbidden code
1011	Forbidden code
1100	Forbidden code
1101	Forbidden code
1110	Forbidden code
1111	Forbidden code

Table 4.5 Binary coded decimal.

Convert 1927 to BCD format
Step 1 Write down decimal digits
Digits   1   9   2   7
Step 2 Convert each digit to BCD
BCD 0001 1001 0010 0111

As you can see, the arithmetic is decimal with the digits 0 to 9 represented by 4-bit codes. When 6 is added to 8 (i.e. 0110 to 1000), the result is not the binary value 1110, but the decimal $6+8=14=0100_2$ (i.e. 4) carry 1.

Although BCD makes decimal to binary conversion easy, it suffers from two disadvantages. The first is that BCD arithmetic is more complex than binary arithmetic simply because the binary tables (i.e. addition, subtraction, multiplication, and division) can be implemented in hardware by a few gates. The decimal tables involve all combinations of the digits 0 to 9 and are more complex. Today's digital technology makes these disadvantages less evident than in the early days of computer technology where each gate was an expensive item.

BCD uses storage inefficiently. As computer owners have to pay for their memory, it is reasonable to use the smallest quantity of memory for a given job. A BCD digit requires four bits of storage, but only 10 symbols are mapped to 10 of the 16 possible binary codes. Consequently, the binary codes 1010 to 1111 (10 to 15) are redundant and represent wasted storage. As we demonstrated earlier in this chapter, natural binary numbers require an average of approximately 3.3 bits per decimal digit.

In spite of the disadvantages of BCD, it is frequently found in applications requiring little storage, such as pocket calculators or digital watches. Microprocessors often have special instructions to aid BCD operations.

There are other ways of representing BCD numbers in addition to the basic BCD code presented above. Each of these codes has desirable properties making it suitable for a particular application (e.g. the representation of negative numbers). These BCD codes are not relevant to this text.

4.4.2 Unweighted codes

The binary codes described earlier are often called *pure* binary, *natural* binary, or *8421 weighted* binary because the 8, 4, 2, and 1 represent the weightings of each of the columns in the positional code. There are many other positional codes that don't have a natural binary weighting. Some codes are called *unweighted* because the value of a bit doesn't depend on its position within a number. Each of these codes does, however, have special properties that make it suitable for a specific application. One such unweighted code is called a *unit distance code*.

Before we can define a unit distance code, we have to introduce the idea of the *distance* between two binary values. The *Hamming distance* between two words is the number of places (i.e. positions) in which they differ. The examples in Table 4.6 should make this clear.

In a *unit* distance code, the distance between consecutive code words is constant and equal to one. That is, no two consecutive code words differ in more than one bit position. Natural binary numbers most certainly don't belong to the domain of unit distance codes. For example, the sequential natural binary numbers $0111=7$ and $1000=8$ differ by a Hamming distance of *four*. The most widely encountered unit distance code is the *Gray* code, the first 16 values of which are given in Table 4.7.

The Gray code is often associated with the *optical encoder*, a mechanism for converting the angle of a shaft or spindle into a binary value. An optical encoder allows you to measure the angular position of a shaft electronically without any physical connection between the shaft and the measuring equipment. A typical example of an optical encoder is found in an automated weather reporting system. The direction from which the wind is blowing is determined by one of the world's oldest measuring devices, the weather vane. The weather vane is mounted on a shaft connected to an optical encoder that provides the angle of rotation (i.e. wind direction) as a digital signal.

Word 1	00101101	0 0101101	0 0101101	00101101	0 0 1 0 1 1 0 1
Word 2	00101100	1 1101100	1 1101101	00100101	1 1 0 1 0 0 1 0
Places different		✓ ✓✓	✓ ✓✓	✓	✓✓✓✓✓✓✓✓
Hamming distance	1	3	2	1	8

Table 4.6 The Hamming distance—the number of positions in which two binary sequences differ.

Decimal value	Natural binary value	Gray code
0	0000	0000
1	0001	0001
2	0010	0011
3	0011	0010
4	0100	0110
5	0101	0111
6	0110	0101
7	0111	0100
8	1000	1100
9	1001	1101
10	1010	1111
11	1011	1110
12	1100	1010
13	1101	1011
14	1110	1001
15	1111	1000

Table 4.7 The 4-bit Gray code (an unweighted unit distance code).

Figure 4.1(a) shows an optical encoder using a natural binary code and Fig. 4.1(b) shows the same arrangement but with a Gray-encoded disk. A transparent glass or plastic disk is attached to the shaft whose angular position is to be measured. As you can see, the disk is covered with concentric tracks, one for each of the bits in the code representing the position of the shaft. A 4-bit code might be suitable for a wind direction indicator, whereas a 10-bit code may be required to indicate the position of a shaft in a machine. Each of these tracks is divided into sectors that are either opaque or transparent.

A light source (LED or incandescent light bulb) is located on one side of the disk over each track. A photoelectric sensor is located on the other side of the disk directly opposite each light source. Thus, for any position of the disk, a particular combination of the photoelectric cells detects a light beam, depending on whether or not there is a transparent sector between the light source and detector.

A natural binary code can create problems when more than one bit of the output code changes as the shaft rotates from one code to the next. In practice, the photoelectric cells can't be perfectly aligned; the light source isn't a point source; and the edges of the sectors don't have perfectly straight edges. When the disk rotates from one sector to the next and two bits change state, one bit may change slightly before the other. For example, the change from the natural binary code 001 to 010 might be observed as the sequence 001, 000, 010. Because the

Sector	Angle	Binary code
0	0–45	0 0 0
1	45–90	0 0 1
2	90–135	0 1 0
3	135–180	0 1 1
4	180–225	1 0 0
5	225–270	1 0 1
6	270–315	1 1 0
7	315–360	1 1 1

Sector	Angle	Gray code
0	0–45	0 0 0
1	45–90	0 0 1
2	90–135	0 1 1
3	135–180	0 1 0
4	180–225	1 1 0
5	225–270	1 1 1
6	270–315	1 0 1
7	315–360	1 0 0

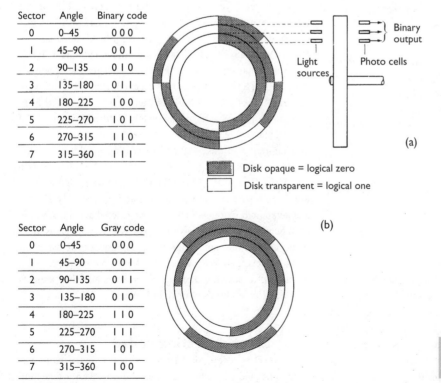

Binary output

Light sources

Photo cells

(a)

Disk opaque = logical zero
Disk transparent = logical one

(b)

Fig. 4.1 (a) A natural binary-encoded optical encoder; **(b)** a Gray-encoded optical encoder.

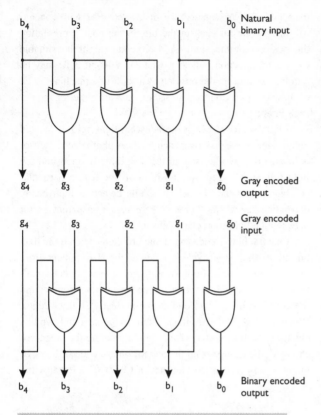

Fig. 4.2 Converting binary codes to Gray codes and vice versa.

least-significant bit changes before the middle bit, the spurious code 000 is generated momentarily. In some applications this can be very troublesome. Figure 4.1(b) shows that a Gray-encoded disk has the property that only one bit at a time changes, solving the problems inherent in the natural binary system. Once the Gray code has been read into a digital system it may be converted into a natural binary code for processing in the normal way.

The EOR gate logic of Fig. 4.2 converts between Gray codes and natural binary codes.

Encoding images

The final topic in this section looks at one way in which the storage space taken up by digitized images can be dramatically reduced. A picture or image can be divided into a number of dots or *pixels*. The smaller you make the pixels, the better the image looks. Unfortunately, it takes a very large number of pixels to create an image of acceptable definition; for example, the average PC has a screen capable of displaying an image made up of 1024×768 pixels.

There are many ways of encoding images. An interesting data compression technique employs a data structure called the *quadtree*, which is illustrated by an 8×8 pixel image in Fig. 4.3. This image can be divided into *four* quadrants, as Fig. 4.3(b) demonstrates (hence the term *quad*tree).

As you can see from Fig. 4.3(b), the four quadrants have different properties. In the top left-hand quadrant, all the pixels are black and are marked 'F' for full. In the bottom left-hand quadrant, all the pixels are white and are marked 'E' for empty. Each of the two right-hand quadrants contains a mixture of black and white pixels—these quadrants are marked 'P' for partially occupied.

The picture of Fig. 4.3(b) can be represented by its four quadrants 0,1,2,3 as E,P,F,P (see Fig. 4.3 for the quadrant numbering scheme). We can partially regenerate the image because we know that one quadrant is all black and another is all white. However, we don't know anything about the two quadrants marked 'P'.

We can, however, subdivide partially filled quadrants 1 and 3 into further quadrants. Consider the upper right-hand quadrant of Fig. 4.3(b) (i.e. quadrant 3). This can be divided into four quadrants, as Fig. 4.3(c) demonstrates. We can describe the structure of Fig. 4.3(c) by E,P,E,P. If we substitute this expansion of quadrant 3 in the original expression for the image, we get: E,P,F, (E,P,E,P).

We haven't yet completely defined quadrant 3 of the image, because there are still subdivisions marked 'P'. Figure 4.3(d) demonstrates how the top right-hand quadrant for Fig. 4.3(c) can be subdivided into the quadrants E,F,E,F. If we now substitute this in the expression for the image we get: E,P,F, (E,(E,F,E,F),E,P). We can do the same thing to quadrant 1 of Fig. 4.3(c) to get: E,P,F, (E,(E,F,E,F),E, (E,F,E,F)). Now we have completely defined quadrant 3 of the original image.

Continuing in this way and expanding quadrant 1 of the original image, we get the expression: E,(E,F,(E,E,F,F), (E,F,F,F)), F,(E,(E,(E,F,E,F),E, (E,F,E,F)). All we have done is to divide an image into four quadrants and successively divided a quadrant into four quadrants until we reach that point at which each quadrant contains only one color. Since many areas of an image contain the same color, the quadtree structure can compress the image. In the case of Fig. 4.3 we have compressed a 64-element block into a string of 29 elements (the elements may be E, F, left bracket, or right bracket).

4.4.3 Error-detecting codes

Error-detecting codes or EDCs can detect that a word has been corrupted (i.e. changed). The subject of error-detecting

(a) Block of 8 × 8 pixels

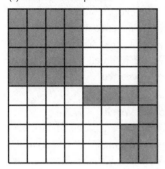

(b) Dividing the block into 4 quadrants

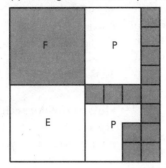

2	3
0	1

Quadrant
numbering

F = full (all elements 1)
E = empty (all elements 0)
P = partially filled

(c) The top right-hand quadrant of b
is divided into four quadrants

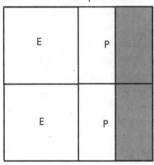

(d) The top right-hand quadrant of c
is divided into four quadrants

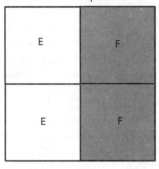

(e) Botton right hand quadrant of a
is divided into four quadrants

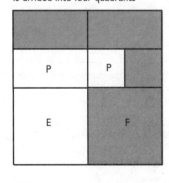

(f) Top right hand quadrant of e
is divided into four quadrants

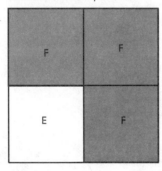

Fig. 4.3 The quadtree.

codes is large enough to fill a number of textbooks. Here we look only at two classes of error-detecting code: codes with a single parity bit and *Hamming codes*. The Hamming code we describe later is not only an EDC, it's also an *error-correcting code*, ECC, that can correct a single-bit error in a corrupted word. Of course, the ECC is also an EDC, whereas the EDC is not necessarily an ECC. Before we can discuss EDCs and ECCs we must introduce two terms: *source word* and *code word*. A source word is an unencoded string of bits and a code

word is a source word that has been encoded. For example, the source code 10110 might be transformed into the code word 111000111111000 by triplicating each bit.

Before we introduce EDCs and ECCs, we must ask ourselves why they are needed. In any electronic system there are always unwanted random signals, collectively called *noise*, that may interfere with the correct operation of the system. These random signals arise from a variety of causes, ranging from the thermal motion of electrons in a digital system to electromagnetic radiation from nearby lightning strikes and power line transients caused by the switching of inductive loads (e.g. starting motors in vacuum cleaners or elevators). The magnitude of these unwanted signals is generally tiny compared with digital signals inside the computer. The two electrical signal levels representing the zero and one binary states are so well separated that one level is almost never spontaneously converted into the other level inside a digital computer under normal operating conditions.

Whenever digital signals are transmitted over a long distance by cables, their magnitude is diminished, making it possible for external noise signals to exceed the level of the digital signals and thus corrupt them. The effect of electrical noise is familiar to anyone who has tuned a radio or television to a distant station—the sound or picture is of a lower quality than when a local station is received. Whenever an error occurs in the reception of digital signals, it is important for the event to be detected so that a request for retransmission of the corrupted data can be made.

ECCs and EDCs are also required by data storage technology. Some of the techniques used to store digital data are prone to errors (albeit with a very low probability); for example, DRAM chips are susceptible to errors caused by alpha-particles due to radioactivity. ECCs and EDCs can determine whether data has been corrupted during the process of storage and retrieval.

Error detection can be implemented by transmitting the desired digital information (i.e. the source word) plus one or more *check bits* whose value is a function of the information bits. Because check bits convey no new information, they are called *redundant bits*.

At the receiving end of a data link the information bits are used to recalculate the check bits. If the received check bits are the same as those locally generated, error free transmission is assumed—otherwise the receiver sends a message back to the transmitter asking it to repeat the lost data.

If an error is detected in a word stored in memory, the error can't be corrected by asking the computer what the stored word should have been because there is no other copy of the word. Consequently the operating system must be informed of the error and then left to take appropriate action (usually by aborting the current task). Memories that use error-correcting codes are able to repair the damage done by an error before the word is passed to the computer.

As an example of the application of check bits, consider a simple two-digit decimal code with a single decimal check digit. The check digit is calculated by adding up the two source digits modulo 10 (modulo 10 simply means that we ignore any carry when we add the digits; for example, the

modulo 10 value of $6+7$ is 3). If the two source digits are 4 and 9, the code word is 493 (the check digit is 3). Suppose that during transmission or storage the code word is corrupted and becomes 463. If we re-evaluate the check digit we get $4+6=10=0$ (modulo ten). As the recorded check digit is 3, we know that an error must have occurred.

How error-detecting codes work

The idea behind EDCs is simple, as Fig. 4.4 demonstrates. An incorrect code word has to be made to reveal itself. Assume we transmit n-bit messages, where m bits are data bits and $r=n-m$ bits are redundant check bits. Imagine an *n-dimensional space* in which each point is represented by the value of an n-bit signal. This n-dimensional space contains 2^n possible elements (i.e. all the possible combinations of n bits). However, an m-bit source code can convey 2^m unique messages. In other words, only 2^m signals are valid out of the 2^n possible signals. Should a code word be received that is not one of these 2^m values, an error may be assumed.

If r check bits are added to the m message digits to create an n-bit code word, there are $2^n=2^{m+r}$ possible code words. The n-dimensional space will contain 2^m *valid* code words, 2^n *possible* code words and $2^n-2^m=2^m(2^{n-m}-1)=2^m(2^r-1)$ *error states*.

If we read a word from memory or from a communication system, we can check its location within the n-dimensional space. If the word is located at one of the 2^m valid points we assume that it's error free. If it falls in one of the 2^n-2^m error states, we can reject it.

Figure 4.5 demonstrates an error-detecting code for $n=3$. Each of the $2^3=8$ possible code words is represented by a corner of the three-dimensional cube. Of the eight possible code

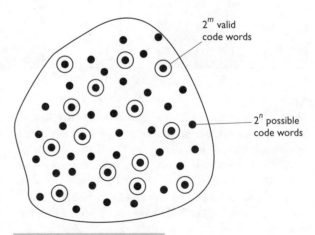

Fig. 4.4 The principle of the EDC.

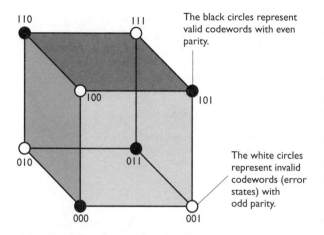

The black circles represent valid codewords with even parity.

The white circles represent invalid codewords (error states) with odd parity.

Fig. 4.5 All possible code words in 3-dimensional space.

words, four have been marked as valid by heavy shading (i.e. 000, 011, 101, 110). If we choose a code word from this group, we can see at once whether it represents a valid code or not (it is valid if there are an even number of 1s in the code word).

In Figure 4.6 we have drawn another three-dimensional cube. However, in this case only one message bit is used and there are two check bits ($m = 1$ and $r = 2$). The only two valid code words are 000 and 111. Note that a Hamming distance of three separates each valid code word from all other valid code words.

Suppose an error occurs and a valid code word (i.e. 000 or 111) is corrupted to become one of the invalid code words {001, 010, 100, 011, 101, 110}. If an invalid code word is detected we can attempt to correct the error by choosing the valid code word *nearest* to the code word in error. Thus, if

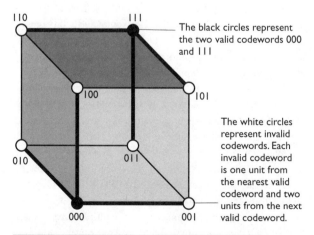

The black circles represent the two valid codewords 000 and 111

The white circles represent invalid codewords. Each invalid codeword is one unit from the nearest valid codeword and two units from the next valid codeword.

Fig. 4.6 An error-correcting code in 3-dimensional space.

the invalid code word we receive is 001, we assume that the correct code was 000 (because 001 is closer to 000 than to 111). In the context of error-correcting codes, *nearest* means the code with the smallest Hamming distance.

Error-correcting codes require that all valid code words be separated from each other by a Hamming distance of at least three. An error-correcting code tries to correct an error by selecting the nearest valid code to the code word in error. Since valid codes are separated by a minimum of three units from each other, a single error moves a code word one unit from its correct value, but it remains two units from any other valid code word. Figure 4.7 illustrates this concept.

Parity EDCs

The simplest error-detecting code uses a single *parity bit*. There are two types of parity: *even* parity and *odd* parity. An error-detecting code with an *even* parity check bit chooses the parity bit to make the total number of 1s in the word (including the parity bit) even. For example, if the source word is 0101101, the parity bit must be 0 because there are four 1s in the word. The code word now becomes **0**0101101. We've appended the parity bit to the most-significant bit position, although there's no reason why the parity bit should be placed at any particular point.

Suppose that this code word is transmitted and is received as **0**0101100 because the least-significant bit has been changed from 1 to 0. The parity of the word calculated at the receiver is odd (there are now three rather than four 1s), and an error is assumed to have occurred. We can't tell from the received word which bit is in error, so we can't correct the error. Had there been two errors, no parity violation would have been detected, and the errors would not be flagged. Single parity check bits are helpful only when errors are relatively infrequent and tend to occur singly.

In a system with odd parity, the parity bit is chosen to make the total number of 1s odd. Table 4.8 gives the eight valid code words for a 3-bit source word, for both even and odd parities. In each case the parity bit is the most-significant bit.

The single parity bit error-detecting code can be extended to create a *block EDC* (also called a *matrix EDC*). A block EDC uses two types of parity check bit: a *vertical* parity bit and a *horizontal* (or longitudinal) parity bit. Imagine a block of data composed of a sequence of source words. Each source word can be written vertically to form a column, and the sequence of source words can be written one after another to create a block. Figure 4.8 demonstrates a simple block of six 3-bit source words.

We can generate a parity bit for each source word (i.e. column) and append it to the bottom of each column to create a new row. Each of these parity bits is called a vertical parity

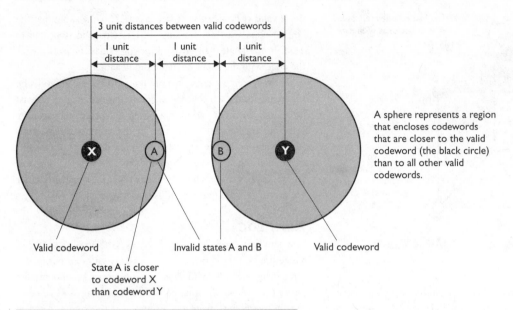

Fig. 4.7 Minimum condition required to correct a single bit error.

Message	Code word (even parity)	Code word (odd parity)
000	0 000	1 000
001	1 001	0 001
010	1 010	0 010
011	0 011	1 011
100	1 100	0 100
101	0 101	1 101
110	0 110	1 110
111	1 111	0 111
	↑	↑
	Even parity bit	Odd parity bit

Table 4.8 Odd and even parity codes.

Bit	Word 1	Word 2	Word 3	Word 4	Word 5	Word 6
D_0	0	1	1	0	1	0
D_1	1	0	0	1	0	1
D_2	1	1	0	1	1	0

The source words are 110, 101, 001, 110, 101, and 010 and have been written down as a block or matrix

Fig. 4.8 Six 3-bit words.

bit. Since a block of source words is made up of a number of columns, a parity word can be formed by calculating the parity across the bits. Each code word (i.e. column) in Fig. 4.9 is composed of four bits: D_0, D_1, D_2, D_3 (where D_3 is the

Bit	Word 1	Word 2	Word 3	Word 4	Word 5	Word 6	Word 7
D_0	0	1	1	0	1	0	1
D_1	1	0	0	1	0	1	1
D_2	1	1	0	1	1	0	0
D_3	0	0	1	0	0	1	0

A vertical even parity bit has been appended to each column to create a new row labeled D_3. Similarly, a horizontal parity bit has been added to each row to create a new column labeled word 7.

Fig. 4.9 Creating a block code error-detecting code.

vertical parity bit). We can now derive a horizontal parity bit by calculating the parity across the columns. That is, we create a parity bit across all the D_0s. Horizontal parity bits for D_1, D_2, and the vertical parity bits, D_3, can be generated in a similar way. Figure 4.9 shows how the source words of Fig. 4.8 are transformed into a block error-detecting code.

Figure 4.10 demonstrates the action of a block error-detecting code in the presence of a single error. A tick marks each row or column where the parity is correct, and a cross where it is not. In this example, the bit in error is detected by the intersection of the row and column in which it creates a parity violation. Thus, although the word 1001 is received incorrectly as 1011 it can be corrected. While the block parity code can detect and correct single errors, it can detect (but not correct) certain combinations of multiple error. Block EDCs/ECCs are sometimes found in data transmission systems and in the storage of serial data on magnetic tape.

Bit	Word 1	Word 2	Word 3	Word 4	Word 5	Word 6	Word 7	
D_0	0	1	1	0	1	0	1	✓
D_1	1	0	1	1	0	1	1	✗
D_2	1	1	0	1	1	0	0	✓
D_3	0	0	1	0	0	1	0	✓
	✓	✓	✗	✓	✓	✓	✓	

By detecting a parity error in a row, we can detect the position of the bit in error (i.e. in this case bit D_1). By detecting a parity error in a column, we can detect the word in error (i.e. in this case word 3). Now we can locate the error which is bit D_1 of word 3. The error can be corrected by inverting this bit.

Fig. 4.10 Detecting and correcting an error in a block code.

4.4.4 Hamming codes

Hamming codes are the simplest class of error-detecting and correcting codes that can be applied to a single code word (in contrast with a block error-correcting code that is applied to a group of words). A Hamming code takes an m-bit source word and generates r parity check bits to create an n-bit code word. The r parity check bits are selected so that a single error in the code word can be detected, located, and therefore corrected.

Hamming codes are designated $H_{n,m}$ where, for example, $H_{7,4}$ represents a Hamming code with a code word of 7 bits and a source word of 4 bits. The following sequence of bits represents an $H_{7,4}$ code word:

Bit position	7	6	5	4	3	2	1
Code bit	I_4	I_3	I_2	C_3	I_1	C_2	C_1

I_i = source bit i, C_i = check bit i.

The information (i.e. source word) bits are numbered I_1, I_2, I_3, and I_4, and the check bits are numbered C_1, C_2, and C_3. Similarly, the bit positions in the code word are numbered from 1 to 7. The check bits are located in binary positions 2^i in the code word (i.e. positions 1, 2, and 4). Note how the check bits are interleaved with the source code bits.

The three check bits are generated from the source word according to the following *parity equations*.

$$C_3 = I_2 \oplus I_3 \oplus I_4$$
$$C_2 = I_1 \oplus I_3 \oplus I_4$$
$$C_1 = I_1 \oplus I_2 \oplus I_4$$

For example, C_3 is the parity bit generated by information bits I_2, I_3, I_4, etc. Suppose we have a source word equal to $I_4, I_3, I_2, I_1 = 1,1,0,1$. The check bits are calculated as

$$C_3 = 0 \oplus 1 \oplus 1 = 0$$
$$C_2 = 1 \oplus 1 \oplus 1 = 1$$
$$C_1 = 1 \oplus 0 \oplus 1 = 0$$

The code word is therefore

$$I_4, I_3, I_2, C_3, I_1, C_2, C_1 = 1,1,0,0,1,1,0$$

Suppose now that the code word is corrupted during storage (or transmission). Assume that the value of I_3 is switched from 1 to 0. The resulting code word is now: 1000110. Using the new code word we can recalculate the check bits to give:

$$C_3 = 0 \oplus 0 \oplus 1 = 1$$
$$C_2 = 1 \oplus 0 \oplus 1 = 0$$
$$C_1 = 1 \oplus 0 \oplus 1 = 0$$

The new check bits are 1,0,0 and the stored check bits are 0,1,0. If we take the exclusive OR of the old and new check bits we get $1 \oplus 0$, $0 \oplus 1$, $0 \oplus 0 = 1,1,0$. The binary value 110 expressed in decimal form is 6 and points to bit position 6 in the code word. It is this bit that is in error. How does a Hamming code perform this apparent magic trick? The answer can be found in the equations for the parity check bits. The check bits are calculated in such a way that any single bit error will change the particular combination of check bits that points to its location.

The Hamming code described above can detect and correct a single error. By adding a further check bit we can create a Hamming code that can detect two errors and correct one error.

4.4.5 Huffman codes

Huffman codes differ from other encoding techniques described in this book because they employ a *variable length* code word. The idea of a Huffman code isn't new. When Samuel Morse devised his famous code he sent his assistant to a printer to count the number of letters in each pigeon hole in which they were stored. Morse argued that the printer's storage bins would provide a crude estimate of how much each letter was used on average. The letter E appears so frequently in English language text that there were many Es, whereas there were relatively few Qs. So, Morse created a code whereby frequently used letters were assigned short codes, and infrequently used letters were assigned longer codes. For example, the letter E has the Morse symbol · and the letter Q has the symbol ----.

A similar arrangement can be extended to binary codes. Huffman codes are applied only to information in which some elements appear more frequently than others. Plain text (e.g. written English) is such a case. To keep things simple, consider the following example. A grocer sells only four items (we did say we were keeping things simple), potatoes, onions, beans, and avocado pears. Being a thoroughly modern trader and a computer scientist the grocer has a computerized business. Every time an item is bought, it is encoded in binary form and stored on disk. The grocer wishes to code transactions in such a way as to use the least possible storage. Initially the grocer tried the 2-bit binary code described in Table 4.9.

If there are *n* transactions, the total storage required to record them is 2*n* bits. At first sight it would seem that there's no way the grocer can get away with fewer than two bits to encode each transaction. However, after a little thought, the grocer realizes that most customers buy potatoes and therefore devises the encoding scheme of Table 4.10.

Table 4.10 uses codes of different lengths. One code has a 1-bit length, one has a 2-bit length, and two have 3-bit lengths. After a week's trading, the total storage space occupied will be

Item	Code
Potatoes	00
Onions	01
Beans	10
Avocado pears	11

Table 4.9 Coding four items with a 2-bit code.

Item	Percent of transactions	Code
Potatoes	75.0	0
Onions	12.50	10
Beans	6.25	110
Avocado pears	6.25	111

Table 4.10 A Huffman code for four items.

the number of transactions for each item multiplied by the length of its code. The average code length will be:

$$1 \times \frac{3}{4} + 2 \times \frac{1}{8} + 3 \times \frac{1}{16} + 3 \times \frac{1}{16} = 1.375$$

By adopting this code, a Huffman code, the average storage has been reduced from two bits per transaction to 1.375 bits per transaction, a saving of 31.25 percent. A Huffman code is often represented in the form of a binary tree, the tree in Fig. 4.11 corresponding to the grocer's example.

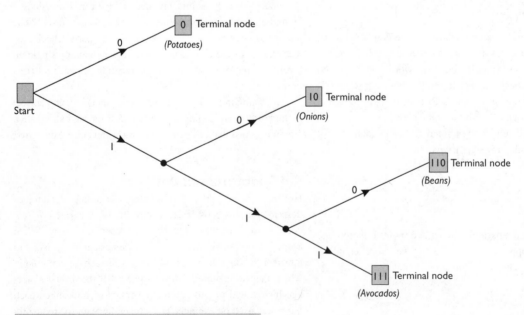

Fig. 4.11 The Huffman code corresponding to Table 4.10.

0	1	2	3	4	5	6	7	8	9
1	2	3	4	5	6	7	8	9	10
2	3	4	5	6	7	8	9	10	11
3	4	5	6	7	8	9	10	11	12
4	5	6	7	8	9	10	11	12	13
5	6	7	8	9	10	11	12	13	14
6	7	8	9	10	11	12	13	14	15
7	8	9	10	11	12	13	14	15	16
8	9	10	11	12	13	14	15	16	17
9	10	11	12	13	14	15	16	17	18

Table 4.11 The decimal addition tables.

0	1	2	3	4	5	6	7	8	9
1	1	2	3	4	5	6	7	8	9
2	2	4	6	8	10	12	14	16	18
3	3	6	9	12	15	18	21	24	27
4	4	8	12	16	20	24	28	32	36
5	5	10	15	20	25	30	35	40	45
6	6	12	18	24	30	36	42	48	54
7	7	14	21	28	35	42	49	56	63
8	8	16	24	32	40	48	56	64	72
9	9	18	27	36	45	54	63	72	81

Table 4.12 The decimal multiplication tables.

Addition	Subtraction	Multiplication
$0+0=0$	$0-0=0$	$0 \times 0=0$
$0+1=1$	$0-1=1$ borrow 1	$0 \times 1=0$
$1+0=1$	$1-0=1$	$1 \times 0=0$
$1+1=0$ carry 1	$1-1=0$	$1 \times 1=1$

Table 4.13 Binary tables.

The diagram in Fig. 4.11 is sometimes called a *trellis* and is read from left to right. From the left, each of the four *terminal nodes* (labeled node 0, node 10, node 110, and node 111) can be reached by following the marked paths. These paths are indicated by a 1 or a 0 depending on the bit to be decoded. Let's look at how a Huffman code is interpreted. Suppose that the grocer's disk contains the following string of bits: 001100101110. What codes does this string correspond to? The first (leftmost) bit of the string is 0. From the trellis we can see that a first bit 0 leads immediately to the terminal node 0. Thus, the first code is 0. Similarly, the second code is also 0. The third code begins with a 1, which takes us to a junction rather than to a terminal. We must examine another bit to continue. This is also a 1, and yet another bit must be read. The third bit is a 0 leading to a terminal node 110. This process can be continued until the string is broken down into the sequence: 0 0 110 0 10 111 0 = potatoes, potatoes, beans, potatoes, onions, avocados, potatoes.

Variations of this type of code are used in data and program compression algorithms to reduce the size of files (e.g. the widely used ZIP compression programs).

Now that we have looked at some general binary codes, we are going to return to numeric codes and examine how a computer performs simple arithmetic operations. The following section ties together binary arithmetic and the digital logic we learned in Chapter 2.

4.5 Binary arithmetic

Now that we've introduced binary numbers and demonstrated how it's possible to convert between binary and decimal formats, the next step is to look at how binary numbers are manipulated. Binary arithmetic follows exactly the same rules as decimal arithmetic, and all that we have to do to work with binary numbers is to learn the binary tables. Table 4.11 gives the decimal addition tables and Table 4.12 gives the decimal multiplications. Table 4.13 gives the binary addition, subtraction, and multiplication tables. As you can see, these are much simpler than their decimal equivalents.

A remarkable fact about binary arithmetic revealed by Table 4.13 is that if we didn't worry about the carry in addition and the borrow in subtraction, then the operations of addition and subtraction would be identical. Such an arithmetic, in which addition and subtraction are equivalent, does exist and has some important applications; this is called *modulo-2 arithmetic*.

Table 4.13 tells us how to add two single digits. We need to add longer words. The addition of n-bit numbers is entirely straightforward, except that when adding the two bits in each column, a carry bit from the previous stage must also added in. Each carry bit results from a carry-out from the column on its right. In the following example, we present the numbers to be added on the left, and on the right we include the carry bits that must be added in.

```
  00110111      →      00110111
+ 01010110      →      01010110
                       111 11      ←carries
  10001101      →      10001101
```

We can carry out octal (or hexadecimal) addition in the same way that we carry out binary addition. All we have to remember is that if we add together two digits whose sum is greater than 7 (or 15), we must convert the result into a carry digit whose value is 8 (or 16) plus the remainder which is the sum less 8 (or 16). For example, if we add 5 and 7 in octal we get 12, which is 4 carry 1 (i.e. 4 plus 8).

Consider the octal addition $12345_8 + 67013_8$.

```
12345    →     12345
67013    →     67013
               11  1    ←carries
101360   →    101360
```

Subtraction can also be carried out in a conventional fashion, although we shall see later that a computer does not subtract numbers in the way we do because negative numbers are not usually represented in a *sign plus magnitude* form but by means of their complements.

```
  01010110          86
 −00101010         −42
                   ——
   1 1     ←borrows 44
  00101100
```

The multiplication of binary numbers can be done by the *pencil and paper* method of shifting and adding, although in practice the computer uses a somewhat modified technique.

```
    01101              13
  × 01010            × 10
    00000            130
   01101
  00000
 01101
00000
 ——————————
0010000010
```

4.5.1 The half adder

Having looked at gates, Boolean algebra, and binary arithmetic, we can now consider the design of circuits to add binary numbers. The most primitive circuit used in binary addition is called the *half adder* or HA, which adds together two bits to give a sum, S, and a carry, C, as described in Table 4.14. The

A	B	S (sum)	C (carry)
0	0	0	0
0	1	1	0
1	0	1	0
1	1	0	1

Table 4.14 Truth table for a half adder.

sum, S, is given by their exclusive OR; that is, $S = \overline{A} \cdot B + A \cdot \overline{B}$. The carry is given by $C = A \cdot B$.

From the chapter on gates we know that this circuit may be realized in at least three different ways, as Fig. 4.12 demonstrates. This circuit, whatever its implementation, is often represented in many texts by the symbol in Fig. 4.13.

We can use Digital Works to construct a half adder and to simulate its behavior. Figure 4.14 shows a screen in which we've constructed a half adder and used the push-button (i.e. input device) to provide inputs A and B. We have connected the adder's sum and carry outputs to LEDs and have linked all inputs and outputs to the **Logic History** function.

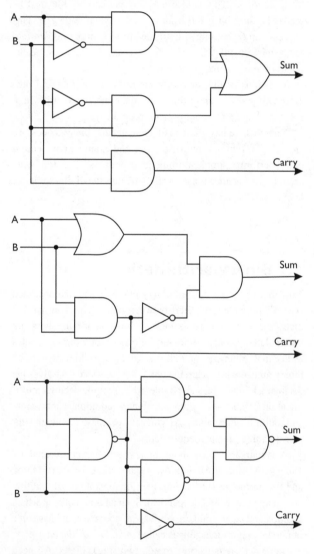

Fig. 4.12 Three ways of implementing a half adder.

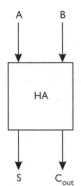

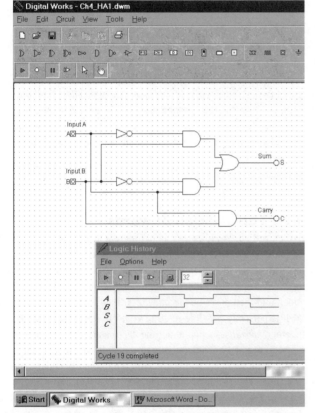

Fig. 4.13 The circuit representation of a half adder.

Fig. 4.14 Using Digital Words to implement and test a half adder circuit.

As you can see from Fig. 4.14, we've run the simulation in the single step mode and have applied all possible inputs to the circuit and have observed the output waveforms.

4.5.2 The full adder

Unfortunately, the half adder is of little use as it stands. When two *n*-bit numbers are added together we have to take account of any *carry bits*. Adding bits a_i of A and b_i of B together must include provision for adding in the carry bit c_{i-1} from the results of the addition in the column to the right of a_i and b_i. This is represented diagrammatically as

$$a_{n-1}\ldots a_2a_1a_0 \;\rightarrow\; a_{n-1}\ldots a_2a_1a_0$$
$$\underline{b_{n-1}\ldots b_2b_1b_0} \qquad b_{n-1}\ldots b_2b_1b_0$$
$$\underline{c_{n-2}\ldots c_1c_0}$$

> This row consists of the carry bits generated by the columns on the right.

When people perform an addition they deal with the carry automatically, without thinking about it. More specifically they say, 'If a carry is generated we add it to the next column, if it is not we do nothing'. In human terms doing nothing and adding zero are equivalent. As far as the logic necessary to carry out the addition is concerned, we always add in the carry from the previous stage, where the carry bit has the value 0 or 1.

The *full adder*, represented by the circuit symbol of Fig. 4.15, adds together two bits A and B, plus a carry-in C_{in} from the previous stage, to generate a sum S and a carry-out C_{out}. In other words, the full adder is a 3-bit adder. Table 4.15 provides the truth table for a full adder.

The conventional way of realizing the circuit for a full adder is to connect two half adders in tandem. Conceptually, a full adder requires that the two bits of A and B be added together and then the carry-in should be added to the result.

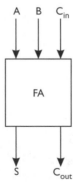

Fig. 4.15 The circuit representation of a full adder.

A	B	C_{in}	S(sum)	C_{out}(carry out)
0	0	0	0	0
0	1	0	1	0
1	0	0	1	0
1	1	0	0	1
0	0	1	1	0
0	1	1	0	1
1	0	1	0	1
1	1	1	1	1

Table 4.15 Truth table for full adder.

Figure 4.16 shows a possible representation of the full adder in terms of two half adders.

The sum output of the full adder is provided by the sum output of the second half adder, HA2. The carry-out from the full adder, C_{out}, is given by ORing the carries from both half adders. To demonstrate that the circuit of Fig. 4.16 does indeed perform the process of full addition a truth table may be used. Table 4.16 provides a truth table for the circuit of Fig. 4.16.

As the contents of the S_2 and C_{out} columns are identical to those of the corresponding columns of the truth table for the full adder (Table 4.15), we must conclude that the circuit of Fig. 4.16 is indeed that of a full adder. Figure 4.17 demon-

strates the use of Digital Works to construct and simulate a full adder built from two half adders.

In practice the full adder is not implemented in this way because the propagation path through the two half adders involves six units of delay. An alternative full adder circuit may be derived directly from the equations for the sum and the carry from the truth table. Let the sum be S, the carry-out C_0, and the carry-in C.

$$S = \overline{C}\cdot\overline{A}\cdot B + \overline{C}\cdot A\cdot\overline{B} + C\cdot\overline{A}\cdot\overline{B} + C\cdot A\cdot B$$

$$\begin{aligned}
\text{and } C_0 &= \overline{C}\cdot A\cdot B + C\cdot\overline{A}\cdot B + C\cdot A\cdot\overline{B} + C\cdot A\cdot B \\
&= \overline{C}\cdot A\cdot B + C\cdot\overline{A}\cdot B + C\cdot A\ (\overline{B} + B) \\
&= \overline{C}\cdot A\cdot B + C\cdot\overline{A}\cdot B + C\cdot A \\
&= \overline{C}\cdot A\cdot B + C\ (\overline{A}\cdot B + A) = \overline{C}\cdot A\cdot B + C\cdot B + C\cdot A \\
&= A\ (\overline{C}\cdot B + C) + C\cdot A = A\ (B + C) + C\cdot B \\
&= C\cdot A + C\cdot B + A\cdot B
\end{aligned}$$

The carry-out represents a *majority logic* function which is true if two or more of the three inputs are true. The circuit diagram of the full adder corresponding to the above equations is given in Fig. 4.18. This circuit contains more gates than the equivalent realization in terms of half adders (12 against 9), but it is faster. The maximum propagation delay is three gates in series.

4.5.3 The addition of words

Even a full adder on its own is not a great deal of help, as we normally wish to add two *n*-bit numbers together. We now look at ways in which two *n*-bit numbers can be added together using full adders, beginning with the *serial* full adder, and then describe the *parallel* full adder.

It is perfectly possible to add two *n*-bit numbers, A and B, together, *serially*, a bit at a time by means of the scheme given in Fig. 4.19. The contents of the shift registers containing the *n*-bit words A and B are shifted into the full adder a bit at a time. The result of each addition is shifted into a result (i.e. sum) register. A single flip-flop holds the carry bit so that the old carry-out becomes the next carry-in. After *n* clock pulses, the sum register, S, contains the sum of A and B. Serial adders aren't used today because parallel adders are much faster.

Parallel adders

A *parallel adder* adds the *n* bits of word A to the *n* bits of word B in one simultaneous operation. Figure 4.20 describes a parallel adder constructed from *n* full adders. The carry-out from each full adder provides the carry-in to the stage on its left. The term *parallel* implies that all *n* additions take place at

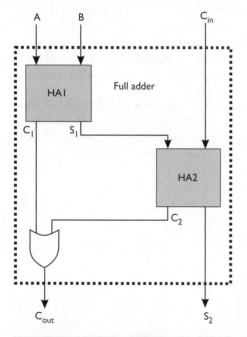

Fig. 4.16 Implementing a full adder by two half adders.

C_{in}	A	B	S_1	C_1	S_2	C_2	C_{out}
0	0	0	0	0	0	0	0
0	0	1	1	0	1	0	0
0	1	0	1	0	1	0	0
0	1	1	0	1	0	0	1
1	0	0	0	0	1	0	0
1	0	1	1	0	0	1	1
1	1	0	1	0	0	1	1
1	1	1	0	1	1	0	1

Table 4.16 Truth table for a full adder implemented by two half adders.

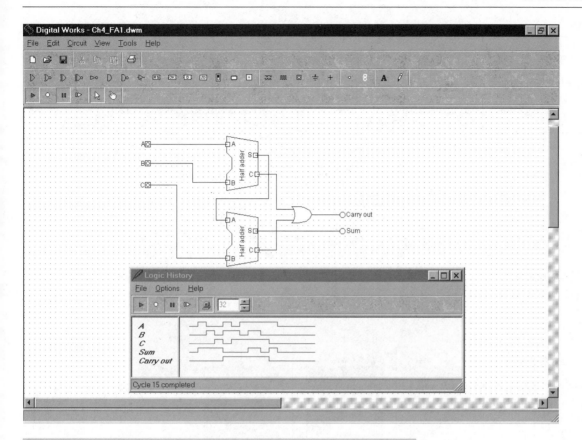

Fig. 4.17 Using Digital Works to implement and test a full adder built from two half adders.

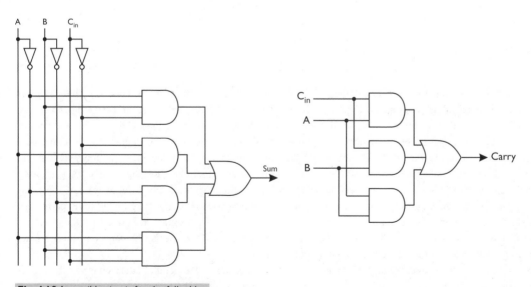

Fig. 4.18 A possible circuit for the full adder.

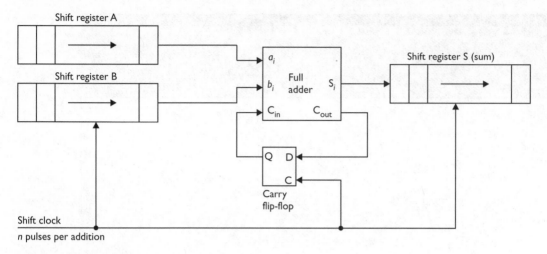

Fig. 4.19 The serial adder.

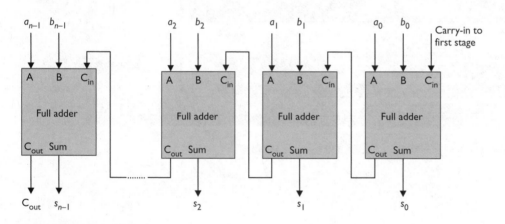

Fig. 4.20 The parallel adder.

the same time and it's tempting to think that the parallel adder is n times faster than the corresponding serial adder. In practice, a real parallel adder is slowed down by the effect of the carry-bit propagation through the stages of the full adder.

Several points are worth noting in Fig. 4.20. Firstly, it might be thought that a half adder could replace the first (i.e. least-significant bit) stage because this stage doesn't have a carry-in (there is no stage to its right). However, by using a full adder for this stage, the carry-in may be set to zero for normal addition, or it may be set to 1 to generate $A + B + 1$ (the '+' here signifying addition and not logical OR). If input B were set to zero, $A + 1$ would be generated and the circuit would function as an incrementer. A facility to add in one to the sum of A plus B will prove very useful when we come to complementary arithmetic.

Another feature of this circuit concerns the carry-out from the most-significant bit stage. If two n-bit words are added and the result is greater than $111 \ldots 1$, then a carry-out is generated. As the computer cannot store words longer than n bits, the sum cannot be stored in the memory as a single entity. The carry-out of the most-significant stage may be latched into a flip-flop (normally forming part of the computer's condition code register). When addition is performed by software as part of a program, it is usual for the programmer to test the carry bit to check whether the result has gone out of range.

A final point about the parallel adder concerns the meaning of the term parallel. The first stage can add a_0 to b_0 to get S_0 as soon as A and B are presented to the input terminals of the full adder. However, the second stage must wait for the first stage's carry-out to be added in to a_1 plus b_1 before it can be sure that its own output is valid. In the worst-case inputs of $111\ldots1+1$, the carry must ripple through all the stages. This type of adder is referred to as a 'ripple-carry adder'.

The full adder we have described here is parallel in the sense that all the bits of A are added to all the bits of B in a single operation without the need for a number of separate clock cycles. Once the values of A and B have been presented to the inputs of the full adders, the system must wait until the circuit has had time to settle down and for all carries to propagate before the next operation is started.

In many digital systems the clock period is determined by the worst-case settling time required by the slowest circuit in the system. Although it's not common, you can design a digital system with a variable clock pulse, where the duration of each pulse is tailored to the worst-case delay possible for the current operation being carried out. It is possible to reduce partially the effect of the ripple-through carry in a parallel adder. Arrangements called *carry look ahead circuits* are used to anticipate a carry over a group of, say, four full adders. That is, the carry-out to stage $i+5$ is calculated by examining the inputs to stages $i+4$, $i+3$, $i+2$, $i+1$, and the carry-in to stage $i+1$, by means of a special high-speed circuit. This anticipated carry is fed to the fifth stage to avoid the delay that would be incurred if a ripple-through carry were used. The exact nature of these circuits is beyond the scope of this book.

The full subtractor

Using the techniques we have applied to the full adder it is possible to design a full subtractor in the same way. As the full subtractor is not used widely we leave its design as an exercise for the reader.

4.6 Signed numbers

Any real computer must be able to deal with *negative* numbers as well as positive numbers. Before we examine how the computer handles negative numbers, we should consider how we deal with them. I believe that people don't, in fact, actually use negative numbers. They use positive numbers (the 5 in -5 is the same as in $+5$), and place a negative sign in front of a number to remind them that it must be treated in a special way when it takes part in arithmetic operations. In other words, we treat all numbers as positive and use a sign (i.e. $+$ or $-$) to determine what we have to do

with the numbers. For example, consider the following two operations.

$$\begin{array}{cc} 8 & 8 \\ +5 & \text{and} \quad -5 \\ \hline 13 & 3 \end{array}$$

In both these examples the numbers are the same, but the operations we performed on them were different; in the first case we added them together and in the second case we subtracted them. This technique can be extended to computer arithmetic to give the *sign and magnitude* representation of a negative number.

4.6.1 Sign and magnitude representation

An n-bit word can have 2^n possible different values from 0 to 2^n-1. For example, an 8-bit word can represent the numbers $0, 1, \ldots, 254, 255$. One way of representing a negative number is to take the most-significant bit and reserve it to indicate the sign of the number. The usual convention is to choose the sign bit as 0 to represent positive numbers and 1 to represent negative numbers. We can express the value of a sign and magnitude number mathematically in the form $(-1)^S \times M$, where S is the sign bit of the number and M is its magnitude. If $S=0$, $(-1)^0=+1$ and the number is positive. If $S=1$, $(-1)^1=-1$ and the number is negative. For example, in 8 bits we can interpret the two numbers 00001101 and 10001101 as

0 0001101 = $+13$ and   1 0001101 = -13

number magnitude (sign bit)

Using a sign and magnitude representation is a perfectly valid way to represent signed numbers, although it is not widely used in integer arithmetic. The range of a sign and magnitude number in n bits is given by

$$-(2^{n-1}-1) \text{ to } +(2^{n-1}-1)$$

All we've done is to take an n-bit number, use one bit to represent the sign, and let the remaining $n-1$ bits represent the number. Thus, an eight-bit number can represent from -127 (11111111) to $+127$ (01111111). One of the objections to this system is that it has two values for zero:

$$00000000 = +0 \quad \text{and} \quad 10000000 = -0$$

I don't see this as a particular problem, given today's ability to produce complex digital devices economically. Possibly the sign and magnitude notation was abandoned when each and every gate was a precious item. A more important reason for rejecting this system is that it requires separate adders and subtractors. We shall soon see that other ways of representing negative numbers remove the need for separate adders and subtractors.

Examples of addition and subtraction in sign and magnitude arithmetic are given below. Remember that the most-significant bit is a sign bit and does not take part in the calculation itself. This is in contrast with two's complement arithmetic (see later) in which the sign bit forms an integral part of the number when it is used in calculations. In each of the four examples below, we perform the calculation by first converting the sign bit to a positive or a negative sign. Then we perform the calculation and, finally, convert the sign of the result into a sign bit.

Sign and magnitude value	Number with sign bit converted into a sign	Number with sign converted into sign bit
1. 001011 +001110	+01011 +01110	
	+11001 $\longrightarrow$	011001
2. 001011 +100110	+01011 −00110	
	+00101 $\longrightarrow$	000101
3. 001011 +110110	+01011 −10110	
	−01011 $\longrightarrow$	101011
4. 001011 −001001	+01011 −01001	
	00010 $\longrightarrow$	000010

4.6.2 Complementary arithmetic

In complementary arithmetic the *negativeness* of a number is contained within the number itself. Because of this, the concept of signs (+ and −) may, effectively, be dispensed with. If we add X to Y the operation is that of addition if X is positive and Y is positive, but if Y is negative the end result is that of subtraction (assuming that Y is represented by its negative form). It is important to point out here that complementary arithmetic is used to represent and to manipulate both positive and negative numbers. To demonstrate that there is nothing magical about complementary arithmetic, let's examine decimal complements.

Ten's complement arithmetic

The 10's complement of an n-digit decimal number, N, is defined as $10^n - N$. The 10's complement may also be calculated by subtracting each of the digits of N from 9 and adding 1 to the result; for example, if $n = 1$, the value of −1 is represented in ten's complement by 9. Consider the four-digit decimal number 1234. Its ten's complement is

a. $10^4 - 1234 = 8766$ or b. $\begin{aligned}9999\\-1234\\\hline 8765 + 1 = 8766\end{aligned}$

Suppose we were to add this complement to another number (say) 8576. We get

$$\begin{aligned}8576\\+8766\\\hline 17342\end{aligned}$$

Now let's examine the effect of subtracting 1234 from 8576 by conventional means.

$$\begin{aligned}8576\\-1234\\\hline 7342\end{aligned}$$

Notice that the results of the two operations are similar in the least-significant four digits, but differ in the fifth digit by 10^4. The reason for this is not hard to find. Consider the subtraction of Y from X. We wish to calculate $Z = X - Y$ which we do by *adding* the ten's complement of Y to X. The ten's complement of Y is defined as $10^4 - Y$. Therefore we get:

$$Z = X + (10^4 - Y) = 10^4 + (X - Y).$$

In other words, we get the desired result, $X - Y$, together with an *unwanted* digit in the leftmost position. This digit may be discarded.

Complementing a number twice results in the original number; for example, $-1234 = 10^4 - 1234 = 8876$. Complementing twice, we get: $-(-1234) = -8876 = 10^4 - 8876 = 1234$.

4.6.3 Two's complement representation

The equivalent of ten's complement in binary arithmetic is *two's complement*. To form the two's complement of an n-bit binary number, N, we evaluate $2^n - N$. For example, in five bits, if $N = 5 = 00101$ then the two's complement of N is given by $2^5 - 00101 = 100000 - 00101 = 11011$. It is important to note here that 11011 represents -00101 (−5) or +27 depending only on whether we interpret the bit pattern 11011 as a two's complement integer or as an unsigned integer.

If we add the two's complement of N (i.e. 11011) to another binary number, we should execute the operation of subtraction. In the following demonstration we add 11011 to 01100 (i.e. 12).

$$
\begin{array}{ll}
01100 & 12 \\
+11011 & +(-5) \\
\hline
100111 & 7
\end{array}
$$

As in the case of ten's complement arithmetic, we get the correct answer together with the $2^n = 2^5$ term, which is discarded. Before continuing further, it is worthwhile examining the effect of adding all the combinations of positive and negative values for a pair of numbers.

Let $X = 9 = 01001$ and $Y = 6 = 00110$.

$$-X = 100000 - 01001 = 10111$$
$$-Y = 100000 - 00110 = 11010$$

$$
\begin{array}{llll}
1. & +X \;\; +9 & 01001 & \\
& +Y \;\; +6 & 00110 & \\
\cline{3-3}
& & 01111 = +15 &
\end{array}
$$

$$
\begin{array}{lll}
2. & +X & 01001 \\
& -Y & +11010 \\
\cline{3-3}
& & 100011 = +3
\end{array}
$$

$$
\begin{array}{lll}
3. & -X & 10111 \\
& +Y & +00110 \\
\cline{3-3}
& & 11101 = -3
\end{array}
$$

$$
\begin{array}{lll}
4. & -X & 10111 \\
& -Y & +11010 \\
\cline{3-3}
& & 110001 = -15
\end{array}
$$

All four examples give the result we'd expect when the result is interpreted as a two's complement number. However, examples 3 and 4 give negative results that require a little further explanation. Example 3 calculates $-9 + 6$ by adding the two's complement of 9 to 6 to get -3 expressed in two's complement form. The two's complement representation of -3 is given by $100000 - 00011 = 11101$.

Example 4 evaluates $-X + -Y$ to get a result of -15 but with the addition of a 2^n term. The two's complement representation of -15 is given by $100000 - 01111 = 10001$. In example 4, where both numbers are negative, we have $(2^n - X) + (2^n - Y) = 2^n + (2^n - X - Y)$. The first part of this expression is the redundant 2^n, and the second part is the two's complement representation of $-X - Y$. The two's complement system works for all possible combinations of positive and negative numbers.

Calculating two's complement values

The two's complement system would not be so attractive if it weren't for the ease with which two's complements can be formed. Consider the two's complement of N, which is defined as $2^n - N$.

Suppose we rearranged the expression by subtracting 1 from the 2^n and adding it to the result.

$$-N \rightarrow (2^n - 1) - N + 1$$
$$\rightarrow \underbrace{111 \ldots 1}_{n \text{ places}} - N + 1$$

For example, in 8 bits ($n = 8$) we have

$$
\begin{aligned}
-N \rightarrow\; & 2^8 - N \\
\rightarrow\; & 100000000 - N \\
\rightarrow\; & 100000000 - 1 - N + 1 \text{ (after rearranging)} \\
\rightarrow\; & 11111111 - N + 1
\end{aligned}
$$

In practice, it's easy to evaluate the two's complement of N. All you have to do is invert the bits and add 1. Why? Because the previous expression demonstrates that $1 - N_i = \overline{N_i}$. If bit i of N is 0, subtracting bit i from 1 gives 1, and if the bit is 1, subtracting bit i from 1 gives 0. For example, in five bits we have

$$7 = 0\,0\,1\,1\,1$$
$$-7 = \overline{0}\,\overline{0}\,\overline{1}\,\overline{1}\,\overline{1} + 1 = 11000 + 1 = 11001$$

Evaluating two's complement numbers in this fashion is attractive because it's easy to perform with hardware. Figure 4.21 demonstrates how an adder/subtractor is implemented. All you need is a little extra logic to convert a parallel binary adder into an adder/subtractor for two's complement numbers.

Each of the EOR gates has two inputs b_i (where $i = 0$ to $n - 1$), and C, a control signal. The output of the EOR gate is $b_i \cdot \overline{C} + \overline{b_i} \cdot C$. If C is 0 then $\overline{C} = 1$ and the output is b_i. If C is 1 then $\overline{C} = 0$ and the output is $\overline{b_i}$. The n EORs form a chain of programmable inverters, complementing the input if $C = 1$ and passing the input unchanged if $C = 0$. Note also that the carry-in input to the first full adder is C. When addition is being performed $C = 0$ and the carry-in is 0. However, when we perform subtraction $C = 1$ so that 1 is added to the result of the addition. We have already inverted B's bits so that adding this 1 forms the two's complement of B, enabling the subtraction of B from A to take place.

Properties of two's complement numbers

1. The two's complement system is a true complement system in that $+X + (-X) = 0$. For example, in five bits $+13 = 01101$ and $-13 = 10011$. The sum of $+13$ and -13 is

$$
\begin{array}{l}
01101 \\
+10011 \\
\hline
100000 = 0
\end{array}
$$

2. There is one unique zero $00 \ldots 0$.

3. If the number is positive the most-significant bit is 0, and if it is negative the most-significant bit is 1. Thus, the most-significant bit is a sign bit.

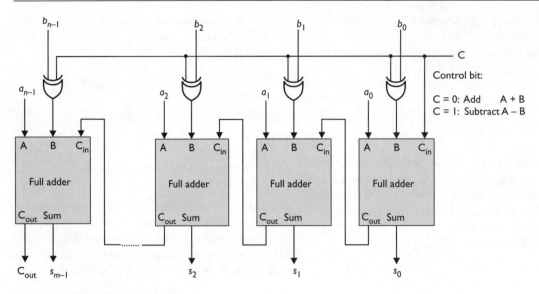

Fig. 4.21 The binary adder/subtractor.

4. The range of two's complement numbers in n bits is from -2^{n-1} to $+2^{n-1}-1$. For $n=5$, this range is from -16 to $+15$. Note that the total number of different numbers is 32 (16 negative, zero, and 15 positive). What this demonstrates is that a 5-bit number can uniquely describe 32 items, and it is up to us whether we choose to call these items the natural binary integers 0 to 31, or the signed two's complement numbers -16 to $+15$.

5. The complement of the complement of X is X (i.e. $-(-X)=X$). In five bits $+12=01100$ and $-12\rightarrow 10011+1=10100$. If we form the two's complement of -12 (i.e. 10100) in the usual fashion by inverting the bits and adding 1, we get $\overline{10100}+1=01011+1=01100$, which is the same as the number we started with. Please note that a negative number is represented by its complement. It is not equal to its complement.

Let's now see what happens if we violate the range of two's complement numbers. That is, we will carry out an operation whose result falls outside the range of values that can be represented by two's complement numbers.

If we choose a 5-bit representation, we know that the range of valid signed numbers is -16 to $+15$. Suppose we first add 5 and 6 and then try 12 and 13.

Case 1

$5=00101$
$+6=00110$

$\overline{}$

$11\quad 01011=11_{10}$

Case 2

$12=01100$
$+13=01101$

$\overline{}$

$25\quad 11001=-7_{10}$ (as a two's complement number)

In case 1 we get the expected answer of $+11_{10}$, but in case 2 we get a *negative* result because the sign bit is '1'. If the answer were regarded as an unsigned binary number it would be $+25$, which is, of course, the correct answer. However, once the two's complement system has been chosen to represent signed numbers, all answers must be interpreted in this light.

Similarly, if we add together two negative numbers whose total is less than -16, we also go out of range. For example, if we add $-9=10111_2$ and $-12=10100_2$, we get

$-9\qquad 10111$
$-12\qquad +10100$

$\overline{}\qquad\overline{}$

$-21\qquad 101011\qquad$ gives a positive result $01011_2=+11_{10}$

Both of these cases represent an out-of-range condition called *arithmetic overflow*. Arithmetic overflow occurs during a two's complement addition if the result of adding two positive numbers yields a negative result, or if the result of adding two negative numbers yields a positive result. If the sign bits of A and B are the same but the sign bit of the result is different, arithmetic overflow has occurred. If a_{n-1} is the sign bit of A, b_{n-1} is the sign bit of B, and s_{n-1} is the sign bit of the sum of A and B, then overflow is defined by

$$V=a_{n-1}\cdot b_{n-1}\cdot \overline{s_{n-1}} + \overline{a_{n-1}}\cdot \overline{b_{n-1}}\cdot s_{n-1}$$

In practice, real systems detect overflow from $C_{in}\neq C_{out}$ to the last stage (we prove this later). Arithmetic overflow is a consequence of two's complement arithmetic and shouldn't be confused with carry-out, which is the carry bit generated by the addition of the two most-significant bits of the numbers. The next two sections look at some of the details of two's complement arithmetic—readers not interested in the underlying theory may omit these sections.

Alternative view of two's complement numbers

We have seen that a binary integer, N, lying in the range $0 \leqslant N < 2^{n-1}$, is represented in a negative form in n bits by the expression $2^n - N$. We have also seen that this expression can be readily evaluated by inverting the bits of N and adding 1 to the result.

Another way of looking at a two's complement number is to regard it as a conventional binary number represented in the positional notation but with the sign of the most-significant bit negative. That is,

$$-N = -d_{n-1}2^{n-1} + d_{n-2}2^{n-2} + \cdots + d_0 2^0$$

where $d_{n-1}, d_{n-2}, \ldots, d_0$ are the bits of the two's complement number D. Consider the binary representation of 14_{10}, and the two's complement form of -14, in five bits.

$+14 = 01110$
$-14 = 2^n - N = 2^5 - 14 = 32 - 14 = 18 = 10010$
or $-14 = \overline{01110} + 1 = 10001 + 1 = 10010$

From what we have said earlier, we can regard the two's complement representation of -14 (i.e. 10010) as

$-1 \times 2^4 + 0 \times 2^3 + 0 \times 2^2 + 1 \times 2^1 + 0 \times 2^0$
$= -16 + (0 + 0 + 2 + 0)$
$= -16 + 2 = -14$

We can demonstrate that a two's complement number is indeed represented in this way. In what follows N represents a positive integer, and D the two's complement form of $-N$. We wish to prove that $-N = D$.

That is, $\displaystyle -N = -2^{n-1} + \sum_{i=0}^{n-2} d_i 2^i \qquad (1)$

In terms of the bits of N and D we have

$$-(N_{n-1}N_{n-2} \ldots N_1 N_0) = d_{n-1}d_{n-2} \ldots d_1 d_0 = D \qquad (2)$$

The bits of D are formed from the bits of N by inverting and adding 1.

$$\overline{N}_{n-1}\,\overline{N}_{n-2} \ldots \overline{N}_1\,\overline{N}_0 + 1 = d_{n-1}d_{n-2} \ldots d_1 d_0 \qquad (3)$$

Substituting equation (3) in equation (1) to eliminate D we get

$$-N = -2^{n-1} + \sum_{i=0}^{n-2} \overline{N}_i 2^i + 1$$

But $\overline{N}_i = 1 - N_i$, so that

$$-\overline{N} = -2^{n-1} + \sum_{i=0}^{n-2}(1 - N_i)2^i + 1$$

$$= -2^{n-1} + \sum_{i=0}^{n-2} 2^i - \sum_{i=0}^{n-2} N_i 2^i + 1$$

$$= -2^{n-1} + (2^{n-1} - 1) - \sum_{i=0}^{n-2} N_i 2^i + 1$$

$$= -2^{n-1} + (2^{n-1} - 1) + 1 - N \quad \left(\text{because } \sum_{i=0}^{n-2} N_i 2^i = N\right)$$

as the most-significant bit of N is zero for N to be within its stated range)

$$= -2^{n-1} + 2^{n-1} - N$$

$$= -N$$

Representing two's complement numbers graphically

We can visualize numbers in the two's complement system by arranging numbers around a circle. Figure 4.22 demonstrates such an arrangement for 4-bit numbers in which a circle has been divided up by 16 radials numbered from 0000 to 1111. Suppose we number the radials according to their two's complement values, so that radials 0000 to 0111 are numbered 0 to 7 and radials 1000 to 1111 are numbered -8 to -1. Notice how stepping one place clockwise increases a number and stepping one place anticlockwise decreases a number. We can now see how adding numbers to a negative value causes the result to move in the direction toward zero. For example, if we add 0011 ($+3$) to 1100 (-4) we get 1111 which is -1. If we had added 0101 ($+5$) to 1100, we would have got (1)0001 which is $+1$ and lies to the right of zero.

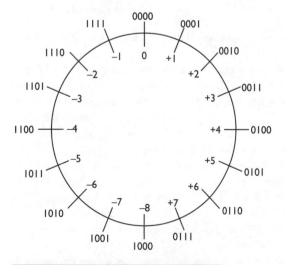

Fig. 4.22 Visualizing two's complement numbers.

4.6.4 **One's complement representation**

An alternative to two's complement arithmetic is *one's complement arithmetic*, in which the representation of a negative number, N, in n bits is given by $2^n - N - 1$. The one's complement representation of a number is one less than the corresponding two's complement representation and is formed more simply by inverting the bits of N. For example, for $n = 5$ consider the subtraction of 4 from 9. The binary value of 4 is 00100 and its one's complement is 11011.

$$
\begin{aligned}
+9 = +01001 &\rightarrow \quad 01001 \\
-4 = -00100 &\rightarrow +11011
\end{aligned}
$$

$$
\begin{aligned}
100100 &\leftarrow \quad \text{result after addition} \\
\llcorner\!\!\rightarrow 1 & \\
00101 &\leftarrow \quad \text{result after adding in the} \\
&\qquad\text{end-around carry}
\end{aligned}
$$

After the addition has been completed, the leftmost bit of the result is added to the least-significant bit of the result in an arrangement called *end-around carry*. This provides us with the final and correct result. Note that if the result of the initial addition yields a carry-out of zero, the result is negative and adding in the carry-out (i.e. zero) also gives the correct answer. Consider the following example.

$$
\begin{aligned}
-9 = -01001 &\rightarrow \quad 10110 \\
+4 = +00100 &\rightarrow +00100
\end{aligned}
$$

$$
\begin{aligned}
011010 &\leftarrow \quad \text{result after addition} \\
\llcorner\!\!\rightarrow 0 & \\
11010 &\leftarrow \quad \text{result after adding in the} \\
&\qquad\text{end-around carry}
\end{aligned}
$$

In one's complement 11010 represents the value -00101 (i.e. -5).

We can demonstrate that end-around carry works in one's complement arithmetic as follows. Suppose we wish to compute $X - Y$. We add the one's complement of Y to X to get: $X + (2^n - Y - 1) = 2^n + (X - Y) - 1$. By transferring the carry-out, 2^n, to the least-significant bit, we correct the result $(X - Y) - 1$ to $(X - Y)$ by canceling the -1 term.

If we add together two one's complement negative numbers we get: $-X + -Y = (2^n - X - 1) + (2^n - Y - 1) = 2^n - 1 + 2^n - 1 - (X + Y)$. If we apply end-around carry to this result, the first 2^n term cancels the first -1 term to leave $2^n - 1 - (X + Y)$. This is, of course, the correct result in one's complement form.

The one's complement system is not a true complement as the value of $X + (-X)$ is not zero. Furthermore, there are two

representations for zero: $00 \ldots 0$ and $11 \ldots 1$. Today, the one's complement system is rarely used to represent signed numbers.

It's instructive to compare the various ways of representing numbers we have encountered so far. Table 4.17 shows how the sequence of 5-bit binary numbers for $n = 5$ for pure binary numbers, sign and magnitude, one's complement, and two's complement representations.

4.7 **Computer arithmetic and assembly language programming**

Having dealt with addition and subtraction at the hardware level in terms of full adders, it's time to see how these operations are carried out by the computer itself at the *assembly language* level. Although we introduce the basics of assembly language here, some readers may wish to skip this section until after they've read the next chapter on the central processing unit and assembly language. We don't wish to preempt the chapter on assembly language, but the following notes should help.

Assembly language is the most primitive language (excepting *machine code*, which is the binary form of assembly language) in which programs can be written and is the native language of the computer. An assembly language uses *mnemonics* to represent the operations that may be performed by the computer. For example, ADD = add, SUB = subtract, MOVE = move, etc. Mnemonics vary from computer to computer, although the meanings of most mnemonics are self-evident. We are going to use a real assembly language, that of Motorola's 68000 microprocessor.

Following the mnemonic is often a *symbolic name* that refers to a variable stored in memory or a register. If we write ADD NUM_1,D0 we mean add the number we've called (or labeled) NUM_1 to the contents of data register D0. NUM_1 refers to the location of the number in memory.

Information in a computer is stored either in a memory location or in a *register*. A memory location is a place in memory where a word is stored. Each memory location has a unique *address* that distinguishes it from all the other memory locations in a memory. A register performs the same function as a memory location (the computer we will be describing has eight registers called D0, D1, ... , D7). Indeed, the only differences between a register and a memory location are:

1. There are only eight registers but millions of memory locations.

2. A register has a short name (D0 to D7), whereas a memory location requires a 32-bit address to specify its location.

Binary code	Natural binary	Sign and magnitude	One's complement	Two's complement
00000	0	0	0	0
00001	1	1	1	1
00010	2	2	2	2
00011	3	3	3	3
00100	4	4	4	4
00101	5	5	5	5
00110	6	6	6	6
00111	7	7	7	7
01000	8	8	8	8
01001	9	9	9	9
01010	10	10	10	10
01011	11	11	11	11
01100	12	12	12	12
01101	13	13	13	13
01110	14	14	14	14
01111	15	15	15	15
10000	16	−0	−15	−16
10001	17	−1	−14	−15
10010	18	−2	−13	−14
10011	19	−3	−12	−13
10100	20	−4	−11	−12
10101	21	−5	−10	−11
10110	22	−6	−9	−10
10111	23	−7	−8	−9
11000	24	−8	−7	−8
11001	25	−9	−6	−7
11010	26	−10	−5	−6
11011	27	−11	−4	−5
11100	28	−12	−3	−4
11101	29	−13	−2	−3
11110	30	−14	−1	−2
11111	31	−15	−0	−1

Table 4.17 The representation of negative numbers.

3. Registers are located on the same chip as the microprocessor and can be accessed rapidly.

4. Many computers allow us to specify only one memory resident operand in an instruction. Consequently, it's necessary to use registers to hold intermediate results.

We are going to use the 68000 microprocessor to illustrate assembly language (in this and other chapters) because:

1. The 68000 can operate on 8-bit data values, which is of manageable size for student examples. A short data word doesn't necessarily restrict the things we can do.

2. The 68000's architecture and assembly language are easy to use and understand. Furthermore, its architecture is not untypical of mainstream computers. Some computers are less typical of computers in general and are therefore less well suited to teaching purposes.

3. The 68000 can operate on byte (8 bit), word (16 bit), or longword (32 bit) values.

An assembly language program to add three numbers

Suppose we wish to perform the operation R = P + Q by adding together the numbers P and Q, and calling the result R. In this expression, P, Q, and R are *symbolic names* referring to physical locations within the 68000's memory. We use symbolic names because we don't want to be bothered with trying to remember the addresses of data. A program that evaluates R = P + Q is written in the form

```
MOVE   P,D0
ADD    Q,D0
MOVE   D0,R
```

Computer instructions are executed sequentially in order. Assembly language instructions are written in the form

```
operation <source>,<destination>
```

where operation defines the action to be carried out, <source> defines where the data comes from, and <destination> defines where the result is stored. Not all computers follow the same convention; for example, the Intel microprocessors uses the convention operation <destination>,<source>.

The first instruction in this tiny program, MOVE P,D0, moves the contents of the memory location we've called P to data register D0. Figure 4.23 shows the location of the program and its data in memory. The mnemonic MOVE means *move a number from its source to its destination* with the effect that MOVE X,Y moves the contents of 'source X' into 'destination Y'.

In a real program the programmer would have to tell the assembler where the addresses P, Q, and R are located in the memory. The MOVE operation doesn't affect the number in P. It is a most important rule that, unless the contents of a memory location or register are modified by writing a new number into it, they do not change. Perhaps it would have been better to call the MOVE instruction COPY, as this expresses the action of MOVE more exactly.

The second instruction, ADD Q,D0, means *add the contents of memory location called Q to the contents of data register D0*.

The final instruction, MOVE D0,R, stores the contents of data register D0 in memory location R.

There's nothing difficult about this example. However, you may be tempted to ask, 'Are we operating with unsigned binary numbers or with two's complement numbers?' The answer is that it doesn't matter. The same addition operation serves both cases: it's how the programmer deals with the result that matters.

We now need to explain how the computer modifies the flow of control (i.e. executes different instructions depending on the result of an operation). At the end of most instructions the computer looks at the result and sets certain *flags* or indicators to indicate the nature of the result. The four most important flags are called the Z-bit, C-bit, N-bit, and V-bit and indicate zero, carry, negative, and overflow, respectively. For example, if you perform SUB P,D0 and the contents of P and D0 are identical, the result of the subtraction will be 0 and the Z-bit will be set.

You can alter the normal sequence of instruction execution with a *conditional branch* instruction that's written BRA$_{condition}$ target. This instruction tests a 'condition' and, if the condition is satisfied, the computer executes the instruction labeled 'target' in the program. Consider now the two programs:

Case 1		Case 2	
MOVE	P,D0	MOVE	P,D0
ADD	Q,D0	ADD	Q,D0
BCS	**ERROR**	**BVS**	**ERROR**
MOVE	D0,R	MOVE	D0,R
.		.	
.		.	
ERROR		ERROR	

In Case 1 we have assumed that the arithmetic is unsigned binary. If, after the ADD Q,D0 operation, the sum of the two numbers is greater than 65 535 (we assume 16-bit arithmetic), a one is propagated from the most-significant bit position into the *carry*. The following instruction, BCS, is a conditional branch that means *Branch if Carry Set*. Thus, if a carry has been generated by the previous instruction, ADD Q,D0, the next instruction (i.e. MOVE D0,R) is not executed. Instead a branch or jump is made to the part of the program labeled by ERROR. This part of the program (not shown here) must be designed to deal with the problem. If a branch is not made, the next instruction immediately following the conditional branch is executed.

In Case 2 the arithmetic has been assumed to be in two's complement form. The program is identical to Case 1 except that after the addition we test to see if the overflow bit has been set. Here we use BVS, which means *Branch if Overflow flag Set*.

We're now going to demonstrate how a computer that uses, say, 32-bit arithmetic can deal with numbers of any arbitrary length.

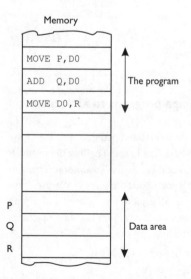

Fig. 4.23 Memory map of a simple program.

Dealing with large integers

The 68000 can deal with 8-bit, 16-bit, and 32-bit numbers. For example, if we wish to perform 8-bit addition we write `ADD.B Q,D0`; if we wish to perform 16-bit addition we write `ADD.W Q,D0`; and if we wish to add 32-bit numbers we write `ADD.L Q,D0`. The 68000 can perform 32-bit arithmetic because its registers are actually 32 bits wide. When we perform a byte operation such as `ADD.B D0,Q`, we are using only the least-significant 8 bits of a 32-bit register. Similarly, 16-bit operations such as `ADD.W D0,D2` involve only the least-significant 16 bits of registers D0 and D2.

Sometimes we need to perform arithmetic on even longer words. In such cases we can create a large word putting together as many units of 32 bits as we need. Unless speed is of the utmost importance, creating large numbers by chaining together smaller units of data is more cost-effective than buying a computer with the required word length.

Suppose we need to deal with unsigned numbers up to 2^{64} (i.e. 1.8447×10^{19}). To create a 64-bit word all we do is to take two 32-bit words in memory and regard them as a 64-bit entity. Using the previous example with P, Q, and R, we can draw the memory map of Figure 4.24.

Our 64-bit word is now composed of two halves. P is represented by P_U (the 32 most-significant bits), and P_L (the 32 least-significant bits). We have drawn the memory map with P_L and P_U adjacent to each other, although there is no reason why this must be done in practice. To add P and Q to get R we must perform the following operations:

$$
\begin{array}{cc}
P_U & P_L \\
+ \, Q_U & Q_L \\
\hline
R_U & R_L
\end{array}
$$

That is, we add P_L to Q_L to get R_L, and then P_U to Q_U to get R_U. The only point to note is that when P_L is added to Q_L any carry generated must be added to the $(P_U + Q_U)$ column. In terms of assembly language the program to add P and Q is

`MOVE.L PL,D0`	Get the low-order 32 bits of P
`ADD.L QL,D0`	and add them to the low-order 32 bits of Q
`MOVE.L D0,RL`	Put the 32-bit sum in the low-order 32 bits of R
`MOVE.L PU,D0`	Now get the high-order 32 bits of P
`ADDX.L QU,D0`	and add them to the high-order 32 bits of Q plus any carry
`MOVE.L D0,RU`	Put the 32-bit sum in the high-order 32 bits of R

The first three lines of this fragment of code calculate the least-significant 32 bits of the result in exactly the same way

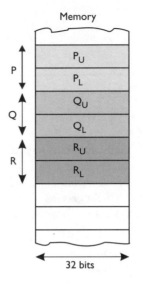

Memory

P

Q

R

32 bits

(a) Memory map

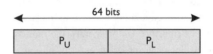

64 bits

P_U | P_L

(b) Conceptualization of P

Fig. 4.24 Memory map of a system for double-precision arithmetic.

we calculated 16-bit answers. When we come to add P_U to Q_U to create the most-significant 32 bits of the result we use a special addition instruction, `ADDX.L`, that automatically adds in any carry bit when P_U is added to Q_U. The instruction `ADDX.L QU,D0` adds the 32 bits in the memory location specified by the symbolic name Q_U to the 32-bit value already in D0, together with the previously generated carry bit. If you are wondering where the 'X' comes from in the mnemonic `ADDX`, it means 'extended' because it is used to extend the effective size of operands.

We can extend this example to deal with numbers made up of an arbitrary number of units. The range of unsigned integers for a given number of bytes is:

Bytes	Range
1	0–255
2	0–65 535
3	0–16 777 215
4	0–4 294 967 296

5	$0-1.099\ 511\ 6 \times 10^{12}$
6	$0-2.814\ 749\ 8 \times 10^{14}$
7	$0-7.205\ 759\ 4 \times 10^{16}$
8	$0-1.844\ 674\ 4 \times 10^{19}$
9	$0-4.722\ 366\ 5 \times 10^{21}$
10	$0-1.208\ 925\ 8 \times 10^{24}$

Subtraction

Subtraction is performed in very much the same way as addition (that is, from the programmer's point of view). The 68000 subtraction instruction has the mnemonic SUB, and SUB X,Y subtracts 16-bit operand X from operand Y and deposits the result in Y. To subtract Q from P to get R, the following program is used:

```
MOVE  P,D0    Put P into data register D0
SUB   Q,D0    Subtract Q from register D0
MOVE  D0,R    Store the result in register D0 in location R
```

In this fragment of code we've added comments to the right of our mnemonic instructions. A program written in a high-level language like Pascal is self-documenting because its meaning is clear and unambiguous (mostly). Unfortunately, the morass of detail in an assembly language program entirely obscures the point of the program. Without a copious quantity of comments the program soon becomes incomprehensible even to its author. In the next section we look at how the CPU deals with really large and microscopically small numbers without demanding excessive amounts of storage to represent them.

4.8 Floating point numbers

Before we go any further we have to admit that floating point arithmetic is not one of the great fun-subjects of computer science. Although the basic idea behind floating point arithmetic is very simple, the exact way in which floating point arithmetic is implemented is rather involved.

So far, we've largely dealt with *integer* values. Let's look at a simple way of handling numbers with both integer and fractional parts (e.g. 13.75_{10} or 1101.11_2). Fortunately, a binary (or decimal) fraction presents no problems. Consider the following two calculations in decimal arithmetic.

Case I Integer arithmetic	Case 2 Fixed point arithmetic
7632135	763.2135
+1794821	+179.4821
9426956	942.6956

Although Case 1 uses *integer* arithmetic and Case 2 uses *fractional* arithmetic, the calculations are entirely identical. The only difference is in the location of the decimal point. We can extend this principle to computer arithmetic. All the computer programmer has to do is to remember where the binary point is assumed to lie. Input to the computer is scaled to match this convention and the output is similarly scaled. The internal operations themselves are carried out as if the numbers were in integer form. This arrangement is called *fixed point arithmetic*, because the binary point is assumed to remain in the same position. That is, there is always the same number of digits before and after the binary point. The advantage of the fixed point representation of numbers is that no complex software or hardware is needed to implement it.

A simple example should make the idea of fixed point arithmetic clearer. Consider an 8-bit fixed point number with the four most-significant bits representing the integer part and the four least-significant bits representing the fractional part.

Let's see what happens if we wish to add the two numbers 3.625 and 6.5, and print the result. An input program first converts these numbers to binary form.

$3.625 \rightarrow 11.101 \rightarrow 0011.1010$ (in 8 bits)
$6.5 \rightarrow 110.1 \rightarrow 0110.1000$ (in 8 bits)

The computer now regards these numbers as 00111010 and 01101000, respectively. Remember that the binary point is only imaginary. These numbers are added in the normal way to give

```
  00111010
+ 01101000
  10100010
```

This result would be equal to 162_{10} if we were to regard it as an unsigned natural binary integer. But it isn't. We must regard it as a fixed point value. The output program now takes the result and splits it into an integer part 1010 and a fractional part .0010. The integer part is equal to 10_{10}, and the fractional part is 0.125_{10}. The result would be printed as 10.125.

In practice, a fixed point number may be spread over several words to achieve a greater range of values than allowed by a single word. The fixed point representation of fractional numbers is very useful in some circumstances, particularly for financial calculations. For example, the smallest fractional part may be (say) 0.1 of a cent or 0.001 dollar. The largest integer part may be $1,000,000. To represent such a quantity in BCD a total of $6 \times 4 + 3 \times 4 = 36$ bits are required. A byte-oriented computer would require five bytes for each number.

Fixed point numbers have their limitations. Consider the astrophysicist who is examining the Sun's behavior. He or she is confronted with numbers ranging from 1 990 000 000 000 000 000 000 000 000 000 000 grams (the Sun's mass) to 0.000 000 000 000 000 000 000 000 000 910 956 grams (the mass of an electron).

If astrophysicists were to resort to fixed point arithmetic, they would require an extravagantly large number of bits to represent the range of numbers used in their trade. A single byte represents numbers in the range 0 to 255. If physicists wanted to work with astronomically large and microscopically small numbers, roughly 14 bytes would be required for the integer part of the number and 12 bytes for the fractional part; that is, they would need a 26-byte (208 bit) number. A clue to a way out of our dilemma is to note that both figures contain a large number of zeros but few significant digits.

4.8.1 Representation of floating point numbers

We can express a decimal number such as 1234.56 in the form $0.123\,456 \times 10^4$ which is called the *floating point format* or *scientific notation*. The computer handle large and small binary values in a similar way; for example, 1101101.1101101 may be represented internally as $0.11011011101101 \times 2^7$ (the 7 is, of course, also stored in a binary format). Before looking at floating point numbers in more detail we should to consider the ideas of *range*, *precision*, and *accuracy* that are closely related to the way numbers are represented in floating point format.

Range   The range of a number tells us how big or how small it can be. In the previous example the astrophysicist was dealing with numbers as large as 2×10^{33} and those as small as 9×10^{-28}, representing a range of approximately 10^{61}, or 61 decades. The range of numbers capable of representation by a computer must be sufficient for the calculations that are likely to be performed. If the computer is employed in a dedicated application where the range of data to be handled is known to be quite small, then the range of valid numbers may be restricted, simplifying the hardware/software requirements.

Precision   The precision of a number is a measure of its exactness and corresponds to the number of significant figures used to represent it. For example, the constant π may be written as 3.142 or 3.141 592. The latter value is more *precise* than the former because it represents π to one part in 10^7 whereas the former value represents π to one part in 10^4.

Accuracy   Accuracy has been included here largely to contrast it with precision, a term often incorrectly thought to mean the same as accuracy. Accuracy is the measure of the

correctness of a quantity. For example, we can say $\pi = 3.141$ or $\pi = 3.241\,592$. The first value is a low-precision number but is more accurate than the higher precision value, which has an error in the second digit. In an ideal world, accuracy and precision would go hand-in-hand. It's the job of the computer programmer to design algorithms that preserve the accuracy that the available precision allows. One of the potential hazards of computation is calculations that take the form

$$\frac{A+B}{A-B}$$

For example, $\dfrac{1234.5687 + 1234.5678}{1234.5687 - 1234.5678} = \dfrac{2469.1365}{0.0009}$

When the denominator of this expression is evaluated we are left with 0.0009, a number with only one decimal place of precision. Although the result might show eight figures of precision, it may be very inaccurate indeed.

A floating point number is represented in the form $a \times r^e$ where a is the *mantissa* (also called the *argument*), r is the *radix* or *base*, and e is the *exponent* or *characteristic*. The computer stores a floating point number by splitting the binary sequence representing the number into the two fields illustrated in Fig. 4.25. The radix r is not stored explicitly by the computer.

Throughout the remainder of this section the value of the radix in all floating point numbers is assumed to be two. Before the IEEE format became popular, some computers used an octal or hexadecimal exponent, so that the mantissa is multiplied by 8^e or 16^e, respectively. For example, if a floating point number has a mantissa 0.101011 and an octal exponent of 4 (i.e. 0100 in 4 bits), the number is equal to 0.101011×8^4 or 0.101011×2^{12}, which is 101011000000_2.

It's not necessary for a floating point number to occupy a single storage location. Indeed, with an 8-bit word, such a representation would be useless. Several words are grouped to form a floating point number (the number of words required is bits-in-floating-point-representation/computer-word-length). The split between exponent and mantissa need not fall at a

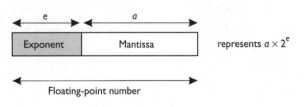

Fig. 4.25 Storing a floating point number.

word boundary. That is, a mantissa might occupy 3 bytes and the exponent 1 byte of a two 16-bit word floating-point number.

When constructing a floating point representation for numbers, the programmer must select

1. The total number of bits

2. The representation of the mantissa (two's complement etc.)

3. The representation of the exponent (biased etc.)

4. The number of bits devoted to the mantissa and exponent

5. The location of the mantissa (exponent first or mantissa first)

Point 4 is worthy of elaboration. Once you've decided on the total number of bits in the floating point representation (an integral number of word lengths), the number must be split into a mantissa and exponent. Dedicating a large number of bits to the exponent results in a floating point number with a very big range. These (exponent) bits have been obtained at the expense of the mantissa, which reduces the precision of the floating point number. Conversely, increasing the bits available for the mantissa improves the precision at the expense of the range.

Because of the flexibility engendered by these five points, the number of ways in which a floating point number may be represented is legion. Once, almost no two machines used the same format. Things improved with the introduction of microprocessors. Today, a standard format for floating point numbers has emerged that now dominates the computer industry. Accordingly, we will largely concentrate on this so-called IEEE standard.

4.8.2 Normalization of floating point numbers

By convention a floating point mantissa is always *normalized* (unless it is equal to zero) so that it is expressed in the form $0.1 \ldots \times 2^e$. If the result of a calculation were to yield $0.01 \ldots \times 2^e$, the result would be normalized to give $0.1 \ldots \times$ 2^{e-1}. Similarly, the result $1.01 \ldots \times 2^e$ would be normalized to $0.101 \ldots \times 2^{e+1}$.

By normalizing a mantissa, the greatest possible advantage is taken of the available precision. For example, the unnormalized 8-bit mantissa 0.00001010 has only four significant bits, whereas the normalized 8-bit mantissa 0.10100011 has eight significant bits. It is worth noting here that there is a slight difference between normalized decimal numbers as used by engineers and scientists, and normalized binary numbers. By convention, a decimal floating point number is normalized so that its mantissa lies in the range $1.00 \ldots 0$ to $9.99 \ldots 9$. A positive floating point normalized binary mantissa x is of the form

$$x = 0.100 \ldots 0 \text{ to } 0.11 \ldots 11$$

That is, $\frac{1}{2} \leqslant x < 1$. A special exception has to be made in the case of zero, as this number cannot, of course, be normalized. A negative, two's complement, floating point mantissa is stored in the form

$$x = 1.01 \ldots 1 \text{ to } 1.00 \ldots 0$$

In this case the negative mantissa, x, is constrained so that $-\frac{1}{2} > x \geqslant -1$. The floating point number is therefore limited to one of the three ranges described by Fig. 4.26.

This form of mantissa representation and normalization was common until the advent of the IEEE standard for floating point numbers. The IEEE standard specifies a *sign and magnitude* representation, so that you might reasonably expect normalized mantissas to lie in the range $0.1000 \ldots 00$ to $0.1111 \ldots 11$ for positive numbers and from $1.1000 \ldots 00$ to $1.1111 \ldots 11$ for negative numbers.

In fact, the IEEE format for floating point numbers uses a leading 1 in front of the binary point. A normalized mantissa must fall in the range $1.000 \ldots 00$ to $1.111 \ldots 11$. Because the IEEE format uses a separate sign bit, a mantissa x is constrained to lie in the ranges

$$-2 < x \leqslant 1, \text{ or } x = 0, \text{ or } 1 \leqslant x < 2$$

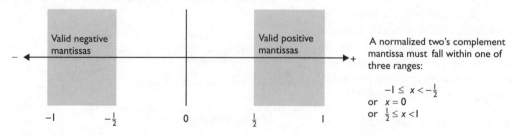

Fig. 4.26 Range of valid normalized two's complement mantissas.

Biased exponents

A floating point representation of numbers must make provision for both positive and negative numbers and positive and negative exponents. The following example in decimal notation demonstrates this concept.

$$+0.123 \times 10^{12}, \ -0.756 \times 10^{9}, \ +0.176 \times 10^{-3}, \ -0.459 \times 10^{-7}$$

The mantissa of an IEEE format floating point number is represented in *sign and magnitude* form. The exponent, however, is represented in a *biased* form. An m-bit exponent provides 2^m unsigned integer exponents from $00\dots0$ to $11\dots1$. Suppose that we relabel these 2^m values from -2^{m-1} to $+2^{m-1}-1$ by subtracting a constant value (or bias) of $B=2^{m-1}$ from each of the numbers. We get a continuous natural binary series from 0 to N representing exponents from $-B$ to $N-B$.

If we use a 3-bit decimal biased exponent with $B=4$, the biased exponents are 0, 1, 2, 3, 4, 5, 6, 7. This sequence represents the actual exponents $-4, -3, -2, -1, 0, 1, 2, 3$. We've invented a way of representing negative numbers by adding a constant to the most negative number to make it equal to zero. In this example, we've added 4 to each number so that -4 is represented by 0, and -3 by $+1$, etc.

We create a biased exponent by adding a constant to the true exponent so that the biased exponent is given by $b'=b+B$, where b' is the biased exponent, b the true exponent, and B a weighting. The weighting B is frequently either 2^{m-1} or $2^{m-1}-1$. Consider what happens for the case where $m=4$ and $B=2^3=8$ (see Table 4.18).

The true exponent ranges from -8 to $+7$, allowing us to represent powers of 2 from 2^{-8} to 2^{-7}, while the biased exponent ranges from 0 to $+15$. The advantage of the biased representation of exponents is that the most negative exponent is represented by zero. Conveniently, the floating point value of zero is represented by $0.0\dots0 \times 2^{\text{most negative exponent}}$ (see Fig. 4.27). By choosing the biased exponent system we arrange that zero is represented by a zero mantissa and a zero exponent as Fig. 4.27 demonstrates.

The biased exponent representation of exponents is also called *excess n*, where n is typically 2^{m-1}. For example, a 6-bit exponent is called excess 32 because the stored exponent exceeds the true exponent by 32. In this case, the smallest true exponent that can be represented is -32 and is stored as an excess 32 value of 0. The maximum true exponent that can be represented is 31 and this is stored as 63.

A second advantage of the biased exponent representation is that the stored (i.e. biased) exponents form a natural binary sequence. This sequence is monotonic so that increasing the exponent by 1 involves adding one to the binary exponent,

Binary representation of exponent	True exponent	Biased form
0000	−8	0
0001	−7	1
0010	−6	2
0011	−5	3
0100	−4	4
0101	−3	5
0110	−2	6
0111	−1	7
1000	0	8
1001	1	9
1010	2	10
1011	3	11
1100	4	12
1101	5	13
1110	6	14
1111	7	15

Table 4.18 Relationship between true and biased exponents.

For example, if $n=1010.1111$, we normalize it to $+1.0101111 \times 2^3$. The true exponent is $+3$ which is stored as a biased exponent of $3+8$ which is 11_{10} or 1011_2 in binary form.

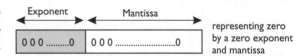

Fig. 4.27 Representing zero in floating point arithmetic.

and decreasing the exponent by 1 involves subtracting one from the binary exponent. In both cases the binary biased exponent can be considered as behaving like an unsigned binary number.

4.8.3 IEEE floating point format

The Institute of Electronics and Electrical Engineers, IEEE, has defined a standard floating point format for arithmetic operations called ANSI/IEEE standard 754-1985. To cater for different applications, the standard specifies three basic formats, called *single*, *double*, and *quad*. Table 4.19 defines the principal features of these three floating point formats.

As we've already said, IEEE floating point numbers are normalized so that their mantissas lie in the range $1 \leqslant F < 2$. This range corresponds to a mantissa with an integer part equal to 1. A non-zero IEEE format floating point number X is

	Single precision	Double precision	Quad precision
Field width in bits			
S = sign	1	1	1
E = exponent	8	11	15
L = leading bit	1	1	1
F = fraction	23	52	111
Total width	32	64	128
Exponent			
Maximum E	255	2047	32 767
Minimum E	0	0	0
Bias	127	1023	16 383

Notes
S = sign bit (0 for a negative number, 1 for a positive number)
L = leading bit (always 1 in a normalized, non-zero mantissa)
F = fractional part of the mantissa
The range of exponents is from Min E + 1 to Max E − 1.
The number is represented by $-1^S \times 2^{E-\text{exponent}} \times L.F$.
A signed zero is represented by the minimum exponent, L = 0, and F = 0, for all three formats.
The maximum exponent has a special function that represents signed infinity for all three formats.

Table 4.19 Basic IEEE floating point formats.

formally defined as

$$X = -1^S \times 2^{E-B} \times 1.F \text{ where,}$$

S = sign bit, 0 = positive mantissa, 1 = negative mantissa
E = exponent biased by B
F = fractional mantissa (note that the mantissa is 1.F and has an implicit leading one)

A single format 32-bit floating point number has a bias of 127 and a 23-bit fractional mantissa. A sign and magnitude representation has been adopted for the mantissa; if S = 1 the mantissa is negative and if S = 0 it is positive.

The mantissa is always normalized and lies in the range 1.000 … 00 to 1.111 … 11. If the mantissa is always normalized, it follows that the leading 1, the integer part, is redundant when the IEEE format floating point number is stored in memory. If we know that a 1 must be located to the left of the fractional mantissa, there is no need to store it. In this way one bit of storage is saved, permitting the precision of the mantissa to be extended by one bit. The format of the number when stored in memory is given in Fig. 4.28.

As an example of the use of the IEEE 32-bit format, consider the representation of the decimal number −2345.125.

$$-2345.125_{10} = -100100101001.001_2$$
(as an equivalent binary number)
$$= -1.00100101001001 \times 2^{11}$$
(as a normalized binary number)

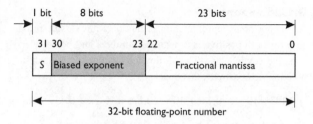

Fig. 4.28 Format of the IEEE 32-bit floating point format.

The mantissa is negative so the sign bit S is 1. The biased exponent is given by $+11 + 127 = 138 = 10001010_2$. The fractional part of the mantissa is

.00100101001001000000000 (in 23 bits)

Therefore the IEEE single format representation of −2345.125 is

11000101000100101001001000000000

In order to minimize storage space in computers where the memory width is less than that of the floating point number, floating point numbers are *packed* so that the sign bit, exponent, and mantissa share part of two or more machine words. When floating point operations are carried out, the numbers are first *unpacked* and the mantissa separated from the exponent. For example, the basic single-precision format specifies a 23-bit fractional mantissa, giving a 24-bit mantissa when unpacked and the leading 1 reinserted. If the processor on which the floating-point numbers are being processed has a 16-bit word length, the unpacked mantissa will occupy 24 bits out of the 32 bits taken up by two words.

If, when a number is unpacked, the number of bits in its exponent and mantissa is allowed to increase to fill the available space, the format is said to be *extended*. By extending the format in this way, the range and precision of the floating point number are considerably increased. For example, a single format number is stored as a 32-bit quantity. When it is unpacked the 23-bit fractional mantissa is increased to 24 bits by including the leading 1 and then the mantissa is extended to 32 bits (either as a single 32-bit word or as two 16-bit words). All calculations are then performed using the 32-bit extended precision mantissa. This is particularly helpful when trigonometric functions (e.g. sin x, cos x) are evaluated. After a sequence of floating operations have been carried out in the extended format, the floating point number is re-packed and stored in memory in its basic form.

In 32-bit single IEEE format, the maximum exponent E_{max} is $+127$ and the minimum exponent E_{min} is -126 rather than $+128$ to -127 as we might expect. The special value $E_{min} - 1$ (i.e. -127) is used to encode zero and $E_{max} + 1$ is used to encode plus or minus infinity or a NaN. A NaN is a special entity catered for in the IEEE format and is *Not a Number*. The use of NaNs is covered by the IEEE standard and they permit the manipulation of formats outside the IEEE standard.

4.8.4 Floating point arithmetic

Unlike integer and fixed point number representations, floating point numbers can't be added in one simple operation. A moment's thought should demonstrate why this is so. Consider an example in decimal arithmetic. Let $A = 12345$ and $B = 567.89$. In decimal floating point form these numbers can be represented by

$$A = 0.12345 \times 10^5 \text{ and } B = 0.56789 \times 10^3$$

If these numbers were to be added by hand, no problems would arise.

```
  12345
+567.89
───────
12912.89
```

However, as these numbers are held in a normalized floating point format we have the following problem.

```
  0.12345 × 10⁵
+ 0.56789 × 10³
```

Addition can't take place as long as the exponents are different. To perform a floating point addition (or subtraction) the following steps must be carried out:

1. Identify the number with the smaller exponent.

2. Make the smaller exponent equal to the larger exponent by dividing the mantissa of the smaller number by the same factor by which its exponent was increased.

3. Add (or subtract) the mantissas.

4. If necessary, normalize the result (post-normalization).

In the above example we have $A = 0.123\,45 \times 10^5$ and $B = 0.567\,89 \times 10^3$.

The exponent of B is smaller than that of A which results in an increase of 2 in B's exponent and a corresponding division of B's mantissa by 10^2 to give $0.005\,678\,9 \times 10^5$. We can now add A to the denormalized B.

```
  A=0.1234500 × 10⁵
+ B=0.0056789 × 10⁵
  ─────────────────
    0.1291289 × 10⁵
```

The result is already in a normalized form and doesn't need post-normalizing. Note that the answer is expressed to a precision of seven significant figures, whereas A and B are each expressed to a precision of five significant figures. If the result were stored in a computer, its mantissa would have to be reduced to five figures after the decimal point (because we were working with five-digit mantissas).

When people do arithmetic they often resort to what may best be called floating precision. If they want greater precision they simply use more digits. Computers use a fixed representation for floating point numbers so that the precision may not increase as a result of calculation. Consider the following binary example of floating point addition.

$$A = 0.11001 \times 2^4$$
$$B = 0.10001 \times 2^3$$

The exponent of B must be increased by 1 and the mantissa of B divided by 2 (i.e. shifted one place right) to make both exponents equal to 4.

```
A=0.11001   × 2⁴
B=0.010001  × 2⁴
  ──────────────
  1.000011  × 2⁴
```

Because the result is no longer normalized, we have to shift its mantissa one place right (i.e. divide it by 2) and add 1 to the exponent to compensate; that is, the result becomes 0.1000011×2^5. We've gained two extra places of precision. We can simply truncate the number to get

$$A + B = 0.10000 \times 2^5$$

A more formal procedure for the addition of floating point numbers is given in Fig. 4.29 as a flowchart. A few points to note about this flowchart are:

1. Because the exponent sometimes shares part of a word with the mantissa, it is necessary to separate them before the process of addition can begin. As we pointed out before, this is called unpacking.

2. If the two exponents differ by more than $p + 1$, where p is the number of significant bits in the mantissa, the smaller number is too small to affect the larger. Hence the result is effectively equal to the larger number and no further action takes place. For example, there's no point in adding 0.1234×10^{20} to 0.4567×10^2, because adding 0.4567×10^2 to 0.1234×10^{20} has no effect on a 4-digit mantissa.

3. During the post-normalization phase the exponent is checked to see if it is less than its minimum possible value or greater than its maximum possible value. This corresponds to testing for *exponent underflow* and *overflow*,

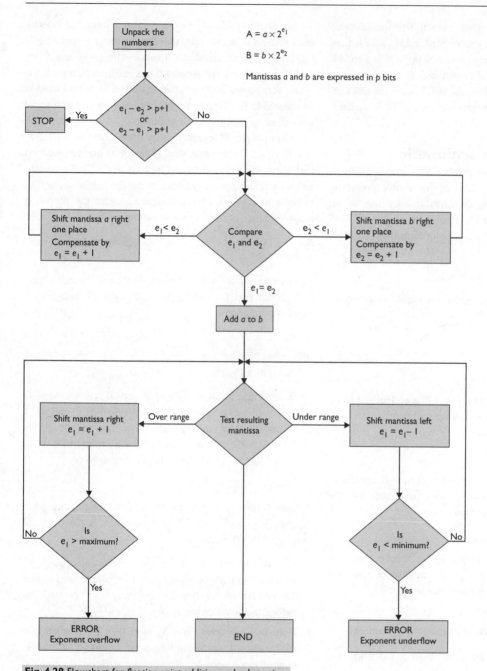

$A = a \times 2^{e_1}$

$B = b \times 2^{e_2}$

Mantissas a and b are expressed in p bits

Fig. 4.29 Flowchart for floating point addition and subtraction.

respectively. Each of these cases represents conditions in which the number is outside the range of numbers that the computer can handle. Exponent underflow would generally lead to the number being made equal to zero, whereas exponent overflow would result in an error condition and may require the intervention of the operating system.

Rounding and truncation

We have seen that some of the operations involved in floating point arithmetic lead to an increase in the number of bits in the mantissa and that some technique must be invoked to keep the number of bits in the mantissa constant. The simplest technique is called *truncation* and involves nothing more than dropping unwanted bits. For example, if we truncate 0.1101101 to four significant bits we get 0.1101. Truncating a number creates an error called an *induced error* (i.e. an error has been induced in the calculation by an operation on the number). Truncating a number causes a *biased* error because the number after truncation is always smaller than the number that was truncated.

A much better technique for reducing the number of bits in a word is *rounding*. If the value of the lost digits is greater than half the least-significant bit of the retained digits, 1 is added to the least-significant bit of the remaining digits. We have been doing this with decimal numbers for years—the decimal number 12.234 is rounded to 12.23, whereas 13.146 is rounded to 13.15. Consider rounding to 4 significant bits the following numbers

$0.1101011 \rightarrow 0.1101$ The three bits removed are 011, so do nothing

$0.1101101 \rightarrow 0.1101 + 1 = 0.1110$ The three bits removed are 101, so add 1

Rounding is always preferred to truncation, partially because it is more accurate and partially because it gives rise to an *unbiased error*. Truncation always undervalues the result, leading to a systematic error, whereas rounding sometimes reduces the result and sometimes increases it. The major disadvantage of rounding is that it requires a further arithmetic operation to be performed on the result.

4.8.5 Examples of floating point calculations

Because of the complexity of floating point arithmetic, due largely to the considerable number of steps involved in the addition or subtraction of two numbers, the following examples have been included. We begin with an example that doesn't use the IEEE standard.

Example 1 Add together 10.125 and 32.1 using floating point arithmetic with the format shown in Fig. 4.30. In each case show how the numbers would be stored in the computer.

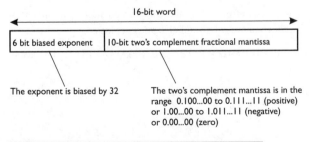

Fig. 4.30 Structure of a hypothetical floating point number.

Solution 1

a. 10.125_{10} is expressed as an unsigned binary number by 1010.001_2.

b. Normalize 1010.001 to get 0.1010001×2^4.

c. The mantissa is expanded to 10 bits as 0.101000100 (the binary point isn't stored).

d. The exponent is 4 or, in biased form, $4 + 32 = 36_{10} = 100100_2$.

e. The floating point representation of 10.125 is 100100 0101000100.

f. If we do the same to 32.1 we get: 100000.00011001100...
$32.1 = 0.100000000110011 \times 2^6$
$= 0.100000001 \times 2^6$ after rounding

The exponent is 6 or, in biased form, $6 + 32 = 38$. The floating point representation of 32.1 is 1001100100000001.

g. As these numbers have different exponents, the smaller mantissa must be scaled. The exponent is increased by two (multiplication by 4) and the mantissa shifted two places right (division by 4) to compensate.

```
100100   0.101000100 = 100110   0.00101000100
  E           M           E             M
```

h. We can now add the mantissas:

```
  0.00101000100
+ 0.100000001
  0.10101001000
```

This resulting mantissa is rounded to 10 bits (0.101010010) and the final answer is

```
100110   0101010010
```

The decimal equivalent of this binary number represents $0.101010010 \times 2^6 = 101010.010_2 = 42.25_{10}$. The correct answer is 42.225. An error has been introduced because the mantissa is restricted to 10 bits.

Example 2 Assuming a system with a 6-bit biased exponent (i.e. excess 32) and a 10-bit two's complement mantissa (as in Fig. 4.30), perform the following operations. In each case compare the calculated result with the true result. Rounding may be employed during the calculation of the 10-bit mantissa. During successive floating point operations (e.g. scaling the mantissa) truncation must be used.

(a) 157.3   (b) 157.3   (c) 157.3   (d) 157.3
    +257.1   −12.6   −142.7   +152.8

Solution 2a
```
  157.3
+ 257.1
  414.4
```

Step 1   Convert 157 to binary

$$157 \div 2 = 78 \quad R=1$$
$$78 \div 2 = 39 \quad R=0$$
$$39 \div 2 = 19 \quad R=1$$
$$19 \div 2 = 9 \quad R=1$$
$$9 \div 2 = 4 \quad R=1$$
$$4 \div 2 = 2 \quad R=0$$
$$2 \div 2 = 1 \quad R=0$$
$$1 \div 2 = 0 \quad R=1$$

Therefore, $157_{10} = 10011101_2$.

Step 2   Convert 0.3 to binary

$$0.3 \times 2 = \underline{0}.6$$
$$0.6 \times 2 = \underline{1}.2$$
$$0.2 \times 2 = \underline{0}.4$$
$$0.4 \times 2 = \underline{0}.8$$
$$0.8 \times 2 = \underline{1}.6$$

Therefore, $0.3_{10} = 0.01001\ldots_2$.

Step 3   Normalize the fixed-point binary number

$$157.3 = 10011101.01001\ldots$$
$$= 0.1001110101001 \times 2^8$$

Step 4   Round the mantissa to 10 bits

0.100111010 1001

$$\longleftrightarrow$$
greater than $\frac{1}{2}$ least-significant bit of
10 remaining bits

0.100111011   rounded mantissa

The floating point representation of 157.3 is 0.100111011×2^8. The exponent is $+8$ (true). In biased form we must add $2^5 = 32$ which gives a biased exponent $= 40 = 101000_2$. The floating point number would be stored as 1010000100111011.

Step 5   Convert 257.1 to a normalized floating point number, rounded to 10 bits

$$257.1 = 0.100000001_2 \times 2^9$$

Step 6   Compare exponents

$$0.100111011 \times 2^8$$
$$0.100000001 \times 2^9$$

Step 7   Make the smaller exponent equal to the larger exponent, and shift its mantissa right for each increment of the exponent.

$$0.0100111011 \times 2^9$$
$$0.100000001 \times 2^9$$

Step 8   Add mantissas

0.010011101×2^9 Note the smaller mantissa has been
0.100000001×2^9 truncated to 10 bits
0.110011110×2^9

The result is already normalized and needs no further processing. This corresponds to $0.110011110 \times 2^9 = 110011110_2 = 414_{10}$ and differs from the exact answer (414.4) by 0.4.

Solution 2b

```
 157.3
-12.6
 144.7
```

Step 1   Convert 157.3 to binary

$157.3_{10} = 0.100111011_2 \times 2^8$ (normalized and rounded)

Step 2   Convert 12.6 to binary

$$12.6_{10} = 1100.10011001100_2$$
$$= 0.110010011011 \times 2^4$$
$$= 0.110010011 \times 2^4 \text{ (floating point rounded binary)}$$

Step 3   Form the two's complement of the mantissa

$0.110010011 \rightarrow 1.001101100$ (invert bits)
$ \rightarrow 1.001101101$ (add 1)

Step 4   Equalize exponents

$1.001101101 \times 2^4 \rightarrow 1.111100110(1101) \times 2^8$
$ \rightarrow 1.111100110 \times 2^8$

Note 1: When shifting negative numbers right the sign bit is propagated.
Note 2: The bits shifted out have been dropped (truncation).

Step 5   Perform addition

0.100111011×2^8
1.111100110×2^8
10.100100001×2^8

Note: The leftmost 1 in the carry-bit position is the result of two's complement arithmetic and is neglected.

Result $= 0.100100001 \times 2^8 = 10010000.1_2 = 144.5$. The exact answer is 144.7_{10}.

Solution 2c

```
 157.3
-142.7
  14.6
```

Step 1 Convert 157.3 to binary

$157.3_{10} = 0.100111011_2 \times 2^8$ (normalized and rounded)

Step 2 Convert 142.7 to binary

$142.7_{10} = 10001110.1011001_2$
$= 0.100011101 \times 2^8$ (normalized and rounded binary)

Step 3 Form the two's complement of the mantissa

$0.100011101 \rightarrow 1.011100010$ (invert bits)
$\rightarrow 1.011100011$ (add 1)

Step 4 Perform addition

```
 0.100111011 × 2⁸
 1.011100011 × 2⁸
10.000011110 × 2⁸
```

The answer is 0.000011110×2^8 (after removing the carry out).

Step 5 Normalize the result

Result $= 0.000011110 \times 2^8 = 0.1111000000_2 \times 2^4 = 15$. The exact answer is 14.6_{10}.

Solution 2d

```
 157.3
−158.3
───────
  −1.0
```

Step 1 $157.3_{10} = 0.100111011_2 \times 2^8$ (normalized and rounded)

Step 2 Convert -158.3 to binary

$158.3_{10} = 10011110.01001_2$
$= 0.1001111001001 \times 2^8$
$= 0.100111101 \times 2^8$ (floating point rounded binary)

Step 3 Form the two's complement of the mantissa

$0.100111101 \rightarrow 1.011000010$ (invert bits)
$\rightarrow 1.011000011$ (add 1)

Step 4 Perform addition

```
0.100111011 × 2⁸
1.011000011 × 2⁸
───────────────────
1.111111110 × 2⁸
```

The answer is negative (sign bit = 1) and un-normalized.

Step 5 Normalize the result

$1.111111110 \times 2^8 = 1.000000000_2 \times 2^0 = -1$. The exact answer is -1_{10}.

Note the operation of the arithmetic shift left.

$1.111111110 \times 2^8 \rightarrow 1.111111100 \times 2^7$
$1.111111100 \times 2^7 \rightarrow 1.111111000 \times 2^6$
$1.111111000 \times 2^6 \rightarrow 1.111110000 \times 2^5$
etc.

Example 3 An IEEE standard 32-bit floating point number has the format: $N = -1^S \times 1.F \times 2^{E-127}$, where S is the *sign* bit, F is the *fractional* mantissa, and E is the *biased* exponent.

(a) (i) Convert the decimal number 123.5 into the IEEE format for floating point numbers.

    (ii) Convert the decimal number 100.25 into the IEEE format for floating point numbers.

(b) Describe the steps that take place when two IEEE floating point numbers are added together. You should start with the two packed floating point numbers and end with the packed sum.

(c) Perform the subtraction of $123.5 - 100.25$ using the two IEEE-format binary floating point numbers you obtained for 123.5 and 100.25 in part (a) of this question. You should begin the calculation with the packed floating point representations of these numbers and end with the packed result.

Solution 3

(a) (i) $123.5_{10} = 1111011.1$
        $= 1.1110111 \times 2^6$

The mantissa is positive, so $S = 0$. The exponent is $+6$, which is stored in biased form as $6 + 127 = 133_{10} = 10000101_2$. The mantissa is 1.1110111, which is stored as 23 bits with the leading 1 suppressed. The number is stored in IEEE format as: 0 10000101 11101110000000000000000.

    (ii) We can immediately write down the IEEE value for 100.25 because it is so close to the 123.5 we have just calculated; that is, 0 10000101 10010001000000000000000.

(b) In order to perform addition (or any other arithmetic operation) the two IEEE-format floating point numbers taking part in the operation must first be unpacked. That is, the sign, the exponent, and the mantissa (with the leading 1 restored) must be reconstituted.

    The two exponents are compared. If they are the same, the mantissas are added. If they are not, the number with the smaller exponent is denormalized by shifting its mantissa right (i.e. dividing by 2) and incrementing its exponent (i.e. multiplying by 2) until the two exponents are equal. Then the numbers are added.

The result is checked. If the mantissa is out of range (i.e. greater than 1.11111...1 or less than 1.0000...0) it must be renormalized. If the exponent goes out of range (bigger than its largest values or smaller than its smallest value) exponent overflow occurs and an error is flagged. The result is repacked and the leading 1 in front of the normalized mantissa removed.

(c) IEEE number
$123.5_{10} =$ 0 10000101 11101110000000000000000
IEEE number
$100.25_{10} =$ 0 10000101 10010001000000000000000

These floating point numbers have the same exponent, so we can subtract their mantissas (after inserting the leading 1).

$$
\begin{array}{r}
1.11101110000000000000000 \\
- 1.10010001000000000000000 \\
\hline
0.01011101000000000000000
\end{array}
$$

The result is not normalized and must be shifted left twice to get: 1.01110100000000000000000. The exponent must be decreased by 2 to get 10000011. The result expressed in floating point format is

0 1000011 01110100000000000000000

4.9 Multiplication and division

In this final part of our excursion into digital arithmetic, we look at what might best be called *advanced* computer arithmetic. Advanced computer arithmetic is concerned with those numerical operations involving multiplication and division. Such operations and their derivatives (reciprocals, square roots, exponentiation, and trigonometric functions) are very important in many areas of computation, especially numerical computation.

Newcomers to computing are sometimes surprised to find that most of the popular 8-bit microprocessors can't perform multiplication directly. Programmers wishing to multiply two numbers with some 8-bit chips must resort to an algorithm involving shifting and adding. Equally, the newcomer might think that the omission of multiplication from the CPU's instruction set is a horrendous oversight entirely devaluing the microprocessor. This is not so. It's remarkable how little multiplication or any similar higher order arithmetic operations appear in many programs (we'll have more to say about this

when we introduce RISC processors). For example, the principal operation carried out by editors, assemblers, compilers, or text processors is the searching of data areas for a match with a given string. In fact the most frequent application of multiplication is not in arithmetic, but in calculating the addresses of array elements. For example, the location of the element $x_{i,j}$ in the m-row by n-column matrix, X, is given by $A + ni + j$, where A is the address of the first element.

Here we consider only multiplication and division, since other mathematical functions can be derived from multiplication. Indeed, division itself will later be defined as an iterative process involving multiplication.

4.9.1 Multiplication
Binary multiplication is no more complex than decimal multiplication. In many ways it's easier as the whole binary multiplication table can be reduced to:

$0 \times 0 = 0$
$0 \times 1 = 0$
$1 \times 0 = 0$
$1 \times 1 = 1$

The multiplication of two bits is identical to their logical AND. When we consider the multiplication of strings of bits, things become more complex, and the way in which multiplication is carried out, or mechanized, varies from machine to machine. The faster and more expensive the computer, the more complex the hardware used to implement multiplication. The simpler machines form the product of two numbers by shifting and adding, very much as people do. High-speed computers perform multiplication in a single operation by means of a very large logic array involving hundreds of gates.

Unsigned binary multiplication
The so-called *pencil and paper algorithm* used by people to calculate the product of two multi-digit numbers involves the multiplication of an n-digit number by a single digit followed by shifting and adding. We can apply the same approach to unsigned binary numbers in the following way. The multiplier bits are examined, one at a time, starting with the least-significant bit. If the current multiplier bit is one the multiplicand is written down; if it is zero then n zeros are written down instead. Then the next bit of the multiplier is examined, but this time we write the multiplicand (or zero) one place to the left of the last digits we wrote down. Each of these groups of n digits is called a *partial product*. When all partial products

have been formed, they are added up to give the result of the multiplication. An example should make this clear.

```
10×13 Multiplier  =1101₂
      Multiplicand=1010₂
   1010
   1101
   ────
   1010      Step 1 first multiplier bit = 1, write down multiplicand
   0000      Step 2 second multiplier bit = 0,  write down zeros shifted left
  1010       Step 3 third multiplier bit = 1, write down multiplicand shifted left
 1010        Step 4 fourth multiplier bit = 1, write down multiplicand shifted left
10000010     Step 5 add together four partial products
```

The result, $10000010_2 = 130_{10}$, is eight bits long. The multiplication of two n-bit numbers yields a $2n$-bit product.

Digital computers don't implement the pencil and paper algorithm in the above way, as this would require the storing of n partial products, followed by the simultaneous addition of n words. A better technique is to add up the partial products as they are formed. A possible algorithm for the multiplication of two n-bit unsigned binary numbers is given in Table 4.20. We will consider the previous example of 1101×1010 using the algorithm of Table 4.20. The mechanization of the product of 1101×1010 is presented in Table 4.21.

Multiplication without a multiplication instruction

The algorithm described in Table 4.20 can readily be applied to a typical microprocessor. The flowchart in Fig. 4.31 illustrates a multiplication algorithm for the 68000 microprocessor. Readers unfamiliar with the 68000 microprocessor and its assembly language may skip this section until they've read Chapters 5 and 6. We are using the 68000's add and shift instructions to perform multiplication, although the 68000 does, in fact, have its own multiply and divide instructions. Table 4.22 provides a suitable 68000 program for 8-bit multiplication.

This program uses both byte and word operations (because the multiplier and multiplicand are 8 bits and the partial product is a 16-bit value). A word operation is indicated by the suffix .W and a byte operation by .B. The partial product in register D0 is shifted one place right by the instruction ROXR.W #1,D0. This special instruction means 'rotate right through extend' and is used because it's necessary to include in the shift any carry out generated by the previous addition.

Signed multiplication

The multiplication algorithm we've just discussed is valid only for unsigned integers or unsigned fixed point numbers. As computers represent signed numbers by means of two's complement notation, it is necessary to find some way of forming the product of two's complement numbers. It is, of course, possible to convert negative numbers into a modulusonly form, calculate the product, and then convert it into a two's complement form if it is negative. That approach wastes time.

Before introducing a suitable algorithm, we demonstrate that the two's complement representation of negative numbers can't be used with the basic shifting and adding algorithm. That is, two's complement arithmetic works for addition and subtraction, but not for multiplication or division (without using special algorithms). Consider the product of X and $-Y$.

Table 4.20 An algorithm for multiplication.

a   Set a counter to n.
b   Clear the $2n$-bit partial product register.
c   Examine the rightmost bit of the multiplier (initially the least-significant bit). If it is one add the multiplicand to the n most-significant bits of the partial product.
d   Shift the partial product one place to the right.
e   Shift the multiplier one place to the right (the rightmost bit is, of course, lost).
f   Decrement the counter. If the result is not zero repeat from step c. If the result is zero read the product from the partial product register.

Table 4.21 Mechanizing unsigned multiplication.

`Multiplier = 1101_2 Multiplicand = 1010_2

Step	Counter	Multiplier	Partial product	Cycle
a and b	4	1101	00000000	
c	4	110<u>1</u>	10100000	1
d and e	4	0110	01010000	1
f	3	0110	01010000	1
c	3	011<u>0</u>	01010000	2
d and e	3	0011	00101000	2
f	2	0011	00101000	2
c	2	001<u>1</u>	11001000	3
d and e	2	0001	01100100	3
f	1	0001	01100100	3
c	1	000<u>1</u>	100000100	4
d and e	1	0000	10000010	4
f	0	0000	10000010	4

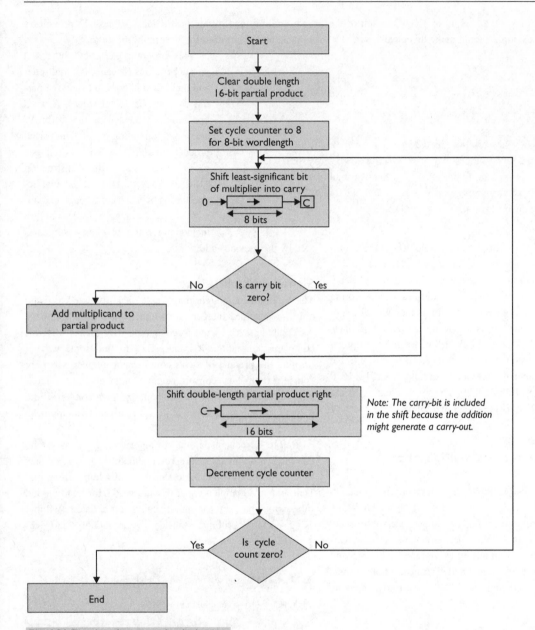

Fig. 4.31 Flowchart for unsigned multiplication.

The two's complement representation of $-Y$ is $2^n - Y$.

If we use two's complement arithmetic, the product $X(-Y)$ is given by $X(2^n - Y) = 2^n X - XY$.

The expected result, $-XY$, is represented in two's complement form by $2^{2n} - XY$. The most-significant bit is 2^{2n} (rather than 2^n) because multiplication automatically yields a double length product. In order to get the correct two's complement result we have to add a correction factor of

$$2^{2n} - 2^n X = 2^n(2^n - X)$$

This correction factor is the two's complement of X scaled by 2^n. As a further illustration consider the product of $X = 15$ and $Y = -13$ in five bits.

$$X = \quad 15 = 01111$$
$$Y = -13 = 10011$$

9	8	7	6	5	4	3	2	1	0	
2^9	2^8	2^7	2^6	2^5	2^4	2^3	2^2	2^1	2^0	
					0	1	1	1	1	X
					1	0	0	1	1	Y (2's complement form)
					0	1	1	1	1	
				0	1	1	1	1		
			0	0	0	0	0			
		0	0	0	0	0				
	0	1	1	1	1					
0	1	0	0	0	1	1	1	0	1	uncorrected result
1	0	0	0	1						correction factor
1	1	0	0	1	1	1	1	0	1	corrected result

The final result in ten bits, $1100111101_2 = -195_{10}$, is correct. Similarly, when X is negative and Y positive, a correction factor of $2^n(2^n - Y)$ must be added to the result.

When both multiplier and multiplicand are negative the following situation exists.

$$(2^n - X)(2^n - Y) = 2^{2n} - 2^nX - 2^nY + XY$$

In this case correction factors of 2^nX and 2^nY must be added to the result. The 2^{2n} term represents a carry-out bit from the most-significant position and can be neglected.

Booth's algorithm

The classic approach to the multiplication of signed numbers in two's complement form is provided by *Booth's algorithm*. This algorithm works for two positive numbers, one negative and one positive, or both negative. Booth's algorithm is broadly similar to conventional unsigned multiplication, but with the following differences. In Booth's algorithm two bits of the multiplier are examined together, to determine which of three courses of action is to take place next. The algorithm is defined below.

1. If the current multiplier bit is 1 and the next lower order multiplier bit is 0, subtract the multiplicand from the partial product.

2. If the current multiplier bit is 0 and the next lower order multiplier bit is 1, add the multiplicand to the partial product.

3. If the current multiplier bit is the same as the next lower order multiplier bit, do nothing.

Note 1: When adding in the multiplicand to the partial product, discard any carry bit generated by the addition.

Note 2: When the partial product is shifted, an arithmetic shift is used and the sign bit propagated.

Note 3: Initially, when the current bit of the multiplier is its least-significant bit, the next lower-order bit of the multiplier is assumed to be zero.

The flowchart for Booth's algorithm is given in Fig. 4.32. In order to illustrate the operation of Booth's algorithm, consider the three products: 13×15, -13×15, and $-13 \times (-15)$. Table 4.23 demonstrates how Booth's algorithm mechanizes these three multiplications.

High-speed multiplication

We don't intend to delve deeply into the subject of high-speed multiplication, as large portions of advanced textbooks are devoted to this topic alone. Here two alternative ways of

Table 4.22 A 68000 program for multiplication.

```
              ORG      $1000       Data origin
P             DS.B     1           Multiplier location (byte)
Q             DS.B     1           Multiplicand location (byte)
R             DS.W     1           Destination of result (word)
              ORG      $2000       Origin of program
              CLR.W    D0          Clear partial product in register D0
              CLR.W    D2          Clear the register used to hold multiplicand Q
              MOVE.B   Q,D2        Get multiplicand in register D2
              LSL.W    #8,D2       Shift multiplicand in D2 left by one byte
              MOVE.B   P,D3        Get multiplier in register D3
              MOVE.B   #8,D1       Set counter to 8
LOOP          LSR.B    #1,D3       Shift multiplier least-significant bit into carry
              BCC      SHIFT       If clear then shift partial product right
              ADD.W    D2,D0       Add multiplicand to most-significant byte
SHIFT         ROXR.W   #1,D0       Shift partial product one place right
              SUB.B    #1,D1       Decrement counter
              BNE      LOOP        Repeat until all 8 bits done
              MOVE.W   D0,R        Store the product in memory
```

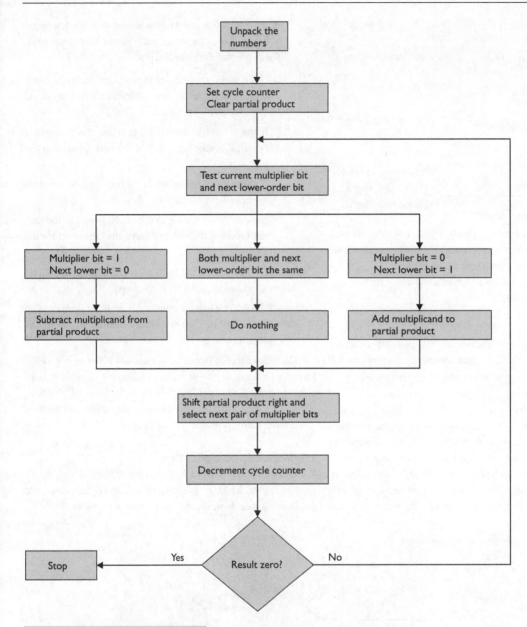

Fig. 4.32 Flowchart for Booth's algorithm.

forming products to the method of shifting and adding are explained.

We have seen in Chapter 2 that you can construct a 2-bit by 2-bit multiplier by means of logic gates. This process can be extended to larger numbers of bits. Figure 4.33 illustrates the type of logic array used to directly multiply two numbers.

An alternative approach is to use a *look-up table* in which all the possible results of the product of two numbers are stored in read-only memory. Table 4.24 shows how two 4-bit numbers may be multiplied by storing all $2^8 = 256$ possible results in a ROM.

The 4-bit multiplier and 4-bit multiplicand together form an 8-bit address that selects one of 256 locations within the ROM. In each of these locations the product of the multiplier (most-significant 4 address bits) and the multiplicand (least-significant 4 address bits) are stored. For example, the product

1. Multiplicand = 01111 = +15
   Multiplier = 01101 = +13

Step	Multiplier bits	Partial product
		0000000000
Subtract multiplicand	011<u>10</u>	1000100000
Shift partial product right		1100010000
Add multiplicand	011<u>01</u>	10011110000
Shift partial product right		0001111000
Subtract multiplicand	01<u>10</u>1	1010011000
Shift partial product right		1101001100
Do nothing	01<u>1</u>01	1101001100
Shift partial product right		1110100110
Add multiplicand	01<u>1</u>01	10110000110
Shift partial product right		0011000011

The final result is 00110000011_2, which is equal to $+195$. Note that the underlined numbers represent the bits to be examined at each stage.

2. Multiplicand = 01111 = +15
   Multiplier = 10011 = −13

Step	Multiplier bits	Partial product
		0000000000
Subtract multiplicand	100<u>10</u>	1000100000
Shift partial product right		1100010000
Do nothing	100<u>1</u>1	1100010000
Shift partial product right		1110001000
Add multiplicand	10<u>01</u>1	10101101000
Shift partial product right		0010110100
Do nothing	1<u>0</u>011	0010110100
Shift partial product right		0001011010
Subtract multiplicand	1<u>0</u>011	1001111010
Shift partial product right		1100111101

The result is 1100111101_2, which corresponds to −195.

3. Multiplicand = 10001 = −15
   Multiplier = 10011 = −13

Step	Multiplier bits	Partial product
		0000000000
Subtract multiplicand	100<u>10</u>	0111100000
Shift partial product right		0011110000
Do nothing	100<u>1</u>1	0011110000
Shift partial product right		0001111000
Add multiplicand	10<u>01</u>1	1010011000
Shift partial product right		1101001100
Do nothing	1<u>0</u>011	1101001100
Shift partial product right		1110100110
Subtract multiplicand	1<u>0</u>011	10110000110
Shift partial product right		0011000011

The result is 0011000011_2, which corresponds to +195.

Table 4.23 Three examples of mechanizing Booth's algorithm.

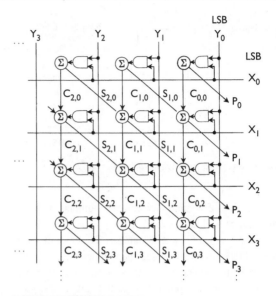

Fig. 4.33 The multiplier array.

Address		Data
Multiplier	Multiplicand	Result
0000	0000	00000000
0000	0001	00000000
:	:	:
:	:	:
0000	1111	00000000
0001	0000	00000000
0001	0001	00000001
:	:	:
:	:	:
0001	1111	00001111
0010	0000	00000000
0010	0001	00000010
:	:	:
:	:	:
0010	1111	00011110
:	:	:
:	:	:
1111	0000	00000000
1111	0001	00001111
:	:	:
:	:	:
1111	1111	11100001

Table 4.24 Multiplication by means of a look-up table.

of 2 and 3 is given by the contents of location 0010 0011, which contains 00000110.

The disadvantage of this technique is the rapid increase in the size of the ROM as the number of bits in the multiplier and multiplicand increases. Table 4.25 provides the relationship

Multiplier bits n	Address bits $2n$	Lines in table 2^{2n}	Total of bits in ROM $2n \times 2^{2n}$
2	4	16	64
3	6	64	384
4	8	256	1 024
5	10	1 024	10 240
6	12	4 096	49 152
7	14	16 384	229 376
8	16	65 536	1 048 576

Table 4.25 Relationship between multiplier size and array size.

between the size of a multiplier and the number of bits a ROM requires to hold the appropriate multiplication table.

The multiplication of two 8-bit numbers requires a memory capacity of 1 048 576 bits. Forming the product of large numbers directly by look-up table is impracticable. Fortunately, it's possible to calculate the product of two $2n$-bit numbers by using an n-bit multiplier.

Before showing how we proceed with binary numbers, let's take a look at the product of two 2-digit decimal numbers, and then extend the technique to binary arithmetic.

$$34 \times 27 = (3 \times 10 + 4)(2 \times 10 + 7)$$
$$= 3 \times 2 \times 10^2 + 3 \times 7 \times 10 + 4 \times 2 \times 10 + 4 \times 7$$
$$= 6 \times 10^2 + 21 \times 10 + 8 \times 10 + 28$$
$$= 6 \times 10^2 + 29 \times 10 + 28$$
$$= 600 + 290 + 28$$
$$= 918$$

Now consider the generation of the product of two 8-bit numbers by means of 4-bit multipliers. Let the two 8-bit numbers A and B be represented by the structure in Fig. 4.34.

A_u represents the 4 most-significant bits of A, and A_l the 4 least-significant bits. We have already encountered the idea of splitting up numbers when we performed 64-bit addition on a 32-bit microprocessor. Eight-bit numbers A and B can be represented algebraically as follows:

$$A = A_u \times 16 + A_l \text{ and } B = B_u \times 16 + B_l$$

Consequently, $A \times B = (A_u \times 16 + A_l)(B_u \times 16 + B_l)$
$$= 256A_uB_u + 16A_uB_l + 16A_lB_u + A_lB_l$$

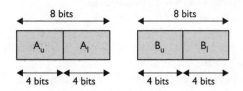

Fig. 4.34 Treating an 8-bit value as two 4-bit units.

This expression requires the evaluation of four 4-bit products (A_uB_u, A_uB_l, A_lB_u, A_lB_l), the shifting of the products by 8 or 4 positions (i.e. multiplication by 256 or 16), and the addition of four partial products. Figure 4.35 shows how this may be achieved.

4.9.2 Division

Division is the inverse of multiplication and is performed by repeatedly subtracting the *divisor* from the *dividend* until the result is either zero or less than the divisor. The number of times the divisor is subtracted is called the *quotient*, and the number left after the final subtraction is the remainder. That is:

Dividend/divisor = quotient + remainder/divisor

Alternatively, we can write:

dividend = quotient × divisor + remainder

Before we consider binary division let's examine decimal division using the traditional pencil and paper technique. The following example illustrates the division of 575 by 25.

```
        quotient
divisor |dividend          25 |575
```

The first step is to compare the two digits of the divisor with the most-significant two digits of the dividend and ask how many times the divisor goes into these two digits. The answer is 2 (i.e. $2 \times 25 = 50$), and 2×25 is subtracted from 57. The number 2 is entered as the most-significant digit of the quotient to produce the situation below.

```
       2
25 |575
      50
       7
```

The next digit of the dividend is brought down, and the divisor is compared with 75. As 75 is an exact multiple of 25, a 3 can be entered in the next position of the quotient to give the following result.

```
      23
25 |575
      50
      75
      75
      00
```

As we have examined the least-significant bit of the dividend and the divisor was an exact multiple of 75, the division is complete, and the quotient is 23 with a zero remainder.

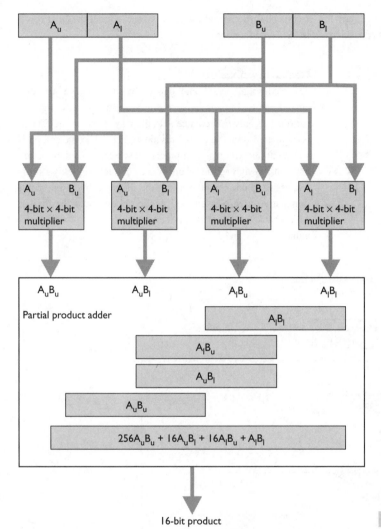

Fig. 4.35 High-speed multiplication.

A difficulty associated with division lies in estimating how many times the divisor goes into the partial dividend (i.e. 57 was divided by 25 to produce 2 remainder 7). Although people do this mentally, some way has to be found to mechanize it for application to computers. Luckily this process is easier in binary arithmetic. Consider the above example using unsigned binary arithmetic.

$$25 = 11001_2 \quad 575 = 1000111111_2$$

$$11001 \overline{)1000111111}$$
$$11001$$

The five bits of the divisor do not go into the first five bits of the dividend, so a zero is entered into the quotient and the divisor is compared with the first six bits of the dividend.

$$
\begin{array}{r}
01 \\
11001 \overline{)1000111111} \\
11001 \\
\hline
010101
\end{array}
$$

The divisor goes into the first six bits of the dividend once, to leave a partial dividend 001010(1111). The next bit of the dividend is brought down to give

$$
\begin{array}{r}
010 \\
11001 \overline{)1000111111} \\
11001 \\
\hline
010101 \\
11001
\end{array}
$$

The partial dividend is less than the divisor, and a zero is entered into the next bit of the quotient. The process continues as follows.

```
           010111
11001 1000111111
       11001
       00101011
         11001
       000100101
          11001
       000011001
          11001
       0000000000
```

In this case the partial quotient is zero, so that the final result is 10111, remainder 0.

Restoring division

The traditional pencil and paper algorithm we've just discussed can be implemented in digital form with little modification. The only real change is to the way in which the divisor is compared with the partial dividend. People do the comparison mentally, whereas computers must perform a subtraction and test the sign of the result. If the subtraction yields a positive result, a one is entered into the quotient, but if the result is negative a zero is entered in the quotient and the divisor added back to the partial dividend to restore it to its previous value.

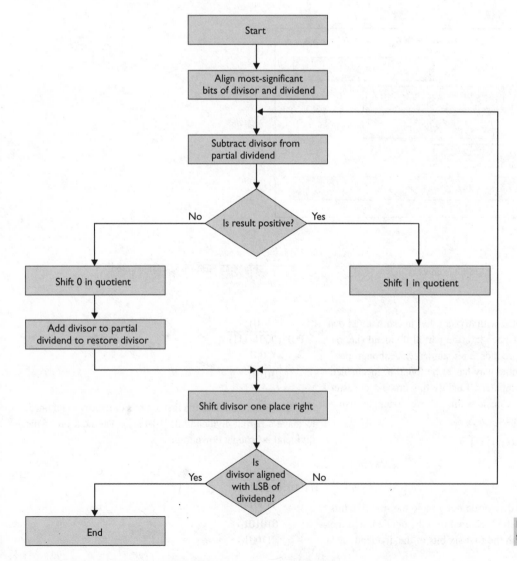

Fig. 4.36 The flowchart for restoring division.

A suitable algorithm for restoring division is as follows:

1. Align the divisor with the most-significant bit of the dividend.

2. Subtract the divisor from the partial dividend.

3. If the resulting partial dividend is negative, place a zero in the quotient and add back the divisor to restore the partial dividend.

4. If the resulting partial dividend is positive, place a one in the quotient.

5. Perform a test to determine end of division. If the divisor is aligned so that its least-significant bit corresponds to the least-significant bit of the partial dividend, stop. The final partial product is the remainder. Otherwise, continue with step 6.

6. Shift the divisor one place right. Repeat from step 2.

The flowchart corresponding to this algorithm is given in Fig. 4.36. As an example of this algorithm consider the division of 01100111_2 by 1001_2, which corresponds to 103 divided by 9 and should yield a quotient 11 and a remainder 4. Figure 4.37 illustrates the division process, step by step.

Non-restoring division

It's possible to modify the restoring division algorithm of Fig. 4.36 to achieve a reduction in the time taken to execute the division process. The *non-restoring* division algorithm is almost identical to the restoring algorithm. The only difference is that the so-called *restoring* operation is eliminated.

From the flowchart for restoring division (Fig. 4.36), it can be seen that after a partial dividend has been restored by adding back the divisor, one half the divisor is subtracted in the next cycle. This is because each cycle includes a shift-divisor-right operation that is equivalent to dividing the divisor by two. The *restore divisor* operation in the current cycle followed by the subtract half the divisor in the following cycle is equivalent to a single operation of add half the divisor to the partial dividend. That is, $D - D/2 = +D/2$, where D is the divisor.

Figure 4.38 gives the flowchart for non-restoring division. After the divisor has been subtracted from the partial dividend, the new partial dividend is tested. If it is negative, zero is shifted into the least-significant position of the quotient and half the divisor is added back to the partial dividend. If it is positive, one is shifted into the least-significant position of the quotient and half the divisor is subtracted from the partial dividend. Figure 4.39 repeats the example of Fig. 4.37 using non-restoring division.

Division by multiplication

Because both computers and microprocessors perform division less frequently than multiplication, some processors implement multiplication but not division. It is, however, possible to perform division by means of multiplication, addition, and shifting.

Suppose we wish to divide a dividend N by a divisor D to obtain a quotient Q, so that $Q = N/D$. The first step is to scale D so that it lies in the range

$$\tfrac{1}{2} \leqslant D < 1$$

Step	Description	Partial dividend	Divisor	Quotient
		01100111	00001001	00000000
1	Align	01100111	01001000	00000000
2	Subtract divisor from partial dividend	00011111	01001000	00000000
4	Result positive—shift in 1 in quotient	00011111	01001000	00000001
5	Test for end			
6	Shift divisor one place right	00011111	00100100	00000001
2	Subtract divisor from partial dividend	−00000101	00100100	00000001
3	Restore divisor, shift in 0 in quotient	00011111	00100100	00000010
5	Test for end			
6	Shift divisor one place right	00011111	00010010	00000010
2	Subtract divisor from partial dividend	00001101	00010010	00000010
4	Result positive—shift in 1 in quotient	00001101	00010010	00000101
5	Test for end			
6	Shift divisor one place right	00001101	00001001	00000101
2	Subtract divisor from partial dividend	00000100	00001001	00000101
4	Result positive—shift in 1 in quotient	00000100	00001001	00001011
5	Test for end			

Fig. 4.37 Example of restoring division for $0100111 \div 1001$.

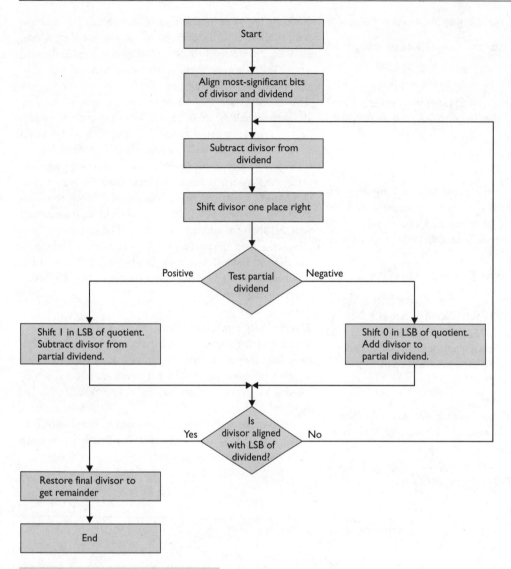

Fig. 4.38 Flowchart for non-restoring division.

This operation is carried out by shifting D left or right and recording the number of shifts—rather like normalization in floating point arithmetic. We define a new number, Z, in terms of D as $Z = 1 - D$. Because D lies between ½ and unity, it follows that Z lies between zero and ½. That is, $0 < Z \leqslant$ ½.

An elementary rule of arithmetic states that the value of the fraction remains unaltered if the top and bottom of the fraction are multiplied by the same number.

Thus, $Q = N/D = KN/KD$. Suppose that $K = 1 + Z$, then

$$Q = \frac{N}{D} = \frac{N(1+Z)}{D(1+Z)} = \frac{N(1+Z)}{(1-Z)(1+Z)} = \frac{N(1+Z)}{1-Z^2}$$

If we now repeat the process with $K = (1 + Z^2)$, we get

$$Q = \frac{N(1+Z)}{1-Z^2} \cdot \frac{1+Z^2}{1+Z^2} = \frac{N(1+Z)(1+Z^2)}{1-Z^4}$$

This process may be repeated n times with the result that

$$Q = \frac{N}{D} = \frac{N(1+Z)(1+Z^2)(1+Z^4)\dots(1+Z^{2^{n-1}})}{1-Z^{2^n}}$$

Since Z is less than unity, the value of Z^{2^n} rapidly approaches zero as n is increased. Consequently, the approximate value of

Step	Description	Partial dividend	Divisor	Quotient
		01100111	00001001	00000000
1	Align divisor	01100111	01001000	00000000
2	Subtract divisor from partial dividend	00011111	01001000	00000000
3	Shift divisor right	00011111	00100100	00000000
4	Test partial dividend—enter 1 in quotient and subtract divisor from partial dividend	−00000101	00100100	00000001
6	Test for end of process	−00000101	00100100	00000001
3	Shift divisor right	−00000101	00010010	00000001
5	Test partial dividend—enter 0 in quotient and add divisor to partial dividend	00001101	00010010	00000010
6	Test for end of process	00001101	00010010	00000010
3	Shift divisor right	00001101	00001001	00000010
4	Test partial dividend—enter 1 in quotient and subtract divisor from partial dividend	00000100	00001001	00000101
6	Test for end of process	00000100	00001001	00000101
3	Shift divisor right	00000100	0000100.1	00000101
4	Test partial dividend—enter 1 in quotient and subtract divisor from partial dividend	−00000000.1	0000100.1	00001011
6	Test for end of process	−00000000.1	0000100.1	00001011
7	Restore last divisor	00000100	0000100.1	00001011

Fig. 4.39 An example of non-restoring division for $01100111 \div 1001$.

Q is given by

$$Q = N(1+Z)(1+Z^2)(1+Z^4) \dots (1+Z^{2^{n-1}})$$

For 8-bit precision n need be only 3, and if $n=5$ the quotient yields a precision of 32 bits. As the divisor was scaled to lie between 1/2 and unity, the corresponding quotient, Q, calculated from the above formula must be scaled by the same factor to produce the desired result.

Examples

Example 1 When two n-bit two's complement integers, A and B, are added together to form a sum S, the possibility of arithmetic overflow exists. The definition of arithmetic overflow is

$$V = \overline{s_{n-1}} \cdot a_{n-1} \cdot b_{n-1} + s_{n-1} \cdot \overline{a_{n-1}} \cdot \overline{b_{n-1}}$$

where s_{n-1}, a_{n-1}, and b_{n-1} are the most-significant bits of the sum, A, and B, respectively. This equation is not used in real computers to detect overflow because it requires the storage of a_{n-1} and b_{n-1}, one of which is normally destroyed by the addition.

The actual method of detecting overflow is to compare the carry-in to the most-significant stage of the parallel adder with the carry out from the same stage. It they are different overflow is said to occur. That is:

$$V = c_n \cdot \overline{c_{n-1}} + \overline{c_n} \cdot c_{n-1}.$$

Prove that the above method of detecting overflow by examining the carry bits of the parallel adder is valid.

Solution 1 The most-significant stage of a parallel adder can be represented by the diagram in Fig. 4.40. The most-significant stage adds together bits a_{n-1}, b_{n-1}, and c_{n-1} to generate a sum bit, s_{n-1}, and a carry-out, c_n. There are four possible combinations of A and B which can be added together:

$+A + +B$
$+A + -B$
$-A + +B$
$-A + -B$

As adding two numbers of differing sign cannot result in arithmetic overflow, we need consider only the cases where A and B are both positive, or both negative.

Case 1 A and B positive, $a_{n-1}=0$, $b_{n-1}=0$.
The final stage adds $a_{n-1} + b_{n-1} + c_{n-1}$ to get c_{n-1}, because a_{n-1} and b_{n-1} are both 0 (by definition if the numbers are positive). That is, the carry-out, c_n, is 0 and $s_{n-1} = c_{n-1}$.

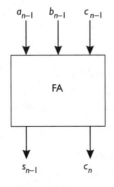

Fig. 4.40 Full adder.

We know overflow occurs if $s_{n-1} = 1$; therefore overflow occurs if the sum is negative and $\overline{c_n} \cdot c_{n-1} = 1$.

Case 2 *A* and *B* negative, $a_{n-1} = 1$, $b_{n-1} = 1$.

The final stage adds $a_{n-1} + b_{n-1} + c_{n-1} = 1 + 1 + c_{n-1}$ to get a sum, $s_{n-1} = c_{n-1}$, and a carry-out $c_n = 1$. Overflow occurs if the sum is positive and $s_{n-1} = 0$. That is, if $c_{n-1} = 0$, or if $c_n \cdot \overline{c_{n-1}} = 1$.

Considering both cases, overflow occurs if $\overline{c_n} \cdot c_{n-1} + c_n \cdot \overline{c_{n-1}} = 1$.

Example 2 A 32-bit IEEE floating point number is represented by $N = -1 \times 2^{E-127} \times 1.F$. The sign bit is bit 31, bits 30 to 23 provide the biased exponent, and bits 22 to 0 provide the 23-bit fractional mantissa.

Carry out the operation $42.6875 - 0.09375$ by first converting these numbers to the IEEE 32-bit format. Use these floating point numbers to perform the subtraction and then calculate the new floating-point value.

Solution 2 $42.6875_{10} = 101010.1011_2$
$$= 1.010101011 \times 2^5$$

This number is positive and $S = 0$. The true exponent is 5 and, therefore, the biased exponent is $5 + 127$ (i.e. actual exponent + bias) $= 132 = 10000100_2$ in 8 bits. The fractional exponent is 010101011(00000000000). Therefore 42.6875 is represented as an IEEE floating point value by 0100001 00010101011000000000000000.

Similarly, $-0.09375_{10} = -0.00011_2 = -1.1 \times 2^{-4}$. The sign bit $S = 1$ because the number is negative, and the biased exponent $E = -4 + 127 = 123 = 01111011_2$. The fractional mantissa is $F = 10000000000000000000000$. The representation of -0.09375 is therefore

10111101110000000000000000000000

These two numbers are stored as

01000010001010101100000000000000 and
10111101110000000000000000000000, respectively.

In order to perform the addition we have to unpack these numbers to sign + biased exponent + mantissa.

First number   0   10000100   01010101100000000000000
Second number 1   01111011   10000000000000000000000

We must insert the leading 1 into the fractional mantissa to get the true mantissa.

First number   0   10000100   **1**01010101100000000000000
Second number 1   01111011   **1**1000000000000000000000000

In order to add or subtract the numbers, the exponents must be the same (we can work with biased exponents). The second number's exponent is smaller by $10000100 - 0111011 = 00001001_2 = 9_{10}$. We increase the second exponent by 9 and shift the mantissa right 9 times to get

First number   0   10000100   **1**01010101100000000000000
Second number 1   10000100   00000000**1**1000000000000000000000000

We can now subtract mantissas to get

101010100011000000000000

The result is positive with a biased exponent of 10000100 and a mantissa 1.0101010011000000000000. This number would be stored as

Result   0   10000100   0101010011000000000000
(we've dropped the leading 1 mantissa)

This number is equal to $+2^5 \times 1.0101010011 = 101010.10011 = 42.59375$.

Summary

In this chapter we have looked at how numerical information is represented inside a digital computer. We have concentrated on the binary representation of numbers, since digital computers handle binary information efficiently. Both positive and negative numbers must be stored and manipulated by a computer. We have looked at some of the ways in which digital computers represent negative numbers.

Since digital computers sometimes have to work with very large and very small numbers, we have covered some of the ways in which the so-called 'scientific notation' is used to encode both large and small numbers. These numbers are stored in the form of a mantissa and a magnitude (i.e. the number of zeros before/after the binary point), and are called floating point numbers. Until recently, almost every computer used its own representation of floating point numbers. Today, the IEEE standard for the format of floating point numbers has replaced most of these *ad hoc* floating point formats.

At the end of this chapter we have briefly introduced the operations of multiplication and division and have demonstrated how they are mechanized in digital computers.

Problems

1. Convert the following decimal integers to their natural binary equivalents.
   a. 15   d. 4090
   b. 42   e. 40 900
   c. 235   f. 65 530

2. Convert the following natural binary numbers to their decimal equivalents.
   a. 110   c. 110111
   b. 1110110   d. 11111110111

3. Complete the table below.

Decimal	Binary	Octal	Hexadecimal	Base 7
37 73				
	10101010 11011011101			
		42 772		
			256 ABC	
				12 666

4. Convert the following base five numbers into their base nine equivalents. For example, $23_5 = 14_9$.
   a. 24   b. 144   c. 444   d. 1234

5. Convert the following decimal numbers to their binary equivalents. Calculate the answer to five binary places and round the result up or down as necessary.
   a. 1.5   d. 1024.0625
   b. 1.1   e. 3.141592
   c. $\frac{1}{3}$ f. $1/\sqrt{2}$

6. Convert the following binary numbers to their decimal equivalents.
   a. 1.1   d. 11011.101010
   b. 0.0001   e. 111.111111
   c. 101.101   f. 10.1111101

7. Calculate the error (both absolute and as a percentage) if the following decimal fractions are converted to binary fractions, correct to five binary places. Convert the decimal number to six binary digits and then round up the 5th bit if the 6th bit is a 1.

a. 0.675   d. 0.1
b. 0.42   e. 0.01
c. 0.1975   f. 0.001

8. Complete the following table. Calculate all values to four places after the radix point.

Decimal	Binary	Octal	Hexadecimal	Base 7
0.37 0.73				
	11011.011101 111.1011			
		0.70 1.101		
			2.56 AB.C	
				1.2 66.6

9. An electronics engineer has invented a new logic device which has three states: $-1, 0, +1$. These states are represented by $\bar{1}$, 0, and 1, respectively. This arrangement may be used to form a balanced ternary system with a radix 3, but where the *trits* represent $-1, 0, +1$ instead of 0, 1, 2. The following examples illustrate how this system works.

Ternary	Balanced ternary	Decimal
11	$1\bar{1}$	4
12	$1\bar{1}1$	5
22	$10\bar{1}$	8
1012	$111\bar{1}$	32

Write down the first 15 decimal numbers in the balanced ternary base.

10. The results of an experiment fall in the range -4 to $+9$. A scientist reads the results into a computer and then processes them. The scientist decides to use a 4-bit binary code to represent each of the possible inputs. Devise a 4-bit code capable of representing numbers in the range -4 to $+9$.

11. Convert the following decimal numbers into BCD.
    a. 1237
    b. 4632
    c. -9417

12. Perform the following additions on the BCD numbers using BCD arithmetic.
    a. 0010100010010001   b. 1001100101111000
        0110100001100100   1001100110000010

13. The 16-bit hexadecimal value $C123_{16}$ can represent many things. What does this number represent, assuming that it is:
    a. An unsigned binary integer?
    b. A signed two's complement binary integer?
    c. A sign and magnitude binary integer?
    d. An unsigned binary fraction?

14. Convert the following 8-bit binary values into their Gray code equivalents.
    a. 10101010
    b. 11110000
    c. 00111011

15. Convert the following 8-bit Gray code values into their binary equivalents.
    a. 01010000
    b. 11110101
    c. 01001010

16. What are the Hamming distances between the following pairs of binary values?
    a. 00101111   b. 11100111
       01011101   01110101

    c. 01010011   d. 11111111
       00011011   00000111

    e. 11011101   f. 0011111
       11011110   0000110

17. Decode the Huffman code below, assuming that the valid codes are $P = 0$, $Q = 10$, $R = 110$, and $S = 111$. How many bits would be required if P, Q, R, and S had been encoded as 00, 01, 10, 11, respectively?
    000001110111000000101111111101010001111100010

18. The hexadecimal dump from part of a microcomputer's memory is as follows.
    0000 4265 6769 6EFA 47FE BB87 2686 3253 7A29
    0010 698F E000

    The dump is made up of a series of strings of characters, each string being composed of nine groups of 4 hexadecimal characters. The first four characters in each string provide the starting address of the following 16 bytes. For example, the first byte in the second string (i.e. $C9) is at address $0010 and the second byte (i.e. $8F) is at address $0011.

    The 20 bytes of data in the two strings represent the following sequence of items:

    a. Five consecutive ASCII-encoded characters
    b. One unsigned 16-bit integer
    c. One two's complement 16-bit integer

d. One unsigned 16-bit fraction
e. One six-digit natural BCD integer
f. One 16-bit unsigned fixed-point number with a 12-bit integer part and a 4-bit fraction.
g. One 4-byte floating point number with a sign bit and true fraction plus an exponent biased by 64.

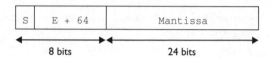

Decode the hexadecimal data, assuming that it is interpreted as above.

19. A message can be coded to protect it from unauthorized readers by EORing it with a binary sequence of the same length to produce an encoded message. The encoded message is decoded by EORing it with the same sequence that was used to decode it. If the ASCII-encoded message used to generate the code is ALANCLEMENTS, what does the following encoded message (expressed in hexadecimal form) mean?

    09 09 0D 02 0C 6C 12 02 17 02 10 73

20. A single-bit error-detecting code appends a parity bit to a source word to produce a code word. An even parity bit is chosen to make the total number of ones in the code word even (this includes the parity bit itself). For example, the source words 0110111 and 1100110 would be coded as 01101111 and 11001100, respectively. In these cases the parity bit has been located in the LSB position.

    Indicate which of the following hexadecimal numbers have parity errors.

    $00, $07, $FF, $A5, $5A, $71, $FE.

21. A single parity bit error-detecting code will detect all single bit errors in a code word. What other classes of error does this type of error detecting code detect? What classes of error will not be detected?

22. A checksum digit is the least-significant digit formed when a series of numbers are added together. For example, the decimal checksum of the sequence 98731 is 8 because $9 + 8 + 7 + 3 + 1 = 28$ and 8 is the least-significant digit. Similarly, the checksum of the hexadecimal sequence A3, 02, 49, FF is ED because $A3 + 02 + 49 + FF = 1ED$.

    The purpose of a checksum is to detect errors in a sequence of digits after they have been transmitted or stored in memory or on tape. The following hexadecimal sequences are terminated by a checksum. Which, if any, are in error?

a. 0001020304050F
b. 11223344556675
c. FFA32415751464

The position of the checksum in the above three strings is the rightmost byte. Does it matter where the checksum is located? What happens if there is an error in the checksum itself?

23. What is the meaning of Hamming distance?

24. The $H_{7,4}$ Hamming code is written $I_4 \, I_3 \, I_2 \, C_3 \, I_1 \, C_2 \, C_1$, where I_i = source bit i, and C_i = check bit i. The three Hamming check bits are calculated from the parity equations:

$C_3 = I_2 \oplus I_3 \oplus I_4$
$C_2 = I_1 \oplus I_3 \oplus I_4$
$C_1 = I_1 \oplus I_2 \oplus I_4$

Show that no two valid codewords differ by less than three bits. Prove that an error in any single bit can be used to locate the position of the error and, therefore, to correct it.

25. Examine the following $H_{7,4}$ Hamming code words and determine whether the word is a valid code word. If it isn't valid, what should the correct code word have been (assuming that only 1 error is present)?
a. 0000000
b. 1100101
c. 0010111

26. Convert the following image into a quadtree.

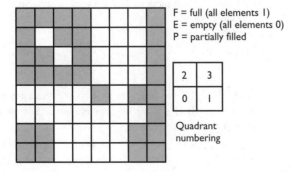

F = full (all elements 1)
E = empty (all elements 0)
P = partially filled

2	3
0	1

Quadrant numbering

27. Convert the following image into a quadtree.

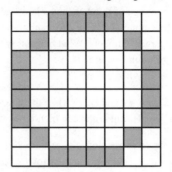

28. Almost all computer hardware courses include a section on number bases and the conversion of numbers between bases. Does the base in which a computer represents numbers really matter to the computer user or even to the student of computer science?

29. Perform the following binary additions:

a. 10110	b. 100111	c. 11011011
+ 101	111001	10111011
	101101	00101011
		01111111

30. Perform the following octal additions:

a. 42	b. 3357	c. 777	d. 437
+ 53	+ 2741	543	426
		+ 420	772
			+ 747

31. Perform the following hexadecimal additions:

a. 42	b. 3357	c. 777	d. ABCD
+ 53	+ 2741	543	F E 1 0
		+ 420	+ 1 2 3 A

32. Using 8-bit arithmetic throughout, express the following decimal numbers in two's complement binary form:
a. −4   d. −25   g. −127
b. −5   e. −42   h. −111
c. 0   f. −128

33. Perform the following decimal subtractions in 8-bit two's complement arithmetic. Note that some of the answers will result in arithmetic overflow. Indicate where overflow has occurred.

a. 20	b. 127	c. 127	d. 5
−5	− 126	− 128	−20

e. 69	f. −20	g. −127	h. −42
−42	−111	−2	+69
			+120

34. Using two's complement binary arithmetic with a 12-bit word, write down the range of numbers capable of being represented (in both decimal and binary formats) by giving the smallest and largest numbers. What happens when the smallest and largest numbers are:
    a. incremented?   b. decremented?

35. Distinguish between *overflow* and *carry* when these terms are applied to two's complement arithmetic on n-bit words.

36. Write down an algebraic expression giving the value of the n-bit integer $N = a_{n-1}, a_{n-2}, \ldots, a_1, a_0$ for the case where N represents a two's complement number.

    Hence prove that (in two's complement notation) the representation of a signed binary number in $n+1$ bits may be derived from its representation in n bits by repeating the leftmost bit. For example, if $n = -12 = 10100$ in five bits, $n = -12 = 110100$ in six bits.

37. Perform the additions below on 4-bit binary numbers.
    a. 0011   b. 1111   c. 0110   d. 1100
      $+1100$ $+0001$ $+0111$ $+1010$

    In each case, regard the numbers as being (i) unsigned integer, (ii) two's complement integer, and (iii) sign and magnitude integer. Calculate the answer and comment on it where necessary.

38. Add together the following pairs of numbers. Each number is represented in a 6-bit sign-and-magnitude format. Your answer should also be in sign-and-magnitude format. Convert each pair of numbers (and result) into decimal form in order to check your answer.
    a. 000111   b. 100111
       010101   010101

    c. 010101   d. 111111
       000111   000001

    e. 110111   f. 011111
       110111   000110

39. Write down the largest base 5 positive integer in n digits and the largest base 7 number in m digits. It is necessary to represent n-digit base 5 numbers in base 7. What is the minimum number m of digits needed to represent all possible n-digit base 5 numbers? *Hint*: the largest m-digit base 7 number should be greater than, or equal to, the largest n-digit base 5 number.

40. A 4-bit binary adder adds together two 4-bit numbers, A and B, to produce a 4-bit sum, S, and a single-bit carry-out C. What is the range of outputs (i.e. largest and smallest values) that the adder is capable of producing? Give your answer in both binary and decimal forms.

    An adder is designed to add together two binary-coded decimal (BCD) digits to produce a single digit sum and a 1-bit carry out. What is the range of valid outputs that this circuit may produce?

    The designer of the BCD adder decides to use a pure binary adder to add together two BCD digits as if they were pure 4-bit binary numbers. Under what circumstances does the binary adder give the correct BCD result? Under what circumstances is the result incorrect (i.e. the 4-bit binary result differs from the required BCD result)?

    What algorithm must the designer apply to the 4-bit output of the binary adder to convert it to a BCD adder?

41. Design a 4-bit parallel adder to add together two 4-bit natural binary-encoded integers. Assume that the propagation delay of a signal through a gate is t ns. For your adder, calculate the time taken to add:
    a. 0000 to 0001
    b. 0001 to 0001
    c. 0001 to 1111

42. Design a full subtractor circuit which will subtract bit X together with a borrow-in bit B_i from bit Y to produce a difference bit $D = Y - X - B_i$, and a borrow-out B_o.

43. In the *negabinary* system an i-bit binary integer, N, is expressed using positional notation as:

    $$N = a_0 \times -1^0 \times 2^0 + a_1 \times -1^1 \times 2^1 + \cdots + a_{i-1} \times -1^{i-1} \times 2^{i-1}$$

    This is the same as conventional natural 8421 binary weighted numbers, except that alternate positions have the additional weighting $+1$ and -1.
    For example, $1101 = (-1 \times 1 \times 8) + (+1 \times 1 \times 4)$
    $$+ (-1 \times 0 \times 2) + (+1 \times 1 \times 1)$$
    $$= -8 + 4 + 1 = -3$$
    The following 4-bit numbers are represented in negabinary form. Convert them to their decimal equivalents.
    a. 0000
    b. 0101
    c. 1010
    d. 1111

44. Perform the following additions on 4-bit negabinary numbers. The result is a 6-bit negabinary value. You must construct your own algorithm.
    a. 0000   b. 1010   c. 1101   d. 1111
      $+0001$ $+0101$ 1011   1111

45. Convert the following signed decimal numbers into their 6-bit negabinary counterparts
    a. 4   b. −7   c. +7   d. 10

46. What is the range of values that can be expressed as an n-bit negabinary value? That is, what is the largest positive decimal number and what is the largest negative decimal number that can be converted into an n-bit negabinary form?

47. A computer has a 24-bit word length, which, for the purpose of floating point operations, is divided into an 8-bit biased exponent and a 16-bit two's complement mantissa. Write down the range of numbers capable of being represented in this format and their precision.

48. Explain the meaning of the following terms (in the context of floating point arithmetic).
    a. Biased exponent
    b. Fractional part
    c. Packed
    d. Unpacked
    e. Range
    f. Precision
    g. Normalization
    h. Exponent overflow/underflow

49. An IEEE standard 32-bit floating point number has the format: $N = -1^S \times 1.F \times 2^{E-127}$, where S is the sign bit, F is the fractional mantissa, and E is the biased exponent.
    a. (i) Convert the decimal number 1000.708 into the IEEE format for floating point numbers.
       (ii) Convert the decimal number 100.125 into the IEEE format for floating point numbers.
    b. Describe the steps that take place when two IEEE floating point numbers are added together. You should start with the two packed floating point numbers and end with the packed sum.
    c. Perform the subtraction 1000.708 − 100.25 using the two IEEE-format binary floating point numbers you obtained for 1000.708 and 100.25 in part a of this question. You should begin the calculation with the packed floating point representations of these numbers and end with the packed result.

50. Convert the 32-bit IEEE format number $C33BD000_{16}$ into its decimal representation.

51. The two's complement fractional part of a normalized floating point number X is constrained to lie within one of the three ranges

$$-1 \leqslant X < -\frac{1}{2} \quad \text{or} \quad X = 0 \quad \text{or} \quad \frac{1}{2} \leqslant X < 1$$

Explain why this is so and illustrate your answer with a 5-bit mantissa.

52. The following numbers are to be represented by three significant digits in the base stated. In each case perform the operation by both truncation and rounding, and state the relative error created by the operation.
    a. 0.1100100_2 b. 0.0011011_2
    c. $0.1A34_{16}$ d. $0.12AA_{16}$

53. We can perform *division by multiplication* to calculate $Q = N/D$. The iterative expression for Q is given by

$$Q = N(1+Z)(1+Z^2)(1+Z^4)\ldots(1+Z^{2^{n-1}})$$

where $Z = 1 - D$.

If $N = 50_{10}$, and $D = 0.74_{10}$, calculate the value of Q. Evaluate Q using 1, 2, 3, and 4 terms in the expression.

Chapter 5

The central processing unit

The *central processing unit* or CPU lies at the heart of all digital computers and is responsible for reading a program's instructions from memory, executing them, and controlling the computer's input/output devices. That is, the CPU includes all the components required to fetch instructions from memory, decode them, execute them, and transfer any data to and from memory or peripherals. The CPU excludes the memory that holds instructions and data and all the input/output devices.

You might see the words *computer*, CPU, *processor*, *microprocessor*, and *microcomputer* in this and other texts. The part of a computer that actually executes a program is called a central processing unit or more simply a *processor*. A *microprocessor* is a CPU fabricated on a single chip of silicon. A computer that is constructed around a *microprocessor* can be called a *microcomputer*. These terms are sometimes used interchangeably.

In this chapter we look at the structure or *architecture* of a hypothetical CPU based on a real microprocessor. We also examine the CPU's control unit, which is responsible for reading an instruction from memory and causing the appropriate actions to take place. A CPU and its control unit can be constructed entirely from the logic elements, flip-flops, and buses using gates with tri-state outputs, which we introduced in Chapters 2 and 3.

To reinforce our description of the CPU we provide a program written in C that simulates a simple CPU. We have written the simulator in a minimal subset of C because most readers will be familiar with at least one high-level language and should be able to follow the code with little difficulty. You can extend the simulator to add further facilities to the architecture and to investigate the design of a processor.

At the end of this chapter we show how the performance of computers can be increased without resorting to new technologies or CPU architectures. We introduce the *multiprocessor* that increases the power of a computer by operating two or more CPUs in parallel.

In the next chapter we look at an actual CPU in much greater detail and show how programs are written in the processor's native language, called *assembly language*. We use the popular 68000 microprocessor to illustrate the CPU. In Chapter 7 we turn our attention to the structure and operation of a different type of CPU called the *reduced instruction set computer* or RISC. Computers based on RISC principles increase performance by employing regular instruction sets, reducing the number of times the processor has to access external memory, and by executing instructions in parallel.

Machine levels

An object can be viewed in more than one way. Consider an airline pilot. Passengers see the pilot as an agent responsible for transferring them from one airport to another. The pilot's colleagues see him or her as a friend with whom they relate at the personal level. The pilot's doctor doesn't see a pilot; the doctor sees a complex biological mechanism. It's exactly the same with computers—you can view a computer in different ways.

Suppose you are using a computer to run a spreadsheet. As far as you're concerned, the machine is a 'spreadsheet machine'; that is, it behaves exactly as if it were an electronic spreadsheet. You could construct an electronic device to *directly* handle spreadsheets, but no one does. Instead they construct a computer and run a program to *simulate* a spreadsheet.

Figure 5.1 illustrates the way in which a computer can be viewed in different ways or levels. The outer level is the *applications* level that the end user sees. This level represents a *virtual* spreadsheet because, to all intents and purposes, the machine looks like a spreadsheet machine. A spreadsheet, a word processor, or a game is probably written in a high-level language such as Pascal, C, or Java. You can view a computer as a machine that directly executes the instructions of a high-level language. In Fig. 5.1 the next layer down is the *high-level language* layer.

Although it's possible to construct a computer that directly executes a high-level language, most practical computers execute *machine code*, which is a primitive language (expressed in binary code) that performs simple operations such as addition and subtraction. The statements and constructs of

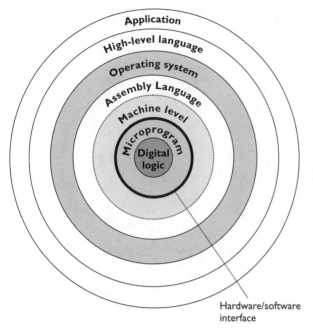

Hardware/software interface

Fig. 5.1 Machine levels and virtual architectures.

These micro-operations are concerned with the transfer of inform-ation between functional units such as register and buses. The sequences of micro-operations that interpret each machine level instruction are stored in *firmware* within the computer. Firmware is a term for read-only memory containing programs or other data that controls the processor's operations and which is not normally modified. In Chapter 7 we will discover that RISC processors don't use a microprogram.

The innermost level of the computer is the *digital logic* level that consists of the gates, flip-flops, and buses. There is no program at this level and the individual logic elements are hardwired to each other; that is, the connections between elements are fixed. You could, in fact, go even deeper into the computer because there is a *physical layer* below the digital logic layer. However, we're not interested in the physical layer because that's the province of the semiconductor engineer and physicist. In this chapter we are concerned with the machine level and microprogram layers.

5.1 Introduction to the CPU

Before we look at the way in which a CPU works, it is important to understand the relationship between the CPU, the memory, and the program. Let's take a simple program to calculate the area of a circle and see how the computer deals with it. In what follows the computer is a hypothetical machine devoid of all the nasty complications associated with reality. Throughout this section we assume that we are operating at the machine level.

We know that the area of a circle, A, can be calculated from the formula $\pi \times r^2$. When people evaluate the area of a circle, they automatically perform many of the calculations at a *subconscious* level. However, when they come to write programs, they must tell the computer exactly what it must do, step by step. To illustrate this point, take a look at the expression πr^2. We write r^2, but we mean a number, which we have given the symbol r, multiplied by itself. We never confuse the *symbol r* with the *value* that we give to r when we evaluate the expression. This may seem an obvious point, but students often have great difficulty when they come to the concepts of an address and data in assembly language. Although people never confuse the symbol for the radius (i.e. r) and its value, say 4 cm, you must remember that an address (i.e. the place where the value of r is stored) and data (i.e. the value of r) are both binary quantities inside the computer.

Figure 5.2 illustrates the relationship between the program, memory, and processor. The memory has been divided into

a high-level language are translated into sequences of machine code instructions by a *compiler*. The machine code layer in Fig. 5.1 is responsible for executing machine code.

Figure 5.1 shows two layers between the machine level and high-level language level. The *assembly language* level sits on top of the machine level and represents the human-readable form of the machine code; for example, the machine code instruction 1100101010101001 might be represented in assembly language as `ADD D0,D1`.

In Fig. 5.1 there is an additional layer between the assembly language layer and the high-level language layer called the *operating system* level. Strictly speaking, this layer isn't like the other layers. The operating system runs on top of the machine code and assembly language layers above provides facilities required by higher-level layers (e.g. memory management and the control of peripherals).

Below the machine-level layer is the *microprogram* layer. A heavy line separates these two layers in Fig. 5.1 because the programmer or user can access all the layers above this line. The two innermost layers (microprogram and digital logic) are not accessible to the programmer.

The microprogram layer is concerned with the primitive operations that take place inside the computer during the execution of a machine code operation. For example, an `ADD D0,D1` machine-level instruction is interpreted by executing a sequence of micro-operations inside the computer.

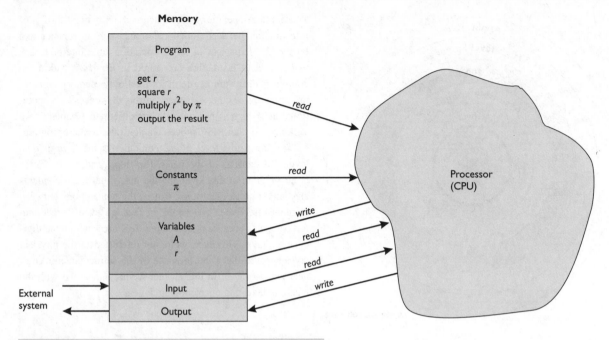

Fig. 5.2 The relationship between the memory, processor, and program.

five parts: program, constants, variables, input, and output. The program is composed of the sequence of operations to be carried out, or *executed*. The constants (in this case there is only one—π) are numbers used by the program but which do not change during its execution. The variables represent numbers created and modified by the program. When the program squares r, it reads the value of the number in the memory location it has called r, squares it, and puts the result back in the same location. Thus the original value of r is lost. If the programmer wishes to retain the original value of r, rather than by overwriting it with r^2, memory locations must be reserved for both r and r^2.

Although the variables (i.e. the values held in memory locations) are often numerical quantities, there is no reason why this must always be so. For example, the variables used by a word processor are the letters (and other symbols) of the text being manipulated. Indeed, it is perfectly possible for the variable to be another program. That is, one program can operate on, or modify, another program.

Any program must be able to communicate with the outside world, otherwise all its efforts are to no effect. We have labeled two memory locations in Fig. 5.2 *input* and *output*. Reading from the input location causes information to be taken from an input device (say a keyboard), and writing to the output location causes information to be moved from the computer to an output device (say a display). Regarding input

and output as memory locations is not entirely fictional—we'll later discover that many computers really do perform all input/output transactions via the memory.

The processor may either read data from a memory location or write data to a memory location. Of the five regions of memory described above, three are *read-only*, one is *write-only*, and one can be read from or written to.

5.1.1 The memory

We can't describe the CPU without a little further discussion of the memory that holds programs and data, and the notation we are going to use to define operations taking place within a computer. We will be taking a much more detailed look at memory systems later in this book.

Figure 5.3 illustrates the so-called *random access memory* system (i.e. RAM). This memory appears as a block of sequential locations, each of which contains a data element. Each location has a unique address that defines the location of the data. For example, in Fig. 5.3 we can say that location number 5 contains the value 27.

5.1.2 Register transfer language

We are going to adopt shorthand called *register transfer language* (RTL) to help us to explain how the CPU operates. Essentially, RTL is an algebraic notation that describes how

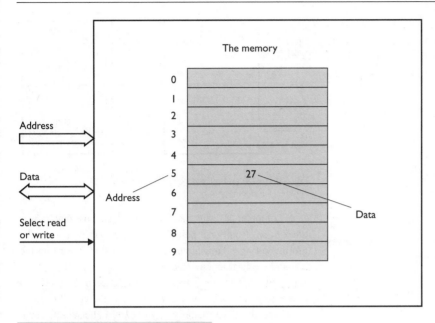

The memory

Address

Data

Address

Data

Select read
or write

Fig. 5.3 The random access memory system.

information is accessed from memories and registers and how it is operated on. RTL is just a *notation* and not a programming language.

RTL uses variables just like any other computer language; for example, one or more letters (or letters followed by numbers) denote registers or storage locations. It's very important to distinguish between a memory location and its contents. RTL uses square brackets to indicate the *contents* of a memory location; for example, the expression [D0]=Monday is interpreted as *the contents of D0 contain the value of Monday*.

A left or *backward* arrow ← indicates the transfer of data. The left-hand side of an expression denotes the *destination* of the data defined by the *source* of the data defined on the right-hand side of the expression. For example, the expression

[MAR] ← [PC]

indicates that the contents of the program counter, PC, are transferred (i.e. copied) into the memory address register, MAR. We will soon see what the terms PC and MAR mean. Note that the contents of the PC are not modified by this operation. In Fig. 5.3 the operation

[3] ← [5]

means copy the contents of location 5 to location 3. If we were writing a program, memory locations 3 and 5 would have been given *symbolic* names, say, x and y, respectively.

A symbolic name is the name given to a number by the programmer—people like to deal with meaningful names rather than, say, the actual numeric addresses of data in memory. The operation [3]←[5] tells us what's happening at the *micro* level—at the high level this operation might be written in the rather more familiar form

x=y;

Consider the RTL expression

[PC] ← [PC]+1

which indicates that the number in the *program counter*, PC, is increased by 1; that is, the contents of the program counter are read, 1 is added, and the result is copied into the PC.

We have used the notation [x] to indicate the contents of memory location x. In future we will refer to the computer's memory as *M* and indicate the contents of location x by the more formal notation

[M(x)]

That is, [M(x)] represents the data stored at address x in the memory. In Fig. 5.3 we can write [M(5)]=27. Suppose the computer executes an operation that stores the contents of the program counter in location 20 in the memory. We can represent this action in RTL as

[M(20)] ← [PC]

While we're on the subject of notation, we should point out that computer programs and computer texts often adopt the convention that a number prefixed by % indicates a binary value and a number prefixed by $ indicates a hexadecimal value. For example, we may write

```
[PC] ← 1026
[PC] ← %10000000010
[PC] ← $402
```

All these expressions mean exactly the same thing. Such conventions for indicating number bases come from a time when computer input and output devices couldn't deal with superscripts and subscripts. Today we can write 400_{16} to indicate the hexadecimal base, but computer languages haven't yet fully exploited all the typographical features now available.

As a final example of RTL notation, consider the following RTL expressions.

(a) $[M(20)] = 6$

(b) $[M(20)] ← 6$

(c) $[M(20)] ← [M(6)]$

(d) $[M(20)] ← [M(6)] + 3$

The first states that the contents of memory location 20 are equal to the number 6. The second example states that the number 6 is put into (copied into, or loaded into) memory location 20. The third example indicates that the contents of memory location 6 are copied into memory location 20. The last example reads the contents of location 6, adds 3 to it, and stores the result in location 20. As you can see, the '←' RTL symbol is equivalent to the '=' symbol in the high-level language Pascal. Remember that RTL is not a computer language; it is a *notation* used to define computer operations.

5.2 Structure of the CPU

Figure 5.4 provides a more detailed view of the *central processing unit* and *memory* system. The same memory system stores both the program and the data acted on or created by the program. It isn't necessary to store both the program and data in the *same* memory. However, for largely economic reasons, most computers do store programs and data in a single memory system. Such computers are called *von Neumann machines* in honor of one of the pioneers of the computer— John von Neumann.

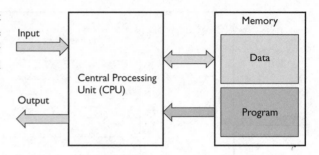

Fig. 5.4 The general-purpose digital computer.

A computer is little more than a black box that moves *information* from one point to another and processes the information as it goes along. By 'information' we mean the data and the instructions held inside the computer. Figure 5.4 shows two *information-carrying* paths between the CPU and its memory. The heavily shaded lower path with the single arrowhead from the memory to the CPU indicates the route taken by the computer's *program*. The CPU reads the sequence of commands that make up a program one by one from its memory.

The upper path (lightly shaded in Fig. 5.4) with arrows at *both* its ends transfers data between the CPU and memory. The *program* being executed controls the flow of information along the data path. This data path is *bi-directional*, because data can flow in two directions. During a *write cycle* data generated by the program flows from the CPU to the memory where it is stored for later use. During a *read cycle* the CPU requests the retrieval of a data item, which is transferred from the memory to the CPU.

Suppose an instruction ADD X,Y,Z corresponding to the operation $x = y + z$ is stored in memory. The CPU must first fetch this instruction from memory and bring it to the CPU. Once the CPU has analyzed or *decoded* the instruction, the CPU has to get the values of '*x*' and '*y*' from memory. The actual values of *x* and *y* are read from the memory and sent to the CPU. The CPU adds these values and sends the result, *z*, back to memory for storage. Remember that X, Y, and Z are symbolic names for the locations of data in memory.

In practice few computers are constructed with two independent information paths between the CPU and its memory as Fig. 5.4 suggests. Most computers have only one path along which information flows between the CPU and its memory—data and instructions have to take turns flowing along this path. Two paths are shown in Fig. 5.4, simply to emphasize that there are two *types* of information stored in the memory (i.e. the *instructions* that make up a program and the *data* used by the program). Indeed, forcing data and instructions to share the same path sometimes creates congestion on the data bus between the CPU and memory that slows the computer down. This effect is called the *von Neumann bottleneck*.

5.2.1 **The address path**

We now look at the structure of a CPU. In order to keep things simple, we will build up a CPU step by step rather than presenting everything all at once. Figure 5.5 provides the block diagram of part of a CPU. In this diagram only the address paths and the paths needed to read an instruction from memory are shown for clarity. That is, we have omitted the data paths required to execute instructions. Address paths are shown in black and the parts of the CPU we're currently interested in are shaded.

The address paths represent highways along which addresses flow from one part of the CPU to another. An address is a number representing the location of an item of data within the memory. In terms of the example in which we evaluated the area of a circle, *r* is the symbolic address of the radius. There are two types of information flow in a

computer: address and data (the latter is usually taken to mean instructions, constants, and variables).

5.2.2 **Reading the instruction**

Before the CPU can execute an instruction, the instruction must first be brought to the CPU from the computer's memory. We begin our description of the way in which a program is executed with the CPU's *program counter*. The expression 'program counter' (also called instruction counter or location counter) is rather a misnomer. The program counter doesn't count programs or anything else, but contains the address of the next instruction in memory to be executed. The program counter can be said to *point to* the next instruction to be executed. If, for example, [PC] = 5 (i.e. the PC contains the number 5), the next instruction to be executed is to be found in memory location 5. The concept of a *pointer* (i.e. a variable that tells you where something is) is a fundamental concept in computer science.

Fetching an instruction begins with the contents of the program counter being moved to the memory address register (i.e. [MAR] ← [PC]). Once the contents of the program counter have been transferred to the memory address register,

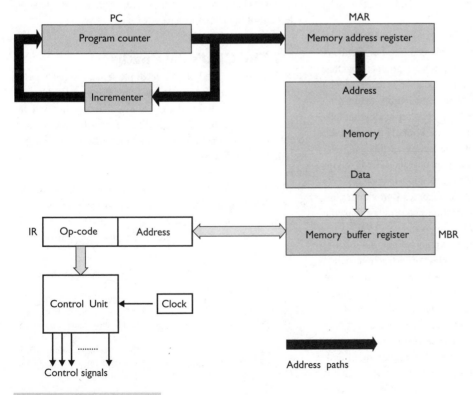

Fig. 5.5 The CPU's address paths.

the contents of the program counter are incremented (increased by 1) and moved back to the program counter; that is,

`[PC] ← [PC] + 1`

After this operation the program counter points to the next instruction while the current instruction is being executed.

The *memory address register*, MAR, holds the address of the location in the memory into which data is being written in a write cycle, or from which data is being read in a read cycle. At this stage, the MAR contains a copy of the (previous) contents of the PC. When a *memory read cycle* is performed, the contents of the memory location specified by the MAR are read from the memory and transferred to the *memory buffer register*, MBR. We can represent this read operation in RTL terms as

`[MBR] ← [M([MAR])]`

We interpret the expression `[M([MAR])]` as *the contents of the memory whose address is given by the contents of the MAR*. The memory buffer register is a temporary holding place for data received from memory in a read cycle, or for data to be transferred to memory in a write cycle. Some texts refer to the MBR as the *memory data register*, MDR. At this point, the MBR contains the bit pattern of the instruction to be executed.

The instruction is next moved from the MBR to the *instruction register*, IR, where it is divided into two fields. A *field* is a part of a word in which the bits are grouped together into a logical entity; for example, a person's name can be divided into two fields: Given name and Family name. One field in the IR contains the *operation code* (op-code) that tells the CPU what operation is to be carried out. The other field, called the *operand field*, contains the address of the data to be used by the instruction. Sometimes the operand field is redundant, as not all op-codes refer to a location in memory. We shall soon see that the operand field can also provide a constant to be employed by the operation code, rather than the address of the data required by the op-code.

Here it is necessary to make two points. First, the instructions we are describing belong to a class of instructions called *one-address* instructions. That is, an instruction consists of only two fields: the op-code and the operand. A typical instruction might be   ADD   x. There are other classes of instruction (e.g. two-address and three-address instructions) that have two or more operands. The second point worth noting is that the CPU we are describing is highly simplified. Some real machines have such long instruction formats that it is necessary to break up an instruction and store it in consecutive memory locations. This means that the CPU must

perform two or more read cycles to fetch an instruction from memory.

The control unit, CU, takes the op-code from the instruction register, together with a stream of clock pulses, and generates signals that control all parts of the CPU. The time between individual clock pulses is in the range 2 ns to 1000 ns (i.e. 2×10^{-9} to 10^{-6} s). The control unit is responsible for moving the contents of the program counter into the MAR, executing a read cycle, and moving the contents of the MBR to the IR. Later we look at the control unit in more detail and demonstrate how it goes about interpreting an op-code.

The sequence of operations in which the next instruction is moved from memory to the instruction register is known as an instruction *fetch phase*. All instructions in a conventional computer are executed in a two-phase operation called a *fetch–execute cycle*. During the fetch phase, the instruction is read from memory and decoded by the control unit. The fetch phase is followed by an *execute phase* in which the control unit generates all the signals necessary to execute the instruction. Table 5.1 puts together the sequence of operations taking place in a fetch phase. In Table 5.1 FETCH is a label that serves to indicate a particular line in the sequence of operations. The notation IR(op-code) means the operation code field of the instruction register.

5.2.3 The CPU's data paths

Now that we've sorted out the fetch phase, let's see what else we need to actually execute instructions. Figure 5.6 adds new data paths to the simplified CPU of Fig. 5.5, together with an address path from the address field of the instruction register to the memory address register. Other modifications to Fig. 5.5 included in Fig. 5.6 are the addition of a data register, D0, and an *arithmetic and logical unit*, ALU.

The *data register* called D0 holds temporary or intermediate results during a calculation. A data register is necessary in a one-address machine, because *dyadic* operations with two operands (e.g. +, −, *, /, etc.) take place on one operand

FETCH	`[MAR] ← [PC]`	Copy contents of the PC to the MAR
	`[PC]  ← [PC] + 1`	Increment the contents of the PC
	`[MBR] ← [M([MAR])]`	Read the instruction from memory
	`[IR]  ← [MBR]`	Move the instruction to the IR
	`CU   ← [IR(op-code)]`	Transmit the op-code to the control unit

Table 5.1 The fetch phase expressed in register transfer language.

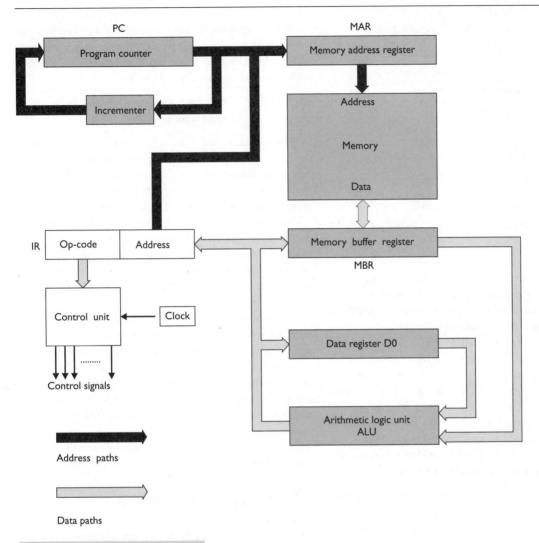

Fig. 5.6 The CPU's address and data paths.

specified by the instruction and the contents of the data register. When we said that an add instruction was represented by the mnemonic ADD x, D0, we didn't say what x was added to. This instruction adds the contents of memory location x to the contents of the data register and deposits the result of the addition in the data register, destroying one of the original operands. In other words, an operation that requires two operands uses the data register to supply one operand and the instruction to supply the other.

Later we shall see that a real microprocessor has more than one data register (the 68000 has eight data registers called D0 to D7). Some of yesterday's computers and many of the first generation 8-bit microprocessors had only one general-purpose data register that was called the *accumulator*.

We can represent an ADD x, D0 instruction by the RTL expression

$$[D0] \leftarrow [D0] + [M(x)]$$

The arithmetic and logic unit is the workhorse of the CPU because it carries out all the calculations. Arithmetic and logical operations are applied either to the contents of the data register or MBR alone, or to the contents of the data register and the contents of the MBR. The output of the ALU is fed back to the data register or to the MBR.

Two types of operation are carried out by the ALU—*arithmetic* and *logical*. The fundamental difference between arithmetic and logical operations is that logical operations don't generate a carry when bit a_i of word A and bit b_i of B are

Operation	Class	Typical mnemonic
Addition	Arithmetic	ADD
Subtraction	Arithmetic	SUB
Negation	Arithmetic	NEG
Multiplication	Arithmetic	MULU
Division	Arithmetic	DIVU
Divide by 2	Arithmetic	ASR
Multiply by 2	Arithmetic	ASL
AND	Logical	AND
OR	Logical	OR
NOT	Logical	NOT
EOR	Logical	EOR
Shift left	Logical	LSL
Shift right	Logical	LSR

Table 5.2 Some typical arithmetic and logical operations.

operated upon. Table 5.2 provides examples of typical arithmetic and logical operations. A logical shift treats an operand as a string of bits that are moved left or right. An arithmetic shift treats a number as a signed two's complement value and propagates the sign bit during a right shift.

Having developed our computer a little further, we can now execute an elementary program. Consider the high-level language operation P = Q + R. Here the *plus* symbol means arithmetic addition. The assembly language program required to carry out this operation is given below and is the same as the program we introduced in Chapter 4 when dealing with addition. Remember that P, Q, and R are symbolic names that refer to the *locations* of the variables in memory.

MOVE Q,D0   Load data register D0 with the contents of memory location Q

ADD R,D0   Add the contents of memory location R to data register D0

MOVE D0,P   Store the contents of data register D0 in memory location P

The one-address machine requires a rather cumbersome sequence of operations just to carry out the simple action of adding two numbers. If we had a computer with a three-address format, we could have written:

ADD Q,R,P   Add the contents of Q to the contents of R and put the result in P

Three-address machines are faster than one-address machines, because they can do in one instruction things that take other machines three operations. However, the power of three-address machines can be achieved only by means of a more complex and expensive CPU and memory system.

The way in which the CPU operates can best be seen by examining the execution of the instruction ADD R,D0 in terms of register-transfer language. Table 5.3 gives the sequence of operations carried out during the fetch and execute phases of an ADD R,D0 instruction. These operations tell us what is actually going on inside the computer.

Two operations sharing the same line in Table 5.3 are executed simultaneously (i.e. the operations ALU ← [MBR] and ALU ← [D0] happen at the same time). Incidentally, operations of the form [PC] ← [MAR] or [D0] ← [D0] + [MBR] are often referred to as *microinstructions*. Each assembly level instruction (e.g. MOVE, ADD) is executed as a series of microinstructions. In general, microinstructions and microprogramming are the province of the computer designer, although some machines are microprogrammable by the user. We take a further look at microinstructions at the end of this chapter.

5.2.4 Executing conditional instructions

So far, we've considered the architecture of the SISD, *single-instruction single-data*, CPU capable of executing programs in a purely *sequential* mode; that is, the computer can execute only a stream of instructions, one-by-one, in strict order. A real

FETCH	[MAR] ← [PC]	Move the contents of the PC to the MAR
	[PC] ← [PC]+1	Increment the contents of the PC
	[MBR] ← [M([MAR])]	Read the instruction from the memory
	[IR] ← [MBR]	Move the contents of the MBR to the IR
	CU ← [IR(op-code)]	Move the op-code from the IR to the CU
ADD	[MAR] ← [IR(address)]	Move the operand address to the MAR
	[MBR] ← [M([MAR])]	Read the data from memory
	ALU ← [MBR]; ALU ← [D0]	Perform the addition
	[D0] ← ALU	Move the output of ALU to the data register

Note: During the fetch phase the op-code is fed to the control unit by CU ← [IR(op-code)] and the CU uses this code to generate all the internal signals required to place the ALU in its addition mode. When the ALU is programmed for addition, it adds together the data at its two input terminals to produce a sum at its output terminals.

Table 5.3 Expressing the fetch–execute cycle in RTL.

computer can make a decision—that's why computers are so powerful. For example, if you're playing a game of computer chess, the computer must decide what move to make in response to your move.

The computer in Fig. 5.6 has no mechanism for making choices or repeating a group of instructions. To do this, the CPU must be able to execute conditional *branches* or *jumps*. A branch is an instruction that forces the CPU to execute an instruction out of the normal sequence. The word *branch* implies selecting one of two courses of action and the word *jump* implies a non-sequential flow of control. Both these terms are used in computer science, often interchangeably. A conditional branch allows high-level constructs such as IF … THEN … ELSE to be implemented. The block diagram of Fig. 5.7 shows the new address and data paths required by the CPU to execute conditional branches.

Three items have been added to our computer in Fig. 5.7:

- a condition code register, CCR
- a path between the CCR and the control unit
- a path between the address field of the instruction register and the program counter.

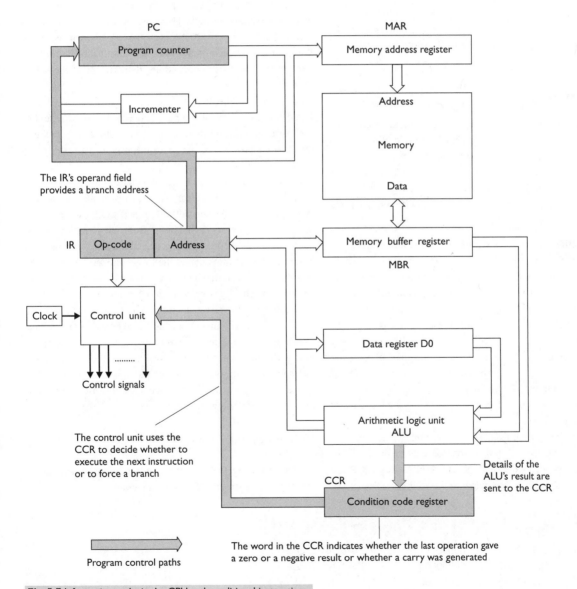

Fig. 5.7 Information paths in the CPU and conditional instructions.

The *condition code register* (sometimes called the *processor status register*, PSR) takes a snapshot of the state of the ALU after each instruction has been executed. A conditional branch instruction forces the control unit to interrogate the CCR's current state. The control unit then either forces the CPU to execute the next instruction in series or to jump (branch) to another instruction somewhere in the program. Let's look at the details of the conditional branch.

The CPU updates the bits of its condition code register after it carries out an arithmetic or a logical operation to reflect the nature of the result. The bits of the CCR of interest here are:

C = Carry   Set if a carry was generated in the last operation. The C bit is, of course, the same as the carry bit in the carry flip-flop.

Z = Zero   Set if the last operation generated a zero result.

N = Negative   Set if the last result generated a negative result, in two's complement terms (i.e. its MSB = 1).

V = Overflow   Set if the last operation resulted in an *arithmetic overflow*. That is, an operation on one or two two's complement values gave a result that was outside its allowable range. (An arithmetic overflow occurs during addition if the sign bit of the result is different from the sign bit of both operands.)

The action of the carry flip-flop is quite straightforward. Whenever, for example, the ALU performs an addition or subtraction, the result goes to the data register and the carry-bit (or borrow-bit) is retained in the carry-bit in the CCR. For example, the addition 00000100 + 00000001 provides a sum 00000101 and a carry bit C = 0, whereas the sum 10000110 + 10001110 provides a sum 00010100 and a carry bit C = 1. Similarly, if the contents of the data register are moved (shifted) left or right by one bit, the bit that would fall off the edge is transferred to the carry flip-flop. For these reasons, the carry bit is sometimes thought of as a 1-bit extension of the data register.

The following examples in 8-bit arithmetic demonstrate the effect of binary addition on the contents of the CCR. In each of the examples the C, Z, N, and V bits of the CCR are presented to show how they relate to the addition.

The CPU doesn't assume anything about the nature of the operation it is carrying out. For example, if you add the ASCII code for the letter 'A' (i.e. $41) to the ASCII code for the letter 'B' (i.e. $42), the result will be $83 or %10000011. The result causes the N-bit of the CCR to be set to one, even though the concept of negativeness is, in this case, quite meaningless.

The condition code register is connected to the control unit, enabling certain types of instruction to interrogate the CCR. For example, some instructions test whether the last operation performed by the central processor yielded a positive result, or whether the carry bit was set, or whether arithmetic overflow occurred. There is, of course, no point in carrying out an interrogation unless the results are acted upon. We need a mechanism that does one thing if the result of the test is true and does another thing if the result of the test is false.

The final modification included in Fig. 5.7 to the CPU of Fig. 5.6 is the addition of a path between the address field of the instruction register and the program counter. It's this feature that enables the computer to respond to the result of its interrogation of the CCR.

A *conditional branch* instruction can test a bit of the CCR and, if the bit tested is clear, the next instruction is obtained from memory in the normal way. But if the bit tested is set, the next instruction is obtained from the location whose address is in the instruction register. The address specified by a branch instruction is called the *target address*. In the above description we said that a branch is made if a certain bit of the CCR is set; equally a branch can be made if the bit is clear (branches can also be made on the state of several CCR bits).

The precise way in which conditional branches are actually implemented inside the computer is discussed later when we deal with the design of the control unit. Table 5.4 illustrates the range of conditional branch instructions implemented by a typical microprocessor. Branch operations can be expressed in register-transfer language in the form

```
IF condition THEN action
```

The following two examples of conditional branches are expressed in terms of RTL. The mnemonic BCC is read as

Operand 1		Operand 2	Result		CCR status bits
00000011	+	00000100	=	00000111	C = 0, Z = 0, N = 0, V = 0
11111111	+	00000001	=	00000000	C = 1, Z = 1, N = 0, V = 0
01100110	+	00110010	=	10011000	C = 0, Z = 0, N = 1, V = 1
11001001	+	10100000	=	01101001	C = 1, Z = 0, N = 0, V = 1

Mnemonic	Branch	Condition	Comment
BCC	Branch on carry clear	$C = 0$	
BCS	Branch on carry set	$C = 1$	
BEQ	Branch on zero result	$Z = 1$	
BNE	Branch on non-zero result	$Z = 0$	
BMI	Branch on minus result (two's comp)	$N = 1$	
BPL	Branch on positive result (two's comp)	$N = 0$	
BVC	Branch on overflow clear (two's comp)	$V = 0$	
BVS	Branch on overflow set (two's comp)	$V = 1$	
BGE	Branch on greater than or equal to	$N \cdot V + \bar{N} \cdot \bar{V} = 1$	Used in two's complement arithmetic
BGT	Branch on greater than	$N \cdot V \cdot \bar{Z} + \bar{N} \cdot \bar{V} \cdot \bar{Z} = 1$	Used in two's complement arithmetic
BHI	Branch if higher than	$\bar{C} \cdot \bar{Z} = 1$	Used in unsigned arithmetic
BLE	Branch if less than	$Z + \bar{N} \cdot V + N \cdot \bar{V} = 1$	Used in two's complement arithmetic
BLS	Branch if lower than or the same	$C + Z = 1$	Used in unsigned arithmetic

Table 5.4 Typical conditional branch instructions.

branch on carry clear and BEQ as *branch on zero* or *branch on equal*.

(i) Branch on carry clear (jump to the target address if the carry bit in the CCR is 0)
BCC adrs: IF [C] = 0 THEN [PC] ← [IR(adrs)]

(ii) Branch on equal (jump to the target address if the Z bit in the CCR is 1)
BEQ adrs: IF [Z] = 1 THEN [PC] ← [IR(adrs)]

A typical example of a conditional branch is as follows (we'll return to this topic in greater detail later).

SUB	x,D0	Subtract *x* from contents of D0
BEQ	Last	If the result was zero then branch to 'Last', otherwise continue
.	.	
.	.	
.	.	
Last		Target address of branch (if taken)

5.2.5 Dealing with literal operands

We have considered operands to be addresses and assumed all instructions (e.g. ADD and BCC) refer to an address somewhere within the CPU's memory. Sometimes we wish to use operands that represent the *actual value* of the data being referred to by the op-code part of the instruction. For example, we may wish to add the number 12 to the contents of data register D0. It is perfectly possible to store the value 12 in memory at location, say, 100, and then execute the instruction ADD 100,D0.

A much better solution is to execute ADD #12,D0, in which the operand is the actual (i.e. *literal*) value used by the

op-code ADD. Although the symbol '#' appears as part of the operand when this instruction is written in mnemonic form, the assembler uses a different code for

ADD #<literal>,<destination>

than it does for ADD <address>,<destination>.

The notation <address> means that the contents of the angle brackets should be replaced by the appropriate address whenever the instruction is actually used by a programmer. Similarly, <destination> means that the programmer should write the appropriate destination for the operand (i.e. in our examples the destination is data register D0). The instruction ADD #12,D0 is defined in RTL as

[D0] ← [D0] + 12

Figure 5.8 shows that an additional data path is required between the operand field of the IR and the data register and ALU to deal with literal operands. In fact, the architecture of Fig. 5.8 can execute any computer program. Any further modifications to this structure improve the CPU's performance without adding any fundamentally new feature.

5.2.6 Example of a simple assembly language program

In order to fit together the things we've learned in this section, an example of a program on our hypothetical computer should help. A suitable basic one-address instruction set for this computer is described in Table 5.5, where M and N are the symbolic names of operands used by instructions. The instructions in Table 5.5 are typical of those of the 68000 microprocessor, except for the IN and OUT instructions. Each instruction in Table 5.5 has a two-digit hexadecimal op-code

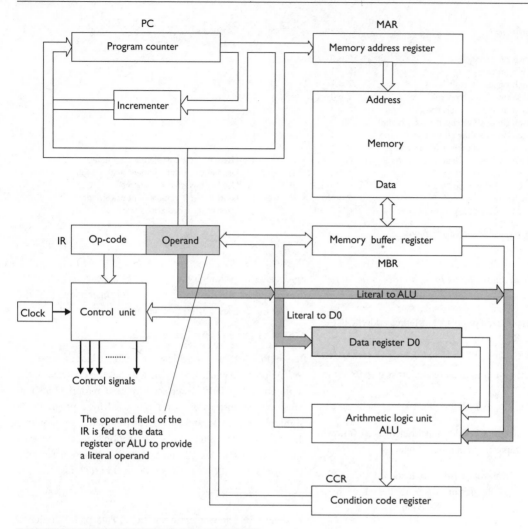

Fig. 5.8 Modifying the CPU to deal with literal operands.

and a two-digit operand. For example, the instruction
MOVE D0,5, which stores the contents of the data register in
memory location 5, is represented by the code 0105. We have
not used actual 68000 operation codes, as the relationship
between a 68000 op-code and its mnemonic is rather complex.

Two operations in Table 5.5 that can't be carried out by
our present computer are the input and output instructions,
IN M,D0 and OUT D0,M, respectively. To implement these
instructions, we would need data paths from the data register
to and from external peripherals.

For the purpose of our example we will assume that the
input device is a keyboard with device number 0 and the output device is a display with device number 1. To read data
from the keyboard we execute the instruction IN 0,D0, and

to display a number on the screen we execute OUT D0,1.
Please note that there is a simple fiction here. For the sake of
simplicity, we have assumed that the keyboard and display
send and receive numbers. This is not true, as keyboards and
displays often operate with ASCII-encoded data. To make our
example more realistic we would have had to transform
data from the keyboard from its ASCII code into its binary
equivalent, and to convert numbers into a sequence of ASCII
characters before sending them to the display.

The problem we wish to solve is:

*Read a series of numbers from the keyboard that are termin-
ated by a zero, add them together, multiply the result by 10,
and print the answer on the display.*

Op-code		Mnemonic		Action
00	M	MOVE	M,D0	Load data register D0 with the contents of memory location M
01	M	MOVE	D0,M	Store the contents of data register D0 in memory location M
02	M	IN	M,D0	Input data from device number M into data register D0
03	M	OUT	D0,M	Output the contents of data register D0 to device number M
04	M	ADD	M,D0	Add the contents of M to data register D0
05	M	SUB	M,D0	Subtract the contents of M from data register D0
06	M	AND	M,D0	Logically AND the contents of M with data register D0
07	M	OR	M,D0	Logically OR the contents of M with data register D0
08		NEG	D0	Complement the contents of data register D0
09		ASL	D0	Shift data register D0 one place left
0A		ASR	D0	Shift data register D0 one place right
0B	M	CMP	M,D0	Compare the contents of M with the contents of data register D0
0C	M	MOVE	#M,D0	Put the number M into data register D0
0D	N	BEQ	N	Branch if Z-bit set to location N (i.e. branch on zero result)
0E	N	BNE	N	Branch if Z-bit clear to location N (i.e. branch on non-zero result)
0F	N	BCC	N	Branch if C-bit clear to location N
10	N	BCS	N	Branch if C-bit set to location N
11	N	BRA	N	Unconditional branch to location N
12		STOP		Stop

Note: The branch on zero and branch on not zero instructions (0D and 0E) are dependent on the state of the Z flag from the ALU. The Z flag is set to one if the result of the last operation performed by the ALU yielded a zero value.

Table 5.5 The instruction set of a hypothetical computer.

BASIC	Pascal	C
10 T=0	Program Sum (Input, Output);	#include <stdio.h>
20 INPUT N	Var N, T: Integer;	void main(void)
30 T=T+N	Begin	{
40 IF N<>0 THEN GOTO 20	T:=0;	int n, T=0;
50 T=T*10	Repeat	scanf(&n);
60 PRINT T	Read (N);	while(n!=0)
70 STOP	T:=T+N	{
	Until N=0;	T+=n;
	T:=T*10;	scanf(&n);
	Write (T)	}
	End.	T*=10;
		printf(T);
		}

Table 5.6 Program to add a sequence of numbers terminated by 0 expressed in BASIC, Pascal, and C.

In a high-level language, this program may be written in the BASIC, Pascal, or C forms in Table 5.6.

Some people who write programs in assembly language first draw a flowchart for their algorithm and then convert it into assembly language; others write the program in a high-level language and then code each of the statements into a number of assembly language instructions. Yet others sit at a terminal and write assembly language directly from the algorithm. These latter people seldom get their programs right and often they fail their exams. You should never write an assembly

language program without first having expressed the algorithm in a suitable form.

Figure 5.9 provides a flowchart for the algorithm to add a sequence of numbers terminated by zero. Flowcharts were once a popular method of representing algorithms in a graphical form before they were coded into either high-level language or assembly language. In general, the use of flowcharts is strongly discouraged today. Although the flowchart can illustrate a simple algorithm quite elegantly, it's unsuited to complex algorithms, because it tends to confuse the structure

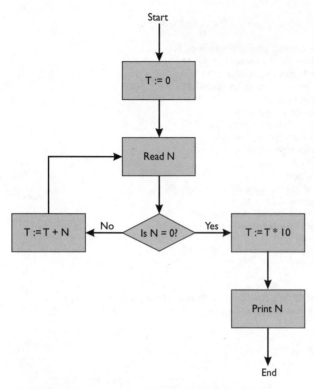

Fig. 5.9 A flow-chart to execute the algorithm of Table 5.7.

```
Module sum_times_ten
  Clear total
  REPEAT
    Get_number
    total:=total+number
  UNTIL number=0
  total:=total * 10
  Print total
End sum_times_ten
```

Table 5.7 Expressing the algorithm of Table 5.6 in pseudocode.

of an algorithm with the implementation of the algorithm. Moreover, a flowchart can be very difficult to modify if the algorithm is ever changed at a later date.

A much better approach to program design is the use of *pseudocode*. A pseudocode version of the algorithm is given in Table 5.7. We will introduce pseudocode briefly here to demonstrate how we can express algorithms. Later we look at pseudocode in more detail.

Pseudocode is an informal notation that allows a programmer to write an algorithm in almost plain English using some of the constructs of structured programming (e.g. IF... THEN... ELSE or WHILE... DO). In the example in Table 5.7, control actions are presented in upper case, variables in lower

case, and plain English actions in bold text. These actions (e.g. Clear, Get_number, Print) all express quite adequately the operation to be carried out. The actions can, themselves, be represented by other sequences of pseudocode operations. When an algorithm has been expressed in pseudocode, the programmer can then translate each of the pseudocode actions or control constructs in an almost semi-automatic fashion.

The algorithm of Fig. 5.9 and Table 5.7 requires a number to be multiplied by 10. As our instruction set lacks any facilities for direct multiplication, we must resort either to repeated addition or write a program to do multiplication. An alternative solution is to note that

$$10T = (2 \times 2T + T) \times 2$$
For example, $10 \times 32 = (2 \times 2 \times 32 + 32) \times 2 = (128 + 32) \times 2$
$$= 160 \times 2 = 320$$

We can multiply by 10 just by using the operations of doubling (i.e. shift the bits left) and adding.

Before we begin to construct the program, we have to decide where to put it in the computer's memory. For convenience we may assume that the program starts at location 0. We don't know yet how long the program will be, but from the pseudocode it should not exceed about 20 instructions. It should therefore be safe to locate any variables at hexadecimal location 20 onwards.

Table 5.8 presents the program in *assembly language* form. Remember that an assembly language program is not executed directly by a computer; it is in a form that can readily be understood by people. Here we must comment on the meaning of *understood* in the previous sentence. Assembly language is easy to understand in the sense that the meaning of each individual instruction is clear to the reader. However, because assembly language is such a low-level language, the meaning (i.e. effect) of a group of instructions is often not clear to the reader. An assembly language program is called *source code* and is assembled or translated by an assembler to produce a binary or machine code form (called object code) that can be directly executed by the computer.

The first column in Table 5.8 containing the numbers 1 to 19 is not part of the program and merely displays the line number for later reference. The second column containing TOTAL, REPEAT, and MULT is the *label* field of the program. These three words are labels or markers that may be referred to by other assembly language instructions. For example, BEQ MULT means branch on a zero result to the address of the instruction labeled MULT. Later, when the program is translated into machine code by an assembler, all references to these labels are automatically translated into the address of the line they label.

```
1.              NAM   EXAMPLE
2.              ORG   $20              Data origin $20 (i.e. 32 decimal)
3.   TOTAL      DS    1                Reserve a word of storage for 'TOTAL'
4.              ORG   0                Origin of the program
5.              MOVE  #0,D0            [D0]←0
6.              MOVE  D0,TOTAL         [TOTAL]←[D0]
7.   REPEAT     IN    0,D0             [D0]←Input
8.              BEQ   MULT             IF last result 0 then branch to MULT
9.              ADD   TOTAL,D0         [D0]←[D0]+[TOTAL]
10.             MOVE  D0,TOTAL         [TOTAL]←[D0]
11.             BRA   REPEAT           [PC]←REPEAT
12.  MULT       MOVE  TOTAL,D0         [D0]←[TOTAL]
13.             ASL   D0               [D0]←[D0]*2          (2 × TOTAL)
14.             ASL   D0               [D0]←[D0]*2          (4 × TOTAL)
15.             ADD   TOTAL,D0         [D0]←[D0]+[TOTAL]    (5 × TOTAL)
16.             ASL   D0               [D0]←[D0]*2          (10 × TOTAL)
17.             OUT   D0,1             Output←[D0]
18.             STOP
19.             END
```

◄──────────────────────►   ◄──────────────────────►

         The program   The comments

Notes:

1. The line number is not part of the program. It is included here to help us to refer to specific lines in the program.
2. The actual start of each line (i.e. column two) is reserved for labels (e.g. TOTAL, REPEAT, and MULT).
3. The comment field to the right of instructions and assembler directives is ignored by the assembler. We have provided comments in RTL form to define the action of each instruction. Real programs use comments in plain English to help the reader understand the meaning of the program.

Table 5.8 The algorithm of Tables 5.6 and 5.7 expressed in assembly language.

At first sight, some of the mnemonics (lines 1, 2, 3, 4, 19) in this program don't appear in the instruction set we defined in Table 5.5. These mnemonics aren't assembly language operations but are called *assembler directives* or pseudo-operations. Assembler directives are not translated into executable instructions. They simply tell the assembler things it needs to know about the program.

The first assembler directive, NAM, names the program (in this case EXAMPLE). The second assembler directive, ORG, sets the *origin* or beginning to $20. Any program or data following this directive is located at address $20 and successive locations. It is perhaps best to imagine an assembler as having a *location counter* that keeps track of where the final machine code is to go in memory. As each new mnemonic is assembled, the location counter is incremented. The effect of an ORG N directive is to reset the value of the location counter to *N*.

The assembler directive DS, *define storage*, reserves one or more memory locations for the named value; for example, TOTAL DS 1 reserves a single word for the item we've called 'TOTAL'. This directive not only reserves storage, it binds a symbolic name to an address. Whenever the programmer writes 'TOTAL' the assembler substitutes the value 20_{16}. The second ORG 0 resets the origin to 0 so that the program will be loaded into memory starting at address 0. The final assembler

directive, END, tells the assembler that the end of the program has been reached. You don't have to worry about assembler directives in high-level languages because the compiler (together with the operating system) decides where programs and data are to be stored. The define storage directive is rather similar to the type declaration in C; for example, int x; performs the same function as x DS 1.

One of the operations in the program of Table 5.8 we haven't yet described is the *arithmetic shift left* instruction, ASL, which shifts the bit pattern of the operand left. ASL D0 shifts the word in data register D0 one place left and introduces a zero into the now vacated least-significant bit position (i.e. the contents of D0 are multiplied by two). Figure 5.10 describes the operation of the ASL instruction; for example, the bit pattern 1100110011111010 becomes 1001100111110100 when shifted one place left (the most-significant bit at the left-hand side is copied into the C-bit of the CCR). By the way, ASL D0 is the same as ADD D0,D0.

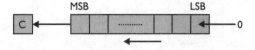

Fig. 5.10 The action of the ASL instruction (arithmetic shift left).

For the sake of simplicity, we assume that the sum of the numbers doesn't produce an out-of-range result when multiplied by ten. That is, we don't have to worry about a carry-out being generated from the most-significant bit (MSB) position when an ASL is executed.

Once the program has been assembled and placed in the computer's memory, it can be executed. The layout or *memory map* of the program is given in Fig. 5.11. A memory map is a snapshot of the contents of a computer's memory and shows the locations of data and programs within the memory.

Each memory location in our hypothetical computer holds four digits. The first two (i.e. most significant) digits of an instruction define the operation code and the second two point to the memory location accessed by the op-code. Exceptions to this are the IN and OUT operations, in which a peripheral is accessed, and the MOVE #<literal>,D0 operation in which the two digits specified by literal are loaded into data register D0. Some op-codes don't require an operand field and their operand fields are indicated by XX in Fig. 5.11 (a real computer would probably replace XX by 00). Now that we have taken a brief look at the CPU of a hypothetical simple computer, we will look at the structure of a more complex CPU.

5.2.7 The architecture of a typical high-performance CPU

It's reasonably true to say that computer architecture has been driven by advances in technology as much as advances in computer science or programming. That is, the programmer gets what the engineer is able to produce economically. If we forget, for a moment, the mainframe and the minicomputer (or work-station), the 1970s saw the introduction of the 8-bit microprocessor with very few internal registers. Advances in semiconductor technology in the 1980s enabled microprocessors to operate with 16- or 32-bit words and more on-chip registers. Progress in the 1990s was more concerned with increasing speed rather than with radically modifying CPU architectures. We are going to take a brief look at the architecture of a CPU that is more representative of today's powerful microprocessors. In the next chapter we will examine Motorola's 68000 microprocessor in much greater detail. Here we are concerned only with three topics—the effect of multiple data registers, the *address* or *pointer* register, and multiple-length operands.

Figure 5.12 illustrates the structure of a CPU with multiple buses and register arrays (rather than the single data register structure of Fig. 5.8). Although Fig. 5.12 is intended only as an example of a CPU, it is very similar to the structure of the 68000 microprocessor that we describe later.

The CPU in Fig. 5.12 has the same basic registers as the more primitive CPUs described earlier (i.e. PC, MAR, MBR). However, the major change is the provision of eight data registers, D0 to D7, and eight address registers, A0 to A7. We have drawn three internal buses in Fig. 5.12 to enable the output from two registers to be fed to the ALU and the output from the ALU to be fed to any of these data and address registers. This bus structure enables the CPU to perform the operation $R3 = f(R1, R2)$, where R1, R2, and R3 are any three registers and f is the function performed by the ALU (such as addition or subtraction).

The provision of 16 user-accessible registers requires a rather different instruction format from the one-address format described earlier. In order to access the data and address registers easily, we need to resort to a *two-address* instruction format. Such an instruction requires three fields: an op-code, an operand address, and a register address. As only one address is a memory address, it is, perhaps, more proper to call this a *one-and-a-half address* format than a two-address format, because many computers have no more than 16 to 32 registers and the register address need occupy no more than four bits. The 68000 uses both a one-and-a-half address and a true two-address format as illustrated by the instruction formats below.

MOVE 1234,2000 copy the contents of memory location 1234 to 2000

MOVE 1234,D0 copy the contents of memory location 1234 to data register D0

MOVE D0,1234 copy the contents of data register D0 to memory location 1234

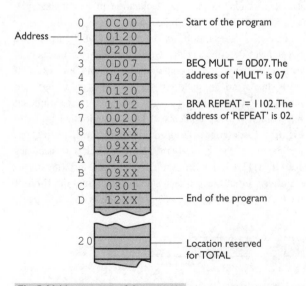

Fig. 5.11 Memory map of the program.

Address —

0	0C00	Start of the program
1	0120	
2	0200	
3	0D07	BEQ MULT = 0D07. The address of 'MULT' is 07
4	0420	
5	0120	
6	1102	BRA REPEAT = 1102. The address of 'REPEAT' is 02.
7	0020	
8	09XX	
9	09XX	
A	0420	
B	09XX	
C	0301	
D	12XX	End of the program

| 20 | | Location reserved for TOTAL |

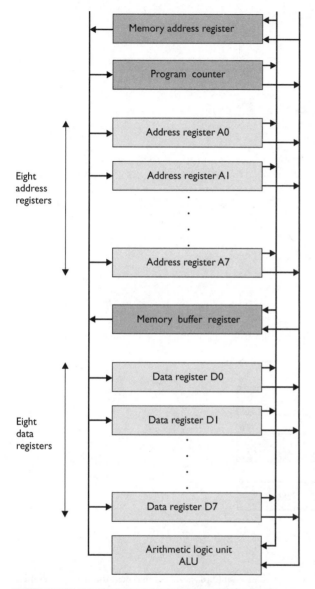

Eight address registers

Eight data registers

Fig. 5.12 Structure of a CPU with multiple address and data registers.

only one general-purpose data register (accumulator). Modern technology allows us to put several data registers on a chip, where once only one or two such registers could be accommodated economically. The only difference between these registers and locations in memory is that the registers are on-chip and can be accessed more rapidly than locations within the memory.

The 68000's registers hold 32 bits (called a *longword*). You can operate on the whole register, the low-order 16 bits of a register (i.e. a *word*), or just the low-order 8 bits of a register (i.e. a *byte*). Figure 5.13 illustrates the organization of a data register. You can view it in one of three ways: as a byte with bits d_0 to d_7, as a word with bits d_0 to d_{15}, or as a longword with bits d_0 to d_{31}. To avoid confusion, we use lower-case d to refer to bits and upper-case D to refer to registers.

Data registers are 32 bits wide. When you use a word or a byte, bits 16 to 31 or bits 8 to 31 remain unaffected, respectively. The programmer indicates the size of an operation by appending .B (byte), .W (word), or .L (longword) to a mnemonic, respectively. We can, for example, write ADD.B D0,D1 or ADD.W D0,D1. By the way, the novice 68000 probably makes more errors by incorrectly mixing .B, .W, and .L operations than any other type of error. The 68000 assembler treats .W as the default operand size—the assembler regards ADD.W and ADD as equivalent.

We don't really need more than one data register (i.e. accumulator) in a one-address machine. However, by providing several data registers, the programmer can store frequently used data values on-chip rather than in the computer's memory. By doing this we can speed up the execution of programs, because data in registers doesn't have to be fetched from the memory. For example, the instruction ADD D0,D1 adds the contents of data register D0 to data register D1 and deposits the result in D1. This instruction requires no references to memory (i.e. there are no external read or write cycles).

The only difficulty associated with the use of multiple registers is the burden it sometimes places on the programmer. That is, the programmer has to decide what register is going to hold what variable. Fortunately, today's programmers invariably write in high-level languages and the job of deciding what register holds what data is left to the compiler, sparing programmers the tricky problem of register allocation.

Address registers

One of the greatest differences between the architecture of the CPU of Fig. 5.12 and that of the simple CPUs described earlier is the addition of eight address registers, A0 to A7.

Although we deal with the 68000 microprocessor in more detail later, we provide an indication of some of the instructions that can be executed by the 68000 in Table 5.9. Each instruction is provided in mnemonic form and briefly described in RTL. These definitions are meant to be illustrative rather than definitive.

Data registers

The 68000's eight data registers, D0 to D7, make this microprocessor more powerful than its predecessors, which had

Mnemonic		Operation
ADD	address,Di	$[Di] \leftarrow [Di] + [M(address)]$
ASL	#number,Di	Shift [Di] left by <number> bits
ASR	#number,Di	Shift [Di] right by <number> bits
DIVU	address,Di	$[Di] \leftarrow [Di] / [M(address)]$
MULU	address,Di	$[Di] \leftarrow [Di] * [M(address)]$
NEG	address	$[M(address)] \leftarrow -[M(address)]$
AND	address,Di	$[Di] \leftarrow [Di] \cdot [M(address)]$
OR	address,Di	$[Di] \leftarrow [Di] + [M(address)]$
NOT	address	$[M(address)] \leftarrow \overline{[M(address)]}$
SUB	address,Di	$[Di] \leftarrow [Di] - [M(address)]$
TST	address	$[M(address)] - 0$
CMP	address,Di	$[Di] - [M(address)]$
EXG	Ri,Rj	$[Ri] \leftarrow [Rj], [Rj] \leftarrow [Ri]$
MOVE	address,Di	$[Di] \leftarrow [M(address)]$
MOVE	Di,address	$[M(address)] \leftarrow [Di]$
MOVE	#data,Di	$[Di] \leftarrow data$
MOVE	#data,address	$[M(address)] \leftarrow data$
LEA	address,Ai	$[Ai] \leftarrow address$
BRA	address	$[PC] \leftarrow address$
BCC	address	IF $C = 0$ THEN $[PC] \leftarrow address$

Table 5.9 Typical 68000 instructions.

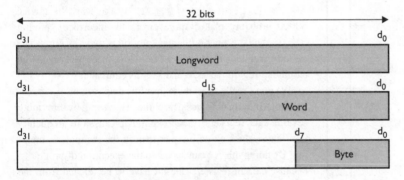

Fig. 5.13 Structure of the 68000's data registers.

Address registers are so called because they are used to hold the addresses of operands to be accessed in memory. We don't intend to go into details about the function of address registers here, because they are described in much more detail later. However, it's worthwhile hinting at how they are actually used.

Up to now, we've regarded the address of an operand as a *constant* (i.e. it doesn't change as the program is executed); for example, we can write P = Q + R, where addresses P, Q, and R are all constants. However, there are many occasions when it is much more convenient to have an address that is *variable* (i.e. can be changed during the execution of a program). Variable addresses arise when you deal with data structures such as tables, lists, arrays, and vectors.

Consider a table of m values that are stored in consecutive memory locations. We can call these values $x_0, x_1, x_2, \ldots, x_i, \ldots x_{m-1}$. The general element in this table is called x_i. Note how the index i corresponds to a variable address (because i can range from 0 to $m - 1$).

The CPU architecture in Fig. 5.12 contains eight address registers that can be used to provide an operand address during a memory access. That is, instead of getting the operand address from the instruction, we can get the operand address from an address register. Figure 5.14 demonstrates the effect of the operation MOVE.B (A0), D0 that gets the source operand from the memory location specified by A0 (note the use of parentheses to indicate that A0 is the source of the operand address). This addressing mode is called

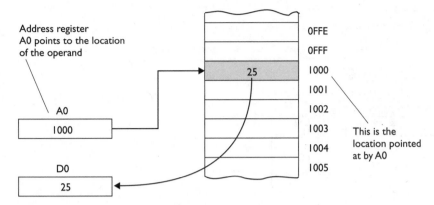

Address register
A0 points to the location
of the operand

A0

1000

D0

25

0FFE
0FFF
1000   25
1001
1002
1003
1004
1005

This is the
location pointed
at by A0

Fig. 5.14 Address register indirect addressing.

address register indirect addressing. The term *indirect* is used because the instruction specifies the address register and the address register specifies the location of the operand.

Once we have loaded the address of an operand into an address register, we don't have to refer to the operand again explicitly. We can access the operand via the address register. For example, the instruction ADD.B (A0), D0 means add the contents of the memory location pointed at by address register A0 to the contents of data register D0. In RTL form, this is represented by

[D0]←[D0] + [M([A0])]

We write ADD.B (A0), D0, rather than ADD.B A0, D0, because we mean that the source operand is not the contents of A0, but the contents of the memory location whose address is in A0. That is, ADD.B A0, D0 means [D0]← [D0] + [A0], whereas ADD.B (A0), D0 means [D0]←[D0] + [M([A0])]. Of course, we have to set up the contents of A0 initially. However, once the appropriate operand address is in A0, we can access the operand simply by specifying the pointer to it in A0.

This *dynamic computation* of addresses by the computer enables us to operate on tables and other data structures, as we shall see in the next chapter.

Before we look at how assembly language programs are written for the 68000 microprocessor (in Chapter 6), we are going to examine the control unit of a CPU. Readers not interested in how an instruction is decoded and executed may skip to Chapter 6. At the end of this chapter we provide a simple CPU simulator in C both to emphasize what we've said about the fetch–execute cycle and to provide readers with the starting point for a more complex simulator.

5.3 The control unit

The precise way in which a digital computer interprets machine code instructions is rather complex. Consequently, the discussion of its control unit, CU, is often relegated to more advanced courses on computer architecture. Here we provide an overview of the control unit's operation and demonstrate how it enables the CPU to carry out the instruction currently in the instruction register. That is, we show how a pattern of bits in the instruction register is used to generate the sequence of actions taking place during the execution of an instruction.

The model of the CPU we are going to use to illustrate the operation of the control unit is presented in Fig. 5.15 (as before we have included a program and data memory in this figure, even though memory is not part of the CPU). We have created a very primitive CPU in order to reduce the level of complexity and have stripped the CPU of any unnecessary detail to make its internal operation easier to understand.

There are two radically different approaches to the design of the control unit. The first, dealt with in Section 5.3.1, is to make the control unit itself a *computer within a computer*, and turn each machine instruction into a sequence of even more primitive instructions called *microinstructions*. The alternative approach (see Section 5.3.2) is to ask what sequence of logical and arithmetic operations are needed to carry out an instruction, and then to design the appropriate logic circuit to bring this about. These two sections are included partially to provide a more complete picture of the CPU and its development and partially to reinforce what we've said about logic. The picture we present of the control unit is highly simplified.

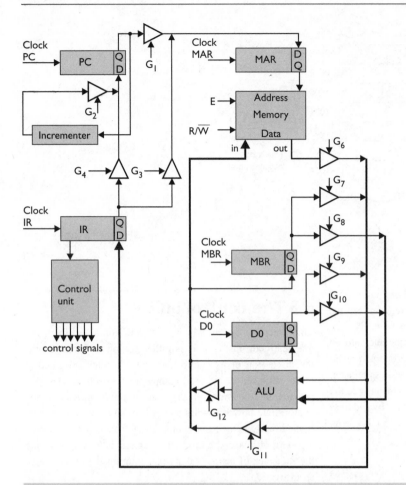

Fig. 5.15 Controlling the flow of data within a CPU (only one data bit shown for simplicity).

5.3.1 Microprogrammed control unit

Before we describe the microprogrammed control unit, we need to define three terms: *macro-level* instruction, *micro-level* instruction, and *interpretation*. The natural or native language of a computer is its machine code, whose mnemonic representation is called *assembly language*. Assembly language instructions are also called macroinstructions. Each macroinstruction is *interpreted* (i.e. executed) by means of a number of very primitive actions called *microinstructions*. In other words, there is a language even more primitive than machine code.

A microinstruction is the smallest event that can take place within a computer and may consist of clocking a flip-flop or moving data from one register to another. The process whereby a macroinstruction is executed by carrying out a series of microinstructions is called *interpretation*. Note that the use of the term *macroinstruction* here has nothing to do with the word *macro* used by programmers.

The internal structure of the primitive CPU illustrated in Fig. 5.15 differs from that we used in Fig. 5.8 to describe the fetch–execute cycle. The CPU in Fig. 5.15 includes the mechanisms by which information is moved within the CPU. Each of the registers (program counter, MAR, data register, etc.) is made up of D flip-flops. When the clock input to a register is pulsed, the data at the register's D input terminals is transferred to its output terminals and held constant until the register is clocked again. The connections between the registers are by means of m-bit wide data highways. The highways in Fig. 5.15 are drawn as a single bold line. The output from each register can be gated onto the bus by enabling the appropriate tri-state buffer.

Suppose our computer performs a fetch–execute cycle in which the op-code is ADD <address>, D0. This instruction adds the contents of the memory location specified by the operand field <address> to the contents of the data register (i.e. D0) and deposits the result in D0. We can write down the sequence of operations that take place during the execution of ADD not only in terms of register transfer language, but also in terms of the enabling of gates and the clocking of flip-flops. Table 5.10 illustrates the sequence of microinstructions executed during the fetch–execute cycle of an ADD instruction. It should be emphasized that the fetch phase of all instructions is identical and it is only the execute phase that varies according to the nature of the op-code read during the fetch phase.

The microprogram

Imagine that the output of the control unit in Fig. 5.15 consists of 12 signals that enable gates G_1 to G_{12}, two signals that control the memory, and five clock signals that pulse the clock inputs of the PC, MAR, MBR, IR, and D0 registers. Table 5.11 presents the 19 outputs of the control unit as a sequence of binary values that are generated during the fetch and execute phases of an ADD instruction.

If, for each of the eight steps in Table 5.11, the 19 signals are fed to the various parts of the CPU in Fig. 5.15, then the fetch–execute cycle will be carried out. Real microprogrammed computers might use 64 to 200 control signals rather than the 19 in this example. One of the most significant differences between a microinstruction and a macroinstruction is that the former contains many fields and may provide several operands, while the macroinstruction frequently specifies only an op-code and one or two operands.

The eight steps in Table 5.11 represent a *microprogram* that interprets a fetch phase followed by an ADD instruction.

Step	Register transfer language	Operations required
1	[MAR] ← [PC]	enable G_1, clock MAR
1a	INC ← [PC]	
2	[PC] ← INC	enable G_2, clock PC
3	[MBR] ← [M([MAR])]	enable memory, R/W̄ = 1, enable G_6, enable G_{11}, clock MBR
4	[IR] ← [MBR]	enable G_7, clock IR
4a	CU ← [IR(op-code)]	
5	[MAR] ← [IR(address)]	enable G_3, clock MAR
6	[MBR] ← [M([MAR])]	enable memory, R/W̄ = 1, enable G_6, enable G_{11}, clock MBR
7	ALU ← [MBR]	enable G_7
7a	ALU ← [D0]	enable G_{10}
8	[D0] ← ALU	enable G_{12}, clock data register D0

Note 1: Where there is no entry in the column labeled 'Operations required', that operation happens automatically. For example, the output of the program counter is always connected to the input of the incrementer and therefore no explicit operation is needed to move the contents of the PC to the incrementer.
Note 2: Any three-state gate not explicitly mentioned is not enabled.
Note 3: Steps 1, 1a are carried out simultaneously, as are 4, 4a and 7, 7a.

Table 5.10 Interpreting a fetch–execute cycle for an ADD instruction in terms of RTL.

Step	Gate control signals												Memory		Register clocks				
	G_1	G_2	G_3	G_4	G_5	G_6	G_7	G_8	G_9	G_{10}	G_{11}	G_{12}	E	R/W̄	PC	MAR	MBR	D0	IR
1	1	0	0	0	0	0	0	0	0	0	0	0	0	x	0	1	0	0	0
2	0	1	0	0	0	0	0	0	0	0	0	0	0	x	1	0	0	0	0
3	0	0	0	0	0	1	0	0	0	0	1	0	1	1	0	0	1	0	0
4	0	0	0	0	0	0	1	0	0	0	0	0	0	x	0	0	0	0	1
5	0	0	1	0	0	0	0	0	0	0	0	0	0	x	0	1	0	0	0
6	0	0	0	0	0	1	0	0	0	0	1	0	1	1	0	0	1	0	0
7	0	0	0	0	0	0	1	0	0	1	0	0	0	x	0	0	0	0	0
8	0	0	0	0	0	0	0	0	0	0	0	1	0	x	0	0	0	1	0

When the memory is accessed by E = 1, a memory read or write cycle may take place. The R/W̄ (i.e. read/write) signal determines the nature of the memory access when E = 1. When R/W̄ = 0 the cycle is a write cycle, and when R/W̄ = 1 the cycle is a read cycle.

Table 5.11 Control signals generated during the fetch and execution phases of an ADD instruction.

We have demonstrated that a macroinstruction is interpreted by executing a microprogram that comprises a sequence of microinstructions. Each of the CPU's instructions has its own microprogram. We now look at the microprogram itself and consider the hardware required to execute it. The microprogram is executed by the same type of mechanism used to execute the macroprogram (i.e. machine code) itself. This is a good example of the common expression 'wheels within wheels'.

Figure 5.16 describes the basic structure of a micro-programmed control unit that has a microprogram counter, a microprogram memory, and a microinstruction register (this structure is typical of the 1980s). The microinstruction address from the microprogram counter is applied to the address input of the microprogram memory and the data output of the memory fed to the microinstruction register. As we've said, the structure of the control unit that executes the macroinstruction is very much like the structure of the CPU itself. However, there is one very big difference between the macroinstruction world and the microinstruction world—the microinstruction register is very much longer than the macroinstruction register, and the microinstruction's structure is much more complex that of the macroinstruction.

Information in the microinstruction register is divided into four fields: next microinstruction address field, micro-program counter load-control field, condition select field, and CPU control field. Most of the bits in the microinstruction register belong to the CPU control field, which controls the flow of information within the CPU by enabling tri-state gates and clocking registers as we've described; for example, all the 19 control signals in Table 5.11 belong to this field. Our next task is to describe one of the principal differences between the micro and macroinstruction. Each microinstruction is also a conditional branch instruction that determines the location of the next microinstruction to be executed. We will now explain how microinstructions are sequenced.

Microinstruction sequence control

If the microprogram counter were to step through the micro-program memory in the natural sequence, 0, 1, 2, 3, … , etc., a stream of consecutive microinstructions would appear in the

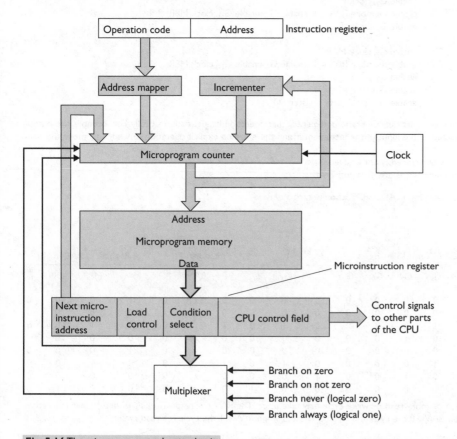

Fig. 5.16 The microprogrammed control unit.

microinstruction register, causing the CPU to behave in the way described by Table 5.10. The CPU control bits of each microinstruction determine the flow of information within the CPU. However, just as in the case of the macroprogram control unit, it is often necessary to modify the sequence in which microinstructions are executed. For example, we might wish to repeat a group of microinstructions *n* times, or we may wish to jump from a fetch phase to an execute phase, or we may wish to call a procedure.

Microinstruction sequence control is determined by the three left-hand fields of the microinstruction register in

condition select field selects one of these flag bits for testing (in this example only the Z bit is used). If the output of the multiplexer is true, a microprogram jump is made to the address specified by the contents of the next microinstruction address field, otherwise the microprogram continues sequentially. In Fig. 5.16 two of the conditions are obtained from the CCR and two bits are permanently true and false. A false condition implies *branch never* (i.e. continue) and a true condition implies *branch always* (i.e. goto).

To emphasize what we've just said, consider the following hypothetical microinstruction:

Next address:	Load control:	Condition select:	CPU control fields:
ADD3:	conditional:	branch on zero:	<CPU control fields>

Fig. 5.16, enabling the microprogram counter to implement both conditional and unconditional branches to locations within the microprogram memory. We shall soon see that this activity is necessary to execute macroinstructions such as BRA, BCC, BCS, and BEQ.

In normal operation, the microprogram counter steps through microinstructions sequentially and the next microprogram address is the current address plus one. By loading the contents of the next microinstruction address field of the current microinstruction field into the microprogram counter, a branch can be made to any point in the microprogram memory. In other words each microinstruction determines whether the next microinstruction is taken in sequence or whether it is taken from the next address field of the current microinstruction. The obvious question to ask is, 'What determines whether the microprogram counter continues in sequence or is loaded from the next microinstruction address field of the current microinstruction?'

The microprogram *load control* field in the microinstruction register tells the microprogram counter how to get the next microinstruction address. This next address can come from the incrementer and cause the microprogram to continue in sequence. The next address can also be obtained from the *address mapper* (see below) or from the address in the next microinstruction address field of the microinstruction register.

The *condition select field* in the microinstruction register implements conditional branches at the macroinstruction level by executing a conditional branch at the microinstruction level. In the simplified arrangement of Fig. 5.16, the condition select field directly controls a 4-to-1 multiplexer that selects one of four flag bits representing the state of the CPU. These flag bits are obtained from the ALU and are usually the flag bits in the condition code register (e.g. Z, N, C, V). The

This microinstruction is interpreted as

$$\text{IF } Z = 1 \text{ THEN } \mu PC \leftarrow ADD3 \text{ ELSE } \mu PC \leftarrow \mu PC + 1$$

where μPC indicates the microprogram counter.

A conditional branch at the macroinstruction level (e.g. BEQ) is interpreted by microinstructions in the following way. The condition select field of the microinstruction selects the appropriate status bit of the CCR to be tested. For example, if the macroinstruction is BEQ, the Z bit is selected. The microprogram counter *load control* field contains the operation 'branch to the address in the microinstruction register on selected condition true'. Thus, if the selected condition is true (i.e. Z = 1), a jump is made to a point in the microprogram that implements the corresponding jump in the macroprogram. If the selected condition is false (i.e. Z = 0), the current sequence of microinstructions is terminated by the start of a new fetch–execute cycle.

Implementing the fetch–execute cycle

The first part of each microprogram executed by the control unit corresponds to a macroinstruction fetch phase that ends with the macroinstruction op-code being deposited in the instruction register. The op-code from the instruction register is first fed to the *address mapper*, which is a look-up table containing the starting address of the microprogram for each of the possible op-codes. That is, the address mapper translates the arbitrary bit pattern of the op-code into the location of the corresponding microprogram that will execute the op-code. After this microprogram has been executed, an unconditional jump is made to the start of the microprogram that interprets the macroinstruction execute phase, and the process continues.

User-microprogrammed processors

Before the advent of today's powerful microprocessors, engineers in the 1980s requiring high performance often constructed their own microprogrammed computers. That is, the engineer constructed a CPU to his or her own specifications. That was fun because you could create your own architecture and instruction set. On the other hand, you ended up with a computer without an off-the-shelf operating system, compilers, or any of the other tools you take for granted when you use a mainstream CPU.

At the heart of many of these systems was the *bit-slice* component that provided a middle path between microcomputer and mainframe. Bit-slice components, as their name suggests, are really sub-sections of a microprocessor that can be put together to create a custom CPU. For example, a 64-bit computer is made by putting together eight 8-bit bit-slice chips.

Bit-slice components are divided into two types corresponding to the functional division within the microprocessor (i.e. the microprogram control and ALU). By using several ALU and microprogram controller bit-slices plus some additional logic and a microprogram in ROM, a CPU with a user-defined instruction set and wordlength may be created. Of course, the designer doesn't have to construct a new CPU out of bit-slice components. You can emulate an existing microprocessor or even add machine level instructions to enhance it.

Figure 5.17 describes a typical bit-slice arithmetic logic unit that can generate one of eight functions of two inputs R and S. These functions vary from R plus S to the exclusive NOR of R and S. The values of R and S may be selected from a register file of 16 general-purpose data registers, an external input, a Q register, or zero.

The bit-slice ALU is controlled (i.e. programmed) by a 9-bit input that selects the source of the data taking part in an arithmetic or logical operation, determines the particular operation to be executed, and controls the destination (together with any shifting) of the result. Typical ALU operations are

$$[R7] \leftarrow [R7] + [R1]$$
$$[R6] \leftarrow [R6] - [R5]$$
$$[R9] \leftarrow [R9] \cdot [R2]$$
$$[R7] \leftarrow [R7] + 1$$

An arithmetic unit of any length (as long as it is a multiple of 4) is constructed by connecting together bit-slice ALUs. Designers can use the ALU's internal registers in any way they desire. For example, they may choose to implement eight addressable data registers, two stack pointers (described later), two index registers, a program counter, and three scratchpad registers. Flexibility is the most powerful feature of bit-slice microprocessors.

This description of the microprogrammed control unit is grossly simplified. In practice the microprogram might include facilities for dealing with interrupts, the memory system, input/output, and so on.

One of the great advantages of a microprogrammed control unit is that it is possible to alter the content of the microprogram memory (sometimes called the *control store*) and hence design your own machine-level instructions. In fact it is perfectly possible to choose a set of microprograms that will execute the machine code of an entirely different computer. In this case the computer is said to *emulate* another computer. Such a facility is useful if you are changing your old computer to a new one whose own machine code is incompatible with your old programs. Emulation applies to programs that exist in binary (object) form on tape or disk. By writing microprograms (on the new machine) to interpret the machine code of the old machine, you can use the old software and still get the advantages of the new machine.

One of the greatest problems in the design of a bit-slice computer lies in the construction and testing of the microprogram. You can, or course, write a program to emulate the bit-slice processor on another computer. A popular method of developing a microprogram is to replace the microprogram ROM with read/write memory and to access this memory with a conventional microprocessor. That is, the microprogram memory is common to both the bit-slice system and the microprocessor. In this way, the microprocessor can input a microprogram in mnemonic form, edit it, assemble it, and then pass control to the bit-slice system. The microprocessor may even monitor the operation of the bit-slice system.

Such a microprogram memory is called a writable control store, and not very long ago a writable control store was regarded as a big selling point of microprogrammed minicomputers and mainframes. However, we have already pointed out that a microprogrammable control store is of very little practical use in most user-microprogrammed computers due to the lack of applications software. Even if a computer user has the expertise to design new microprogrammed macroinstructions, it is unlikely that the system software and compilers will be able to make use of these new instructions. Finally, RISC technology (as we shall see) does not use microprogramming and interest in microprogramming is much less than it once was.

5.3.2 The random logic control unit

The type of control unit we've just described interprets a machine-code instruction by means of a microprogram stored in a read-only memory. The complexity of a microprogrammed

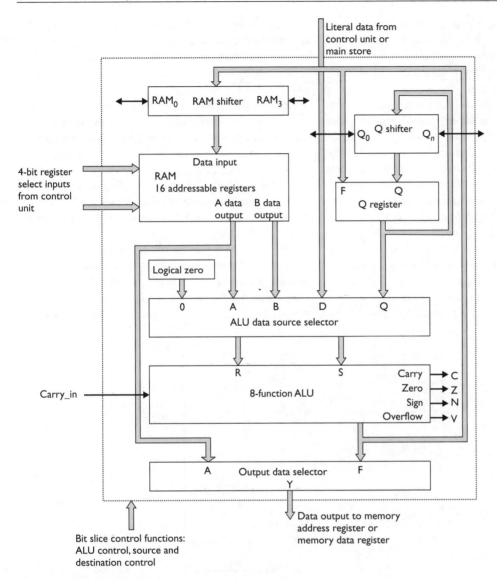

Fig. 5.17 The microprogrammed ALU.

control unit is not directly related to the complexity of the machine code instructions it interprets, just as the complexity of a computer at the machine-code level is not related to the complexity of the high-level language programs being run on it. This statement is correct to a first approximation, but it must be admitted that some designers have attempted to provide machine-level instructions that are close to some of the more complex facilities offered by high-level languages. In such cases, there is indeed a relationship between the complexity of the high-level language and the complexity of the control unit.

When engineers design a *random logic control unit*, RALU, they ask 'What sequence of microinstructions is needed to execute each machine code instruction and what logic elements do we need to implement them?' In other words, designers resort to the Boolean techniques we described in Chapter 2. The word *random* in the expression *random logic element* implies that the arrangement of gates from which the control unit is constructed varies widely from computer to computer. The same microprogrammed control unit can readily be adapted to suit many different computers with relatively little modification, whereas the random logic control unit is dedicated to a specific CPU and cannot easily be modified.

Before designing a random logic control unit, let's consider an ultra-simple CPU. We could use one of the CPU structures described earlier in this section. However, by adopting another design we hope to show the reader that the structure of the CPU is chosen by an engineer and is not rigidly fixed. When designing any computer, the engineer has to weigh up the trade-off between computational power, speed, and cost. The architecture of the computer we're going to consider is essentially the same as that of the CPU described earlier. However, its implementation is rather different because the internal bus structure has been much simplified. Note that we use the term *architecture* to describe the functional capabilities of a computer. A computer's architecture is independent of the way in which the computer is physically implemented (i.e. organized).

Figure 5.18 presents the structure of a primitive CPU. It is primitive because the number of buses and functional units

has been reduced to the bare minimum, making the CPU cheap to produce but reducing its speed. As there is only one internal bus, several microinstructions cannot be carried out simultaneously in order to execute operations in parallel. For example, there is no separate incrementer for the program counter, forcing the ALU to be used to increment the contents of the PC. Consequently, the ALU and associated data paths are not available for other operations while the program counter is being incremented.

In Fig. 5.18 a single system bus is connected to all registers and the memory permitting the transfer of only one data word at a time from a source to a destination. The ALU has two inputs P and Q. The P input comes only from data register D0 and the Q input comes only from the system bus.

The memory receives the address of the memory location to be accessed directly from the MAR, whose output is permanently connected to the memory's address input. A dedicated connection between the MAR and memory is possible because the memory never receives an address input from any

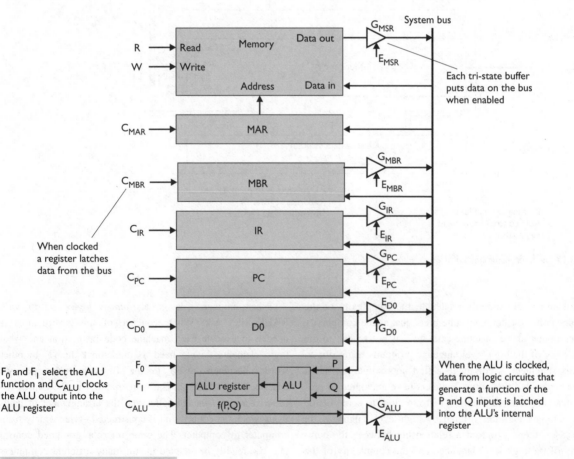

Fig. 5.18 Structure of a single-bus CPU.

source other than the memory address register. A permanent connection removes the need for bus control circuits.

Two data paths link the memory to the system bus. In a read cycle (R true), data is transferred from the memory to the system bus via tri-state gate G_{MSR}. During a memory write cycle (W = 1), data is transferred from the system bus directly to the memory.

The MBR, data register, program counter, and instruction register are each connected to the system bus in the same way. When one of these registers wishes to place data on the bus, its tri-state gate is enabled. Conversely, data is copied into a register from the bus by clocking the register. The instruction register, IR, is arranged so that it can receive data from the memory directly, without the data having to pass through the MBR as indicated earlier in this chapter.

The ALU receives data from two sources, the system bus and data register D0, and places its own output on the system bus. This arrangement begs the question, 'If the ALU gets data from the system bus, how can it put data on the same bus at the same time it is receiving data from this bus?'

Figure 5.18 shows that the ALU contains an internal ALU register. When this register is clocked by C_{ALU}, the output from the ALU is captured and can be put on the system bus when gate G_{ALU} is enabled.

The ALU is controlled by a 2-bit code, F_1, F_0, that determines its functions as defined in Table 5.12. These operations are representative of real instructions, although a practical ALU would implement, typically, 16 different functions.

In order to keep the design of a random logic control unit as simple as possible, we will construct a 3-bit operation code giving a total of eight instructions. The repertoire of instructions in Table 5.13 presents a very primitive instruction set indeed, but it does include many of the types of instructions found in real first-generation processors. We have defined explicit LOAD and STORE instructions rather than a single MOVE instruction that does the work of both LOAD and STORE.

Having constructed an instruction set, the next step is to define each of the instructions in terms of RTL, and determine the sequence of operations necessary to carry them out on the computer in Fig. 5.18. Table 5.14 lists all the clock

Op-code	Mnemonic	Operation
000	LOAD N	[D0]←[M(N)]
001	STORE N	[M(N)]←[D0]
010	ADD N	[D0]←[D0] + [M(N)]
011	SUB N	[D0]←[D0] − [M(N)]
100	INC N	[M(N)]←[M(N)] + 1
101	DEC N	[M(N)]←[M(N)] − 1
110	BRA N	[PC]←N
111	BEQ N	IF Z=1 THEN [PC]←N

Note that N is the operand field used by the instruction.

Table 5.13 A primitive instruction set for the CPU of Fig. 5.18.

signals, denoted by $C_{<register>}$, and all the tri-state bus controller signals, denoted by $E_{<source\ of\ data>}$, required to execute each of the CPU's instructions. The symbol Z is the zero-flag bit from the CCR, which is assumed to be part of the ALU.

Because the ALU block contains a register, we use the notation [ALU] to mean the contents of the ALU's output register.

From op-code to operation

In order to execute an instruction we have to do two things: convert the 3-bit op-code into one of eight possible sequences of action and then cause these actions to take place.

Figure 5.19 shows how the instructions are decoded, and is similar in operation to the 3-line to 8-line decoder described in Chapter 2. For each of the eight possible 3-bit op-codes, one and only one of the eight outputs is placed in an active-high condition. For example, if the op-code corresponding to ADD (i.e. 010) is loaded into the instruction register during a fetch phase, Output 2 from the AND gate array, ADD, is asserted high while all other AND gate outputs remain low.

It's no good simply detecting and decoding a particular instruction. The control unit has to carry out the sequence of microinstructions that will execute the instruction. To do this we require a source of signals to trigger each of the microinstructions. A circuit that produces a stream of trigger signals is called a *sequencer* and Fig. 5.20 provides the logic diagram of a suitable eight-step sequencer.

The outputs of three JK flip-flops arranged as a 3-bit binary up-counter counting 000, 001, 010, ..., 111 are connected to eight 3-input AND gates to generate timing signals T_0 to T_7. Figure 5.21 illustrates the timing pulses created by this circuit. Note that the timing decoder is similar to the instruction decoder of Fig. 5.18. As not all macroinstructions require the same number of microinstructions to interpret them, the sequencer of Fig. 5.20 has a reset input that can be used to reset the sequencer by returning it to state T_0.

F_1	F_0	Function
0	0	add P to Q
0	1	subtract Q from P
1	0	increment Q
1	1	decrement Q

Table 5.12 Decoding the ALU control code, F_0, F_1.

Instruction	Op-code	Operations (RTL)	Control actions		
Fetch		$[MAR] \leftarrow [PC]$	$E_{PC}=1$	C_{MAR}	
		$[IR] \leftarrow [M([MAR])]$	$R=1,\ E_{MSR}=1,$	C_{IR}	
		$[ALU] \leftarrow [PC]$	$E_{PC}=1$	$F_1,F_0=1,0,\ C_{ALU}$	
		$[PC] \leftarrow [ALU]$	$E_{ALU}=1$	C_{PC}	
LOAD	000	$[MAR] \leftarrow [IR]$	$E_{IR}=1$	C_{MAR}	
		$[DO] \leftarrow [M([MAR])]$	$R=1,\ E_{MSR}=1,$	C_{DO}	
STORE	001	$[MAR] \leftarrow [IR]$	$E_{IR}=1$	C_{MAR}	
		$[M([MAR])] \leftarrow [DO]$	$E_{DO}=1$	$W=1$	
ADD	010	$[MAR] \leftarrow [IR]$	$E_{IR}=1$	C_{MAR}	
		$[MBR] \leftarrow [M([MAR])]$	$R=1,\ E_{MSR}=1,$	C_{MBR}	
		$[ALU] \leftarrow [MBR]$	$E_{MBR}=1$	$F_1,F_0=0,0,\ C_{ALU}$	
		$[DO] \leftarrow [ALU]$	$E_{ALU}=1$	C_{DO}	
SUB	011	$[MAR] \leftarrow [IR]$	$E_{IR}=1$	C_{MAR}	
		$[MBR] \leftarrow [M([MAR])]$	$R=1,\ E_{MSR}=1,$	C_{MBR}	
		$[ALU] \leftarrow [MBR]$	$E_{MBR}=1$	$F_1,F_0=0,1,\ C_{ALU}$	
		$[DO] \leftarrow [ALU]$	$E_{ALU}=1$	C_{DO}	
INC	100	$[MAR] \leftarrow [IR]$	$E_{IR}=1$	C_{MAR}	
		$[ALU] \leftarrow [M([MAR])]$	$R=1,\ E_{MSR}=1,$	C_{MBR}	
		$[ALU] \leftarrow [MBR]$	$E_{MBR}=1$	$F_1,F_0=0,1,\ C_{ALU}$	
		$[M([MAR])] \leftarrow [ALU]$	$E_{ALU}=1$	$W=1$	
DEC	101	$[MAR] \leftarrow [IR]$	$E_{IR}=1$	C_{MAR}	
		$[ALU] \leftarrow [M([MAR])]$	$R=1,\ E_{MSR}=1,$	C_{MBR}	
		$[ALU] \leftarrow [MBR]$	$E_{MBR}=1$	$F_1,F_0=1,1,\ C_{ALU}$	
		$[M([MAR])] \leftarrow [ALU]$	$E_{ALU}=1$	$W=1$	
BRA	110	$[PC] \leftarrow [IR]$	$E_{IR}=1$	C_{PC}	
BEQ	111	IF Z=1 THEN	$E_{IR}=1$ IF Z=1 THEN	C_{PC}	
		$\quad [PC] \leftarrow [IR]$			

Table 5.14 Interpreting the instruction set of Table 5.13 in RTL and microinstructions.

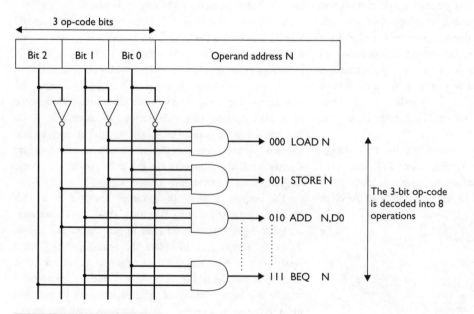

Fig. 5.19 The instruction decoder.

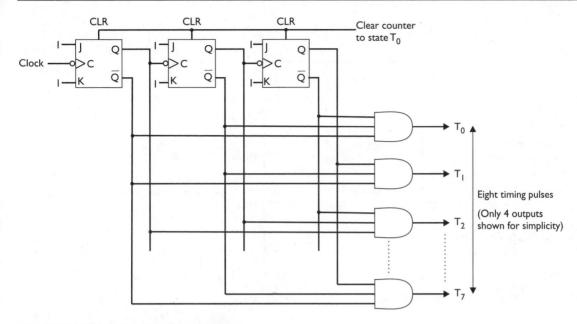

Fig. 5.20 The timing pulse generator (sequencer).

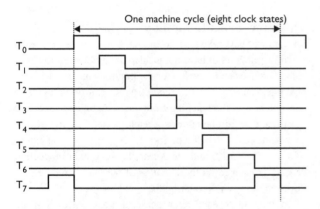

Fig. 5.21 The outputs from the timing-pulse generator.

The sequencer of Fig. 5.20 is illustrative rather than practical, because, as it stands, the circuit may generate spurious timing pulses at the timing pulse outputs due to the use of an asynchronous counter. All outputs of an asynchronous counter don't change state at the same instant, and therefore the bit pattern at its output may pass through several states (if only for a few nanoseconds) before it settles down to its final value. Unfortunately, these transient states or *glitches* may last long enough to create spurious timing signals, which, in turn, may trigger undesired activity within the control unit. A solution to

these problems is to disable the output of the timing pulse generator until the counter has settled down (or to use a synchronous counter).

The next step in designing the control unit is to combine the signals from the instruction decoder with the timing signals from the sequencer to generate the actual control signals. Figure 5.22 shows one possible approach.

There are nine vertical lines in Fig. 5.22 (only three are shown). One vertical line corresponds to the fetch phase and each of the other eight lines is assigned to one of the eight instructions. At any instant one of the vertical lines from the instruction decoder (or fetch) is in a logical one state, enabling the column of 2-input AND gates to which it is connected. The other inputs to the column of AND gates are the timing pulses from the sequencer.

As the timing signals, T_0 to T_7, are generated, the outputs of the AND gates enabled by the current instruction synthesize the control signals required to implement the random logic control unit. The output of each AND gate corresponding to a particular microinstruction (e.g. C_{MAR}) triggers the actual microinstruction (i.e. micro-operation). As we pointed out earlier, not all macroinstructions require eight clock cycles to execute them.

Each microinstruction is activated by one or more control signals from the nine columns of AND gates. Figure 5.23 shows the array of OR gates that combine the outputs from the AND gates to generate the control signals.

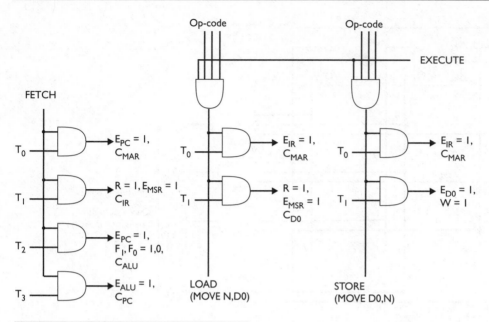

Fig. 5.22 The outputs from the timing-pulse generator.

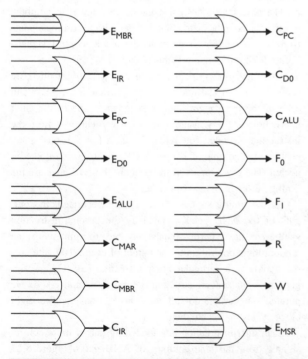

Fig. 5.23 The OR gate array used to generate the actual micro-instructions.

The fetch–execute flip-flop

So far we have devised a mechanism to interpret each macroinstruction but have not tackled the problem of the two-phase fetch–execute cycle. As the control unit is always in one of two states (fetch or execute), an RS flip-flop provides a convenient way of switching from one state to another. When $Q = 0$ the current operation is a fetch phase, and when $Q = 1$ an execute phase is being performed. Figure 5.24 is an extension of Fig. 5.22 and demonstrates how the instruction decoder is enabled by the Q output of the fetch–execute flip-flop, and the fetch decoder by the $\overline{Q}$ output.

At the end of each fetch phase, a clock pulse from the timing generator sets the fetch–execute flip-flop, permitting the current op-code to be decoded and executed. The timing pulse generator is reset at the end of each fetch. At the end of each execute phase, the fetch–execute flip-flop is cleared and the sequencer reset, enabling the next fetch phase to begin.

Table 5.15 shows how the machine-level instructions can be represented in terms of both timing signals and micro-instructions. Note that we've included the micro-operation $[MAR] \leftarrow [IR]$ in the fetch phase.

The microinstructions are the bus driver enables, the register clocks, the ALU function select bits, the memory controls (R and W), and the reset and set inputs of the fetch–execute flip-flop. For each of the microinstructions we can write down a Boolean expression in terms of the machine-level instruction

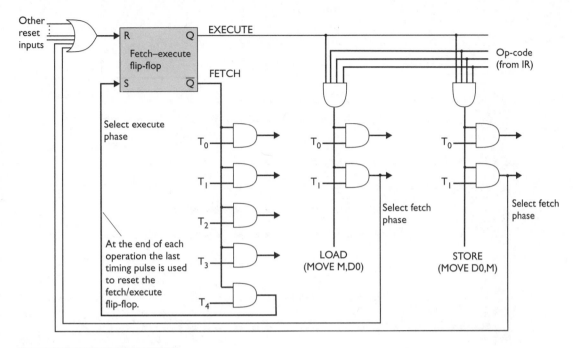

Fig. 5.24 The fetch–execute flip-flop.

and the sequence of timing pulses. For example, consider expressions for E_{MBR}, E_{IR}, C_{MAR}.

$$E_{MBR} = ADD \cdot T_1 + SUB \cdot T_1 + INC \cdot T_1 + DEC \cdot T_1$$
$$E_{IR} = Fetch \cdot T_4 + BRA \cdot T_0 + BEQ \cdot T_0$$
$$C_{MAR} = Fetch \cdot T_0 + Fetch \cdot T_4$$

We should note, of course, that this CPU and its microprogram is very highly simplified and illustrates the nature of the random logic CU rather than its exact design.

Table 5.15 could also be used to implement a microprogrammed control unit, in which case the lines of the table represent consecutive words in the control store.

Microprogramming and random logic control units—a summary

We have now covered the two approaches to the design of a control unit. We can't go into the details of control unit design here, and will therefore point out the most significant features of microprogrammed and random logic control units.

1. Random logic control units are faster than their microprogrammed counterparts. This must always be so because the random logic control unit is optimized for its particular application. Moreover, a microprogrammed control unit is slowed by the need to read a microinstruction from the microprogram memory. Memory accesses are generally slower than basic Boolean operations.

2. Microprogramming offers a flexible design. As the microprogram lives in read-only memory, it can easily be modified at either the design or the production stage. A random logic control unit is strictly special-purpose and cannot readily be modified to incorporate new features in the processor (e.g. additional machine-level instructions), and sometimes it is difficult to remove design errors without considerable modification of the hardware.

3. The high point of microprogramming was the early 1970s, when main memory had an access time of 1–2 μs and the control store used to hold microprograms had an access time of 50–100 ns. It was then sensible to design complex machine-level instructions that were executed very rapidly as microcode. Today, things have changed, and memories with access times of below 50 ns are the norm rather than the exception. Faster memory makes microprogramming less attractive because hard-wired random logic control units execute instructions much more rapidly than microcoded control units. Today's generation of RISC (reduced instruction set computers) and post-RISC architectures are not microprogrammed.

In the next section we are going to demonstrate how a simple CPU can be simulated in C.

Instruction	Time	Enables						Clocks						ALU		Memory		Fetch/Execute	
		MBR	IR	PC	D0	MSR	ALU	MAR	MBR	IR	PC	D0	ALU	F_i	F_0	R	W	R	S
Fetch	T_0	○	○	—	○	○	○	—	○	○	○	○	○	×	×	○	○	○	○
	T_1	○	○	○	○	—	○	○	○	—	○	○	○	×	×	—	○	○	○
	T_2	○	○	—	○	○	○	○	○	○	—	○	—	—	○	○	○	○	○
	T_3	○	—	○	○	○	—	○	○	○	○	○	○	×	×	○	○	○	○
	T_4	○	○	○	○	○	○	○	○	○	○	○	○	×	×	○	○	○	—
LOAD	T_0	○	○	○	○	—	○	○	○	○	○	—	○	×	×	—	○	—	○
STORE	T_0	○	○	○	—	○	○	○	○	○	○	○	○	×	×	○	—	—	○
ADD	T_0	○	○	○	○	—	○	○	—	○	○	○	○	×	×	—	○	○	○
	T_1	—	○	○	○	○	○	○	○	○	○	○	○	○	○	○	○	○	○
	T_2	○	○	○	○	○	—	○	○	○	○	—	—	×	×	○	○	—	○
SUB	T_0	○	○	○	○	—	○	○	—	○	○	○	○	×	×	—	○	○	○
	T_1	—	○	○	○	○	○	○	○	○	○	○	○	○	—	○	○	○	○
	T_2	○	○	○	○	○	—	○	○	○	○	—	—	×	×	○	○	—	○
INC	T_0	○	○	○	○	—	○	○	—	○	○	○	○	×	×	—	○	○	○
	T_1	—	○	○	○	○	○	○	○	○	○	○	○	○	—	○	○	○	○
	T_2	○	○	○	○	○	—	○	○	○	○	—	—	×	×	○	—	—	○
DEC	T_0	○	○	○	○	—	○	○	—	○	○	○	○	×	×	—	○	○	○
	T_1	—	○	○	○	○	○	○	○	○	○	○	○	—	—	○	○	○	○
	T_2	○	○	○	○	○	—	○	○	○	○	○	—	×	×	○	—	—	○
BRA	T_0	○	—	○	○	○	○	○	○	○	—	○	○	×	×	○	○	—	○
BEQ	T_0	○	—	○	○	○	○	○	○	○	N	○	○	×	×	○	○	—	○

Table 5.15 The interpretation of machine-code instructions.

5.4 Simulating a CPU

One way of learning how a processor operates is to build one. We present a program in C that simulates a very simple 8-bit CPU. In order to make the simulator as accessible to as many readers as possible, we have written the simulator in C but have avoided all but C's most basic elements. All data types are 8 bits and the only C constructs we use are `while`, `if...then...else`, and the `switch` construct, which selects one of several courses of action.

We are going to construct two simulators—the first is a very primitive CPU with an 8-bit instruction that simply demonstrates the fetch–execute cycle, and the second simulator is not too dissimilar to typical first-generation 8-bit microprocessors.

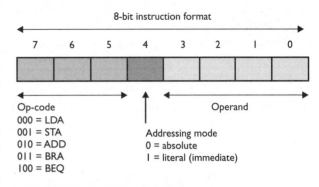

Fig. 5.25 Format of an 8-bit instruction.

5.4.1 CPU with an 8-bit instruction

Our first computer has a single data register (i.e. accumulator) called D0 and all instructions are memory-to-register apart from the store and the branch instructions. Only the store instruction performs a write to memory.

Choosing an instruction set requires many compromises; for example, if the number of bits in an instruction is fixed, increasing the number of different instructions reduces the number of bits left for other functions such as addressing modes or register selection.

We can define an instruction set for our primitive 8-bit machine as

The first step in constructing a simulator is to describe the action of the computer in pseudocode.

```
PC = 0
REPEAT
  Read the instruction pointed at by the PC
  Increment the program counter
  Split the instruction into
          1. an operation code
          2. an addressing mode
          3. an operand
  IF the addressing mode is direct
          THEN get the operand from memory
          ELSE the operand is a literal
     Execute the instruction
FOREVER
```

Instruction	Mnemonic	RTL definition			
Load D0 from memory	LDA N	[D0]	←	[M(N)]	
Store D0 in memory	STA N	[M(N)]	←	[D0]	
Add memory to D0	ADD N	[D0]	←	[D0] + [M(N)]	
Branch to location N	BRA N	[PC]	←	N	
If D0 = zero then branch to N	BEQ N	IF [D0] =	0	THEN [PC]←N	

We have provided only five instructions because these are illustrative of all instructions. This computer has an 8-bit instruction format that includes both the op-code and the operand. If we choose a 3-bit op-code (8 instructions) and a 4-bit operand (a 16-bit memory), the remaining bit can be used to specify the addressing mode (absolute or literal). Real 8-bit microprocessors solve the problem of instruction set design by using one byte to provide an operation code and then 0, 1, or 2 succeeding bytes to provide an operand.

Figure 5.25 defines the structure of an 8-bit instruction for our simulated machine.

We can now write a program to implement this algorithm. The following fragment of code is largely self-explanatory. Note that we have not provided any input or output (when testing the code, I initialized the memory to contain a sequence of instructions and used `printf` statements to display the value of the PC, D0, and other variables).

The instruction in the 8-bit instruction register (IR) is decoded by the three operations

```
opcode = IR >> 5;
     /* get the op-code        */
amode = (IR & 0x10) >> 4;
     /* extract the address mode bit */
operand = IR & 0x0F;
     /* extract the operand      */
```

C allows you to operate on the individual bits of a byte; for example, the operator $>>$ n performs a right shift by n bits. The opcode is obtained from the three most-significant bits of the IR by shifting right five times. A bitwise logical AND can be performed between a variable and a hexadecimal value; for example, IR & 0x0F ANDs the IR with 00001111_2 to extract the operand bits in the four least-significant bit positions.

Once we've extracted the addressing mode (bit 4 of the instruction register) with amode = (IR & 0x10) >> 4, we can calculate the source operand for the load and add instruction by

```
if (amode==0) source=memory[operand];
else source=operand;
```

The following listing provides the C code for this CPU simulator.

```c
#define LDA   0
#define STA   1
#define ADD   2
#define BRA   3
#define BEQ   4
#define STOP  8

void main(void)

{
    unsigned short int PC=0;          /* program counter              */
    unsigned short int D0=0;          /* data register                */
    unsigned short int MAR;           /* memory address register      */
    unsigned short int MBR;           /* memory buffer register       */
    unsigned short int IR;            /* instruction register         */
    unsigned short int operand;       /* the 8-bit operand from the IR */
    unsigned short int source;        /* source operand               */
    unsigned short int opcode;        /* the 3-bit op-code from the IR */
    unsigned short int amode;         /* the 1-bit addressing mode     */
    unsigned short int memory[16];    /* the memory                   */
    unsigned short int run=1;         /* execute program while run is 1 */
/* Instruction format:                          */
/* 7  6  5  4  3  2  1  0                        */
/* Bits 3 to 0 4-bit operand                    */
/* Bit  4       1-bit addressing mode           */
/* Bits 7 to 5 3-bit instruction code           */

/* main loop */

    while (run)
    {
        MAR = PC;                     /* PC to MAR                    */
        PC  = PC+1;                   /* increment PC                 */
        MBR = memory[MAR];            /* get next instruction         */
        IR  = MBR;                    /* copy MBR to IR               */

        opcode  = IR >> 5;            /* get the op-code              */
        amode   = (IR & 0x10) >> 4;   /* extract the address mode bit */
        operand = IR & 0x0F;          /* extract the operand          */
```

```
    if (amode==0) source=memory[operand]; else source=operand;

    switch (opcode)  /* now execute the instruction */
      { case LDA:    { D0=source;                      break;}
        case STA:    { memory[operand]=D0;             break;}
        case ADD:    { D0=D0+source;                   break;}
        case BRA:    { PC=operand;                      break;}
        case BEQ:    { if (D0==0) PC=operand;          break;}
        case STOP:   { run=0;                           break;}
      }
   }
}
```

Most of the work done in the simulator takes place in the `switch` construct at the end of this program where each instruction is interpreted.

5.4.2 CPU with a 16-bit instruction

We now describe a CPU that is much closer to the architecture of typical 8-bit microprocessors. The simulator uses an 8-bit memory with 256 locations. Each instruction occupies two consecutive memory locations—an 8-bit instruction followed by an 8-bit operand. This arrangement provides us with a much richer instruction set than the previous example. However, each fetch cycle requires *two* memory accesses. The first access is to fetch the op-code and the second to fetch the operand; that is:

FETCH	[MAR]	← [PC]	Copy contents of the PC to the MAR
	[PC]	← [PC]+1	Increment contents of the PC
	[MBR]	← [M([MAR])]	Read the instruction from memory
	[IR]	← [MBR]	Move the instruction to the IR
	opcode	← [IR]	Save the op-code
	[MAR]	← [PC]	Copy contents of the PC to the MAR
	[PC]	← [PC]+1	Increment contents of the PC
	[MBR]	← [M([MAR])]	Read the operand from memory
	[IR]	← [MBR]	Move the operand to the IR
	operand	← [IR]	Save the operand

This multi-byte instruction format is used by 8-bit and 16-bit microprocessors. Indeed, the 68000 has one 10-byte instruction.

The architecture of this computer is memory-to-register or register-to-memory; for example, it supports both ADD D0,M and ADD M,D0 instructions. In addition to the direct and literal addressing modes, we have provided address register indirect addressing with a single A0 register. We have also provided program counter-relative addressing (discussed in the next chapter) in which the operand is specified with respect to the current value of the program counter; for example, MOVE D0,12(PC) means store the contents of data register D0 12 bytes on from the location pointed at by the program counter.

The instruction itself is divided into four fields as Fig. 5.26 demonstrates. A 4-bit op-code in bits 7, 6, 5, 4 provides up to 16 instructions. A 2-bit addressing mode in bits 1, 0 selects the way in which the current operand is treated. When the addressing mode is 00, the operand provides the address of the data to be used by the current instruction. When the addressing mode is 01 the operand provides the actual (i.e. literal) operand. Modes 10 and 11 provide indexed and program counter-relative addressing respectively (i.e. the operand is added to the A0 register or the PC, respectively).

Bit 2 of the instruction is a direction bit that determines whether the source operand is in memory or is provided by the data register; for example, the difference between MOVE D0,123 and MOVE 123,D0 is determined by the value of the direction bit.

We can express the basic fetch cycle and decode instruction phase in C as

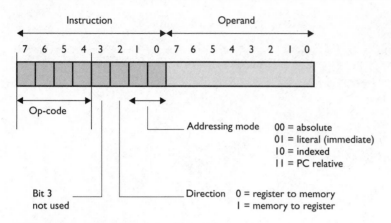

Fig. 5.26 Format of the CPU's instruction.

```
while (run)

  {
  MAR = PC;                        /*PC to MAR                      */
  PC  = PC+1;                      /*increment PC                   */
  MBR = memory[MAR];               /* get next instruction          */
  IR  = MBR;                       /* copy MBR to IR                */
  opcode = IR;                     /* store the op-code bits        */

  MAR = PC;                        /* PC to MAR                     */
  PC  = PC+1;                      /* increment PC                  */
  MBR = memory[MAR];               /* get the operand               */
  IR  = MBR;                       /* copy MBR to IR                */
  operand = IR;                    /* store the operand bits        */
  amode   = opcode & 0x03;         /* extract the address mode bits */
  direction = (opcode & 0x04) >> 2; /* get data direction 0=register to memory
                                             1=memory to register */

  opcode = opcode >> 4;            /* get the 4-bit instruction code   */

    /* use the address mode to get the operand */

      switch (amode)
        { case 0: {source=memory[operand];        break; /* absolute */
                  }
          case 1: {source=operand;                break; /* literal   */
                  }
          case 2: {source=memory[A0+operand];     break; /* indexed   */
                  }
          case 3: {source=memory[PC+operand];     break; /* PC relative */
                  }
        }

    }
```

 Each instruction is executed by means of the `switch` construct. Note that the CCR has only a zero flag (it would have been more complex to have provided a C and V bit). The following provides the complete code for the processor.

```
#define MOVE 0
#define ADD  1
#define SUB  2
#define BRA  3
#define CMP  4
#define BEQ  5
#define BNE  6
#define EXG  7 / *EXG exchanges the contents of two registers */
#define STOP 15

void main(void)
{
   unsigned short int PC =0;          /* program counter                    */
   unsigned short int D0 =0;          /* data register                      */
   unsigned short int A0 =0;          /* address register                   */
   unsigned short int CCR=0;          /* condition code register            */
   unsigned short int MAR;            /* memory address register            */
   unsigned short int MBR;            /* memory buffer register             */
   unsigned short int IR;             /* instruction register               */
   unsigned short int operand;        /* the 8-bit operand from the IR       */
   unsigned short int source;         /* source operand                     */
   unsigned short int destination;    /* the destination value              */
   unsigned short int opcode;         /* the 4-bit op-code from the IR       */
   unsigned short int amode;          /* the 2-bit addressing mode          */
   unsigned short int direction;      /* the 1-bit data direction flag       */
   unsigned short int memory[256];    /* the memory                         */
   unsigned short int run=1;          /* execute program while run is 1     */
/*  Instruction format:                                  */
/* 7  6  5  4  3  2  1  0                                 */
/* Bit 1 and 0  2-bit address mode                       */
/*                     00 address mode=absolute      */
/*                     01 address mode=literal       */
/*                     10 address mode=indexed       */
/*                     11 address mode=relative      */
/* Bit 2        1-bit direction (source/operand)     */
/* Bit 3        not used                             */
/* Bit 7 to 4  4-bit instruction code                */
/* main loop */
   while (run)
   {
     MAR =PC;                    /* PC to MAR                        */
     PC  =PC+1;                  /* increment PC                     */
     MBR =memory[MAR];           /* get next instruction             */
```

(*program continued*)

```
IR  =MBR;                  /* copy MBR to IR                  */
opcode=IR;                 /* store the op-code bits          */
MAR=PC;                    /* PC to MAR                       */
PC  =PC+1;                 /* increment PC                    */
MBR=memory[MAR];           /* get the operand                 */
IR  =MBR;                  /* copy MBR to IR                  */
operand=IR;                /* store the operand bits          */
amode  =opcode & 0x03;     /* extract the address mode bits   */
direction=(opcode & 0x04) >> 2; /* get data direction 0=register to memory
                                               1=memory to register */
opcode=opcode>>4;          /* get the 4-bit instruction code  */

/* use the address mode to get the source operand */

switch (amode)
  { case 0: {source=memory[operand];        break;}  /* absolute    */
    case 1: {source=operand;                break;}  /* literal     */
    case 2: {source=memory[A0+operand];     break;}  /* indexed     */
    case 3: {source=memory[PC+operand];     break;}  /* PC relative */
  }

/* now execute the instruction */

switch (opcode)
  {case MOVE: {if (direction==0) destination=D0;
                  else D0=source;
                  if (D0==0) CCR=1; else CCR=0; /* update CCR */
               break;
              }

  case ADD:   {if (direction==0)
                  { destination=D0+source;
                    if (destination==0) CCR=1; else CCR=0;
                  }
               else
                  { D0=D0+source;
                    if (D0==0) CCR=1; else CCR=0;
                  }
               break;
              }

  case SUB:   {if (direction==0)
                  { destination=D0-source;
                    if (destination==0) CCR=1; else CCR=0;
                  }
               else
                  { D0=D0-source;
                    if (D0==0 ) CCR=1; else CCR=0;
                  }
               break;
              }
```

```
    case BRA:    {if (amode==0)   PC=operand;
                  if (amode==1)  PC=PC+operand; break;
                 }

    case CMP:    { MBR=D0-source;
                   if (MBR==0)  CCR=1;
                   else CCR=0; break;
                 }

    case BEQ:    {if (CCR==1)
                      { if (amode==0)  PC=operand;
                        if (amode==1)  PC=PC+operand;
                      } break;
                 }

    case BNE:    {if (CCR !=1)
                      { if (amode==0)  PC=operand;
                        if (amode==1)  PC=PC+operand;
                      } break;
                 }

    case EXG:    {MBR=D0;  D0=A0;  A0=MBR;  break;
                 }

    case STOP:   {run=0; break;
                 }
    }

/* save result in memory if register to memory */
if (direction==0)
    switch (amode)
    { case 0: { memory[operand]=destination;    break; /* absolute    */
              }

      case 1: {                                 break; /* literal     */
              }

      case 2: { memory[A0+operand]=destination; break; /* indexed     */
              }

      case 3: { memory[PC+operand]=destination; break; /* PC relative */
              }

    }
  }
}
```

We have now covered the basic von Neumann machine. In the next chapter we look at some of the fine details of a high-performance CISC (complex instruction set computer) and demonstrate how assembly language programs are written. In Chapter 7 we describe some of the techniques developed in the 1980s to increase the speed of processors and introduce the ARM RISC processor. However, before we leave the CPU we briefly examine one of the ways in which computers can be made more powerful without adopting new technology—by operating several CPUs in parallel.

5.5 Multiprocessor systems

A *multiprocessor system* is a computer in which two or more processors work together to achieve a greater throughput than is possible with one processor alone. These processors communicate at high speed with each other and share the same hardware facilities such as memory. Multiprocessor systems using between 2^6 and 2^{16} *processing elements* can achieve a level of performance ranging from the super-minicomputer to the supercomputer. The processing elements, PEs, in a multiprocessor system may be simple arithmetic devices like multipliers and adders, or complete computers. Multiprocessing is a vast subject and here we only scratch the surface of this topic.

5.5.1 The performance of multiprocessor systems

A processor's execution rate can be measured in *mips* (millions of instructions per second), or in *megaflops* (millions of floating point instructions per second). Multiprocessor systems have two additional figures of merit called *speedup* and *efficiency*.

The speedup, S_p, of a multiprocessor system using p processors is defined as $S_p = T_1/T_p$, where T_1 is the time taken to perform the computation on a single processor and T_p is the time taken to perform the same computation on p processors. The value of S_p must fall in the range $1 \leqslant S_p \leqslant p$. The lower limit on S_p corresponds to a problem in which parallelism can't be exploited and only one processor can be used. In practice, this inequality is slightly incorrect because a program runs more slowly on one processor in a parallel processor than it would on a single processor. The upper limit on S_p

corresponds to a problem that can be divided equally between the p processors.

The efficiency, E_p, of a multiprocessor system is defined as the ratio between the speedup ratio and the number of processors, that is $E_p = S_p/p = T_1/pT_p$. The efficiency, E_p, must fall in the range 1 (all processors used fully) to $1/p$ (only one processor out of p used).

The speedup ratio is profoundly affected by the parts of a problem that cannot be computed in parallel. Figure 5.27 shows how a problem may have components or tasks that must be executed serially, P_s, and tasks that can be executed in parallel, P_p. If each task in Fig. 5.27 requires t seconds, the total time required by a serial processor is $8t$. Since three pairs of tasks can be carried out in parallel, the total time taken on a parallel system is $4t$. Consider, for example, the product $(P+Q)(P-Q)$. The operations $P+Q$ and $P-Q$ can be carried out simultaneously in parallel, whereas their product can be carried out serially only after $P+Q$ and $P-Q$ have been evaluated.

Suppose a program consists of two components: a part that must be computed serially and a part that can be computed by processors operating in parallel. The fraction of the task that is executed serially is f, and the fraction that is executed in parallel is $(1-f)$. The time taken to process the task on a parallel processor is $fT_1 + (1-f)T_1/p$, where T_1 is the time required to execute the task on a single processor and p is the number of processors. The speedup ratio is $S_p = T_1/(fT_1 + (1-f)T_1/p) = p/(1+(p-1)f)$. This equation is known as *Amdahl's law* and tells us that increasing the number of processors in a system is futile unless the value of f can be made very low.

Figure 5.28 demonstrates the relationship between the speedup ratio, $S(f)$, and f (the fraction of serial processing)

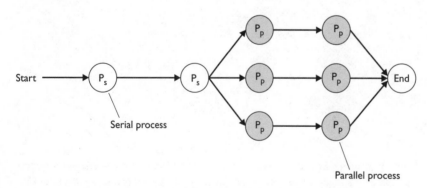

If each process takes t seconds, the total time taken is $4t$

Fig 5.27 Executing a problem in serial and parallel.

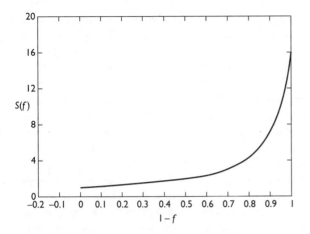

Fig. 5.28 The effect of f on the speedup ratio ($p = 16$).

for a system with 16 processors. The horizontal axis is the fraction of a task that is executed in parallel, $1 - f$. As you can see, the speedup ratio rises very rapidly as the value of $1 - f$ approaches 1.

Multiprocessor systems design is not easy because there are a lot of factors to take into account; for example, the distribution of tasks between processors, the interconnection of the processors (i.e. the *topology* of the multiprocessor system), the management of the memory resources, the avoidance of *deadlock*, and the control of input/output resources. Deadlock occurs when two or more processors cannot continue because each is blocking the other.

The distribution of tasks between processors is of crucial importance in selecting the architecture of the processor system itself. In turn, the distribution of tasks is strongly determined by the nature of the problem to be solved by the computer. In other words, the architecture of a multiprocessor system can be optimized for a certain type of problem. Conversely, a class of programs that runs well on one multiprocessor system may not run well on another.

5.5.2 Topics in multiprocessor systems design

A key parameter of a multiprocessor system is its *topology*, which defines how the processors are arranged with respect to each other and how they communicate. An equally important parameter of a multiprocessor system is the degree of *coupling* between the various processors. We will discuss processor coupling first and then look at multiprocessor topologies.

Processors with facilities for exchanging large quantities of data very rapidly are said to be *tightly coupled*. Such computers share resources like buses or blocks of memory. The advantage of tightly coupled systems is their potential speed, because one processor doesn't have to wait long periods while data is transferred from another. Their disadvantage arises from the complexity of the hardware and software necessary to coordinate the processors. If they share a bus or memory, an *arbiter* is needed to determine which processor is permitted to access the resource at any time.

Multiprocessor organization

Although there is an endless variety of multiprocessor architectures, we can identify broad groups whose members have certain features in common. One possible approach to the classification of multiprocessor systems, attributed to Flynn, is to consider the type of the parallelism (i.e. architecture or topology) and the nature of the interprocessor communication. Flynn's four basic multiprocessor architectures are referred to by the abbreviations SISD, SIMD, MISD, and MIMD, and are described later. However, Flynn's topological classification of multiprocessor systems is not the only one possible, as multiprocessors may be categorized by a number of different parameters.

SISD (Single Instruction Single Data-stream) The SISD machine is nothing more than the conventional single processor system. It is called *single instruction* because only one instruction is executed at a time, and *single data-stream* because there is only one task being executed at any instant.

SIMD (Single Instruction Multiple Data-stream) The SIMD architecture executes instructions *sequentially*, but on data in *parallel*. The idea of a single instruction operating on parallel data is not as strange as it may sound. Consider vector math-ematics. A vector is a multi-component data structure; for example, the 4-component vector A might be 0.2, 4.3, 0.2, 0.1. A very frequent operation in most branches of engineering is the calculation of the *inner product* of two n-component vectors, A and B. The inner product of vectors A and B is defined as

$$s = A \cdot B = \sum a_i b_i$$

For example, if A is $(1, 4, 3, 6)$ and B is $(4, 6, 2, 3)$, the inner product $A \cdot B$ is $1 \times 4 + 4 \times 6 + 3 \times 2 + 6 \times 3 = 4 + 24 + 6 + 18 = 52$. The inner product can be expressed as single operation (i.e. $s = A \cdot B$), but involves multiple data elements (i.e. the $\{a_i \cdot b_i\}$). Such calculations are used extensively in computer graphics and image processing. One way of speeding up the calculation of an inner product is to assign a processor to the generation of each of the individual elements, the $\{a_i \cdot b_i\}$.

The simultaneous calculation of $a_i \cdot b_i$ for $i = 1$ to n requires n processors, one for each component of the vector.

Such an arrangement consists of a single controller that steps through the program (i.e. the single instruction-stream) and an array of processing elements (PEs) acting on the components of a vector in parallel (i.e. the multiple data-stream). Often, such PEs are number crunchers or high-speed ALUs, rather than the general-purpose microprocessor we have been considering throughout this text.

The SIMD architecture, or *array processor*, has a high performance/cost ratio and is very efficient as long as the task running on it can be decomposed largely into vector operations. Consequently, the array processor is best suited to processing radar signals in air-traffic control, processing weather information (this involves partial differential equations), and computerized *tomography* where the output of a body-scanner is processed almost entirely by vector arithmetic.

MISD (Multiple Instruction Single Data-stream) The MISD architecture performs multiple operations concurrently on a single stream of data and is associated with the *pipeline processor*. A pipeline processor is best described in terms of an analogy with an automobile assembly line, where a single stream of components is operated on by a number of sequential processes to produce the finished automobile. For example, four cars may be in the pipeline at any instant with a different operation being applied to each car. A complete car is produced after a car has passed through each of the stages in the pipeline and has been operated on at each stage. We look at pipelining in more detail when we discuss the RISC processor.

In multiprocessor terms, the various processors are arranged in-line and are synchronized so that each processor accepts a new input every t seconds. If there are n processors, the total execution time of a task is nt seconds. At each epoch, a processor takes a partially completed task from a downstream processor and hands on its own task to the next upstream processor. As a pipeline processor has N processors operating concurrently and each task may be in one of the N stages, it requires a total of $Nt + (K-1)t$ time slots to process K tasks. The MISD architecture is a special case of the multiprocessor and is not dealt with further, as it is not suited to multiprocessor systems based on general-purpose microprocessors. MISD systems are highly specialized and require special-purpose architectures and are not discussed further here. In fact, MISD architectures have never been developed to the same extent as SIMD and MIMD architectures.

MIMD (Multiple Instruction Multiple Data-stream) The MIMD architecture is the most general-purpose form of multiprocessor system and is represented by systems in which each processor has its own set of instructions operating on its own data structures. In other words, the processors are acting in a largely autonomous mode. Each individual processor may be

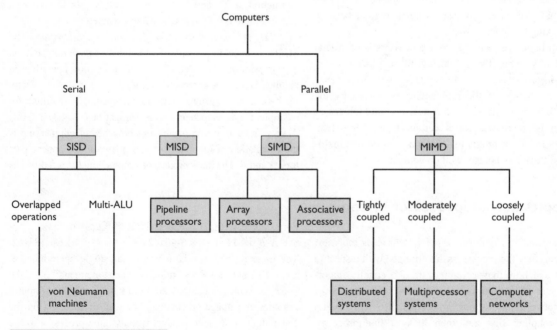

Fig. 5.29 Multiprocessor categories.

working on part of the main task and does not necessarily need to get in touch with its neighbors until it has finished its subtask.

Because of the generality of the MIMD architecture, it can be said to encompass the relatively tightly coupled arrangements to be discussed shortly, and the very loosely coupled geographically distributed LANs. Figure 5.29 provides a graphical illustration of the classification of multiprocessor systems according to Fathi and Krieger.

5.5.3 MIMD architectures

The major design consideration in the production of such a multiprocessor concerns the *topology* of the system, which describes the arrangement of the communications paths between the individual processors.

Figures 5.30–5.33 depict classic MIMD topologies, which are the same as those available to the designer of local area networks (apart from the hypercube). Multiprocessor structures are described both by their topology and by their interconnection level. The level of interconnection is a measure of the number of switching units through which a message must pass when going from processor X to processor Y. Basic topologies are the bus, the ring, and the star, although, of course, there are many variants of each of these pure topologies.

The bus topology

The bus, Fig. 5.30, is the simplest of topologies because each processor is connected to a single common data highway—the bus. The bus is a simple topology, not least because it avoids the problem of how to route a message from processor X to processor Y. All traffic between processors must use the bus. The disadvantage of the bus as a method of implementing a multiprocessor system lies in the problem of controlling access to the bus. As only one processor at a time can use the bus, it is necessary to design an *arbiter* to determine which processor may access the bus at any time. Arbitration between two or more contending processors slows down the system and leads to bottlenecks. A bus offers a relatively high degree of coupling but is more suitable for schemes in which the quantity of data exchanged between the individual processors is small.

The ring topology

The ring topology of Fig. 5.31 is arranged so that each processor is connected only to its two nearest neighbors. One neighbor is called the *upstream* neighbor and the other the *downstream* neighbor. A processor receives information from its downstream neighbor and passes it on to its upstream neighbor. In this way, information flows round the ring in one direction only, and a packet of information passes through each of the processors in the ring. The information passed to a processor contains a destination address. When a processor receives a packet, it checks the address and, if the packet address corresponds to the processor's own address, the processor reads the packet. Similarly, a processor is able to add packets of its own to the stream of information flowing round the ring.

The ring topology offers certain advantages for some classes of loosely coupled multiprocessor network and represents one of the most popular forms of local area network. It is less widely used as a method of interconnecting processors in a tightly coupled MIMD architecture. A ring network is vulnerable to a break in the ring. Some systems employ a *double ring* that does not fail if one of the rings fails.

The star topology

The star topology of Fig. 5.32 employs a central processor as a switching network, rather like a telephone exchange,

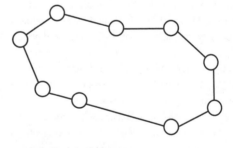

Fig. 5.31 The ring topology.

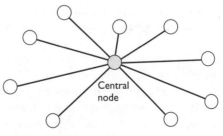

Fig 5.32 The star topology.

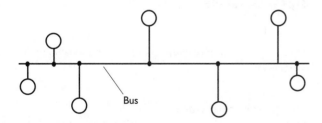

Fig. 5.30 The bus topology.

between the other processors, which are arranged logically (if not physically) around the central node. The advantage of the star is that it reduces bus contention, as there are no shared communication paths. Moreover, the star does not require the large number of buses needed by unconstrained topologies.

On the other hand, the star network is only as good as its central node. If this node fails, the entire system fails. Consequently, the star topology does not display any form of graceful degradation. The central network must be faster than the nodes using its switching facilities, if the system is to be efficient. In many ways, both the ring and the star topologies are better suited to local area networks, where the individual signal paths are implemented by serial data channels, rather than by the parallel buses of the tightly coupled multiprocessor.

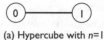

(a) Hypercube with $n=1$

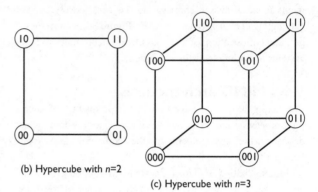

(b) Hypercube with $n=2$

(c) Hypercube with $n=3$

The hypercube topology

An n-dimensional hypercube multiprocessor connects together $N=2^n$ processors in the form of an n-dimensional binary cube. Each corner (vertex or *node*) of the hypercube consists of a suitable processing element and its associated memory. Because of the topology of a hypercube, each node is directly connected to exactly n other neighbors; that is, the number of links per node depends on the dimension of the cube. Figure 5.33 illustrates the hypercube topology for $n=1, 2, 3$, and 4.

Each processor in a hypercube has an n-bit address in the range $0\ldots00$ to $1\ldots11$ (i.e. 0 to 2^n-1), and each node has n nearest neighbors with an address that differs from the node's address by only one bit. For example, if $n=4$ and a node has an address 0100, its four nearest neighbors have addresses 1100, 0000, 0110, and 0101. The maximum path length between any two nodes in a hypercube is n.

A hypercube of dimension n is constructed *recursively* by taking a hypercube of dimension $n-1$ and prefixing all its node addresses by 0 and adding to this another hypercube of dimension $n-1$ whose node addresses are all prefixed by 1. In other words, a hypercube of dimension n can be subdivided into two hypercubes of dimension $n-1$, and these two subcubes can, in turn, be divided into four subcubes of dimension $n-2$ and so on.

The hypercube is of interest because it has a topology that makes it relatively easy to map certain groups of algorithm on to the hypercube. In particular, the hypercube is well suited to problems involving the evaluation of *fast Fourier transforms* (FFTs)—used in sound and video signal processing. The first practical hypercube multiprocessor was built at Caltech in 1983. This was called the Cosmic Cube and was

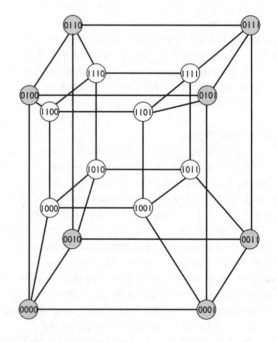

(d) Hypercube with $n=4$

Fig. 5.33 The hypercube.

based on 64 8086 microprocessors plus 8087 floating point coprocessors.

The crossbar network

Another possible topology described in Fig. 5.34 is the so-called *crossbar* switching architecture, which has its origin in

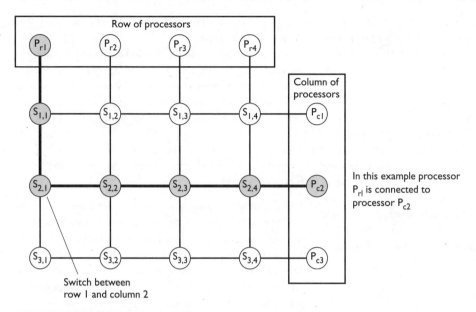

Row of processors

Column of processors

In this example processor P_{rl} is connected to processor P_{c2}

Switch between row 1 and column 2

Fig. 5.34 The crossbar switching network.

the telephone exchange, where it is employed to link subscribers to each other.

The processors are arranged as a single column (processors P_{c1} to P_{cm}) and a single row (processors P_{r1} to P_{rn}). That is, there are a total of $m+n$ processors. Note that the processors may be processing elements or just simple memory elements. Each processor in a column is connected to a horizontal bus and each processor in a row is connected to a vertical bus. A switching network, $S_{r,c}$, connects the processor on row r to the processor on column c. This arrangement requires $m \times n$ switching networks for the $m+n$ processors.

The advantage of the crossbar matrix is the speed at which the interconnection between two processors can be set up. Furthermore, it can be made highly reliable by providing alternative connections between nodes should one of the switch points fail. Reliability is guaranteed only if the switches are fail-safe and always fail in the off or no-connection position.

If the switches at the crosspoints are made multi-way (vertical to vertical, horizontal to horizontal, or horizontal to vertical), we can construct a number of simultaneous pathways through the matrix. The provision of multiple pathways considerably increases the bandwidth of the system.

In practice, the crossbar matrix is not widely found in general-purpose systems because of its high complexity. Another penalty associated with this arrangement is its limited expandability. If we wish to increase the power of the system by adding an extra processor, we must also add another bus, together with its associated switching units.

The binary tree

An interesting form of multiprocessor topology is illustrated in Fig. 5.35. For obvious reasons this structure is called a *binary tree*. Any two processors (nodes) in the tree communicate

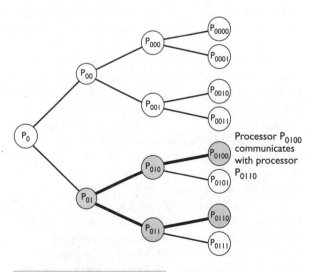

Processor P_{0100} communicates with processor P_{0110}

Fig. 5.35 The binary tree topology.

with each other by traversing the tree right-to-left until a processor common to both nodes is found, and then traversing the tree left-to-right. For example, Fig. 5.35 shows how processor P_{0110} communicates with processor P_{0100}, by establishing backward links from P_{0110} to P_{01} via P_{011} and then forward links from P_{01} to P_{010} to P_{0100}.

The topology of the binary tree has the facility to set up multiple simultaneous links (depending on the nature of each of the links), because the whole tree is never needed to link any two points. In practice, a real system would implement additional pathways to relieve potential bottlenecks and to guard against the effects of failure at certain switching points. The failure of a switch in a right-hand column, for example P_{0010}, causes the loss of a single processor, whereas the failure of a link at the left-hand side, for example P_0, immediately removes half the available processors from the system.

Coupling

Up to now we have been looking at the topology of multiprocessor systems with little or no consideration of the nuts and bolts of the actual connections between the processors. Possibly more than any other factor, the required degree of coupling between processors in a multiprocessor system determines how the processors are to be linked. A tightly coupled multiprocessor system passes data between processors either by means of shared memory or by allowing one processor to access the other processor's data, address, and control buses directly. When shared memory, sometimes called *dual-port RAM*, is employed to couple processors, a block of read/write memory is arranged to be common to both processors. One processor writes data to the block and the other reads that data. Data can be transferred as fast as each processor can execute a memory access.

The degree of coupling between processors is expressed in terms of two parameters: the *transmission bandwidth*, and the *latency* of the interprocessor link. The transmission bandwidth is defined as the rate at which data is moved between processors and is expressed in bits per second. For example, if a microprocessor writes a byte of data to an 8-bit parallel port every $0.5\,\mu s$, the bandwidth of the link is 8 bits/$0.5\,\mu s$ or 16 Mbit/s. However, if a 16-bit port is used to move words at the same rate, the bandwidth rises to 32 Mbit/s.

The latency of an interprocessor link is defined as the time required to initiate a data transfer. That is, latency is the time that elapses between a processor requesting a data transfer and the time at which the transfer actually takes place. A high degree of coupling is associated with large transmission bandwidths and low latencies. As might be expected, tightly coupled microprocessor systems need more complex hardware than loosely coupled systems.

We have now covered the way in which the CPU operates and have described parallel systems using several CPUs operating together. In the next chapter we look at a typical processor in detail, and in the chapter after that we look at another form of parallelism—*instruction level parallelism*, ILP.

Summary

In this chapter we've introduced the heart of the computer, the CPU, which is responsible for reading instructions from memory and executing them. In particular, we have looked at the von Neumann machine, which operates in a two-phase mode. First it reads an instruction from memory and then it gets the data required by the instruction from the same memory. This dual use of memory leads to the so-called *von Neumann bottleneck* on the bus between the CPU and memory.

In addition to describing the 'fetch–execute' cycle we have demonstrated how the CPU deals with literal operands and implements the conditional execution required to synthesize high-level constructs such as IF … THEN.

The middle part of this chapter has provided an overview of the way in which the CPU's control unit is implemented. We've done this for two reasons. The first is to explain in detail how the CPU goes about executing instructions and the second is to demonstrate how the digital logic we covered in Chapters 2 and 3 is used to implement a computer.

We described two ways of implementing a control unit. The first was microprogramming, in which a machine level instruction is interpreted by executing a sequence of primitive operations that control registers and buses. These primitive operations are stored in a microprogram read-only memory. The second way of implementing a control unit is to use a combination of counters, decoders, and basic logic elements to generate the sequence of operations required to implement each machine level instruction.

The final part of this chapter introduced the concept of multiprocessing, in which more than one CPU can be combined to increase the power of a computer.

Problems

1. What is the largest memory space (i.e. program) that can be addressed by processors with the following number of address bits?

(a) 12 bits

(b) 16 bits

(c) 24 bits

(d) 32 bits

(e) 48 bits

(f) 64 bits

2. The von Neumann stored program computer locates program and data in the same memory. What are the advantages and disadvantages of a system with a combined program and data memory?

3. What does the expression $[100] \leftarrow [50] + 2$ mean?

4. What does the expression $[100] \leftarrow [50+2] + 2$ mean?

5. What is an operand?

6. What is the CCR?

7. What is a literal operand?

8. What is the difference between the instructions MOVE #4,D3 and MOVE 4,D3?

9. For the memory map of Fig. 5.36 explain the meaning of the following RTL expressions in plain English.

(a) $[M(1000)] = 120$

(b) $[M(1003)] = [M(1001)] + 1$

(c) $[M(1004)] \leftarrow 5$

(d) $[M(1000)] \leftarrow [M(1005)]$

(e) $[M(1001)] \leftarrow [M(1002)] + [M(1003)]$

(f) $[M(1000)] \leftarrow [M([M(1001)] + 1)]$

10. Suppose a problem in an algebra text says 'Let $x = 5$'. What exactly is x? Answer this question from the point of view of a computer scientist.

11. In the context of a CPU, what is the difference between a data path and an address path?

12. Why is the program counter a *pointer* and not a *counter*?

13. What's the difference between a memory location and a data register?

14. Explain the function of the following registers in a CPU:

(a) PC

(b) MAR

(c) MBR

(d) IR

1000	120
1001	1003
1003	8
1004	0
1005	23

Fig. 5.36 Memory map for Problem 9.

15. Does a computer need data registers?

16. Some machines have a one-address format, some a two-address format, and some a three-address format; for example, ADD P1, ADD P1,P2, and ADD P1,P2,P3, respectively. What are the relative merits of each of these instruction formats?

17. What is the difference between the C, Z, V, and N flags in a computer's condition code register?

18. For each of the following 4-bit operations calculate the values of the C, Z, V, and N flags.

(a)	0011	(b)	1111	(c)	0000
	+0101		+0001		−1111

(d)	1011	(e)	0000	(f)	1110
	+0111		−0001		+1111

19. A CPU has an instruction format op-code source, destination. If we use '#' to represent the literal mode, why is ADD #4,P a legal instruction whereas ADD P,#4 is an illegal instruction?

20. Some microprocessors have one general-purpose data register, some two, some eight, and so on. What do you think determines the number of such general-purpose data registers in any given computer?

21. What is the difference between a dedicated and a general-purpose computer?

22. What is a bus?

23. What is the so-called von Neumann bottleneck?

24. What is the difference between machine code and assembly language?

25. What is the difference between the program counter (part of the CPU) and the location counter (used by an assembler)?

26. What is the advantage of a computer with many registers over one with few registers?

27. What are the advantages and disadvantages of one-, two-, and three-operand instructions? Under what circumstances do you think that a four-operand instruction might be useful?

28. What is an address register and what is its role in a CPU?

29. What is an assembler directive and why is it called a *pseudo-operation*?

30. How does the assembly language programmer decide what data goes in memory locations and what data goes in data registers?

31. Using the instructions

```
MOVE  Source,Dn
MOVE  Dn,Destination
ADD   Source,Dn
SUB   Source,Dn
BEQ   Address
BNE   Address,
```

   (a) Write an assembly language program to store the numbers $1, 2, 3, ..., 30$ in consecutive memory locations starting at 100.
   (b) Translate the algorithm

```
IF X>12 THEN X := 2*X+4
        ELSE X := X+Y
```

   into assembly language.

32. What is a microinstruction?

33. Microprogramming has now fallen into disfavor. Why do you think this is so?

34. For the structure of Fig. 5.18 write a microprogram to implement the operation

$$(A+B+C+1)$$

Assume that only one operand, A, is required by the instruction and that operands B and C are in the next consecutive two memory locations, respectively.

35. Write a program in a suitable high-level language to simulate the microprogrammed architecture of Fig. 5.18. You should be able to present microinstructions to your program and observe their effect on the simulated architecture.

36. Consider the calculation $(A+B+C+D)(P+Q+R+S)$. If this were performed on a multiprocessor system with four CPUs, what is the maximum efficiency that can be achieved?

Chapter 6

Assembly language programming and the 68K family

Following our examination of the CPU and its control unit, the next step is to look at a real architecture, the 68000, in greater detail. The 68000 is the first member of a *family* of microprocessors and is compatible with the 68020, 68030, 68040, and 68060 processors in the sense that assembly language programs written for the 68000 will run on later members of the 68000 family. Programs written in 68020 assembly language will not necessarily run on the 68000, because the newer and more powerful members of the 68000 family have enhanced instruction sets. In this chapter we use '68K' to refer to the 68000 and later members of this family. We've decided to use the 68K as a vehicle for teaching microprocessor architecture for three reasons. First, the 68K family is found in a wide variety of microcomputers. Second, the 68K has a sophisticated architecture, incorporating facilities once found only on more powerful minicomputers and mainframe computers. Third, the 68K's assembly language is relatively easy to learn.

This chapter looks at the 68K's architecture and provides an introduction to assembly language programming. Some of the material we cover in this chapter was introduced when we looked at the CPU. We have decided to provide a little overlap in order to ensure that the reader doesn't have to keep referring to earlier material when reading this chapter.

The *architecture* of a processor is the assembly language programmer's view of it. An architecture is made up of the processor's registers, its instruction set, and its addressing modes. Once we've described the 68K's architecture, we demonstrate the design of simple assembly language programs. We begin this chapter by looking at the structure of an assembly language program composed of both instructions and commands, called *assembler directives*, that control the way in which storage is allocated to data (rather like declarations in high-level language). We also describe how the 68K works with data elements that may be 1, 2, or 4 bytes long. Much of this chapter is concerned with various types of operation that the 68K can perform and the way in which data elements are accessed in memory. We devote a section to subroutines (also called *procedures* or *functions*) and the way in which information is moved between a subroutine and the body of a program. This topic is important because an understanding of how subroutines work at the machine level helps you to understand the nature of high-level languages—particularly C.

As assembly language programming is a practical activity, we provide a 68K cross-assembler and simulator with this book. The simulator runs on a PC and allows you to execute 68K programs. In particular, you can execute a program instruction-by-instruction and observe the effect of each instruction on memory and registers as it is executed. We will use this simulator a lot in this chapter to indicate the way in which the 68K operates. However, before we continue, we are going to demonstrate what an assembly language program looks like.

6.1 Structure of an assembly language program

Figure 6.1 provides the *listing* of a very simple assembly language program written to run on the Teesside 68K cross-assembler. This program implements the high-level language operation $R = P + Q$ (where variables $P = 2$ and $Q = 4$). Fortunately, very few rules govern the layout of a 68K assembly language program. The leftmost column is reserved for user-defined labels—in this case, P, Q, and R. If a line begins with an asterisk in the first column, the assembler ignores the rest of the line. Consequently, you can put an asterisk in column 1 to create a comment. Another rule is that the mnemonic and its operand must be separated by at least one space and that no embedded spaces must be located within either the mnemonic or operand fields.

Assemblers allow you to express numbers in different bases—numbers prefixed by $ in Fig. 6.1 are hexadecimal. The prefix % is used to indicate that the following number is expressed in binary form; for example, the three operations

```
MOVE 25,D0
MOVE $19,D0
MOVE %11001,D0
```

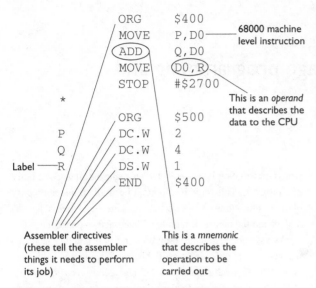

```
        ORG    $400
        MOVE   P,D0      ─── 68000 machine
        ADD    Q,D0          level instruction
        MOVE   D0,R
        STOP   #$2700
  *                          This is an operand
                             that describes the
        ORG    $500          data to the CPU
  P     DC.W   2
  Q     DC.W   4
Label ─R DS.W  1
        END    $400
```

Assembler directives
(these tell the assembler
things it needs to perform
its job)

This is a *mnemonic*
that describes the
operation to be
carried out

Fig. 6.1 Structure of an assembly language program.

are all equivalent. The assembler translates each of these into exactly the same machine code.

In Fig. 6.1 you can also see another prefix, the # symbol. Prefixing an operand with # indicates the *immediate* addressing mode; that is, the operand is a literal or actual value. We will return to this point later.

Figure 6.2 shows the structure of a typical 68K instruction. Instructions with two operands are always written in the form source,destination, where source is where the operand comes from and destination is where the result goes to.

6.1.1 Assembler directives

Assembly language statements can be divided into two types: *executable statements* and *assembler directives*. An executable statement is an instruction in mnemonic form that the assembler translates into the machine code of the target microprocessor. In the example in Fig. 6.1, the executable instructions are

```
MOVE    P,D0
ADD     Q,D0
MOVE    D0,R,     and
STOP    #$2700
```

The meanings of the first three instructions are obvious. The last instruction, STOP #$2700, terminates the program by halting further instruction execution. Don't worry too much about the operand #$2700—the # symbol tells the assembler that the following value is a number and not an address and the $ indicates a hexadecimal number. We use this STOP instruction to terminate programs running on the Teesside simulator. This instruction also loads the 68K's status register with the value 2700 (a special code that initializes the 68K).

An *assembler directive* tells the assembler something it needs to know about the program it is assembling; for example, the assembler directive ORG means *origin* and tells the assembler where the instructions or data are to be loaded in memory. The expression ORG $400 tells the assembler to load instructions in memory starting at address 400_{16}. We used the value 400_{16} because the 68K reserves the first 1024 bytes of memory in locations 0 to $3FF_{16}$ for a special purpose. Therefore, 68K assembly language programs normally begin at 400_{16}. This statement is not true of all 68K-based systems.

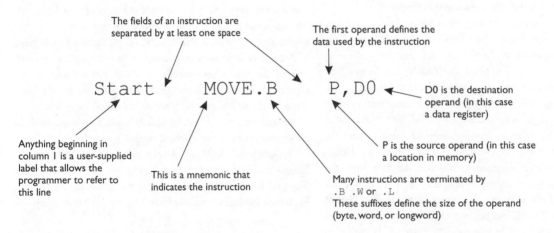

Fig. 6.2 Anatomy of an assembly language instruction.

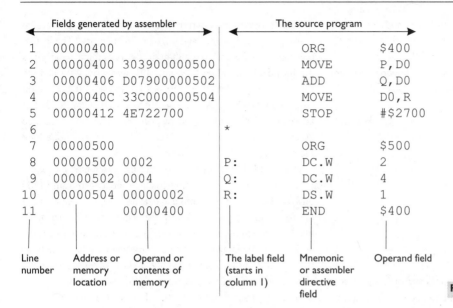

Line number	Address or memory location	Operand or contents of memory	The label field (starts in column 1)	Mnemonic or assembler directive field	Operand field
1	00000400			ORG	$400
2	00000400	303900000500		MOVE	P,D0
3	00000406	D07900000502		ADD	Q,D0
4	0000040C	33C000000504		MOVE	D0,R
5	00000412	4E722700		STOP	#$2700
6			*		
7	00000500			ORG	$500
8	00000500	0002	P:	DC.W	2
9	00000502	0004	Q:	DC.W	4
10	00000504	00000002	R:	DS.W	1
11		00000400		END	$400

Fig. 6.3 Assembling a program.

We can better understand what's happening by looking at the output produced when the program is assembled by the Teesside cross-assembler—see Fig. 6.3.

This listing has six columns. The first column contains the line number that makes it easy to locate a particular line in the program. The second column provides the address in memory into which an instruction or data is loaded. All instructions, addresses, and data from the assembler are expressed in hexadecimal form. The third column contains the instruction or the data. The rightmost three columns in Fig. 6.3 are the instructions or assembler directives themselves. As you can see, the instruction MOVE D0,R is located on line 4 and is stored in memory location $40C_{16}$. This instruction is translated into the machine code $33C000000504_{16}$, where the operation code is $33C0_{16}$ and the address of operand R is 00000504_{16}. Such a listing is used only to debug a program.

The assembler maintains a variable, called the *location counter*, that keeps track of where the next instruction or data element is to be located in memory. When you write an ORG directive, you preset the value of the location counter to that specified by the ORG. Let's look as some of the other assembler directives in this program.

The *define constant* assembler directive, DC, allows you to load a constant in memory; that is, it provides a means of presetting memory locations with data *before* a program is executed. This directive is written DC.B to store a byte, DC.W to store a word, and DC.L to store a longword. In the program of Fig. 6.3, the assembler directive P DC.W 2 places the value 2 in memory, and labels the location 'P'. Since this directive is located immediately after the ORG $500 assembler directive,

the integer 2 is located at memory location 500_{16}. This memory location (i.e. 500_{16}) can be referred to as P. When you wish to read the value of P (i.e. the contents of memory location 500_{16}), you use P as a source operand; for example, MOVE P,D0. Because the size of the operand is a word, the value 0000000000000010_2 is stored in location 500_{16}.

The next assembler directive, Q DC.W 4, loads the constant 4 in the next available location—502_{16}. Why 502_{16} and not 501_{16}? Because the operands are word sized (i.e. 16 bits) and the 68K's memory is byte addressed. Each word occupies two bytes—P takes up 500_{16} and 501_{16}.

The *define storage* directive, DS, tells the assembler to reserve memory locations and also takes a .B, .W, or a .L qualifier. For example, R DS.W 1 tells the assembler to reserve a word in memory and to equate the address of the first word with 'R'. The difference between DC.B N and DS.B N is that the former stores the 8-bit value N in memory, whereas the latter reserves N bytes of memory by advancing the location counter by N.

The final assembler directive, END $400, tells the assembler that the end of the program has been reached and that there is nothing else left to assemble. The Teesside cross-assembler requires the END directive to take a parameter that is the address of the first instruction of the program to be executed. In this case, execution begins with the instruction at address 400_{16}.

Another important assembler directive is EQU, which equates a symbolic name to a numeric value. If you write Tuesday EQU 3, you can use the symbolic name Tuesday instead of its value, 3. For example, ADD #Tuesday,D0 is identical to ADD #3, D0. We now provide another example of the use of assembler directives.

Example   Draw a memory map for the following fragment of code, which calculates the perimeter of an object, and indicate what each of the statements does.

```
           ORG      $1000
Size       DC.B     25
Width      DC.B     14
Perim      DS.B     1
           ORG      $1200
           MOVE.B   Size,D0
           ADD.B    Width,D0
           ADD.B    D0,D0
           MOVE.B   D0,Perim
           STOP     #$2700
           END      $1200
```

Figure 6.4 displays this program in three forms: the source program, the assembled program, and the memory map corresponding to the program.

This program uses two define constant directives to set up constants called Size and Width in memory. These two constants are 25 and 14, although the assembled code gives the hexadecimal values $19 and $0E, respectively. Since the first assembler directive, ORG $1000, sets the location counter to $1000, these two one-byte variables are loaded at addresses $1000 and $1001, respectively. The define storage assembler directive, Perim DS.B 1, reserves a one-byte location called Perim at $1002.

The second ORG directive resets the assembler's *location counter* to $1200. Successive instructions are loaded from $1200 onward (we can put programs and data anywhere we want within the 68K's memory). The 68K's instructions vary in size from two bytes to ten bytes—so you can't easily estimate the size of a program just by knowing how many instructions it has. The fragment of code in Fig. 6.4 shows the address of each instruction and the encoding of each instruction (e.g. the machine code for MOVE.B Size, D0 is 10381000_{16}). In general, programmers are rarely interested in the actual locations or values of instructions.

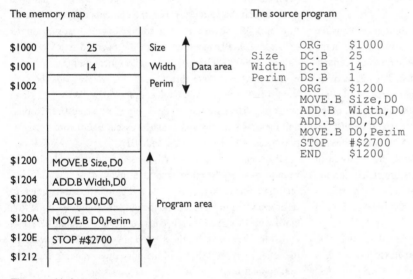

The memory map

$1000	25	Size
$1001	14	Width
$1002		Perim

Data area

$1200	MOVE.B Size,D0
$1204	ADD.B Width,D0
$1208	ADD.B D0,D0
$120A	MOVE.B D0,Perim
$120E	STOP #$2700
$1212	

Program area

The source program

```
           ORG      $1000
Size       DC.B     25
Width      DC.B     14
Perim      DS.B     1
           ORG      $1200
           MOVE.B   Size,D0
           ADD.B    Width,D0
           ADD.B    D0,D0
           MOVE.B   D0,Perim
           STOP     #$2700
           END      $1200
```

The assembled program

```
 1   00001000                    ORG       $1000
 2   00001000  19        SIZE:   DC.B      25
 3   00001001  0E        WIDTH:  DC.B      14
 4   00001002  00000001  PERIM:  DS.B      1
 5   00001200                    ORG       $1200
 6   00001200  10381000          MOVE.B    SIZE,D0
 7   00001204  D0381001          ADD.B     WIDTH,D0
 8   00001208  D000              ADD.B     D0,D0
 9   0000120A  11C01002          MOVE.B    D0,PERIM
10   0000120E  4E722700          STOP      #$2700
11             00001200          END       $1200
```

Fig. 6.4 Relationship between a source program, assembled program, and memory map.

The program is very simple—it calculates the perimeter of a rectangular object with dimensions Size × Width. The first instruction MOVE.B Size,D0, copies the contents of memory location Size to data register D0. Because we have used a define constant directive with the label 'Size', the assembler substitutes the address $1000 for the name 'Size' when the program is assembled. In other words, you write MOVE.B Size,D0 and the assembler 'sees' MOVE.B $1000,D0. When the program is executed, the contents of memory location $1000 (i.e. 25) are copied to D0.

The next instruction adds the contents of memory location 'Width' to the contents of D0. To calculate the length of the perimeter, we have to double the result. In this case, we can use ADD.B D0,D0 to double the contents of D0. The operation MOVE.B D0,Perim copies the result into the memory location we've called 'Perim'. The instruction ADD D0,D0 offers a simple means of multiplying a number by 2. The last instruction STOP #$2700 terminates the program. The Teesside cross-assembler requires the assembler directive END $1200 to terminate the program and indicate the point at which instruction execution is to begin.

6.1.2 Operand size and the 68K

It would be nice if the 68K operated on *things* and we didn't have to worry about the size of these *things*. Alas, *things* have to be sent down buses, stored in memory, and processed by ALUs. Consequently, real computers operate on chunks of data composed of a particular number of bits. We now look at the implications of these statements for the programmer.

The 68K has a 32-bit *architecture* and a 16-bit *organization*. You can think of a computer's architecture as an expression of *what* it does, and its organization as an expression of *how* it does it. The 68K's internal registers hold 32 bits and it can perform operations on 32-bit data elements (i.e. it looks like a 32-bit machine to the programmer). However, the 68K has a 16-bit external data bus, so that 32-bit operands must be moved to and from memory as two consecutive 16-bit words. Some of the 68K's internal data paths are only 16 bits wide (this is the way in which its architecture is organized). Later members of the 68K family have both 32-bit architectures and organizations. So, as far as the programmer is concerned, the 68K operates on 32-bit operands. However, the situation is rather more complex because the 68K can also handle 16-bit and 8-bit values.

The 68K has a *byte-addressable* architecture. Successive bytes in memory are stored at consecutive byte addresses (0, 1, 2, 3, ...) and any byte in memory can be individually read from or written to. Since a 16-bit word is composed of two bytes, successive words are stored at consecutive even addresses: 0, 2, 4, 6, ... Similarly, successive 32-bit longwords are stored at addresses 0, 4, 8, ... Figure 6.5 illustrates how the 68K's memory space is organized.

Figure 6.5 poses an interesting question. If you store a 32-bit longword at, say, memory location $1000, where do the

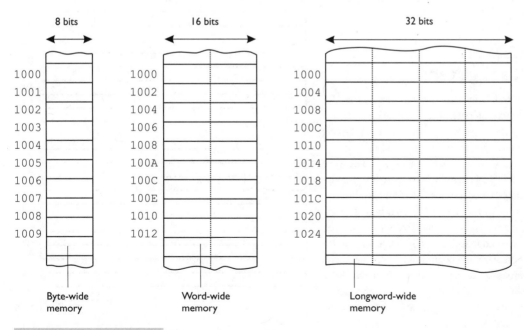

Fig. 6.5 The 68K's memory space.

four bytes go? For example, if the longword is $12345678, does byte $12 go into address $1000 or does byte $78 go into address $1000?

The 68K stores the most-significant byte of an operand at the lowest address (in this case $12 is stored at $1000). This storage order is called *Big-Endian* (because the 'big end' of a number goes in first). The term Big-Endian has been borrowed from *Gulliver's Travels*. Intel processors are Little-Endian and store bytes in the reverse order to the 68K family.

The 68K stores the most-significant byte of a word (i.e. bits d_{08} to d_{15}) at the *even* address, and the least-significant byte of a word (i.e. bits d_{00} to d_{07}) at the *odd* address. For example, if we execute the operation MOVE.W D0,1234, bits d_{00} to d_{07} of D0 are stored at byte address 1235 and bits d_{08} to d_{15} of D0 are stored at byte address 1234. To avoid confusion between registers and bits, we use 'D' to indicate a register and 'd' to indicate a bit.

All addresses processed and stored by the 68K are 32-bit values. However, in order to permit the 68K to be fitted in a 64-pin package, not all its 32 address lines are connected to pins. Address bits A_{24} to A_{31} are not connected to pins and cannot be used to access memory. In other words, the 68K's address bus is effectively 24 bits wide and can access only 2^{24} bytes (i.e. 16 Mbyte) of addressable memory. Later members of the 68K family support a full 32-bit address bus and a 2^{32}-byte (i.e. 4 Gbyte) address space. Don't worry about this feature—it has no effect on either programming or understanding the 68K.

6.2 The 68K's registers

We now look at the 68K's internal registers that it uses for temporary or *scratchpad* storage. The 68K needs registers because it has a *register-to-memory architecture*. A typical instruction specifies one operand in memory and the other as a register; for example, ADD $1234,D0 adds the contents of memory location $1234 to data register D0. Figure 6.6 provides a simplified programmer's model of the 68K's architecture.

A microprocessor can be viewed in three different ways. Designers see its internal structure and organization; they have created the device and must have an intimate knowledge of all its aspects, particularly the control unit. Engineers who interface the microprocessor to all the other components of a system are interested in its electrical properties and wish to know about the voltages and currents at each of the pins, the timing requirements, and the protocols observed by the various signals entering or leaving the chip. Programmers aren't

interested in such fine detail and require little more than a programming model of the machine. That is, programmers need to know its instruction set and the arrangement of its internal registers; they are interested in what it does and not in how it does it. A knowledge of a microprocessor's architecture and the way in which its instructions operate allow the programmer to write compact code or fast code when such circumstances are necessary.

The 68K has eight 32-bit general-purpose data registers, eight 32-bit address registers, an 8-bit condition code register, an 8-bit status byte, and a 32-bit program counter. The status byte is not discussed further in this section because it is accessed only by the operating system and is invisible to the user programmer—the status byte simply defines the 68K's operating mode and controls the way in which interrupts are dealt with.

6.2.1 Data registers

Figure 6.6 shows that the 68K has eight *general-purpose* data registers, numbered D0 to D7. Any operation that can be applied to data register Di can also be applied to Dj. In other words, there are no special-purpose data registers reserved for certain types of instruction. Some microprocessors do not permit all instructions to be applied to each of their registers.

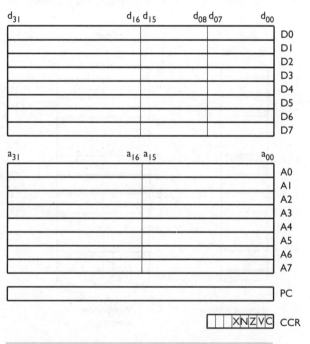

Fig. 6.6 The programmer's model of the 68K microprocessor.

In such cases, learning assembly language is rather like learning to conjugate irregular foreign verbs.

Why has the 68K got eight data registers? Why not one or 16 or 32? The advantage of multiple data registers is that frequently used data can be kept on-chip rather than in the system's main store, in order to speed up the processing. The number of registers on any real chip is determined by the cost of the silicon they take up and by the number of bits needed to address them. Since the 68K has eight data registers, it takes three bits to specify one of these eight registers. All the 68K's instructions are an integer multiple of 16-bit words and most instructions contain the op-code and operand register in a single 16-bit word. Any increase in the number of data registers would require a reduction in the number of bits dedicated to the op-code. In other words, there is a trade-off between the number of different instructions and the number of registers that can be specified by a given op-code length.

There's little difference between on-chip registers and memory locations as far as the programmer is concerned. On-chip registers can be accessed more rapidly than locations in main store. Because it takes three bits to specify a register and 32 bits to specify a memory location, instructions that access registers are shorter than those that access memory. It's good practice to keep frequently used data in registers rather than in memory.

Programmers writing in high-level languages don't have to worry about how data is allocated to registers or to memory, because the compiler performs data allocation automatically (although C lets you allocate variables to registers). When writing in assembler language, the programmer must decide what data goes in memory and what should be stored in the registers. Any register can be used to hold any variable and what goes where is left entirely up to the programmer. I usually allocate variables in the order D0, D1, etc. Whenever I have a global variable (i.e. one that applies to the main program and the subroutines called by it), I usually allocate registers starting at D7 and work backwards. For example, I often use D7 as a global error register. This is my personal style and I find it helps me to read my own assembly language programs.

Some assemblers (not the Teesside assembler) permit data registers to be renamed to reflect the variables they hold. For example, D0 might be renamed `Monday` and the operation `MOVE.B 12,D0` written `MOVE.B 12,Monday`.

The 68K's data registers are written D0 to D7. To refer to the sequence of consecutive bits i to j in register Dn we write D$n(i:j)$. For example, we indicate bits 8 to 31, inclusive, of

D4 by D4(8:31). This notation is an extension of RTL and is not part of the 68K's assembly language.

A particularly interesting feature of the 68K is its ability to perform operations on byte, word, or longword operands. The 68K assembly language indicates byte, word, or longword operations by appending .B, .W, or .L, respectively, to a mnemonic. When a byte operation is applied to the contents of a data register, only bits D_{00} to D_{07} of the register are affected. Similarly, a word operation affects bits D_{00} to D_{15} of the register. Only the lower-order byte (word) of a register is affected by a byte (word) operation. For example, applying a byte operation to data register D1 affects only bits 0 to 7 and leaves bits 8 to 31 unchanged. CLR.B D1 forces the contents of D1 to XXXXXXXXXXXXXXXXXXXXXXXX00000000, where the Xs represent the old bits of D1 before the CLR.B D1 was executed. If [D1]=\$12345678 before the CLR.B D1, then [D1]=\$12345600 after it.

Some further examples should make the action of byte, word, and longword operations clearer. In each case we give the 68K form of the instruction and its definition in RTL.

Assembly form	RTL definition
ADD.L D0,D1	[D1(0:31)] ← [D1(0:31)]+[D0(0:31)]
ADD.W D0,D1	[D1(0:15)] ← [D1(0:15)]+[D0(0:15)]
ADD.B D0,D1	[D1(0:7)] ← [D1(0:7)] + [D0(0:7)]

We won't employ the slice notation unless we specifically wish to emphasize that we are operating on a slice of a register. If the slice of a register isn't specified by $(0:m)$, we generally mean the bits of the register appropriate to the operand size (i.e. .B, .W, .L). For example, D3 and D3(0:31) are equivalent when referring to a longword operand.

If the initial contents of D0 and D1 are \$12345678 and \$ABCDEF98, respectively, the ADD operation has the following effects on the contents of D1 and the carry bit, C.

ADD.L D0,D1	results in [D1]=BE024610 and [C]=0
ADD.W D0,D1	results in [D1]=ABCD4610 and [C]=1
ADD.B D0,D1	results in [D1]=ABCDEF10 and [C]=1

The state of the carry bit and other bits of the CCR are determined only by the result of operations on bits 0–7 for a byte operation, by the result of operations on bits 0–15 for a word operation, and by the result of operations on bits 0–31 for a longword operation.

One of the most common errors made by 68K programmers is using inconsistent operations on a data register, as the following example demonstrates.

```
MOVE.B   XYZ,D0    Get the contents of memory location XYZ
SUB.B    #5,D0     and subtract 5 to get [XYZ]−5
CMP.W    #12,D0    Is ([XYZ]−5)>12
BGT      Test
```

This example implements IF ([XYZ]−5)>12 THEN.... But note that the operand XYZ is treated as a *byte* value and yet it is compared with a *word* value. This fragment of code might work correctly sometimes if the contents of bits 8 to 15 of D0 are zero. However, if these bits are not zero, this code will not operate correctly.

6.2.2 Address registers

The 68K has eight 32-bit address registers, called A0 to A7, which act as *pointer registers*. These address registers hold the *address* of a variable in memory. A data register holds the *value* of a variable, whereas an address register holds the *location* of a variable. Because you can modify the contents of an address register, you can change the location of a variable. This facility lets you deal with tables, vectors, arrays, matrices, and lists. If address register A0 contains the location of element x_i, then incrementing A0 causes it to point at the location of x_{i+1}.

Registers A0–A6 are identical in that whatever we can do to A*i*, we can also do to A*j*. Address register A7 has an additional function to those of A0 to A6, because A7 is used by the 68K as a *stack pointer* for the storage of subroutine addresses. We describe the use of the stack pointer in detail later in this chapter.

In some ways, address registers can be used in almost exactly the same way as data registers. For example, we can move data to or from address registers and we can add data to them. However, there are a number of important differences between the 68K's address and data registers. Operations on the address registers do not (normally) affect the status of the 68K's condition code register. The 68K's manufacturers have argued that programmers should be allowed to carry out address calculations without modifying the value of the CCR, because the CCR should reflect the status of the CPU due to operations on data. For example, if you are in the process of adding up a series of numbers, you shouldn't have to worry about modifying the CCR every time you have to calculate the address of the next number in the series. When we look at the ARM processor in the next chapter we will find that the CCR is updated only when the programmer requests it.

Because the contents of an address register are considered to be a *single entity*, byte and word divisions are meaningless. It's not difficult to appreciate the reason for the decision to treat the contents of an address register as a single entity. If an address register points to the location of an item in memory, the concept of separate and independent fields within the address register is quite meaningless.

All operations on an address register are longword operations—but things are a bit more complex than this statement suggests. You can apply a .L operation to an address register but not a .B operation. No instruction may operate on the low-order byte of an address register. However, word, .W, operations are permitted on the contents of an address register because a .W operation is automatically extended to .L, as we shall now demonstrate.

Addresses are treated as signed two's complement values. If we perform an operation on the lower-order word of an address register, the sign bit is extended from A_{15} to bits A_{16} to A_{31}. For example, the operation MOVEA.W #$8022,A3 has the effect

[A3] ← $FFFF8022

Note how the 16-bit value $8022 is sign extended to the 32-bit value $FFFF8022. Similarly, the operation MOVEA.W #$7022,A3 has the effect

[A3] ← $00007022

The concept of a two's complement (i.e. negative address) seems strange. However, if you think of a positive address as meaning forward and a negative address as meaning backward, everything becomes clear. Suppose address register A1 contains the value 1280. If address register A2 contains the value −40 (stored as the appropriate two's complement value), adding the contents of A1 to the contents of A2 by ADDA.L A1,A2 to create a composite address results in the value 1240, which is 40 locations back from the address pointed at by A1.

Although some of the operations that can be applied to the contents of data registers can also be applied to the contents of address registers, the 68K's assembler employs special mnemonics for operations that modify the contents of an address register. The following examples illustrate some of these mnemonics. In each case, the *destination* operand is an address register.

```
ADDA.L   D1,A3    ADDA =add to address register
MOVEA.L  D1,A2    MOVEA=move to an address register
SUBA.W   D1,A3    SUBA =subtract from an address register
```

Some assemblers for the 68K permit only the use of the `ADD` mnemonic for both `ADD.W  A1,D1` and for `ADD.W  D1,A1`. Other assemblers demand that the programmer write `ADDA.W D1,A1` and will reject `ADD.W D1,A1`. The purpose of forcing programmers to write `MOVEA`, `ADDA`, and `SUBA` instead of `MOVE`, `ADD`, and `SUB` when specifying address registers as destinations is to remind them that they are dealing with addresses and that these addresses are treated differently from data values (e.g. because of sign-extension). Practical applications of the 68K's address registers are provided when we discuss addressing modes.

Example Address register A0 points to the beginning of a data structure in memory. This data structure is made up of 50 items numbered from 0 to 49. Each of these 50 items is composed of 12 bytes. Data register D0 contains the number of the item we wish to access. Suppose we need to put the address of this item in A1. In what follows we will need the operation `MULU #n,Di` that multiplies the 16-bit low-order word in Di by n and puts the 32-bit product in Di.

Figure 6.7 illustrates this data structure. We need to find where the required item falls within the data structure. In order to do this we multiply the contents of D0 by 12 (because each item takes up 12 bytes). Then we add this offset to the contents of A0 and deposit the result in A1. That is:

```
MULU       #12,D0    Calculate the offset into the data structure
MOVEA.L    A0,A1     Copy A0 to A1
ADDA.L     D0,A1     Add the offset to A1
```

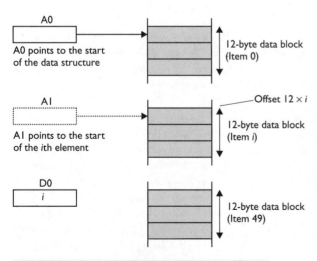

Fig. 6.7 Using an address register to access a data element.

6.3 An introduction to the 68K's instruction set

We now describe some of the 68K's instructions. Our intention is to demonstrate the type of things a microprocessor can do, rather than to provide an assembly language primer. A more detailed definition of the 68K's instruction set is given in the Appendix.

The 68K's instruction set is more primitive than you might imagine, although, in fact, the 68K represents a great leap forward over earlier microprocessors. When we say that the 68K has a primitive instruction set, we mean that it's not able to carry out floating point operations directly or that it can't perform the string matching operations found in editors and text processors. Complex operations are implemented by sequences of primitive machine code instructions—just as a computer is made up of a large number of basic gates. The 68040 and later members of the 68K family include an on-chip floating point unit.

6.3.1 Data movement instructions

The most important class of computer instructions is composed of the *data movement* instructions that copy data from one place to another. These instructions comprise between 50 and 70 percent of the instructions in a typical program. Other types of machine code instruction are arithmetic, logical, branch, and control.

We'll introduce some of the 68K's data movement instructions as soon as we've cleared up a few matters of terminology. To avoid unnecessary complexity, we have dropped the operand size qualifier `.B`, `.W`, and `.L` from instructions, because we're more interested in what these instructions do rather than in whether the instruction is applied to a byte, word, or longword. Assemblers usually allow you to omit the qualifier after an instruction by assuming a default value of `.W` (i.e. `ADD D1,D2` is the same as `ADD.W D1,D2`). Similarly, we have dropped the notation Di(0:15) whenever it's clear that Di means the 'lower-order word' of Di.

Remember that all two-operand instructions are written in the form *operation source, destination*, where *source* refers to the source operand and *destination* refers to the location of the destination operand. For example, `MOVE D3,D4` copies the contents of data register D3 (i.e. the source operand) into data register D4 (i.e. the destination operand).

Typical 68K data and address movement instructions are

Assembly form		RTL definition
MOVE	Di,Dj	[Dj] ← [Di]
MOVE	P,Di	[Di] ← [M(P)]
MOVE	Di,N	[M(N)] ← [Di]
EXG	Di,Dj	[Temp] ← [Di], [Di] ← [Dj], [Dj] ← [Temp]
SWAP	Di	[Di(0:15)] ← [Di(16:31)], [Di(16:31)] ← [Di(0:15)]
LEA	P,Ai	[Ai] ← P

The EXG instruction exchanges the contents of two registers (it's intrinsically a longword operation). EXG may be used to transfer the contents of an address register into a data register and vice versa. SWAP exchanges the upper- and lower-order words of a given data register. The LEA (load effective address) instruction generates an address and puts it in an address register.

Let's write a program that executes some of these data movement instructions and then use the Teesside simulator to observe what happens as we trace through it. This program is just a random selection of data movement instructions—it doesn't actually do anything.

68K's registers (the simulator is on the CD accompanying this book). We begin by using the DF (*display formatted registers*) command to display the contents of the simulated computer's registers immediately after the program is loaded. Figure 6.8 shows the screen output in response to DF. Note that the 68K has *two* A7 address registers labeled SS and US in all simulator output. SS is the *supervisor* state stack pointer A7 and US is the *user* state stack pointer A7. When the 68K is first powered up, the supervisor stack pointer is selected (we will discuss the difference between these later). Throughout this chapter, all references to the stack pointer refer to the supervisor stack pointer, SP (i.e. A7). In Fig. 6.8, PC is the program counter, SR the status register (containing the 68K's CCR and status bits), and X, N, Z, V, C are the CCR's flag bits.

The DF command also reads the instruction currently pointed at by the program counter, 'disassembles' it, and prints it. Because the simulator doesn't know about 'symbolic

```
      ORG       $400
      MOVE.L    #$12345678,D0   Copy a 32-bit literal to a register
      MOVE.B    D0,D1           Copy a byte from a register to a register
      MOVE.W    D0,D2           Copy a word from a register to a register
      MOVE.L    D0,D3           Copy a longword from a register to a register
      EXG       D0,A0           Exchange the 32-bit contents of two registers
      SWAP      D3              Swap the upper and lower words of a register
      MOVEA.L   Data,A1         Copy the contents of a memory location into an address register
      LEA       Data,A1         Copy the address "Data" into an address register
      STOP      #$2700
Data  DC.L      $ABCDDCBA       Store a longword constant in memory at address "Data"
      END       $400
```

The above source file produces the following listing file when assembled by the Teesside assembler.

```
1   00000400                              ORG       $400
2   00000400  203C12345678              MOVE.L    #$12345678,D0
3   00000406  1200                      MOVE.B    D0,D1
4   00000408  3400                      MOVE.W    D0,D2
5   0000040A  2600                      MOVE.L    D0,D3
6   0000040C  C188                      EXG       D0,A0
7   0000040E  4843                      SWAP      D3
8   00000410  227900000420              MOVEA.L   DATA,A1
9   00000416  43F900000420              LEA       DATA,A1
10  0000041C  4E722700                  STOP      #$2700
11  00000420  ABCDDCBA       DATA:      DC.L      $ABCDDCBA
12            00000400                  END       $400
```

We now use the Teesside 68K simulator to run this program in the *trace mode* and observe the contents of the simulated

names', all addresses, data values, and labels are printed as hexadecimal values. In the above example, the program counter is pointing at location 400_{16} and the instruction at this address is MOVE.L #$12345678,D0.

We now execute this program, instruction by instruction. We use the TR (trace) function to execute a single instruction and dump the registers to the screen. Once we have entered the trace mode, hitting the return/enter key executes an instruction at a time. The trace mode is exited by entering a period or full stop. In the following output, we have emboldened registers that have changed for the purpose of clarity. This example demonstrates the use of the simulator and shows how registers are modified as instructions are executed.

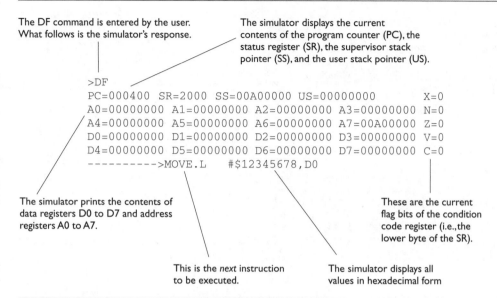

The DF command is entered by the user. What follows is the simulator's response.

The simulator displays the current contents of the program counter (PC), the status register (SR), the supervisor stack pointer (SS), and the user stack pointer (US).

```
>DF
PC=000400  SR=2000  SS=00A00000  US=00000000        X=0
A0=00000000  A1=00000000  A2=00000000  A3=00000000  N=0
A4=00000000  A5=00000000  A6=00000000  A7=00A00000  Z=0
D0=00000000  D1=00000000  D2=00000000  D3=00000000  V=0
D4=00000000  D5=00000000  D6=00000000  D7=00000000  C=0
---------->MOVE.L   #$12345678,D0
```

The simulator prints the contents of data registers D0 to D7 and address registers A0 to A7.

These are the current flag bits of the condition code register (i.e., the lower byte of the SR).

This is the *next* instruction to be executed.

The simulator displays all values in hexadecimal form

Fig. 6.8 Structure of the output from the simulator's DF and TR commands.

```
>tr
PC=000406  SR=2000  SS=00A00000  US=00000000        X=0
A0=00000000  A1=00000000  A2=00000000  A3=00000000  N=0
A4=00000000  A5=00000000  A6=00000000  A7=00A00000  Z=0
D0=12345678  D1=00000000  D2=00000000  D3=00000000  V=0
D4=00000000  D5=00000000  D6=00000000  D7=00000000  C=0
----->MOVE.B   D0,D1
```

The only registers that have changed are D0 and the program counter. The next instruction to be executed, MOVE.B D0,D1, copies a byte of D0 to D1.

```
Trace>
PC=000408  SR=2000  SS=00A00000  US=00000000        X=0
A0=00000000  A1=00000000  A2=00000000  A3=00000000  N=0
A4=00000000  A5=00000000  A6=00000000  A7=00A00000  Z=0
D0=12345678  D1=00000078  D2=00000000  D3=00000000  V=0
D4=00000000  D5=00000000  D6=00000000  D7=00000000  C=0
----->MOVE.W   D0,D2
```

As you can see, only the least-significant byte of D0 has been copied to D1. The next two instructions, MOVE.W D0,D2 and MOVE.L D0,D3, demonstrate the transfer of a word and a longword, respectively.

```
Trace>
PC=00040A  SR=2000  SS=00A00000  US=00000000        X=0
A0=00000000  A1=00000000  A2=00000000  A3=00000000  N=0
A4=00000000  A5=00000000  A6=00000000  A7=00A00000  Z=0
D0=12345678  D1=00000078  D2=00005678  D3=00000000  V=0
D4=00000000  D5=00000000  D6=00000000  D7=00000000  C=0
----->MOVE.L   D0,D3
```

```
Trace>
PC=00040C  SR=2000  SS=00A00000  US=00000000        X=0
A0=00000000  A1=00000000  A2=00000000  A3=00000000  N=0
A4=00000000  A5=00000000  A6=00000000  A7=00A00000  Z=0
D0=12345678  D1=00000078  D2=00005678  D3=12345678  V=0
D4=00000000  D5=00000000  D6=00000000  D7=00000000  C=0
----->EXG    D0,A0
```

The next instruction, EXG D0,A0, exchanges the contents of a pair of registers to give

```
Trace>
PC=00040E  SR=2000  SS=00A00000  US=00000000        X=0
A0=12345678  A1=00000000  A2=00000000  A3=00000000  N=0
A4=00000000  A5=00000000  A6=00000000  A7=00A00000  Z=0
D0=00000000  D1=00000078  D2=00005678  D3=12345678  V=0
D4=00000000  D5=00000000  D6=00000000  D7=00000000  C=0
----->SWAP    D3
```

The SWAP instruction swaps the upper and lower order words of a data register.

```
Trace>
PC=000410  SR=2000  SS=00A00000  US=00000000        X=0
A0=12345678  A1=00000000  A2=00000000  A3=00000000  N=0
A4=00000000  A5=00000000  A6=00000000  A7=00A00000  Z=0
D0=00000000  D1=00000078  D2=00005678  D3=56781234  V=0
D4=00000000  D5=00000000  D6=00000000  D7=00000000  C=0
----->MOVEA.L  $0420,A1
```

The MOVEA.L Data,A1 and LEA Data,A1 instructions have the following effects.

```
Trace>
PC=000416  SR=2000  SS=00A00000  US=00000000        X=0
A0=12345678  A1=ABCDDCBA  A2=00000000  A3=00000000  N=0
A4=00000000  A5=00000000  A6=00000000  A7=00A00000  Z=0
D0=00000000  D1=00000078  D2=00005678  D3=56781234  V=0
D4=00000000  D5=00000000  D6=00000000  D7=00000000  C=0
----->LEA.L   $0420,A1
```

```
Trace>
PC=00041C  SR=2000  SS=00A00000  US=00000000        X=0
A0=12345678  A1=00000420  A2=00000000  A3=00000000  N=0
A4=00000000  A5=00000000  A6=00000000  A7=00A00000  Z=0
D0=00000000  D1=00000078  D2=00005678  D3=56781234  V=0
D4=00000000  D5=00000000  D6=00000000  D7=00000000  C=0
----->STOP    #$2700
```

As you can see, a MOVEA.L Data,A1 instruction loads address register A1 with the *contents* of the operand Data, whereas LEA Data,A1 loads A1 with the *address* of the operand (the significance of this will become clear later). We now look at instructions that do more than move data from one place to another.

6.3.2 Arithmetic and logical operations

Arithmetic operations are those that act on numeric data (i.e. signed and unsigned integers). We have seen that ADD M,Di adds the contents of memory location M to the contents of data register Di and stores the result in Di. Other arithmetic operations implemented by the 68K are SUB (subtract), DIVU and DIVS (unsigned and signed divide), MULU and MULS (unsigned and signed divide), and NEG (negate). The 68K's

```
          MOVE.B   Data1,D0     Pick up the ASCII character for 'A'
          MOVE.B   Data1,D1     Pick up the ASCII character for 'B'
          ADD.B    D0,D1        Add 'A' to 'B'

Data1     DC.B     'A'          Store an ASCII character in memory at address "Data1"
Data1     DC.B     'B'          Store an ASCII character in memory at address "Data2"
```

logic (i.e. Boolean) operations AND, OR, EOR, NOT act on the individual bits of a word. In contrast, an arithmetic operation acts on the whole number, rather than on its individual bits.

The following instructions illustrate some of the arithmetic and logical instructions found on the 68K. Note that [X] represents the contents of the X bit in the CCR and is, for most practical purposes, a copy of the carry bit.

Instruction	Assembly form	RTL definiton
Add	ADD Di,Dj	[Dj] ← [Di]+[Dj]
Add with extend	ADDX Di,Dj	[Dj] ← [Di]+[Dj]+[X]
Subtract	SUB Di,Dj	[Dj] ← [Dj]−[Di]
Subtract with extend	SUBX Di,Dj	[Dj] ← [Dj]−[Di]−[X]
Multiply	MULU Di,Dj	[Dj(0:31)] ← [Di(0:15)]×[Dj(0:15)]
Divide	DIVU Di,Dj	[Dj(0:15)] ← [Dj(0:31)]/[Di(0:15)]
		[Dj(16:31)] ← remainder
Logical AND	AND Di,Dj	[Dj] ← [Di]·[Dj]
Logical OR	OR Di,Dj	[Dj] ← [Di]+[Dj]
Logical EOR	EOR Di,Dj	[Dj] ← [Di]⊕[Dj]
Logical NOT	NOT Di	[Di] ← $\overline{[Di]}$

The action of most of these instructions is self-evident. However, the multiplication instruction multiplies a 16-bit source operand by a 16-bit destination operand and deposits the 32-bit product in the destination operand. The division instruction divides a 32-bit destination operand by a 16-bit source operand. The result is a 16-bit quotient (in the least-significant bits of the destination operand) and a 16-bit remainder in the most-significant bits of the destination operand. For example, if D0 contains \$1234, the effect of MULU #\$5678,D0 gives [D0] = \$06260060. Similarly, if D0 contains \$00003664, the effect of DIVU #\$3,D0 is [D0] = \$00011221 (i.e. \$1221 remainder 1).

Before we look at the use of arithmetic and logical operations, we need to make a point. The computer executes instructions without any regard

for the meaning of the data it is processing. Consider the following fragment of perfectly legal code

We've just added the ASCII representation for the character 'A' to 'B', which is a legal machine-level operation because the processor doesn't prevent operations on inappropriate data types. In this case, the end result in D1 is \$83 (i.e. \$41 + \$42). Many high-level languages are *strongly typed* because an operation may only be applied to the appropriate data type; for example, Java does not allow you to add an integer to a real value. When writing an assembly language program, you must be careful to check that the operation you are performing on a data element is appropriate to its type.

Using arithmetic operations

Now that we've introduced some basic 68K operations, we can write a program to perform a calculation. Suppose we wish to calculate the value of $Z = (X^2 + Y^2)/(X − Y)$. We will assume that X and Y are 16-bit values. Note that the 68K supports 16-bit × 16-bit multiplication, but not 32-bit × 32-bit multiplication. The following program uses unsigned multiplication and division (i.e. we will assume that X and Y are positive values and that $X > Y$).

```
        ORG      $400       Start of the program
        MOVE.W   X,D0       Put the value of X in D0
        MULU     D0,D0      Calculate X²
        MOVE.W   Y,D1       Put the value of Y in D1
        MULU     D1,D1      Calculate Y²
        ADD.L    D0,D1      Add X² to Y² and put the 32-bit result in D1
        MOVE.W   X,D2       Put the value of X in D2
        SUB.W    Y,D2       Subtract Y from D2 to get D2 = X−Y
        DIVU     D2,D1      Divide D1 by D2 to get (X²+Y²)/(X−Y)
        MOVE.W   D1,Z       Put the result now in D1 into Z
        STOP     #$2700

        ORG      $500       Put the data here
X       DC.W     50         Initial dummy value for variable X
```

(program continued)

```
Y       DC.W    12          Initial dummy value for variable Y
Z       DS.W    1           Reserve space for the result
        END     $400        End of program and address of entry point
```

Note that you can't perform a *memory-to-memory* subtraction—the operation SUB X, Y does not exist. You have to load one of the operands onto a data register.

We assemble this program, called PROG1.X68, with the Teesside cross-assembler. The DOS command line X68K PROG1 -L performs the assembly and creates a listing file, PROG1.LIS. This listing file contains

```
Source file: PROG1.X68
Assembled on: 96-09-04 at: 15:26:29
            by: X68K PC-2.2 Copyright © University of Teesside 1989, 96
Defaults: ORG $0/FORMAT/OPT A,BRL,CEX,CL,FRL,MC,MD,NOMEX,NOPCO

 1   00000400                    ORG     $400        ;Start of the program
 2
 3   00000400 303900000500       MOVE.W  X,D0        ;Put the value of X in D0
 4   00000406 C0C0               MULU    D0,D0       ;Calculate X²
 5   00000408 323900000502       MOVE.W  Y,D1        ;Put the value of Y in D1
 6   0000040E C2C1               MULU    D1,D1       ;Calculate Y²
 7   00000410 D280               ADD.L   D0,D1       ;Add X² to Y² and put result in D1
 8   00000412 343900000500       MOVE.W  X,D2        ;Put the value of X in D2
 9   00000418 947900000502       SUB.W   Y,D2        ;Subtract Y from D2 to get X−Y
10   0000041E 82C2               DIVU    D2,D1       ;Divide D1 by D2 to get (X²+Y²)/(X−Y)
11   00000420 33C100000504       MOVE.W  D1,Z        ;Put the result now in D1 into Z
12   00000426 4E722700           STOP    #$2700
13
14   00000500                    ORG     $500        ;Put the data here
15
16   00000500 0032        X:     DC.W    50          ;Initial dummy value for X
17   00000502 000C        Y:     DC.W    12          ;Initial dummy value for Y
18   00000504 00000002    Z:     DS.W    1           ;Reserve space for the result
19
20            00000400           END     $400        ;End of program and address of entry point
Lines: 20, Errors: 0, Warnings: 0.
```

We can use the Teesside simulator to run this program line-by-line and observe its execution. The simulator is invoked by the DOS command E68K PROG1. If we enter LOG PROG1.LOG when the simulator is running, all screen input/output is stored in a log file called PROG1.LOG that can be printed or displayed later. In what follows, the monospaced output was generated by the computer—the other output in italics is my commentary.

If we enter MD 500, the simulator displays the 16 bytes stored at memory location 500_{16} onward. The MD (i.e. memory display) command displays the contents of the simulator's memory.

```
>MD 500

000500    00 32 00 0C 00 00 00 00 00 00 00 00 00 00 00 00.
```

The first six digits 000500 give the first location on the line, and the following 16 pairs of digits give the contents of 16 consecutive bytes starting at the first location. As you can see, location 500_{16} contains $32_{16} = 50$, and location 502_{16} contains $0C_{16} = 12$. These values were set up by the DC.W (define constant) assembler directives.

If we enter the command DF (display formatted registers), the simulator will display the contents of the simulated 68K's registers. These include the PC (preset to 400_{16}) and the next instruction to be executed.

```
>DF
PC=000400 SR=2000 SS=00A00000 US=00000000        X=0
A0=00000000 A1=00000000 A2=00000000 A3=00000000  N=0
A4=00000000 A5=00000000 A6=00000000 A7=00A00000  Z=0
D0=00000000 D1=00000000 D2=00000000 D3=00000000  V=0
D4=00000000 D5=00000000 D6=00000000 D7=00000000  C=0
----->MOVE.W   $0500,D0
```

In this simple program we are going to enter the TR (trace) command, which executes a line of the program at a time and displays the contents of the registers. In this way we can follow the execution of the program.

```
>TR
PC=000406 SR=2000 SS=00A00000 US=00000000        X=0
A0=00000000 A1=00000000 A2=00000000 A3=00000000  N=0
A4=00000000 A5=00000000 A6=00000000 A7=00A00000  Z=0
D0=00000032 D1=00000000 D2=00000000 D3=00000000  V=0
D4=00000000 D5=00000000 D6=00000000 D7=00000000  C=0
----->MULU.W   D0,D0
```

As you can see, the instruction MOVE.W $0500,D0 has been executed and the contents of memory location 500_{16} have been copied into data register D0. Once you have entered the trace mode, simply hitting the enter key traces an instruction at a time.

```
Trace>
PC=000408 SR=2000 SS=00A00000 US=00000000        X=0
A0=00000000 A1=00000000 A2=00000000 A3=00000000  N=0
A4=00000000 A5=00000000 A6=00000000 A7=00A00000  Z=0
D0=000009C4 D1=00000000 D2=00000000 D3=00000000  V=0
D4=00000000 D5=00000000 D6=00000000 D7=00000000  C=0
----->MOVE.W   $0502,D1
```

We have just executed MULU D0,D0 and the content of D0 is $9C4_{16}$. This is $50 \times 50 = 2500 = 9C4_{16}$.

```
Trace>
PC=00040E SR=2000 SS=00A00000 US=00000000        X=0
A0=00000000 A1=00000000 A2=00000000 A3=00000000  N=0
A4=00000000 A5=00000000 A6=00000000 A7=00A00000  Z=0
D0=000009C4 D1=0000000C D2=00000000 D3=00000000  V=0
D4=00000000 D5=00000000 D6=00000000 D7=00000000  C=0
----->MULU.W   D1,D1
```

```
Trace>
PC=000410 SR=2000 SS=00A00000 US=00000000        X=0
A0=00000000 A1=00000000 A2=00000000 A3=00000000  N=0
A4=00000000 A5=00000000 A6=00000000 A7=00A00000  Z=0
D0=000009C4 D1=00000090 D2=00000000 D3=00000000  V=0
D4=00000000 D5=00000000 D6=00000000 D7=00000000  C=0
----->ADD.L    D0,D1
```

At this stage D1 contains $C_{16}^2 = 12 \times 12 = 144 = 90_{16}$.

```
Trace>
PC=000412 SR=2000 SS=00A00000 US=00000000        X=0
A0=00000000 A1=00000000 A2=00000000 A3=00000000  N=0
A4=00000000 A5=00000000 A6=00000000 A7=00A00000  Z=0
D0=000009C4 D1=00000A54 D2=00000000 D3=00000000  V=0
D4=00000000 D5=00000000 D6=00000000 D7=00000000  C=0
----->MOVE.W   $0500,D2
```

(*program continued*)

At this stage we have calculated $X^2 + Y^2$ and deposited the result in data register D1.

```
Trace>
PC=000418 SR=2000 SS=00A00000 US=00000000        X=0
A0=00000000 A1=00000000 A2=00000000 A3=00000000 N=0
A4=00000000 A5=00000000 A6=00000000 A7=00A00000 Z=0
D0=000009C4 D1=00000A54 D2=00000032 D3=00000000 V=0
D4=00000000 D5=00000000 D6=00000000 D7=00000000 C=0
----->SUB.W  $0502,D2

Trace>
PC=00041E SR=2000 SS=00A00000 US=00000000        X=0
A0=00000000 A1=00000000 A2=00000000 A3=00000000 N=0
A4=00000000 A5=00000000 A6=00000000 A7=00A00000 Z=0
D0=000009C4 D1=00000A54 D2=00000026 D3=00000000 V=0
D4=00000000 D5=00000000 D6=00000000 D7=00000000 C=0
----->DIVU.W  D2,D1

Trace>
PC=000420 SR=2000 SS=00A00000 US=00000000        X=0
A0=00000000 A1=00000000 A2=00000000 A3=00000000 N=0
A4=00000000 A5=00000000 A6=00000000 A7=00A00000 Z=0
D0=000009C4 D1=00160045 D2=00000026 D3=00000000 V=0
D4=00000000 D5=00000000 D6=00000000 D7=00000000 C=0
----->MOVE.W  D1,$0504
```

The 68K instruction DIVU D2,D1 divides the 32-bit contents of data register D1 by the lower-order 16 bits in data register D2. The result is a 16-bit quotient in the lower-order word of D1 and a 16-bit remainder in the upper-order word of D1. That is; $A54_{16}/9C4_{16} = 45_{16}$ remainder 16_{16}. The contents of D1 are \$00160045.

```
Trace>
PC=000426 SR=2000 SS=00A00000 US=00000000        X=0
A0=00000000 A1=00000000 A2=00000000 A3=00000000 N=0
A4=00000000 A5=00000000 A6=00000000 A7=00A00000 Z=0
D0=000009C4 D1=00160045 D2=00000026 D3=00000000 V=0
D4=00000000 D5=00000000 D6=00000000 D7=00000000 C=0
----->STOP    #$2700
```

The instruction MOVE.W D1,\$0504 stores the low-order 16-bit result in D1 in memory location 504_{16} (i.e. Z). Note that we have used a wordlength operation and have discarded the remainder in the upper-order word of D1.

```
Trace >
Processor halted at: 00042A
```

When we hit return again, the STOP instruction is executed. We can end the trace mode by entering a period. Then we use MD (memory display) again to re-examine the memory.

```
Trace>.
>MD 500

000500   00 32 00 0C 00 45 00 00 00 00 00 00 00 00 00 00.
```

As you can see, memory location 504_{16} now contains the integer result of $(50^2 + 12^2)/(50 - 12) = 45_{16} = 69$. You can exit the 68K simulator mode and return to the DOS command level by entering a Q (quit) command.

6.3.3 Shift operations

All a shift operation does is to move a group of bits one or more places left or right. The 68K has a full complement of both arithmetic and logical shifts operations, that are described in Figs. 6.9 and 6.10. Shift operations can be applied to bytes, words, and longwords. The difference between the various shift operations determines what happens to the bits at each end of a word when it is shifted.

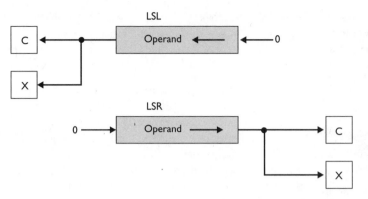

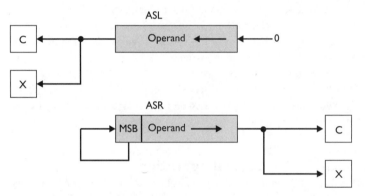

Fig. 6.9 The 68 K's logical and arithmetic shift instructions.

Suppose the 8-bit value 11001010 is shifted one place right. What is the new value? A logical shift right operation, LSR, introduces a zero into the leftmost bit position vacated by the shift, and the new value is 01100101.

Arithmetic shifts treat the data shifted as a signed two's complement value. Therefore, the sign bit is propagated by an arithmetic shift right. In this case, the number $11001010 = -54$ is negative and, after an arithmetic right shift, ASR, the new result is 11100101 (i.e. -27).

When a word is shifted right, the old least-significant bit is shifted out and 'lost'. In fact, Figs. 6.9 and 6.10 show that this bit isn't entirely lost because it's copied into the CCR's C (i.e. carry) bit. Note that most shift operations also copy the bit shifted out into the X-bit (i.e. extend bit) of the CCR.

An arithmetic shift left is equivalent to multiplication by 2, and an arithmetic shift right is equivalent to division by 2.

The assembly language forms of the 68K's logical and arithmetic instructions are

```
LSL #n,Di
LSR #n,Di
ASL #n,Di
ASR #n,Di
```

The integer n indicates the number of places to be shifted; that is, you can shift the bits in register Di by more than one place in a single operation. Like other operations on data registers, these instructions can be applied to bytes, words, and longwords. If you shift a word by more than one place, the end value of the carry bit is determined by the final shift. Consider the following examples:

Initial contents of D0	Operation	Final contents of D0
11001100	LSL.B #1,D0	10011000
11001100	LSR.B #1,D0	01100110
11001100	ASL.B #1,D0	10011000
11001100	ASR.B #1,D0	11100110
1010111100001100	ASR.W #3,D0	1111010111100001
0011100001111101	ASR.W #4,D0	0000001110000111

A typical application of a logical shift operation is to extract certain bits in a word. Consider an 8-bit byte in D0 with the format xxyyyzzz, where the 'x's, 'y's, and 'z's are three groups of bits that have been *packed* into a byte. Suppose we wish to extract the three 'y's from this byte. We can use the sequence

```
LSR.B #3,D0              Shift D0 right 3 places to get 000xxyyy in D0
AND.B #%00000111,D0      Clear bits 3 to 7 of D0
```

The first instruction LSR.B #3,D0 shifts xxyyyzzz right to get 000xxyyy in D0. We remove the 'x's by means of the logical operation AND.B #%00000111,D0 to get 00000yyy in D0.

Circular shifts and rotates

Figure 6.10 describes the 68K's *circular* shifts. A circular shift or *rotate* operation treats the data being shifted as a ring with the most-significant bit adjacent to the least-significant bit. Circular shifts result in the most-significant bit being shifted into the least-significant bit position (left shift), or vice versa for a right shift. No data is lost during a circular shift.

The 68K supports two types of *circular* shift. The rotate left and rotate right operations (ROL and ROR) shift the bits of a register left or right. The bit that is shifted out at one end is shifted into the other end and also copied into the carry bit. Consider the following examples:

Initial D0	Shift	D0 after the shift
11001110	ROL.B #1,D0	10011101
11001110	ROR.B #1,D0	01100111
11110000	ROL.B #2,D0	11000011

Figure 6.10 also shows the 68K's two circular shift operations that include the extend bit (X-bit) in the condition code register. The mnemonics for these instructions are ROXL and ROXR (rotate left through extend and rotate right through extend). You may wonder why the X-bit is included in the form of circular shift in Fig. 6.10. Suppose you want to perform a 64-bit quadword logical shift left. The 68K is a 32-bit machine with 32-bit registers. We will assume that the lower-order 32 bits of the quadword are in D0 and the higher-order 32 bits are in D1.

We can shift the 32 bits of D0 one place left by means of the operation LSL.L #1,D0. If you look at Fig. 6.10 you will see that the most-significant bit of D0 is shifted into the X-bit. If we now execute ROXL.L #1,D1, the 32 bits of D1 are rotated left and the X-bit is moved into the least-significant bit position. The X-bit is, of course, the most-significant bit from D0.

6.3.4 Logical operations

Like shift operations, logical operations allow you to directly manipulate the individual bits of a word. The 68K implements four logical operations; NOT, AND, OR and EOR. The NOT

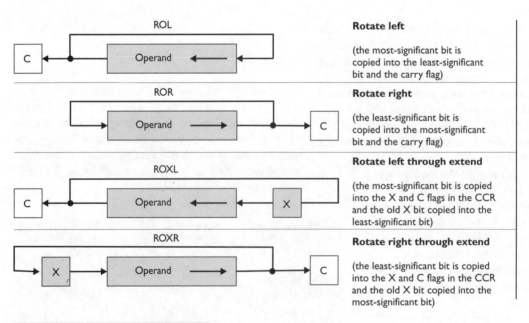

Fig. 6.10 The 68 K's circular shift instructions.

operation simply inverts the bits of an operand; for example, if [D0] = 11001010, the operation NOT.B D0 results in [D0] = 00110101.

The AND operation is *dyadic* and is applied to a source and destination operand. Bit *i* of the source is ANDed with bit *i* of the destination and the result is stored in bit *i* of the destination. If [D0] = 11001010, the operation

```
AND.B #%11110000,D0
```

results in [D0] = 11000000.

The AND operation is used to mask the bits of a word. If you AND bit *x* with bit *y*, the result is 0 if *y* = 0, and *x* if *y* = 1. A typical example of the AND instruction is to strip the parity bit off a byte. That is,

```
AND.B #%01111111,D0
```

clears bit 7 of D0 to zero, and leaves bits 0 to 6 unchanged. Note that we have expressed the source operand in binary form because it best indicates the nature of the operation.

The OR operation is used to set one or more bits of a word to 1. ORing a bit with 0 has no effect, and ORing the bit with 1 sets it. For example, if [D0] = 11001010, the operation

```
OR.B #%11110000,D0
```

results in [D0] = 11111010.

The EOR operation is used to toggle one or more bits of a word. EORing a bit with 0 has no effect, and EORing it with 1 inverts it. For example, if [D0] = 11001010, the operation

```
EOR.B #%11110000,D0
```

results in [D0] = 00111010.

By using the NOT, AND, OR, and EOR instructions, you can perform any logical operations on a word. Suppose you wish

to clear bits 0, 1, and 2, set bits 3, 4, and 5, and toggle bits 6 and 7 of the byte in D0. You could write:

```
AND.B   #%11111000,D0   Clear bits 0, 1, and 2
OR.B    #%00111000,D0   Set bits 3, 4, and 5
EOR.B   #%11000000,D0   Toggle bits 6 and 7.
```

If [D0] initially contains 01010101, its final contents will be 10111000. We will look at a more practical application of bit manipulation after we have covered branch operations in a little more detail.

6.3.5 Branch instructions

A branch instruction modifies the flow of control and causes the program to continue execution at the *target address* specified by the branch. The simplest branch instruction is the *unconditional* branch instruction, BRA target, that always forces a jump to the instruction at the target address. In the following fragment of code, the BRA Here instruction forces the 68K to execute next the instruction on the line which is labeled by Here.

```
        BRA Here
        .
        .
        .
Here    MOVE D0,D4
```

The 68K provides 14 conditional branch instructions of the form Bcc, where cc is one of 14 possible combinations—see Table 6.1. Conditional branch instructions test one or more bits of the condition code register. If the result of the test is true, a branch is made to the target address. Otherwise, the instruction following the branch is executed. Without branch instructions we would not be able to implement high-level

Mnemonic	Instruction	Type	Branch on condition
BCC	branch on carry clear	Flag test, unsigned	$\overline{C}$
BCS	branch on carry set	Flag test, unsigned	C
BEQ	branch on equal	Flag test	Z
BNE	branch on not equal	Flag test	$\overline{Z}$
BGE	branch on greater than or equal	Flag test, signed	$N \cdot V + \overline{N} \cdot \overline{V}$
BGT	branch on greater than	Flag test, signed	$N \cdot V \cdot \overline{Z} + \overline{N} \cdot \overline{V} \cdot \overline{Z}$
BHI	branch on higher than	Flag test, unsigned	$\overline{C} \cdot \overline{Z}$
BLE	branch on less than or equal	Flag test, signed	$Z + \overline{N} \cdot V + N \cdot \overline{V}$
BLS	branch on lower than or same	Flag test, unsigned	$C + Z$
BLT	branch on less than	Flag test, signed	$\overline{N} \cdot V + N \cdot \overline{V}$
BMI	branch on minus (i.e. negative)	Flag test, signed	N
BPL	branch on plus (i.e. positive)	Flag test, signed	$\overline{N}$
BVC	branch on overflow clear	Flag test, signed	$\overline{V}$
BVS	branch on overflow set	Flag test, signed	V

Table 6.1 The 68K's branch instructions.

language constructs such as IF...THEN...ELSE or DO...WHILE.

When the CPU executes most instructions, the CCR's flag bits are automatically updated. Each flag bit in the CCR may be set by an instruction, cleared by it, or remain unaffected. The Z-bit is set if the result of an operation yields a zero result. The N-bit is set if the most-significant bit of the result is one. The carry bit is set if the carry out of the most-significant bit of the result is one. The V-bit is set if the operation yields an out of range result when the operand(s) and result are all regarded as two's complement values. Remember that for the purpose of setting or clearing bits of the CCR, the term most-significant bit refers to bit 7, 15, or 31, depending on whether the current operation is a byte, word, or longword operation, respectively. You can also directly modify the contents of the CCR by special instructions like MOVE #N,CCR.

Table 6.1 shows that some branch instructions test a single bit in the CCR, whereas others test two or three bits. Some tests are applied to unsigned numbers and some to signed numbers. Consider the numbers P = 11110000 and Q = 00110000. If these numbers are unsigned, P = 240 and Q = 48, and P > Q. However, if these numbers are regarded as signed, P = −16 and Q = 48, and P < Q. If we wish to branch on '>' we would use BGT with signed numbers and BHI with unsigned numbers.

The relationship between the CCR and the CPU is unique in the sense that each type of CPU treats its CCR in a different way to other CPUs; for example, a 68K MOVE instruction updates the CCR, whereas some other processors don't update the CCR following a move operation. Consequently, the assembly language programmer must be aware of the relationship between the CCR and the instruction set. Table 6.2 indicates the relationship between some of the 68K's instructions and its CCR. For example, an exchange register instruction, EXG, has no effect on the CCR and the bits of the CCR remain in the state they were in before the EXG was executed. On the other hand, an add instruction, ADD, affects every bit of the CCR. The new values of the CCR bits depend on the result of the addition.

Using conditional branches

The target address used by a branch instruction is automatically calculated by the assembler. All you have to write is Bcc <target> and then label the appropriate target instruction with <target>. Consider the following example:

```
ADD     D1,D2   Add D1 to D2 and branch
                IF the result is minus
BMI     ERROR
```

Operation	X	N	Z	V	C
ADD	*	*	*	*	*
ADDX	*	*	*	*	?
AND	—	*	*	0	0
ASL	*	*	*	*	*
ASR	*	*	*	*	*
BTST	—	—	*	—	—
CHK	—	*	U	U	U
CLR	—	0	I	0	0
CMP	—	*	*	*	*
DIVS/DIVU	—	*	*	*	0
EOR	—	*	*	0	0
EXG	—	—	—	—	—
EXT	—	*	*	0	0
LEA	—	—	—	—	—
LSL	*	*	*	0	*
LSR	*	*	*	0	*
MOVE	—	*	*	0	0
MOVEQ	—	*	*	0	0
MULS/MULU	—	*	*	0	0
NEG	*	*	*	*	*
NEGX	*	*	*	*	*
NOT	—	*	*	0	0
OR	—	*	*	0	0
ROL	—	*	*	0	*
ROR	—	*	*	0	*
ROXL	*	*	*	0	*
ROXR	*	*	*	0	*
SUB	*	*	*	*	*
TST	—	*	*	0	0

Note: — = not affected
U = undefined
? = other
* = general case (updated according to the instruction)

Table 6.2 The way in which the 68K's instructions modify the CCR.

```
        .           )
        .           ) ELSE part
        .           )
        .           )
ERROR   .           ) THEN part
        .           )
```

The operation ADD D1,D2 adds the contents of D1 to D2, deposits the results in D2 and updates the condition code register accordingly.

When the BMI instruction is executed, the branch is taken (the THEN part) if the N-bit of the CCR is set because the addition gave a negative result. In this case, a negative result forces a branch to the line labeled by ERROR, and the intervening code between BMI ERROR and ERROR... is not executed.

If the branch is not taken because the result of ADD D1,D2 was not negative, the code immediately following the BMI ERROR is executed. This code corresponds to the ELSE part of our IF THEN ELSE construction.

Unfortunately, there's an error in the above example. Suppose that the condition $N = 1$ is not met and the ELSE part is executed. Once this code has been executed, we fall through to the THEN part, which is not what we want to do. After the ELSE part has been executed, it's necessary to skip round the THEN part by means of a BRA instruction.

```
         ADD    D1,D2
         BMI    ERROR
         .                 ) ELSE part
         .                 )
         BRA    EXIT    Skip past the THEN part
ERROR    .                 )
         .                 ) THEN part
         .                 )
EXIT
```

The *unconditional branch* instruction, BRA EXIT, forces the computer to execute the next instruction at EXIT and skips past the 'ERROR' clause.

By the way, like most other computers the 68K uses *relative branching* so that the operand following a Bcc represents the 'distance' to be branched from the current instruction rather than the absolute address. When you write a program, the assembler automatically calculates the appropriate relative address—we'll return to this later.

Remember we said earlier that not all the 68K's instructions affect the CCR. For example, consider the following two examples

```
         ADD    D1,D2    Add the contents of D1 to the
                         contents of D2
         BMI    ERROR    If the result is negative, branch to
                         ERROR
and
         ADD    D1,D2    Add the contents of D1 to the
                         contents of D2
         EXG    D3,D4    Exchange the contents of D3 and D4
         EXG    D5,D6    Exchange the contents of D5 and D6
         BMI    ERROR    If the result of the addition was
                         negative, branch to ERROR
```

Both these fragments of code have the same effect as far as the BMI ERROR is concerned. However, the second case might prove confusing to the reader of the program who may well imagine that the state of the CCR prior to the BMI ERROR is determined by the EXG D5,D6 instruction.

We now look at a more extended example of conditional behavior. Suppose you want to write a subroutine to convert a 4-bit hexadecimal value into its ASCII equivalent. Table 6.3 illustrates the relationship between the binary value of a number (expressed in hexadecimal form), and its ASCII equivalent (also expressed in hexadecimal form). For example, if the internal binary value in a register is 00001010, its

ASCII character	Hexadecimal value	Binary value
0	30	0000
1	31	0001
2	32	0010
3	33	0011
4	34	0100
5	35	0101
6	36	0110
7	37	0111
8	38	1000
9	39	1001
A	41	1010
B	42	1011
C	43	1100
D	44	1101
E	45	1110
F	46	1111

Table 6.3 Relationship between ISO/ASCII characters and hexadecimal values.

hexadecimal equivalent is A_{16}. In order to print the letter 'A' on a terminal, you have to transmit the ASCII code for the letter 'A' (i.e. \$41) to it. Once again, note that there is a difference between the internal binary representation of a number within a computer and the code used represent the symbol for that number. The number six is expressed in eight bits by the binary pattern 00000110 and is stored in the computer's memory in this form. On the other hand, the symbol for a six (i.e. '6') is represented by the binary pattern 00110110 in the ASCII code. If we want a printer to make a mark on paper corresponding to '6', we must send the binary number 00110110 to it. Consequently, numbers held in the computer must be converted to their ASCII forms before they can be printed.

From Table 6.3 we can derive an algorithm to convert a 4-bit internal value into its ASCII form. A hexadecimal value in the range 0 to 9 is converted into ASCII form by adding hexadecimal 30 to the number. A hexadecimal value in the range \$A to \$F is converted to ASCII by adding hexadecimal \$37. If we represent the number to be converted by HEX and the number to be converted by ASCII, we can write down a suitable algorithm in the form

```
IF HEX < $A THEN ASCII := HEX+$30
            ELSE ASCII := HEX+$37
```

Alternatively, we can rewrite the algorithm as

```
ASCII := HEX+$30
IF ASCII > $39 THEN ASCII := ASCII+7
```

The alternative algorithm can be translated into low level language as

carry out the two tests in succession because no intervening instruction modifies the state of the CCR.

```
*                           Note: D0.B holds HEX value on subroutine entry
*                                 D0.B holds the ASCII character code on return
*                                 No other register is modified by this subroutine
*      ADD.B   #$30,D0             ASCII := HEX+$30
       CMP.B   #$39,D0             IF ASCII ≤ $39 THEN EXIT
       BLE     EXIT
       ADD.B   #7,D0                         ELSE ASCII  := ASCII+7
EXIT RTS
```

We have used a new instruction `CMP` (compare). The effect of `CMP source,destination` is to subtract the source operand from the destination operand and then set the flag bits of the CCR accordingly; that is, a `CMP` is the same as a `SUB` except that the result is not recorded.

We now look at another example of branch operations. Here, we demonstrate how you might use implement the following algorithm:

```
*   IF x=y THEN y=6
*   IF x>y THEN y=y+1
*
       CMP.B    D0,D1      Assume that x is in D0 and y in D1
       BNE      NotEqu     IF x=y THEN
       MOVE.B   #6,D1                y=6
       BRA      exit                 and leave the algorithm
NotEqu BGE      exit       IF x≤y   THEN exit
       ADD.B    #1,D1              ELSE y=y+1
exit   .                   exit point for the algorithm
```

Note that we perform two tests after the comparison `CMP.B D0,D1`. One is a `BNE` and the other a `BGE`. We can

Although the conditional test performed by a high-level language can be quite complex (e.g. IF $X+Y-Z>3t$), the conditional test at the assembly language level is rather more basic, as this example demonstrates.

Templates for control structures

We can readily represent some of the control structures of high-level languages as templates in assembly language. A template is a pattern or example that can be modified to suit the actual circumstances. In each of the following examples, the high-level construct is provided as a comment to the assembly language template by means of asterisks in the first column. The condition tested is [D0]=[D1] and the actions to be carried out are `Action1` or `Action2`. The templates can be used by providing the appropriate test instead of `CMP D0,D1` and providing the appropriate sequence of assembly language statements instead of `Action1` or `Action2`.

```
*              IF [D0]=[D1] THEN Action1
*
       CMP   D0,D1      Perform test
       BNE   EXIT       IF [D0]≠[D1] THEN exit
Action1   .                        ELSE execute Action1
          .
EXIT                    Exit point for construct
```

```
*              IF [D0]=[D1] THEN Action1 ELSE Action2
*
       CMP   D0,D1      Compare D0 with D1
       BNE   Action2    IF [D0]≠[D1] perform Action2
Action1   .             Fall through to action1 if [D0]=[D1]
          .
       BRA   EXIT       Skip round Action2
Action2   .             Action2
          .
EXIT                    Exit point for construct
```

```
*           FOR K=I TO J
*               .
*           ENDFOR
*
        MOVE    #I,D2       Load loop counter, D2, with I
Action1     .               Perform Action1
            .
        ADD     #1,D2       Increment loop counter
        CMP     #J+1,D2     Test for end of loop
        BNE     Action1     IF not end THEN go round again
EXIT                                ELSE exit
```

```
*           WHILE [D0]=[D1] Perform Action1
*
Repeat  CMP     D0,D1       Perform test
        BNE     EXIT        IF [D0]≠[D1] THEN exit
Action1     .                       ELSE carry out Action1
            .
        BRA     Repeat      REPEAT loop
EXIT                        Exit from construct
```

```
*           REPEAT Action1 UNTIL [D0]=[D1]
*
Action1     .               Perform Action1
            .
        CMP     D0,D1       Carry out test
        BNE     Action1     REPEAT as long as [D0]≠[D1]
EXIT                        Exit from loop
```

```
*           CASE OF I
*               I=0 Action0
*               I=1 Action1
*               I=2 Action2
*               I=3 Action3
*                 .
*                 .
*               I=N ActionN
*               I>N Exception
*
        CMP.B       #N,I        Test for I out of range
        BGT         EXCEPTION   IF I>N THEN exception
        MOVE.W      I,D0        Pick up value of I in D0
        MULU        #4,D0       Each address is a longword
        LEA         Table,A0    A0 points to table of addresses
        LEA         (A0,D0),A0  A0 now points to case I in table
        MOVEA.L     (A0),A0     A0 contains address of case I handler
        JMP         (A0)        Execute case I handler
*
Table   ORG         <address>   Here is the table of exceptions
Action0 DC.L        <address0>  Address of case 0 handler
Action1 DC.L        <address1>  Address of case 1 handler
Action2 DC.L        <address2)  Address of case 2 handler
   .
   .
   .
Action  NDC.L       <addressN>  Address of case N handler
*
EXCEPTION           ...         Exception handler here
```

Note that the case number *I* (stored in D0) must be multiplied by four before it can be added to the address in A0. This action is necessary since the case numbers are consecutive integers 0, 1, 2, 3 while the addresses of the case handlers are consecutive longword addresses (i.e. A0+0, A0+4, A0+8, ...).

Applying logical operations

It's immediately obvious how arithmetic operations are applied to real applications, as everyone is familiar with numerical calculations in everyday life. The application of logical operations is less obvious. In Chapter 2 we saw how a group of bits can represent the status of devices connected to the computer. The examples provided were pumps, heaters, and valves that are turned on or off by the value of a particular bit in a control word. Logical operations are needed for the manipulation of the individual bits within a word.

Consider the control of a system with eight single-bit inputs (P, Q, R, S, T, U, V, W), and eight single-bit outputs (A, B, C, D, E, F, G, H). We're not interested in the details of input/output techniques here and assume that reading a memory location whose address is INPUT loads the values of P to W into a data register. Similarly, writing the contents of a data register to memory location OUTPUT sets up the eight output bits A to H. The formats of the input and output control words are defined in Fig. 6.11.

Suppose that a system has to implement the following control operation:

```
IF ((P=1) AND (Q=0)) OR ((P=0) AND (S=1))
  THEN
    BEGIN
      C:=1; E:=0
    END
  ELSE
    BEGIN
      C:=0; E:=1
    END
ENDIF
```

We now have to translate this algorithm into 68K code. The above action involves the testing of three bits of INPUT (P, Q, and S), and then setting or clearing two bits of OUTPUT (C and E). An important consideration is that the bits of OUTPUT not involved in the algorithm must not be affected in any way by operations on bits C and E. The following sequence of instructions execute the desired action.

```
              MOVE.B  INPUT,D0          Get input status
              AND.B   #%11000000,D0     Mask out all bits but P and Q
              CMP.B   #%10000000,D0     Test for P=1, Q=0
              BEQ     TRUE              Goto action on test true
              MOVE.B  INPUT,D0          Get input status again
              AND.B   #%10010000,D0     Mask out all bits but P and S
              CMP.B   #%00010000,D0     Test for P=0, S=1
              BEQ     TRUE              Goto action on test true
      FALSE   MOVE.B  OUTPUT,D0         Get the output control word
              AND.B   #%11011111,D0     Clear bit C
              OR.B    #%00001000,D0     Set bit E
              MOVE.B  D0,OUTPUT         Set up new output control word
              BRA     EXIT              Branch past actions on test true
      TRUE    MOVE.B  OUTPUT,D0         Get the output control word
              AND.B   #%11110111,D0     Clear bit E
              OR.B    #%00100000,D0     Set bit C
              MOVE.B  D0,OUTPUT         Set up new output control word
      EXIT                              Continue
```

Remember that the assembly language symbol % indicates that the following number is to be interpreted by the assembler as a binary value, and the symbol $ means that the following number is interpreted as a hexadecimal value. Once more the advantage of programming in binary (in certain circumstances) is self-evident, as AND.B #%11000000,D0 tells the reader much more than the hexadecimal and decimal forms of the operand, AND.B #$C0,D0 and AND.B #192,D0, respectively.

The assembly language symbol # (pronounced 'hash') informs the assembler that the following value is not the address of a memory location containing the operand, but the actual operand itself. Thus, AND.B #%11000000,D0 means calculate the logical AND between the binary value 11000000 and the contents of D0. If we had made a mistake in the program and had written AND.B %11000000,D0 (rather than AND.B #%11000000,D0), the instruction would have ANDed D0 with the contents of memory location %11000000 (i.e. 192). The use of the # symbol is called immediate addressing and is dealt with in more detail later in this chapter.

Let's look again at the compare instruction, CMP, which compares the two operands specified by the instruction and sets the bits of the CCR accordingly. CMP.B #%00010000,D0 compares the contents of D0 with the binary value 00010000, which is done by subtraction (i.e. [D0] – 00010000). The

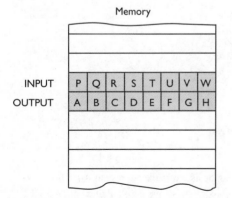

Fig. 6.11 The memory map of two input/output ports.

result of the subtraction is discarded, leaving the contents of D0 unaffected by the CMP operation. Only the bits of the CCR are modified. If D0 contains 00010000, the subtraction yields zero, setting the Z (zero) flag of the CCR. The following operation, BEQ TRUE, results in a branch to the instruction whose address is labeled TRUE. All 68K comparison instructions are of the form CMP source,destination which results in the comparison: destination – source. The difference between CMP Di,Dj and SUB Di,Dj is that the former evaluates Dj – Di and throws away the result, whereas the latter evaluates Dj – Di and puts the result in Dj.

The label FALSE is a dummy label and is not in any way used by the assembly program. It merely serves as a reminder to the programmer of the action to be taken as a result of the test being false. At the end of this sequence is an instruction BRA EXIT. A BRA (branch) is equivalent to a GOTO in a high level language and causes a branch round the action taken if the result of the test is true.

6.3.6 System control instructions

System control instructions can't be described in any detail here, as they relate to topics not yet introduced. Broadly speaking, control instructions are used by the operating system rather the applications programmer. We have already met one control instruction, STOP #$2700, that can be used to bring the 68K to a halt.

Typical system control instructions set the priorities of interrupt request handlers or they determine the operating status of the processor. We examine interrupts in both Chapter 8 and Chapter 10.

6.4 Addressing modes

Addressing modes are concerned with *how* an operand is located by the CPU. A computer's addressing modes are almost entirely analogous to human addressing modes, as the following examples demonstrate.

- Here's $100 (literal value)
- Get the cash from 12 North Street (absolute address)
- Go to 10 East Street and they'll tell you where to get the cash (indirect address)
- Go to 2 North Street and get the cash from the fifth house to the right (relative address)

These four 'addressing modes' show that we can provide data itself (i.e. the $100 cash), say exactly where it is, or explain

how you go about finding where it is. Now let's apply the same principles to the computer.

Up to this point we've dealt largely with the absolute addressing mode, in which the actual address in memory of an operand is specified by the instruction, or with register direct addressing in which the address of an operand is a register. We now introduce other ways of specifying the location of an operand. Because the address of an operand can be calculated in several ways, we use the term *effective address* as a general expression for the address of an operand. At first sight, the topic of addressing modes often seems confusing. It isn't—the programmer uses different addressing modes to deal with operands that never change, operands whose values are variables, and operands that belong to data structures such as lists, tables, and arrays.

6.4.1 Absolute addressing

In *absolute* or *direct* addressing the operand field of the instruction provides the address of the operand in memory. For example, the instruction MOVE 1234,D0 copies the contents of memory location 1234 into data register D0. We have used this addressing mode in many of the preceding examples. Let's look at a few examples of instructions with absolute addresses:

```
MOVE    1234,D0      [D0]    ← [1234]
MOVE    D0,1234      [1234]  ← [D0]
MOVE    1234,1224    [1224]  ← [1234]
ADD     1234,D0      [D0]    ← [D0] + [1234]
SUB     TEMP,D2      [D2]    ← [D2] − [TEMP]
```

Note that [1234] is a short-hand form of [M(1234)] and means the contents of memory location 1234.

Assembly language programmers seldom use numeric addresses (e.g. 1234) and invariably use *symbolic* addresses (e.g. WEEK_DAY). In the high-level language expression, x := y + z, the letters x, y, and z are all symbolic values (as opposed to the actual locations of these variables in memory). We sometimes use numeric values as addresses in this chapter, because we are trying to demonstrate what happens when machine code instructions are executed.

Figure 6.12 demonstrates absolute addressing at the high-level language level, the low-level language level, and the machine code level.

Absolute addressing is used whenever the address of a variable is constant. A constant address implies that the same location in memory always holds the same variable (e.g. 1234 might always be used to hold a variable TEMP_X). This may sound like a statement of the obvious, but we'll soon see that there are occasions when we have to use *variable* addresses.

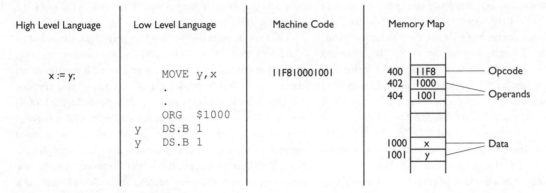

Fig. 6.12 Four views of absolute addressing.

6.4.2 Immediate addressing

We've already met immediate addressing, which is also known as *literal* addressing. Immediate addressing is provided by all microprocessors and allows the programmer to specify a constant as an operand. The value following the op-code in an instruction is not a reference to the address of an operand but is the actual operand itself. In 68K assembly language, the symbol # precedes the operand to indicate immediate addressing. The four instructions below demonstrate how absolute and immediate addressing modes are represented in 68K assembly language and in RTL, respectively.

Assembly language form	RTL form	Name
MOVE 1234,D0	[D0] ← [1234]	absolute addressing
MOVE #1234,D0	[D0] ← 1234	immediate addressing
ADD 1234,D0	[D0] ← [D0]+[1234]	absolute addressing
ADD #1234,D0	[D0] ← [D0]+1234	immediate addressing

The symbol # is not part of the instruction. It is a message to the assembler telling it to select that code for 'move data' that uses the immediate addressing mode. Don't confuse the symbol # with the symbols $ or %. The $ indicates only that the following number is hexadecimal and the % indicates that the following number is binary. The symbols $ and % are necessary, because most computers cannot deal with subscripts, and therefore the conventional way of indicating the base by a subscript is impossible. For example, the three instructions MOVE #25,D0, MOVE #$19,D0, and MOVE #%00011001,D0 have identical effects.

Application of immediate addressing

Immediate addressing is used whenever the value of the operand required by an instruction is known at the time the program is

written. That is, it is used to handle constants as opposed to variables. Immediate addressing is faster than absolute addressing, because only one memory reference is required to read the instruction during the fetch phase. For example, when the instruction MOVE #5,D0 is read from memory in a fetch cycle, the operand, 5, is available immediately without a further memory access to location 5 to read the actual operand. Some of the applications of immediate addressing are given below.

1. As an arithmetic constant

```
MOVE    NUM,D0      [D0]     ← [M(NUM)]
ADD     #22,D0      [D0]     ← [D0]+22
MOVE    D0,NUM      [M(NUM)] ← [D0]
```

This sequence of instructions is equivalent to the high-level language construct NUM := NUM+22 and increases the value in memory location NUM by 22. That is, [M(NUM)] ← [M(NUM)]+22. The 68K can, in fact, add an immediate operand to a memory location directly without using a data register by means of the special add immediate instruction ADDI. For example, ADDI #22,NUM adds the constant value 22 to the contents of the location called NUM.

2. In a comparison with a constant
Consider the test on a variable, NUM, to determine whether it lies in the range 7 < NUM < 25.

```
        MOVE    NUM,D0   Get NUM in D0
        CMP     #8,D0    Compare it with 8
        BMI     FALSE    IF negative NUM≤7
        CMP     #25,D0   Compare it with 25
        BPL     FALSE    IF positive NUM>24
TRUE    ...
          .
          .
FALSE   ...
```

3. As a method of terminating loop structures
A typical loop structure is illustrated in BASIC, Pascal, and C below.

```
BASIC

10  FOR I = 1 TO N
    .
    .
    .
50  NEXT I
```

```
Pascal

FOR I: = 1 TO N DO
    BEGIN
    .
    .
    .
    END;
```

```
C

for(int i: = 0; i < N+1; i++)
    {
    .
    .
    .
    }
```

The high-level language FOR... construct may readily be translated into 68K assembly language. In the following example, the loop counter is stored in data register D0.

```
N       EQU     10          Define the loop size - we've used N=10 here
        .
        .
        MOVE    #1,D0       Load D0 with initial value of the loop counter
NEXT    ...                 Start of loop

                            Body of loop
        .
        ADD     #1,D0       Increment the loop counter
        CMP     #N+1,D0     Test for the end of the loop
        BNE     NEXT        IF not end THEN repeat loop
```

At the end of the loop, the counter is incremented by means of the instruction ADD #1,D0. The counter, D0, is then compared with its terminal value by CMP #N+1,D0. By the way, if you write an expression such as N+1, the assembler evaluates it and replaces it by the calculated value—in this example #N+1 is replaced by 11. We use the comparison with N+1, because the counter is incremented before it is tested. On the last time round the loop, the variable I becomes N+1 after incrementing and the branch to NEXT is not taken, allowing the loop to be exited. This loop construct can be written in a more elegant fashion, but at this point we're interested only in the application of immediate addressing as a means of setting up counters.

6.4.3 Address register indirect addressing

So far we've dealt with addresses that don't change during the execution of a program. A fixed or absolute address is used to access a variable. We now demonstrate that it's difficult to access data structures such as *tables*, *lists*, or *arrays* unless the

computer has a means of changing addresses during the execution of a program.

We know how to add together several numbers. Just imagine the effort required to add together 100 numbers stored in consecutive locations using the addressing modes we've used up to now.

```
MOVE  NUM1,D0    Put first number in D0
ADD   NUM2,D0    Add second number to D0
ADD   NUM3,D0    Add third number to running total
.
.
ADD   NUM99,D0   Add the 99th number
ADD   NUM100,D0  Add the last number
```

Clearly, there has to be a better solution to this problem. What we want is an instruction that adds in number 1 when we execute it the first time, number 2 when we execute it the second time, and number i when we execute it the ith time.

Address register indirect addressing lets you generate lots of different addresses when a program is executed. Address register indirect addressing is so called because it uses an address register to *point* at the location of the operand in memory; that is, the address of an operand is obtained *indirectly* via an address register. Instead of telling the computer where the operand is, you tell it where the address of the operand can be found.

In address register indirect addressing, the operand field of an instruction holds the address of the address register (i.e. A0 to A7) to be used in calculating the true address of the operand. The actual address of the operand is given by the contents of the address register specified in the instruction. Address register indirect addressing is indicated to the 68K assembler by enclosing the address register in round parentheses. For example, if A0 contains 1000, the instruction CLR (A0) clears the contents of memory location 1000. That is, in address register indirect addressing the effective address of an operand is provided by the contents of the address register specified by the instruction.

Figure 6.13 illustrates the effect of the operation MOVE.B (A0),D0 when $[A0] = 1000_{16}$. The computer first reads the contents of address register A0 and then reads the contents of memory pointed at by A0. The contents of A0 are 1000, so the processor reads the contents of memory location 1000 to get the actual operand, 25.

Figure 6.14 illustrates the type of instruction you'd use to add up a sequence of numbers, ADD.B (A0),D0. The computer reads the contents of address register A0 (i.e. 1000) and then reads the contents of memory location 1000 (i.e. 25). This operand is then added to the contents of D0.

The following instructions illustrate address register indirect addressing and provide RTL definitions for the action to be carried out, together with a plain language description.

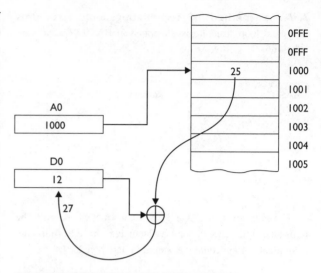

Fig. 6.14 Using address register indirect addressing.

Some texts call this addressing mode 'indexed addressing' or 'modifier-based addressing'. The manufacturers of the 68K reserve the term *indexed addressing* to indicate a particular variant of address register indirect addressing in which the effective address of an operand is calculated by adding the contents of two modifier registers, as we shall see later.

Assembly language form	RTL definition	Description
MOVE (A0),D0	[D0] ← [M([A0])]	Move the contents of the main store pointed at by A0 to D0
MOVE D1,(A2)	[M([A2])] ← [D1]	Move the contents of D1 to the location pointed at by A2
ADD (A1),D2	[D2] ← [D2] + [M([A1])]	Add the contents of the location pointed at by A1 to the contents of D2
MOVE (A1),(A2)	[M([A2])] ← [M([A1])]	Move the contents of the location pointed at by A1 to the location pointed at by A2

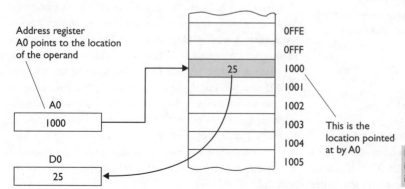

Fig. 6.13 An illustration of address register indirect addressing—the MOVE.B (A0),D0 instruction.

We can deal with the problem of adding 100 numbers by means of address register indirect addressing in the following way. This isn't efficient code—we'll write a better version later.

```
        ORG     $001000     Start of the program
        CLR     D0          D0 is the number counter
        MOVEA   #NUM1,A0    A0 points to the first number
        CLR     D1          Clear the total in D1
LOOP    ADD     (A0),D1     Add in the number pointed at by A0
        ADDA    #2,A0       Point to the next number in the list
        ADD     #1,D0       Increment the number counter
        CMP     #100,D0     Have we added the 100 numbers?
        BNE     LOOP        If not then repeat
        STOP    #$2700      Halt the program
        ORG     $2000       Data region
NUM1    DC.W    1,2,3,4,5   Some dummy data (only 5 numbers given here)
        END     $400
```

In the preceding code, the pointer in address register A0 is incremented by 2 on each pass round the loop—the increment of 2 is required because the memory elements are words and each word occupies two bytes in memory. After assembling this program we can run it on the Teesside simulator. We display the initial state of the simulated 68K and then execute the first few instructions to demonstrate what is happening. The purpose of this demonstration is to show how address register indirect addressing is used.

```
>df
PC=001000 SR=2000 SS=00A00000 US=00000000      X=0
A0=00000000 A1=00000000 A2=00000000 A3=00000000 N=0
A4=00000000 A5=00000000 A6=00000000 A7=00A00000 Z=0
D0=00000000 D1=00000000 D2=00000000 D3=00000000 V=0
D4=00000000 D5=00000000 D6=00000000 D7=00000000 C=0
------>CLR.W      D0

>tr
PC=001002 SR=2004 SS=00A00000 US=00000000      X=0
A0=00000000 A1=00000000 A2=00000000 A3=00000000 N=0
A4=00000000 A5=00000000 A6=00000000 A7=00A00000 Z=1
D0=00000000 D1=00000000 D2=00000000 D3=00000000 V=0
D4=00000000 D5=00000000 D6=00000000 D7=00000000 C=0
------>MOVEA.W   #$2000,A0
```

The *MOVEA.W #$2000* instruction loads the address register with the constant $2000, which is sign-extended to the 32-bit value $00002000.

```
Trace>
PC=001006 SR=2004 SS=00A00000 US=00000000      X=0
A0=00002000 A1=00000000 A2=00000000 A3=00000000 N=0
A4=00000000 A5=00000000 A6=00000000 A7=00A00000 Z=1
D0=00000000 D1=00000000 D2=00000000 D3=00000000 V=0
D4=00000000 D5=00000000 D6=00000000 D7=00000000 C=0
------>CLR.W      D1

Trace>
PC=001008 SR=2004 SS=00A00000 US=00000000      X=0
A0=00002000 A1=00000000 A2=00000000 A3=00000000 N=0
A4=00000000 A5=00000000 A6=00000000 A7=00A00000 Z=1
D0=00000000 D1=00000000 D2=00000000 D3=00000000 V=0
D4=00000000 D5=00000000 D6=00000000 D7=00000000 C=0
------>ADD.W     (A0),D1
```

The next instruction to be executed adds the contents of the memory location pointed at by address register A0 into data register D1. Initially, D1 contains 0 and A0 points at location 2000_{16} (which contains the value 1). The next two operations increment the address pointer and the element counter in D0.

```
Trace>
PC=00100A SR=2000 SS=00A00000 US=00000000         X=0
A0=00002000 A1=00000000 A2=00000000 A3=00000000 N=0
A4=00000000 A5=00000000 A6=00000000 A7=00A00000 Z=0
D0=00000000 D1=00000001 D2=00000000 D3=00000000 V=0
D4=00000000 D5=00000000 D6=00000000 D7=00000000 C=0
------>ADDA.W    #$02,A0
```

```
Trace>
PC=00100E SR=2000 SS=00A00000 US=00000000         X=0
A0=00002002 A1=00000000 A2=00000000 A3=00000000 N=0
A4=00000000 A5=00000000 A6=00000000 A7=00A00000 Z=0
D0=00000000 D1=00000001 D2=00000000 D3=00000000 V=0
D4=00000000 D5=00000000 D6=00000000 D7=00000000 C=0
------>ADDQ.W    #$01,D0
```

```
Trace>
PC=001010 SR=2000 SS=00A00000 US=00000000         X=0
A0=00002002 A1=00000000 A2=00000000 A3=00000000 N=0
A4=00000000 A5=00000000 A6=00000000 A7=00A00000 Z=0
D0=00000001 D1=00000001 D2=00000000 D3=00000000 V=0
D4=00000000 D5=00000000 D6=00000000 D7=00000000 C=0
------>CMPI.W    #$64,D0
```

The next two instructions, CMPI.W #$64,D0 and BNE $1008, test the contents of the loop counter and branch back to address $1008 if D0 does not contain $64_{16} = 100_{10}$. Because the simulator doesn't know about symbolic names, the branch target address is given as $1008 rather than 'LOOP'. The mnemonic for the conditional branch is expressed as BNE.S. Don't worry about the '.S' extension. The 68K assembler uses two different forms of branch, one for short distances up to about 128 bytes and the other for branches to instructions further away.

```
Trace>
PC=001014 SR=2009 SS=00A00000 US=00000000         X=0
A0=00002002 A1=00000000 A2=00000000 A3=00000000 N=1
A4=00000000 A5=00000000 A6=00000000 A7=00A00000 Z=0
D0=00000001 D1=00000001 D2=00000000 D3=00000000 V=0
D4=00000000 D5=00000000 D6=00000000 D7=00000000 C=1
------>BNE.S     $1008
```

Since D0 doesn't contain 64_{16}, we branch back to address 1008_{16}.

```
Trace>
PC=001008 SR=2009 SS=00A00000 US=00000000         X=0
A0=00002002 A1=00000000 A2=00000000 A3=00000000 N=1
A4=00000000 A5=00000000 A6=00000000 A7=00A00000 Z=0
D0=00000001 D1=00000001 D2=00000000 D3=00000000 V=0
D4=00000000 D5=00000000 D6=00000000 D7=00000000 C=1
------>ADD.W     (A0),D1
```

We've been here before—except that the loop counter is now 1 and A0 points at location 2002_{16}. The next addition adds the next number in series as the following operation demonstrates.

```
Trace>
PC=00100A SR=2000 SS=00A00000 US=00000000         X=0
A0=00002002 A1=00000000 A2=00000000 A3=00000000 N=0
A4=00000000 A5=00000000 A6=00000000 A7=00A00000 Z=0
D0=00000001 D1=00000003 D2=00000000 D3=00000000 V=0
D4=00000000 D5=00000000 D6=00000000 D7=00000000 C=0
------->ADDA.W    #$02,A0
```

This process continues and A0 is incremented by 2 on each of the 99 passes round the loop.

We can modify the program to add the hundred numbers further. Notice just how compact the following code is.

```
        LEA     NUM1,A0   A0 points at the list of numbers
        CLR     D0        Clear the total
        MOVE    #99,D1    Set up the counter for 100 cycles
LOOP    ADD     (A0),D0   Add in a number
        ADDA.L  #2,A0     Point to next number
        DBRA    D1,LOOP   Repeat until all numbers added
```

We've just introduced two new instructions. The first instruction, LEA NUM1,A0, means 'load effective address NUM1 into address register A0'. This instruction loads an address into an address register and has the same effect as MOVEA #NUM1,A0. The LEA instruction doesn't require a # symbol to indicate a literal operand because the source operand is always an address.

The 68K's *decrement and branch* instruction DBRA D1,LOOP provides a convenient means of implementing a loop. This instruction subtracts 1 from the contents of D1 and branches back to the line labeled by LOOP. If, however, D1 is decremented and goes from 0 to −1, the loop is not taken and the next instruction in sequence is executed. Because the branch terminates on −1 rather than 0, loading Di with N causes DBRA Di,LOOP to execute $N+1$ times.

The following provides an RTL definition for DBRA D1,LOOP.

```
LOOP:
              .
              .

          [D0] ← [D0]−1
          IF [D0] = −1 THEN
                      [PC] ← Exit
                      ELSE [PC] ← LOOP
Exit:         .
```

Address register indirect addressing with displacement

A more general form of the 68K's address register indirect addressing mode is called *address register indirect addressing mode with displacement*. The effective address is written d(Ai), where d is a constant and Ai an address register. The effective address of an operand is calculated by adding the contents of the address register specified by the instruction to the signed two's complement constant that forms part of the instruction. Figure 6.15 illustrates how the effective address is calculated for the instruction MOVE.B 4(A0),D0. This instruction means 'load register D0 with the contents of the memory location four bytes onward from the location pointed at by address register A0'.

We can define the operation MOVE d(A0),D0 in RTL as [D0] ← [M(d+[A0])], where d is a 16-bit two's complement value in the range −32K to 32K. This constant is called a *displacement* (or *offset*) because it indicates how far the operand is located from the location pointed at by A0. The displacement can be negative; for example; MOVE.B −4(A0),D0 specifies an operand four bytes back from the location pointed at by A0.

Why would you wish to use this addressing mode? Consider the data structure of Fig. 6.16, where three variables P, Q, and R have consecutive locations on memory. If we load address register A0 with the address of the first variable, P, we can access each variable via A0.

In this fragment of code we define the displacements P, Q, and R as 0, 1, and 2, respectively.

```
P    EQU        0
Q    EQU        1
R    EQU        2
     .
     .
     .
     MOVEA.L    #Block,A0   A0 points to 'Block'
     MOVE.B     P(A0),D0    Evaluate R=P+Q
     ADD.B      Q(A0),D0
     MOVE.B     D0,R(A0)
```

This fragment of code adds two numbers and stores their sum in memory. But where in memory? The location of the three numbers is Block+P, Block+Q, and Block+R, respectively. Since the value of Block can be changed by the programmer, we can locate the variables P, Q, and R in any three consecutive locations anywhere in memory. Why would we want to do that? If we access variables by specifying their location with respect to a pointer, we can move the program about in memory without having to recalculate all addresses. We now look at a typical example of this addressing mode.

Using address register indirect addressing with displacement

Let's look at a more sophisticated example of this addressing mode that involves vectors. A vector is composed of a sequence of components; for example, the vector X might be composed of four elements x_0, x_1, x_2, x_3. One of the most common of all mathematical calculations (because it crops up in many different areas—particularly graphics) is the evaluation of the inner or scalar product of two vectors. Suppose A and B are two n-component vectors; the inner product S, of

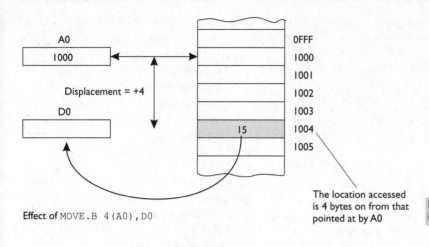

Effect of MOVE.B 4(A0),D0

The location accessed is 4 bytes on from that pointed at by A0

Fig. 6.15 An illustration of address register indirect addressing with displacement.

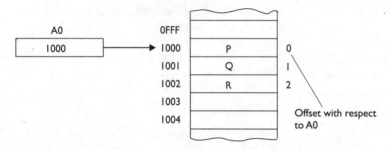

Offset with respect to A0

Fig. 6.16 Using address register indirect addressing with displacement.

A and B, is given by

$$S = \sum a_i b_i = a_0 b_0 + a_1 b_1 + \cdots + a_{n-1} b_{n-1}$$

For example, if $A = (1, 3, 6)$ and $B = (2, 3, 5)$, the inner product S is given by $1 \times 2 + 3 \times 3 + 6 \times 5 = 41$. Consider the case in which the components of vectors A and B are 16-bit integers.

```
N       EQU   $10            16 components (N=16)
        ORG   $001000        Origin of program
        CLR   D0             [D0] ← 0
        SUBA  A0,A0          [A0] ← 0
LOOP    MOVE  VEC1(A0),D1    [D1] ← [M([A0]+VEC1)]
        MULU  VEC2(A0),D1    [D1] ← [D1]*[M([A0]+VEC2)]
        ADD   D1,D0          [D0] ← [D0]+[D1]
        ADDA  #2,A0          [A0] ← [A0]+2
        CMPA  #2*N,A0        [A0]-2N note N words=2N bytes
        BNE   LOOP           IF Z=0 THEN [PC] ← LOOP
        MOVE  D0,S           [S] ← [D0]
*
        ORG   $002000        Origin of data
S       DS    1              Reserve a word for the product
VEC1    DS    $20            Reserve 16 words for Vector1
VEC2    DS    $20            Reserve 16 words for Vector2
```

The instruction MULU <ea>,Di multiplies the 16-bit word at the effective address specified by <ea> by the lower-order word in Di. The 32-bit longword product is loaded into Di(0:31). MULU operates on unsigned values and uses two 16-bit source operands to yield a 32-bit destination operand. As the 68K lacks a 'clear address register' instruction, we have to use either MOVEA #0,A0 or the faster SUBA A0,A0 to clear A0.

Note the strange-looking instruction CMPA #2*N,A0. This instruction contains the expression 2*N that is automatically evaluated by the assembler. The assembler looks up the value of N (equated to $10) and multiples it by 2 to get $20. Consequently, the assembler treats CMPA #2*N,A0 as CMPA #$20,A0.

Variations on a theme

The 68 K supports two important variations on address register indirect addressing. One is called *address register indirect addressing with predecrementing* and the other is called *address register indirect addressing with postincrementing*. The former addressing mode is written in assembly language as $-(\text{Ai})$ and the latter $(\text{Ai})+$. Both these addressing modes use address register indirect addressing to access an operand exactly as we've described. However, the postincrementing mode automatically increments the address register *after* it's been used, whereas the predecrementing mode automatically decrements the address register *before* it's used. Figure 6.17 demonstrates the operation ADD.B $(\text{A0})+,\text{D0}$. This instruction adds the contents of the location pointed at by A0 (i.e. P) to the contents of data register D0. After A0 has been used to access P, the value of A0 is incremented to point at the next element, Q.

An important application of address register indirect addressing is the sequential accessing of tables of information. If we access an item of data by a MOVE.B $(\text{Ai}),\text{Dj}$ instruction, the next item (i.e. byte) in the table can be accessed by first updating the address pointer, Ai, by ADDA #1,Ai and then repeating the MOVE.B $(\text{Ai}),\text{Dj}$. Clearly, it is sensible to combine these two instructions in order to reduce the size of the program. The 68K's automatic postincrementing mode increments an address register after it has been used to access an operand. This addressing mode is indicated by $(\text{Ai})+$. The following are examples of address register indirect addressing with postincrementing.

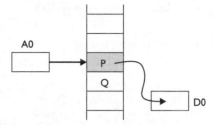

(a) Initially, address register A0 points at element P in memory which is accessed and loaded into D0

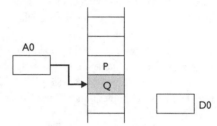

(b) After accessing element P, A0 is incremented to point at the next element, Q

Fig. 6.17 Address register indirect addressing with postincrementing.

Assembly language form		RTL definition
ADD.B	(A2)+,D2	[D2] ← [D2]+[M([A2])]; [A2] ← [A2]+1
MOVE.B	D0,(A1)+	[M([A1])] ← [D0]; [A1] ← [A1]+1
CLR.W	(A0)+	[M([A0])] ← 0; [A0] ← [A0]+2
MOVE.W	(A2)+,A(3)+	[M([A3])] ← [M([A2])];
		[A2] ← [A2]+2; [A3] ← [A3]+2

The pointer register is automatically incremented by 1 for byte operands, 2 for word operands, and 4 for longword operands. Consider the following examples:

ADD.W	(A2)−,D2	illegal—postdecrementing not allowed
MOVE.W	D0,(12,A1)+	illegal—offset (i.e. 12) not allowed with postincrementing
MOVE.W	−(A2),(A3)+	legal
SUB.W	D3,+(A4)	illegal—preincrementing not allowed
CMP.W	(A6)+,D3	legal

MOVE.B	(A0)+,D5	[D5(0:7)] ← [M([A0])]; [A0] ← [A0]+1
MOVE.L	(A0)+,D5	[D5(0:31)] ← [M([A0])]; [A0] ← [A0]+4

The 68 K provides a *predecrementing* address register indirect addressing mode with the assembly language form $-(\text{Ai})$, where the contents of Ai are decremented before they are used to access the operand at the address pointed at by Ai. As above, the predecrement is by 1, 2, or 4, depending on whether the operand is a byte, word, or longword, respectively. Note that both predecrementing and postincrementing addressing modes do not permit the use of an offset in the

calculation of an effective address; that is, only $(\text{Ai})+$ and $-(\text{Ai})$ are legal. To make this clear, we present several 68K instructions—some of these represent legal and some represent illegal addressing modes.

Predecrementing and postincrementing are complementary operations in the sense that one undoes the other. Suppose we use MOVE D3,$-(\text{A2})$ to store the contents of D3 on a stack in memory (we discuss the stack in detail later in this chapter). MOVE D3,$-(\text{A2})$ decrements A2 and then copies D3 to the top of the stack pointed at by A2. After this instruction has been executed, A2 is pointing to the top item on the stack. If later we wish to remove D3 from the stack and put it in D5, we can execute MOVE $(\text{A2})+,\text{D5}$. Postincrementing leaves A2 pointing to the new top item on the stack.

Examples of register indirect addressing with postincrementing

Let's revisit the program to add together 100 numbers stored in consecutive locations.

```
        LEA     NUM1,A0     A0 points at list of numbers
        CLR.W   D0          Clear the total
        MOVE.W  #99,D1      Set up the counter for 100 cycles
LOOP    ADD.W   (A0)+,D0    Add in a number and move the pointer to next
        DBRA    D1,LOOP     Repeat until all numbers added
```

This example uses the instruction ADD.W (A0)+,D0 to add the number pointed at by A0 to the contents of D0 and then move the pointer to point to the next number in the sequence.

Let's look at another example of this postincrementing addressing mode. Suppose we have a table of N unsigned integer bytes and wish to locate the value of the largest. The number of bytes is less than 256. A simple pseudocode algorithm to do this is:

```
largest=0
FOR i=1 to N
    read number_i
    if (number_i > largest) THEN largest=number_i
END_FOR
```

This pseudocode uses the notation number i to indicate the ith element in a sequence. We can express this in 68K assembly language as

```
        ORG     $400
N       EQU     10          Assume a dummy value of N=10 (number of elements)
        CLR.B   D0          Use D0 as largest and set it to 0
        MOVE.W  #N-1,D1     Use D1 as a counter and preset it to N-1
        LEA     List,A0     Use A0 as a pointer to the list
Next    MOVE.B  (A0)+,D2    Read a number
        CMP.B   D0,D2       Is new number>largest?
        BLE     Last        It isn't, so check for end of loop
        MOVE.B  D2,D0       It is, so record the new largest number
Last    DBRA    D1,Next     Repeat until count exhausted
        STOP    #$2700
        ORG     $1000       Let's put some test values here
List    DC.B    1,4,8,6,2,3,7,6,9,3
        END     $400
```

Indexed addressing

The 68K provides yet another variant on the address register indirect addressing mode called *indexed addressing*, which uses two registers to calculate the effective address of an operand. The assembly language form of the effective address is written d(Ai,Xj), where d is an 8-bit signed constant forming part of the instruction, Ai is one of the eight address registers, and Xj is either one of D0–D7 or A0–A7. The effective address is calculated from the expression d8 + [Ai] + [Xi]; for example, the effect of CLR 28(A3,D6) is to clear the contents of the location whose effective address is given by the contents of A3 plus the contents of D6 plus 28, that is, $[M(28 + [A3] + [D6])] \leftarrow 0$.

Although indexed addressing seems complex, it's really just a modest variation on address register indirect addressing. Instead of using one pointer register, the effective address is given by the sum of the contents of two registers and a displacement. Note that the displacement in indexed addressing lies in the range −128 to +127, whereas the displacement in address register indirect addressing is −32K to +32K.

An important application of indexed addressing is in the accessing of two-dimensional tables in which the location of an element is specified by its row position and its column position. Figure 6.18 illustrates the effect of MOVE.B Offset(A0,D0),D1. You can regard A0 as pointing at the beginning of a data structure. In this example, we've shown three blocks of data. By adding the contents of D0 to A0 we can select a specific data block in the structure. In the example of Fig. 6.18, the contents of D0 would be 6 (if each data block occupies 3 bytes).

By adding a constant to the effective address created by adding the two registers, we can access a particular element of one of the data blocks. In Fig. 6.18, the offset is 1.

A simple example of indexed addressing is provided by a data structure representing the days of the week. Suppose the structure consists of a number of weeks, each of which is divided into seven days. An item of data is accessed by locating the head of the data structure, counting off the appropriate number of weeks and then accessing the required day. If the

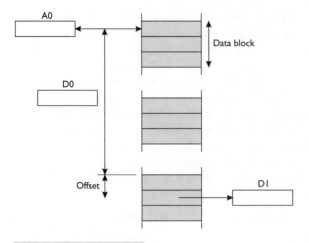

Fig. 6.18 Indexed addressing.

location of the array in memory is called `DIARY` and we wish to access the location corresponding to `Tuesday` of week five, we need to access location `DIARY + (WEEK-1) *7 + Tuesday`. If `Tuesday = 2`, the location of the required element is `DIARY + 28 + 2 = DIARY + 30`.

The data structure can be accessed using indexed addressing by loading A0 with `DIARY` and D0 with the location of the start of the desired week, and then using the desired day as a constant as demonstrated in the following fragment of code.

```
SUNDAY      EQU    0
MONDAY      EQU    1
TUESDAY     EQU    2
WEDNESDAY   EQU    3
.
.
            LEA    DIARY,A0          A0 points to head of structure
            MOVE   WEEK,D0           D0 contains week number
            SUB    #1,D0             Calculate (Week-1)*7
            MULU   #7,D0             D0 now contains number of days
            MOVE.B TUESDAY(A0,D0),D1 Access the required item
```

Note that modern 68K assemblers permit you to write either `TUESDAY(A0,D0)` or `(TUESDAY,A0,D0)`.

6.4.4 Relative addressing

Before we introduce this addressing mode, we'll pose a problem. Consider the operation `MOVE $1234,D0`, which uses the absolute address `$1234`. If you were to take the program containing this instruction and its data and locate it in a different region of memory, it wouldn't work. Why? Because the data is no longer in location `$1234`. The only way to run this program is to change all the addresses of operands to their new locations. We'll soon see that relative addressing provides a means of relocating programs without changing addresses.

Relative addressing is similar to address register indirect addressing because the effective address of an operand is given by the contents of a register plus a displacement. However, relative addressing uses the *program counter* to calculate the effective address, rather than an address register; that is, the location of the operand is specified relative to the current instruction. If we denote relative addressing by means of `d16(PC)`, the operation 'Load data register D0 relative' is written

`MOVE d16(PC),D0`

and is defined in RTL as: $[D0] \leftarrow [M([PC] + d16)]$. As before, `d16` is a 16-bit two's complement offset that is normally written in symbolic form and whose value is calculated by the assembler. Figure 6.19 demonstrates the relationship between the PC, the instruction, and the operand address. Actually, Fig. 6.19 is slightly simplified because the 68K's program counter is automatically incremented by 2 after the instruction fetch phase.

Relative addressing is important because it allows the programmer to write *position-independent code*, PIC, which avoids absolute addresses. The machine code version of a program written in PIC is independent of the physical location of the program in memory. You can move (i.e. relocate) PIC

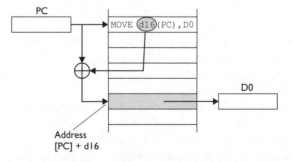

Fig. 6.19 Program counter relative addressing—the effect of `MOVE d16(PC),D0`.

programs in memory without modifying them. For example, MOVE 36(PC),D0 means load data register D0 with the contents of the memory location 36 locations on from this instruction. It doesn't matter where the operation MOVE 36(PC),D0 lies in memory, because the data associated with it will always be stored in the 36th location following the instruction.

Calculating the displacement required by an instruction using program counter relative addressing is virtually impossible because you don't normally know the value of the PC and the address of the operand. Fortunately, you never have to perform this calculation—the assembler does it for you. Consider the following example:

```
          ORG     $400
          MOVE.B  Value1,D0      Put Value1 in D0
          MOVE.B  Value1(PC),D1  Put Value1 in D1
          STOP    #$2700
Value1    DC.B    $23
          END     $400
```

Let's assemble this code and see what happens.

```
1  00000400                          ORG     $400
2  00000400 10390000040E             MOVE.B  VALUE1,D0       ;Put Value1 in D0
3  00000406 123A0006                 MOVE.B  VALUE1(PC),D1   ;Put Value1 in D1
4  0000040A 4E722700                 STOP    #$2700
5  0000040E 23            VALUE1:     DC.B    $23
6           00000400                 END     $400
```

As you can see, the address of operand Value1 is $0000040E (as a 32-bit longword). The instruction on line 2, MOVE.B Value1,D0, contains an opcode ($1039) and the absolute address of the operand ($0000040E).

Now look at the instruction on line 3, MOVE.B Value1(PC),D1. In this case the opcode is $123A and the operand is the 16-bit value $0006. When the 68K reads an instruction, the program counter is automatically incremented by 2. That is, once MOVE.B Value1(PC),D1 has been read from memory, the program counter is incremented by 2 from $00000406 to $00000408. If we add the offset $0006 to $00000408, we get $0000040E, which is the address of the operand Value1.

The 68K lets you use relative addressing for *source* operands, but not for *destination* operands. That is, you can use relative addressing to specify where an operand comes from but not where it is going to (this restriction is a design decision made by those who created the 68K and not a fundamental limitation). For example, both the instructions MOVE 12(PC),D3 and ADD 8(PC),D2 are legal instructions, whereas MOVE D3,12(PC) and ADD D2,8(PC) are illegal instructions. Fortunately, we can get round the problem of writing completely position independent code for the 68K by loading the address of the operand into an address register using position independent code and then using address register indirect addressing. To achieve this we use the LEA (load effective address) instruction that loads an address into an address register. Consider the following examples of this instruction.

Assembly language form	RTL definition
LEA $1000,A0	[A0] ← 1000_{16}
LEA (A1),A0	[A0] ← [A1]
LEA 10(A1),A0	[A0] ← [A1]+10
LEA 10(PC),A0	[A0] ← [PC]+10

As you can see, LEA generates an address and then simply deposits it in an address register. The two instructions MOVEA.L #Temp7,A0 and LEA Temp7,A0 are, effectively, equivalent.

The following fragment of code demonstrates how the LEA instruction can be used to support position independent code.

```
     LEA    VALUE1(PC),A0   Calculate the relative address of
                            VALUE1 and store it in A0
     .
     .
     MOVE   D2,(A0)         Store D2 at the address pointed at by A0
     .
     MOVE   (A0),D3         Move the word pointed at by A0 to D3
     .
VALUE1 DS   1              Reserve one word of memory for data
```

When the instruction LEA VALUE1(PC),A0 is assembled, the assemblers take the value of VALUE1 and subtract the current value of the program counter from it to evaluate the offset required by the instruction.

We now look at one of the most important applications of program counter relative addressing, relative branching.

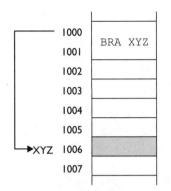

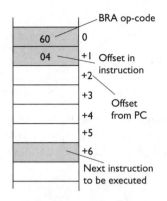

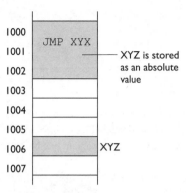

(a) Assembly language form of the instruction. A branch is made to the instruction at address XYZ

(b) Machine-code form of the instruction. The stored offset is 4 because the destination is 4 bytes from the end of the current instruction

(c) Equivalent form using the JMP instruction with an absolute address.

Fig. 6.20 Relative branching.

Relative branching

We've already met the branch instructions (e.g. BEQ, BNE), which can force a branch to the target address. What we haven't said is that the target address is expressed relative to the current value of the program counter. Most microprocessors have a relative branching mode in which the destination of a branch instruction is expressed with reference to the current address in the program counter. Figure 6.20 illustrates relative addressing by means of a memory map.

In Fig. 6.20(a) we write BRA XYZ, where XYZ is the target address. In the machine code form, Fig. 6.20(b), we see that the offset that forms part of the instruction is stored as 4 because the target address is 4 bytes beyond the end of the branch instruction. Remember that the program counter is automatically incremented by two after the BRA instruction is read during an instruction fetch.

Figure 6.20(c) demonstrates the instruction JMP XYZ, which uses an absolute address; that is, XYZ is stored as $1006.

The offset used by a relative branch is an 8-bit signed two's complement number in the range -128 to $+127$. As 2

is automatically added to the PC at the start of an instruction, relative branching is possible within the range -126 to $+129$ bytes from the start of the current instruction (i.e. the branch). The 68K also supports a long branch with a 16-bit offset that provides a range of -32K to $+32$K bytes.

Fortunately, the programmer doesn't usually have to worry too much about short and long branches, or about calculating the branch offset. If you write BRA ABC, the assembler computes the offset as ABC $-$ [PC] $-$ 2.

Figure 6.20 also illustrates the importance of relative branching in the production of position independent code. The program containing the instruction BRA XYZ can be relocated merely by moving it in memory, whereas the program containing JMP XYZ must be modified if it is relocated.

The following program provides an example of both relative branching and relative addressing. A block of data is moved from one region of memory to another. The first location of the block to be moved is FROM, and the first location of its destination is TO. The number of words to be moved is given by SIZE.

```
          ORG     $400          Start of program
SIZE      EQU     16            Let's use a 16-byte block
          LEA     FROM(PC),A0   A0 points to the source
          LEA     TO(PC),A1     A1 points to the destination
          MOVE.B  #SIZE,D0      D0 is the loop counter
REPEAT    MOVE.B  (A0)+,(A1)+   REPEAT move byte from source to destination
          SUB.B   #1,D0
          BNE     REPEAT        UNTIL all bytes moved
          STOP    #$2700
```

```
(program continued)
*
        ORG     $001000
FROM    DS.B    16              Locate source and destination blocks here
TO      DS.B    16
        END     $400
```

Note how we use relative addressing to load the address of the source and destination blocks into address registers A0 and A1, respectively. This program can be assembled to give

In absolute addressing the location of the operand required by the current operation is provided by the instruction. This address is the effective address of the operand. In indirect

```
Source file: PROG8.X68
Assembled on: 96-10-08 at: 18:23:13
        by: X68K PC-2.2 Copyright (c) University of Teesside 1989,96
Defaults: ORG $0/FORMAT/OPT A,BRL,CEX,CL,FRL,MC,MD,NOMEX,NOPCO

 1 00000400                        ORG     $400            ;Start of program
 2          00000010 SIZE:         EQU     16              ;Let's use a 16-byte block
 3 00000400 41FA0BFE               LEA     FROM(PC),A0     ;A0 points to the source
 4 00000404 43FA0C0A               LEA     TO(PC),A1       ;A1 points to the destination
 5 00000408 103C0010               MOVE.B  #SIZE,D0        ;D0 is the loop counter
 6 0000040C 12D8      REPEAT:      MOVE.B  (A0)+,(A1)+     ;REPEAT move byte from source to dest
 7 0000040E 5300                   SUB.B   #1,D0
 8 00000410 66FA                   BNE     REPEAT          ;UNTIL all bytes moved
 9 00000412 4E722700               STOP    #$2700
10                   *
11 00001000                        ORG     $001000
12 00001000 00000010 FROM:         DS.B    16              ;Locate source and dest blocks here
13 00001010 00000010 TO:           DS.B    16
14          00000400               END     $400
```

Remember that the programmer doesn't have to worry about the calculation of relative branch offsets because the assembler performs this process automatically. For example, in Fig. 6.21, the instruction BNE REPEAT causes a branch backwards to instruction MOVE (A0)+,(A1)+ in the event of the zero bit in the CCR not being set. From the memory map of Fig. 6.21, we see that the address of the branch operation is $00 0410 and the address of the operation MOVE (A0)+,(A1)+ is $00 040C. We therefore have to branch 4 locations from the start of the BNE, or 6 locations from the end of the BNE. As the CPU always increments the PC by 2 at the start of a branch, the stored offset is −6. In two's complement form this is $FA.

6.4.5 Indirect addressing
We now look at the final and most complex addressing mode, *memory indirect addressing*. As this addressing mode is supported by very few processors, some students may wish to skip ahead to the next section. However, memory indirect addressing is interesting because it enables you to access complex data structures efficiently.

addressing the effective address of the operand is given by the contents of the memory location pointed at by the address following the op-code. In other words, the instruction provides the address of the address of the data. Figure 6.22 illustrates this concept with the instruction MOVE.B [2000],D0. This is a hypothetical instruction because the 68000 doesn't support indirect addressing, although the more powerful 68020 and later members of the 68K family do provide indirect addressing.

The instruction MOVE.B [2000],D0 causes the processor to read the contents of location 2000 to get the address of the operand (i.e. 3078). Location 3078 contains the value 27, which is the actual value loaded into D0. Remember that this form of instruction is not implemented by the 68K family and we are now talking about a hypothetical processor. We can represent MOVE.B [2000],D0 in RTL terms by

$$[D0] \leftarrow [M([M(2000)])]$$

This operation can be more easily understood by splitting it into two consecutive actions:

```
Temp ← [M(2000)]
[D0] ← [M(Temp)]
```

000400	41FA	LEA	FROM(PC),A0
000402	0BFE		
000404	43FA	LEA	TO(PC),A1
000406	0C0A		
000408	103C	MOVE.B	#SIZE,D0
00040A	0010		
00040C	12D8	MOVE.B	(A0)+,(A1)+
00040E	5300	SUB.B	#1,D0
000410	66FA	BNE	REPEAT
000412	4E72	STOP	#$2700
000414	2700		

001000		FROM	
001010		TO	

Fig. 6.21 Moving a block of data in memory.

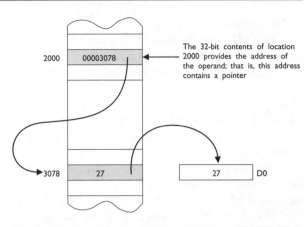

Fig. 6.22 Indirect addressing—effect of MOVE.B [2000],D0 instruction.

We can regard indirect addressing as part of a natural progression starting with immediate addressing. Table 6.4 provides the RTL definitions of immediate addressing, absolute addressing, and indirect addressing. We have also included

indirect indirect addressing to show that the process can be continued indefinitely. However, no widely used processor supports this addressing mode.

From the preceding definition of indirect addressing, it should be apparent that memory indirect addressing is similar to address register indirect addressing. As we've said, indirect addressing is not provided on all microprocessors because it's not absolutely necessary if indexed addressing is available.

Indirect addressing allows the calculation of addresses at run-time during the execution of a program. The following program shows how indirect addressing is used to add together 100 numbers. Remember that this program cannot be run on a 68K microprocessor, because the general form of indirect addressing is not available.

```
          ORG    $400            Origin of program
          CLR    D1              Clear total
NEXT_ONE  ADD    [POINTER],D1    Add in the number pointed at
          ADD    #2,POINTER      Increment the pointer
          CMP    #NUMB+200,POINTER  Test for end of list
          BNE    NEXT_ONE        Continue until all added in
          .
          .
          ORG    $2000           Data origin
POINTER   DC.L   NUMB            POINTER=address of list of numbers
NUMB      DS.W   100             Reserve 100 words for the numbers
```

Addressing Mode	Assembly Language Form	RTL Form
Immediate	MOVE #VALUE,D0	[D0] ← VALUE
Absolute	MOVE ADDRESS,D0	[D0] ← [ADDRESS]
Indirect	MOVE [ADDRESS],D0	[D0] ← [[ADDRESS]]
Indirect indirect	MOVE [[ADDRESS]],D0	[D0] ← [[[ADDRESS]]] and so on

Table 6.4 RTL definitions of addressing modes.

This program is intended only to illustrate the application of indirect addressing. We have assumed that the wordlength is sufficient to deal with the sum of the numbers without overflow. The only instruction in the above program not available on the 68K is ADD [POINTER],D1.

In this program the variable called POINTER contains the address of the first number to be added to the total in D1. Initially, POINTER is set to $2004, by means of the assembler directive POINTER DC.L NUMB, where NUMB is the address of the first item in the list of 100 numbers. After each number in the list is added to the total in D1 by ADD [POINTER],D1, the value of POINTER is incremented by two. When the contents of POINTER have increased by 200 (i.e. one hundred 2-byte words), the addition is complete.

The 68020's memory indirect addressing modes

The 68020 and later members of the 68K family implement two forms of indirect addressing. One is called memory indirect with preindexing and has the syntax ([bd,Ai,Xi],od). The other is memory indirect with postindexing and has the syntax ([bd,Ai],Xi,od). Here bd and od are two signed integer constants and register Xi may be either an address register or a data register. The 68020 supports several variations on these two modes because any combination of bd, od, Ai, and Xi are optional may be omitted from the effective address.

The 68020's memory indirect address is calculated by adding the contents of the square brackets to get a pointer to memory. The contents of the location pointed at are read and od and Xi added to generate the address of the actual operand. Sounds complex, doesn't it? Suppose that the effective address of an operand is ([20,A0,D0],12), and [A0] = 1000 and [D0] = 400. The contents of the square brackets are 20 + [A0] + [D0] = 20 + 1000 + 400 = 1420. The contents of memory location 1420 are then accessed—suppose the value of [M(1420)] is 8234. The value of od is added to the pointer to get 8234 + 12 = 8246. This is the effective address of the operand.

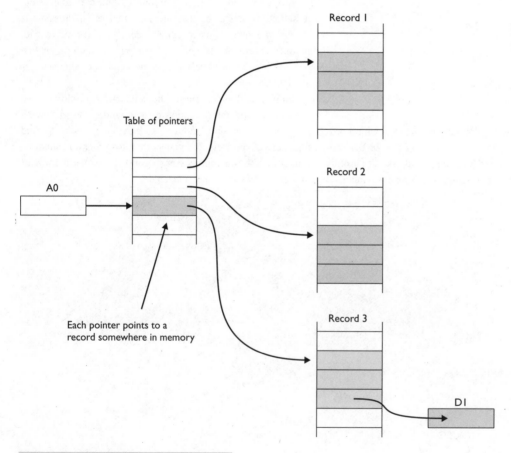

Fig. 6.23 Example of memory indirect addressing.

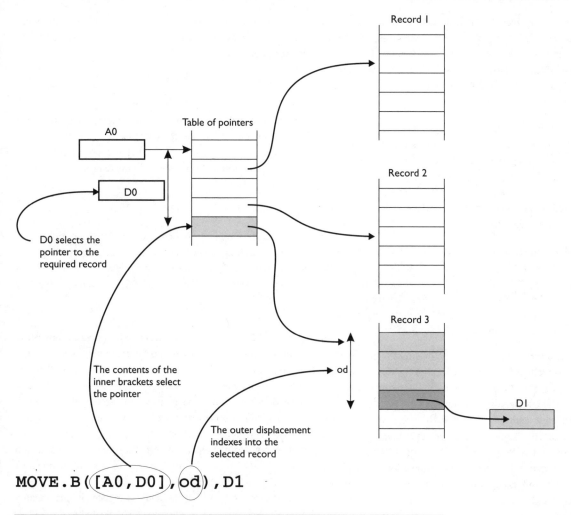

MOVE.B (([A0,D0],od),D1

Fig. 6.24 Interpreting the effective source operand address in MOVE.B ([A0,D0],od),D1.

The RTL definitions of these two effective addresses are

([bd,Ai,Xi],od) ea=[M([M(bd+[Ai]+[Xi])]+od)]
([bd,Ai],Xi,od) ea=[M([M(bd+[Ai])]+[Xi]+od)]

Let's look at what the 68020's memory indirect addressing mode really means. Figure 6.23 demonstrates the effect of the instruction MOVE.B ([A0]),D1. In this example we have omitted the index register, Xi, and offsets bd and od.

Figure 6.23 demonstrates how address register A0 points to a table of pointers. The value in A0 selects one of the pointers in the table. The operand accessed by this instruction is obtained indirectly via the selected pointer. The example of Fig. 6.23 only hints at the power of the 68020's memory indirect addressing mode.

Figure 6.24 provides a better example of the 68020's memory indirect addressing mode; the instruction is MOVE.B ([A0,D0],od),D1. In this case, the contents of D0 are added to A0 and the pointer at that address read from memory. By adding a data register to an address register, we can select one of several pointers at run time.

Each of these pointers points to a record. By adding an offset to the starting address of a record, we can access a specific item in the record.

6.4.6 68K addressing modes summary

The topic of addressing modes causes students more problems than any other aspect of assembly language programming. Addressing modes are not really all that complex; they simply tell the computer where to find the data it needs. Here, we provide a short summary of the 68K's addressing modes to present a unified picture of how they all fit together. Figure 6.25 summarizes the 68K's addressing modes graphically—we don't include the 68020's memory indirect addressing modes in this figure.

1. Data or address register direct The address of an operand is specified by a data or address register. The data taking part in the operation is in the specified register. For example, MOVE.B D3,D4 means [D4]←[D3] and MOVEA.L D3,A2 means [A2]←[D3]. The main store is not accessed by this addressing mode. This addressing mode is used to access frequently used variables.

2. Immediate addressing The actual operand forms part of the instruction and is indicated to the assembler by a # symbol. For example, MOVE.B #123,D4 means load data register D4 with the number 123, or [D4]←123. Immediate addressing is used to specify a constant that does not vary while the program is running.

3. Absolute addressing In absolute or direct addressing the operand is specified by its actual location in the main store. For example, MOVE.B D3,1234 means store the contents of data register D3 in memory location 1234, or [M(1234)] ← [D3]. Absolute addressing is used to access variables; for example, ADD.B Date,D3 accesses the contents of memory location Date. Programmers often avoid using absolute addressing because it doesn't provide position independent code. Absolute addressing can't be used to access elements in data structures such as arrays, lists, and tables.

4. Address register indirect addressing In address register indirect addressing, the address of the desired operand is stored in one of the 68K's eight address registers. This addressing mode is indicated to the assembler by enclosing the register in round brackets. The instruction MOVE.B (A0),D3 means read the contents of address register A0, use the number found in A0 to access memory, and then move the data at that address to D3. In terms of register transfer language, MOVE (A0),D3 is defined as [D3] ← [M([A0])]. The 68K supports the following four variations on address register indirect addressing.

(a) Address register indirect with a displacement We frequently wish to access data whose location is expressed with respect to some datum which is in an address register. That is, the effective address of the operand is given by the contents of the address register specified by the instruction plus an offset forming part of the instruction. For example,

suppose A0 points to the start of a table with 20 entries and we wish to access the seventh entry. We could execute the following code to do this.

```
ADDA    #7,A0      Move A0 seven bytes onward
MOVE.B  (A0),D1    Get the desired entry
```

Unfortunately, there is a flaw in this scheme. After the operation has been carried out, the contents of A0 no longer point to the head of the data structure. A better approach is to use an offset to point to the desired entry in the data structure.

```
MOVE.B   7(A0),D1  Get the item seven bytes
                   on from A0
```

In address register indirect addressing with offset, the effective address of an operand is written in as d16(Ai), where d16 is a 16-bit two's complement offset and Ai is a pointer register. The location of the operand is given by [M([Ai] + d16)].

(b) Address register indirect with postincrementing Address register indirect with postincrementing is identical to plain address register indirect addressing, except that the address register used to generate the effective address is incremented *after* it has been used to access the operand. Automatic postincrementing allows you to step through a table of sequential elements without having to increment the pointer register manually. The effect of the single instruction MOVE.B (A3)+,D2 is the same as the pair of instructions MOVE.B (A3),D2 and ADDA #1,A3.

The amount by which the address register is incremented after it has been used is automatically selected as 1, 2, or 4, depending on whether the operand accessed was a byte, a word, or a longword, respectively. That is, the address register steps through the memory in units of a byte, word, or longword, according to the nature of the data.

In the next section, we show how this addressing mode can be used to retrieve an item of data from the stack pointed at by the address register.

(c) Address register indirect with predecrementing Address register indirect with predecrementing is identical to address register indirect with postincrementing except that the address register is *decremented* before the operand is accessed. For example, the single instruction MOVE.B −(A0),D3 is identical to the instruction pair SUBA #1,A0 and MOVE.B (A0),D3. This addressing mode is used to step through tables in the reverse way from address register indirect with postincrementing.

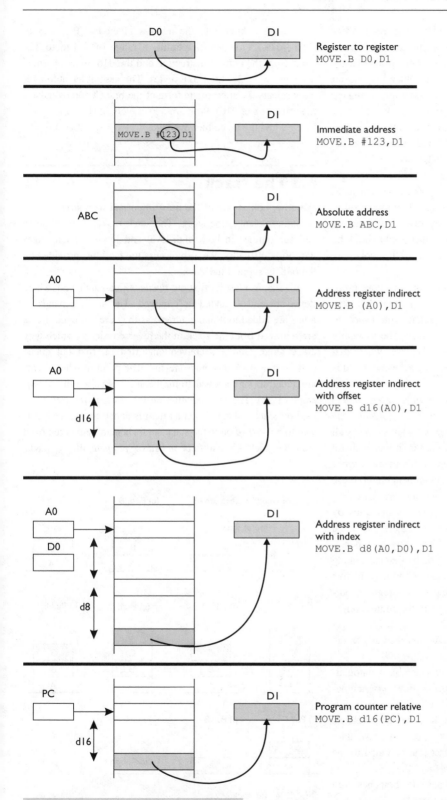

Fig. 6.25 Summary of the 68K's addressing modes.

(d) Indexed addressing   Indexed addressing lets us specify the effective address of an operand as the sum of the contents of two registers and a constant offset. One of the register pair must be an address register and the other may be an address register or a data register. The assembly language form of this effective address is written d8(Ai,Aj) or (d8,Ai,Dj), where d8 is an 8-bit two's complement value in the range −128 to +127. The operand accessed by this addressing mode is expressed in RTL as [M([Ai]+ [Xj]+d8)], where Xj is either Aj or Dj.

Indexed addressing can be used to access two-dimensional tables with one register being used to calculate a row position and the other a column position. Equally, one register can be used to point to a region of data and the other used to hold the address of the desired operand from the start of this table.

5. Relative addressing   Relative addressing or, more properly, *program counter relative addressing* permits the programmer to specify the address of an operand with respect to the current contents of the program counter. The assembly language form of a relative address is d16(PC), where d16 is a 16-bit signed constant. The operand accessed by this addressing mode is [M([PC]+d16)].

Relative addressing is important to 68K programmers because it enables them to write *position independent code* (i.e. code that does not use absolute memory addresses). As all operands are specified with respect to the PC, it means that a section of code can be located anywhere within memory without having to recalculate addresses. Programmers prefer to use relative addressing rather than the absolute addressing mode.

The 68K is not able to specify *destination* operands by means of relative addressing. ADD Variable(PC),D3 is a legal instruction, whereas ADD D3,Variable(PC) is not. Programmers may overcome this limitation by first calculating the relative address of an operand by means of a load effective address instruction, LEA, and then using address register indirect addressing with the effective address in the address register. That is, we can write LEA Variable(PC),A3 to get the relative address of Variable in A3 and then access the operand by means of, for example, ADD D3,(A3).

It's important to appreciate that all assemblers automatically calculate relative address offsets—the programmer doesn't have to evaluate the appropriate value of d16. For example, if a variable Day_2 were to be accessed by means of the instruction MOVE Day_2(PC),D2, the assembler would automatically calculate the offset that is added to the PC to generate the effective address of Day_2.

The 68K permits conditional and absolute branches with relative addresses. All branches of the form Bcc d8 or Bcc

d16 cause a branch to the address given by [PC]+d8 or [PC]+d16. A d8 branch permits a range of −126 to 129 bytes from the current instruction and the d16 branch permits a range of −32K to +32K bytes. The assembler automatically selects the appropriate form of the branch and calculates the offset (d8 or d16). Programmers merely have to write Bcc label and the assembler evaluates ([PC] - label).

6.5 The stack

We now look at one of the most important data structures in computer science, the stack. The stack makes it possible to call subroutines in both high-level and low-level languages with little difficulty. We also discuss the facilities provided by the 68K to support the stack.

A stack is a last in, first out *queue* with a single end, where items are always added or removed. The stack expands as items are added to it and contracts as they are removed. Items are removed from the stack in the reverse order to which they are entered. Unlike a conventional first in, first out queue (FIFO), the stack has only one end. The point at which items are added to, or removed from, the stack is called the *top-of-stack* (TOS). The next position on the stack is referred to as *next-on-stack* (NOS). When an item is added to the stack it is said to be *pushed* on to the stack, and when an item is removed from the stack it is said to be *pulled* (or *popped*) off the stack.

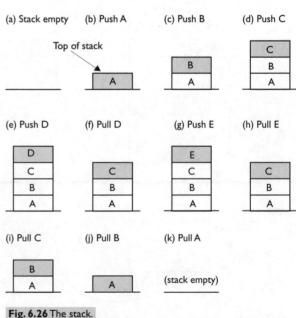

Fig. 6.26 The stack.

Figure 6.26 presents a series of diagrams illustrating the operation of a stack as items A, B, C, D, and E, are added to it and removed from it.

The stack has many important applications. Consider a computer that can transfer data between memory and the stack, and perform monadic operations on the top item of the stack, or dyadic operations on the top two items of the stack—such special computers do exist. A dyadic operation (e.g. +, *, AND, OR) removes the top two items on the stack and pushes the result of the operation.

Consider how an ADD instruction might be executed by a stack-based computer. Figure 6.27(a) shows a system with four data elements on the stack. When the ADD is executed, the element at the top of the stack is pulled (Fig. 6.27(b)) and sent to the adder. As you can see, the next element (i.e. C) is now the new TOS (i.e. the old NOS). In Fig. 6.27(c) the new TOS is pulled and sent to the adder. Finally, the output of the adder, D+C, is pushed onto the stack to create a new TOS.

Note how this ADD instruction doesn't have an operand (unlike all the instructions we've described so far). A stack-based computer has so-called *addressless* instructions because they act on elements at the top of the stack.

The following example illustrates the evaluation of the expression (A+B)(C−D) on a hypothetical stack-based computer. We will assume that the instruction PUSH pushes the contents of D0 onto the stack, ADD, SUB, and MULU all act on the top two items on the stack, and PULL places the top item on the stack in D0.

```
 1. MOVE A,D0   Get A in D0
 2. PUSH        Push it on the stack
 3. MOVE B,D0   Get B in D0
 4. PUSH        Push it on the stack
 5. ADD         Pull the top two items off the stack, add
                them, and push the result
 6. MOVE C,D0   Get C in D0
 7. PUSH        Push it on the stack
 8. MOVE D,D0   Get D
 9. PUSH        Push it on the stack
10. SUB         Pull the top two items off the stack, subtract
                them, and push the result
11. MULU        Pull the top two items off the stack, multiply
                them, and push the result
12. PULL        Pull the result off the stack and put it in D0
```

(a) Initial state of the stack with four items

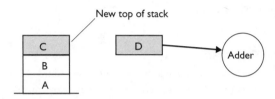

(b) First element pulled off the stack

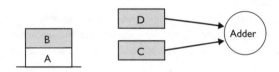

(c) Second element pulled off the stack

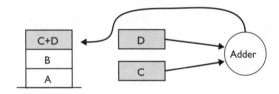

(d) Result pushed on the stack

Fig. 6.27 Executing an ADD operation on a stack machine.

Figure 6.28 represents the state of the stack at various stages in the above procedure. The number below each diagram in Fig. 6.28 corresponds to the line number in the program. Although the 68K and all other similar microprocessors

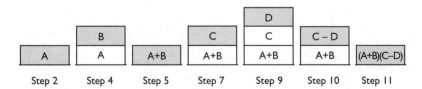

Fig. 6.28 Executing a program on a stack machine.

do not permit operations on the stack in the form we've just described (e.g. ADD, SUB, MULU), some special-purpose microprocessors have been designed to support stack-based languages like FORTH.

We will soon see that the 68K implements instructions that enable it to access a stack. However, the 68K is not a stack machine. Pure stack machines do exist, although they have never been developed to the same extent as 2-address machines like the 68K.

6.5.1 The 68K stack

When a stack is implemented in hardware, the addition of a new item to the top-of-stack causes all other items on the stack to be pushed down. Such a hardware stack is frequently implemented as a modified shift register. Similarly, when an item is removed from the stack, the NOS becomes TOS and all items move up.

Microprocessors don't implement a stack in this way. When a stack is implemented by a microprocessor, the items on the stack don't move. The stack is located in a region of conventional read/write memory in the main store, and a *stack pointer* points to the top of the stack. This stack pointer performs the same function as an address register and is modified to point to the top of stack as the stack grows and contracts. In some microprocessors, the stack pointer points to the next free location on the stack, whereas in others, it points to the current top of stack.

Figure 6.29 demonstrates how the program illustrated in Fig. 6.28 is executed by a computer with a stack in memory and a stack pointer, SP.

The 68K doesn't have a special stack pointer—it uses address register A7 as a *system* stack pointer. We call A7 the *system* stack pointer because the stack pointed at by A7 stores return addresses during subroutine calls (as we shall see later). 68K assemblers let you write either A7 or SP; for example, the instructions MOVE.W D0,(A7) and MOVE.W D0,(SP) are equivalent.

The 68K can maintain up to seven other stacks simultaneously, because all its address registers can be used as stack pointers.

We must point out a technicality here. The 68K actually has two A7 registers and, therefore, two system stack pointers. One A7 is called the *supervisor stack pointer* and is associated with the operating system. The other is called the *user stack pointer* and is associated with user programs running under the operating system. Because the operating system controls the allocation of the computer's resources (memory and I/O), the operating system should be protected from errors caused by the less reliable user programs. A stack pointer dedicated solely to the operating system prevents user programs accessing and possibly corrupting the operating system's stack. Only one of these two A7s is accessible at a time, because the 68K is either running an operating system or it isn't.

In what follows, we use the 68K's stack pointer to illustrate the operation of a stack. Intuitively, you might expect the assembly language form of the instruction to push the contents of data register D0 on the stack to be PUSH D0, and the corresponding mnemonic to pull an item from the stack and put it in D0 to be PULL D0. These explicit PUSH and PULL instructions are not defined. Instead, you have to resort to the *address register indirect with predecrementing* addressing

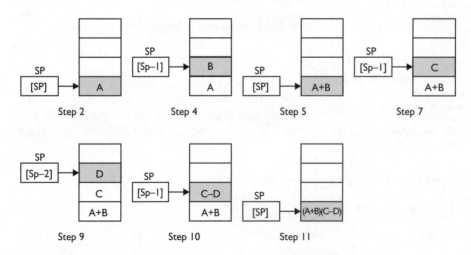

Fig. 6.29 Executing the program of Fig. 6.28 on a practical stack machine.

mode and the *address register indirect with postincrementing* addressing mode, respectively.

Figure 6.30 illustrates the effect of a PUSH D0 instruction which is implemented by MOVE.W D0,-(SP), and PULL D0, which is implemented by MOVE.W (SP)+,D0. The 68K's stack grows towards lower addresses as data is pushed on it. For example, if the stack pointer contains $80014C and a word is pushed onto the stack, the new value of the stack pointer will be $80014A.

The 68K's push operation MOVE.W D0,-(SP) is defined in RTL as

[SP] ← [SP]-2	Predecrement the stack pointer to point to next free element
[M([SP])] ← [D0]	Copy contents of D0 to the stack

and the 68K's pull operation MOVE.W (SP)+,D0 is defined as

[D0] ← [M([SP])]	Copy the element on top of the stack to D0
[SP] ← [SP]+2	Postincrement the stack pointer to point to the new TOS

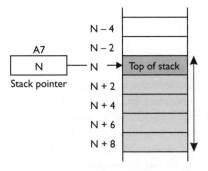

(a) Snapshot of the 68000's stack

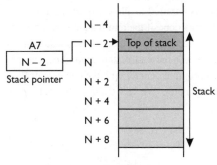

(b) State of the stack after pushing a word by MOVE.W D0,-(A7)

Fig. 6.30 The 68K's stack.

These push and pull operations may be used with word or longword operands. A longword operand automatically causes the SP to be decremented or incremented by 4. Address registers A0 to A6 may be used to push or pull byte, .B, operands—but not the system stack pointer, A7.

The 68K's stack pointer is decremented *before* a push and incremented *after* a pull. Consequently, the stack pointer always points at the item at the *top* of the stack; for example, MOVE (SP)+,D3 pulls the top item off the stack and deposits it in D3. Note that MOVE (SP),D3 copies the TOS into D3 *without* modifying the stack pointer.

When the stack shrinks after a MOVE.W (SP)+,D0 operation, the items on the stack are not physically deleted, they are still there in the memory until overwritten by, for example, a MOVE.W D0,-(SP) operation.

Some applications of the stack in computer science involve the manipulation and evaluation of algebraic expressions and are beyond the scope of this text. The stack has a rather more prosaic use as a temporary data store. Executing a MOVE.W D0,-(SP) saves the contents of D0 on the stack, and executing a MOVE.W (SP)+,D0 returns the contents of D0. The application of the stack as a temporary storage location avoids storing data in explicitly named memory locations. More importantly, if further data is stored on the stack, it does not overwrite the old data.

The 68K has a special instruction called *move multiple registers* MOVEM that saves or retrieves an entire group of registers. For example, MOVEM.L D0-D7/A0-A6,-(A7) pushes all registers on the stack pointed at by A7 (see Fig. 6.31). The register list used by MOVEM is written in the form Di-Dj/Ap-Aq and specifies data registers Di to Dj inclusive and address registers Ap to Aq inclusive. Groups of registers are pulled off the stack by, for example, MOVEM.L (A7)+,D0-D2/D4/A4-A6.

The most important applications of the stack are in the implementation of subroutines (discussed in the following section), and in the handling of *interrupts*.

6.5.2 The stack and subroutines

Suppose a particular sequence of operations is to be performed two or more times during the execution of a program. Writing out the same block of assembly language instructions over and over again is both tedious to the programmer and wasteful of memory space. The *subroutine* provides a solution

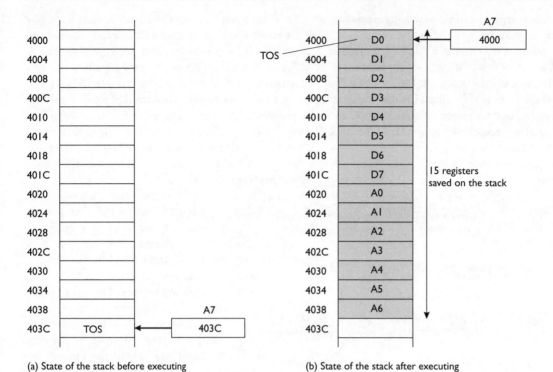

(a) State of the stack before executing
   MOVEM.L D0-D7/A0-A6,-(A7)

(b) State of the stack after executing
   MOVEM.L D0-D7/A0-A6,-(A7)

Fig. 6.31 The 68K's move multiple registers instruction.

to this problem. In high-level languages the subroutine is frequently known as a *procedure* or *function*.

A subroutine is a piece of code that can be called or invoked from any point in a program. When a subroutine is called, a branch is made to the first executable instruction of the subroutine. After the subroutine has been executed, a return is made to the instruction following the point at which it was called. Figure 6.32 illustrates this concept with a simple subroutine called ABC that calculates the value of $2x^2$ (where x is a 16-bit

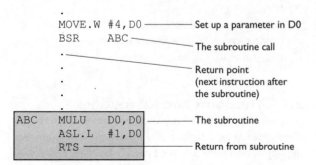

Fig. 6.32 The subroutine.

value passed in D0). This subroutine is called by the instruction BSR ABC (branch to subroutine), and a return from subroutine is made by an RTS (return from subroutine) instruction.

Figure 6.33 displays the program of Fig. 6.32 in the form of a memory map and demonstrates the flow of control between the calling program and the subroutine ABC.

The key to understanding subroutines is the *return mechanism*. If a piece of code can be called from anywhere in a program, a mechanism is required to allow a return to the correct place. Some processors deposit the return address in a register before the jump to subroutine is executed. Suppose that this register is called Rx. At the end of the subroutine, the programmer loads the program counter with the contents of Rx to return to the calling point. We can express this call–return mechanism as

Save PC and jump: [Rx] ← [PC]
                         [PC] ← subroutine target
                                   address

Return from subroutine: [PC] ← [Rx]

Unfortunately, register Rx cannot be used by the programmer while a subroutine call is in progress. This is not entirely

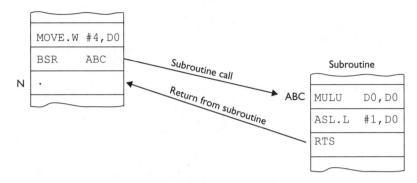

Fig. 6.33 Memory map of a subroutine call and flow of control.

true, because you can save the contents of Rx in memory to make Rx available to the programmer for use by another subroutine. However, this does force the programmer to keep track of the subroutine return address. In the next chapter we will look at the ARM processor, which does indeed use a register to hold subroutine return addresses.

A much better way of handling the return addresses of subroutines is to store them on the stack. This is done by most microprocessors in the following way.

1. Subroutine call
   Push the contents of the PC on the stack
   Jump to the subroutine.

2. Return from subroutine
   Pull the return address off the stack
   Put the return address in the program counter.

The value of the PC pushed on the stack during a subroutine call is usually the return address (i.e. the address of the next instruction following the subroutine call). The effect of these operations on the stack is illustrated by Fig. 6.34. Since the last item stored on the stack is the first item to be removed from it, the stack is well suited to nested subroutines. That is, a subroutine is able to call another subroutine, and this process is repeated indefinitely. Actually, it can continue only until all the memory allocated to the stack is exhausted, at which time *stack overflow* is said to occur. Note that Fig. 6.34 is simplified because we have assumed that the return address takes only one location on the stack (the 68K stores a 32-bit return address).

Figures 6.35 and 6.36 demonstrate how multiple subroutine calls are made from different points in the program. As you can see from Fig. 6.36, subroutine ABC is called from two different points in the program. In each case, a return is

made to the instruction following the subroutine call by means of the instruction RTS at the end of the subroutine.

Writing a subroutine in assembly language is simplicity itself. All you need do to turn a block of code into a subroutine is to append the instruction *return from subroutine*, RTS, to the end of the block. Suppose you have to divide the 16-bit integer in data register D3 by two and add three to the result several times during the course of a program (i.e. [D3] ← [D3]/2 + 3). The following subroutine will accomplish this.

```
DIV2PLUS3  ASR.W  #1,D3    Divide by 2
           ADD.W  #3,D3    Add 3
           RTS             Return
```

A subroutine is called by executing the instruction BSR <label> or JSR <label>, where BSR means *branch* to subroutine and JSR means *jump* to subroutine. The difference between BSR and JSR is that BSR uses a *relative* address and JSR an *absolute* address. Remember that the programmer simply supplies the label of the subroutine and the assembler automatically calculates the appropriate relative or absolute address. To call the above subroutine, all we have to do is write either BSR DIV2PLUS3 or JSR DIV2PLUS3. BSR is preferred to JSR because it permits the use of position independent code, although the range of branching with BSR is −32K bytes to +32K bytes from the present instruction. JSR uses an absolute address and cannot therefore be used to generate position-independent code.

6.5.3 Example of the use of subroutines

We now look at a more extended example of how subroutines are used. The following program inputs text from the keyboard until an @ symbol is typed. Successive characters are stored in a buffer in memory. When an @ is encountered, the

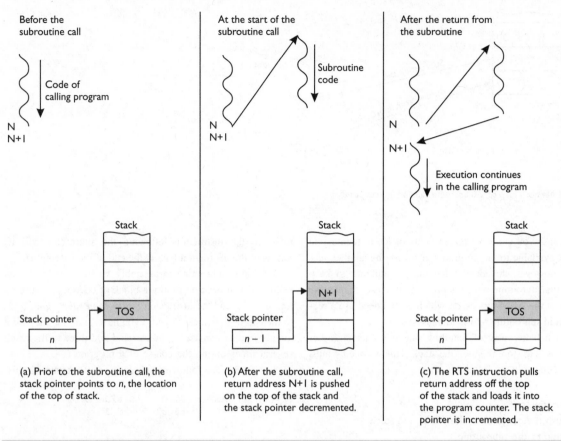

Before the subroutine call

Code of calling program

N
N+1

At the start of the subroutine call

Subroutine code

N
N+1

After the return from the subroutine

Execution continues in the calling program

N
N+1

Stack

Stack pointer

TOS

n

(a) Prior to the subroutine call, the stack pointer points to *n*, the location of the top of stack.

Stack

Stack pointer

N+1

n − 1

(b) After the subroutine call, return address N+1 is pushed on the top of the stack and the stack pointer decremented.

Stack

Stack pointer

TOS

n

(c) The RTS instruction pulls return address off the top of the stack and loads it into the program counter. The stack pointer is incremented.

Fig. 6.34 The stack and the subroutine call. (Note that the 68K's stack pointer is decremented by 4 rather than 1 because an address requires 4 bytes.)

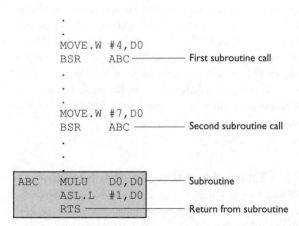

```
       .
       .
       MOVE.W  #4,D0
       BSR     ABC ──────────── First subroutine call
       .
       .
       MOVE.W  #7,D0
       BSR     ABC ──────────── Second subroutine call
       .
       .
 ABC   MULU    D0,D0 ──────────── Subroutine
       ASL.L   #1,D0
       RTS ──────────── Return from subroutine
```

Fig. 6.35 Multiple subroutine calls (the code).

text is displayed on the screen. As it would be very tedious to write a subroutine to input a character from the keyboard or send a character to the screen, we use input and output subroutines.

In this example we use the character input and output mechanisms built into the Teesside 68K simulator. All I/O is performed by means of a TRAP #15 instruction, which is a call to the operating system. We have not yet covered the 68K's TRAP instructions, but all we need say here is that a TRAP calls a function that forms part of the computer's operating system. Before the TRAP is executed, you have to tell the O/S what operation you want by putting a parameter in data register D0. A '5' indicates character input, and a '6' indicates character output. When a character is input, it is deposited in D1. Similarly, the character in D1 is displayed by the output routine. This use of TRAP #15 applies only to the Teesside 68K simulator.

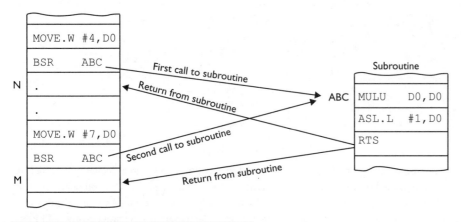

Fig. 6.36 Multiple subroutine calls (the flow of control).

We can express the algorithm in pseudocode as

```
Initialize a pointer to point to the top of the character buffer
REPEAT
        Read a character from the keyboard
        Store it in the buffer at the address given by the pointer
        Update the pointer
UNTIL character = "@"
Reset the pointer to point to the top of the character buffer
REPEAT
        Read a character from the buffer at the address given by the pointer
        IF character = "@" THEN exit
        Display the character on the screen
        Update the pointer
UNTIL exit
```

In the following program, the `BUFFER` is a region of memory reserved for the data to be stored.

```
          ORG       $000400         Define the origin for data
          LEA       BUFFER(PC),A0   Preset A0 as a pointer register
NEXTIN    BSR       GET_CHAR        Get a character
          MOVE.B    D1,(A0)+        Store character and move pointer to next
          CMP.B     #'@',D1         IF character = '@' THEN print
          BNE       NEXTIN          ELSE repeat
PRINT     LEA       BUFFER(PC),A0   Reset pointer to start of buffer
NEXTOUT   MOVE.B    (A0)+,D1        Get a character and update pointer
          CMP.B     #'@',D1         IF character = '@' THEN EXIT
          BEQ       DONE
          BSR       PUT_CHAR                              ELSE print character
          BRA       NEXTOUT         Repeat
DONE      STOP      #$2700          Halt the 68K
*
GET_CHAR  MOVE.B    #5,D0           Input routine
          TRAP      #15             Load input command in D0 and call O/S
          RTS                       Return
*
```

(*program continued*)

```
PUT_CHAR  MOVE.B    #6,D0           Output routine
          TRAP      #15             Load output command in D0 and call O/S
          RTS                       Return
*
          ORG       $500
BUFFER    DS.B      40              Reserve 40 bytes of storage
          END       $400
```

The instruction CMP.B #'@',D1 means 'compare the contents of the lower-order byte of data register D1 with the byte whose ISO/ASCII code corresponds to the symbol @'. Enclosing a character between apostrophes indicates that the character should be replaced by its ISO/ASCII value. For example, MOVE.B #'A',D0 and MOVE.B #$41,D0 are equivalent. The instruction LEA BUFFER(PC),A0 generates position independent code because it calculates the address of the buffer relative to the program counter. If we had written LEA BUFFER,A0, we would have generated code that is not position independent.

When an RTS instruction is encountered at the end of a subroutine, the longword address on the top of the stack is pulled and placed in the program counter in order to force a return to the calling point. The following code is produced by assembling this program. We will need this output when we trace the program (in particular the addresses of the subroutines and the return addresses of subroutine calls).

We have loaded this program into the simulator and have traced part of it. The following trace output demonstrates the flow of control as subroutine calls and subroutine returns are made—when you read the trace look at the program counter and the stack pointer (A7 = SS). Remember that the PC is incremented between 2 and 4 bytes after each instruction.

```
Source file: PROG5.X68
Assembled on: 96-09-30 at: 19:02:46
          by: X68K PC-2.2 Copyright (c) University of Teesside 1989,96
Defaults: ORG $0/FORMAT/OPT A,BRL,CEX,CL,FRL,MC,MD,NOMEX,NOPCO

 1  00000400                         ORG     $000400       ;Define the origin for data
 2  00000400 41FA00FE                LEA     BUFFER(PC),A0 ;Preset A0 as pointer register
 3  00000404 61000022   NEXTIN:      BSR     GET_CHAR      ;Get a character
 4  00000408 10C1                    MOVE.B  D1,(A0)+      ;Store character and move pointer to next
 5  0000040A 0C010040                CMP.B   #'@',D1       ;IF character = '@' THEN print
 6  0000040E 66F4                    BNE     NEXTIN        ;ELSE repeat
 7  00000410 41FA00EE   PRINT:       LEA     BUFFER(PC),A0 ;Reset pointer to start of buffer
 8  00000414 1218       NEXTOUT:     MOVE.B  (A0)+,D1      ;Get a character and update pointer
 9  00000416 0C010040                CMP.B   #'@',D1       ;IF character = '@' THEN EXIT
10  0000041A 67000008                BEQ     DONE
11  0000041E 61000010                BSR     PUT_CHAR      ;ELSE print character
12  00000422 60F0                    BRA     NEXTOUT       ;Repeat
13  00000424 4E722700   DONE:        STOP    #$2700        ;Halt the 68K
14                      *
15  00000428 103C0005   GET_CHAR:    MOVE.B  #5,D0         ;Input routine
16  0000042C 4E4F                    TRAP    #15           ;Load input command in D0 and call O/S
17  0000042E 4E75                    RTS                   ;Return
18                      *
19  00000430 103C0006   PUT_CHAR:    MOVE.B  #6,D0         ;Output routine
20  00000434 4E4F                    TRAP    #15           ;Load output command in D0 and call O/S
21  00000436 4E75                    RTS                   ;Return
22                      *
23  00000500                         ORG     $500
24  00000500 00000028   BUFFER:      DS.B    40            ;Reserve 40 bytes of storage
25  00000400                         END     $400
```

```
>df
PC=000400  SR=2000  SS=00A00000  US=00000000           X=0
A0=00000000  A1=00000000  A2=00000000  A3=00000000  N=0
A4=00000000  A5=00000000  A6=00000000  A7=00A00000  Z=0
D0=00000000  D1=00000000  D2=00000000  D3=00000000  V=0
D4=00000000  D5=00000000  D6=00000000  D7=00000000  C=0
----->LEA.L    $FE(PC),A0

>tr
PC=000404  SR=2000  SS=00A00000  US=00000000           X=0
A0=00000500  A1=00000000  A2=00000000  A3=00000000  N=0
A4=00000000  A5=00000000  A6=00000000  A7=00A00000  Z=0
D0=00000000  D1=00000000  D2=00000000  D3=00000000  V=0
D4=00000000  D5=00000000  D6=00000000  D7=00000000  C=0
----->BSR.L    $0428
```

We've set A0 to point to the buffer for input data. The next instruction calls the subroutine to input a character. Note the change in the PC.

```
Trace>
PC=000428  SR=2000  SS=009FFFFC  US=00000000      X=0  009FFFFC:00000408 s
A0=00000500  A1=00000000  A2=00000000  A3=00000000  N=0
A4=00000000  A5=00000000  A6=00000000  A7=009FFFFC  Z=0
D0=00000000  D1=00000000  D2=00000000  D3=00000000  V=0
D4=00000000  D5=00000000  D6=00000000  D7=00000000  C=0
----->MOVE.B    #$05,D0

Trace>
PC=00042C  SR=2000  SS=009FFFFC  US=00000000      X=0  009FFFFC:00000408 s
A0=00000500  A1=00000000  A2=00000000  A3=00000000  N=0
A4=00000000  A5=00000000  A6=00000000  A7=009FFFFC  Z=0
D0=00000005  D1=00000000  D2=00000000  D3=00000000  V=0
D4=00000000  D5=00000000  D6=00000000  D7=00000000  C=0
----->TRAP      #$0F

Trace>
```

> This is the character entered from the keyboard and captured by the Trap #15

(Z)

```
PC=00042E  SR=2000  SS=009FFFFC  US=00000000      X=0  009FFFFC:00000408 s
A0=00000500  A1=00000000  A2=00000000  A3=00000000  N=0
A4=00000000  A5=00000000  A6=00000000  A7=009FFFFC  Z=0
D0=00000005  D1=0000005A  D2=00000000  D3=00000000  V=0
D4=00000000  D5=00000000  D6=00000000  D7=00000000  C=0
----->RTS
```

Having got the input (in this case Z) in D1, we return from the subroutine. Watch the program counter again. It is currently $42E and will be replaced by $408 (i.e. the address of the instruction after the subroutine call).

```
Trace>
PC=000408  SR=2000  SS=00A00000  US=00000000           X=0
A0=00000500  A1=00000000  A2=00000000  A3=00000000  N=0
A4=00000000  A5=00000000  A6=00000000  A7=00A00000  Z=0
D0=00000005  D1=0000005A  D2=00000000  D3=00000000  V=0
D4=00000000  D5=00000000  D6=00000000  D7=00000000  C=0
----->MOVE.B    D1,(A0)+
```

We now store the character in D1 in memory and increment the pointer in A0.

```
Trace>
PC=00040A  SR=2000  SS=00A00000  US=00000000           X=0
A0=00000501  A1=00000000  A2=00000000  A3=00000000  N=0
A4=00000000  A5=00000000  A6=00000000  A7=00A00000  Z=0
D0=00000005  D1=0000005A  D2=00000000  D3=00000000  V=0
D4=00000000  D5=00000000  D6=00000000  D7=00000000  C=0
----->CMPI.B    #$40,D1
```

```
Trace>
PC=00040E SR=2000 SS=00A00000 US=00000000          X=0
A0=00000501 A1=00000000 A2=00000000 A3=00000000 N=0
A4=00000000 A5=00000000 A6=00000000 A7=00A00000 Z=0
D0=00000005 D1=0000005A D2=00000000 D3=00000000 V=0
D4=00000000 D5=00000000 D6=00000000 D7=00000000 C=0
----->BNE.S    $0404
```

We test the character in D1 for equality with '@' = $40 and then branch back to $0404 if we haven't input an '@'.

```
Trace>
PC=000404 SR=2000 SS=00A00000 US=00000000          X=0
A0=00000501 A1=00000000 A2=00000000 A3=00000000 N=0
A4=00000000 A5=00000000 A6=00000000 A7=00A00000 Z=0
D0=00000005 D1=0000005A D2=00000000 D3=00000000 V=0
D4=00000000 D5=00000000 D6=00000000 D7=00000000 C=0
----->BSR.L    $0428
```

We haven't, so we continue by reading another character.

```
Trace>
PC=000428 SR=2000 SS=009FFFFC US=00000000          X=0 009FFFFC:00000408 s
A0=00000501 A1=00000000 A2=00000000 A3=00000000 N=0
A4=00000000 A5=00000000 A6=00000000 A7=009FFFFC Z=0
D0=00000005 D1=0000005A D2=00000000 D3=00000000 V=0
D4=00000000 D5=00000000 D6=00000000 D7=00000000 C=0
----->MOVE.B    #$05,D0
```

To avoid more tracing, we'll jump ahead to the point at which a '@' has been input in D0.

```
Trace>
PC=00042C SR=2000 SS=009FFFFC US=00000000          X=0 009FFFFC:00000408 s
A0=00000501 A1=00000000 A2=00000000 A3=00000000 N=0
A4=00000000 A5=00000000 A6=00000000 A7=009FFFFC Z=0
D0=00000005 D1=0000005A D2=00000000 D3=00000000 V=0
D4=00000000 D5=00000000 D6=00000000 D7=00000000 C=0
----->TRAP     #$0F

Trace>
@
PC=00042E SR=2000 SS=009FFFFC US=00000000          X=0 009FFFFC:00000408 s
A0=00000502 A1=00000000 A2=00000000 A3=00000000 N=0
A4=00000000 A5=00000000 A6=00000000 A7=009FFFFC Z=0
D0=00000005 D1=00000040 D2=00000000 D3=00000000 V=0
D4=00000000 D5=00000000 D6=00000000 D7=00000000 C=0
----->RTS

Trace>
PC=000408 SR=2000 SS=00A00000 US=00000000          X=0
A0=00000502 A1=00000000 A2=00000000 A3=00000000 N=0
A4=00000000 A5=00000000 A6=00000000 A7=00A00000 Z=0
D0=00000005 D1=00000040 D2=00000000 D3=00000000 V=0
D4=00000000 D5=00000000 D6=00000000 D7=00000000 C=0
----->MOVE.B    D1,(A0)+

Trace>
PC=00040A SR=2000 SS=00A00000 US=00000000          X=0
A0=00000503 A1=00000000 A2=00000000 A3=00000000 N=0
A4=00000000 A5=00000000 A6=00000000 A7=00A00000 Z=0
D0=00000005 D1=00000040 D2=00000000 D3=00000000 V=0
D4=00000000 D5=00000000 D6=00000000 D7=00000000 C=0
----->CMPI.B    #$40,D1
```

```
Trace>
PC=00040E  SR=2004  SS=00A00000  US=00000000         X=0
A0=00000503  A1=00000000  A2=00000000  A3=00000000  N=0
A4=00000000  A5=00000000  A6=00000000  A7=00A00000  Z=1
D0=00000005  D1=00000040  D2=00000000  D3=00000000  V=0
D4=00000000  D5=00000000  D6=00000000  D7=00000000  C=0
----->BNE.S      $0404
```

Since D1 contains the ASCII code for '@', the test for equality will yield true and we will not take the branch back to $0404.

```
Trace>
PC=000410  SR=2004  SS=00A00000  US=00000000         X=0
A0=00000503  A1=00000000  A2=00000000  A3=00000000  N=0
A4=00000000  A5=00000000  A6=00000000  A7=00A00000  Z=1
D0=00000005  D1=00000040  D2=00000000  D3=00000000  V=0
D4=00000000  D5=00000000  D6=00000000  D7=00000000  C=0
----->LEA.L      $EE(PC),A0
```

The next instructions reset the pointer to the top of the buffer, read a character, and compare it to '@'.

```
Trace>
PC=000414  SR=2004  SS=00A00000  US=00000000         X=0
A0=00000500  A1=00000000  A2=00000000  A3=00000000  N=0
A4=00000000  A5=00000000  A6=00000000  A7=00A00000  Z=1
D0=00000005  D1=00000040  D2=00000000  D3=00000000  V=0
D4=00000000  D5=00000000  D6=00000000  D7=00000000  C=0
----->MOVE.B     (A0)+,D1
```

```
Trace>
PC=000416  SR=2000  SS=00A00000  US=00000000         X=0
A0=00000501  A1=00000000  A2=00000000  A3=00000000  N=0
A4=00000000  A5=00000000  A6=00000000  A7=00A00000  Z=0
D0=00000005  D1=0000005A  D2=00000000  D3=00000000  V=0
D4=00000000  D5=00000000  D6=00000000  D7=00000000  C=0
----->CMPI.B     #$40,D1
```

```
Trace>
PC=00041A  SR=2000  SS=00A00000  US=00000000         X=0
A0=00000501  A1=00000000  A2=00000000  A3=00000000  N=0
A4=00000000  A5=00000000  A6=00000000  A7=00A00000  Z=0
D0=00000005  D1=0000005A  D2=00000000  D3=00000000  V=0
D4=00000000  D5=00000000  D6=00000000  D7=00000000  C=0
----->BEQ.L      $0424
```

If it isn't an '@', we will print it by calling the output routine.

```
Trace>
PC=00041E  SR=2000  SS=00A00000  US=00000000         X=0
A0=00000501  A1=00000000  A2=00000000  A3=00000000  N=0
A4=00000000  A5=00000000  A6=00000000  A7=00A00000  Z=0
D0=00000005  D1=0000005A  D2=00000000  D3=00000000  V=0
D4=00000000  D5=00000000  D6=00000000  D7=00000000  C=0
----->BSR.L      $0430
```

```
Trace>
PC=000430  SR=2000  SS=009FFFFC  US=00000000         X=0  009FFFFC:00000422 s
A0=00000501  A1=00000000  A2=00000000  A3=00000000  N=0
A4=00000000  A5=00000000  A6=00000000  A7=009FFFFC  Z=0
D0=00000005  D1=0000005A  D2=00000000  D3=00000000  V=0
D4=00000000  D5=00000000  D6=00000000  D7=00000000  C=0
----->MOVE.B     #$06,D0
```

In this case we have branched to address $0430.

```
Trace>
PC=000434 SR=2000 SS=009FFFFC US=00000000        X=0 009FFFFC:00000422 s
A0=00000501 A1=00000000 A2=00000000 A3=00000000 N=0
A4=00000000 A5=00000000 A6=00000000 A7=009FFFFC Z=0
D0=00000006 D1=0000005A D2=00000000 D3=00000000 V=0
D4=00000000 D5=00000000 D6=00000000 D7=00000000 C=0
----->TRAP      #$0F
```

We call the operating system with the TRAP. Note that the contents of D1 will be printed as the ASCII character Z. Then we return to the body of the program.

```
Trace>
```

This is the character entered from the keyboard and captured by the Trap #15

Z

```
PC=000436 SR=2000 SS=009FFFFC US=00000000        X=0 009FFFFC:00000422 s
A0=00000501 A1=00000000 A2=00000000 A3=00000000 N=0
A4=00000000 A5=00000000 A6=00000000 A7=009FFFFC Z=0
D0=00000006 D1=0000005A D2=00000000 D3=00000000 V=0
D4=00000000 D5=00000000 D6=00000000 D7=00000000 C=0
----->RTS
```

Note the change in the value of the PC.

```
Trace>
PC=000422 SR=2000 SS=00A00000 US=00000000        X=0
A0=00000501 A1=00000000 A2=00000000 A3=00000000 N=0
A4=00000000 A5=00000000 A6=00000000 A7=00A00000 Z=0
D0=00000006 D1=0000005A D2=00000000 D3=00000000 V=0
D4=00000000 D5=00000000 D6=00000000 D7=00000000 C=0
----->BRA.S    $0414
```

And so on....

6.5.4 Subroutines, the stack, and parameter passing

A subroutine is designed to carry out some particular function. In order to do this, it is almost always necessary to transfer data between the calling program and the subroutine. Up to now we have passed data to and from the subroutine via data registers.

In the previous example, we called the subroutine GET_CHAR to input a character from the keyboard. When this subroutine is invoked by the operation BSR GET_CHAR, a branch is made to the entry point of the subroutine. This subroutine reads the keyboard until a key is pressed. A return to the calling point is made with the ASCII code of the character in data register D1. As only a single byte is passed from the subroutine to the calling program, a data register provides a handy vehicle to transfer the character.

You can even use the C bit in the CCR to pass information from a subroutine to its calling program. A single bit may not

seem like an awful lot of information. However, problems sometimes arise within the subroutine and the calling program must be informed about them. Suppose a subroutine had been called to read data from a terminal and the terminal was faulty or not switched on. By setting the carry bit prior to a return from subroutine, the calling program can be informed that an error exists. The following fragment of a program illustrates this point.

```
       BSR  GETDATA  Call subroutine and return with data in D0
       BCS  ERROR    IF carry flag set THEN something went wrong
       .
       .                        ELSE deal with the data
       .
ERROR                Recover from error condition
```

Unfortunately, you can't use registers to transfer large quantities of data to and from subroutines, owing to the limited number of registers. You can pass parameters to a subroutine by means of a mailbox in memory. Consider the following.

```
        MOVE.W      Param1,Mbox1    Put first parameter in mail box 1
        MOVE.W      Param2,Mbox2    Put second parameter in mail box 2
        BSR         Sub             Now call the subroutine
         .                          Return here...
         .
         .
Sub     MOVE.W      Mbox1,D0        Retrieve the first parameter
        MOVE.W      Mbox2,D1        Retrieve the second parameter
         .
         .
         .
        RTS                         Return to the calling program
```

Such a solution is not popular, because the subroutine cannot be interrupted or called by another program. Any data stored in explicitly named locations could be corrupted by the interrupting program. Section 8.2 deals in detail with the interrupt mechanism and its implementation.

For the purposes of this chapter, a brief description of the interrupt will suffice. An interrupt is a method of diverting the processor from its intended course of action, and is employed to deal with errors and external events that must be attended to as soon as they occur. Whenever a processor receives an interrupt request from a device, the processor finishes its current instruction and then jumps to the program that handles the cause of the interrupt. After the interrupt has been serviced, a return is made to the point immediately following the last instruction executed before the interrupt was dealt with. The return mechanism of the interrupt is almost identical to that of the subroutine—the return address is saved on the stack.

Suppose a subroutine is interrupted during the course of its execution. If the interrupt handling routine also wishes to use the same subroutine (yes, that's possible), any data stored in explicitly named memory locations will be overwritten (corrupted) by the reuse of the subroutine. If the data had been stored in registers and the contents of the registers pushed on the stack by the interrupt handling routine, no data in the subroutine would have been lost by its reuse. After the subroutine has been reused by the interrupt handling routine, the contents of the registers stored on the stack are restored and a return from interrupt made with the state of the registers exactly the same as at the instant the interrupt was serviced.

We are now going to look at the preferred means of transferring data between a subroutine and its calling program.

Passing parameters on the stack

An ideal way of passing information between the subroutine and calling program is via the stack. Suppose two 16-bit parameters, P1 and P2, are needed by the subroutine. The parameters are pushed on the stack immediately before the subroutine call by the following code:

```
MOVE.W    P1,−(A7) Push the first parameter
MOVE.W    P2,−(A7) Push the second parameter
```

The state of the stack initially, prior to the subroutine call, and immediately after it, is given in Fig. 6.37. Note that the return address is a longword and takes up two words on the stack.

On entering the subroutine, the parameters can be retrieved from the stack in several ways. We must make one point clear before we go any further. You must never change the stack pointer in such a way that you move it down the stack. Consider Fig. 6.37(c) where the stack pointer is pointing at the return address. If you add 4 to the stack pointer, it will point to parameter P2 on the stack. You can now get P2 with, say, MOVE.W (A7),D0. However, the return address is

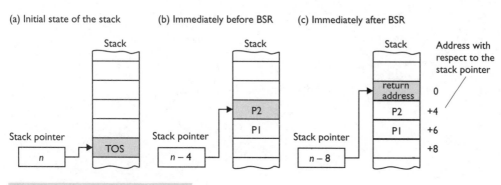

Fig. 6.37 Passing parameters on the stack.

no longer on the stack (it's still there in memory above the top of the stack). If an interrupt occurs or you call a subroutine, the new return address will be pushed on the top of the stack, overwriting the old return address. There is, of course, nothing stopping you moving the stack pointer up—that creates space on the stack and does not cause a problem. So, never move the stack pointer below the top-of-stack.

You can avoid moving the stack pointer by making a copy of it in another address register with LEA (A7),A0. Now you can use A0 to get the parameters; for example, P1 can be loaded into D1 by MOVE 6(A0),D1. The offset 6 is required because the parameter P1 is buried under the return address (4 bytes) and P2 (2 bytes). Similarly, P2 can be loaded into D2 by MOVE.W 4(A0),D2.

After returning from the subroutine with RTS, the contents of the stack pointer are [A7]−4, where A7 is the value of the stack pointer before P1 and P2 were pushed on the stack. The stack pointer can be restored to its original value or cleaned up by executing the instruction LEA 4(A7),A7 to move the stack pointer down by three words. Note that LEA 4(A7),A7 is the same as ADD.L #4,A7. P1 and P2 are, of course, still in the same locations in memory, but they will be overwritten as new data is pushed on the stack.

By using the stack to pass parameters to a subroutine, the subroutine may be interrupted and then used by the interrupting program without the parameters being corrupted. As the data is stored on the stack, it is not overwritten when the subroutine is interrupted because new data is added at the top of the stack, and then removed after the interrupt has been serviced.

Let's look at another example of parameter passing in detail. In the following program two numbers are loaded into D0 and D1, and then the contents of these registers are pushed on the stack. A subroutine, AddUp, is called to add these two numbers together. In this case the result is pushed on the stack.

```
        ORG     $400
        LEA     $1000,A7        Set up the stack pointer
        MOVE.W  #1,D0           Set up two parameters in D0 and D1
        MOVE.W  #2,D1
        MOVE.W  D0,-(A7)        Push parameter 1 on the stack
        MOVE.W  D1,-(A7)        Push parameter 2 on the stack
        BSR     AddUp           Call adder routine
        MOVE.W  (A7)+,D4        Read the result from the stack
        LEA     2(A7),A7        Clean up the stack
        STOP    #$2700          Stop
*
AddUp   MOVE.W  4(A7),D2        Get parameter 2 from the stack
        MOVE.W  6(A7),D3        Get parameter 1 from the stack
        ADD     D2,D3           Add them
        MOVE.W  D3,4(A7)        Store the result in the parameter 2 slot
        RTS
```

If we assemble this program, we get

```
 1  00000400              ORG     $400
 2  00000400 4FF81000     LEA     $1000,A7      ;Set up the stack pointer
 3  00000404 303C0001     MOVE.W  #1,D0         ;Set up two parameters in D0 and D1
 4  00000408 323C0002     MOVE.W  #2,D1
 5  0000040C 3F00         MOVE.W  D0,-(A7)      ;Push parameter 1
 6  0000040E 3F01         MOVE.W  D1,-(A7)      ;Push parameter 2
 7  00000410 6100000C     BSR     ADDUP         ;Call adder routine
 8  00000414 381F         MOVE.W  (A7)+,D4      ;Read the result
 9  00000416 4FEF0002     LEA     2(A7),A7      ;Clean up stack
10  0000041A 4E722700     STOP    #$2700        ;Stop
11                   *
12  0000041E 342F0004 ADDUP: MOVE.W  4(A7),D2   ;Get parameter 2
13  00000422 362F0006     MOVE.W  6(A7),D3      ;Get parameter 1
14  00000426 D642         ADD     D2,D3         ;Add them
15  00000428 3F430004     MOVE.W  D3,4(A7)      ;Store result in the parameter 2 slot
16  0000042C 4E75         RTS
17                   *
18          00000400      END     $400
```

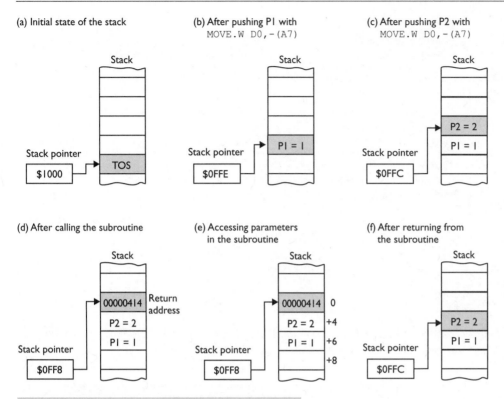

(a) Initial state of the stack

(b) After pushing PI with
MOVE.W D0,-(A7)

(c) After pushing P2 with
MOVE.W D0,-(A7)

(d) After calling the subroutine

(e) Accessing parameters
in the subroutine

(f) After returning from
the subroutine

Fig. 6.38 The state of the stack during the execution of a program.

We will now load the program and trace it line by line. Figure 6.38 shows the state of the stack at various points during the execution of this program.

```
>DF
PC=000400  SR=2000  SS=00A00000  US=00000000        X=0
A0=00000000  A1=00000000  A2=00000000  A3=00000000  N=0
A4=00000000  A5=00000000  A6=00000000  A7=00A00000  Z=0
D0=00000000  D1=00000000  D2=00000000  D3=00000000  V=0
D4=00000000  D5=00000000  D6=00000000  D7=00000000  C=0
----->LEA.L      $1000,SP

>TR
PC=000404  SR=2000  SS=00001000  US=00000000        X=0  00001000:00000000  s
A0=00000000  A1=00000000  A2=00000000  A3=00000000  N=0  00001004:00000000  s+4
A4=00000000  A5=00000000  A6=00000000  A7=00001000  Z=0  00001008:00000000  s+8
D0=00000000  D1=00000000  D2=00000000  D3=00000000  V=0  0000100C:00000000  s+12
D4=00000000  D5=00000000  D6=00000000  D7=00000000  C=0  00001010:00000000  s+16
----->MOVE.W     #$01,D0
```

Note the five new entries to the right of the register display. These lines display the five longwords at the top of the stack. Each line contains the stack address, the longword in that address, and the address with respect to the current stack pointer.

```
Trace>
PC=000408  SR=2000  SS=00001000  US=00000000        X=0  00001000:00000000  s
A0=00000000 A1=00000000 A2=00000000 A3=00000000 N=0  00001004:00000000  s+4
A4=00000000 A5=00000000 A6=00000000 A7=00001000 Z=0  00001008:00000000  s+8
D0=00000001 D1=00000000 D2=00000000 D3=00000000 V=0  0000100C:00000000  s+12
D4=00000000 D5=00000000 D6=00000000 D7=00000000 C=0  00001010:00000000  s+16
----->MOVE.W    #$02,D1


Trace>
PC=00040C  SR=2000  SS=00001000  US=00000000        X=0  00001000:00000000  s
A0=00000000 A1=00000000 A2=00000000 A3=00000000 N=0  00001004:00000000  s+4
A4=00000000 A5=00000000 A6=00000000 A7=00001000 Z=0  00001008:00000000  s+8
D0=00000001 D1=00000002 D2=00000000 D3=00000000 V=0  0000100C:00000000  s+12
D4=00000000 D5=00000000 D6=00000000 D7=00000000 C=0  00001010:00000000  s+16
----->MOVE.W    D0,-(SP)


Trace>
PC=00040E  SR=2000  SS=00000FFE  US=00000000        X=0  00000FFE:00010000  s
A0=00000000 A1=00000000 A2=00000000 A3=00000000 N=0  00001002:00000000  s+4
A4=00000000 A5=00000000 A6=00000000 A7=00000FFE Z=0  00001006:00000000  s+8
D0=00000001 D1=00000002 D2=00000000 D3=00000000 V=0  0000100A:00000000  s+12
D4=00000000 D5=00000000 D6=00000000 D7=00000000 C=0  0000100E:00000000  s+16
----->MOVE.W    D1,-(SP)
```

Note how the previous instruction, MOVE.W D0,- (SP), has modified the stack. The top of the stack is no longer $1000, but $0FFE. You can also see that the contents of D0.W (i.e. 0001) have been pushed on the stack.

```
Trace>
PC=000410  SR=2000  SS=00000FFC  US=00000000        X=0  00000FFC:00020001  s
A0=00000000 A1=00000000 A2=00000000 A3=00000000 N=0  00001000:00000000  s+4
A4=00000000 A5=00000000 A6=00000000 A7=00000FFC Z=0  00001004:00000000  s+8
D0=00000001 D1=00000002 D2=00000000 D3=00000000 V=0  00001008:00000000  s+12
D4=00000000 D5=00000000 D6=00000000 D7=00000000 C=0  0000100C:00000000  s+16
----->BSR.L     $041E


Trace>
PC=00041E  SR=2000  SS=00000FF8  US=00000000        X=0  00000FF8:00000414  s
A0=00000000 A1=00000000 A2=00000000 A3=00000000 N=0  00000FFC:00020001  s+4
A4=00000000 A5=00000000 A6=00000000 A7=00000FF8 Z=0  00001000:00000000  s+8
D0=00000001 D1=00000002 D2=00000000 D3=00000000 V=0  00001004:00000000  s+12
D4=00000000 D5=00000000 D6=00000000 D7=00000000 C=0  00001008:00000000  s+16
----->MOVE.W    $04(SP),D2
```

At this point the return address, $00000414, has been pushed on the stack and the stack pointer is now pointing at $00000FF8.

```
Trace>
PC=000422  SR=2000  SS=00000FF8  US=00000000        X=0  00000FF8:00000414  s
A0=00000000 A1=00000000 A2=00000000 A3=00000000 N=0  00000FFC:00020001  s+4
A4=00000000 A5=00000000 A6=00000000 A7=00000FF8 Z=0  00001000:00000000  s+8
D0=00000001 D1=00000002 D2=00000002 D3=00000000 V=0  00001004:00000000  s+12
D4=00000000 D5=00000000 D6=00000000 D7=00000000 C=0  00001008:00000000  s+16
----->MOVE.W    $06(SP),D3


Trace>
PC=000426  SR=2000  SS=00000FF8  US=00000000        X=0  00000FF8:00000414  s
A0=00000000 A1=00000000 A2=00000000 A3=00000000 N=0  00000FFC:00020001  s+4
A4=00000000 A5=00000000 A6=00000000 A7=00000FF8 Z=0  00001000:00000000  s+8
D0=00000001 D1=00000002 D2=00000002 D3=00000001 V=0  00001004:00000000  s+12
D4=00000000 D5=00000000 D6=00000000 D7=00000000 C=0  00001008:00000000  s+16
----->ADD.W     D2,D3
```

```
Trace>
PC=000428 SR=2000 SS=00000FF8 US=00000000        X=0 00000FF8:00000414 s
A0=00000000 A1=00000000 A2=00000000 A3=00000000 N=0 00000FFC:00020001 s+4
A4=00000000 A5=00000000 A6=00000000 A7=00000FF8 Z=0 00001000:00000000 s+8
D0=00000001 D1=00000002 D2=00000002 D3=00000003 V=0 00001004:00000000 s+12
D4=00000000 D5=00000000 D6=00000000 D7=00000000 C=0 00001008:00000000 s+16
----->MOVE.W   D3,$04(SP)

Trace>
PC=00042C SR=2000 SS=00000FF8 US=00000000        X=0 00000FF8:00000414 s
A0=00000000 A1=00000000 A2=00000000 A3=00000000 N=0 00000FFC:00030001 s+4
A4=00000000 A5=00000000 A6=00000000 A7=00000FF8 Z=0 00001000:00000000 s+8
D0=00000001 D1=00000002 D2=00000002 D3=00000003 V=0 00001004:00000000 s+12
D4=00000000 D5=00000000 D6=00000000 D7=00000000 C=0 00001008:00000000 s+16
----->RTS

Trace>
PC=000414 SR=2000 SS=00000FFC US=00000000        X=0 00000FFC:00030001 s
A0=00000000 A1=00000000 A2=00000000 A3=00000000 N=0 00001000:00000000 s+4
A4=00000000 A5=00000000 A6=00000000 A7=00000FFC Z=0 00001004:00000000 s+8
D0=00000001 D1=00000002 D2=00000002 D3=00000003 V=0 00001008:00000000 s+12
D4=00000000 D5=00000000 D6=00000000 D7=00000000 C=0 0000100C:00000000 s+16
----->MOVE.W   (SP)+,D4

Trace>
PC=000416 SR=2000 SS=00000FFE US=00000000        X=0 00000FFE:00010000 s
A0=00000000 A1=00000000 A2=00000000 A3=00000000 N=0 00001002:00000000 s+4
A4=00000000 A5=00000000 A6=00000000 A7=00000FFE Z=0 00001006:00000000 s+8
D0=00000001 D1=00000002 D2=00000002 D3=00000003 V=0 0000100A:00000000 s+12
D4=00000003 D5=00000000 D6=00000000 D7=00000000 C=0 0000100E:00000000 s+16
----->LEA.L    $02(SP),SP

Trace>
PC=00041A SR=2000 SS=00001000 US=00000000        X=0 00001000:00000000 s
A0=00000000 A1=00000000 A2=00000000 A3=00000000 N=0 00001004:00000000 s+4
A4=00000000 A5=00000000 A6=00000000 A7=00001000 Z=0 00001008:00000000 s+8
D0=00000001 D1=00000002 D2=00000002 D3=00000003 V=0 0000100C:00000000 s+12
D4=00000003 D5=00000000 D6=00000000 D7=00000000 C=0 00001010:00000000 s+16
----->STOP      #$2700
```

As you can see, the 68K ends with the result $1+2=3$ in data register D4, and the stack pointer is $1000 (the same as its starting value). Passing a parameter to a subroutine by value is easy. Getting a result back from the subroutine is more tricky, as we'll soon see.

are two copies of the parameter: the original in the calling program and its copy on the stack. If a parameter is passed by value, changing it within the subroutine doesn't change its value in the calling program—as the next example demonstrates.

Passing parameters by reference

In the previous examples, we passed a copy of a parameter to the subroutine by pushing its value on the stack. This mechanism is called passing parameters by value. Note that there

```
*      Program to call a subroutine that swaps two numbers A and B
*
       ORG     $400
       LEA     $1000,A7      Set up the stack pointer
       MOVE.W  A,-(A7)       Push value of parameter A
       MOVE.W  B,-(A7)       Push value of parameter B
       BSR     SWAP          Call subroutine to swap A and B
       LEA     4(A7),A7      Clean up the stack
       STOP    #$2700        Stop
*
```

(*program continued*)

```
SWAP  MOVE.W  4(A7),D1      Get first parameter in D0
      MOVE.W  6(A7),4(A7)   Copy second parameter to first parameter
      MOVE.W  D1,6(A7)      Copy first parameter to second parameter
      RTS
*
A     DC.W    $1234
B     DC.W    $5678
*
      END     $400
```

This program calls a subroutine to swap two numbers, A and B. The two parameters are first pushed on the stack in the main program. In the subroutine the two parameters are retrieved from their locations on the stack and swapped over. However, once a return from subroutine is made and the stack cleaned up, the parameters on the stack are lost. Parameters A and B in the main program were never swapped.

You can also pass a parameter to a subroutine by reference by passing its address on the stack. That is, you don't say 'Here's a parameter'; instead you say, 'Here's where the parameter is located'. In this case, there is only one copy of the parameter.

Let's repeat the example in which we added two numbers together, and, this time, pass the parameters to the subroutine by reference.

The following program introduces a new instruction, push effective address, PEA, that pushes an address in the stack; for example, the operation PEA PQR pushes the address PQR on the stack. The instruction PEA PQR is equivalent to

```
MOVE.L #PQR,-(A7) Push address PQR on the stack
```

Here is the code:

```
        ORG     $400
        LEA     $1000,A7     Set up the stack pointer
        PEA     X            Push address of variable X
        PEA     Y            Push address of variable Y
        PEA     Z            Push address of variable Z (the result)
        BSR     AddUp        Call adder routine
        MOVE.W  Z,D2         Read the result (a dummy operation)
        LEA     12(A7),A7    Clean up stack
        STOP    #$2700       Stop
*
AddUp   MOVEA.L 12(A7),A0    Get address of parameter X
        MOVEA.L 8(A7),A1     Get address of parameter Y
        MOVE.W  (A0),D2      Get value of X
        MOVE.W  (A1),D3      Get value of Y
        ADD     D2,D3        Add them
        MOVEA.L 4(A7),A3     Get address of parameter Z
        MOVE.W  D3,(A3)      Put result in variable Z
        RTS
*
        ORG     $500
X       DC.W    1
Y       DC.W    2
Z       DS.W    1
```

The following is the assembled version of this program.

```
 1 00000400                        ORG    $400
 2 00000400 4FF81000               LEA    $1000,A7   ;Set up the stack pointer
 3 00000404 487900000500           PEA    X          ;Push address of X
 4 0000040A 487900000502           PEA    Y          ;Push address of Y
 5 00000410 487900000504           PEA    Z          ;Push address of Z
 6 00000416 61000010               BSR    ADDUP      ;Call adder routine
 7 0000041A 343900000504           MOVE.W Z,D2       ;Read the result
 8 00000420 4FEF000C               LEA    12(A7),A7  ;Clean up stack
 9 00000424 4E722700               STOP   #$2700     ;Stop
10                          *
```

```
11 00000428 206F000C    ADDUP:    MOVEA.L  12(A7),A0   ;Get address of parameter X
12 0000042C 226F0008              MOVEA.L  8(A7),A1    ;Get address of parameter Y
13 00000430 3410                  MOVE.W   (A0),D2     ;Get value of X
14 00000432 3611                  MOVE.W   (A1),D3     ;Get value of Y
15 00000434 D642                  ADD      D2,D3       ;Add them
16 00000436 266F0004              MOVEA.L  4(A7),A3    ;Get address of parameter Z
17 0000043A 3683                  MOVE.W   D3,(A3)     ;Put result in variable Z
18 0000043C 4E75                  RTS
19                       *
20 00000500                       ORG      $500
21 00000500 0001         X:       DC.W     1
22 00000502 0002         Y:       DC.W     2
23 00000504 00000002     Z:       DS.W     1
24                       *
25          00000400              END      $400
```

We can now run this program line by line. In this case, note how the addresses of the variables are pushed on the stack and then loaded in address registers in the subroutine. We will use the MD 500 command to view the data area initially (it should contain the two 16-bit constants 1 and 2.

```
>MD 500
000500 00 01 00 02 00 00 00 00 00 00 00 00 00 00 00 00.

>DF
PC=000400 SR=2000 SS=00A00000 US=00000000        X=0
A0=00000000 A1=00000000 A2=00000000 A3=00000000 N=0
A4=00000000 A5=00000000 A6=00000000 A7=00A00000 Z=0
D0=00000000 D1=00000000 D2=00000000 D3=00000000 V=0
D4=00000000 D5=00000000 D6=00000000 D7=00000000 C=0
----->LEA.L     $1000,SP

>TR
PC=000404 SR=2000 SS=00001000 US=00000000        X=0 00001000:00000000 s
A0=00000000 A1=00000000 A2=00000000 A3=00000000 N=0 00001004:00000000 s+4
A4=00000000 A5=00000000 A6=00000000 A7=00001000 Z=0 00001008:00000000 s+8
D0=00000000 D1=00000000 D2=00000000 D3=00000000 V=0 0000100C:00000000 s+12
D4=00000000 D5=00000000 D6=00000000 D7=00000000 C=0 00001010:00000000 s+16
----->PEA      $0500
Trace>
PC=00040A SR=2000 SS=00000FFC US=00000000        X=0 00000FFC:00000500 s
A0=00000000 A1=00000000 A2=00000000 A3=00000000 N=0 00001000:00000000 s+4
A4=00000000 A5=00000000 A6=00000000 A7=00000FFC Z=0 00001004:00000000 s+8
D0=00000000 D1=00000000 D2=00000000 D3=00000000 V=0 00001008:00000000 s+12
D4=00000000 D5=00000000 D6=00000000 D7=00000000 C=0 0000100C:00000000 s+16
----->PEA      $0502
```

As you can see, the operation PEA $0500 has pushed the address $00000500 on the stack and moved the stack pointer up by 4.

```
Trace>
PC=000410 SR=2000 SS=00000FF8 US=00000000        X=0 00000FF8:00000502 s
A0=00000000 A1=00000000 A2=00000000 A3=00000000 N=0 00000FFC:00000500 s+4
A4=00000000 A5=00000000 A6=00000000 A7=00000FF8 Z=0 00001000:00000000 s+8
D0=00000000 D1=00000000 D2=00000000 D3=00000000 V=0 00001004:00000000 s+12
D4=00000000 D5=00000000 D6=00000000 D7=00000000 C=0 00001008:00000000 s+16
----->PEA      $0504
```

```
Trace>
PC=000416 SR=2000 SS=00000FF4 US=00000000      X=0  00000FF4:00000504  s
A0=00000000 A1=00000000 A2=00000000 A3=00000000 N=0  00000FF8:00000502  s+4
A4=00000000 A5=00000000 A6=00000000 A7=00000FF4 Z=0  00000FFC:00000500  s+8
D0=00000000 D1=00000000 D2=00000000 D3=00000000 V=0  00001000:00000000  s+12
D4=00000000 D5=00000000 D6=00000000 D7=00000000 C=0  00001004:00000000  s+16
----->BSR.L    $0428


Trace>
PC=000428 SR=2000 SS=00000FF0 US=00000000      X=0  00000FF0:0000041A  s
A0=00000000 A1=00000000 A2=00000000 A3=00000000 N=0  00000FF4:00000504  s+4
A4=00000000 A5=00000000 A6=00000000 A7=00000FF0 Z=0  00000FF8:00000502  s+8
D0=00000000 D1=00000000 D2=00000000 D3=00000000 V=0  00000FFC:00000500  s+12
D4=00000000 D5=00000000 D6=00000000 D7=00000000 C=0  00001000:00000000  s+16
----->MOVEA.L  $0C(SP),A0


Trace>
PC=00042C SR=2000 SS=00000FF0 US=00000000      X=0  00000FF0:0000041A  s
A0=00000500 A1=00000000 A2=00000000 A3=00000000 N=0  00000FF4:00000504  s+4
A4=00000000 A5=00000000 A6=00000000 A7=00000FF0 Z=0  00000FF8:00000502  s+8
D0=00000000 D1=00000000 D2=00000000 D3=00000000 V=0  00000FFC:00000500  s+12
D4=00000000 D5=00000000 D6=00000000 D7=00000000 C=0  00001000:00000000  s+16
----->MOVEA.L  $08(SP),A1


Trace>
PC=000430 SR=2000 SS=00000FF0 US=00000000      X=0  00000FF0:0000041A  s
A0=00000500 A1=00000502 A2=00000000 A3=00000000 N=0  00000FF4:00000504  s+4
A4=00000000 A5=00000000 A6=00000000 A7=00000FF0 Z=0  00000FF8:00000502  s+8
D0=00000000 D1=00000000 D2=00000000 D3=00000000 V=0  00000FFC:00000500  s+12
D4=00000000 D5=00000000 D6=00000000 D7=00000000 C=0  00001000:00000000  s+16
----->MOVE.W   (A0),D2


Trace>
PC=000432 SR=2000 SS=00000FF0 US=00000000      x=0  00000FF0:0000041A  s
A0=00000500 A1=00000502 A2=00000000 A3=00000000 N=0  00000FF4:00000504  s+4
A4=00000000 A5=00000000 A6=00000000 A7=00000FF0 Z=0  00000FF8:00000502  s+8
D0=00000000 D1=00000000 D2=00000001 D3=00000000 V=0  00000FFC:00000500  s+12
D4=00000000 D5=00000000 D6=00000000 D7=00000000 C=0  00001000:00000000  s+16
----->MOVE.W   (A1),D3


Trace>
PC=000434 SR=2000 SS=00000FF0 US=00000000      X=0  00000FF0:0000041A  s
A0=00000500 A1=00000502 A2=00000000 A3=00000000 N=0  00000FF4:00000504  s+4
A4=00000000 A5=00000000 A6=00000000 A7=00000FF0 Z=0  00000FF8:00000502  s+8
D0=00000000 D1=00000000 D2=00000001 D3=00000002 V=0  00000FFC:00000500  s+12
D4=00000000 D5=00000000 D6=00000000 D7=00000000 C=0  00001000:00000000  s+16
----->ADD.W    D2,D3


Trace>
PC=000436 SR=2000 SS=00000FF0 US=00000000      X=0  00000FF0:0000041A  s
A0=00000500 A1=00000502 A2=00000000 A3=00000000 N=0  00000FF4:00000504  s+4
A4=00000000 A5=00000000 A6=00000000 A7=00000FF0 Z=0  00000FF8:00000502  s+8
D0=00000000 D1=00000000 D2=00000001 D3=00000003 V=0  00000FFC:00000500  s+12
D4=00000000 D5=00000000 D6=00000000 D7=00000000 C=0  00001000:00000000  s+16
----->MOVEA.L  $04(SP),A3
```

```
Trace>
PC=00043A SR=2000 SS=00000FF0 US=00000000        X=0  00000FF0:0000041A  s
A0=00000500 A1=00000502 A2=00000000 A3=00000504 N=0  00000FF4:00000504  s+4
A4=00000000 A5=00000000 A6=00000000 A7=00000FF0 Z=0  00000FF8:00000502  s+8
D0=00000000 D1=00000000 D2=00000001 D3=00000003 V=0  00000FFC:00000500  s+12
D4=00000000 D5=00000000 D6=00000000 D7=00000000 C=0  00001000:00000000  s+16
----->MOVE.W    D3,(A3)

Trace>
PC=00043C SR=2000 SS=00000FF0 US=00000000        X=0  00000FF0:0000041A  s
A0=00000500 A1=00000502 A2=00000000 A3=00000504 N=0  00000FF4:00000504  s+4
A4=00000000 A5=00000000 A6=00000000 A7=00000FF0 Z=0  00000FF8:00000502  s+8
D0=00000000 D1=00000000 D2=00000001 D3=00000003 V=0  00000FFC:00000500  s+12
D4=00000000 D5=00000000 D6=00000000 D7=00000000 C=0  00001000:00000000  s+16
----->RTS

Trace>
PC=00041A SR=2000 SS=00000FF4 US=00000000        X=0  00000FF4:00000504  s
A0=00000500 A1=00000502 A2=00000000 A3=00000504 N=0  00000FF8:00000502  s+4
A4=00000000 A5=00000000 A6=00000000 A7=00000FF4 Z=0  00000FFC:00000500  s+8
D0=00000000 D1=00000000 D2=00000001 D3=00000003 V=0  00001000:00000000  s+12
D4=00000000 D5=00000000 D6=00000000 D7=00000000 C=0  00001004:00000000  s+16
----->MOVE.W    $0504,D2

Trace>
PC=000420 SR=2000 SS=00000FF4 US=00000000        X=0  00000FF4:00000504  s
A0=00000500 A1=00000502 A2=00000000 A3=00000504 N=0  00000FF8:00000502  s+4
A4=00000000 A5=00000000 A6=00000000 A7=00000FF4 Z=0  00000FFC:00000500  s+8
D0=00000000 D1=00000000 D2=00000003 D3=00000003 V=0  00001000:00000000  s+12
D4=00000000 D5=00000000 D6=00000000 D7=00000000 C=0  00001004:00000000  s+16
----->LEA.L     $0C(SP),SP

Trace>
PC=000424 SR=2000 SS=00001000 US=00000000        X=0  00001000:00000000  s
A0=00000500 A1=00000502 A2=00000000 A3=00000504 N=0  00001004:00000000  s+4
A4=00000000 A5=00000000 A6=00000000 A7=00001000 Z=0  00001008:00000000  s+8
D0=00000000 D1=00000000 D2=00000003 D3=00000003 V=0  0000100C:00000000  s+12
D4=00000000 D5=00000000 D6=00000000 D7=00000000 C=0  00001010:00000000  s+16
----->STOP      #$2700
```

If we look at memory again, we will find that the sum of X and Y has been stored in location Z.

```
>MD 500
000500 00  01  00  02  00  03  00  00  00  00  00  00  00  00  00  00.
```

We have passed the parameters by reference. In practice, a programmer would pass parameters that aren't changed in the subroutine by value, and only pass parameters that are to be changed by reference.

6.5.5 Example of a 68K program

We now put together some of the things we've learned about the 68K's instruction set, and write a simple program to implement a text matching algorithm that determines whether a string contains a certain substring. The problem can be solved by sliding the substring along the string until each character of the substring matches with the corresponding character of the string, as illustrated in Fig. 6.39.

The string starts at address $002000 and is terminated by a carriage return (ASCII code $0D). The substring is stored at location $002100 onwards, and is also terminated by a carriage return. In what follows, the string of characters is referred to as STRING, and the substring as TEXT.

We will construct a main program that calls a subroutine, MATCH, to scan the string for the first occurrence of the substring. Because STRING and TEXT are both strings of consecutive characters, we will pass them to MATCH by reference. The subroutine should return the address of the first

String	THIS	THAT	THEN	THE	OTHER
Substring	THEN	THE			

Step	Matches	THIS	THAT	THEN	THE	OTHER
1	2	THEN THE				
2	0	THEN THE				
3	0	THEN THE				
4	0	THEN THE				
5	0	THEN THE				
6	2	THEN THE				
7	0	THEN THE				
8	0	THEN THE				
9	1	THEN THE				
10	0	THEN THE				
11	**8**	**THEN THE**				
12	0	THEN THE				
13	0	THEN THE				

Fig. 6.39 Matching a string and a substring.

character in the string matching the first character of the substring. This address is to be returned on the stack. If the match is unsuccessful, the null address, $00000000, is pushed on the stack.

```
CRET       EQU      $0D                  ASCII code for carriage return
*
           ORG      $400                 Start of the main program
           LEA      $1000,A7             Set up the stack pointer
           PEA      STRING               Push the address of the string
           PEA      TEXT                 Push the address of the substring
           LEA      -4(A7),A7            Make room on the stack for the result
           BSR      MATCH                Perform the match
           MOVE.L   (A7)+,D0             Let's have a look at the result
           LEA      8(A7),A7             Clean up the stack (remove the 2 parameters)
           STOP     #$2700
*
*
*          MATCH matches the substring whose location is pointed at by
*          A0 with the string whose location is pointed at by A1.
*          Both strings are terminated by a carriage return.
*
*          The match is carried out by comparing the first character of
*          the substring with the characters of the string, one by one.
*          If a match is found, the rest of the characters of the
*          substring are matched with the corresponding characters of
*          the string. If they all match up to the substring terminator,
*          the search is successful. As soon as a mismatch is found, we
*          return to matching the first character of the substring with
*          a character from the string. If the terminator of the string
*          is reached, the search has been unsuccessful.
*
MATCH      MOVEM.L D0/A0-A3,-(A7)        Save all working registers
           MOVEA.L 32(A7),A0            Get STRING address off the stack
           MOVEA.L 28(A7),A1            Get TEXT (substring) address off the stack
```

```
*
NEXT        MOVE.B    (A0)+,D0           Get a character from the string
            CMP.B     #CRET,D0           Is this character a carriage return?
            BEQ       FAIL               If carriage return then no match so exit
            CMP.B     (A1),D0            Match character with char from substring
            BNE       NEXT               If no match then move along the string
*
*           We have found the first match.
*           We have to save the two pointers before performing the
*           submatch in case we have to return to matching the pairs
*           of first characters.
*
            MOVEA.L   A0,A2              Save A0 in A2 in case of no full match
            MOVEA.L   A1,A3              Save A1 in A3
            ADDA.L    #1,A1              Increment pointer to substring
*
LOOP        MOVE.B    (A1)+,D0           Get next character from substring
            CMP.B     #CRET,D0           If terminator found then success
            BEQ       SUCCESS
            CMP.B     (A0)+,D0           Else compare it with next char from string
            BEQ       LOOP               Repeat while they match
*
*           No submatch found so prepare to continue matching pairs
*           of first characters.
*
            MOVEA.L   A2,A0              Restore A0 and A1
            MOVEA.L   A3,A1              to their values before the submatch
            BRA       NEXT               Try again
*
SUCCESS     SUBA.L    #1,A2              Undo work of auto increment
            MOVE.L    A2,24(A7)          Push address of match on stack
            BRA       RETURN
*
FAIL        MOVE.L    #0,24(A7)          Push null address on stack for fail
*
RETURN      MOVEM.L   (A7)+,D0/A0-A3     Restore all working registers
            RTS
*
            ORG       $002000            Location of the string
STRING      DC.B      'THIS THAT THEN',$0D
            ORG       $002100            Location of substring to be matched
TEXT        DC.C      'THEN THE',$0D
*
            END       $400
```

Now that we have looked at the 68K's instruction set and addressing modes, the next step is to consider how we might go about designing a 68K assembly language program.

6.6 Designing assembly language programs

We're now going to briefly discuss the design of simple assembly language programs. We don't intend to cover assembly programming in detail, as that would depart too far

from the scope of this text. Equally, it is unreasonable to introduce the CPU and assembly language without at least indicating how assembly language programs are put together. Most students will never write extensive assembly language programs—not least because of the availability of so many high-level languages.

6.6.1 Writing programs in pseudocode

A convenient way of transforming a requirement (e.g. for a word processor or a database) into a program is to use pseudocode as an intermediate step. Pseudocode is so called because it is not a formal computer language, but offers programmers a way of expressing algorithms in a top-down and structured fashion without all the complexity of a real language like Pascal or Java.

As an example of pseudocode, consider how we might express the sequence of actions involved in getting up and going to work. We can do this most easily by initially concentrating only on what we want to do and leaving the details of how we actually carry out individual actions until a later stage.

Our first-level pseudocode may be written in the form

```
Go_To_Work
      Get_Up
      Wash
      Dress
      Have_Breakfast
      Drive_To_Work
End Go_To_Work
```

At this stage we have simply defined the major sequence of activities involved in getting up and going to work. As yet, we have not filled in any of the details. It is possible to use any of a large number of conventions to represent actions in pseudocode. Some use bold text to represent actions, some use underscores to link words (e.g. `Drive_to_work`), as I have done here, and some concatenate the words and start each new word with an upper-case character.

A second-level pseudocode elaborates on each of the individual actions. For example, `Have_Breakfast` can be elaborated as

```
Have_Breakfast
      Make_Coffee
      Boil_Egg
      Butter_Bread
      Eat_Breakfast
      Wash_Dishes
End Have_Breakfast
```

The process of elaboration may be continued until we reach the point at which each action at the pseudocode level can be replaced by a relatively small number of instructions in the appropriate computer language.

6.6.2 Conditional behavior

In this section we take a step backwards and go over material we have already introduced. This apparently retrograde step is necessary because converting a problem into assembly language is not a trivial task. In particular, beginners sometimes have more problems with conditional behavior than with any other aspect of assembly language programming (apart from addressing modes).

Conventional computers execute programs sequentially instruction-by-instruction. This is true of both low-level assembly language programs and high-level language programs. However, there are three occasions when a computer does not follow this pattern and executes instructions out of their natural sequence. The first is when an interrupt originating in hardware affects the sequence of operations. For example, a disk drive may interrupt the flow of operation by demanding attention, because it is ready to receive new data.

A second case of non-sequential behavior is caused by unconditional branch and jump instructions. Examples are GOTO (in high-level languages) and BRA (branch) or JMP (jump) in low-level languages.

The third case of non-sequential behavior is the conditional branch that forces the computer to take one of two or more courses of action, depending on the result of a prior action or calculation. We are going to show how conditional behavior is implemented in a low-level language. But before we do this, we look at conditional behavior in a broader context.

Conditional behavior is a part of everyday life. Consider the following example:

```
Wake_Up
Dress
Have_Breakfast
If before 8 am Walk_To_Work
If after 8 am Drive_To_Work
Start_Work
```

In this example, two possible activities may take place after the activity Have_Breakfast. Either we walk to work or we drive to work. Conditional behavior requires that we test a variable (i.e. the time) and then execute one of two actions.

Typical high-level languages express conditional behavior in the form of an IF THEN ELSE construct.

```
Wake_Up
Dress
Have_Breakfast
IF before 8 am THEN Walk_To_Work
               ELSE Drive_To_Work
Start_Work
```

In more formal terms, we can write the expression in the form IF L THEN S1 ELSE S2, where L is a Boolean expression that has the value true or false, and S1 and S2 are executable actions. Thus, if the Boolean expression L is true, action S1 is executed and, if L is false, action S2 is executed. In the previous example, L is 'Is the time before 8 am', S1 is 'Walk_To_Work' and S2 is 'Drive_To_Work'.

Note that there is a joining up after the conditional behavior—it doesn't matter how we get to work; once there, we `Start_Work`.

High-level languages permit quite complex expressions for the Boolean value L. For example, we may write

`IF x > 3.6 OR y+2 < x2 THEN S1 ELSE S2`

Summary

In this chapter we have both looked at the programming model of a typical high-performance microprocessor family and introduced the way in which assembly language programs can be constructed. Probably the most difficult aspect of any microprocessor's assembly language is its addressing modes. Although the 68K has a larger range of addressing modes than earlier 8-bit devices, its addressing modes are not particularly difficult to understand, since they follow a regular pattern. However, it is not just the addressing modes themselves that are difficult to understand but the way in which they are used. Perhaps one of the best ways of approaching addressing modes is to ask 'what problems do they solve?' Thus, instead of learning how indexed addressing operates, it is better to consider a problem such as accessing an element in an array that could not be solved easily without resorting to indexed addressing.

Problems

Because assembly language is a core subject in this text, we have provided a series of tutorials rather than a simple list of end-of-chapter problems. These tutorials include background material as well as the problems themselves. We have also provided some solutions to the problems.

Tutorial 1

1. **The memory map** For the memory map below, evaluate the following expressions, where [M(N)] means *the contents of the memory location whose address is N*. All addresses and their contents are decimal values.

Addr	Value
00	12
01	17
02	7
03	4
04	8
05	4
06	4
07	6
08	0
09	5
10	12
11	7
12	6

(a) [M(7)]
(b) [M([M(4)])]
(c) [M([M([M(0)])])]
(d) [M(2+10)]
(e) [M([M(9)]+2)]
(f) [M([M(9)]+[M(2)])]
(g) [M([M(5)]+[M(8)]+2 * [M(6)])]
(h) [M(0)] * 3+[M(1)] * 4
(i) [M(9)] * [M(10)]

The 68K microprocessor has eight data registers D0 to D7, and eight address registers A0 to A7. Data registers are used as *general-purpose* storage elements during calculations. Address registers are used as pointers. That is, an address register contains the *address* of an operand in memory and is used to *point* to this item in memory. In 68K assembly language, the use of an address register as a *pointer* is indicated by enclosing the address register in round brackets. The assembly language notation (A2) means *the memory location pointed at by the contents of address register A2;* for example, MOVE (A2),D3.

An operand in an assembly language instruction normally represents a *location (i.e. address)* in memory; for example, MOVE source,destination means copy the contents of the *source* location to the *destination* location. Similarly, MOVE 1234,2222 causes the 68K to read the contents of location 1234 and to put the value read from that location in address 2222. The instruction ADD source,destination adds the contents of the *source* location to the contents of the *destination* location and puts the sum in the *destination* location. A number prefixed by the hash symbol, '#' (e.g. #12), represents an *actual* or *literal* value and is not a reference to a memory location. ADD #4,D3 adds the value 4 to the contents of data register D3.

2. Register Transfer Language

Describe the action of the following 68K assembly language instructions in RTL, register transfer language. That is, translate the assembly language syntax of the 68K instruction into the RTL notation that defines the action of the instruction.

(a)	MOVE	3,4	(g)	MOVE	(A0),D3
(b)	MOVE	D0,D4	(h)	MOVE	#12,(A0)
(c)	MOVE	3,D0	(i)	MOVE	(A1),(A2)
(d)	MOVE	D0,3	(j)	ADD	D2,D1
(e)	MOVE	#4,D4	(k)	ADD	#13,D4
(f)	MOVE	#4,5	(l)	ADD	(A3),1234

3. Misconceptions

This question asks you to explain why some assembly language operations, and some RTL expressions, are incorrect. Before attempting the question, the following notes will help you.

- Address and data registers are not part of the CPU's external memory. However, registers hold *data* or *information* exactly like memory locations.
- The 68K CPU accesses a memory location by giving the memory an *address*; for example, CLR 1234 clears (i.e. sets to zero) the contents of memory location 1234. A data or address register doesn't have an address because the *name* of the register is, effectively, its address, for example CLR D2.
- A computer doesn't *need* data registers. However, data registers are very useful because they can be accessed more rapidly than locations in memory.

- The instruction MOVE.L A3,D0 is translated into RTL as [D0] ← [A3], and means *copy the contents of address register A3 into data register D0*. If you see the instruction MOVE.L (A3),D0 in a program it can't possibly have the effect [D0] ← [A3]. You cannot have *identical* instructions with *different syntaxes* that do the *same* things. The instruction MOVE (A3),D0 has the effect [D3] ← [M([A0])].

- The instruction MOVE (A0),D6 means *copy the data pointed at by the contents of address register A0 into D6*. In the figure below, address register A0 contains the value 1005 and therefore points to location 1005 in memory. If you use the effective address, (A0), in an assembly language instruction you will access memory location 1005. For example, CLR.B 1005 and CLR.B (A0) have the same effect (assuming A0 contains 1005).

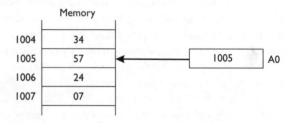

- In 68K assembly language the symbol '#' is used as a prefix to indicate that the following value is a *literal* (i.e. immediate or constant) value and not a reference to a memory location. This symbol is not used in RTL.

Assembly language	RTL definition	In English
MOVE 4,D6	[D6] ← [M(4)]	Copy contents of location 4 into D6
MOVE #4,D6	[D6] ← 4	Put the value 4 in D6
MOVE (A0),D6	[D6] ← [M([A0])]	Put the value pointed at by A0 in D6

- The RTL expression [D3] means *the contents of data register D3* (i.e. whatever is in data register D3). The contents of a data register or a memory location are a string of ones and zeros that may represent anything you want (an instruction, a number, one or more characters, part of an image, etc.).
- You cannot write the expression A3 = 4 in RTL, as it would mean that address register A3 is the same as the number 4. The correct expression is [A3] = 4 which means that address register 3 holds the value 4. The RTL expression D3 ← 4 is also meaningless. The expression should be [D3] ← 4 which means that 4 is copied into D3.

Consider the following 68K assembly language instructions expressed in both RTL and plain English.

Explain why the following assembly language and RTL constructs are incorrect.

(a)	MOVE D3,#4		(d)	[D3] ← A0 + 3
(b)	MOVE [D3],D2		(e)	[D3] ← #3
(c)	MOVE (D3),D2		(f)	3 ← [D3]

4.

Use an ASCII editor to create a simple 68K program called ADDER.X68. The program is to be assembled with the 68K cross-assembler and then run on the 68K simulator. Your program should add together the numbers: 6, 4, 12, 16, 17, and 50. After you have created your program, cross-assemble it with the command X68K ADDER -L to create a binary (i.e. an object) file and a listing file. Run the binary file you have created in the simulation mode with the command E68K ADDER.

In the simulation mode of E68K you can:

- Modify the contents of memory locations with MM (memory modify)
- Ready the contents of memory locations with MD (memory display)
- Read the 68K's registers with DF (display registers)
- Modify the contents of a register with .reg value (e.g., PC 1000)

- Step through the program an instruction at a time with TR (trace)
- Use the HE (help) facility to see what the simulator offers

5. Give examples of valid 68K assembly language instructions that use:

a. register-to-register addressing
b. register-to-memory addressing
c. memory-to-register addressing
d. memory-to-memory addressing

Using the 68K cross-assembler

The following 68K assembly language program illustrates what an assembler does. This is not a real program—it is designed only to illustrate some points. The source program is followed by its assembled listing file produced by X68K. Examine both the source code and listing file, and try to follow what is happening.

The following code was produced by the 68K cross-assembler from the above source code.

```
               ORG     $400
Test    EQU    6                Dummy equates
Alan    EQU    7
XXX     DS.W   2                Save two words of storage
YYY     DC.L   $12345678        Put the longword $12345678 in memory
Name    DC.B   'Clements'       Put an ASCII string in memory
        DC.B   $FF
        DC.L   Test+Name        Store a 32-bit constant
        DC.B   4                Put 4 in memory
        MOVE.L #Name,A0
Next    MOVE.B (A0)+,D0          Pick up a character
        CMP.B  #$FF,D0           Test for end of string
        BEQ    Exit              And exit on terminator
        BSR    Print             Print a character
        BRA    Next              Repeat
Exit    STOP   #$2700            Halt the 68K
*
Print   NOP                      Dummy subroutine
        NOP
        RTS                      Return
*
        END    $400              END needed ($400 is start address)
```

Source file: ASDIR.X68
Assembled on: 94-02-27 at: 18:19:31
        by: X68K PC-2.1 Copyright (c) University of Teesside 1989,93
Defaults: ORG $0/FORMAT/OPT A,BRL,CEX,CL,FRL,MC,MD,NOMEX,NOPCO

```
 1 00001000                     ORG     $400
 2          00000006    TEST:   EQU    6             ;Dummy equates
 3          00000007    ALAN:   EQU    7
 4 00001000 00000004    XXX:    DS.W   2             ;Save two words of storage
 5 00001004 12345678    YYY:    DC.L   $12345678     ;Put longword $12345678 in memory
 6 00001008 436C656D656E NAME:  DC.B   'Clements'    ;Put an ASCII string in memory
          7473
 7 00001010 FF                  DC.B   $FF
 8 00001012 0000100E            DC.L   TEST+NAME     ;Store a 32-bit constant
 9 00001016 04                  DC.B   4             ;Put 4 in memory
10 00001018 207C00001008        MOVE.L #NAME,A0
11 0000101E 1018        NEXT:   MOVE.B (A0)+,D0       ;Pick up a character
12 00001020 0C0000FF            CMP.B  #$FF,D0        ;Test for end of string
13 00001024 67000008            BEQ    EXIT           ;And exit on terminator
14 00001028 61000008            BSR    PRINT          ;Print a character
```

```
15 0000102C 60F0                        BRA     NEXT        ;Repeat
16 0000102E 4E722700       EXIT:   STOP    #$2700      ;Halt the 68K
17                         *
18 00001032 4E71           PRINT:  NOP                 ;Dummy subroutine
19 00001034 4E71                   NOP
20 00001036 4E75                   RTS                 ;Return
21                         *
22         00000400                END     $400        ;END needed ($400 is start address)
```

Lines: 22, Errors: 0, Warnings: 0.

The first column provides the line number. The second column defines the location in memory into which data and instructions go. The third column contains the instructions and the constants generated by the assembler. The remainder is the original assembly language program. Consider line 8:

```
8 00001012 0000100E             DC.L      TEST+NAME                ;Store a 32-bit constant
```

The constant is TEST+NAME. In line 2 TEST was equated to 6 (i.e. the assembler automatically substitutes 6 for TEST). But what is 'NAME'? On line 6, NAME is used as a label and refers to the address (or location in memory) of the code on this line. This address is $1008. Therefore, the constant to be stored is 6+$1008=$100E. You can see that this really is the value stored from column 3 in line 8. Line 10 has the location $1018 and not $1017 because all word (and longword) addresses MUST be even. The following notes will help you understand the assembly process.

- The PC 68K simulator system requires an ORG $400 statement. This is the point at which code or data can be located in the 68K's memory.
- You must not locate data in the middle of a section of code. The microprocessor executes instructions sequentially and will regard embedded data as instructions. Put data between the end of the executable instructions of a program and the END assembler directive. For example:

```
       MOVE.B  D3,D4            The last instruction `
       STOP    #$2700           This stops the 68K dead in its tracks
Data1  DC.B    'This is data'
Test   DS.B    4                Save 4 bytes of storage
       END     $400             The END directive is that last item in a program
```

The only way that you can locate data in the middle of a program is by jumping past it like this:

```
         MOVE.B  D3,D4            An instruction
         BRA     Continue         Jump past the data
Data1    DC.B    'This is data'   Put the string here
Test     DS.B    4                Save 4 bytes of storage
Continue ADD.B   #1,D6            Back to the instructions....
```

- You can halt a 68K by executing the STOP #<data> instruction that stops the 68K and loads the 16-bit value <data> into its status register. The conventional value for <data> is $2700.
- I saw a student's program that began with the operation MOVE.B (A0),D0 which loads D0 with the byte pointed at by address register A0. But what is the *initial* value of A0? You have to set up A0 before you can use it (or any other variable). In spite of advances in modern technology and Mr Motorola's exceedingly good chips, none of them have clairvoyant registers that can read a student's mind.
- You call a subroutine with a BSR Name or a JSR Name instruction. This is the *only* way you call a subroutine. You cannot call a subroutine with a conditional branch (BEQ, BNE, BCC, etc.).
- Operations on data values are 8-bit, 16-bit, or 32-bit, and instructions take .B, .W, or .L extensions. Make sure that you always use the correct data size and use it consistently. Operations on address registers are always .L because an address register holds a 32-bit *pointer*. A .W operation is permitted on an address register but the result is treated as a two's complement value and sign-extended to 32 bits.

- The END address assembler directive terminates the assembly process (i.e. no instructions beyond this point are assembled). The address provides the location from which the 68K begins executing code.

Basic 68K instructions

The 68K microprocessor has a very rich instruction set. However, you will find that the following instructions can be used to write a surprisingly large range of programs. The expression <ea> means *effective address* and denotes any legal addressing mode for that instruction.

```
MOVE      <ea>,Di          Move source to destination
MOVE      Di,<ea>
MOVEA     <ea>,Ai          Move source to destination address register
ADD       <ea>,Di          Add source to destination
ADD       Di,<ea>
SUB       <ea>,Di          Subtract source from destination
SUB       Di,<ea>
CMP       <ea>,Di          Compare source with destination
CMP       Di,<ea>
BEQ       address          Branch on zero (i.e. Z-bit of CCR=1)
BNE       address          Branch on not zero (i.e. Z-bit of CCR=0)
BRA       address          Branch unconditionally (i.e. goto)
MULU      <ea>,Di          Multiply 16-bit source by 16-bit destination. Put 32-bit result in destination
CLR       <ea>             Clear contents of destination
LEA       Value,Ai         Put an address in an address register
LEA       Value(Aj),Ai
```

Partial solutions to Tutorial 1

1. (a) $[M(7)]=6$
   (c) $[M([M([M(0)])])]=[M([M(12)])]$
   $\qquad =[M(6)]=4$
   (e) $[M([M(9)]+2)]=[M(5+2)]=[M(7)]=6$
   (g) $[M([M(5)]+[M(8)]+2*[M(6)])]$
   $\qquad =[M(4+0+2*4)]=[M(12)]=6$
   (i) $[M(9)] * [M(10)]=5 * 12=60$

2. **Mnemonic form**   **RTL form**

   (a) MOVE 3,4 $[M(4)] \leftarrow [M(3)]$
   (c) MOVE 3,D0 $[D0] \leftarrow [M(3)]$
   (e) MOVE #4,D4 $[D4] \leftarrow 4$
   (g) MOVE (A0),D3 $[D3] \leftarrow [M([A0])]$
   (i) MOVE (A1),(A2) $[M([A2])] \leftarrow [M([A1])]$
   (k) ADD #13,D4 $[D4] \leftarrow [D4]+13$

3. (a) MOVE D3,#4   You cannot move a value into a literal

   (c) MOVE (D3),D2   You can't use a data register as a pointer to a memory location
   (e) $[D3] \leftarrow$ #3   The symbol # indicates a literal in *assembly language* not in *RTL*.

Tutorial 2

1. By means of a memory map explain the effect of the following sequence of 68K assembly language directives. Note that the 68K can operate with three sizes of operand: byte (8 bits); word (16 bits); and longword (32 bits).

```
        ORG    $600
        DS.L   2
        DC.L   2
        DC.B   '123'
Time    DC.B   6
Top     DS.B   6
BSc1    EQU    2
IT1     EQU    3
SE1     DS.B   IT1+BSc1
```

2. What would the following 68K assembly language fragment store at address $1002?

```
        ORG    $1000
P       EQU    5
Q       DS.B   2
One     DC.W   P+Q
```

3. What is wrong with each of the following 68K assembly language operations?

    (a) `MOVE     Temp,#4`
    (b) `ADD.B    #1,A3`

    (c) `CMP.L    D0,#9`
    (d) `MOVE.B   #500,D5`
    (e) `DS.B     1,2`
    (f) `ADD.W    +(A2),D3`
    (g) `ORG      #400`
    (h) `BEQ.B    Loop_3`

4. *Translating common high-level constructs into assembly language* The four blocks of code below will help you to answer the following question. Remember that ORG, DC.W, and DS.W are assembler directives and not 68K assembly language instructions.

```
Example (a) Z := X+Y

        ORG    $400      Start of data area
X       DC.W   $1234     Put the constant 1234₁₆ in memory
Y       DC.W   1234      Put the constant 1234 in memory
Z       DS.W   1         Reserve one word of memory for Z
        ORG    $500      Put code here
        MOVE.W X,D0      Copy X to D0
        ADD.W  Y,D0      Add Y to D0
        MOVE.W D0,Z      Put D0 in Z
```

```
Example (b) Z := X+Y+4

        ORG    $400
X       DC.W   $1234
Y       DC.W   1234
Z       DS.W   1
        MOVE.W X,D0
        ADD.W  Y,D0
        ADD.W  #4,D0     Add 4 to D0
        MOVE.W D0,Z
```

```
Example (c) FOR I := 0 to 9
              X(I) := X(I)+6
            END_FOR

        ORG    $400        Start of data
X       DS.W   10          Save 10 words for array X
        ORG    $500        Start of program
        CLR.W  D0          Use D0 as counter I
        LEA    X,A0        A0 points to start of array X
LOOP    MOVE.W (A0),D1     Get element X(I)
        ADD.W  #6,D1       Add 6 to get X(I)+6
        MOVE.W D1,(A0)+    Put it back in memory and point to next
        ADD.W  #1,D0       Increment element counter
        CMP.W  #10,D0      REPEAT
        BNE    LOOP
```

```
Example (d) IF Q=4 THEN
                            X := 5
                    ELSE
                            X := Y
        ORG       $400
X       DS.W      1         Reserve a word for X
Y       DS.W      1         Reserve a word for Y
Q       DS.W      1         Reserve a word for Q
        ORG       $500
        CMPI.W    #4,Q      Compare Q with 4
        BNE       ELSE      IF Q ≠ 4 THEN goto 'ELSE'
        MOVE.W    #5,X      IF Q = 4 THEN X := 5
        BRA       EXIT      Skip past 'ELSE' part
ELSE    MOVE.W    Y,X       ELSE part (X := Y)
EXIT    ............        Leave the program
```

The value of Q is compared with the literal '4' by CMPI.W #4,Q. A comparison instruction causes the Z-bit, N-bit, and C-bit of the conditional code register to be updated. If the two values being compared are the same, the result of the subtraction is zero and the Z-bit is set to 1 to indicate a zero result. CMPI.W #4,Q is a *literal-to-memory* operation ('I' indicates 'immediate' to memory').

The instruction BNE ELSE forces a branch to the line beginning with 'ELSE' if the result of the comparison was not zero (i.e. Q ≠ 4). The line beginning ELSE sets the value of X to Y (i.e. causes the ELSE part of the instruction to be executed).

If the value of Q is equal to 4, the result of the comparison sets the Z-bit of the CCR. When the BNE ELSE instruction is executed, the branch is not taken and the following instruction, MOVE.W #5,X, is executed. This action corresponds to the THEN part of the code.

(a) Read through the above blocks of code and answer the following questions.

   (i) What is the effect of the assembler directive ORG $400?

   (ii) What is the effect of the assembler directive DS.W 20?

   (iii) What is the effect of the assembler directive DC.W 1234?

   (iv) What is the effect of the assembler directive DC.W $1234?

   (v) What is the effect of the '+' in the effective address (A0)+?

(b) What is wrong with the following fragment of 68K assembly language (the error is one of semantics; that is, the meaning of the code is incorrect).

```
        CMP.W     #4,Q      IF Q=4 THEN X := 5 ELSE X := Y
        BNE       ELSE      IF Q≠4 THEN goto 'ELSE'
THEN    MOVE.W    #5,X      IF Q=4 THEN X := 5
ELSE    MOVE.W    Y,X       ELSE part (i.e. X := Y)
EXIT    ...                 Leave the program
```

(c) Translate the following fragment of high-level language into 68K assembly language.

```
IF T=5
    THEN X=4
END_IF
```

Assume that T and X are in memory. Write a program to implement this fragment of code and run it on the 68K simulator. Select your own values for variables T and X. Use the simulator's trace mode to observe the behavior of the program.

(d) Translate the following fragment of high-level language into 68K assembly language. Use the 68K simulator to test your program.

```
IF T=5
    THEN X=4
    ELSE Y=5
END_IF
```

5. The 68K can operate with *byte*, *word*, and *longword* operands. What does this mean? Which type of operand do you use in any particular circumstance?

6. Explain what the following 68K program does. Use the 68K simulator to test your observations.

```
        MOVE.B    #20,D0
Again   MOVEA.L   #$1000,A0
        CLR.B     (A0)
        ADDA.L    #1,A0
        SUB.B     #1,D0
        BNE       Again
```

Partial solutions to Tutorial 2

2. What would the following code store at address $1002?

```
        ORG   $1000
P       EQU   5
Q       DS.B  2
One     DC.W  P+Q
```

The operation ORG $1000 sets the *location counter* to 1000_{16}. The line P EQU 5 equates the symbolic name 'P' with the value 5. In future, if you write 'P' the assembler regards it as '5'. Note that the EQU directive does not generate any code or affect memory allocation. The line Q DS.B 2 reserves two bytes of storage in memory. The addresses of these two bytes are 1000_{16} and 1001_{16}. The label 'Q' in the first column assigns the value of the current address to 'Q'; that is, Q = 1000. Finally, the line One DC.W P+Q stores the 16-bit constant given by P+Q in memory. P = 5 and Q = 1000, therefore, the value 1005_{16} is stored in memory. This is stored at memory location 1002_{16} because the previous directive, DS.B 2, takes up two bytes. The following listing was produced by the 68K cross-assembler.

```
1  00001000                    ORG    $1000
2            00000005   P:      EQU    5
3  00001000  00000002   Q:      DS.B   2
4  00001002  1005       ONE:    DC.W   P+Q
```

3. What is wrong with each of the following 68K assembly language operations?

(a) MOVE	Temp,#4	You cannot move a value to a literal (operand order wrong)
(b) ADD.B	#1,A3	You cannot perform a byte operation on an address register
(c) CMP.L	D0,#9	Same as (a). The instruction should be CMP.L #9,D0
(d) MOVE.B	#500,D5	The operand is a byte, yet the literal is too big to hold in a byte
(e) DS.B	1,2	You can't have multiple operands with this directive
(f) ADD.W	+(A2),D3	The addressing mode +(A2) is illegal. (A2)+ is legal
(g) ORG	#400	This assembler directive should be ORG $400
(h) BEQ.B	Loop_3	A BEQ takes no .B extension. There is a legal .S extension to BEQ. The form BEQ.S forces a 'short' 8-bit displacement.

sequence of equal length is stored at memory location $700 onward. Each sequence ends with the character $0D (i.e. the ASCII value for a *carriage return*). Write a 68K assembly language program to determine whether or not these two strings are identical. If they are identical, place the value $00 in data register D0. If they are not, place the value $FF in D0.

Use the 68K cross-assembler and simulator to write the program and test it.

Modify your program to use the simulator's character input routine to input the two strings into memory. The simulator's character input code that puts a byte into D1 is

```
Get_char  MOVE.B  #5,D0
          TRAP    #15
```

2. A sequence of ASCII-encoded characters is stored at memory location $600 onwards and is terminated by a $0D. Write a program to reverse the order of the sequence (i.e. the first value at location $600 will now be $0D which was the old end of the string).

Use the 68K simulator to input a string and print it in reverse order.

The simulator's character output code that prints the byte in D1 is

```
Put_char  MOVE.B  #6,D0
          TRAP    #15
```

Tutorial 3

1. A sequence, or *string* of one-byte ASCII characters, is stored at memory location $600 onward. A second

3. The following program contains both syntax and semantic errors. What is the difference between these two types of error? Locate both types of error.

```
* This is a program designed to locate the smallest number in a table
*
        ORG     #400
Numbers DS.B    42,3,060,20,8,9,$A,$C,7,2,$F,5AF,8,600,0A,9,40,6,#FF
        MOVE.B  #Numbers,A0   A0 points to table of numbers
        CLR.B   D0            Current smallest number
N_2     MOVE.B  (A0),D1       Get a number
        ADD.B   #1,A1         Point to next number
```

```
        CMP.B   D0,D1           Is new number lower?
        BGE     N_1
        MOVE.B  D1,D0           Keep new low number
N_1     CMP.B   D1,#$FF         Check for end
        BNE     N_2
        BRA     Print           Print it
        END     $400
*
Print   MOVE.B  #5,D1
        TRAP    #15
        RTS
        STOP    #$2700
```

4. Examine the following fragment of pseudocode and its translation into 68K assembly language. Work through this code and ensure that you understand it. Is the program correct? Can you improve it?

```
*           X := 5
*           Y := 7
*           FOR I := 1 TO 9
*                   Y := Y + I
*                   IF T(I) = J(I) + X THEN J(I) := T(I) * 4-Y
*                                      ELSE J(I) := J(I) - T(I)
*           END_FOR
*
            ORG   $400
            MOVEA #T,A0     A0 points at base of array T
            MOVEA #J,A1     A1 points at base of array J
            MOVE  #1,D0     Use D0 as a counter to hold I
            MOVE  #5,D1     X := 5; D1 is X
            MOVE  #7,D2     Y := 7; D2 is Y
Next        ADD   D0,D2     Y := Y + I
            MOVE  (A0),D3   Read T(I) into D3
            MOVE  (A1),D4   Read J(I) into D4
            MOVE  D4,D5     D5 is a temp copy of J(I)
            ADD   D1,D5     Compute J(I) + X in D5
            CMP   D5,D3     IF T(I) = J(I) + X
            BNE   Else
            MULU  #4,D3     THEN compute T(I) * 4 - Y
            SUB   D2,D3
            MOVE  D3,(A1)   J(I) := T(I) * 4 - Y
            BRA   End_Loop
Else        SUB   D3,D4     J(I) := J(I) - T(I)
            MOVE  D4,(A1)
End_Loop    ADDA  #2,A0     Point to next element in T
            ADDA  #2,A1     Point to next element in J
            ADD   #1,D0     Increment the loop counter
            CMP   #10,D0    Repeat until I = 10
            BNE   Next
```

5. Write a 68K program to run on the simulator that:

- inputs a single ASCII-encoded numeric character
- converts the character into binary numeric form
- inputs and converts a second character
- adds the two numbers
- converts the numeric result into character form
- prints the result as ASCII characters

If the input characters are 5 and 7, the displayed result should be 12.

Discussion of strings

A string is a sequence of *consecutive* characters. The characters are normally ASCII-encoded, and each character in the string occupies one byte. Computer languages indicate a string in different ways. Some enclose the string in single quotes (e.g. 'This is a string') and some enclose the string in double quotes (e.g. "This is also a string"). Remember that the *space* is also a valid ASCII character, with the hexadecimal value $20. A string is, essentially, an array of characters.

If a string is composed of *n* characters, it occupies at least *n* bytes in memory. In practice, strings require some means of indicating their end or their size. You could store a string as *n*, *char_1*, *char_2*, ..., *char_n*, where *n* is the length of the string. For example, the ASCII-encoded string 'ABC' might be stored in memory as the sequence of bytes $03, $41, $42, $43.

Equally, you can use a *terminator* or marker to indicate the end of a string. Of course, the terminator must not occur naturally in the string. If the terminator is the null byte, the string 'ABC' would be stored as the sequence $41, $42, $43, $00. Some strings use the terminator $0D because this is the ASCII code for a carriage return.

A string, when stored in memory, has an *address*. The address of the string is usually the address of the first character in the string. Figure 6.40 shows a string 'The String' located at location 1000_{16} in memory. The string is composed of 10 characters and is terminated by a *null* byte (i.e. 0).

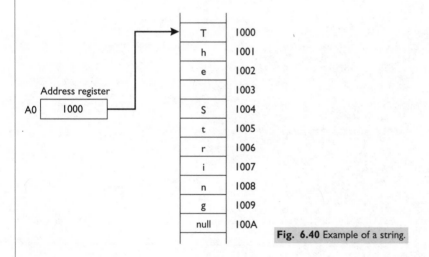

Fig. 6.40 Example of a string.

Most microprocessors don't permit direct operations on strings (e.g. you can't compare two strings using a single instruction). The 68K operates on byte, word, and longword data structures only. In general, you have to process a string by using byte operations to access individual characters, one by one. The characters of a string can be accessed by means of *address register indirect addressing*. In Fig. 6.40, address register A0 contains the value 1000_{16}, which is the address or location of the first character in the string.

The operation MOVE.B (A0),D0 copies the byte pointed at by the contents of address register A0 into data register D0. Applying this instruction to Fig. 6.40 would copy the character 'T' into data register D0 (the actual data loaded into D0 is, of course, the ASCII code for a letter 'T').

The 68K supports *address register indirect addressing with postincrementing*, which is indicated by placing a '+' after the address register in parentheses. After the address register has been used to access an operand (i.e. the location at which the address register is pointing), the contents of the address register are automatically incremented. In this case, the instruction would be written MOVE.B (A0)+,D0, and the contents of address register A0 incremented to 1001 after the character located at 1000 has been accessed. This addressing mode is useful because the address register points at the next character in a string after the current character has been accessed. Consider the following example.

Suppose we want to count the number of characters in the string pointed at by address register A1 and return the string length in D3 (assume that A1 initially points at the first character in the string). The string is terminated by the null character which we regard as being part of the string (i.e. it is included in the character count).

```
        MOVE.B  #0,D3       Preset the character counter to 0
Again   MOVE.B  (A1)+,D0    Get a character into D0
        ADD.B   #1,D3       Increment the character counter
        CMP.B   #0,D0       Is the character a null?
        BNE     Again       Repeat until zero found
```

At the end of this code, address register A1 will be pointing at the next location immediately following the string. Suppose we want to count the number of times 'A' occurs in a string that starts at address Find_A.

```
        LEA     Find_A,A0   A0 points at the start of the string
        CLR.B   D1          Clear the A's counter
Next    MOVE.B  (A0)+,D0    REPEAT Get a character
        CMP.B   #'A',D0            IF 'A'
        BNE     Test
        ADD.B   #1,D1                   THEN increment A's counter
        BRA     Next
Test    CMP.B   #$0,D0      UNTIL terminator found
        BNE     Next
```

Note that the instruction CMP.B #'A',D0 compares the contents of D0 (i.e. the last character read from the string) with the source operand, #'A'. The # symbol means the *actual value* and the 'A' means the number whose value is the ASCII code for the letter A. If you omit the # symbol, the processor will read the contents of memory location 41_{16} (because 'A' = 41_{16}). By the way, since the 68K's MOVE instruction sets its CCR, we can test for the terminator as soon as we pick up a character, as the following code demonstrates.

```
        LEA     Find_A,A0   A0 points at the start of the string
        CLR.B   D1          Clear the A's counter
Next    MOVE.B  (A0)+,D0    REPEAT Get a character
        BEQ     Exit               Exit on null character
        CMP.B   #'A',D0            IF 'A'
        BNE     Next
        ADD.B   #1,D1                   THEN increment A's counter
        BRA     Next        END REPEAT
Exit
```

Tutorial 4

1. Write a program to arrange a sequence of eight numbers in *descending* order. You can store the numbers in memory before the program is executed by means of the DC.B assembler directive. For example,

```
List DC.B 1,2,5,4,8,5,4,2
```

There are many ways of performing this sorting operation. One of the simplest is to search the list for the largest number and put it at the top of the list. Then do the same to the remaining numbers, and so on. Use the 68K cross-assembler and simulator to test your program.

2. Why is it best to pass parameters to and from a subroutine by means of the stack?

3. Write a subroutine to carry out the operation X * (Y + Z), where X, Y, and Z are all wordlength (i.e. 16-bit) values. The three parameters, X, Y, and Z, are to be passed on the stack to the procedure. The subroutine is to return the result of the calculation via the stack. Remember that the 68K instruction MULU D0,D1 multiplies the 16-bit unsigned integer in D0 by the 16-bit unsigned integer in D1 and puts the 32-bit product in D1.

Write a subroutine, call it, and pass parameters X, Y, and Z on the stack. Test your program by using the 68K simulator's debugging facilities.

Discussion of passing parameters via the stack

The effective address (Ai) is called *address register indirect addressing* because the address of the operand is obtained indirectly via address register A*i*. The effective address d16(Ai) is called *address register indirect addressing with offset* because the address of the operand is given by [Ai] + d16, where d16 is a *signed two's complement 16-bit constant* in the range −32K to +32K. The contents of the address register are not modified by this addressing mode, and predecrementing or postincrementing variations are not permitted. This addressing mode was originally written in the form d16(Ai), but can also be written (d16,Ai), because the syntax of 68K assembly language has been modified. If A0 contains $1000, the instruction MOVE.B 12(A0),D0 loads the contents of memory location $1012 into D0. The contents of A0 remain $1000.

Assume that a subroutine, ABC, requires two parameters XXX and YYY. Assume also that XXX is a *word* and YYY a *longword*. The parameters can be pushed on the stack before calling the subroutine.

```
        MOVE.W   XXX,D0       Get XXX               The stack is initially in state a.
        MOVE.W   D0,-(A7)     Push XXX              The stack is in state b.
        MOVE.L   YYY,D0       Get YYY
        MOVE.L   D0,-(A7)     Push YYY              The stack is in state c.
        BSR      ABC          Call subroutine       The stack is in state d.
        ADD.L    #6,A7        Clean up the stack    The stack is in state f = state a.
        .
        .
        .
ABC     MOVE.L   4(A7),D0     Get YYY from the stack  Parameter YYY is under return address
        MOVE.W   8(A7),D1     Get XXX from the stack  Parameter XXX is under YYY
        .
        .
        RTS                                         The stack is in state e after the RTS
```

Figure 6.41 shows the state of the stack during the calling of a subroutine and the return from a subroutine. Note that some elements on the stack take 2 bytes and some 4 bytes.

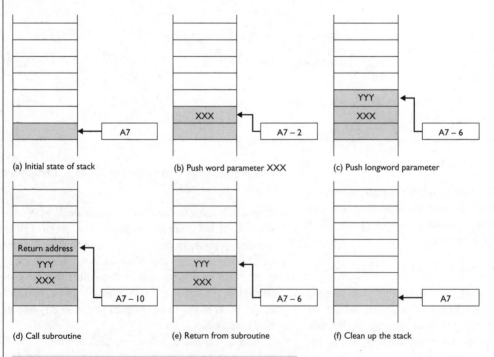

(a) Initial state of stack (b) Push word parameter XXX (c) Push longword parameter

(d) Call subroutine (e) Return from subroutine (f) Clean up the stack

Fig. 6.41 The state of the stack during the execution of a program.

Parameters are pushed on the stack before calling the subroutine and then retrieved from the stack by the subroutine. The subroutine can use *address register indirect addressing with offset* to get at the parameters. If the subroutine is called again (e.g. after an interrupt), data on the stack is not corrupted.

Parameters can be passed back to the calling program by putting them on the stack (to replace one of the parameters passed on the stack).

You can pass parameters by *value* (as we have done), or by *reference* (i.e. by their address). In the latter case, you pass the *address* of the parameter to the subroutine.

Tracing the execution of the program

We can follow the execution of the above program by using the simulator and tracing an instruction at a time. First, we need to turn the above code fragment into a program and assemble it.

```
 1  00000400                    ORG      $400
 2  00000400  4FF82000          LEA      $2000,A7      ;Dummy value for stack pointer
 3  00000404  303900000432      MOVE.W   XXX,D0        ;Get XXX
 4  0000040A  3F00              MOVE.W   D0,-(A7)      ;Push XXX
 5  0000040C  203900000434      MOVE.L   YYY,D0        ;Get YYY
 6  00000412  2F00              MOVE.L   D0,-(A7)      ;Push YYY
 7  00000414  6100000E          BSR      ABC           ;Call subroutine
 8  00000418  DFFC00000006      ADD.L    #6,A7         ;Clean up the stack
 9  0000041E  4E71              NOP
10  00000420  4E722700          STOP     #$2700
11  00000424  202F0004    ABC:  MOVE.L   4(A7),D0      ;Get YYY from the stack
12  00000428  322F0008          MOVE.W   8(A7),D1      ;Get XXX from the stack
13  0000042C  4E71              NOP                    ;Don't care what happens in sub
14  0000042E  4E71              NOP
15  00000430  4E75              RTS                    ;Return
16  00000432  1234        XXX:  DC.W     $1234         ;Dummy value for XXX
17  00000434  87654321    YYY:  DC.L     $87654321     ;Dummy value for YYY
18            00000400          END      $400
```

We have provided dummy data and included NOP (no operation) instructions as fillers. We are interested only in parameter passing. The next step is to use the simulator to trace through the program, instruction by instruction. The following listing demonstrates how the registers change as the program is executed.

```
>DF
PC=000400 SR=2000 SS=00A00000 US=00000000         X=0
A0=00000000 A1=00000000 A2=00000000 A3=00000000   N=0
A4=00000000 A5=00000000 A6=00000000 A7=00A00000   Z=0
D0=00000000 D1=00000000 D2=00000000 D3=00000000   V=0
D4=00000000 D5=00000000 D6=00000000 D7=00000000   C=0
----->LEA.L     $2000,SP

>TR
PC=000404 SR=2000 SS=00002000 US=00000000         X=0
A0=00000000 A1=00000000 A2=00000000 A3=00000000   N=0
A4=00000000 A5=00000000 A6=00000000 A7=00002000   Z=0
D0=00000000 D1=00000000 D2=00000000 D3=00000000   V=0
D4=00000000 D5=00000000 D6=00000000 D7=00000000   C=0
----->MOVE.W    $00000432,D0

Trace>
PC=00040A SR=2000 SS=00002000 US=00000000         X=0
A0=00000000 A1=00000000 A2=00000000 A3=00000000   N=0
A4=00000000 A5=00000000 A6=00000000 A7=00002000   Z=0
D0=00001234 D1=00000000 D2=00000000 D3=00000000   V=0
D4=00000000 D5=00000000 D6=00000000 D7=00000000   C=0
----->MOVE.W    D0,-(SP)
```

```
Trace>
PC=00040C  SR=2000  SS=00001FFE  US=00000000          X=0
A0=00000000  A1=00000000  A2=00000000  A3=00000000  N=0
A4=00000000  A5=00000000  A6=00000000  A7=00001FFE  Z=0
D0=00001234  D1=00000000  D2=00000000  D3=00000000  V=0
D4=00000000  D5=00000000  D6=00000000  D7=00000000  C=0
----->MOVE.L    $00000434,D0

Trace>
PC=000412  SR=2008  SS=00001FFE  US=00000000          X=0
A0=00000000  A1=00000000  A2=00000000  A3=00000000  N=1
A4=00000000  A5=00000000  A6=00000000  A7=00001FFE  Z=0
D0=87654321  D1=00000000  D2=00000000  D3=00000000  V=0
D4=00000000  D5=00000000  D6=00000000  D7=00000000  C=0
----->MOVE.L    D0,-(SP)

Trace>
PC=000414  SR=2008  SS=00001FFA  US=00000000          X=0
A0=00000000  A1=00000000  A2=00000000  A3=00000000  N=1
A4=00000000  A5=00000000  A6=00000000  A7=00001FFA  Z=0
D0=87654321  D1=00000000  D2=00000000  D3=00000000  V=0
D4=00000000  D5=00000000  D6=00000000  D7=00000000  C=0
----->BSR.L     $00000424

Trace>
PC=000424  SR=2008  SS=00001FF6  US=00000000          X=0
A0=00000000  A1=00000000  A2=00000000  A3=00000000  N=1
A4=00000000  A5=00000000  A6=00000000  A7=00001FF6  Z=0
D0=87654321  D1=00000000  D2=00000000  D3=00000000  V=0
D4=00000000  D5=00000000  D6=00000000  D7=00000000  C=0
----->MOVE.L    4(SP),D0

Trace>
PC=000428  SR=2008  SS=00001FF6  US=00000000          X=0
A0=00000000  A1=00000000  A2=00000000  A3=00000000  N=1
A4=00000000  A5=00000000  A6=00000000  A7=00001FF6  Z=0
D0=87654321  D1=00000000  D2=00000000  D3=00000000  V=0
D4=00000000  D5=00000000  D6=00000000  D7=00000000  C=0
----->MOVE.W    8(SP),D1

Trace>
PC=00042C  SR=2000  SS=00001FF6  US=00000000          X=0
A0=00000000  A1=00000000  A2=00000000  A3=00000000  N=0
A4=00000000  A5=00000000  A6=00000000  A7=00001FF6  Z=0
D0=87654321  D1=00001234  D2=00000000  D3=00000000  V=0
D4=00000000  D5=00000000  D6=00000000  D7=00000000  C=0
----->NOP

Trace>
PC=00042E  SR=2000  SS=00001FF6  US=00000000          X=0
A0=00000000  A1=00000000  A2=00000000  A3=00000000  N=0
A4=00000000  A5=00000000  A6=00000000  A7=00001FF6  Z=0
D0=87654321  D1=00001234  D2=00000000  D3=00000000  V=0
D4=00000000  D5=00000000  D6=00000000  D7=00000000  C=0
----->NOP

Trace>
PC=000430  SR=2000  SS=00001FF6  US=00000000          X=0
A0=00000000  A1=00000000  A2=00000000  A3=00000000  N=0
A4=00000000  A5=00000000  A6=00000000  A7=00001FF6  Z=0
D0=87654321  D1=00001234  D2=00000000  D3=00000000  V=0
D4=00000000  D5=00000000  D6=00000000  D7=00000000  C=0
----->RTS
```

```
Trace>
PC=000418 SR=2000 SS=00001FFA US=00000000        X=0
A0=00000000 A1=00000000 A2=00000000 A3=00000000 N=0
A4=00000000 A5=00000000 A6=00000000 A7=00001FFA Z=0
D0=87654321 D1=00001234 D2=00000000 D3=00000000 V=0
D4=00000000 D5=00000000 D6=00000000 D7=00000000 C=0
----->ADDA.L    #6,SP


Trace>
PC=00041E SR=2000 SS=00002000 US=00000000        X=0
A0=00000000 A1=00000000 A2=00000000 A3=00000000 N=0
A4=00000000 A5=00000000 A6=00000000 A7=00002000 Z=0
D0=87654321 D1=00001234 D2=00000000 D3=00000000 V=0
D4=00000000 D5=00000000 D6=00000000 D7=00000000 C=0
----->NOP
```

At the end of the program let's look at the state of the stack.

```
>MD 1FF0
001FF0 00 00 00 00 00 00 00 00 04 18 87 65 43 21 12 34
```

As you can see, the stack contains the values 1234, 87654321, and the subroutine return address 00000418 (in reverse order).

Tutorial 5

1. Write a subroutine ADDABC that performs the operation C : = A + B. Variables A, B, and C are all *word* (i.e. 16-bit) values. Test your program on the 68K simulator.

Your calling code and subroutine should have the following features:

- Parameters A and B should be passed on the stack to the procedure by *reference* (i.e. by *address*).

- Since parameters A and B are adjacent in memory, you need pass only the *address* of parameter A to the subroutine (because the address of parameter B is two bytes on from parameter A).

- Parameter C should be passed back to the calling program on the stack by *value*.

- Before you call the subroutine, make room on the stack for the returned parameter (i.e. parameter C).

- After calling the subroutine, read the parameter off the stack into data register D0 (i.e. D0 should end up containing the value of A + B).

- The subroutine ADDABC must not *corrupt* any registers. Save all working registers on the stack on entry to the subroutine and restore them before returning from the subroutine.

- When you write your code, preset the stack pointer to a value like $1500 (by using either MOVEA.L #$1500,A7 or LEA $1500,A7). Doing this will make it easier to follow the movement of the stack while your program is running.

- Make certain that you are operating with the correct operand sizes! Use .W for data values and .L for addresses/pointers.

- Some of the important instructions you might need are provided below. Make sure you understand exactly what they do.

```
MOVEM.L    RegList,-(A7)    Push a group of registers on stack
MOVEM.L    (A7)+,RegList    Pull a group of registers off stack
LEA        X(Ai),Aj         Load Aj with the contents of register Ai+X
MOVEA.L    (Ai),Aj          Load Aj with longword pointed at by Ai
```

Your program should be of the general form

```
        ORG   $400
        LEA   $1500,A7    Set up the stack pointer with an easy value
        ...               Pass the parameters
        BSR   ADDABC      Call the subroutine
        ...               Get the result, C, in D0
        ...               Clean up the stack
        STOP  #$2700      Halt execution
*
ADDABC  ...
        ...
        RTS
*
        ORG   $1200       Put the test data here
A       DC.W  $1234       This is the first parameter
B       DC.W  $ABAB       This is the second parameter
        END   $400
```

This is not an easy or trivial problem. You will need to draw a map of the stack at every stage and take very great care not to confuse pointers (addresses) and actual parameters.

Tutorial 6

1. Suppose you wish to preload memory with the value 1234 *before* executing a program. Which of the following operations is correct?

   (a) DC.B   #1234
   (b) DC.W   1234
   (c) DC.W   #1234
   (d) DS.B $1234
   (e) MOVE.W #1234,Location

2. The register transfer language definition of MOVE.B (A2)+,D3 is one of the following.

   (a) D3 ← [M([A2])];   [A2] ← [A2]+1
   (b) [D3] ← [M([A2])];   [A2] ← [A2]+1
   (c) D3 ← [M([A2])];   [A2] ← [A2]+1
   (d) [A2] ← [A2]+1;   [D3] ← [A2];

3. When a parameter is passed to a subroutine by reference (i.e. not by value),

   (a) the parameter can be put in an address register
   (b) the address of the parameter can be put in an address register
   (c) the address of the parameter can be pushed on the stack
   (d) the parameter can be pushed on the stack
   (e) parts (a) and (d) are correct
   (f) parts (b) and (c) are correct

4. Consider the following code:

   ```
   MOVE.W  X,-(A7)    Push X
   MOVE.L  Y,-(A7)    Push Y
   BSR     PQR        Call PQR
   Clean_up           Clean up the stack
   ```

   (a) Why do you have to clean up the stack after returning from the subroutine?
   (b) What code would you use to clean up the stack?
   (c) Draw a memory map of the stack immediately before executing the RTS in the subroutine PQR.

5. Why is it best to pass parameters to and from a subroutine by means of the stack?

6. Explain why the following assembly language and RTL constructs are incorrect.

   (a) MOVE D4,#$64
   (b) MOVE (D3),D2
   (c) [D3] ← A0+3
   (d) [D3] ← #3

7. Write a 68K assembly language program to implement the following construct:

   IF X=4 THEN X=X+2.

8. You cannot (should not?) exit a subroutine by jumping out of it by means of a branch instruction. You must exit it with an RTS instruction. Why?

9. Assume that a string of ASCII characters is located in memory starting at location $2000. The string ends with the character 'Z'. Design and write a 68K assembly language program to count the number of 'E's, if any, in the string.

10. Express the following sequence of 68K assembly language instructions in register transfer language and explain in plain English what each instruction does.

   (a) `LEA       4(A2),A1`
   (b) `MOVEA.L   A3,A2`
   (c) `MOVE.B    (A1),D3`
   (d) `MOVE.B    #5,(A1)`
   (e) `BCS       ABC`
   (f) `MOVE.B    (A1)+,-(A3)`

11. The following fragment of 68K assembly language has several serious errors. Explain what the errors are. Explain how you would correct the errors.

```
        MOVE.B  X,D0        Get X in a data register
        CMP.B   #4,D0       IF X=4 THEN X := X+6
        BEQ     Add_6
        MOVE.B  D0,X        Restore X in memory
        PEA     X           Push X on the stack
        BSR     Sqr         Calculate X²
X       DS.W    1           Save space for X
        STOP    #$2700
*
ADD_6   ADD.B   #6,D0       X := X+6
        RTS                 Return
Sqr     MOVE.L  (A7)+,D2    Get X
        MULU    D2,D2       Square X
        MOVE.L  D2,-(A7)    Put X*X on the stack
        RTS                 Return
```

12. Suppose you are given an algorithm and asked to design and test a program written in 68K assembly language. How would you carry out this activity? Your answer should include considerations of program design and testing, and the necessary software tools.

```
        LEA     String,A0   A0 points at the string
        CLR     D0          D0 is the 'E's counter: E_Count=0
Next    MOVE.B  (A0)+,D1    REPEAT Get next character
        CMP.B   #'E',D0         IF character='E'
        BNE     Not_E
        ADD.B   #1,D0           THEN E_Count=E_Count+1
Not_E   CMP.B   #'Z',D0
        BNE     Next        UNTIL Character='Z'
        STOP    #$2700
String DC.B     Length
```

4. (a) The two parameters take up 6 bytes on the stack and this space must be reclaimed.
   (b) You can clean up the stack by `LEA 6(A7),A7` or `ADDA.L #6,A7`.

5. If the subroutine is interrupted and reused by the interrupt handler no data will be corrupted if it is stored on the stack.

6. (a) You cannot move a value into a literal
   (b) A data register cannot be used as a pointer
   (c) In RTL a register must be enclosed by [ ] (i.e. [A0])
   (d) In RTL the symbol # has no meaning

7.
```
        MOVE.B  X,D0
        CMP.B   #4,D0
        BNE     Exit
        ADD.B   #2,D0
        MOVE.B  D0,X
Exit
```

8. When you call a subroutine you push the return address on the stack. If you jump out of a subroutine, you leave the return address on the top of the stack (and possibly screw up the next `RTS`).

9.

10. (a) [A1] ← [A2]+4
   Copy the contents of address register A2 plus 4 into address register A1
   (b) [A2] ← [A3]
   Copy the contents of address register A3 into address register A2
   (c) [D3] ← [M([A1])]
   Copy the contents of the memory location pointed at by address register A1 into data register D3

Solutions to Tutorial 6

1. (a) `DC.B    #1234`   Wrong: no hash symbol and .B is incorrect
   (b) `DC.W    1234`   Correct
   (c) `DC.W    #1234`   Wrong: no hash is necessary
   (d) `DS.B    $1234,location` Wrong: $1234 is greater than a byte
   (e) `MOVE.W  #1234,Location` Wrong: this is a run-time operation

2. (b)

3. (f)

(d) `[M([A1])] ← 5`

Copy the value 5 into the memory location pointed at by address register A1

(e) `IF [C]=1 THEN [PC] ← ABC`

If the carry bit of the CCR is set then branch to location ABC

(f) `[A3] ← [A3]−1; [M([A3])]←[M([A1])];`
`[A1] ← [A1]+1;`

Decrement address register A3 and copy the contents of the memory location pointed at by A1 into the memory location pointed at by A3. Then increment A1.

11. There are three errors:

(a) The `BEQ Add_6` instruction is used to call a subroutine. A 68K conditional branch does not store a return address on the stack. The problem can be fixed by

```
CMP.B  #4,D0   IF X=4 THEN X := X+6
BNE    No_Add
BSR    Add_6
No_Add
```

(b) The address of X is pushed on the stack with the `PEA` instruction. However, the value of X is lifted off the stack in subroutine `Sqr`. The simplest correction is to push the value of X on the stack.

(c) The data element X is stored with the executable code (the value of X would be read by the CPU and 'executed').

Typical assembly language errors

Here is a list of some of the assembly language errors I found in the various scripts I marked. Apart from simple typographical errors, one of the most common errors is to invent new instructions and addressing modes.

Error		Comment
`MOVE`	`$1000,A0`	The instruction itself is not wrong—but the intention is. The student really wants to put the number $1000 in A0, not the contents of $1000. The instruction should be `MOVE #$1000,A0` or `LEA $1000,A0`.
`MOVE(A0),D2`		This should be `MOVE (A0),D2`. A space is required between the op-code and operand field of all instructions.
`BEQ`	`RUN COUNT`	No space is permitted in label (or variable) names. `BEQ RUNCOUNT`.
`BEQ`	`NEXT`	The conditional branch forces a branch to `NEXT` if the Z-bit is zero.
`.`		However, you cannot return from a branch by means of an `RTS` instruction.
`NEXT.`		An `RTS` (return from subroutine) can be used only with a `BSR`
`.`		or a `JSR` instruction.
`RTS`		
`LEA`	`TABLE,A1+`	The addressing mode does not exist and neither does `LEA TABLE,(A1)+`.
`CMPM`	`(A),(A1)`	This is not a legal addressing mode for `CMP`. The special compare memory with memory instruction has the single legal addressing mode `CMPM (Ai)+,(Aj)+`.
`CMP`	`#44B,A1`	This literal should be `CMP #$44B,A1`. The $ symbol is needed to show that the number is hexadecimal.
`MOVE.B`	`(ARRAY),A1`	This is an illegal addressing mode—it does not exist.
`MOVE.B`	`(ARRAY)+1,A0`	This is a doubly illegal addressing mode!
`ADD1`	`D0`	Illegal instruction; the writer obviously means `ADD #1,D0`.
`MOVE.B`	`#$1 , D1`	No space around delimiter; it should be `MOVE.B #$1,D0`.
`ADDA`	`#$1,A7`	This is not wrong technically. Address register A7 is normally reserved as the stack pointer. The stack pointer must always be on an even boundary.

```
      LEA.B     X,A0
```
LEA (load effective address) cannot be used with a byte operand, as LEA loads an address register with a longword.

```
      LEA       #Number,A1
```
This instruction should be LEA Number,A1. I know that this is confusing, but LEA loads an address into an address register. The 68K instruction MOVEA.L #Number,A0 is, effectively, the same as LEA Number,A0.

```
      LEA       Table[#1],A0
```
Illegal addressing mode.

```
      CLR.B     D1
Tab DS.B        100
      MOVE.B    #1,D2
```
You cannot locate data in the middle of a program.
The computer would execute CLR.B and then read the first location of the table and try and execute it.

Further examples of string manipulation

Suppose we wish to test whether two strings are identical. Figure 6.42 shows two strings in memory. One is located at 1000_{16} and the other at 2000_{16}. In this case both strings are identical.

In order to compare the strings we have to read a character at a time from each string. If, at any point, the two characters do not match, the strings are not identical. If we reach two null characters, the strings are the same. We use A0 to point at one string and A1 to point at the other. We will set D7 to a zero if the strings are not the same and one if they are the same.

A common string manipulation problem is the removal of multiple spaces in text. If you enter a command into a computer like delete X,Y,Z the various component parts (i.e. fields) of the command are first analyzed. A 'command line processor' might remove multiple spaces before

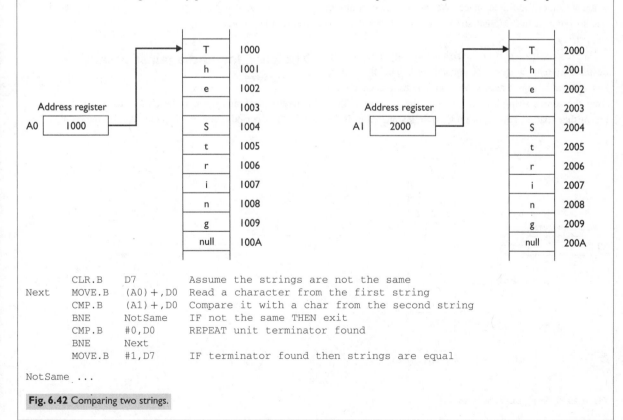

```
        CLR.B    D7          Assume the strings are not the same
Next    MOVE.B   (A0)+,D0    Read a character from the first string
        CMP.B    (A1)+,D0    Compare it with a char from the second string
        BNE      NotSame     IF not the same THEN exit
        CMP.B    #0,D0       REPEAT unit terminator found
        BNE      Next
        MOVE.B   #1,D7       IF terminator found then strings are equal

NotSame ...
```

Fig. 6.42 Comparing two strings.

processing the command. Figure 6.43 shows how we might go about dealing with this problem. On the left, the string has three spaces. On the right, the same string has been rewritten with only one space.

are searching for multiple spaces, we will move one character beyond the space because of the autoincrementing addressing mode. Therefore, we have to adjust the pointer before continuing.

```
           LEA      String,A0    Set both pointers to the start of the string
           LEA      String,A1
Next       MOVE.B   (A0)+,D0     Get a character from the source string
           MOVE.B   D0,(A1)+     Copy it to its destination
           CMP.B    #0,D0        If it is a null, then exit
           BEQ      Exit
           CMP.B    #' ',D0      Was the character a space?
           BNE      Next         If not a space, continue copying across
Loop       MOVE.B   (A0)+,D0     Get another character from the source string
           CMP.B    #' ',D0      Is this a space too?
           BEQ      Loop         Continue until a non-space is found
           LEA      -1(A0),A0    Wind the source pointer back to the last char
           BRA      Next         Go back to the string
Exit    .                        Exit point
```

Since the final string will be the same size or shorter than the original string, we can simply 'move up' characters when we find a multiple space. We can use two pointers: one to point at the original string and one to point at the final string.

We read characters from the string and copy them to their destination until a space is encountered. The first space encountered is copied across. We continue to read characters from the source string but do not copy them across if they are further spaces. This algorithm requires some care. If we

Figure 6.44 demonstrates the operation of this algorithm. By the way, there is a flaw in this program. What happens if the end of the string is a space followed by a null? How can you fix the problem?

The case for and against assembly language

Broadly speaking, you can divide the history of computers into four periods: the mainframe, the minicomputer, the

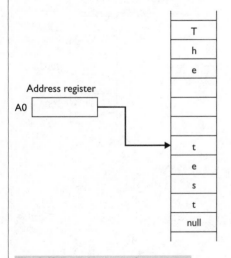
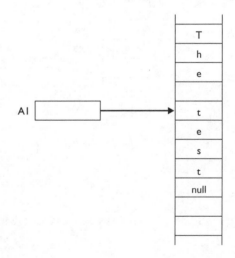

Fig. 6.43 Removing spaces from a string.

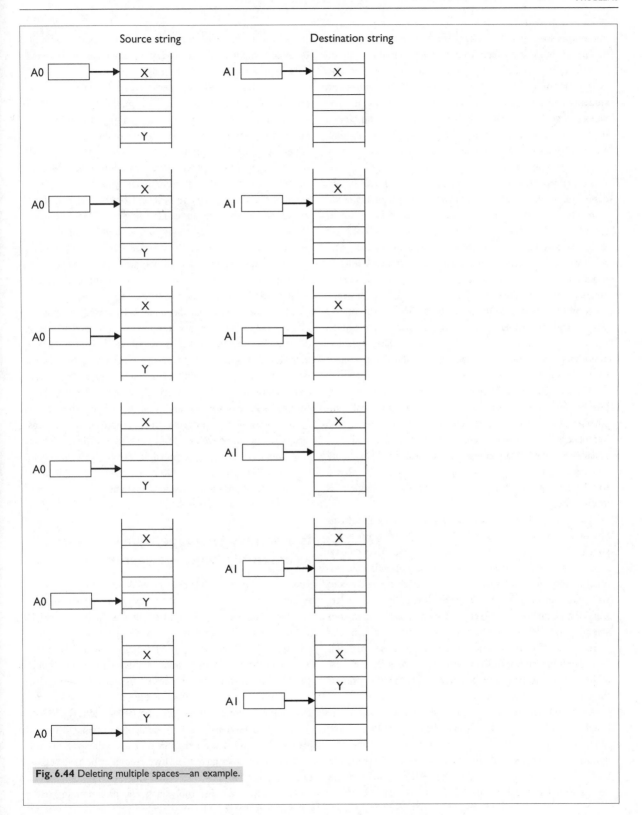

Fig. 6.44 Deleting multiple spaces—an example.

microprocessor, and the modern post-microprocessor. The *mainframe* era was characterized by computers that required large buildings and teams of technicians and operators to keep them going. More often than not, both academics and students had little direct contact with the mainframe—you handed a deck of punched cards to an operator and waited for the output to appear hours later. During the mainframe era, academics concentrated on languages, compilers, algorithmics, and operating systems.

The *minicomputer* era put computers in the hands of students and academics, because university departments could now buy their own minis. As minicomputers were not as complex as mainframes and because students could get direct hands-on experience, many departments of computer science and electronic engineering taught students how to program in the native language of the computer—assembly language. In those days, the mid-1970s, assembly language programming was used to teach both the control of I/O devices and the writing of programs (i.e. assembly language was taught rather like high-level languages). The explosion of computer software had not taken place, and if you wanted software you had to write it yourself.

The late 1970s saw the introduction of the *microprocessor*. For the first time, each student was able to access a real computer. Unfortunately, microprocessors appeared before the introduction of low-cost memory (both primary and secondary). Students had to program microprocessors in assembly language because the only storage mechanism was often a ROM with just enough capacity to hold a simple single-pass assembler.

The advent of the low-cost microprocessor system (usually on a single board) ensured that virtually every EE or CS student took a course on assembly language. Even today, most courses in computer science include a module on computer architecture and organization, and teaching students to write programs in assembly language forces them to understand the computer's architecture. However, some computer scientists who had been educated during the mainframe era were unhappy with the microprocessor, because they felt that the 8-bit microprocessor was a retrograde step—its architecture was far more primitive than the mainframes they had studied in the 1960s.

The 1990s are the *post-microprocessor* era. Today's personal computers—the PCs, Apples, and PowerPCs—have more power and storage capacity than many of yesterday's mainframes, and they have a range of powerful software tools that were undreamed of in the 1970s. Moreover, the computer science curriculum of the 1990s has exploded.

In 1970 a student could be expected to be familiar with all fields of computer science. Today, a student can be expected only to browse through the highlights.

The availability of high-performance hardware and the drive to include more and more new material in the CS curriculum has put pressure on academics to justify what they teach. In particular, many are questioning the need for courses on assembly language.

If you regard computer science as being primarily concerned with the *use* of the computer, you can argue that assembly language is an irrelevance. Does the surgeon study metallurgy in order to understand how a scalpel operates? Does the pilot study thermodynamics to understand how a jet engine operates? Does the news reader study electronics to understand how the camera operates? The answer to all these questions is 'no'. So why should we inflict assembly language and computer architecture on the student?

First, *education* is not the same as *training*. The student of computer science is not simply being trained to use a number of computer packages. A university course leading to a degree should also cover the *history* and *theoretical basis* of the subject. Without a knowledge of computer architecture, the computer scientist cannot understand how computers have developed and what they are capable of.

In spite of the progress in microprocessor systems design, some embedded systems such as washing machine controllers are still programmed in assembly language to help minimize the size of the code. However, C is now widely used to program embedded systems.

Is assembly language today the same as assembly language yesterday?

Two factors have influenced the way in which we teach assembly language—one is the way in which microprocessors have changed, and the other is the use to which assembly language teaching is put. Over the years, microprocessors have become more and more complex, with the result that the architecture and assembly language of a modern state-of-the-art microprocessor is radically different from that of an 8-bit machine of the late 1970s. When we first taught assembly language in the 1970s and early 1980s, we did it to demonstrate how computers operated and to give students hands-on experience of a computer. Since all students now either have their own computer or have access to a computer lab, this role of the single-board computer is obsolete. Moreover, assembly language programming once attempted to ape high-level language programming—students were taught algorithms such as sorting and searching in assembly language, as if assembly language were no more than the (desperately) poor man's C.

The argument for teaching assembly language programming today can be divided into two components: the underpinning of computer architecture and the underpinning of computer software.

Assembly language teaches how a computer works at the machine (i.e. register) level. It is therefore necessary to teach assembly language to all those who might later be involved in computer architecture—either by specifying computers for a particular application, or by designing new architectures. Moreover, the von Neumann machine's sequential nature teaches students the limitation of conventional architectures and, indirectly, leads them on to unconventional architectures (parallel processors, Harvard architectures, dataflow computers, and even neural networks).

It is probably in the realm of software that you can most easily build a case for the teaching of assembly language. During a student's career, he or she will encounter a lot of *abstract* concepts in subjects ranging from programming languages to operating systems to real-time programming to AI. The foundation of many of these concepts lies in assembly language programming and computer architecture. You might even say that assembly language provides *bottom-up* support for the *top-down* methodology we teach in high-level languages. Consider some of the following examples (taken from the teaching of Motorola's 68K series assembly language).

- **Data types**—Students come across data types in high-level languages and the effects of strong and weak data typing. Teaching an assembly language that can operate on bit, byte, word, and longword operands helps students understand data types. Moreover, the ability to perform any type of assembly language operation on any type of data structure demonstrates the need for strong typing.

- **Addressing modes**—A vital component of assembly language teaching is addressing modes (literal, direct, and indirect). The student learns how pointers function and how pointers are manipulated. This aspect is particularly important if the student is to become a C programmer. Because an assembly language is unencumbered by data types, the students' view of pointers is much simplified by an assembly language. The 68020 has complex addressing modes that support double indirection and the manipulation of tables of pointers.

- **The stack and subroutines**—In my teaching I now emphasize how procedures are called, and parameters passed and returned from procedures. By using an assembly language you can readily teach the passing of parameters by *value* and by *reference*. The use of *local variables* and *re-entrant* programming can also be taught. This supports the teaching of task-switching kernels in both operating systems and real-time programming.

- **Recursion**—The recursive calling of subroutines often causes a student problems. You can use an assembly language, together with a suitable system with a tracing facility, to demonstrate how recursion operates. The student can actually observe how the stack grows as procedures are called.

- **Run-time support for high-level languages**—A high-performance processor like the 68020 provides facilities that support run-time checking in high-level languages. For example, the CHK2 instruction provides automatic checking of array bounds at run-time (if an array element is out of bounds, an operating system call is made). The 68K also provides run-time checking for errors such as an attempt to divide a number by zero.

- **Protected-mode operation**—Members of the 68K family operate in either a *supervisor* mode or a *user* mode. The operating system operates in the supervisor mode and all user (applications) programs run in the user mode. This mechanism can be used to construct *secure* or *protected* environments in which the effects of an error in one application can be prevented from harming the operating system (or other applications).

- **Input/output**—Many high-level languages make it difficult to access I/O ports and devices directly. By using an assembly language we can teach students how to write device drivers and how to control interfaces. Most real interfaces are still programmed at the machine level by accessing registers within them.

All these topics can, of course, be taught in the appropriate courses (e.g. high-level languages, operating systems). However, by teaching them in an assembly language course, they pave the way for future studies, and also show the student exactly what is happening within the machine.

Conclusion

A strong case can be made for the continued teaching of assembly language within the computer science curriculum. However, an assembly language cannot be taught just as if it were another general-purpose programming language as it was once taught 10 years ago. Perhaps more than any other component of the computer science curriculum, teaching an assembly language supports a wide range of topics at the heart of computer science. An assembly language should not be used just to illustrate algorithms, but to demonstrate what is actually happening inside the computer.

Chapter 7

An introduction to RISC processors and the ARM

The previous chapter introduced a typical high-performance CISC architecture. We now describe how microprocessor manufacturers took a new look at processor architectures in the 1980s and started designing simpler but faster processors. We begin by explaining why chip designers turned their backs on the conventional complex instruction set computer (CISC) such as the 68K and the Intel 86X families and started producing *reduced instruction set computers* (RISCs) such as MIPS and the PowerPC. RISC processors have simpler instruction sets than CISC processors (although this is a rather crude distinction between these families, as we shall soon see).

By the mid-1990s many of these so-called RISC processors were considerably more complex than some of the CISCs they replaced. That isn't a paradox. The RISC processor isn't really a cut-down computer architecture—it represents a new approach to architecture design. In fact, the distinction between CISC and RISC is now so blurred that virtually all processors now have both RISC and CISC features. We assume that readers are broadly familiar with the material in Chapter 6 (e.g. instruction types, addressing modes, and assembly language) before they read this chapter.

We illustrate the RISC architecture with the ARM processor, which is found in systems ranging from workstations to mobile cellphones. The ARM processor family has a remarkably elegant architecture, making it an ideal candidate for the role of a teaching machine. In spite of the ARM's simplicity, it has many interesting features that demonstrate the power of RISC architectures. We use the development tools supplied with this book to demonstrate the ARM's operation. The material on the ARM assembler assumes that you have already covered the material in Chapter 6.

7.1 The RISC revolution

Before we look at the ARM, we describe the history and characteristics of RISC architecture. From the introduction of the microprocessor in the 1970s to the mid-1980s there seems to have been an almost unbroken trend towards more and more complex (you might even say *Baroque*) architectures. Some of these architectures developed rather like a snowball rolling downhill. Each advance in chip fabrication technology allowed designers to add more and more layers to the microprocessor's central core. Intel's 8086 family illustrates this trend particularly well, because Intel took its original 16-bit processor and added more features in each successive generation. This approach to chip design leads to cumbersome architectures and inefficient instruction sets, but it has the tremendous commercial advantage that end users don't have to pay for new software when they buy the latest reincarnation of a microprocessor.

A reaction against the trend toward greater architectural complexity began at IBM with their 801 architecture and continued at Berkeley where Patterson and Ditzel coined the term *RISC* to describe a new class of architectures that reversed earlier trends in microcomputer design. According to popular wisdom, RISC architectures are streamlined versions of traditional complex instruction set computers. This notion is both misleading and dangerous, because it implies that RISC processors are in some way cruder versions of existing architectures. In brief, RISC architectures redeploy to better effect some of the silicon real estate used to implement complex instructions and elaborate addressing modes in conventional microprocessors of the 68000 and 8086 generation. The mnemonic 'RISC' should really stand for *regular* instruction set computer.

Those who designed first-generation 8-bit architectures in the 1970s were striving to put a computer on a chip, rather than to create the perfect computing engine. The designers of 16-bit machines added sophisticated addressing modes and new instructions, and provided more general-purpose registers. The designers of RISC architectures have taken the design process back to fundamentals by studying what many computers actually do and by starting from a blank sheet (as opposed to modifying an existing chip á la Intel).

Two factors influencing the architecture of first- and second-generation microprocessors were *microprogramming* and the desire to help compiler writers by providing ever more complex instruction sets. The latter is called *closing the semantic gap* (i.e. reducing the difference between high-level and low-level languages). By complex instructions we mean instructions like MOVE 12 (A3, D0), D2 and ADD -(A6), D3 that carry out multistep operations in a single machine-level instruction. MOVE 12 (A3, D0), D2 generates an effective address by adding the contents of A3 to the contents of D0 plus the literal 12. The resulting address is used to access the source operand that is loaded into register D2.

Microprogramming achieved its high-point in the 1970s, when ferrite core memory had a long access time of 1 μs or more and semiconductor high-speed random access memory was very expensive. Quite naturally, computer designers used the slow main store to hold the complex instructions that made up the machine-level program. These machine-level instructions are interpreted by microcode in the much faster microprogram control store within the CPU. Today, main stores use semiconductor memory with an access time of 50 μs or less, and most of the advantages of microprogramming have evaporated. Indeed, the goal of a RISC architecture is to execute an instruction in a single machine cycle. A corollary of this statement is that complex instructions can't be executed by RISC architectures. Before we look at RISC architectures, we have to describe some of the research that led to the search for better architectures.

7.1.1 Instruction usage

Computer scientists carried out extensive research over a decade or more in the late 1970s into the way in which computers execute programs. Their studies demonstrated that the relative frequency with which different classes of instructions are executed is not uniform and that some types of instruction are executed far more frequently than other types. Fairclough divided machine-level instructions into eight groups according to type and compiled the statistics shown in Table 7.1. The 'mean value of instruction use' gives the percentage of times that instructions in that group are executed averaged over both program types and computer architecture. These figures relate to early 8-bit processors.

The eight instruction groups in Table 7.1 are:

1. Data movement

2. Program flow control (i.e. branch, call, return)

3. Arithmetic

4. Compare

5. Logical

6. Shift

7. Bit manipulation

8. Input/output and miscellaneous.

Table 7.1 convincingly demonstrates that the most common instruction type is the data movement primitive of the form P := Q in a high-level language or MOVE P, Q in a low-level language. Similarly, the program flow control group, which includes both conditional and unconditional branches (together with subroutine calls and returns), forms the second most common group of instructions. Taken together, the data movement and program flow control groups account for 74 percent of all instructions. A corollary of this statement is that we can expect a large program to contain only 26 percent of instructions that are not data movement or program flow control primitives.

An inescapable inference from such results is that processor designers might be better employed devoting their time to optimizing the way in which machines handle instructions in groups 1 and 2 than in seeking new *powerful* instructions that are seldom used. In the early days of the microprocessor, chip manufacturers went out of their way to provide special instructions that were unique to their products. These instructions were then heavily promoted by the company's sales force. Today, we can see that their efforts should have been directed towards the goal of optimizing the most frequently used instructions. RISC architectures have been designed to exploit the programming environment in which most instructions are data movement or program control instructions.

Another aspect of computer architecture that was investigated was the optimum size of *literal operands* (i.e. constants). Tanenbaum reported the remarkable result that 56 percent of all constant values lie in the range −15 to +15 and that

Instruction group	1	2	3	4	5	6	7	8
Mean value of instruction use	45.28	28.73	10.75	5.92	3.91	2.93	2.05	0.44

Table 7.1 Instruction usage as a function of instruction type.

98 percent of all constants lie in the range −511 to +511. Consequently, the inclusion of a 5-bit constant field in an instruction would cover over half the occurrences of a literal. RISC architectures have sufficiently long instruction lengths to include a literal field as part of the instruction that caters for the majority of literals.

Programs use subroutines heavily, and an effective architecture should optimize the ways in which subroutines are called, parameters are passed to and from subroutines, and workspace is allocated to local variables created by subroutines. Research showed that in 95 percent of cases 12 words of storage are sufficient for parameter passing and local storage. A computer with 12 registers should be able to handle all the operands required by most subroutines without accessing main store. Such an arrangement reduces the processor-memory bus traffic associated with subroutine calls. We look at the way in which RISCs deal with subroutines in Section 7.2.1.

7.1.2 Characteristics of RISC architectures

Having described the ingredients that go into an efficient architecture, we now look at the attributes of first-generation RISCs before covering RISC architectures in more detail. The characteristics of an efficient RISC architecture are:

1. RISC processors have sufficient on-chip registers to overcome the worst effects of the processor–memory bottleneck. Registers can be accessed more rapidly than off-chip main store. Although today's processors rely heavily on fast on-chip cache memory to increase throughput (see Chapter 10 for a discussion of cache), registers still offer the highest performance.

2. RISC processors have three-address, register-to-register architectures with instructions in the form OPERATION Ra, Rb, Rc, where Ra, Rb, and Rc are general-purpose registers.

3. Because subroutine calls are so frequently executed, (some) RISC architectures make provision for the efficient passing of parameters between subroutines.

4. Instructions that modify the flow of control (e.g. branch instructions) are implemented efficiently because they comprise about 20–30 percent of a typical program.

5. RISC processors aim to execute one instruction per clock cycle. This goal imposes a limit on the maximum complexity of instructions.

6. RISC processors don't attempt to implement infrequently used instructions. Complex instructions waste silicon real-estate and conflict with the requirements of point 8. Moreover, the inclusion of complex instructions increases the time taken to design, fabricate, and test a processor.

7. A corollary of point 5 is that an efficient architecture should not be microprogrammed, because microprogramming interprets a machine-level instruction by executing microinstructions. In the limit, a RISC processor is close to a microprogrammed architecture in which the distinction between machine cycle and microcode has vanished.

8. An efficient processor should have a single instruction format (or at least very few formats). A typical CISC processor such as the 68000 has variable-length instructions (e.g. from 2 to 10 bytes). By providing a single instruction format, the decoding of a RISC instruction into its component fields can be performed by a minimum level of decoding logic. It follows that a RISC's instruction length should be sufficient to accommodate the operation code field and one or more operand fields. Consequently, a RISC processor may not utilize memory space as efficiently as does a conventional CISC microprocessor.

Two fundamental aspects of the RISC architecture that we cover later are its *register set* and the use of *pipelining*. Multiple overlapping register windows were implemented by the Berkeley RISC to reduce the overhead incurred by transferring parameters between subroutines. Pipelining is a mechanism that permits the overlapping of instruction execution (i.e. internal operations are carried out in parallel). Many of the features of RISC processors are not new, and were employed long before the advent of the microprocessor. The RISC revolution happened when all these performance-enhancing techniques were brought together and applied to microprocessor design.

7.2 The Berkeley RISC

Although many CISC processors were designed by semiconductor manufacturers, one of the first RISC processors came from the University of California at Berkeley. The Berkeley RISC wasn't a commercial machine, although it had a tremendous impact on the development of later RISC architectures. Figure 7.1 describes the format of a Berkeley RISC instruction. Each of the 5-bit operand fields (Destination, Source 1, Source 2) permits one of 32 internal registers to be accessed.

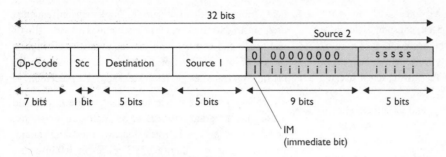

Fig. 7.1 Format of the Berkeley RISC instruction.

The single-bit *set condition code field*, Scc, determines whether the condition code bits are updated after the execution of an instruction. The 14-bit Source 2 field has two functions. If the IM bit (immediate) is 0, the Source 2 field specifies one of 32 registers. If the IM bit is 1, the Source 2 field provides a 13-bit literal operand.

Since five bits are allocated to each operand field, it follows that this RISC has $2^5 = 32$ internal registers. This last statement is emphatically not true, since the Berkeley RISC has 138 user-accessible general-purpose internal registers. The reason for the discrepancy between the number of registers directly addressable and the actual number of registers is due to a mechanism called *windowing*, which gives the programmer a view of only a subset of all registers at any instant. Register R0 is hardwired to contain the constant zero. Specifying R0 as an operand is the same as specifying the constant 0.

7.2.1 Register windows

An important feature of the Berkeley RISC architecture is the way in which it allocates new registers to subroutines; that is, when you call a subroutine, you get some new registers. If you can create 12 registers out of thin air when you call a subroutine, each subroutine will have its own workspace for temporary variables, thereby avoiding relatively slow accesses to main store.

Although only 12 or so registers are required by each invocation of a subroutine, the successive nesting of subroutines rapidly increases the total number of on-chip registers assigned to subroutines. You might think that any attempt to dedicate a set of registers to each new procedure is impractical, because the repeated calling of nested subroutines will require an unlimited amount of storage. Subroutines can indeed be nested to any depth, but research has demonstrated that on average subroutines are not nested to any great depth over short periods. Consequently, it is feasible to adopt a modest number of local register sets for a sequence of nested subroutines.

Figure 7.2 provides a graphical representation of the execution of a typical program in terms of the *depth of nesting* of subroutines as a function of time. The trace goes up each time a subroutine is called and down each time a return is made. If subroutines were never called, the trace would be a horizontal line. This figure demonstrates that even though subroutines may be nested to considerable depths, there are periods or runs of subroutine calls and returns that do not require a nesting level of greater than about five.

A mechanism for implementing local variable workspace for subroutines adopted by the designers of the Berkeley RISC is to support up to eight nested subroutines by providing on-chip workspace for each subroutine. Any further nesting forces the CPU to dump registers to main memory, as we shall soon see.

Memory space used by subroutines can be divided into four types:

Global space	Global space is directly accessible by all subroutines and holds constants and data that may be required from any point within the program. Most conventional microprocessors have only global registers.
Local space	Local space is private to the subroutine. That is, no other subroutine can access the current subroutine's local address space from outside the subroutine. Local space is employed as working space by the current subroutine.
Imported parameter space	Imported parameter space holds the parameters imported by the current subroutine from its parent that called it. In Berkeley RISC terminology these are called the high registers.

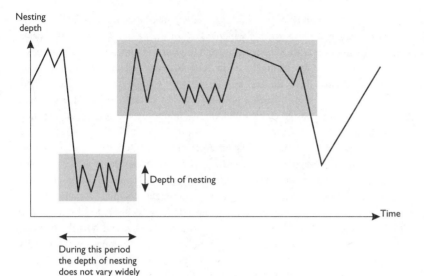

Nesting depth

Depth of nesting

Time

During this period the depth of nesting does not vary widely

Fig. 7.2 Depth of subroutine nesting as a function of time.

Exported parameter space Exported parameter space holds the parameters exported by the current subroutine to its child. In RISC terminology these are called the low registers.

Consider the following fragment of C code. Don't worry if you aren't a C programmer—the fine details don't matter. What we are going to do is to demonstrate the way in which memory is allocated to parameters. The main program creates three variables x, y, and z. Copies of x and y are passed to the function (i.e. subroutine) `calc`. The result is returned to the main program and assigned to z. Figure 7.3 illustrates a possible memory structure for the program.

Parameters x, y, and z are local to function `main`, and copies of x and y are sent to function `calc` as imported

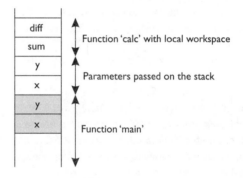

Fig. 7.3 Parameter space.

parameters. We will assume that copies of these parameters are placed on the stack before `calc` is called. The value returned by function `calc` is an exported parameter, and sum and `diff` are local variables in `calc`.

```
void main (void)
   {
    int x=204, y=25, z;
    z=calc (x, y);          /* let's calculate (x+y)/(x−y) */
   }
int calc (int a, int b)     /* this function calculates (a+b)/(a−b) */
   {
    int sum, diff;
    sum=a+b;                /* calculate a+b */
    diff=a−b;               /* calculate a+b */
    return (sum/diff)
   }
```

Windows and parameter passing

One of the reasons for the high frequency of data movement operations is the need to pass parameters to subroutines and to receive them from subroutines. Figure 7.3 has already demonstrated how parameters x and y are copied to the stack and then to the function that uses them.

The Berkeley RISC architecture deals with parameter passing by means of *multiple overlapped windows*. A window is the set of registers visible to the current subroutine. Figure 7.4 illustrates the structure of the Berkeley RISC's overlapping windows. Only three consecutive windows $(i-1, i, i+1)$ of the eight windows are shown in Fig. 7.4. The vertical columns represent the registers seen by the corresponding window. Each window sees 32 registers, but they aren't all the same 32 registers.

The Berkeley RISC has a special-purpose register, called the *window pointer*, WP, that indicates the current active window. Suppose that the processor is currently using the *i*th window set. In this case the WP contains the value *i*. The registers in each of the eight windows are divided into four groups, as shown in Table 7.2.

All windows consist of 32 addressable registers, R0 to R31. A Berkeley RISC instruction of the form ADD R3, R12, R25 implements [R25]←[R3]+[R12], where R3 lies within the window's *global address space*, R12 lies within its import from (or export to) parent subroutine space, and R25 lies within its *local address space*. RISC arithmetic and logical instructions always involve 32-bit values (there are no 8-bit or 16-bit operations).

The Berkeley RISC's subroutine call is CALL Rd, ⟨address⟩ and is similar to a typical CISC instruction BSR ⟨address⟩. Whenever a subroutine is invoked by CALLR Rd,⟨address⟩ the contents of the window pointer are incremented by 1 and the current value of the program counter saved in register Rd of the new window. The Berkeley RISC doesn't employ a conventional stack in external main memory to save subroutine return addresses.

Once a new window has been invoked (in Fig. 7.4 this is window *i*), the new subroutine sees a different set of registers from the previous window. Global registers R0 to R9 are an exception because they are common to all windows. Window R10 of the child (i.e. called) subroutine corresponds to (i.e. is the same as) window R26 of the calling (i.e. parent) subroutine. Suppose you wish to send a parameter to a subroutine. If the parameter is in R10 and you call a subroutine, register R26 in this subroutine will contain the parameter. There hasn't been a physical transfer of data because register R26 in the current window is simply register R10 in the previous window.

The physical arrangement of the Berkeley RISC's window system is given in Fig. 7.5. On the left-hand side of the diagram is the actual register array that holds all the on-chip general-purpose registers. The eight columns associated with windows 0 to 7 demonstrate how each window is mapped to the physical memory array on the chip and how the overlapping regions are organized. The windows are logically arranged in a circular fashion so that window 0 follows window 7 and window 7 precedes window 0. For example, if the current window pointer is 3 and you access register R25, location 74 is accessed in the register file. However, if you access register R25 when the window pointer is 7, you access location 137.

The total number of physical registers required to implement the Berkeley windowed register set is

$$10 \text{ global} + 8 \times 10 \text{ local} + 8 \times 6 \text{ parameter transfer registers}$$
$$= 138 \text{ registers}$$

Window overflow

Unfortunately, the total quantity of on-chip resources of any processor is finite and, in the case of the Berkeley RISC, the registers are limited to eight windows. If subroutines are nested to a depth greater than or equal to 7, window overflow is said to occur, as there is no longer a new window for the next subroutine invocation. When an overflow takes place, the only thing left to do is to employ external memory to hold the overflow data. In practice, the oldest window is saved rather than the new window created by the subroutine just called.

If the number of subroutine returns minus the number of subroutine calls exceeds 8, window underflow takes place. Window underflow is the converse of window overflow and

Register name	Register type
R0 to R9	The global register set is always accessible.
R10 to R15	Six registers used by the subroutine to receive parameters from its parent and to pass results back to its parent.
R16 to R25	Ten local registers accessed only by the current subroutine that cannot be accessed directly by any other subroutine.
R26 to R31	Six registers used by the subroutine to pass parameters to and from its own child (i.e. a subroutine called by itself).

Table 7.2 Berkeley RISC register types.

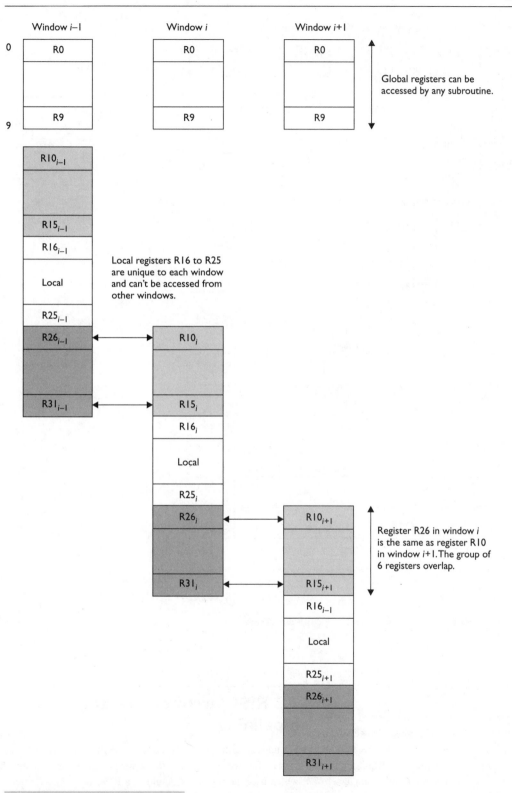

Fig. 7.4 Berkeley windowed register sets.

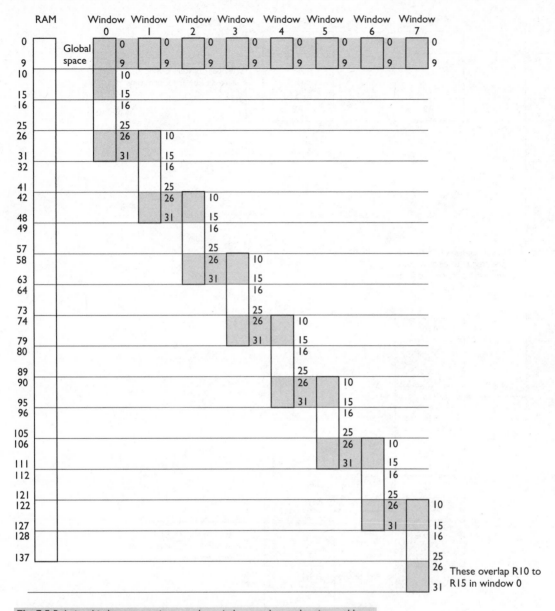

Fig. 7.5 Relationship between register number, window number, and register address.

the youngest window saved in main store must be returned to a window.

A considerable amount of research was carried out into dealing with window overflow efficiently. However, the imaginative use of windowed register sets in the Berkeley RISC was not adopted by many of the later RISC architectures. Modern RISC processors generally have a single set of 32 general-purpose registers.

7.3 RISC architecture and pipelining

We now describe *pipelining*, one of the most important techniques for increasing the throughput of a digital system, which uses the regular structure of a RISC to carry out internal operations in parallel.

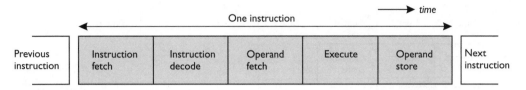

Fig. 7.6 Instruction execution.

Figure 7.6 illustrates the machine cycle of a hypothetical microprocessor executing an `ADD  P` instruction (i.e. `[A]←[R]+[M(P)]`, where A is an on-chip general purpose register and P is a memory location. The instruction is executed in five phases:

Instruction fetch Read the instruction from the system memory and increment the program counter.

Instruction decode Decode the instruction read from memory during the previous phase. The nature of the instruction decode phase is dependent on the complexity of the instruction encoding. A regularly encoded instruction might be decoded in a few nanoseconds with two levels of gating, whereas a complex instruction format might require ROM-based look-up tables to implement the decoding.

Operand fetch The operand specified by the instruction is read from the system memory or an on-chip register and loaded into the CPU.

Execute The operation specified by the instruction is carried out.

Operand store The result obtained during the execution phase is written into the operand destination. This may be an on-chip register or a location in external memory.

Each of these five phases may take a specific time (although the time taken would normally be an integer multiple of the system's master clock period). Some instructions require fewer than five phases; for example, `CMP  R1,R2` compares R1 and R2 by subtracting R1 from R2 to set the condition codes and does not need an operand store phase.

The inefficiency in the arrangement of Fig. 7.6 is immediately apparent. Consider the *execution phase* of instruction

interpretation. This phase might take one fifth of an instruction cycle, leaving the instruction execution unit idle for the remaining 80 percent of the time. The same rule applies to the other functional units of the processor, which also lie idle for 80 percent of the time. A technique called *instruction pipelining* can be employed to increase the effective speed of the processor by overlapping in time the various stages in the execution of an instruction. In the simplest of terms, a pipelined processor executes one instruction while fetching another instruction.

The way in which a RISC processor implements pipelining is described in Fig. 7.7. The RISC processor executes the instruction in four steps or phases: instruction fetch from external memory, operand fetch, execute, and operand store (we're using a 4-stage system because a separate 'instruction decode' phase isn't normally necessary). The internal phases take approximately the same time as the instruction fetch, because these operations take place within the CPU itself and operands are fetched from and stored in the CPU's own register file. Instruction 1 in Fig. 7.7 begins in time slot 1 and is completed at the end of time slot 4.

In a non-pipelined processor, the next instruction doesn't begin until the current instruction has been completed. In the pipelined system of Fig. 7.7, the instruction fetch phase of instruction 2 begins in time slot 2, at the same time that the operand is being fetched for instruction 1. In time slot 3, different phases of instructions 1, 2, and 3 are being executed simultaneously. In time slot 4, all functional units of the system are operating in parallel and an instruction is completed in every time slot thereafter. An n-stage pipeline can increase throughput by up to a factor of n.

Pipeline bubbles

A pipeline is an ordered structure that thrives on regularity. At any stage in the execution of a program, a pipeline contains components of two or more instructions at varying stages in their execution. Consider Fig. 7.8, in which a sequence of instructions is being executed in a four-stage pipelined processor. When the processor encounters a *branch* instruction, the

	Time 1	Time 2	Time 3	Time 4	Time 5	Time 6	Time 7	Time 8
Instruction 1	Instruction fetch	Operand fetch	Execute	Operand store				
Instruction 2		Instruction fetch	Operand fetch	Execute	Operand store			
Instruction 3			Instruction fetch	Operand fetch	Execute	Operand store		
Instruction 4				Instruction fetch	Operand fetch	Execute	Operand store	
Instruction 5					Instruction fetch	Operand fetch	Execute	Operand store

In time slot 3, instruction 1 is being executed, instruction 2 is in the operand fetch phase, and instruction 3 is being fetched from memory

Fig. 7.7 Pipelining and instruction overlap.

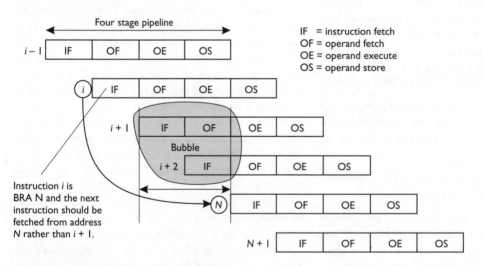

IF = instruction fetch
OF = operand fetch
OE = operand execute
OS = operand store

Instruction i is BRA N and the next instruction should be fetched from address N rather than i + 1.

Fig. 7.8 The pipeline bubble caused by a branch.

following instruction is no longer found at the next sequential address but at the target address in the branch instruction. The processor is forced to reload its program counter with the value provided by the branch instruction. This means that all the useful work performed by the pipeline must now be thrown away, since the instructions immediately following the branch are not going to be executed.

When information in a pipeline is rejected or the pipeline is held up by the introduction of idle states, we say that a *bubble* has been introduced.

As we have already stated, program control instructions are very frequent. Consequently, any realistic processor using pipelining must do something to overcome the problem of bubbles caused by instructions that modify the flow of control (branch, subroutine call and return). The Berkeley RISC reduces the effect of bubbles by refusing to throw away the instruction following a branch. This mechanism is called a *delayed jump* or a branch-and-execute technique because the instruction immediately after a branch is always executed. Consider the effect of the following sequence of instructions:

```
ADD     R1,R2,R3    [R3]←[R1]+[R2]
JMPX    N           [PC]←[N]           Goto address N
ADD     R2,R4,R5    [R5]←[R2]+[R4]  This is executed
ADD     R7,R8,R9    Not executed because the branch is taken
```

The processor calculates R5 := R2 + R4 *before* executing the branch. This sequence of instructions is most strange to the eyes of a conventional assembly language programmer, who is not accustomed to seeing an instruction executed after a branch has been taken.

Unfortunately, it's not always possible to arrange a program in such a way as to include a useful instruction immediately after a branch. Whenever this happens, the compiler must introduce a no operation instruction, NOP, after the branch and accept the inevitability of a bubble. Figure 7.9 demonstrates how a RISC processor implements a *delayed jump*. The branch described in Fig. 7.9 is a computed branch whose target address is calculated during the execute phase of the instruction cycle.

Another problem caused by pipelining is *data dependency*, in which certain sequences of instructions run into trouble because the current operation requires a result from the previous operation and the previous operation has not yet left the pipeline. Figure 7.10 demonstrates how data dependency occurs.

Suppose a programmer wishes to carry out the apparently harmless calculation

```
X:=(A+B) AND (A+B-C)
```

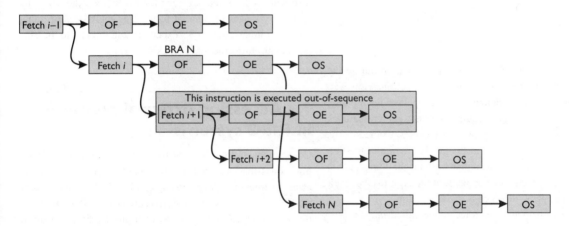

Fig. 7.9 Delayed branch.

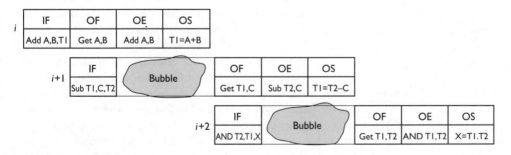

Fig. 7.10 Data dependency.

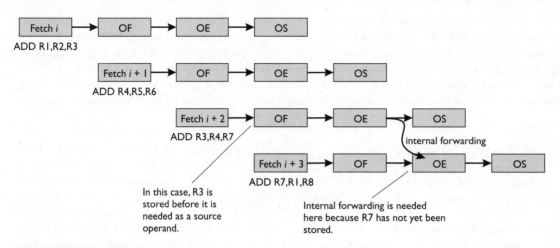

Fig. 7.11 Internal forwarding.

Assuming that A, B, C, X, and two temporary values, T1 and T2, are in registers in the current window, we can write

```
ADD  A,B,T1     [T1]←[A]+[B]
SUB  T1,C,T2    [T2]←[T1]−[C]
AND  T1,T2,X    [X] ←[T1]·[T2]
```

Instruction $i+1$ in Fig. 7.10 begins execution during the operand fetch phase of the previous instruction. However, instruction $i+1$ cannot continue on to its operand fetch phase, because the very operand it requires does not get written back to the register file for another two clock cycles. Consequently, a bubble must be introduced in the pipeline while instruction $i+1$ waits for its data. In a similar fashion, the logical AND operation also introduces a bubble, as it too requires the result of a previous operation which is in the pipeline.

Figure 7.11 demonstrates a technique called *internal forwarding*, which is designed to overcome the effects of data dependency. The following sequence of operations is to be executed.

```
1.  ADD  R1,R2,R3    [R3]←[R1]+[R2]
2.  ADD  R4,R5,R6    [R6]←[R4]+[R5]
3.  ADD  R3,R4,R7    [R7]←[R3]+[R4]
4.  ADD  R7,R1,R8    [R8]←[R7]+[R1]
```

In this example, instruction 3 (i.e. ADD R3,R4,R7) uses an operand generated by instruction 1 (i.e. the contents of register R3). Because of the intervening instruction 2, the destination operand generated by instruction 1 has time to be written into the register file before it is read as a source operand by instruction 3.

Instruction 3 generates a destination operand R7 that is required as a source operand by the next instruction. If the processor were to read the source operand requested by instruction 4 from the register file, it would see the old value of R7. By means of internal forwarding the processor transfers R7 from instruction 3's execution unit directly to the execution unit of instruction 4 (see Fig. 7.11).

7.4 Accessing external memory in RISC systems

Conventional CISC processors have a wealth of addressing modes that are used in conjunction with memory reference instructions. For example, the 68020 implements ADD D0,-(A5), which adds the contents of D0 to the top of the stack pointed at by A5 and then pushes the result on to this stack.

In their ruthless pursuit of efficiency, the designers of the Berkeley RISC severely restricted the way in which it accesses external memory. The Berkeley RISC permits only two types of reference to external memory: a load and a store. All arithmetic and logical operations carried out by the RISC apply only to source and destination operands in registers. Similarly, the Berkeley RISC provides a limited number of addressing modes with which to access an operand in the main store. It's not hard to find the reason for these restrictions on external memory accesses—an external memory reference takes longer than an internal operation. We now discuss some of the general principles of Berkeley RISC load and store instructions.

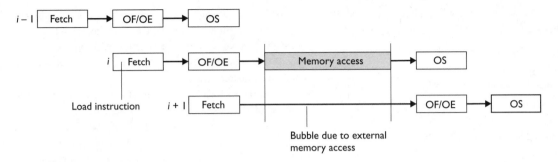

Fig. 7.12 The load operation.

Consider the load register operation of the form `LDXW (Rx)S2,Rd`, which has the effect `[Rd] ← [M([Rx]+S2)]`. The operand address is the contents of the memory location pointed at by register Rx plus offset S2. Figure 7.12 demonstrates the sequence of actions performed during the execution of this instruction. During the source fetch phase, register Rx is read from the register file and used to calculate the effective address of the operand in the execute phase. However, the processor can't progress beyond the execute phase to the store operand phase, because the operand hasn't been read from the main store. Therefore the main store must be accessed to read the operand and a store operand phase executed to load the operand into destination register Rd. Because memory accesses introduce bubbles into the pipeline, they are avoided wherever possible.

The Berkeley RISC implements two basic addressing modes: indexed and program counter relative. All other addressing modes can (and must) be synthesized from these two primitives. The effective address in the indexed mode is given by

$$EA = [Rx] + S2$$

where Rx is the index register (one of the 32 general-purpose registers accessible by the current subroutine) and S2 is an offset. The offset can be either a general-purpose register or a 13-bit constant (see Fig. 7.1).

The effective address in the program counter relative mode is given by

$$EA = [PC] + S2$$

where PC represents the contents of the program counter and S2 is an offset as above.

These addressing modes include quite a powerful toolbox: zero, one, or two pointers and a constant offset. If you wonder how we can use an addressing mode without an index (i.e. pointer) register, remember that R0 in the global register set permanently contains the constant 0. For example, `LDXW (R12)R0,R3` uses simple address register indirect addressing, whereas `LDXW (R0)123,R3` uses absolute addressing (i.e. memory location 123).

There's a difference between the addressing modes permitted by load and store operations. A load instruction permits the second source, S2, to be either an immediate value or a second register, whereas a store instruction permits S2 to be a 13-bit immediate value only. This lack of symmetry between the load and store addressing modes is because a 'load base × index' instruction requires a register file with *two* ports, whereas a 'store base + index' instruction requires a register file with *three* ports. Two-ported memory allows two simultaneous accesses. Three-ported memory allows three simultaneous accesses and is harder to design.

Figure 7.1 defines just two basic Berkeley RISC instruction formats. The short immediate format provides a 5-bit destination, a 5-bit source 1 operand, and a 14-bit short source 2 operand. The short immediate format has two variations: one that specifies a 13-bit literal for source 2 and one that specifies a 5-bit source 2 register address. Bit 13 specifies whether the source 2 operand is a 13-bit literal or a 5-bit register pointer.

The long immediate format provides a 19-bit source operand by concatenating the two source operand fields. Thirteen-bit and 19-bit immediate fields may sound a little strange at first sight. However, since $13 + 19 = 32$, the Berkeley RISC permits a full 32-bit value to be loaded into a window register in two operations. In the next section we will discover that the ARM processor deals with literals in a different way. A typical CISC microprocessor might take the same number of instruction bits to perform the same action (i.e. a 32-bit operation code field followed by a 32-bit literal).

The following describes some of the addressing modes that can be synthesized from the RISC's basic addressing modes.

1. **Absolute addressing**
   EA = 13-bit offset
   Implemented by setting Rx = R0 = 0, S2 = 13-bit constant.

2. **Register indirect**
   EA = [Rx]
   Implemented by setting S2 = R0 = 0.

3. **Indexed addressing**
   EA = [Rx] + Offset
   Implemented by setting S2 = 13-bit constant.

4. **Two-dimensional byte addressing (i.e. byte array access)**
   EA = [Rx] + [Ry]
   Implemented by setting S2 = [Ry].
   This mode is available only for load instructions.

Conditional instructions (i.e. branch operations) do not require a destination address and therefore the five bits 19–23, normally used to specify a destination register, are used to specify the condition (one of 16 since bit 23 is not used by conditional instructions).

The Berkeley RISC instruction set is described below. The purpose of this instruction set is to demonstrate that many instructions are similar to those of a CISC. Note the inclusion of a subtract *reverse* operation—all this does is to perform a subtraction except that the order of the operands is reversed (i.e. it calculates B − A rather than A − B). All data operations act on 32-bit values (the Berkeley RISC doesn't provide the luxury of byte, word, and longword operands). However, this processor does include several memory reference operations designed to access 8-, 16-, and 32-bit values.

Berkeley RISC register to register operations		
SLL	Rs,S2,Rd	shift left logical by S2
SRA	Rs,S2,Rd	shift right arithmetic by S2
SRL	Rs,S2,Rd	shift right logical by S2
AND	Rs,S2,Rd	logical AND
OR	Rs,S2,Rd	logical OR
XOR	Rs,S2,Rd	logical exclusive OR
ADD	Rs,S2,Rd	add
ADDC	Rs,S2,Rd	add with carry
SUB	Rs,S2,Rd	subtract
SUBC	Rs,S2,Rd	subtract with borrow
SUBI	Rs,S2,Rd	subtract reverse
SUBCI	Rs,S2,Rd	subtract reverse with borrow
Load instructions		
LDXW	(Rx)S2,Rd	load long (32-bit load)
LDXHU	(Rx)S2,Rd	load short unsigned (16 bit load)
LDXHS	(Rx)S2,Rd	load short signed (16 bit load, sign-extended)
LDXBU	(Rx)S2,Rd	load byte unsigned (8 bit load)
LDXBS	(Rx)S2,Rd	load byte signed (8 bit load, sign-extended)
LDRW	Y,Rd	load relative long
LDRHU	Y,Rd	load relative short unsigned
LDRHS	Y,Rd	load relative short signed
LDRBU	Y,Rd	load relative byte unsigned
LDRBS	Y,Rd	load relative byte signed
Store instructions		
STXW	Rm,(Rx)S2	store long
STXH	Rm,(Rx)S2	store short
STXB	Rm,(Rx)S2	store byte
STRW	Rm,Y	store relative long

STRH	Rm,Y	store relative short
STRB	Rm,Y	store relative byte
Control transfer instructions		
JMPX	COND,(Rx)S2	conditional jump
JMPR	COND,Y	conditional relative jump
CALLX	Rd,(Rx)S2	call subroutine and change window
CALLR	Rd,Y	call relative and change window
RET	COND,(Rx)S2	return and change window
CALLI	Rd	call an interrupt
RETI	COND,(Rx)S2	return from interrupt
Miscellaneous instructions		
LDHI	Rd,Y	load immediate high
GETLPC	Rd	load PC into register
GETPSW	Rd	load PSW into register
PUTPSW	Rm	put contents of register in PSW

We will look at the instruction set of a modern RISC processor in much more detail later in this chapter.

7.5 Reducing the branch penalty

If we're going to reduce the effect of branches on the performance of RISC processors, we need to determine the effect of branch instructions on the performance of the system. Because we cannot know how many branches a given program will contain, or how likely each branch is to be taken, we have to construct a *probabilistic model* to describe the system's performance. We will make the following assumptions:

1. Each non-branch instruction is executed in one cycle

2. The probability that a given instruction is a branch is p_b

3. The probability that a branch instruction will be taken is p_t

4. If a branch is taken, the additional penalty is b cycles

5. If a branch is not taken, there is no penalty

6. If p_b is the probability that an instruction is a branch, $1-p_b$ is the probability that it is not a branch

The average number of cycles executed during the execution of a program is the sum of the cycles taken for non-branch instructions, plus the cycles taken by branch instructions that are taken, plus the cycles taken by branch instructions that are not taken. We can derive an expression for the average number of cycles per instruction as

$$T_{ave} = (1-p_b) \cdot 1 + p_b \cdot p_t \cdot (1+b) + p_b \cdot (1-p_t) \cdot 1 = 1 + p_b \cdot p_t \cdot b$$

This expression, $1 + p_b \cdot p_t \cdot b$, tells us that the number of branch instructions, the probability that a branch is taken, and the overhead per branch instruction all contribute to the branch penalty. We are now going to examine some of the ways in which the value of $p_b \cdot p_t \cdot b$ can be reduced.

7.5.1 Branch prediction

If we can predict the outcome of the branch instruction *before* it is executed, we can start filling the pipeline with instructions from the branch target address (assuming the branch is going to be taken). For example, if the instruction is BRA N, the processor can start fetching instructions at locations N, $N+1$, $N+2$, etc., as soon as the branch instruction is fetched from memory. In this way, the pipeline is always filled with useful instructions.

This prediction mechanism works well with an unconditional branch like BRA N. Unfortunately, conditional branches pose a problem. Consider a conditional branch of the form BCC N (branch to N on carry bit clear). Should the RISC processor make the assumption that the branch will not be taken and fetch instructions in sequence, or should it make the assumption that the branch will be taken and fetch the instruction at the branch target address N?

As we have already said, conditional branches are required to implement various types of high-level language construct. Consider the following fragment of high-level language code.

```
if (J<K) I=I+L;
(for T=1; T<=I; T++)
    {
      :
    }
```

The first conditional operation compares J with K. Only the nature of the problem will tell us whether J is often less than K.

The second conditional in this fragment of code is provided by the FOR construct that tests a counter at the end of the loop and then decides whether to jump back to the body of the construct or to terminate to loop. In this case, you could bet that the loop is more likely to be repeated than exited. Loops can be executed thousands of times before they are exited. Some computers look at the type of conditional branch and then either fill the pipeline from the branch target if you think that the branch will be taken, or fill the pipeline from the instruction after the branch if you think that it will not be taken.

If we attempt to predict the behavior of a system with two outcomes (branch taken or branch not taken), there are four possibilities:

1. Predict branch taken and branch taken—successful outcome
2. Predict branch taken and branch not taken—unsuccessful outcome
3. Predict branch not taken and branch not taken—successful outcome
4. Predict branch not taken and branch taken—unsuccessful outcome

Suppose we apply a branch penalty to each of these four possible outcomes. The penalty is the number of cycles taken by that particular outcome, as Table 7.3 demonstrates. For example, if we think that a branch will not be taken and get instructions following the branch and the branch is actually taken (forcing the pipeline to be loaded with instructions at the target address), the branch penalty in Table 7.3 is c cycles.

We can now calculate the average penalty for a particular system. To do this we need more information about the system.

Prediction	Result	Branch penalty
Branch taken	Branch taken	a
Branch taken	Branch not taken	b
Branch not taken	Branch taken	c
Branch not taken	Branch not taken	d

Table 7.3 The branch penalty.

The first thing we need to know is the probability that an instruction will be a branch (as opposed to any other category of instruction). Assume that the probability that an instruction is a branch is p_b. The next thing we need to know is the probability that the branch instruction will be taken, p_t. Finally, we need to know the accuracy of the prediction. Let p_c be the probability that a branch prediction is correct. These values can be obtained by observing the performance of real programs. Figure 7.13 illustrates all the possible outcomes of an instruction. We can immediately write:

$(1 - p_b)$ = probability that an instruction is not a branch.
$(1 - p_t)$ = probability that a branch will not be taken.
$(1 - p_c)$ = probability that a prediction is incorrect.

These equations are obtained by using the principle that if one event or another must take place, their probabilities must add up to unity. The average branch penalty per branch instruction is therefore

$$C_{ave} = a \cdot (p\text{branch\_predicted\_taken\_and\_taken})$$
$$+ b \cdot (p\text{branch\_predicted\_taken\_but\_not\_taken})$$
$$+ c \cdot (p\text{branch\_predicted\_not\_taken\_but\_taken})$$
$$+ d \cdot (p\text{branch\_predicted\_not\_taken\_but\_not\_taken})$$

$$C_{ave} = a \cdot (p_t \cdot p_c) + b \cdot (1 - p_t) \cdot (1 - p_c)$$
$$+ c \cdot p_t \cdot (1 - p_c) + d \cdot (1 - p_t) \cdot p_c$$

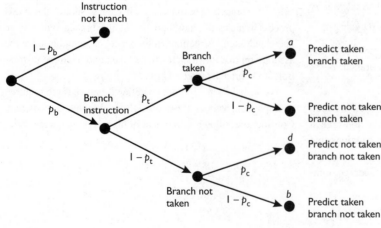

Fig. 7.13 Branch prediction.

The average number of cycles added due to a branch instruction is

$$C_{ave} \cdot p_b = p_b \cdot (a \cdot p_t \cdot p_c + b \cdot (1 - p_t) \cdot (1 - p_c) + c \cdot p_t \cdot (1 - p_c) + d \cdot (1 - p_t) \cdot p_c)$$

We can make two assumptions to help us to simplify this general expression. The first is that $a = d = N$ (i.e. if the prediction is correct the number of cycles is N). The other simplification is that $b = c = B$ (i.e. if the prediction is wrong the number of cycles is B). The average number of cycles per branch instruction is therefore

$$p_b \cdot (N \cdot p_t \cdot p_c + B \cdot p_t \cdot (1 - p_c) + B \cdot (1 - p_t) \cdot (1 - p_c) + N \cdot (1 - p_t) \cdot p_c) = p_b \cdot (N \cdot p_c + B \cdot (1 - p_c))$$

This formula can be used to investigate trade-offs between branch penalties, branch probabilities, and pipeline length. There are several ways of implementing branch prediction (i.e. increasing the value of p_c). Two basic approaches are *static branch prediction* and *dynamic branch prediction*. Static branch prediction makes the assumption that branches are always taken or never taken. Since observations of real code have demonstrated that branches have a greater than 50 percent chance of being taken, the best static branch prediction mechanism would be to fetch the next instruction from the branch target address as soon as the branch instruction is detected.

A better method of predicting the outcome of a branch is by observing its op-code, because some branch instructions are taken more or less frequently than other branch instructions. Using the branch op-code to predict that the branch will or will not be taken results in 75 percent accuracy. An extension of this technique is to devote a bit of the op-code to the static prediction of branches. This bit is set or cleared by the compiler depending on whether the compiler estimates that the branch is most likely to be taken. This technique provides branch prediction accuracy in the range 74–94 percent.

Dynamic branch prediction techniques operate at run-time and use the past behavior of the program to predict its future behavior. Suppose the processor maintains a table of branch instructions. This branch table contains information about the likely behavior of each branch. Each time a branch is executed, its outcome (i.e. taken or not taken) is used to update the entry in the table. The processor uses the table to determine whether to take the next instruction from the branch target address (i.e. branch predicted taken) or from the next address in sequence (branch predicted not taken).

Single-bit branch predictors provide an accuracy of over 80 percent and 5-bit predictors provide an accuracy of up to 98 percent. A typical branch prediction algorithm uses the last two outcomes of a branch to predict its future. If the last two outcomes are X, the next branch is assumed to lead to outcome X. If the prediction is wrong it remains the same the next time the branch is executed (i.e. two failures are needed to modify the prediction). After two consecutive failures, the prediction is inverted and the other outcome assumed. This algorithm responds to trends and is not affected by the occasional single *different* outcome.

We are now going to look at the architecture of a real RISC processor. We have decided to use the ARM processor because it is both interesting and fairly easy to understand.

7.6 The ARM processor

One of the strongest arguments made by the supporters of RISC processors in the 1980s was that it is relatively easy to design and produce a RISC processor. From 1983 onward Acorn Computers created a series of chips solidly based on RISC principles that demonstrated the proof of this statement. The same company later set up Advanced RISC Machines, of Cambridge, England, to develop further generations of RISC processors (called the ARM family). In 1998 the company was floated on the stockmarket and became ARM Ltd. We are going to use the ARM processor to illustrate the RISC philosophy because the ARM is easy to understand and incorporates some very interesting architectural features. In this section we provide an overview of the ARM architecture and concentrate on its innovative features.

ARM's registers

Like most mainstream RISC architectures, the ARM is a 32-bit machine with a register-to-register, three-operand instruction set. First-generation ARMs supported 32-bit words and unsigned bytes, whereas later members of the ARM range provide 8-bit signed bytes and 16-bit signed and unsigned half-words. The ARM processor doesn't implement delayed branches and therefore the instruction following a branch is not automatically executed.

All operands are 32-bits wide, except for some multiplication instructions that generate a 64-bit product in two registers, and byte and halfword accesses (64-bit and halfword accesses are available only on some members of the ARM family). The ARM has only 16 user-accessible general-purpose registers called r0 to r15 and a current program status register, CPSR, that's similar to the condition code register we've described earlier.

The ARM doesn't divide registers into address and data register like the 68000—you can use any register as an

User registers	Supervisor registers	Abort registers	Undefined registers	Interrupt registers	Fast interrupt registers
r0	r0	r0	r0	r0	r0
r1	r1	r1	r1	r1	r1
r2	r2	r2	r2	r2	r2
r3	r3	r3	r3	r3	r3
r4	r4	r4	r4	r4	r4
r5	r5	r5	r5	r5	r5
r6	r6	r6	r6	r6	r6
r7	r7	r7	r7	r7	r7
r8	r8	r8	r8	r8	r8_FIQ
r9	r9	r9	r9	r9	r9_FIQ
r19	r10	r10	r10	r10	r10_FIQ
r11	r11	r11	r11	r11	r11_FIQ
r12	r12	r12	r12	r12	r12_FIQ
r13	r13_SVC	r13_abort	r13_undef	r13_IRQ	r13_FIQ
r14	r14_SVC	r14_abort	r13_undef	r14_IRQ	r14_FIQ
r15 =PC	r15 =PC	r15 =PC	r15 =PC	r15 =PC	r15 =PC

— Shaded registers are banked

There are 16 registers r0 to r15. When an exception occurs, some of the registers are changed. For example, if an interrupt occurs, the current value of register r13 is switched out and a new r13 switched in. The new r13 can be written r13_IRQ to indicate it exists only during interrupt handling.

Program Status Register

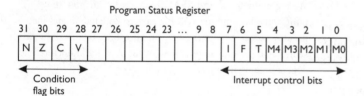

31	30	29	28	27	26	25	24	23	...	9	8	7	6	5	4	3	2	1	0
N	Z	C	V									I	F	T	M4	M3	M2	M1	M0

Condition flag bits

Interrupt control bits

Fig. 7.14 The ARM's register set.

address register or a data register. By reducing the number of bits in an op-code used to specify a register, more bits are available to select an instruction. The ARM doesn't provide lots of different instructions like a CISC processor. Instead, it provides flexibility by allowing instructions to do two or more things at once (as we shall soon see). In some ways, the ARM is rather like a microprogrammed CPU.

The ARM's registers are not all general-purpose. Register r15 contains the program counter, and register r14 is used to save subroutine return addresses (r14 is also called the *link register*, lr). Because r15 (which can be written 'PC' in ARM assembly language) is as accessible to the programmer as any other register, you can easily perform computed gotos. By convention, ARM programmers use register r13 as a stack pointer, although that is not mandatory.

The ARM has more than one *program status register* (CPSR—see Fig. 7.14). In normal operation the CPSR contains the current values of the condition code bits (N, Z, C, and V) and eight system status bits. The I and F bits are used to disable interrupt requests and fast interrupt requests, respectively. We discuss interrupts and exceptions in the next chapter. Status bits M0 to M4 indicate the processor's current operating mode. The T flag is implemented only by the Thumb-compatible versions of the ARM family. Such processors implement *two* instruction sets, the 32-bit ARM instruction set and a compressed 16-bit Thumb instruction set.

When an interrupt occurs, the ARM saves the pre-exception value of the CPSR in a stored program status register (there's one for each of the ARM's five interrupt modes).

Unlike conventional CISC processors, the ARM doesn't dump registers on a stack in response to an exception.

There are, in fact, more than 16 general-purpose registers because the ARM performs a very limited type of windowing. The ARM runs in its user mode except when it switches to one of its other five operating modes. These modes correspond to interrupts and exceptions and are not of interest to us in this chapter. Interrupts and exceptions switch in new r13 and r14 registers (the so-called *fast interrupt* switches in new r8 to r14 registers as well as r13 and r14). When a mode switch occurs, registers r0 to r12 are unmodified. For our current purposes we will assume that there are just 16 user-accessible registers r0 to r15. Figure 7.14 describes the ARM's register set.

The *current program status register* is accessible to the programmer in all modes. However, user-level code can't modify the I, F, and M0–M4 bits (this restriction is necessary to enable the ARM to support a protected operating system). When a context switch occurs between states, the CPSR is saved in the appropriate SPSR (saved program status register). In this way, a context switch does not lose the old value of the CPSR.

Summary of the ARM's register set

- The ARM has 16 accessible 32-bit registers called r0 to r15 at any one time

- r15 acts as the program counter and r14 (called the *link register*) stores the subroutine return address

- You can write PC for r15 in ARM assembly language, lr for r14, and sp for r13

- The ARM has a current program status register, CPSR, that holds condition codes

- Some registers are not unique because processor exceptions create new instances of r13 and r14

- Because the return address is not necessarily saved on the stack by a subroutine call, the ARM is very fast at implementing subroutine return calls

As most readers will have read the chapter on the CISC processor and are now familiar with instruction sets and addressing modes, we provide only a short introduction to the ARM's instruction set before introducing some of its development tools and constructing simple ARM programs.

7.6.1 ARM instructions

The basic ARM instruction set is not, at first sight, exciting. A typical three-operand register-to-register instruction has the format

```
ADD  r1,r2,r3
```

and is interpreted as $[r1] \leftarrow [r2] + [r3]$. Note the order of the operands—the destination appears first (left-to-right), then the first source operand, and finally the second source operand. Table 7.4 describes some of the ARM's data processing instructions.

Although the ARM's basic instruction set is very straightforward, it does include some interesting features. The ARM provides so called *reverse* instructions; for example, the normal subtract instruction SUB r1,r2,r3 is defined as $[r1] \leftarrow [r2] - [r3]$, whereas the reverse subtract operation RSB r1,r2,r3 is defined as $[r1] \leftarrow [r3] - [r2]$. You may be wondering why anyone would want a reverse subtraction instruction, because all you need do is to use normal subtraction with swapped operands. As we shall see, the ARM doesn't treat the two source operands symmetrically.

A slightly unusual logical operation is the *bit clear* instruction BIC. The BIC performs the operation AND NOT (e.g. $A \cdot \overline{B}$), so that BIC r1,r2,r3 is defined as $[r1] \leftarrow [r2] \cdot \overline{[r3]}$. The BIC performs a logical AND between the first operand and the complement of the second operand. If this seems confusing, consider the effect of BIC r1,r2,r3 on the two operands $[r2] = 11001010$ and $[r3] = 11110000$. The result loaded into r1 is 00001010 because each bit in the second operand set to 1 clears the corresponding bit of the first operand.

The ARM has a regular instruction set (by comparison with CISC processors). However, the multiply instruction, MUL, has two peculiarities. First, the destination (i.e. result) register must not be the same as the first source operand register; for example, MUL R0,R0,R1 is illegal (although MUL R0,R1,R0 is legal). Second, the MUL instruction may not specify an immediate value as the second operand.

A particularly interesting operation is the *multiply and accumulate* instruction, MLA, that has the rather fearsome four-operand form MLA Rd,Rm,Rs,Rn. This instruction performs a multiplication and adds the result to a running total. A common operation in many branches of computing is the calculation of the *inner product* of two vectors (the inner product is also known as the *scalar* product). This operation is found in both graphics and signal-processing and is one of the most important instructions provided by special-purpose digital signal processing chips. If vector A consists of the n components $a_1, a_2, a_3, \ldots, a_n$ and vector B consists of the n components $b_1, b_2, b_3, \ldots, b_n$, the inner-product of A and B is the scalar value $s = A \cdot B = a_1 \cdot b_1 + a_2 \cdot b_2 + a_3 \cdot b_3 + \cdots + a_n \cdot b_n$. For example, if $A = 0, 1, 4, 2, 3$ and $B = 1, 1, 2, 5, 2$, the inner product $A \cdot B = 0 \times 1 + 1 \times 1 + 4 \times 2 + 2 \times 5 + 3 \times 2 = 25$. The RTL definition of MLA is

$$[R_d] \leftarrow [R_m] \times [R_s] + [R_n]$$

The result is truncated to 32 bits.

The ARM provides two compare instructions, each of which has two operands. CMP R_n, R_s evaluates $[R_n] - [R_d]$ and sets the condition codes in the CPSR. The compare negated instruction, CMN R_n, R_s, also performs a comparison, except that the second operand is negated before the comparison is made.

The ARM has an unusual test equivalence instruction, TEQ R_n, R_s, that tests whether two values are equivalent. If the two operands are equivalent, the Z-bit is set to 1. This instruction is very similar to the CMP, except that the V-bit isn't modified by a TEQ.

The test, TST R_n, R_s, instruction performs a test on two operands by ANDing the operands bit-by-bit and then setting the condition code bits. A conventional single-operand CISC TST instruction is the same as compare with zero and is used to test an operand for zero or negative. The ARM's two-operand TST instruction allows you to mask out bits of the operand you wish to test. For example, if R0 contains $0...0001111_2$, the effect of TST R1,R0 is to mask the contents of R1 to 4 least-significant bits and then to compare those bits with 0.

The ARM's built-in shift mechanism

We are going to look at one of the ARM's most unusual features (in comparison with both conventional CISC and other RISC architectures). The instructions in Table 7.4 lack operations that modify the flow of control (i.e. branches and subroutine calls). We will deal with these instructions later. Table 7.4 also lacks *shift* instructions. There is a good reason for this omission—almost all ARM instructions are shift instructions; that is, a normal instruction can also perform shifting.

Figure 7.15 illustrates the format of a data processing instruction. Before continuing, we should note one important aspect of Fig. 7.15. Bit 20 of an instruction, the S-bit, is used to force an update of the condition code register, CPSR. If an instruction has the suffix 'S', the CPSR is updated—otherwise it is not; for example, ADDS r3,r1,r2 adds r1 to r2, puts the result in r3, and sets the condition code flags accordingly. However, ADD r3,r1,r2 performs exactly the same addition but does not update the condition codes in the CPSR. This feature (common to several other RISC processors) allows the programmer to update the condition codes only when they are needed.

As you can see from Fig. 7.15, the encoding of an ARM instruction follows the general pattern of other RISC architectures: an opcode, some control bits, and three operands. Operands Rn and Rd specify registers. Operand 2 in bits 0 to 11 of the op-code in Fig. 7.15 selects either a third register or a literal. The ARM's designers have been ingenious and used

Mnemonic	Operation	Definition
ADD	Add	$[Rd] \leftarrow Op1 + Op2$
ADC	Add with carry	$[Rd] \leftarrow Op1 + Op2 + C$
SUB	Subtract	$[Rd] \leftarrow Op1 - Op2$
SBC	Subtract with carry	$[Rd] \leftarrow Op1 - Op2 + C - 1$
RSB	Reverse subtract	$[Rd] \leftarrow Op2 - Op1$
RSC	Reverse subtract with carry	$[Rd] \leftarrow Op2 - Op1 + C - 1$
MUL	Multiply	$[Rd] \leftarrow Op1 \times Op2$
MLA	Multiply and accumulate	$[Rd] \leftarrow Rm \times Rs + Rn$
AND	Logical AND	$[Rd] \leftarrow Op1 \wedge Op2$
ORR	Logical OR	$[Rd] \leftarrow Op1 \vee Op2$
EOR	Exclusive OR	$[Rd] \leftarrow Op1 \oplus Op2$
BIC	Logical AND NOT	$[Rd] \leftarrow Op1 \wedge \overline{Op2}$
CMP	Compare	Set condition codes on $Op1 - Op2$
CMN	Compare negated	Set condition codes on $Op1 + Op2$
TST	Test	Set condition codes on $Op1 \wedge Op2$
TEQ	Test equivalence	Set condition codes on $Op1 \oplus Op2$
MOV	Move	$[Rd] \leftarrow Op2$
MVN	Move negated	$[Rd] \leftarrow \overline{Op2}$
LDR	Load register	$[Rd] \leftarrow [M(ea)]$
STR	Store register	$[M(ea)] \leftarrow [Rd]$
LDM	Load register multiple	Load a block of registers from memory
STM	Store register multiple	Store a block of registers in memory
SWI	Software interrupt	$[r14] \leftarrow [PC]$, $[PC] \leftarrow 8$, enter supervisor mode

Table 7.4 The ARM data processing and data move instructions.

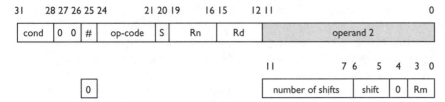

Fig. 7.15 Format of the ARM'S data processing instructions.

this field to provide a shift function on all data processing instructions.

When bit 25 of an op-code is 0, operand 2 both selects a second operand register and a shift operation. Bits 5 to 11 specify one of five types of shift and the number of places to be shifted. The shifts supported by the ARM are LSL (logical shift left), LSR (logical shift right), ASR (arithmetic shift right), ROR (rotate right), and RRX (rotate right extended by one place). The RRX shift is similar to the 68000's ROXL (rotate right extended) in which the bits are rotated and the carry bit is shifted into the vacated position. These shifts are similar to the corresponding 68000 shifts and are defined as:

LSL   The operand is shifted left by 0 to 31 places. The vacated bits at the least-significant end of the operand are filled with zeros.

LSR   The operand is shifted right 0 to 31 places. The vacated bits at the most-significant end of the operand are filled with zeros.

ASL   The arithmetic shift left is identical to the logical shift left. This multiplies a number by 2 for each shift.

ASR   The operand is shifted right 0 to 31 places. The vacated bits at the most-significant end of the operand are filled with zeros if the original operand was positive, or with 1s if it was negative (i.e. the sign-bit is replicated). This divides a number by 2 for each place shifted.

ROR   The operand is rotated by 0 to 31 places right. The bit shifted out of the least-significant end is copied into the most-significant end of the operand. This shift preserves all bits. No bit is lost by the shifting.

RRX   The operand is rotated by 1 place right. The bit shifted out of the least-significant end of the operand is shifted into the C-bit. The old value of the C-bit is copied into the most-significant end of the operand; that is, shifting takes place over 33 bits (i.e. the operand plus the C-bit).

The ARM combines a shift operation with every data processing instruction at no extra cost in terms of code and little

additional cost in terms of time. However, the number of addressable registers provided by the ARM is 16 rather than the 32 offered by most other RISC architectures.

The shift is applied to *operand 2* rather than the result. For example, the ARM instruction

ADD r1,r2,r3, LSL #4

performs a logical shift left by four places on the 32-bit operand in register r3 before adding it to the contents of register r2 and depositing the result in register r1. In RTL terms, this instruction is defined as

$$[r1] \leftarrow [r2] + [r3] \times 16$$

You can use this shifting facility to perform clever short cuts; for example, suppose you want to multiply the contents of r3 by 9. The operation

ADD r3,r3,r3, LSL #3

logically shifts the second operand in r3 three places left to multiply it by 8. This value is added to operand 1 (i.e. r3) to generate $8 \times R3 + R3 = 9 \times R3$. However, instructions such as ADD r3,r3,r3, LSL #3 take an extra cycle to complete because the ARM can read only two registers from the register file in a single cycle.

This ability to scale operands is useful when dealing with tables. Suppose that a register contains a pointer to a table of 4-byte elements in memory and we wish to access element number *i*. What is the address of element *i*? The address of the *i*th element is the pointer plus $4 \times i$. If we assume that the pointer is in register r0 and the offset is in r1, the pointer to the required element, r2, is given by $[r0] + 4 \times [r1]$. In ARM assembly language, we can load this pointer into r2 by

ADD r2,r0,r1, LSL #2

As you can see, we have added the offset to r0 in a conventional way, but we've also been able to scale the offset by 4 because each integer requires 4 bytes. This instruction performs the operation $[r2] \leftarrow [r0] + [r1] \times 4$.

The ARM permits *dynamic shifts* in which the number of places shifted is specified by the contents of a register. In this case the instruction format is similar to that of Fig. 7.15, except that bits 8 to 11 specify the register that defines the number of shifts, and bit 4 is 1 to select the dynamic shift mode. If register r4 specifies the number of shifts, we can write

```
ADD r1,r2,r3, LSL r4
```

which has the RTL definition $[r1] \leftarrow [r2] + [r3] \times 2^{[r4]}$.

Later we will demonstrate how the ability to shift operand 2 can be used to generate constants.

How do you shift an operand itself without using a data processing operation such as an addition? You can apply a shift to the source operand of the move instruction; for example,

```
MOV r0,r1,LSL #2;   ;shift the contents of r1 left twice
                     and copy result to 0
MOV r0,r1,LSL #6;   ;multiply [r1] by 64 and copy
                     result to r0
MOV r0,r1,ASR #2;   ;divide [r1] by 4 and copy result
                     to r0
```

We look at the MOV instruction in more detail later.

7.6.2 ARM branch instructions

One of the ARM's most interesting features is that each instruction is *conditionally executed*. Again, this is a standard feature of microprogrammed instruction sets. Bits 28 to 31 of each ARM instruction provide a condition field that defines whether the current instruction is to be executed—see Table 7.5.

The 16 conditions described in Table 7.5 are virtually the same as those provided by many other microprocessors. One condition is the default case *always*, which means that the current instruction is to be executed. The special case *never* is reserved by ARM for future expansion and should not be used. In order to indicate the ARM's conditional mode to the assembler, all you have to do is to append the appropriate condition to a mnemonic. Consider the following example in which the suffix EQ is appended to the mnemonic ADD to get

```
ADDEQ r1,r2,r3
```

The addition is now performed only if the Z-bit in the CPSR is set. The RTL form of this operation is

```
IF Z=1 THEN [r1] ← [r2] + [r3]
```

Consider the high-level expression

```
IF x=y THEN p=q+r
```

If we assume that x, y, p, q, and r are in registers r0, r1, r2, r3, and r4, respectively, we can express this algorithm as

```
CMP     r0,r1
ADDEQ   r2,r3,r4
```

The ARM's ability to make the execution of each instruction conditional makes it easy to write compact code. Consider the following extension of the previous example:

```
CMP    r0,r1     ;compare x and y
ADDEQ  r2,r3,r4  ;IF x=y THEN p=q+r
SUBLS  r2,r3,r4  ;        ELSE IF x<y THEN p=q-r
```

Op-code bits 31 – 28	Mnemonic prefix	Condition	Flags
0000	EQ	equal	$Z=1$
0001	NE	not equal	$Z=0$
0010	CS/HS	carry set/unsigned higher or same	$C=1$
0011	CC/LO	carry clear/unsigned lower	$C=0$
0100	MI	negative	$N=1$
0101	PL	positive or zero	$N=0$
0110	VS	overflow set	$V=1$
0111	VC	overflow clear	$V=0$
1000	HI	higher than (unsigned)	$(C=1) \cdot (Z=0)$
1001	LS	lower or same (unsigned)	$(C=0) + (Z=1)$
1010	GE	greater than or equal (signed)	$N=V$
1011	LT	less than (signed)	$N \neq V$
1100	GT	greater than (signed)	$(Z=0) \cdot (N=V)$
1101	LE	less than or equal (signed)	$(Z=1) + (N \neq V)$
1110	AL	always (default)	don't care
1111	NV	never (do not use)	none

Table 7.5 The ARM's condition codes.

Other languages would require explicit branch instructions to implement such an algorithm. Let's look at a high-level construct first encoded into ARM assembly language and then 68000 assembly language.

```
IF    (P=Q)
      THEN  X=P−Y
```

If we assume that r1 = P, r2 = Q, r3 = X, and r4 = Y, we can write

```
CMP    r1, r2
SUBEQ  r3, r1, r4
```

The equivalent 68000 code is

```
      CMP.L  D1,D2
      BNE    Not
      SUB.L  D1,D4
      MOVE.L D4,D3
Not ...
```

There is, of course, nothing to stop you combining conditional execution and shifting because the branch and shift fields of an instruction are independent. You can write

```
ADDCC  r1,r2,r3 LSL  r4
```

which is interpreted as

```
IF C=0 THEN [r1]←[r2]+[r3]×2^[r4]
```

The following example from Steve Furber demonstrates the ARM's ability to generate very effective code for the construct:

```
IF (a=b) AND (c=d)
   THEN e:=e+1;
```

Assume that a is in register r0, b is in register r1, c is in register r2, d is in register r3, and e is in register r4.

```
CMP    r0,r1       Compare a and b

CMPEQ  r2,r3       If a=b THEN compare c
                   and d

ADDEQ  r4,r4,#1    if c=d then increment e
                   by 1
```

In this example, the first instruction, CMP r0,r1, compares a and b. The next instruction, CMPEQ r2,r3, performs a comparison only if the result of the first line was true (i.e. a=b). The third line, ADDEQ r4,r4,#1, is evaluated only if the previous line was true (i.e. c=d). The third line adds the literal 1 to r4 to implement the e:=e+1 part of the expression.

7.6.3 Immediate operands

Like other RISC and CISC processors, ARM instructions can specify an immediate operand as well as a register. Figure 7.16 demonstrates how an immediate operand is encoded. When bit 25 of an instruction is 0, the ARM specifies a register that may or may not be shifted before it is used as operand 2 (as we've already described). When bit 25 is 1, the 12-bit operand 2 field *could* provide a 12-bit literal. But it doesn't. Those who designed the ARM argued that *range* is more important than *precision* and provided an 8-bit literal in the range 0 to 255 that can be *scaled* to provide a 32-bit value.

In Fig. 7.16 the four most-significant bits of the operand 2 field specify the literal's alignment within a 32-bit frame. If the 8-bit literal is N and the 4-bit alignment is n in the range 0 to 12, the value of the literal is given by $N \times 2^{2n}$. Note that the scale factor is $2n$. This mechanism is, of course, analogous to the way in which floating point numbers are represented. Scaling is performed automatically by the assembler. If you write

```
ADD r1,r2,#65536
```

This assembler deals with the out-of-range literal by scaling it.

Summary of data processing instructions

The ARM's instruction set is both simple and powerful. It's simple because instructions are regular and the instruction set is very small. The instruction set is powerful because you can apply three attributes to each instruction. You can choose whether to update the condition codes by appending an S to the op-code. You can make the instruction's execution conditional by appending the condition to the instruction (note that

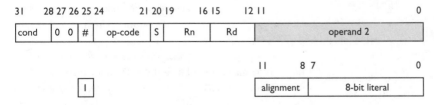

Fig. 7.16 Format of the ARM'S instructions with immediate operands.

the conditional suffix precedes the update flags suffix). You can specify a register or a literal as operand 2 and then shift the operand before it is used. Consider the following examples:

Op-code		Operation
ADD	r1,r2,r3	$[r1] \leftarrow [r2]+[r3]$
ADDS	r1,r2,r3	$[r1] \leftarrow [r2]+[r3]$, **update flags**
ADDEQ	r1,r2,r3	IF Z $=1$ THEN $[r1] \leftarrow [r2]+[r3]$
ADDEQS	r1,r2,r3	IF Z $=1$ THEN $[r1] \leftarrow [r2]+[r3]$, **update flags**
ADD	r1,r2,r3, LSL #2	$[r1] \leftarrow [r2]+[r3] \times 4$
ADD	r1,r2,r3, LSL r4	$[r1] \leftarrow [r2]+[r3] \times 2^{[r4]}$
ADD	r1,r2, #125	$[r1] \leftarrow [r2]+125$
ADD	r1,r2, #0xFF00	$[r1] \leftarrow [r2]+255*2^8$
ADDCSS	r1,r2,r3, LSL r4	IF C $=1$ THEN $[r1] \leftarrow [r2]+[r3] \times 2^{[r4]}$, **update flags**

7.6.4 Sequence control

We've already seen that the ARM implements the conditional execution of instructions. The ARM also implements a conventional branching mechanism using the conditions described in Table 7.5. For example, the instruction BNE LOOP forces a branch if the Z-bit of the condition code register (i.e. CPSR) is clear. The branch instruction is encoded in 32 bits, which includes an 8-bit op-code and a '24'-bit signed offset that is added to the contents of the program counter. The 24-bit signed offset is actually a 26-bit value which is stored as a word offset in 24 bits because ARM instructions can only ever be word-aligned. Consequently, the byte and halfword parts of the offset do not have to be stored, as they will always be zero.

The simple unconditional branch has the single-letter mnemonic B, as the following demonstrates:

```
B  Next  ;branch to 'Next'
```

You can implement a loop construct in the following way:

```
      MOV  R0, #20    ;load the loop counter R0 with 20
Next .
      .
      .
      SUBS R0,R0,#1   ;decrement loop counter
      BNE  Next       ;repeat until loop count=zero
```

This fragment of code is exactly like that of many CISC processors, but note that you have to explicitly update the condition codes when you decrement the loop counter with SUBS R0,R0,#1.

The ARM also implements a so-called *branch with link* instruction that is similar to the subroutine call. A branch operation can be transformed into a 'branch with link' instruction by appending L to its mnemonic. Consider the following:

```
BL  Next  ;branch to 'Next' with link
```

The ARM copies the program counter held in register r15 into the link register r14. That is, the branch with link preserves the return address in r14. We can express this instruction in RTL as

```
[r14] ← [PC]  ;copy to link register
[r15] ← Next  ;jump to 'Next'
```

Note that in practice, the value loaded into r14 is really $[PC]-4$ because the PC actually points to the instruction being fetched into the pipeline, rather than the instruction being currently executed.

A return from subroutine is made by copying the saved value of the program counter to the program counter. You can use the move instruction, MOV, to achieve this:

```
MOV  PC,r14  ;copy r14 to r15 (restore PC)
```

Because the subroutine return address is stored in r14 rather than on the stack in external memory, the ARM's subroutine call and return mechanism is very fast indeed. However, you have to be careful not to accidentally overwrite the return address in r14. Moreover, if a subroutine calls another subroutine, you have to save the previous return address in r14 on the stack.

Because the branch with link instruction can be made conditional, the ARM implements a full set of conditional subroutine calls. You can write, for example,

```
CMP   r9,r4  ;if r9<r4
BLLT  ABC    ;then call subroutine ABC
```

The mnemonic `BLLT` is made up of `B` (branch unconditionally), `L` (branch with link), and `LT` (execute on condition less than).

7.6.5 Data movement and memory reference instructions

In keeping with the RISC philosophy, the ARM processors support only register-to-register operations and load and store operations between registers and memory. However, the ARM's data movement instructions do have some interesting features.

The ARM implements two instructions that copy data from one register to another (or a literal to a register). `MOV` r_i, r_j simply copies the contents of register r_j into register r_i. The instruction `MVN` r_i, r_j copies the *logical complement* of the contents of register r_j into register r_i. The logical complement of a value is calculated by inverting its bits (i.e. it's the one's complement rather than the arithmetic two's complement).

The `MOV` instruction can be used conditionally and combined with a shifted literal (like the data processing instructions). Consider the following examples:

```
MOV     r0,#0           ; [r0] ←0; Clear r0
MOV     r0,r1, LSL #4    ; [r0] ←[r1] * 16
MOVNE   r3,r2, ASR #5    ; IF Z = 0 THEN [r3] ← [r2]/32
MOVS    r0,r1, LSL #4    ; [r0] ←[r1]*16;  update condition codes
MVN     r0,#0           ; [r0] ←−1;  the 1's complement of 0 is 111 … 1
MVN     r0,r0           ; [r0] ←[r0];  complement the bits of r0
MVN     r0,#0xF         ; [r0] ←0xFFFFFFF0
```

The ARM provides a special move instruction that lets you examine or modify the contents of the current processor status register, CPSR. The operation `MRS  Rd,  CPSR` copies the value of the current processor status register into general register Rd. Similarly, the `MSR_f CPSR, Rm` instruction copies general register Rm into the CPSR (note that bits 28, 29, 30, 31 of the CPSR hold the V, C, Z, and N flags, respectively). This instruction is privileged and can't be executed in the user mode (to prevent users changing to a privileged mode).

Loading an address into a register

Up to now, we have assumed that an address is already in a register. As you know, we cannot load a 32-bit literal value into a register (because 32-bit literals aren't supported and the ARM doesn't implement multiple-length instructions). However, we can load an 8-bit literal shifted by an even power of 2 into a register. The ARM assembly language programmer can use the `ADR` (load address into register) instruction to load a register with a 32-bit address; for example

```
ADR  r0,table
```

loads the contents of register r0 with the 32-bit address 'table'. If you look through the ARM's instruction set, you will not find the `ADR` instruction listed because it doesn't exist. Don't let this worry you. The ARM assembler treats the `ADR` as a *pseudo-instruction* and then generates the code that causes the appropriate action to be carried out. The `ADR` instruction attempts to generate a `MOV`, `MVN`, `ADD`, or `SUB` instruction to load the address into a register.

Figure 7.17 demonstrates how the ARM assembler treats an `ADR` instruction. We have used ARM's development system to show the source code, the disassembled code, and the registers during the execution of the program (we'll return to this system later). As you can see, the instruction `ADR r5,table1` has been assembled into the instruction `ADD r5,pc,0x18`, because `table1` is 18_{16} bytes onward from the current contents of the program counter in r15. That is, the address `table1` has been synthesized from the value of the PC plus the constant 18_{16}.

The ARM assembler also supports a similar pseudo-operation. The construct `LDR  rd, =value` is used to load value into register rd. The `LDR` pseudo-instruction uses the `MOV` or `MVN` instructions, or it places the constant in memory and uses program counter relative addressing to load the constant.

Accessing memory

The ARM implements two remarkably flexible memory-to-register and register-to-memory data transfer operations, `LDR` and `STR`. Figure 7.18 illustrates the structure of the ARM's memory reference instructions. Like all ARM instructions, the memory access operations `LDR` and `STR` have a conditional field and can, therefore, be executed conditionally.

An important element of the ARM's design philosophy is that all instructions are 32 bits and no instruction is composed of two or more longwords. A corollary of this statement is you can't specify an absolute address or load a 32-bit literal into a register. The ARM's load and store instructions use what we called (in the previous chapter) *address register indirect addressing* to access memory. ARM literature refers to address register indirect addressing as '*indexed addressing*'.

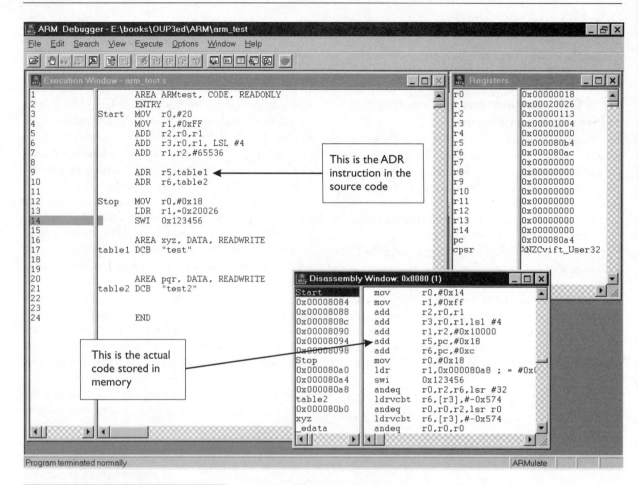

Fig. 7.17 Effect of the ADR pseudo instruction.

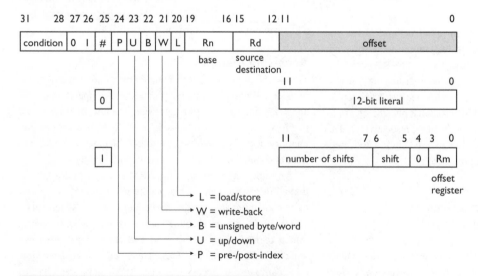

Fig. 7.18 Format of the ARM's memory reference instructions.

Remember that any of the ARM's 16 registers can act as an address (i.e. index) register.

Bit 20 of the op-code (see Fig. 7.18) determines whether the instruction is a load or a store, and bit 25, the bit, determines the type of the offset used by indexed addressing. Let's look at some of the various forms of these instructions. Simple versions of the load and store operations that provide indexing can be written

```
LDR r0,[r1] ;load r0 with the word pointed at by r1
STR r2,[r3] ;store the word in r2 in the location pointed at by r3
```

These addressing modes correspond exactly to the 68000's address register indirect addressing modes `MOVE.L (A1),D0` and `MOVE.L D2,(A3)`, respectively.

The simple indexed addressing mode can be extended by providing an offset to the base register; for example,

```
LDR r0, [r1, #8]  ;load r0 with the word pointed at by [r1]+8
```

The ARM goes further and permits the offset to be *permanently* added to the base register in a form of autoindexing (rather like the 68000's predecrementing and postincrement-

ing addressing modes). This mode is indicated by using the ! suffix as follows:

```
LDR r0,[r1,#8]!  ;load r0 with the word pointed at by [r1]+8
                 ;and post-index by adding 8 to r1
```

In this example, the effective address of the operand is given by the contents of register r1 plus the offset 8. However, the index (i.e. pointer register) is also incremented by 8. By modifying the above syntax slightly, we can perform post-indexing by accessing the operand at the location pointed at by the base register and then incrementing the base register, as the following demonstrates:

```
LDR r0,[r1],#8 ;load r0 with the word pointed at by r1
               ;and post-index by adding 8 to r1
```

We can summarize these three forms as

```
LDR r0,[r1,#8]   ;effective address=[r1]+8, r1 is unchanged
LDR r0,[r1,#8]!  ;effective address=[r1]+8, [r1]←[r1]+8
LDR r0,[r1],#8   ;effective address=[r1], [r1]←[r1]+8
```

Let's look at Fig. 7.18 in greater detail. The base register, r*n*, acts as a memory pointer (much like other RISC processors) and the U-bit defines whether the final address should be calculated by adding or subtracting the offset. The B-bit can be set to force a *byte* operation rather than a word. Whenever a byte is loaded into a 32-bit register, bits 8 to 31 are set to zero (i.e. the byte is not sign-extended).

The P- and W-bits control the ARM's autoindexing modes. When W = 1 and P = 1, pre-indexed addressing is performed. When W = 0 and P = 0, post-indexed addressing is performed.

Consider the following example that calculates the total of a table of bytes terminated by zero.

```
        MOV    r0,    #Table   ;r0 points to Table
        MOV    r2,    #0       ;clear the running total
Next LDRB r1,    [r0],#1  ;get a byte and increment the pointer
        ADD    r2,    r1, r2   ;calculate the new total
        CMP    r1,    #0       ;test for end
        BNE    Next
```

As there is no 'clear register' instruction we have to synthesize one by `SUB r2,r2,r2` or by `MOV r2,#0`.

Example

Let's provide a simple example to consolidate some of the things we've learned. Suppose A and B are two *n*-component vectors. As we have already stated, the inner product of

A and B is the scalar value $s = A \cdot B = a_1 \cdot b_1 + a_2 \cdot b_2 + a_3 \cdot b_3 + \cdots + a_n \cdot b_n$. We can now write the code:

```
      MOV   r4,#0            ;clear initial sum in r4
      MOV   r5,#24           ;load loop counter with n (assume 24 here)
      ADR   r0,A             ;r0 points at vector A
      ADR   r1,B             ;r1 points at vector B
Next  LDR   r2,[r0],#4       ;Repeat: get Ai and update pointer to A
      LDR   r3,[r1],#4       ;        get Bi and update pointer to B
      MLA   r4,r2,r3,r4      ;            s=s+Ai×Bi
      SUBS  r5,r5,#1         ;            decrement loop counter
      BNE   Next             ;repeat n times
```

This block of ARM *RISC* code is not too dissimilar to the corresponding 68000 *CISC* code.

```
      CLR.L    D2            ;clear initial sum in D2
      MOVE.B   #24,D0        ;load loop counter with n (assume 24 here)
      LEA      A,A0          ;A0 points at vector A
      LEA      B,A1          ;A1 points at vector B
Next  MOVE.W   (A0)+,D1      ;Repeat: get Ai and update pointer to A
      MULU     (A1)+,D1      ;            Ai×Bi and update pointer to B
      ADD.L    D1,D2         ;            s=s+Ai×Bi (sum in D2)
      SUB      #1,D0         ;            decrement loop counter
      BNE      Next          ;repeat n times
```

All ARM processors can operate with 32-bit values. The ARMv4 also supports byte and halfword (i.e. 16-bit) operations. A 16-bit unsigned word can be loaded into a register and stored in memory, or a 16-bit or 8-bit value can be loaded and sign-extended. Typical load/store instruction are

LDHR   Load unsigned halfword (i.e. 16 bits)
LDRSB   Load signed byte
LDHSH   Load signed halfword
STHR   Store halfword

Multiple register movement

A RISC's strict register-to-register instruction set with memory access limited to load and store operations isn't very efficient when blocks of data have to be copied between memory and registers. Fortunately, the ARM supports the transfer of multiple registers between the processor and memory. The format of a *move multiple register* instruction is similar to that of Fig. 7.18, except that the 16 bits 15 to 0 specify the list of registers to be moved. The ARM's two block transfer instructions are

$$\text{LDM}_{mode} \text{ Rn,register\_list or}$$
$$\text{LDM}_{mode} \text{ Rn!,register\_list}$$

and

$$\text{STM}_{mode} \text{ Rn,register\_list or}$$
$$\text{STM}_{mode} \text{ Rn!,register\_list or v}$$

The subscript 'mode' indicates one of eight addressing modes (IA = increment after, IB increment before, DA = decrement after, DB = decrement before, FD = full descending, FA = full ascending, ED = empty descending, EA = empty ascending). These modes fall into two groups: IA, IB, DA, and DB are block-copying modes, whereas FD, ED, FA, and EA are stack modes.

The stack modes describe how the stack on to which registers are pushed or pulled is to behave. If the stack is *ascending* it grows toward higher addresses; if it is descending it grows toward lower addresses like the 68000's stack. The *empty* and *full* modes select whether the stack pointer points at the item on the top of the stack (full mode), or at the next item above the top of stack (empty mode). The 68000's stack is a *full mode* stack.

The optional '!' after the base register indicates whether the base register is modified (i.e. updated) after the instruction has been executed. Consider the following example of a load multiple registers from memory instruction:

LDMIA r1!,{r2−r5, r7−r10}

The instruction `LDMIA r1!,{r2−r5, r7−r10}` copies registers r2 to r5 and r7 to r10 inclusive from memory, using r1 as a pointer with auto-indexing. Transfers from memory start at the base address specified by r1 and registers are transferred in numerical order, beginning with the lowest numbered register at the lowest address. For example, if r1 contains 1000_{16}, register r2 is loaded from 1000_{16}, r3 from 1004_{16}, r4 from 1008_{16}, and so on. After the instruction has been executed, the value of r1 is 32 greater than it was (8 registers × 4 bytes).

The difference between the `LDMIA` and `LDMIB` is that `LDMIA` increments the base register *after* it has been used to address memory, whereas the `LDMIB` increments the base register *before* it is used. In terms of the notation we used to describe the 68000's assembly language, `LDMIA` corresponds to `(rd)+` and `LDMIB` corresponds to `+(rd)`. Another example of a multiple register transfer is:

```
STMIA r0,{r3,r4,r5,r9}    ;store r3 at location pointed at by r0
                          ;store r4 at location pointed at by r0+4
                          ;store r5 at location pointed at by r0+8
                          ;store r9 at location pointed at by r0+12
```

In this case, the suffix 'IA' indicates that the index register is incremented *after* each transfer. Had the instruction `LDMDA` been used, the index register would have been decremented.

Suppose you want to compare two 16-byte strings in memory. You can use a block load and conditional execution to generate some compact and fast code:

```
        ADR     r0,String1    ;r0 points to the first string
        ADR     r1,String2    ;r1 points to the second string
        LDMIA   r0,{r2−r5}    ;get first 16-byte string in r2 to r5
        LDMIA   r1,{r6−r9}    ;get second 16-byte string in r6 to r9
        CMP     r2,r6         ;compare two 4-byte chunks
        CMPEQ   r3,r7         ;if previous 4 bytes same then compare next 4
        CMPEQ   r4,r8         ;and so on
        CMPEQ   r5,r9
        BEQ     Equal         ;if final 4 same then strings are equal
NotEq   .                     ;if we end here then string not same

        .

Equal   .
```

The swap instruction

The ARM also provides a swap instruction, `SWP`, that exchanges the contents of a register with a memory location;

for example, the effect of `SWP r0,r1,[r2]` is

`[temp]←[M([r2])]` ;read the contents of memory pointed at by r2

`[M([r2])]←[r1]` ;store the contents of r1 in the location pointed at by r2

`[r0]←[temp]` ;copy saved memory contents of r0

At the end of this swap operation, r1 has been stored in memory and the memory element has been stored in r0. If the same register is specified (i.e. `SWP r1,r1,[r2]`) a true swap takes place. This instruction can be used computationally in a program, but its real purpose is in multiprocessor systems to facilitate communication between processors.

Subroutines and the block move instruction

Although r0 to r13 are interchangeable general-purpose registers, programmers normally reserve register r13 as a stack pointer (however, there are no hardware restrictions or requirements). As we have already said, a subroutine call is implemented by the branch and link instruction, `BL`, that saves the return address in the *link register* called r14 or lr. If a subroutine calls another subroutine, we have to save the previous return address in r14 before it gets overwritten by the new return address. Moreover, if the new subroutine uses registers containing active data, we can save them on the stack prior to the subroutine call. Consider the following code:

```
ABC    .                     ;this is the first subroutine
       .

       STMFD r13,(r0-r4,lr)  ;save working registers and link register
       BL    PQR             ;call subroutine PQR
       .

       .

       LDMFD r13,(r0-r4,pc)  ;restore working registers and return
       .

       .

PQR                          ;a subroutine called from ABC
       .

       .

       MOV   pc, lr          ;return (copy link register to PC)
```

Note how we have saved registers r0 to r4 and the link register on the stack pointed at by r13 in subroutine ABC prior to calling subroutine PQR. When we call PQR, a new return address is loaded in the link register. After a return from PQR is made, subroutine ABC is executed to completion. By using a block load instruction, we can both restore registers r0 to r4 and return to the calling program. Remember that the register list we saved was r0–r4 and lr. When we restore registers, we restore r0–r4, pc which means that r0 to r4 are restored, whereas the value of the link register on the stack is copied to the program counter.

7.6.6 Further features of the ARM
The ARM processors operate in a user/supervisor mode rather like members of the 68K family. The ARM's operating modes are *user*, *FIQ* (fast interrupt), *IRQ* (interrupt), *SVC* (software interrupt), *Abort* (memory faults), *Undef* (undefined instructions), and *System* (operating system tasks). Each of these modes (except user and system) has its own *saved program status register*, SPSR, that is used to hold a copy of the CPSR at the time that the exception occurred.

The ARM's software interrupt instruction, SWI, is rather like the 68000's TRAP and is used to call an operating facility. Executing an SWI saves the return address in r14_svc, saves the CPSR in SPSR_svc, enters the supervisor mode, disables interrupt requests, and forces a jump to memory location 08_{16}. The interrupt handler must ensure that the program counter and condition codes are correctly restored at the end of exception handling.

The SWI is a conditional instruction and takes a 24-bit immediate operand. The operand is not used by the instruction itself, but the exception handler may access it to determine, say, the type of software interrupt.

7.7 Using the ARM

We are now going to look at ARM's development system that allows you to write programs in assembly language, assemble them, and then run the programs. The software needed to carry out these operations is provided on the CD that accompanies this book. This software consists of three parts: an *assembler*, a *linker* (that generates binary code), and a *simulator* (that lets you execute the binary code on a PC). Let's begin with its assembly language.

7.7.1 The ARM assembler
All assembly languages and their assemblers are roughly similar (there isn't the same difference between the 68000 and the ARM assembly languages as there is between, for example, Pascal and LISP). Most assemblers follow the layout

```
label mnemonic operand comment
```

There are, however, differences in the conventions they employ and in the way in which assembler directives are implemented. Figure 7.19 shows a simple ARM assembly language program (that does nothing other than manipulate a few numbers).

As you can see, the program in Fig. 7.19 begins with the assembler directive

```
AREA TestProg, CODE, READONLY
```

This directive provides the name of the section of code and describes its properties. The ENTRY directive on the next line provides the code's unique entry point. An END directive terminates the code.

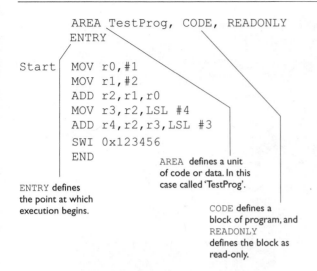

```
        AREA TestProg, CODE, READONLY
        ENTRY
Start   MOV r0,#1
        MOV r1,#2
        ADD r2,r1,r0
        MOV r3,r2,LSL #4
        ADD r4,r2,r3,LSL #3
        SWI 0x123456
        END
```

ENTRY defines the point at which execution begins.

AREA defines a unit of code or data. In this case called 'TestProg'.

CODE defines a block of program, and READONLY defines the block as read-only.

Fig. 7.19 Structure of an ARM assembly language program.

We have used the software interrupt, SWI, instruction to terminate the program. This instruction provides a convenient means of halting execution (SWI is an operating system call).

Once a program has been written, you can assemble it with the ARM assembler. An ARM assembly language program has the extension .s to denote *source code*. If the program is called ARMtest1.s, you enter the command (from the DOS prompt)

```
armasm -g ARMtest1.s
```

Assembling the program produces an object file called ARMtest1.o. The ARM development system requires that a program be *linked* before you can execute its code. *Linking* is performed in both high-level language compilation and low-level language assembly and involves bringing together separately compiled/assembled units of code. To link the object file generated by the assembler you enter

```
armlink ARMtest1.o -o ARMtest1
```

The command armlink takes the object file ARMtest1.o and creates an executable file ARMtest1.

Now that we've created the binary code, we can run it in the debugger that can be called from DOS or from Windows. We've used the Windows version (see Fig. 7.20).

After invoking the simulator, we've loaded the program ARMtest1 and opened a window that displays the disassembled source code and shows the contents of the registers. In Fig. 7.20

we have stepped through the program line by line by clicking on the single-step icon. The program has ended with an error message caused by the SWI instruction. Note the values of the registers. We are now going to provide a tutorial on the use of the ARM development system. The full development system provides a very powerful set of tools and is available from ARM Ltd. Here we are interested only in writing an assembly language program and observing its execution.

7.7.2 A tutorial: using the ARM development system

We now provide a tutorial that goes through the steps necessary to develop and debug a program written in ARM assembly language. We begin by writing a simple program to determine whether a given string is a palindrome or not. A palindrome is a string that reads the same from left-to-right as from right-to-left—in this example the string is 'ANNA'. All we have to do is to remove a character from each end of the string and compare this pair of characters. If they are the same the string might be a palindrome; if they differ the string isn't a palindrome. We then repeat the same operation on the remaining string (i.e. substring), and so on. If we reach the middle of the string, the string is a palindrome.

The algorithm to determine whether a string is a palindrome requires at least three variables. We need a pointer to the character at the left-hand end of the string, a pointer to the character at the right-hand end of the string, and a flag that indicates whether the string is a palindrome or not.

The following fragment of pseudocode provides a first-level solution to the problem. The variables left_pointer and right_pointer point at the characters at the ends of the string currently being examined, and Palindrome is true if the string is a palindrome and false otherwise. We begin by assuming that the string is a palindrome and set the flag Palindrome=false if ever a pair of characters don't match.

```
Palindrome=true
Set left_pointer to point at leftmost character
Set right_pointer to point at rightmost character
REPEAT
    Get left character at left_pointer position
    Get right character at right_pointer position
    IF left character≠right character
      THEN Palindrome=false
    left_pointer=left_pointer+1
    right_pointer=right_pointer−1
UNTIL middle of string OR Palindrome=false
```

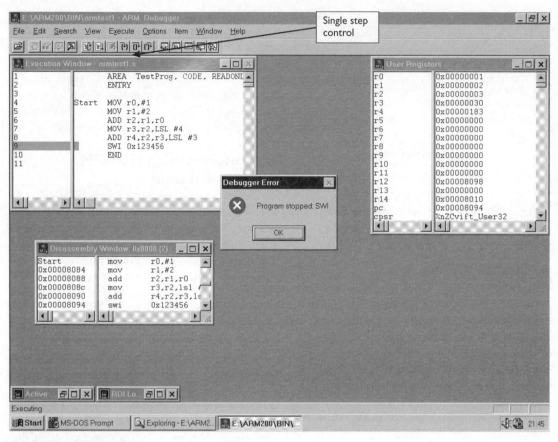

Fig. 7.20 Running the simulator.

The only tricky part of this problem is determining when we reach the middle. Consider the palindromes ABCCBA and ABCBA. The first palindrome has an even number of letters and the second an odd number of letters. Consider the following:

Step	Even length	Pointers at end of test	Odd length	Pointers at end of test
1	**A**BCCB**A**		**A**BCB**A**	
2	A**B**CC**B**A		A**B**C**B**A	
3	AB**CC**BA	Left_pointer = right_pointer + 1	AB**C**BA	Left_pointer = right_pointer

The middle of the string is located when either the left pointer is one less than the right pointer or the left pointer is equal to the right pointer.

We can easily write a fragment of code that scans the string. In the following code (written in the form of a subroutine), register r0 points to the left-hand end of the string and register r1 points to the right-hand end of the string.

Remember that the ARM instruction LDRB r3,[r0],#1 means 'load register r3 with the byte pointed at by r0 and add 1 to the contents of r0'.

```
again    LDRB  r3,[r0],#1    ;get left hand character and update pointer
         LDRB  r4,[r1],#-1   ;get right hand character and update pointer
         CMP   r3,r4         ;compare characters at the ends of the string
         BNE   notpal        ;if characters different then fail
```

```
        .                           ;test for middle of string
        .
        .
        BNE   again                 ;if middle not found then repeat
waspal                              ;end up here if string is palindrome
notpal  MOV   pc,lr                 ;return from subroutine
```

We can test for the middle of a string in the following way:

```
        CMP   r0,r1                 ;if r2=r1 then odd length palindrome
        BEQ   waspal                ;if same then exit with palindrome found
        ADD   r2,r0,#1              ;copy left pointer to r2 and move right
        CMP   r2, r1                ;if r2=r1 then even length palindrome
        BEQ   waspal                ;if same then exit with palindrome found
```

However, this code causes a problem. The code we wrote to scan the palindrome automatically updates the pointers when they are used to fetch characters (e.g. the left pointer is used and updated by LDRB r3,[r0],#1 and the right pointer is updated by LDRB r4,[r1],#-1). This means that both pointers are updated during the character-fetch operations and therefore we have to take account of this when comparing the pointers). We can fix the problem in three ways: update the

pointers only *after* the test for the middle, take copies of the pointers and move them back before comparing them, or perform a new test on the copies for left_pointer= right_pointer+2 and left_pointer=right_ pointer+1. We will use the first option to get

```
                                    ;r0 points at left hand end of string
                                    ;r1 points at right hand end of string
pal     MOV   r10,#0x0              ;r10=Palindrome=0=set fail flag
again   LDRB  r3,[r0]               ;get left-hand character
        LDRB  r4,[r1]               ;get right-hand character
        CMP   r3,r4                 ;compare the ends of the string
        BNE   notpal                ;if different then fail
                                    ;test for middle of string
        CMP   r0,r1                 ;if r0=r1 then odd length palindrome
        BEQ   waspal                ;if same then exit with palindrome found
        ADD   r2,r0,#1              ;copy left pointer to r2 and move right
        CMP   r2,r1                 ;if r2=r1 then even length palindrome
        BEQ   waspal                ;if same then exit with palindrome found
        ADD   r0,r0,#1              ;move left pointer right
        SUB   r1,r1,#1              ;move right pointer left
        B     again                 ;REPEAT
waspal  MOV   r10,#0x1              ;r10=1=success flag
notpal  MOV   pc,lr                 ;return
```

The following code provides the complete program to test a string. We begin by scanning the string (which is terminated by a 0) to find the location of the right hand character.

```
                AREA palindrome, CODE, READONLY
                ENTRY
start                                   ;locate the ends of the string
                LDR     r0,=string      ;r0 points to start of string to test
                MOV     r1,r0           ;copy left pointer to right pointer in r1
loop            LDRB    r2,[r1],#1      ;get char and update right pointer
                CMP     r2,#0           ;repeat until terminator located
                BNE     loop
                SUB     r1,r1,#2        ;fix right pointer to point to end of string
                BL      pal             ;call subroutine to test for palindrome
stop            MOV     r0,#0x18        ;stop program execution by calling the O/S
                LDR     r1,=0x20026     ;the three lines of 'magic' code in this
                SWI     0x123456        ;block are an operating system call

                                        ;test for palindrome
                                        ;r0 points at left hand end of string
                                        ;r1 points at right hand end of string
pal             MOV     r10,#0x0        ;r10=Palindrome=0=set fail flag
again           LDRB    r3,[r0]         ;get left hand character
                LDRB    r4,[r1]         ;get right hand character
                CMP     r3,r4           ;compare the ends of the string
                BNE     notpal          ;if different then fail
                                        ;test for middle of string
                CMP     r0,r1           ;if r0=r1 then odd length palindrome
                BEQ     waspal          ;if same then exit with palindrome found
                ADD     r2,r0,#1        ;copy left pointer to r2 and move right
                CMP     r2,r1           ;if r2=r1 then even length palindrome
                BEQ     waspal          ;if same then exit with palindrome found
                ADD     r0,r0,#1        ;move left pointer right
                SUB     r1,r1,#1        ;move right pointer left
                B       again           ;REPEAT
waspal          MOV     r10,#0x1        ;r10=1=success flag
notpal          MOV     pc,lr           ;return
```

The subroutine either returns 0 in r10 (not palindrome) or 1 (is palindrome).

Note the three lines of '*magic code*' labeled by stop. We use the term 'magic code' to indicate that it's meaning isn't clear because it's a system requirement. In this case, I copied the code from ARM's literature because it offers a means of halting program execution by calling an operating system function. This code applied to the specific system I was using. Other versions of the ARM simulator may require different termination mechanisms. You can always terminate a program by implementing an infinite loop:

```
Finish  B  Finish
```

Having written the program (using an ASCII editor), we assemble it with the command ARMASM. If the program is called PROG1.s, it is assembled by

```
ARMASM -g PROG1.s
```

The assembly process produces a new object file called PROG1.o. The '-g' option generates debugging information for later use. If no errors are found during the assembly phase, the object code must be linked to produce the binary code that can be executed by an ARM processor (or simulated on a PC). The command used to link a program is ARMLINK. In this case we write

```
ARMLINK PROG1.o -o PROG1
```

The linker creates a new file called PROG1 that can be loaded into the ARM simulator.

Once we have created a file to run, we can call the Windows-based ARM debugger by clicking on the ADW icon (assuming you've loaded ARM's package on your system). This loads the development system and creates the window shown in Fig. 7.21. By selecting the **File** item on the top toolbar, you get a pull-down menu whose first item is 'Load image' (see Fig. 7.22). Clicking on **Load image** invokes the window used to open a file and lists the available files (see Fig. 7.23). In this case, we select the file called prog1. Figure 7.24 shows the situation after this program has been loaded.

The **Execution Window** in Fig. 7.24 shows the code loaded into the debugger. Note that the ARM development system creates a certain amount of header code in addition to your program. We are not interested in this code. Figure 7.24

shows address 0x00008008 highlighted—this is the point at which execution is to begin (i.e. the initial value of the program counter). However, you can also start the program by setting a breakpoint to 0x8080 and then running the code to the breakpoint. Doing this executes the startup code and then stops the simulation at the appropriate point.

We can view other windows beside the **Execution Window**. In Fig. 7.25 we have selected the **View** command on the top toolbar and have chosen **Registers** from the pull-down list to give a second pull-down list of registers.

Figure 7.26 shows the debugger with the register window active. You can modify the contents of any register in this window by double clicking on the appropriate register. Figure 7.27 shows how the current contents of a register appear in a **Modify Item** window. In this diagram the PC contains 0x00008008 which we alter to 0x00008080 (the address of

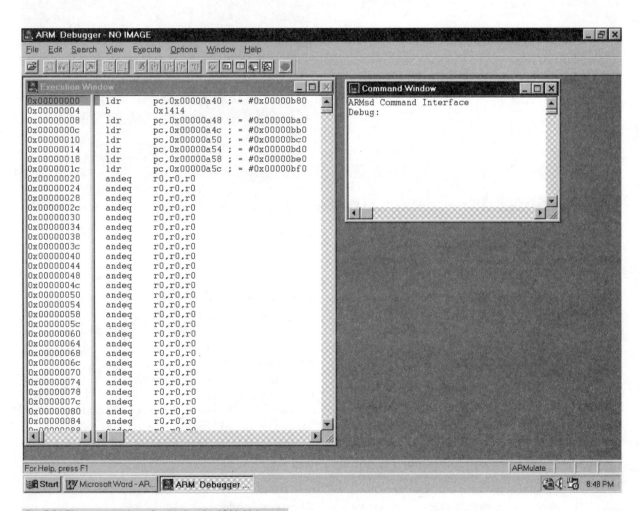

Fig. 7.21 The initial window after loading the ARM ddebugger.

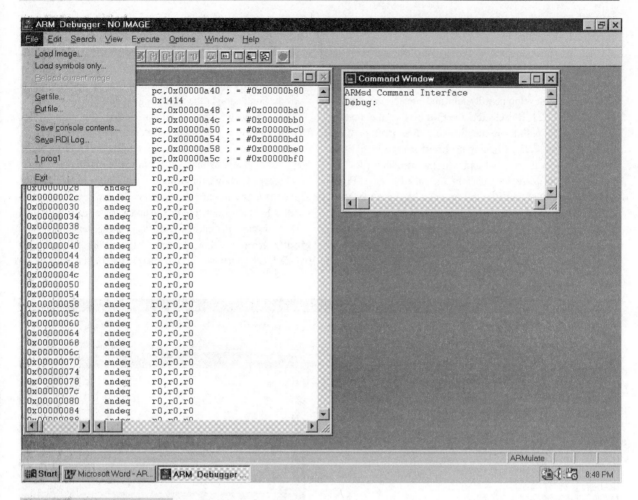

Fig. 7.22 The File pull-down menu.

the start of prog1). This address (i.e. 8080) is a feature of the ARM development system I used.

Figure 7.28 shows the state of the system after the PC has been reloaded. As you can see, the code that we originally entered is now displayed.

In Fig. 7.28 we have resized the windows to make best use of the available space in order to see as much as possible of the program's comment field (without losing the **Registers** window). The first instruction to be executed is highlighted.

We can now begin to execute the program's instructions to test whether a string is a palindrome. There are several ways of running a program in the ARM debugger; for example, we can run the whole program until it terminates, execute a group

of instructions, or execute a single instruction at a time. If you click on the *step-in* icon on the toolbar, a single instruction at a time is executed. The effect of program execution can be observed by monitoring the contents of the registers in the **Registers** window.

In Fig. 7.29 we have begun execution and have reached the second instruction of the subroutine 'pal'. In Fig. 7.30 we have executed some more instructions and have reached line number 26 in the code.

Let's return to the **View** pull-down menu on the toolbar to display more information about the program. In Fig. 7.31 we have pulled down the menu and in Fig. 7.32 we have selected the **Disassembly** mode and have been given the **Disassembly Address** window.

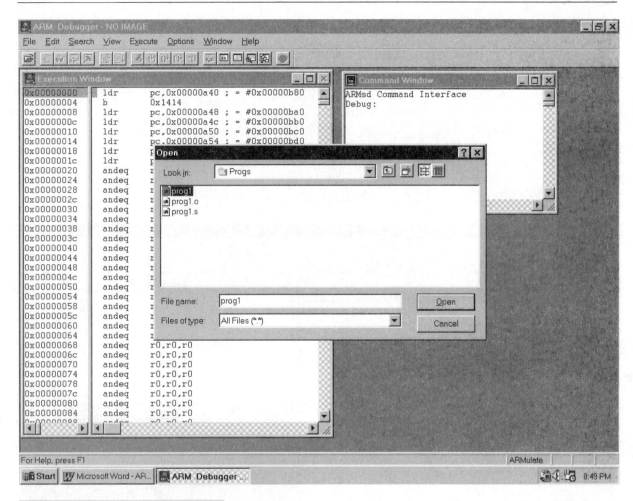

Fig. 7.23 Loading a program into the simulator.

Disassembly display

Figure 7.33 shows the **Disassembly Window**. You can see the contents of the memory locations starting at 0x00008080. Note that the symbolic labels are displayed, although the text string is interpreted as instructions.

Simplifying the code

We can simplify the code we've developed to test for a palindrome; that's one of the advantages of writing a program in assembly language. The following provides an improved version (without the header, data, and termination mechanism, which don't change).

```
start   LDR    r0,=string     ;r0 points to start of string to test
        MOV    r1,r0          ;copy left pointer to right pointer in r1
loop    LDRB   r10,[r1],#1    ;get character and update right pointer
        CMP    r10,#0         ;repeat until terminator located
        BNE    loop
        SUB    r1,r1,#2       ;fix right pointer to point to end of string
        BL     pal            ;call subroutine to test for palindrome
stop                          ;stop program execution
```

(program continued)

```
pal      LDRB    r3,[r0],#1      ;get left-hand character
         LDRB    r4,[r1],#-1     ;get right-hand character
         CMP     r3,r4           ;compare the ends of the string
         BNE     notpal          ;if different then fail
         SUBS    r3,r1,r0        ;get difference between pointers
         BEQ     waspal          ;if same then exit with palindrome found
         BMI     waspal          ;if left pointer past right then palindrome
         B       pal             ;REPEAT
waspal   MOV     r10,#0x1        ;r10=1=success flag
notpal   MOV     pc,lr           ;return
```

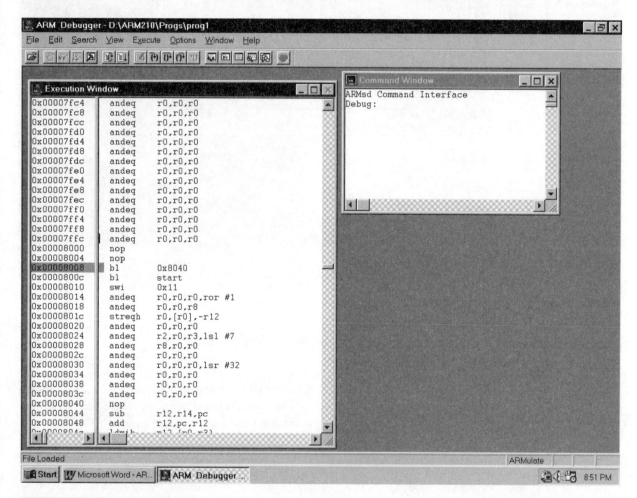

Fig. 7.24 The screen after loading prog1.

We've used two improvements. The first is to use r10 (the success/fail flag) to test for the terminator at the end of the string. In this way, we begin the subroutine with [r10]=0 and save an instruction. The major change is in the test for the middle of the string. If we automatically increment the left pointer and decrement the right pointer when they are used, we will have one of two situations when we reach the middle. If the string is even, the left- and the right-hand

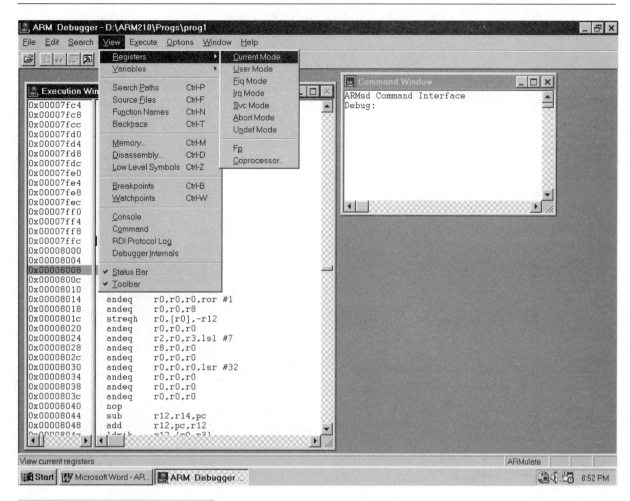

Fig. 7.25 Selecting the set of register to view.

pointers will have swapped over. If the string is odd, the two pointers will be pointing at the same character. The code subtracts the left pointer from the right pointer and stops on zero or negative.

Further simplification
Steve Furber at Manchester University pointed out that the code can be simplified even further. Look at the way I handled a return if the string wasn't a palindrome.

```
        CMP   r3,r4      ;compare the ends of the string
        BNE   notpal     ;if different then fail
        .
        .
notpal  MOV   pc,lr      ;return
```

We test two characters and then branch to notpal if they aren't the same. From notpal, we perform a return by placing the return address in the link register into the PC. Steve uses conditional execution to combine these two instructions; that is,

```
CMP    r3,r4     ;compare the ends of the string
MOVNE pc,lr      ;if not same then return
```

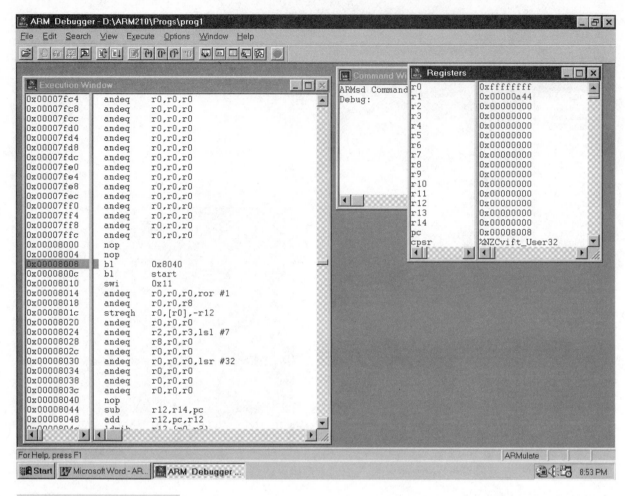

Fig. 7.26 Viewing the ARM's registers.

Steve's final version is

```
pal  LDRB  r3,[r0],#1    ;get left-hand character
     LDRB  r4,[r1],#-1   ;get right-hand character
     CMP   r3,r4         ;compare the ends of the string
     MOVNE pc,lr         ;if not same then return
     CMP   r0,r1         ;compare pointers
     BMI   pal           ;not finished
     MOV   r10,#1
     MOV   pc,lr         ;return (success)
```

The Thumb mode

Before we leave the ARM, we should mention another interesting feature of some members of the ARM family of processors. Anyone reading papers on processor design will eventually come across the expression 'code density' that indicates the ratio of computation to code. A program running on a processor with a high code density is smaller than a program that performs the same function running on a processor with a low code density.

'Thumb' is a special subset of the ARM architecture that supports a very high code density. An ARM processor that supports the Thumb mode can be switched into this mode of the branch and execute instruction, BX. There isn't room to cover the Thumb architecture in detail—all we'll do here is point out some of its features. Thumb instructions are 16, rather than 32, bits, which improves code density at the expense of

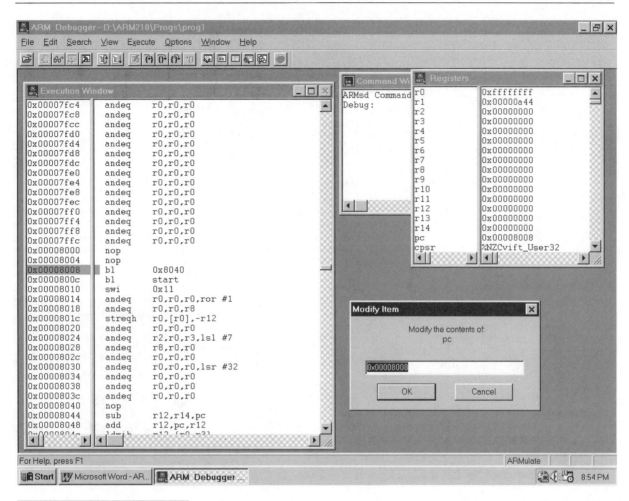

Fig. 7.27 Reloading the simulated PC.

functionality. Most Thumb instructions are executed unconditionally, whereas all ARM instructions are executed conditionally. Because instructions are only 16 bits wide, most Thumb instructions use a two-address format like the 68000 and similar CISC processors. Finally, the Thumb instruction set is less regular than the ARM instruction set.

Summary

In this chapter we've looked at the way in which engineers re-evaluated the CISC processor in the 1980s and came up with a new set of principles that were used to construct RISC processors. These principles were the use of a regular instruction set, pipelining, and the abandoning of microprogramming.

Although RISC processors can achieve spectacular throughputs by means of pipelining, they are highly sensitive to the effects of branch instructions. We have looked at how branch instructions degrade the performance of RISC processors and have discussed some of the ways in which the outcome of branch instructions can be predicted and the next instruction fetched from the branch target address if the branch is predicted as taken.

By the 1990s, RISC principles had been incorporated into most processors and the difference between RISC and CISC processors had become almost (but not entirely) meaningless.

We could have used one of several RISC processors to illustrate the features of a RISC instruction set; for example, MIPS or the PowerPC. Instead, we chose the ARM processor because it has many of the features of a typical RISC processor and is fairly easy to understand. However, we have also

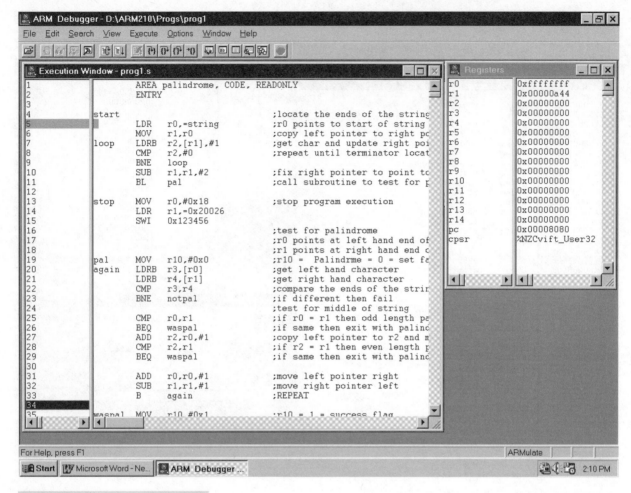

Fig. 7.28 The system after resetting the PC.

decided to introduce the ARM because it has some interesting features that are not found on other processors. In particular, the ARM supports the conditional execution of all instructions, and the processing of the second operand by scaling.

Problems

1. What are the characteristics of a CISC processor?

2. The most frequently executed class of instruction is the data move instruction. Why is this?

3. The Berkeley RISC has a 32-bit architecture and yet provides only a 13-bit literal. Why is this and does it really matter?

4. What are the advantages and disadvantages of register windowing?

5. What is pipelining and how does it increase the performance of a computer?

6. A pipeline is defined by its length (i.e. the number of stages that can operate in parallel). A pipeline can be short or long. What do you think are the relative advantages of long and short pipelines?

7. What is *data dependency* in a pipelined system and how can its effects be overcome?

8. RISC architectures don't permit operations on operands in memory other than load and store operations. Why?

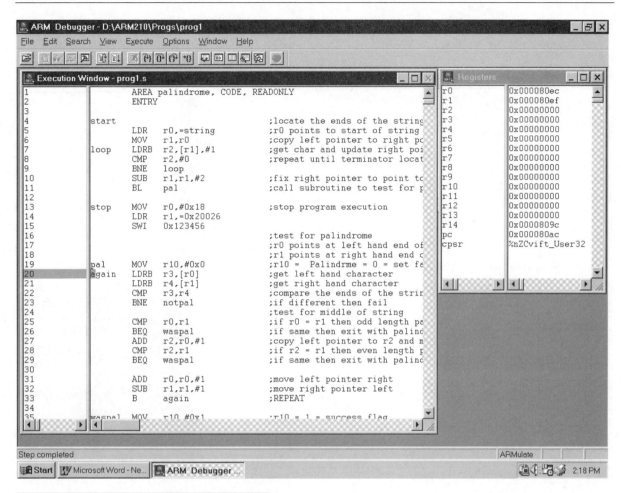

Fig. 7.29 The situation after executing several instructions.

9. The average number of cycles required by a RISC processor to execute an instruction is given by

$$T_{ave} = 1 + p_b \cdot p_t \cdot b$$

where:

The probability that a given instruction is a branch is p_b

The probability that a branch instruction will be taken is p_t

If a branch is taken, the additional penalty is b cycles

If a branch is not taken, there is no penalty

Draw a series of graphs of the average number of cycles per instruction as a function of $p_b \cdot p_t$ for $b = 1$, 2, 3, and 4.

10. What is branch prediction and how can it be used to reduce the so-called branch penalty in a pipelined system?

11. In what significant ways does the ARM differ from the 68K?

12. Most RISC processors have 32 user-accessible registers, whereas the ARM has only 16. Why is this so?

13. Construct an instruction set that has the best features of a CISC processor like the 68K and a RISC processor like the ARM. Write some test programs for your architecture and compare them with the corresponding pure 68K and ARM programs.

14. All ARM instructions are conditional, which means that they are executed only if a defined condition is met; for example, ADDEQ means 'add if the last result set the zero flag'.

Explain how this feature can be exploited to produce very compact code. Give examples of the use of this feature to implement complex conditional constructs.

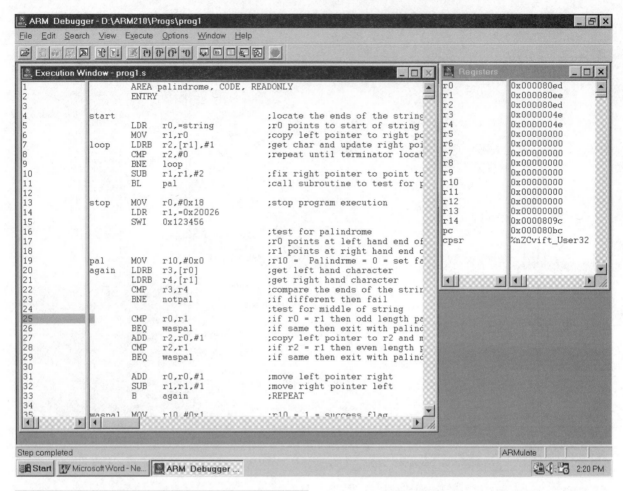

Fig. 7.30 The situation after executing part of the subroutine `pal`.

15. What is the effect of the following ARM instructions?
    (a) `MOV   r1,#0xFF`
    (b) `MVN   r1,#0xFF`
    (c) `MVN   r1,#25`
    (d) `MVN   r1,#0xF`
    (e) `MOVS  r1,#0xF`
    (f) `MLA   r3,r5,r6,r2`
    (g) `LDR   r1,[r3,#8]!`
    (h) `LDR   r1,[r3,#8]`

16. The ARM has a wealth of move multiple register instructions that copy data between memory and several registers. The load versions of these instructions are

```
LDMIA,  LDMIB,  LDMDA,  LDMDB,  LDMFD,
LDMFA,  LDMED,  LDMEA
```

What do these instructions do?

17. How are subroutines handled in ARM processors?

18. Implement a *jump table* in ARM assembly language. A jump table is used to branch to one of a series of addresses stored in a table. For example, if register r3 contains the value *i*, a jump (i.e. branch) will be made to the address of the *i*th entry in the table. Jump tables can used to implement the 'case' or 'switch' construct in high-level languages.

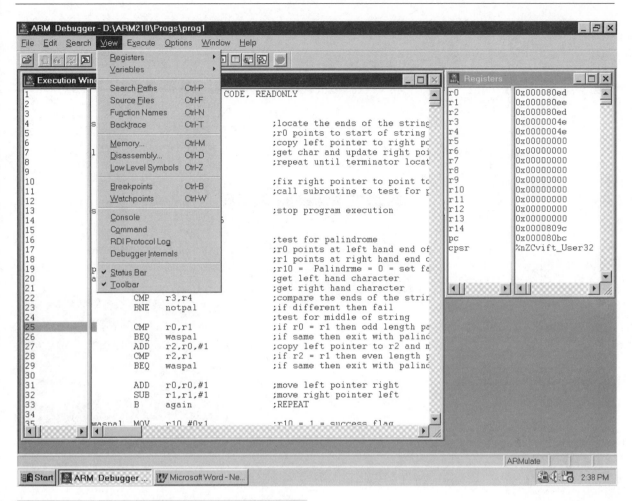

Fig. 7.31 Using the <u>V</u>iew function to select the <u>D</u>isassembly display.

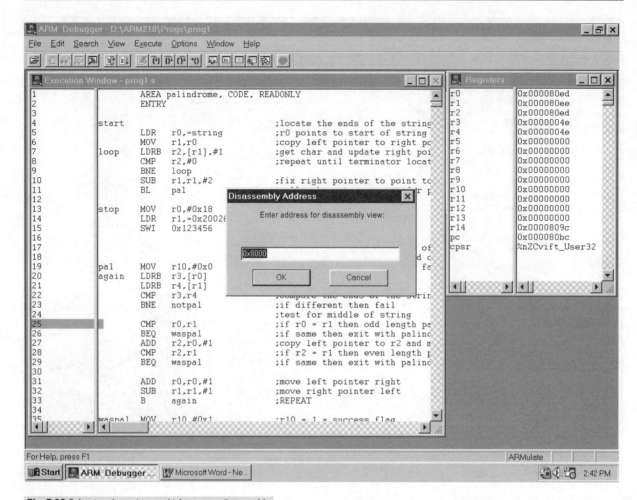

Fig. 7.32 Selecting the point at which to start disassembly.

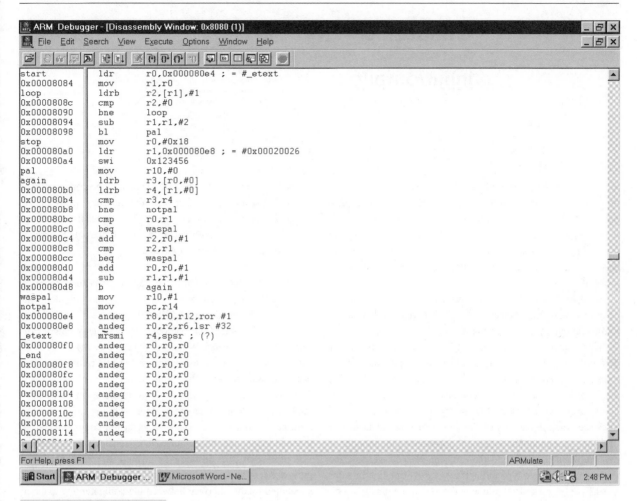

Fig. 7.33 The disassembled code.

Chapter 8

Input/output

So far we've examined the internal structure and operation of the computer's central processing unit. However, if a computer is to be of any real value to people it must have some way of communicating with them. After all, there's no point in creating a supercomputer the size of a paperback that can solve the ultimate question of life, the universe, and everything, if it can't tell us the answer. In this chapter we look at the *ways and means* by which information gets into and out of a computer and the devices or *peripherals* that are connected to the computer (e.g. the printer and the display).

This chapter covers three major areas. We begin by demonstrating how the CPU implements input and output transactions. The CPU doesn't dirty its hands with the fine details of input/output (I/O) operations. Instead, the CPU often hands over the details of I/O operations to special-purpose interface chips; for example, the computer sends data to one of these chips and logic within the chip handles the transfer of data between the chip and the *external* device. We describe the operation of two typical interface chips—one that handles I/O a byte (or a word) at a time and one that handles I/O a bit at a time.

We also look at some of the peripherals themselves—beginning with the peripherals found in all personal computers (the mouse, keyboard, display, and printer). At the end of this chapter, we provide a glimpse of some of the more esoteric peripherals found in embedded computer systems.

I/O fundamentals

Computer I/O is wide-ranging subject and is best subdivided into three areas:

1. The *strategy* by which data is moved into or out of the computer.

2. The interface circuit that actually moves the data into or out of the computer.

3. The *input/output devices* themselves that convert data into a form that can be used by an external system or which take data from the outside world and convert it into a form

that can be processed digitally. Data may be converted into an almost infinite number of representations, from a close approximation to human speech to a signal that opens or closes a valve in a chemical factory. Input/output devices are frequently called *peripherals*.

The difference between these three aspects of I/O can be illustrated by two examples. Consider first a computer connected to a keyboard and television display (i.e. CRT). Data is moved into or out of the computer by a strategy called *programmed data transfer*. Whenever the computer wants to send data to the display, an instruction in the program writes data into the *output port* that communicates with the CRT. Similarly, when the computer requires data, an instruction reads data from the *input port* connected to the keyboard. The term *port* indicates a gateway between the computer and an external I/O device. Programmed data transfer or programmed I/O represents the *strategy* by which the information is moved, but tells us nothing about *how* the data is moved—that is handled by the interface between the computer and external peripheral. In this example the keyboard and display are the I/O devices proper (i.e. peripherals).

To keep our example simple, let's just consider data that's sent from a computer to a remote display terminal (see Fig. 8.1). When the computer sends data to its output port, the output port transmits that data to the display. The output port is frequently a sophisticated integrated circuit whose complexity may even approach that of the CPU itself. Such a semi-intelligent device relieves the computer of the tedious task of communicating with the CRT terminal directly, and frees it to do useful calculations.

The connection between a computer and a display terminal may consist of a twisted-pair (two parallel wires twisted at regular intervals). As the data written into the output port by the CPU is in parallel form (say eight bits), the output port must serialize the data and transmit it a-bit-at-a-time over the twisted pair to the CRT terminal. Moreover, the output port must supply start and stop bits to enable the CRT terminal to synchronize itself with the stream of bits from the computer.

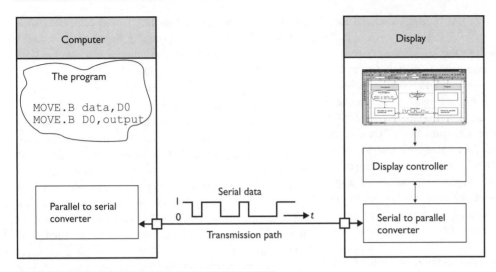

Fig. 8.1 Relationship between a computer and a peripheral.

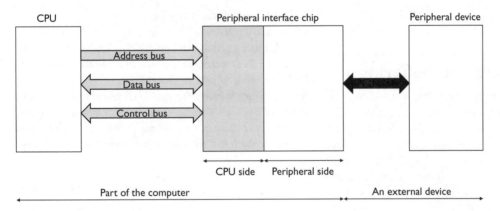

Fig. 8.2 Structure of an interface.

Chapter 11 deals in more detail with serial data transmission. We can now see that the output port is the device that is actually responsible for moving the data between the processor and the peripheral.

The display terminal is the output device proper. It accepts serial data from the computer, reconstitutes it into a parallel form and uses the data to select a character from a table of symbols. The symbols are then displayed on a television-style (raster-scan) screen. Sometimes the transmitted character performs a control function (e.g. carriage return, line feed, or backspace) that affects the layout of the display. Figure 8.1 illustrates the relationship between the concepts expressed in this example.

Figure 8.2 illustrates the relationship between the CPU, the peripheral interface chip, and the peripheral device itself.

As you can see, the peripheral interface chip looks just like a memory location to the CPU (i.e. you read or write data to it). However, this chip contains specialized logic that allows it to communicate with the peripheral.

As another example of the relationship between I/O strategy, the I/O interface, and the peripheral, consider the way in which a block of data is written to a disk drive. It's often impractical to use programmed data transfers for disk I/O because programmed transfers are too slow. The output strategy most frequently used is *direct memory access* (DMA), in which the data is transferred from the computer's memory to a peripheral, or vice versa, without passing through the CPU's registers. The CPU simply tells the DMA hardware to move a block of data and the DMA hardware gets on with the task, allowing the CPU to continue its main function of information processing. This strategy (i.e. DMA) requires special hardware to implement it.

An interface chip called a *DMA controller* (DMAC) is responsible for moving the data between the memory and the peripheral. The DMAC must provide addresses for the source or destination of data in memory, and signal to the peripheral that data is needed or is ready. Furthermore, the DMAC must grab the computer's internal data and address buses for the duration of a data transfer. Data transfer by DMA must be done while avoiding a conflict with the CPU for the possession of the buses. In this example the peripheral is a disk drive—a complex mixture of electronics and high-precision mechanical engineering designed to store data by locally affecting the magnetic properties of the surface of a disk rotating at a high speed.

Before dealing with input/output strategies, we must introduce the concepts of *handshaking* and *buffering*, as they are important in all but the simplest I/O systems.

8.1 Handshaking and buffering

Irrespective of the strategy by which data is moved between the processor and peripheral, all data transfers fall into one of two classes: *open-loop* or *closed-loop*. In an open-loop I/O transaction the data is sent on its way and its safe reception assumed. Open-loop data transfers correspond to the basic level of service offered by the mail system. A letter is written and dropped into a mailbox. The sender believes that after a reasonable delay, the letter will be received. However, the sender doesn't know whether the letter was received.

In many circumstances the open-loop transfer of data is perfectly satisfactory. The probability of data getting lost or corrupted is very small, and its loss may be of little importance. If Aunt Mabel doesn't get a birthday card, the world doesn't come to an end. Consider now the following exchange of information between a control tower and an aircraft.

Approach control 'Cherokee Nine Four Six November cleared for straight in approach to runway 23. Wind 270 degrees 10 knots. Altimeter 32.13. Report field in sight.'

Aircraft 'Straight in runway 23. Altimeter 32.13. Cherokee Nine Four Six November.'

The aircraft acknowledges the receipt of the message and reads back any crucial data (i.e. the identification of the runway is 23 and the pressure setting required by the altimeter is 32.13 inches of mercury). This data transfer demonstrates the operation of a *closed-loop* system. In the computer world, a closed-loop data transfer simply indicates that data has been received (the data itself isn't read back).

Open-loop data transfer

Figure 8.3 illustrates a simple open-loop data transfer between a computer and a peripheral. At point A data from the computer becomes valid (the shading before point A indicates that the data is invalid). At point B the computer asserts a control signal called DAV (*data valid*) to indicate that the data from the computer is valid. The peripheral must read the data before it vanishes at point D. DAV is negated at point C to inform the peripheral that the data is no longer valid. This data transfer is called *open-loop* because the peripheral doesn't communicate with the CPU and doesn't indicate that it has received the data.

Closed-loop data transfer

Figure 8.4 illustrates a *closed-loop* data transfer between a computer and a peripheral. Initially, the computer (i.e. originator of the data) makes the data available and then asserts data DAV at point B to indicate that the data is valid, just as in an open-loop data transfer. The peripheral receiving the data sees that DAV has been asserted, indicating that new data is ready, and reads the data. In turn the peripheral asserts DAC, *data accepted*, which is a reply to the computer. DAC informs the

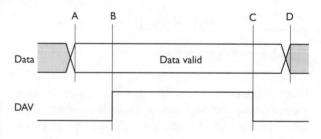

(a) Timing diagram

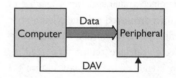

(b) Arrangement

Fig. 8.3 Open-loop data transfer between computer and peripheral.

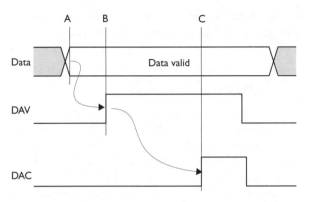

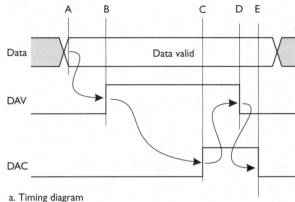

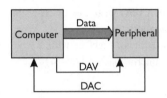

a. Timing diagram

b. Arrangement

Fig. 8.4 Closed-loop data transfer between computer and peripheral.

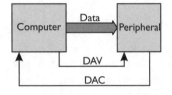

a. Timing diagram

b. Arrangement

Fig. 8.5 Fully interlocked handshaking.

computer that the data has been accepted. The computer then de-asserts DAV to complete the data exchange. This sequence of events is known as *handshaking*. Apart from indicating the receipt of data, handshaking also caters for slow peripherals, because the transfer is held up until the peripheral indicates its readiness by asserting DAC.

In this example, we have talked about data transfer between computer and peripheral. Data can also be transferred in the reverse direction between peripheral and computer. In our next example we will use the terms *transmitter* and *receiver* to indicate the originator and receptor of the data.

Figure 8.5 shows how the handshaking process can be taken a step further in which the acknowledgement is itself acknowledged to create a *fully interlocked* data transfer. The term 'fully interlocked' means that each stage in the handshaking procedure can continue only when the previous stage has been acknowledged. At point A in Fig. 8.5 the data becomes valid and at point B the transmitter asserts DAV indicating the availability of data. At C the receiver asserts DAC, indicating that DAV has been observed and the data accepted. So far, this is the same procedure as in Fig. 8.4.

The transmitter sees that DAC is asserted and de-asserts (i.e. negates) DAV at D, indicating that data is no longer valid

and that it is acknowledging that the receiver has accepted the data. Finally, at E the receiver de-asserts DAC to complete the cycle and to indicate that it has seen the transmitter's acknowledgement of its receipt of data.

The difference between Figs. 8.4 and 8.5 (i.e. between handshaking and fully interlocked handshaking) should be stressed again. Handshaking merely involves an acknowledgement of data, which implies that the assertion of DAV is followed by the assertion of DAC. What happens after this is undefined. In fully interlocked handshaking each action (i.e. the assertion or negation of a signal) takes place in a strict sequence which ends only when all signals have finally been negated. Interlocked handshaking is a two-way process because the receiver acknowledges the assertion of DAV by asserting DAC whereas the transmitter acknowledges the assertion of DAC by negating DAV. Moreover, because fully interlocked handshaking also acknowledges negations, it is said to be *delay insensitive*.

Many real systems employing closed-loop data transfers make the entire handshaking sequence automatic in the sense that it is carried out by special-purpose hardware. The computer itself doesn't get involved in the process. Only if something goes wrong does the processor take part in the handshaking.

In any data transfer involving handshaking, a problem arises when the transmitter asserts DAV but DAC isn't asserted by the receiver in turn (because the equipment is faulty or the receiver is not switched on). When the transmitter wishes to send data, it starts a timer concurrently with the assertion of DAV. If DAC isn't asserted by the receiver after a given time has passed, the operation is aborted. The period of time between the start of an action and the declaration of a failure state is called a *timeout*. When a timeout occurs, an interrupt (see Section 8.3) is generated, forcing the computer to take action. In a poorly designed system without a timeout mechanism, the non-completion of a handshake causes the transmitter to wait for DAC forever and the system is then said to hang-up.

8.1.1 Buffered I/O

How fast should an interface operate? As fast as it can—any faster and it wouldn't be able to keep up with the data; any slower and it would waste time waiting for data. Unfortunately, most real interfaces don't transfer data at anything like an optimum speed. In particular, data can sometimes arrive so fast that it's impossible to process one element before the next is received.

Doctors have a similar problem. If a doctor took exactly m minutes to treat a patient and a new patient arrived every m minutes, all should be well. However, even if patients arrive on average every m minutes and a consultation takes on average m minutes, the system wouldn't work because some patients arrive at approximately the same time. Doctors solved this problem long ago by putting new patients in a waiting room until they can be dealt with. Sometimes the waiting room becomes nearly full when patients enter more rapidly than average.

The same solution can be applied to any I/O process. Data is loaded into a special device called a FIFO (first in, first out) memory. The FIFO behaves almost exactly like a doctor's waiting room. Data arrives at the memory's input port and is stored in the same sequence in which it arrives. Data leaves the memory's output port when it is required. Like the doctor's waiting room, the FIFO can fill with data during periods in which data arrives faster than it can be processed. It's up to the designer to provide a FIFO with sufficient capacity to deal with the worst-case input burst. (There is, however, one significant difference between the FIFO and waiting room. FIFOs aren't littered with piles of tattered ten-year-old copies of *National Geographic*.)

Saving data in a store until it is required is called *buffering* and the FIFO store is often called a buffer. Some interfaces include a buffer on-chip. We are now going to examine the strategies by which I/O is performed in greater detail.

8.2 Programmed I/O

Programmed I/O takes place when an instruction in the program initiates the data transfer; for example, a programmer might write the instruction MOVE.B Keyboard,D0, which reads a byte of data from the keyboard and puts it in D0. Some microprocessors have special instructions that are used only for I/O; for example, when a microprocessor executes an OUT 123 operation, the contents of a data register are placed on the data bus. At the same time, the number 123 is placed on the eight least-significant bits of the address bus and a pulse is generated on the system's I/O write line. Each of the I/O ports in such a system monitors the address lines. When an I/O interface sees its own address, together with a read-port or a write-port signal, the interface acts on that signal and executes an I/O data transfer.

Memory-mapped I/O

Many microprocessors lack explicit I/O instructions like the OUT <port> we've just described. In fact, most microprocessors have no special input or output instructions whatsoever. If these microprocessors are to use programmed I/O, they have to resort to *memory-mapped I/O*, in which the processor treats interface ports as an extension to memory. Part of the CPU's normal memory space is dedicated to I/O operations, and all I/O ports look exactly like normal memory locations.

Memory-mapped I/O ports are accessed by conventional memory reference instructions such as MOVE D0,IO_PORT (to output data) and MOVE IO_PORT,D0 (to input data). A disadvantage of memory-mapped I/O is that part of the memory space available to programs and data is lost to the I/O system.

Figure 8.6 describes the organization of a memory-mapped I/O port and provides a memory map. An output port located at address $008000 is connected to a display device. Data is transmitted to the display by storing it in memory location $008000. As far as the processor is concerned, it's merely storing data in memory. The program in Table 8.1 sends 128 characters (starting at $002000) to the display.

The numbers in the right-hand column in Table 8.1 give the time to execute each instruction in microseconds, assuming a clock rate of 8 MHz. To output the 128 characters takes approximately $128 \times (8+8+8+10)/8 = 544\,\mu s$, which is a little over $\frac{1}{2}$ thousandth of a second. Data is transferred at a rate of one character per $4\frac{1}{4}\,\mu s$.

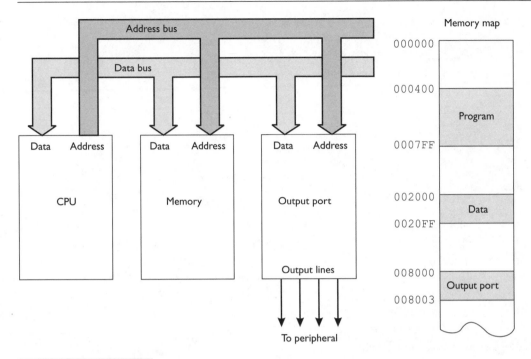

Fig. 8.6 Memory mapped I/O.

```
* FOR i=1 to 128
*      Move data from Tableᵢ to output_port
* ENDFOR
*                                                                    Cycles
PORT    EQU     $008000      Location of memory-mapped port
COUNT   EQU     128          Size of block to be output
        ORG     $000400      Origin of program
*
        MOVE    #COUNT,D1    [D1] ← 128              Set up loop counter
        LEA     TABLE,A0     [A0] ← TABLE            A0 points to the table
        LEA     PORT,A1      [A1] ← Port1            A1 points to the port
*
LOOP    MOVE.B  (A0)+,D0     [D0] ← [M([A0])]        Get data to be output    8
                             [A0] ← [A0]+1
        MOVE.B  D0,(A1)      [M([A1])] ← [D0]        Output the data          8
        SUB     #1,D1        [D1] ← [D1]−1           Decrement counter        8
        BNE     LOOP         Repeat until counter=0                           10

        ORG     $002000      Origin for data area
TABLE   DS.B    128          Reserve 128 bytes for the table of data
```

Table 8.1 A hypothetical example of a programmed output transfer.

Although the program in Table 8.1 looks as if it should work, it's unsuited to almost all situations involving programmed output. Most peripherals connected to an output port are relatively slow devices, and sending data to them at this rate would simply result in almost all the data being lost. As we've said, some interfaces are able to deal with short bursts of high-speed data because they store data in a buffer. They can't, however, deal with a continuous stream of data at high speeds because the 'waiting room' fills up and soon overflows.

A solution to the problem of dealing with such a mismatch in speed between computer and peripheral is found by asking the peripheral if it's ready to receive or to transmit data, and not sending data to it until it is ready to receive it. That is, we

```
*   FOR i=1 TO 128
*           REPEAT
*               Read Port_status_byte
*           UNTIL Port_not_busy
*           Move data from Table_i to output_port
*   ENDFOR
*
1.  PORTDATA   EQU     $008000         Location of memory-mapped port
2.  PORTSTAT   EQU     $008002         Location of port's status byte
3.  COUNT      EQU     128             Size of block to be output
4.             ORG     $000400         Origin of program
5.             MOVE    #COUNT,D1       Set up character counter in D1
6.             LEA     TABLE,A0        A0 points to table in memory
7.             LEA     PORTDATA,A1     A1 points to data port
8.             LEA     PORTSTAT,A2     A2 points to port status byte
9.  LOOP       MOVE.B  (A0)+,D0        Get a byte from the table
10. WAIT       MOVE.B  (A2),D2          REPEAT Read the port's status
11.            AND.B   #1,D2              Mask all but lsb of status
12.            BEQ     WAIT             Until port ready
13.            MOVE.B  D0,(A1)         Store data in peripheral
14.            SUB     #1,D1           Decrement loop counter
15.            BNE     LOOP            Repeat until COUNT=0
16. *
17.            ORG     $002000         Start of data area
18. TABLE      DS.B    128             Reserve 128 bytes of data
```

Table 8.2 Using the polling loop to control the flow of data.

introduce a form of software handshaking procedure between the peripheral and the interface.

Almost all memory-mapped I/O ports occupy two or more memory locations. One location is reserved for the actual data to be input or output, and one holds a *status byte* associated with the port. For example, let $008000 be the location of the port to which data is sent and let $008002 be the location of the status byte. Suppose that bit 0 of the status byte is a 1 if the port is ready for data and a 0 if it is busy. The fragment of program in Table 8.2 implements memory-mapped output at a rate determined by the peripheral. The comments at the beginning of the program describe the data transfer in pseudocode.

The program in Table 8.2 is identical to the previous example in Table 8.1 except for lines 8–12 inclusive. In line 8 an address register, A2, is used to point to the status byte of the interface at address $008002. In line 10 the status byte of the interface is read into D2 and masked down to the least-significant bit (by the action of AND.B #1,D2 in line 11). If the least-significant bit of the status byte is zero, a branch back to line 10 is made by the instruction in line 12. When the interface becomes free (as indicated by the least-significant bit of the status byte being 1), the branch to WAIT is not taken and the program continues exactly as in Table 8.1.

Lines 10, 11, and 12 constitute a *polling loop*, in which the output device is continually polled (questioned) until it

indicates it is free, allowing the program to continue. A typical slow printer operates at 30 characters/second, or approximately 1 character per 33 000 µs. Because the polling loop takes about 3 µs, the loop is executed 11 000 times per character.

Operating a computer in a polled input/output mode is grossly inefficient because so much of the computer's time is wasted waiting for the port to become free. If the microcomputer has nothing better to do while it is waiting for a peripheral to become free (i.e. not busy), polled I/O is perfectly acceptable. Many of the first generation of personal computers were operated in this way. However, a more powerful computer working in a multiprogramming environment can attend to another task or program during the time the I/O port is busy. In this case a better I/O strategy is to ignore the peripheral until it is ready for a data transfer and then let the peripheral ask the CPU for attention. Such a strategy is called *interrupt-driven I/O*. Note that all the I/O strategies we are describing use memory-mapped I/O.

By the way, if you are designing a computer with memory-mapped I/O and a memory cache, you have to tell the cache controller not to cache the port's status register. If you don't do this, the cache memory would read the status once, cache it, and then return the cached value on successive accesses to the status. Even if the status register in the peripheral changes, the old value in the cache is frozen.

8.3 Interrupt-driven I/O

A computer executes instructions sequentially unless a jump or a branch is made. There is, however, an important exception to this rule called an *interrupt*. An interrupt is an *event* that forces the CPU to modify its sequence of actions. This 'event' may be an external signal from a peripheral (i.e. a *hardware interrupt*) or an internally generated call to the operating system (i.e. a *software interrupt*). Today, the term *exception* is often used to describe all these events.

Most microprocessors have an active-low *interrupt request* input called $\overline{IRQ}$ that can be asserted by a peripheral to request attention. Note that the word *request* carries with it the implication that the interrupt request may or may not be granted. Figure 8.7 illustrates the organization of a system with a simple interrupt-driven I/O mechanism.

In Fig. 8.7 an interrupt request line runs from the CPU to all the peripherals. Each peripheral capable of generating an interrupt is connected to this $\overline{IRQ}$ line. A peripheral asserts its $\overline{IRQ}$ output when it requires attention. Figure 8.7 demonstrates that few components are needed to implement interrupt-driven I/O in a microprocessor system. This system is analogous to the emergency handle in a train. When the handle is pulled in one of the carriages, the driver knows that a problem has arisen but doesn't yet know who pulled the handle. Similarly, the CPU doesn't know which peripheral caused the interrupt or why.

When the CPU detects that its $\overline{IRQ}$ input has gone active-low, the following (simplified) sequence of events takes place.

- The CPU finishes its current instruction. Most microprocessors cannot be stopped in mid-instruction, because individual machine code instructions are *indivisible* and must always be executed to completion.

- The contents of the program counter and the condition code register are pushed onto the stack. The *processor status word*, PSW, must be saved because the interrupt routine will almost certainly modify the condition code bits.

- Further interrupts are disabled to avoid an interrupt being interrupted (we will elaborate on this partially true statement later).

- The CPU deals with the cause of the interrupt by executing a program called an *interrupt handler*.

- The CPU executes a *return from interrupt* instruction at the end of the interrupt handler. Executing this instruction pulls the PC and PSW off the stack and execution then continues normally—as if the interrupt had never happened.

Figure 8.8 illustrates the sequence of actions taking place when an interrupt occurs. Note that (in a 68000 system) the processor status word consists of the system byte plus the condition code register, CCR. The system byte is used by the operating system and interrupt processing mechanism.

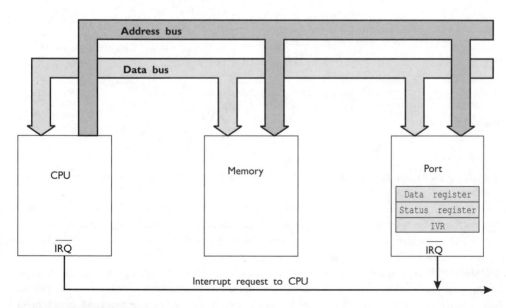

Fig. 8.7 Interrupt organization.

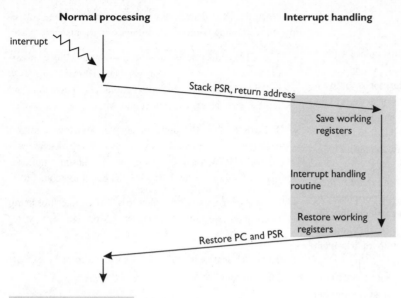

Normal processing

Interrupt handling

interrupt

Stack PSR, return address

Save working
registers

Interrupt handling
routine

Restore working
registers

Restore PC and PSR

Fig. 8.8 Interrupt sequence.

```
* Pick up pointer to next free entry in the table (buffer)
* Read a byte from the table and transmit it to the interface
* Move the pointer to the next entry in the table
* and save the pointer in memory
* Return from interrupt
*
OUTPUT     EQU       $008000      Location of memory-mapped output port
           ORG       $000400      Start of the program fragment
*
           MOVEA.L   POINTER,A0   Load A0 with the pointer to the buffer
           MOVE.B    (A0)+,D0     Read a character from the buffer
           MOVE.B    D0,OUTPUT    Send this character to the output port
           MOVE.L    A0,POINTER   Save the updated pointer
           RTE                    Return from interrupt

           ORG       $002000      Data origin
BUFFER     DS.B      1024         Reserve 1024 bytes for the table
POINTER    DC.L      BUFFER       Reserve a longword for the pointer
```

Table 8.3 A simple interrupt handler.

Interrupt-driven I/O requires a more complex program than programmed I/O because the information transfer takes place not when the programmer wants or expects it, but when the data is available. The software required to implement interrupt-driven I/O is frequently part of the operating system. A fragment of a hypothetical interrupt-driven output routine in 68000 assembly language is provided in Table 8.3. Each time the interrupt handling routine is called, data is obtained from a buffer and passed to the memory-mapped output port at $008000. In a practical system

some check would be needed to test for the end of the buffer.

Because the processor executes this code only when a peripheral requests an I/O transaction, interrupt-driven I/O is very much more efficient than the polled-I/O we described earlier.

Although the basic idea of interrupts is common to most computers, there are considerable variations in the precise nature of the interrupt-handling structure from computer to computer. We are now going to look at how the 68000 deals with interrupts, because this microprocessor has a particularly comprehensive interrupt handling facility.

8.3.1 Prioritized interrupts

Computer interrupts are almost exactly analogous to interrupts in everyday life. Suppose two students interrupt me when I'm lecturing—one with a question and the other because he or she feels unwell. I will respond to the more urgent of the two requests. Once I've dealt with the student who's unwell, I answer the other student's question and then continue my teaching. Computers behave in the same way.

Most computers have more than one interrupt request input. Some interrupt request pins are connected to peripherals requiring immediate attention (e.g. a disk drive), whereas others are connected to peripherals requiring less urgent attention (e.g. a keyboard). For the sake of accuracy, we should point out that the processor's interrupt request input is connected to the peripheral's interface, rather than the peripheral itself. If the disk drive is not attended to (i.e. serviced) when its data is available, the data will soon be lost. Data from the disk is lost because it is replaced by new data. In such circumstances, it is reasonable to assign a priority to each of the interrupt request pins.

The 68000 supports seven interrupt request inputs from $\overline{IRQ7}$, the most important, to $\overline{IRQ1}$ the least important. Suppose an interrupt is caused by the assertion of $\overline{IRQ3}$ and no other interrupts are pending. The interrupt on $\overline{IRQ3}$ will be serviced. If an interrupt at a level higher than $\overline{IRQ3}$ occurs, it will be serviced before the level 3 interrupt service routine is completed. However, interrupts generated by $\overline{IRQ1}$ or $\overline{IRQ2}$ will be stored pending the completion of $\overline{IRQ3}$'s service routine.

The 68000 does not have seven explicit $\overline{IRQ1}$ to $\overline{IRQ7}$ interrupt request inputs (simply because such an arrangement would require seven precious pins). Instead, the 68000 has a 3-bit encoded interrupt request input, $\overline{IPL0}$ to $\overline{IPL2}$. The 3-bit value on $\overline{IPL0}$ to $\overline{IPL2}$ reflects the current level of interrupt request from 0 (i.e. no interrupt request) to 7 (the highest level corresponding to $\overline{IRQ7}$). Figure 8.9 illustrates some of the elements involved in the 68000's interrupt handling structure. A *priority encoder* chip is required to convert an interrupt request on $\overline{IRQ1}$ to $\overline{IRQ7}$ into a 3-bit code in $\overline{IPL0}$ to $\overline{IPL2}$. The priority encoder automatically prioritizes interrupt requests, and its output reflects the highest interrupt request level asserted.

The 68000 doesn't automatically service an interrupt request. A *processor status byte* in the CPU in Fig. 8.9 controls the way in which the 68000 responds to an interrupt. Figure 8.10 describes the *status byte* in more detail. The 3-bit

interrupt mask field in the processor status byte, I_2, I_1, I_0, determines how the 68000 responds to an interrupt. The current interrupt request is serviced if its level is greater than that of the interrupt mask; otherwise the request is ignored. For example, if the interrupt mask has a current value of 4, only interrupt requests on $\overline{IRQ5}$ to $\overline{IRQ7}$ will be serviced.

When the 68000 services an interrupt, the interrupt mask bits are reset to make them equal to the level of the interrupt currently being serviced. For example, if the interrupt mask bits were set to 2 and an interrupt occurred at level $\overline{IRQ5}$, the mask bits would be set to 5. Consequently, the 68000 can now be re-interrupted only by interrupt levels 6 and 7. After the interrupt has been serviced, the old value of the processor status byte saved on the stack (and therefore the interrupt mask bits) is restored to its original level.

Non-maskable interrupts

Microprocessors sometimes have a special interrupt request input called a *non-maskable interrupt request*. The term *non-maskable* means that the interrupt cannot be turned off (i.e. delayed or suspended) and must be serviced immediately. Non-maskable interrupts are found in two particular applications. The first includes circumstances in which the interrupt is caused by a critical event that must not be missed. A typical event is an interruption of the power supply. When this happens the system still functions for a few milliseconds on energy stored in capacitors (energy storage devices found in all power supplies). A non-maskable interrupt generated at the first sign of a power loss is used to shut down the computer in an orderly fashion so that it can be restarted later with little loss of data and no corruption (accidental overwriting) of disk files.

A second application of non-maskable interrupts is in real-time systems. Suppose that the temperature and pressure at various points must be measured periodically in a chemical process. If these points aren't polled on a programmed basis, a stream of regularly spaced non-maskable interrupts will do the trick. At each interrupt, the contents of a counter register are updated and, if a suitable span of time has elapsed, the required readings are taken.

The 68000 reserves its level 7 interrupt ($\overline{IRQ7}$) as a non-maskable interrupt because an interrupt on $\overline{IRQ7}$ is *always* serviced by the 68000. If a level 7 interrupt is currently being serviced by the 68000, a further active transition on $\overline{IRQ7}$ (i.e. a high-to-low edge) results in the 68000 servicing the new level 7 interrupt.

8.3.2 Vectored interrupts

Remember that all interfaces capable of generating an interrupt are connected to a single interrupt request line (but forget

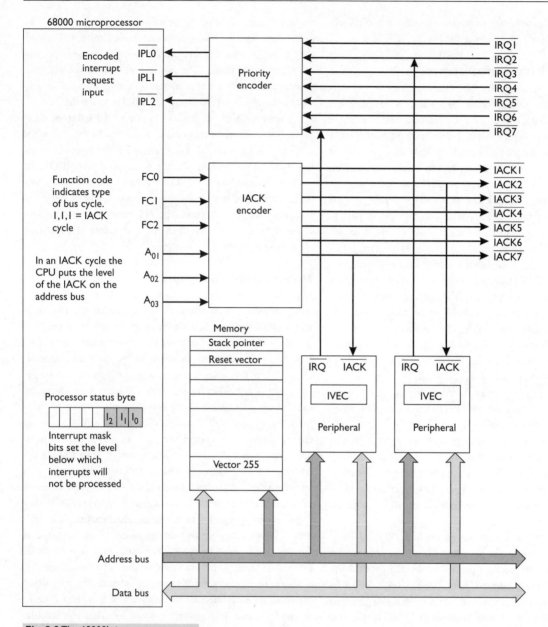

Fig. 8.9 The 68000's interrupt structure.

for a moment the 68000's 7-level interrupt request system). When an interrupt occurs, the microprocessor reads the contents of a certain memory location containing a pointer to the interrupt handler, and jumps to the address stored in this location. Which location does the processor read to get the interrupt vector (i.e. pointer)? The answer depends on the actual processor and is *design dependent*. Some designers put the interrupt vector at the top end of memory and some put it at the bottom end.

A predetermined fixed address holding a pointer to an interrupt handling routine has several disadvantages. In particular, it's not possible to distinguish between interrupts originating from one of several peripherals. Before we look at how the 68000 solves the problem of multiple interrupt

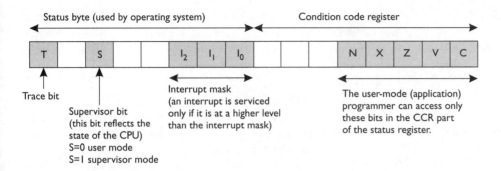

Trace bit

Supervisor bit
(this bit reflects the
state of the CPU)
S=0 user mode
S=1 supervisor mode

Interrupt mask
(an interrupt is serviced
only if it is at a higher level
than the interrupt mask)

The user-mode (application)
programmer can access only
these bits in the CCR part
of the status register.

Fig. 8.10 The 68000's status word.

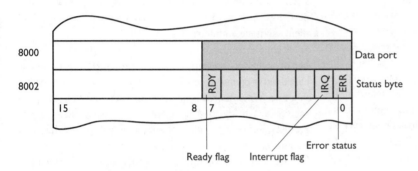

Ready flag   Interrupt flag

Error status

Fig. 8.11 A memory-mapped data and status port.

sources, it's instructive to consider how first-generation microprocessors performed the task of isolating the cause of an interrupt request.

Following the detection and acceptance of an interrupt, first-generation microprocessors resorted to a simple method of locating the appropriate interrupt-handling routine. These processors used software to ask each of the possible interrupters, in turn, whether they were responsible for the interrupt. This operation is called *polling* (the same mechanism used for programmed I/O).

Figure 8.11 shows the structure of a typical memory-mapped I/O port with a data port at address $8000 and a status byte at location $8002. We have defined three bits in the status byte

- RDY (ready) indicates that the port is ready to take part in a data transaction

- IRQ indicates that the port has generated an interrupt

- ERR indicates that an error has occurred (i.e. the input or output is unreliable).

A purely polled I/O system simply tests the RDY bit of a peripheral until it is ready to take part in an I/O transaction.

A system with interrupt-driven I/O and device polling waits for an interrupt and then reads the IRQ bit in the status register of each peripheral. This technique is fairly efficient as long as there are few devices capable of generating an interrupt.

Because the programmer chooses the order in which the interfaces are polled following an interrupt, a limited measure of prioritization is built into the polling process. However, a well-known law of the universe states that when searching through a pile of magazines for a particular copy, the desired issue is always at the opposite end to the point at which the search was started. Incidentally, beginning the search at the other end of the pile doesn't seem to defeat this law. Likewise, the device that generated the interrupt is the last device to be polled. Consequently, a system with polled interrupts could lead to the situation in which a certain device requests service but never gets it. We next demonstrate how some processors allow the peripheral that requested attention to identify itself by means of a mechanism called the *vectored interrupt*.

The vectored interrupt

In a system with *vectored interrupts* the interface itself identifies its associated interrupt-handling routine, thereby removing the need for interrupt polling. Let's look at how the 68000 implements vectored interrupts. Whenever the 68000 detects an interrupt, the 68000 acknowledges it by transmitting an *interrupt acknowledge* (called IACK) message to all the interfaces that might have originated the interrupt.

The 68000 doesn't have an explicit 'IACK' pin. Instead, it uses its three *function code outputs*, FC0, FC1, FC2, to inform peripherals that it's acknowledging an interrupt (see Fig. 8.9). These three function code outputs tell external devices (memory and interfaces) what the 68000's doing. For example, the function code tells the system whether the 68000 is reading an instruction or an operand from memory. The special function code 1,1,1 indicates an interrupt acknowledge.

Because the 68000 has seven levels of interrupt request, it's necessary to acknowledge only the appropriate level of interrupt. It would be unfair if a level 2 and a level 6 interrupt occurred nearly simultaneously and the interface requesting a level 2 interrupt thought that its interrupt was about to be serviced. The 68000 indicates which level of interrupt it's acknowledging by providing the level of the interrupt being serviced on the three least-significant bits of its address bus (A_{01} to A_{03}). External logic detects FC0, FC1, FC2 = 1,1,1 and uses A_{01} to A_{03} to generate seven interrupt acknowledge signals $\overline{IACK0}$ to $\overline{IACK7}$.

After issuing an interrupt request, the interface waits for an acknowledgement on its $\overline{IACK}$ input. When the interface detects $\overline{IACK}$ asserted, it puts out an *interrupt vector number* on data lines d_{00} to d_{07}. That is, the interface responds with a number ranging from 0 to 255. When the 68000 receives this interrupt vector number, it multiplies it by four to get an entry into the 68000's *interrupt vector table*; for example, if an interface responds to an IACK cycle with a vector number of 100, the CPU multiplies it by 4 to get 400. In the next step, the 68000 reads the contents of memory location 400 to get a pointer to the location of the interrupt handling routine for the interface that initiated the interrupt. This pointer is loaded into the 68000's program counter to start interrupt processing.

Because an interface can supply one of 256 possible vector numbers, it's theoretically possible to support 256 unique interrupt-handling routines for 256 different interfaces. We say theoretically, because it's unusual for 68000 systems to dedicate all 256 vector numbers to interrupt handling. In fact, the 68000 itself uses vector numbers 0 to 63 for purposes other than handling hardware interrupts (these vectors are reserved for other types of exception).

Why does the 68000 multiply the vector number by four? The answer to this is easy: the interrupt vector loaded into the 68000's PC is a 32-bit value that occupies four bytes in memory. Therefore, each vector number is associated with a four-byte (i.e. longword) block of memory. The interrupt vector table itself takes up $4 \times 256 = 1024$ bytes of memory. Figure 8.12 illustrates the way in which the 68000 responds to a level 6 vectored interrupt.

Daisy-chaining

The scheme for vectored interrupts we've just described seems to have an important flaw. Although there are 256 possible interrupt vector numbers, the 68000 supports only seven levels of interrupt. Why then do we need to cater for so many interrupt handlers? In the first case, it is not necessary for all interfaces to be active at the same time. We could envisage a scheme with say 20 interfaces with 20 interrupt handlers. It is perfectly possible to program the interfaces so that only 7 of them can issue an interrupt at any instant.

A simple means of providing an effectively infinite number of levels of interrupt request is provided by a technique called *daisy-chaining*, in which peripherals are linked together in a line. When the CPU acknowledges an interrupt, the message is sent to the first peripheral in the daisy chain. If this peripheral doesn't require attention, it passes the interrupt acknowledgement down the line to the next peripheral.

Figure 8.13 shows how interrupt requesters at a given priority level can be prioritized by daisy-chaining. Each peripheral has an $\overline{IACK\_IN}$ input on its left and an $\overline{IACK\_OUT}$ output on its right. The $\overline{IACK\_OUT}$ pin of each peripheral is wired to the $\overline{IACK\_IN}$ pin of the peripheral on its right. Thus, the $\overline{IACK\_OUT}/\overline{IACK\_IN}$ pins constitute a daisy chain. Suppose an interrupt request at level 6 is issued and acknowledged by the 68000. The interface at the left-hand side of the daisy chain closest to the 68000 receives the $\overline{IACK}$ signal first from the CPU. If this interface generated the interrupt, it responds with an interrupt vector. If the interface did not request service, it passes the $\overline{IACK}$ signal to the device on its right. That is, $\overline{IACK\_IN}$ is passed out on $\overline{IACK\_OUT}$. The $\overline{IACK}$ signal ripples down the daisy chain until a device responds with an interrupt vector.

Daisy-chaining interfaces permits an unlimited number of interfaces to share the same level of interrupt and each interface to have its own interrupt vector number. Individual interfaces are prioritized by their position with respect to the CPU. The closer to the CPU an interface is, the more chance it has of having its interrupt request serviced in the event of multiple interrupt requests at this level.

Interrupts considered harmful

Each aspect of life can be divided into one of two categories: a good thing or a bad thing. Some computer scientists are

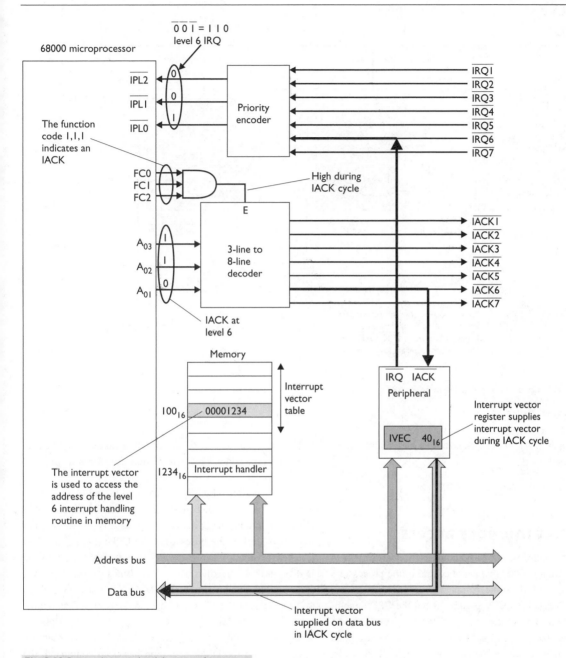

Fig. 8.12 Responding to a level 6 vectored interrupt.

firmly convinced that interrupts are a bad thing. A single interface generating the occasional interrupt causes few headaches. But imagine a system with many interfaces, all generating their interrupts asynchronously (i.e. at random). The entire system no longer behaves in a deterministic way, but becomes stochastic (non-deterministic) and is best described by the mathematics of random processes. This system is analogous to a large group of people in a bar—there is always someone who never gets served.

Some safety-critical systems rely on polling to determine whether I/O devices are ready to take part in I/O transactions rather than interrupts. The programmer has control of all

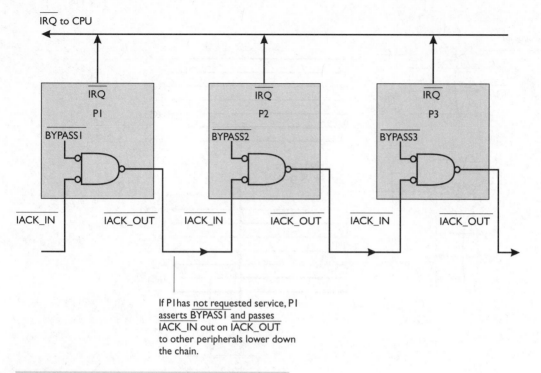

IRQ to CPU

If P1 has not requested service, P1 asserts BYPASS1 and passes IACK_IN out on IACK_OUT to other peripherals lower down the chain.

Fig. 8.13 Daisy-chaining interrupts at the same level of priority.

polled I/O operations and can choose how and when peripherals are polled.

8.4 Direct memory access

A computer computes, so why should it become involved with input/output activity that is not central to the processor's activity? The third I/O strategy, called *direct memory access*, DMA, moves data between a peripheral and the CPU's memory without the direct intervention of the CPU itself. DMA provides the fastest possible means of transferring data between an interface and memory, as it carries no CPU overhead and leaves the CPU free to do useful work. As in most walks of life, if something is worth having, it's expensive. DMA is no exception to this rule, because it is quite complex to implement and requires a relatively large amount of hardware. Figure 8.14 illustrates the operation of a system with DMA.

DMA works by grabbing the data and address buses from the CPU and using them to transfer data directly between the peripheral and memory. During normal operation of the computer in Fig. 8.14, bus switch 1 is closed, and bus switches 2 and 3 are open. The CPU controls the buses, providing an address on the address bus and reading data from memory or writing data to memory via the data bus.

When a peripheral wishes to take part in an I/O transaction it asserts the TransferRequest input of the DMA controller (DMAC). In turn, the DMA controller asserts DMArequest to request control of the buses from the CPU; that is, the CPU is taken off-line. When the CPU returns DMAgrant to the DMAC, a DMA transfer takes place. Bus switch 1 is opened and switches 2 and 3 closed. The DMAC provides an address to the address bus and hence to the memory. At the same time, the DMAC provides a TransferGrant signal to the peripheral, which is then able to write to, or read from, the memory directly. When the DMA operation has been completed, the DMAC hands back control of the bus to the CPU.

A real DMA controller is a very complex device. It has several internal registers, at least one to hold the address of the next memory location to access and one to hold the number of words to be transferred. Many DMACs are able to handle several interfaces, which means that their registers must be duplicated. Each interface is referred to as a *channel*, and typical single-chip DMA controllers handle up to four channels (i.e. peripherals) simultaneously.

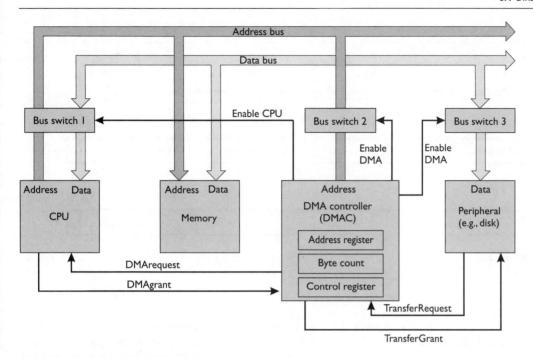

Fig. 8.14 Input/output by means of DMA.

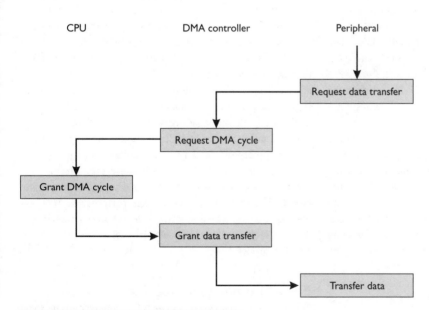

Fig. 8.15 Protocol flowchart for a DMA operation.

Figure 8.15 provides a protocol flowchart for the sequence of operations taking place during a DMA operation. This figure shows the sequence of events that take place in the form of a series of transactions between the peripheral, the DMAC, and the CPU.

DMA operates in one of two modes: *burst mode* or *cycle stealing*. In the burst mode the DMA controller seizes the system bus for the duration of the data transfer operation (or at least for the transfer of a large number of words). Burst mode DMA allows data to be moved into memory as fast as the

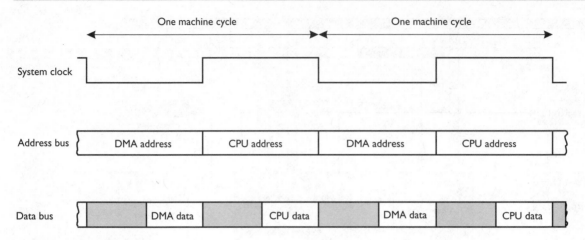

Fig. 8.16 DMA by cycle stealing.

weakest link in the chain memory/bus/interface permits. The CPU is effectively halted in the burst mode because it cannot use its data and address buses.

In the cycle steal mode described by Fig. 8.16, DMA operations are interleaved with the computer's normal memory accesses. As the computer does not require access to the system buses for 100 percent of the time, DMA can take place when they are free. This free time occurs while the CPU is busy generating an address ready for a memory read or write cycle.

When the system clock is low, the CPU doesn't need the use of the buses, so the DMAC grabs them and carries out a data transfer. When the clock goes high the CPU carries out its normal memory access cycle. DMA by cycle stealing is said to be *transparent* because the computer is oblivious of it. That is, the transfer is invisible to the computer and no processing time is lost. A DMA operation is initiated by the CPU writing a start address and the number of words to be transferred into the DMAC's registers. When the DMA oper- ation has been completed, the DMAC generates an interrupt, indicating to the CPU that the data transfer is over and that a new one may be initiated or results of the current transfer made use of.

In systems with a cache memory, DMA can take place in parallel with normal CPU activity; that is, the CPU can access data and code that's been cached while the I/O interface is copying data between a peripheral and the main memory.

8.5 Parallel and serial interfaces

Having described how I/O transactions can be programmed, interrupt driven, or use DMA, we now look at two real

integrated circuits that implement an interface between the CPU and the outside world. These devices look like a block of memory locations to the CPU and implement the protocol required to communicate with the external system. Although we've decided to describe two actual devices, the general principles apply to virtually all interface devices. Readers not interested in the fine details of I/O systems may skip this section.

The first interface to be described is the peripheral interface adapter that transfers data between an external system and a processor via an 8-bit highway, and the second interface is the asynchronous communications adapter that transfers data on a single-bit serial highway. Both interfaces are basic first-generation circuits intended for applications involving 8-bit microprocessors. We have selected these particular devices (i.e. 6820 PIA and 6850 ACIA) because they illustrate the fundamental principles and are not as complex as the current crop of interfaces optimized for high-performance 16/32-bit microprocessors. Other interfaces found in microprocessor systems include: Ethernet controllers, disk controllers, and video controllers.

8.5.1 The parallel interface

The *peripheral interface adapter*, PIA, contains all the logic needed to move data between the CPU and two 8-bit I/O ports. A port's eight pins may be programmed individually to act as inputs or outputs; for example, a port can be configured with two inputs and six outputs. The PIA can automatically perform handshaking with the device connected to its ports.

Figure 8.17 gives a block diagram of the PIA, from which it can be seen that the two I/O ports, referred to as the A side

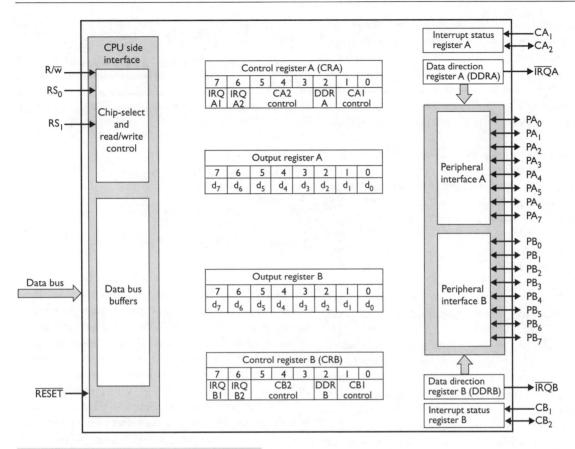

Fig. 8.17 Structure of the parallel interface adapter, PIA.

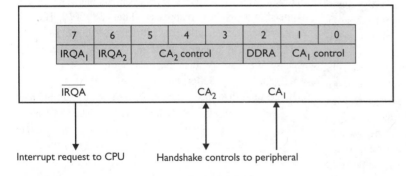

Fig. 8.18 Structure of the PIA's side A control register.

and the B side, appear symmetrical. In general this is true, but small differences in the behavior of these ports are described when necessary. Each port has two control pins associated with it that can transform the port from a simple I/O latch into a device capable of performing a handshake or initiating interrupts, as required.

The interface between the PIA and the CPU is quite conventional, as Fig. 8.18 demonstrates. The PIA's CPU-side pins make the PIA look to the CPU like a block of four locations in RAM. These pins comprise a data bus and its associated control circuits. Two register-select pins RS_0 and RS_1 are connected to the lower-order bits of the CPU's address bus and discriminate between the PIA's internal registers. The PIA has a clock input, E, for internal synchronization, a read/write control input, a reset input that can be used to force it into a known state when the system is first powered up, three chip-select inputs, and two interrupt request outputs. The chip-select inputs CS0, CS1, $\overline{\text{CS2}}$ must be 1, 1, 0 to enable the PIA. Modern peripherals have a single active-low chip-select input.

The PIA has two independent interrupt request outputs. $\overline{\text{IRQA}}$ indicates an interrupt generated by the PIA's A side and $\overline{\text{IRQB}}$ indicates an interrupt generated by side B. You can wire $\overline{\text{IRQA}}$ and $\overline{\text{IRQB}}$ together and poll the PIA's status registers to determine which side generated the interrupt. When the PIA is first powered up, a pulse is applied to its $\overline{\text{RESET}}$ input to force the contents of all its internal registers into a zero state. In this mode the PIA is in a safe state with all its programmable pins configured as inputs. It would be highly dangerous to permit the PIA to assume a random initial configuration, since any random output signals might cause havoc elsewhere.

To appreciate how the PIA operates, we have to understand the function of its six internal registers. The PIA has two *peripheral data registers* (PDRA and PDRB), two *data-direction registers* (DDRA, DDRB), and two *control registers* (CRA and CRB). A location within the PIA is addressed by accessing the PIA with the appropriate 2-bit address on RS_0, RS_1. However, as RS_0 and RS_1 can distinguish between no more than four of the six internal registers, some mechanism must be provided to obtain the necessary discrimination. Such a mechanism is implemented by making bit 2 of the control registers (written CRA_2 or CRB_2) act as a pointer to either the data register or the data-direction register. Table 8.4 shows how this addressing arrangement works.

Table 8.4 shows that RS_1 determines which of the two sides (i.e. 8-bit I/O ports) of the PIA is selected, and RS_0 determines whether the control register or one of the pair of registers formed by the peripheral data register and the data register is selected. Thus, the control registers can always be unconditionally accessed when $RS_0 = 1$, but to select a peripheral data register or a data-direction register, bit 2 of the appropriate control register must be set or cleared, respectively.

The peripheral data registers act as the interface between the PIA and the outside world. When one of the PIA's 16 I/O pins is programmed as an input, data is moved from the relevant pin through the peripheral data register onto the CPU's data bus during a read cycle. Conversely, when acting as an output, the CPU latches a 1 or 0 into the appropriate bit of the peripheral data register to determine the state of the corresponding output pin.

RS_1	RS_0	CRA_2	CRB_2	Location selected	Address
0	0	1	X	Peripheral data register A	BASE
0	0	0	X	Data direction register A	BASE
0	1	X	X	Control register A	BASE + 2
1	0	X	1	Peripheral data register B	BASE + 4
1	0	X	0	Data direction register B	BASE + 4
1	1	X	X	Control register B	BASE + 6

X = don't care
BASE = base address of the memory-mapped PIA
RS_0 = register select 0
RS_1 = register select 1
CRA_2 = bit 2 of control register A
CRB_2 = bit 2 of control register B

Table 8.4 The register selection scheme of the PIA.

The *data-direction registers* determine the direction of data transfer on the PIA's I/O pins. If a zero is written into bit i of DDRA, bit i of the A-side peripheral data register is configured as an input. Conversely, writing a one into bit i of DDRA configures bit i of the A-side peripheral data register as an output. In this way the I/O pins of the PIA's A-side or B-side ports may be defined as inputs or outputs by writing an appropriate code into DDRA or DDRB, respectively. The PIA's I/O pins can be defined dynamically and the direction of data transfer altered during the course of a program. The DDR's bits are cleared during a power-on-reset to avoid accidentally forcing any pin into an erroneous output mode.

The example in Table 8.5 demonstrates how side A is configured as an input and side B as an output. The PIA is assumed to be memory-mapped at address $80\,0000. The registers are accessed at addresses $80\,0000, $80\,0002, $80\,0004, and $80\,0006. Consecutive addresses differ by 2 rather than 1 because the 68000's data bus is 16 bits wide (2 bytes), whereas the PIA is 8 bits wide.

Once the PIA has been configured, data can be read from side A of the PIA into data register D0 by a MOVE.B PDRA,D0 instruction, and data may written into side B by writing to the PIA with a MOVE.B D0,PDRB.

Controlling the PIA

In addition to determining whether a data-direction register or a peripheral data register can be directly accessed from the data bus, the control registers are responsible for controlling the special-purpose pins associated with each port of the PIA. Pins CA_1, CA_2 control the flow of information between the peripheral's A-side and the PIA by providing any required handshaking between the peripheral and PIA. Similarly, side-B has control pins CB_1 and CB_2. The operation of CA_1, CA_2 and

```
PDRA     EQU     $800000     Base address of PIA (data register side A)
DDRA     EQU     $800000     Data direction register shares PDRA address
CRA      EQU     $800002     Control register address (side A)
PDRB     EQU     $800004
DDRB     EQU     $800004
CRB      EQU     $800006

*        Select side A DDR by setting CRA2 to 0 (we clear all bits)
         CLR.B   CRA

*        Configure side A data register as input by writing 0s into DDRA
         MOVE.B  #0,DDRA

*        Select side B data direction register B by setting CRB2 to 0
         CLR.B   CRB

*        Select side B as an output by writing 1s into DDRB
         MOVE.B  #%11111111,DDRB

*        Select PDRA as an input port by setting bit CRA2 to 1
         ORI.B   #%00000100,CRA

*        Select PDRB as an output port by setting bit CRB2 to 1
         ORI.B   #%00000100,CRB
```

Table 8.5 Configuring a PIA.

CRA_1	CRA_0	Transition of CA_1 control input	$IRQA_1$ interrupt flag status	Status of PIA $\overline{IRQA}$ output
0	0	negative edge	set on negative edge	masked (remains high)
0	1	negative edge	set on negative edge	enabled (goes low)
1	0	positive edge	set on positive edge	masked (remains high)
1	1	positive edge	set on positive edge	enabled (goes low)

For example, if CRA_1, CRA_0 is set to 0,1, a negative (falling) edge at the CA_1 control input sets the $IRQA_1$ status flag in control register CRA to one, and the PIA's $\overline{IRQA}$ interrupt request output is asserted to interrupt the host processor. CRA_1 determines the sense of the transition on CA_1 that sets the interrupt flag status, and CRA_0 determines whether the PIA will interrupt the host processor when the interrupt flag is set.

Table 8.6 Effect of CA_1 control bits.

CB_1, CB_2 is similar—but important differences do exist. A description of control register A and CA_1 and CA_2 is given, and any difference in the behavior of the corresponding B-side pins is dealt with as necessary.

The bits of control register A, CRA, can be divided into four groups according to their function. Bits CRA_0 to CRA_5 are chosen by the programmer to define the PIA's operating mode (Fig. 8.18). Bits CRA_6 and CRA_7 are interrupt status bits that are set or cleared by the PIA itself. Bit CRA_6 is interrupt request flag 1, $IRQA_1$, and is set by an active transition at the CA_1 input pin. Similarly, CRA_7 corresponds to the $IRQA_2$ interrupt request flag and is set by an active transition at the CA_2 input pin. We now examine the control register in more detail.

CA_1 control Bits CRA_0 and CRA_1 determine how the PIA responds to a change of level (0-to-1 or 1-to-0) at the CA_1 control input. The relationship between the CA_1 control input, CRA_0, CRA_1 and the interrupt flag $IRQA_1$ is described in Table 8.6. CRA_1 determines the sense (i.e. 'up' or 'down') of the transition on CA_1 that causes the CRA_7 interrupt flag (i.e. $IRQA_1$) to be set. CRA_0 determines whether an active transition on CA_1 generates an interrupt request by asserting the $\overline{IRQA}$ output. CA_1 can be used as an auxiliary input if bit CRA_0 is clear, or as an interrupt request input if bit CRA_0 is set.

Whenever an interrupt is caused by an active transition on CA_1, the interrupt flag in the control register, $IRQA_1$, is set and the $\overline{IRQA}$ output pin goes low. After the CPU has read the contents of peripheral data register A, interrupt flag $IRQA_1$ is automatically reset. In a typical application of the PIA, CA_1 is connected to a peripheral's RDY output so that the peripheral can request attention when it is ready to take part in a data transfer.

CRA$_5$	CRA$_4$	CRA$_3$	Transition of CA$_2$ control input	IRQA$_2$ interrupt flag status	Status of PIA $\overline{\text{IRQA}}$ output
0	0	0	negative edge	set on negative edge	masked (remains high)
0	0	1	negative edge	set on negative edge	enabled (goes low)
0	1	0	positive edge	set on positive edge	masked (remains high)
0	1	1	positive edge	set on positive edge	enabled (goes low)

Table 8.7 Effect of CA$_2$ control bits when CRA$_5$ = 0.

Case	CRA$_5$	CRA$_4$	CRA$_3$	Output CA$_2$	
0	1	0	0	Low on the falling edge of E after a CPU read side A data operation.	High when interrupt flag bit CRA$_7$ is set by an active transition of CA$_1$ input.
1	1	0	1	Low on the falling edge of E after a CPU read side A data operation.	High on the negative edge of the first E pulse occurring during a deselect state of the PIA.
2	1	1	0	Low when CRA$_3$ goes low as a result of a CPU write to CRA.	Always low as long as CRA$_3$ is low. Will go high on a CPU write to CRA which changes CRA$_3$ to a 1.
3	1	1	1	Always high as long as CRA$_3$ is high. Will be cleared on a CPU write to CRA that clears CRA$_3$.	High when CRA$_3$ goes high as a result of a CPU write to CRA.

Table 8.8 Effect of CA$_2$ control bits when CRA$_5$ = 1.

Data direction access control (CRA$_2$) When register select input RS$_0$ = 0, the data-direction access control bit determines whether data-direction register A or peripheral data register A is selected. When the PIA is reset, CRA$_2$ = 0 so that the data-direction register is always available after a reset.

CA$_2$ control (CRA$_3$, CRA$_4$, CRA$_5$) The CA$_2$ control pin may be programmed as an input that generates an interrupt request (in a similar way to CA$_1$), or it may be programmed as an output. Bit 5 of the control register determines CA$_2$'s function. If bit 5 = 0, CA$_2$ is an interrupt request input (Table 8.7) and if bit 5 = 1, CA$_2$ is an output (Table 8.8). Table 8.7 demonstrates that the behavior of CA$_2$, when acting as an interrupt-request input, is entirely analogous to that of CA$_1$.

When CA$_2$ is programmed as an output with CRA$_5$ = 1 it behaves in the manner defined in Table 8.8. It is in this mode that sides A and B of the PIA differ—a separate table (Table 8.9) describes the behavior of CB$_2$ as a function of CRB$_4$ and CRB$_3$ when CRB$_5$ = 1. As the significance of the entries in Table 8.8 is not immediately apparent, further explanation is given case by case.

Case 1 CRA$_5$ = 1, CRA$_4$ = 0, CRA$_3$ = 0. This is known as the *handshake mode* and is used when a peripheral is transmitting data to the CPU via the PIA. A timing diagram of the action of the handshake mode of CA$_2$ is given in Fig. 8.19, together with an explanation of the steps involved. In handshake mode CA$_2$ goes high whenever a peripheral has data ready for reading and remains high until the CPU has read the data from the PIA's data register.

Case 2 CRA$_5$ = 1, CRA$_4$ = 0, CRA$_3$ = 1. This mode is sometimes called the *pulsed mode*, *input-programmed handshaking mode*, or *autohandshaking mode*, and is illustrated in Fig. 8.20. CA$_2$ automatically produces a single pulse at a low level after the side-A peripheral data register has been read by the CPU. Because the peripheral receives a pulse on CA$_2$ after the CPU has read the PIA, the peripheral knows that its data has been received and that the PIA is ready for new data.

Case 3 CRA$_5$ = 1, CRA$_4$ = 1, CRA$_3$ = 0. In this mode CA$_2$ is set low and remains in that state until CRA$_3$ is set. That is, CA$_2$ is cleared under program control.

Case 4 CRA$_5$ = 1, CRA$_4$ = 1, CRA$_3$ = 1. Now CA$_2$ is set to a high level and remains in that state until CRA$_3$ is cleared. Cases 3 and 4 demonstrate the use of CA$_2$ as an additional output, set or cleared under program control.

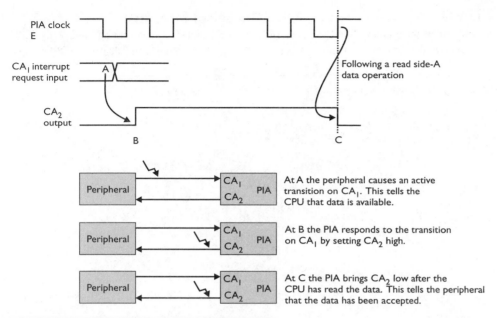

Following a read side-A data operation

At A the peripheral causes an active transition on CA_1. This tells the CPU that data is available.

At B the PIA responds to the transition on CA_1 by setting CA_2 high.

At C the PIA brings CA_2 low after the CPU has read the data. This tells the peripheral that the data has been accepted.

Fig. 8.19 The PIA input handshake mode (case 0 in Table 8.8).

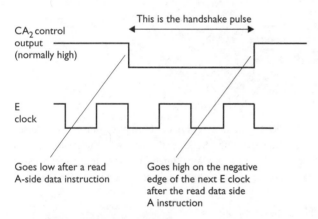

This is the handshake pulse

CA_2 control output (normally high)

E clock

Goes low after a read A-side data instruction

Goes high on the negative edge of the next E clock after the read data side A instruction

Fig. 8.20 The PIA pulsed input mode.

Differences between side-A and side-B ports

The significant difference between side A and side B occurs in the behavior of control pins CA_2 and CB_2 when programmed in the handshake or autohandshake modes. Side A performs handshaking operations when data is *read* from the PIA by the CPU. Side B performs handshaking operations when data is *written* into the PIA from the CPU. This difference becomes apparent when you look at the behavior of CB_2 when it is programmed as an output (i.e. $CRB_5 = 1$). Table 8.9 describes the side A and side B differences.

Case 1 CRB_5, CRB_4, CRB_3. In this handshaking mode CB_2 goes high whenever a peripheral is ready to receive data, and remains high until the CPU has written data into the PIA's side B data register. Figure 8.21 gives the timing diagram of this mode of operation.

Case 2 $CRB_5 = 1$, $CRB_4 = 0$, $CRB_3 = 1$. In this mode the PIA tells the peripheral that data is available by putting a pulse on the CB_2 pin after data has been written into the PIA's side B data register. Case 2, which corresponds to output with autohandshaking, is illustrated in Fig. 8.22.

Cases 3 and 4 These cases are entirely analogous to those of the A side.

Using the PIA

We now look at a typical application of a PIA. Figure 8.23 demonstrates how the PIA might be employed to interface a computer to a printer. The printer receives data from the host processor via its data bus, d_0 to d_7. When the printer is ready to receive a new character, it asserts its active-low $\overline{RDY}$ output and when a valid character is on d_0 to d_7, the host processor must assert the active-low strobe input to the printer, $\overline{STB}$.

Since the host processor is being used to send data *to* the printer, it is reasonable to employ side B of a PIA to interface the printer, as side B provides an output handshake facility. If the printer's $\overline{\text{RDY}}$ line is connected to the PIA's CB_1 control input, the PIA can be programmed to interrupt the host processor whenever the printer is ready.

8.5.2 The serial interface

The serial interface transfers data into and out of the CPU a bit at a time along a single wire; that is, the 8-bit value

```
* Setup_PIA
*    CR=IRQB1,IRQB2,CB2 control,DDR/DR select,CB1 control
*       x,    x,    1 0 1,      0,              0 0
*       output handshake, select DDR, CB1 negative-edge sensitive
*    Configure Side B as an output port by loading DDRB with all one's
*    Select data register by setting bit 2 of control register CRB
* End Setup_PIA

* Poll_PIA
*    REPEAT
*       Test IRQB1
*    UNTIL Printer ready and IRQB1 is asserted
*    Transmit data to PIA
* End Poll_PIA

PIA     EQU     <PIA location>        Location of memory mapped PIA
PDRB    EQU     4                     Offset for peripheral data register B
DDRB    EQU     4                     Offset for data direction register B
CRB     EQU     6                     Offset for control register B
IRQB    EQU     7                     IRQ1 = bit 7 of CRB
CRSET   EQU     %00101000             Data to setup control register
CRB2    EQU     4                     Bit 2 of CRB controls DDRB/PDRB
*
        LEA     PIA,A0                A0 points to PIA
        MOVE.B  #CRSET,CRB(A0)        Set up control register B
        MOVE.B  #%11111111,DDRB(A0)   Configure side B as output
        ORI.B   #CRB2,CRB(A0)         Select PDRB
*
Poll    BTST.B  #IRQB,CRB(A0)         Test CB1 (STB) status
        BEQ     Poll                  Until STB asserted
        MOVE.B  D0,PDRB(A0)           Transmit a byte to the printer...
```

Similarly, by connecting the PIA's CB_2 control output to the printer's $\overline{\text{STB}}$ input, an autohandshaking procedure can be implemented.

10110001_2 would be sent in the form of eight (or more) pulses one after the other. Serial data transfer is much slower than the parallel data transfer offered by a PIA, but is inexpensive because it requires only a single connection between the serial

Case	CRB_5	CRB_4	CRB_3	Output CB_2	
0	1	0	0	Low on the rising edge of the first E pulse after a CPU write side A data operation.	High when interrupt flag bit CRB_7 is set by an active transition of CB_1 input.
1	1	0	1	Low on the falling edge of E after a CPU write side B data operation.	High on the negative edge of the first E pulse occurring during a deselect state of the PIA.
2	1	1	0	Low when CRB_3 goes low as a result of a CPU write to CRB.	Always low as long as CRB_3 is low. Will go high on a CPU write to CRB which changes CRB_3 to a 1.
3	1	1	1	Always high as long as CRB_3 is high. Will be cleared on a CPU write to CRB that clears CRB_3.	High when CRB_3 goes high as a result of a CPU write to CRB.

Table 8.9 Effect of CB_2 control bits when $CRB_5 = 1$.

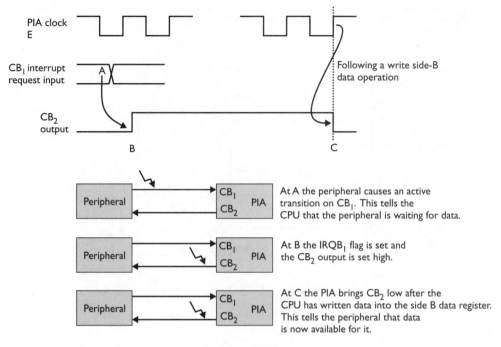

Fig. 8.21 The PIA output handshake mode (case 0 in Table 8.9).

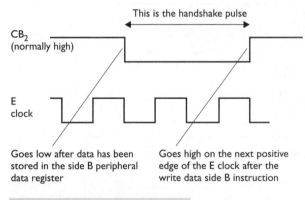

Fig. 8.22 The PIA input handshake mode.

interface and the external world (apart from a ground-return). Serial data transmission is used by data transmission systems that operate over distances greater than a few meters, and Chapter 11 will have much more to say on the subject of data transmission. Here we're more interested in the *asynchronous communications adapter* (ACIA) interface that connects a CPU to a serial data link.

We are not concerned with fine details of the ACIA's internal operation, but rather in what it does and how it is used to transmit and receive serial data. When discussing serial transmission we often use the term *character* to refer to a unit of

data rather than a byte, because many transmission systems are designed to transmit information in the form of ISO/ASCII-encoded characters.

Figure 8.24 demonstrates how a 7-bit character is transmitted bit by bit *asynchronously* (there are other ways of implementing serial transmission systems). During a period in which no data is being transmitted from an ACIA, the serial output is at a high level, which is called the *mark* condition. When a character is to be transmitted, the ACIA's serial output is put in a low state (a mark-to-space transition) for a period of one bit time. The bit time is the reciprocal of the rate at which successive serial bits are transmitted and is measured in *baud*. In the case of a two-level binary signal, the baud corresponds to bits/second. The initial bit is called the *start bit* and tells the receiver that a stream of bits, representing a character, is about to be received. If data is transmitted at 9600 baud, each bit period is $1/9600 = 0.1042$ ms.

During the next seven time slots (each of the same duration as the start bit) the output of the ACIA depends on the value of the character being transmitted. The character is transmitted bit-by-bit. This data format is called *non-return to zero* (NRZ) because the output doesn't go to zero between individual bits. After the character has been transmitted, a further two bits (a *parity bit* and a *stop bit*) are appended to the end of the character.

423

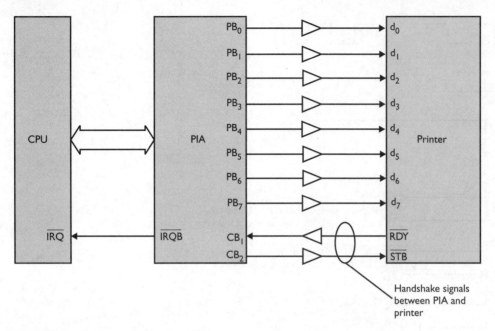

Fig. 8.23 Using the PIA to control a printer.

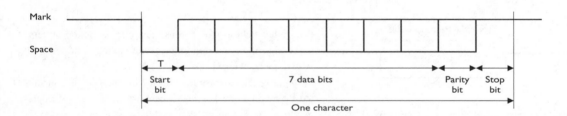

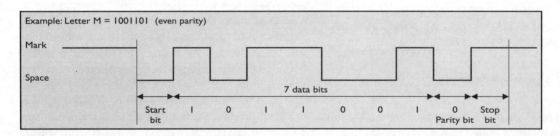

Fig. 8.24 Format of an asynchronous serial character.

At the receiver, a new parity bit is generated locally from the incoming data and then compared with the received parity bit. If the received and locally generated parity bits differ, an error in transmission is assumed to have occurred. A simple parity bit cannot correct an error once it has occurred, nor detect a pair of errors in a character. Not all serial data transmission systems employ a parity bit as an error detector.

The stop bit (or optionally two stops bits) indicates the end of the character. Following the reception of the stop bit(s), the transmitter output is once more in its mark state and is ready to send the next character. The character is composed of ten bits but contains only seven bits of useful information.

The key to asynchronous data transmission is that once the receiver has detected a start bit, it need maintain synchronization only for the duration of a single character. The receiver examines successive received bits by sampling the incoming signal at the center of each pulse. Because the clock at the receiver is not synchronized with the clock at the transmitter, each received data bit will not be sampled exactly at its center.

Figure 8.25 provides the internal arrangement of the ACIA, a highly programmable interface whose parameters can be defined under software control. The ACIA has a single receiver input pin and a single transmitter output pin. The ACIA's CPU side is very much the same as that of the PIA, as Fig. 8.25 demonstrates. This ACIA doesn't have a $\overline{\text{RESET}}$ input (due to a lack of pins) and must be reset by a software command after the initial power-up sequence.

The ACIA's peripheral side pins

The ACIA communicates with a peripheral via seven pins, which may be divided into three groups: receiver, transmitter, and modem control. At this point, all we need say is that the modem is a black box that interfaces a digital system to the public switched telephone network and therefore permits digital signals to be transmitted across the telephone system. A modem converts digital signals into audio (analog) tones. We'll look at the modem in more detail in Chapter 11.

Receiver The receiver part of the ACIA has a clock input and a serial data input. The receiver clock is used to sample the incoming data bits and may be 64, 16, or 1 times that of the bit rate of the received data; for example, an ACIA operating at 9600 bits/s might use a 16× receiver clock of 153 600 Hz. The serial data input receives data from the peripheral to which the ACIA is connected. Most systems require a special interface chip between the ACIA and the

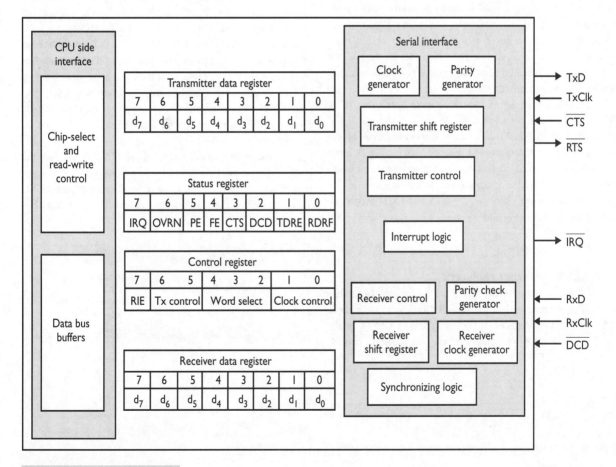

Fig. 8.25 Organization of the ACIA.

serial data link to convert the signal levels at the ACIA to the signal levels found on the data link.

Transmitter The transmitter part of the ACIA has a clock input from which it generates the timing of the transmitted data pulses. As in the case of the receiver, the transmitter clock may be operated at 64, 16, or 1 times the rate of the data. In many cases the transmitter and receiver clocks are derived from the same oscillator. The transmitter data output provides a serial signal at a TTL level.

Modem control The ACIA communicates with a *modem* or similar equipment via three active-low pins (two inputs and one output). The ACIA's *request to send* ($\overline{\text{RTS}}$) output may be set or cleared under software control and is used by the ACIA to tell the modem that it is ready to transmit data to it.

The two active-low inputs to the ACIA are *clear-to-send* ($\overline{\text{CTS}}$) and *data-carrier-detect* ($\overline{\text{DCD}}$). The $\overline{\text{CTS}}$ input is a signal from the modem to the ACIA that inhibits the ACIA from transmitting data if the modem is not ready (because the telephone connection has not been established or has been broken). If the $\overline{\text{CTS}}$ input is high, a bit is set in the ACIA's status register, indicating that the modem (or other terminal equipment) is not ready for data.

The modem uses the ACIA's $\overline{\text{DCD}}$ input to tell the ACIA that the carrier has been lost (i.e. a signal is no longer being received) and that valid data is no longer available at the receiver's input. A low-to-high transition at the $\overline{\text{DCD}}$ input sets a bit in the status register and may also initiate an interrupt if the ACIA is so programmed. In applications of the ACIA that don't use a modem, the $\overline{\text{CTS}}$ and $\overline{\text{DCD}}$ inputs are connected to a low-level and not used.

directly accessed by the CPU. However, as the status and receiver data registers are always read from, and the transmitter data register and control register are always written to, the ACIA's $R/\overline{W}$ input is used to distinguish between the two pairs of registers. The addressing arrangement of the ACIA is given in Table 8.10.

The control register is a write-only register that defines the operational properties of the ACIA, particularly the format of the transmitted or received data. Table 8.11 defines the control register's format. The counter division field, CR_0 and CR_1, determines the relationship between the transmitter and receiver bit rates and their respective clocks (Table 8.12).

When CR_1 and CR_0 are both set to one, the ACIA is reset and all internal status bits, with the exception of the CTS and DCD flags, are cleared. The CTS and DCD flags are entirely dependent on the signal level at the respective pins. The ACIA is initialized by first writing ones into bits CR_1 and CR_0 of the control register, and then writing one of the three division ratio codes into these positions. In the majority of systems $CR_1 = 0$ and $CR_0 = 1$ for a divide by 16 ratio.

The word select field, CR_2, CR_3, CR_4, defines the format of the received or transmitted characters. These three bits allow the selection of eight possible arrangements of number of bits per character, type of parity, and number of stop bits (Table 8.13). For example, if you require a word with 8 bits, no parity, and 1 stop bit control bits CR_4, CR_3, CR_2 must set to 1, 0, 1.

The transmitter-control field, CR_5 and CR_6, determines the level of the request to send ($\overline{\text{RTS}}$) output, and the generation of an interrupt by the transmitter portion of the ACIA. Table 8.14 gives the relationship between these controls bits

The ACIA's internal registers

The ACIA has four internal registers: a transmitter data register (TDR), a receiver data register (RDR), a control register (CR), and a status register (SR). Since the ACIA has a single register-select input RS, only two internal registers can be

RS	R/$\overline{W}$	Type of register	ACIA register
0	0	Write only	Control
0	1	Read only	Status
1	0	Write only	Transmitter data
1	1	Read only	Receiver data

Table 8.10 Register selection scheme of the ACIA.

7	6	5	4	3	2	1	0
Receive interrupt enable	Transmitter control		Word select			Counter division	

Table 8.11 Format of the ACIA's control register.

CR_1	CR_0	Division ratio
0	0	$\div 1$
0	1	$\div 16$
1	0	$\div 64$
1	1	Master reset

Table 8.12 Relationship between CR_1, CR_0, and the division ratio.

CR_4	CR_3	CR_2	Word length	Parity	Stop bits	Total bits
0	0	0	7	Even	2	11
0	0	1	7	Odd	2	11
0	1	0	7	Even	1	10
0	1	1	7	Odd	1	10
1	0	0	8	None	2	11
1	0	1	8	None	1	10
1	1	0	8	Even	1	11
1	1	1	8	Odd	1	11

Table 8.13 The word select bits.

CR_6	CR_5	RTS	Transmitter interrupt
0	0	Low	Disabled
0	1	Low	Enabled
1	0	High	Disabled
1	1	Low	Disabled—a break level is placed on the transmitter output

Table 8.14 Function of transmitter control bits CR_5, CR_6.

and their functions. $\overline{\text{RTS}}$ can be employed to tell the modem that the ACIA has data to transmit.

The transmitter interrupt mechanism can be enabled or disabled depending on whether the CPU is operating in an interrupt-driven or in a polled data mode. If the transmitter interrupt is enabled, a transmitter interrupt is generated whenever the transmitter data register (TDR) is empty, signifying the need for new data from the CPU. If the ACIA's clear-to-send input is high, the TDR empty flag bit in the status register is held low, inhibiting any transmitter interrupt.

The effect of setting both CR_6 and CR_5 to a logical one requires some explanation. If both these bits are high a *break* is transmitted until the bits are altered under software control. That is, the transmitter output of the ACIA is held at its space level. A break can be used to generate an interrupt at the receiver because the asynchronous format of the serial data

precludes the existence of a space level for more than about 10 bit periods.

The receiver interrupt enable field consists of bit CR_7 which, when clear, inhibits the generation of interrupts by the receiver portion of the ACIA. Whenever bit CR_7 is set, a receiver interrupt is generated by the receiver data register (RDR) flag of the status byte going high, indicating the presence of a new character ready for the CPU to read. A receiver interrupt can also be generated by a low-to-high transition at the data-carrier-detect ($\overline{\text{DCD}}$) input, signifying the loss of a carrier. CR_7 is a composite interrupt enable bit. It is impossible to enable either an interrupt caused by the RDR being empty or an interrupt caused by a positive transition on the $\overline{\text{DCD}}$ pin alone.

Configuring the ACIA

The following 68000 assembly language listing demonstrates how the ACIA is initialized before it can be used to transmit and receive serial data.

```
* Setting up an ACIA
*
ACIA      EQU     $800000            Location of ACIA in memory
CR        EQU     0                  Control register offset
          LEA     ACIA,A0            A0 points to ACIA
*
* Perform a software reset by writing 1,1 to CR1, CR0
          MOVE.B  #%00000011,CR(A0)
* Select counter division ratio as clk/16 CR1,CR0=0,1
* Select character format CR4,CR3,CR2=1,0,1
* Select operating mode
*     CR6,CR5=0,1=assert RTS and enable transmitter interrupt
* Select receiver interrupt mode CR7=1 to enable Rx interrupt
          MOVE.B  #%10110101,CR(A0) Set up ACIA
```

The status register

The status register has the same address as the control register, but is distinguished from it by being a read-only register. Table 8.15 gives the format of the status register. Let's look at the function of these bits.

Bit 0—Receiver Data Register Full (RDRF) When set the RDRF bit indicates that the receiver data register is full and a character has been received. If the receiver interrupt is enabled, the interrupt request flag, bit 7, is also set whenever RDRF is set. Reading the data in the receiver data register clears the RDRF bit. Whenever the $\overline{\text{DCD}}$ input is high, the RDRF bit remains at a logical zero, indicating the absence of any valid input.

7	6	5	4	3	2	1	0
IRQ	PE	OVRN	FE	CTS	DCD	TDRE	RDRF

Table 8.15 Format of the ACIA's control register.

The RDRF bit is used to detect the arrival of a character when the ACIA is operated in a polled input mode.

```
*   Subroutine to receive a character
*   REPEAT
*      Read ACIA status
*   UNTIL RDRF=1
*   Read ACIA data
*
ACIA      EQU      $800000
RDRF      EQU      0          Rx data ready=bit 0 of SR
SR        EQU      0          Offset for status register
DR        EQU      2          Offset for data register
          LEA      ACIA,A0    A0 points to ACIA
POLL      TST.B    #RDRF,SR(A0)  REPEAT Test Rx status bit
          BEQ      POLL       UNTIL character received
          MOVE.B   DR(A0),D0  Move input from ACIA to D0
RTS
```

Bit 1—Transmitter Data Register Empty (*TDRE*) This flag is the transmitter counterpart of RDRF. A logical 1 in TDRE indicates that the contents of the transmitter data register (TDR) have been transmitted and the register is now ready for new data. The IRQ bit is also set whenever the TDRE flag is set if the transmitter interrupt is enabled. The TDRE bit is at a logical zero when the TDR is full, or when the $\overline{\text{CTS}}$ input is high, indicating that the terminal equipment is not ready for data. The fragment of code below demonstrates how the TDRE flag is used when the ACIA is operated in a polled output mode.

```
*   Subroutine to transmit a character
*   REPEAT
*      Read ACIA status
*   UNTIL TDRE=1
*   Write data to ACIA
*
ACIA      EQU      $800000
TDRE      EQU      1          Transmitter data register empty=bit 1
SR        EQU      0          Offset for status register
DR        EQU      2          Offset for data register
          LEA      ACIA,A0    A0 points to ACIA base
POLL      BTST.B   #TDRE,SR(A0)  Test transmitter for empty state
          BEQ      POLL       Repeat until transmitter ready
          MOVE.B   D0,DR(A0)  Move byte from D0 to ACIA
          RTS
```

Bit 2—Data Carrier Detect (*DCD*) The *data-carrier-detect* bit is set whenever the $\overline{\text{DCD}}$ input is high, indicating that a carrier is not present. The $\overline{\text{DCD}}$ pin is normally employed only in conjunction with a modem. When the signal at the $\overline{\text{DCD}}$ input makes a low-to-high transition, the DCD bit in the status register is set and the IRQ bit is also set if the receiver interrupt is enabled. The DCD bit remains set even if the $\overline{\text{DCD}}$ input returns to a low state. To clear the DCD bit, the CPU must read the contents of the ACIA's status register and then the contents of the data register.

Bit 3—Clear to Send (*CTS*) The *clear-to-send* bit directly reflects the status of the ACIA's $\overline{\text{CTS}}$ input. A low level on the $\overline{\text{CTS}}$ input indicates that the modem is ready for data. If the CTS bit is set, the transmitter data register empty bit is inhibited (clamped at zero), and no data may be transmitted by the ACIA.

Bit 4—Framing Error (*FE*) The *framing error* bit is set whenever a received character is incorrectly framed by a start bit and a stop bit. A framing error is detected by the absence of the first stop bit and indicates a synchronization (timing) error, a faulty transmission, or a break condition. The framing error flag is set or cleared during receiver data transfer time and is present throughout the time that the associated character is available.

Bit 5—Receiver Overrun (*OVRN*) The receiver overrun flag bit is set when a character is received, but hasn't been read by the CPU before a subsequent character is received. The new character overwrites the previous character which is now lost. Consequently, the receiver overrun bit indicates that one or more characters in the data stream have been lost. Synchronization is not affected by an overrun error—the error is caused by the CPU not reading a character, rather than by a fault in the transmission process. The overrun bit is cleared after reading the data from the RDR or by a master reset. Modern ACIAs usually have FIFO buffers to hold several characters to give the CPU more time to read them.

Bit 6—Parity Error (PE)   The parity error is set whenever the received parity bit does not agree with the parity bit generated locally at the receiver from the preceding data bits. Odd or even parity may be selected by writing the appropriate code into bits 2, 3, and 4 of the control register. If no parity is selected, then both the transmitter parity generator and the receiver parity checker are disabled. Once a parity error has been detected and the parity error bit set, it remains set as long as a character with a parity error is in the receiver data register.

```
ACIAC    EQU      $800000      Base address of ACIA
ACIAD    EQU      ACIA+2       Address of data register
RDRF     EQU      0            Receiver data register full
TDRE     EQU      1            Transmitter data register empty
DCD      EQU      2            Data carrier detect
CTS      EQU      3            Clear to send
FE       EQU      4            Framing error
OVRN     EQU      5            Overrun
PE       EQU      6            Parity error
INPUT    MOVE.B   ACIAC,D0     Get status from ACIA
         BTST     #RDRF,D0     Test for received character
         BNE      ERROR_CK     If character received then test SR
         BTST     #DCD,D0      Else test for loss of signal
         BEQ      INPUT        Repeat loop while DCD clear
         BRA      DCD_ERR      Else deal with loss of signal
ERR_CK   BTST     #FE,D0       Test for framing error
         BNE      FE_ERR       If framing error, deal with it
         BTST     #OVRN,D0     Test for overrun
         BNE      OV_ERR       If overrun, deal with it
         BTST     #PE,D0       Test for parity error
         BNE      PE_ERR       If parity error deal with it
         MOVE.B   ACIAD,D0     Load the input into D0
         BRA      EXIT
*
DCD_ERR                       Deal with loss of signal
         BRA      EXIT
*
FE_ERR   Deal with framing error
         BRA      EXIT
*
OV_ERR   Deal with overrun error
         BRA      EXIT
*
PE_ERR   Deal with parity error
*
EXIT     RTS
```

Bit 7—Interrupt Request (IRQ)   The *interrupt request* bit is a composite interrupt request flag because it is set whenever the ACIA wishes to interrupt the CPU, for whatever reason. The IRQ bit may be set by any of the following:

- Receiver data register full (SR bit 0 set);
- Transmitter data register empty (SR bit 1 set);
- DCD bit set (SR bit 2).

Whenever IRQ = 1 the ACIA's $\overline{\text{IRQ}}$ pin is forced active-low to request an interrupt from the CPU. The IRQ bit is cleared by a read from the receiver data register or a write to the transmitter data.

Programming the ACIA

We are now going to look at a more complete program that uses some of the ACIA's error detecting facilities when receiving data.

So far we've examined how information in digital form is read by a computer, processed in the way dictated by a program, and then output in digital form. We haven't yet considered how information is converted between real-world form and digital form. In the next section we describe some of the most frequently used computer interfaces, such as the keyboard, the display, and the printer.

8.6 Input devices for personal computers

The ASCII code for the upper-case letter we call 'A' is 01000001_2. In order to convert this computer representation of 'A' into the actual letter 'A' on paper we have to use a peripheral called a *printer*. Similarly, we have to strike a key on a keyboard with the symbol 'A' on it in order to get the code 01000001_2 into the computer. We now look at peripherals in typical personal computers that input and output data—beginning with the keyboard. Following the keyboard we describe the video display and printer, respectively. This chapter concludes with some of the interfaces associated with computers used in more general applications.

8.6.1 The keyboard

The keyboard and video display are the principal input and output devices for the majority of microcomputer systems. The CRT display is so popular because it is an almost entirely electronic device and is relatively inexpensive to produce. It is cheap because it relies on semiconductor technology for its electronics and on tried and tested television technology for its display.

A CRT terminal can be separated into two parts: an input device (the keyboard) and an output device (the display). The terms *input* and *output* refer here to the device as seen from the CPU. That is, a keyboard provides an output, which in turn becomes the CPU's input. We look first at the keyboard that consists of an array of switches and a means of converting the input from a specific key into a binary code.

The switch

A keyboard is composed of two parts: a set of keys that detect the pressure of a finger and an encoder that converts the output of a key into a unique binary code representing that key.

The key switch that detects the pressure of a finger, called a *keystroke*, is often a mechanical device (see Fig. 8.26(a)). A typical keyswitch contains a plunger that is moved by a finger against the pressure of a spring. As it moves down, the plunger forces two wires together to make a circuit—the output of this device is inherently binary (on or off). A small stainless steel snap-disk located between the plunger and base of the switch produces an audible click when bowed downwards by the plunger. A similar click is made when the plunger is released. Consequently, the act of depressing a keyswitch has a positive feel because of its tactile feedback. One of the differences between low-cost and professional keyboards is the presence, or otherwise, of this feedback.

Figure 8.26(b) describes the *membrane switch*, which provides a very low cost mechanical switch for applications such as microwave oven control panels. A thin plastic membrane is coated with a conducting material and spread over a printed circuit board. Either by forming the plastic membrane into slight bubbles or by creating tiny pits in the PCB, it is possible to engineer a tiny gap between contacts on the PCB and the metal-coated surface of the membrane. Pressure on the surface of the membrane due to a finger pushes the membrane against a contact to close a circuit. The membrane switch can be hermetically sealed for ease of cleaning and is well suited to applications in hazardous or dirty environments (e.g. mines). Equally, the membrane switch suffers all the disadvantages of other types of low-cost mechanical switch.

Although the mechanical switch has some excellent ergonomic properties, it has rather less good electrical properties. In particular, the contacts may get dirty and make intermittent contact or they may tend to bounce when brought together, producing a series of pulses rather than a single, clean contact. This effect is called *contact bounce*. You can eliminate the effects of contact bounce by connecting the switch to the S input of an RS flip-flop. When the switch first closes, the flip-flop is set and its Q output goes high. Even if the contacts bounce and S goes low, the Q output remains high.

Another form of mechanical switch employs a plunger with a small magnet embedded in one end. As this magnet is pushed downwards, it approaches a *reed relay* composed of two gold-plated iron contacts in a glass tube. These contacts become magnetized by the field from the magnet, attract each other and close the circuit—Fig. 8.26(c). Because the contacts are in a sealed tube, the reed relay is one of the most reliable types of mechanical switches.

Non-mechanical switches

Non-mechanical switches have been devised to overcome some of the problems inherent in mechanical switches. Three of the most commonly used non-mechanical switches are the *Hall effect* switch, the *elastometric* switch, and the *capacitive* switch. The *Hall effect switch* consists of a magnet that is pushed against the force of a spring towards a Hall cell. The Hall cell is a semiconductor device through which a steady current flows. When a magnetic field is applied at right angles to the current, a voltage is produced across the terminals of the cell at right angles to both the magnetic field and the current flow. Figure 8.27 illustrates the operation of such a switch. By detecting the Hall effect voltage due to the magnetic field you can generate a digital output corresponding to the states switch-open or switch-closed. The Hall effect switch does not suffer from contact bounce, but is relatively expensive.

The *capacitive switch* relies on the change in capacitive coupling between two metallic contacts when a finger is pressed against them. The great advantage of a capacitive switch keyboard is its extremely low cost and small size, because it is often nothing more than a printed circuit board with contacts etched on the surface. Some capacitive switches use a single contact to sense a keystroke and rely on the capacitive coupling between the contact and ground via the finger.

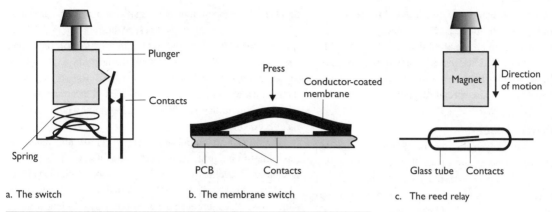

a. The switch   b. The membrane switch   c. The reed relay

Fig. 8.26 The mechanical switch: (a) basic switch, (b) membrane switch, (c) reed relay.

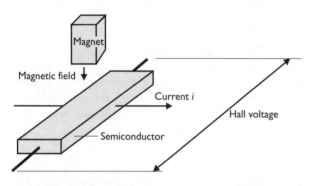

Fig. 8.27 The Hall effect switch.

Unfortunately, the capacitive switch keyboard has no tactile feedback and is rather unpleasant to use. Designers can get round the lack of tactile feedback by providing audio feedback. Each time a keystroke is made, a short audio bleep is sounded from a loudspeaker. The capacitive switch is found in some very low-cost personal computers, television touch-sensitive tuners, and in professional equipment that must be hermetically sealed for operation in hazardous environments.

Elastometric switches employ certain types of material that change their electrical resistance when subjected to pressure. When a finger is pressed against the material, the drop in its electrical resistance is detected by a suitable interface. As above, this type of switch lacks any tactile feedback and its feel is said to be *mushy* and *ill defined*.

Keyboard layout

Because of the influence of the typewriter, the layout of most electronic keyboards closely follows that of the QWERTY keyboard. QWERTY isn't a mnemonic—it's the order of letters on the back row of characters (from left to right) on a typewriter. Historically, the QWERTY layout was devised to minimize the probability of keys jamming together on a mechanical keyboard when certain letter combinations were struck nearly simultaneously. Keys are arranged on a QWERTY keyboard so that commonly occurring letter pairs (e.g. th) are not adjacent. Keyboards for languages other than English don't use a QWERTY layout because jamming is caused by an entirely different sequence of characters.

The QWERTY layout is no longer relevant to electronic keyboards and the keys should, ideally, be repositioned to suit the typist. Because it would be expensive to retrain a whole generation of typists, it appears that we're stuck with the QWERTY layout for the foreseeable future.

Some keyboards have a separate numeric keypad containing the digits 0 to 9, decimal point, and cursor control characters (backspace, line feed, carriage return, etc.). Modern keyboards are often fitted with so called function keys (e.g. F0, F1,..., F12 in the case of the PC) that carry out special actions depending on the program being run.

In order to reduce the total number of keys and hence the size and cost of the keyboard, many of the keys have two, three, or even four different functions. Multifunction keys are implemented by using three special keys (shift, control, and alternate) whose purpose is to modify the meaning of the other keys. The *shift key* behaves in a fashion entirely analogous to the corresponding key on a typewriter and either converts a lower-case character into its upper-case equi-valent, or selects between one of two alternative symbols e.g. ':' or '*').

The *control key*, CTRL, permits the normal alphanumeric keys to be used to generate the non-printing ISO/ASCII control characters; for example, pressing the control key and C at the same time often means, 'cancel the last operation'. Some control characters are used to control a data link between a computer and a remote device. The *alternate key*, ALT, permits new functions to be specified that are not covered by the shift and control functions. Indeed, computers use combinations of these modifier keys (e.g. shift and control simultaneously) to create even more special functions.

The keyboard encoder

The conversion of a keystroke into its ISO/ASCII-encoded equivalent can be performed by a special-purpose chip called a *keyboard encoder*. Figure 8.28 illustrates the operation of such a chip, which contains all the circuitry necessary to convert a signal from an array of switches into a binary code together with a *strobe* (i.e. a pulse that indicates a new character). It's perfectly possible to design a keyboard encoder with the PIA described earlier in this chapter.

Figure 8.29 demonstrates how the keyboard encoder operates. Eight horizontal lines are connected to the pins of an 8-bit output port. Similarly, eight lines that run vertically are connected to an 8-bit input port. A switch is located at each of the $8 \times 8 = 64$ cross-points between horizontal and vertical lines. When a key is pressed, a connection is made between the vertical line and the corresponding horizontal line. As long as no key is pressed, there is no connection between any vertical and any horizontal line. Clearly, if a switch is pressed we can determine which key it was by determining its row and its column.

The eight vertical input lines are each terminated in a resistor connected to $+5$ volts, so that these lines are pulled up to a logical one. That is, if a byte were read from the input port, it would

be 11111111. Suppose now the output port puts the binary value 11111110 onto its eight output lines, as illustrated in Fig. 8.29. If the CPU reads from its input port with, say, the top right-hand key pressed, it will see 11111110. If the next key to the left on the same row is pressed it will see 11111101. Pressing a key on the topmost row causes a 0 to be read into the vertical position corresponding to that key. Pressing a key in any other row has no effect on the data read.

The CPU next outputs the byte 11111101 and reads the input lines to interrogate the second row of keys. This process is continued cyclically, with the CPU outputting 11111110, 11111101, 11111011, 11110111 … to 01111111, as the 0 is shifted one place left each time. In this way all eight rows of the switch matrix are interrogated one by one. The assembly language program in Table 8.16 gives an idea of the software necessary to operate the keyboard.

8.6.2 Pointing devices

Although the keyboard is an excellent device for inputting text, it can't be used efficiently as a *pointing device* to select an arbitrary point on the screen. Personal computers invariably employ one of three pointing devices: the joystick, the mouse, and the trackball.

The joystick

The joystick is a low-cost, low-resolution input found largely in games applications. Its principal advantage over the mouse or trackball is that it can provide four axes (the conventional left–right up–down axes, plus a twist or rotate axis), and a

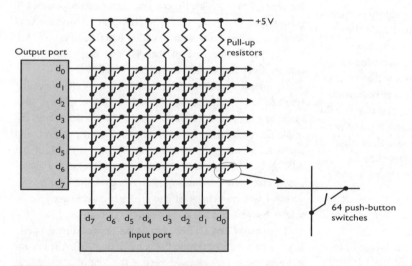

Fig. 8.28 Structure of the keyboard encoder.

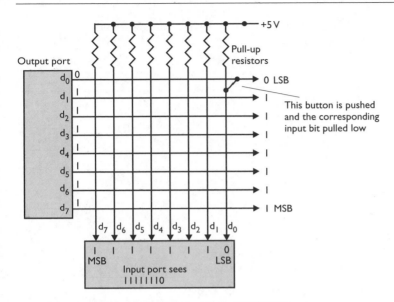

Fig. 8.29 State of the keyboard encoder with one key pressed.

fourth pseudo-axis can be incorporated as a pushbutton on the joystick's top.

The joystick is so called because it mimics the joystick used to control military aircraft and some light aircraft. This device consists of a handle that can be moved simultaneously in the left–right and front–back directions. The computer reads the position of the stick and uses it to move a cursor on the screen in sympathy—you don't look at the joystick when moving it; you look at the cursor on the screen. Without this visual feedback between the hand and the eye, people wouldn't be able to use pointing devices.

Figure 8.30 illustrates the operation of the joystick, which uses two *potentiometers* to sense the position of the control column. A potentiometer consists of a thin film of a partially conducting material and a metallic contact (the slider) that can move along the thin film. Mechanical linkages between the joystick and potentiometers move the arms of the two sliders. The potentiometers employ a fixed resistance (i.e. the thin film) that has a constant voltage across its two terminals. If the resistance is linear, the voltage at any point along the resistance is proportional to its distance from its end. Consequently, the slider supplies an analog voltage output that is an approximately linear function of its position. Note that two analog-to-digital converters are needed to transform the two analog outputs into X and Y digital position inputs required by the computer.

A joystick usually has a dead zone of up to 10 percent of its full-scale output about its neutral position. The dead zone is a property of a joystick's construction, which means that small movements of the joystick about its central neutral position generate no change in its X and Y outputs. This effect has the advantage that the joystick produces a null output in its 'hands off' neutral position and is unaffected by small movements. However, a dead zone makes it harder to make precise movements when the joystick is near to its neutral position.

The mouse

The mouse is probably the most popular pointing device in PCs. A *mechanical* mouse consists of a housing that fits comfortably in the hand and a ball that rotates in contact with the surface of a desk—you could say that a mouse is a larger version of the ball-point pen. As the mouse is dragged along the desk, the ball rotates. Circuits in the mouse translate the ball's movement into a signal that can be read by the computer. An *electronic* mouse doesn't use a ball to detect motion. It requires a special pad that has a grid of horizontal and vertical lines. The mouse reflects a light beam off the grid and counts the number of horizontal and vertical lines crossed as the mouse moves about the pad.

When the computer receives a signal from the mouse, the signal is processed and used to move a cursor on the screen (exactly like all the other pointing devices in this group). The software that controls the mouse may allow you to modify the mouse's sensitivity; that is, you can determine how much the cursor moves for a given movement of the mouse.

A modern mouse is comfortable to hold and can be used to move the cursor rapidly to any point on the screen. Once the

```
*  Set X to 11111110
*  Set X counter to -1
*  REPEAT
*   Rotate X left
*   Output X
*   Read Y
*  UNTIL Y≠0 (i.e. a key is pressed)
*
*  Compress Y value to 3-bit code
*  Set Y counter to -1
*  REPEAT
*   Increment Y counter
*   Compare Y with 11111110
*   Shift Y right
*  UNTIL Y=11111110
*  Concatenate X and Y to get 6-bit value key location
*
           ORG     $002000          Subroutine origin
XLINES  EQU     $008000          Output port for horizontal lines
YLINES  EQU     $008002          Input port for vertical lines
*
           MOVE.B  #%01111111,D0    Preset the initial value of X output
           MOVE.B  #-1,D1           Preset X counter to -1
XLOOP   ROL.B   #1,D0            Rotate value of X output one place left
           ADD.B   #1,D1            Increment X counter in step
           AND.B   #%00000111,D1    X counter value is modulo 8
           MOVE.B  D0,XLINES        Send X value to output port
           MOVE.B  YLINES,D2        Read value of Y from input lines
           CMP.B   #%11111111,D2    Has a key been pressed?
           BEQ     XLOOP            Repeat if Y is all ones
*
           CLR.B   D3               Preset Y counter to 0
YLOOP   CMP.B   #%11111110,D2    Test for Y=0
           BEQ     CONCAT           Exit to concatenate X and Y values
           ROR.B   #1,D2            Rotate value of Y one place right
           ADD.B   #1,D3            Increment Y counter
           BRA     YLOOP            Repeat
*
CONCAT  LSL.B   #3,D2            Shift value of Y counter 3 places left
           OR.B    D2,D1            Add in value of X counter
           RTS                      Return with key value in D1
```

Table 8.16 Reading data by scanning a keyboard.

mouse is at the correct point, you depress one of two buttons that fit naturally under your fingers as you move the mouse. Some versions of the mouse have one or three buttons. Pressing a button activates some pre-defined application-dependent function on the screen. Typical mouse-based systems require you to click the button *once* to select an application (i.e. highlight it), and *twice* to launch an application (i.e. run it). Clicking a button twice in this way is called *double-clicking* and is not always easy to perform because the interval between the clicks must fall within a given range.

Figure 8.31 demonstrates the principle of an *optical* mouse. As the ball rotates (due to the friction between itself and the desk), its motion is resolved into two axes by means

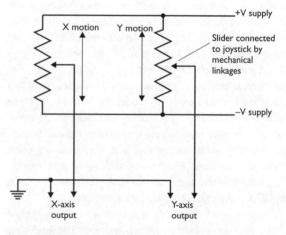

Fig. 8.30 Operation of the joystick.

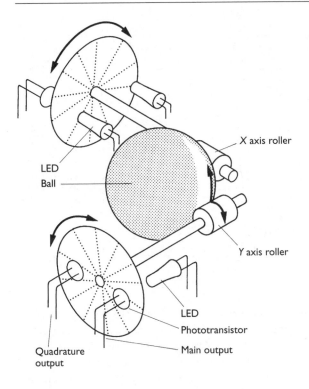

LED
Ball

X axis roller

Y axis roller

LED
Phototransistor

Quadrature
output

Main output

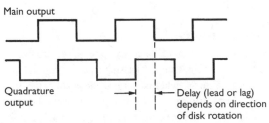

Main output

Quadrature
output

Delay (lead or lag)
depends on direction
of disk rotation

Fig. 8.31 Operation of the optical mouse.

of the rollers located at right angles to each other. If the mouse is moved upwards or from left to right, only one roller rotates. If the mouse is moved diagonally both rollers rotate and their relative speed is a function of the diagonal angle.

Each roller is connected to a shaft that rotates an optical encoder (i.e. an opaque disk with holes in its surface). When the encoder rotates, it interrupts a beam of light between an LED and a detector. Each pulse is fed to the computer, and by adding up the number of pulses received it is possible to determine how far the mouse has moved along that axis. In practice, two beams of light are necessary because a single beam would make it impossible to determine whether the mouse was moving in a positive or a negative direction. A second detector is required to produce a *quadrature* signal that is out of phase with the main signal. If the ball is rotated

one way, the quadrature signal leads the main signal, and if the rotation is reversed the quadrature signal lags the main signal.

The trackball

A trackball is an upside-down mouse—it remains stationary on the desk and you rotate a 1″ to 6″ ball to move the cursor on the screen. Unlike the mouse, the trackball requires no desk space and can be fitted on the keyboard of a laptop or portable computer. Trackballs are often built in to electronic equipment that requires an operator to select a point on a screen (e.g. a target on a radar screen). Some computer users prefer the trackball to the mouse.

The trackball or a tiny joystick is now routinely built into laptop and notebook computers. Some manufacturers go a long way to make the pointing device easy to use. Other manufacturers carefully position the pointing device to ensure that it cannot be operated efficiently by a left-handed user.

Two other input sensors worth mentioning are the 'eraser tip' pointer and track pads used by some laptop computers. The eraser tip pointer is rather like a tiny joystick that juts out of a keyboard. It is operated like a joystick except that it doesn't move. It senses pressure and uses a pressure-to-voltage converter to move the cursor. The track pad consists of a small flat region that senses the position of a finger and uses the finger as if it were a mouse. Both these devices are not as precise as the mouse, but they don't require desk space.

8.7 The CRT and LED displays

We now describe how the *cathode ray tube* (CRT) display that lies at the heart of most display systems operates. A CRT is little more than a special type of the vacuum tube (called a *valve* in the UK) that was once used in all radios and TVs before they were replaced by transistors.

Figure 8.32 describes the construction of the cathode ray tube, the earliest and still the most common means of generating electronic images. It is a remarkably simple device that uses a technology discovered early in the 20th century. The CRT is a glass tube from which all the air has been removed. A wire coil, called a *heater*, is located at one end of the CRT. When a sufficiently large current flows through the heater, it becomes red-hot—exactly like the element in an electric fire that's heated to about 600 °C. The heater raises the temperature of a cylinder (called the *cathode*) coated with a special substance that gives off electrons when it is hot. The negatively charged electrons that leave the surface of the cathode

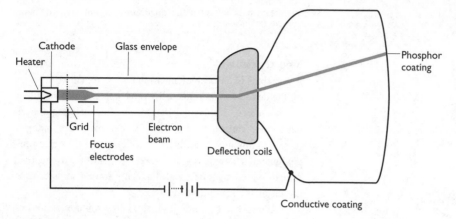

Fig. 8.32 Structure of the CRT.

are launched into space and are unimpeded by air molecules because of the high vacuum in the CRT.

The negatively charged electrons from the CRT's cathode don't get very far because they are pulled back to the cathode. When the electrons boil off into space, they leave behind a positive charge that attracts them back. To overcome this effect, the surface and sides of the glass envelope at the front of the CRT are coated with a conducting material connected to a very high positive voltage with respect to the cathode. The high positive voltage (over 20 000 V) attracts electrons from the cathode to the screen. As the electrons travel along the length of the CRT, they accelerate and gain kinetic energy. When they hit the front of the screen, their kinetic energy is dissipated—in the form of light.

When certain compounds, called *phosphors*, are bombarded by electrons, they convert the kinetic energy of the electrons into light. The color and intensity of the light depend on chemical characteristics of the phosphor coating and the speed and quantity of the electrons. For the time being, we will assume that the composition of the phosphor gives out a white light; that is, the display is black and white or *monochrome*.

The beam of electrons from the cathode flows through a series of cylinders and wire meshes located near the cathode. Using the principle that 'like charges repel and unlike charges attract' various electrical potentials are applied to these cylinders and meshes to control the flow of the beam from the cathode to the screen and to focus the electrons to a tight spot—the smaller the spot, the better the *resolution* of the display. The cathode and focusing electrodes are called a *gun*.

A wire mesh called a *control grid* is placed in the path of the electron beam and connected to a negative voltage with

respect to the cathode. The stronger the negative voltage on the grid, the more the electrons from the cathode are repelled, and the fewer get through to the screen. By changing or *modulating* the voltage on the grid, the number of electrons hitting the screen and, therefore, the brightness of the spot, can be controlled.

Raster-scan displays

Two scanning coils (also called a *yoke*) are placed around the neck of the CRT at right angles. Passing a current through one coil creates a magnetic field that deflects the beam in the horizontal axis, and passing a current through the other coil causes a deflection in the vertical axis. Because there are two coils at right angles, the beam can be deflected up/down and left/right to strike any point on the screen.

The magnetic field in the coil that causes the beam to be deflected in the horizontal axis is increased *linearly* to force the spot to trace out a horizontal line across the face of the CRT. This line is called a scan line or a *raster*. When the beam reaches the right-hand side, it is rapidly moved to the left-hand edge, ready for the next horizontal scan.

While the beam is being scanned in the horizontal direction, another linearly increasing current is applied to the vertical deflection coils to move the beam downward. However, the rate at which the beam moves vertically is a tiny fraction of the rate at which it moves horizontally. During the time it takes the beam to scan from top to bottom, it makes hundreds of scans in the horizontal plane. A scan in the vertical axis is called a *frame*. Figure 8.33(a) shows the combined effects of the fast horizontal and slow vertical scans—eventually, the beam covers or scans the entire surface of the screen.

As the beam scans the surface of the screen, the voltage on the grid is modulated to vary the brightness of the spot between black and white to draw an image. Figure 8.33(b) demonstrates how the letter 'A' can be constructed by switching the beam on and off as it scans the screen. The scanning process is carried out at such a rate that the human viewer cannot see the moving spot and perceives a continuous image. Typically, the horizontal scan rate is in the region of 31 000 lines/second and the vertical scan rate is 50 to 100 fields/second. We will return to the scanning process later when we describe the system used to store images.

The simplest design of a CRT screen would be a *hemisphere*, because any point on its surface is a constant distance from the focusing mechanism. Such a screen is unacceptable because of the difficulty of viewing it, and, over the years, the CRT screens have become both flatter and squarer—at the cost of ever more sophisticated focusing mechanisms. The CRT's screen is, in fact, not square; its width : height ratio (or *aspect* ratio) is the same as a television, 4 : 3. We will soon describe the CRT's lighter and less power-hungry competitor, the *liquid crystal display*.

The CRT is an *analog* device that employs electrostatic and electromagnetic fields to focus an electron beam to any point on a screen—designing a good CRT is even harder than baking the perfect loaf. The engineering problems increase rapidly with the size of the screen. Consequently, large CRTs

are difficult to construct and are very expensive. The weight of the CRT also increases dramatically with screen size. In the early 1990s the cost of a 17 inch screen was about 4 times that of a 14 inch screen and a 19 inch screen cost over 10 times as much as a 14 inch screen. The CRT was one of the last components of the computer to experience falling prices. However, by the late 1990s 19 inch screens were selling for the price of a mid-1990s 17 inch screen.

8.7.1 Generating a display

Now that we've described two basic display devices, the next step is to explain how an image is generated. Figure 8.34 provides a more detailed description of the *raster-scan* display based on the CRT (or the LCD). A *sawtooth* waveform is applied to the vertical scan coils of a CRT to cause the spot to move from the top of the screen to the bottom of the screen at a constant linear rate. When the spot reaches the bottom of the screen, it rapidly flies back to the top again. At the same time, a second sawtooth waveform is applied to the horizontal scanning coils to cause the beam to scan from the left-hand side to the right hand side before flying back again. A negative pulse is applied to the grid during the flyback period to turn off the beam.

Since the computer display grew out of the television, let's look at some of the details of a TV display. In the USA a TV image uses 60 vertical scans a second and each vertical scan (called a *field*) is composed of 262½ lines. A frame is made up of two consecutive fields containing 262½ odd numbered lines and 262½ even numbered lines. The total number of lines per frame is $2 \times 262\frac{1}{2} = 525$. In Europe there are 50 vertical scans a second and each vertical scan is composed of 312½ lines. The total number of lines per frame is $2 \times 312\frac{1}{2} = 625$.

A display composed of consecutive fields of odd and even lines is called an *interlaced display* and is used to reduce the rate at which lines that have to be transmitted. However, interlaced displays are effective only with broadcast TV and tend to generate unacceptable flicker when used to display text in a computing environment.

As the beam is scanned across the surface of the screen, passing every point, the voltage on the grid can be changed to modify the brightness of the spot. Although at any instant a TV screen consists of a single spot, the viewer perceives a complete image for two reasons. First, the phosphor coating continues to give out light for a short time after the beam has struck it, and, second, a phenomenon called the *persistence of vision* causes the brain to perceive an image for a short time after it has been removed.

A raster-scan display system can be constructed by mapping the screen to memory inside a computer. As the beam

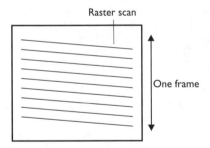

a. The raster scan display

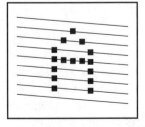

b. Modulating the beam to create an image

Fig. 8.33 The raster scan.

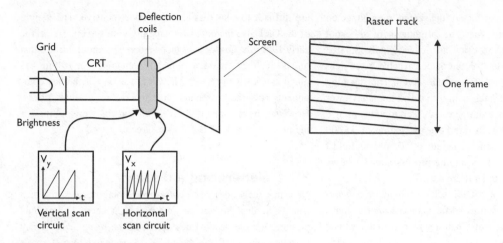

Fig. 8.34 Details of the raster-scan display.

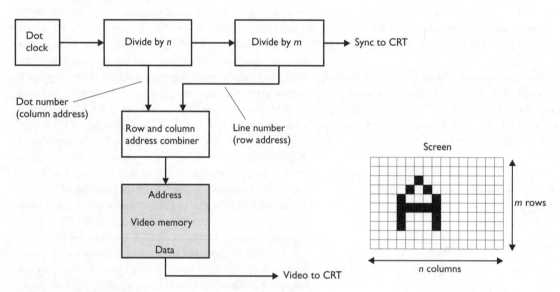

Fig. 8.35 The display controller.

scans the physical display screen, the corresponding location in the computer memory is interrogated and the resulting value used to determine the brightness of the spot. Figure 8.35 provides a highly simplified arrangement of a system that generates an n column by m row display.

In Fig. 8.35 a clock called a *dot clock* produces pulses at the dot rate (i.e. it generates a pulse for each dot or pixel on the display). The dot clock is fed into a divide-by-n circuit that produces a single pulse every time n dots along a row are counted. It also produces a dot number in the range $0, 1, 2, \ldots, n-1$. The output of the divide-by-n circuit is a pulse at

the row rate (i.e. raster) rate, which is fed to a divide-by-m circuit.

The output of the divide-by-m circuit is a pulse at the *frame rate* (i.e. a pulse for each complete scan of the screen). This pulse is fed to the CRT's control circuits and is used to lock or *synchronize* the scanning circuits in the CRT unit with the dot clock. The divide-by-m circuit produces an output in the range $0, 1, 2, \ldots, m-1$ corresponding to the current row. The *column and row address combiner* takes the current column and row addresses from the two dividers and generates the address of the corresponding pixel in the video memory.

The pixel at this address is fed to the CRT to either turn the beam on (a white dot), or turn the beam off (no dot).

A real display system differs from that of Fig. 8.35 in several ways. Probably the most important component of the display generator is the *video memory* (sometimes called *VRAM*) that holds the image to be displayed. Figure 8.36 shows the structure of a *dual-ported* video memory. We call this memory dual-ported because it can be accessed by both an external CPU and the display generator *simultaneously*. The CPU needs to access the video memory in order to generate and modify the image being displayed.

One of the problems of video display design is the sheer rate at which pixels are accessed. Consider a super-VGA display with a resolution of 1024×768 pixels and a refresh rate (frame rate) of $70\,Hz$. In one second, the system must access $1024 \times 768 \times 70 = 55\,050\,240$ pixels. The time available to access a single pixel is approximately $1/55\,000\,000\,s = 18\,ns$, which is far too short for typical video memory. In practice, even less time is available to access pixels, because some time is lost to left- and right-hand margins and the flyback.

The only way in which a practical video display system can be constructed is to read a group of pixels from video memory at a time and then send them to the CRT one-at-a-time. Figure 8.36 shows how the video memory performs this operation. The address from the display generator selects a row of pixels that are loaded into a *shift register* once per row clock. This arrangement means that the video memory is accessed by the display generator only once per row, rather than once per pixel. Consequently, the memory doesn't

require such a low access time. The individual pixels of a row are read out of the shift register at the dot (i.e. pixel) rate. A shift register is capable of much higher speed operation than memory.

Modern display systems permit more sophisticated images than the simple on/off dot displays of a few years ago. In practice, several video memories (called *planes*) are operated in parallel, with each memory plane contributing one bit of the current pixel. If there are q memory planes, the q bits can be fed to a q-bit digital-to-analog converter to generate one of 2^q levels of brightness (i.e. a gray scale), or they can be used to select one of 2^q different colors (we discuss color later).

8.7.2 The liquid crystal display

Few devices have been written off more times than the CRT. For decades we've been awaiting the flat, paper-thin, light-weight screen that can be hung on the wall to replace the conventional CRT display. Up to now, the CRT has remained the most popular display mechanism. The late 1980s witnessed the rapid growth of a rival to the CRT, the *liquid crystal display*, or *LCD*. By the mid-1990s color LCDs were widely found in laptop portables. However, the resolution of these displays is less than many CRTs, their maximum size is about 21 inches, and they cost much more than CRTs. First-generation LCDs had a resolution of 640×480 pixels. By the mid-1990s, 800×600 pixel displays were rapidly taking over, and the 14 inch 1024×768 pixel display was being introduced in top-of-the-range systems.

Light is a form of *electromagnetic radiation* that shares some of the properties of *waves*; for example, the vibration

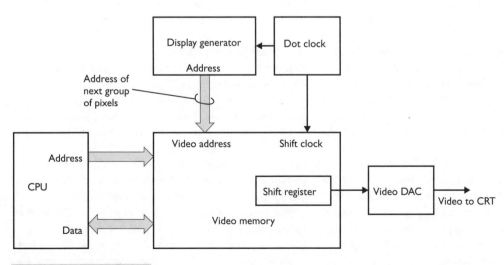

Fig. 8.36 The video memory.

of a light wave is at right angles to the direction of its propagation. Light from an incandescent bulb is composed of large numbers of individual light waves, all arranged with their axes of vibration at random. Such light is said to be *unpolarized* because the vibrations do not favor a specific axis. If the vibrations are all along the same axis, the light is *polarized*.

When light passes through a *polarizing filter*, only light whose axis of vibration has a certain angle is transmitted through the filter—polarizing sunglasses employ this principle to reject polarized light. If you take two polarizing filters and arrange them in series with their axes of polarization at right angles, no light can pass through the pair. One polarizing filter blocks light polarized in one plane and the other filter blocks the light polarized in the other plane. You can carry out this experiment with two pairs of Polaroid sunglasses. The polarization of light and the polarizing filter can be used as the basis of a display system—all you need is a material that can be polarized on demand.

Unlike the molecules in a solid crystal, the molecules of a liquid are arranged at random. *Liquid crystals* are liquid, but their molecules have a preferred alignment; that is, they are liquids that display some of the properties of solids. A particu-lar group of substances known as *nematic* liquid crystals are affected by an electric field. When an electric field is applied to a nematic liquid crystal, the molecules *twist* or rotate under the influence of the field. The polarization of light passing though such a *twisted* liquid crystal is either unmodified or rotated through 90°, depending on whether a field is applied across the liquid crystal. So-called *super-twisted nematic crystals* can rotate the polarization of light by over 90°. Figure 8.37 illustrates a liquid crystal cell that can be switched between the two states: no rotation and rotation by 90°.

The liquid crystal display mimics the behavior of the CRT; that is, it creates a pixel that can be switched on or off. All we have to do is to make a sandwich of a polarizing substance and a liquid crystal—light will pass through them if the liquid crystal is polarized in the same plane as the polarizing material. Otherwise, the two polarizing filters block the transmission of light.

We now have all the ingredients of a *flat panel display*: a polarizing filter that transmits light polarized in one plane only and a liquid crystal cell that can rotate the polarization of light by 90° (or more) electronically. Figure 8.38 demonstrates the structure and operation of a single-pixel LCD cell.

In Fig. 8.38 light is passed first through a polarizer arranged with its axis of polarization at 0°, then through the liquid crystal, and finally through a second polarizer at 90°. If the liquid crystal does not rotate the plane of polarization of the light, all the light is blocked by the second polarizer. If, however, an electrostatic field is applied to the two electrodes, the liquid crystal rotates the polarization of the light by 90° and the light passes through the second polarizer. Consequently, a light placed behind the cell will be visible or invisible.

An entire LCD is made by creating rows and columns of cells like those described in Fig. 8.38. Each cell is selected or *addressed* by applying a voltage to the row and the column in which it occurs. The voltage is connected to each cell by depositing transparent conductors on the surface of the glass sandwich that holds the liquid crystals.

Because an LCD cell can be only on or off, it's impossible to achieve directly different levels of light transmission (i.e. you can display only black or white). However, because you can rapidly switch a cell on and off, you can generate intermediate light levels by modulating the time for which a cell transmits light. Typical LCDs can achieve 64 gray levels.

LCDs can be operated in a *reflective* mode by means of the ambient light that falls on the cell, or in a *transmissive* mode by means of light that passes through the cell. Ambient light displays have a very low *contrast ratio* (i.e. there's not a lot of difference between the on state and the off state) and are often difficult to read in poor light, but they do consume very little power indeed. Typical reflective LCDs are found in pocket calculators, low-cost toys, and some personal organizers. Displays operating in a transmissive mode using *back-lighting* are much easier to read, but require a light source (often a fluorescent tube) that consumes a considerable amount of power. Ultimately, it's the power taken by this fluorescent tube that limits the life of a laptop computer's battery.

8.7.3 Drawing lines

This book is about computer hardware. However, as we've come so far in describing display systems, we'd just like to demonstrate how dots can be transformed into lines by software. There are two types of image: the *bitmapped* image and the *parametrized* image. All images in the video memory are bitmapped in the sense that each pixel in the display corresponds to a pixel in the video memory (strictly speaking, perhaps we should use the term *pixel-mapped*). Photographs and TV pictures are examples of bitmapped images.

A *parametrized* image is defined in terms of an *algorithm*; for example, you might describe a line as running from point (−4,12) to point (30,45) in a display, or as the equation $y = 4x + 25$ for $-9 < x < 70$. The graphics software is responsible for taking the parametrized image and converting it into a

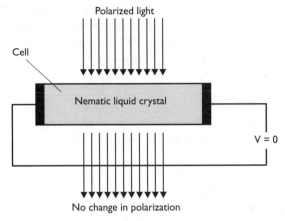

a. Polarization of light not affected by the cell

b. Polarization of light rotated by 90°

Fig. 8.37 The LCD cell.

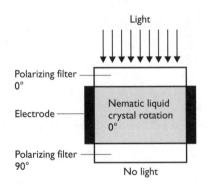

(a) The crossed polarizers block light

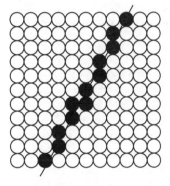

Fig. 8.39 Drawing a line.

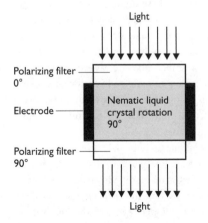

(b) The liquid crystal rotates the polarization through 90° and light is transmitted

Fig. 8.38 Displaying a pixel.

bitmapped image in the display's memory. You can therefore store video information either as an actual pixel-by-pixel image or as a *recipe* that can be used to construct an image. We are now going to look at the parametrized image because it can be specified with relatively few bits and it can easily be manipulated.

Figure 8.39 demonstrates how a line is mapped to a display by evaluating the *equation* of the line and then selecting every pixel that passes through the line. In a practical system, relatively few pixels will lie exactly on the line, and it is necessary to select pixels close to the line. Because the line is such a fundamental component of graphics, considerable research has gone into the construction of high-speed line-drawing algorithms.

Jack Bresenham invented the classic line-drawing algorithm in 1965. Any straight line can be expressed in the form $ay = bx + c$, where x and y are variables, and a, b, and c constants that define the line. The *slope* of the line is given by

b/a, and the point at which the line goes through the x origin is given by $y = c/a$. For the sake of simplicity, consider a line that goes through the origin, so that $ay = bx$, where $a = 1$ and $b = +0.5$. Figure 8.40 illustrates how the line corresponding to this equation goes through some pixels (shown black in Fig. 8.40). All other pixels are either *above* or *below* the line. If the equation of the line is rearranged in the form $ay - bx = 0$, the pixels above the line (white in Fig. 8.40) satisfy the relation $ay - bx > 0$, and those below the line (gray in Fig. 8.40) satisfy the relation $ay - bx < 0$.

The Bresenham algorithm draws lines with a slope $m = b/a$ in the range 0 to 1. This algorithm evaluates the *sign* of $ay - bx$ at regular intervals. By monitoring the *sign* of the function, you can determine whether you are above or below the line. The line is drawn from its starting point from, say, left to right. Suppose we select a pixel somewhere along this line. Bresenham's algorithm tells us how to go about selecting the next pixel. Figure 8.41 demonstrates that the new pixel is selected to be either the pixel directly to the right of the current pixel or the pixel both above and to the right of the current pixel.

The algorithm evaluates the value of the function at the midpoint between the two candidates for the new pixel along the line. The pixel selected to be the next pixel is the one that lies closest to the line, as Fig. 8.41 demonstrates.

The fine details of the Bresenham algorithm are more complex than we've described. The algorithm must handle lines that don't pass through the origin and lines that don't have the slope in the range 0 to 1 that we've described in Fig. 8.41. Further modifications reduce the number of multiplications required to calculate the location of the midpoint between the candidates for next pixel.

Let's construct a fragment of C code to implement the Bresenham line-drawing algorithm. We will assume that a

straight line is to be drawn from $x1,y1$ to $x2,x2$, and that the slope of the line is between 0 and 1. At each step in drawing the line we increment the value of the x coordinate by x_step (in practice this might be one pixel along the x-axis). The corresponding change in y is

$$x\_step * (y2 - y1)/(x2 - x1)$$

The Bresenham algorithm eliminates this calculation by either making or not making a fixed step along the y-axis.

```
void DrawLine(x1,y1,x2,y2)
int x, y, e, dx, dy;      .
{
    dx  = x2-x1;
    dy  = y2-y1;
    e   = 2*dy-dx;
    y   = y1;
    for (x=x1; x1 ≤ x2; x++)
      { plot (x, y);
        if (e<0)
            e=e+2*dy;
        else {
              e  = e+2*(dx-dy);
              y  = y+1;
            }
      }
}
```

If the line's slope is greater than 1, we can use the *same* algorithm by simply swapping x and y.

Antialiasing

The Bresenham and similar algorithms provide effective line drawing mechanisms, but all these algorithms generate lines that suffer from a *step-like* appearance due to the nature of the line-following mechanism. These steps are often termed *jaggies* and spoil the line's appearance. The effect of finite pixel size and jaggies is termed *aliasing*, a term taken from the world of signal processing to indicate the error introduced when analog signals are sampled at too low a rate to preserve fidelity. Figure 8.42 demonstrates how we can remove some of the worst effects of aliasing.

The antialiasing technique in Fig. 8.42 uses pixels with gray-scale values to create a line that appears less jagged to the human eye. A pixel that is on the line is made fully black. Pixels that are partially on the line are displayed as less than 100 percent black. When the human eye sees the line from a distance, the eye–brain combination perceives a line free of jaggies. That is, the brain averages or smoothes the image.

Now that we've looked at how images are created on a screen, we examine how they are printed on paper.

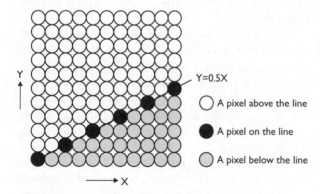

Fig. 8.40 The equation of a straight line.

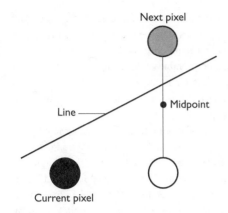

(a) Select next pixel up and right

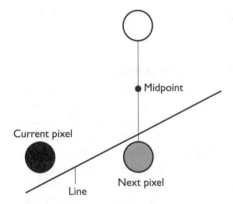

(b) Select next pixel right

Fig. 8.41 Searching along a line.

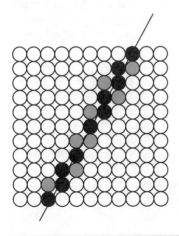

Fig. 8.42 Improving a line by antialiasing.

8.8 The printer

The printer produces a hard copy output from a computer by converting digital information into marks on paper. Because printers rely on precisely machined moving mechanical parts, they can be more expensive and less reliable than the purely electronic CRT displays. Moreover, the range of prices of printers is greater than that of CRT-based displays.

For all practical purposes, there are only two types of display: CRT and LCD. The same isn't true of the printer, which employs a variety of printing mechanisms, each of which represents a particular trade-off between cost, speed, reliability, and quality of printing. However, all printers must perform the following basic functions.

1. Move the paper to a given line

2. Move the print head to a given point along a line

3. Select a character to be printed

4. Make a mark on the paper corresponding to that character

The first and last of these functions are relatively easy to explain and are dealt with first. Depending on the application, paper is available in single sheet, continuous roll, or fan-fold form. Paper can be moved by *friction feed*, in which the paper is trapped between a motor-driven roller and pressure rollers that apply pressure to the surface of the paper. As the roller (or platen) moves, the paper is dragged along with it. Figure 8.43(a) shows the operation of a friction feed drive. Such a drive is not perfect and may allow paper to slip, or at least prevent the precise alignment of the paper.

An alternative paper-feeding mechanism is the tractor feed or sprocket feed (Fig. 8.43(b)) where rings of conical pins are located round the ends of the platen. The edges of the paper (invariably fan-fold paper) are perforated with holes on the same pitch (spacing) as the pins. The pins fit through the holes and, as the platen rotates, the paper is accurately and precisely pulled through the printer.

The rise of the personal computer has seen the decline of fan-fold paper. Most printers found in the home or small office now use plain paper. Some banks and similar institutions still employ fan-fold paper to print statements (and other pre-printed forms).

Printing a character

Printers are often described by the way in which marks on the paper are made; for example, the golf-ball, the cylinder, the daisy wheel, the line printer, the drum printer, and the inkjet printer. Although making a mark on paper is intimately connected with the way a character is formed, we can identify

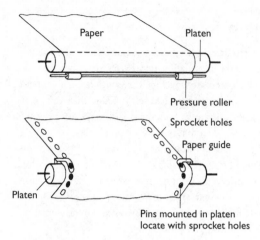

Fig. 8.43 Moving paper: (a) the pressure feed, (b) the tractor feed.

several fundamental principles. One of the earliest methods of marking paper is based on the impact of a hard object against an ink-coated ribbon, which is then forced onto the paper to make a mark in the shape of the object. This is how the mechanical office typewriter operates. However, the tremendous reduction in the cost of laser and inkjet printers in the early 1990s has rendered many impact printers obsolete.

Some printers form characters on paper without physically striking the paper, and are therefore known as non-impact printers. One group of non-impact printers employs special paper, coated with a material that turns black or blue when heated to about 110 °C. Such printers are called thermal printers and form a character by heating a particular combination of dots within a matrix of, typically, 7 by 5 points (like the CRT terminal). Thermal printers are very cheap (until you think about the cost of the special paper) and are relatively silent in operation. A similar mechanism uses black paper coated with a thin film of shiny aluminum. When a needle electrode is applied to the surface and a large current passed through it, the aluminum film is locally vaporized to reveal the dark coating underneath. Both these mechanisms are seldom found outside specialist applications such as mobile ticket printing.

Another method of printing involves spraying a fine jet of ink at the paper. As this technique also includes the way in which the character is selected and formed, it will be dealt with in more detail later.

The hardware that actually prints the character is called the *print head*. There are two classes of print head: the single print head and the multiple print head found in line printers. Typewriters employ a fixed print head and the paper and platen move as each new character is printed. A fixed print

head is unsuitable for high-speed printing, as the platen and paper have a large mass and hence a high inertia, which means that the energy required to perform a high-speed carriage return would be prohibitive. Since the mass of the print head is very much less than that of the platen, most printers are arranged so that the paper stays where it is and the print head moves along the line.

One way of moving the print head is to attach it to a nut on a threaded rod (the lead screw). At the end of the rod is a stepping motor, which can rotate the rod through a fixed angle at a time. Each time the rod rotates the print head is moved left or right (depending on the direction of rotation). In another arrangement the print head is connected to a belt, moved by the same technique as the paper itself. The belt passes between two rollers, one of which moves freely and one of which is controlled by a stepping motor.

We are now going to look at various types of printer in terms of the way in which they form characters on paper.

8.8.1 The dot matrix printer

A dot matrix printer forms individual characters from a matrix of dots in much the same way as a CRT draws its characters. The dots are generated by a number of wires (called *needles*) pressing an inked ribbon onto the paper, or the needles may be used with spark erosion techniques, or may be replaced by heating elements in a thermal printer. The dot matrix printer was very popular in the 1970s and 1980s, when it offered the only low-cost means of printing. Today's inkjet and laser printers have largely eclipsed the dot matrix printer.

Figure 8.44 illustrates the operation of a dot matrix print head. Seven solenoids individually control seven wires. The solenoid is a coil which, when energized by a current, creates a strong magnetic field inside it. Because the wires are made of iron they can be moved in or out of the solenoid by passing a current through it. The seven wires are brought together by a

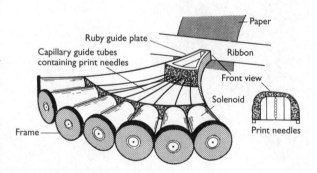

Fig. 8.44 The dot matrix print head.

ruby guide-plate to form a column of seven dots. By energizing a particular combination of solenoids, that group of needles is propelled towards the ribbon producing a pattern of dots on the paper. After each column of dots has been printed, the head is moved one dot position to print another column. After five (or seven) columns have been printed a complete character has been formed.

First-generation dot matrix printers sometimes used seven dots per column and their quality was rather poor. Twenty-four dot print heads produce an output approaching the quality of the office typewriter. Some matrix printers operate in a near letter quality, NLQ, mode by merging and overlapping dots to produce characters that look as if they were made by an office typewriter (provided, of course, you have poor sight).

Since dot matrix printers work by forming characters out of patterns of dots, there is no reason why they can't be directed to print any pattern of dots and therefore draw pictures (i.e. operate in a graphics mode). Most of today's printers (of all types) are controlled by a dedicated processor that interprets the incoming characters from the host computer as printing characters or as control characters. Certain sequences of control character force the printer to print specified sequences of dots (rather than ISO/ASCII characters). As much of the work in generating graphics has been led by companies making printers, it should come as no surprise to learn that not all printers use the same code sequences to describe graphics. Indeed, when you buy one of today's complex word processors, you usually get dozens of printer driver programs and must select the appropriate driver for your printer. Fortunately, many printers use codes developed by Epson, and some printers can be forced to abandon their own codes and to emulate another printer.

Other impact printers

Computer users in the 1970s could buy one of several types of impact printer (in addition to the matrix printer). Impact printers using cylinders, golf-balls, and daisy wheels generate correspondence quality output, but they are slow and the number of characters is limited. Most of these printers are little used today (apart from the high-volume line printer).

Cylinder golf-ball printers and daisy wheel printers Figure 8.45 illustrates the operation of the cylinder, the golf-ball and the daisy wheel print heads. The cylinder print head is a metallic cylinder with four rows of sixteen symbols embossed around it. The ribbon and paper are positioned immediately in front of the cylinder, and the hammer is located behind it. The cylinder is rotated about its vertical axis and is moved up or down until the desired symbol is positioned next to the ribbon. A hammer, driven by a solenoid, then strikes the back of the cylinder, forcing the symbol at the front onto the paper through the inked ribbon.

The golf-ball head was originally used in IBM electric typewriters. Characters are embossed on the surface of a metallic sphere. For a given volume the sphere has more usable space than the cylinder. The golf-ball rotates in the same way as a cylinder, but is tilted rather than moved up or down to access different rows of characters. Unlike the cylinder, the golf-ball is propelled towards the ribbon and the paper by a cam mechanism, rather than by a hammer striking it at the back.

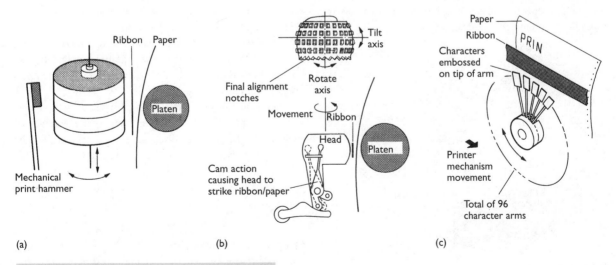

Fig. 8.45 The cylinder, golf-ball, and daisy wheel print heads.

Like its namesake, the daisy wheel printer has a disk with slender petals arranged around its periphery. An embossed character is located at the end of each of these spokes. The wheel is made of plastic or metal and is very lightweight, giving it a low inertia. A typical daisy wheel has 96 spokes, corresponding to the upper- and lower-case subsets of the ISO/ASCII code.

The daisy wheel rotates in the vertical plane, at high speed, in front of the ribbon. As the wheel rotates, each of the characters passes between a solenoid-driven hammer and the ribbon. When the desired character is at a print position, the solenoid is energized and the hammer forces the spoke against the ribbon to mark the paper. Some printers control the amount of current in the solenoid (and hence the force of the hammer) according to the size of the character to give each character a uniform density.

The line printer A line printer is so called because it prints a whole line of text at one go, rather than by printing characters sequentially. Line printers are expensive, often produce low quality output, and are geared to high-volume, high-speed printing. Figure 8.46 illustrates the construction of the drum printer.

In front of the ribbon is a drum extending along the entire width of the paper. The character set to be printed is embossed along the circumference of the drum. This character set is repeated, once for each of the character positions, along the drum. A typical line printer has 132 character positions and a set of 64 characters. Consequently, there are $132 \times 64 = 8448$ characters embossed on the drum. As the drum rotates, the rings of characters pass over each of the 132 print positions, and a complete set of characters passes each printing point once per revolution. Unlike other printers, a mark is made on the paper by a hammer hitting the paper and driving it into the head through the ribbon. By controlling the instant at which the hammer is energized, any particular character may be printed. As there is one hammer per character position, a whole line may be printed during the course of a single revolution of the drum.

Suppose the line to be printed contains the single word ALAN, and that in each ring of characters the first character is A followed by B etc. The paper is assumed to have been advanced to the current line by a tractor mechanism. As the drum rotates, a timing signal is generated and sent to the electronics controlling the hammers. When a synchronizing pulse is produced by the first letter (i.e. A), hammers one and three are energized and the pattern A A is printed. After the drum has stepped to its twelfth position, the second hammer is energized and the line now contains ALA . Another two steps of the drum and the fourth hammer is energized to generate the finished line ALAN. After the drum has completed a full revolution, the paper is advanced one line and the sequence repeated.

8.8.2 The inkjet printer

Inkjet printers were originally developed for professional applications and the technology migrated to low-cost PC applications. We first describe the original continuous inkjet and then the modern drop-on-demand variety. The continuous inkjet printer owes more to the CRT for its operation than the impact printer. The basic features of an inkjet printer are illustrated in Fig. 8.47. A fine jet of ink is emitted from a tiny nozzle to create a high-speed stream of ink drops. The nozzle is vibrated ultrasonically so that the ink stream is broken up into individual drops. As each drop leaves the nozzle it is given an electrical charge, so that the stream of drops can be deflected electrostatically, just like the beam of electrons in a CRT. By moving the beam, characters can be written on the surface of the paper. The paper is arranged to be off the central axis of the beam, so that when the beam is undeflected, the ink drops do not strike the paper and are collected in a reservoir for reuse.

Continuous inkjet printers are high-speed devices, almost silent in operation, and are used in high-volume commercial applications. Early inkjet printers were very expensive and were regarded with suspicion because they suffered a number of problems during their development. In particular, they were prone to clogging of the nozzle. Many of the early problems have now been overcome.

Drop-on-demand printing

The modern drop-on-demand inkjet printer is very much simpler than its continuous jet predecessor. In fact, it's identical

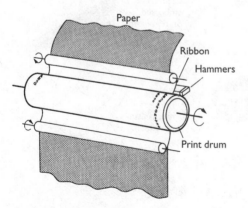

Fig. 8.46 The line printer.

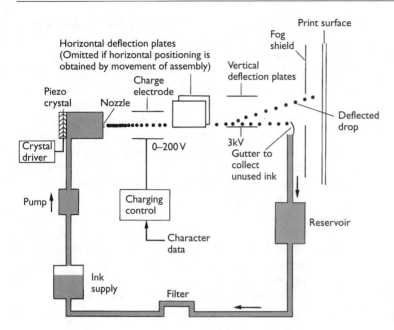

Fig. 8.47 The continuous inkjet printer.

to a dot matrix printer apart from the print head itself. The print head that generates the inkjet also includes the ink reservoir. When the ink supply is exhausted after about 1000 pages, the head assembly is thrown away and a new head inserted. Although this looks wasteful, it costs little more than a conventional ribbon and both reduces maintenance requirements and increases reliability. Some inkjet printers do have permanent print heads and just change the ink cartridge.

The inkjet printer provides a print quality almost as good as a laser printer for the cost of a dot-matrix printer. In the 1980s, inkjet printers had a maximum resolution of 300 dpi (dots per inch). By the late 1990s inkjet printers with resolution of over 1400 dpi were available at remarkably low cost. Later we will look at the color inkjet printer, which created the mass market in desktop digital photography.

The drop-on-demand print head uses multiple nozzles, one for each of the dots in a dot matrix array. The head comes into contact with the paper and there's no complex ink delivery and focusing system. The holes or *capillary nozzles* through which the ink flows are too small to permit the ink to leak out. Ink is forced through the holes by creating a shockwave in the reservoir that expels a drop of ink though the nozzle to the paper.

One means of creating a shockwave is to place a thin film of piezoelectric crystal transducer in the side of the reservoir (see Fig. 8.48(a)). When an electric field is applied across a piezoelectric crystal, the crystal flexes. By applying an electrical pulse across such a crystal in a print head, it flexes and

creates the shockwave that forces a single drop of ink through one of the holes onto the paper (see Fig. 8.48(b)). Note that there is a separate crystal for each of the holes in the print head.

Some inkjet printers use an even simpler technique for ejecting a drop of ink. They employ a fine wire behind the nozzle to instantaneously heat the ink to boiling point, which creates bubbles that force out a tiny drop. These printers were sometimes called *bubblejet* printers.

Inkjet printers are capable of good quality and high resolution (over 1000 dpi). However, the ink drops can spread out on paper due to the capillary action of fibers on the paper's surface (this effect is called *wicking*). Specially coated paper considerably reduces the effect of wicking, although such paper can be very expensive.

8.8.3 The laser printer

The dot matrix printer brought word processing to the masses because it was able to produce acceptable quality text for a wide range of applications at a low cost. The laser printer has now brought the ability to produce high-quality text and graphics to those who, only a few years ago, could afford no more than a medium-quality dot matrix printer. In fact, the quality of the laser printer is sufficiently high to enable a small office to create artwork similar to that once produced by the professional typesetter; that is, desktop publishing (DTP).

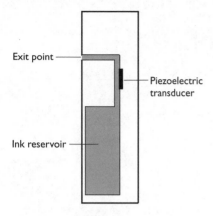

Exit point

Piezoelectric transducer

Ink reservoir

a. Structure of head assembly (only one nozzle shown)

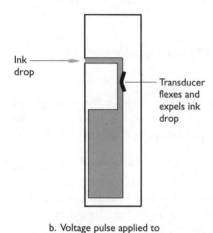

Ink drop

Transducer flexes and expels ink drop

b. Voltage pulse applied to transducer to eject a drop of ink

Fig. 8.48 Structure of the bubblejet.

The laser printer is just a photocopier specially modified to accept input from a host computer. The principle of the photocopier and the laser printer is both elegant and simple, although its practical implementation is very complex. At the heart of a laser printer lies a precisely machined metal drum, which is as wide as the sheet of paper to be printed. The secret of the drum lies in its *selenium* coating. Selenium is an electrical insulator with an important property—when selenium is illuminated by light, it becomes conductive.

A photocopier works by first charging up the surface of the drum to a very high electrostatic potential (typically 1000 V with respect to ground). By means of a complex arrangement of lenses and mirrors, the original to be copied is scanned by a very bright light and the image projected on the rotating drum. After one rotation, the drum contains an invisible image of the original document. If the image is invisible we are entitled to ask ourselves, 'What form does this image take?' Black regions of the source document reflect little light and the corresponding regions on the drum receive no light. The selenium coating in these regions is not illuminated, doesn't become conducting, and therefore retains its electrical charge.

White regions of the document reflect light onto the drum, causing the selenium to become conducting and to lose its charge. In other words, the image on the drum is painted with an electrostatic charge, ranging from high voltage (black) to zero voltage (white).

One of the effects of an electrostatic charge is its ability to attract nearby light objects. In the next step the drum is rotated in close proximity to a very fine black powder called the *toner*. Consequently, the toner is attracted to those parts of the drum with a high charge. Now the drum contains a true positive image of the original. The image is a positive image because black areas on the original are highly charged and pick up the black toner.

The drum is then rotated in contact with the paper, which is given an even higher electrostatic charge. The charge on the paper causes the toner to transfer itself from the drum to the paper. In the final stage, the surface of the paper is heat-treated to fix the toner on to it. Unfortunately, not all toner is transferred from the drum to the paper. Residual toner is scraped off the drum by rotating it in contact with a very fine blade. Eventually, the drum becomes scratched or the selenium no longer functions properly and it must be replaced. In contrast with other printers, the laser printer requires the periodic replacement of some of its major components. Low-cost laser printers sometimes combine the drum and the toner, which means that the entire drum assembly is thrown away once the toner has been exhausted. This approach to printer construction reduces the cost of maintenance while increasing the cost of consumables.

Unlike the photocopier, the laser printer has no optical imaging system. The image is written directly on the drum by means of an electromechanical system. As the drum rotates, an image is written onto it line by line in very much the same way that a television picture is formed in a cathode ray tube.

Figure 8.49(a) illustrates the organization of the laser scanner and Fig. 8.49(b) provides details of the scanning mechanism. A low-power semiconductor laser and optical system produces a very fine spot of laser light. By either varying the intensity of the current to the laser or by passing the beam through a liquid crystal whose opacity is controlled electronically (i.e. modulated), the intensity of the light spot falling on the drum can be varied.

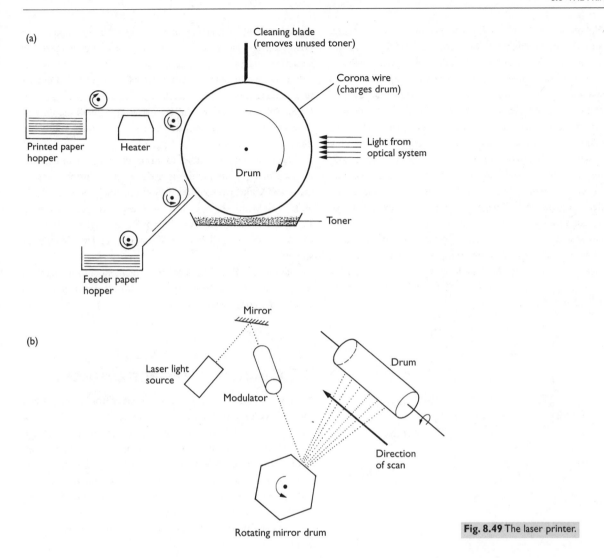

Fig. 8.49 The laser printer.

The light beam strikes a multi-sided rotating mirror. As the mirror turret rotates, the side currently in the path of the light beam‵sweeps the beam across the surface of the selenium-coated drum. By modulating the light as the beam sweeps across the drum, a single line is drawn. This scanning process is rather like the raster-scan mechanism found in a CRT display. After a line has been drawn, the next mirror in the rotating turret is in place and a new line is drawn below the previous line, because the selenium drum has moved by one line.

The combined motions of the rotating mirror turret and the rotating selenium drum allow the laser beam to scan the entire surface of the selenium drum. Of course, the optical circuits required to perform the scanning are very precise indeed. The resolution imposed by the optics and the laser beam size provided low-cost first-generation laser printers with a resolution of about 300 dots per inch. Such a resolution is suitable for moderately high-quality text, but is not entirely suitable for high-quality graphics. Second-generation laser printers with resolutions of 600 or 1200 dpi became available in the mid-1990s. Not all drums are now coated with selenium because organic compounds have been found that mimic selenium's properties.

It has been suggested that a dot density of about 800 dots/inch is required for the highest quality image. There's little point in increasing dot density beyond 800 dots/inch, as the human eye can't resolve any further increase in picture quality. Interestingly enough, the first television system devised by Logie Baird used a purely mechanical scanning system which was rather like the optical arrangement now found in a laser printer or photocopier.

449

Not all laser printers employ the same optical arrangement, because the rotating mirror turret is complex and requires careful alignment. One alternative technique designed by Epson uses an incandescent light source behind a stationary liquid crystal shutter. The liquid crystal shutter has a linear array of 2000 dots, each of which can be turned on and off to build up a single line across the drum. By writing a complete line in one operation, the only major moving part involved in the scanning process is the photosensitive drum itself. Technically, a laser printer without a laser scanner isn't really a laser printer. However, the term 'laser printer' is used to describe any printer that generates an image by using an electrostatic charge to deposit a fine powder (the toner) on paper.

Other ways of avoiding the complex rotating drum mirror turret are a linear array of light-emitting diodes (LEDs) in an arrangement similar to the liquid crystal shutter, or a CRT projection technique that uses a CRT to project a line on the photosensitive drum (Fig. 8.50).

Laser printers generate images (i.e. the arrangement of dots) electronically by converting the codes for characters into suitable patterns of dots stored in read-only memories. By changing the character generator ROMs (often housed in user insertable/removable cassettes), it is possible to change font types. Some laser printers allow you to download the bit patterns for character sets into RAM inside the printer in order to increase the print speed.

Laser printers are able to print dot-map pictures; that is, each pixel of the picture is assigned a bit in the printer's memory. A linear resolution of 300 dots/inch requires $300 \times 300 = 90\,000$ dots/square inch. A sheet of paper measuring 11 inches by 8 inches (i.e. 88 square inches) can hold up to $88 \times 90\,000 = 7\,920\,000$ dots, or just under 1 Mbyte of storage.

Having introduced the principles of monochrome displays and printers, we are going to look at how color displays and printers are constructed.

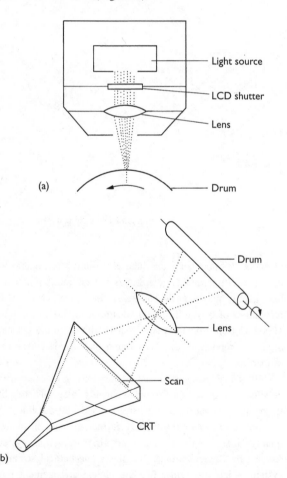

(a)

(b)

Fig. 8.50 The print drum.

8.9 Color displays and printers

It's been possible to print color images for a long time, although color printers were astronomically expensive until relatively recently. Low-cost printers began to appear in the early 1990s (largely based on inkjet technology), although the quality was suitable only for draft work. By the late 1990s high-quality, low-cost color printers were widely available and the new term *photorealistic* was coined to describe printers that were almost able to match the quality of color photographs. Before we discuss color printers we need to say a little about the nature of color.

8.9.1 Theory of color

Light is just another type of electromagnetic radiation, like X-rays and radio waves. The eye is sensitive to electromagnetic radiation in the visible spectrum and light waves of different frequencies are perceived as different colors. This visible spectrum extends from violet to red (i.e. wavelengths from 400 nm to 700 nm). Frequencies lower than red are called infrared and those higher than violet are called ultraviolet. Both these frequencies are invisible to the human eye, although they play important roles in our life.

A single frequency has a pure color or *hue*, and we perceive its intensity in terms of its brightness. In practice, we see few pure colors in everyday life. Most light sources contain visible radiation over a broad spectrum. If a light source contains approximately equal amounts of radiation across the entire visual spectrum we perceive the effect as *white light*. In practice light often consists of a mixture of white light together with light containing a much narrower range of frequencies. The term *saturation* describes the ratio of colored light to white light; for example, pink is unsaturated red at about 700 nm plus white light. An unsaturated color is sometimes referred to as a *pastel* shade.

Note that most light sources contain a broad range of frequencies (e.g. sunlight and light from an incandescent lamp). Sources of a narrow band of visible frequencies are gas discharge lamps and LEDs; for example, the sodium light used to illuminate streets at night emits light with two very closely spaced wavelengths at about 580 nm (i.e. yellow).

Whatever jumble of frequencies the eye detects, the brain perceives a single color. Suppose a particular light source contains the colors red and green. We don't see these two colors; we perceive a single color whose frequency is intermediate between red and green; that is, we see yellow. By mixing various quantities of the three primary colors red, green, and blue we can create any other color. Moreover, since we can add red, green, and blue to create white light, we can control the level of saturation.

Color can be specified in one of several ways. The RGB model can be used to define the percentages of red, green, and blue in a color. The HSB model attempts to define light in the way we perceive it (H = hue or color, S = saturation, B = brightness or intensity). A totally different technique of specifying color is the *Pantone Matching System*. This is an entirely arbitrary and proprietary commercial system. A very large number of colors are defined and given reference numbers. You define a color by matching it against the colors in the Pantone system.

8.9.2 Color CRTs

The majority of general-purpose computers employ color displays—partially because we see the world in color, and partially because we already have color TV and the cinema. In principle the operation of a color CRT is very simple, although it's very difficult to construct large color CRTs. Figure 8.51 illustrates the construction of the color CRT, which is similar to a monochrome CRT. Instead of having a *single* gun assembly, the color CRT has *three* gun assemblies, one for each of the primary colors red, green, and blue—Fig. 8.51(a). The focusing system aims each beam at the same spot on the screen, and the three beams are deflected in unison by the scanning coils.

The key to the color CRT is the *shadow mask* located immediately in front of the screen. The *shadow mask* is made

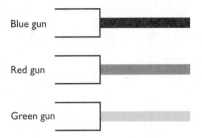

(a) Three independent electron guns produce three beams

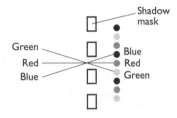

(b) Each beam hits only its own phosphor

Fig. 8.51 Generating a color image.

of metal and has a very large number of tiny holes punched in it—Fig. 8.51(b). Behind the shadow mask on the surface of the CRT's screen are millions of tiny dots of phosphor. These phosphors are arranged as triplets. One dot produces a green light when bombarded by electrons; one a red light; and one a blue light. Because of the geometry of the shadow mask, the phosphor dots on the screen, and the electron guns, the electron beam from the green gun can hit only green phosphors (the red and blue phosphors are shielded by the shadow mask). The same is true for beams from the other two guns. Some CRTs employ a different type of shadow mask; for example, the *Trinitron* shadow mask employs vertical stripes rather than dots to generate a brighter image.

By applying three independent control voltages to each of the three guns, you can control the intensities of each of the beams. Consequently, you can control the intensity of each of the three pixels—red, green, and blue. Any color can be generated by adding suitable intensities of green, red, and blue light, and, therefore, the human eye sees each pixel not as three different colors, but as a single color.

In order to provide today's realistic color displays, very large numbers of colors are required—more than can be provided economically at current memory prices. Figure 8.52 demonstrates how a lot of colors can be specified with relatively few bits.

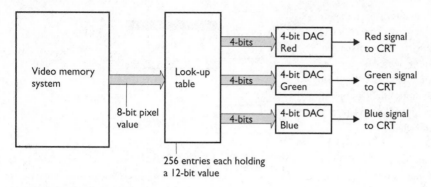

Fig. 8.52 The color look-up table.

The output of the video memory specifies the current pixel's attributes. In the example of Fig. 8.52, the pixel is defined by an 8-bit integer that provides one of $2^8 = 256$ possible values. The 8-bit pixel value is sent to a *look-up table* that produces one of 256 12-bit outputs; that is, each of the 256 locations contains a *12-bit* value. Each 12-bit output is divided into three 3-bit fields representing the primary colors red, green, and blue. In turn, each of these 4-bit values is fed to a DAC to generate one of $2^4 = 16$ levels of brightness. This system can select 1 of 16 levels of red, 1 of 16 levels of green, and 1 of 16 levels of blue. The pixel can therefore have any one of $16 \times 16 \times 16 = 4096$ values (i.e. colors).

So, an 8-bit pixel code from the video memory can perform the apparently impossible act of selecting one of 4096 different pixels. The paradox is resolved by the nature of the look-up table. It has 256 entries, each of which can select one of 4096 colors; that is, at any instant the look up table allows the display to address 256 colors out of a *palette* of 4096 colors. The look-up table is loaded with the values appropriate to the application being run.

Because the surface of the screen is made up of dots, the resolution of a color CRT is limited—the smallest element that can be displayed on the screen is a single dot. The resolution of color CRTs is often specified in terms of the *pitch* or distance between clusters of the three dots. Typical CRT resolutions lie in the range 0.28 to 0.31mm. The total number of dots is governed by the size of the CRT. Table 8.17 relates image size to resolution for some popular configurations.

Color LCDs

Color LCDs operate on a similar principle to the color CRT and generate a color pixel from three cells with three primary colors. The individual cells of a color LCD include red, green, or blue filters to transmit light of only one color. As in the

Monitor size	Image size	Resolution (pixels)	Dots per inch
15 inch	270×200 mm	640×480	60
		800×600	75
		1024×768	96
17 inch	315×240 mm	640×480	51
		800×600	63
		1024×768	85
21 inch	385×285 mm	640×480	42
		800×600	52
		1024×768	85
		1280×1024	84
		1600×1200	106

Table 8.17 Monitor size, image size, and resolution.

case of the color CRT, the three primary colors are clustered to enable other colors to be synthesized by combining red, green, or blue. Color LCDs are divided into two types: *active* and *passive*. Both active and passive displays employ the same types of LCD cells—the difference lies in the ways in which the individual cells of a matrix are selected.

The so-called *passive* liquid crystal matrix of Fig. 8.53 (this arrangement applies to both monochrome and color displays) applies a large pulse to all the cells (i.e. pixels) of a given row. This pulse is marked 2 V in Fig. 8.53 and is currently applied to row 2. A smaller pulse, which may be *either* positive or negative, is applied to each of the columns in the array. The voltages from the row and the column pulses are applied across each cell in a row, and are summed to either polarize the cell or leave it unpolarized. This arrangement displays an entire row of pixels at a time. Once a row has been drawn, a pulse is applied to the next row, and so on.

Each cell (shown shaded in Fig. 8.53) is connected to one row line and to one column line. In Fig. 8.53 a pulse of level 2 V is applied to one terminal of all the cells in row 2 of the

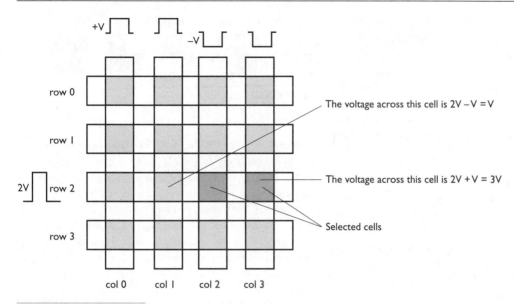

Fig. 8.53 The passive matrix.

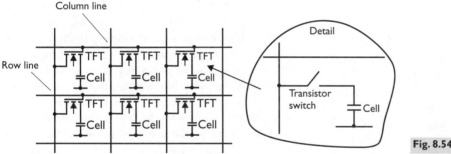

Fig. 8.54 The active matrix.

matrix. A pulse of level $+V$ or $-V$ is then applied in turn to each of the column cells, 0, 1, 2, and 3. The voltage *across* each cell in the matrix must be either 0 (neither row nor column selected), V (row selected with $+2V$, column selected with $+V$), or 3 V (row selected with $+2V$, column selected with $-V$). The matrix is designed so that the 3 V pulse across a cell is sufficient to polarize the liquid crystal and turn the cell on.

The passive matrix suffers from the problem of *cross-talk* caused by the pulse on one row leaking into cells on adjacent rows. Furthermore, if the matrix has m rows, each row is driven (i.e. accessed) for only $1/m$ of the available time. These limitations produce a display that has low contrast, suffers from smearing when moving images (e.g. the cursor) are displayed, and has a less bright image than the TFT active matrix alternative to be described next.

A much better arrangement is the *active matrix* of Fig. 8.54; the cell structure is exactly the same as that of a passive display, only the means of addressing a cell is different. A transistor, which is simply an *electronic switch*, is located at the junction of each row and column line; that is, there is one transistor for each cell. The transistor can be turned on or off by applying a pulse to its row and column lines. However, the electrical capacitance of each cell is able to store a charge and maintain the cell in the on or off condition while the matrix is addressing another transistor. That is, a transistor can be accessed and turned on or off, and that transistor will maintain its state until the next time it is accessed. The active matrix array produces a sharper and more vivid picture. The lack of cross-talk between adjacent cells means that the active matrix suffers less smearing than the passive array equivalent.

453

The transistors that perform the switching are not part of a silicon chip but are laid down in thin films on a substrate—hence the name TFT (*thin film transistor*). It takes $3 \times 640 \times 480$ thin film transistors to make an active matrix display, and, if just a few of these transistors are faulty, the entire display has to be rejected. The manufacturing yield of good arrays is not 100 percent, which means that the cost of a TFT active matrix array is considerably higher than the passive equivalent.

8.9.3 Color printers

You might be surprised to find that color printers don't employ the same RGB (red, green, blue) principle used by the color CRT. Suppose we look at an object that we call 'red', which is illuminated by white light. The red object absorbs some of the white light and reflects some of the light to the observer. If all the light is reflected we call the object *white* and if all the light is absorbed we call the object *black*. However, if the object is red, all frequencies are absorbed *except* red. In other words, if we wish to print images we have to consider what light is absorbed rather than what light is generated (as in a CRT).

The RGB model is called *additive* because a color is created by adding three primary colors. The CMY (for cyan, magenta, yellow) color model used in printing is called *subtractive* because a color is generated by subtracting the appropriate components from white light. Cyan (blue–green) is the absence of red, magenta the absence of green, and yellow the absence of blue. Mixing equal amounts of cyan, magenta, and yellow subtracts all colors from white light to leave black. To create a color such as purple the printer generates a pattern of magenta and cyan dots. The saturation can be controlled by leaving some of the underlying white paper showing through.

In practice, adding the three subtractive primaries together doesn't produce a satisfactory black; it creates a dark muddy-looking color. Although the human eye is not terribly sensitive to slight color shifts, it is very sensitive to any color shift in black (black must be true black). Many printers use a four-color model, CMYK, where K indicates *black*. Including a pure black as well as the three subtractive primaries considerably improves the image.

Printing color is much more difficult than displaying color on a CRT. Each of the red, green, and blue beams can be modulated to create an infinite range of colors (although, in practice, a digital system is limited to a finite number of discrete colors). When you print an image on paper, you have relatively little control over the size of the dot. Moreover, it's not easy to ensure that the dots created from the different subtractive

Fig. 8.55 Dithering.

primaries are correctly lined up (or *registered*). A common means of generating different levels or *shades* of a color is by means of *dithering* (a technique that can also be applied to black and white printers to create shades of gray).

Dithering operates by dividing the print area into an array of, say, 2×2 matrices of 4 dots. Figure 8.55 provides a simple example of dithering in black and white. Because the dots in the matrices are so small, the eye perceives a composite light level and the effect is to create one of five levels of gray from black to white.

Dithering isn't free. If you take a 3×3 matrix to provide 10 levels of intensity, the effective resolution of an image is divided by three; for example, a 300 dpi printer can provide a resolution of 300 dpi or a resolution of 100 dpi with a 10-level gray scale. In other words, there's a trade-off between resolution and the range of tones that can be depicted.

The principle of dithering can be extended to *error diffusion* where dots are placed at random over a much larger area than the 2×2 matrix. This technique is suited to printing areas of color that require subtle changes of gradation (e.g. skin tones).

An alternative approach to dithering that provides more tones without reducing resolution is to increase the number of colors. This technique was introduced by some manufacturers to provide the photorealism required to print the output from digital cameras. An example of enhanced subtractive inkjet printing used six inks: cyan, magenta, yellow, light magenta, light cyan, and black. The lighter colors make it possible to render skin tones more realistically.

Color inkjet printers

The color inkjet printer is virtually the same as its black and white counterpart. The only difference lies in the multiple heads. Typical color printers use a separate black cartridge and a combined color cartridge. Since the head and ink reservoirs form a combined unit, the cartridge has to be thrown away when the first of the color inks runs out. Some printers use separate print heads and reservoirs and only the ink cartridge need be replaced.

The ink used in an inkjet printer can be dye-based or pigment-based. A dye is a soluble color dissolved in a solvent and is used by most printers. A pigment is a tiny insoluble particle that is carried in suspension. Pigment-based inks are superior to dyes because pigments are more resistant to fading and can provide more highly saturated colors. Unfortunately pigment-based inks have less favorable characteristics from the point of view of the designer; for example, the pigments can separate out of the liquid.

Inkjet printers can be prone to *banding*, an effect where horizontal marks appear across the paper due to uneven ink distribution from the print head.

Apart from its cost, the advantage of color inkjet printing is the bright, highly saturated colors. However, good results can be achieved only with suitable paper. The type of plain paper used in laser printers gives poor results. The drops of ink hit the paper and soak into its surface to mix with adjacent drops. This mixing effect reduces the brightness and quality of the colors.

Thermal wax and dye sublimation printers

The thermal wax printer is rather like a dot matrix printer with heat sensitive paper. The print head extends the length of the paper and contains a matrix of thousands of tiny pixel-size heaters. Instead of a ribbon impregnated with ink, a sheet of material coated with colored wax is placed between the head and the paper. When the individual elements are heated to about 80 °C, the wax is melted and sticks to the paper. An entire line of dots is printed at a time. The paper must make three or more passes under the print head to print dots in each of the primary (subtractive) colors. The sheet containing the wax consists of a series of bands of color.

Dye sublimation is similar to the thermal wax technique but is more expensive and is capable of a higher quality result. The heating elements in the print head are heated to 400 °C, which doesn't melt the wax but vaporizes it. Special waxes are used that undergo *sublimation* when heated; that is, they go directly from the solid state to the gaseous state without passing through the liquid state.

By controlling the amount of heating the quantity of wax transferred to the paper can be modified. This makes it possible to generate precise colors without having to resort to techniques such as dithering. Unlike the thermal wax process, which deposits drops of wax on the paper, dye sublimation impregnates the paper with the wax. Dye sublimation can create very high quality images on special paper. The cost of the consumables (waxed sheets and special paper) make sublimation printing much more expensive than inkjet printing.

The phase-change printer

The phase-change printer falls somewhere between the inkjet printer and the thermal wax printer. The basic organization is that of the inkjet printer. The fundamental difference is that the print head contains a wax that is heated to about 90 °C to keep it in liquid form. The wax is bought in the form of sticks that are loaded into the print head.

The print head itself uses a piezoelectric crystal to create a pressure wave that expels a drop of the molten wax onto the paper. The drops freeze on hitting the paper. This causes them to adhere well without spreading out. Consequently, you can print highly saturated colors on plain paper. Because the paper is covered with lumpy drops, some phase-change printers pass the paper through pressure rollers to flatten the drops.

The color laser printer

Color laser printers are almost identical to monochrome laser printers. Instead of using a black toner, they use a toner in one of the subtractive primary colors. However, the entire printing mechanism has to be replicated for each of these primary colors. Each stage (i.e. scan) uses a light with a different primary color. Consequently, color laser printers are large and expensive and are currently largely found only in professional applications. A lower cost arrangement that avoids replicating the drum is to scan the image onto a single drum using a toner with the first primary color and then transfer it to paper. The same process is repeated three (or four) times except that a different color toner is used after each scan.

8.10 Other peripherals

We've looked at some of the peripherals most commonly found in a personal computer. We now describe some of the many possible peripherals that can be connected to a digital computer. The purpose of this section is to demonstrate a range of peripherals rather than to provide a comprehensive coverage of the subject.

Computers are used mainly in embedded control systems—the PC is just the tip of a very large iceberg. Embedded controllers take information from the outside world, process it, and control something. We begin by looking at some of the sensors that can measure an amazingly large range of variables.

At the beginning of this book we used the example of an embedded computer in an automobile's ignition control system that measured the temperature, air pressure, and oxygen concentration to compute the optimum ignition timing. How does a computer measure variables such as temperature, pressure, and oxygen concentration?

8.10.1 Measuring temperature

One of the most common of all sensors or *transducers* is the temperature probe. The everyday temperature transducer is the *thermometer* that converts the temperature into the length of a column of liquid. Mercury or alcohol in a glass bulb expands with temperature and is driven up a fine transparent tube against a scale calibrated in degrees.

Computers don't measure temperature via the thermal expansion of a liquid. Temperature is measured in terms of a voltage or current (the level of the voltage or current is an analog value that can easily be converted into digital form, as we shall demonstrate in Chapter 12). Three effects can be used to convert temperature into a voltage. The first is the *thermoelectric* effect, in which two wires of dissimilar metals are connected together to form a *thermocouple* (e.g. copper and constantan, or chromel and alumel). If the junction is heated a voltage appears across it (about $50\,\mu V/\,^{\circ}C$). This technique can be used to measure a wide range of temperatures; for example, a platinum/platinum–rhodium alloy thermocouple can measure up to $1500\,^{\circ}C$ (e.g. those found in furnaces).

Figure 8.56 illustrates the structure of a temperature-compensated thermocouple where the potential difference between a junction composed of chromel and alumel alloy wires is measured. Since these two wires must be connected to the measuring system, two further junctions are used and put in an ice bath to provide a reference junction.

The output of a thermocouple is not a linear function of temperature. Fortunately, the manufacturers of thermocouples publish algorithms (and the associated coefficients) to convert the output of a thermocouple into accurate temperatures.

Another temperature-measuring technique is to use the resistance of a metal that changes with temperature. A platinum resistance temperature detector, RTD, has a resistance of $10\,\Omega$ that changes by $0.385\%/\,^{\circ}C$. The RTD is more linear than the thermocouple but is unsuited to the measurement of temperatures over about $800\,^{\circ}C$.

Some semiconductor devices called *thermistors* have an electrical resistance that varies with temperature. These devices are very sensitive to small changes in temperature. The temperature coefficient is negative so that the thermistor conducts more as the temperature rises. Because of their sensitivity thermistors can be used to measure temperature precisely over a small range.

Another temperature-measuring element is the *band-gap* device, which employs a *semiconductor junction* (i.e. the region between two differently doped areas of silicon in a transistor). The bandgap detector operates over a relatively narrow range of temperatures, but can provide an accuracy of $0.1\,^{\circ}C$.

Most of the temperature sensors we've just described can be made very small indeed (e.g. 1 mm or less across).

8.10.2 Measuring light

Light intensity has been measured for hundreds of years. For example, when it was noticed that compounds of silver and iodine darken on exposure to light, the effect was exploited as photography. In the early 1900s Max Planck proposed that light consists of individual packets, containing a discrete amount of energy, called *photons*. When a photon hits an atom, an electron may be knocked out of its orbit round the nucleus. If this atom is metallic, a current will flow in the metal. Several light detectors operate by detecting the flow of electrons when light interacts with the atoms of a material.

The *photodiode* is a semiconductor photosensor comprising a junction between two differently doped regions of silicon. The photons of light falling on the junction create a current in the device. These devices are sensitive to light in the region 400 nm to 1000 nm (this includes infrared as well as visible light). Another means of measuring light intensity exploits the *photovoltaic effect* in silicon and selenium.

Light intensity can also be measured by the photoresistor. Certain substances, such as cadmium sulphide, change their electrical resistance when illuminated.

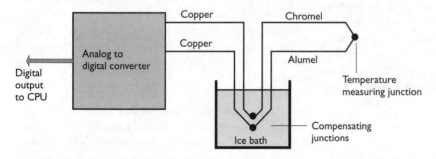

Fig. 8.56 Temperature-compensated thermocouple.

8.10.3 **Measuring pressure**

The effect of pressure or *stress* on a material is to deform it by compression or expansion, an effect we call *strain*. Strain is defined as the change in length per unit length. We can measure stress (pressure) from the effect of the strain it causes.

The *strain gauge* consists of a zigzag path of wire embedded in a substrate such as plastic. When the strain gauge is deformed by bending, the resistance of the wire increases slightly (because it has been stretched). The change in resistance in response to strain is usually very small indeed—the resistance of a 200 Ω strain gauge might change by only a few millionths of an ohm.

A strain gauge might be bonded to, say, the wing of an aircraft to measure how much it deflects in flight.

A modern form of the pressure sensor is constructed with semiconductor technology. Four resistors are deposited on a 1 mm diameter wafer of silicon in the form of a bridge. When the silicon flexes due to stress, the voltage across two of the terminals changes. If one side of the wafer is adjacent to a vacuum (created beneath the silicon disk during the manufacturing process), the device measures the absolute pressure on the other side. This type of pressure transducer is very versatile and can measure very tiny pressures or very high pressures. It is used in some electronic engine management systems to measure the manifold pressure (required to calculate engine power).

8.10.4 **Rotation sensors**

If you sometimes feel you're going round in circles, a rotation sensor can at least confirm it. At first sight it's hard to imagine a sensor that can tell you how fast something is turning.

One way of measuring rotation is to exploit the mechanism that creates the world's weather patterns—the *Coriolis* force. Air at the equator is heated by the Sun and flows North and South. Figure 8.57 shows the direction of air flowing to the North. It doesn't travel due North. Let's consider what happens to the northward-moving stream of air. The Earth rotates on its North–South axis once every 24 hours. Since the circumference of the Earth is 24 000 miles, the Earth is moving at 1000 mph at the equator. And so is the air above the equator, because the Earth drags the air around with it.

The circumference of the Earth falls as you move away from the equator and the speed at which the Earth's surface moves reduces. If you live in North America you're moving at about 600 mph. The stream of air flowing North from the equator it is also moving West-to-East at 1000 mph. However, because the rotational speed of the Earth drops as you go North, an observer on the ground sees the air deflected toward

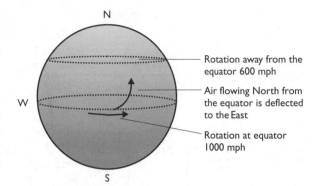

Fig. 8.57 The Coriolis force.

the East. That is, the air appears to come from the South-west. Because it takes a force to deflect an object, we say that the wind has been deflected by a force called the Coriolis force (this force does not actually exist).

Figure 8.58 demonstrates how the Coriolis force is used to measure the rate of rotation of a body. A triangular prism has three piezoelectric transducers bonded to its sides. A piezoelectric crystal flexes when a voltage is applied across its face; equally, a voltage is generated when it is flexed (i.e. the piezoelectric effect is reversible). An alternating voltage is applied to one of the transducers to create a high-frequency sound wave that propagates through the prism. The two facing piezoelectric transducers convert the vibrations into two equal alternating voltages when the prism is stationary.

When the prism rotates the vibrations spread out from the transducer through the medium that is rotating. The motion of the vibrations and the motion of the rotating prism interact and the direction of the vibrations is altered by the Coriolis force. Consequently, the two sensors don't pick up equal amounts of vibration in a rotating prism. The difference between the outputs of the sensors can be used to generate a signal whose amplitude depends on the rate of rotation. Figure 8.58 illustrates the effect of a left rotation. The output from the left transducer (a) is greater than that from the right transducer (b).

You might wonder who would want to sense rotation. As in many other areas of electronics, the introduction of a new device often leads to applications that couldn't have been imagined in the past. Low-cost rotation sensors can be used in automatic applications to follow the motion of a car. If you know how far the car has traveled (from the odometer) and the angular velocity (from which you can calculate the angular position), you can work out where the car is (if you know its initial position). This technology can be used to provide in-car navigation systems—especially when coupled with a

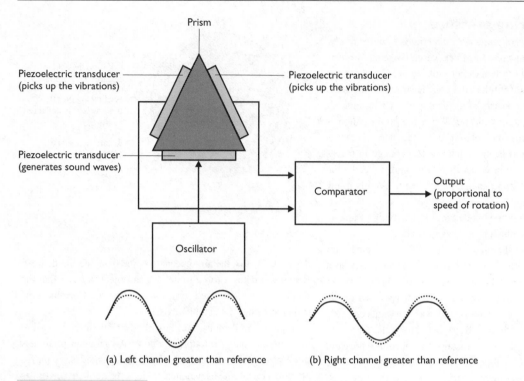

Prism

Piezoelectric transducer
(picks up the vibrations)

Piezoelectric transducer
(picks up the vibrations)

Piezoelectric transducer
(generates sound waves)

Comparator

Output
(proportional to
speed of rotation)

Oscillator

(a) Left channel greater than reference

(b) Right channel greater than reference

Fig. 8.58 Measuring rotation.

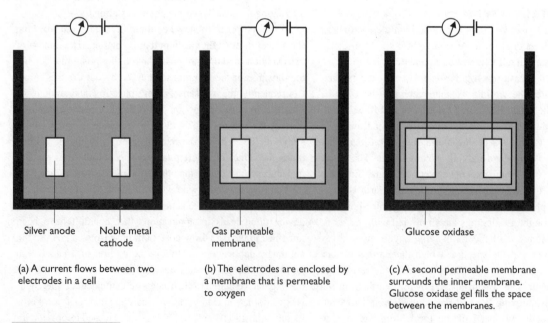

Silver anode   Noble metal
                cathode

Gas permeable
membrane

Glucose oxidase

(a) A current flows between two
electrodes in a cell

(b) The electrodes are enclosed by
a membrane that is permeable
to oxygen

(c) A second permeable membrane
surrounds the inner membrane.
Glucose oxidase gel fills the space
between the membranes.

Fig. 8.59 The biosensor.

Global Positioning System (GPS). Another application of a rotation sensor is in stabilizing platforms, for example a video camera.

8.10.5 Biosensors

One of the greatest revolutions in the late 20th century is *biotechnology*, which may eventually dwarf the computer revolution. If computers are to be used in biotechnology systems, it's necessary to be able to detect biological parameters *electronically*. Until relatively recently, the only way of measuring a biological quantity such as the level of glucose or oxygen in blood was to take a sample and send it to a laboratory for chemical analysis. In circumstances where time is critical, such as during an operation, a knowledge of a biological parameter like the blood oxygen level is vital.

It's difficult to describe biosensors in a few paragraphs because they require an understanding of biochemical reactions. Here, we describe only the underlying principles. The first biosensor was developed by Clark in the 1950s to measure the amount of dissolved oxygen in blood.

Suppose you connect two electrodes to a voltage supply and immerse them in a liquid (see Fig. 8.59(a)). A current will flow between the electrodes if there's a means of transporting electrons. Unfortunately, blood contains many molecules capable of carrying a charge, and their combined effect would swamp the current carried by oxygen molecules. Clark's solution was to surround the electrodes with a plastic *gas permeable membrane* (a form of molecular sieve). Now only oxygen is able to pass through the membrane and carry a charge between the electrodes. By measuring the current flow you can determine the oxygen concentration (Fig. 8.59(b)) in the liquid surrounding the cell.

This technique can be extended to detect more exotic molecules, such as glucose. A third membrane can be used to surround the membrane containing the electrodes. Between the outer and inner membranes is a gel of glucose oxidase enzyme that reacts with glucose and oxygen to generate gluconic acid. The amount of glucose in the liquid under test is inversely proportional to the amount of oxygen detected (Fig. 8.59(c)).

Since these techniques were developed in the 1960s, the number of detectors has vastly increased and the size of the probes reduced to the point at which they can be inserted into veins.

Summary

In this chapter we've looked at the way in which computers communicate with the world outside their CPUs. Because this topic is so large, we have divided it into three parts: the *strategy* by which data is moved into and out of the computer, the *interfaces* that actually carry out the data transfer, and the output devices or *peripherals* that receive data from, or transmit data to, the computer.

One of the reasons that the computer has become such a part of everyday life is the growth in low-cost peripherals. We have described the operation of the video displays and printers that allow ordinary people in developed countries to do things that once could only be attempted by large commercial organizations. However, we have also briefly introduced some of the devices that enable us to control the world around us: temperature, pressure, and even rotation sensors. In the final chapter we will examine how the signals from these sensors are processed by the computer.

Problems

1. What is an input/output strategy, as opposed to an input/output device?

2. What is programmed I/O?

3. Define the meaning of the following terms in the context of I/O operations:
   (a) Port
   (b) Peripheral
   (c) FIFO
   (d) Handshake
   (e) Interlocked handshake
   (f) Polling loop

4. What is the difference between an unintelligent I/O device (e.g. a flip-flop) and an intelligent I/O device (e.g. a PIA)?

5. Why does the CPU have to save the processor status (i.e. status byte and CCR) before responding to an interrupt?

6. What is a non-maskable interrupt and how is it used?

7. Explain how daisy-chaining can be used to improve the way in which interrupts are handled in a system with many peripherals.

8. What is the role of the 68000's interrupt mask in its prioritized interrupt handling system?

9. What is a prioritized interrupt?

10. What is a vectored interrupt?

11. To what extent are interrupts and subroutines the same and to what extent do they differ?

12. In a particular computer, the overhead involved in an interrupt call is 5 μs and the overhead involved in a return from interrupt is 6 μs. Suppose that this computer executes 10 instructions/microsecond. How many instructions can be used in an interrupt-handling routine if the overall interrupt-handling efficiency is to be greater than 70 percent?

13. What is DMA and why is it so important in high-performance systems?

14. What are the advantages and disadvantages of memory-mapped I/O in comparison with dedicated I/O that uses special instructions and signals?

15. The PIA has six internal registers and two register select lines. How does the PIA manage to select six registers with only two lines?

16. Can you think of any other way of implementing a register select scheme (other than the one used by the PIA)?

17. In the context of the PIA, what is a data direction register, DDR, and how is it used?

18. How does the PIA use its CA_1 and CA_2 control lines to implement handshaking?

19. How are the characters transmitted over a serial data link divided into individual characters and bits?

20. What are the functions of the ACIA's $\overline{DCD}$ and $\overline{CTS}$ inputs?

21. What is the difference between a framing error and an overrun error?

22. Why are mechanical switches unreliable?

23. What is the difference between additive and subtractive color models?

24. Use the Internet or a current computer magazine to calculate the ratio of the cost of a 17 inch monitor to a basic color printer. What was the value of this ratio 12 months ago?

25. Why does an interlaced CRT monitor perform so badly when used as a computer monitor?

Chapter 9

Computer memory

In this chapter we look at memory and describe how information is stored inside a computer. Memory systems are divided into two broad classes: *immediate* access memory and *secondary* storage. We examine first the high-speed immediate access main store based on semiconductor technology and demonstrate how memory components are interfaced to the CPU. In the second part of this chapter we look at secondary stores that hold data not currently being processed by the CPU. Most secondary storage systems employ either magnetic or optical storage technologies.

It is difficult to discuss memory systems in any detail without introducing the relationship between memory and the operating system. In particular, the operating system is responsible for allocating physical (i.e. actual) memory to programs and to controlling the operation of disk drives. However, because the operating system performs other important functions and deserves more than a short mention in this chapter, we cover cache memories and memory management in the next chapter.

Before we begin our discussion of storage devices proper, we introduce some of the terminology and underlying concepts associated with memory systems.

What is memory?

Everyone knows what memory is, but it's rather more difficult to say exactly what we mean by *memory*. We can define memory as the long- or short-term change in the physical properties of matter caused by an event. For example, ice forms on a pond during a spell of cold weather and remains for a short time after the weather gets warmer. The water has changed state from a liquid to a solid under the influence of a low temperature and now remembers that it has been cold, even though the temperature has risen above freezing point. To construct a computer memory, we have to choose a property of matter that can be modified (i.e. written) and later detected (i.e. read).

Without human memory we wouldn't be able to follow a movie, because anything that happened prior to the current

point in time would have vanished. As we watch the film, optical signals from the retina at the back of the eye cause changes within the brain—the event has passed but its effect remains. The film itself is yet another memory device. The photons of light once generated by a scene alter the chemical structure of a thin coating of silver compounds on a film of plastic.

Both human memory and photographic film share a property called *forgetfulness*. Human memory gradually fades unless it's refreshed (i.e. we need *reminding* about the event). Similarly, color film slowly fades when exposed to bright sunlight because UV light breaks down the pigments. Later, we describe *dynamic memory*, which also forgets the data stored in it unless it is periodically refreshed.

Computers employ two fundamental types of memory: *immediate* access store (which we've also called main store) and *secondary* storage. The very concept of the von Neumann stored program computer is based on the sequential execution of instructions. Clearly, the program must be stored if the individual instructions are to be carried out one after the other. Furthermore, as computation yields temporary values, memory is needed to hold them. Such memory is called immediate access memory because it must be able to access its contents at the same rate the CPU executes instructions.

A typical personal computer executes lots of different programs. Programs not currently being executed have to be stored somewhere. Moreover, most computer users often have large quantities of data that have to be retained until needed. Secondary storage devices hold vast amounts of information cheaply, but cannot retrieve data at anything like the rate at which a computer executes instructions. Immediate access stores are approximately 1 000 000 times faster than secondary stores.

Because digital logic devices operate on binary signals, it's reasonable to expect computer memories to behave in a similar fashion. Memory systems store information in binary form by exploiting a two-valued property of the storage medium. Humans sometimes do this in non-computer applications; consider; for example, tying the proverbial knot in a piece of string. The information is stored as one bit: knot or no-knot. I've always wondered why people don't tie different types of knot to increase the string's information-carrying capacity.

The most important requirement of a memory element is that it must be able to assume one of two *stable* states, and that an energy barrier must separate these states; that is, it must require energy to change the state of the memory. If there were no energy barrier separating the states, it would be possible for a stored binary value to change its state at the least provocation. In the case of our piece of string, it requires a considerable energy input either to tie a knot or to untie it.

Before we look at actual memory devices, we are going to introduce some of the terminology used to describe memory systems.

Memory terminology

There are many types of storage mechanism, each with its own characteristics. We begin with the fundamental parameters of memory systems.

Memory cell A *memory cell* is the smallest unit of information storage and holds a single 0 or 1. Memory cells are often grouped together to form words. The location of each cell in the memory is specified by its *address*, which is called a *physical* address to distinguish it from the *logical* address of an operand generated by the computer.

Capacity A memory's *capacity* is expressed as the number of bits or bytes that it can hold. Semiconductor devices are specified in terms of bits (e.g. a 256 Mbit DRAM chip), whereas CDs and disks are specified in terms of bytes (e.g. a 600 Mbyte CD or a 4 Gbyte hard disk). Some manufacturers use the convention that $1K = 1000$ and $1M = 1\,000\,000$—we will use the normal convention that $1K = 2^{10} = 1024$ and $1M = 2^{20} = 1\,048\,576$.

Density The *density* of a memory system is a measure of how much data can be stored per unit area or per unit volume; that is, density = capacity/size.

Access time A memory component's most important parameter is its *access time*, which is the time taken to read data from a given memory location, measured from the start of a read cycle. Access time is made up of two parts: the time taken to locate the required memory cell within the memory array plus the time taken for the data to become available from the memory cell. Strictly speaking, we should refer to *read* cycle access time and *write* cycle access time. Since many semiconductor memories have almost identical read and write access times, we regard access time as the read or write access time. This is not true of all forms of memory, because

some devices have quite different read and write access times. Some memories are also specified in terms of *cycle time*, which is the time that must elapse between two successive read or write accesses. Access time and cycle times are often identical. However, this statement is not true for semiconductor dynamic memories and flash EPROMs.

Random access When memory is organized so that the access time of any cell within it is constant and is independent of the actual location of the cell, the memory is said to be *random access memory* (RAM). That is, the access time of random access memory doesn't depend on where the data being accessed is located. This means that the CPU doesn't have to worry about the time taken to read a word from memory, because all read cycles have the same duration.

If a memory is random access for the purpose of read cycles, it is invariably random access for the purpose of write cycles. It is unfortunate that the term RAM is often employed to describe read/write memory where data may be read from the memory or written into it (as opposed to read-only memory). This usage is incorrect, because the term *random* access indicates only the property of constant access time and has nothing to do with the memory's ability to modify (i.e. write) its data. Another term for random access is *immediate* access. The dialed telephone system is a good example of random access system in everyday life. The time taken to connect with (access) any subscriber is constant and independent of their physical location.

Serial access In a *serial access* memory, the time taken to access data is dependent on the physical location of the data within the memory, and can vary over a wide range for any given system. Examples of serial access memories are magnetic tape transports, disk drives, CD drives, shift registers, and magnetic bubble memories. Serial access is also referred to as *sequential access*. It's easy to see why serial access memories have variable access times. If data is written on a magnetic tape, the time taken to read the data is the time taken for the piece of tape containing the data to move to the read head. This data might be 1 or 2400 ft from the beginning of the tape.

Bandwidth The *bandwidth* of a memory system indicates the speed at which data can be transferred between the memory and the host computer and is measured in bytes/second. Bandwidth is determined by the access time of the memory, the type of data path between the memory and the CPU, and the interface between the memory and CPU. For example, a hard disk might have a bandwidth of 40 Mbyte/s; that is, 40 Mbyte can be transferred between the disk and CPU in a second.

Latency Bandwidth indicates how fast you can transfer data once you have the data to transfer. *Latency* refers to the delay between beginning a memory access and the start of the transfer. When speaking of disk drives, latency refers to the time taken for the disk to rotate until the desired data is under the read/write head. When speaking of buses, *latency* refers to the time required to take control of a bus before a data transfer can take place.

Volatile memory This loses its stored data when the source of power is removed. Most semiconductor memories in which data is stored as a charge on a capacitor or as the state of a transistor (on or off) in a bistable circuit are volatile. Some semiconductor devices such as EPROM and flash memory are non-volatile and retain data when the power is off. Memories based on magnetism are generally non-volatile because their magnetic state doesn't depend on a continuous supply of power.

Read-only memory The contents of a *read-only memory* (ROM) can be read but not modified (under normal operating conditions). True read-only memories are, by definition, non-volatile. Read-only memory is frequently used to hold operating systems and other system software in small microprocessor systems (e.g. palmtop personal organizers).

Static memory Once data has been written into a *static* memory cell, the data remains there until it is either altered by over-writing it with new data, or by removing the source of power if the memory is volatile.

Dynamic memory These, called DRAMs, store data in the form of an electronic charge on the inter-electrode capacitance of a field effect transistor. Because this capacitor is not perfect, the charge gradually leaks away, discharging the capacitor and losing the data. Dynamic memories require additional circuits to restore the charge on the capacitors periodically (every 2–16 ms) in an operation known as *memory refreshing*. DRAMs are much cheaper than static memories of the same capacity.

Memory technology

It's probably true to say that memory systems employ a wider range of technologies than any other component of a digital computer. Each technology has advantages and disadvantages; for example, cost, speed, density (bits/mm^3), power consumption, physical size, and reliability. We now provide a brief overview of some of these memory technologies—we will cover these technologies in much greater detail when we look at specific memory devices. A few of the following technologies are obsolete.

Structure modification We can store information by modifying the *structure*, shape, or dimensions of an object. Three decades ago this storage technology was found in punched cards and paper tape systems that use the 'there/not-there' principle in which holes are made or not made in paper. The gramophone record is a structural memory that stores analog information by deforming the sides of a spiral groove cut into the surface of a plastic disk. At any instant the analog information is a function of the depth of the cut in the side of the groove. Both computer and analog structural memories have now virtually disappeared because of their low storage capacities and great sensitivity to physical damage. You could consider CD-ROM to be structural memory because information is stored as a string of dots on a sheet of plastic.

Delay lines Superman employs a neat trick to view the past—he just zooms away from Earth at a speed faster than light and then views past events from their light, which has been streaming away from the Earth at a constant speed of 300 000 km/s. A stream of photons moving through space represents the memory of the event. We can call this *spatial memory* because data is stored as a wave traveling through a medium. Early computers converted data into ultrasonic sound pulses traveling down tubes filled with mercury. When the train of pulses representing the stored binary sequence travels from one end of the tube to the other end, it is detected, amplified, and then recirculated. This type of memory is also called a *delay-line* memory and is no longer found in digital computers.

Feedback Data can be held in an electronic device by means of *feedback*. For example, if the output of a gate is in a 1 state, the 1 can be fed back to the input to maintain the same output. We have already met the flip-flop, which is held in a stable logical state by feeding its output back to its input. Some modern semiconductor devices based on feedback have a very low access time and are found in cache memory systems. Semiconductor memory based on feedback can be designed to consume very little power. Such memory is used in portable systems (or those with a battery backup mode).

Charge storage Dynamic memory devices store data as an electrical charge (i.e. a surfeit or deficit of electrons with respect to a body's surroundings). If a conductor is electrically insulated from its surroundings, it can be given an electrical charge. Binary information is stored by regarding one state as electrically charged and the other state as not charged. The insulation prevents the charge from rapidly draining away. Such a memory element is known as a *capacitor* and was used in one of the world's first computers (Williams used a cathode ray tube to store a bit as a charge on the screen). The most popular form of immediate memory found in today's PCs and workstations, DRAM, employs charge storage.

Magnetism The most common storage mechanism used to implement low-cost, high-capacity memories is magnetism. An atom consists of a nucleus around which electrons orbit. The electrons themselves have a spin that can take one of two values, called *up* and *down*. Electron spin generates a magnetic field and the atom can be in one of two possible magnetic states. Atoms themselves are continually vibrating due to heat (thermal motion). In most substances, the spin axes of the electrons are randomly oriented, because of the much stronger thermal vibrations of the atoms. Consequently, most substances demonstrate no overall magnetic effect.

A class of materials exhibits a property called *ferromagnetism*, in which adjacent electrons align their spin axes parallel with one another. Under these circumstances all the atoms in the bulk material are oriented with their spins in the same direction and the material is magnetized. Because we can magnetize material with its electron spins in one of two states and then detect these states, magnetic materials are used in computer memories. Both hard and floppy disk drives employ magnetic storage techniques. Up to the 1960s, immediate access memories stored data in tiny ferromagnetic rings called *ferrite cores* (hence the term *core stores*). Ferrite core stores are virtually obsolete today. In the early 1970s a class of magnetic memory called *bubble memory* looked as if it might replace disk and tape stores. However, bubble memories have never had a significant impact on memory technology and we will not discuss them further.

Optical The most modern and the oldest mechanism used to store data is *optical technology*. Printed text is an optical memory because ink modifies the optical (i.e. reflective) properties of the paper. The same mechanism stores digital information in *barcodes*. More recently, two technologies have been combined to create high-density optical storage devices. The *laser* creates a tiny beam of light that illuminates a correspondingly tiny dot that has been produced by *semiconductor fabrication* techniques. These dots store information rather like the holes in punched cards and paper tape. A purist would point out that punched cards used *transmitted* light, whereas laser-based systems use *reflected* light.

Memory hierarchy

As we've just pointed out, several technologies can be used to create storage devices. Consider the various types of memory found in a typical personal computer that employs four or more memory technologies. Internal registers within the CPU itself (data and address registers, stack pointers, the program counter, and so on) have access times of the order of one nanosecond and are implemented in the same semiconductor technology used to fabricate the CPU.

The main store that holds the programs in a typical computer ranges from 32 to over 512 Mbyte and has an access time of about 50 ns. Even this memory is sometimes partitioned into a high-speed cache memory and a slower main store. We discuss cache memory in the next chapter. The program that starts the computer running is called the *BIOS* and is stored in semiconductor read-only memory. Finally, the PC may have one or more hard disks, a floppy disk, a CD-ROM (or DVD) drive and a tape transport. If all these devices store data, why do we need so many of them?

As in every aspect of life, economics plays a dominant role in memory systems design. The characteristics a computer designer would like to see in a memory device are often mutually exclusive. The ideal memory has the following (highly improbable) characteristics:

High speed A memory's access time should be very low, preferably 1 ns, or less.

Small size Memory should be physically small. One hundred thousand megabytes (i.e. 100 Gbyte) per cubic centimeter would be nice.

Low power consumption The entire memory system should run off a watch battery for 100 years.

Highly robust The memory should not be prone to errors; a logical one should never spontaneously turn into a logical zero or vice versa. It should also be able to work at temperatures of −60 °C or at 200 °C—the military are very keen on this aspect of systems design.

Low cost Memory should cost nothing and, ideally, should be given away free with software (e.g. buy Windows 2010® and get the 100 Gbyte of RAM needed to run it free).

Figure 9.1 illustrates the memory hierarchy found in many computers. Memory devices at the top of the hierarchy are expensive, fast, and have small capacities. Devices at the bottom of the hierarchy are cheap and store vast amount of data, but are abysmally slow. This diagram isn't exact because, for example, the CD-ROM has a capacity of 600 Mbyte and (from the standpoint of capacity) should appear above hard disks in this figure.

Let's look at the characteristics of typical real memory devices in a PC. At the tip of the memory hierarchy in Fig. 9.1 we have internal CPU memory. Registers in CPUs have very low access times and are built with the same technology as

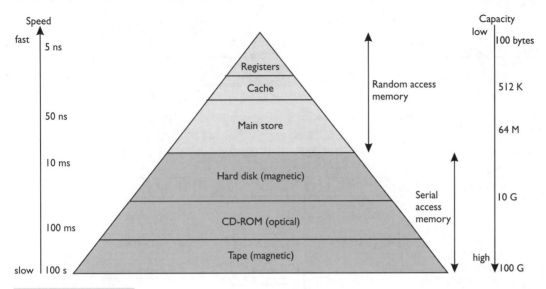

Fig. 9.1 Memory hierarchy.

the CPU itself. They are very expensive (in terms of the silicon resources they take up), limiting the number of internal registers and scratchpad memory within the CPU itself. This is especially true when the CPU is fabricated on a silicon chip, although the number of registers that can be included on a chip has increased dramatically in recent years.

Immediate access store (also called RAM or main store) holds programs and data during their execution and is relatively fast (10 ns–50 ns). Main store is invariably implemented as semiconductor static or dynamic memory. Up to the 1970s ferrite core stores and plated wire memories were found in main stores. Random access magnetic memory systems are now all but obsolete because they are slow, costly, consume relatively high power, and are physically bulky. Figure 9.1 shows that there are two types of random access memory: cache and main store. Cache memory holds copies of frequently used data (we discuss cache in detail in the next chapter).

The magnetic disk stores large quantities of data in a small space and has a very low cost per bit. Unfortunately, accessing data on a particular track is a *serial process* and a disk's access time, although fast in human terms, is orders of magnitude slower than immediate access store. A typical disk drive can store 16 Gbyte (i.e. 2^{34} bytes) and has an access time of 8 ms. In the late 1990s an explosive growth in disk technology took place and low-cost hard disks became available with greater storage capacities than CD-ROMs and tape systems.

The CD-ROM was developed by the music industry to store sound on thin plastic disks called CDs (*compact disks*).

CD-ROM technology uses a laser beam to read tiny dots embedded on a layer inside the disk. Unlike hard disks, CD-ROMs use interchangeable media. CDs are inexpensive and store up to about 600 Mbyte, but have longer access times than conventional hard disks. In general, the CD-ROM is used to distribute software. Writable CD drives and their media are more expensive and are used to back up data or to distribute data. When we cover magnetic media and CDs in detail, we will find that magnetic media require that the read/write head be very close to the media's surface, whereas the CD uses optical technology and the read head doesn't come into contact with the surface. This makes the CD a good interchangeable medium. The CD-ROM was developed into the higher capacity DVD in the late 1990s.

Magnetic tape provides an exceedingly cheap serial access medium that can store several gigabytes on a tape costing a few dollars. Unfortunately, the average access time of tape drives is very long in comparison with other storage technologies, and it is therefore largely used for archival purposes. Writable CDs have now replaced tapes in many applications.

By combining all these types of memory in a single computer system, the computer engineer can get the best of all worlds. You can construct a relatively low-cost memory system with a performance only a few percent lower than that of a memory constructed entirely from expensive high-speed RAM. The key to computer memory design is having the right data in the right place at the right time. A large computer system may have thousands of programs and millions of data files. Fortunately, the CPU requires few programs and files at

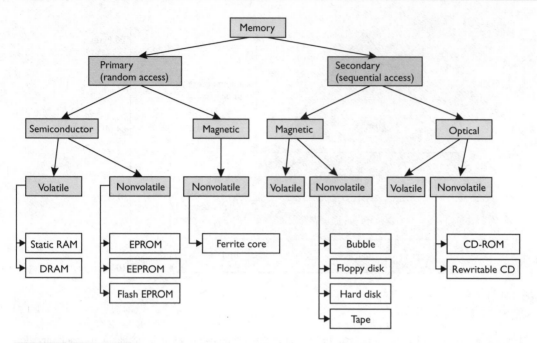

Fig. 9.2 Classes of memory.

any one time. By designing an operating system that moves data from disk into the main store so that the CPU always (or nearly always) finds the data it wants in the main store, the system has the speed of a giant high-speed store at a tiny fraction of the cost. Such an arrangement is called a *virtual memory* because the memory appears to the user as, say, a 4000 Mbyte main store, when in reality there may be a real main memory of only 32 Mbyte and 4000 Mbyte of disk storage. We examine virtual memory systems in the next chapter. Figure 9.2 summarizes the various types of memory currently available according to type (this list is not complete).

We now introduce *semiconductor memory*, the memory used to implement high-speed random-access main stores. We begin by describing its characteristics and then demonstrate how it is interfaced to a typical processor. We also look at some members of the family of semiconductor memory. After that, we describe the technologies used to implement secondary storage systems. Readers who are not interested in the fine details of memory systems may skip this section.

9.1 Semiconductor memory

Semiconductor random access memory is fabricated on silicon chips by the same process used to manufacture microprocessors. Without the availability of low-cost semiconductor memory, the microprocessor revolution would have been seriously delayed had microprocessors been forced to use the slow, bulky, and expensive ferrite core memory of 1960s and 1970s mainframes. The principal features of semiconductor memory are its high density (measured in bits per chip) and ease of use. There are two major classes of semiconductor memory: *static* and *dynamic*.

9.1.1 Static semiconductor memory

Static semiconductor memory is created by fabricating an array of latches on a single silicon chip. This memory has a very low access time, but is about four times more expensive than dynamic memory. Furthermore, a static RAM stores only one quarter as much data as a dynamic memory of the same silicon area. Static RAM is easy to use from the engineer's point of view and is found in small memories. Some memory systems use static memory devices because of their greater reliability than dynamic memory. Large memories are constructed with dynamic memory because of its lower cost. Some static memories use less power than DRAM and some use more power.

Figure 9.3 illustrates a typical semiconductor memory chip, a 4M CMOS RAM. The acronym *CMOS* means *complementary metal oxide semiconductor* and indicates the

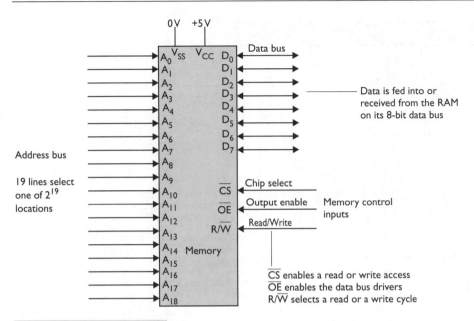

Fig. 9.3 The 512K × 8 static RAM.

semiconductor technology used to manufacture the chip, and the 4M denotes the memory's capacity in bits; in this case 2^{22} bits. All semiconductor memories are specified in terms of their *capacity* (e.g. 1K, 4K, 16K, 64K, 256K, 1M, 4M, 16M, and 64M, where M stands for Mbit, or megabit) and their *organization* (e.g. $16M \times 1$ or $4M \times 4$). The memory in Fig. 9.3 is organized as $512K \times 8$ bits and has a capacity of 4 Mbit.

A memory's organization describes how its cells are arranged in terms of width and depth. Memory components are organized as *n* words by *m* bits (the total capacity is defined as $m \times n$ bits). Bit-organized memory components have a 1-bit width; for example, a bit-organized 256K chip is arranged as 256K locations each of one bit. Some devices are nibble organized; for example, a 256K chip is arranged as 64K locations, each containing 4 bits. The device in Fig. 9.3 is byte-organized as 512K words of 8 bits. Such byte-wide chips are suited to small memories in microprocessor systems in which one or two chips may be sufficient for all the processor's read/write memory requirements.

The chip in Fig. 9.3 is interfaced to the rest of the computer via its 32 pins, of which 19 are the address inputs needed to select one of $2^{19} = 524\,288$ (i.e. 512K) unique locations. Eight data lines transfer data from the memory during a read cycle, and receive data from the processor during a write cycle. Electrical power is fed to the chip via two pins. The three control pins, $\overline{CS}$, $\overline{OE}$, and R/$\overline{W}$, determine the operation of the memory component as follows.

Pin	Name	Function
$\overline{CS}$	Chip select	When low, $\overline{CS}$ selects the chip for a memory access
R/$\overline{W}$	Read/not write	When high, R/$\overline{W}$ indicates a read cycle; when low it indicates a write cycle
$\overline{OE}$	Output enable	When low in a read cycle, $\overline{OE}$ allows data to be read from the chip and placed on the data bus

In Fig. 9.3 power is fed to the memory via its V_{ss} and V_{cc} pins. Like many semiconductor components, memories run off a 5 V supply (although the use of 3.3 V systems has become popular since the 1990s).

In order for the chip to take part in a read or write operation, its $\overline{CS}$ pin must be in a low state. When discussing computers, the terms '*read*' and '*write*' refer to the computer's perspective (data read from the memory is written into the computer and vice versa). Whenever $\overline{CS}$ is inactive-high, the memory component ignores all signals at its other pins. Disabling the memory by turning off its internal tri-state bus drivers permits several memories to share the data bus as long as only one device is enabled at a time. The R/$\overline{W}$ input determines whether the chip is storing the data at its eight data pins (R/$\overline{W} = 0$), or is transferring data to these pins (R/$\overline{W} = 1$).

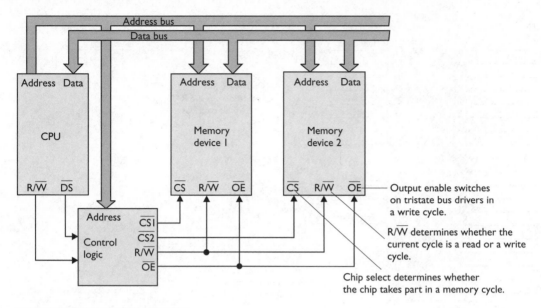

Fig. 9.4 Interfacing memory to a CPU.

The output enable pin, $\overline{\text{OE}}$, is used to turn on the memory's tristate bus drivers during a read cycle and off at all other times. Not all memory chips have a separate output control. Many chips combine $\overline{\text{OE}}$ with $\overline{\text{CS}}$ and $\text{R}/\overline{\text{W}}$ so that the output data buffers are automatically enabled when $\overline{\text{CS}} = 0$ and $\text{R}/\overline{\text{W}} = 1$.

Data is stored in a static RAM chip in flip-flops, each composed of four or six transistors. All the address decoding and read/write electronics is located on the chip, making the design of modern memory systems very easy. Figure 9.4 demonstrates how this device can be connected to a CPU. Because the chip is 8 bits wide (i.e. it provides 8 bits at a time), two chips would be connected in parallel in a system with a 16-bit data bus, and four chips in a system with a 32-bit data bus.

The arrangement of Fig. 9.4 is very simple. The CPU's data bus is connected to the memory's data pins and the CPU's address bus is connected to the memory's address pins. The memory's $\overline{\text{CS}}$, $\text{R}/\overline{\text{W}}$, and $\overline{\text{OE}}$ control inputs are connected to signals from the block labeled *control logic*. This block takes control signals from the CPU and generates the signals required to control a read or a write cycle.

Suppose the memory device is connected to a CPU with a 32-bit address bus that can access 2^{32} locations. This RAM has only 19 address inputs and provides only a fraction of the address space that the CPU can access (i.e. 512 kbyte out of 4 Gbyte). Extra logic is required to map this block of RAM onto an appropriate part of the processor's address space. The high-order address lines from the CPU (in this case, A_{19} to A_{31}) are connected to a control logic block that uses these address lines to perform the mapping operation. Essentially, there are $4\text{G}/512\text{K} = 2^{32}/2^{19} = 2^{13}$ slots into which the RAM can be mapped. We'll explain how this is done later in this chapter.

9.1.2 Accessing memory—timing diagrams

The computer designer is interested in the relationship between the memory and the CPU. In particular, the memory must provide data when the CPU wants it, and the CPU must provide data when the memory wants it. The most important tool used to relate the memory to the CPU is the *timing diagram*. A timing diagram is a cause and effect diagram that illustrates the sequence of actions taking place during a read or write cycle. The designer is concerned with the relationship between information on the address and data buses and the memory's control inputs. Figure 9.5 shows the simplified timing diagram of a static RAM memory chip during a read cycle.

The timing diagram illustrates the state (i.e. logic level) of the signals involved in a memory access as a function of time. Each signal may be in a 0 or a 1 state and sloping edges indicate a change of level. In Fig. 9.5 the timing diagram of the address bus appears as two parallel lines crossing over at points A and B. The use of two parallel lines is a convention and means that some of the address lines may be high and

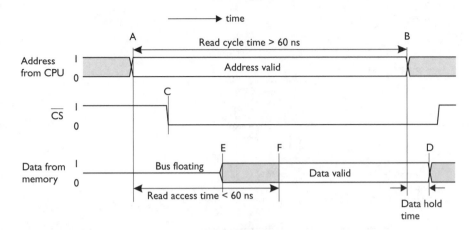

Fig. 9.5 Timing diagram of the read cycle of a static RAM.

some low. It's not the actual logical values of the address lines that interest us, but the time at which the contents of the address bus become stable for the duration of the current memory access cycle. We haven't drawn the R/W̅ line because it must be in its electrically high state for the duration of the entire read cycle.

Let's walk through this diagram from left to right. At point A in Fig. 9.5, the contents of the address bus have fully changed from their previous value and are now stable; that is, the old address from the CPU has been replaced by a new address. This point is taken as a reference for some of the memory's timing parameters. Because logic transitions from 0 to 1 or 1 to 0 are never instantaneous, changes of state are depicted by sloping lines. Some timing diagrams use the high-to-low transition of C̅S̅ as the principal reference point.

Between points A and B the address bus contains the address of the memory location currently being read from. During this time the address from the CPU must not change. The time between A and B is the minimum cycle time of the memory. If the minimum cycle time is quoted as 60 ns, another memory access cannot begin until at least 60 ns after the start of the current cycle.

Consider now the operation of the memory component in a read cycle. The CPU puts out an address on its address bus corresponding to a location within the memory. The higher-order address lines from the CPU cause a chip-select output of the address decoder in the control logic to be asserted and to select a memory component as described in Fig. 9.4. At point C in Fig. 9.5 the memory's active-low chip select input, C̅S̅, goes low and turns on the three-state bus driver outputs connected to the data pins. Up to point E the contents of the data bus are represented by a single line midway between the two

logic levels. This convention indicates that the data bus is floating and is disconnected from the data output circuits of the memory.

When a low level on C̅S̅ turns on the memory's three-state output circuits at point E, the data bus stops floating and data appears at the output terminals. Unfortunately, sufficient time has not yet elapsed for the addressed memory word to be located and its contents retrieved. Consequently, the contents of the data bus between points E and F are not valid and cannot be used. At point F the data is valid and the time between points A and F is called the chip's *read access time*. Some static RAMs measure the read access time from C̅S̅ low to data valid.

At the end of the read cycle at point B, the contents of the address bus begin to change. Because of propagation delays in the chip, the data at its output pins does not change until some guaranteed minimum time has elapsed. This delay is called the *data hold time* and is the duration between points B and D. The preceding description of a read cycle has been simplified. For a fuller account of timing diagrams see the bibliography.

The write cycle

A static RAM's write cycle is similar to its read cycle, except that R/W̅ must be in a low state, and data placed on the chip's data input lines by the CPU. Figure 9.6 shows the simplified write cycle timing diagram of a static RAM. We haven't provided O̅E̅ timing (we'll assume that O̅E̅ is inactive-high throughout the write cycle to avoid the memory going into a read cycle when R/W̅ is high).

During the write cycle described by Fig. 9.6, data from the CPU is presented to the memory at its data inputs, R/W̅ is set low to indicate a write access, and C̅S̅ asserted. Data is

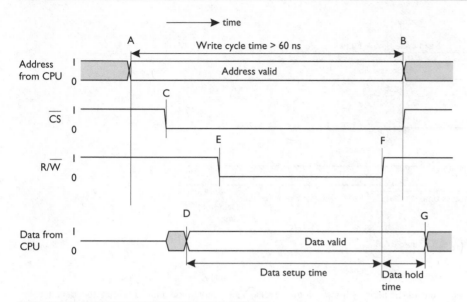

Fig. 9.6 Timing diagram of the write cycle of a static RAM.

latched into the memory cell by the rising edge of the R/W̄ input. The critical timing parameters in a write cycle are the duration of the write pulse width (i.e. the minimum time for which R/W̄ must be low) and the data *setup time* with respect to the rising edge of R/W̄. Data setup time is the time for which data must be present at the input terminals of a memory before the data is latched into the memory.

9.1.3 Dynamic memory

Dynamic random access read/write memory or, more simply, DRAM, is the most compact and lowest cost form of semiconductor memory available. Not only is dynamic RAM both cheaper and denser in terms of bits/chip than static memory, DRAM chips consume less power than some of their static memory counterparts. A typical DRAM chip has a capacity of 64M × 1 bits.

A static RAM stores data in an RS flip-flop constructed from four transistors. Dynamic memory devices store one bit of information in a single transistor memory cell. For a given number of transistors per chip, a dynamic memory can store about four times as much data as its static counterpart.

Data in a dynamic memory cell is stored as an electrical charge on a terminal of a field effect transistor. This charge generates an electrostatic field that modifies the flow of current between the transistor's other two terminals. A dynamic memory chip contains all the electronics needed to access a given cell, to write a one or a zero to it in a write cycle, and to read its contents in a read cycle.

Figure 9.7 illustrates the internal arrangement of a typical 16M × 1 dynamic memory chip (i.e. the chip has 16M locations each holding one bit). You might think that a 16M × 1-bit DRAM requires 24 address lines, because a 16M memory space is spanned by 24 address lines (i.e. $2^{24} = 16M$). In order to reduce the size of the DRAM's package, its address bus is *multiplexed*; that is, an address is input in two halves. One half of the address is called the *row address* and the other half is called the *column address*. A DRAM requires two control signals to handle the address: a row address strobe ($\overline{RAS}$) that captures the row address and a column address strobe ($\overline{CAS}$) that captures the column address.

Multiplexing the address bus increases the complexity of the interface between the DRAM and the CPU. As the 16M × 1 memory component contains only a single bit in each of its 16M addressable locations, 16 of these chips are required to construct a 16-bit wide memory module.

Unfortunately, the electrical charge on the transistor in a memory cell gradually leaks away and the cell loses its stored data. A typical dynamic memory cell is guaranteed to retain data for up to 16 ms after it has been written. In order to retain data for longer than 16 ms, data must be rewritten into every cell periodically in an operation called *refreshing*. In practice, simply accessing a memory cell refreshes it (and all cells in the same row). The need to refresh dynamic memories periodically increases the complexity of the CPU–DRAM interface.

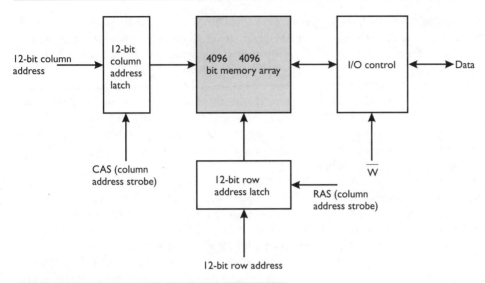

Fig. 9.7 The internal organization of a 16M × 1 dynamic RAM.

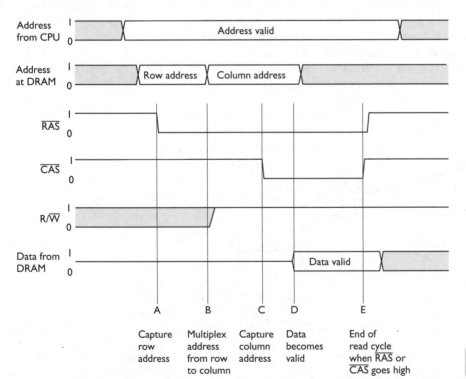

Fig. 9.8 Timing diagram of the read cycle of a dynamic RAM.

The DRAM read cycle

Figure 9.8 provides the simplified timing diagram of a DRAM read cycle, which is more complex than a static RAM's timing diagram. There are two address traces in Fig. 9.8. One trace describes the address from the CPU and the other the address at the DRAM's address inputs. A read cycle starts with the *row address* of the current memory location being applied to the address inputs of the DRAM. An address multiplexer in the memory control system transmits bits A_{00} to A_{11} from the CPU to address inputs A_{00} to A_{11} at the DRAM. The chip's row address strobe, $\overline{RAS}$, is then asserted active-low to latch the row address into the chip (point A in Fig. 9.8).

The next step is to switch over the address from row to column (point B) and apply the column address to the chip. In this case, address lines A_{12} to A_{23} from the CPU are connected to address lines A_0 to A_{11} at the DRAM. The column address strobe, $\overline{CAS}$, is asserted at point C to capture the column address. At this point, the entire 24-bit address has been captured by the DRAM and the address bus plays no further role in the read cycle. The data in the cell accessed by the address then appears on the data-output line after a delay of typically 30–70 ns from the point at which $\overline{RAS}$ went low (point D). A read cycle ends when the first of either $\overline{RAS}$ or $\overline{CAS}$ returns inactive-high.

Figure 9.8 also shows the role of the $R/\overline{W}$ signal from the CPU. This signal must go high before $\overline{CAS}$ is asserted and remain high for the rest of the cycle. Designing a DRAM memory system is quite complex because the designer must generate the correct sequence of control signals (their timing with respect to each other can be quite critical).

Unlike the static RAM, which has an access time equal to its cycle time, the dynamic RAM's cycle time is longer than its access time because certain internal operations must take place within the DRAM before another access can begin. A DRAM might have an access time of 30 ns and a cycle time of 60 ns. Cycle time is important because it places a limitation on the speed of the system.

Figure 9.9 indicates the logic needed to control a dynamic memory. The DRAM control must carry out the address multiplexing and generate the necessary $\overline{RAS}$ and $\overline{CAS}$ signals. You can obtain much of the logic needed to implement a dynamic memory controller on a single chip.

The DRAM write cycle

A DRAM write cycle, described in Fig. 9.10, is similar to a read cycle except that the DRAM's $R/\overline{W}$ input must go low before $\overline{CAS}$ goes low, and the data to be stored in the addressed cell must be applied to the data-in line.

The timing of the DRAM's address, $\overline{RAS}$, and $\overline{CAS}$ signals is the same in both read and write cycles. However, in a write cycle the data from the CPU must be available and the $R/\overline{W}$ control signal must be low before the DRAM's $\overline{CAS}$ input is asserted (some DRAMs support other write modes).

Refreshing DRAM

As we've said, the data in each DRAM memory cell must be periodically rewritten if it's not to be lost. DRAMs are designed so that you don't have to refresh all cells individually.

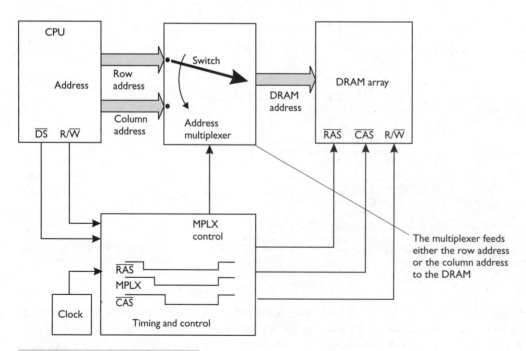

Fig. 9.9 Controlling the dynamic memory.

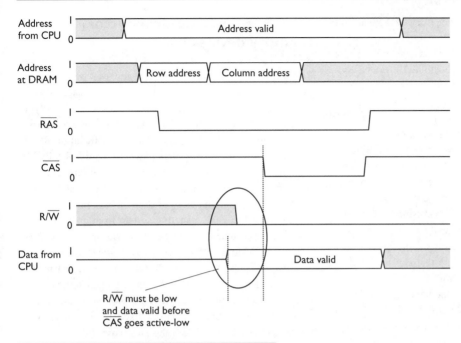

Fig. 9.10 The write-cycle timing diagram of a dynamic RAM.

Simply accessing a row simultaneously refreshes all cells in that row. A typical refresh controller performs all row refresh cycles every 16 ms.

A few years ago, refreshing a DRAM was a complex process because you had to provide the logic to generate the row address of each row to be refreshed. All that needs be done to refresh a modern DRAM is to assert $\overline{CAS}$ while $\overline{RAS}$ is high. This mode is called *CAS-before-RAS* refresh to distinguish it from a normal read or write access when $\overline{CAS}$ goes low *after* $\overline{RAS}$. The DRAM automatically generates row refresh addresses internally. The DRAM refresh logic stops the processor and carries out a burst of refresh cycles at a time.

DRAM reliability

Semiconductor dynamic memory suffers from two peculiar weaknesses. When a memory cell is accessed and the inter-electrode capacitor charged the dynamic memory draws a very heavy current from the power supply causing a voltage drop along the power supply lines. This voltage drop can be reduced by careful layout of the circuit of the memory system. Another weakness of the dynamic memory is its sensitivity to *alpha particles*. Semiconductor chips are encapsulated in plastic or ceramic materials that contain tiny amounts of radioactive material. One of the products of radioactive decay is the alpha particle (helium nucleus), which is highly ionizing

and corrupts data in cells through which it passes. When an alpha particle passes through a DRAM cell, a *soft* error occurs. An error is called soft if it is not repeatable (i.e. the cell fails on one occasion but has not been permanently damaged). The quantity of alpha particles can be reduced by careful quality control in selecting the encapsulating material, but is never reduced to zero. By the way, all semiconductor memory is prone to alpha particle errors—it's just that DRAM cells have a low stored energy/bit and are more prone to these errors than other devices.

A random soft error that corrupts a bit once a year in a personal computer is an irritation. In professional and safety-critical systems the consequences of such errors might be more severe. The practical solution to this problem lies in *error-correcting codes*. Five *check bits* are appended to a 16-bit data word to create a 21-bit code word. If one of the bits in the code word read back from the DRAM is in error, you can calculate which bit it was and correct the error.

9.1.4 Limits to memory density

Since their introduction in the 1960s, the density of semiconductor memories has steadily grown. Early semiconductor memories had a capacity of 16 bits. Today, some have capacities of 256 Mbit. These figures represent a growth factor of 2^{24} in three decades. You can, in fact, buy much larger memory modules, but these are composed of several chips bonded to a circuit board.

It seems reasonable to ask whether this growth in memory density can continue forever without limit. Unfortunately, it can't continue because there are limits to memory density. Consider the following factors.

Feature size   Semiconductor devices are manufactured by a process that involves a step called *photolithography*. Silicon is coated with a photosensitive material and an image projected onto the silicon. This image is developed and used to create the transistors that make up the memory. If you can create a smaller image, you can make smaller transistors and therefore build memories with more cells on a silicon chip. The smallest line or *feature* that can be etched on the silicon is, of course, governed by the smallest line that can be projected. The minimum width of a line projected onto the silicon is determined by the wavelength of the light used by the projector, because a beam of light spreads out due to an effect called *diffraction*. Even blue light with its short wavelength cannot generate features small enough for modern chips. Today, electron beams are sometimes used to draw features on the silicon.

Quantum mechanical effects   One of the consequences of quantum mechanics is that an object can spontaneously penetrate a barrier without having the energy to go through it. The probability of penetrating a barrier depends on the barrier's width and the size of the object—the thinner the barrier the more likely the penetration. If the insulators that separate one transistor from another in a memory become too thin, electrons will spontaneously be able to tunnel through the insulators.

Statistical nature of a current   An electrical current is composed of a flow of electrons. In normal systems the number of electrons flowing in a circuit is staggeringly large. If memories are made smaller and smaller, the number of electrons flowing will diminish. At some point, the random nature of a current flow will have to be taken into account.

Energy   It requires a finite amount of energy to cause a memory cell to change from one state to another. However, the minimum amount of energy that can be used in switching is limited by quantum mechanics (i.e. there is a fixed minimum level of energy that can be used to perform switching).

These restrictions impose an ultimate limit on how much information we can store in a semiconductor device. However, we have not yet approached this limit and progress is likely to continue at the present rate until at least 2010.

9.1.5 Read-only semiconductor memory devices

As much as any other component, the ROM (*read-only memory*) was responsible for the growth of low-cost personal computers in the 1980s when secondary storage mechanisms such as disk drives were still very expensive. In those days a typical operating system and BASIC interpreter required approximately 8 to 64 kbyte of memory and could fit into a ROM. Although all personal computers now have hard disks, ROMs are still found in diskless palmtop computers and personal organizers. Even in an era of low-cost disk drives, all computers require read-only memory to store the so-called *bootstrap* program that loads the operating system from disk when the computer is switched on. In the PC world, this ROM-based program is called the BIOS (*basic input/output system*).

Another application of the ROM is in dedicated microprocessor-based controllers. When a microcomputer is assigned to a specific task, such as the ignition control system in an automobile, the software is fixed for the lifetime of the device. A ROM provides the most cost-effective way of storing this type of software.

From an engineering point of view, semiconductor ROMs are very easy to use because interfacing ROM to a CPU is even easier than interfacing static RAM. Because the ROM is never written to, a ROM chip requires nothing more than the address of the location to be accessed and a chip-select signal to operate the output circuits of the chip's data bus.

Semiconductor technology is eminently well suited to the production of high-density, low-cost read-only memories. We now describe the characteristics of some of the read-only memories in common use: mask-programmed ROM, PROM, EPROM, flash EPROM, and EEPROM.

Mask-programmed ROM

Mask-programmed ROM is the cheapest type of read-only semiconductor memory—when bought in bulk. These devices are programmed during their manufacture and are so called because a mask (i.e. stencil) projects the pattern of connections required to define the contents. Mask-programmed ROMs cannot be altered because the data is built into its physical structure. They are used only when large numbers of devices are required because the cost of setting up the mask is very high. The other read-only memories we describe next are all programmable and some are reprogrammable.

PROM

A transistor is a switch that can pass or block the passage of the current through it. Each memory cell in a PROM (*programmable read-only memory*) contains a transistor that can be turned on or off to store a 1 or a 0. The transistor's state (on or off) is determined by the condition of a tiny metallic link that connects one of the transistor's inputs to a fixed voltage. When you buy a PROM, it is filled with all 1s because each link forces the corresponding transistor into a 1 state. A PROM is programmed by passing such a large current through a link that the link melts and changes the state of the transistor from a 0 to a 1. For obvious reasons, these links are often referred to as *fuses*. A PROM is programmed once and once only, because if you fuse a link it stays that way. The PROM has a low access time (5–50 ns) and is largely used as a logic element rather than as a means of storing programs.

EPROM

The EPROM is an *erasable* programmable read-only memory that is also programmed in a special machine costing from about a hundred dollars upwards (an EPROM programmer is different from a PROM programmer). Data is stored in an EPROM memory cell as an electrostatic charge on a highly insulated conductor. The charge can remain for periods in excess of ten years without leaking away. Essentially, an EPROM is a dynamic memory with a refresh period of tens of years.

We do not intend to cover semiconductor technology in this text, but it is worth looking at how EPROMs operate. All we need state is that semiconductors are constructed from pure silicon and that the addition of tiny amounts of impurities (called *dopants*) changes the electrical characteristics of silicon. Silicon doped with an impurity is called *n*-type or *p*-type silicon depending on how the impurity affects the electrical properties of the silicon.

Figure 9.11 illustrates an EPROM memory cell consisting of a single NMOS field effect transistor. A current flows in the N+ channel between the transistor's positive and negative terminals, V_{dd} and V_{ss}. By applying a negative charge to a gate electrode, the negatively charged electrons flowing

through the channel are repelled and the current turned off. That is, the transistor has two states: a state with no charge on the gate and a current flowing through the channel and a state with a charge on the gate that cuts off the current in the channel.

A special feature of the EPROM is the *floating gate* that is insulated from any conductor by means of a thin layer of silicon dioxide—an almost perfect insulator. By placing or not placing a charge on the floating gate, the transistor can by turned on or off to store a one or a zero in the memory cell.

If the floating gate is entirely insulated, how do we put a charge on it in order to program the EPROM? The solution is to place a *second* gate close to the floating gate but insulated from it. By applying typically 12–25 V to this second gate, some electrons cross the insulator and travel to the floating gate (in the same way that lightning crosses the normally non-conducting atmosphere).

You can program an EPROM, erase it, and reprogram it many times. Illuminating the silicon chip with ultraviolet light erases the data stored in it. Photons of UV light hit the floating gate and cause the stored charge to drain away through the insulator. The silicon chip is located under a quartz window that is transparent to UV light.

EPROMs are suitable for small-scale projects and for development work in laboratories because they can be programmed, erased, and reprogrammed by the user. The disadvantage of EPROMs is that they have to be removed from a computer, placed under a UV light to erase them, and then placed in a special-purpose programmer to reprogram them. Finally, they have to be re-inserted in the computer.

Flash EPROM

One of the most popular read-only memories is the *flash EPROM* that can be erased and reprogrammed electronically. Typical applications of the flash EPROM are personal

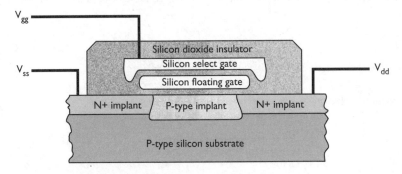

Fig. 9.11 The structure of an EPROM memory cell.

organizers and system software in personal computers (e.g. the BIOS in PCs).

The structure of a conventional EPROM memory cell and a cell in a flash EPROM is very similar. The difference lies in the thickness of the insulating layer (silicon oxynitride) between the floating gate and the surface of the transistor. The insulating layer of a conventional EPROM is about 300 Å thick, whereas a flash EPROM's insulating layer is only 100 Å thick. Note that $1\,\text{Å} = 1 \times 10^{-10}\,\text{m}$ (or 10 nanometers).

When a conventional EPROM is programmed, the charge is transferred to the floating gate by a mechanism called the *avalanche effect*. The voltage difference between the gate and the surface of the transistor causes electrons to burst through the oxynitride insulating layer in the same way that lightning bursts through the atmosphere. These electrons are called *hot electrons* because of their high levels of kinetic energy (i.e. speed). The charge on the floating gate is removed during exposure to UV light which gives the electrons enough energy to cross the insulating layer.

A flash EPROM is programmed in exactly the same way as an EPROM (i.e. by hot electrons crashing through the insulator). However, the insulating layer in a flash EPROM is so thin that a new mechanism is used to transport electrons across it when the chip is erased. This mechanism is known as *Fowler–Nordheim tunneling* and is a quantum mechanical effect. When a voltage in the range 12–20 V is applied across the insulating layer, electrons on the floating gate are able to tunnel through the layer, even though they don't have enough energy to cross the barrier.

A flash EPROM is divided into sectors with a capacity of typically 1024 bytes. Some devices let you erase a sector or the whole memory, while others permit only a full chip erase. The flash EPROM can't be programmed, erased, and reprogrammed without limit. Repeated write and erase cycles eventually damage the very thin insulating layer. Some first-generation flash EEPROMs are guaranteed to perform only 100 erase/write cycles, although devices are now available with lifetimes of at least 10 000 cycles.

EEPROM

The electrically erasable and reprogrammable ROM (called EEPROM or E²PROM) is similar to the flash EPROM and can be programmed and erased electrically. An EEPROM can be programmed inside a computer and doesn't have to be removed and placed under a UV light. The difference between the EEPROM and the flash EPROM is that the flash EPROM uses *Fowler–Nordheim tunneling* to erase data and *hot electron injection* to write data, whereas pure EEPROMs use the tunneling mechanism to both write and erase data. Table 9.1 illustrates the difference between the EPROM, flash EPROM, and EEPROM.

EEPROMs are more expensive than flash EPROMs and generally have smaller capacities. The size of the largest state-of-the-art flash memory is usually four times that of the corresponding EEPROM. Modern EEPROMs operate from single 5 V supplies and are rather more versatile than flash EPROMs. Like the flash memory, they are *read-mostly* devices, with a lifetime of 10 000 erase/write cycles. EEPROMs have access times as low as 35 ns but still have long write cycle times (e.g. 5 ms).

You might be forgiven for asking what the difference is between a read/write RAM and an EEPROM. First, the EEPROM is non-volatile, unlike the typical semiconductor RAM. Second, the EEPROM has a very long write cycle time (i.e. it takes much longer to write data than to read it). Third, the EEPROM can be written to only a finite number of times. Successive erase and write operations put a strain on its internal structure and eventually destroy it. Finally, EEPROM is much more expensive than semiconductor RAM. The EEPROM is found in special applications where data must be retained when the power is off. A typical application is in a radio receiver that can store a number

Device	EPROM	Flash EPROM	EEPROM
Normalized cell size	1.0	1.0–1.2	3.0
Programming mechanism	Hot electron injection	Hot electron injection	Tunneling
Erase mechanism	UV light	Tunneling	Tunneling
Erase time	20 min	1 s	5 ms
Minimum erase	Entire chip	Entire chip (or sector)	Byte
Write time (per cell)	< 100 µs	< 100 µs	5 ms
Read access time	200 ns	200 ns	35 ns

Table 9.1 Programmable ROM differences.

of different frequencies and recall them when the power is reapplied.

9.2 Interfacing memory to a CPU

We now look at how the semiconductor memory components that constitute a memory subsystem are interfaced to the microprocessor. Readers who are not interested in microprocessor systems design may skip this section.

9.2.1 Memory organization

A microprocessor operates on a word of width w bits. The microprocessor communicates with memory over a bus of width b bits. Memory components of width m bits are connected to the microprocessor via this bus. In the best of all possible worlds, the values of w, b, and m are all the same. This was often true of 8-bit microprocessors, but is rarely true of today's high-performance processors. Consider the 68000 microprocessor, which has an internal 32-bit architecture and a 16-bit data bus interface. When you read a 32-bit value in memory, the processor automatically performs two 16-bit read cycles. The programmer doesn't have to worry about this, because the memory accesses are carried out automatically. Memory components are normally 1, 4, or 8 bits wide. If you use 4-bit-wide memory devices in a 68000 system, you have to arrange them in groups of 4 because a memory block must provide the bus with 16 bits of data. Figure 9.12 shows the organization of 8-bit, 16-bit, and 32-bit systems.

A memory system must be as wide as the data bus. That is, the memory system must be able to provide an 8-bit bus with 8 bits of data, a 16-bit bus with 16 bits of data,

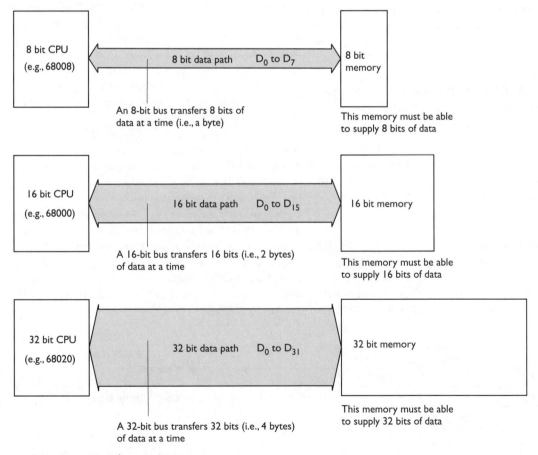

Fig. 9.12 CPU, bus, and memory organization.

a 32-bit bus with 32 bits of data, etc. Consider the following examples.

- **Example 1** An 8-bit computer with an 8-bit bus uses memory components that are 4 bits wide. Two of these devices are required to supply 8 bits of data.
- **Example 2** A 16-bit computer with a 16-bit bus uses memory components that are 1 bit wide. Sixteen of these devices are required to supply 16 bits of data.

The amount of data in a block of memory, in bytes, is equal to the width of the data bus (in bytes) multiplied by the number of locations in the block of memory.

- **Example 3** An 8-bit computer uses memory components organized as $64K \times 4$ bits; that is, there are $64K = 2^{16}$ different addressable locations in the chip. Two of these chips are required to provide the CPU with 8 data bits. The total size of the memory is 64 kbyte.
- **Example 4** A 16-bit computer uses memory components that are $64K \times 4$ bits. Four of these chips must be used to provide the CPU with 16 bits of data. Therefore, each of the 64K locations provides 16 bits of data or two bytes (i.e. each of the 4 chips provides 4 of the 16 bits). The total size of the memory is 2 bytes $\times 64K = 128$ kbyte.
- **Example 5** A 16-bit computer uses $64K \times 16$-bit memory components. Only one of these chips is required to provide 16 bits of data (2 bytes). Therefore, each chip provides $2 \times 64K = 128$ kbyte.

Figure 9.13 demonstrates how three 16-bit wide blocks of memory can be constructed from 4-bit wide, 8-bit wide, and 16-bit wide memory components.

9.2.2 Address decoders

If the memory in a microprocessor system were constructed from memory components with the same number of uniquely addressable locations as the processor, the problem of address decoding would not exist. For example, an 8-bit CPU with

address lines A_{00}–A_{23} would simply be connected to the corresponding address input lines of the memory component. This would, of course, require a memory device with $16M \times 8$-bit locations (i.e. 2^{24} bytes). Microprocessor systems often have memory components that are smaller than 16 Mbyte. Moreover, there are different types of memory: read/write memory, read-only memory, and memory-mapped peripherals. We now look at some of the ways in which memory components are interfaced to a microprocessor.

In order to simplify matters, we will assume an 8-bit processor with a 16-bit address bus spanned by address lines A_0 to A_{15}. We are not going to use the 68000 because it has a 23-bit address bus, a 16-bit data bus, and special byte selection logic. All these features of the 68000 make it more powerful than earlier processors, but they do get in the way of illustrating the basic principles. The examples we use are applicable to 8-bit devices like the 6800 or the Z80. We will provide several 68000-based examples at the end of this chapter.

Consider the situation illustrated by Fig. 9.14, in which two $1K \times 8$ memory components are connected to the address bus of an 8-bit microprocessor. This processor has 16 address lines A_0–A_{15}. Ten address lines A_0–A_9 from the CPU are connected to the corresponding address inputs of the two memory components, M1 and M2. Whenever a location (one of $2^{10} = 1K$) is addressed in M1, the corresponding location is addressed in M2. The data outputs of M1 and M2 are connected to the system data bus. Because the data outputs of both memory devices M1 and M2 are connected together, the data bus drivers in the memory components must have tri-state outputs. That is, only one of the memory components may put data on the system data bus at a time.

Both memory devices in Fig. 9.14 have a chip-select input ($\overline{CS1}$ for block 1 and $\overline{CS2}$ for block 2). Whenever the chip-select input of a memory is active-low, that device takes part in a memory access and puts data on the data bus if $R/\overline{W} = 1$. When $\overline{CS1}$ or $\overline{CS2}$ is inactive (i.e. in a high state) the appropriate data bus drivers are turned off, and no data is put on the data bus by that chip.

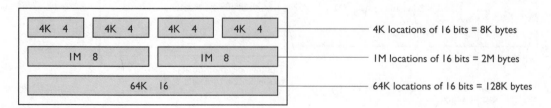

Fig. 9.13 16-bit memory organization.

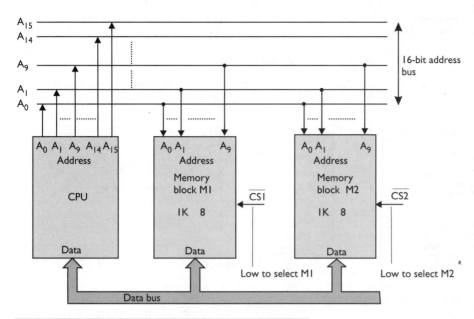

Fig. 9.14 Connecting two 1 kbyte memories to a 16-bit address bus.

Let CS1 be made a function of the address lines A_{10} to A_{15}, so that $\overline{CS1} = f1(A_{15}, A_{14}, A_{13}, A_{12}, A_{11}, A_{10})$. Similarly, let $\overline{CS2}$ be a function of the same address lines, so that $\overline{CS2} = f2(A_{15}, A_{14}, A_{13}, A_{12}, A_{11}, A_{10})$. Suppose we choose functions $f1$ and $f2$ subject to the constraint that there are no values of A_{15}, A_{14}, A_{13}, A_{12}, A_{11}, A_{10} that cause both $\overline{CS1}$ and $\overline{CS2}$ to be low simultaneously. Under these circumstances, the conflict between M1 and M2 is resolved, and the memory map of the system now contains two disjoint 1K blocks of memory. There are several different strategies for decoding A_{10}–A_{16} (i.e. choosing functions $f1$ and $f2$). These strategies may be divided into three groups: *partial address decoding*, *full address decoding*, and *block address decoding*.

Partial address decoding

Partial address decoding is the simplest and most inexpensive form of address decoding to implement. Figure 9.15 demonstrates how two 1 kbyte blocks of memory are connected to the address bus in such a way that both blocks of memory are never accessed simultaneously. The conflict between M1 and M2 is resolved by connecting $\overline{CS1}$ directly to A_{15} of the system address bus and by connecting $\overline{CS2}$ to A_{15} via an inverter. In this way M1 is selected whenever $A_{15} = 0$, and M2 is selected whenever $A_{15} = 1$. Although we have succeeded in distinguishing between M1 and M2 for the cost of a single inverter, a heavy price has been paid. Because $A_{15} = 0$ selects M1 and $A_{15} = 1$ selects M2, it follows that either M1 or M2

will always be selected. Although the system address bus can specify $2^{16} = 64K$ unique addresses, only 2K different locations can be accessed. Address lines A_{10}–A_{14} take no part in the address-decoding process and consequently have no effect on the selection of a location within either *M1* or *M2*.

Figure 9.16 gives the memory map of the system corresponding to Fig. 9.15. As you can see, M1 is repeated 32 times in the lower half of the memory space and M2 is repeated 32 times in the upper half of the memory space, because the five address lines A_{10} to A_{14} take no part in address decoding. In this section, all addresses will be given in hexadecimal form (we don't need to use a subscript).

Partial address decoding is sometimes found in dedicated microcontroller systems where low cost is of paramount importance. The penalty paid when a partial address-decoding scheme is employed is that it prevents full use of the microprocessor's address space and frequently makes it difficult to expand the memory system at a later date.

Full address decoding

A microprocessor system is said to have full address decoding when each addressable location within a memory component responds to a single address on the system's address bus. That is, all the microprocessor's address lines, A_{00}–A_{15}, are used to access each physical memory location, either by specifying a given memory device or by specifying an address within it.

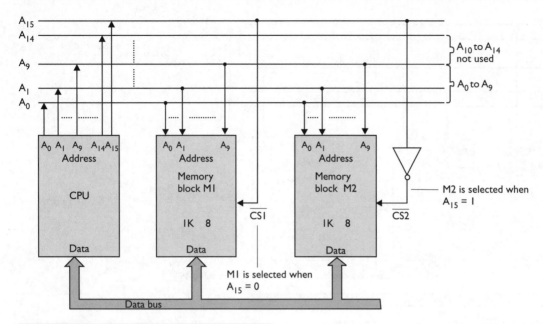

Fig. 9.15 Resolving contention by partial address decoding.

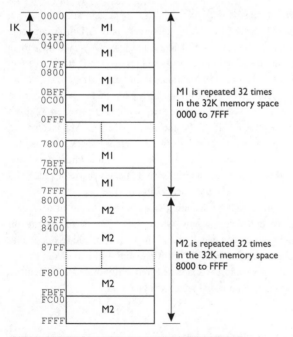

Fig. 9.16 The memory map corresponding to Fig. 9.15.

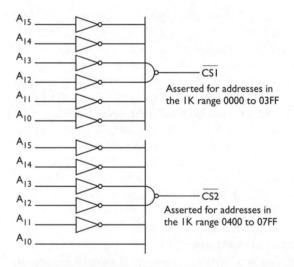

Fig. 9.17 A full address decoder for two 1 K memory blocks of Fig. 9.15.

memory. Address lines A_0 to A_9 select a location in one of the memory components, leaving A_{10} to A_{15} to be decoded. Suppose we select M1 when A_{15}, A_{14}, A_{13}, A_{12}, A_{11}, $A_{10} = 0, 0, 0, 0, 0, 0$ and M2 when A_{15}, A_{14}, A_{13}, A_{12}, A_{11}, $A_{10} = 0, 0, 0, 0, 0, 1$. These address values correspond to the 1K address blocks 0000 to 03FF and 0400 to 07FF. Figure 9.17 demonstrates how we might perform the address decoding with random logic.

Full address decoding represents the ideal but is sometimes impractical because it may require an excessive quantity of hardware to implement it. We will design an address decoder for the pervious example of a system with two 1K blocks of

Block address decoding

Block address decoding is a compromise between partial address decoding and full address decoding. It avoids the inefficient memory usage of partial address decoding, by dividing the memory space into a number of *blocks* or *pages*. Block address decoding is implemented by dividing the processor's address space into a number of equal-sized blocks. This operation is easy to perform because you can buy logic devices that carry out this function (called decoders).

In a typical application of block address decoding, an 8-bit microprocessor's 64K memory space is divided into 4 blocks of 16K. An inexpensive 2-line-to-4-line decoder logic element converts the two high-order address lines, A_{15}–A_{14}, into four lines. Each of these four lines is associated with one of the binary states of address lines A_{15} and A_{14}. The four outputs of this address decoder are used as the chip-select inputs of memory components. The advantage of block address decoding is that no memory component can occupy a memory space larger than a single block. In practice, real microprocessor systems often employ a combination of partial address decoding, full address decoding, and block address decoding. You can further decode these 16K blocks and divide the memory space between several peripheral devices. Figure 9.18 describes how this arrangement might be implemented.

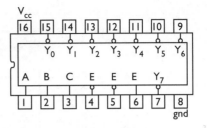

Fig. 9.19 Pinout of the 74138 3-line to 8-line decoder.

Address decoding using *m*-line to *n*-line decoders

The problems of address decoding can be greatly diminished by means of data decoders that decode an *m*-bit binary input into one of *n* outputs, where $n = 2^m$. Figure 9.19 gives the pin-out of a typical 3-line to 8-line decoder, the 74138, and Table 9.2 gives its truth table. This decoder has active-low outputs, making it especially suitable for address-decoding applications, because the majority of memory components have active-low chip-select inputs. Note that a real logic device would be expressed as *74LS138* or *74HC138* depending on the semiconductor technology used to manufacture it (each *technology* has different electrical properties).

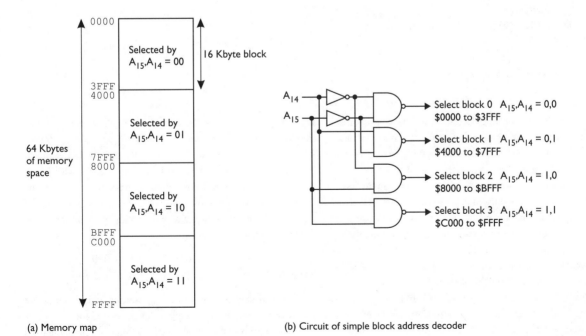

(a) Memory map

(b) Circuit of simple block address decoder

Fig. 9.18 Dividing 64K memory space into four blocks.

Enable inputs			Control inputs			Outputs							
$\overline{E1}$	$\overline{E2}$	E3	C	B	A	$\overline{Y0}$	$\overline{Y1}$	$\overline{Y2}$	$\overline{Y3}$	$\overline{Y4}$	$\overline{Y5}$	$\overline{Y6}$	$\overline{Y7}$
1	1	0	X	X	X	1	1	1	1	1	1	1	1
1	1	1	X	X	X	1	1	1	1	1	1	1	1
1	0	0	X	X	X	1	1	1	1	1	1	1	1
1	0	1	X	X	X	1	1	1	1	1	1	1	1
0	1	0	X	X	X	1	1	1	1	1	1	1	1
0	1	1	X	X	X	1	1	1	1	1	1	1	1
0	0	0	X	X	X	1	1	1	1	1	1	1	1
0	0	1	0	0	0	0	1	1	1	1	1	1	1
0	0	1	0	0	1	1	0	1	1	1	1	1	1
0	0	1	0	1	0	1	1	0	1	1	1	1	1
0	0	1	0	1	1	1	1	1	0	1	1	1	1
0	0	1	1	0	0	1	1	1	1	0	1	1	1
0	0	1	1	0	1	1	1	1	1	1	0	1	1
0	0	1	1	1	0	1	1	1	1	1	1	0	1
0	0	1	1	1	1	1	1	1	1	1	1	1	0

Table 9.2 Truth table of the 74LS138.

Device	Size	Address range	A_{15}	A_{14}	A_{13}	A_{12}	A_{11}	A_{10}	A_9	A_8	A_7	A_6	A_5	A_4	A_3	A_2	A_1	A_0
ROM1	4K	0000–0FFF	0	0	0	0	x	x	x	x	x	x	x	x	x	x	x	x
ROM2	4K	1000–1FFF	0	0	0	1	x	x	x	x	x	x	x	x	x	x	x	x
ROM3	4K	2000–2FFF	0	0	1	0	x	x	x	x	x	x	x	x	x	x	x	x
ROM4	4K	3000–3FFF	0	0	1	1	x	x	x	x	x	x	x	x	x	x	x	x
RAM	8K	4000–5FFF	0	1	0	x	x	x	x	x	x	x	x	x	x	x	x	x
P1	32	6000–601F	0	1	1	0	0	0	0	0	0	0	0	x	x	x	x	x
P2	32	6020–603F	0	1	1	0	0	0	0	0	0	0	1	x	x	x	x	x
.	.	.	.	.	.	.	.	.	.	.	.	.	.	.	.	.	.	.
P8	32	60E0–60FF	0	1	1	0	0	0	0	0	1	1	1	x	x	x	x	x

Table 9.3 Address table of a microprocessor system.

The 74138 3-line to 8-line decoder was a popular address-decoding device in first-generation microprocessor systems. Because the 74138 has three enable inputs (two active-low and one active-high), it is particularly useful when decoders are to be connected in series, or when the enable inputs are to be connected to address lines in order to reduce the size of the block of memory being decoded.

Consider an example of address decoding in an 8-bit microprocessor system using the 74138 3-line to 8-line decoder. A microprocessor system is to be designed with 16 kbyte of ROM in the range $0000–$3FFF using 4 kbyte EPROMs and 8 kbyte of read/write memory in the range $4000–$5FFF using a single 8 kbyte chip. Provision must be made for at least eight memory-mapped peripherals in the 256 byte range $6000–$60FF.

The first step is to work out what address lines have to be decoded to select each memory block. We can do this in two ways. First, if we know the size of the block we can calculate how many address lines are required to select it out of all possible blocks of the same size. Consider the 8K RAM block. The memory space is 64K, so there are 64K/8K = 8 blocks. Since $8 = 2^3$, the three high-order address lines have to be decoded. Alternatively, we can write down the first and last addresses in the block and note which address values are common to all locations; that is,

$4000 = 0\ 1\ 0\ 0\ 0\ 0\ 0\ 0\ 0\ 0\ 0\ 0\ 0\ 0\ 0\ 0$
$5FFF = 0\ 1\ 0\ 1\ 1\ 1\ 1\ 1\ 1\ 1\ 1\ 1\ 1\ 1\ 1\ 1$

As you can see, only the three high-order address lines are common to every location within this memory block.

Table 9.3 gives the address table for this system and shows how one 74LS138 divides the memory space into eight 4 K blocks. A second decoder subdivides one of these blocks to

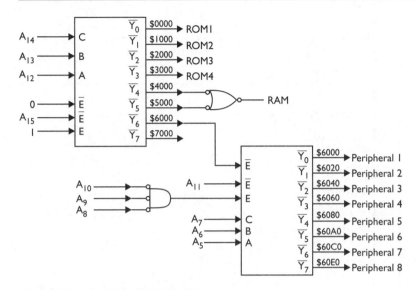

Fig. 9.20 Circuit of an address decoder for Table 9.3.

provide memory space for the peripherals. Figure 9.20 gives a circuit diagram of the address decoder and Fig. 9.21 illustrates its memory map. It is easy to see the advantages of block address decoding. First, RAM, ROM or peripheral devices can be added without further alterations to the address-decoding circuitry by employing the unused outputs of the three decoders. Second, the system is flexible. By modifying the connections between the decoder circuits and the memory components they select, the effective address of those memory components may be altered.

Note how we've selected the 8 K block of RAM in Fig. 9.20. Since the RAM is selected if either of the two 4 K blocks selected by $\overline{Y4}$ or $\overline{Y5}$ is selected, we can OR (in negative logic terms) $\overline{Y4}$ and $\overline{Y5}$ to select the RAM. Because the peripherals don't occupy a 4 K block, we have used address lines A_8 to A_{11} to select a second 3-line to 8-line decoder that decodes the peripheral address space.

Address decoding with the PROM

Address decoding is the art of generating the chip-select signal of a memory component from a number of address lines. Some address decoders employ random logic gates or use m-line to n-line decoders. An alternative to logic synthesis techniques is the programmable read-only memory (PROM) look-up table. Instead of calculating whether the current address selects this or that device, you just read the result from a table. The PROM was a popular address decoder because of its low access time (10–50 ns) and its ability to perform most (if not all) the address decoding required with a

single chip. The PROM address decoder saves valuable space on the microprocessor board and makes the debugging or modification of the system easier. Because PROMs consume more power than modern devices, they've largely been replaced by CMOS PAL (programmable array logic) devices.

The PROM's n address inputs select one of 2^n unique locations. When accessed, each of these locations puts a word on the PROM's m data outputs. This word is the value of the various chip-select signals themselves. That is, the processor's higher-order address lines directly look up a location in the PROM containing the values of the chip selects.

Let's look at a very simple example of a PROM-based address decoder. Table 9.4 describes a 16-location PROM that decodes address lines A_{12} to A_{15} in an 8-bit microcomputer. Address lines A_{12} to A_{15} are connected to the PROM's A_0 to A_3 address inputs. Whenever the CPU accesses its 64 K memory space, the contents of one (and only one) of the locations in the PROM are read. Suppose that the processor reads the contents of memory location $E124. The binary address of this location is 1110000100100100_2 whose four higher-order bits are 1110. Memory location 1110 in the PROM is accessed and its contents applied to the PROM's data pins D0 to D7 to give the values of the 8 chip selects $\overline{CS0}$ to $\overline{CS7}$. In this case, the device connected to D5 (i.e. $\overline{CS5}$) is selected. Figure 9.22 demonstrates how the PROM-based address decoder is used. This is a simplified diagram—in practice we would have to ensure that the PROM was enabled only during a valid memory access (for example, by using the processor's data strobe to enable the decoder).

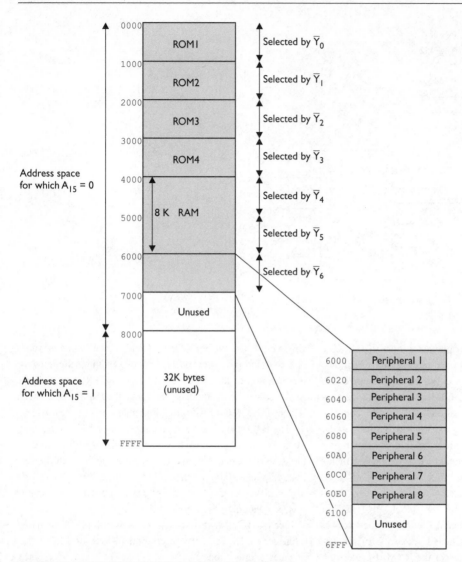

Fig. 9.21 Memory map for the system of Table 9.3 and Fig. 9.20.

Table 9.4 divides the CPU's memory space into 16 equal-sized blocks. Because the processor has a 64 kbyte memory space, each of these blocks is 64 K/16 = 4 kbyte. Consequently, this address decoder can select 4 kbyte devices. If we wanted to select devices as small as 1 kbyte, we would require a PROM with 64 locations (and 6 address inputs). If you examine the D4 ($\overline{\text{CS4}}$) output column, you find that there are two adjacent 0s in this column. If the processor accesses either the 4 K range 6000–6FFF or 7000–7FFF, $\overline{\text{CS4}}$ goes low. In other

words, we have selected an 8 K block by putting a 0 in two adjacent entries. Similarly, there are four 0s in the $\overline{\text{CS5}}$ column to select a 4 × 4 K = 32 K block.

As we have just observed, the PROM can select blocks of memory of differing size. In a system with a 16-bit address bus, a PROM with n address inputs (i.e. 2^n bytes) can fully decode a block of memory with a minimum size of $2^{16}/2^n = 2^{16-n}$ bytes. Larger blocks of memory can be decoded by increasing the number of active entries (in our case, 0s) in

Inputs					Outputs							
(A_{15}) A_3	(A_{14}) A_2	(A_{13}) A_1	(A_{12}) A_0	Range	$\overline{CS0}$ D_0	$\overline{CS1}$ D_1	$\overline{CS2}$ D_2	$\overline{CS3}$ D_3	$\overline{CS4}$ D_4	$\overline{CS5}$ D_5	$\overline{CS6}$ D_6	$\overline{CS7}$ D_7
0	0	0	0	0000–0FFF	0	1	1	1	1	1	1	1
0	0	0	1	1000–1FFF	1	0	1	1	1	1	1	1
0	0	1	0	2000–2FFF	1	1	0	1	1	1	1	1
0	0	1	1	3000–3FFF	1	1	1	0	1	1	1	1
0	1	0	0	4000–4FFF	1	1	1	1	1	1	1	1
0	1	0	1	5000–5FFF	1	1	1	1	1	1	1	1
0	1	1	0	6000–6FFF	1	1	1	1	0	1	1	1
0	1	1	1	7000–7FFF	1	1	1	1	0	1	1	1
1	0	0	0	8000–8FFF	1	1	1	1	1	1	1	1
1	0	0	1	9000–9FFF	1	1	1	1	1	1	1	1
1	0	1	0	A000–AFFF	1	1	1	1	1	1	1	1
1	0	1	1	B000–BFFF	1	1	1	1	1	1	1	1
1	1	0	0	C000–CFFF	1	1	1	1	1	0	1	1
1	1	0	1	D000–DFFF	1	1	1	1	1	0	1	1
1	1	1	0	E000–EFFF	1	1	1	1	1	0	1	1
1	1	1	1	F000–FFFF	1	1	1	1	1	0	1	1

Table 9.4 Address decoding with a PROM.

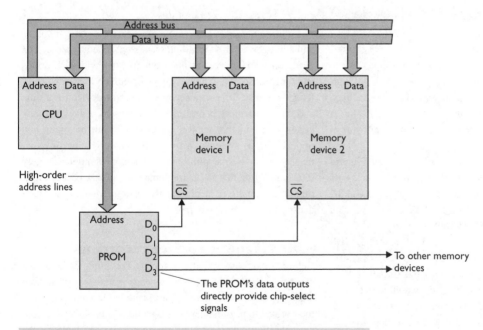

Fig. 9.22 Simplified circuit of a PROM-based decoder corresponding to Table 9.4.

the data column of the PROM's address/data table. The size of the block of memory decoded by a data output is equal to the minimum block size multiplied by the number of active entries in the appropriate data column.

Today, the systems designer can also use programmable logic elements such as PALs and PLAs to implement address decoders.

The structure of 68000-based memory systems

To conclude this section on memory organization, we look at how memory components are connected to a 68000 micro-processor. This processor has a 16 Mbyte memory space and a 16-bit wide data bus. Because the 68000 has a 16-bit wide data bus with data lines d_{00} to d_{15}, memory blocks must be

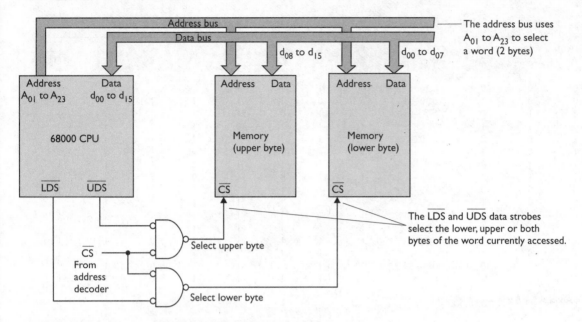

Fig. 9.23 Dealing with byte and word accesses in a 68000-based system.

16 bits wide in order to support both word and byte accesses. The address bus is not composed of 24 address lines A_{23} to A_{00}, but 23 address lines A_{23} to A_{01}. These address lines select a 16-bit word (i.e. 2 bytes), rather than a single byte. Two control signals, $\overline{\text{UDS}}$ (upper data strobe) and $\overline{\text{LDS}}$ (lower data strobe), distinguish between the upper and lower bytes of a 16-bit word, respectively.

Figure 9.23 shows the arrangement of a 68000-based system. If the 68000 accesses a byte on d_{00} to d_{07}, it asserts address strobe $\overline{\text{LDS}}$. If the 68000 accesses a byte on d_{08} to d_{15} it asserts address strobe $\overline{\text{UDS}}$. If the 68000 accesses a word on d_{00} to d_{15} it asserts both $\overline{\text{LDS}}$ and $\overline{\text{UDS}}$ simultaneously. This mechanism provides a pseudo A_{00} (i.e. $\overline{\text{LDS}}$ asserted, $\overline{\text{UDS}}$ negated $= A_{00} = 1$, and $\overline{\text{LDS}}$ negated, $\overline{\text{UDS}}$ asserted $= A_{00} = 0$). If the 68000 accesses a word on d_{00} to d_{15} it asserts both $\overline{\text{LDS}}$ and $\overline{\text{UDS}}$ simultaneously. By means of its two address strobes and 23-bit address bus, the 68000 can address a word and then access either of the bytes at the word address or both bytes at this address. Note that in 68000 systems, the byte on data lines d_{00} to d_{07} is at the *odd* address and the byte on data lines d_{08} to d_{15} is at the even address. We provide several address decoding examples at the end of this chapter.

9.3 Secondary storage

We've already seen that a computer's memory can be partitioned into a high-speed, high-cost, low-capacity main store and a low-speed, low-cost, high-capacity secondary store. The term *secondary store* was once synonymous with disk drives and tape transports, although magnetic bubble memories challenged the disk drive as a secondary storage device for a time and optical memory is replacing disk and tape drives in many applications. In this section we examine both magnetic and optical storage systems. We will also be describing tiny distances—1 μin is one millionth of an inch or approximately 0.025 μm. Note that units are sometimes mixed because disk literature often gives head dimensions in metric units and data density in bits per square inch.

9.3.1 Magnetic surface recording

Before looking at specific magnetic recording devices, we examine the nature of the *ferromagnetic* materials used to store data. The origin of magnetism lies in the motion of electrons in their orbits. In most matter the magnetic effects of electron spin are entirely overcome by the stronger force generated by the thermal vibration of the atoms, which prevents any magnetic interaction between adjacent atoms. The strong interaction between electron spins in ferromagnetic materials such as iron and some of its compounds results in the alignment of electrons over a region of the material called a *domain*. Domains range from 1 mm to several centimeters in size. Because the electron spins are aligned within a domain, the domain exhibits a strong spontaneous magnetization and behaves like a tiny magnet with a North Pole at one end and a South Pole at the other end.

Within a large piece of ferromagnetic material, the magnetic axes of individual domains are arranged at random. Because of the random orientations of the domains, there is no overall magnetic field in the bulk material.

We now describe how a ferromagnetic material can be magnetized into a specific state and used to store data—these basic principles apply to all magnetic recording systems. Suppose we thread a wire through a hole in a ring (called a *toroid*) of a ferromagnetic material and pass a current, *i*, through the wire. The current generates a vector magnetic field, *H*, in the surrounding space, where *H* is proportional to *i*. A magnetic field, *B*, is produced inside the ring by the combined effects of the external field, *H*, and the internal magnetization of the core material. A graph of the relationship between the internal magnetic field *B* and the external magnetic field *H* for a ferromagnetic material is given in Fig. 9.24. This curve is called a *hysteresis loop*.

Suppose that the external field round the wire is initially zero; that is, $H = 0$ because the current flowing through the wire, *i*, is zero. Figure 9.24 demonstrates that there are two possible values of *B* when $H = 0$: $+B_r$ and $-B_r$. These two states represent a logical one and a logical zero. The suffix r in B_r stands for *remnant*, and refers to the magnetism remaining in the ring when the external field is zero. Like the flip-flop, this magnetic material has two stable states and can remain in either of the states indefinitely. Unlike the flip-flop, the ferromagnetic material is a non-volatile store and requires no power source to retain data.

Assume that initially the ferromagnetic material is magnetized in a logical zero state and has an internal field $-B_r$. If a negative external field is applied (i.e. negative *i*, therefore negative *H*), the value of the internal magnetization *B* goes slightly more negative than $-B_r$ and we move towards point P in Fig. 9.24. If *H* is now reduced to zero, the remnant magnetization returns to $-B_r$. In other words, there is no net change in the state of the ferromagnetic material.

Now consider applying a small positive internal field *H*. The internal magnetization is slightly increased from $-B_r$ and we move along the curve towards point Q. If the external magnetization is reduced we move back to $-B_r$. However, if *H* is increased beyond the value $+H_m$, the magnetization of the material flips over at Q, and we end up at point R. Now, when we reduce the external field *H* to zero, we return to $+B_r$ and not to $+B_r$. That is, if the material is initially in a negative state, increasing the external magnetization beyond H_m causes it to assume a positive state. A magnetic field of less than H_m is insufficient to change the material's state.

Similarly, if the ferromagnetic material is in a one state $(+B_r)$, a positive value of *H* has little effect, but a more negative value of *H* than $+H_m$ will switch the material to a zero state $(-B_r)$.

The switching of a ferromagnetic material from one state to another is done by applying a pulse with a magnitude greater than I_m to the wire. A pulse of $+I_m$ always forces the material into a logical one state, and a pulse of $-I_m$ forces it into a logical zero state.

The hysteresis curve can readily be explained in terms of the behavior of domains. Figure 9.25 shows a region of a ferromagnetic material at three stages. At stage (a) the magnetic material is said to be in its virgin state with the domains

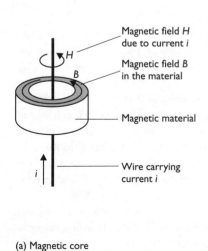

(a) Magnetic core

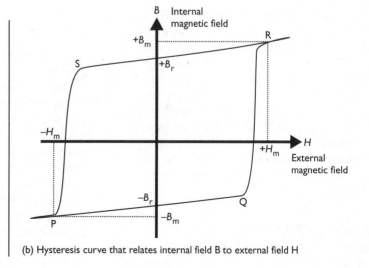

(b) Hysteresis curve that relates internal field B to external field H

Fig. 9.24 The hysteresis curve.

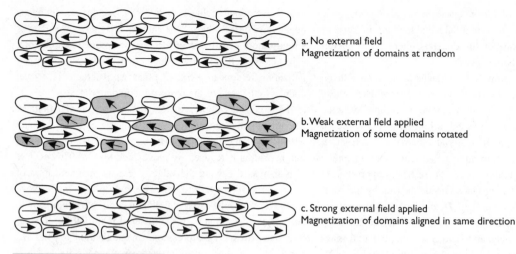

a. No external field
Magnetization of domains at random

b. Weak external field applied
Magnetization of some domains rotated

c. Strong external field applied
Magnetization of domains aligned in same direction

Fig. 9.25 The behavior of domains.

oriented at random, and has no net magnetization. This corresponds to the origin of the hysteresis curve, where $H = 0$ and $B = 0$.

At stage (b) an external magnetic field has been applied and some of the domains have rotated their magnetic axes to line up with the external field. As the external field is increased, more and more domains flip over, and there comes a point where the domains already aligned with the external field reinforce it, causing yet more domains to flip over. This process soon develops into an avalanche as the internal field rapidly builds up, and all domains are aligned with the external field. At this point, stage (c), the bulk material is fully magnetized and is said to be saturated.

The precise form of the hysteresis curve of Fig. 9.24 (also called a B–H curve) differs from one magnetic material to another. In general, the best B–H curve for the purpose of storing data is square, so that the transition from one state to another (i.e. from $-B_r$ to $+B_r$) takes place for an infinitesimally small change in H. Such a magnetic material is said to have a *square-loop B–H characteristic*. Magnetic materials displaying strong hysteresis effects are called *hard*, whereas those displaying little or no hysteresis are called *soft*. Now that we have described the basic principles of magnetization, we are going to look at how it is applied in practice.

Magnetizing a flat surface

The operating principles of disk drives (both hard and floppy) and tape units are virtually the same: the former records data on a flat platter (i.e. *disk*) coated with a magnetic material,

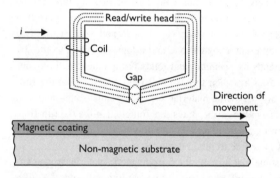

Fig. 9.26 Surface recording.

whereas the latter records data on a thin band of flexible plastic coated with magnetic material. Figure 9.26 illustrates the generic recording process—the same model serves both disk and tape systems.

The write head used to store data consists of a ring of *high-permeability* soft magnetic material with a coil wound round it. High permeability means that the material offers a low resistance to a magnetic field. The material of the write head is magnetically soft and does not have a square-loop hysteresis. Consequently it does not exhibit residual or remnant magnetization.

The most important feature of the write head is a tiny *air-gap* in the ring. When a current flows in the coil a magnetic flux is created within the ring. This flux flows round the core, but when it encounters the air-gap, it spreads out into the surrounding air as illustrated in Fig. 9.27.

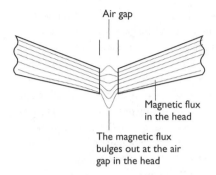

Fig. 9.27 The air gap.

Because the head is either close to or in contact with the recording medium, the magnetic field round the air gap passes through the magnetic material coating the backing. If this field is strong enough, it causes the magnetic particles (i.e. domains) within the coating to become aligned with the field from the head. Since the magnetic surface is moving, a continuous strip of surface is magnetized as it passes under the write head. If the direction of the current in the coil is changed the field reverses and the magnetic particles in the coating are magnetized in the opposite direction. Figure 9.28 shows how the domains in the surface material might be magnetized (North–South or South–North) after passing under the write head. We have also plotted the current in the write head on the same figure.

Reading data

Having recorded data in the form of a magnetized band along a track, we have to reverse the process to retrieve the data.

A read head is essentially the same as a write head (sometimes a single head serves as both read and write head). When the magnetized material moves past the gap in the read head, a *magnetic flux* is induced in the head. The flux, in turn, induces a voltage across the terminals of the coil that is proportional to the rate of change of the flux, rather than the absolute value of the magnetic flux itself. Figure 9.29 shows the waveforms associated with writing and reading data on a magnetic surface. The voltage from the read head is given by

$$v(t) = K \, d\Phi/dt$$

K is a constant depending on the physical parameters of the system, and Φ is the flux produced by the moving magnetic medium. Since the differential of a constant is zero, only transitions of magnetic flux can be detected. The output from a region of the surface with a constant magnetization is zero, making it difficult to record digital data directly on tape or disk, as we shall soon see.

As time has passed, engineers have produced greater and greater packing densities (over 10 million bits per square inch). Using vertical recording (see later) densities of over 15 million bits per square inch are possible. One of the main sources of improvement has been in the composition of the magnetic medium used to store data. The size of the particles has been reduced and their magnetic properties improved. Some tapes employ a thin metallic film, rather than individual particles. Metal oxide coatings are about 800 µm thick with oxide particles approximately 25 µm by 600 µm with an ellipsoidal shape. A thin film coating is typically only 100 µm thick.

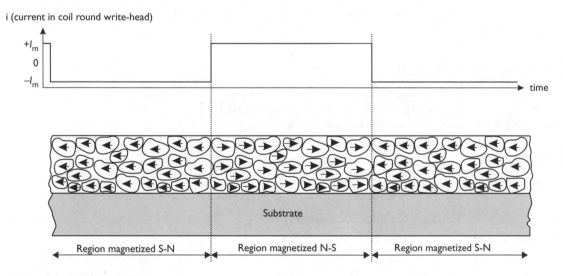

Fig. 9.28 The magnetized layer.

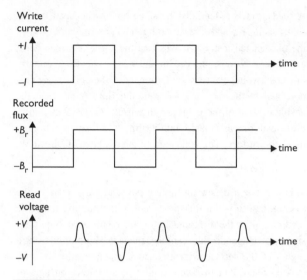

Fig. 9.29 Read/write waveforms.

Vertical recording

The basic recording process we have just described uses horizontal recording, in which the magnetic domains on the surface of the recording medium are magnetized in the horizontal plane (i.e. the same plane as the medium itself).

Unfortunately, increasing the packing density of bits by reducing the size of the magnetized regions introduces a phenomenon called *demagnetization* that makes it harder to read the stored data. Figure 9.30 illustrates the effects of demagnetization. When the tiny magnets representing the stored data are placed end to end with North Pole to North Pole, the magnetic fields from the magnets tend to cancel each other out (hence the term demagnetization).

An alternative form of recording employs *vertical magnetization* in which the domains are magnetized in the plane perpendicular to the surface of the medium (see Fig. 9.31). Vertical recording requires a special magnetic medium and a special read/write head. However, not only can we use vertical recording to create very tiny data cells, but the effects of demagnetization are reduced and there is a very sharp change of field at cell boundaries making it easier to read back the recorded data. Unfortunately, it is not quite as easy to design magnetic media suitable for vertical recording as it is to design media for conventional horizontal recording.

Thin film heads

The conventional read/write head uses a ring of magnetic material with a tiny air gap. In 1978 IBM developed the *thin film head*, Fig. 9.32, that employs a permalloy head (permalloy is a magnetically soft alloy of nickel and iron) around which is wound a spiral of copper. Thin film heads are constructed by the same type of technology used in the manufacture of semiconductors. Consequently, the thin film read/write head can be made with great precision, mass produced at relatively low cost, and made as small as necessary. When not energized (i.e. no current flowing in the coil), the magnetization of the permalloy is parallel to the surface of the recording medium. When a write current flows through the coil, the magnetic field from the head is rotated through 90° and therefore magnetizes the surface. A thin film head permits data to be recorded and played back at a higher speed than a conventional read/write head.

Later, when we describe modern disk drives, we will introduce other technologies that have been used to increase the density of bits.

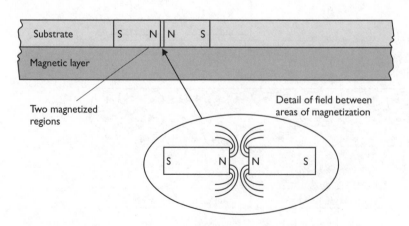

Fig. 9.30 Horizontal recording and demagnetization.

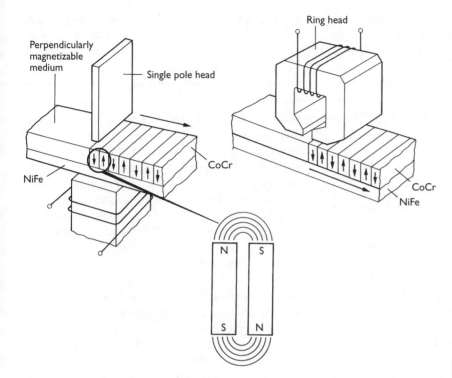

Fig. 9.31 Vertical recording.

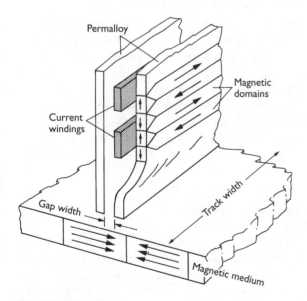

Fig. 9.32 Thin film head.

9.3.2 Data encoding techniques

Now that we've described the basic process by which information is recorded on a magnetic medium, we are going to look at some of the ways in which digital data is encoded before

it is recorded. All magnetic secondary stores record data serially, a bit a time, along the path described by the motion of the magnetic medium under the write head. Tape transports have multiple parallel read/write heads and record several parallel tracks simultaneously across the width of the tape. However, the data recorded along each track is recorded serially.

You can't transmit the sequence of logical 1s and 0s to be recorded directly to the write head. If you were to record a long string of 0s or 1s by simply saturating the surface at $-B_r$ or $+B_r$, no signal would be received during playback. Why? Because only a *change* in flux creates an output signal. A process called encoding or *modulation* must first be used to transform the data pattern into a suitable code. Essentially, the source data has to be encoded so that the recorded data is always changing even if the source is all 1s or 0s. Similarly, when the information is read back from the tape it must be decoded or *demodulated* to extract the original digital data. The actual encoding/decoding process chosen is a compromise between the desire to pack as many bits of data as possible into a given surface area while preserving the reliability of the system and keeping its complexity within reasonable bounds.

Let's look at some of the possible recording codes (beginning with a code that illustrates the problem of recording long strings of 1s and 0s). However, before we can compare various encoding techniques we need to describe some of the parameters or properties of a code. In what follows the term *flux reversal* indicates a change of state in the recorded magnetic field in the coating of the tape or disk. Simply reversing the direction of the current in the write head causes a flux reversal. Some of the criteria by which a recording code may be judged are as follows.

1. **Efficiency**   The storage efficiency of a code is defined as the number of stored bits per flux reversal and is expressed as a percentage. The maximum value is 100 percent and corresponds to one bit per flux reversal.

2. **Inter-symbol correlation**   The symbols representing the data to be stored should be as unlike each other as possible to make it easy to distinguish between the symbols even if they are badly distorted due to defects in the recording/playback process. In a two-valued digital system, the symbols should be identical but of opposite sign (i.e. inverted). This is defined as 100 percent correlation.

3. **Bandwidth**   The bandwidth occupied by a signal is a measure of its rate of change. The French mathematician Fourier demonstrated that any waveform can be expressed as an infinite series of sine waves and cosine waves with frequencies of f, $2f$, $3f$, ... etc. The bandwidth occupied by a signal is the range of frequencies over which it extends. Bandwidth is measured in units called hertz (Hz) which correspond to the old *cycles per second*. For example, the telephone network has a bandwidth of 300–3300 Hz and does not transmit frequencies above and below these limits. As human speech has a wider bandwidth, the telephone distorts it by cutting off low and high frequencies. Consequently, the quality of telephone speech is rather poor. In engineering terms, very low and very high frequencies are difficult to handle. A recording code with a narrow bandwidth is preferable to one with a wide bandwidth. In particular, a code with very low frequency components approaching D.C. (direct current or zero frequency) should be avoided.

4. **Self-clocking**   The encoded data must ultimately be decoded and separated into individual bits. A code that provides a method of splitting the bits off from one another is called self-clocking and is highly desirable. A non-self-clocking code provides no timing information and makes it difficult to separate the data stream into individual bits.

5. **Complexity**   The simpler the encoding and decoding processes are the less they cost. Because the recording and playback processes involve time-varying analog signals, the precision and tolerance of the circuitry should not be so great that its cost is prohibitive. Although the signals involved in digital recording are nominally digital (i.e. two-state), in practice the signal read off the tape or disk has all the properties of an analog signal.

6. **Noise immunity**   An ideal code should have the largest immunity to extraneous signals (i.e. noise). Noise in magnetic recording systems is caused by imperfections in the magnetic coating leading to *drop-outs* and *drop-ins*. A drop-out is a loss of signal caused by missing magnetic material, and a drop-in is a noise pulse. Another source of noise is *cross-talk* which is the signal picked up by the head from adjacent tracks. Cross-talk is introduced because the tracks are very close together and because the read/write head might not be perfectly aligned with the track on the surface of the recording medium. Noise can also be caused by imperfect erasure. Suppose a track is recorded and later erased. If the erase head didn't pass exactly over the center of the track, it's possible that the far edge of the track might not have been fully erased. When the track is re-recorded and later played back, a spurious signal from the unerased portion of the track will be added to the wanted signal.

7. **Bit pattern sensitivity**   Bit pattern sensitivity is the susceptibility of a code to certain bit patterns occurring in the data to be encoded and is also known as *pulse crowding* and *intersymbol interference*. Some encoding schemes can be very susceptible to errors if the data stream contains long strings of 1s or 0s. Schemes exist for reducing the bit pattern sensitivity of a code by an arrangement called write precompensation, which involves predistorting the write signal to the record head to take account of the properties of particular sequences of digits.

Return-to-zero encoding

In its pure form, return-to-zero, RZ, recording requires that the surface be unmagnetized to store a zero and magnetized by a short pulse to store a 1. Because no signal is applied to the write head when recording a zero, any 1s already written on the tape or disk are not erased or overwritten. Consequently, RZ encoding is not a practical proposition. A slight modification of RZ recording is return-to-bias recording, RB, in which a 0 is recorded by saturating the magnetic coating in one direction, and a 1 by saturating it in the opposite direction by a short pulse of the opposite polarity.

Figure 9.33 illustrates the principles of return-to-bias recording and playback. The actual pulse width used depends

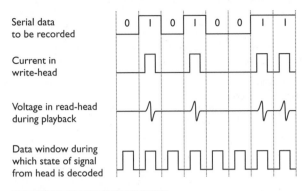

Fig. 9.33 Return-to-bias recording.

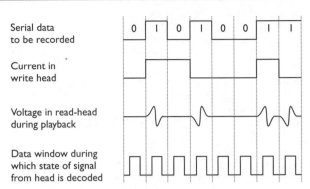

Fig. 9.34 Non-return to zero one recording (NRZ1).

on the characteristics of the head and the magnetic medium. A wide pulse reduces the maximum packing density of the recorded data and is wasteful of tape or disk surface but is easy to detect, whereas a very narrow pulse may be difficult to detect.

The recording technique in Fig. 9.33 is very simple: the current in the write head saturates the surface to $-B_r$ and each time the recorded data is a 1, a positive pulse saturates the surface to $+B_r$.

Data is read from the disk/tape by first generating a data window, which is a time-slot during which the signal from the read head is to be sampled. The signal from the read head is sampled at the center of this window. Unfortunately, a sequence of 0s generates no output from the read head, and there is no simple way of making sure that the data window falls exactly in the middle of a data cell. For this reason return-to-bias is said to be non-self-clocking. The worst-case efficiency of RB recording is 50 percent (when the data is a string of 1s), the correlation fair, but the noise sensitivity poor. A low-frequency response is needed to handle the signal from the disk/tape. For all these reasons, RB recording is not popular and is seldom employed.

Non-return to zero encoding

One of the first widely used data encoding techniques was called *modified non-return to zero* or NRZ1. Each time a logical one is to be recorded, the current flowing in the head is reversed. When reading data each change in flux is interpreted as a logical one. Figure 9.34 illustrates NRZ1 recording. NRZ1 requires a maximum of one flux transition per bit of stored data, and represents the optimum packing density of 100 percent. NRZ1 has a poor correlation, requires a low-frequency bandwidth, and has fair sensitivity to noise. The greatest drawback of NRZ1 is that it isn't self-clocking and

it's impossible to reliably retrieve a long string of 0s (i.e. a period with no signal from the read-head).

Phase encoding

Several codes are based on a recording technique called *phase* (or *Manchester*) *encoding* that was once widely used by magnetic tape transports. A flux transition is located at the center of each and every bit cell: a low-to-high transition indicates a one and a high-to-low transition a zero. Because there's always a flux transition at the center of each data cell, a clock signal can be derived from the recorded data and therefore this encoding technique is self-clocking. A stream of alternate 1s and 0s requires one flux transition per bit, whereas a stream of 1s or 0s requires two flux changes per bit.

Figure 9.35 illustrates how the sequence 01010011 is phase encoded. Phase encoding has a low efficiency of 50 percent because up to two transitions per bit required. The correlation is 100 percent because there is a maximum difference between 1s and 0s. The bandwidth requirements are good because there is no low frequency component in the recorded signal. However, as up to two flux transitions are required per bit, the maximum recorded frequency is twice that of NRZ1 at an equivalent bit density. The circuit complexity is greater than that of NRZ1, although suitable encoder/decoders are available as single chips. Finally, phase encoding has a good immunity to noise. Because of these attributes phase encoding is widely used in digital data transmission systems as well as magnetic recording systems.

Frequency modulation

Frequency modulation, FM, was once widely used to encode data in floppy disk systems. Like phase encoding, this technique is self-clocking. The encoded waveform is created by marking the boundary of each data cell with a clock pulse.

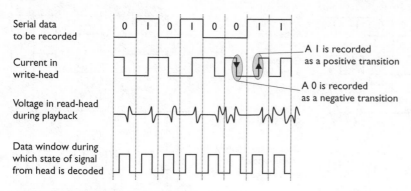

Fig. 9.35 Phase encoded recording (PE).

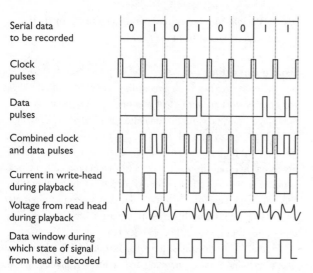

Fig. 9.36 Frequency modulation (FM).

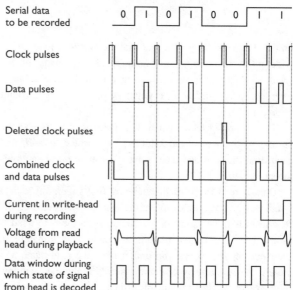

Fig. 9.37 Modified frequency modulation (MFM).

A pulse is then placed at the center of a cell to denote a logical one, otherwise the cell is left empty. Figure 9.36 shows the clock pulses, data pulses, and combined clock and data pulse waveform. This waveform is then used to record the information by reversing the current flowing in the write head (and therefore the flux in the magnetic medium) at each pulse. FM recording is identical to PE in all its properties except that a one or zero is recorded by the presence or absence of a transition at the center of a cell rather than by the direction of the transition. Frequency modulation is somewhat a misnomer. True fréquency modulation is described in Chapter 11 when we deal with data transmission.

Modified frequency modulation

Modified frequency modulation, MFM, has replaced FM as the standard for the recording of data on floppy disks. The terms FM and MFM are little used outside technical literature. In general, FM is referred to as *single density* recording and MFM as *double density* recording, because MFM stores twice the amount of data for a given surface area. MFM is therefore 100 percent efficient and needs only one flux transition per bit.

MFM is an attempt to raise the efficiency of FM encoding to the level of NRZ1, while maintaining FM's self-clocking properties. Figure 9.37 demonstrates that the encoded FM signal may be divided conceptually into two separate signals: a timing signal consisting of a pulse at each cell boundary, and a data signal consisting of a pulse at the center of each data cell containing a logical one. It is tempting to ask whether we can remove the clock signal, because it carries no useful information.

As in FM, a data pulse is placed at the center of each cell containing a one. Unlike FM, the clock pulses at the boundary

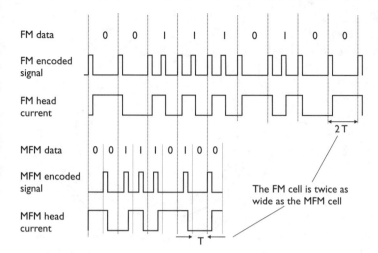

Fig. 9.38 FM and MFM drawn to the same time-scale.

of the cells are deleted, but with one exception. Whenever two zeros are to be recorded in succession, a clock pulse is placed between them (see Fig. 9.37). MFM has similar properties to FM and PE, although its correlation is lower. Because the maximum gap between flux transitions is no more than $2T$, where T is the width of a data cell, MFM is self-clocking.

Floppy disk drives store information at a constant bit rate, so MFM provides twice the storage capacity of FM because the clock pulses of FM have been replaced by data pulses in MFM. The ability of MFM to store twice as much data as FM is not clear from Figs. 9.36 and 9.37, as their scales are intrinsically different. Figure 9.38 presents the same data waveforms for FM and MFM on identical time-scales. It can now be appreciated that MFM stores twice the information on the same surface area. The greater recording density of MFM has important implications when system reliability is considered because of the greater susceptibility of MFM to pulse crowding and imperfections in the magnetic medium.

Group codes and RLL codes

Another encoding technique found in both magnetic disk and tape secondary stores is the *group code* that gained popularity in the early 1970s when IBM first adopted it for one of their tape systems. Simple coding schemes assign a particular waveform to each bit to be recorded, which proves incompatible with some of the requirements of an optimum code in terms of bandwidth, intersymbol correlation, and flux density. A group code takes n bits to represent an m-bit source word, where $n > m$. Thus, although there are 2^n possible code words, only 2^m of these 2^n values are used to create 2^m different waveforms for recording on the tape or disk. Waveforms with

poor recording and playback characteristics can be removed from the code words to be stored on the tape or disk; that is, only the 'best' waveforms are used to store data. For example, the 4/5 group code in Table 9.5 uses five bits to encode four bits of data. The algorithm that maps the four bits of data onto the 5-bit group code to be recorded avoids the occurrence of more than two 0s in succession. Therefore, this group code guarantees at least one flux transition per three recorded bits, making the code self-clocking.

Another recording code is the RLL or *run-length limited* code. Instead of inserting clock pulses to provide timing information as in FM and MFM recording, RLL codes limit the longest sequence of 0s that can be recorded in a burst. Because the maximum number of 0s in succession is fixed,

Input code	Output code
0 0 0 0	1 1 0 0 1
0 0 0 1	1 1 0 1 1
0 0 1 0	1 0 0 1 0
0 0 1 1	1 0 0 1 1
0 1 0 0	1 1 1 0 1
0 1 0 1	1 0 1 0 1
0 1 1 0	1 0 1 1 0
0 1 1 1	1 0 1 1 1
1 0 0 0	1 1 0 1 0
1 0 0 1	0 1 0 0 1
1 0 1 0	0 1 0 1 0
1 0 1 1	0 1 0 1 1
1 1 0 0	1 1 1 1 0
1 1 0 1	0 1 1 0 1
1 1 1 0	0 1 1 1 0
1 1 1 1	0 1 1 1 1

Table 9.5 ANSI X3.54 4/5 group code.

timing circuits can be designed to reliably locate the center of each bit cell. A run-length limited code is expressed as Rm,n, where m defines the minimum number of 0s and n the maximum number of 0s between two 1s.

A typical RLL code is RLL 2,7 which means that each 1 is separated from the next 1 by two to seven 0s. In RLL a maximum of four 0s may precede a 1 and three 0s may follow a 1. Because RLL records only certain bit patterns, the source data must be encoded before it can be passed to the RLL coder; for example, the source pattern 0011 would be converted to 00001000.

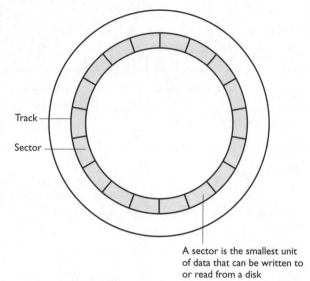

A sector is the smallest unit of data that can be written to or read from a disk

Fig. 9.39 Structure of a disk.

9.4 Disk drive principles

We now look at the construction and characteristics of the two fundamental ways of arranging magnetic memories—the disk drive and the tape transport. We describe first the hard disk drive and then the floppy disk.

The hard disk is a flat, circular, rigid sheet of aluminum coated with a thin layer of magnetic material. This disk rotates continually about its central axis in much the same way as a black vinyl disc rotates in a gramophone player (for readers old enough to remember the days before the CD). The read/write head is positioned at the end of an arm above the surface of the disk. As the disk rotates, the read/write head traces a circular path or *track* around the disk. Digital information is stored along concentric tracks round the disk (Fig. 9.39). We will soon see that data is written in blocks called *sectors* along the track. Hard disks vary in size from 8 in (older miniframes) to 3½ and 5¼ in (personal computers) to 1.3–2½ in (laptop portable computers). The rotational speed of disks in personal computers was 3600 r.p.m., although 7200 r.p.m. is now common and some disks rotate at over 10 000 r.p.m. Track spacing is of the order of 2500 tracks/in. As time passes, track spacing will continue to improve significantly, whereas the speed of rotation will not grow at anything like the same rate. It is possible that glass disks will replace aluminum disks because glass is less temperature-sensitive than aluminum and is more durable.

Figure 9.40 illustrates the structure of a disk drive. A significant difference between the gramophone disk (but not the CD) and the magnetic disk is that the groove on the audio disc is physically cut into its surface, whereas the tracks on a magnetic disk are simply the circular paths traced out by the motion of the disk under the read/write head. Passing a current through the head magnetizes the moving surface of the disk and writes data along the track. Similarly, when reading

data, the head is moved to the required track and the motion of the magnetized surface induces a tiny voltage in the coil of the read head.

A precision servomechanism called an *actuator* moves or 'steps' the arm holding the head horizontally along a radius from track to track. An actuator is an electromechanical device that converts an electronic signal into mechanical motion. Remember the difference between the magnetic disk and the gramophone record. In the former the tracks are concentric and the head steps from track to track, whereas in the latter a continuous spiral groove is cut into the surface of the disk and the stylus gradually moves towards the center as the disk rotates.

The characteristics of disk drives vary from manufacturer to manufacturer and are continually being improved on at an immense rate. A high-performance disk drive of the late 1990s had a rotational speed of 5400 r.p.m. (i.e. 90 revolutions per second), a capacity of 18 Gbyte (approximately 10^{10} bits), an average seek time of 8 ms (*seek time* is the time taken to locate a given track), and could transfer data to the computer at over 10 Mbyte per second. Only a decade earlier, a typical hard disk in a PC had a capacity of 20 Mbyte and an access time of over 70 ms. During the 1990s, average disk storage densities were increasing at a rate of about 60 percent per year compounded (this is a phenomenal rate of growth). However, the improvement in performance (access time and data rate) over the same period grew at a more modest 7 percent per year.

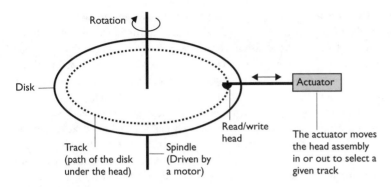

Fig. 9.40 Principle of the disk drive.

Prior to the mid-1990s, disk drives were relatively expensive items and often cost more than the CPU and main memory. Even today, a high-capacity, fast, state-of-the-art hard disk is one of the most expensive components in a computer. The cost of a disk drive lies in its complex and precise mechanical structure. Manufacturers have reduced the effective cost per megabyte of disk drives by stacking two or more disks on a common spindle and using multiple heads as described by Fig. 9.41. A drive might have three disks with six surfaces and six heads that move together when driven by the common actuator. The motion of the heads over the corresponding tracks on each of the surfaces describes a *cylinder*.

The parameters of a rigid disk are impressive. The magnetic layer is only 0.01 μm thick (i.e. about 2000 atoms deep) and the read/write head is positioned 0.2 μm above the surface of the platter. On top of the magnetic layer is a lubricating layer of a fluorocarbon that is about one molecule thick. The structure of the heads themselves is quite complex. Not only must they have the correct electrical and magnetic properties (the air gap in the read/write head may be only 50 μm wide), but also the correct mechanical properties. If the head were actually in physical contact with the disk surface, the abrasive magnetic coating would soon wear it out because its velocity over the surface of the disk is of the order of 100 km/hour. The head is mounted in a holder called a slipper positioned above the disk at about 0.2 μm from the surface. We cannot directly achieve such a level of precision with current engineering technology. However, by exploiting the head's aerodynamic properties it can be made to fly in the moving layer of air just above the surface of the disk.

When an object moves, the air near its surface, called the *boundary layer*, moves with it. At some distance above the surface the air is still. Consequently a velocity gradient exists

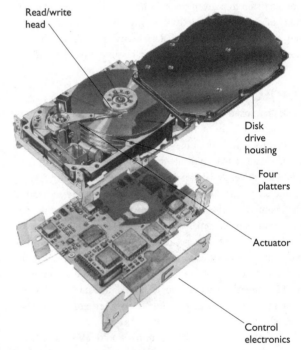

Fig. 9.41 The multiple platter disk drive.

between the surface and the still air. At a certain point above the disk's surface, the velocity of the air flowing over the head generates enough lift to match the pressure of the spring pushing the head towards the disk. At this point, the head is in equilibrium and floats above the disk. Modern slippers fly below 70×10^{-9} m (i.e. 0.07 μm) and have longitudinal grooves cut in them to dump some of the lift. The precision of a modern slipper is so great that the acid in a fingerprint caused by careless handling can destroy its aerodynamic contour.

The height at which the head flies above the surface of the disk is related to the surface finish or roughness of the magnetic coating. If the magnetic material is polished, the surface to head gap can be reduced by 50 percent in comparison with an unpolished surface.

Occasionally, the head does hit the surface and is said to *crash*. A crash can damage part of the track and this track must be labeled *bad* and the lost data rewritten from a backup copy of the file.

The disk controller (i.e. the electronic system that controls the operation of a disk drive) specifies a track and sector and either reads its contents into a buffer (i.e. temporary store) or writes the contents of the buffer to the disk. Some computer scientists call a disk drive a random access device because you can step to a given track without having to read the contents of each track. Strictly speaking, disk drives are sequential access devices because it is necessary to wait until the desired sector moves under the head before it can be read.

9.4.1 Operational parameters

Disk drive users are often most interested in three parameters: the *total capacity* of the system, the *rate* at which data is written to or read from the disk, and its average *access time*. In the late 1990s typical storage capacities ranged from 4 Gbyte to over 20 Gbyte, data rates were several megabytes/s and average access times from 8 ms to 12 ms. By the end of the century, data densities will have reached 10 Gbit/in^2 and track widths of the order of 1 μm.

A disk drive's average access time is composed of three parts: the time required to step to the desired track (*seek* time), the time taken for the disk to rotate so that the sector to be read is under the head (*latency*), and the time taken to read the data. In practice, the reading time is often left out of published access times.

The average time to step from track to track is quite difficult to determine because the head doesn't move at constant velocity and considerations such as head-settling time need to be taken into account. Each seek consists of four distinct phases:

- *acceleration* (the arm is accelerated until it reaches approximately halfway to its destination track)
- *coasting* (after acceleration on long seeks the arm moves at its maximum velocity)
- *deceleration* (the head must slow down and stop at its destination)
- *settling* (the head has to be exactly positioned over the desired track).

Designing head-positioning mechanisms isn't easy. If you make the arm on which the head is mounted very light (to make it easy to accelerate the head assembly), the arm might be too flimsy and twist. If you make the arm stiffer (and therefore heavier), it may be impossible to seek a track without an exorbitantly expensive actuator.

The average number of steps per access depends on the arrangement of the data on the disk and on what happens to the head between successive accesses. If the head is parked at the periphery of the disk, it must move further on average than if it is parked at the center of the tracks. Figure 9.42 shows a file composed of six sectors arranged at random over the surface of the disk. Consequently, the head must move from track to track at random when the file is read sector by sector.

In the absence of any other information, a crude estimate of the average stepping time is one third the number of tracks multiplied by the time taken to step from one track to the adjacent track. This figure is based on the assumption that the head moves a random distance from its current track to its next track each time a seek operation is carried out. If the head were to be retracted to track 0 after each seek, the average access time would be half the total number of tracks multiplied by the track to track stepping time. If the head were to be parked in the middle of the tracks after each seek, the average access time would be $\frac{1}{4}$ of the number of tracks multiplied by the track to track stepping time.

Very short seeks (1 to 4 tracks) are dominated by head-settling time. Short seeks in the range 200 to 400 tracks are dominated by the constant acceleration (speedup) phase and

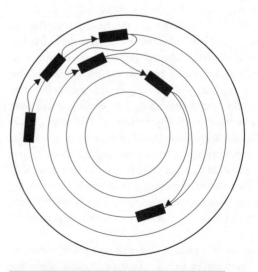

Fig. 9.42 The arrangement of the sectors of a file.

the seek time is proportional to the square root of the number of tracks to step plus the settle time. Finally, long seeks are dominated by the constant velocity (coast) phase and the seek time is proportional to the number of tracks.

The access time of a disk is made up of its seek time and the time to access a given sector once a track has been reached (the *latency*). The latency is easy to calculate. If you assume that the head has just stepped to a given track, the minimum latency is zero (the sector is just arriving under the head). The worst case latency is one revolution (the head has just missed the sector and has to wait for it to go round). On average, the latency is $\frac{1}{2}t_{\text{rev}}$, where t_{rev} is the time for a single revolution of the platter. If a disk rotates at 7200 r.p.m., its latency is given by

$$\frac{1}{2} \times \frac{1}{(7200 \div 60)} = 0.004\,17\,\text{s} = 4.17\,\text{ms}$$

Another important parameter is the rate at which data is transferred to and from the disk. If a disk rotates at R revolutions per minute, has s sectors per track, and each sector contains B bits, the capacity of a track is $B \cdot s$ bits. These $B \cdot s$ bits are read (or written) in $60/R$ seconds. Therefore, the data rate is given by $B \cdot s/(60/R) = B \cdot s \cdot R/60$ bits/s. This is, of course, the actual rate at which data is read from the disk. Buffering the data in the drive's electronics allows it to be transmitted to the host computer at a different rate.

The length of a track close to the center of a disk is much less than that of a track near to the outer edge of the disk. In order to maximize the storage capacity, some systems use *zoning* in which the outer tracks have more sectors than the inner tracks.

Modern disk drives must be tolerant to *shock* (i.e. acceleration caused by movement). This requirement is particularly important for disk drives in portable equipment such as laptop computers. Two shock parameters are normally quoted. One refers to the tolerance to shock when the disk is inoperative and the other to shock while the disk is running. Shock can cause two problems. One is physical damage to the surface of the disk if the head crashes into it (this is called *head slap*). The other is damage to data structures if the head is moved to another track during a write operation. Shock sensors can be incorporated in the disk drive to detect the beginning of a 'shock event' and disable any write operation in progress.

recording/playback mechanism (i.e. how data is transferred has no effect on how data is physically recorded). When hard disk drives first appeared, data was transferred between the computer and drive in the form it was to be written or read (i.e. the *raw* digital pulses). Disk drives were 'unintelligent' and lacked sophisticated control systems. The signal processing electronics was located on an interface card in the computer. All signal processing is now carried out by circuits located in the disk drive housing.

If you pick up a catalog of disk drives from a retailer, you will find that the drives are often listed in terms of the interface between the disk drive and the computer. In the personal computer word, the interface is usually IDE (integrated drive electronics) or SCSI (small computer system interface).

The IDE interface is little more than a parallel data highway that copies data between the PC's AT bus and the disk drive. The software (or *firmware* because it is in read-only memory) that controls the IDE interface is part of the PC's BIOS. Over the years, the performance of PCs has increased and the IDE interface has been improved to take account of improvements in both processor and disk technology. The IDE interface was introduced in 1986 to support disks up to 528 Mbyte and a data rate up to 3 Mbyte/s. In the late 1990s the E-IDE (*enhanced IDE*) interface was designed to handle disks up to 9.4 Gbyte and data rates up to 20 Mbyte/s.

The general-purpose SCSI interface connects up to eight independent disk drives or similar peripherals to a computer; that is, more than one device can be connected to the same SCSI cable. SCSI interfaces are usually associated with high-performance computers because a special controller is required to operate the SCSI bus. The SCSI-1 standard, adopted in 1986, defines how data is transferred over the SCSI bus. As in the case of the IDE interface, the SCSI standard has been amended to provide a higher level of performance. The original SCSI interface had an 8-bit data path and operated at 2 Mbit/s (2 million bits/s). A new standard, SCSI-2, was introduced in 1990 to provide synchronous data transfers at 10 Mbit/s. A SCSI-2 option called *wide SCSI* provides a 16-bit data path and a maximum transfer rate of 20 Mbit/s. The SCSI-3 standard now supports data rates up to 80 Mbyte/s.

9.4.2 The disk electrical interface

A disk drive's electrical interface defines the way in which it communicates with the host computer. In principle, there is little or no relationship between the interface and the

9.4.3 Winchester disk drives

Hard disk drives in the early 1980s found in compact, low-cost minicomputers and high-performance microprocessor systems were often called *Winchester* disks. The generic term

'Winchester' describes a wide range of small disk drives and there appears to be no single feature that makes a drive a Winchester. The term is associated with IBM and some say it's related to the Winchester rifle and others to the town of Winchester. Winchester technology was originally applied to 14 inch disks and then extended to 8, $5\frac{1}{4}$, $3\frac{1}{4}$, and the $2\frac{1}{4}$ inch drives found in laptop computers. Although modern drives incorporate the features of the original Winchester drives, the term 'Winchester' is seldom used today.

As the recording density increased and the inter-track spacing reduced, it became more and more necessary to find ways of ensuring that the head flies exactly over the track it is accessing. This led to increasingly complex head-positioning mechanisms and their associated electronics. Winchester technology solved the problem of head tracking by making the disks, read/write heads, and positioner an integral unit. Earlier large hard drives had replaceable disk packs. Winchester disks cannot be changed, so the problem of trying to follow a track on a disk written by another unit doesn't arise. Because the head disk assembly requires no head alignment, the track spacing can be reduced and the storage density increased. The Winchester disk drive is a sealed chassis that stops the entry of dirt and dust. Most drives have a small hole in the unit protected by an air-filter to equalize internal and external air pressures. As the disk rotates in a clean environment, the flying height of the head can be reduced and the recording density increased.

Unlike earlier hard disk drives, it is not necessary to retract the heads beyond the outer rim of the disks when the unit is not in use. Because the heads fly only when the disks are rotating and aren't retracted when the disk is stationary, it's necessary to allocate a portion of the disk's surface as a *landing area*. That is, the heads are permitted to come into contact with (i.e. land on) a part of the disk where data is not stored. In order to make this possible it is necessary to lubricate the surface of the disk. Such disks must be brought up to speed (and stopped) as quickly as possible to reduce the time for which the heads are in contact with the disks.

Some Winchester disk drives use a *rotary head positioner* to move the read/write heads rather than the linear (in and out) positioners found on earlier hard disk drives. Figure 9.43 shows how a rotary head positioner called a *voice-coil actuator* rotates an arm about a pivot, causing the head assembly to track over the surface of the disks. A voice-coil is so called because it works like a loudspeaker. A current is passed through a coil positioned within a strong magnetic field provided by a permanent magnet. The current in the coil generates a magnetic field, causing the coil to be attracted to, or repelled by, the fixed magnet, moving the pivoted arm.

An important parameter of the disk drive is its *mean time between failure* (MTBF), which is the average time between failures. The MTBF ranges from over 1 000 000 hours for large drives to 100 000 hours for smaller and older drives. A 100 000 hour MTBF indicates that the drive can be expected to operate for about $11\frac{1}{2}$ years continually without failure—a value that is longer than the average working life of a PC. A disk with an MTBF of 1 000 000 hours can be expected to run for over 100 years.

The audio-visual drive

In the mid-1990s three things happened to PCs; their speed increased to the point at which they could process audio and video signals, the capacity of hard disks became sufficient to store over an hour of video, and computing entered an *audio-visual* age. Although hard disks can store video

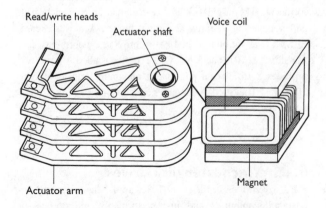

Read/write heads

Actuator shaft

Voice coil

Actuator arm

Magnet

When a current flows through the 'voice coil', it is either attracted to the magnet or repelled (depending on the direction of the current). One end of an arm is connected to the voice coil and the other end of the arm carries the read/write heads. The arm is pivoted on a shaft so that the heads move across the disk and the voice coil moves in or out.

Fig. 9.43 A Winchester head assembly positioning mechanism.

information, conventional drives suffer from *data discontinuity*. Data processing applications require a low average access time and it doesn't matter if there are infrequent short gaps in the data stream. However, when the data represents sound or moving pictures, the ear and the eye can detect even tiny interruptions.

Disk manufacturers have created the so-called *audiovisual* (A/V) drive, which employs the same storage technology as conventional drives but has improved control systems and interfaces. What then causes data discontinuities in conventional drives? Because the stored data elements are very small, even tiny imperfections in the magnetic media cause errors in the data stream when data is read from a disk. The controller in a disk drive is responsible for dealing with these errors. Powerful error-correcting codes are used to protect the stored data. On readback, the data from the disk is processed and errors automatically corrected. Unfortunately, a conventional disk might take 800 ms to recover from an error. A/V disks employ high-speed error correction hardware and algorithms to overcome this problem. Similarly, some hard disks respond to a soft error by re-reading the sector. The A/V disk avoids sector re-reads by means of its powerful error-correcting codes.

As the density of bits on platters has increased, the thermal characteristics (i.e. expansion or contraction with temperature changes) of the disk and read/write mechanism have become more important. Temperature changes affect the head's ability to follow a track. Some disk drives include a thermal calibration mechanism that periodically compensates for temperature changes. This calibration takes place every few minutes and is invisible to the user. However, it does cause an interruption of about 0.1 s in the data flow. A/V disks perform thermal calibration intelligently and delay calibration if a data request is pending. If thermal calibration is taking place and data is requested, the drive reschedules the recalibration process and immediately begins to access the data.

9.4.4 The floppy disk drive

The floppy disk is a removable secondary storage medium that can be transported from one system to another. Floppy disks have long access times and low storage capacities and bear the same relationship to hard disks as microlights to jumbo jets. This isn't intended as a disparaging comparison, because the floppy disk was often the only secondary storage device in early PCs. Today, floppy disks are used exclusively to backup data and to install programs. However, the sheer size of modern operating systems and applications has forced many vendors to provide their products on CD-ROMs. The conventional floppy disk will probably be phased out because data transfer between machines can be achieved by writable CDs, removable hard drives, and electronic mail.

The floppy disk drive is an IBM invention dating back to the 1960s, when it was first used to load microcode into IBM's 370 computers and later to store information in the IBM 3740 Data Entry System. The original floppy disk was made of plastic coated with a magnetic material enclosed in an 8 in square protective envelope. Figure 9.44 shows the

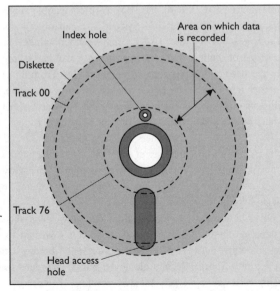

Fig. 9.44 The first generation floppy disk.

arrangement of the floppy disk, with a central hub aperture, a cutout to allow the head to access the disk, and an index hole. The floppy disk is so called because the plastic disk is very thin and is therefore not rigid. A floppy disk can readily be bent and the stored data easily destroyed. They should therefore be handled with great care.

The 8 in floppy disk is now obsolete and was replaced by the 5¼ in minifloppy disk. In turn, the 5¼ in floppy has been largely replaced by the 3½ in floppy disk, which is smaller and comes in a more robust rigid plastic case. The capacity of an 8 in floppy disk in the mid-1970s was 300 kbyte and the capacity of a first-generation 5¼ in floppy disk was 80 kbyte. High-density 5½ in floppy disks store 1.2 Mbyte and 3½ in floppies 1.44 Mbyte (some have capacities of 2.88 Mbyte).

Floppy disks rotate at 360 r.p.m., or about 5–10 percent the speed of a hard disk drive. Such a low speed simplifies the drive mechanism and reduces the frictional heating of the disk in its envelope, but at the cost of increasing the rotational latency to 166 ms.

A small hole called the *index hole* is cut in the 5¼ in disk to provide a means of detecting the start of a track when formatting the disk (we describe formatting shortly). Whenever the hole passes between a light source on one side of the disk and a photoelectric cell on the other, an electrical pulse is generated, informing the disk controller that the start of a track has been located. The 3½ in disc uses a positive locking mechanism to hold the disk in place and determine the start of a track (i.e. the disk slots onto the spindle and the start of a track is defined with respect to the spindle).

A floppy disk's read/write head is moved to the desired track by a stepping mechanism that we shall describe shortly. The head is positioned over the disk and is able to access its surface through a cutout in the cardboard envelope of a 5¼ in disk or under a sliding metal window in a 3½ in disk. Modern floppy drives have two heads and data is recorded on both sides of the disk. Unlike the hard disk, where the head flies above the surface, the head in a floppy disk comes into contact with the surface. In order to prevent undue wear on the head and the disk's surface, the drive motor may be stopped after a period of disk inactivity.

Figure 9.45 shows two head-positioning mechanisms. In Fig. 9.45(a) a stepper motor is connected to a disk (called a cam) that rotates as the motor rotates. A spiral groove is cut in the cam and a rod attached to the head carriage slots in the groove. As the cam rotates, the *cam follower* moves in or out, carrying the head assembly with it. The stepping motor, unlike conventional motors, does not rotate smoothly but moves in a jerky fashion a few degrees at a time. Short electrical pulses are applied to the motor causing it to step a

precise number of degrees, moving the head assembly to the selected track. In Fig. 9.45(b) a stepper motor is connected to a *lead screw*. A nut is threaded on the screw and attached to the head carriage. As the screw rotates, the nut moves the head in or out.

Because the floppy disk drive is a relatively low-precision device that makes extensive use of low-cost plastic parts, the track-to-track spacing is much greater than that found in hard disks. First-generation 8 in floppy disks had 77 tracks each containing 26 sectors at a density of 48 tracks/in and an overall capacity of 300 kbyte. The more modern 3½ in 1.44 Mbyte floppy disk has eighty 0.115 mm wide tracks of 18 sectors spaced at 135 tracks per inch. Data is recorded at an average density of about 17 000 bits/in. The capacity is expressed as formatted capacity and represents the data available to users. It does not include data that performs housekeeping tasks such as labeling the track and sector number of each sector stored on the disk. In hard disk terms this capacity is tiny indeed. We now look at how data is formatted when stored on a disk (the same basic principles apply to both floppy and hard disks).

9.4.5 Organization of data on disks

Having described the principles of magnetic recording systems we now explain how data is actually arranged on a disk. This section provides an overview of some of the principles behind data organization, but doesn't describe a complete system in detail. Although there is an almost infinite number of ways in which digital data may be organized or *formatted* on a disk, two systems developed by IBM have become standard: the IBM 3740-compatible single-density recording and the IBM System 34-compatible double-density recording. In the 1970s some microcomputer manufacturers used their own *ad hoc* formats making it impossible to swap data between different systems. From the end user's point of view, the free exchange of software between computers is highly beneficial. From the software distributor's point of view, the choice of a non-standard format makes it more difficult for others to copy their software. Equally, it often forced the user of such non-standard equipment to remain dependent on one or two suppliers. The growth of the PC in the 1980s swept away many of the non-standard recording formats.

Floppy disks are now invariably *soft-sectored* and the sectors are data structures written to the disk to hold data. A disk must be formatted before it can be used by writing sectors along the tracks in order to let the controller know when to start reading or writing information. Formatting

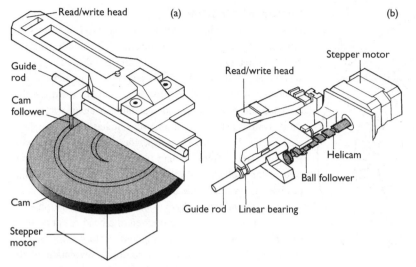

(a) A steeper motor rotates a cam through a given angle. A groove is cut in the cam and a rod sits in the groove. When the cam rotates, the rod is dragged in or out by the groove

(b) A stepper motor rotates a shaft with a helical groove cut into it. A ball bearing sits in the groove and drags the read/write head assembly along as the shaft rotates.

Fig. 9.45 Head-positioning mechanisms.

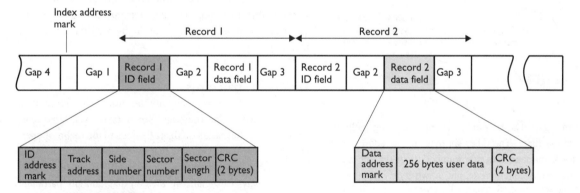

Fig. 9.46 Structure of a track.

involves writing a series of sector headers followed by empty data fields that can later be filled with data as required.

Figure 9.46 describes the structure of a track formatted according to the IBM 34 format double-density system. You can understand Fig. 9.46 if you appreciate two points. First, *gaps* are required between data structures to allow for variations in the disk's speed and time to switch between read and write operations. The disk drive is a mechanical device and doesn't rotate at an exactly constant speed. Consequently, the exact size of a sector will be slightly different each time you write it. Second, the drive electronics needs a means of locating the beginning of each sector.

A track consists of an index gap followed by a sequence of sectors. The number and size of sectors varies from operating system to operating system. Each sector includes an identity field (ID field) and a data field. The various information units on the disk are separated by gaps. A string of null bytes is written at the start of the track followed by an *index address mark* to denote the start of the current track. The address mark is a special byte, unlike any other. We've already seen that the MFM recording process uses a particular algorithm to encode data. That is, only certain recorded bit patterns are valid. By deliberately violating the recording algorithm and recording a bit pattern that does not conform to the set of valid patterns, uniquely identifiable bit patterns can be created to act as special markers. Such special bit patterns are created by omitting certain clock pulses.

The sectors following the index gap are made up of an ID (identification) address mark, an ID field, a gap, a data field,

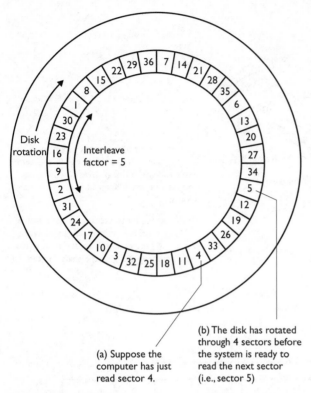

Disk rotation

Interleave factor = 5

(a) Suppose the computer has just read sector 4.

(b) The disk has rotated through 4 sectors before the system is ready to read the next sector (i.e., sector 5)

Fig. 9.47 Sector interleaving.

and a further gap. The ID field is seven bytes long including the ID address mark. The other six bytes of the address field are the track number, the side number (0 or 1), the sector address, the sector length code, and a two-byte *cyclic redundancy check* (CRC) code. The 16-bit CRC provides a powerful method of detecting an error in the sector's ID field and is the 16-bit remainder obtained by dividing the polynomial representing the field to be protected by a standard generator polynomial.

The beginning of the data field itself is denoted by one of two special markers: a *data address mark* or a *deleted data address mark* (these distinguish between data that is active and data that is no longer required). Following the data address mark comes a block of user data (typically 128 to 1024 bytes) terminated by a 16-bit CRC to protect the data field from error. The data field is bracketed by two gaps to provide time for the write circuits in the disk to turn on to write a new data field and then turn off before the next sector is encountered. Gap 2 must have an exact size for correct operation with a floppy disk controller, whereas gaps 1, 3, and 4 are simply delimiters and must only be greater than some specified minimum.

Sector interleaving

Disks have physical and logical sectors. Physical sectors are the actual sectors and are numbered sequentially $1, 2, \ldots$, up to the maximum number of sectors per disk. The logical sectors are those seen by the operating system and are also numbered $1, 2, 5 \ldots$, etc. At first sight it might seem sensible to make the physical and logical numbering of sectors the same. Unfortunately, this simple scheme has a problem. Once a sector has been read from disk, the operating system must perform various housekeeping functions (e.g. calculating the next sector address, data validation, transferring the data to its destination in main memory). If the logical sectors are mapped to contiguous physical sectors, by the time physical sector i has been read and processed, the head might be over, say, physical sector $i+2$. Contiguous sectors can't be read consecutively, and more than a complete revolution of the disk takes place between each sector read. By *interleaving* the logical sectors, we can greatly reduce access time by arranging that the next logical sector will be the next physical sector to be read. Figure 9.47 demonstrates the effect of sector interleaving. Modern systems avoid sector interleaving by reading the whole track into a buffer (i.e. high-speed random access memory).

Disk data structures

Up to now we've considered only the structure of information stored on disk at the track and sector level. The large-scale structure of information on disks belongs to the realm of operating systems. However, now that we've come so far, it would be churlish to end without saying something about files. There are many ways of organizing files on disk and any particular method has its advantages and disadvantages. Conceptually, we can imagine that a filing system might require three data structures: a list of sectors available to the filing system (i.e. the free sectors), a directory of files, and the files themselves.

The free sector list

A simple method of dealing with the allocation of sectors to files is to provide a *bit-map* (usually in track 0, sector 1). Each bit in the bit-map represents one of the sectors on the disk and is clear to indicate a free sector and set to indicate an allocated sector. 'Free' means that the sector can be given to a new file, and 'allocated' means that the sector already belongs to a file. If all bits of the bit-map are set, there are no more free sectors and the disk is full. Figure 9.48 illustrates the free sector list.

Suppose the disk file manager creates a file. It first searches the bit-map for free sectors, and then allocates the

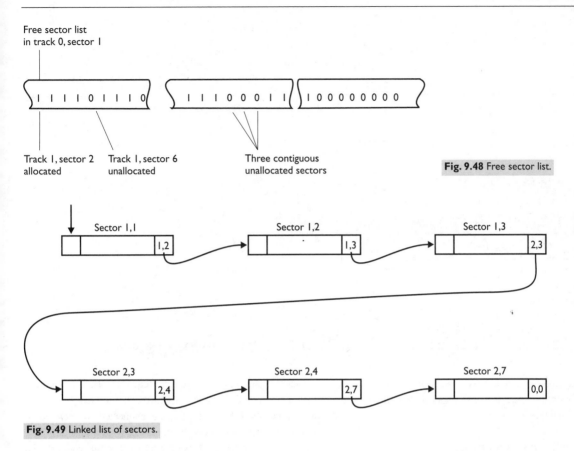

Free sector list
in track 0, sector 1

| 1 1 1 1 0 1 1 1 0 | 1 1 1 0 0 0 1 1 | 1 0 0 0 0 0 0 0 0 |

Track 1, sector 2
allocated

Track 1, sector 6
unallocated

Three contiguous
unallocated sectors

Fig. 9.48 Free sector list.

Sector 1,1 | 1,2 → Sector 1,2 | 1,3 → Sector 1,3 | 2,3

Sector 2,3 | 2,4 → Sector 2,4 | 2,7 → Sector 2,7 | 0,0

Fig. 9.49 Linked list of sectors.

appropriate number of free sectors to the new file. When a file is deleted, the disk file manager returns the file's sectors to the pool of free sectors simply by clearing the corresponding bits in the bit-map. The sectors comprising the deleted file are not overwritten when the file is deleted by the operating system. You can recover so-called deleted files as long as they haven't been overwritten since they were removed from the directory and their sectors returned to the pool of free sectors.

There's little point in storing data on a disk unless it can be accessed with a minimum of effort. To achieve this objective, a data structure called a *directory* holds information about the nature of each file and where the file can be found. Information in directories varies from the minimum required (the filename plus the location of the first sector of the file) to an extensive description of the file including attributes such as file ownership, access rights, date of creation, and date of last access.

The sectors of a file can be arranged as a *linked list* in which each sector contains a pointer to the next sector in the list, as Fig. 9.49 demonstrates. The final sector contains a null

pointer because it has no next sector to point to. Two bytes are required for each pointer: one for the track number and one for the sector number. The advantage of a linked list is that the sectors can be randomly organized on the disk (randomization occurs because new files are continually being created and old files deleted).

Linked lists create *sequential* access files rather than *random access* files. The only way of accessing a particular sector in the file is by reading all sectors of the list until the desired sector is located. Such sequential access is, of course, highly inefficient. Sequential access files are easy to set up and a sequential file system is much easier to design than one that caters for random access files.

As time passes and files are created, modified, and deleted, files on a disk may become very fragmented (i.e. the locations of their sectors are, effectively, random). Once the sectors of a file are located at almost entirely random points on the disk, disk accesses become very long because of the amount of head movement required. Defragmentation programs are used to clean up the disk by reorganizing files to make

(a) The table

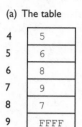

4	5
5	6
6	8
7	9
8	7
9	FFFF

(b) Clusters on the disk

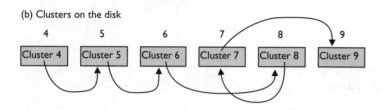

(c) Clusters of the file

Fig 9.50 The file allocation table.

consecutive logical sectors have consecutive addresses. We now briefly describe the structure of a popular filing system used by MS-DOS.

The MS-DOS file structure

MS-DOS extends the simple bit-map of Fig. 9.48 to a linked list of *clusters*. DOS associates each entry in a *file allocation table*, FAT, with a cluster of two to eight sectors (the size of the clusters is related to the size of the disk drive). That is, the smallest unit of storage by which a file can grow is a cluster of sectors. Using a cluster map rather than a bit-map reduces both the size of the map and the number of times that the operating system has to search the map for new sectors. However, the cluster map increases the *granularity* of files because files are forced to grow in minimum increments of a whole cluster. If sectors hold 1024 bytes, 4-sector clusters mean that the minimum increment for a file is 4×1024 bytes $= 4$ kbyte. If the disk holds many files, the total wasted space can be quite large.

Each entry in the FAT corresponds to an actual cluster of sectors on the disk. Figure 9.50 illustrates the structure of a FAT with entries 4 to 9 (corresponding to clusters 4 to 9). Assume that a file starts with cluster number 4 and each cluster points to the next cluster in a file. The FAT entry corresponding to this cluster contains the value 5, which indicates that the next cluster is 5. Note how entry 6 contains the value 8, indicating that the cluster after 6 is 8. Clusters aren't allocated sequentially (leading to the fragmentation we described

earlier). Figure 9.50(b) shows the sequence of clusters on the disk corresponding to this FAT. We have used lines with arrows to show how clusters are connected to each other. Figure 9.50(c) shows how the operating system sees the file.

Cluster 9 in the FAT belonging to this file contains the value $FFFF_{16}$, which indicates that this is the last cluster in a file. Another special code used by DOS, $FFF7_{16}$, indicates that the corresponding cluster is unavailable because it is damaged (i.e. the magnetic medium is defective). The FAT is set up when the disk is formatted and defective sectors are noted. The first two entries in a file allocation table provide a media descriptor that describes the characteristics of the disk.

When MS-DOS was designed, 12-bit FAT entries were sufficient for disks up to 10 Mbyte and 16-bit FAT entries for disks above 10 Mbyte. The maximum size disk that can be supported is the number of clusters multiplied by the number of sectors per cluster multiplied by the number of bytes per sector. Because the FAT16 system supports only 65 525 clusters, the maximum disk size is limited (assuming a limit on the size of sectors and clusters). These figures demonstrate how rapidly the face of computing changed in the 1990s—a 10 Mbyte hard disk was once considered large, whereas today it's difficult to find a disk less than about 4 Gbyte. The rapid growth in disk capacity forced Microsoft to adopt a 32-bit FAT with Windows NT, later releases of Windows 95, and Windows 98. FAT32 allows the operating system to handle disks up to 2 terabytes.

DOS storage media hold four types of data element. The first element is called the *boot record* and identifies the operating system and the structure of the disk (number of sectors and clusters, size of clusters), and can provide a boot program used when the system is first powered up. Following the boot sector are two FATs (one is a copy of the other provided for security). After the FATs a *root directory* provides the details of the files. These details include the filename, file characteristics (when created etc.), and the address of the file's first cluster in the FAT. The remainder of the disk is allocated to the files themselves.

9.4.6 High-performance drives

We now look at the technology and performance of typical late 1990s disk drives and describe IBM's 8.4 Gbyte Deskstar, which employs magnetoresistive head technology, partial response maximum likelihood data demodulation (PRML), and no-ID sector formatting. Figure 9.51 shows the increase in areal densities (the term *areal* means 'per unit area') for IBM disk drives since 1980 and the recent 60 percent compound growth rate made possible largely through the use of magnetoresistive heads. The Deskstar uses four platters, each contributing more than 2 Gbyte, and has an areal density of 1.74 Gbit/in². Its average seek time is 9.5 ms and it supports a sustained data rate of 5.8 Mbyte/s with a peak data transfer rate up to 33.3 Mbyte/s. The SMART

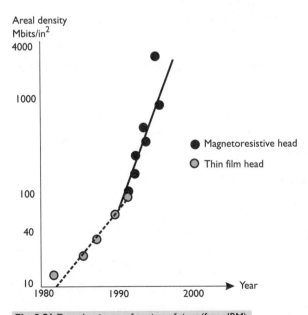

Fig. 9.51 Data density as a function of time (from IBM).

protocol (Self-Monitoring Analysis and Reporting Technology) ensures data availability and helps alert the system to potential drive failures. We will describe all these techniques that increase the drive's *areal density* and performance. This information was extracted from IBM's literature.

The magnetoresistive head

The ultimate performance of a disk drive using the traditional head we described earlier is limited because the recording head has to perform the conflicting tasks of writing data on the disk and retrieving previously written data. As the bit patterns recorded on the surface of disks have grown smaller, the amplitude of the signal from the read head has been reduced, making it difficult for the drive's electronics to identify the recorded bit patterns. You can increase the read signal enough to determine the magnetic pattern recorded on the disk by adding turns around the magnetic core of the head, because the read signal is proportional to the number of turns. However, increasing turns also increases the head's inductance—the resistance of a circuit to a change in the current flowing through it. A high inductance limits the frequency with which the current reversals can occur during write operations.

Magnetoresistive head technology provides separate read and write heads. An inductive head, optimized for writing information, is integrated with a magnetoresistive structure optimized for reading. Each of the two elements can be optimized to perform its particular function—reading or writing data. An MR write head can use as few as 10 turns of wire to achieve an optimally low level of inductance for write operations. That compares with as many as 50 turns for thin-film inductive heads. The lower inductance of the MR write element makes it easier to write the signal at very high data frequencies.

Separate read and write elements in MR heads reduce the noise problems associated with head misalignments over tightly spaced data tracks. During read operations, the disk drive's servo system positions the head accurately over the centerline of the data track that has just been written. Because of the electromechanical nature of these servo systems, some misalignment is unavoidable. As areal densities are increased by packing data tracks closer together, head misalignment can cause the head to pick up noise from adjacent tracks, and thereby produce a read signal with an unacceptably low signal-to-noise ratio. Even slight misalignments of thin-film inductive heads can offset the head from the written track, reducing signal amplitude and adding noise. With MR heads, the separate read element can be fabricated to be narrower than the written track. As a result, the read element can remain entirely over a written track even when the head is slightly misaligned.

Another advantage of MR heads is that the resistive read element produces a strong signal even when reading bits that are spaced just ten millionths of an inch apart and one hundred millionths of an inch wide, *regardless of linear disk speed*. This velocity-independent signal output permits drive vendors to increase areal densities without spinning the disks faster to prevent read signal degradation.

With either a thin-film inductive head or an MR head, most of the head's mass and size comes from the slider and the suspension mechanisms, which are the aerodynamic components that permit the head to fly over a disk. The head's active elements are extremely small by comparison. The write element of an MR head is designed much the same way as a thin-film inductive head. A current flowing through the coil produces a magnetic fringe field round the gap that writes data to a disk by reversing the direction of the magnetic fields on the disk's surface.

A magnetoresistive head operates in a different way from conventional read heads. In a conventional head, a change in magnetic flux from the disk induces a voltage in a coil. In a magnetoresistive head, the flux modifies the electrical resistance of a conductor (i.e. more current flows through the conductor when you apply a voltage across it). Lord Kelvin discovered this phenomenon, called *anisotropic magnetoresistance*, in 1857. The MR head's separate read element consists of a minute stripe of a permalloy material (a nickel iron compound, NiFe) placed next to one of the write element's magnetic pole pieces. The electrical resistance of the permalloy changes by a few percent when it is placed in the vicinity of a magnetic field, or when it is exposed to a magnetic field in a certain direction. This change in the material's resistance allows the MR head to detect the magnetic flux transitions associated with recorded bit patterns. During a read operation, a small current is passed through the stripe of resistive material. As the MR stripe is exposed to the magnetic field from the disk, an amplifier measures the resulting voltage drop across the stripe.

The read element is located in the space between two highly permeable magnetic shields. The shields focus the magnetic field from the disk and reject stray fields. Shielding layers protect the magnetoresistive elements from other magnetic fields. The second shield also functions as one pole of the inductive write head, thus giving rise to the term 'merged magnetoresistive head'.

Figure 9.52 shows the basic design of a magnetoresistive head consisting of separate read and write elements formed over each other and sharing common material layers. The write element is a conventional thin-film inductive head. Figure 9.53 shows the idealized diagram of the magnetic recording process using a merged magnetoresistive head flying over a rotating disk.

No-ID formatting

IBM has developed a special *No-ID sector* format that allows disk drives to be formatted more efficiently, improving their capacity, reliability, and performance. The ID (or header) information is stored in semiconductor memory instead of on the disk surface, resulting in increased track capacity without changing the linear bit density. When combined with a magnetoresistive head, the No-ID sector format also increases the track density.

We have already described how tracks are formatted on floppy disks (see Fig. 9.46). Similar principles apply to hard

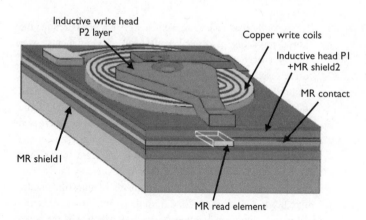

Fig. 9.52 The magnetoresistive head (from IBM).

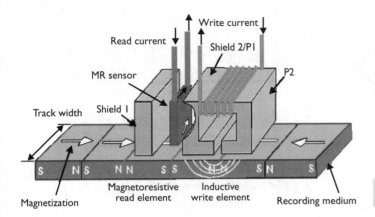

Fig. 9.53 Magnetic recording and the magnetoresistive head (from IBM).

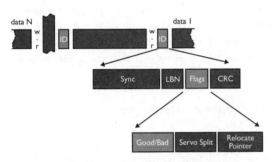

Fig. 9.54 Format of a disk with ID fields (from IBM).

disks. Modern high-density disk drives employ embedded controllers that actively maintain the head over the required track. Tracks are divided into data and *servo* fields. The servo fields contain the positioning information used to locate the head over a given track. User data is stored in the data fields, each with its associated ID field. The ID fields contain information that identifies the data sector and flags to indicate defective sectors (see Fig. 9.54).

Clearly, the ID field (and servo field) take up space that could be devoted to storing user data. A track's *format efficiency* can be improved by reducing this overhead. IBM's No-ID sector format eliminates the ID fields to provide a marked improvement in the format efficiency.

The majority of disk drives use an addressing scheme where the data sectors are identified to the host system by a *logical block number* (LBN). The host computer sends a list of logical block numbers to be written or read and the disk drive converts these values into zone, cylinder, head, and sector (ZCHS) values. The servo system seeks the desired zone, cylinder, and head, and the disk drive begins reading ID fields until a match is found. Once the appropriate ID field has been read, the drive can read or write the following data field.

The ID fields allow flexibility in the format and provide a simple mechanism for handling defects, but they occupy up to 10 percent of a track. Moreover, because each sector's ID field must be read prior to a read or write operation, an additional 5 percent space is required to allow for write-to-read recovery prior to each ID field (this corresponds to the gaps we described earlier).

Defect management is accomplished by reserving a fixed number of spare sectors at some chosen interval. If a sector is determined to be defective, its data is relocated in one of the spare sectors. The relocation process ranges from shifting all the sectors between the defect and the spare to using a specific spare sector to replace the defective sector. Performance degradation can occur if the sectors are not at their expected locations, requiring an additional seek operation. To reduce the likelihood of sector relocation, a large number of sectors are reserved as spares, reducing the format efficiency.

IBM's No-ID sector format uses the servo control system to locate physical sectors and a defect map stored in RAM to identify logical sectors. This allows the disk data controller to convert logical block numbers (LBNs) to physical block numbers (PBNs). The LBN ranges from 0 to the number of addressable blocks on the disk drive. The PBN is a number from 0 to the number of physical blocks on the disk drive, but with the defective and spare sectors mapped out. Once the PBN is computed, it is converted to the exact Zone/Cylinder/Head/Sector (ZCHS) value for the sector. Since the defect information is known in advance, the proper logical block is guaranteed to be located at the computed ZCHS. The defect map is stored in a compressed format, optimized for small size and rapid lookup. The servo system is used to locate the physical sector, based upon knowledge of the track formats in each zone.

The No-ID sector format enhances a disk drive's reliability because the header information is stored in RAM, not on the

Fig. 9.55 Magnetoresistive head geometry (from IBM).

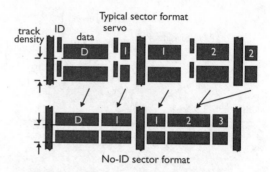

Fig. 9.56 Sector format compensation (from IBM).

disk. Current disk drives rely on CRC or ECC to reduce the vulnerability to errors in the ID fields.

The No-ID sector format provides a significant improvement for disk drives employing conventional thin-film heads and an even greater advantage with magnetoresistive heads. Figure 9.55 shows the basic geometry of a magnetoresistive head, as seen from the disk surface. As we said earlier, the read element is narrower than the write element. In practice, there is an offset between the center of the read and write elements due to the longitudinal separation of the elements. When used with a rotary actuator, the head is skewed with respect to the tracks as the actuator moves across the disk. The result is a lateral offset between the read and write head centerlines. Optimum performance is achieved by centering the read head over the data track for read operations and centering the write head over the data track for write operations. This operation will cause the read head to be partially off-track during a write operation.

This offset presents a problem when ID fields are present, since they must be accurately read for both read and write operations. ID fields may be written partially off-track, requiring increased write width to ensure the read head can reliably read the ID field. The increased write width imposes limits on the track density. By removing the ID field, No-ID effectively eliminates the limit on track density. Since all the header and data field split information is stored in RAM, there's no information to be read from the disk relating to the data sector identities or locations. The servo system need only know the write-to-read element offset to center the write head on the track during write operations. Therefore, the lateral location of the read head is not important during a write operation.

Figure 9.56 compares a typical sector format with a No-ID sector format. Since the format no longer imposes constraints on the read and write head offsets, manufacturing yields for magnetoresistive heads are improved. The removal of offset ID fields allows the tracks to be placed closer together, resulting in greater capacity. The performance is enhanced by the increased throughput (reduced overhead) and by the

knowledge of the absolute sector locations. Power management is enhanced since there is no need to turn on the read electronics to read ID fields when searching for a sector. No-ID sector formatting with magnetoresistive heads increases capacity by up to 30 percent.

Partial response maximum likelihood encoding

As the recorded bit density has increased due to advances in head technology, the signals from adjacent bits begin to interfere with each other. The overlap of analog signals from the read head is known as *intersymbol interference* (we met this concept when we introduced recording codes—we'll meet it again when we come to modems and data transmission).

One way of dealing with the effects of intersymbol interference is called *partial response maximum likelihood* (PRML) decoding and was originally developed for data communication with deep space probes. PRML detection was used to process data from the Viking Lander on its mission to Mars. It's also not too far from the subject of my own PhD thesis.

Conventional disk drives use *peak detection* to decode signals from the read head. The electronics subsystem is concerned only with the location of the peak of the pulses received from the read head. Figure 9.57 illustrates how peak detection operates. A signal from the read head is differentiated, which causes it to cross the zero voltage threshold when the input is at a maximum or minimum peak. This processed signal is then 'squared up' to create the binary pulses required by the computer.

PRML detection involves a much more sophisticated process that requires both analog and digital signal processing techniques. PRML can handle more tightly packed bits than conventional systems and employs a technique called

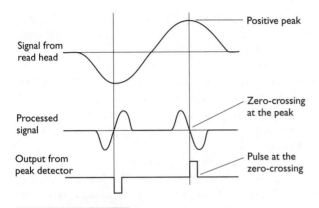

Fig. 9.57 Peak detection.

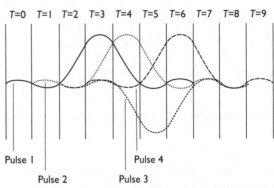

Fig. 9.60 Transmitting four bits that overlap.

maximum likelihood detection to determine the sequence of bits that were written on the disk.

Consider the signal from a read head corresponding to a flux transition (Fig. 9.58). This signal (i.e. pulse) can be modelled by the sequence 0,0,0,1,1,0,0,0 (i.e. it occupies 7 bit periods of duration T). Figure 9.59 shows a sequence of four such consecutive flux transitions with the values $+1$, $+1$, -1, $+1$ from the read head. Each new signal is transmitted every $7T$

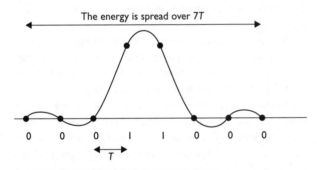

Fig. 9.58 Sampled impulse response of a pulse.

seconds and doesn't interfere with its neighbors (i.e. there is no signal overlap). We have used a different line style for each of the signals.

Suppose that bits are packed much more closely together so that a flux transition transmits a new pulse every T seconds. Figure 9.60 shows the four pulses transmitted at $T=0$, $T=1$, $T=2$, and $T=3$, respectively. Each of these pulses is depicted by a different line style to distinguish it from its neighbors.

Because the pulses in Fig. 9.60 overlap in time, the voltage at the read head is the sum of the voltages due to each of the individual pulses. Figure 9.61 shows the actual voltage due to this pulse sequence that appears at the output of the read head. As you can see, the merging of the pulses (intersymbol interference) generates a waveform that doesn't resemble the original sequence of binary pulses.

PRML uses the fact that a flux transition generates a pulse with a known shape to separate a pulse from its neighbors. A filtering process called *equalization* is used to separate the pulses.

Maximum likelihood detection uses the *Viterbi* algorithm to make a best estimate of the data received from the disk.

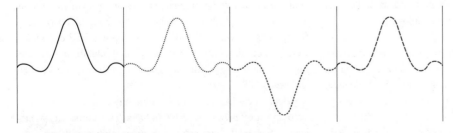

Fig. 9.59 Four bits transmitted at widely separated intervals.

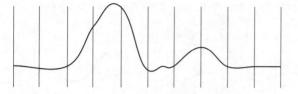

Fig. 9.61 The composite signal produced from four overlapping bits.

Essentially, the algorithm works by generating locally the signal it would expect to see from the disk for various patterns of 1s and 0s and comparing this signal with the actual signal received from the disk. The detector selects the best match with the data from the read head. The pattern that has the least error (difference) is the one with the maximum likelihood of being correct.

SMART technology

A new function provided by disk drives that emerged in the late 1990s was a sophisticated form of self-testing called *Self-Monitoring, Analysis and Reporting Technology* (SMART). The following description of SMART is taken from a paper by Ottem and Plummer of Seagate.

Today's computer users expect data storage reliability and don't even consider the possibility of losing data due to a hard disk drive failure. Reliability prediction technology anticipates the failure of a disk drive with sufficient notice to allow you to backup data prior to a drive's failure. SMART was pioneered by Compaq and developed by Seagate Technology Inc., IBM, Conner Peripherals Inc., Western Digital Corporation, and the Quantum Corporation.

Reliability prediction technology emerged from a need to protect mission-critical information stored on disk drives. As system storage capacity requirements increased and multiple disk array systems started to appear, industry leaders decided to create an early warning system that would allow time to backup data, should a failure become imminent. In order to understand how SMART evolved, it is necessary to look at SMART's roots, which are based in technology developed by IBM and Compaq.

IBM's reliability prediction technology is called *Predictive Failure Analysis* and operates by measuring several attributes, including head flying height, to predict failures. When the disk drive detects the degradation of an attribute such as flying height it informs the host that a failure may occur.

Compaq later announced a breakthrough in diagnostic design called IntelliSafe which was developed in conjunction with Seagate, Quantum, and Conner. This technique monitors a range of attributes and sends attribute and threshold information to host software. The disk drive then decides if an alert is warranted, and sends that message to the system, along with the attribute and threshold information. The attribute and threshold level implementation of IntelliSafe varies with each disk drive vendor, but the interface, and the way in which status is sent to the host, are consistent across all vendors.

Compaq placed IntelliSafe in the public domain by presenting their specification for the ATA/IDE environment, SFF-8035, to the Small Form Factor Committee on 12 May 1995. Compaq, Seagate, Conner, IBM, Quantum, and Western Digital collaborated in the development of a new version, appropriately named SMART, which combines conceptual elements of Compaq's IntelliSafe and IBM's PFA.

Features of SMART technology include a series of attributes, or diagnostics, chosen specifically for each individual drive model. Attribute individualism is important because drive architectures vary from model to model. Attributes and thresholds that detect failure in one model may not be suited to another model. The architecture of the drive determines which attributes should be measured and which thresholds are appropriate. Although not all failures will be predicted, we can expect an evolution of SMART as technology and experience improve our ability to predict reliability.

A disk drive must be able to monitor many elements in order to have a comprehensive reliability management capability. One of the most crucial elements is understanding failures. Failures can be seen from two standpoints: predictable, and unpredictable. Unpredictable failures occur quickly, like electronic and mechanical problems, such as a power surge that can cause chip or circuit failure. Improvements in quality, design, process, and manufacturing can reduce the incidence of non-predictable failures.

Predictable failures are characterized by degradation of an attribute over time, before the disk drive fails. This creates a situation where attributes can be monitored, making it possible for predictive failure analysis. Many mechanical failures are considered predictable, such as the degradation of head flying height, which would indicate a potential head crash. Certain electronic failures may show degradation before failing, but more commonly mechanical problems are gradual and predictable.

Mechanical failures, which are mainly predictable failures, account for 60 percent of drive failures. This number is significant because it demonstrates a great opportunity for reliability prediction technology. With the emerging technology of SMART, an increasing number of failures will be predicted and data loss will be avoided.

SMART technology is like a jigsaw puzzle: it takes many pieces, put together in the right way, to make a pattern. One piece of the puzzle is understanding failures. Another piece of the puzzle is the way in which attributes are determined. Attributes are reliability prediction parameters, customized by the manufacturer for different types of drives. To determine attributes, Seagate design engineers review returned drives, consider the design points, and create attributes to signal the types of failures that they are seeing. Information gained from field experience can be used to predict reliability exposures and, over time, attributes can be incorporated into the new reliability architecture. Some of the attributes that can be used to predict failure are:

- head flying height
- data throughput performance
- spin-up time
- reallocated sector count
- seek error rate
- seek time performance
- spin try recount
- drive calibration retry count

SMART technology is proprietary because the actual attributes used to monitor reliability depend on the particular disk construction.

Now that we've covered some of the modern aspects of disk technology we can present the major parameters of IBM's 8.4 Gbyte Deskstar disk drive (Table 9.6), which represented a typical high-performance drive in the late 1990s.

9.4.7 RAID systems

Having looked in some detail at individual disk drives, we now introduce a technology called *RAID*, which combines separate disk drives into a single system. There are high-capacity disk drives and there are low-capacity disk drives. In the 1980s and 1990s low-capacity disks were relatively cheaper than their high-capacity counterparts—largely due to the low cost of mass-produced disk drives targeted at the PC market. Consequently, it was more cost-effective to create a large memory system by using several low-capacity drives than by using a single high-capacity drive. The term SLED (single large expensive disk) was coined to describe systems that did not employ several low-cost disk drives.

In 1987 three computer scientists at the University of California in Berkeley (Gibson, Katz, and Patterson) devised

Interface	ATA-3
Device capacity (formatted)	8.45 Gbyte
Sector size	512 bytes
Recording zones	8
User cylinders	9784
Data heads	8
Disks	4
Areal density (maximum)	1.74 Gbit/in^2
Recording density (maximum)	162.6 kbpi
Track density	10 700 TPI
Performance	
Data buffer	512 KB
Rotational speed	5400 r.p.m.
Latency (average)	5.6 ms
Media transfer rate	76.2 (inner) Mbit/s
	127.4 (outer) Mbit/s
Interface transfer rate	33.3 Mbyte/s
(maximum AT)	Ultra DMA Mode-2
	16.6 Mbyte/s PIO Mode-4,
	MW DMA Mode-2
Sustained data transfer rate	5.8 to 10.2 Mbyte/s
Seek time (typical read)	
Average	9.5 ms
Track-to-track	2.2 ms
Full track	15.5 ms
Reliability	
Error rates (non-recoverable)	≤1 per 10^{13} bits transferred
Contact start stop cycles	40 000
Power requirements	+5 VDC +12 VDC
Dissipation (typical)	
Startup (maximum peak)	0.80 A (5 V), 2.13 A (12 V)
Idle (average)	4.7 W
Power consumption efficiency index	0.0006 W/Mbyte
Physical size	
Height	25.4 mm
Width	101.6 mm
Depth	146 mm
Weight (maximum)	580 g
Environmental characteristics	
Operating	
Ambient temperature	5–55 °C
Relative humidity (non-condensing)	8–90%
Maximum wet bulb (non-condensing)	29 °C
Shock (half sine wave)	10 g/11 ms
Vibration (random (RMS))	0.67 g (5–500 Hz)
Non-operating	
Ambient temperature	−40–65 °C
Relative humidity (non-condensing)	5–95%
Maximum wet bulb (non-condensing)	35 °C
Shock (half sine wave)	75 g/11 ms
Vibration (random (RMS))	1.04 g (2–200 Hz)

Table 9.6 Parameters of the Deskstar 8.4.1

a new technology called *RAID* (redundant array of inexpensive disks) that used several low-cost disk drives to create a large and reliable disk store. There are several variations of the RAID technologies, called RAID 1, RAID 2, ... , RAID 5. We discuss only RAID 1, RAID 3, and RAID 5 systems here.

RAID 1 systems are very simple. Two hard drives are connected to a single disk controller to provide *disk mirroring*. Two copies are made of all files and each copy can be read independently of the other. RAID 1 technology improves read access time because the controller can obtain data from the first drive that has it ready. Furthermore, RAID 1 systems improve reliability because there are two copies of each file. If the probability of one drive failing is p, the probability of both drives failing is p^2, which greatly enhances reliability. RAID 1 technology is inefficient because the amount of disk space required is doubled.

RAID 3 technology transfers data in parallel to a set of disks in parallel. RAID 3 systems have n data disks and a separate parity disk (n is typically 4). Data in a RAID 3 system is said to be *striped* so that a stripe is sent in parallel to each of the n drives. A parity byte (generated across the n stripes) is stored on the parity disk. If an error occurs in any of the stripes, the missing data can be regenerated from the parity information. An error in a data block of one of the disks can be detected by the error-detecting code used whenever data is stored on disk.

Let's illustrate the RAID 3 system with a simple example, where P represents a parity bit across bits (i.e. disks) 1 to 4. Table 9.7 shows four stripes across the five disks. The value of stripe 1 is 0100 and its even parity bit is 1, which is stored on the parity disk number 5.

Suppose disk drive 3 in the array fails to give the situation in Table 9.8. As you can see, the error-detecting codes on disk 3 indicate that the data has been corrupted but cannot tell you what the data should have been. However, because we still have the data on disks 1, 2, 4, and the parity disk, we can reconstruct the missing data. For example, stripe 2 is 11?00. In order to maintain correct parity the missing bit must be 0 and the corrected stripe is 11000. RAID 3 systems require that the heads of the disk be synchronized.

Another popular implementation of RAID technology is the RAID 5 array, which is similar to a RAID 3 array because n drives are used to store stripes of data and one is used to store a parity stripe. However, the stripes in a RAID 5 system are sectors rather than bytes, and the parity stripes are distributed across the array rather than stored on a specific drive. RAID 5 systems are more suited to smaller blocks of data (e.g. in network systems) and are simpler because they don't require the read/write heads of each of the drives to be synchronized.

Both RAID 3 and RAID 5 systems can tolerate the complete failure of one of the disks in the array. When that happens, their error-correcting property vanishes, although the array can operate (assuming no further errors) until a new drive is swapped in. The operator can pull out the failed drive and plug in a spare drive to keep the system running smoothly.

The *mean time between failure* of an array of disks is less than that of a single disk. If you have five drives, it's five times more likely that one of them will fail over a given period than if you had just one drive. However, the use of redundancy (i.e. the ability to tolerate a single failure) in a RAID system more than compensates for the increased

Stripe	Disk 1 bit 1	Disk 2 bit 2	Disk 3 bit 3	Disk 4 bit 4	Disk 5 P
1	0	1	0	0	1
2	1	1	0	0	0
3	0	1	1	1	1
4	1	0	1	0	0

Table 9.7 Principle of the RAID 3 array.

Stripe	Disk 1 bit 1	Disk 2 bit 2	Disk 3 bit 3	Disk 4 bit 4	Disk 5 P
1	0	1	?	0	1
2	1	1	?	0	0
3	0	1	?	1	1
4	1	0	?	0	0

Table 9.8 Correcting an error in a RAID 3 array.

probability of a single disk failure because *two* disks have to fail to bring the system down. We will look at reliability in more detail in Chapter 12. Now that we have described the hard disk drive, we are going to look at the tape transport.

9.5 The tape transport

Tape-based secondary systems were popular in the 1970s and 1980s and were largely associated with mainframe computers. Anyone who has ever seen a science fiction film made in the 1960s or 1970s can't fail to have noticed the banks of jerkily rotating tape spools in monster-sized tape drives that symbolized high technology in those days. Today, tape is mainly found in small cartridge-based systems where it provides backup and archival storage. The increase in the capacity and decrease in the cost of hard drives together with the growth of optical storage systems make tape much less attractive than it once was. Readers not interested in the development of the tape transport may skip ahead to the section on *The streaming tape drive*.

Figure 9.62 describes the arrangement of a classical digital tape drive that records information on a thin strip of polyester tape coated with a magnetic material. The tape is $\frac{1}{2}$ in wide

and is stored in (typically) 10.5 in reels of 2400 feet. The construction of a tape transport (or tape drive) for digital data is not greatly different from a high-quality domestic reel-to-reel recorder.

The function of a tape transport is to move tape at a constant speed past a read/write head. When searching for a particular block of data, the tape is moved at a relatively high speed and stopped when the start of the block is found. Because of their inertia, tape spools can't be halted instantaneously without snapping (or stretching) the tape. In high performance tape transports the movement of the tape past the heads is decoupled from the motion of the pay-out and take-up spools. How this is actually achieved is described shortly.

Tape is pulled past the read/write head(s) by a capstan and idler-wheel arrangement. A capstan is a cylinder of precisely machined and polished hard metal rotating at a constant speed. As the tape passes the capstan, it is pushed against the capstan by an idler wheel (or pinch roller). Friction between the capstan, tape, and idler causes the tape to be pulled. The idler wheel rotates because of the motion of the tape against it and is not driven by any mechanism itself. When the tape is stopped, a solenoid pulls the idler wheel away from the tape. Brake pads are also applied to the tape to stop it.

The tape between the capstans and spools hangs in a loop in the two vacuum columns below each of the tape spools. By sucking air out of the bottom of the column, the tape loop is kept hanging down. Photoelectric sensors are located at the top and bottom of the vacuum columns to detect the presence or absence of the tape loop. By using these sensors to control the speed of the spool motors, the length of the loop in the vacuum column can be kept approximately constant. For example, if the left-hand reel is paying out tape too fast, the loop grows downwards. When it reaches the lower sensors the motion of the left-hand spool is slowed down and the loop starts to shorten.

The purpose of the vacuum columns is to allow the almost instantaneous stopping of the tape as it moves past the tape heads. When the idler wheel disengages from the capstan, the tape brakes are applied and the spool motors stopped. The tape under the heads stops almost instantaneously, but the spools momentarily continue either to pay out tape or take it up. This simply leads to one of the tape loops growing and the other shrinking. Vacuum column buffers have their disadvantages. A power failure can lead to tape spillages when the power is reapplied. Vacuum column buffers also consume considerable power and are relatively error prone. They can't be used in aircraft because of the low ambient air pressure. The vacuum system sucks dust from the air

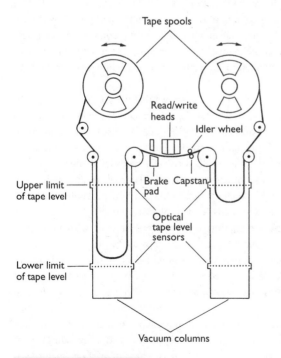

Fig. 9.62 The tape transport.

and deposits it where it is least wanted—on the tape. Finally, the constant hiss of the air into the vacuum columns is annoying.

Early tape transports used a technique widely found on domestic tape decks in the 1970s, the tension arm buffer. Figure 9.63 illustrates the tension arm, which takes up slack tape or pays out tape when the tape tension increases. This arrangement proves satisfactory for low to medium tape speeds up to 45 in/s.

The tension arm was developed to allow tape speeds of 75 in/s in an arrangement called the *floating shuttle* and is illustrated in Fig. 9.64. Tension arms tend to work in unison, with one taking up slack and the other paying out tape. By combining the two loops in a freely moving shuttle, improved performance is possible because the shuttle can be

kept light (15 grams). The shuttle is a small block with two pulleys around which are routed the take-up and pay-out loops from the reels. A sophisticated motor control system is needed to keep the shuttle within two or three inches of its center position.

Parameters of tape transport mechanisms

Tape unit parameters vary widely in terms of both tape speed and recording format. Typical speeds vary from 12.5 to 250 in/s. The details of a popular recording format (nine-track phase-encoded data) are given in Fig. 9.65. We provide this diagram to demonstrate just how many parameters have to be specified if a system is to become an international standard.

Figure 9.65 corresponds to the ISO standard ISO 3788–1976 (E) for '9-track, 12.7 mm wide magnetic tape recorded at 1600 rpi, phase encoded'. Note that 'rpi' means 'reversals per inch'. Information is stored by magnetizing the surface, with the magnetic domains pointing either up the tape or down the tape. We have to specify the physical dimensions of the tape if it is to be interchangeable. Tape is generally 12.7 mm (0.5 in) wide or 6.30 mm (0.25 in) wide. Magnetic tape systems record data in parallel along a number of tracks. For example, ISO 3788–1976 (E) specifies the nine parallel tracks illustrated in Fig. 9.65. Nine tracks provide a byte of data plus an odd parity track. If the nine tracks are considered to form a column of data, the bit in the parity track is chosen to make the total number of 1s in the column odd. A single parity bit helps to detect errors, because if a column with an even number of 1s is found at least one error must have occurred.

A glance at Fig. 9.65 shows that the position of the tracks along the surface has been standardized and that data is arranged into blocks. It is not enough just to record information on tape; the information has to be arranged in a meaningful fashion. ISO 3788–1976 (E) specifies a block structure that consists of between 18 and 2048 rows of data and is preceded by a preamble and succeeded by a postamble. Forming of data into units called blocks (blocking) is necessary, because the tape drive cannot read or write a single row of bits efficiently. Each block is separated from its neighbors by an interblock gap which is nominally 15 mm (0.6 in) long.

Standard ISO 3788–1976 (E) covers data encoding and specifies that the data be *phase encoded* and a 1 bit is defined as 'a flux transition to the polarity of the interblock gap when reading in the forward direction'. Having settled on the dimensions of the tape, the recording (i.e. encoding) technique, and the track structure, we have at least one major variable left: the recording density. As the tape moves past the

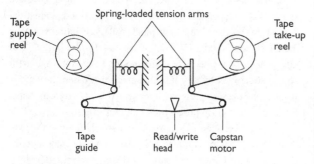

Fig. 9.63 The tension arm tape buffer.

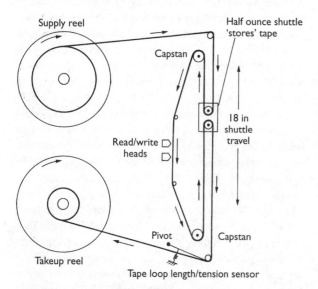

Fig. 9.64 The floating shuttle.

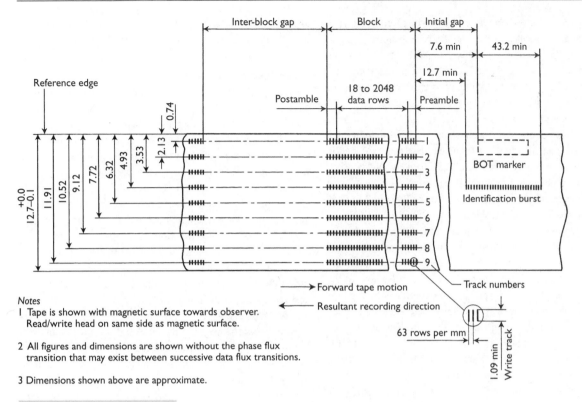

Fig. 9.65 Format of nine-track tape.

write head, data is written onto the surface at a density that depends on the speed of the tape and on the number of bits per second sent to the write head. The greater the packing density (in bits per inch), the greater the efficiency of data storage. ISO 3788–1976 (E) specifies a packing density of 1600 bits per inch (63 bits per mm).

Up to now, we've said nothing about the information stored on the tape, other than to say that it is recorded in blocks of 8-bit columns with an interblock gap between blocks. ISO 3788–1976 (E) prescribes that the data be recorded in the form of ISO 7-bit character codes or, optionally, the 8-bit extended ISO code. The structure of files on magnetic tape is rather dependent on the operating system that created them. However, ISO 1991–1979 (E) does specify the file structures necessary for data interchange on magnetic tape.

Data is recorded in *blocks* because it is impossible to read a single byte at a time by starting and stopping the tapes. Between the blocks is an interblock gap (typically $\frac{3}{4}$ in), giving the tape time to stop after a read/write operation and to accelerate to normal speed before the next operation. Each block is preceded by a preamble and followed by a postamble,

which are used to synchronize the electronics during a read operation. By making the preamble and postamble symmetric it is possible to read the tape in either direction.

Tapes have markers at their ends to indicate the physical start and end of the tape. The markers take the form of a piece of metallic foil attached to the tape, or small holes. There are also software markers recorded on the tape, BOT (beginning of tape) and EOT (end of tape).

The tape transports we have just discussed were the classic secondary stores of mainframe computers. By the early 1970s tape transports were using recording densities of 6250 bytes/in, speeds of 200 in/s, a 0.3 in interrecord gap, and were able to start and stop within 1 ms.

The streaming tape drive

Today's low-cost, high-performance microcomputers have large hard disks and provide ample amounts of secondary storage. Since hard drives employ fixed media, we need a way of transferring programs between computers and preserving the contents of the hard disk in the event of a system failure leading to the corruption of part of the surface of the disk. The floppy disk provides a convenient way of transporting small programs, but is not as well suited to the role of a backup store, owing to its limited capacity. A 1 Gbyte drive would require about seven hundred $3\frac{1}{2}$ in floppy disks to back it up (note that data compression techniques can be used to reduce the amount of space required by a program or data by a factor of 2 to 10).

A solution to the problem of efficiently and cheaply backing up hard disks is provided in the shape of the *streaming tape drive*. The cost of a high-performance tape transport lies in the mechanism needed to stop and start the tape quickly. Such a complex tape control mechanism has been abandoned in the tape streamer, resulting in a mechanism small enough to fit in the same space as a hard disk drive.

The tape streamer can't stop and start the tape within an interblock gap and has to use an alternative mechanism to position the tape. Figure 9.66 shows how a tape is nominally stopped at the end of a block but overshoots it because of the lack of any sophisticated tape buffering mechanism. The tape must then be rewound and positioned before the interblock gap so that when the tape is restarted it will come up to speed by the time the next block is passing the read/write head. This process takes approximately one second and is a thousand times slower than a vacuum-buffered tape transport.

The inability to stop and start on an interblock gap is not as bad as it sounds. The tape streamer is frequently used to store large blocks of data from the disk and therefore runs continuously, rather than by skipping from one data block to another. Some of the latest tape streamers solve the stop/start problem by providing a *massless buffer*. As the cost of semiconductor memory is now so low, it is possible to read a large chunk of data from the tape into memory local to the streamer. The host computer then reads data not from the tape directly, but from the semiconductor memory. In this way it is possible to skip almost instantaneously from block to block, because the data is now held in random access memory.

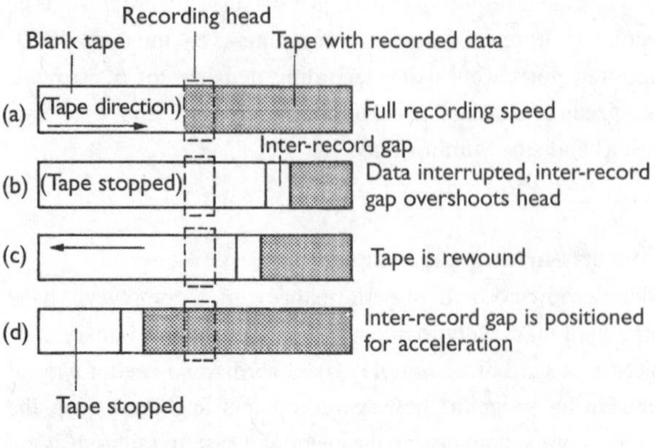

Cassettes and cartridges

The digital cassette recorder is comparable in size with the domestic cassette player. The cassettes themselves are identical to those used to record music except that they are made to a much higher standard, and are free from imperfections such as dropout. Figure 9.67 shows the structure of a cassette drive, which hardly differs from the domestic version.

A typical cassette recorder records digital data at a density of 1600 bpi. Note that a cassette drive records data along one track serially, unlike the nine-track reel-to-reel tape transport. The data is phase encoded. Some systems have a two-track head, but the tracks are not used concurrently. They merely double the effective length of the tape by allowing one head to access the upper surface and one head the lower surface. The tape moves at 15 in/s in the read or write modes, and data is transferred at 24 kbit/s.

The read/write head has a dual gap allowing simultaneous reading and writing. A combined read/write head permits the recorded data to be read back immediately after it has been recorded and any record errors detected. If an error is found, the writing of the current block may be aborted, the tape backed up, and the block rewritten.

The cartridge is merely an upmarket version of the cassette. A typical cartridge uses $\frac{1}{4}$ in magnetic tape, holds 10 times as much data as a cassette, and generally exceeds the performance of a cassette drive in all respects. A low-cost cartridge drive stores about 500 Mbyte of data.

During the late 1980s technology of the VCR (video-cassette recorder) was applied to magnetic cartridge drives. The VCR employs a tape whose *effective length* is many times longer than its actual length, because the video track is recorded as a series of parallel diagonal stripes. The mechanism

Fig. 9.66 Repositioning tape in a streaming drive.

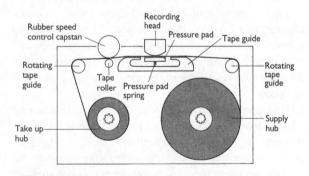

Fig. 9.67 The cassette tape.

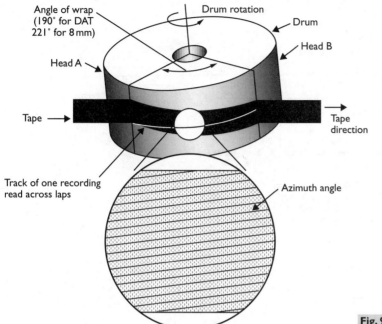

Fig. 9.68 Helical scan recording.

used to record data is called *helical scan* technology because the recording head rotates and traces out a *helix*. Figure 9.68 illustrates the principle of helical scan recording. Helical scan technology is now used in DAT (digital audiotape) systems and has been applied to digital data storage. DAT recording systems are used to archive large amounts of data (e.g. 5 Gbyte).

A typical DAT recorder uses $\frac{1}{4}$ in (8 mm) tape and stores data at about 61 000 bits/in. The linear speed of the tape is only 0.32 in/s, but the effective speed is much greater because of the helical scanning mechanism. Because the speed of a DAT tape is so much lower than that of tape in a conventional cartridge (90 in/s against 0.32 in/s), the DAT tape is more durable. A DAT is good for over 1000 passes, whereas a conventional cartridge might begin to wear out after 100 passes.

9.6 Optical memory technology

Optical storage is the oldest method of storing information known to humanity. Early systems employed indentations in stone or pottery that were eventually rendered obsolete by flexible optical storage media (better known as *papyrus* and later *paper*). Yesterday's computers employed punched cards and paper tape optical storage, where the presence or absence of holes in the card or paper tape records the data. Both punched cards and paper tape were often read by mechanical means rather than optical means.

Between the 1950s and the 1980s, the principal secondary storage systems employed by general-purpose digital computers used magnetic devices to store information. Optical storage systems were not widely used until the 1990s, because it was difficult to perform all the actions required to store and retrieve data economically until improvements had been made in a wide range of technologies.

The optical disk or *CD-ROM* has dramatically changed secondary storage technology and made it possible to store large quantities of information in a small area at a low cost. A CD-ROM can store over 500 Mbyte of user data on one side of a single 120 mm (4.72 in) disc, which is equivalent to around 200 000 pages of text or 400 high-density $3\frac{1}{2}$ in floppy disks. The optical disk is a rigid plastic disk (Fig. 9.69(a)), whose surface is covered with a long spiral track. The track is laid down on a substrate inside the disk and is covered with a transparent plastic protective layer. Like the magnetic disk, information is stored along a track in binary form. Unlike the magnetic disk, the track in an optical disk is a continuous spiral (like that of a gramophone record). The spiral on a CD begins at the innermost track and spirals outward, whereas the track on a gramophone record begins at the edge and spirals inward.

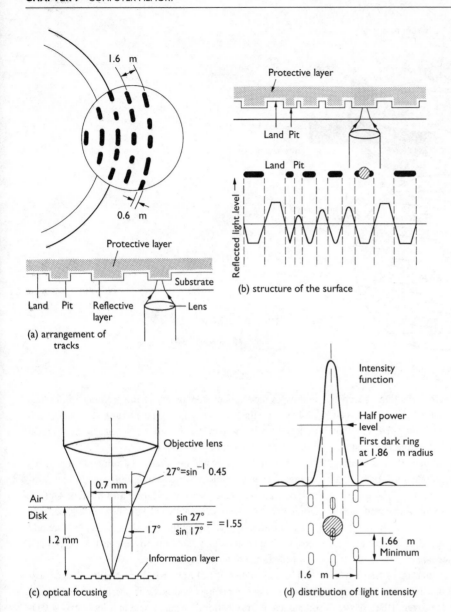

(a) arrangement of tracks

(b) structure of the surface

(c) optical focusing

(d) distribution of light intensity

Fig. 9.69 The optical disk system.

Although the principles of the optical disk are almost trivial, the details of its operation are very complex. The fundamental problems of optical storage are reliability, detecting the presence of tiny dents called *pits* on the surface of the disk, optically tracking the reflective elements, and encoding/decoding the data.

9.6.1 Storing and reading information

An optical disk stores information by means of reflecting or non-reflecting metallic dots along the track. A beam of light produced by a semiconductor laser is focused on the surface of the track and a photosensitive transistor or diode detects the light reflected back from the surface. Figure 9.69(b) illustrates the structure of the surface of an optical disk and shows that the amount of light reflected back from a laser depends on the 'height' of the reflecting surface. The base of this reflecting surface is called the *land* and indentations in it are known as *pits* (when viewed from above the disk).

Data is recorded as a series of variable length *pits* along a spiral track at a constant pitch (1.6 μm). A CD has 20 000 tracks and a track is 30 times narrower than a single human hair. The *pits* and *land* are coated on a substrate and covered with a protective transparent layer. The disk is produced by stamping from a master disk that is, itself, produced by the same type of technology employed to fabricate microprocessors. It's very expensive to make one CD-ROM, but very cheap to make thousands. Indeed, by the late 1990s CD-ROMs were used to distribute advertising material and software from Internet service providers so freely that computer magazines were full of readers' letters asking what they should do with all these unwanted CDs.

Light from the laser is focused first through an objective lens and then by the air–disk interface onto the pits and land as Fig. 9.69(c) demonstrates. This arrangement means that the spot of light on the surface is very much larger (by three orders of magnitude) than the pits. Consequently, surface imperfections and dust particles don't interfere with the readback process. In other words, you can tolerate a speck of dust on the surface of a CD that's over 100 times larger than the pit on which the beam is focused without getting a read error. (By the way, many CD users put a CD down with the clear side up because they think the clear side must be protected. That's not so. The side with the pits and lands is covered with a very thin (0.02 mm) protective coating and is much more vulnerable to scratches than the clear side.)

In order to understand how data from a CD is read, you have to know something about the nature of laser light. The individual light waves in light from the sun or from a lamp are *incoherent* or random; that is, the light source is composed of a very large number of random waves. Light from a laser is *coherent* and all the waves are synchronized—they go up and down together. If you take two laser beams with identical frequencies and shine them on the same spot the beams add up. If the beams are in-phase (i.e. the light waves go up and down at the same time) the resulting spot will be four times as bright (not twice as bright because the beam's energy is the square of its amplitude). However, if the beams are 180° out of phase with one wave going up as the other goes down, the waves will cancel and the spot will disappear.

When light from the laser hits the *land* (i.e. the area between the pits), the light is reflected back and can be detected by a light-sensitive diode. When the light from the laser hits a pit, about half falls on the pit and the other half on the land around the pit. The height of the pit is approximately 0.13 μm above the surrounding land so that light that hits the land has to travel an extra 2×0.13 μm further to get to the detector. However, 0.13 μm corresponds to $\frac{1}{4}$ of the wavelength of the light in the plastic medium and the light reflected back from around a pit travels $\frac{1}{2}$ wavelength further than the light reflected from the top of a pit. The light from the pit and light reflected from the surrounding land *destructively interfere* and the light waves cancel each other out. Figure 9.69(b) demonstrates how the pits modulate the relative intensity of the light. A change in the level of light intensity reflected from the surface of the disk represents a change from land to pit or from pit to land. Figure 9.70 from Philips shows in more detail how light from land and pits is detected.

The spot of laser light that follows a track should be as small as possible in order to pack as many pits (and therefore as much data) onto the disk as possible. The minimum size of the spot is determined by a number of practical engineering considerations. The resolution (i.e. the smallest element that can be seen) of the optical system is determined by the wavelength of the laser light (780 nm) and the *numerical aperture* of the objective lens (0.45). Numerical aperture, NA, is defined as lens diameter/focal length and the value of 0.45 is a compromise between resolution and *depth of focus* (increasing the resolution and hence storage capacity makes it harder

(a) Organization of the track with land/pits

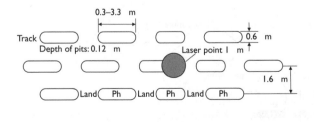

(b) Light reflected from land and pits

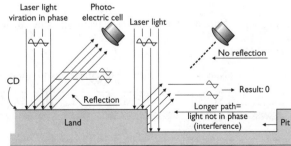

Fig. 9.70 Detecting light from land and pits. (a) Organization of the track with land/pits; (b) light reflected from land and pits.

to focus the beam on the disk). These values of wavelength and NA provide a minimum resolution of $1\,\mu m$. Note that there is sometimes confusion about the wavelength of the laser light. The wavelength is 780 nm in air, but when the laser beam travels through the plastic material of the disk its wavelength is reduced to 500 nm.

Figure 9.69(d) shows the distribution of light intensity from a beam of light falling on a pit within an array of pits (formed by adjacent tracks). At the microscopic level, a beam of light doesn't have a hard edge but instead displays an *intensity distribution*. The sizes of the pits are such that half the energy of the spot falls on a pit and half falls on the land. The reflected energy is ideally zero if the light from the pits and land interferes destructively. The optimum separation of the pits is determined by the wavelength of the light used by the laser.

The data stored on the CD-ROM has to be encoded to achieve both maximum storage density and freedom from errors. Moreover, the encoding technique must be self-clocking to simplify the data recovery circuits. Figure 9.71 illustrates the basic encoding scheme chosen by the designers of the CD-ROM. The length of the pits themselves is modulated and the transition of a pit to land (or from land to pit) represents a one bit.

The source data is encoded so that each 8-bit byte is transformed into a 14-bit code. Although there are $2^{14} = 16\,384$ possible 14-bit patterns, only $2^8 = 256$ of these patterns are actually used. The encoding algorithm chooses 14-bit code words that do not have two consecutive 1s separated by fewer than two 0s. Moreover, the longest permitted run of 0s

is 10. These two restrictions mean that the 14-bit code has 267 legal values, of which 256 are actually used. The 14-bit codes corresponding to the first ten 8-bit codes are given in Table 9.9.

The groups of 14-bit code words are not simply joined end-to-end, but are separated by three so-called *merging bits*. The function of the merging bits is to ensure that the encoding rules are not violated when the end of one group is taken in conjunction with the start of the next. These merging bits carry no useful data and are simply separators. The following example demonstrates the need for merging bits:

Source data: 0010   1000........

These two patterns generate the sequence ...00101000.... Note how the end of the first group and the start of the second

	Source data bits	Encoded bits
0	00000000	01001000100000
1	00000001	10000100000000
2	00000010	10010000100000
3	00000011	10001000100000
4	00000100	01000100000000
5	00000101	00001000010000
6	00000110	00010000100000
7	00000111	00100100000000
8	00001000	01001001000000
9	00001001	10000001000000
10	00001010	10010001000000

Table 9.9 Converting 8-bit values to a 14-bit code.

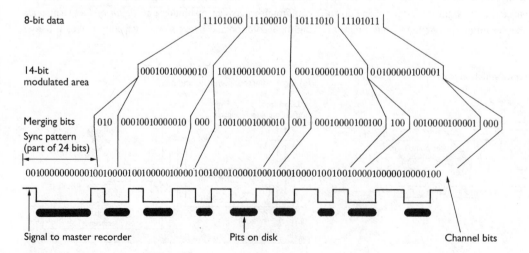

8-bit data |11101000|11100010|10111010|11101011|

14-bit modulated area |00010010000010|10010001000010|00010000100100|00100000100001|

Merging bits
Sync pattern (part of 24 bits) |010|00010010000010|000|10010001000010|001|00010000100100|100|00100000100001|000|

00100000000001001000010010000010000100100010000100010001000010010010000100000100000100

Signal to master recorder   Pits on disk   Channel bits

Fig. 9.71 Encoding data on an optical disk.

group create the forbidden pattern 101, which has a 1 separated from another 1 by fewer than two 0s. We can solve the problem by inserting the separator 000 between the groups to get

Encoded data: ....00100001000.......

Three 0s (i.e. merging bits) have been inserted between the two code words to eliminate the possibility of a forbidden sequence of bits.

Another factor in the choice of the pattern of bits to be used as the merging bits is the need to keep the lengths of the track and land along the surface of the tracks equal (when averaged). This restriction is necessary because the CD drive's focusing and tracking mechanism uses the average energy reflected from the surface, and it is therefore necessary to avoid changes in average energy due to data dependency.

The channel clock derived from the signal recovered from the pits and land is 4.3218 MHz, because this is the maximum rate of change of signal from the pits and land at the standard CD scanning speed of 1.3 m/s. The bit density is 1.66 bit/μm or 42 kbit/in. At a track pitch of 1.6 μm this corresponds to 6×10^8 bit/in^2 or 10^6 bit/mm^2.

So far, we've talked about the encoding of the data to achieve a maximum density of bits. Due to the way in which pits are laid down and the unbelievably high precision required by the system, it's impossible to avoid large numbers of errors. Since we can't realistically reduce the number of errors, we have to employ powerful error-correcting codes to nullify the effect of the errors. Due to the complexity of these codes (not to mention the mathematical background), all we can do here is to describe their characteristics.

The Cross Interleaved Reed–Solomon code (CIRC) takes groups of 24 bytes of data and encodes them into groups of 32 bytes. Information is *interleaved* (spread out over the surface of a track) so that a burst of errors at one physical location affects several code groups. The following hypothetical example should clarify this concept. Suppose data is recorded in groups of 4 bytes $a_1a_2a_3a_4$ $b_1b_2b_3b_4$ $c_1c_2c_3c_4$ $d_1d_2d_3d_4$ and that a group is not corrupted unless two bytes are lost in a group (because of some form of error-correcting mechanism). Since errors tend to occur in groups (because of, say, a scratch), large amounts of data will be lost. If we interleave the bytes, we might get $a_1b_1c_1d_1$ $a_2b_2c_2d_2$ $a_3b_3c_3d_3$ $a_4b_4c_4d_4$. In this case, if we lose two consecutive bytes, we will be able to correct the error because the bytes are from different groups.

One of the differences between the CD used to store audio information and the CD-ROM used by computers is

that the latter employs an extra layer of encoding to reduce further the undetected error rate to one in 10^{13} bits. Moreover, the sophisticated CIRC encoding makes it possible to correct an error burst of up to 450 bytes (which would take up 2 mm of track length). The capacity of a CD-ROM is 553 Mbyte of user data (an audio CD can store 640 Mbyte of sound).

The spiral track of the CD-ROM is divided into sectors and each sector is individually addressable. The address of a sector is expressed *absolutely* with respect to the start of the track and is in the form of minutes, seconds, and blocks from the start (this format is the same as that of the audio CD). A sector or block is composed of 12 synchronizing bytes (for clock recovery), a 4 byte header that identifies the sector, a block of 2048 bytes of user data and 288 auxiliary bytes largely made up of the error-correcting code.

Because the size of the pits is constant and they are recorded along a spiral on a disk, the number of pits per revolution must vary between the inner and outer tracks. Contrast this with the magnetic disk, in which the bit density changes between inner and outer tracks because the *bits* must be smaller on inner tracks if there are to be the same number as in outer tracks.

A consequence of constant-size pits is that the speed of the disk depends on the location of the sector being read (i.e. the disk moves with a *constant linear velocity*, rather than a *constant angular velocity*). Think about it: if the pits have a constant length, there are more pits around an outer track and therefore the disk must rotate slowly to read them at a constant rate. As the read head moves in towards the center, the disk must speed up since there are fewer pits around the circumference. First-generation CD-ROMs (and audio CDs) spin at between about 200 and 500 r.p.m. As you might imagine, this arrangement severely restricts the access time of the system. Moreover, the relatively heavy read head assembly also reduces the maximum track-to-track stepping time. These factors together limit the average access time of a CD-ROM to the region of 100–200 ms (an order of magnitude worse than hard disks). We used the expression *track-to-track stepping*, even through the track is really a continuous spiral. When in the seek mode, the head steps across the spiral and reads an address block to determine whether it has reached the correct part of the spiral. As the technology used to manufacture CD drives improved through the 1990s, drive speeds were increased. Speeds went up from twice to 40 times the nominal CD rotation speed by the end of the 1990s and average access times dropped to 80 ms.

9.6.2 **Tracking and focusing**

We have described how data is stored on a CD, but have said little about the mechanism used to read it from the surface of the disk. To give you an idea of the precision involved, the objective lens is positioned about 1 mm above the surface of the disk and the depth of focus of the spot is 2 μm. The lens must be positioned to an accuracy of about one millionth of a meter above the disk in a system costing a few dollars. We now look at the way in which data is read and focusing and tracking are achieved.

Figure 9.72 demonstrates how data is read from a CD. Coherent light from the laser at a wavelength of approximately 780 nm is focused on the surface of the disk. The light is passed through a *quarter wave plate* that rotates the plane of its polarization by 45°. Light from the surface of the disk is reflected back along the same axis as the incident light and is reflected by a polarizing prism, which rotates its polarization by 45° to the detector. Since the polarization of the light has now been rotated by 90° with respect to the light from the laser, it is possible to ensure that only the light reflected from the disk's surface reaches the detector.

Figure 9.73 is a line drawing from Philips that illustrates the structure of a CD-ROM read and tracking head. Note that the laser itself isn't moved to perform focusing or fine-tracking. A voice coil moves the much lighter objective lens through which the light passes.

Because the optical system requires a degree of positioning that is accurate to within a fraction of the wavelength of light, a precise positioning mechanism is necessary. Precision servomotors determine the horizontal position of the read head and its position from the surface of the disk is determined by a coil in a magnetic field (changing the current in

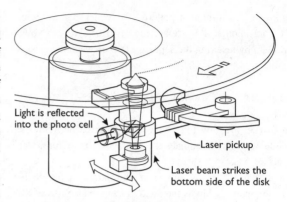

Fig. 9.73 Organization of CD optics.

the coil changes the force between the coil and the magnet). Figure 9.74(a) illustrates the principle of the vertical positioning (i.e. focusing) mechanism. Light from the surface is split into two equal halves by an optical wedge and these beams are focused on a pair of photodiodes.

When the beam is correctly focused on the surface (position B in Fig. 9.74(a)), the two beams are focused on the center of each of the photodiode pairs. Each diode produces an equal output and no position correction is necessary. However, if the head moves towards the disk surface (position C), the reflected beam is wider and the optical wedge causes the split beams to focus behind the photodiodes in position C_1. As a result of this, inner diodes D_2 and D_3 receive less light than the outer diodes. If the head moves away from the surface, the converse situation arises. It is possible to derive a focusing signal from

$$F_{error} = (D_1 + D_4) - (D_2 + D_3)$$

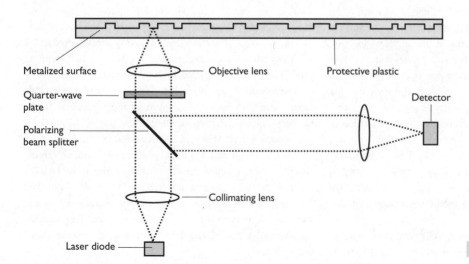

Metalized surface

Quarter-wave plate

Polarizing beam splitter

Objective lens

Protective plastic

Detector

Collimating lens

Laser diode

Fig. 9.72 Structure of CD optics.

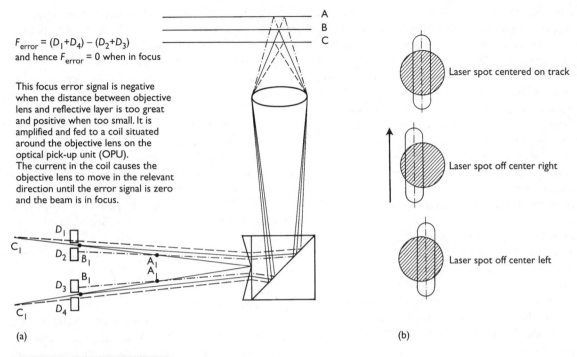

$F_{error} = (D_1 + D_4) - (D_2 + D_3)$
and hence $F_{error} = 0$ when in focus

This focus error signal is negative when the distance between objective lens and reflective layer is too great and positive when too small. It is amplified and fed to a coil situated around the objective lens on the optical pick-up unit (OPU).
The current in the coil causes the objective lens to move in the relevant direction until the error signal is zero and the beam is in focus.

Laser spot centered on track

Laser spot off center right

Laser spot off center left

(a)

(b)

Fig. 9.74 CD focusing mechanism.

Radial focusing (i.e. making sure that the beam falls exactly in the center of the track) is performed in a similar way to focusing in the vertical plane. Figure 9.74(b) demonstrates the effect of a beam focused exactly on the pits and beams that are offset to the left and to the right of a track. When a beam is correctly focused, both pairs of diodes D_1, D_2 and D_3, D_4 receive equal amounts of light. If the beam drifts off track, one pair will receive more light than the other. A radial error can be obtained by comparing the outputs from the pairs of detectors.

$$R_{error} = (D_1 + D_2) - (D_3 + D_4)$$

The radial error can be used to move the head to the left or the right. This focusing arrangement is elegant because it employs the same hardware to focus in two dimensions simultaneously.

The received data rate is compared with an accurate crystal clock and any difference is used to speed up or to slow down the disk's drive motor.

Optical disks will not completely replace magnetic disks in the near future. As we said above, optical disks rotate at a relatively low speed and the laser head has a much greater mass than a flying thin-film magnetic read/write head. Taken together these make the access time of optical disks relatively slow. Furthermore, it is relatively difficult to write to optical

disks, which means that low-cost systems are read-only and are best suited to information retrieval systems (e.g. programs, encyclopedias, literature surveys, and legal and medical information).

9.6.3 Writable CDs

Because it is easier to write information on a CD than to erase it, some optical storage systems operate in a *write-once, read-mostly* mode called WORM. Typical WORMs store about 550 Mbyte of data (single-sided) and have an access time of the order of 100 ms. Although you can't erase data on a WORM, a 550 Mbyte capacity is sufficiently large to add a new file each time an existing file is updated. In the early 1990s a WORM drive cost about $3000 and media cost $100. By the end of the 1990s, the cost of these drives and their media had declined by a factor of over 20.

There is no single leading WORM technology, and the various manufacturers employ different techniques to write to the CD (the principles of reading and tracking are the same as the CD-ROM). Some WORMs simply ablate (i.e. blast away) the surface of a non-reflecting layer of material above a reflecting background to create a pit. Some WORMs employ a powerful laser to melt a region of a coating of tellurium to create a pit. Another type of writable disk is called CD-R, which uses an organic dye within a layer in the disk. When the dye is hit by a laser during the write operation, the dye's optical properties are modified. The write laser has a power of 30 mW, which is about six times more powerful than the laser used to read data from a CD.

It is possible to create true read/write optical storage systems that are able to write data onto the disk, read it, and then erase it in order to write over it. Clearly, any laser technology that burns or ablates a surface cannot be used in an erasable system. Erasable CDs employ a rather complex technology that exploits several fundamental principles in physics (the optical properties of the CD and the *magneto-optical* properties of matter).

Figure 9.75 illustrates the principle of the erasable CD. The CD substrate is pre-stamped with the track structure and the track or groove coated with a number of layers (some are for the protection of the active layer). The active layer uses a material like terbium iron cobalt (TeFeCo) that changes the polarization of the reflected laser light. The magnetization of the TeFeCo film determines the direction of the reflected light's polarization.

Initially the film in Fig. 9.75(a) is subjected to a uniform magnetic field to align the TeFeCo molecules and therefore provide a *base direction* for the polarization of the reflected

light. This base can be thought of as a continuous stream of zero bits. During the write phase, Fig. 9.75(b), a short pulse of laser light hits the surface and heats the film changing its magnetic properties. By simultaneously activating an electromagnet under the surface of the disk, the direction of the film's magnetization can be reversed with respect to the base direction. This action creates a 1 state. When the spot cools down (Fig. 9.75(c)), the drop in temperature fixes the new direction of magnetization.

The disk is read by focusing a much weaker polarized beam on the disk and then detecting whether the reflected beam was rotated clockwise or anticlockwise (Fig. 9.75(c)). To erase a bit, the area that was written to is pulsed once again with the light power laser and the direction of the magnetic field from the electromagnet reversed to write a zero. Table 9.10 describes the characteristics of a typical magneto-optical disk drive.

High-capacity CDs

Not very long ago, the 600 Mbyte $5\frac{1}{4}$ in CD-ROM was the state of the art. Progress in everything from laser technology to head positioning to optical technology soon meant that the CD-ROM was no longer at the cutting edge of technology. Like all the other parts of the computer, the CD-ROM has evolved. In the late 1990s a new technology called the DVD-ROM (*digital versatile disk*) appeared. The DVD-ROM has a minimum capacity 6 times that of a CD-ROM and a potential capacity much more than that. Part of the driving force behind the DVD-ROM has been the desire to put video (i.e. feature-length films) on disk in digital format.

The DVD-ROM looks like a conventional CD-ROM, and the underlying technology is exactly the same. Only the parameters have changed. Improvements in optical tracking have allowed the track spacing to be reduced and hence the length of the track to be considerably increased. DVD tracks are 0.74 mm apart (conventional CD-ROMs use 1.6 mm spacing). Lasers with shorter wavelengths (635 nm) have permitted the use of smaller pits.

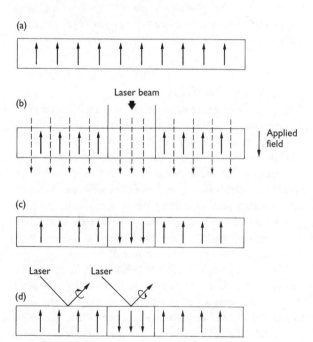

Fig. 9.75 Principle of the rewritable optical disk.

Capacity	1.3 Gbyte
Bytes/sector	1024
Seek time	39.6 ms (max)
	0.35 ms (track-to-track)
	19.8 ms (random seek)
Average latency	8.9 ms
Rotation speed	3375 r.p.m.
Transfer rate	23.95 Mbit/s
MTBF	1 000 000 hours
Unrecoverable errors	Fewer than 1 per 10^{13} bits read

Table 9.10 Characteristics of a magneto-optical disk drive.

The DVD-ROM can be double-sided, which instantly doubles its data capacity. Moreover, by using semitrans-parent layers, it is possible to have several optical layers within the disk. Focusing the laser on a particular layer accesses data in that layer. Other layers are out of focus.

Summary

The von Neumann machine needs memory to store programs and data—lots of memory. As computer technology has advanced, the size of user programs and operating systems has more than kept up. In the early 1980s a PC with a 10 Mbyte hard disk was state-of-the-art. Today, even a modest 'utility' might require over 10 Mbyte.

In this chapter we have looked at some of the aspects of a computer's memory system. We began with a description of the characteristics of fast semiconductor memory and then moved on to the characteristics of slower but much cheaper se ondary storage. Today, there is a bewildering number of memory technologies. We have briefly covered some of them: from semiconductor dynamic memory to devices based on magnetism to optical storage technology. Memory technology is important because, to a great extent, it determines the way in which we use computers. Faster CPUs make it possible to process data rapidly, enabling us to tackle problems like high-speed real-time graphics. Faster, denser, and cheaper memories make it possible to store and process large volumes of data. For example, the optical disk makes it possible to implement very large on-line databases. Low-cost high-capacity hard disks now enable people to carry more than 4 Gbyte of data in a portable computer or over 20 Gbyte in a desktop machine. In just two decades the capacity of hard disks in personal computers has increased by a factor of 2000.

Tutorial problems

Problem 1

An 8-bit microprocessor with a 16-bit address bus accesses addresses in the range 101xxxxxxxxxxxxx (where the bits marked 101 are selected by the address decoder and the xs refer to locations within the memory block).

(a) What range of addresses does this block correspond to?
(b) How big is this block?

Solution

(a) The lowest address is 1010000000000000 and the highest address is 1011111111111111. This corresponds to the range $A000 to $BFFF.
(b) Three address lines are decoded to divide the address space spanned by A_0 to A_{15} into eight blocks. The size of one block is $64K/8 = 8K$. You could also calculate the size of the block because you know it is spanned by 13 address lines and $2^{13} = 8K$.

Problem 2

An 8-bit microprocessor with a 16-bit address bus addresses a block of 32 kbyte of ROM.

(a) How many memory components are required if the memory is composed of 8 kbyte chips?
(b) What address lines from the processor select a location in the 32 kbyte ROM?
(c) What address lines have to be decoded to select the ROM?
(d) What is the range of memory locations provided by each of the chips (assuming that the memory blocks are mapped contiguously in the region of memory space starting at address $0000)?

Solution

(a) The number of chips required is (memory block)/(chip size) = $32K/8K = 4$.
(b) Each chip has $8K = 2^{13}$ locations which are accessed by the 13 address lines A_0 to A_{12} from the processor.
(c) Address lines A_0 to A_{12} from the CPU select a location in the chip leaving A_{13} to A_{15} to be decoded.
(d) The memory blocks are

$0000 to $1FFF
$2000 to $3FFF
$4000 to $5FFF
$6000 to $7FFF

Problem 3

Draw an address decoding table to satisfy the following memory map

RAM1	00 0000—00 FFFF
RAM2	01 0000—01 FFFF
I/O_1	E0 0000—E0 001F
I/O_2	E0 0020—E0 003F

Solution

```
Address lines
23 22 21 20 19 18 17 16 15 14 13 12 11 10 9  8  7  6  5  4  3  2  1  0   Device Range
 0  0  0  0  0  0  0  0  x  x  x  x  x  x x  x  x  x  x  x  x  x  x  x   RAM1   00 0000—00 FFFF
 0  0  0  0  0  0  0  1  x  x  x  x  x  x x  x  x  x  x  x  x  x  x  x   RAM2   01 0000—01 FFFF
 1  1  1  0  0  0  0  0  0  0  0  0  0  0 0  0  0  0  0  0  x  x  x  x  x   I/O1   E0 0000—E0 001F
 1  1  1  0  0  0  0  0  0  0  0  0  0  0 0  0  0  0  0  1  x  x  x  x  x   I/O2   E0 0020—E0 003F
```

Problem 4

A 68000 microprocessor system implements the following memory blocks:

(a) 1 Mbyte of ROM using $256K \times 16$-bit chips
(b) 8 Mbyte of DRAM using $2M \times 4$-bit chips

Construct a suitable address-decoding table and design an address decoder for this system.

Solution

A 16-bit wide chip provides two bytes of data per location. Therefore, a single $256K \times 16$-bit ROM provides 512 kbyte of data. We need two of these chips to provide 1 Mbyte (Fig. 9.76). A 1 Mbyte block of data contains 2^{20} bytes and is spanned by address lines A_{00} to A_{19}. In a 68000-based system address lines A_{20} to A_{23} must be decoded to select this block. Assume that the block of ROM is located at address \$00 0000 and that $A_{23},A_{22},A_{21},A_{20}=0,0,0,0$. This 1 Mbyte block is composed of two 512 kbyte sub-blocks. Therefore one of these sub-blocks is selected when $A_{19}=0$ and the other when $A_{19}=1$.

The 8 Mbyte of DRAM are spanned by A_{00} to A_{22} (i.e. 2^{23} bytes). This block of memory must be on an 8 Mbyte boundary (i.e. \$00 0000 or \$80 0000 in a 68000-based system).

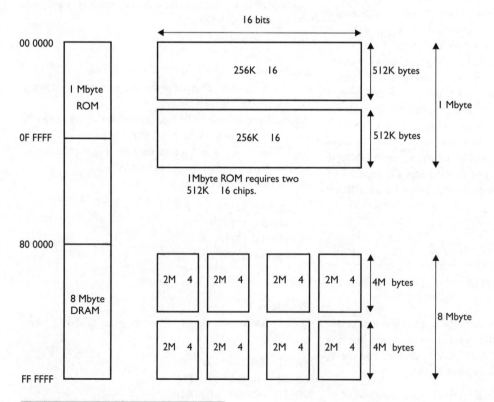

Fig. 9.76 Memory map of system in Problem 4.

Since $00\,0000$ is occupied by ROM, we'll put the DRAM at $80\,0000$ for which $A_{23} = 1$. This block is composed of 2M-location by 4-bit-wide devices. Four 4-bit-wide chips are required in-line to provide 16 bits (2 bytes) of data. The amount of data provided by these four chips per location is 2M locations $\times 2$ bytes $= 4M$. We need two of these sub-blocks to get 8Mbyte. The first sub-block is selected by $A_{22} = 0$ and the second by $A_{22} = 1$.

The second step is to construct an address-decoding table. Note that a memory block must be on a boundary equal to its own size. The following address-decoding table shows address lines A_{23} to A_{00}. Although the 68000 lacks an A_{00} line because it uses data strobes for byte selection, it's easier to add an A_{00} line to the table so that we can operate in bytes (rather than words).

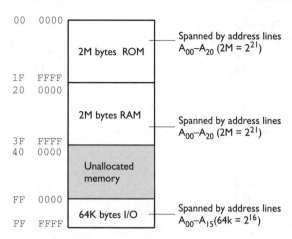

Fig. 9.77 Memory map for Problem 5.

Address decoding table for Problem 4

Device	Range		A_{23}	A_{22}	A_{21}	A_{20}	A_{19}	A_{18}	...	A_{00}
ROM1	00 0000–07	FFFF	0	0	0	0	0	x	...	x
ROM2	08 0000–0F	FFFF	0	0	0	0	I	x	...	x
DRAM1	80 0000–BF	FFFF	I	0	x	x	x	x	...	x
DRAM2	C0 0000–FF	FFFF	I	I	x	x	x	x	...	x

Note that if you didn't treat the 8 Mbyte block of DRAM as a single block, but as two separate 4 Mbyte blocks, you could put each of these 4 Mbyte sub-blocks on any 4 Mbyte. The following address decoding table is also a legal solution.

Solution

First draw a memory map (Fig. 9.77). A block of memory must be located on a byte boundary equal to its own size (e.g. 1 Mbyte block must fall on $00\,0000$, $10\,0000$, $20\,0000$, ..., $F0\,0000$ boundaries).

Device	Range		A_{23}	A_{22}	A_{21}	A_{20}	A_{19}	A_{18}	...	A_{00}
ROM1	00 0000–07	FFFF	0	0	0	0	0	x	...	x
ROM2	08 0000–0F	FFFF	0	0	0	0	I	x	...	x
DRAM1	40 0000–7F	FFFF	0	I	x	x	x	x	...	x
DRAM2	80 0000–BF	FFFF	I	0	x	x	x	x	...	x

Problem 5

Design an address decoder for the following 68000 memory map:

(a) 2 Mbyte of EPROM starting at address $00\,0000$ using $512K \times 8$ chips

(b) 2 Mbyte of RAM using $256K \times 8$ chips

(c) 64 kbyte I/O space starting at $FF\,0000$

The next step is to decide how the memory blocks are organized. The EPROM block is composed of $512K \times 8$-bit chips. Two chips are needed side-by-side to span the 68000's 16-bit data bus (i.e. the basic unit of storage is 1024 kbyte). Two 1024 kbyte blocks are required. The RAM is composed of $256K \times 8$-bit chips. Two of these side-by-side make a block of 512 kbyte (four 512 kbyte blocks are needed in all).

We can now draw an address decoding table. Address lines used to access a location within a memory are marked X. Address lines used to select the block are marked by 0 or 1

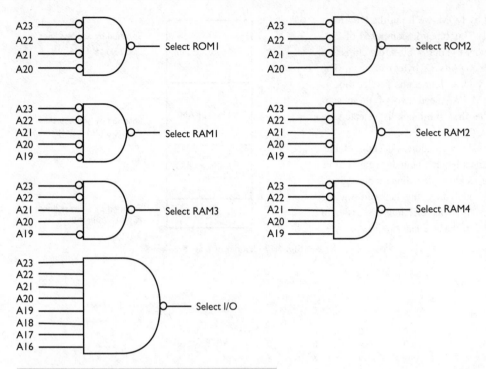

Fig. 9.78 Circuit diagram of address decoder for Problem 5.

(according to the location of the block within the memory map).

	A_{23}	A_{22}	A_{21}	A_{20}	A_{19}	A_{18}	A_{17}	A_{16}	A_{15}	A_{14}	A_{13}	A_{12}	A_{11}	A_{10}	A_{09}	A_{08}	A_{07}	A_{06}	A_{05}	A_{04}	A_{03}	A_{02}	A_{01}	A_{00}
ROM1	0	0	0	0	X	X	X	X	X	X	X	X	X	X	X	X	X	X	X	X	X	X	X	X
ROM2	0	0	0	1	X	X	X	X	X	X	X	X	X	X	X	X	X	X	X	X	X	X	X	X
RAM1	0	0	1	0	0	X	X	X	X	X	X	X	X	X	X	X	X	X	X	X	X	X	X	X
RAM2	0	0	1	0	1	X	X	X	X	X	X	X	X	X	X	X	X	X	X	X	X	X	X	X
RAM3	0	0	1	1	0	X	X	X	X	X	X	X	X	X	X	X	X	X	X	X	X	X	X	X
RAM4	0	0	1	1	1	X	X	X	X	X	X	X	X	X	X	X	X	X	X	X	X	X	X	X
I/O	1	1	1	1	1	1	1	1	X	X	X	X	X	X	X	X	X	X	X	X	X	X	X	X

The final step is to design the circuit (Fig. 9.78). This circuit uses random logic. All outputs are active-low because most memory components are selected by active-low chip-select signals.

Problem 6

Design an address decoder using a PROM to implement the following 68000 memory map.

(a) 4 Mbytes of ROM at address $00 0000 using 1 M × 8-bit chips.

(b) 8 Mbytes of RAM at address $80 0000 using 4M × 4-bit chips.

(c) 1 Mbyte of ROM at address $60 000 using 512M × 8-bit chips.

Solution

We begin by working out the sub-blocks of memory required from the size of the specified memory components.

(a) A pair of 1M × 8-bit chips gives 2 Mbyte. We need two sub-blocks to get 4Mbyte.

(b) Four 4M × 4-bit chips gives 8 Mbyte. This provides all our needs.

(c) A pair of 512K × 8-bit chips gives 1 Mbyte. This provides all our needs.

Address decoding table

Device	Range	A_{23}	A_{22}	A_{21}	A_{20}	A_{19}	A_{18}	...	A_{00}	Size
ROM 1	00 0000–1F FFFF	0	0	0	x	x	x	...	x	2 Mbyte
ROM 2	20 0000–3F FFFF	0	0	I	x	x	x	...	x	2 Mbyte
RAM 1	80 0000–FF FFFF	I	x	x	x	x	x	...	x	8 Mbyte
RAM 2	60 0000–6F FFFF	0	I	I	0	x	x	...	x	I Mbyte

If we use a PROM to perform the address decoding, each line (location) in the PROM must select a block equal to the smallest block to be decoded. In this case, the smallest block is 1 Mbyte; that is, the PROM must decode A_{23} to A_{20}. In the following table, D_0 from the PROM selects ROM1, D_1 selects ROM2, D_2 selects RAM2, and D_3 selects RAM1.

Solution

Two byte-wide RAM chips are required to span the 68000's 16-bit data bus. The minimum block of memory is therefore $2 \times 128\,\text{kbyte} = 256\,\text{kbyte}$. This address space is accessed by the 18 address lines A_{17}–A_{00}. We require 1 Mbyte of RAM, or four 256 kbyte blocks. Address lines A_{19}–A_{18} select one

PROM decoding table

Device	Range	A_{23}	A_{22}	A_{21}	A_{20}	D_0	D_1	D_2	D_3
ROM 1	00 0000–0F FFFF	0	0	0	0	0	I	I	I
ROM 1	10 0000–1F FFFF	0	0	0	I	0	I	I	I
ROM 2	20 0000–2F FFFF	0	0	I	0	I	0	I	I
ROM 2	30 0000–3F FFFF	0	0	I	I	I	0	I	I
	40 0000–4F FFFF	0	I	0	0	I	I	I	I
	50 0000–5F FFFF	0	I	0	I	I	I	I	I
RAM 2	60 0000–6F FFFF	0	I	I	0	I	I	0	I
	70 0000–7F FFFF	0	I	I	I	I	I	I	I
RAM 1	80 0000–8F FFFF	I	0	0	0	I	I	I	0
RAM 1	90 0000–9F FFFF	I	0	0	I	I	I	I	0
RAM 1	A0 0000–AF FFFF	I	0	I	0	I	I	I	0
RAM 1	B0 0000–BF FFFF	I	0	I	I	I	I	I	0
RAM 1	C0 0000–CF FFFF	I	I	0	0	I	I	I	0
RAM 1	D0 0000–DF FFFF	I	I	0	I	I	I	I	0
RAM 1	E0 0000–EF FFFF	I	I	I	0	I	I	I	0
RAM 1	F0 0000–FF FFFF	I	I	I	I	I	I	I	0

Problem 7

A memory board in a 68000-based system with a 16-bit data bus has 1 Mbyte of RAM composed of $128\text{K} \times 8$ RAM chips located at address $C0\,0000 onward. The board also has a block of 256 kbyte of ROM composed of $128\text{K} \times 8$ chips located at address $D8\,0000. Design an address decoder for this board.

of these four blocks. Finally, the remaining four address lines A_{23}–A_{20} select this 1 Mbyte block out of the 16 possible 1 Mbyte blocks (A_{23}–$A_{20} = 1100$). The ROM is implemented as a single 256 kbyte block using two 128 kbyte chips. The following table can be used to construct a suitable decoder.

Address decoding table for Problem 7

Device	A_{23}	A_{22}	A_{21}	A_{20}	A_{19}	A_{18}	A_{17}	A_{01}	A_{00}	
RAM1	I	I	0	0	0	0	x...	x	x	C0 0000–C3 FFFF
RAM2	I	I	0	0	0	I	x...	x	x	C4 0000–C7 FFFF
RAM3	I	I	0	0	I	0	x...	x	x	C8 0000–CB FFFF
RAM4	I	I	0	0	I	I	x...	x	x	CC 0000–CF FFFF
ROM	I	I	0	I	I	0	x...	x	x	D8 0000–DB FFFF

Problem 8

Design an address decoder that locates three blocks of memory in the ranges: $00 0000–$7F FFFF, $A0 8000–$A0 8FFF, and $F0 0000–$FF FFFF.

Solution

Address range		$A_{23}–A_{20}$	$A_{19}–A_{16}$	$A_{15}–A_{12}$	$A_{11}–A_8$	$A_7–A_4$	$A_3–A_0$	Block size
000000–7FFFFF	First location	0000	0000	0000	0000	0000	0000	8 Mbyte spanned by
	Last location	0111	1111	1111	1111	1111	1111	24 lines
A08000–A08FFF	First location	1010	0000	1000	0000	0000	0000	4 kbyte spanned by
	Last location	1010	0000	1000	1111	1111	1111	12 lines
F00000–FFFFFF	First location	1111	0000	0000	0000	0000	0000	1 Mbyte spanned by
	Last location	1111	1111	1111	1111	1111	1111	20 lines

From the table, you can see that the first block is selected by address line A_{23}, the second block by address lines $A_{23}–A_{12}$, and the third block by address lines $A_{23}–A_{20}$.

Problem 9

The following address decoding PROM selects three blocks of memory in a 68000-based system. How large is each block, and what address range does it occupy?

CPU Address line	A_{23}	A_{22}	A_{21}	$\overline{CS2}$	$\overline{CS1}$	$\overline{CS0}$
PROM Address line	A_2	A_1	A_0	D_2	D_1	D_0
	0	0	0	0	1	1
	0	0	1	1	1	1
	0	1	0	1	0	1
	0	1	1	1	0	1
	1	0	0	1	1	0
	1	0	1	1	1	0
	1	1	0	1	1	0
	1	1	1	1	1	0

Solution

The PROM decodes the 68000's three highest-order address lines A_{23} to A_{21}. These address lines partition the 68000's 16 Mbyte address space into eight 2 Mbyte blocks. $\overline{CS2}$ selects the 2 Mbyte block for which $A_{23},A_{22},A_{21}=0,0,0$. This is the address space $00 0000 to $1F FFFF. $\overline{CS1}$ selects two 2 Mbyte blocks for which $A_{23},A_{22}=0,1$. This is the 4 Mbyte address space $40 0000 to $7F FFFF. $\overline{CS0}$ selects the four 2 Mbyte blocks for which $A_{23}=1$. This is the 8 Mbyte address space $80 0000 to $FF FFFF.

Problem 10

A 3½ in floppy disk drive uses two-sided disks and records data on 80 tracks per side. A track has 9 sectors and each holds 512 bytes of data. The disk rotates at 360 r.p.m., the seek time is 10 ms track-to-track, the head-settling time is 10 ms, and the head-load time is 200 ms. From the above information calculate:

(a) The total capacity of the floppy disk in bytes.
(b) The average rotational latency.
(c) The average time to locate a given sector assuming that the head is initially parked at track 0, and is in an unloaded state. The head is loaded after the required track has been located.
(d) The time taken to read a single sector once it has been located.
(e) The average rate at which data is moved from the disk to the processor during the reading of a sector. This should be expressed in bits per second.
(f) An estimate of the packing density of the disk in terms of bits per inch around a track located at 1½ inches from the center.

Solution

(a) Total capacity $=$ sides × tracks × sectors × bytes/sector
$$= 2 \times 80 \times 9 \times 512 = 737\,280 \text{ bytes}$$
(called 720 kbyte).

(b) Average rotational latency $= ½$ period of revolution.
360 r.p.m. corresponds to $360/60 = 6$ revolutions per second.
One revolution $= 1/6$ second.
Average latency is therefore $1/12$ second $= 83.3$ ms.

(c) Average time to locate sector $=$ latency + head load time + head settling time + seek time
$$= 83.3 \text{ ms} + 200 \text{ ms} + 10 \text{ ms} + 80/2 \times 10 \text{ ms}$$
$$= 693.3 \text{ ms}.$$

(d) In one revolution (1/6 second) 9 sectors pass under the head.

Therefore, time to read one sector is $1/6 \times 1/9 = 18.52$ ms.

(e) During the reading of a sector, 512 bytes are read in 18.52 ms.

The average data rate is the number of bits read divided by the time taken

$= (512 \times 8)/0.018\,52 = 221\,166$ bits/second.

(f) Packing density = total number of bits divided by track length

$$= 9 \times 512 \times 8/(2 \times 3.142 \times 1\frac{1}{2})$$
$$= 1977.7 \text{ bits/in.}$$

Problems

1. Why is memory required in a computer system?

2. Briefly define the meaning of the following terms associated with memory technology:

   (a) Random access
   (b) Non-volatile
   (c) Dynamic memory
   (d) Access time
   (e) EPROM

3. What properties of matter are used to store data?

4. A computer has a 64-bit data bus and 64-bit-wide memory blocks. If a memory access takes 50 ns, what is the bandwidth of the memory system?

5. A computer has a 64-bit data bus and 64-bit-wide memory blocks. The memory devices have an access time of 45 ns. A clock running at 50 MHz controls the computer and all operations take an integral (i.e. whole number) of clock cycles. What is the effective bandwidth of the memory system?

6. What is the purpose of a semiconductor memory's $\overline{\text{CS}}$ (chip select) input?

7. A dynamic RAM chip costs $\$n$ and is organized as $16M \times 1$ bits. A memory composed of 128 Mbyte is to be built with these chips. If each word of the memory is 64 bits wide, how many chips are required? What is the cost of the memory, if the cost of the other components is estimated to be 20 percent of the cost of the memory chips themselves? Note that one Mbyte is 2^{20} bytes.

8. What are the principal characteristics of *random* access and *serial* access memory?

9. Why is all semiconductor ROM RAM but not all semiconductor RAM ROM?

10. If *content addressable memory*, CAM, could be manufactured as cheaply as current semiconductor memories, what impact do you think it would have on computers? We haven't covered CAM in this text—you'll have to look it up (try the WWW).

11. What is *flash* memory and why is it widely used to store a PC's *BIOS* (basic input/output system)?

12. Use a copy of a current magazine devoted to personal computing to work out the cost of memory today (price per megabyte for RAM, hard disk, CD-ROM, and DVD).

13. Give the size (i.e. the number of addressable locations) of each of the following memory blocks as a power of 2. The blocks are measured in bytes.

    (a) 4K   (b) 16K
    (c) 2M   (d) 64K
    (e) 16M   (f) 256K

14. What address lines are required to span (i.e. address) each of the memory blocks in the previous problem? Assume that the processor is byte-addressable and has 24 address lines A_{00} to A_{23}. What address lines must be decoded to select each of these blocks?

15. What is an *address decoder* and what role does it carry out in a computer?

16. A computer's memory can be constructed from memory components of various capacities (i.e. total number of bits) and organizations (i.e. locations $\times$ width of each location). For each of the following memory blocks, calculate how many of the specified memory chips are required to implement it.

Memory block	Chip organization
(a) 64 kbyte	$8K \times 8$
(b) 1 Mbyte	$32K \times 4$
(c) 16 Mbyte	$256K \times 8$

17. What is partial address decoding and what are its advantages and disadvantages over full address decoding?

18. An address decoder in an 8-bit microprocessor with 16 address lines selects a memory device when address lines A_{15}, A_{14}, A_{13}, $A_{11} = 1$, 1, 0, 1. What is the size of the

memory block decoded and what range of addresses does it span (i.e. what is the first and last addresses in this block)?

19. An address decoder in a 68000-based microprocessor selects a memory device when address lines A_{23}, A_{22}, A_{21}, $A_{20} = 1, 1, 0, 1$. What is the size of the memory block decoded and what range of addresses does it span (i.e. what is the first and last addresses in this block)?

20. Design address decoders to implement each of the following 68000 address maps. In each case, the blocks of memory are to start from address $00 0000.

    (a) 4 blocks of 64 kbyte using 32K × 8-chips
    (b) 8 blocks of 1 Mbyte using 512K × 8-bit chips
    (c) 4 blocks of 128 kbyte using 64K × 8-bit chips

21. A memory system in a 68000-based computer includes blocks of ROM, static RAM, and DRAM. The sizes of these three blocks are

    ROM: 4 Mbyte
    SRAM: 2 Mbyte
    DRAM: 8 Mbyte

    These memory blocks are implemented with the following memory components:

    ROM: 1M × 16-bit chips
    SRAM: 512K × 8-bit chips
    DRAM: 4M × 4-bit chips

    (a) Show how the blocks of memory are organized in terms of the memory devices used to implement them.
    (b) Draw a memory-map for this system and indicate the start and end address of all blocks.
    (c) Draw an address decoding table for this arrangement.
    (d) Design an address decoder for this system using simple logic gates logic.
    (e) Construct an address decoder using a PROM for this system and design a decoding table to show its contents.

22. A computer's memory system is invariably non-homogeneous. That is, it is made up of various types of storage mechanism, each with its own characteristics. Collectively, these storage mechanisms are said to form a *memory hierarchy*. Explain why such a memory hierarchy is necessary, and discuss the characteristics of the memory mechanisms that you would find in a modern high-performance personal computer.

23. In the context of memory systems, what is the meaning of hysteresis?

24. Can you think of any examples of the effects of hysteresis in everyday life?

25. Why does data have to be encoded before it can be recorded on a magnetic medium?

26. Explain how data is recorded using PE encoding and draw a graph of the current in the write head generated by the data stream 10101110.

27. A disk is a serial (sequential) access device that can implement random access files. Explain this apparent contradiction of terminology.

28. How do the following elements of a track-seek time affect the optimum arrangement of data on a disk: acceleration, coasting, deceleration, and settling?

29. What is an audio-visual drive and how does it differ from a conventional hard drive?

30. What are the advantages of the SCSI interface over the IDE interface?

31. What are the limits on ultimate performance in:

    (a) The hard disk
    (b) The floppy disk
    (c) The CD-ROM?

32. What are the operational characteristics of the serial access devices found in a PC? Use one or more of the magazines devoted to the PC to answer this question.

33. An image consists of 64 columns by 64 rows of pixels. Each pixel is a 4-bit 16-level gray-scale value. A sequence of these images is stored on a hard disk. This hard disk rotates at 7200 r.p.m. and has 64 1024-byte sectors per track.

    (a) Assuming that the images are stored sequentially, how fast can they be transferred from disk to screen?
    (b) If the images are stored *randomly* throughout the disk, what is the longest delay between two consecutive images if the disk has 1500 tracks, and the head can step in or out at a rate of one track per millisecond?

34. A hard disk drive has 10 disks and 18 surfaces available for recording. Each surface is composed of 200 concentric tracks and the disks rotate at 7200 r.p.m.. Each track is divided into 8 blocks of 256 32-bit words. There is one read/write head per surface and it is possible to read the 18 tracks of a given cylinder simultaneously. The time to step from track to track is 1 ms (10^{-3} s). Between data transfers the head is parked at the outermost track of the disk.

Calculate:

(a) The total capacity in bits of the disk drive

(b) The maximum data rate in bits/second

(c) The average access time in milliseconds

(d) The average transfer rate when reading 256 word blocks located randomly on the disk

(e) The recording density (bits/in) of the innermost and the outermost tracks if the disk has a 6 in diameter and the outermost track comes to 1 in from the edge of the disk. The track density is 200 tracks/in.

35. Derive an expression for the average distance moved by a head from one cylinder to another (in terms of the number of head movements). Movements are made at random and the disk has N concentric cylinders numbered from 0 to $N - 1$ with the innermost cylinder numbered 0. Assume that when seeking the next cylinder, all cylinders have an equal probability of being selected. Show that the average movement approaches $N/3$ for large values of N.

Hint: Consider the Kth cylinder and calculate the number of steps needed to move to the Jth cylinder, where J varies from 0 to $(N - 1)$.

36. A floppy disk drive has the following parameters:

Sides:	2
Tracks:	80
Sectors/track:	9
Bytes/sector:	1024
Rotational speed:	360 r.p.m.
Track-to-track step time:	1 ms

Using the above data, calculate:

(a) Total capacity of the disk

(b) Average time to locate a sector

(c) Time to read a sector once it has been located

(d) Data transfer rate during the reading of a sector

37. Why does a floppy disk have to be formatted before data can be written to it? How do you think that sector size affects the performance of a disk system?

38. What is a CRC?

39. Several books state that if you get the interleave factor of a disk wrong, the operating system's performance will be dramatically degraded. Why?

40. What are the advantages of MS-DOS's file allocation table (FAT) over the free-sector bit-map and linked list of sectors?

41. Interpret the meaning of the following extract from a FAT.

1	2
2	4
3	7
4	FFFF
5	6
6	8
7	5
8	FFFF
9	FFF7

42. Why are gaps required when a data structure is set up on a floppy disk during formatting?

43. Why are error-detecting systems so important in secondary storage systems (in comparison with primary storage systems)?

44. What are the advantages of a magnetoresistive head over a thin-film head?

45. Use the Internet to find the properties of today's large hard disk drives.

46. SMART technology is used to predict the failure of a hard disk. To what extent can this technology be applied to other components and subsystems in a computer?

47. To what extent can SMART technology be used to construct a computer that uses redundant components to protect against failure?

48. A magnetic tape has a packing density of 800 characters per inch, an interblock gap of $\frac{1}{2}$ inch, and is filled with records. Each contains 400 characters. Calculate the fraction of the tape containing useful data if the records are written as:

(a) Single record blocks

(b) Blocks containing 4 records

49. Data is recorded on magnetic tape at 9600 bpi along each track of 9-track tape. Information is organized as blocks of 20 000 bytes and an *interblock gap* of 0.75 in is left between blocks. No information is recorded in the interblock gaps. What is the *efficiency* of the storage system?

50. An engineer proposes to use a video recorder (VCR) to store digital data. Assume that the useful portion of each line can be used to store 256 bits. What is the storage capacity of a one-hour tape (in bits), and at what rate is data transferred? A TV picture is transmitted as 525 lines, repeated 30 times per second, in the USA and 625 lines, repeated 25 times a second, in the UK.

51. Do standards in memory technology help or hinder progress?

52. Does magnetic tape have a future as a secondary storage medium?

53. What are the relative advantages and disadvantages of magnetic and optical storage systems?

54. Why is a laser needed to read the data on a CD-ROM?

55. Why is it relatively harder to write data on a CD than to read it?

56. Discuss the ethics of this argument: *Copying software ultimately benefits the manufacturer of the copied software, because it creates a larger user-base for the software and, in turn, creates new users that do pay for the software.*

57. Data is recorded along a continuous spiral on a CD-ROM. Data is read from a CD-ROM at a constant bit rate (i.e. the number of bits/s read from the CD-ROM is constant). What implications do you think that this statement has for both the designer and the user of a CD-ROM?

Chapter 10

The CPU, memory, and the operating system

We now look at one of the most important components of a modern computer, the *operating system*. Some might argue that a section on operating systems in an introductory architecture and hardware course is a little out of place. We include this topic here for two reasons. First, the operating system is intimately connected with the hardware that it controls and that it allocates to user programs. Second, students taking a course in computer architecture often take a parallel course in high-level languages and data structures, but don't encounter the formal treatment of operating systems until later in their studies. We have therefore provided this short introduction to operating systems. Operating systems can be very large programs indeed (e.g. 100 Mbyte), although the *kernel* or business end of the operating system that is the subject of this chapter might require only a few kbyte of code.

We begin with an overview of operating systems and then concentrate on four areas in which hardware and software overlap: multitasking, exception handling, memory management (virtual memory), and cache memory.

Multitasking permits a computer to run several programs at the same time. Exception handling is concerned with the way in which the operating system communicates with user applications and external hardware. Memory management translates addresses from the computer into the actual addresses of data within the CPU's memory system. Cache memory enables a computer with a small quantity of high-speed memory and a large amount of slower memory to operate as if the computer were almost entirely composed of high-speed memory. Strictly speaking, cache memories aren't normally regarded as being closely related to operating systems. We include cache memory here because it has some of the characteristics of virtual memory.

Before continuing, we need to make a comment about terminology. The terms *program* and *job* are used synonymously in texts on operating systems and mean the same thing. Similarly, the terms *task* and *process* are also equivalent. A process (i.e. task) is an instance of a program that includes the code, data, and volatile data values in registers. The ability of a computer to execute several processes concurrently is called *multitasking* or *multiprogramming*. However, the term *multiprocessing* describes a system with several processors (CPUs) that run parts of a process in parallel. We do not cover multiprocessing here. In this chapter we will use the terms *process* and *multitasking*.

10.1 The operating system

The relationship between an operating system, OS, and a computer is similar to the relationship between a conductor and an orchestra. The great conductor is an international celebrity who gets invited to take part in talk shows on television and is showered with society's highest awards. And yet the conductor doesn't add a single note to a concert. The importance of conductors is well known—they coordinate the players. Moreover, a good conductor knows the individual strengths and weaknesses of players and can apply them in such a way as to optimize their collective performance.

An operating system is probably the most important piece of software in a computer system, and yet it solves no user-oriented problems. Its role is to coordinate the functional parts of the computer (including software) to maximize the efficiency of the system. We can define *efficiency* as the fraction of time for which the CPU is executing user programs. It would be more accurate if we were to say that the operating system is designed to remove inefficiency from the system. Suppose a program prints a document. While the printer is busy printing the document, the CPU is idling with nothing to do. The operating system would normally intervene to give the CPU something else to do while it's waiting for the printer to finish.

A second and equally important role of the operating system is to act as the interface between the user and the computer. Programmers communicated with first-generation operating systems via a *job control language*, JCL, that looked rather like any other conventional computer language. Many of today's operating systems, such as Microsoft's Windows, have rejected JCLs in favor of graphically oriented operating systems. These operating systems make use of *WIMP* (windows, icons, mouse, and pointer) and *GUI* (graphical user interface) environments and are well suited to those who are not professional computer programmers.

From the user's point of view an operating system should behave like the perfect bureaucrat. It should be efficient, helpful, and (like all the best bureaucrats) remain in the background. For example, a poorly designed operating system, when asked to edit a file, might reply 'ERROR 53'. The programmer now has to find the operating system manual to look up the meaning of ERROR 53. It's all a waste of time really because the last user ripped out the page with the translation of error messages because he or she got fed up with having to refer to them. A really good operating system would have replied: 'Hi there. Sorry, but my disk is full. I've noticed you've got a lot of backup copies, so if you delete a couple I think we'll be able to find room for your file. Have a nice day.' Finkel, in his book *An operating systems vade mecum*, calls this aspect of an operating system the *beautification principle*, which he sums up by '... an operating system is a collection of algorithms that hides the details of the hardware and provides a more pleasant environment'.

Figure 10.1 shows how the components of the operating system relate to each other and to the other programs that run under the operating system's supervision. The diagram is depicted as a series of concentric circles for a good reason— programs in the outer rings use facilities provided by programs in the inner rings. At the center of the circle lies the *scheduler* that switches from one task to another in a multitasking environment. The scheduler is smaller than programs in the outer ring, such as database managers and word processors.

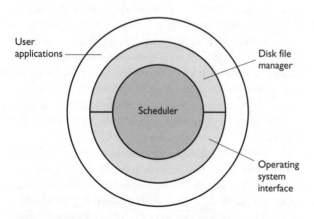

Fig. 10.1 Hierarchical model of an operating system.

User applications

Disk file manager

Scheduler

Operating system interface

A scheduler is often said to be *tightly coded* because it uses a small amount of code optimized for speed.

Sophisticated operating systems employ hardware and software mechanisms to protect the important inner rings from accidental or illegal access by other components. If a user task corrupts part of the kernel, the operating system may crash and the system halt.

Not all computers have an operating system. When a computer acts as a controller or is dedicated to a single process, there is no need for an operating system. The code that executes the process is held in memory in machine code form. Whenever functions normally performed by an operating system are required, they are incorporated into the process itself.

General-purpose operating systems were once found only on large computers, but are now available on all personal computers. Before we look at the details of an operating system, consider the following example. A student wishes to edit and then run a program on a workstation. The student goes to a terminal and logs on. By logging on the student makes his or her presence known to the computer (a request for service), and at the same time the operating system is able to verify the user's identity by means of a password. The logging-on sequence prevents unauthorized users from gaining access to the system, and may also perform an accounting function by measuring the total resources consumed.

If the computer has several terminals, another operating system function is to allocate processing time and memory space to each of the users. The operating system must also prevent one user from accidentally (or maliciously) interfering with another user's programs. In order for the student to edit the program, an editor program must be invoked and the editor told the name of the program to be edited and what the new version is to be called. If any of these activities cannot be completed, the operating system reports back to the user.

When editing is complete, the student submits the job for running. As the program is in source code form (high-level or assembly-level), it must be compiled into object code (binary machine code) before it can be executed. In the days of JCLs the student had to enter several lines of code to compile and run a program. Today's graphically oriented systems allow you to click on a *compile* icon followed by an *execute* icon.

At the end of the session the student logs off, freeing the terminal and the resources allocated to the current job. The operating system returns these resources to its pool and prepares the necessary accounting information and statistics for the student's job. These statistics include the time for which he or she has been connected to the terminal, the actual CPU processing time used, the amount of disk space allocated, and the number of lines of output generated.

10.1.1 Types of operating system

Operating systems can be divided into several categories: single-user, batch mode, demand mode, real-time, and client–server. Like a few other computer concepts, the distinction between operating system classes can be vague, and a real operating system may have attributes common to several classes. We now briefly describe the various types of operating system (although the modern high-performance PC and the local area network have rendered some of them obsolete today).

The *single-user* operating system (e.g. MS-DOS) is the most primitive type and allows only one user or process to access the system at a time. First-generation mainframe operating systems worked in a *batch mode*. Jobs to be executed were fed into the computer, originally in the form of punched cards. Each user's program began with job control cards telling the operating system which of its facilities were required. The operating system scheduled the jobs according to the resources they required and their priority, and eventually generated an output.

Batch mode operation is analogous to a dry cleaning service. Clothes are handed in and are picked up when they've been cleaned. The disadvantage of batch mode systems is their lengthy turn-around time. It was very frustrating in the 1970s to wait five hours for a printout only to discover that the job didn't run because of a simple mistake in one of the cards. Although punched cards are a thing of the past, batch mode operation is still implemented in some systems by creating a file consisting of a sequence of operating system commands.

Demand mode operating systems allow you to access the computer from a terminal, which is a great improvement over batch mode operation because you can complete each step before going on to the next one. Such an arrangement is also called *interactive* because the operating system and the user are engaged in a dialog. Each time the user correctly completes an operation, he or she is informed of its success and invited to continue by some form of prompt message. If a particular command results in an error, the user is informed of this by the operating system and can therefore take the necessary corrective action.

Real-time operating systems belong, largely, to the world of industrial process control. The primary characteristic of a real-time operating system is that it must respond to an event within a well-defined time. Consider a computer-controlled petrochemical plant. The conditions at many parts of the plant are measured and reported to the computer on a regular basis. Control actions must be taken as conditions in the plant change; for example, a sudden build-up of pressure in a reaction vessel cannot be ignored. The computer running the plant invariably has a real-time operating system that responds to interrupts generated by external events.

Real-time operating systems are found wherever systems are computer-controlled and the response time of the computer must closely match that of the system it is controlling. Real-time operating systems are so called because the computer is synchronized with what people call clock time. Other operating systems operate in computer time. A job is submitted, and its results delivered after some elapsed time. There is no particular relationship between the elapsed time and the time of day. The actual elapsed time is a function of the loading of the computer and the particular mix of jobs it is running. In a real-time system the response time of the computer to any stimulus is guaranteed.

Modern multimedia systems that use sound and video are also real-time systems—not least because a pause in a video clip (while the computer is carrying out another process) is most disconcerting. Consequently, real-time operating system technology will probably have a strong influence on the way in which future processors develop; for example, Intel's so-called multimedia extensions (MMX) added special-purpose instructions to the Pentium microprocessor's instruction set.

Some modern operating systems are called *client–server* and, in general, run on distributed systems. A typical client–server system may be found in a university where users all have their own computer (or *host*) with a CPU, memory, and a hard disk drive. These computers are linked to a *server* by a local area network. Processes running on one of the terminals are called *client processes* and are able to make requests to the server. Thus, the operating system is distributed between the client and the server. A client on one host is able to use the resources of a server on another host (the programmer may not even be aware of the location of the server).

10.2 Multitasking

Multitasking is the ability of a computer to handle more than one job at once. Students often ask me in a slightly surprised tone, 'How can a computer execute more than one program at a time when it has only one program counter and one ALU?' The answer I give is that they are, strictly speaking, correct. A computer cannot execute two or more programs simultaneously, but it can give the impression that it is running several programs concurrently. The following example demonstrates how such an illusion is possible.

Consider an exhibition of simultaneous chess. A first-class player is pitted against several weaker opponents and steps from board to board making a move at a time. As the master player is so much better than his or her opponents, one of the master's moves takes but a fraction of the time they take. Consequently, all players share the illusion that they have a single opponent of their own.

The organization of the games of simultaneous chess can readily be applied to the digital computer. All we need is a periodic signal to force the CPU to switch from one job to another and a mechanism to tell the computer where it was up to when it last executed a particular job. The jobs are referred to as *tasks* or *processes*, and the concept of executing several processes together is called *multiprogramming* or *multitasking*. A *process* is a program together with its associated program counter, stack, registers, and any resources it's using.

Before we look at how multitasking is implemented we discuss some of its advantages. If each process required only CPU time, multitasking would have little advantage over running processes consecutively (at least in terms of the efficient use of resources). If we re-examine simultaneous chess, we find that its success is based on the great speed of the master player when compared with that of his or her opponents. While each player is laboriously pondering his or her next move, the master player is busy making many moves.

A similar situation exists in the case of computers. While one user is busy reading information from a disk drive and loading it into memory or is busy printing text on a printer, another user can take control of the CPU. A further advantage of multiprogramming is that it enables several users to gain access to a computer at the same time. This is very important today when 40 or more students wish to have access to a computer (i.e. server) at any given instant.

Consider two processes, A and B, each of which requires several different activities to be performed during the course of its execution (e.g. video display controller, code execution, disk access). The sequence of activities carried out by each of these two processes as they are executed is given in Fig. 10.2.

If process A were allowed to run to completion before process B were started, valuable processing time would be wasted while activities not involving the CPU were carried out. Figure 10.3 shows how the processes may be scheduled to make more efficient use of resources. The boxes indicate the period of time for which a given resource is allocated to a particular process. For example, after process A has first used the CPU, it accesses the disk. While the disk is being accessed by process A, process B is able to gain control of the processor.

The fine details of multiprogramming operating systems are beyond the scope of an introductory book. However, the following principles are involved:

1. The operating system schedules a process in the most efficient way and makes best use of the facilities available. The algorithm may adapt to the type of jobs that are running, or the operator may feed system parameters into the computer to maximize efficiency.

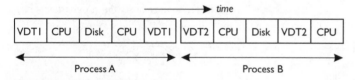

VDT1	CPU	Disk	CPU	VDT1	VDT2	CPU	Disk	VDT2	CPU

Process A ← → Process B

Fig. 10.2 Example of multitasking.

Resource	Activity					
	Slot 1	Slot 2	Slot 3	Slot 4	Slot 5	Slot 6
VDT 1	Process A				Process A	
VDT 2	Process B				Process B	
Disk			Process A	Process B		
CPU		Process A	Process B	Process A		Process B

time

Fig. 10.3 Applying multitasking to the system of Fig. 10.2.

2. Operating systems perform memory management. If several processes run concurrently, the operating system must allocate memory space to each of them. Moreover, the operating system should locate the processes in memory in such a way as to make best possible use of the memory.

3. If the CPU is to be available to one process while another is accessing a disk or using a printer, these devices must be capable of autonomous operation. That is, they must either be able to take part in DMA (direct memory access) operations without the active intervention of the CPU, or they must be able to receive a chunk of high-speed data from the CPU and process it at their leisure.

4. One of the principal problems that a complex multitasking operating system has to overcome is that of *deadlock*. Suppose process A and process B both require CPU time and a printer to complete their activity. If process A has been allocated the CPU and the printer by the operating system, all is well and process B can proceed once process A has been completed. Now imagine the situation that occurs if process A requests CPU time and the printer but receives only the CPU, and process B makes a similar request and receives the printer but not the CPU. In this situation both processes have one resource and await the other. As neither process will give up its resource, the system is deadlocked and hangs up indefinitely. Much work has been done on operating system resource allocation algorithms to deal with this problem.

10.2.1 **What is a process?**

A task or *process* is a piece of executable code that can be executed by the processor (i.e. CPU). Each process runs in an *environment* made up of the contents of the processor's registers, its program counter, its status register, SR, and the state of the memory allocated to this process. The environment defines the current state of the process and tells the computer where it's up to in the execution of a process.

At any instant a process is in one of three states: *running*, *runnable*, or *blocked*. Figure 10.4 provides a *state diagram* for a process in a multitasking system. When a process is created, it is in a runnable state waiting its turn for execution. When the scheduler passes control to the process, it is running (i.e. being executed). If the process has to wait for a system resource such as a printer before it can continue, it enters the *blocked* state. The difference between runnable and blocked is simple—a runnable process can be executed when its turn comes; a blocked process cannot enter the runnable state until the resources it requires become free.

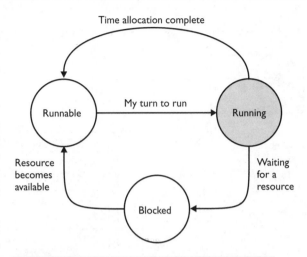

Fig. 10.4 State diagram of a process in a multitasking system.

10.2.2 **Switching processes**

We now outline the way in which process switching takes place by using two hardware mechanisms described earlier—the *interrupt* and the *stack*. A clock connected to the CPU's interrupt request input generates a pulse, say, every 0.01 seconds. Whenever the IRQ line is asserted at each 0.01 s interval, the CPU responds to the interrupt. At the moment the interrupt occurs, the information that defines the process is in the CPU (i.e. processor status word, program counter, and registers currently being used by the process). This information is called the process's *context* or *volatile portion*. An interrupt results in the program counter and machine status being saved on the stack, and a jump made to the interrupt handling routine. At the end of the interrupt handling routine an RTE (return from exception) instruction is executed and the program then continues from the point at which it was interrupted.

The 68K's RTE instruction is similar to the RTS (return from subroutine) instruction. When a subroutine is called, the return address is pushed on the stack. When an exception (i.e. interrupt) is generated, *both* the return address and the current value of the processor status word (containing the CCR) are pushed on the stack. The RTE instruction restores both the program counter and the status word. Consequently, an exception doesn't affect the status of the processor.

Suppose now that the interrupt handling routine modifies the stack pointer before the return from exception is executed. That is, the stack pointer is changed to point at another process's volatile portion. Now, when the RTE is executed, the value of the program counter retrieved from the stack isn't that belonging to the program being executed just before the interrupt. The value of the PC loaded by the return from

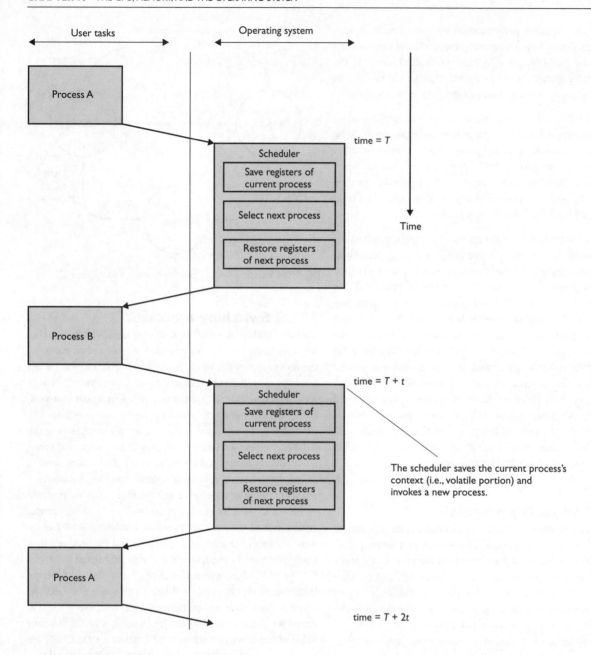

Fig. 10.5 Switching processes.

exception belongs to a different process that was saved earlier when another program was interrupted—that process will now be executed.

Figure 10.5 demonstrates the sequence of events that take place during process switching. Initially process A, at the top of Fig. 10.5, is running. At time T, the program is interrupted by a real-time clock and control passed to the scheduler in the operating system. The arrow from the program to the scheduler shows the flow of control from the program to the operating system. The scheduler stores the current values of the process's registers, program counter, and status in memory. Process switching is sometimes called *context switching* because it involves switching from the volatile portion of one process to the volatile portion of another process. The *scheduler* component of the operating system responsible for switching processes is called the *first-level interrupt handler*.

In Fig. 10.5 an interrupt occurs at T, $T+t$, $T+2t$, ..., and every t seconds switching takes place between processes A and B. We have ignored the time required to process the interrupt. In some real-time systems, the process-switching overhead is very important.

Figure 10.6 provides a demonstration of how process switching works (a real system is more complex). Two

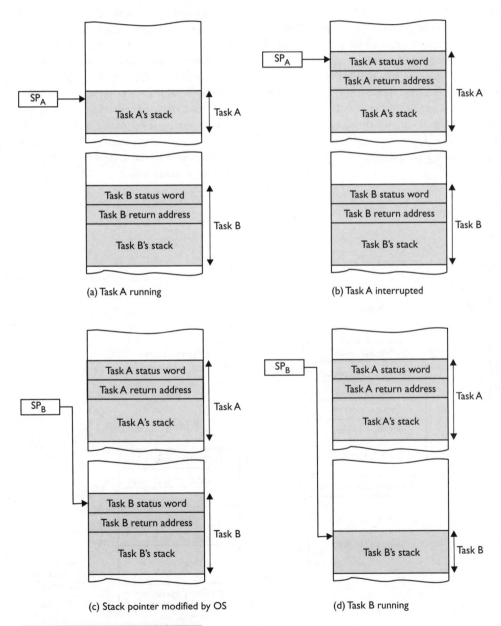

(a) Task A running

(b) Task A interrupted

(c) Stack pointer modified by OS

(d) Task B running

Fig. 10.6 Process switching and the stack.

processes, A and B, are located in memory. To keep things simple, we will assume that the regions of memory allocated to these processes do not change during the course of their execution. Each process has its own stack, and at any instant the stack pointer may be pointing to either A's stack or B's stack.

In Fig. 10.6(a) process A is running and process A's stack pointer SP_A is pointing at the top of the stack. In Fig. 10.6(b) a process-switching interrupt has occurred and the contents of the program counter and machine status have been pushed on to the stack (i.e. A's stack). For the sake of simplicity Fig. 10.6 assumes that all items on the stack occupy a single location.

In Fig. 10.6(c) the operating system has changed the contents of the system stack pointer so that it is now pointing at process B's stack (i.e. the stack pointer is SP_B). Finally, in Fig. 10.6(d) the operating system executes an RTE, and process B's program counter is loaded from its stack, which causes process B to be executed. Thus, at each interrupt, the operating system swaps the stack pointer before executing an RTE and a new process is run.

In a more realistic system the operating system maintains a table of processes to be executed. Each entry in the table is called a *task control block*, TCB, that contains all the information the operating system needs to know about the process. Typically, the TCB includes details about the process's priority, its maximum run time, and whether or not it is currently runnable (as well as its registers).

Figure 10.7 illustrates the structure of a possible task control block. In addition to the process's environment, the TCB in Fig. 10.7 contains a *pointer* to the next TCB in the chain of TCBs; that is, the TCBs are arranged as a *linked list*. A new process is created by inserting its TCB into the *linked list*.

Some operating systems allow processes to be prioritized so that a process with a high priority will always be executed in preference to a process with a lower priority. A runnable process is executed when its turn arrives (subject to the limitations of priority). If the process is not runnable (i.e. blocked), it remains in the computer but is bypassed each time its turn comes. When the process is to be run, its run flag is set and it will be executed next time round.

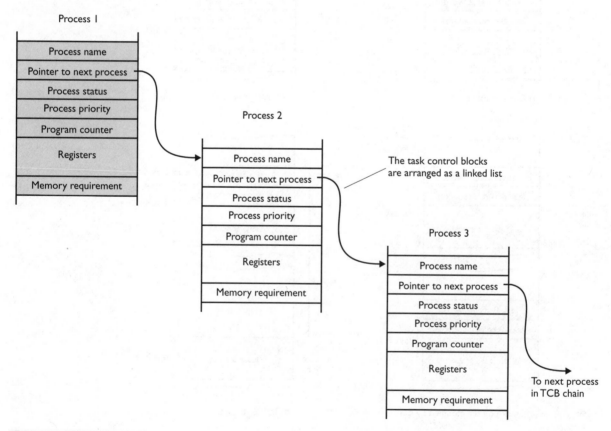

Fig. 10.7 The task control block.

10.3 Operating system support from the CPU

We now describe how processors can be designed to support operating system functions. What type of support can a CPU offer the operating system? It's possible to design processors that are protected from certain types of error or that provide hardware support for multitasking. First-generation 8-bit microprocessors didn't provide the operating systems designer with any special help. Here we concentrate on members of the 68K family because these devices provide particularly strong support to operating systems.

At any instant a processor can be in one of several states or levels of *privilege*; for example, members of the 68K family provide two levels of privilege. One of the 68K's states is called the *supervisor state* and the other the *user state*. The operating system runs in the supervisor state and applications programs running under the control of the operating system run in the user state. We will soon see that separating the operating system from user applications makes the system very robust and difficult to crash. When an applications program crashes (e.g. due to a bug), the crash doesn't affect the operating system running in its protected supervisor environment.

Switching states

Let's start from the assumption that the supervisor state used by the operating system is somehow special and confers first-class privileges on the operating system—we'll find out what these privileges are shortly.

When the 68K is operating in its user state, any interrupt or exception forces it into its supervisor state (remember that the terms *exception* and *interrupt* are sometimes employed interchangeably). That is, an exception causes a transition to the supervisor state and, therefore, calls the operating system.

Figure 10.8 illustrates two possible courses of action that may take place in a 68K system when an exception is generated. Both these diagrams are read from the top down. In each case, the left-hand side is shaded to represent user or applications programs running in the *user state* and the right-hand side is unshaded to represent the operating system running in the *supervisor state*.

In Fig. 10.8(a) a user program is running and an exception occurs (e.g. a disk drive may request a data transfer). A jump is made to the exception handler that forms part of the operating system. The exception handler deals with the request and a return is made to the user program. However, the exception might have been generated by a *fatal* error condition that arises during the execution of a program. Figure 10.8(b) shows the

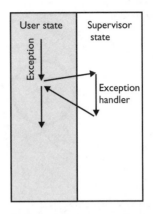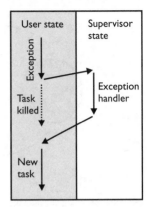

(a) Normal program execution continues after an exception

(b) The operating system kills the current task and starts another

Fig. 10.8 Taking action after an exception.

situation in which an exception caused by a fatal error occurs. In this case, the operating system terminates the 'faulted' user program and then runs another user program.

Figures 10.8(a) and (b) show user programs and the operating system existing in separate compartments or environments—this is not fiction. We now explain why user programs and the operating system sometimes really do live in different universes. In simple 68K-based systems, the processor's supervisor and user state mechanism isn't exploited, and all code is executed in the supervisor state. More sophisticated systems with an operating system do make good use of the 68K's user and supervisor state mechanisms.

When power is first applied to the 68K, it automatically enters its supervisor state. This action makes sense, because you would expect the operating system to initially take control of the computer while it sets everything up and loads any user processes that it's going to run.

The three big questions we've now got to answer are:

- How does the 68K know which state it's in?

- How is a transition made from one state to another?

- What does it matter anyway?

The answer to the first question is easy—the 68K uses a special flag bit, called an *S-bit*, in its status register to indicate what state it's currently operating in. If $S = 1$, the 68K is in its supervisor state and if $S = 0$, the 68K is in its user state. The S-bit is located in bit 13 of the 68K's 16-bit *status register*, SR. The lower-order byte of the status register is the condition code register, CCR. The upper byte of the status register containing the S-bit is called the *system byte* and defines the operating state of the processor.

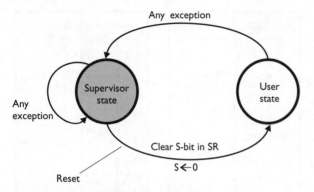

Fig. 10.9 Switching between user and supervisor states.

The second question we asked was 'How is a transition made from one state to another?' The *state diagram* in Fig. 10.9 describes the relationship between the 68K's user and supervisor states. Lines with arrows indicate *transitions* between states (text against a line explains the action that causes the transition). Figure 10.9 shows that a transition from the supervisor state to the user state is made by clearing the S-bit in the status register. Executing a MOVE #0, SR instruction clears the S-bit (and the other bits) of the status byte and puts the 68K in the user state. You could clear only the S-bit with the instruction ANDI #$DFFF, SR.

When the operating system wishes to execute an applications program in the user state, it clears the S-bit and executes a jump to the appropriate program; that is, the operating system invokes the less privileged user state by executing an instruction that clears the S-bit to 0.

Figure 10.9 demonstrates that once the 68K is running in its user state, the only way in which a transition can be made to the supervisor state is by means of an exception—any exception. A return can't be made to the supervisor state by using an instruction to set the S-bit to 1. If you could do this, anyone would be able to access the supervisor state's privileged features and the security mechanism it provides would be worthless. Let's say that again—a program running in the user state *cannot* deliberately invoke the supervisor state directly.

Suppose a user program running in the user state tries to enter the privileged supervisor state by executing MOVE $2000, SR to set the S-bit. Any attempt by the user state programmer to modify the S-bit results in a *privilege violation* exception. This exception forces the 68K into its supervisor state, where the exception handler deals with the problem.

We can now answer the third question we asked earlier—what's the benefit of the 68K's two-state mechanism? Some

instructions such as STOP and RESET can be executed only in the supervisor state and are said to be *privileged*. The STOP instruction brings the processor to a halt and the RESET acts on external hardware such as disk drives. You might not want the applications programmer to employ these powerful instructions, which may cause the entire system to crash if used inappropriately. Other privileged instructions are those that operate on the system byte (including the S-bit) in the status register. If the applications programmer were permitted to access the S-bit, he or she could change it from 0 (user state) to 1 (supervisor state) and bypass the processor's security mechanism.

If the 68K's user/supervisor mode mechanism were limited to preventing the user-state programmer executing certain instructions, it would be a nice feature of the processor, but of no earth-shattering importance. The user/supervisor state mechanism has two important benefits: the provision of dual stack pointers and the support for *memory protection*. These two features protect the operating system's memory from either accidental or deliberate modification by a user application. We now describe how the 68K's supervisor state protects its most vital region of memory—the stack.

10.3.1 The 68K's two stacks

Many computers manage subroutine return addresses by means of a *stack*. The processor's *stack pointer* points to the top of the stack and is automatically updated as items are pushed onto the stack or are pulled off it. When a subroutine is called by an instruction like BSR XYZ, the address immediately after the subroutine call (i.e. the *return* address) is pushed on the stack. The final instruction of the subroutine, RTS (return from subroutine), pulls the return address off the stack and loads it in the program counter.

If you corrupt the contents of the stack by overwriting the return address or if you corrupt the stack pointer itself, the RTS instruction will load an undefined address into the program counter. Instead of making a return to a subroutine's calling point, the processor will make a jump to a random point in memory and start executing code at that point. The result might lead to an illegal instruction error or to an attempt to access non-existent memory. Whatever happens, the program will crash.

Consider the following fragment of code, which is both badly written and contains a serious error. Don't worry about the fine details—it's the underlying principles that matter. Remember that the 68K's stack pointer is address register A7.

```
        MOVE.W  D3,-(A7)      Push the parameter in register D3 onto the stack
        BSR     Sub_X         Call a subroutine
        .                     Return here
        .
Sub_X   ADDA.L  #4,A7         Step over the return address on the top of the stack
        MOVE.L  (A7)+,D0      Read the parameter from the stack
        SUBA.L  #6,A7         Restore the stack pointer
        .                     The body of the subroutine goes here....
        RTS                   Return from subroutine
```

The programmer first pushes the 16-bit parameter in data register D3 onto the stack by means of the instruction MOVE.W D3,-(A7), and then calls a subroutine at location Sub_X. Figure 10.10(a) illustrates the state of the stack at this point. As you can see, the stack contains the 16-bit parameter (one word) and the 32-bit return address (two words) on top of the buried parameter.

When the subroutine is executed, the programmer attempts to retrieve the parameter from the stack by first stepping past the 4-byte return address on the top of the stack. The instruction ADDA.L #4, A7 adds 4 to the stack pointer to leave it pointing at the required parameter, Fig. 10.10(b). This is a terrible way of accessing the parameter because you should never move the stack pointer down the stack when there are valid items on the stack above the stack pointer—do remember that we're providing an example of how *not* to do things.

The programmer then reads the parameter from the stack by means of the operation MOVE.L (A7)+, D0. This instruction pulls a longword off the stack and increments the stack pointer by the size of the operand (4 for a longword) (Fig. 10.9(c)). Since the stack pointer has been moved down by first stepping past the return address and then pulling the parameter off the stack, it must be adjusted by 6 to point to the subroutine's return address once more (i.e. a 4-byte return

address plus a 2-byte parameter), Fig. 10.9(d). Finally, the return from subroutine instruction, RTS, pulls the 32-bit return address off the stack and loads it in the program counter.

This fragment of code fails because it contains a serious error. The parameter initially pushed on the stack was a *16-bit value*, but the parameter read from the stack in the subroutine was a *32-bit value*. The programmer really intended to write the instruction MOVE.W (A7)+, D0 rather than MOVE.L (A7)+,D0; the error in the code is just a single letter. The effect of this error is to leave the stack pointer pointing at the *second word* of the 32-bit return address, rather than the first word. The SUBA.L #6, A7 instruction was intended to restore the stack pointer to its original value. However, because the stack pointer is pointing 2 bytes above the correct return address, the RTS instruction loads the program counter with an erroneous return address resulting in a jump to a *random* region of memory. We have demonstrated that this blunder not only gives the wrong result, but also generates a fatal error. We now demonstrate how the user/supervisor mechanism helps us to deal with such a situation.

The 68K's user and supervisor stack pointers

There's very little the computer designer can do to prevent programming errors that corrupt either the stack or the stack

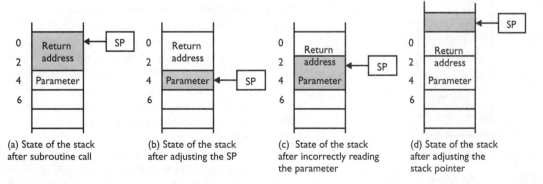

(a) State of the stack after subroutine call

(b) State of the stack after adjusting the SP

(c) State of the stack after incorrectly reading the parameter

(d) State of the stack after adjusting the stack pointer

Fig. 10.10 The effect of an error on the stack.

pointer. What the computer designer can do is to limit the effects of possible errors. Members of the 68K family approach the problem of stack security by providing *two* identical stack pointers, each of which is called address register A7 (see Fig. 10.11). However, both stack pointers can't be active at the same time because either one or the other is in use (it's a bit like Clark Kent and Superman—you never see them together).

One of the 68K's two stack pointers is called the *supervisor stack pointer* or SSP and is active whenever the processor is in the *supervisor state*. The other stack pointer, the *user stack pointer* or USP, is active when the processor is in the *user state*. Because the 68K is always in either the user state or the supervisor state, only one of the two stack pointers is available at any instant. The supervisor stack pointer is entirely invisible to the user programmer—there's no way in which the user programmer can modify (or even read) the supervisor stack pointer. However, the supervisor state programmer (i.e. the operating system) can use a special privileged instruction to access the user stack pointer. This instruction is MOVE USP,Ai or MOVE Ai,USP

Let's summarize what we've just said. When the 68K is operating in its supervisor state, its S-bit is 1 and the supervisor stack pointer is active. The supervisor stack pointer points at the stack used by the operating system to handle its subroutine and exception return addresses. Because an

exception sets the S-bit to 1, the return address is always pushed on the supervisor stack even if the 68K was running in the user mode at the time of the exception. When the 68K is operating in its user state, its S-bit is 0 and the user stack pointer is active. The user stack pointer points at the stack used by the current applications program to store subroutine return addresses.

Consider the previous example of the faulty applications program running in the user state (see Fig. 10.11). When the return from subroutine instruction is executed, an incorrect return address is pulled off the stack and a jump to a random location made. An *illegal instruction exception* will eventually occur when the processor tries to execute a data pattern that doesn't correspond to a legal op-code. An illegal instruction exception forces a change of state from user to supervisor mode. The illegal instruction exception handler runs in the supervisor state, whose own stack pointer has not been corrupted. That is, the applications programmer can corrupt his or her own stack pointer and crash the program, but the operating system's own stack pointer will not be affected by the error. When a user program crashes, the operating system mounts a rescue attempt.

You may wonder what protects the supervisor stack pointer. The answer is: nothing. It is assumed that a well-constructed and debugged operating system rarely corrupts its stack and crashes (at least in comparison with user programs and programs under development).

The 68K's two-stack architecture doesn't directly prevent the user programmer from corrupting the contents of the operating system's stack. Instead, it separates the stack used by the operating system and all exception-processing software from the stack used by the applications programmer by implementing two stack pointers. Whatever the user does in his or her own 'environment' cannot prevent the supervisor stepping in and dealing with the problem.

Use of two stacks in process switching

Earlier in this chapter we described the notion of multitasking. The 68K's two stack pointer mechanism is particularly useful in implementing multitasking. Each user (applications) program has its own private stack. When the process is running, it uses the USP to point to its stack. When the process is waiting or blocked, its own stack pointer is saved alongside the other elements of its volatile portion (i.e. environment) in its task control block.

The supervisor stack pointer is used by the operating system to manage process switching and other operating system functions. In this way, each application can have its own user

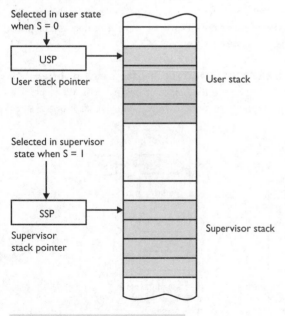

Fig. 10.11 The 68K's two stack pointers.

stack pointer and the operating system's stack can be separated from the user processes.

Suppose an applications program (i.e. process) is running and a process-switching interrupt occurs. A jump is made to the scheduler, the S-bit is set, the supervisor stack pointer becomes active, and the return address and status word are saved on the supervisor stack.

the process's registers from the TCB to the supervisor stack and then pulling the registers off the stack immediately before executing an RTE instruction. Note that restoring a process's volatile environment is the mirror image of saving a process's volatile environment.

The behavior of the part of an operating system that switches processes can readily be expressed as pseudocode.

```
Module TaskSwitch
    Disable all further interrupts
    Push registers D0 to D7 and A0 to A6 on the supervisor stack
    Get the process's stack pointer in the USP and put it on the stack
    Transfer all registers, PC, and SR from the stack to TaskControlBlock_i
    Locate Process_j the next process to run
    Copy registers of next process from TaskControlBlock_j to the stack
    Copy process's stack pointer from TCB to USP
    Pull registers D0 to D7 and A0 to A6 from the stack
    Enable interrupts
    Return from exception (i.e., restore SR and PC)
End module
```

At this stage, the scheduler can't really do anything because the 68K's address and data registers may contain information required by the process that was just interrupted. These registers constitute the process's volatile portion. The first thing the scheduler must do is to save the registers on the stack (i.e. the supervisor stack). A 68K-based kernel might employ MOVEM.L D0-D7/A0-A6,-(A7) to push registers D0 to D7 and A0 to A6 onto the stack pointed at by A7. We don't save A7 because that's the supervisor stack pointer. However, we need to save the user stack pointer because that belongs to the process. We can access the USP by, say, MOVE USP, A0 and then save A0 on the supervisor stack with the other 15 registers (PC and SR).

Now that the last process's volatile portion has been saved, the scheduler can go about its job of switching processes. The next step would be to copy these registers from the stack to the process's entry in its task control block. Typically, the scheduler might remove the process's volatile environment from the top of the supervisor stack and copy these registers to the process's task control block.

The scheduler can now locate the next process to run according to an appropriate algorithm (e.g. first come, first served, highest priority first, smallest process first). Once the next process has been located it can be restarted by copying

We represent this algorithm in the following 68K program. In order to test the task-switching mechanism, we've created a dummy environment with two processes. Process 1 prints the number 1 on the screen whenever it is executed. Process 2 prints the sequence 2, 3, 4, …, 9, 2, 3, … when it is called. If we allow each process to complete one print cycle before the next process is called, the output should be 12131415… 18191213….

In a real system, a real-time clock might be used to periodically switch tasks. In our system we use a TRAP #0 instruction to call the task switcher. This instruction acts like a hardware interrupt that is generated internally by an instruction in the program (i.e. the program counter and status registers are pushed on the supervisor stack and a jump is made to the exception handling routine whose address is in memory location $00 0080).

The program is entered at $400, where the supervisor stack pointer is initialized and dummy values loaded into A6 and A0 for testing purposes (because much of the program involves transferring data between registers, the stack, and task control blocks, it's nice to have visible markers when you are debugging a program by single-stepping it).

We have highlighted the body of the task switcher in bold. The subroutine NEW selects the next process to run. In this case, there are only two processes and the code is:

```
IF task 1 running THEN next task=task 2
                 ELSE next task=task 1

          ORG        $80              TRAP #0 vector
          DC.L       TRAP0            Address of trap 0 handler

          ORG        $400             Entry point of program
          LEA        $4000,A7         Preset the SSP
          LEA        $A6A6A6A6,A6      Dummy value in A6 to help in tracing
          MOVEA.L    #$12121212,A0     Dummy value for USP
          MOVE.L     A0,USP
          BRA        TASK1            Jump into a task 1

*         The task switcher is entered from TRAP #0

TRAP0     MOVEM.L    A0—A7/D0—D7,—(SP) Dump all registers on the stack
          MOVEA.L    CURRENT,A0       Get pointer to current TCB

          MOVE.W     #34,D0           Copy SR, PC, and registers to TCB
SAVE      MOVE.W     (SP)+,(A0)+       This is 35 words (SR+PC+16 registers)
          DBRA       D0,SAVE

          MOVE.L     USP,A1           Get task's A7 = USP
          MOVE.L     A1,—10(A0)        Save USP in A7 slot in TCB

*         All current task's environment now saved in its TCB

          BSR        NEW              Switch tasks

*         Now restore the new task

          MOVEA.L    CURRENT,A0       Get pointer to the new TCB
          LEA        70(A0),A0        Point to past end of TCB

          MOVE.W     #34,D0           Copy SR, PC, registers from TCB
RESTORE   MOVE.W     —(A0),—(SP)       This is 35 words (1+2+16×2)
          DBRA       D0,RESTORE

          MOVEA.L    60(A0),A1        Get USP from TCB
          MOVE.L     A1,USP           Restore USP

          MOVEM.L    (SP)+,A0—A6/D0—D7 Restore registers from stack
          LEA        4(SP),SP         Skip past A7 on stack
          RTE                         Load SR and PC to return from exception

*         Switch tasks (simple routine goes 1,2,1,2,...)
NEW       MOVEA.L    CURRENT,A0       Get current task pointer
          CMPA.L     #TCB1,A0         If it's 1 then make it 2
          BNE        NOT1
          MOVE.L     #TCB2,CURRENT
          BRA        FINISH
NOT1      MOVE.L     #TCB1,CURRENT    If it's 2 then make it 1
FINISH    RTS
```

```
TASK1    MOVE.B    #'1',D1              A dummy task that prints 1 and ends
         MOVE.B    #6,D0                Call OS to print
         TRAP      #15
         TRAP      #0                   Switch tasks
         BRA       TASK1                Repeat

TASK2    ADD.B     #1,D1                A dummy task that prints a number and ends
         MOVE.B    #6,D0                Call OS to print
         TRAP      #15
         TRAP      #0                   Switch tasks
         CMP.B     #'9',D1
         BNE       TASK2
         MOVE.B    #'1',D1              Reset sequence
         BRA       TASK2                Repeat

         ORG       $1000
CURRENT  DC.L      TCB1                 Pointer to current TCB

         ORG       $2000
TCB1     DS.W      35                   Space for task 1 TCB

         ORG       $2080                Task 2 TCB (preset)
TCB2     DC.L      $D0D0D0D0            Dummy D0
         DC.L      $00000031            Initial D1 (ASCII '1')
         DS.L      6
         DC.L      $A0A0A0A0            Dummy A0
         DS.L      6
         DC.L      $77777770            Dummy A7 = USP
         DC.W      $00FF                Dummy SR
         DC.L      TASK2                Address of TASK2 for PC

         END       $400
```

Let's look at how task switching takes place. When an exception takes place (in this case a `TRAP #0` exception), the program counter (return address) and status register are pushed on the supervisor stack to give the situation of Fig. 10.12(a).

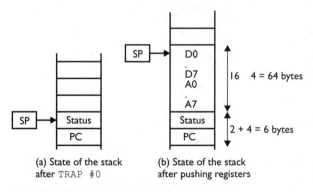

(a) State of the stack after `TRAP #0`

(b) State of the stack after pushing registers

Fig. 10.12 Use of the stack during process switching.

The first instruction in the process switcher, `MOVEM.L A0-A7/D0-D7,-(SP)` pushes all the 68K's address and data registers on the supervisor stack. Together with the PC and SR, we now have the process's entire volatile environment on the stack. Well, not entirely. Remember that the 68K has a user stack pointer. So, we copy it into A1 and then put it in the 'A7' slot on the stack (thereby overwriting the copy of the supervisor stack pointer in that slot).

The next step is to copy all these registers to the task control block pointed at by `CURRENT` (the variable that points to the active TCB). The task control block is changed by calling `NEW` and the registers copied to the stack. Finally the registers are restored from the stack and the new process invoked.

Now that we've described the 68K's user and supervisor modes and the role of exceptions in process switching, we can introduce one of the most important aspects of an operating system, *memory management*.

10.4 Memory management

Up to now we've assumed that the computer's central processing unit generates the address of an instruction or data and that this address corresponds to the actual location of the data in memory. For example, if a computer executes an instruction such as MOVE $1234,D0, the source operand is found in location number $1234 in the computer's random access memory. Although this statement is true of simple microprocessor systems, it's not true of computers with operating systems such as Unix and Windows. An address generated by the CPU doesn't necessarily correspond to the actual location of the data in memory. Why this is so is the subject of this section.

Memory management is a general term that covers all the various techniques by which an address generated by a CPU is translated into the actual address of the data in memory. Memory management plays several roles in a computer system. First, memory management permits computers with small main stores to execute programs that are far larger than the main store. Second, memory management is used in multitasking operating systems to make it look as if each process has sole control of the CPU. Third, memory management can be employed to protect one process from being corrupted by another process. Finally, memory management, in conjunction with the operating system, deals with the allocation of memory to variables.

If all computers had an infinite amount of random access memory, life would be much easier for the operating system designer. When a new program is loaded from disk, you could place it immediately after the last program you loaded into memory. Moreover, with an infinitely large memory you never have to worry about loading programs that are too large

for the available memory. In practice, real computers often have too little memory. In this section we are going to look at how the operating system manages the available memory.

Figure 10.13(a) demonstrates a multitasking system in which three processes are initially loaded into memory—process A, process B, and process C. This diagram shows the *physical* memory or main store where the programs are located. In Fig. 10.13(b) process B has been executed to completion and deleted from memory to leave a *hole* in the memory. In Fig. 10.13(c) a new process, process D, is loaded in part of the unused memory and process A deleted. Finally, in Fig. 10.13(d) a new process, process E, is loaded in memory in two parts because it can't fit in any single free block of memory space.

A multitasking system rapidly runs into the *memory allocation* and *memory fragmentation* problems described by Fig. 10.13. Operating systems solve these problems by means of *memory management*, which maps the computer's programs to the available memory space. Memory management is carried out by means of special-purpose hardware called a *memory management unit*, MMU (see Fig. 10.14). Some microprocessors include an MMU on the same chip as the CPU and some microprocessors use external MMUs.

Whenever the CPU generates the address of an operand or an instruction, it places the address on its address bus. This address is called a *logical address*—it's the address that the programmer sees. The MMU translates the logical address into the location or *physical address* of the operand in memory. In Fig. 10.14 part of the address from the CPU goes to the memory management unit, where it is changed or mapped into a new address; for example, the logical address $12345678 might get mapped onto the physical address $ABC678.

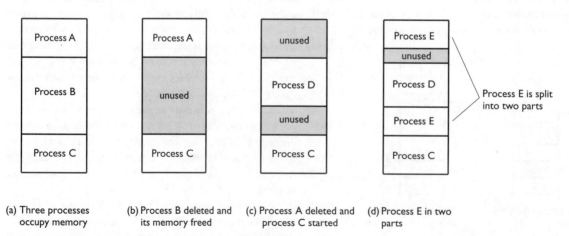

(a) Three processes occupy memory

(b) Process B deleted and its memory freed

(c) Process A deleted and process C started

(d) Process E in two parts

Fig. 10.13 Memory fragmentation in a multitasking environment.

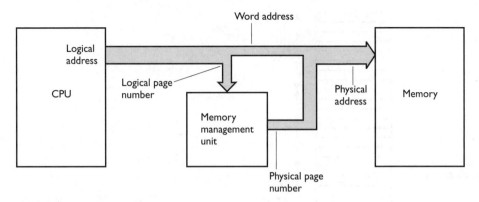

Fig. 10.14 The memory management unit.

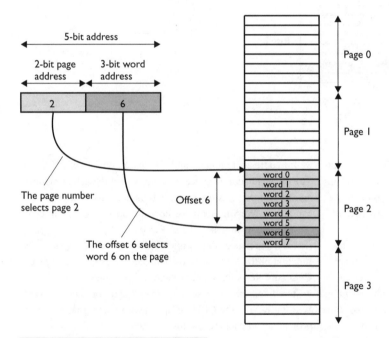

Fig. 10.15 The structure of paged memory.

The logical address consists of two parts: a *page* address and a *word* address. In the previous example, page $12345 gets translated into page $ABC and the word address $678 remains unchanged. Figure 10.15 illustrates the relationship between word address and page address for a very simple computer system with four pages of eight words (i.e. $4 \times 8 = 32$ locations).

The logical address from the CPU in Fig. 10.15 consists of a 2-bit page address that selects one of $2^2 = 4$ pages, and a 3-bit word address that provides an *offset* (or index) into the currently selected page. A 3-bit offset can access $2^3 = 8$ words

within a page. If, for example, the CPU generates the address 10110_2, location 6 on *logical* page 2 is accessed.

In a system with memory management the 3-bit word address from the CPU goes directly to the memory, but the 2-bit page address is sent to the memory management unit (see Fig. 10.16). The logical page address from the CPU selects an entry in a *table* of pages in the MMU, as Fig. 10.16 demonstrates. Suppose the processor accesses logical page 2 and the corresponding page table entry contains the value 3. This value (i.e. 3) corresponds to the *physical* page address of the location being accessed in memory; that is, the MMU has

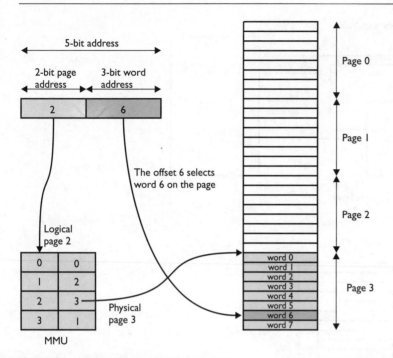

Fig. 10.16 Mapping logical pages to physical pages.

translated logical page 2 into physical page 3. The physical address corresponds to the location of the actual operand in memory. If you compare Figs. 10.15 and 10.16 you can see that the same logical address has been used to access two different physical addresses.

Why should the operating system go to the trouble of taking an address from the processor and using an MMU to convert it into a *new* address in order to access physical memory? To answer this question we have to look again at how programs are arranged in memory. Figure 10.17 shows the structure of both *logical* memory and *physical* memory at some point during the execution of processes A, B, C, and D. As far as the processor is concerned, the processes all occupy single blocks of address space that are located consecutively in logical memory, Fig. 10.17(a).

If you examine the physical memory (Fig. 10.17(b)), the actual processes are distributed in real memory in an almost random fashion. Both processes B and C are split into non-consecutive regions and two regions of physical memory are currently unallocated. Note also that the logical address space seen by the processor is *larger* than the physical address space—process D is currently located on the hard disk and is not in the computer's RAM.

A processor's logical address space is composed of all the addresses that the processor can specify. If the processor has a 32-bit address, its logical address space consists of 2^{32} bytes. The physical address space is composed of the actual memory and its size depends on how much memory the computer user can afford. We will soon see how the operating system deals with situations in which the processor wishes to run programs that are larger than the available physical address space. The function of the MMU is to map the addresses generated by the CPU onto the actual memory and to keep track of where data is stored as new processes are created and old ones removed. With an MMU, the CPU doesn't have to worry about where programs and data are actually located.

Consider a system with 4 kbyte logical and physical pages and suppose the processor generates the logical address 881234_{16}. This 24-bit address is made up of a 12-bit logical page address 881_{16} and a 12-bit word address 234_{16}. The 12 low-order bits, 234_{16}, define the same relative location within both logical and physical address pages. The logical page address is sent to the MMU, which looks up the corresponding physical page address in entry number 881 in the page table. The physical page address found in this location is passed to memory.

Let's look at the way in which the MMU carries out the mapping process. Figure 10.18 demonstrates how the pages or *frames* of logical address space are mapped to the frames of physical address space. The corresponding address mapping

CPU memory space

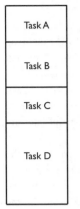

(a) Logical address space

Actual memory space

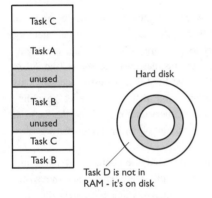

Task D is not in
RAM - it's on disk

(b) Physical address space

Fig. 10.17 Logical and physical address space.

Logical address space   Physical address space

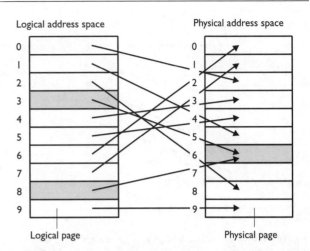

Logical page   Physical page

Fig. 10.18 Mapping logical address space onto physical address space

Logical page	Physical page
0	2
1	5
2	8
3	6
4	3
5	4
6	0
7	1
8	6
9	9

Table 10.1 Logical to physical address mapping table corresponding to Fig. 10.18.

table is described in Table 10.1. Notice that logical page 3 and logical page 8 are both mapped to physical page 6. This situation might arise when two programs share a common resource (e.g. a compiler or an editor). Although each program thinks that it has a unique copy of the resource, both programs access a shared copy of the resource.

10.4.1 Virtual memory

We've already said that a computer can execute programs larger than its physical memory. In a virtual memory system the programmer sees a large array of physical memory (the virtual memory) which appears to be entirely composed of high-speed main store. In reality, the physical memory is composed of a relatively small high-speed RAM and a much larger but slower disk store. Virtual memory has two advantages. It allows the execution of programs larger than the physical memory would normally permit and frees the programmer from worrying about choosing logical addresses falling within the range of available physical addresses. Programmers are at liberty to choose any logical address they desire for their program and its variables. The actual addresses selected by a programmer don't matter, because the logical addresses are automatically mapped to the available physical memory space as the operating system sees fit.

The means of accomplishing such an apparently impossible task is called *virtual memory* and was first used in the Atlas computer at the University of Manchester, England, in 1960. Figure 10.19 illustrates a system with ten logical address pages but only five physical address pages. Consequently, only 50 percent of the logical address space can be mapped to

555

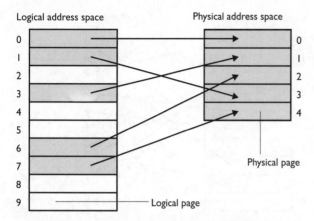

Fig. 10.19 A system with a smaller physical address space than a logical address space.

Logical page	Present bit	Physical page
0	1	0
1	1	3
2	0	
3	1	1
4	0	
5	0	
6	1	2
7	1	4
8	0	
9	0	

Table 10.2 Logical-to-physical address mapping table corresponding to Fig. 10.19.

physical address space at any instant. Table 10.2 provides a logical page to physical page *mapping table* for this situation. Each entry in the logical address page table has two entries: one is the *present bit*, which indicates whether the corresponding page is available in physical memory; the other is the logical page to physical page mapping.

Part of a program that's not being used resides on disk. When this code is to be executed, it is copied from disk to the computer's immediate access memory. Sometimes it's impossible to fit all of the program (and the data required by the program) in main memory. Consequently, only part of the program can be loaded into random access memory. The operating system divides the program into pages and loads some of these pages into its random access memory. As pages are loaded, the operating system updates the page table in the MMU so that each logical page can be mapped to the corresponding physical page in RAM.

Consider what happens when such a program that resides partially in memory and partially on disk is executed. When the processor generates a logical address, the memory management unit reads the mapping table in the MMU to look up the corresponding physical page address. If the page is present in RAM, a logical-to-physical address translation takes place and the information is accessed. However, if the logical page is currently not in RAM, an address translation cannot take place. In this case, the MMU sends a special type of interrupt to the processor called a *page fault*.

When the processor detects a page fault from the MMU, the operating system intervenes and copies a page of data from the disk to the random access memory. Finally, the operating system updates the page-mapping table in the MMU, and reruns the faulted memory access. This arrangement is called *virtual memory* because the processor appears to have a physical memory as large as its logical address space.

Virtual memory works effectively only if, for most of the time, the data being accessed is in physical memory. Fortunately, accesses to programs and their data are highly clustered. Operating systems designers speak of the *80:20 rule*—for 80 percent of the time the processor accesses only 20 percent of a program. Note that the principles governing the operation of virtual memory are, essentially, the same as those governing the operation of cache memory (described later).

When a page fault is detected, the operating system transfers a new page from disk to physical memory and overwrites a page in physical memory. So, which page gets the chop when a new page is loaded in memory? The most sensible way of selecting an old page for removal is to take the page that is not going to be required in the near future. Unfortunately, this algorithm is impossible to implement. A simple page replacement algorithm is called the *not-recently-used algorithm*, NRU. The NRU algorithm is not optimum, but it is very easy to implement.

When a new page replaces an old page, any data in the old page frame that has been modified since it was created must be written back to disk. A typical virtual memory system clears a *dirty bit* in the page table when the page is first created. Whenever the processor performs a write operation to an operand on this page, the dirty bit is set. When this page is swapped out (i.e. overwritten by a new page), the operating system looks at its dirty bit. If this bit is clear, nothing need be done; if it is set, the page must be copied to disk.

Virtual memory allows the programmer to write programs without having to know anything about the characteristics of real memory and where the program is to be located.

10.4.2 Virtual memory and the 68K family

Members of Motorola's 68K family (68010, 68020, 68060, etc.) are well suited to virtual memory technology. We should point out here that the 68000 was the first member of the 68K family and lacks some of the facilities required to support virtual memory efficiently. The 68020 and later members of this family are much better suited to virtual memory systems than the plain vanilla 68000.

We've already stated that the architecture of the 68K family provides several mechanisms to support operating systems. The 68K's *protected state* when S = 1 separates operating system and application-level programs (aided by the dual stack pointer mechanism). Members of the 68K family have a *function control* output that tells an external system such as a memory management unit whether the CPU is executing an instruction in the user or the supervisor state.

Figure 10.20 illustrates the dialog that takes place between the CPU, the memory management unit (MMU), and the memory system during a read or a write cycle. The MMU is configured by the operating system when the computer is first powered up. The operating system sets up logical address to physical address translation tables and defines the type of access that each page may take part in (we'll see the reason for this shortly).

At the start of a memory access the CPU generates a logical address and sends it to the MMU together with the control signals that define the type of the access (i.e. read or write, program or data, user or supervisor mode). If the location being accessed is not currently in the main store or is an *illegal* access, the MMU sends an error message to the CPU to abort the current access and to begin exception processing and error recovery. An illegal access occurs when a process attempts to write to a page that has been designated read-only, or when a user program is attempting to access a page assigned to supervisor space and the operating system.

By dividing memory space into regions of different characteristics, you can provide a considerable measure of security. A user program cannot access memory space belonging to the operating system, because an attempt to access this memory space would result in the MMU generating an interrupt. Not only does the 68K protect the supervisor stack pointer from illegal access by a user program, but the 68K and MMU combination protects the supervisor stack (and any other address space allocated to the supervisor) from illegal access.

Figure 10.21 illustrates the structure of a memory management system in a 68K-based computer that checks whether the address space currently being accessed is legal. The 68010 and 68020 use external MMUs. Later members of the 68K family (e.g. 68030) have on-chip MMUs. Each entry in the MMU's page translation table contains the details about the page's access rights. Whenever the 68K performs a memory access, it indicates the type of access on its *function code* output pins (e.g. user/supervisor, code/data). For example, the 68020 may say

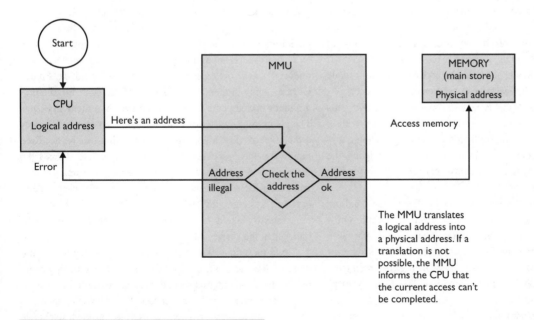

Fig. 10.20 Dialog between the CPU, MMU, and memory.

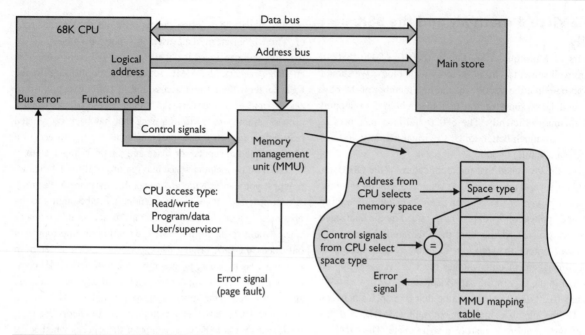

Fig. 10.21 Memory space matching hardware.

'I'm operating in the user state performing a read access to data with a logical address $12345678'. The MMU compares the CPU's function code and the read/write signal with the information in the currently accessed page in its mapping table. If the access is legal, a memory access takes place. If either the corresponding physical page is not in memory or the access is illegal, a page fault is generated and a signal returned to the 68K's bus error input. In terms of the previous example, the logical address $12345678 might generate a page address $12345. If this page is in the MMU and it can be accessed by a user-mode write, a logical-to-physical page translation can take place.

A bus error is a special type of exception and the 68K calls the appropriate handler in the operating system to deal with it. A missing physical page results in the operating system copying a page from disk to main store and then updating the MMU. An illegal access would probably run in the offending process being suspended.

The 68K's user/supervisor modes, exception-handling facilities, and memory management make it a very robust processor. Errors in a user program that would otherwise bring the system to a halt force a switch to the 68K's supervisor state and allow the operating system to either repair the damage or terminate the faulty program. The memory management mechanism protects the operating system from illegal access by applications programs and even protects one user program from access by another.

10.5 Cache memory

The basic concepts underlying virtual memory can be extended to any hierarchical memory structure. We are now going to look at *cache memory*, which can dramatically increase the performance of a computer system at relatively little cost.

Cache memory provides system designers with a way of exploiting high-speed processors without incurring the cost of large high-speed memory systems. The word *cache* is pronounced 'cash' or 'cash-ay' and is derived from the French word meaning hidden. Cache memory is hidden from the programmer and appears as part of the system's memory space. There's nothing mysterious about cache memory—it's simply a quantity of very high-speed memory that can be accessed rapidly by the processor. The element of magic stems from the ability of systems with cache memory to employ a tiny amount of high-speed memory (e.g. 16 kbyte of cache memory in a system with 16 Mbyte of DRAM) and expect the processor to make over 95 percent of its accesses to the cache rather than the slower DRAM.

Up to the mid-1990s, cache sizes of 8–32 kbyte were common. By the end of the 1990s, PCs had internal on-chip caches of 128 kbyte and external second level caches of up to 1 Mbyte.

Cache memory can be understood in everyday terms by its analogy with a diary or notebook used to jot down telephone numbers. A telephone directory contains hundreds of thousands of telephone numbers and nobody carries a telephone directory around with them. However, lots of people have a notebook with a hundred or so telephone numbers that they keep with them. Although the fraction of all possible telephone numbers in someone's notebook might be less than 0.01 percent, the probability that their next call will be to a number in the notebook is high because they frequently call the same people. Cache memory operates on exactly the same principle, by locating frequently accessed information in the cache memory rather than in the much slower main memory. Unfortunately, unlike the personal notebook, the computer cannot know, in advance, what data is most likely to be accessed. You could say that computer caches operate on a learning principle. By experience they learn what data is most frequently used and then transfer it to the cache.

The general structure of a cache memory is provided in Fig. 10.22. A block of cache memory sits on the processor's address and data buses in parallel with the much larger main memory. Note that the implication of *parallel* in the previous sentence is that data in the cache is also maintained in the main memory. To return to the analogy with the telephone notebook, writing a friend's number in the notebook does not delete their number in the directory.

Cache memory relies on the same principle as the notebook with telephone numbers. The probability of accessing the next item of data in memory isn't a random function. Because of the nature of programs and their attendant data structures, the data required by a processor is often highly clustered. This aspect of memories is called the *locality of reference* and makes the use of cache memory possible (it is of course the same principle that underlies virtual memory).

A cache memory requires a *cache controller* to determine whether the data currently being accessed by the CPU resides in the cache or whether it must be obtained from the main memory. When the current address is applied to the cache controller, the controller returns a signal called *hit*, which is asserted if the data is currently in the cache. Before we look at how cache memories are organized, we will demonstrate their effect on a system's performance.

Effect of cache memory on computer performance

The principal parameter of a cache system is its *hit ratio*, h, which defines the ratio of hits to all accesses. The hit ratio is determined by statistical observations of the operation of a real system and cannot readily be calculated. Furthermore, the hit ratio is dependent on the specific nature of the programs being executed. It is possible to have some programs with very high hit ratios and others with very low hit ratios. Fortunately, the effect of *locality of reference* usually means that the hit ratio is very high—often in the region of 95 percent. Before calculating the effect of a cache memory on a processor's performance, we need to introduce some terms.

Access time of main store	t_m
Access time of cache memory	t_c
Hit ratio	h
Miss ratio	m
Speedup ratio	S

The figure of merit of a computer with cache is called the *speedup ratio*, which indicates how much the cache accelerates the memory's access time. The *speedup ratio* is defined as the ratio of the memory system's access time without cache to its access time with cache.

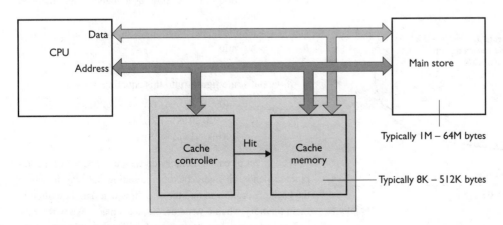

Fig. 10.22 Structure of a cache memory.

N accesses to a system without cache memory require Nt_m seconds. N accesses to a system with cache require $N(ht_c + mt_m)$ seconds; that is, the time spent in accessing the cache plus the time spent accessing the main memory multiplied by the total number of memory accesses. We can express m in terms of h as $m = (1 - h)$, since if an access is not a hit it must be a miss. Therefore the total access time for a system with cache is given by: $N(ht_c + (1 - h)t_m)$.

The speedup ratio is therefore given by

$$S = \frac{Nt_m}{N(ht_c + (1 - h)mt_m)} = \frac{t_m}{(ht_c + (1 - h)t_m)}$$

As we're not interested in the absolute speed of the main and cache memories, we can introduce a new parameter, k, that defines the ratio of the access time of cache memory to main memory. That is, $k = t_c/t_m$. Typical values for t_m and t_c might be 50 ns and 10 ns, respectively, which gives a value for k of 0.2. Therefore,

$$S = \frac{t_m/t_m}{(ht_c/t_m + (1 - h)t_m/t_m)} = \frac{1}{hk + (1 - h)} = \frac{1}{1 - h(1 - k)}$$

Figure 10.23 provides a plot of S as a function of the hit ratio, h. As you might expect, when $h = 0$ and all accesses are made to the main memory the speedup ratio is 1. Similarly, when $h = 1$ and all accesses are made to the cache the speedup ratio is $1/k$. The most important conclusion to be drawn from Fig. 10.23 is that the speedup ratio is a sensitive function of the hit ratio. Only when h approaches about 90 percent does the effect of the cache memory become really significant. This result is consistent with common sense. If h drops below about 90 percent, the accesses to main store take a disproportionate amount of time and accesses to the cache have little effect on system performance.

Life isn't as simple as these equations suggest. Computers are clocked devices and run at a speed determined by the clock. Consequently, memory accesses take place in one or more whole clock cycles. If a processor accesses main store in one clock cycle, adding cache memory is not going to make the system faster. If we assume that a computer has a clock cycle time t_{cyc}, and accesses cache memory in p clock cycles (i.e. access time $= pt_{cyc}$) and main store in q clock cycles, its speedup ratio is

$$S = \frac{t_m}{(ht_c + (1 - h)t_m)} = \frac{qt_{cyc}}{(pht_{cyc} + (1 - h)qt_{cyc})}$$

$$= \frac{q}{(ph + (1 - h)q)} = \frac{1}{ph/q + 1 - h}$$

If $q = 4$ and $p = 2$, the speedup ratio is given by $1/(2h/4 + 1 - h) = 2/(2 - h)$.

In practice, we are more concerned with the performance of the entire system. A computer doesn't spend all its time accessing memory. The following expression gives a better picture of the average cycle time of a computer because it takes into account the average number of cycles the processor spends performing internal (i.e. non-memory reference) operations.

$$t_{average\ cycle\ time} = Internal.t_{cyc}$$
$$+ Memory(h.t_{cache} + (1 - h)(t_{cache} + t_{delay}))$$

where

Internal = fraction of cycles the processor spends doing internal operations
t_{cyc} = processor cycle time
Memory = fraction of cycles processor spends doing memory accesses
t_{delay} = additional delay required caused by cache miss
h = hit ratio
t_{cache} = cache memory access time

If we put some figures into this equation, we get

$$t_{average\ cycle\ time} = 40\% \times 100\,ns + 60\%(0.9 \times 20\,ns$$
$$+ 0.1(20\,ns + 100\,ns))$$
$$= 40\,ns + 18\,ns = 58\,ns$$

The effect of cache memory on the performance of a computer depends on many factors, including the way in which the cache is organized and the way in which data is written to main memory when a write access takes place. We will return to some of these considerations when we have described how cache systems are organized.

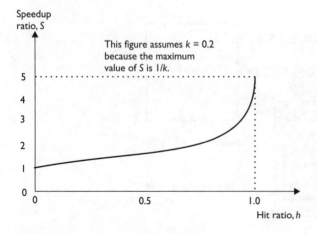

Speedup ratio, S

This figure assumes $k = 0.2$ because the maximum value of S is $1/k$.

Hit ratio, h

Fig. 10.23 Speedup as a function of hit ratio.

10.5.1 Cache organization

There are at least three ways of organizing a cache memory: direct-mapped, associative-mapped, and set associative-mapped cache. Each of these systems has its own performance:cost trade-off.

Direct-mapped cache

The easiest way of organizing a cache memory employs *direct mapping*, which relies on a simple algorithm to map data block i from the main memory into data block j in the cache. For the purpose of this section we will regard the smallest unit of data held in a cache as a *line* that is made up of typically two or four consecutive words. The line is the basic unit of data that is transferred between the cache and main store and varies between 4 and 32 bytes.

Figure 10.24 illustrates the structure of a highly simplified direct-mapped cache. As you can see, the memory space is divided into *sets* and the sets into *lines*. This memory is composed of 32 words and accessed by a 5-bit address bus from the CPU. For the purpose of this discussion we need only consider the set and line (as it doesn't matter how many words there are in a line). The address in this example has a 2-bit *set* field, a 2-bit *line* field, and a 1-bit *word* field. The cache memory holds $2^2 = 4$ lines of two words. When the processor

generates an address, the appropriate line in the cache is accessed. For example, if the processor generates the 5-bit address 10100_2, line 2 in set 2 is accessed.

A glance at Fig. 10.24 reveals that there are four possible lines numbered two: a line 2 in set 0, a line 2 in set 1, a line 2 in set 2, and a line 2 in set 3. In this example the processor accessed line 2 in set 2. The obvious question is, 'How does the system know whether the line 2 accessed in the cache is the line 2 from set 2 in the main memory?'

Figure 10.25 shows how a direct-mapped cache resolves the contention between lines. Each line in the cache memory has a *tag* or label that identifies which set this particular line belongs to. When the processor accesses line 2, the tag belonging to line 2 in the cache is sent to a comparator. At the same time the set field from the processor is also sent to the comparator. If they are the same, the line in the cache is the desired line and a hit occurs.

If they are not the same, a miss occurs and the cache must be updated. The old line 2 from set 1 is either simply discarded or rewritten back to main memory, depending on how the updating of main memory is organized.

Figure 10.26 provides a skeleton structure of a direct-mapped cache memory system. The cache memory itself is nothing more than a block of very high-speed random access read/write memory. The cache tag RAM is a fast combined memory and comparator that receives both its address and data inputs from the processor's address bus. The cache tag RAM's address input is the line address from the processor, which is used to access a unique location (one for each of the possible lines). The data in the cache tag RAM at this location is the tag associated with that location. The cache tag RAM also has a data input that receives the tag field from the processor's address bus. If the tag field from the processor matches the contents of the tag (i.e. set) field being accessed, the cache tag RAM returns a hit signal.

As Fig. 10.26 demonstrates, the cache tag RAM is nothing more than a high-speed random access memory with a built-in data comparator. Some of the major semiconductor manufacturers have implemented single-chip cache tag RAMs.

The advantage of the direct-mapped cache is almost self-evident. Both the cache memory and the cache tag RAM are widely available devices that, apart from their speed, are no more complex than other mainstream devices. Moreover, the direct-mapped cache requires no complex line replacement algorithm. If line x in set y is accessed and a miss takes place, line x from set y in the main store is loaded into the frame for line x in the cache memory and the tag set to y. That is, there is no decision concerning which line has to be rejected when a new line is to be loaded.

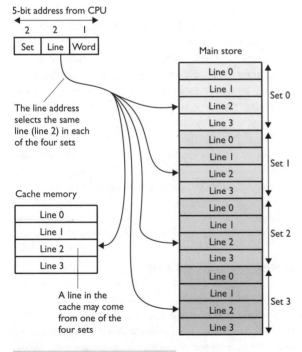

Fig. 10.24 The direct, mapped cache.

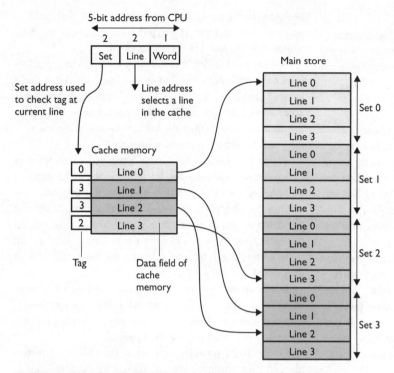

Fig. 10.25 Resolving contention between lines in a direct-mapped cache.

Another important advantage of direct-mapped cache is its inherent parallelism. Since the cache memory holding the data and the cache tag RAM are entirely independent, they can both be accessed simultaneously. Once the tag has been matched and a hit has occurred, the data from the cache will also be valid (assuming the two cache data and cache tag memories have approximately equal access times).

The disadvantage of direct-mapped cache is almost a corollary of its advantage. A cache with n lines has one restriction—at any instant it can hold only one line numbered x. What it cannot do is hold a line x from set p and a line x from set q. This restriction exists because there is one page frame in the cache for each of the possible lines. Consider the following fragment of code:

```
REPEAT
    Get_data
    Compare
UNTIL match OR end_of_data
```

This innocuous fragment of code reads a string of data from a buffer and then compares it with another string until a match is found. Suppose that in the compiled version of this code part of the Get_data routine is in set x, line y and that part of the Compare routine is in set z, line y. Because a direct-mapped cache can hold only one line y at a time, the frame corresponding to line y must be reloaded twice for each path through the loop. Consequently, the performance of a direct-mapped cache can be very poor under certain circumstances. However, statistical measurements on real programs indicate that the very poor worst-case behavior of direct mapped caches has no significant impact on their average behavior.

Suppose a cache is almost empty and most of its lines have not yet been loaded with active data. Certain lines may have to be swapped out of the cache frequently because data in the main store just happens to share the same line numbers. In spite of this objection to direct-mapped cache, it is very popular because of its low cost of implementation and high speed.

Associative mapped cache

One way of organizing a cache memory that overcomes the limitations of direct-mapped cache is described in Fig. 10.27. Ideally, we would like a cache that places no restrictions on what data it can contain. The *associative* cache is such a memory.

An address from the processor is divided into three fields: the *tag*, the line, and the word. Like the direct-mapped cache,

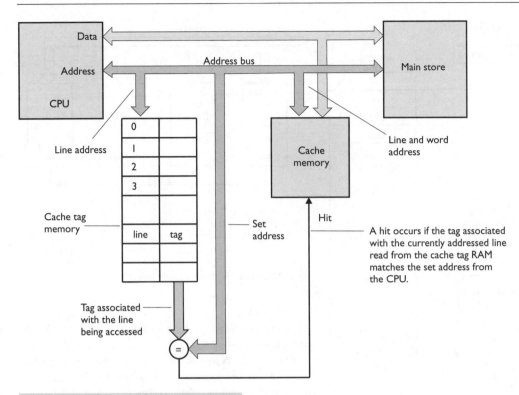

Fig. 10.26 Implementation of direct-mapped cache.

the smallest unit of data transferred into and out of the cache is the line. Unlike the direct-mapped cache, there's no predetermined relationship between the location of lines in the cache and lines in the main memory. Line p in the memory can be put in line q in the cache with no restrictions on the values of p and q. Consider a system with 1 Mbyte of main store and 64 kbyte of associatively mapped cache. If the size of a line is four 32-bit words (i.e. 16 bytes), the main memory is composed of $2^{20}/16 = 64$K lines and the cache is composed of $2^{16}/16 = 4096$ lines. Because an associative cache permits any line in the main store to be loaded into one of its lines, line i in the associative cache can be loaded with any one of the 64K possible lines in the main store. Therefore, line i requires a 16-bit tag to uniquely label it as being associated with line i from the main store.

When the processor generates an address, the word bits select a word location in both the main memory and the cache. The line address from the processor can't be used to address a line in the associative cache (unlike the direct-mapped cache memory). Why? Because each line in the direct-mapped cache can come only from one of n lines in the main store (where n is the number of sets). The tag resolves which of the lines is actually present. In an associative cache *any* of the 64K lines in the main store

can be located in any of the lines in the cache. Consequently, the associative cache requires a 16-bit tag to identify one of the 2^{16} lines from the main memory. More importantly, as the cache's lines are not ordered, the tags are not ordered and cannot be stored in a simple look-up table like the direct-mapped cache. In other words, when the CPU accesses line i, it may be anywhere in the cache or it may not be in the cache.

Associative cache systems employ a special type of memory called *associative* memory. An associative memory has an n-bit input but not necessarily 2^n unique internal locations. The n-bit address input is a *tag* that is compared with a tag field in each of its locations simultaneously. If the input tag matches a stored tag, the data associated with that location is output. Otherwise the associative memory produces a miss output. An associative memory is not addressed in the same way that a computer's main store is addressed. Conventional computer memory requires the explicit address of a location, whereas an associative memory is accessed by asking, 'Do you have this item stored somewhere?'

Associative cache memories are efficient because they place no restriction on the data they hold. In Fig. 10.27 the tag that specifies the line currently being accessed is compared with the tag of each entry in the cache simultaneously. In other

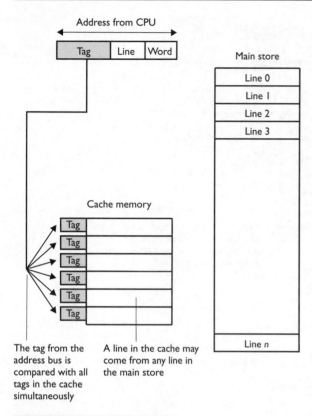

Fig. 10.27 Associative-mapped cache.

The tag from the address bus is compared with all tags in the cache simultaneously

A line in the cache may come from any line in the main store

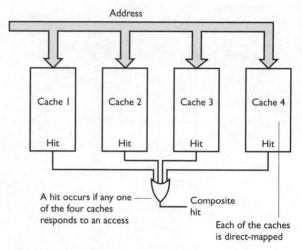

A hit occurs if any one of the four caches responds to an access

Composite hit

Each of the caches is direct-mapped

Fig. 10.28 Set associative-mapped cache.

words, all locations are accessed at once. Unfortunately, large associative memories are not yet cost-effective. Once the associative cache is full, a new line can be brought in only by overwriting an existing line that requires a suitable line replacement policy (as in the case of virtual memories).

Set associative-mapped cache

Most computers employ an arrangement that is a compromise between the direct-mapped cache and the fully associative cache. This compromise system is called a *set associative cache*.

A set associative cache memory is nothing more than several direct-mapped caches operated in parallel. The simplest arrangement is called a 2-way set associative cache and consists of two direct-mapped cache memories. Each line in the cache system is duplicated; for example, there are two line 5s in the cache. Consequently, it is now possible to store two line 5s, one line 5 from set *x* and one line 5 from set *y*. A set associative cache memory is therefore associative *within* a set. If the cache has *n* parallel sets, an *n*-way comparison is performed in parallel against all members of the set. Because

n is small (typically 2 to 16), the logic required to perform the comparison is not complex.

Figure 10.28 describes the common 4-way set associative cache. When the processor accesses memory, the appropriate line in each of four direct-mapped caches is accessed simultaneously. Since there are four lines, a simple associative match can be used to determine which (if any) of the lines in cache are to supply the data. In Fig. 10.28 the *hit* output from each direct-mapped cache is fed to an OR gate which generates a hit if any of the caches generates a hit.

Level 2 caches

The hierarchy cache, main store, hard disk can be further expanded by dividing the cache into a level 1 and a level 2 cache. A level 1 cache normally lives on the same chip as the CPU itself; that is, it is integrated with the processor. Level 1 caches grow in size as semiconductor technology advances and more memory devices can be integrated on a chip. A level 2 cache lives off the processor chip and is larger than a level 1 cache. Level 2 caches are typically 0.5 Mbyte.

When the processor makes a memory access, the level 1 cache is first searched. If the data isn't there, the level 2 cache is searched. If it isn't in the level 2 cache, the main store is accessed. The average access time is given by

$$t_{ave} = h_{L1}t_{c1} + h_{L2}t_{c2} + (1 - h_{L1} - h_{L2})t_{memory}$$

where h_{L1} and h_{L2} are the hit rates of the level 1 and level 2 caches, and t_{c2} and t_{c2} are the access times of the level 1 and level 2 caches, respectively.

10.5.2 **Considerations in cache design**

Apart from choosing the structure of a cache system and the line replacement policy (if it is an associative cache or set-associative cache), the designer has to consider how write cycles are to be treated. Should write accesses be made only to the cache and then the main store updated when the line is replaced? Should the main memory also be updated each time a word in the cache is modified? The latter policy is called *write through* and allows the cache to be written to rapidly and the main memory updated over a longer span of time (if there is *write buffer* to hold the data until the bus becomes free). A write through policy can lead to more memory write accesses than are strictly necessary.

When a cache miss occurs, a line of data is fetched from the main store. Consequently, the processor may read a byte from the cache and then the cache requires a line of, say, eight bytes from the main store. As you can imagine, the cost of a miss on an access to cache carries an additional penalty because an entire line has to be filled from memory. Fortunately, modern memories, CPUs, and cache systems support a *burst-fill* mode in which a burst of consecutive data elements can be transferred between the main store and cache memory. Let's look at cache access times again.

If data is not in the cache, it must be fetched from memory and loaded in the cache. If we assume that t_l is the time taken to reload the cache on a miss, the effective average access time of the memory system is given by

$$t_{ave} = ht_c + (1-h)t_m + (1-h)t_l$$

The term $(1-h)t_l$ is the additional time required to reload the cache following each miss. This expression can be rewritten as

$$t_{ave} = ht_c + (1-h)(t_l + t_m)$$

The term $(t_l + t_m)$ corresponds to the time taken to access main memory and to load a line in the cache following a miss. However, because both accessing the element that caused the miss and filling the cache take place in parallel, we can note that $t_l > t_m$ and simplify the equation to get

$$t_{ave} = ht_c + (1-h)t_l$$

Relatively few memory accesses are write operations (about 5–30 percent of memory accesses). If we take into account the action taken on a miss during a read access and on a miss during a write access, the average access time for write though memory is given by

$$t_{ave} = ht_c + (1-h)(1-w)t_l + (1-h)wt_c$$

where w is the fraction of write accesses and t_l is the time taken to reload the cache on a miss. The $(1-h)(1-w)t_l$ term

represents the time taken to reload the cache on a read access, and the term $(1-h)wt_c$ represents the time taken to access the cache on a write miss. This equation is based on the assumption that writes occur infrequently and therefore the main store has time to store write through data between two successive write operations.

Another aspect of cache memories that has to be taken into account in sophisticated systems is *cache coherency*. As we know, data in the cache also lives in the main memory. When the processor modifies data it must modify both the copy in the cache and the copy in the main memory (although not necessarily at the same time). There are circumstances when the existence of two copies (which can differ) of the same item of data causes problems. For example, an I/O controller using DMA might attempt to move an old line of data from the main store to disk without knowing that the processor has just updated the copy of the data in the cache, but has not yet updated the copy in the main memory. Cache coherency is also known as data consistency.

10.5.3 **Disk cache**

Although we've discussed caching main memory, the same techniques can be applied to hard disks to improve their performance. Read caching increases the effective speed of disk drives, since drives are millions of times slower than main memory. Because computers often access disk drives in a predictably ordered manner, performance can be greatly increased by reading data into a memory cache before the computer asks for it. If a computer requests data from a certain location, there's an 80 percent to 90 percent chance that the next request will be for data in the following location. Because the caching program reads information into memory before it is needed, it is often also called a *look-ahead buffer*. A disk cache can be implemented in software in the computer or in hardware in the hard disk, leaving the host computer free from the burden of managing the cache.

Adaptive caching

Cache misses (i.e. $1-h$) can be reduced by the use of *adaptive* strategies and *segmentation*. Suppose a drive has 1 Mbyte of cache memory. A simple cache strategy would be to fill all 1 Mbyte of cache with look-ahead data. If none of the data is required for the next request, all of this data must be purged. Suppose the 1 Mbyte buffer is partitioned into two 512 kbyte buffers, allowing the drive to behave as if it had two caches. Data for one application can be stored in the first 512 kbyte segment, and the data for a second program can be stored in the second 512 kbyte segment. Most drives from Seagate have either two or four fixed cache segments. More than four segments are usually unnecessary.

Another type of caching uses an adaptive algorithm. Assume that the drive has an 800 kbyte read look-ahead buffer arranged as four 200 kbyte segments. Now suppose that an application asks for data that is not in any of the four segments. The drive must read this data from the platters, and decide where to place it in the cache. To do this a decision must be made to determine which segment of the cache gets purged. Ideally we would not want to purge the data in a segment that is about to be used, since we would have to reload that data again. The optimum segment to replace is one that contains data that is no longer needed. Adaptive algorithms make the decision on what data to replace based on an analysis of what the least-utilized data is.

We now look at the details of a real system. Quantum has developed a buffer segmentation method using *adaptive segmentation* firmware that uses the available buffer space more efficiently. The buffer isn't divided into fixed length segments. An algorithm determines the size of the data transfer, regardless of whether the operation is a read or write, and calculates the optimum amount of the buffer to allocate. Buffer space is optimized because the drive can write data to the buffer contiguously.

As the example in Fig. 10.29 illustrates, a 128 kbyte buffer with adaptive segmentation can provide as much or more usable buffer space as a 256 kbyte buffer with fixed segmentation. After the three data requests, R1, R2, and R3, the buffer with

fixed segmentation is full. At the next request, if the data is not already in the buffer, at least one 64 kbyte segment will be overwritten with new data. With the same three requests, the buffer with adaptive segmentation still has space available. In addition, when this buffer is filled, the drive will overwrite only the amount of buffer space required.

Quantum's DisCache firmware uses a *look-ahead* design and an on-board cache buffer to optimize disk drive performance. When the host CPU requests data, DisCache not only provides the requested data, but also adapts its cache algorithm based on the next request. If the next request is for sequential data, the look-ahead caching scheme continues filling the buffer with new sequential data. Thus, especially for long sequences of sequential commands, the continuous prefetch provides round-robin filling and emptying of the buffer, resulting in increased throughput.

Typically, over 50 percent of all disk requests are sequential. So, once DisCache fills the buffer with sequential data, there is a high probability that data requested by the CPU will be in the on-board cache. If it is, DisCache eliminates both the seek time and rotational latency delays that dominate non-cached disk transactions. Because the host CPU doesn't have to access the disk drive to transfer the data, the data retrieval process occurs almost instantaneously.

In a multitasking environment, where a hard disk services multiple CPU operations, the disk must divide available time among all the operations, even though each might be requesting data sequentially from the disk. In conventional disk drive

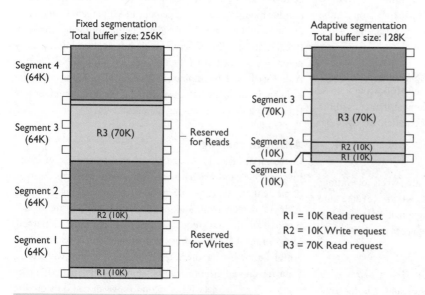

Fig. 10.29 Adaptive versus fixed disk cache segmentation.

systems, the read/write heads seek from one location to another to service multiple data requests. With DisCache, however, the number of seeks required will typically be reduced. After the first seek and read has been performed for each process, DisCache can often transfer the data directly from the high-speed on-board cache memory to the host CPU.

Ordinary disk drive technology allows host-to-buffer and buffer-to-disk transfers to occur simultaneously during data writing operations. Quantum's proprietary WriteCache technology takes caching a step further by allowing the host-to-buffer transfer of disk drive data to occur while the buffer-to-disk transfer of a prior command still is executing. When a write command is executed with WriteCache, the drive stores the data to be written in its cache buffer and immediately sends a *command complete* message to the host before the data is actually written to the disk. The host is then free to perform other host-to-buffer processes. This process eliminates rotational latencies during sequential access, and overlaps rotational latency and seek time with system processing during random access. As a result, sustained data transfer rates increase by up to a factor of 10 for sequential writes and up to 30 percent for random writes.

Summary

The operating system is probably a unique topic in computer science, because nowhere else do hardware and software so closely meet. Although most computers today see the operating system as the GUI and the file manager, there is another part of the operating system that lies hidden from the user. This is the kernel, which performs process switching in a multitasking system and allocates logical address space to the available memory.

In this chapter we have shown how the multitasking can be implemented by saving one process's 'volatile portion' and then restoring another task by loading its volatile portion in the processor's registers.

One of the most important functions carried out by operating systems is the management of the memory. We have shown how logical addresses in the program can be mapped to locations in the immediate access memory. We have also looked at the 68K's user/supervisor mode facility and described how it can be used to create secure operating systems.

The final topic in this chapter was the cache memory that can radically improve the performance of a computer system for relatively little cost. Cache memory operates on the same principle as virtual memory (frequently accessed data is

placed in a very high-speed store). Although cache memory has less of an impact on the operating system than virtual memory, we included cache memory in this chapter because of its similarity to virtual memory.

Problems

1. What is an operating system?

2. What is the difference between a modern operating system and one typical operating system from the 1970s?

3. What is the difference between operating systems on large and small computers?

4. WIMP-based operating systems have largely replaced JCL-based operating systems on personal computers. Do JCL-based operating systems such as Microsoft's MS-DOS 6 and Unix have any advantages over WIMP-based systems?

5. Is it necessary for a CPU to support interrupts in order to construct an operating system?

6. A process in a multitasking system can be in one of the three states: running, runnable, or blocked. What does this statement mean and what are the differences between the three states?

7. What is a process control block and what is the minimum amount of information that it must store?

8. What are the 68K's *user* and *supervisor* states and why have they been implemented?

9. Explain why the stack is such an important data structure and how stack errors can cause the system to crash.

10. The 68K provides a greater degree of protection from user (applications) errors by implementing two stack pointers. Explain how this protection mechanism works.

11. If two stack pointers are a good thing, what about two PCs or two sets of data registers, and so on?

12. What is the difference between a physical address and a logical address?

13. When a new physical page is swapped into memory, one of the existing pages has to be rejected. How is the decision to reject an existing page made?

14. What is the difference between *virtual* memory and *cache* memory?

15. Write a program in 68K assembly language that periodically switches between two processes (assume these are fixed processes permanently stored in memory).

16. A computer has main memory with an access time of 60 ns and cache memory with an access time of 15 ns. If the average hit ratio is 92 percent, what is the maximum theoretical speedup ratio?

17. A computer has main memory with an access time of 60 ns and cache memory with an access time of 15 ns. The computer has a 50 MHz clock and all operations require at least two clock cycles. If the hit ratio is 92 percent, what is the theoretical speedup ratio for this system?

18. A computer has main memory with an access time of 60 ns and cache memory with an access time of 15 ns. The computer has a 50 MHz clock and all operations require at least two clock cycles. On average the computer spends 40 percent of its time accessing memory and 60 percent performing internal operations (an internal operation is a non-memory access). If the hit ratio is 92 percent, what is the speedup ratio for this system?

19. What is the fundamental limitation of a direct-mapped cache?

20. How can the performance of a direct-mapped cache memory be improved?

21. A computer has main memory with an access time of 60 ns and cache memory with an access time of 15 ns.

The cache has a line size of 16 bytes and the computer's memory bus is 32 bits wide. The cache controller operates in a burst mode and can transfer 32 bits between cache and main memory in 80 ns. Whenever a miss occurs the cache must be reloaded with a line. If the average hit ratio is 92 percent, what is the speedup ratio?

22. What is cache coherency and why is it important only in sophisticated systems?

23. What are the similarities and differences between memory cache and so-called disk cache?

24. What is the speedup ratio of a typical disk cache?

25. For the following ideal systems, calculate the hit ratio h required to achieve the stated speedup ratio S.

   (a) $t_m = 60$ ns $t_c = 10$ ns $S = 1.1$
   (b) $t_m = 60$ ns $t_c = 10$ ns $S = 1.5$
   (c) $t_m = 60$ ns $t_c = 10$ ns $S = 3.0$
   (d) $t_m = 60$ ns $t_c = 10$ ns $S = 4.0$

26. Draw a graph of the speedup ratio for an ideal system for $k = 0.5$, $k = 0.2$, $k = 0.1$ (plot the three lines on the same graph). The value of k defines the ratio of cache to main store access times, t_c/t_m.

Chapter 11

....

Computer communications

Two of the greatest technologies of our age are telecommunications and computer engineering. Telecommunications is concerned with moving information from one point to another, or from one point to many other points. It's probably no exaggeration to say that we take the telecommunications industry for granted. If you were to ask someone what the greatest technological feat of 1969 was, they'd probably reply, 'The first manned landing on the Moon.' You could say that a more magnificent achievement was the ability of millions of people half a million kilometers away to watch events on the Moon in their own homes. However, even if many aren't conscious of the immense developments in the telecommunications industry, they won't have missed the microprocessor revolution. Computers are now everywhere and the average American or European is probably never more than a few feet away from a computer.

It's hardly surprising that these two technologies with their widely differing origins, histories, and traditions merged to allow computers to communicate and share resources. Until recently most developments in telecommunications didn't greatly affect the average person in the same way that computer technology had revolutionized every facet of life. Better communications simply meant lower telephone bills and, alas, the portable 'cell' phone.

Computer networks began as part of a general trend towards distributed computing with multicomputer systems and distributed databases. From the 1970s onward computer networks were implemented to allow organizations such as the military, the business world, and the academic communities to share data. Easy access to a communications medium called the *Internet* and the invention of the software *browser* created a revolution almost as big as the microprocessor revolution of the 1970s. From the mid-1990s onward, the Internet grew at such a rate that you couldn't watch TV or read a newspaper without seeing a reference to it. The success of the Internet drove developments in communications equipment.

This chapter examines the way in which computers communicate with each other. However, since the subject of this book is computer hardware, we will concentrate more on the hardware-related aspects of computer communication than the software.

The first part of Chapter 11 provides a short history of communications, concentrating on the development of long-distance signaling systems. We then introduce the idea of *protocols* and *standards* that play a vital role in any communications system. Simply moving data from one point to another isn't the whole story. Protocols are the mutually agreed rules or procedures enabling computers to exchange data in an orderly fashion. By implementing a suitable protocol we ensure that the data gets to its correct destination and deal with the problems of lost or corrupted data.

The next step is to examine how digital data in serial form is physically moved from one point to another. We look at two types of data path: the telephone network and the RS232C interface that links together computers and peripherals.

Two important protocols for the transmission of serial data are briefly examined—a *character-oriented* protocol that treats data as blocks of ASCII-encoded characters and a *bit-oriented* protocol that treats data as a continuous stream of bits.

The next part of this chapter is devoted to *local area networks* and describes the features of some of the LANs in current use. An important aspect of LANs is the way in which the computers and peripherals are able to share the same network without apparent conflict. The final topic in this chapter is the *wide area network* (WAN) that connects computers together over distances longer than about a mile—WANs are used to implement the Internet.

11.1 Introduction

To understand how computer networks evolved you have to appreciate the situation in the 1960s and 1970s. In those days the personal computer hadn't been invented and minicomputers were very expensive. Consider the following scenario from the early 1970s. A scientist uses a minicomputer to control an experiment. One day the scientist has to perform a numerical calculation so complex that it would require all the minicomputer's time for several days. During the time that the minicomputer is devoted to number crunching, the experiment has to be shut down. If the equipment must be run continuously, the scientist has to buy a new and more powerful computer capable of handling both experiment and calculation.

Such an approach is terribly wasteful, because, once the calculation has been completed, the new computer is underused. A much better solution was to buy time on a large mainframe and pay only for the work actually done. The scientist could obtain access to the computational facilities he or she needed in one of two ways. One was to physically take the problem to the mainframe on magnetic tape or disk. The other was to transmit the data over a network from the minicomputer to the mainframe and then download the results from the mainframe.

It's very expensive to construct data links between computers separated by distances ranging from the other side of town to the other side of the world. There is, however, one network that has spanned the globe for over 50 years, the *public switched telephone network*, PSTN. Some authors now refer to the PSTN by the acronym POTS (*plain old telephone system*). The PSTN has become the backbone of many computer networks. The telephone network doesn't provide an ideal solution to the linking of computers, because it was not originally designed to handle high-speed digital data.

During the 1980s a considerable change in the way computers were used took place. The flood of low-cost microcomputers generated a corresponding increase in the number of peripherals capable of being controlled by a computer. It is now commonplace to connect together many different computers and peripherals on one site (e.g. a factory), enabling data to be shared, control centralized, and efficiency improved. Such a network is called a *local area network* (LAN).

When the personal computer became popular, low-cost hardware and software were used to link PCs to the global network called the *Internet*. By the late 1990s networks were no longer the province of the factory or university—any schoolchild with a PC at home could access NASA's database to see pictures of the latest spaceshots before they got on the evening news. Moreover, the child didn't need to know anything about computer science other than how to operate a mouse.

Figure 11.1 illustrates the concept of a computer network with two interconnected local area networks. A network performs the same function as a telephone exchange and routes

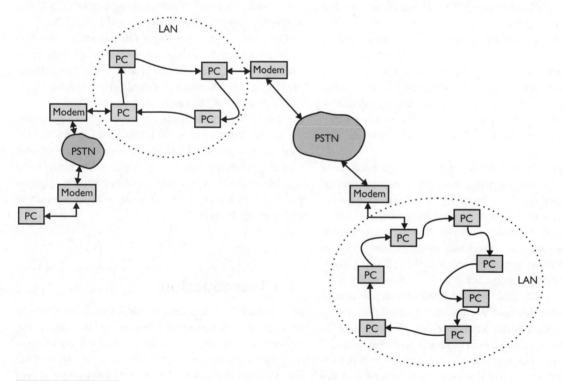

Fig. 11.1 The network.

data from one computer to another. The LANs in Fig. 11.1 might be used to share data in, for example, a university environment. The local area networks are themselves connected to the telephone system (PSTN) via hardware called a *modem* (you don't need a modem if you have an ISDN connection). Figure 11.1 also demonstrates that a single computer can be connected to the other networks via the PSTN.

A LAN lets you communicate with a mainframe on a distant site or with one of the many microprocessors and peripherals on your own site. The local area network has made possible the *paperless* office, in which people pass memos to each other via the network. (Actually, people seem to create a memo on the screen, print it, correct it, print it, correct it, ..., and then send it electronically. The paperless office often uses far more paper than the conventional office ever did.)

11.1.1 History of computer communications

Before we describe *computer* networks, it's instructive to take a short look at the history of data transmission. Some of my students think that electronics began in the 1960s or even later. Telecommunications predates the electronic digital computer by over a century and its history is just as exciting as the *space race* of the 1960s. Some of the key players were engineers who were every bit as great as Newton or Einstein.

As early as 1809 King Maximilian asked the Bavarian Academy of Sciences to suggest a scheme for high-speed communication over long distances, because he had seen how the French visual semaphore system had helped Napoleon's military campaigns. As a result, Sömmering designed a crude telegraph that used 35 conductors (one for each character). How was information transmitted in a pre-electronic age? If you pass electricity through water containing a little acid the electric current breaks down the water into oxygen and hydrogen. Sömmering's telegraph worked by detecting the bubbles that appeared in a glass tube containing acidified water when

electricity was passed through it. Sömmering's telegraph wasn't exactly suited to high-speed transmission—but it was a start.

H. C. Oersted made probably the greatest leap forward in electrical engineering in 1819 when he discovered that an electric current creates a magnetic field round a conductor. Conversely, a moving magnetic field induces an electric current in a conductor.

One of the driving forces behind early telecommunications systems was the growth of the rail network. A system was required to warn stations down the line that a train was arriving. Shortly after the connection between electricity and magnetism had been established by Oersted, Wheatstone and Cooke invented an effective telegraph in 1828. They used the magnetic field round a wire to deflect a compass needle. By 1840 a 40-mile stretch between Slough and Paddington in London had been linked using the Wheatstone and Cooke telegraph.

Figure 11.2 illustrates the operation of a different type of *telegraph* that produces a sound rather than the deflection of compass needles. When the key is depressed, a current flows in the circuit and energizes the solenoid (i.e. it magnetizes the iron core inside the coil). The magnetized core attracts a small iron plate that produces an audible click as it strikes the core. Information is transmitted to this type of telegraph in the form of the *Morse code*.

Morse constructed his code from four symbols: the dot, the dash (whose duration is equal to three dots), the space between dots and dashes, and the space between words. Unlike simple codes, the Morse code is a *variable length* code. The original Morse key didn't send a 'bleep'—a dot was the interval between two closely spaced clicks and a dash the interval between two more widely spaced clicks. In other words, the operator had to listen to the space between clicks.

In 1843 Samuel Morse sent his assistant Alfred Vail to the printer's to count the relative frequencies of the letters they were using to set up their press. Morse gave frequently

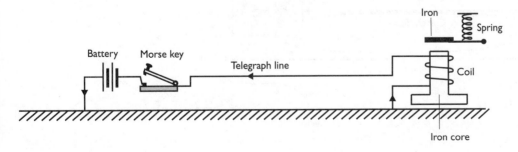

Fig. 11.2 The telegraph.

occurring letters short codes and infrequently occurring letters were given long symbols; for example, the code for E is · and Q is — — · —. It's interesting to note that the Morse code is relatively close to the optimum Huffman code for the English language. We met variable-length Huffman codes in Chapter 4.

The very first long distance telecommunications networks were designed to transmit *digital* information from point-to-point (i.e. on–off telegraph signals). Information was transmitted in binary form using two signal levels (current = *mark*, no current = *space*). The transmitter was the Morse key and the receiver the Morse telegraph.

The first long-distance data links

We take wires and cables for granted. In the early nineteenth century, plastics hadn't been invented and the only materials available for insulation and waterproofing were things like asphaltum. In 1843 a form of rubber called *gutta percha* was discovered and was used to insulate the signal-carrying path in cables. The Atlantic Telegraph Company created an insulated cable for underwater use containing a single copper conductor made of seven twisted strands, surrounded by gutta percha insulation. This cable was protected by 18 surrounding iron wires coated with hemp and tar.

Submarine cable telegraphy began with a cable crossing the English Channel to France in 1850. Alas the cable failed after only a few messages had been exchanged. A more successful attempt was made the following year.

Transatlantic cable-laying from Ireland began in 1857 but was abandoned when the strain of the cable descending to the ocean bottom caused it to snap under its own weight. The Atlantic Telegraph Company tried again in 1858. Again, the cable broke after only three miles but the two cable-laying ships managed to splice the two ends. After several more

breaks and storm damage, the cable reached Newfoundland in August 1858.

It soon became clear that this cable wasn't going to be a commercial success because the signal was too weak to detect reliably (the receiver used the magnetic field from current in the cable to deflect a magnetized needle). The original voltage used to drive a current down the cable was approximately 600 V. So, they raised the voltage to about 2000 V to drive more current along the cable. Such a high voltage burned through the primitive insulation, shorted the cable, and destroyed the first transatlantic telegraph link after about 700 messages had been transmitted in three months.

In England, the Telegraph Construction and Maintenance Company developed a new 2300 mile long cable weighing 9000 tons that was three times the diameter of the failed 1858 cable. Laying this cable required the largest ship in the world. After a failed attempt in 1865 a transatlantic link was established in 1866.

Telegraph distortion

During the 19th century the length of cables increased as technology advanced. It soon became apparent that signals suffer *distortion* during transmission. The 1866 transatlantic telegraph cable could transmit only 8 words per minute. By the way, it cost $100 *in gold* to transmit 20 words (including the address) across the first transatlantic cable.

A sharply rising pulse at the transmitter end of a cable is received at the far end as a highly distorted pulse with long rise and fall times. Figure 11.3 illustrates the effect of this so-called *telegraph distortion*. The sponsors of the transatlantic cable project were worried by the effect of this distortion and the problem was eventually handed to William Thomson at the University of Glasgow.

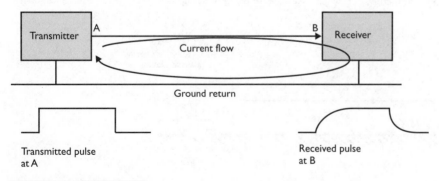

Fig. 11.3 Telegraph distortion.

Thomson was one of the 19th century's greatest scientists, who published more than 600 papers. He developed the second law of thermodynamics and created the absolute temperature scale. The unit of temperature with absolute zero at 0 K is called the kelvin in his honor—Thomson later became Lord Kelvin. Thomson worked on the dynamical theory of heat and carried out fundamental work in hydrodynamics. His mathematical analysis of electricity and magnetism covered the basic ideas for the electromagnetic theory of light. I'm not certain what he did in his spare time. One of Thomson's most quoted statements that still applies today was:

I often say when you can measure what you are speaking about and express it in numbers, you know something about it, but when you cannot measure it, when you cannot express it in numbers, your knowledge of it is of a meagre and unsatisfactory kind.

In 1855 Thomson presented a paper to the Royal Society analyzing the effect of pulse distortion that became the cornerstone of what is now called *transmission line theory*. The cause of the problems investigated by Thomson lies in the physical properties of electrical conductors and insulators. At its simplest, the effect of a transmission line is to reduce the speed at which signals can change state. Thomson's theories enabled engineers to construct data links with much lower levels of distortion.

Origins of the telephone network

In 1872 Alexander Graham Bell, who had recently emigrated to the USA, started work on a method of transmitting several signals simultaneously over a single line. Bell's project was called the *harmonic telegraph*. This project failed, but it did lead to a spin-off in 1876 called the *telephone*. In one real sense the invention of the telephone was a disaster for the future of data transmission systems, because the telephone network that sprang up in the 1880s was designed to transmit only speech signals in analog form.

A network designed to transmit intelligible speech (as opposed to hi-fi) must transmit analog signals in the frequency range 300 to about 3300 Hz (i.e. the so-called voice band). Consequently, the telephone network now linking millions of subscribers across the world can't be used to directly transmit digital data that requires a bandwidth extending to zero frequency (i.e. d.c.). If the computer had been invented before the telephone, we wouldn't have had this problem. Transmission paths that transmit or pass signals with frequency components from d.c. to some upper limit are called

baseband channels. Transmission paths that transmit frequencies between a lower and an upper frequency are called *bandpass* channels.

Digital information from computers or peripherals must be converted into analog form before it is transmitted across a bandpass channel such as the PSTN. At the receiving end of the network, this analog signal is reconverted into digital form. The device that converts between digital and analog signals over a data link is called a *modem* (i.e. *mo*dulator–*dem*odulator). Ironically enough, all the long-haul links on modern telephone networks now transmit digital data, which means that the analog signal derived from the digital data must be converted to digital form before transmission over these links. It is probable that the PSTN will become entirely digital (as it was in the 1840s) and speech will be converted to digital form within the subscriber's own telephone. Indeed, the only analog link in many telephone systems is just the connection between the subscriber and the local exchange. This link is sometimes called the *last mile*.

Although the first telegraph systems operated from point-to-point, the introduction of the telephone led to the development of switching centers, or telephone exchanges. The first generation of switches employed a telephone operator who manually plugged a subscriber's line into a line connected to the next switching center in the link. By the end of the 19th century the infrastructure of the computer networks was already in place.

In 1897 an undertaker called Strowger invented the automatic telephone exchange, which used electromechanical devices to route calls between exchanges. When a number was dialed, a series of pulses were sent down the line to a rotary switch. If you dialed, for example "5", the five pulses would move a switch five steps to connect you to line number five, which routed your call to the next switching center. Consequently, when you called someone the number you dialed depended on the route though the system. A system was developed where each user could be called with the same number from anywhere and the exchange would automatically translate this number to the specific numbers required to perform the routing. Mechanical switching was gradually replaced by electronic switching and the pulse dialing that actually operated the switches gave way to the use of tones (i.e. messages to the switching computers).

By the time the telegraph was well established, radio was being developed. James Clerk Maxwell predicted radio waves in 1864 following his study of light and electromagnetic waves. Heinrich Hertz demonstrated the existence of radio waves in 1887 and Marconi is credited with being the first to use radio to span the Atlantic in 1901.

In 1906 Lee deForest invented the vacuum tube amplifier. Without a vacuum tube (or transistor) to amplify weak signals, modern electronics would have been impossible (although primitive computers using electromechanical devices could have been built without electronics).

The telegraph, telephone, and vacuum tube were all steps on the path to the development of computer networks. As each of these practical steps was taken, there was a corresponding development in the accompanying theory (in the case of radio, the theory came before the discovery). Table 11.1 provides a list of some of the most significant dates in the early development of long-distance communications systems.

Computer communications is a complex branch for computing because it covers so many areas. A programmer drags an icon from one place to another on a screen. This action causes the applications program to send a message to the operating system that might begin a sequence of transactions resulting in data being retrieved from a computer halfway around the world. Data sent from one place to another has to be encapsulated, given an address, and sent on its way. Its progress has to be monitored and its receipt acknowledged.

It has to be formatted in the way appropriate to the transmission path. All these actions have to take place over many different communications channels (telephone, radio, satellite, and fiber optic cable). Moreover, all the hardware and software components from different suppliers, constructed with different technologies, have to communicate with each other.

The only way we can get such complex systems to work is to define rules or *protocols* that define how the various components communicate with each other. In the next section we look at these rules and the bodies that define them.

11.2 Protocols and computer communications

To an outsider the world of computer communications must seem like an entirely hardware-oriented subject. After all, computer communications just involves moving data from point A to point B—doesn't it? It therefore follows that computer communications is all about data transmission hardware.

1837	Charles Wheatstone patents the electric telegraph.
1844	Samuel Morse demonstrates a Baltimore to Washington DC telegraph link.
1847	An inelastic latex called gutta percha is discovered. It serves as a reliable insulator in water.
1850	Morse patents his telegraph.
1858	First transatlantic telegraph.
1861	First USA transcontinental telegraph cable begins service.
1864	James C. Maxwell predicts electromagnetic radiation.
1868	First successful transatlantic telegraph cable completed between UK and Canada.
1874	Baudot invents a division multiplexing scheme for telegraphs.
1875	Typewriter invented.
1876	Bell patents the telephone.
1887	Heinrich Hertz discovers radio waves and verifies Maxwell's theory.
1906	Lee deForest invents the vacuum tube triode (an amplifier).
1915	USA transcontinental telephone service begins between New York and San Francisco.
1920s	Catalina Island telephone service to mainland via radio system.
1921	Radio telephone calls between England and Norway implemented.
1927	First commercial transatlantic radio telephone service begins.
1945	Arthur C. Clarke proposes using Earth-orbiting satellite as a communications relay.
1947	The transistor invented at Bell Laboratories.
1948	Claude Shannon publishes his work on information theory (related to channel capacity).
1949	High-performance submarine cable developed by AT&T using polyethylene and butyl rubber dielectric.
1956	First transatlantic telephone cables (one in each direction). A total of 102 repeaters (vacuum tube) amplifiers were used.
1957	USSR launches first satellite, Sputnik 1.
1962	First television satellite launched, Telstar 1.
1965	First commercial communications satellite launched, Early Bird (INTELSAT 1).
1966	Fiber optics first proposed.
1971	First large-scale computer network, ARPANET, comes into service.
1970s	ALOHA local area network developed for the Hawaiian islands.
1973	Metcalfe develops the Ethernet.
1980	OSI 7-layer reference model (for networks) adopted.
1980	Bell Systems develops fiber optic cables.

Table 11.1 Key dates in the early developments in telecommunications.

Consequently, communication between computers is possible provided that they employ standard hardware conforming to agreed standards. In fact, much of computer communications is largely concerned with how computers go about exchanging data, rather than with just the mechanisms used to transmit data. Therefore the standards used in computer communications relate not only to the hardware parts of a communication system (i.e. the plugs and sockets connecting a computer to a transmission path, the transmission path itself, the nature of the signals flowing along the transmission path), but to the procedures or protocols followed in transmitting the information.

Most readers will have some idea of what is meant by a standard, but they may not have come across the term 'protocol' as it is used in computer communications. When any two parties communicate with each other (be they people or machines), they must both agree to abide by a set of unambiguous rules. For example, they must speak the same language and one may start speaking only when the other indicates a readiness to listen.

Consider another example. Suppose you have a bank overdraft and send a check to cover it. If after a few days you receive a threatening letter from the manager, what do you conclude? Was your check received after the manager's letter was sent? Has one of your debits reached your account and increased the overdraft? Was the check lost in the post? This confusion demonstrates that the blind transmission of information can lead to unclear and ill-defined situations. It is necessary for both parties to know exactly what messages each has and has not received. What we need is a set of rules to govern the interchange of letters.

Such a set of rules is called a *protocol* and, in the case of people, is learned as a child. When computers communicate with each other, the protocol must be laid down more formally. If many different computers are to communicate with each other, it is necessary that they adhere to standard protocols that have been promulgated by national and international standards organizations, trade organizations, and other related bodies.

In the 1970s and 1980s the number of computers and the volume of data to be exchanged between computers increased dramatically. Manufacturers were slow to agree on and to adopt standard protocols for the exchange of data, which led to incompatibility between computers. To add insult to injury, it was often difficult to transfer data between computers that were nominally similar. Computers frequently employed different dialects of the same high-level language, formatted data in different ways, encoded it in different ways, and transmitted it in different ways. Even the builders of the Tower of Babel

had only to contend with different languages. The development of standard protocols has much improved the situation.

By demonstrating how protocols are used in computer communications, we hope that you will appreciate the role of standards in computer communications and will take them into account when you specify, purchase, or design such equipment. It is a sad fact that many working hours are lost in both manufacturing and service industries simply because engineers have to waste time interfacing non-standard equipment to computers or providing for communications between incompatible systems.

The issue of standardization arises not only in the world of computer communications. Standardization is an important part of all aspects of information technology. For example, the lack of suitable standards or the non-compliance with existing standards has a dampening effect on the progress of information technology. Independent manufacturers do not wish to enter a chaotic market that demands a large number of versions of each product or service produced to cater for all the various non-standard implementations. Similarly, users do not want to buy non-standard equipment or services that do not integrate with their existing systems.

Standards bodies

If a computer user in Middlesbrough, England, is to access a computer in Phoenix, Arizona, the two computers must cooperate. The commands and data sent by one computer must be recognized and complied with by the other computer. The *rules* governing the communications process are called a *protocol* and are formalized in a document called a *standard*. All aspects of the communications system must be standardized—from the communications protocol to the nature of the signals on the communications path to the plugs and sockets that connect the computer to the network.

How do all these components of a network get standardized? There are two basic types of standard. One is called a *de facto* or *industrial* standard and is imposed by a manufacturer. A good example of an industrial standard is Microsoft's Windows operating system. The success of Windows in the market-place has encouraged its adoption as a standard by most PC manufacturers and software houses.

The other type of standard is a *national* or *international* standard that has been promulgated by a recognized body. There are international standards for the binary representation of numbers. When the decimal number nine is transmitted over a network, it is represented by its universally agreed international standard, the binary pattern 00111001.

The world of standards is very complex because it involves lots of different parties with vested interests at local, national, and international levels. Typically, a standard begins life in a working party in a professional organization such as the Institute of Electrical and Electronics Engineers (IEEE) or the Electronic Industries Association (EIA). A standard generated by one of these professional bodies is forwarded to the appropriate national standards body (e.g. the American National Standards Institute (ANSI) in the USA or the British Standards Institution (BSI) in the UK). Finally, the standard might reach the International Organization for Standardization (ISO), made up of members from the world's national standards organizations.

11.2.1 Open systems and standards

Before we look at protocols for computer communications, we must make an important point. In the descriptions of systems that follow, we use analogies in order to illustrate difficult or abstract concepts. In general, these are analogies with only limited application and cannot be extended too far.

It's impossible to read a book on computer communications without encountering the so-called *International Organization for Standardization Basic Reference Model for Open Systems Interconnection* or, more mercifully, the ISO model for OSI (ISO 7498). A system, in the ISO context (and jargon), is defined as

a set of one or more computers together with the software, peripherals, terminals, human operators, physical processes and means of data transfer that go with them, which make up a single information processing unit.

The reference model for OSI isn't a set of protocols for a communications system. It's a *framework* for the identification and design of protocols for existing or future communications systems. It enables engineers to identify and to relate together different areas of standardization. The OSI framework doesn't imply any particular technology or method of implementing systems. In other words, the reference model helps engineers to design protocols for computer communications systems.

The expression *open system* simply means a system that is open to communication with other open systems. A system is open only if it employs agreed (i.e. standardized) protocols when it communicates with the outside world. Of course, it does not have to employ standard protocols for communications within the system itself. An analogy with an open system is a television receiver, because it is open to the reception of sound and pictures from transmitters using the agreed protocol (e.g. 525 lines/frame, 60 fields/second, NTSC color in the USA or 625 lines/frame, 50 fields/second, PAL color in

the UK). A pocket calculator is a closed system because it is unable to receive inputs from other systems.

Before the development of the ISO reference model, equipment manufacturers often designed communications systems on an *ad hoc* basis. A manufacturer produced a package of hardware and software to provide communications facilities between two points in their client's network.

The purpose of the ISO reference model is to isolate the specific functions performed by the communications system from all other aspects of the system. Once these functions have been isolated, it is possible to devise standards for them. In this way, any manufacturer can produce equipment or software that performs a particular function. If designers use hardware and software conforming to well-defined standards, they can create an information transmission system by putting together all the necessary parts. These parts may be obtained from more than one source. As long as their functions are clearly defined and the way in which they interact with other parts is explicitly stated, they can be used as the building blocks of a system. Alternatively, a manufacturer can produce these building blocks for incorporation in other people's systems.

Standard ISO 7498, which describes the reference model, isn't an easy document to understand. The standard was written for the implementers of standards and is addressed to them. This document provides a formal and precise framework for the description of standards related to computer communications and identifies the set of standards needed to allow open computer communications to take place.

Figure 11.4 illustrates the structure of the ISO reference model for OSI, where two parties, A and B, are in communication with each other. The most important feature of the ISO model is the way in which it divides the task of communicating between two points between seven *layers* of protocol. Each layer carries out an action or service required by the layer above it. The actions performed by any given layer of the reference model are precisely defined by the service for that layer and require an appropriate protocol for the layer between the two points that are communicating. This view conforms to current thinking about software and is strongly related to the concept of modularity.

In everyday terms, consider an engineer in one factory who wishes to communicate with an engineer in another factory. The engineer in the first factory describes to an assistant the nature of some work that is to be done. The assistant then dictates a letter to a secretary who, in turn, types the letter and hands it to a courier. Here, the original task (i.e. communicating the needs of one engineer to another) is broken down into subtasks, each of which is performed by a different person. The engineer doesn't have to know about the actions carried

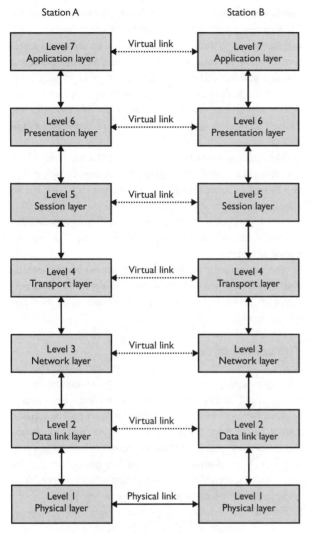

Fig. 11.4 The basic reference model for open systems interconnection.

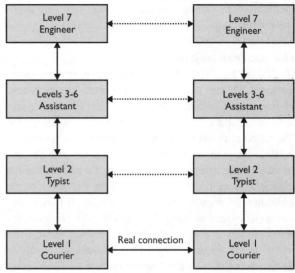

Fig. 11.5 Illustrating the concept of layered protocols.

out by other people involved in the exchange of data. Indeed, it does not matter to the engineer how the information is conveyed to his or her counterpart.

In the ISO model, communication between layers within a system takes place between a layer and the layers immediately above and below it. Layer X in System A communicates only with layers $X+1$ and $X-1$ in System A (see Fig. 11.4). Layer 1 is an exception, because there's no layer below it. Layer 1 communicates only with layer 2 in A and with the corresponding layer 1 in B at the other end of the communications link. In terms of the previous analogy, the secretary who types the letter communicates only with the assistant who

dictates it and with the courier who transports it. Figure 11.5 illustrates this example in terms of ISO layers, although this rather simple example doesn't correspond exactly to the ISO model. In particular, layers 3 to 6 are represented by the single layer called 'assistant'.

Another characteristic of the ISO model is the *apparent* or *virtual* link between corresponding layers at each end of the communication channel (this link is also called *peer-to-peer*). Two corresponding layers at two points in a network are called peer subsystems and communicate using layer protocols. Therefore, a message sent by layer X at one end of the link is in the form required by the corresponding layer X at the other end. It appears that these two layers are in direct communication with each other, as they are using identical protocols. In fact, one layer X is using the layers below it to transmit the message across the link. At the other end, layer 1 and higher layers process the message until it reaches layer X in the form it left layer X at the other end of the link. Returning to our analogy, the secretary at one factory appears to communicate directly with the secretary at the other factory, because the language used in the letter is appropriate to the task being performed by the two secretaries.

An engineer in Factory A is communicating with an engineer in Factory B. Each engineer appears to be in direct communication with his or her counterpart, even though there is no actual link between the engineers themselves.

We now look at the functions performed by the seven layers of the ISO reference model for open systems interconnection, starting with the uppermost layer, the application layer.

The application layer

The highest layer of the ISO reference model is the *application layer*, which is concerned with protocols for applications programs (e.g. file transfer, electronic mail). This layer represents the interface with the end user. Strictly speaking, the OSI reference model is concerned only with *communications* and does not represent the way in which the end user employs the information. The protocol observed by the two users in the application layer is determined entirely by the nature of the application. Consider the communication between two lawyers when they are using the telephone. The protocol used by the lawyers is concerned with the semantics of legal jargon. Although one lawyer appears to be speaking directly to another, he or she is using another medium involving other protocols to transport the data. In other words, there is no real person-to-person connection but a virtual person-to-person connection built upon the telephone network.

Another example of an application process is the operation of an automatic teller at a bank. The operator is in communication with the bank and is blissfully ignorant of all the technicalities involved in the transaction. The bank asks the user what transaction he or she wishes to make and the user indicates the nature of the transaction by pushing the appropriate button. The bank may be 10 m or 1000 km away from the user. The details involved in the communication process are entirely hidden from the user; in the reference model the user is operating at the applications level.

The presentation layer

The application layer in one system passes information to the presentation layer below it and receives information back from this layer. Remember that a layer at one end of a network can't communicate directly with the corresponding layer at the other end. Each layer (except one) communicates with only the layer above it and with the layer below it. At one end of the communications system the presentation layer translates data between the local format required by the application layer above it and the format used for transfer. At the other end, the format for transfer is translated into the local format of data for the application layer. By 'format' we mean the way in which the computer represents information such as characters and numbers.

To take another analogy, a Russian diplomat can phone a Chinese diplomat at the UN, even though neither speaks the other's language. Suppose the Russian diplomat speaks to a Russian-to-English interpreter who speaks to an English-to-Chinese interpreter at the other end of a telephone link, who, in turn, speaks to the Chinese diplomat. The diplomats represent the applications layer process and talk to each other about political problems. However, they don't speak to each other directly and have to use a presentation layer to format the data before it is transmitted between them. In this example, the Chinese-to-English and English-to-Russian translators represent the presentation layer.

This analogy illustrates an important characteristic of the OSI reference model. The English-to-Chinese translator may be a human or a machine. Replacing one with the other has no effect on the application layer above it or on the information transfer layers below it. All that is needed is a mechanism that translates English to Chinese, subject to specified performance criteria.

The presentation layer's principal function is the translation of data from one code to another. However, this layer performs other important functions such as data encryption and text compression.

The session layer

Below the presentation layer sits the session layer. The session layer organizes the dialog between two presentation layers. It establishes, manages, and synchronizes the channel between two application processes. This layer provides dialog control of the type, 'Roger, over', in radio communications, and the mechanisms used to synchronize application communications (but synchronization actions must be initiated at the application layer). The session layer resolves collisions between synchronization requests. An example is: '... did you follow that? ... ', '... then I'll go over it again'.

The transport layer

The four layers below the session layer are responsible for carrying the message between the two parties in communication. The transport layer isolates the session and higher layers from the network itself. At first sight, it may seem surprising that as many as four layers are needed to perform such an apparently simple task as moving data from one point in a network to another point. However, we are talking about establishing and maintaining connections across interlinked LANs and wide area networks with, possibly, major differences in technology and performance—not just communications over a simple wire. The reference model has been designed to include both LANs and WANs that may involve communication paths across continents and include several different communications systems. Figure 11.6 shows how the

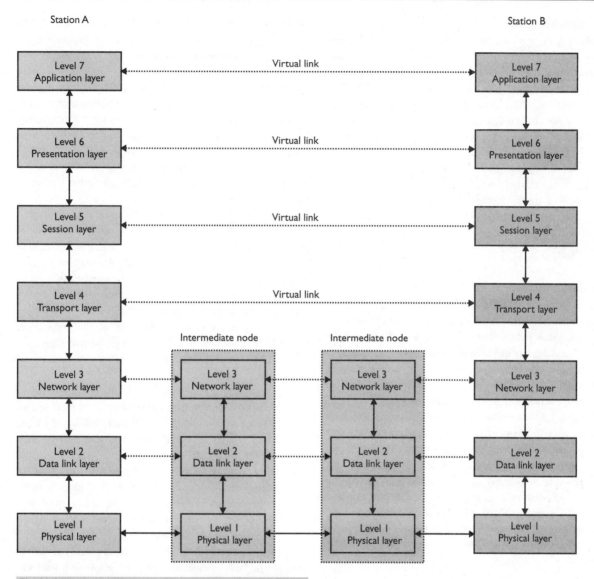

Fig. 11.6 Networks with intermediate nodes between end stations.

ISO model for OSI caters for communications systems with intermediate nodes.

The transport layer is responsible for the reliable transmission of messages between two application nodes of a network and for ensuring that the messages are received in the order in which they were sent. The transport layer isolates higher layers from the characteristics of the real networks by providing the reliable economic transmission required by an application independent of the characteristics of the underlying facilities (for example, error detection/correction, multiplexing to reduce cost, splitting to improve throughput, and message reordering). In brief, the transport layer doesn't have to know anything about how the network is organized.

Packet switching networks divide information into units called *packets* and then send them across a complex network of circuits. Some packets take one route through the network and others take another. Consequently, it is possible for packets to arrive at their destination out of sequence. The transport layer must assemble packets in the correct order, which involves storing the received out-of-sequence packets until the system is ready for them.

The network layer

The network layer serves the transport layer above it by conveying data between the local transport layer and the remote transport layer. Consequently, the network layer is system dependent unlike the layers above it. Complex communications systems may have many paths between two points. The network layer chooses the optimum path for a message to cross the network or for the establishment of a *virtual connection*. As an analogy, consider the postal system. Mail sent to a nearby sorting office might be directed to a more distant sorting office if the local office is congested and cannot cope with the volume of traffic. Similarly, in a data transmission network, transmission paths are chosen to minimize the transit time of packets and the cost of transmission. We will look at routing in networks later.

The data link layer

The data link layer establishes an error-free (to a given probability) connection between two adjacent points in a network. Information may be transmitted from one end of a network to the other end directly or via intermediate nodes in a series of hops. The data link layer at one node receives a message from the network layer above it and sends it via the physical layer below it to the data link layer at the adjacent node.

The data link layer also detects faulty messages and automatically asks for their retransmission. Protocols for the data link layer and the physical layer below it were the first protocols to be developed and are now widely adopted. Data link layer protocols cover many different technologies: LANs (for example, Ethernet-type networks using CMSA/CD), and WANs (for example, X.25). Systems often divide this layer into two parts, a higher level *logical link control* (LLC) and a lower level *medium access control* (MAC).

The physical layer

The lowest layer is called the *physical layer* and is unique because a physical connection between any two points in a network exists only at this level. The physical layer is responsible for receiving the individual bits of a message from the data link layer and for transmitting them over some physical medium to the adjacent physical layer which detects the bits and passes them to the data link layer above it. The physical layer ensures that bits are received in the order they are transmitted.

The role of the physical layer can be divided into two areas. The transmission layer handles the physical medium (e.g. wire, radio, and optical fiber) and ensures that a stream of bits gets from one place to another. The physical layer also implements the *connection strategy*. There are three fundamental connection strategies. *Circuit switching* establishes a permanent connection between two parties for the duration of the information transfer. The telephone system was once based on circuit switching. *Message switching* stores a message temporarily at each node and then sends it on its way across the network. Circuit switching uses a single route through the network, whereas in message switching different messages may travel via different routes. *Packet switching* divides a message into units called *packets* and transmits them across the network. Packet switching doesn't maintain a permanent connection through the network and is similar to message switching.

Packet switching comes in two flavors, the *datagram* and the *virtual circuit*. A datagram service transmits packets independently and they have to be reassembled at their destination (they may arrive out of order). A virtual circuit first establishes a route through the network and then sends all the packets, in order, via this route. The difference between circuit switching and a virtual circuit is that message switching requires a connection for the duration of the connection, whereas the virtual circuit can be used by other messages.

The physical layer doesn't guarantee reliable delivery of its messages. The service offered by this layer is known as a *best effort service*. Information sent on the physical medium might be lost or corrupted in transit because of electrical or electromagnetic noise interfering with the transmitted data. On radio or telephone channels the error rate may be very high (one bit lost in 10^3 transmitted bits), whereas on fiber optic links it may be very low (one bit lost in 10^{12}). It is the responsibility of layers on top of the physical layer to make up for imperfections in this layer. The physical communication paths themselves may be copper wires, optical fibres, microwave links, or satellite links.

Remember that the ISO reference model permits modifications to one layer without changing the whole of a network. For example, the physical layer between two nodes can be switched from a coaxial cable to a fiber optic link without any alterations whatsoever taking place at any other level. After all, the data link layer is interested only in giving bits to, or receiving them from, the physical layer. It's not interested in how the physical layer goes about its work.

Message encapsulation

Figure 11.7 demonstrates how information is transported across a network by means of a system using layered protocols. In Fig. 11.7(a) we have the application-level data that is to be transmitted from one computer to another. For the sake of simplicity, we'll assume that there aren't any presentation or session layers. The applications layer passes the data to the transport layer, which puts a *header* in front of the data and a *trailer* after it. The data has now been encapsulated in the same way that we put a letter into an envelope. The header and trailer include the address of the sender and the receiver.

Data

(a) Data at the applications layer

| Transport layer header | Data | Trailer |

(b) Data at the transport layer

| Network layer header | Transport layer header | Data | Trailer |

(c) Data at the network layer

Fig. 11.7 Encapsulated frames.

The packet from the transport layer is handed to the network layer, which, in turn, adds its own header and trailer. This process continues all the way down to the physical layer.

Now look at the process in reverse. When a network layer receives a packet from the data link layer below it, the network layer strips off the network layer header and trailer and uses them to check for errors in transmission and to decide how to handle this packet. The network layer then hands the packet to the transport layer about it, and so on.

Standards and the ISO reference model for OSI

The ISO reference model for ISO is just a framework for the development of standards. Figure 11.8 shows how standards for the layers of the reference model have grown. This figure is hourglass shaped. The bottom is broad to cater for the many low-level protocols introduced to deal with diverse types of channel, technology, and network, whereas the middle is narrow because it's desirable to have as few protocols as possible

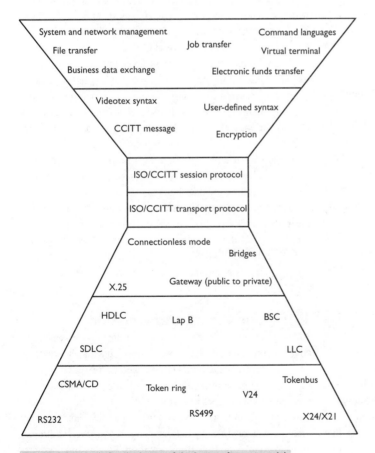

Fig. 11.8 Standards for the layers of the basic reference model.

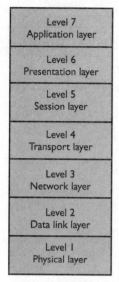

| Level 7 Application layer |
| Level 6 Presentation layer |
| Level 5 Session layer |
| Level 4 Transport layer |
| Level 3 Network layer |
| Level 2 Data link layer |
| Level 1 Physical layer |

(a) ISO protocol stack

| Application layer |
| Transmission control |
| Internet protocol |
| Network access protocol |

(b) Internet protocol stack

Fig. 11.9 ISO and Internet layers.

to move information around a network. The top is wide because it reflects the great range of applications of LANs.

The ISO reference model for OSI isn't quite as popular today as it was in the 1980s. It was anticipated that most (if not all) standards for networks would fit within the OSI framework. That hasn't happened. Many of today's standards are proprietary (*ad hoc* or industrial) and don't conform closely to the OSI model. However, some of the current standards such as the Internet TCP/IP protocol are *layered* even if the layers don't correspond exactly to the seven layers we've just described. Figure 11.9 shows the Internet *protocol stack* alongside the ISO reference model.

Since this is a text devoted to the hardware aspects of computers, we are now going to look more closely at the bottom two layers of the reference model—the physical layer and the data link layer.

11.3 The physical layer

Figure 11.10 illustrates the physical links connecting together two stations, User A and User B. A station is a point in a network that communicates with another point in the network. Alternative words for station are *node*, *receiver*, *transmitter*, or *host*. Before we can consider the factors influencing the design of a physical channel, it's necessary to look at the function it performs. You may find the repetition of the word

physical a little boring. We employ this word to distinguish between two very different entities—a *physical* channel and a *logical* channel. A physical channel is the *actual* transmission path connecting two stations, and may be a wire link, a radio link, or any other suitable medium. A logical channel is an *apparent* transmission path linking two stations but which may not actually exist. Of course, a logical channel is made up of one or more physical channels operating in tandem. However, the characteristics of a logical channel may be very different from those of the physical channels of which it is composed.

We can describe a physical channel under three headings: the signal path itself, the mechanical interface to the signal path, and the functionality of the channel. The signal path is concerned with the way in which data is to be transmitted electronically over a channel, and the nature of the signal flowing across the channel must be defined; for example, we must ask what signal levels constitute logical 1s and logical 0s.

A second and less obvious consideration concerns the mechanical arrangement of the link. What types of plugs and sockets does it use to connect the node with the transmission path? Standard connectors are as vital as standard signal levels if the equipment at the end of a link is to be readily interchangeable with equipment from several different manufacturers.

The third aspect of a physical layer link of importance is its *functionality*. In other words, what does the channel do apart from transmit data? The telephone channel, for example, not only permits voice signals to be sent from one subscriber to another, but also transmits the dialing pulses or tones needed to set up the connection between the subscribers. In the same way, a serial data link must normally include provision for carrying supervisory signals or messages that take part in controlling the data link.

Some authors describe a fourth component of the physical layer that they call the *procedural* aspect. The procedural aspect governs the sequence of events that take place when a channel is set up, maintained, and closed. We include the procedural element of a standard in the functional element.

11.3.1 Serial data transmission

Although we introduced serial data transmission when we covered computer interfaces, we have included a short section on serial transmission here because we are interested in other aspects. Ideally, information should be moved from one computer to another a word at a time, with all the *m* bits of a word transmitted simultaneously. An *m*-bit parallel data highway requires *m* wires to carry the data, and two or three additional wires to control the flow of information. Parallel links are feasible only for computers separated by up to several meters.

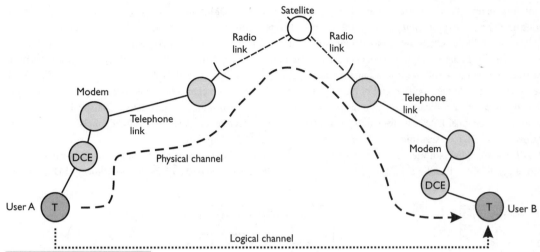

Fig. 11.10 The physical channel.

Networks transmit data serially a bit at a time and require only two lines—one to carry the data and one to act as the ground return. Remember that a voltage has a meaning only when specified with respect to some reference point such as the ground or the earth. If a single path links two points, data can be moved in only one direction at a time. Fiber optic links require a single fiber; and radio links don't need a physical connection.

There are three types of transmission path between stations. The most basic transmission path is called *simplex* and permits the transmission of information in one direction only; that is, there's a single transmitter at one end of the transmission path and a single receiver at the other end with no reverse flow of information. The other two arrangements are more interesting and are called *half-duplex* and *full-duplex*, respectively, and are illustrated by Figs. 11.11(a) and 11.11(b). A half-duplex data link transmits information in only one direction at a time (i.e. from A to B or from B to A). Two-way transmission is achieved by *turning round* the channel.

The radio in a taxi represents a half-duplex system. Either the driver speaks to the base station or the base station speaks to the driver. They can't have a simultaneous two-way conversation. When the driver has finished speaking, he or she says 'Over' and switches the radio from transmit mode to receive mode. On hearing 'over', the base station is switched from receive mode to transmit mode.

Full-duplex data link permits simultaneous transmission in both directions. The telephone channel is an example of a full-duplex system, because you can both speak and listen at the same time. Some data transmission systems use the telephone network in a half-duplex mode.

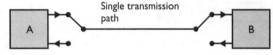

(a) Half-duplex transmission

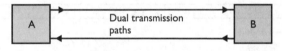

(b) Full-duplex transmission

Fig. 11.11 Implementing a two-way transmission path.

Multiplexing signals

One of the problems facing those who wish to transmit information over long distances is the cost of the physical transmission path. Whether it's the cost of constructing a line of telegraph poles from coast to coast in the 19th century or the cost of launching a satellite today, long-distance communications channels don't come cheap. Consequently, engineers have done everything they can to squeeze the last drop of capacity out of a communications channel.

Later we will point out that the information-carrying capacity of a channel is determined by two parameters—the bandwidth of the channel and the level of noise (i.e. unwanted signals) on the channel. If you have a channel that's transporting less data than its maximum capacity permits, you are not using it fully.

The efficient use of a communications channel can be increased by a technique called *multiplexing* in which two or more streams of information share the same channel. Figure 11.12(a) demonstrates *time division multiplexing*, TDM, in which the outputs of several transmitters are fed to a communications channel sequentially. In this example, the channel carries a burst of data from transmitter 1 followed by a burst of data from transmitter 2, and so on. At the receiving end of the link, a switch routes the data to receiver 1, receiver 2, ..., in order.

If the capacity of the channel is at least four times that of each of the transmitters, all four transmitters can share the same channel. All that's needed is a means of synchronizing the switches at both ends of the data link.

A simple TDM system gives each transmitter (i.e. channel) the same amount of time whether it needs it or not. Such an arrangement leads to an inefficient use of the available bandwidth. *Statistical* time division multiplexing allocates time slots only to those channels that have data to transmit. Each time slot requires a channel number to identify it, because channels aren't transmitted sequentially. Statistical multiplexing is very effective provided that all channels don't want to transmit at the same time.

Figure 11.12(d) demonstrates an alternative form of multiplexing called *frequency division multiplexing*, FDM. In this

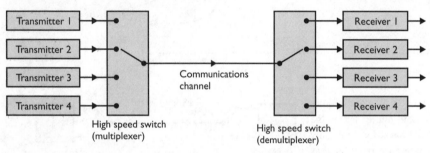

(a) Time-division multiplexing

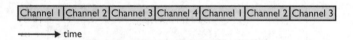

(b) A time-division multiplexed signal consists of a sequence of time slots

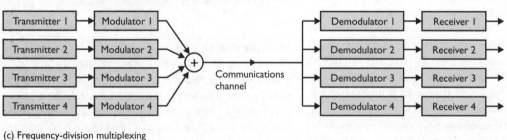

(c) Frequency-division multiplexing

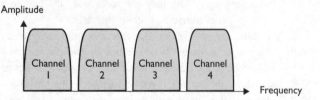

(d) A frequency-division multiplexed signal consists of a series of frequency bands

Fig. 11.12 Time and frequency division multiplexing.

case the *bandwidth* of the channel is divided between the four transmitters. Unlike in TDM, each transmitter has continuous access to the channel, but it has access to only one quarter of the channel's bandwidth.

We're already familiar with frequency division multiplexing. All a radio station does is to change the frequency range of speech and music signals to a range that can be transmitted over the airwaves. A radio receiver filters out one range of frequencies from all the other frequencies and then converts them back to their original range.

Suppose that the bandwidth of the data from each transmitter extends from 0 to 20 kHz and the communications link has a bandwidth of 80 kHz. The output of the first transmitter is mapped to 0–20 kHz (no change), the output of the second transmitter is mapped to 20–40 kHz, the output of the third transmitter to 40–60 kHz, and so on. A device that maps one range of frequencies to another range of frequencies is called a *modulator* (we will have more to say about modulators when we introduce the *modem* later in this chapter).

At the receiver end of the link, filters separate the incoming signal into four bands and the signals in each of these bands are converted back to their original ranges of 0–20 kHz. In practice it is necessary to leave gaps between the frequency bands because filters aren't perfect. Moreover, a bandpass channel doesn't usually start from a 'zero' frequency. A typical FDM channel might be from, say, 600 MHz to 620 MHz in 400 slices of 50 kHz each.

Serial data transmission begs an obvious question. How is the stream of data divided up into individual bits and the bits divided into separate words? The division of the data stream into bits and words is handled in one of two ways: asynchronously and synchronously. These are treated separately.

Asynchronous serial transmission

We've already met asynchronous serial systems when we described the ACIA. The following introduction is included here for the sake of completeness. In an asynchronous serial transmission system the clocks at the transmitter and receiver responsible for dividing the data stream into bits are not synchronized. Figure 11.13 shows the waveform corresponding to a single 7-bit character. The output from the transmitter sits at a mark state whenever data is not being transmitted and the line is idle. The term *mark* belongs to the early days of data transmission and is represented by –12 V in many systems operating over short distances.

In what follows, a bit period is the shortest time for which the line may be in a mark or a space state. When the transmitter wishes to transmit a word, it places the line in a space state for one bit period. A space is represented by +12 V. When the receiver sees this level, called a *start bit*, it knows that a character is about to follow. The incoming data stream can then be divided into seven bit periods and the data sampled at the center of each bit. The receiver's clock is not synchronized with the transmitter's clock and the bits are not sampled exactly in the center. However, if the receiver's clock is within approximately 4 percent or so of the transmitter's clock, the system works well.

After seven data bits have been sent, a *parity bit* is transmitted to give a measure of error protection. If the receiver finds that the received parity doesn't match the calculated parity, an error is flagged and the current character rejected. The parity bit is optional and need not be transmitted.

One or two *stop bits* at a mark level follow the parity bit. The stop bit carries no information and serves only as a spacer between consecutive characters. After the stop bit has been transmitted, a new character may be sent at any time. Asynchronous serial data links are used largely to transmit data in character form.

If the duration of a single bit is T seconds, the length of a character is given by the start bit plus seven data bits plus the parity bit plus the stop bit = 10T. Asynchronous transmission is clearly inefficient, since it requires 10 data bits to transmit seven bits of useful information. Several formats for asynchronous data transmission are in common use; for example, eight data bits, no parity, one stop bit.

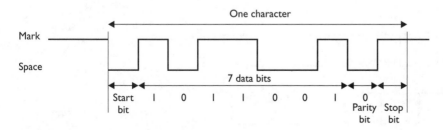

Fig. 11.13 Asynchronous serial transmission.

Bit rate and baud rate

The speed at which a serial data link operates is expressed in *bits per second* and is typically in the range 110 to over 56 600 bps. When I was a student in the early 1970s, computer science departments had teletypes operating at 110 bits per second. Today, you can connect to the Internet via your own telephone at 56 kbit/s.

Two units of speed are employed in data transmission. Once is *bits per second* (bps) and the other *baud* (after J. M. E. Baudot, a pioneer in the days of the telegraph). Bit rate defines the rate at which information flows across a data link. Baud rate defines the switching speed of a signal (i.e. the baud rate indicates how often a signal changes state).

For a binary two-level signal, a data rate of one bit per second is equivalent to one baud; for example, a modem transmitting binary data at 300 bps is said to operate at 300 baud. Suppose a data transmission system uses signals with 16 possible discrete levels. Each signal element can have one of $16 = 2^4$ different values; that is, a signal element encodes a 4-bit value. If the 16-level signals are transmitted at 1200 baud, the data rate is $4 \times 1200 = 4800$ bps.

Once the receiver has assembled all the bits of a character, the computer reads the character using any of the techniques discussed in Chapter 8. In fact, because the transmission and reception of serial data is performed entirely by special-purpose integrated circuits, the computer itself doesn't have to worry about the fine details of serial data transmission.

Synchronous serial transmission

Asynchronous data links are largely used to link peripherals, printers, and modems to computers. When information has to be passed between the individual computers of a network, *synchronous* serial transmission is generally employed. In a synchronous serial data transmission system, information is transmitted continuously with no gaps between adjacent groups of bits. We use the expression *groups of bits* because synchronous systems often transmit entire blocks of pure

binary information at a time, rather than a sequence of ASCII-encoded characters.

Two problems face the designer of a synchronous serial system. One is how to divide the incoming data stream into individual bits and the other is how to divide the data bits into meaningful groups. We briefly look at the division of serial data into bits and return to the division of serial data into blocks when we introduce character-oriented and bit-oriented protocols.

Bit synchronization If a copy of the transmitter's clock were available at the receiver there would be no difficulty in breaking up the data stream into individual bits. Unfortunately, providing the receiver with a copy of the transmitter's clock requires an additional transmission path for the clock and thereby increases the cost of the data link. A better solution is found by encoding the data in such a way that a synchronizing signal is included with the data signal. We introduced ways of encoding digital data for recording on magnetic media in Chapter 9—similar techniques can readily be applied to data transmission. If the data stream is *phase encoded*, a separate clock can be derived from the received signal and the data extracted. Figure 11.14 shows a phase-encoded signal in which the data signal changes state in the center of each bit cell. A low-to-high transition signifies a 1 and a high-to-low transition signifies a 0.

11.4 Data transmission across the PSTN

The most widely used transmission path for wide area digital data networks is the telephone system—often called the *public switched telephone network*, PSTN, to distinguish it from private networks. We first discuss some of the characteristics of the telephone network and then describe the modem used to interface digital equipment to the network.

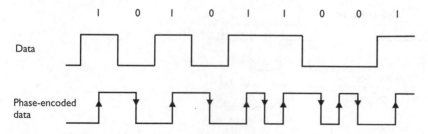

Fig. 11.14 Phase-encoded synchronous serial transmission.

11.4.1 **Channel characteristics**

One way of characterizing a telephone channel is to apply a tone (a sine wave) of constant amplitude to the transmitter end of a telephone link and then to measure its amplitude at the receiver. Figure 11.15 describes the *sine wave*, the fundamental waveform of electronics. The *gain* of the telephone channel is expressed as a *logarithm*; that is, $10 \log_{10}(P_o/P_i)$, where P_i is the transmitted power level and P_o the received power level. The unit of gain is the *decibel* (in honor of Bell) and is positive if the signal is *amplified* (i.e. $P_o > P_i$) and negative if the signal is *attenuated* (i.e. $P_o < P_i$). In a system without amplifiers, the gain is always less than 1.

By varying the frequency of the sine wave and recording the gain of the channel for each frequency, the relationship between the gain of the channel and the transmitted frequency can be derived. Such a graph is called the *amplitude–frequency distortion* characteristic of the channel (see Fig. 11.16). The frequency axis (the horizontal axis) is invariably plotted on a logarithmic scale. An ideal channel has a flat frequency response over all the frequencies of interest; that is, the gain should not vary with frequency. A similar type of graph is used to characterize hi-fi equipment. Figure 11.16 describes the frequency response of a hypothetical ideal telephone channel. The attenuation of the channel in its passband is referred to a 0 dB level (i.e. a gain of unity) and attenuation at other frequencies is measured with respect to this value.

Figure 11.16 demonstrates how some frequencies are transmitted with little attenuation and how frequencies below f_l (the lower *cut-off* point) and above f_u (the upper cut-off point) are severely attenuated as the frequency moves away from the respective cut-off point. Most telephone channels are not as well behaved as the ideal channel of Fig. 11.16. The passband (between f_l and f_u) is not usually as flat and the passband may sometimes be very much less than 300 Hz to 3300 Hz. Although most of the energy in human speech is below 3300 Hz, certain sounds have significant energy components above this frequency; for example, a cut-off point of

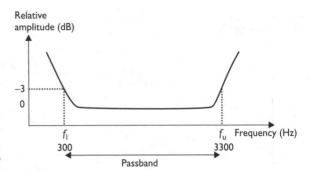

Fig. 11.16 Characteristics of the telephone network.

3300 Hz makes it very difficult to distinguish between the sibilant sounds 'f' and 's'.

Unfortunately, the graph of Fig. 11.16 doesn't tell the whole story. Signals suffer not only from amplitude–frequency distortion but also from *phase* distortion. Readers without a knowledge of signal theory are unlikely to be familiar with this concept. Any signal can be decomposed into a series of sine waves and cosine waves of different frequencies. Phase distortion is related to the *time delay* experienced by the various sine and cosine waves making up a particular digital sequence. When a pulse sequence travels along a cable, the various sine and cosine waves from which the signal is composed suffer different delays. The signals at the receiving end of the network add up to produce a waveform with a very different shape from the one that was originally transmitted.

All we need say here is that the phase distortion introduced by a telephone channel distorts the *shape* of transmitted pulses, making it difficult to distinguish between signals representing a logical 0 and those representing a logical 1. Equipment can be designed to overcome some of the effects of the amplitude and phase distortion introduced by a telephone channel. Such equipment is called an *equalizer* and is associated with high-speed transmission systems where the effects of distortion are more severe.

Figure 11.17 defines the limits of acceptance of attenuation–frequency distortion for a telephone channel between a single transmitter and receiver. The shaded area represents the forbidden region of unacceptable attenuation. If a real telephone channel has an amplitude–frequency distortion characteristic that falls outside the envelope of Fig. 11.17, the telephone company should try to correct the faulty line or equipment.

You might think that *any* signal can be transmitted across a telephone channel, as long as its frequency components fall within the envelope described by Fig. 11.17. In practice, there

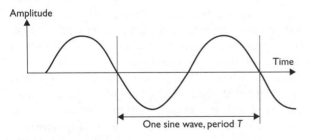

Fig. 11.15 The sine wave.

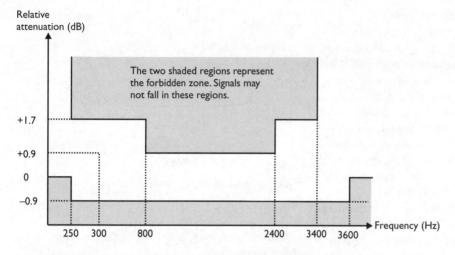

Relative attenuation (dB)

The two shaded regions represent the forbidden zone. Signals may not fall in these regions.

Fig. 11.17 Limits of acceptance for attenuation–frequency distortion.

are restrictions on the nature of a transmitted signal because the channel is used to carry more than user data. The analog channel provided by the PSTN is a *linear channel* in the sense that its output is the sum of all the inputs to the channel. This means that you can transmit two signals in different parts of the channel's bandwidth and then separate them at the receiver. Digital systems don't have this property—it's not generally possible to add two digital signals together at one end of a channel and then separate them at the other end.

Because analog channels can transmit more than one signal simultaneously, the PTTs have allocated certain parts of the telephone channel's bandwidth to signaling purposes. Human speech doesn't contain appreciable energy within these signaling bands and a normal telephone conversation doesn't affect the switching and control equipment using these frequencies.

A consequence of the use of certain frequencies for signaling purposes is that data transmission systems mustn't generate signals falling within specified bands. Figure 11.18 shows the internationally agreed restriction on signals transmitted by equipment connected to the PSTN. Any signals transmitted in the ranges 500–800 Hz and 1800–2600 Hz must have levels 38 dB below the maximum in-band signal level.

Noise

A perfect telephone channel would deliver to the receiver an exact copy of the signal presented at the transmitter. We've just seen that the amplitude–frequency and phase–frequency characteristics of the channel distort the shape of the transmitted signal. Another source of signal impairment is called

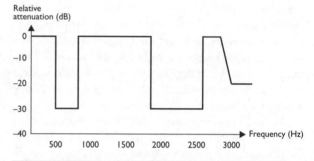

Relative attenuation (dB)

Fig. 11.18 Restriction on energy content of transmitted signals.

noise. Noise is the generic term for unwanted signals that are added to the received signal.

The most common source of noise is called *thermal noise* and is caused by the random motion of electrons in matter. Thermal noise appears to human listeners as the background hiss on telephone, radio, and TV circuits, and is frequently referred to as *Gaussian noise* because of its statistical properties. Once thermal noise has been added to a signal there's no way you can remove it. The amount of thermal noise depends on the temperature of the system and its bandwidth. Only by cooling the system or by reducing its bandwidth can we reduce the effects of thermal noise. Receivers designed to pick up the weak signals received from distant space vehicles are cooled in liquid nitrogen to minimize the effects of thermal noise on the received signal. In general, the contribution of thermal noise to all other forms of noise is not usually the limiting factor in terrestrial switched telephone networks.

Telephone channels are prone to far more harmful sources of noise than thermal noise. *Cross-talk* is noise picked up from other circuits due to unwanted electrical, capacitive, or magnetic coupling. In everyday terminology, we can think of cross-talk as crossed lines. Careful shielding of cables and isolation of circuits can reduce cross-talk. Another form of noise is *impulsive noise*, which produces the clicks and crackles on telephone circuits. Impulsive noise is caused by transients when heavy loads such as elevator motors are switched near telephone circuits, lightning, and dirty and intermittent electrical connections. Impulsive noise accounts for the majority of transmission errors in telephone networks and is worse in switched circuits than in private leased lines. Figure 11.19 describes thermal and impulsive noise.

Another form of noise is caused by *echoes*. When the transmitted signal reaches the receiver at the end of a cable, some of its energy is echoed back to the transmitter. Echo cancelers at each end of a telephone channel remove echoes, but they are sometimes poorly adjusted and permit a transmitted signal to be echoed from the receiver back to the transmitter and then back again to the receiver. The receiver then gets the transmitted signal plus a time-delayed and attenuated version of this signal. Echoes can be sufficiently large to affect the operation of the receiver.

A channel is characterized by the ratio between the unwanted noise and the wanted signal. The *signal-to-noise* ratio of a channel is defined as

$$10 \log_{10}(S/N)$$

where S is the signal power and N the noise power. Because the signal-to-noise ratio is a logarithmic value, adding 10 dB means that the ratio increases by a factor of 10.

These forms of noise are called *additive* because they are added to the received signal. Another class of noise is called multiplicative noise and is caused by *multiplying* the received signal by a noise signal. The most common multiplicative noise is called *phase jitter* and is caused by random errors in the phase of the clock used to sample the received signal. All these sources of noise make it harder to distinguish between signal levels in a digital system.

Channel capacity

Highways and communication channels have two things in common—they're often expensive to construct and they have a finite capacity. So, what is the capacity of a communications channel?

Because a channel has a finite bandwidth, the switching speed (i.e. baud rate) is limited. The maximum data rate is given by $2 \times f \times \log_2 L$, where f is the channel's bandwidth and L is the number of signal levels. If the bandwidth of a channel is 3000 Hz and you are using a signal with 1024 discrete signal levels, the maximum data rate is $2 \times 3000 \times \log_2 1024 = 6000 \times 10 = 60$ kbps. This figure relates the capacity of a *noiseless* channel to its bandwidth.

You can increase the capacity of the channel by using more signal levels. However, there comes a point at which the noise on the channel makes it difficult to distinguish between two adjacent signal levels. In other words, a channel's capacity is limited by both its bandwidth and the noise level.

Claude Shannon investigated the theoretical capacity of a noisy channel in the late 1940s. Shannon proved that the theoretical capacity of a communications channel is given by

$$\text{capacity (in bps)} = f \times \log_2(1 + S/N)$$

where f is the bandwidth, S the signal power, and N the noise power. Consider a telephone line with a bandwidth of 3000 Hz and a signal-to-noise ratio of 30 dB (i.e. $S/N = 1000$). The maximum capacity is given by $3000 \times \log_2(1 + 1000) = 3000 \times 9.97 = 29\,900$ bps.

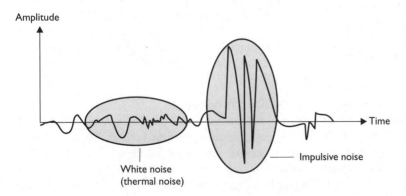

White noise
(thermal noise)

Impulsive noise

Fig. 11.19 Noise characteristics.

Shannon's theorem provides an absolute limit that can't be bettered. However, modern modems can apparently do better than theory suggests. First, data such as text or an image contains a lot of redundancy and can be compressed before transmission; for example, a 1 Mbit file might be compressed to 100 kbits and transmitted in 10 seconds at 10 kbps, corresponding to an effective transmission rate of 100 kbps. Second, the noise on telephone lines tends to be impulsive or *bursty*. The theoretical calculations relating channel capacity to noise all assume that the noise is white noise (e.g. thermal noise). By requesting the retransmission of data blocks containing errors due to noise bursts, you can increase the average data rate.

11.4.2 Modulation and data transmission

We are now going to look at a topic called *modulation*, the means of modifying signals to make them suitable for transmission over a particular channel.

Signals and modulation

A bandpass channel like a telephone channel can transmit sine waves within its bandwidth but can't transmit digital pulses that are composed of sine waves with an infinite range of frequencies. If a sequence of binary signals were presented to one end of a telephone network, the various sine waves making up the binary pulses would be attenuated. Since the telephone network does not attenuate each frequency component equally, the sine waves at the receiving end of the network would not add up to produce the same waveform that was presented to the transmitting end. In fact, the digital signals would be so severely distorted that they would be unrecognizable at the receiving end of the circuit.

Because the telephone network can transmit voice-band signals in the range 300–3300 Hz, various ways of converting digital information into speech-like signals have been investigated. Figure 11.20 shows how the digital data can be used to change, or *modulate*, the amplitude of a sine wave in sympathy with a digital signal. This technique is known as *amplitude modulation* or AM. The equipment needed to generate such a signal is called a modulator, and that required to extract the digital data from the resulting signal is called a demodulator. The interface between a computer and a telephone system is called a *modem* (*mod*ulator–*dem*odulator). Because AM is more sensitive to noise (i.e. interference) than other modulation techniques, it is not widely used in data transmission.

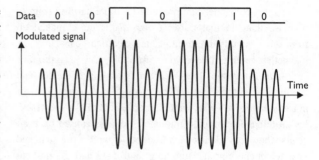

Data 0 0 1 0 1 1 0
Modulated signal

Time

Fig. 11.20 Amplitude modulation.

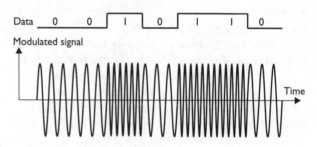

Data 0 0 1 0 1 1 0
Modulated signal

Time

Fig. 11.21 Frequency modulation.

Instead of modulating a sine wave by changing its amplitude, it's possible to change its frequency in sympathy with the digital data. In a binary system, one frequency represents one binary value and a different frequency represents the other. Figure 11.21 shows the frequency modulation (FM) of a signal. FM is widely used because it has a better tolerance to noise than AM (i.e. it is less affected by various forms of interference). As two frequencies are used to represent the two binary states, frequency modulation is sometimes referred to as *frequency shift keying*, FSK.

Figure 11.22 illustrates another form of modulation called *phase modulation* (PM). In this case, the *phase* of the sine wave is changed in sympathy with the digital signal. PM is widely used and has fairly similar characteristics to FM. If the phase change corresponding to a logical 1 is 180°, and 0° (no change) corresponds to a logical 0, one bit of information can be transmitted in each time slot (Fig. 11.22). If, however, the phase is shifted by multiples of 90°, two bits at a time can be transmitted (Fig. 11.23).

High-speed modems

Modems operate over a wide range of bit rates. Until the mid-1990s most modems operated at between 300 and 9600 bps. Low bit rates were associated with the switched telephone network, where some lines were very poor and signal impairments reduced the data rate to 2000 bps or below. The higher rates of

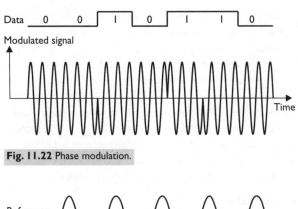

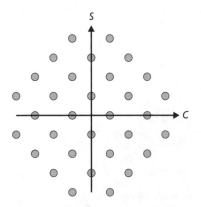

Fig. 11.24 The 32-point QAM constellation.

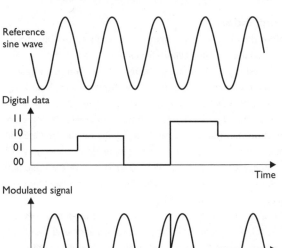

Fig. 11.22 Phase modulation.

Fig. 11.23 Differential phase modulation.

is called *quadrature amplitude modulation* (QAM). A QAM signal can be represented mathematically by the expression $S \times \sin(\omega t) + C \times \cos(\omega t)$, where S and C are two constants. The term *quadrature* is used because a sine wave and a cosine wave of the same frequency and amplitude are almost identical. The only difference is that a sine wave and a cosine wave are 90° out of phase (90° represents $\frac{1}{4}$ of 360°—hence *quad*rature). Figure 11.24 demonstrates a 32-point QAM constellation in which each point represents one of 32 discrete signals. A signal element encodes a 5-bit value which means a modem with a signaling speed of 2400 baud can transmit at 12 000 bps.

Figure 11.25 demonstrates that the points in a QAM constellation are spaced equally. Each circle includes the space that is closer to one of the signal elements than to any other element. When a signal element is received, the values of S and C are calculated and the value of the signal element determined. If noise or other impairments cause a point to be shifted (i.e. there are errors in the received values of constants S and C), an error doesn't occur unless the values of S and C move the received point outside a circle. Figure 11.26 shows how amplitude and phase errors modify the position of a point in the QAM constellation.

QAM is not the ultimate modulation technique. A better system used by some high-speed modems is called *Trellis Code Modulation* (TCM). This is a more complex type of encoding that spreads the energy of a data element over several neighboring elements. When you receive a signal element, you can't say that the corresponding bit was either 0 or 1 because that element contains energy from several transmitted bits. Why should you want to smear each transmitted element over several elements? The answer is simple. If you put all an element's energy into one time slot, a noise pulse might obliterate it. If you spread the element out, a noise spike might obliterate only a fraction of its energy. The theory of

4800 bps and 9600 bps were generally found on privately leased lines where the telephone company offered a higher grade of service.

The growth of the Internet provided a mass market for high-speed modems. Improved modulation techniques and better signal processing technology has had a massive impact on modem design. By the mid-1990s, low-cost modems operated at 14.4 kbaud or 28.8 kbaud. By 1998, modems capable of operating at 56 kbaud over conventional telephone lines were available for the price of a 1200 bps modem only a decade earlier.

High-speed modems operate by simultaneously changing the amplitude and phase of a signal. This modulation technique

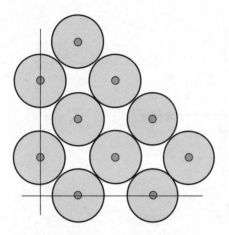

Fig. 11.25 The packing of points in a QAM constellation.

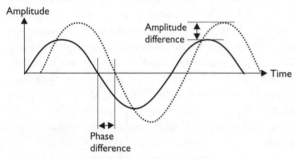

(a) Phase and amplitude difference

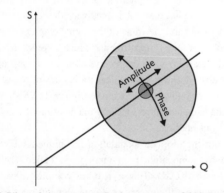

(b) Effect of phase and amplitude errors on a QAM signal

Fig. 11.26 Effect of errors on a QAM point.

trellis modulation (also called *convolutional encoding*) has been around since the 1960s. It's only today's low-cost signal processing chips that make it possible to implement the necessary coders and decoders. TCM is a combined system of

encoding and modulation—the encoding process smears an element across its neighbors and QAM is used to modulate each element before transmission.

The decoder for trellis modulation is called a *Viterbi* decoder. As a sequence of data elements arrives at the receiver, the demodulator attempts to guess the corresponding transmitted sequence—remember that the received signal contains noise and isn't a perfect copy of the transmitted data. The Viterbi decoder guesses that several possible transmitted sequences might have produced the received sequence and then selects the sequence that was most likely to have produced the received signal.

Equalization

One of the effects of the distortion introduced by the attenuation–frequency and phase–frequency characteristics of a transmission path is to cause the *time dispersion* of a transmitted signal element. Time dispersion simply means that a signal is spread out in time and has a longer duration at the receiver than it had at the transmitter (remember the telegraph distortion that played havoc with signals on the first transatlantic cables). Despite its fancy name, time dispersion is a commonplace event. When you go to a concert in a large hall, the music from the instruments suffers time dispersion—an effect we call *reverberation*.

If a short pulse were to be applied to a modem at one end of the telephone channel, the pulse would appear at the output of the modem at the other end of the channel as a continuous rounded waveform with a duration greater than about 1/3 ms (Fig. 11.27). The value of 1/3 ms is given by the reciprocal of the bandwidth of the channel (i.e. 1/3300 Hz). The waveform of Fig. 11.27 is known as the *impulse response* of the channel. Figure 11.27 represents a hypothetical case—the actual pulse is different for each channel.

Tests over telephone circuits have shown that the time dispersion experienced by a pulse doesn't normally exceed 6 ms, although it can occasionally be very much greater. Even at a relatively low signaling rate of 600 baud, an individual signal element is likely to be lengthened so that it overlaps up to five of its immediately neighboring elements. This overlap is called *intersymbol interference*. Fortunately, the dispersed signal energy represents usually only a fraction of the energy of

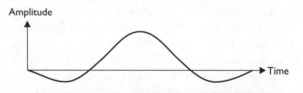

Fig. 11.27 The received signal from a single transmitted pulse.

the signal in the correct time slot, so that the effect of the intersymbol interference is negligible. At higher transmission rates, intersymbol interference becomes the limiting factor in correctly decoding the received data.

We're going to demonstrate the effect of intersymbol interference on the transmission of a simple pulse train. Suppose a data transmission system produces pulses with an interval of T seconds between adjacent pulses. Assume that each of these pulses may have an amplitude of $+1$ or -1 units.

When a signal is processed by a digital system, the signal is sampled periodically and its sample values digitized. Figure 11.28 demonstrates how the pulse in Fig. 11.27 is sampled at integer multiples of T seconds. A received pulse can be represented numerically by the vector $0 \quad \frac{-1}{4} \quad \frac{1}{4} \quad 1 \quad \frac{1}{4} \quad \frac{-1}{4} \quad 0$ which is called the *sampled impulse response* of the channel.

Suppose a message consisting of the bits $-1, 1, 1, 1, -1, 1$ is transmitted and each new pulse is transmitted every T seconds. We can view the transmitted data as six consecutive waveforms, as Fig. 11.29 demonstrates.

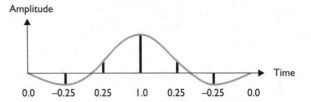

Fig. 11.28 The sampled impulse response of a channel.

The signal at the receiver due to the six pulses in Fig. 11.29 is made up of the sum of the six time-shifted impulse responses, each of which is multiplied by $+1$ or -1 depending on the polarity of the transmitted signal element. Figure 11.30 illustrates the received waveform. As you can see, its meaning isn't easy to interpret.

Let's look at the same signal numerically. We will write down the sequence due to each of the data bits and then calculate its sum.

Pulse	T=0	T=1	T=2	T=3	T=4	T=5	T=6	T=7	T=8	T=9	T=10	T=11
−1	0	$\frac{1}{4}$	$-\frac{1}{4}$	-1	$-\frac{1}{4}$	$\frac{1}{4}$	0					
1		0	$-\frac{1}{4}$	$\frac{1}{4}$	1	$\frac{1}{4}$	$-\frac{1}{4}$	0				
1			0	$-\frac{1}{4}$	$\frac{1}{4}$	1	$\frac{1}{4}$	$-\frac{1}{4}$	0			
1				0	$-\frac{1}{4}$	$\frac{1}{4}$	1	$\frac{1}{4}$	$-\frac{1}{4}$	0		
−1					0	$\frac{1}{4}$	$-\frac{1}{4}$	-1	$-\frac{1}{4}$	$\frac{1}{4}$	0	
1						0	$-\frac{1}{4}$	$\frac{1}{4}$	1	$\frac{1}{4}$	$-\frac{1}{4}$	0
Sum	0	$\frac{1}{4}$	$-\frac{1}{2}$	-1	$\frac{3}{4}$	2	$\frac{1}{2}$	$-\frac{3}{4}$	$\frac{1}{2}$	$\frac{1}{2}$	$-\frac{1}{4}$	0

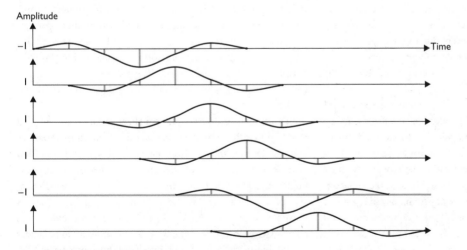

Fig. 11.29 Transmitting six pulses at intervals of T seconds.

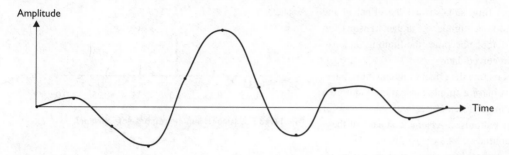

Fig. 11.30 The received signal after transmitting $-1, 1, 1, 1, -1, 1$ over the channel $(0, -\frac{1}{4}, \frac{1}{4}, 1, \frac{1}{4}, -\frac{1}{4}, 0)$.

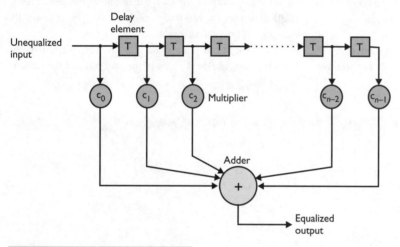

Fig. 11.31 The linear transversal equalizer.

You can see that the original message is recoverable simply by sampling at the correct instant (i.e. sampling the received signal when the component due to a transmitted signal element is 1). Where the intersymbol interference is worse than in this example, simple circuits alone cannot recover the transmitted data.

A process called *equalization* can eliminate the effects of intersymbol interference. Conceptually, an equalizer may be thought of as a filter whose attenuation–frequency and group-delay frequency responses are the inverse of those of the channel. Equalization can be performed within the modem. Another term for equalization is *line conditioning*. In fact, the equalization of a telephone channel is analogous to the use of a graphic equalizer in a hi-fi system to correct the frequency distortion introduced by loudspeaker and the acoustics of the room.

On a fixed telephone channel (i.e. a non-dialed line), it is possible to set up the equalizer once and for all and then to forget it. Unfortunately, on a switched line (especially at high data rates) every time a channel is obtained by dialing a new path through the telephone network a different transmission is set up, requiring a unique form of equalization. For this reason, *automatic adaptive equalizers* have been designed to follow any changes in the nature of the distortion introduced by the channel.

It's difficult to describe the equalizer in any detail without resorting to discrete mathematics and the Z-transform. Here we will just describe the equalizer that is just a type of digital filter (see Chapter 12). One of the simplest forms of equalizer is implemented by means of a *linear transversal filter*, which consists of a series of delay units and multipliers and an adder, as illustrated in Fig. 11.31. A practical equalizer is usually more complex than this. Conceptually, you can think of an equalizer as undoing the effects of time dispersion by canceling out the effects of neighboring pulses on a received pulse.

11.4.3 Modems

We now look at the modems used to transmit digital data over the PSTN. If digital data is to be transmitted from one point to another across a telephone channel, it is necessary that the modems at each end of the transmission path be compatible. Because of the variation in the quantity of telephone channels and the economics of modems, there are a number of different types of modem. Like many of the other components of a computer system, the performance of modems has increased while their cost has plummeted. However, it's probable that the progress made in the 1990s will not continue at the same rate because the performance of modems is approaching the theoretical limit described by Shannon.

Modem standards

There are two sets of standards for modems. In the USA, the scene has been dominated by the Bell Telephone Company, which has devised a series of *de facto* standards for modems. Outside the USA, modem standards have been determined by the *International Consultative Committee on Telegraphy and Telephony* (CCITT). Both these organizations have produced standards for the same transmission rates, but the modulation techniques employed by Bell are not compatible with those of the CCITT. For example, a CCITT modem operating at 1200 bps uses FSK (i.e. frequency-shift keying) with a 1300 Hz signal representing a logical 1 and a 2100 Hz signal representing a logical 0. The Bell 202C modem operates with frequencies of 1070 Hz and 1270 Hz. Modern high-speed modems follow the CCITT standards. See examples below

1. Transmission rate   The transmission rate of a modem is a measure of the speed at which it transmits or receives digital information. A modem's transmission rate should not be confused with the frequencies used in the modulation process. Typical transmission rates are 75, 300, 600, 1200, 2400, 4800, 9600, 14 400, 19 200, 28 800, 36 600, and 56 000 baud.

2. Modulation method   Low- and medium-speed modems use frequency modulation to transport information. However, the frequencies chosen to represent a logical 1 or a logical 0 vary with a number of factors. High-speed modems employ phase modulation and QAM (quadrature amplitude modulation) in an attempt to raise the baud rate without increasing the modulation frequency or switching speed.

3. Channel type   Some modems operate in a half-duplex mode, permitting a communication path in only one direction at a time. Others support full-duplex operation with simultaneous, two-way communication. Full-duplex operation does not necessarily imply two identical channels. Some systems permit a high data rate (e.g. 1200 baud) in one direction and a low data rate in the other, or reverse, direction (e.g. 75 baud).

4. Originate/answer modems   Whenever information is exchanged between two modems, one modem is called the *originating* modem because it is at the end of the channel that carried out the dialing and set up the channel. The *answer* modem is at the end of the channel that receives the call. Many modems can both originate calls and answer calls, but some modems are answer-only and cannot originate a call. Originate and answer modems employ different frequencies to represent 1s and 0s (when using frequency modulation).

5. Modem standards   As stated above, modem standards fall into two groups. Those standardized by the CCITT and those standardized by the Bell Telephone Company. These standards deal with how data is transmitted and received. The influence of the PC has given rise to a *de facto* standard for the computer control of modems. This is the Hayes standard, and the set of operations defined by the standard are called the *AT commands*.

6. Asynchronous/synchronous   An asynchronous data transmission system transmits information in the form of, typically, 8-bit characters with periods of inactivity between characters. A synchronous system transmits a continuous stream of bits without pauses, even when the bits are carrying no user information. Modems are designed to operate with either asynchronous or synchronous data streams. Low-speed transmission systems usually adopt an asynchronous transmission system and high-speed transmission systems (over 2400 baud) can operate in either synchronous or asynchronous modes.

Examples of modem standards

1.	Bell 202
Mode:	1200 baud, half-duplex, asynchronous, FSK
Transmit frequency:	Space = 2200 Hz, Mark = 1200 Hz
Receive frequency:	Space = 2200 Hz, Mark = 1200 Hz
2.	CCITT V.21
Mode:	300 baud, full-duplex, asynchronous, FSK
Transmit frequency (originate):	Space = 1180 Hz, Mark = 980 Hz
Receive frequency (originate):	Space = 1850 Hz, Mark = 1650 Hz
Transmit frequency (answer):	Space = 1850 Hz, Mark = 1650 Hz

Receive frequency (answer): Space = 1180 Hz,
 Mark = 980 Hz

3. CCITT V.23
Mode: 1200 baud, half-duplex,
 asynchronous, FSK

Transmit frequency: Space = 2100 Hz,
 Mark = 1300 Hz

Receive frequency: Space = 2100 Hz,
 Mark = 1300 Hz

4. CCITT V.32
Mode: 2400 baud, 4800 or
 9600 bps, QAM

5. CCITT V.33
Mode: 2400 baud, 14 400 bps,
 QAM

6. CCITT V.34
Mode: 2400 baud, 28 800 bps,
 QAM

Some half-duplex modems have a narrowband *back* or *reverse* channel. A reverse channel is a low-speed communication path in the opposite direction to the main channel. For example, the Bell 202 1200 baud modem has a 5 baud reverse channel and the CCITT V23 mode 2, 1200 baud, modem has a 75 baud reverse channel. You might be forgiven for wondering what the difference is between a full-duplex modem and a half-duplex modem with a reverse channel. The answer is that a full-duplex channel is able to transmit equally in both directions. Modems with reverse channels are able to transmit only limited information across the reverse channel. A reverse channel offers an excellent mechanism for error control because requests to retransmit lost data can be made via the reverse channel. Another application of reverse channels is in accessing databases or similar software. The forward or main channel is used by the computer to display data on the user's screen. The reverse channel is used by the terminal to computer link because the user is sending relatively little data to the computer.

11.4.4 High-speed transmission over the PSTN

The backbone of the POTS (*plain old telephone system*) is anything but plain. Data can be transmitted across the world via satellite, terrestrial microwave links, and fiber optic links at very high rates. The factor that limits the rate at which data can be transmitted is known as the *last mile*; that is, the connection between your phone and the global network at your local switching center.

ISDN

A technology called ISDN (*integrated services digital network*) was developed in the 1980s to help overcome the bandwidth limitations imposed by the *last mile*. ISDN was intended for professional and business applications and is now available to anyone with a personal computer. There are two variants of ISDN—basic rate services and primary rate services. The basic rate service is intended for small businesses and provides three fully duplex channels. Two of these so-called B channels can carry voice or data and the third D channel is used to carry control information. B channels operate at 64 kbps and the D channel at 16 kbps.

ISDN's popularity is due to its relatively low cost and the high quality of service it offers over the telephone line. You can combine the two B channels to achieve a data rate of 128 kbps. You can even use the D control channel (simultaneously) to provide an auxiliary channel at 9.6 kbps. Note that ISDN can handle both voice and data transmission simultaneously.

Several protocols have been designed to control ISDN systems. V.110 and V.120 are used to connect an ISDN communications device to high-speed ISDN lines. ISDN took a long time from its first implementation to its adoption by many businesses. However, newer technologies have been devised to overcome the *last mile* problem, and ISDN will probably never become as commonplace as some had anticipated.

ADSL

If there's one thing you can guarantee in the computing world, it's that yesterday's state-of-the-art technology will become the current standard and a new state-of-the-art technology will emerge. Just as ISDN was becoming popular in the late 1990s, a system called ADSL (*asymmetric digital subscriber line*) was being developed as a new high-speed, *last mile* system.

As we've said, telephone lines have a bandwidth of 3000 Hz that limits the maximum rate at which data can be transmitted. In fact, the twisted wire pair between your home and the telephone company has a much higher bandwidth. The bandwidth of a typical twisted pair less than about 3 miles (5 km) is over 1 MHz.

Asymmetric digital subscriber line technology exploits the available bandwidth of the local connection. The bandwidth of the telephone link is divided into a number of 4 kHz slices, as Fig. 11.32 demonstrates. The first slice from 0 to 4 kHz represents the conventional telephone bandwidth. Frequencies between 4 kHz and 24 kHz aren't used in order to provide a guard band to stop the higher frequencies interfering with conventional telephone equipment.

The spectrum between 24 kHz and 1.1 MHz is divided into 249 separate 4 kHz channels in the same way as the FM band

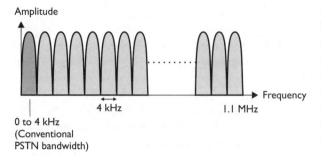

Fig. 11.32 Dividing a 1.1 MHz bandwidth into 4 kHz slots.

is divided into slots for the various broadcasting stations. A data signal can be assigned one of these slices and its spectrum tailored to fit its allocated 4 kHz slot. At the other end of the link, the signal in that 4 kHz slot is converted back into the data signal. Until recently it was very difficult to perform these operations. The advent of low-cost digital signal processing has made it much easier to process signals (i.e. to shift their range of frequencies from one band to another).

The characteristics of these slots vary with frequency; for example, there is much more attenuation of signals in slots close to 1.1 MHz. The terminal equipment is able to use the better channels to carry high data rates and to allocate the higher frequency channels to slower bit rates.

11.4.5 The RS232C physical layer protocol

The first really universal standard for the physical layer was published in 1969 by the Electronic Industry Association (EIA) in the USA and is known as RS232C (Recommended Standard 232 version C). Since then the standard has been revised (e.g. RS232D and RS232E). Because 1969 is such a long time ago in the world of electronics and predates the microprocessor revolution, RS232 was not developed for

today's world. This standard was originally intended for links between modems and computers, but has now been adapted by many manufacturers to suit various types of links (e.g. printer interfaces and even mouse interfaces). The development of such an early standard is good because RS232C was there ready to be used when today's new microcomputer equipment first appeared. Unfortunately, it was not optimized for such a role. We cover this standard here because it is implemented by all personal computers.

Early in the development of data transmission systems, RS232 was created as a standard for the connection between computer equipment and modems. Any manufacturer's computer equipment can be simply plugged into another manufacturer's modem, as long as both systems conform to RS232. Such a standard allows one manufacturer to produce equipment for a different manufacturer's computers. Although it is sometimes said that standards limit progress by enforcing a rigid conformity, the converse is true. Without agreed standards, a manufacturer is very wary of entering a new market.

RS232 specifies the plug and socket at the modem and the digital equipment (i.e. their mechanics), the nature of the transmission path, and the signals required to control the operation of the modem (i.e. the functionality of the data link).

From the point of view of the standard, the modem is known as *data communications equipment* (DCE) and the digital equipment to be connected to the modem is known as *data terminal equipment* (DTE). Figure 11.33 illustrates the role played by the RS232 standard in linking DCE to DTE. A corollary is that RS232 specifies a link between a DTE and a DCE rather than a link between two similar devices. This is important because the RS232 standard is now largely used to link together two similar pieces of equipment (i.e. both ends of the data link are DTEs). We will soon see the significance of this.

Because RS232 was intended for DTE to DCE links, its functions are very largely those needed to control a modem. The control functions provided by RS232 data links are not always suited to, or needed by, links between two DTEs. In

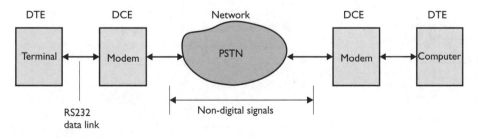

Fig. 11.33 Linking DTE to DCE with the RS232 data link.

practice, this means that a computer manufacturer and a printer manufacturer may both supply equipment with interfaces sold as conforming to RS232. Yet each manufacturer may choose to implement a subset of the many functions provided by RS232, as not all the functions are required by their particular applications. Unfortunately, they may choose slightly different subsets, making it impossible to plug the printer into the computer with a cable and connector conforming to RS232.

RS232C control lines

The next step in our examination of the RS232 standard is to describe the functions carried out by the RS232 signals flowing between the DTE and the DCE. It's this aspect of RS232 that causes all the trouble when printer X is connected to computer Y.

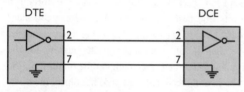

(a) DTE connnected to DCE
in half-duplex mode

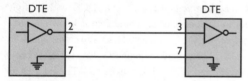

(b) DTE connnected to DTE
in half-duplex mode

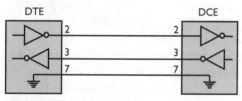

(c) DTE connnected to DCE
in full-duplex mode

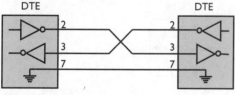

(d) DTE connnected to DTE
in full-duplex mode

Fig. 11.34 The RS232 minimal subset.

The absolute minimum service provided by an RS232 data link is the point-to-point transmission of data without any associated control functions. Figure 11.34 illustrates such a subset. Information is transmitted between DTE and DCE (or DTE and DTE) in a single direction (half-duplex) or in two directions (full-duplex) providing the four variations in Fig. 11.34.

When DTE is connected to DCE (Fig. 11.34(a)), the corresponding pins of the DTE and DCE are connected together (i.e. pins 2 to 2, 3 to 3) because the data-out pin of the DTE is the corresponding data-in pin of the DCE. When DTE is connected to DTE (Figs. 11.34(b) and 11.34(d)), it is necessary to cross over pins 2 and 3 as shown.

Relatively few data links use the absolute minimum subset of functions provided by the connection in Fig. 11.34. However, even modest peripherals such as printers require some form of control. Figure 11.35 illustrates the most widely used control lines. The arrows at the end of signal lines show the direction of data transmission with respect to the DTE. The function of these control lines is described next. Here we reintroduce two terms: *asserted* and *negated*. When a signal is said to be *asserted*, it is placed in the state that causes its named action to take place. Conversely, when a signal is *negated*, it is placed in the state that stops or defeats its named action. For example, asserting request to send indicates that a device is ready to transmit data. When it is negated, it indicates that the transmitter is unable to send data. These terms have been adopted because they remove the need to remember whether a logical 1 or a logical 0 causes some action to take place. *Asserted* simply means place in the active state, irrespective of whether that state is electrically high or low.

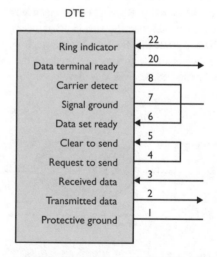

Fig. 11.35 The most widely used lines of RS232.

RS232 control signals are asserted by placing them in an electrically high state.

We met some of the RS232 control signals in Chapter 8 when we introduced the ACIA—the asynchronous communications adapter that interfaces a computer to a serial data link. Note that the ACIA uses active-low control signals (e.g. RTS), whereas the RS232 link uses active-high control signals (e.g. RTS). For this reason, the control inputs and outputs of the ACIA are interfaced to RS232C lines via inverting buffers. The following control signals implement most of the important functions of an R232 DTE to DCE link.

Request to send (RTS) This is a signal from the DTE to the DCE. When asserted, RTS indicates to the DCE that the DTE wishes to transmit data to it.

Clear to send (CTS) This is a signal from the DCE to the DTE and, when asserted, indicates that the DCE is ready to receive data from the DTE.

Data set ready (DSR) This is a signal from the DCE to the DTE which indicates the readiness of the DCE. When this signal is asserted, the DCE is able to receive from the DTE. DSR indicates that the DCE (usually a modem) is switched on and is in its normal functioning mode (as opposed to its self-test mode).

Data terminal ready (DTR) This is a signal from the DTE to the DCE. When asserted, DTR indicates that the DTE is ready to accept data from the DCE. In systems with a modem, it maintains the connection and keeps the channel open. If DTR is negated, the communication path is broken. In everyday terms, negating DTR is the same as hanging up a phone.

The way in which the RTS and CTS pair of control signals is applied is illustrated by Fig. 11.36. In Fig. 11.36(a), DTE is connected to DCE without any lines being crossed over. In Fig. 11.36(b), DTE is connected to DTE and pins 4 (RTS) and 5 (CTS) are crossed over. CTS and RTS must be crossed over because the RTS output of one side of the data link serves as the CTS input at the other side.

Sometimes, DTE is connected to a DCE or a DTE and the RTS/CTS handshaking procedure between the pair is not required (or is not implemented), but the DTE requires a response to the assertion of its RTS output. Figure 11.36(c) shows how this situation can be handled. The RTS output is connected directly to the CTS input at the connector so that the DTE automatically receives a handshake whenever it asserts its RTS output. Of course, in this mode the DTE may think that the remote DCE/DTE is ready to receive data when it is not. A cable that connects a DTE to a DTE is sometimes called a *null modem*.

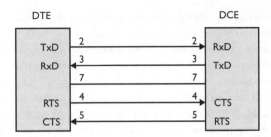

(a) DTE to DCE

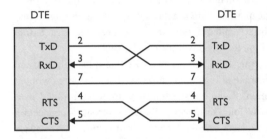

(b) DTE to DTE

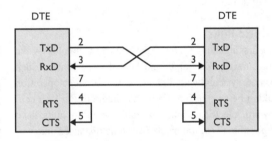

(c) DTE to DTE locally

Fig. 11.36 Connecting RTS to CTS.

11.4.6 Other physical channels

The majority of transmission paths are composed of twisted pairs, coaxial cable, radio links, or fiber optic links.

A *twisted pair* is nothing more than two insulated wires that are twisted around each other (as opposed to running parallel to each other). Why are the wires *twisted*? A wire acts as an antenna and picks up signals (i.e. interference). If two wires are intertwined, a signal induced in one wire is canceled by the signal induced in the other wire. Twisted pairs are used to transport low-frequency signals over relatively short distances; for example, a twisted pair connects a telephone to its local exchange.

Coaxial cable consists of an inner conductor entirely surrounded by an outer conductor and is the type of cable used to connect televisions to antennas. Between the two conductors lies an insulating material, called a *dielectric*. Sometimes the outer conductor is braided or woven from fine copper wire and sometimes it's a solid conductor. Figure 11.37 illustrates the structure of coaxial cable (often abbreviated to co-ax), whose thickness may vary between 5 and 25 mm. Coaxial cables are able to operate at high data rates (greater than 100 Mbit/s) and are used over short to medium distances. Coaxial cable is used to transmit voice-band telephone signals (permitting up to 10 000 channels per cable), television signals (as in cable TV), and digital signals in many local area networks (particularly *Ethernets*). Transmission over distances greater than 1 km is achieved by feeding the signal into an amplifier (called a *repeater*) and regenerating it before sending it on its way down the coaxial cable.

Fiber optic links use a cable that transmits light and are able to operate at high data rates over long distances without regeneration. Radio links permit data to be transmitted over medium to long distances without a physical connection between adjacent stations (apart from the *ether* or free space that separates all objects). We look at fiber optic links first and then return to radio links.

Fiber optic links

The very first signaling systems used optical technology—the signal fire, the smoke signal, and later the semaphore. Such transmission systems were limited to line-of-sight operation and couldn't be used in fog. From the middle of the 19th century onward, electrical links via cable or radio links have made it possible to communicate over long distances independently of weather conditions.

Today, the confluence of different technologies has, once again, made it possible to use light to transmit messages.

Semiconductor technology has given us the laser and the LED (light-emitting diode), which can directly convert pulses of electricity into pulses of light in both the visible and infrared parts of the spectrum. Similarly, semiconductor electronics has created devices that can turn light directly into electricity so that we can detect the pulses of light from a laser or LED. The relatively new science of materials technology has given us the ability to create a fine thread of transparent material called an *optical fiber*. The optical fiber provides a simple method of piping light from its source to its detector, just as the coaxial cable pipes electronic signals from one point to another.

Seemingly, light can be transmitted only in a straight line and therefore can't be used for transmission over paths that turn corners or go round bends. Fortunately, one of the properties of matter (i.e. the speed of light in a given medium) makes it possible to transmit light down a long thin cylinder of material (i.e. the optical fiber). Figures 11.38(a) and (b) demonstrate the effect of a light beam striking the surface of an optically dense material in a less dense medium, such as air. Light rays striking the surface at nearly right angles to the surface pass from the material into the surrounding air after being bent (or refracted) as Fig. 11.38(a) demonstrates. The relationship between the angle of incidence θ_2 and the angle of refraction θ_1 is $\cos(\theta_2)/\cos(\theta_1) =$ index of refraction.

Light rays striking the surface at a shallow angle suffer *total internal reflection* and are reflected just as if the surface (i.e. the boundary between the optically dense material and the air) were a mirror. The critical angle, θ_C, at which total internal reflection occurs, is a function of the *refractive index* of the material through which the light is propagated and the

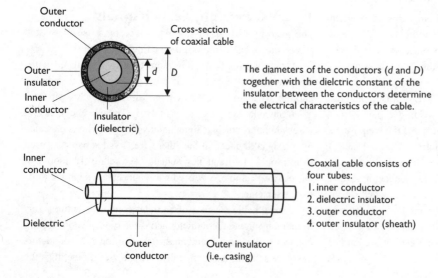

The diameters of the conductors (*d* and *D*) together with the dielctric constant of the insulator between the conductors determine the electrical characteristics of the cable.

Coaxial cable consists of four tubes:
1. inner conductor
2. dielectric insulator
3. outer conductor
4. outer insulator (sheath)

Fig. 11.37 Coaxial cable.

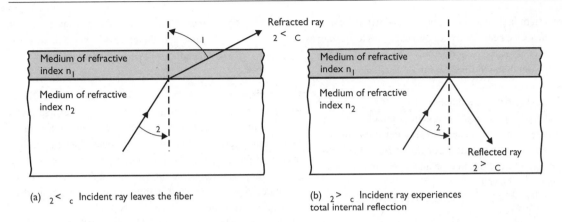

(a) $\theta_2 < \theta_c$ Incident ray leaves the fiber

(b) $\theta_2 > \theta_c$ Incident ray experiences total internal reflection

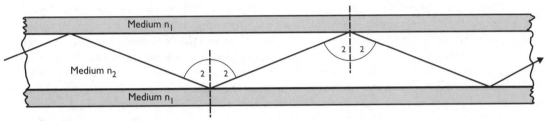

(c) Propagation of a ray along a fiber by repeated total internal reflection

Fig. 11.38 Total internal reflection.

surface material at which the reflection occurs. The same phenomenon takes place when a diver looks upward. Total internal reflection at the surface of the water makes the surface look like a mirror. Figure 11.38(c) demonstrates how light is propagated along the fiber by internal reflections from the sides.

By drawing out a single long thread of a transparent material such as plastic or glass, we can create an optical fiber as illustrated in Fig. 11.39. The optical fiber consists of three parts:

- the core itself, which transmits the light

- a cladding that has a different index of reflection to the core and hence causes total internal reflection at its interface with the core

- a sheath that provides the optical fiber with protection and mechanical strength.

The diameter of the optical fiber is very small indeed—often less than $100\,\mu$m. Sometimes there is an abrupt junction between the core and cladding (a step-index fiber) and sometimes the refractive index of the material varies continuously from the core to the cladding (a graded index fiber). Graded

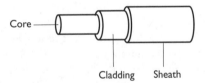

Fig. 11.39 The optical fiber.

index fibers are difficult to produce and therefore more expensive than step-index fibers, but they offer lower attenuation and a higher bandwidth.

Fiber optic links can be created from many materials, but a fiber drawn from high-quality fused quartz has the least attenuation and the greatest bandwidth (e.g. the attenuation can be less than $1\,$dB/km). The bandwidth of fiber optic links can range from $200\,$MHz to over $10\,$GHz ($10^9\,$Hz), which represents very high data rates indeed.

There are several types of optical fiber, each with its own special properties (e.g. attenuation per km, bandwidth, and cost). Two generic classes of optical fiber are the multimode and single mode fibers. Multimode fibers operate as described by bouncing the light from side to side as it travels down the fiber. Since a light beam can take many paths down the cable, the transit time of the beam is spread out and a single pulse of light is received as a considerably broadened pulse. Consequently, a multimode fiber cannot be used at very high pulse rates.

A single-mode fiber has a diameter only a few times that of the wavelength of the light being transmitted (a typical diameter is only 5 μm). As a single mode fiber does not support more than one optical path through the fiber, the transmitted pulse is not spread out in time and a very much greater bandwidth can be achieved.

The advantages of a fiber optic link, Fig. 11.40, over more conventional technologies are:

Bandwidth	The bandwidth offered by the best fiber optic links is approximately 1000-fold greater than that offered by coaxial cable or microwave radio links.
Attenuation	High-quality optical fibers have a lower attenuation than coaxial cables and therefore fewer repeaters are required over long links such as undersea cables.
Mechanics	The optical fiber itself is truly tiny and therefore lightweight. All that is needed is a suitable sheath to protect it from mechanical damage or corrosion. It is therefore cheaper to lay fiber optic links than coaxial links
Immunity to EM interference	Fiber optic links are not affected by electromagnetic interference and therefore they do not suffer the effect of noise induced by anything from nearby lightning strikes to cross-talk from adjacent cables. Furthermore, since they do not use ele tronic signals to convey information,

there's no signal leakage from an optical fiber and therefore it's much harder for unauthorized persons to eavesdrop.

Radio links

Radio links transmit information through the ether and don't require a physical medium to be laid down between the transmitter and receiver. Radio links are characterized by the frequency of the radio signals used to transport data and whether or not they are terrestrial or satellite links. Figure 11.41 illustrates a portion of the electromagnetic spectrum used to transmit information.

Radio signals in the frequency range 100 kHz to about 1000 MHz (i.e. 1 GHz) are used for conventional purposes such as terrestrial radio and television broadcasting. Frequencies above 1 GHz are called *microwaves* and are used for many applications ranging from radar to information transmission to heating. Microwaves have two important properties. They travel in straight lines and they can be modulated at high frequencies to carry high data rates.

Because microwaves travel in straight lines, the Earth's curvature limits direct links to about 100 km or so (depending on the terrain and the height of the transmitter and receiver dishes). Longer communications paths require repeaters—microwaves are picked up by an antenna on a tower, amplified, and transmitted to the next tower in the chain. Few industrial cities are without some tall landmark festooned with microwave dishes.

Since the late 1960s satellite microwave links have become increasingly more important. A satellite placed in geostationary orbit 35 700 km above the equator takes 24 hours to orbit the Earth. Because the Earth itself rotates once every 24 hours, a satellite in a geostationary orbit appears to hang motionless in space and remain over the same spot. Such a satellite can be used to transmit messages from one point on

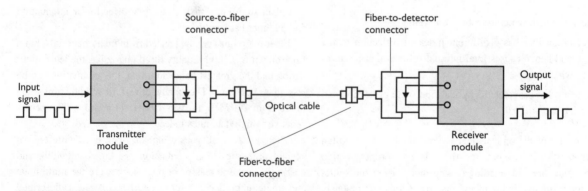

Fig. 11.40 The fiber optic link.

Frequency band	Name	Typical applications
3–30 kHz	Very low frequency (VLF)	Long-range navigation, submarine communications
30–300 kHz	Low frequency (LF)	Navigational aids and radio beacons
300–3000 kHz	Medium frequency (MF)	Maritime radio, direction finding, commercial AM radio
3–30 MHz	High frequency (HF)	Short wave broadcasting, transoceanic ship and aircraft communication, telegraph, facsimile
30–300 MHz	Very high frequency (VHF)	FM radio, air traffic control, police, taxi, and utilities
0.3–3 GHz	Ultra-high frequency (UHF)	UHF television, navigational aids, cell phones
3–30 GHz	Super-high frequency (SHF)	Microwave links, radar, satellite communications
30–300 GHz	Extra-high frequency (EHF)	

Note: kHz = kilohertz = 10^3 Hz, MHz = megahertz = 10^6 Hz, GHz = gigahertz = 10^9 Hz

Fig. 11.41 The radio frequency spectrum.

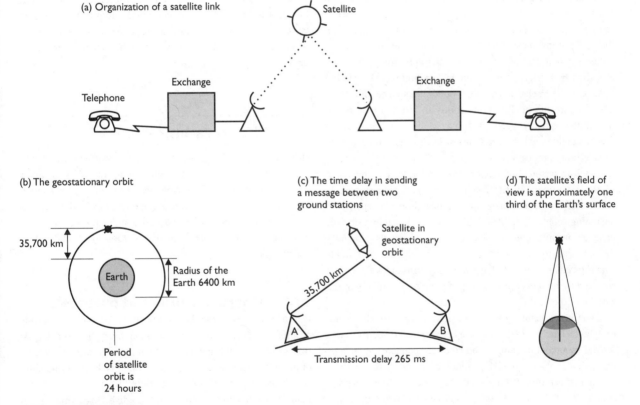

(a) Organization of a satellite link

Satellite

Exchange   Exchange

Telephone

(b) The geostationary orbit

35,700 km

Earth

Radius of the Earth 6400 km

Period of satellite orbit is 24 hours

(c) The time delay in sending a message between two ground stations

Satellite in geostationary orbit

35,700 km

A   B

Transmission delay 265 ms

(d) The satellite's field of view is approximately one third of the Earth's surface

Fig. 11.42 The satellite link

the Earth's surface to another point up to approximately 12 000 km away, as illustrated in Fig. 11.42.

Theoretically, three satellites each separated by 120° could completely cover a band around the Earth. However, receivers at extreme limits of reception would have their dishes poin ing along the ground at a tangent to the surface of the Earth.

As the minimum practical angle of elevation is about 5°, satellites should not be more than about 110° apart for reliable operation. Data is transmitted to the satellite on the uplink frequency, regenerated, and transmitted down again at the downlink frequency (the uplink frequency is higher than the downlink frequency). Table 11.2 describes some of the

Band	Frequency range	Characteristics
L-band	1.53–2.7 GHz	Signals penetrate buildings and structures. Low power transmitters required.
Ku-band	11.7–17.8 GHz	Signals penetrate some structures. High data rates possible.
Ka-band	18–31 GHz	There is a lot of available unallocated spectrum and very high data rates are possible. The signals have little penetrating power and are attenuated by rain.

Table 11.2 Frequencies used in satellite communications.

frequency bands used by satellites. Suitable microwave or coaxial links transmit data from a local source to and from the national satellite terminals.

Satellites are used to transmit television signals, telephone traffic, and data signals. Data signals can be transmitted at rates greater than 50 Mbps, which is many times faster than that offered by the public switched telephone network but rather less than that offered by the fiber optic link (and much less than that offered by the super data highways). Satellite links can be replaced by fiber optic links. The only real advantage of the satellite is its ability to broadcast from one transmitter to many receivers. It may well be that, in years to come, satellites will be used almost exclusively for domestic broadcasting purposes.

Satellite systems are generally very reliable. The sheer size of the investment in the satellite and its transport vehicle means that engineers have spent much time and energy in designing reliable satellites. Unfortunately, a satellite doesn't have an infinite lifespan. Its solar power panels gradually degrade due to the effects of the powerful radiation fields experienced in space, and it eventually runs out of the fuel required by its rocket jets to keep it pointing accurately at the surface of the Earth.

Satellites operate mostly in the 1 to 10 GHz band. Frequencies below 1 GHz are subject to interference from terrestrial sources of noise and the atmosphere attenuates frequencies above 10 GHz. Satellite users have to take account of a problem imposed by the length of the transmission path (about 70 000 km). Microwaves traveling at the speed of light (300 000 km/s) take approximately 250 ms to travel from the source to their destination. Consequently it is impossible to receive a reply from a transmission in under 0.5 s. Data transmission modes using half-duplex become difficult to operate due to the long transit delay and the large turn-around time. Satellite data links are better suited to full-duplex operation.

High geosynchronous orbits are not the only option available. Figure 11.43 shows that satellites can be placed in one of three types of orbit. Satellites in low and medium Earth orbits appear to move across the sky, which means that when your satellite drops below the horizon you have to switch the link to another satellite. Low Earth orbits require lots of satellites for reliable communications, but the latency is very low. Fewer satellites are required to cover the world from medium Earth orbits and the latency is about 0.05–0.14 s.

11.5 The data link layer

Now that we've looked at some of the ways in which bits are moved from one point to another by the physical layer, the next step is to show how the data link layer handles entire messages and overcomes imperfections in the physical layer. We are going to look at two popular protocols for the data link layer—a *character-oriented* protocol and a *bit-oriented* protocol.

11.5.1 Character-oriented protocols

One of the tasks of the data link layer is to divide the stream of bits it receives from the physical layer into blocks. At first sight, it might appear that dividing a continuous stream of bits into meaningful units is a difficult task. Infactitisquiteaneasytasktoformbitsintowords. Here we've removed the inter-word spacing from plain English text, making it harder, but not impossible, to read. Readers are able to make sense of the above sequence of characters by looking for recognizable groups of characters corresponding to words. A similar technique can be applied to streams of characters (character-oriented protocols) or to streams of bits (bit-oriented protocols).

In character-oriented transmission the data to be transmitted is encoded in the form of (usually) ASCII characters. For example, the string 'Alan' is sent as the sequence of four

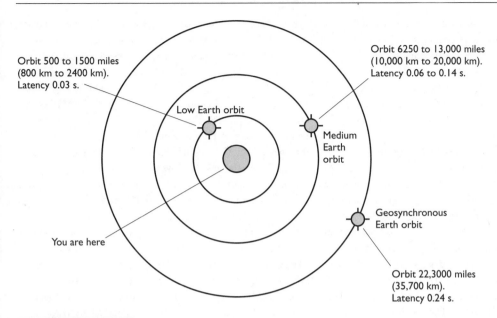

Orbit 500 to 1500 miles
(800 km to 2400 km).
Latency 0.03 s.

Orbit 6250 to 13,000 miles
(10,000 km to 20,000 km).
Latency 0.06 to 0.14 s.

Low Earth orbit

Medium Earth orbit

Geosynchronous Earth orbit

You are here

Orbit 22,3000 miles
(35,700 km).
Latency 0.24 s.

Fig. 11.43 Satellite orbits.

	Character sequence			Bit sequence
Case 1	*0101100*	**0010110**	*0100111*	*01011000010110*0100111
Case 2	*0100010*	*1101101*	*0100111*	*0100010110*11010100111
Case 3	*0101100*	**0010110**	**0010110**	*0101100*00101100<u>0010110</u>

Fig. 11.44 Use of the SYN character to frame a message.

7-bit characters below. The individual letters are coded in hexadecimal form as

'A' $= 41 = 100\ 0001$
'l' $= 6C = 110\ 1100$
'a' $= 61 = 110\ 0001$
'n' $= 6E = 110\ 1110$

The transmitted data stream is given by 100000100110111 0000110111011. This string of bits is read from left to right, with the first bit (i.e. leftmost bit) representing the least significant bit of the 'A'.

What we need is a method of identifying the beginning of a message. Once this has been done, the bits can be divided into groups of seven (or eight if a parity bit is used) for the duration of the message.

The ASCII code provides several characters whose function is to control a data link. The *synchronous idle* character SYN ($16 or 0010110_2) is used to denote the beginning of a message. The receiver reads the incoming bits and ignores them until it sees a SYN character. Figure 11.44 demonstrates the use of the SYN character. On the left we have provided three consecutive characters with spaces between successive characters. On the right we've removed spaces to show the bit stream. The bits representing a SYN have been made bold. Case 1 shows how the SYN is detected.

Unfortunately, this simple scheme is flawed because the end of one character plus the start of the next may look like a SYN character. Case 2 in Fig. 11.44 shows how a spurious SYN might be detected. To avoid this problem, two SYN characters are transmitted sequentially. If the receiver does detect a SYN, it reads the next character. If this is also a SYN the start of a message is assumed to have been located, otherwise a false synchronization is assumed and the search for a valid SYN character continued. See Fig. 11.44, case 3.

Character-oriented protocols provide point-to-point communication between two stations. Like all data link layer protocols, they both control the flow of information (message sequencing and error recovery) and they set up and maintain the transmission path.

Character-oriented protocols employ an alphabet of characters to represent data supplied from (or delivered to) higher levels and to carry out control functions. These protocols are also called *byte control-oriented* protocols (BOPs). A consequence of reserving special characters for control functions is that the transmitted data stream must not contain certain combinations of bits, as these will be interpreted as control characters. Fortunately, there are ways of getting round this problem. Character-oriented protocols may employ either synchronous or asynchronous serial transmission techniques.

Function of the ASCII control characters

The most commonly used character set for character-oriented protocols is the ASCII set. ASCII stands for *American Standard Code for Information Interchange* and uses an 8-bit code. Seven bits define one of 128 characters and the eighth bit is an optional parity bit. The ASCII code has become an international standard and is also known as the *CCITT Alphabet Number 5*. British standard BS4730:1974 specifies the UK version of the ASCII code. Table 11.3 lists the 128 characters of the ASCII character code, 32 of which are dedicated to system control functions. The meaning of some of these control characters is given below.

Example of a byte-oriented protocol

An early and widely used character-oriented protocol was the *binary synchronous protocol*, or BiSync, originally devised by IBM. Information at the physical layer is transmitted

synchronously in the form of individual characters and the data link layer is responsible for dividing the data from the physical layer into separate characters and the stream of characters into individual blocks or frames.

The BiSync message format is presented in Fig. 11.45. BiSync uses ASCII control codes to sequence messages and control the data link. Two synchronizing characters, SYN, denote the start of the message. The next field is the *header* that begins with the SOH (start of header) character. The header field regulates the flow of data. After the header field comes the text field preceded by an STX (start of text) character. Following the text field is an ETX (end of text) character and an error detecting code (BCC).

Figure 11.46 shows how the exchange of messages between two systems, A and B, can be presented graphically. The vertical axis represents increasing time, so that the diagram is read from top to bottom. Initially computer A sends a message, Block 1, to computer B. A's message is acknowledged by B, which returns an acknowledge character, ACK, to A.

The second message block from A is corrupted by noise and B sends a negative acknowledge message, NAK, inviting A to repeat its transmission. The Block 2 is repeated and acknowledged. In this example, block 3 is received satisfactorily by B, but B's acknowledgement gets lost. If nothing were done, the system would hang up, with A waiting for a

		0	1	2	3	4	5	6	7
		000	001	010	011	100	101	110	111
0	0000	NULL	DCL	SP	0	@	P	`	p
1	0001	SOH	DC1	!	1	A	Q	a	q
2	0010	STX	DC2	"	2	B	R	b	r
3	0011	ETX	DC3	#	3	C	S	c	s
4	0100	EOT	DC4	$	4	D	T	d	t
5	0101	ENQ	NAK	%	5	E	U	e	u
6	0110	ACK	SYN	&	6	F	V	f	v
7	0111	BEL	ETB	'	7	G	W	g	w
8	1000	BS	CAN	(	8	H	X	h	x
9	1001	HT	EM	)	9	I	Y	i	y
A	1010	LF	SUB	*	:	J	Z	j	z
B	1011	VT	ESC	+	;	K	[	k	}
C	1100	FF	FS	,	<	L	\	l	|
D	1101	CR	GS	-	=	M	]	m	}
E	1110	SO	RS	.	>	N	^	n	~
F	1111	SI	US	/	?	O	_	o	DEL

NULL   null   This is a fill-in character that may be added to or removed from a data stream without affecting the information content of the data stream.

SOH   start of heading   This is the first character of a heading of an information message.

STX   start of text   A character that precedes a text and which is used to terminate a heading.

ETX   end of text   A transmission control character which terminates a text.

EOT   end of transmission   A transmission control character which indicates the conclusion of the transmission of one or more texts.

Table 11.3 The ASCII code.

ENQ	enquiry	A transmission control character used as a request from a remote station.
ACK	acknowledge	A transmission control character transmitted by a receiver as an affirmative response to the sender.
BEL	bell	A control character that rings a bell, signaling the need for attention.
BS	backspace	A format effector that moves the active position (the position at which the next character is to be printed) one character position backwards on the same line.
HT	horizontal tabulation	A format effector that advances the active position to the next predetermined character position on the same line.
LF	line feed	A format effector that advances the active position to the same character position of the next line.
VT	vertical tabulation	A format effector that advances the active position to the same character position in the next predetermined line.
FF	form feed	A format effector that advances the active position to the same character position on a predetermined line of the next form or page.
CR	carriage return	A format effector that moves the active position to the first character position on the same line.
SO	shift out	A control character used in conjunction with *shift in* and *escape* to extend the graphic set of the code. It may alter the meaning of the bit combinations that follow it until a *shift in* character is reached. The characters space and delete are not affected by shift out.
SI	shift in	A control character that is used in conjunction with *shift out* and *escape* to extend the graphic character set of the code. It may reinstate the standard meaning of the bit combinations that follow it.
DLE	data link escape	A transmission character that changes the meaning of a limited number of consecutively following characters. It is used exclusively to provide supplementary data transmission control functions. Only graphic characters and transmission control characters can be used in *DLE* sequences.
DC1	device control 1	A *device control* character primarily intended for turning on an ancillary device. It may also be used to restore a device to its basic mode of operation.
DC2	device control 2	A *device control* character primarily intended for turning on an ancillary device. It may also be used to set a device mode of operation (in which case DC1 is used to restore the device to the basic mode), or for any other device control function not provided by other DCs.
DC3	device control 3	A *device control* character primarily intended for turning off or stopping an ancillary device. This function may be a secondary-level stop, e.g. wait, pause, standby, or halt (in which case DC1 is used to restore normal operation). If not used in this mode it may be used for any other device control function.
DC4	device control 4	A *device control* character primarily intended for turning off, stopping, or interrupting an ancillary device. If not required for this purpose it may be used for any other device control function not provided by other DCs.
NAK	negative acknowledge	A transmission control character transmitted by a receiver as a negative response to the sender.
SYN	synchronous idle	A transmission control character used by a synchronous transmission system in the absence of any other character (the idle condition) to provide a signal from which synchronism may be achieved or retained between data-terminal equipment.
ETB	end of transmission block	A transmission control character used to indicate the end of a transmission block of data where data is divided into such blocks.
CAN	cancel	A character, or the first character of a sequence, indicating that the data preceding it is in error. As a result this data must be ignored.
EM	end of medium	A control character that may be used to identify the physical end of a medium, or the end of the used portion of a medium, or the end of the wanted portion of data recorded in a medium. The position of this character does not necessarily correspond to the physical end of the medium.
SUB	substitute character	A control character used in place of a character that has been found to be invalid or in error. SUB is intended to be introduced by automatic means.
ESC	escape	A control character used to provide an additional control function. It alters the meaning of a limited number of consecutively following bit combinations that constitute the escape sequence.
FS	file separator	These four control characters are used to qualify data logically. The specific meaning of any character has to be defined for each application. These characters delimit information in the form of a file, group, record, and unit respectively.
GS	group separator	
RS	record separator	
US	unit separator	

Table 11.3 (Continued)

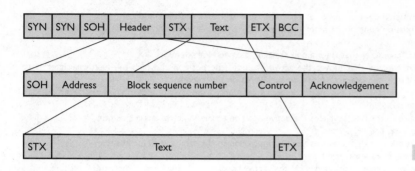

Fig. 11.45 The format of a BiSync message.

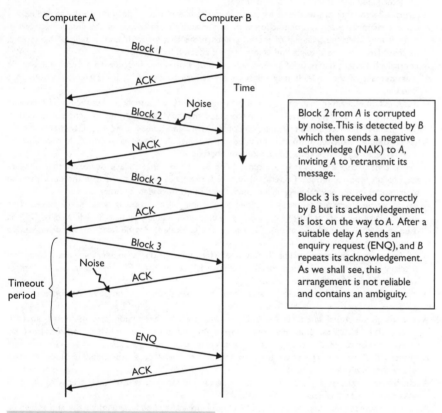

Block 2 from *A* is corrupted by noise. This is detected by *B* which then sends a negative acknowledge (NAK) to *A*, inviting *A* to retransmit its message.

Block 3 is received correctly by *B* but its acknowledgement is lost on the way to *A*. After a suitable delay *A* sends an enquiry request (ENQ), and *B* repeats its acknowledgement. As we shall see, this arrangement is not reliable and contains an ambiguity.

Fig. 11.46 Two-way communication with BiSync.

reply forever. To get out of this deadlock, A starts a timer whenever it sends a message. If a reply isn't received within a reasonable interval, a *timeout* is generated, forcing A to send a reply request or enquiry (ENQ) message to B. When B detects the ENQ, it replies with an ACK or a NAK depending on whether it received the last message.

This simple scheme contains a potential ambiguity. If A sends a message that is entirely lost in transmission, computer A will receive no ACK or NAK from B, and after a timeout it will send a reply request. When B gets the reply request, it sends an acknowledgement to the last message it received. This is not A's most recent message but the one before it. The last message sent by A has been lost and neither A nor B is aware of this. When A receives the ACK from B it sends its next message instead of repeating the last message.

A way round this ambiguity is to resort to numbered acknowledgements. The simplest arrangement employs two acknowledgement codes, ACK-0 and ACK-1, that are used alternately. Figure 11.47 demonstrates how the two ACKs resolve this ambiguity.

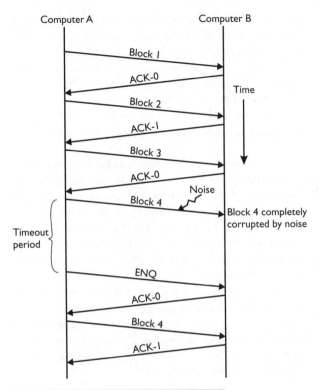

Fig. 11.47 Two-way communication with BiSync.

In this case two alternate values for the acknowledgement message are used. These are ACK-0, ACK-1, ACK-0, ACK-1, ACK-0,.... After receiving an ACK-0, A sends Block 4 which is severely corrupted and is not received by B. After a timeout, A sends an enquiry request and receives ACK-0 as a response. A knows that ACK-0 is a response to Block 3. If Block 4 had been received, A would have seen an ACK-1.

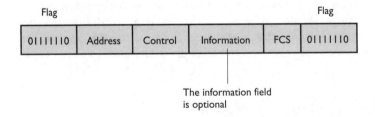

The information field is optional

Fig. 11.48 The HDLC frame format.

This treatment of a character-oriented protocol is intended only to give an idea of how messages are exchanged in an orderly fashion. The setting up of calls and their clearing-down after a transmission are not included here. Readers wishing to pursue this further should consult the bibliography.

11.5.2 Bit-oriented protocols

The ASCII code is excellent for handling text, but is ill fitted to representing pure binary data. Binary data can be anything from a core dump (a block of memory) to a program in binary form to floating point numbers. When data is stored in character form, it is easy to choose one particular character (e.g. SYN or ACK) as a special marker. When the data is stored in a pure binary form it's apparently impossible to choose any particular data sequence as a reserved marker or *flag*, because that sequence may also appear as valid data. We next explain how the impossible can be achieved.

As in the case of character-oriented protocols, the key to understanding the HDLC protocol is the HDLC *frame* format. A frame is the smallest unit of data that can be sent across a network by the data link layer. Frames are indivisible in the sense that they cannot be subdivided into smaller frames, just as an atom can't be divided into other atoms. However, a frame is composed of several distinct parts just as an atom is made up of neutrons, protons, and electrons. Figure 11.48 illustrates the HDLC format of a single frame.

Each frame begins and ends with a unique 8-bit flag, 01111110. Whenever a receiver detects the sequence 01111110, it knows that it has located the start or the end of a frame. Of course, an error in transmission may generate a spurious flag by converting (say) the sequence 01101110 into 01111110. In such cases, the receiver will lose the current frame. Due to the unique nature of the flag, the receiver will automatically resynchronize when the next opening flag is detected.

One of the key features of HDLC is its ability to transmit information entirely transparently. When we say that information is transparent, we mean that it is invisible to the data link layer and has no special tag or code associated with it to indicate that it is data and not something else. Remember that character-oriented protocols employ some characters to carry user-supplied data, whereas other characters are reserved for system functions. HDLC puts no restrictions whatsoever on the nature of the data carried across the link. Consequently, higher levels of the reference model can transmit any bit sequence they wish without affecting the operation of the data link layer.

I hope that by now you've noticed an apparent contradiction in what I said previously—'A frame is delimited by a unique flag (01111110)' and 'any binary pattern may be transmitted as data'. This contradiction is resolved by a delightfully simple scheme called *zero insertion and deletion* or *bit stuffing*.

Figure 11.49 shows how bit stuffing is used to make data transparent. Data from the block marked *transmitter* is passed to an encoder marked *zero insertion* that operates according to a simple algorithm. A bit at its input is passed unchanged to its output unless the five preceding bits have all been 1s. In the latter case, two bits are passed to the output: a 0 followed by the input bit. As an example consider the sequence 010111111011 containing the forbidden flag sequence. If the first bit is the leftmost bit, the output of the encoder is 0101111101011.

This bit insertion mechanism guarantees that any binary sequence can appear in the input data, but a flag sequence can't occur in the output data because five 1s are always terminated by 0. Flags intended as frame delimiters are appended to the data stream after the encoding block (see Fig. 11.49).

At the receiving end of the link, opening and closing flags are detected and removed from the data stream by the flag removal circuit. The data stream is then passed to the block marked *zero deletion* for decoding, which operates in the reverse way to zero insertion: if five 1s are received in succession, the next bit (which must be a 0) is deleted. For example, the received sequence 0101111101011111000 is decoded as 01011111101111100.

Now that we've described how a data stream is divided into individual bits and the bits into frames, the next step is to look at the HDLC frame. Figure 11.48 demonstrates that the HDLC frame is divided into four logical fields: an address field, a control field, an optional information field, and a frame check sequence (FCS).

Address field

The data link layer protocol can be configured to operate in one of several modes and Fig. 11.50 illustrates the *master–slave* mode. In this mode, one station is designated as the *master* station and all the other stations connected to the

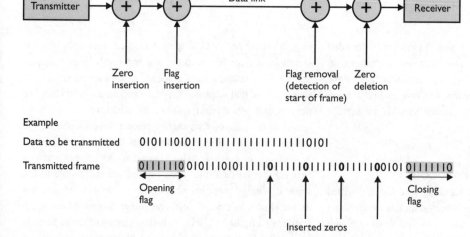

Fig. 11.49 Bit insertion and deletion.

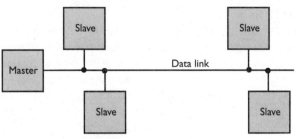

All communication is between a slave and the master. Direct slave-to-slave communication is not permitted.

Fig. 11.50 Master–slave transmission with HDLC.

master are called *slaves*. Such an arrangement is found in, for example, banks, where a central master communicates with a slave station at each teller position. As the cost of computers has fallen, this type of arrangement with one computer and many so-called *dumb terminals* has declined. A characteristic of the master–slave mode is that only the master may send messages when it wishes. A slave is not permitted to transmit until it is invited to do so by the master.

In a master–slave arrangement, the HDLC's address field provides the address of the slave (even if there is only one slave in the system). The master doesn't need an address because there's a unique master. When a master sends a frame, the address field contains the address of the slave for which the frame is intended. If the slave is transmitting a frame, the address is its own, identifying itself to the master.

Any slave receiving a frame whose address doesn't match its own address ignores the message. Unlike humans, computers don't listen to third-party traffic.

The address field is eight bits wide, permitting 127 slaves to be directly identified. If the least-significant bit of the address field bit is a logical 0, the following byte is an extension of the address field. If the least-significant bit of the extension address is also a 0, the following byte is a further extension of the address. Clearly, this arrangement permits an infinitely extendable address field.

Two special-purpose addresses have been defined. The address 11111111 is a global address indicating that the frame is a broadcast frame and is intended for all stations on the network. The special address 00000000 (null) causes the frame to be ignored by all stations! A null address is included for test purposes.

Control field

The real power of the HDLC protocol lies in its 8-bit control field, which determines the type of the frame being transmitted and controls the flow of messages across the data link layer. Table 11.4 defines the three types of control field used by an HDLC frame. Note that the control field bits are numbered 1 to 8 (bit 1 is the least-significant bit) and are written with the least-significant bit on the left. This contradicts the conventional numbering of bits from 0 to $m-1$ with the least-significant bit on the right. We have used the format of Table 11.4 because that is the format used by the standard.

The two least-significant bits of a C-field define one of three types of frame: I-frame, S-frame, or U-frame. An I-frame or *information frame* contains an information field and is used to transport data from a higher level layer than the data link layer.

The S-frame or *supervisory frame* controls the flow of information on the link. Typical functions include acknowledging I-frames or requesting the retransmission of frames lost during transmission. There are four types of S-frame; the type is indicated by the two bits labeled 'S' in Table 11.4. We shall look more closely at the S-frame later.

Frame type	1	2	3	4	5	6	7	8
I frame	0		N(S)		P/F		N(R)	
S frame	I	0	S	S	P/F		N(R)	
U frame	I	I	M	M	P/F	M	M	M

N(S) = send sequence number
N(R) = receive sequence number
P/F = poll/final bit
SS = two supervisory bits
MMMMM = five modifier bits

Table 11.4 The format of the HDLC control field.

The *unnumbered frame* (U-frame) provides control functions not available with the I- or C-frames. U-frames perform functions like setting up or changing the operating mode of the data link layer and connecting or disconnecting two stations.

All three types of control fields have a *poll/final* (P/F) bit, which is a dual-purpose bit. When transmitted by a master station, it is called a *poll bit* (P-bit) and indicates that the master is polling (i.e. asking) the secondary station for a response. Remember that in the master–slave mode, the secondary station cannot transmit until it is invited to do so by the master. A control field with P/F = 1 sent by the master indicates such an invitation.

When a control field is sent by a secondary station, the P/F bit is defined as a *final bit* and, when set, indicates that the current field is the last frame of the series. In other words, a slave sets P/F = 1 when it has no more frames to send.

Much of the power of the control field lies in two state variables $N(S)$ and $N(R)$. They are called *state variables* because they define the state of the system at any instant. Both are 3-bit numbers in the range 0–7. $N(S)$ is called the send sequence number and $N(R)$ is called the receive sequence number.

Only I-frames contain a send sequence number, $N(S)$, which uniquely labels the current information frame. For example, if $N(S) = 101$ the frame is numbered 5. When this frame is received the value of $N(S)$ is examined and compared with the previous value. If the previous value was 4, the message is received in sequence. But if the value was not 4, there is a gnashing of teeth and grieving over a lost message. Note that the sequence count is modulo 8, so that it goes 67012345670.... Consequently, if eight messages are lost, the next value of $N(S)$ will apparently be correct.

The receive sequence number, $N(R)$, is available in both S and I control fields. $N(R)$ indicates the number of the next I-frame that the receiver expects to see. That is, an $N(R)$ acknowledges I-frames up to and including $N(R) - 1$. Suppose station A is sending an information frame with $N(S) = 3$, $N(R) = 6$ to B. The interpretation of this frame is that A is sending frame number 3 and has safely received frames up to 5 from B. It is saying that it expects to see an information frame from B with the value of $N(S)$ equal to 6. By means of the $N(R)$ and $N(S)$ state variables, it's impossible to lose a frame without detecting an error, as long as there are not more than seven outstanding I-frames that have not been acknowledged. If eight or more frames are sent, it is impossible to tell whether a value of $N(R) = i$ refers to frame i or to frame $i - 8$. It is up to the system designer to ensure that this situation never happens. We will soon look at how $N(S)$ and $N(R)$ are used in more detail.

FCS field

We've already said that the data link layer is built on top of an imperfect physical layer. Bits transmitted across a physical medium may become corrupted by noise, with a 1 being transformed to a 0 or vice versa. The error rate over point-to-point links in a dedicated local area network may be of the order of one bit lost in every 10^{12} bits. Error rates over other channels may be very much worse than this. Section 11.7.5 looks at some of the ways in which errors can be detected and their effects made good. Here we simply describe the FCS field for completeness.

HDLC chooses its message coding and decoding scheme to provide the maximum possible error protection. At the receiver, the bits of the address field, control field, and I-field are treated as the coefficients of a long polynomial, which is divided by a special polynomial called a *generator*. The HDLC protocol uses the CCITT generator 10001000000100001 or $x^{16} + x^{12} + x^5 + 1$. The result of the division yields a quotient (which is thrown away) and a 16-bit remainder, which is the 16-bit FCS appended to the frame.

At the receiver, the message bits forming the A-, C-, and I-fields are also divided by the generator polynomial to yield a locally calculated remainder. The calculated remainder is compared with the received remainder in the FCS field. If they match, the frame is assumed to be valid. Otherwise the frame is rejected.

You may wonder how the FCS is detected, because the I-field, when present, may be of any length, and no information is sent to indicate its length directly. In fact, the FCS field cannot be detected. The receiver assembles data until the closing flag is detected and then works backward to obtain the FCS and the I-field.

11.5.3 HDLC message exchange

The HDLC protocol caters for several configurations and operating modes. Here we consider only the *unbalanced normal response mode* (NRM). A data link is unbalanced when it is operated in a master–slave mode. In the NRM, a secondary station (i.e. slave) may initiate transmission only as a result of receiving explicit permission from the primary station (i.e. master). That is, a master can send data to a slave at any time, but a slave may respond only when invited to do so by the master.

Before we continue, it's necessary to define the four messages associated with a supervisory frame. Table 11.5 shows how the four S-frames are encoded.

The RR (receiver ready) frame indicates that the station sending it is ready to receive information frames and is equivalent to saying, 'I'm ready'. The REJ (reject) frame indicates

Control bit								S-frame type	
I	2	3	4	5	6	7	8		
I	0	0	0	P/F	←	N(R)	→	RR	receiver ready
I	0	0	I	P/F	←	N(R)	→	REJ	reject
I	0	I	0	P/F	←	N(R)	→	RNR	receiver not ready
I	0	I	I	P/F	←	N(R)	→	SREJ	selective reject

Table 11.5 The format of the S-frame.

an error condition and usually implies that one or more frames have been lost in transmission. The REJ frame rejects all frames, starting with the frame numbered $N(R)$. Whenever a station receives an REJ frame, it must go back and retransmit all messages after $N(R)-1$. Sending all these messages is sometimes inefficient, because not all frames in a sequence may have been lost.

The RNR (receiver not ready) frame indicates that the station is temporarily unable to receive information frames. RNR is normally used to indicate a busy condition (e.g. the receiver's buffers may all be full). The busy condition is cleared by the transmission of an RR, REJ, or SREJ frame. An I-frame sent with the P/F bit set also clears the busy condition.

The SREJ (selective reject) frame rejects the single frame numbered $N(R)$ and is equivalent to 'Please retransmit frame number $N(R)$'. The use of SREJ is more efficient than REJ, because the latter requests the retransmission of all frames after $N(R)$ as well as $N(R)$. The REJ command is necessary when either a number of frames have been lost, or the receiver is not capable of storing frames.

Figure 11.51 demonstrates the operation of the HDLC protocol by means of a sequence of frame exchanges between A (the master) and B (the slave) operating in a half-duplex mode. Each frame is denoted by *type*, $N(S)$, $N(R)$, P/F, where type is I (for an information field), RR, REJ, RNR, or SREJ. Typical HDLC frames are

	Type,	N(S), N(R), P/F
I,5,0	I-frame,	$N(S)=5$, $N(R)=0$
I,5,0,P	I-frame,	$N(S)=5$, $N(R)=0$, Poll bit set by master
REJ,,4,F	S-frame,	$N(R)=4$, Reject, Final bit set by slave

Note that a double comma indicates the absence of an $N(S)$ field.

Initially in Fig. 11.51, the master station sends three I-frames. The poll bit in the third frame is set to force a response from the slave. The slave replies by sending two I-frames that are terminated by setting the F bit of the C-field. If the slave had no I-frames to send, it would have responded with RR,,3,F. Note that the values of $N(S)$ and $N(R)$ in a frame are those appropriate to the *sender* of the frame.

The master sends a further two I-frames, terminated by a poll bit. However, the first frame in this pair (I,3,2) is corrupted by noise and rejected by the receiver (slave). When the slave responds to the poll from the master, it sends a supervisory frame, REJ,,3,F, rejecting the I-frame numbered 3 and all succeeding frames. This causes the master station to repeat the two frames numbered $N(S)=3$ and $N(S)=4$.

When the master station sends an I-frame numbered I,5,2,P, it also is corrupted in transmission and rejected by the receiver. Now the secondary station cannot respond to this polled request. When the master sends a message with P = 1, it starts a timer. If a response is not received within a certain period, the timeout, the master station takes action. In this case, it sends a supervisory frame (RR,,2,P) to force a response. The secondary station replies with another supervisory frame (REJ,,5,F) and the master then repeats the lost message.

Students are often confused by the provision both of REJ and SREJ supervisory frames. A selective reject frame, SREJ,,$N(R)$, rejects only the message whose send sequence count is $N(R)$. Therefore, SREJ,,$N(R)$ is equivalent to 'Please repeat your message with $N(S)=N(R)$'. If a sequence of messages are lost, it is better to use REJ,,$N(R)$ and have $N(R)$ and all messages following $N(R)$ repeated.

However, even if only one message is lost, it's sometimes necessary to use an REJ. Suppose that the current value of $N(S)$ is 6 and that the message $N(S)=3$ has been lost. If a response REJ,,3 is received, messages with $N(S)=3$, 4, 5, and 6 must be repeated. Although this process is inefficient and time-consuming, it has a valid application. If the receiver can't store incoming messages, an error will always force it back to the lost message. Remember that HDLC was designed before low-cost microprocessor systems had become available. By having the REJ procedure, it is not necessary to build *intelligence* into the slave part of the data link.

Figure 11.52 shows the operation of an HDLC system operating in full-duplex mode, permitting the simultaneous exchange of messages in both directions.

We have explained only part of the HDLC data link layer protocol. Unnumbered fields are used to perform operations

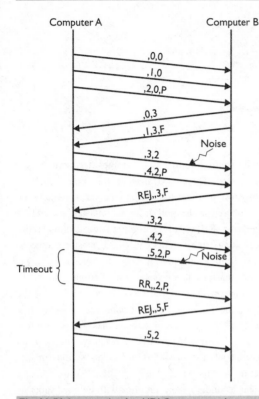

Computer A   Computer B

,0,0
,1,0
,2,0,P
,0,3
,1,3,F
Noise
,3,2
,4,2,P
REJ,,3,F
,3,2
,4,2
,5,2,P   Noise
Timeout
RR,,2,P,
REJ,,5,F
,5,2

A message is denoted by type, N(S),N(R),P/F. For example, ,3,0,P indicates an information frame numbered 3, with an N(R) count of 0, and the poll bit set indicating that a response is required. Note that message 3 from A (i.e., ,3,2) is lost. Therefore, when A sends the message ,4,2,P with the poll bit set, B responds with REJ,,3,F. this indicates that B is rejecting all messages from A numbered 3 and above, and that the F bit is set, denoting that B has no more messages to send to A.

Fig. 11.51 An example of an HDLC message exchange sequence

related to the setting up or establishing of the data link layer channel and the eventual clearing-down of the channel.

Before we move on to local area networks, we are going to examine the way in which errors introduced by the physical layer can be detected and corrected.

11.5.4 Error detection and correction

A transmission error occurs whenever one or more bits in a message are so severely corrupted by noise that they are incorrectly detected at the receiver. Because a data transmission system is intended to convey information from one point to another *reliably*, a mechanism is required to deal with the errors that inevitably occur on any real physical channel. Although we introduced error-detecting and error-correcting code in Chapter 4 when we were looking at coding techniques, we will cover this topic again here with a somewhat different emphasis.

Error detection is a process that determines whether or not an error has occurred in the transmission of a message. For exa ple, if you receive the message. 'My birthday falls on February 30', you know that a transmission error has occurred

because February 30 isn't a valid date. However, you don't know what the correct message should have been.

Once we know that a message is in error, we can deal with the situation in one of two ways. Either we must request a retransmission of the faulty message or we must repair the damage done to the message. Data transmission codes that derive a correct message from a faulty message are known as *error-correcting codes*, ECCs.

The best way of illustrating the concepts involved in error-detecting and error-correcting codes is to introduce some examples. Consider four codes:

Code 1   The input sequence is copied to the output sequence without modification

Code 2   Each input element is duplicated. Inputting a 1 causes a 11 to be output and inputting a 0 causes a 00 to be output.

Code 3   Each input element is repeated three times. Inputting a 1 causes a 111 to be output and inputting a 0 causes a 000 to be output.

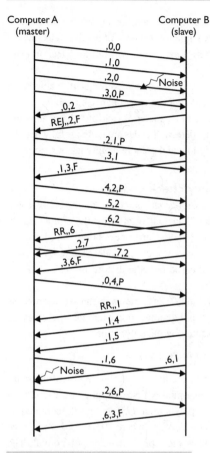

Computer A
(master)

Computer B
(slave)

,0,0

,1,0

,2,0   Noise

,3,0,P

,0,2

REJ,,2,F

,2,1,P

,3,1

,1,3,F

,4,2,P

,5,2

,6,2

RR,,6

,2,7

,7,2

,3,6,F

,0,4,P

RR,,1

,1,4

,1,5

,1,6   ,6,1

Noise

,2,6,P

,6,3,F

- A sends a frame ,0,0 (information frame numbered 0, A is expecting a frame from B numbered 0).
- A sends frame ,1,0 (information frame numbered 1, A is still expecting a frame from B numbered 0).
- A sends frame ,2,0. This frame is corrupted by noise and is not correctly received by B.
- B sends frame ,0,2 (information frame numbered 0, B is expecting a frame from A numbered 2). Note that because A's frame ,2,0 has been lost, B is still expecting to see a frame from A labeled with $N(S)=2$.
- A sends ,3,0,P (information frame numbered 3, A is expecting a frame numbered 0 from B). A is also polling B for a response. At this point A does not know that its previous message has been lost, and A has not received B's last message.
- B sends a reply to A's poll. This is REJ,,2,F indicating that all A's messages numbered 2 and above have been rejected. The final bit, F, is set indicating that B has nothing more to send at the moment.
- A now sends ,2,1 (information frame 2, and A is expecting to see a frame from B numbered 1). This frame is a repeat of A's information frame numbered 2 which was lost earlier.

Fig. 11.52 HDLC full-duplex transmission.

Code 4 This is similar to Code 3 because each input element is triplicated. However, in this case the output sequence is rearranged so that the three output bits corresponding to each input are spread out over three groups of three bits. For example, if the input sequence is a,b,c, the output sequence is a,b,c, a,b,c, a,b,c.

The codes introduced here serve only for illustrative purposes and don't represent practical codes used by typical data transmission systems. Suppose that the bit pattern 100 is applied to the transmitter and that the third received bit is corrupted. Each of the four codes defined above can be represented as:

Coder	Input sequence	Transmitted sequence	Received sequence
1	100	100	101
2	100	110000	111000
3	100	111000111	110000111
4	100	100100100	101100100

Although the data received from Coder 1 is in error, there's no way of detecting the error because each received code is as valid (i.e. legal) as any other code.

The data received from Coder 2 is in error because the second group is 10, which is an illegal bit pattern as only the patterns 00 and 11 are valid. Clearly we have detected an error, but we cannot correct it because there is no way of telling which bit has been corrupted.

When we examine the data from Coder 3, it's clear that the first group, 101, is in error as it is not one of the two valid codes (000 and 111). If we make the assumption that one error is much more likely than two errors, we can say that the transmitted code was probably a 1. Now we have both detected *and* corrected an error.

The output of Coder 4 must be rearranged to yield the sequence 111 000 100 and the offending error detected and corrected. That is, Coder 4 behaves exactly like Coder 3 under these circumstances.

Now let's consider the effect of two errors in the transmitted sequence. Assume that both the second and third transmitted bits are corrupted.

Coder	Input sequence	Transmitted sequence	Received sequence
1	100	100	111
2	100	110000	101000
3	100	111000111	100000111
4	100	100100100	111100100

In this case, the two errors go undetected by Coder 1 and both errors are detected by Coder 2. Coder 3 detects that an error has taken place but incorrectly corrects the error because the received code, 100, is assumed to represent 0.

Because Coder 4 scrambles the order of the bits, the two errors fall in adjacent groups and can be both detected and corrected. That is, the output sequence is 111100100, or 111 100 100 after descrambling. This yields 111 000 000 after correction to give the final output 1 0 0.

These examples teach us that some codes detect errors and others both detect and correct errors. Moreover, they tell us that multiple errors may entirely defeat error-correcting codes. The most important thing to note is that an error-detecting or error-correcting code adds bits to the data to be transmitted. Coder 4 tells us that we can improve error correction just by reordering bits.

Single-bit parity error-detecting codes

The principle behind an error-correcting code is quite simple. A message word is transformed into a code word by the addition of redundant bits that are a function of the message. These bits are called *redundant* because they carry no new information, as they are derived from the message according to some algorithm. All they do is to help detect errors.

Consider an unencoded source message with a length m bits. There are 2^m possible valid messages of m bits. Now suppose that we create an n-bit code word by adding r redundant bits to the message. That is, $n = m + r$.

Although the code word has $2^n = 2^{m+r}$ possible values, only 2^m of these values are valid. When a code word is received, it is checked to see whether it represents a valid message. If it is valid, no error is assumed to have occurred.

The simplest error-correcting code is the single-bit parity check code. In this case, $r = 1$. In an even parity code, a parity bit, P, is appended to the message. P is chosen to make the total number of ones in the code word even. If, for example, the parity bit is at the right, the 4-bit messages 0010 and 0110 are coded as 00101 and 01100, respectively. When a code word is received, the total number of ones is counted. If the result is even, no error is assumed. Otherwise the message is rejected as faulty. A single parity bit will always detect a single or an odd number of errors but will fail to detect an even number of errors.

Single-bit parity error checking is frequently associated with character-oriented codes, where a parity bit can be conveniently attached to a 7-bit character to yield an 8-bit code word. Single-bit parity error-detecting codes are quite useful when the error rate is relatively low and great reliability is not required.

Cyclic redundancy check codes

Modern data transmission systems require more sophisticated error-detecting codes than that offered by the simple parity bit. Like most of today's error-correcting or detecting codes, the cyclic redundancy check code requires a certain amount of mathematical knowledge before its operation can be understood.

The stream of 1s and 0s of a message can be regarded as the coefficients of a polynomial. For example, the message 1101 may be represented by the polynomial

$$1101 \rightarrow 1 \cdot x^3 + 1 \cdot x^2 + 0 \cdot 2^1 + 1 \cdot x^0 = x^3 + x^2 + 1$$

Suppose we take a polynomial of order m, representing an m-bit message. The polynomial is first multiplied by x^r and then divided by an r-bit polynomial G. The result obtained is $x^r \cdot M(x) = Q(x) \cdot G(x) + x^r \cdot R(x)$, where $M(x)$ is the message polynomial and $R(x)$ is the r-bit remainder polynomial. The remainder polynomial, $R(x)$, is the *cyclic check code* and is appended to the message before transmission.

At the receiver, the m bits of the message are divided by the same generator polynomial, $G(x)$, and a locally calculated remainder is obtained. This is compared with the received CRC and an error flagged if they are not the same.

The power of the cyclic redundancy check error-detecting code is twofold. It's very easy to implement in hardware and it detects a very large fraction of all possible errors.

The standard generator polynomial specified by CCITT X.25 is

$$G(x) = x^{16} + x^{12} + x^5 + 1$$

This polynomial detects any burst error with a length less than or equal to r bits. Burst errors with a length greater than r bits will be detected with a probability of $1 - 2^{-r}$.

Error-correcting codes

Many communication systems rely entirely on error-detecting codes to deal with physical channel impairments. Whenever the receiver detects a message in error the receiver asks the transmitter to repeat the lost message. Such a system is called *automatic repeat request*, ARQ. An alternative approach is to use a *forward error correcting code*, FEC, which provides the receiver with a means of correcting transmission errors without incurring the delay associated with ARQ. Such a delay may be vital in real-time applications or in deep space communications links.

We've already looked at a very primitive error-detecting and correcting code. Simply triplicating each transmitted bit enables us to detect and correct a single error. Such a scheme is grossly inefficient and requires two check bits for each message bit. In any case, it cannot deal with multiple errors. There are many practical error-detecting and correcting codes in use today, although they are too complex to cover here. One of the simplest practical error-detecting and correcting codes is the Hamming code introduced in Chapter 4.

The vast majority of data transmission systems do not employ forward error-correcting codes, but rely on the very powerful error-detecting properties of the CRC codes and request the retransmission of any faulty messages. Sometimes both FECs and ARQ codes are combined. By using an FEC with a cyclic redundancy check code, it is possible to automatically correct single-bit errors in the received data and to request the retransmission of messages that are then found to have incorrect CRCs.

11.6 Local area networks

Local area networks have changed the face of modern computing. The high performance and low cost of today's LAN makes it feasible for even the smallest organizations to link together all their computers and allied digital equipment.

When only modest quantities of data were being transmitted over long, often intercontinental, distances, the impact of data transmission on computing was minimal. With the advent of low-cost microprocessor and minicomputer systems together with the clustering of a number of such devices in a relatively small area (an office, factory, university, or laboratory), the need for a specialized form of inexpensive communications network was felt. Because of this pressure, a branch of data transmission dealing with the transfer of large quantities of information at high speed between geographically distributed computers arose. This new field is, of course, known as *local area networks*. Data transmission systems operating over much greater areas than LANs (and using public communications facilities) are called *wide area networks*, WANs.

We begin this section by defining LANs in terms of their properties and then introduce the concept of LAN topology, which is a measure of the way in which the nodes of a LAN are connected together. Finally, we look at particular types of LAN and show how they pass messages between their various nodes.

What is a LAN?

Local area networks and beauty have at least one thing in common: they both exist only in the eye of the beholder. There's no absolute definition of a local area network. Equally, everybody knows (or thinks they know) what is meant by a LAN. Writers avoid the problem of trying to define a LAN by listing its properties. We will follow in their footsteps.

1. A LAN is local Here's where the difficulty of defining a LAN begins. What is local to one person is frequently distant to another. In the UK, a trip of 30 km is sometimes regarded as a major excursion. In the USA, it's often no more than a hop to your nearest neighbor. The term *local* implies a *single* site—even if the site is very large. The site may be a laboratory, a factory, or an entire complex of factories. The term MAN, *metropolitan area network*, has been coined to indicate a network extending over a relatively large area, such as a number of separate sites or even part of a city.

2. A LAN is private A LAN belongs to the owner of the site on which it is operated and does not use public data transmission equipment such as the telephone network. Therefore, the owner of the LAN doesn't have to comply with the very complex legal restrictions and obligations associated with a public network. This goes hand-in-hand with point 1. The LAN extends over a single site because public carriers are not necessary. As soon as separate sites are linked, they invariably require the use of a public network. A LAN on one site can be connected to a LAN on another site by means of the PSTN (or POTS if you prefer that acronym). The interface between the LAN and the PSTN is called a *gateway*. A gateway is an interconnection between two or more separate networks. In everyday terms, the Leicester Square underground station is a gateway because it allows travelers on the Northern line to move on to the Piccadilly line.

3. A LAN offers a high data rate The rate at which information can be transmitted across a physical channel depends on the length and the electrical properties of the transmission path. LANs have relatively short transmission paths and often use coaxial cable or a twisted pair, permitting data rates up to 100 Mbit/s. This data rate is very much greater than the 9600 to 56 kbit/s supported by most telephone channels.

4. A LAN is reliable   Most LANs are relatively simple systems with a coaxial cable connecting the various nodes of the network. There are no complex switching systems like those associated with telephone networks. LANs are reliable because they link systems over short distances and aren't subject to the types of interference that plague the long-haul transmission paths of the telephone network. Furthermore, the LAN does not employ the fault- and noise-prone mechanical or electronic message-switching techniques associated with the telephone system. Consequently, a well-designed LAN should offer a very long MTBF (mean time between failure) and a short MTTR (mean time to repair) if it does fail. A repair may involve little more than replacing one of the nodes that has failed. LANs are normally designed so that the failure of a single node has no effect on the performance of the system.

5. A LAN is cheap   LANs have been devised to connect low-cost systems, and therefore the use of expensive technology or transmission media can't be tolerated. LANs are not only cheap, but require little labor in their installation. One of the most clearly defined trends to emerge from the microprocessor world is the tendency for the price of anything associated with microprocessors to fall dramatically as time passes. We've already witnessed remarkable drops in the price of DRAM memory, hard disk drives, and peripherals (printers and modems). If low-cost microprocessor systems are to be linked, the local area network chosen to do this must be cost-effective. Nobody is going to pay $20 000 to link together two $1000 microcomputers. Not even in Texas.

6. A LAN is fair to the users   A LAN should offer all its nodes full connectivity, which means that any given node should be able to communicate with any other node. Equally, each node should have the same access rights to the transmission medium, so that all nodes have the same probability that their message will be delivered across the network. The fairness criterion exists only at levels 1 and 2 of the ISO model for OSI. A higher level may limit the scope of a particular node's access rights.

7. The nodes of a LAN should be equal   This criterion is, perhaps, a little more tendentious than the others and is not a characteristic of every LAN. When we say that all nodes should be equal we mean that they should have the same software and the same hardware. A corollary of this statement is that it should be possible to add new nodes to an existing system without modifying the software at all the other nodes.

11.6.1 Network topology

The topology of a network describes the way in which the individual users of the network are linked together. There are four basic topologies suitable for use in a LAN: the unconstrained topology, the star network, the bus, and the ring. These topologies are the same topologies used to implement the multiprocessor systems we introduced in Chapter 4.

The unconstrained network

The most general topology is the unconstrained network of Fig. 11.53. The individual nodes are connected together in an arbitrary fashion. Its advantage is that additional links can be provided to reduce bottlenecks where heavy traffic passes between a group of nodes. Further nodes and links can readily be added without disturbing the hardware of the existing system. The road network of most countries is an unconstrained topology, with new roads being added when and where necessary.

The disadvantage of the unconstrained topology is that a decision must be made at each node on the best way to route a message to its destination. In terms of the analogy with the road system, the driver must have a road map to enable him or her to drive from one place to another. A message cannot just be transmitted from one node to each other node to which it is connected, as this would lead to the message being multiplied at each node and propagated round the network forever. Instead, each node must have its own road map and make a decision on which link the message is to be transmitted on the way to its destination.

Calculating the best route through the network for each message has the computational overhead of working out routing algorithms. Furthermore, whenever a new link or node is added to the network, the routing information must be changed at each node. Figure 11.54 shows how a message may be routed through an unconstrained topology. We will return to the topic of routing at the end of this chapter.

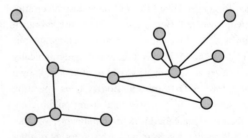

Fig. 11.53 The unconstrained topology.

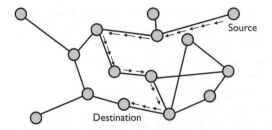

Fig. 11.54 Routing a message through an unconstrained topology.

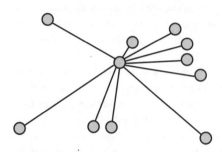

Fig. 11.55 The star topology.

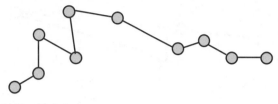

(a) The simple bus

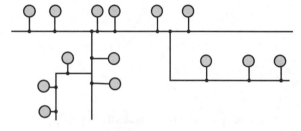

(b) A more general form of bus

Fig. 11.56 The bus topology.

The star network

Figure 11.55 shows how the star network routes all messages from source to destination via one central node and eliminates the need for nodes to make routing decisions. The star has a simple topology and has advantages when the network's physical topology matches its logical topology. Clearly, there are circumstances where the nodes are distributed in such a way that the links between some of the nodes and the central node are economically unviable.

The star network has two obvious disadvantages. As all messages pass through the central node, the loss of the central node brings down the network. Other networks may offer a degraded but useful service if part of the network fails. Furthermore, because all traffic passes through the central node, it must be capable of working at a sufficiently high speed to handle all nodes to which it is connected.

The bus

The *bus topology* is illustrated in Fig. 11.56. Both the bus and the ring are attempts to minimize the complexity of a network by both removing a special-purpose central node and the need for individual nodes to make routing decisions.

In a bus all nodes are connected to a common data highway. The bus may be a single path linking all nodes—see Fig. 11.56(a). A more general form of bus is described by Fig. 11.56(b) and consists of several interlinked buses. Such a

topology is called an unrooted tree. When a message is put on the bus by a node, it flows outwards in all directions and eventually reaches every point in the network. The bus has one topological and one practical restriction. Only one path may exist between any two points, otherwise there would be nothing to stop a message flowing round a loop forever. The practical limitation is that the bus cannot normally exceed some maximum distance from end to end.

The principal problem faced by the designers of a bus is how to deal with a number of nodes wanting to use the bus at the same time. This is called *bus contention* and is dealt with later.

The ring

Figure 11.57 illustrates the ring topology, in which the nodes are connected together in the form of a ring. Like the bus, this topology provides a decentralized structure, because no central node is needed to control the ring. Each node simply receives a message from one neighbor and passes it on to its other neighbor. Messages flow in one direction round the ring.

The only routing requirement placed on each node is that it must be able to recognize a message intended for itself. The ring does not suffer from contention like the bus topology. However, a node on the ring has the problem of how to inject a new message into the existing traffic flow.

A ring is prone to failure because a broken link makes it impossible to pass messages all the way round the ring. Some networks employ a double ring structure with two links between each of the nodes. If one of the links is broken it is possible for the ring to reconfigure itself and bypass the failure.

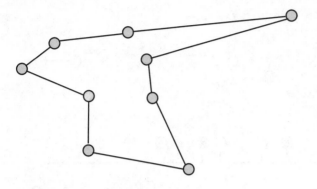

Fig. 11.57 The ring topology.

11.6.2 Flow control mechanisms in buses

One of the earliest local area networks and one that has had a profound effect on the development of today's LANs was called ALOHA. ALOHA was designed to link remote terminals spread out over the Hawaiian islands, with central processing facilities at Honolulu on the island of Oahu. The central processor was called the *Menahune*, which is a Hawaiian name for an imp. The word *imp* is a reference to the IMPs (interface message processors) that formed the nodes of the ARPANET wide area network.

From a topological viewpoint, ALOHA has a star structure with a central master, the Menahune, surrounded by slaves. The physical link layer was implemented by UHF radio channels. Full-duplex operation was achieved by using frequencies of 407.35 MHz for slave to master communication and 413.75 MHz for master to slave communication.

Communication between the master (Menahune) and a slave (i.e. a user terminal) is entirely straightforward. The master just transmits a packet of information consisting of a 32-bit header, a 16-bit header parity check field, and up to 80 bytes of data followed by a 16-bit data parity check field. The maximum packet size is 88 bytes (i.e. 704 bits) which takes 73 ms to transmit at 9600 bps. A packet from the master is received by all slaves, but only the slave whose own address matches that in the packet's header responds to it.

Things are very different when a message is sent from a slave to the master. Although the network's geographical topology looks like a star, it behaves as a bus, as far as slave-to-master traffic is concerned. The reason for this is quite simple. Each slave uses the same medium (radio at 407.35 MHz) and all slaves are linked together by the ether. Consequently, whenever a slave transmits, its message spreads out to all other slaves, as well as to the master.

Such a bus network introduces the problem of *contention*. No two nodes can access the same channel simultaneously without the messages interfering destructively with each other. When two messages overlap in time, the event is called a *collision* and both messages are lost.

ALOHA deals with the problem of contention in a rather simple but crude fashion. Any slave wishing to communicate with the master just goes ahead and transmits its message. Of course, if another slave is transmitting at the same time or joins in before the message is finished, both messages are lost. The loss of a message is detected by an equally crude technique—if the slave doesn't receive an acknowledgement within a timeout period, it is assumed that its message has been corrupted in transmission.

When a message from a slave node collides with a message from another slave, both messages are lost. If the duration of a message is T seconds and two messages just collide, the total time lost is up to $2T$ seconds. Assuming that the probability of a station wanting to transmit a packet has a *Poisson distribution*, it can be shown that the maximum throughput of this system approaches 18 percent of the maximum channel capacity. A Poisson distribution is a statistical model of events like the rate at which people use the telephone.

To make the effect of collisions clearer, consider the analogy with revolving doors. Suppose a revolving door has a maximum capacity of 1000 people per hour when all the people follow one after the other (i.e. polite behavior without contention). If people arrive at these doors at random (an example of a Poisson distribution), then with people using a random wait every time they collide, the maximum throughput cannot exceed 180 people per hour.

A modification of ALOHA's crude contention control is called *slotted ALOHA*. The channel time is divided into fixed slots with a duration equal to the maximum packet length. A packet may be transmitted only at the start of a time slot and the probability of a collision is much reduced. If packets are transmitted at random, the beginning of one packet can collide with the end of another and a period of time equal to two packet lengths is lost. If all packets are transmitted in fixed time slots, a collision cannot affect two adjacent slots, and a time equal to only one packet length is lost. Of course, this arrangement requires that all transmitters have access to an accurate clock in order to schedule their messages to fall within the time slots. Slotted ALOHA has a maximum efficiency of 36 percent.

In a contention net any node wishing to transmit just goes ahead and puts its message on the bus. As there is no control over when a node may transmit, there is nothing to prevent two or more nodes transmitting simultaneously. If this does happen, all messages being transmitted are irretrievably scrambled and lost. The simplest form of contention control is to let the transmitters retransmit their messages. Unfortunately, such a scheme wouldn't work, because the competing nodes would keep retransmitting the messages that would keep getting scrambled. The problem of collisions in a bus network is identical to that of two people approaching the same revolving door together—they can't both get in, they step back, and advance together causing a collision, so they step back again, advance together, collide, ...

A better strategy on detecting a collision is to *back off* or wait a random time before trying to retransmit the frame. It is unlikely that the competing nodes would reschedule the transmissions for the same time. In terms of the revolving door analogy, as soon as the two people collide, they each immediately throw a die and then wait the number of seconds the die shows before trying again. It is unlikely that they would each get the same number, so they can go through the door separately. Networks operating under this form of contention control are well suited to bursty traffic. That is, the arrangement works as long as the average traffic density is very low (much less than the maximum capacity of the bus). If the amount of traffic rises, there comes a point where collisions generate repeat messages that generate further collisions and further repeats, and the system eventually collapses.

A better form of contention control is to allow the node to listen to the bus before trying to send its frame. Obviously, if one node is already in the process of sending a message, other nodes are not going to attempt to transmit. A collision will occur only if two nodes attempt to transmit at nearly the same instant. Once a node has started transmitting and its signal has propagated throughout the network, no other node can interrupt. For almost all systems, this danger zone, the propagation time of a message from one end of the network to the other, is very small and is only a tiny fraction of the duration of a message.

A further modification of this arrangement is to allow the transmitters to listen to the bus while they are transmitting. Suppose a transmitter, thinking the bus was free, had started transmitting, and at the same time another transmitter had done likewise. After a very short time both transmitters would become aware that the bus is in use and abort their messages. In this way the effect of a collision is reduced, because the transmitters stop as soon as they detect the collision. In the absence of a listen-while-transmitting mechanism, a collision is detected indirectly by the absence of any acknowledgement to the message.

Ethernet

One of the most popular derivatives of ALOHA is Ethernet, which was proposed by Robert Metcalfe in the early 1970s. Metcalfe joined the Xerox Corporation and developed Ethernet (the name comes from the *ether*, a medium that was once thought to fill all space). Xerox formed a consortium with DEC and Intel who approached the IEEE and proposed the Ethernet as a standard.

Ethernet wasn't the only possible standard at that time. During the late 1970s, it became apparent that LANs were going to become a major area of growth and that the introduction of a large number of *ad hoc* protocols for LANs would have, ultimately, a bad effect on the computer industry. In 1980 the IEEE established its Standards Project 802 to provide a framework for LAN standards. The 802 committee set itself the goal of designing a standard for the new LANs that would take account of existing and prospective technology, and the needs of the various LAN users. The 802 committee didn't intend to produce standards for all seven layers of the ISO basic reference model, but limited themselves to standards for the physical and data link layers.

While the IEEE was organizing its 802 project, the Ethernet LAN was rapidly becoming a *de facto* standard for contention buses, and therefore the IEEE had to incorporate it in their work. At the same time, engineers were involved in a vigorous debate about the relative merits of buses and rings as LAN topologies. The IEEE 802 committee reflected the nature of the real world, so they devised a set of standards that took account of both bus and ring topologies. They wanted the greatest happiness of the greatest number of people. The IEEE 802 draft standard includes standards for an Ethernet bus, a token ring, and a token bus. Figure 11.58 illustrates the scope of the 802 standards.

The physical layer of Ethernet uses a baseband coaxial cable with phase encoded data at 10 Mbps. The term *baseband* means that the digital data is transmitted directly without the need for modems. The contention mechanism adopted by Ethernet is called *Carrier Sense Multiple Access with Collision Detect* (CSMA/CD). When an Ethernet station wishes to transmit a packet, it listens to the state of the bus. If the bus is in use, it waits for the bus to become free. In Ethernet terminology this is called *deference*. Once a station has started transmitting it acquires the channel, and after a delay equal to the end-to-end round trip propagation time of the network, a successful transmission without collision is guaranteed.

Before the packet has propagated throughout the network, a collision window exists during which two stations may begin transmitting unknown to each other. When a station

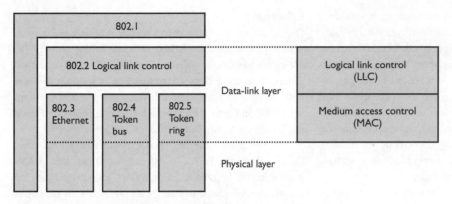

Fig. 11.58 Scope of the IEEE 802 standards for LANs.

Preamble (8 bytes)	Destination address (6 bytes)	Source address (6 bytes)	Type (2 bytes)	Data (variable)	CRC (4 bytes)

Fig. 11.59 Ethernet packet format.

Preamble (7 bytes)	SFD (1 byte)	Destination address (6 bytes)	Source address (6 bytes)	Length (2 bytes)	Data (variable)	CRC (4 bytes)

Fig. 11.60 IEEE 802.3 packet format.

realizes that its packet is being corrupted by another packet, it reinforces the collision by transmitting a *jam packet*. If it stopped transmitting immediately, the other transmitter might not detect the collision. The collision would be detected indirectly much later by the error-detecting code that forms part of the transmitted frame. This process is inefficient and wastes time. Sending a short jam packet makes the collision obvious to all listeners. After the jam packet has been sent, another attempt is made after a random delay. If repeated attempts fail, the random delay is increased as the sender tries to adapt to a busy channel.

The Ethernet's 10 Mbps data rate is low by today's standards. A new standard, IEEE 802.3u, operating at 100 Mbps was ratified in 1995, and work began on a standard for a gigabit Ethernet in the late 1990s.

Figure 11.59 describes an Ethernet packet that consists of six fields. The 8-byte preamble is a synchronizing pattern used by the electronics to detect the start of a frame and to derive a clock signal from it. The preamble consists of 7 bytes of alternating 1s and 0s followed by the pattern 10101011. Two address fields are provided, one for the source and one for the destination. A 6-byte (48-bit) address allows sufficient address space for each Ethernet node to have a unique address.

The *type* field is reserved for use by higher level layers to specify the protocol. The data field has a variable length, although the size of an Ethernet packet must be at least 64 bytes. The data field must be between 46 and 1500 bytes. The final field is a 4-byte cyclic redundancy checksum, CRC, which provides a very powerful error-detecting mechanism.

Figure 11.60 describes the format of a packet conforming to the IEEE's 802.3 standard, which is very similar to the original Ethernet packet. The preamble and start-of-frame delimiter are identical to the corresponding Ethernet preamble. The principal difference is that the 802.3 packet has a field that indicates the length of the data portion of the frame.

The 802.3 protocol covers layer 1 of the OSI reference model (the physical layer) and part of the data link layer called the *medium access control*, MAC. The IEEE 802 standards divide the data link layer into a medium access layer and a *logical link control*, LLC.

11.6.3 Flow control mechanisms in rings

A ring network connects all stations to each other in the form of a continuous loop. Unlike the stations of a bus network that listen passively to data on the bus unless it is meant for them, the stations of the ring must take an active part in all data transfers. When receiving incoming data a station must test the packet and decide whether to keep it for itself or to pass it on to its next neighbor. In general, the mechanisms used to determine which station may gain access to the ring are more varied than those for buses. Three popular control techniques are *token passing*, *register insertion*, and *slotted rings*. Contention control in the sense of bus networks is not found in rings.

Token rings

One of the fascinating things about LANs is the way in which many of their seemingly abstract technological aspects can be related to everyday life. A classic railway problem is the control of trains on a single line. Collisions occur if two trains travel in opposite directions from the ends of a single line. These collisions tend to be more harmful than those on data networks. One of the early solutions was to provide a metal ring or token for the stretch of line. Only the driver in possession of the token has a right to use the line. If a driver arrives at one end of the line and the token is not there the train must wait; if it is there the driver can pick it up, enter the line, and hang up the token at its other end. As long as the driver has the token, no one can enter the line behind the train or ahead of it. After the driver has hung up the token, another train can take it and go back down the line.

Token rings pass a special bit pattern (the token) round the ring from station to station. The station currently holding the token is the station that can transmit data if it so wishes. If it does not wish to take the opportunity to send data itself,

it passes the token on round the ring. For example, suppose the token has the special pattern 11111111, with zero stuffing used as in the case of HDLC to keep the pattern unique. A station on the ring wishing to transmit monitors its incoming traffic. When it has detected seven ones it inverts the last bit of the token and passes it on. Thus a pattern called a *connector* (11111110) passes on down the ring. The connector is created to avoid sending the eighth '1' and thereby passing on the token. The station holding the token may now transmit its data. After it has transmitted its data, it sends a new token down the ring. As there is only one token, contention cannot arise on the ring unless, of course, a station becomes antisocial and sends out a second token. In reality, a practical system is rather more complex, because arrangements must be included for dealing with lost tokens.

Register insertion rings

The structure of a node in a register insertion ring is illustrated in Fig. 11.61. A message to be transmitted is first loaded into a shift register. This shift register is, initially, not part of the ring. When the station detects that the ring is either idle or is at a point between two separate messages, it breaks the loop and inserts the shift register. The message to be transmitted is clocked out of its shift register at the same rate that data is moved round the ring. As the message leaves the shift register at one end, any data on the ring is shifted in at the other end. In effect, the register has lengthened the ring. Since the shift register is now part of the ring, it can neither be removed nor used to send other messages.

When the message has moved round the ring it eventually arrives in the originating shift register. At this instant the register can be switched out of the circuit and the message swallowed. If the message is ever damaged on its journey round the ring, the sender must wait for the ring to become idle before the shift register can be switched out.

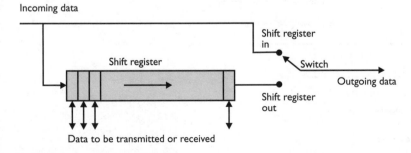

Fig. 11.61 The register insertion ring.

Slotted rings

In a *slotted ring* one or more packet carriers (the slots) are passed round the ring. The slotted ring is also known as a *Cambridge ring* because it was developed at the University of Cambridge. A carrier is not a physical entity like a railway carriage. It is just a special type of packet whose bits can be modified by the nodes through which it passes. Up to now we have considered that all packets (i.e. frames) are only generated or received, but never modified. Each carrier has a header, a tail, and a full/empty bit. Whenever an empty carrier passes a station wishing to transmit data, the station fills the packet with data and marks the carrier as full by setting the full/empty bit. At its destination the data is removed from the carrier and the full flag is cleared.

Figure 11.62 shows the format of packets used by the Cambridge ring. The first bit is a synchronization bit that denotes the start of the packet—rather like the start bit of asynchronous systems. The second bit is the full/empty bit. The third bit is used by a station called the *monitor*. A ring structure is moderately democratic but it needs a special station, the monitor, to generate empty packets on power-up and to ambush corrupted packets.

The packet includes an 8-bit destination address, followed by a 16-bit data field. Following the data field are a 2-bit control field and a single parity bit. Compared to the HDLC format or the Ethernet format, the packets flowing round the Cambridge ring are relatively crude.

Many papers were published on the relative advantages and disadvantages of ring- and bus-based local area networks in the 1980s. Some writers preferred the Ethernet, others the token ring. Some like the bus because it's very easy to extend; others wouldn't use it because it cannot guarantee the receipt of a message within a finite period, as it is theoretically possible for a message to suffer an infinite sequence of collisions. Other (wiser) engineers say that the form of a LAN is often unimportant as the interface between the user program and the LAN (i.e. the operating system) is normally much slower than the most primitive forms of LAN.

The IEEE 802.5 token ring

The IEEE has created a standard for the token ring LAN called 802.5. Figure 11.63 describes the format of an IEEE 802.5 frame. Two types of frame are supported—a three-octet frame (Fig. 11.63(a)) and a variable-length frame (Fig. 11.63(b)). Note that some of the standards for contention buses and token rings use the term *octet* rather than byte to describe an 8-bit element. Each frame begins and ends with a starting and ending delimiter that marks the frame's boundaries. The second octet provides access control (i.e. a token bit, a monitor bit, and priority bits). The short

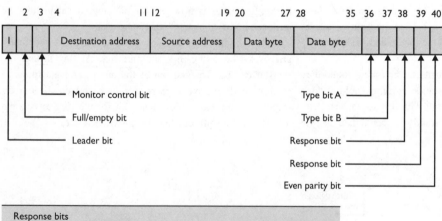

Response bits		
38	39	Response
0	0	Busy—destination node can't deal with packet
0	1	Accept—destination node accepts packet
1	0	Not selected
1	1	Ignore—no node has read the packet

Fig. 11.62 The format of data on the Cambridge ring.

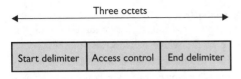

(a) Token format

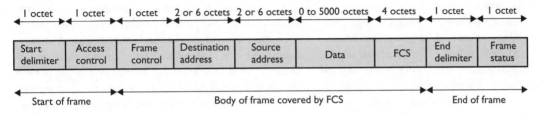

(b) Frame format

Fig. 11.63 Formats for 802.5 packets.

three-octet frame format is used to pass the control token round the ring from one node to the next. The IEEE 802.5 standard provides for prioritization. When a station wishes to transmit data it waits for a free token whose priority is less than its own.

The variable-length frame is used to control the ring and to carry data. Token ring addresses use the same 48-bit structure as the corresponding Ethernet frames.

An offshoot of the IEEE 802.5 standard is the FDDI (*fiber distributed data interface*) standard ISO 9314 that covers high-speed rings using fiber optic technology at 100 Mbps. An FDDI network uses *two* rings in parallel, allowing either simultaneous dual-ring operation to increase throughput or protection against a break in the ring.

A more recent network is the *Fiber Channel* adopted by IBM, Sun, and Hewlett-Packard. The Fiber Channel provides for data rates of up to 800 Mbps in a fully duplex mode. The maximum transmission path is determined by the data rate—the longer the path the lower the maximum data rate.

11.7 Routing techniques

How does a message get from one point in a network to its destination? Routing in a network is analogous to routing in everyday life; for example, you sometimes have to study a road map to find the optimum route to your destination. The analogy between network and computer routing is close in at least one sense—the shortest route isn't always the best.

Drivers avoid highly congested highways. Similarly, a network strives to avoid sending packets along a link that is either congested or costly.

Figure 11.64 describes a hypothetical network consisting of six nodes A to F and 10 data links. Suppose you wish to route a message from F to C. Some of the available routings are:

F–A–C

F–A–B–C

F–A–D–C

F–E–C

F–E–D–C

F–E–D–A–C

F–E–D–A–B–C

F–E–B–C

F–E–B–A–C

F–E–B–A–D–C

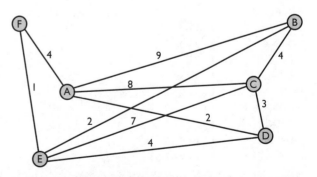

Fig. 11.64 Cost of routing in a network.

One of the simplest (and least efficient) ways of implementing routing involves a crude technique called *flooding*. When a node wishes to send a message, it sends the message on each of its links to adjacent nodes. Each node receiving the message copies the message to all its outgoing links (apart from the link to the node on which the message was received).

You can now see where the term flooding came from—a message is replicated at each junction and it soon becomes a flood or avalanche. Because messages multiply at each node, you have to provide a means of stopping the process. Messages are stamped with a 'best-before date' and deleted by nodes if they exceed it. Although flooding is the simplest possible routing strategy, it is inefficient because it wastes bandwidth. Flooding is not used by today's networks.

Suppose now we apply a *cost* to each of the routings. This cost is a figure-of-merit that might be determined by the reliability of a link, its latency (i.e. delay), or its actual cost (it might be rented). We have provided a number against each link in Fig. 11.64 to indicate its cost. If we now apply these costs to the routines, we get the figure shown in Table 11.6.

Table 11.6 indicates that the cheapest route is F to E to B to C, which is slightly cheaper than the more direct route F to E to C.

We've now explained that using the cheapest route between any two nodes can optimize the performance of a network. However, how do you find the cheapest route though the network, and what happens if the cost of a link changes (if every node attempts to use the same link its performance will fall and increase its cost)? Much research has been carried out into the routing of messages around complex networks. Here we can only mention some of the basic concepts of routing.

Centralized routing

A network with centralized routing uses a master station that has a knowledge of the whole network and the best routes between all nodes. The master station broadcasts the routing information to the other nodes. Let's see how this applies to the example of Fig. 11.64. Table 11.7 provides routing tables for nodes A to F. In each case we have calculated the cheapest route and the next node. Table 11.8 summarizes the information in Table 11.7 and gives the next node for any destination.

Consider the routing of a message from node A to B. At node A the router looks up the next destination for a message consigned to B and sends the packet to node F. Node F receives this packet and looks up the next node for a packet bound for B, which is E. At node E the packet is sent on the best route to D which is direct to B. The packet reaches B having followed the optimum route A to F to E to B.

Distributed routing

Getting a complete knowledge of a complex network is not easy. Another way of dealing with routing is to allow each node to build up its own database for the rest of the network. Initially each node knows only about its immediate neighbors and the cost to reach them. After a time, a node can request information from its immediate neighbors about their neighbors, and so on. Eventually, a complete picture of the network can be constructed.

The optimum route between any two points in a network isn't necessarily constant because the network itself is constantly changing. Nodes are added and removed. Links can be broken or become hopelessly congested. Maintaining a fixed table of optimum routes (called *static routing*) is less efficient than constantly updating routing information to cope best with the current conditions. This strategy is called *adaptive routing*.

11.7.1 IP (Internet protocol)

Although networks were originally developed for highly specialized applications such as reliable military communications systems and academic research tools, it's the Internet that's caught people's attention because of its impact on everyday life. The Internet began as a development of the US Defense Advanced Research Projects Agency, DARPA, in the 1960s. This project created and developed a small experimental network using packet switching called ARPANET (the 'D' for 'defense' has been dropped from the acronym). Research into the ARPANET was carried out at many universities and this network gradually evolved into what we now call the Internet. The protocol used for ARPANET's transport layer forms the basis of the Internet's *transmission control protocol*, TCP.

Route	Cost per segment	Total cost
F–A–C	4+8	12
F–A–B–C	4+9+4	17
F–A–D–C	4+2+3	9
F–E–C	1+7	8
F–E–D–C	1+4+3	8
F–E–D–A–C	1+4+2+8	15
F–E–D–A–B–C	1+4+2+9+4	20
F–E–B–C	1+2+4	7
F–E–B–A–C	1+2+9+8	20
F–E–B–A–D–C	1+2+9+2+3	17

Table 11.6 The cost of routing a message from node F to C in Fig. 11.64.

Node A			Node B		
Destination	Next node	Cost	Destination	Next node	Cost
B	F	7	A	E	7
C	D	5	C	C	4
D	D	2	D	E	6
E	F	5	E	E	2
F	F	4	F	E	3

Node C			Node D		
Destination	Next node	Cost	Destination	Next node	Cost
A	D	5	A	A	2
B	B	4	B	E	6
D	D	3	C	C	3
E	B	6	E	E	4
F	B	7	F	E	5

Node E			Node F		
Destination	Next node	Cost	Destination	Next node	Cost
A	F	5	A	A	4
B	B	2	B	E	3
C	B	6	C	E	7
D	D	4	D	E	5
F	F	1	E	E	1

Table 11.7 Routing tables for nodes A to F.

Source code	Destination node					
	A	B	C	D	E	F
A		F	D	D	F	F
B	E		C	E	E	C
C	D	B		D	B	B
D	A	E	C		E	E
E	F	B	B	D		F
F	A	E	E	E	E	

Table 11.8 Routing matrix (next node table).

The Internet links together millions of networks and individual users. In order to access the Internet, a node must use the TCP/IP protocol (transmission control protocol/Internet protocol) that corresponds to layers 4 and 3 of the OSI reference model, respectively. Some of the higher level protocols that make use of TCP/IP are TELNET (a remote login service that allows you to access a computer across the Internet), FTP (*file transfer protocol*) that allows you to exchange files across the Internet, and SMTP (*simple mail transfer protocol*) that provides electronic mail facilities. Here we provide only an overview of the TCP/IP layers.

Internet's network layer protocol, IP, routes a packet between nodes in a network. The packets used by the IP are *datagrams* and are handled by appropriate data link layer protocols—typically Ethernet protocols on LANs and X.25 protocols across public data networks (i.e. the telephone system).

Figure 11.65 describes the format of an IP packet (or frame) that is received from the data link layer below it and passed to the TCP transport layer above it.

IP's *version* field defines the version of the Internet protocol that created the current packet. This facility allows room for growth because improvements can be added as the state-of-the-art improved while still permitting older systems to access the network. The IP version widely used in the late 1990s was IPv4 and IPv6 was developed to deal some of the problems created by the Internet's increasing size and to provide for time-critical services such as real-time video and speech.

The *header length* defines the size of the header in multiples of 32-bit words (i.e. all fields preceding the data). The minimum length is five. Because the header must be a multiple of 32-bits, IP's padding field is used to supply 0 to 3 octets to force the header to fit a 32-bit boundary. The *datagram*

version	header length	service type	datagram length	
identification			flags	fragment offset
time-to-live		protocol	header checksum	
source IP address				
destination IP address				
options				padding
data (up to 64 K octets total in IP packet)				

Fig. 11.65 Structure of the IP layer packet.

length is a 16-bit value that specifies the length of the entire IP packet, which limits the maximum size of a packet to 64K octets. In practice, typical IP packets are below 1 kbyte.

The *service type* field tells the transport layer how the packet is to be handled; that is, priority, delay, throughput, and reliability. The service request allows the transport layer to choose between, for example, a link with a low delay or a link that is known to be highly reliable.

The *flags* and *fragment offset* fields are used to deal with *fragmentation*. Suppose a higher level layer uses larger packets than the IP layer. A packet has to be split up (i.e. fragmented) and transmitted in chunks by the IP. The fragmentation flags indicate that an IP packet is part of a larger unit that has to be reassembled, and the fragment offset indicates where the current fragment fits (remember that IP packets can be received out-of-order).

The *time-to-live* field corresponds to the packet's 'best-before date' and is used to specify the longest time that the packet can remain on the Internet. When a packet is created, it is given a finite life. Each time the packet passes a node, the time-to-live count is decremented. If the count reaches zero, the packet is discarded. This facility prevents packets circulating round the Internet endlessly.

The *protocol* field specifies the higher-level protocol that is using the current packet; for example, the TCP protocol has the value 6. This facility enables the destination node to pass the IP packet to the appropriate service.

The *header checksum* is used to detect errors in the header. Error checking in the data is performed by a higher level protocol. The checksum is the one's complement of the sum of all 16-bit integers in the header. When a packet is received the checksum is calculated and compared with the transmitted value. A checksum is a very crude means of providing error protection (it's not in the same league as the FCS) but it is very fast to compute.

The *source* and *destination IP address* fields provide the address of where the packet is coming from and where it's going. We will return to IP addressing later. The *options* field is, well, optional and allows the packet to request certain facilities. For example, you can request that the packet's route through the Internet be recorded or you can request a particular route though the network. Finally, the *data* field contains the information required by the next higher protocol.

IP routing

Both the IP source and destination addresses are 32 bits in version 4 of the Internet protocol. Version 6 will provide 128 bit addresses (that's probably enough to give each of the Earth's molecules its own Internet address).

An IPv4 address is unique and permits 2^{32} (over 4000 million) different addresses. When specifying an Internet address it's usual to divide the 32 bits into four 8-bit fields and convert each 8-bit field into a decimal number delimited by a period; for example, the IP address 11000111 10000000 01100000 00000000 corresponds to 199.128.96.0.

Although an IP address provides 2^{32} unique values, it doesn't allow up to 4000 million nodes (or users) to exist on the Internet because not all addresses are available. An IP address is a hierarchical structure designed to facilitate the routing of a packet through the Internet and is divided into four categories, as Fig. 11.66 demonstrates.

Internet addresses have two fields—a network address and a node address. Class A Internet protocol addresses use a 7-bit network identifier and then divide each network into 2^{24} different nodes. Class B addresses can access one of $2^{14} = 16$K networks each with 64K nodes, and class C addresses select one of $2^{12} = 4096$ networks with 254 nodes.

You can easily see how inefficient this arrangement is. Although only 128 networks can use a class A address, each network gets 16 million node addresses, whether they are needed or not. Class A and B addresses have long since been allocated (removing large numbers of unique addresses from the pool). This leaves only a rapidly diminishing pool of class C addresses (until the IPv6 protocol becomes more widely used).

The end user doesn't directly make use of a numeric Internet address. Logical Internet addresses are written in

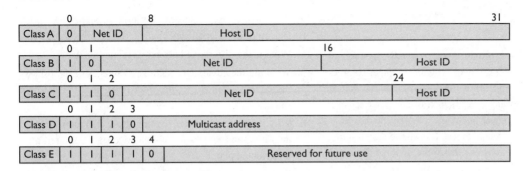

Fig. 11.66 Structure of an IP address.

Source port		Destination port	
Sequence number			
Acknowledgement number			
Data offset	Reserved	Flags	Window
Checksum		Urgent pointer	
Options			Padding
Data			

Fig. 11.67 Structure of TCP header.

the form *user@host.department.institution.domain*. The way in which these logical addresses are mapped to physical addresses is beyond the scope of this chapter.

Transmission control protocol

TCP performs a level 4 transport layer function by interfacing to the user and host's applications processes at each end of the Net. In many ways the TCP is rather like an operating system because it carries out functions such as opening, maintaining, and closing the channel. The TCP takes data from the user at one end of the Net and hands it to the IP layer below for transmission. At the other end of the Net, the TCP takes data from the IP layer and passes it to the user. Figure 11.67 describes the transport header.

The *source* and *destination* port addresses provide application addresses. Each node (host) might have several application programs running on it, and each application is associated with a port. This means you can run several applications, each using the Internet, on a computer at any instant.

The *sequence number* ensures that messages can be assembled in sequence because it contains the byte number of the first byte in the data. The *acknowledgement number* indicates the byte sequence number the receiving TCP node expects to receive and, therefore, acknowledges the receipt of all

previous bytes. This arrangement is analogous to the HDLC protocol used by layer 2 protocols.

The *offset* defines the size of the TCP header and, therefore, the start of the data field. The *flags* field contains 6 bits that control the operation of the TCP; for example, by indicating the last data segment or by breaking the link. The *window* field tells the receiving node how many data bytes the sending node can accept in return. The *checksum* provides basic error correction for the transport layer. The *options* field defines TCP options. The *padding* field ensures that the header fits into a 32-bit boundary.

The *urgent pointer* field is used in conjunction with the URG flag bit. If the URG bit is set, the urgent pointer provides a 16-bit offset from the sequence number in the current TCP header. This provides the sequence number of the last byte in urgent data (a facility used to provide a sort of interrupt facility across the Internet). The host receiving a message with its URG bit set should pass it to the higher layers ahead of any currently buffered data.

Although the TCP protocol forms the backbone of the Internet, it is rather old and has its origin in the days of the ARPANET. In particular, the TCP's error-detecting checksum is almost worthless because it isn't as powerful as the data link layer's FCS error-detecting mechanism. TCP plus IP headers are 40 bytes or more and these add a significant overhead to short data segments.

Summary

In this chapter we have provided an overview of some of the aspects of interest to those involved with computer communications networks. Computer networks is a subject that is advancing as rapidly as any other branch of computer science, because it increases the power of computer systems and exploits many of today's growing technologies. It is all too easy to think of computer communications as a hardware-oriented discipline centered almost exclusively on the transmission of signals from point A to point B. Modern computer communications networks have software components that far outweigh their hardware components in terms of complexity and sometimes even cost. In this chapter we have introduced the ideas behind the seven layers of the ISO basic reference model for open systems interconnection and have described protocols for the bottom two layers.

Problems

1. If the cost of a computer and all its peripherals is so low today, why is the field of computer communications expanding so rapidly?

2. What is the meaning of a *protocol* and why are protocols so important in the world of communications?

3. What is the difference between a WAN and a LAN?

4. What is an *open* system?

5. Why has the ISO model for OSI proved so important in the development of computer communications?

6. What are the differences between the transport and network layers of the ISO reference model?

7. Why is the physical layer of the OSI model different from all the other layers?

8. What is a virtual connection?

9. What are the differences between half-duplex and full-duplex transmission modes? How is it possible to make a half-duplex system look like a full-duplex system?

10. What is the difference between phase and frequency modulation?

11. What are the types of noise that affect a data link? Which types of noise are artificial and what are natural? If you were comparing a satellite link and a telephone link, what do you think are the effect, type, and consequences of noise on each link?

12. If a channel has a sampled impulse response of 0.3 1.0 −0.3 0.3, and the vector 1, 1, 1, −1, −1, 0−1, 1, 0, −1 is transmitted over this channel, what is the received vector?

13. Why cannot users transmit any type of signal they wish (i.e. amplitude, frequency characteristics) over the PSTN?

14. What is the difference between DTE and DCE?

15. What are the advantages and disadvantages of the following communications media: fiber optic link, twisted pair, satellite link?

16. Why is a SYN character required by a character-oriented data link, and why is a SYN character not required by a bit-oriented data link?

17. What is bit stuffing and how is it used to ensure transparency?

18. What are the advantages and disadvantages of LANs based on the ring and bus topologies?

19. What is the meaning of CSMA/CS in the context of a mechanism for handling collisions on a LAN?

20. The maximum range of a line-of-sight microwave link, d, is given by the formula $d^2 = 2r \cdot h + h^2$, where r is the radius of the Earth and h is the height of the antenna above the Earth's surface. This formula assumes that one antenna is at surface level and the other at height h. Show that this formula is correct. *Hint*: it's a simple matter of trigonometry.

21. For each of the following bit rates determine the period of one bit in the units stated.

Bit rate	Unit
(a) 100 bps	ms
(b) 1 kbps	ms
(c) 56 kbps	μs
(d) 100 Mbps	ns

22. Each of the following time values represents one bit. For each value give the corresponding bit rate expressed in the units stated.

Element duration	Unit of bit rate
(a) 1 s	bps
(b) 10 μs	kbps
(c) 10 μs	Mbps
(d) 15 ns	Gbps

23. For each of the following systems calculate the bit rate.

(a) 300 baud	2-level signal
(b) 600 baud	4-level signal
(c) 9600 baud	256-level signal

24. The ISO reference model has seven layers. Is that too many, too few, or just right?

25. Define an open system and provide three examples of open systems.

26. If a signal has a signal-to-noise ratio of 50 dB and the power of the signal is 1 mW, what is the power of the noise component?

27. For the network of Fig. 11.68 calculate the lowest cost route between any pairs of nodes.

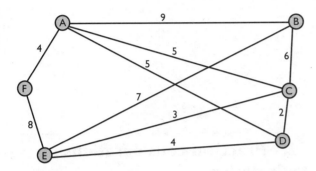

Fig. 11.68 Routing in a network.

28. Suppose the network of Fig. 11.68 used *flooding* to route its packets. Show what would happen if a packet were to be sent from node F to node C.

29. A network has a bandwidth of 3400 Hz and a signal-to-noise ratio of 40 dB. What is the maximum theoretical data rate that the channel can support?

30. Shannon's work on the capacity of a channel relates to so-called white Gaussian noise (e.g. thermal noise). Many telephone channels suffer from impulse noise (switching transients that appear as clicks). Do you think that (for the same noise power) such a channel would have a better information-carrying capacity than predicted by Shannon?

31. Why is a *checksum* error detector so much worse than a *cyclic redundancy code*?

Chapter 12

....

Advanced topics

In this final chapter we look at four aspects of computer hardware that don't fit well into the mainstream of this text—the electrical characteristics of gates, testing logic circuits, reliability, and the analog–digital interface. The first three topics deal with practical aspects of systems and the final topic demonstrates how computers process analog information. Although these topics are often omitted from introductory texts, we have included an overview here because of their importance.

We begin with the *electrical characteristics* of gates. Gates aren't perfect logical devices—these devices have real-world characteristics that set limits on their performance. We show how a range of electrical signals represent the logical 0 and 1 levels and how gates distort digital signals. Like any other product, gates can sometimes fail. We therefore include a short introduction to some of the ways in which circuits can be tested.

How often do systems fail? An astronaut, when asked how it felt to be strapped into his space capsule atop thousands of tons of explosive propellants, replied, 'How would you feel sitting on top of a million critical components, each supplied by the company that put in the lowest tender?' Systems designers need to be able to predict how likely their systems are to fail. *Reliability theory* tells us how we can predict the behavior of large numbers of components over a given time span and enables us to determine how likely a system is to fail if we know the reliability of its individual components. Moreover, we can use reliability theory to construct systems that are less likely to fail.

When we looked at input and output devices in Chapter 8, we mentioned that the real world uses analog signals. The last part of this chapter shows how analog signals are converted into digital form for processing in a computer and how digital signals can be converted back into analog signals. In particular we introduce one of today's most important areas of digital engineering, *digital signal processing* (DSP).

12.1 Practical considerations in logic design

A student undertaking an introductory course in logic design or reading an elementary text on Boolean algebra might be left with the impression that designing a digital system involves little more than simplifying a few Boolean equations, turning the results into a circuit diagram, and then putting it all together. In practice this is not so.

The real-world designer is subject to several constraints. Logic elements are not only characterized in terms of Boolean algebra—they have other important properties that can't be neglected. Moreover, the designer isn't interested in just any solution, he or she is interested in the cheapest solution. The blind application of conventional Boolean algebra does not always lead to the most cost-effective solution to a problem.

We now take a brief look at some of the characteristics of logic elements that are of greatest interest to the design engineer. This section isn't a rigorous approach covering all the practical aspects of digital design, but is intended as an informal guide to some of the areas of digital design that concern the engineer.

12.1.1 Electrical characteristics of gates

A glance at a manufacturer's data sheet for even the simplest logic element reveals several pages of information. This data sheet is really a set of promises from the manufacturer to the user that indicate how the gate will perform. Table 12.1 gives the basic parameters of a typical logic element.

Logic elements are produced by a number of different manufacturing processes. One of the first types of logic element was called TTL, *transistor–transistor logic* (the term 'transistor–transistor' indicates that the transistors in the circuit are directly connected to each other). Over the years, different versions of this family were produced—some are fast

Temperature range (commercial)	−40°C to 85°C			
Temperature range (military)	−55°C to 125°C			
Operating voltage	2 V to 5.5 V			
Maximum ratings				
Storage temperature	−65°C to 150°C			
Supply voltage	−0.5 V to 7 V			
D.C. input current	−20 mA			

D.C. characteristics (at Vcc = 5 V)		Min	Typ	Max	Unit
V_{OH}	output high voltage	4.4	4.5		V
V_{OL}	output low voltage			0.1	V
V_{IH}	input high voltage	3.85			V
V_{IL}	input low voltage			1.65	V
I_{IH}	input high current			1	μA
I_{IL}	input low current			−1	μA
I_{OH}	output high current			−8	mA
I_{OL}	output low current			8	mA
Switching characteristics			Typ	Max	Unit˙
t_{LH}	low-to-high delay		3.7	5.5	ns
t_{HL}	high-to-low delay		3.7	5.5	ns

Table 12.1 Electrical characteristics of an AHC logic element.

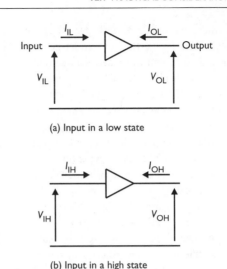

(a) Input in a low state

(b) Input in a high state

Fig. 12.1 Voltages and current flow in logic circuits.

and some use low power. A widely used form of TTL is called low-power Schottky TTL or '*LS TTL*'. Microprocessors and memory elements are manufactured by NMOS and CMOS technologies whose properties differ from TTL. Fortunately, NMOS and CMOS chips can be connected to TTL logic elements because they employ similar signal levels to represent 1s and 0s.

The specific details of the manufacture and the properties of various logic families are well beyond the scope of this book so we will just look at a representative member of a typical family. We describe the characteristics of the *Advanced High-Speed CMOS* logic family, AHC, that has superseded LS TTL.

The operating temperature range tells designers how cold or how hot they can let their equipment become without the characteristics of the logic element drifting outside their stated ranges. Considerations of temperature are often of little importance to the designers of domestic equipment that is maintained at approximately 10 °C to 25 °C. However, automobile manufacturers may regard the thermal behavior of logic elements as one of their most important parameters. Companies have to sell their automobiles in markets as far apart as Alaska and the Sahara.

Figure 12.1 shows a simple buffer element in both logical 0 and 1 output states. We have indicated the voltages at the inputs and outputs and the current that flows in the inputs and outputs. Note that, *by convention*, current is defined as flowing into a gate. For example, in Fig. 12.1(a) the current flowing into an input in a low state is defined as I_{IL}. However, in real TTL gates the current flows *out* of an input when

the input is in a low state. Consequently, the value of I_{IL} is negative (i.e. current flowing into a gate is positive and current flowing out of a gate is negative).

The voltage characteristics of a logic element define the *worst-case* input and output conditions. The term 'worst-case' means that no device will have parameters less good than the quoted worst-case values (if it does, it is faulty). Ideally, we would like logic elements to have logical 0 outputs of 0 V and logical 1 outputs of +5 V (i.e. the same values of power supply levels) to provide the greatest discrimination between digital signals. The ACH logic element in Table 12.1 doesn't display the maximum discrimination between its logical 0 and logical 1 output states. For example, V_{OL} is defined as the maximum output voltage when the output is in a 0 state. V_{OL} is quoted as 0.1 V, which implies that the output for a logical 0 may lie anywhere in the range 0 V to 0.1 V. The low-level output will never be greater than 0.1 V unless, of course, the device is faulty.

Similarly, V_{IL} defines the maximum input voltage that an element will reliably recognize as a logical 0. A V_{IL} of 1.65 V means that inputs in the range 0 V to 1.65 V are guaranteed to be interpreted as a logical 0. Note that V_{IL} is quoted as 1.65 V and V_{OL} as 0.1 V. The difference between these two figures is called the *noise margin* of the device. If we know that an output in a low state will be 0.1 V or less, and that an input will see a voltage of up to 1.65 V as a low state, then up to $1.65 − 0.1 = 1.55$ V may be added to the output without any error occurring. The additional 1.55 V allows for noise in the system. Noise is the general term given to all unwanted signals.

Another important group of electrical parameters in Table 12.1 is those concerning the flow of current between gates. In an ideal world no current flows between the output of a gate and the input to which it is connected. Unfortunately, in order to maintain a given logic level, a gate's input must absorb some current from the output driving the input; that is, current flows between an output and one or more inputs. Because an output can supply only a limited current, the number of inputs that can be connected to an output is finite.

Table 12.1 tells us that the maximum current flowing into the input terminal of a gate in a high state, I_{IH}, is $1\,\mu A$ $(1.0 \times 10^{-6}\,A)$. The maximum current flowing into the output terminal of a gate in a logic 1 state, I_{OH}, is given as $-8\,mA$. Remember that, by convention, current flowing into a gate is defined as positive and the minus sign indicates that current flows out of the gate. Current flows into an output in a logical 0 state and out of an output in a logical 1 state. However, we frequently forget the sign of the current into or out of a gate, since we are usually more concerned with the magnitude of a current rather than its sign (i.e. direction).

A fundamental difference exists between I_{IH} and I_{OH}. I_{IH} represents the maximum current taken by the input of a gate, whereas I_{OH} represents the maximum current that may be supplied by the output circuit of a gate. The actual output current of a gate will always be a value between 0 and I_{OH} or I_{OL}. When the output of a gate is connected to the input of another gate the output current of one gate must be exactly equal to the input current of the gate to which it is connected. A basic law of electronics states that the current flowing along a given path must be the same at all points along the path. Figure 12.2(a) illustrates the electrical conditions of a gate with a logical 0 output driving two inputs and Fig. 12.2(b) illustrates the electrical conditions of a gate with a logical 1 output driving four inputs.

When several inputs are connected to one output, the total current drawn by the inputs must not exceed the maximum current that the output can supply. If there are n inputs, it follows that I_{OH} must be greater than nI_{IH} for reliable operation. For ACT logic in the high-level state, one output can supply enough current to drive $8\,mA/1\,\mu A = 8000$ inputs. Older LS TTL logic elements have typical values of $I_{OH}=400\,\mu A$ and $I_{IH}=-40\,\mu A$ giving a maximum drive capacity of only 10 inputs.

The four basic equations that govern the electrical operation of gates are:

$$V_{OL} < V_{IL}$$
$$V_{OH} > V_{IH}$$
$$I_{OL} > nI_{IL} \text{ for } n \text{ inputs connected to one output}$$
$$I_{OH} > nI_{IH} \text{ for } n \text{ inputs connected to one output.}$$

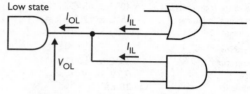

Low state

(a) An output in a low state drives two inputs

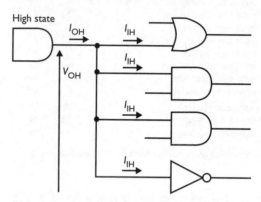

High state

(b) An output in a high state drives three inputs

Fig. 12.2 Current flow between inputs and outputs.

12.1.2 Effect of finite propagation delays on logic elements

Another important set of properties of all logic elements is their *timing characteristics*. Up to now we've assumed that if a number of Boolean values are applied to the input terminals of a circuit, the correct output will appear instantaneously at the output of the circuit. In other words, the circuit's output is determined only by the Boolean equations of the gates. In practice this is not so. All real gates suffer from an effect called *propagation delay* and it takes about 5 ns for a change in an input signal to affect the gate's output. One nanosecond is an unbelievably short period of time in human terms—but not in electronic terms. The speed of light is $3 \times 10^8\,m/s$ and electrical signals in computers travel at about 70 percent of the speed of light. In one nanosecond a signal travels about 20 cm.

The propagation delay introduced by logic elements is one of the greatest problems designers have to contend with. We have already seen some of the effects of delays when we introduced clocked flip-flops. Figure 12.3 illustrates the effect of propagation delay on a single inverter where a pulse with sharp (i.e. vertical) rising and falling edges is applied to the input of an inverter. An inverted pulse is produced at its output and is delayed with respect to the input pulse. Moreover, the edges of the output pulse are no longer vertical. The time t_{HL}

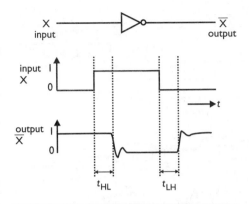

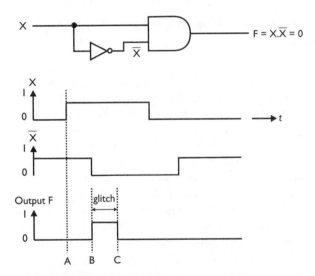

Fig. 12.3 Effect of propagation delay on an inverter.

Fig. 12.4 Side effect of propagation delay.

AND gate are both true, and its output rises to a logical 1 from points B to C (after its own internal delay). The short pulse at the output of the AND gate is called a *glitch*, and can be very troublesome in digital systems. There are two solutions to this problem. One is to apply special design techniques to the Boolean logic to remove the glitch. The other is to connect the output to a flip-flop, and to clock the flip-flop after any glitches have died away.

12.1.3 Testing digital circuits

A significant part of the cost of a digital system is its testing. Why should testing be so expensive? After all, a system either works or it doesn't. If it doesn't work it can easily be scrapped and replaced more economically than repairing it.

Although it's easy to test a light bulb by plugging it into a socket, it's much more difficult to test all but the most primitive of digital systems. Consider a small memory element with 10 address lines and 8 data outputs (i.e. 1 kbyte). How many tests do we need to perform to verify that the memory is working correctly? Obviously the memory can be tested by writing a pattern into each of its $2^{10} = 1024$ locations and then reading the pattern back. That is, the test requires a total of 1024 read and 1024 write cycles.

But wait a moment. How do we know that the memory will store every possible data pattern in each possible word location? The test must be extended by writing all possible data values into a location before testing the next location. In this case there are $2^8 = 256$ tests per location, or $2^8 \times 2^{10} = 2^{18}$ tests altogether.

At last we have now thoroughly tested the memory component. No we have not! Some memories display a fault called *pattern sensitivity*, in which writing data to one location affects the contents of another location. You can test for pattern sensitivity by writing a data pattern to the location we wish to test and then filling all other locations with a different data pattern. We then reread the data in the location under test to see whether it has changed. So for each of our 2^{18} tests, we must write a different pattern in all the other $2^{10} - 1$ word cells. This gives us a total of $2^{18} \times 2^{10}$ or 2^{28} tests. If we were to consider a 1 Mbyte memory, it would require $2^8 \times 2^{20} \times 2^{20} = 2^{48}$ tests (a gigantic number).

This example demonstrates that it's effectively impossible to test any reasonably complex digital system with external inputs and internal states. Even if tests could be carried out at a rate of over 10 million/second, most complex digital systems (e.g. a microprocessor chip) would take longer to test than the anticipated life of the entire universe. A way out of this dilemma is to perform a test that provides a reasonable

represents the time delay between the rising edge of the input pulse and the point at which the output of the gate has reached V_{OL}. Similarly, t_{LH} represents the time between the falling edge of the input and the time at which the output reaches V_{OH}.

You might think that the effect of time delays on the passage of signals through gates simply reduces the speed at which a digital system may operate. Unfortunately, propagation delays have more sinister effects as demonstrated by Fig. 12.4. By the rules of Boolean algebra the output of the AND gate is $X \cdot \overline{X}$ and should be permanently 0.

Now examine its timing diagram. At point A the input, X, rises from 0 to 1. However, the X input to the AND gate does not fall to 0 for a time which is equal to the propagation delay of the inverter. Consequently, for a short time the inputs of the level of confidence in its ability to detect a large fraction of possible faults without requiring an excessive amount of time. The first step in devising such a test is to distinguish between the idea of a *defect* and a *fault*. A real system fails because of a *defect* in its manufacture. For example, a digital system may fail because of a defect at the component level (a crystal defect in a silicon chip), or at the system level (a solder splash joining together two adjacent tracks on a printed circuit board). The observed failure is termed a *fault*.

Although there are an infinite number of possible *defects* that might cause a system to fail, their effects (i.e. faults) are relatively few. In simpler terms, an automobile may suffer from many defects, but many of these defects result in a single observable *fault*—the car doesn't move. That is, a fault is the observable effect due to a defect. A digital system can be described in terms of a fault model (i.e. the list of observable effects of defects). Typical faults are:

1. Stuck-at-1   The input or output of a circuit remains in a logical 1 state independently of all other circuit conditions. This is usually written s_a_1.

2. Stuck-at-0   In this case the input or output is permanently stuck in a 0 state (i.e. s_a_0).

3. Bridging faults   Two inputs or outputs of a circuit are effectively connected together and cannot assume independent logic levels. That is, they must both be 0 or 1.

It is possible to devise a longer list of fault models, but the stuck-at fault model is able to detect a surprisingly large number of defects. In other words, if we test a system by considering all possible stuck-at-1 and stuck-at-0 faults, we are likely to detect almost all of the probable defects.

The sensitive path test

A *sensitive path* between an input and an output is constructed to make the output a function of the input being tested (i.e. the output is sensitive to a *change* in the input). Figure 12.5(a) illustrates a circuit with three gates and six inputs A to J. The sensitive path to be tested is between input A and output K.

Figure 12.5(b) demonstrates how we have chosen the sensitive path by ensuring that a change in input A is propagated through the circuit. By setting AND gate 1's B and C inputs high, input A is propagated through this gate to the E input of AND gate 2. The second input of AND gate 2, F, must be set high to propagate E through gate 2. Output G of AND gate 2 is connected to input H of the three-input OR gate 3. In this case, inputs I and J must be set low to propagate input H (i.e. A) through OR gate 3.

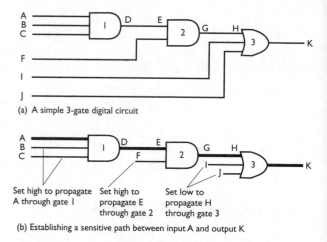

(a) A simple 3-gate digital circuit

Set high to propagate   Set high to   Set low to
A through gate I   propagate E   propagate H
     through gate 2   through gate 3

(b) Establishing a sensitive path between input A and output K

Fig. 12.5 Using sensitive path analysis to test digital circuits.

By setting inputs B, C, F, I, J to 1, 1, 1, 0, 0 the output becomes K = A and, therefore, by setting A to 0 and then to 1, we can test the sensitive path between A and K and determine whether any A stuck_at fault exists.

A *fault list* can be prepared for the circuit, which, in this case, might consist of A s_a_0, A s_a_1, B s_a_0, B s_a_1, ... A convenient notation for the fault list is: A/0, A/1, B/0, B/1, ..., etc. The '/' is read as 'stuck at'.

To test for A s_a_0 (i.e. A/0), the other inputs are set to the values necessary to create a sensitive path and A is switched from 0 to 1. If the output changes state, A is not stuck at zero. The same test also detects A/1.

Fault tests are designed by engineers (possibly using CAD techniques) and can be implemented either manually or by means of computer controlled *automatic test equipment* (ATE). This equipment sets up the appropriate input signals and tests the output against the expected value. We can specify the sensitive path for A in the circuit of Fig. 12.5(b) as $A \cdot B \cdot C \cdot F \cdot \bar{I} \cdot \bar{J}$.

It's not always possible to test digital circuits by this sensitive path analysis because of the *topological* properties of some digital circuits. For example, a digital signal may take more than one route through a circuit and certain faults may lead to a situation in which an error is canceled at a particular node. Similarly, it's possible to construct logic circuits that have an undetectable fault. Figure 12.6 provides an example of such a circuit. This type of undetectable fault is due to *redundancy* in the circuit and can be eliminated by redesigning the circuit. Alternatively, a circuit can be made easier to test by connecting some of its internal nodes to pins so that they can be directly examined.

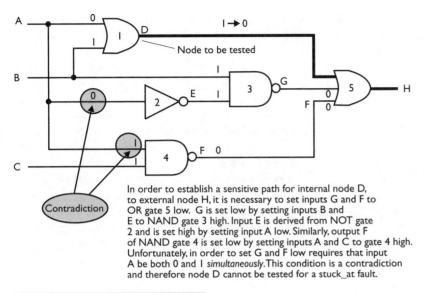

In order to establish a sensitive path for internal node D, to external node H, it is necessary to set inputs G and F to OR gate 5 low. G is set low by setting inputs B and E to NAND gate 3 high. Input E is derived from NOT gate 2 and is set high by setting input A low. Similarly, output F of NAND gate 4 is set low by setting inputs A and C to gate 4 high. Unfortunately, in order to set G and F low requires that input A be both 0 and 1 *simultaneously*. This condition is a contradiction and therefore node D cannot be tested for a stuck_at fault.

Fig. 12.6 Circuit with an undetectable fault.

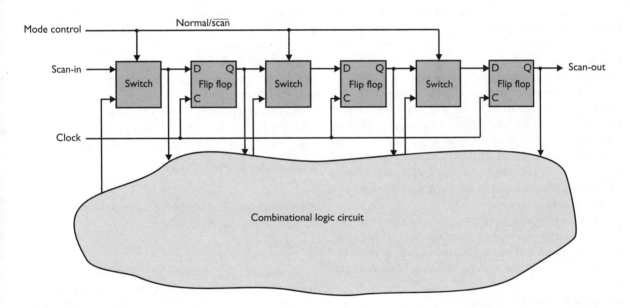

Fig. 12.7 Testing sequential circuits.

Sequential circuits are particularly difficult to test, partially because flip-flops exhibit more complex behavior than simple gates, but mainly because they have *internal states* that can't normally be observed from outside the circuit. One solution to the testing of sequential circuits is to design them with in-built test facilities. The sequential circuit has a means of preloading its internal registers with known values and a means of observing the outputs of the flip-flops. In practice, four control signals might be used: a run/test input to force the normal mode or the test mode, a clock input that shifts data into or out of the circuit, a serial input that can be used to preload the internal flip-flops, and an output that can be used to observe the outputs of the internal flip-flops. Figure 12.7 illustrates the structure of a sequential circuit with built-in test facilities.

The type of testing described by Fig. 12.7 is called *boundary scan* because the circuits that perform the test are located just inside a chip's input and output pins. In the mid-1980s the Joint Test Action Group (JTAG) was set up to promote a standard for testing logic circuits. This standard became IEEE Standard 1149.1.

12.2 Computers and reliability

Reliability is one of the major factors in both the selection of components for incorporation in a computer and in its actual design. The domestic consumer is not normally directly conscious of the importance of reliability. When I go into a camera shop, the salesperson says 'Nice camera, F1.4, self-focusing, automatic exposure, motor drive…'. I buy it. It breaks down a week later.

When you buy computer equipment, you don't ask the salesperson about irrelevant or frivolous features. Instead, you are concerned with parameters such as its *mean time between failure* (MTBF) and its *mean time to repair* (MTTR), because professional equipment has to operate continuously for long periods of time. The failure of computer equipment can be expensive, embarrassing, or even disastrous. The failure of a computer in an online hotel reservation system leads to a direct loss of income and an additional loss in the form of goodwill, whereas the total failure of a computer operating control rods in a nuclear reactor is too frightening to contemplate. Before we deal with reliability formally, note the word *total* in the previous sentence—later we shall see how systems can be made more reliable by choosing designs that tolerate a partial failure of the system.

We take a brief look at the concept of reliability in the next section. The first part of this section uses a little mathematics—you can skip that part if you wish because it's the conclusions that matter rather than the derivation of the formulas.

Introduction to reliability

There are two widely held personal theories of reliability. The first theory states that demons live in all manufactured devices and that their aim is to cause a breakdown at the worst possible time (for example, an aircraft's weather radar would never dream of failing unless the aircraft was about to fly into a thunderstorm). The second theory is that a device is designed by its manufacturers to fail at the precise moment its guarantee ends.

Neither of these theories is entirely true. A device may fail from one of many causes and it's almost impossible to say when any particular device is going to fail. However, when dealing with large numbers of nominally identical devices, we can say something about the *average* device. The reliability of a device is defined as $1-p$, where p is the probability of its failure in a given time. For example, if there is a one in ten chance of a particular component failing within a year (i.e. $p=0.1$), it may be said to be $1-0.1=0.9$ or 90 percent reliable. We will assume that the value of the failure rate is *constant*. Later, we point out that this statement is only approximately true.

Consider the reliability of a very large number of identical components (e.g. memory chips). After a time t, N of these chips are still working and the rest have failed. The change of N as a function of time is represented by dN/dt, and is negative because N is decreasing. The ratio of the rate of decrease of N to the population of working devices is called the *failure rate*, L, and is denoted by:

$$L = -\frac{dN}{dt}/N$$

The failure rate is often expressed in units of failures percent per 1000 hours, although the period of time varies from application to application. For example, if a component is said to exhibit a failure rate of 0.003 percent per 1000 hours, a batch of 1 000 000 components can be expected to show 30 failures after 1000 hours of use.

We can write this expression for the failure rate in the form $dN/N = -L dt$. Assuming (for the moment) that the failure rate is constant, the expression can be integrated to give

$\log N = -Lt + C$, where C is a constant of integration or $N = e^{-Lt+C} = e^{-Lt} \times e^C = Ke^{-Lt}$, where $K = e^C$.

K represents the initial number of components at $t=0$ and is normally written N_0. We now have

$$N = N_0 e^{-Lt}$$

Incidentally, this equation also describes the decay of radioactive material (i.e. it calculates how much radioactive material remains as time passes). Figure 12.8 illustrates the effect of this so-called *exponential decay*, where half the remaining population fails after every T units of time. The value of T is called the component's 'half-life'.

If we define the reliability, $r(t)$, of a batch of N_0 components as N/N_0 (that is, the current survivors divided by the original population) then we can write

$$r(t) = e^{-Lt}$$

A more useful concept than failure rate is *mean time between failure*, MTBF, because it gives an idea of the

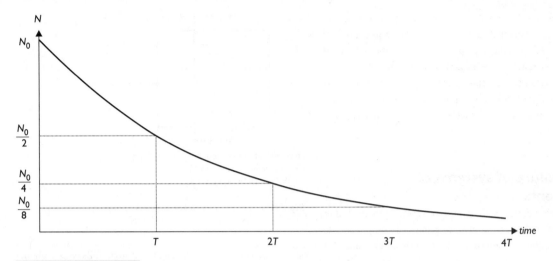

Fig. 12.8 Exponential decay.

expected lifetime of a component. MTBF is obtained by adding together the lifetime of every component and taking the average value. For N_0 components, we calculate the MTBF as

$$\frac{\sum_{i=1}^{N_0} \text{life of component } i}{N_0} = \int_0^\infty r(t)\mathrm{d}t$$

Integrating this expression yields $\text{MTBF} = m = 1/L$. We can now express the reliability of a batch of components as $r(t) = \mathrm{e}^{-t/m}$. The value of the mean time between failure, m, is obtained by *measurement*; that is, the failure rate of a batch of components must be measured by observing their behavior. Of course, the component you buy may not be a student of statistics and may therefore fail at the earliest inconvenient moment.

Although it's desirable to have components with a large MTBF, it's just as important to have components or systems that can be rapidly repaired when they do fail. Another useful parameter is the MTTR (*mean time to repair*), also called MTRF (*mean time to repair a fault*). These two parameters can be combined to give the *availability* or *uptime ratio* of a system; that is,

$$\text{availability} = \frac{\text{MTBF}}{\text{MTBF} + \text{MTTR}}$$

For example, if $\text{MTBF} = 8000\,\text{h}$ and $\text{MTTR} = 4\,\text{h}$, the availability is $8000/(8000 + 4) = 0.9995 = 99.95$ percent.

We have assumed that that the failure rate, L, and therefore m, is a constant. In practice, this is not entirely true. Figure 12.9 shows the classic *bathtub curve* of the failure rate of a component as a function of time. The left-hand part of the curve describes the component's *infant mortality* and

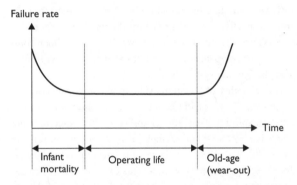

Fig. 12.9 The reliability curve.

corresponds to the initial high failure rate in a batch of components due to defects in manufacturing. The flat portion of the curve corresponds to a constant failure rate and represents the useful life of the batch of components. The rise in failure rate at the end of the batch's lifetime corresponds to old age and is due to the wearing out of components.

It's now common for manufacturers to *burn in* some of their components before selling them. That is, the components are powered up and operated for several days before they are sold in order to get them through the infant mortality region. The burn-in process may take place at a higher than normal operating temperature to accelerate the ageing. Components failing during the burn-in period are discarded and the buyer gets a more reliable component. Of course, components that have been burnt-in are appreciably more expensive than components straight off the production line.

The failure of components is a function of temperature and it has been observed that an increase in the temperature of components reduces their reliability. Since the effect of temperature on reliability is remarkably predictable (this has been demonstrated by experiments and is in line with the thermal behavior of molecules), it is possible to carry out accelerated ageing tests on components simply by raising their temperature.

12.2.1 Failure of systems of components

Everything we've just said would be useless to computer engineers if it couldn't be applied to groups of components to enable the designer to determine the overall failure rate of a system made up of many components with known failure rates.

Suppose a system is composed of two components, r_1 and r_2. If we know that the reliability of these components is r_1 and r_2, respectively, we can calculate the reliability of the system. Assume that the system, as a whole, fails if either component r_1 or component r_2 fails. For example, a car will fail if either the ignition system fails or the fuel system fails.

The reliability of a system made up of components operating 'in series' (i.e. one out, all out) is the *product* of their individual reliabilities. Thus, the reliability of our two-component system is $r = r_1 \times r_2$. For example, if r_1 is 99 percent reliable and r_2 is 95 percent reliable, the overall reliability is $0.99 \times 0.95 = 0.94$, or 94 percent. This formula is reassuringly in line with common sense. The overall reliability is dependent on the lowest reliability in the expression—that is, the system is as good as its weakest link. The reliability of a system made up of links of components operating in series is given in Fig. 12.10.

12.2.2 Increasing reliability through redundancy

It is possible to design a system that fails only when more than one component fails. Such a system involves *redundancy* or *backup* and is represented by Fig. 12.11, where components

The reliability of components in series is the product of the individual reliabilities; that is, $r = r_1 r_2 \dots r_n$

Fig. 12.10 The reliability of components in series.

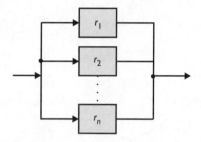

The reliability of components in parallel is 1− unreliability and is given by
$r = 1 - (1 - r_1)(1 - r_2)\dots(1 - r_n)$

Fig. 12.11 The reliability of components in parallel.

operate in parallel and the whole system fails when all the components have failed.

When components operate in parallel, a failure occurs only when all components fail. If the reliability of the ith component is given by r_i, then its unreliability, or probability of failure, is given by $(1 - r_i)$. For example, with two components, the probability of both components failing is $(1 - r_1)(1 - r_2)$. If there are n components in parallel, the probability of them all failing is $(1 - r_1)(1 - r_2) \dots (1 - r_n)$. Therefore, the reliability of a system with n components in parallel is given by

$$1 - \text{system unreliability} = 1 - (1 - r_1)(1 - r_2) \dots (1 - r_n)$$

Consider now the two components r_1 and r_2 with reliabilities 99 percent and 98 percent operating in parallel. The overall system reliability is

$$1 - (1 - 0.99)(1 - 0.98) = 1 - (0.01)(0.02) = 1 - 0.0002$$
$$= 0.9998 \text{ or } 99.98 \text{ percent}$$

Notice how the use of parallel components can have a dramatic effect on overall reliability. In practice there are slight penalties to be paid for using parallel systems, because the components and pathways linking the parallel modules may themselves fail.

In a real system the reliability can be calculated and redundancy added, where necessary, to strengthen weak links in the chain. Consider the system illustrated in Fig. 12.12, which has a CPU, memory module, three terminals, two disk controllers, and two disk drives. Table 12.2 defines the reliabilities of the individual components.

If we assume that the system will still give a reduced, but acceptable, level of service with just a CPU, memory module, and a single disk controller and associated drive, then Fig. 12.13 shows the system from a reliability point of view. The overall reliability is determined by four groups in series: the

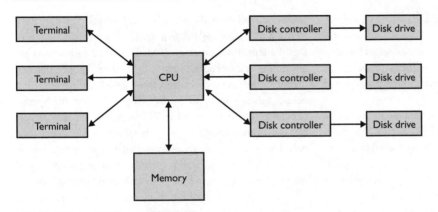

Fig. 12.12 The reliability of a computer system.

Component	Reliability
Terminal	0.98
CPU	0.999
Memory	0.8
Disk controller	0.995
Disk drive	0.8

Table 12.2 Reliability of components in Fig. 12.12.

terminals, the CPU, the memory, the disk controllers, and the disk drives. Because the terminals are in parallel, a system failure occurs only when all three terminals fail. Similarly, each disk controller or its associated disk drive must fail before the system fails.

The reliability of each of these four links is

Terminal	$1-(1-0.98)(1-0.98)(1-0.98)$
	$=1-0.000\,008=0.999\,992$
CPU	0.999
Memory	0.8

Disk drive and
controller
$$1-(1-0.995\times0.8)(1-0.995\times0.8)$$
$$\times(1-0.995\times0.8)$$
$$=1-(1-0.796)(1-0.796)(1-0.796)$$
$$=1-0.008\,495=0.9915$$

The overall system reliability is given by the product of the individual reliabilities of the four links operating in series:

$$0.999\,992\times0.999\times0.8\times0.9915=0.7924 \text{ or } 79 \text{ percent}$$

This result is almost entirely dominated by the low reliability of the memory module. Suppose the manufacturer puts two memory modules in parallel. The reliability of the memory system would now be $1-(1-0.8)(1-0.8)$, or 0.96, and the overall reliability of the system 0.9509, or 95 percent.

From what we've just said, reliability may look like a science. It's not. It's a black art. The computer designer or any other engineer should not grow too complacent. Reliability calculations are based on two assumptions. The first is that the reliability of a component is constant for most of its life (Fig. 12.8). This assumption ignores new modes of failure in

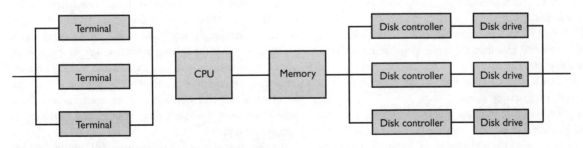

Fig. 12.13 Calculating the reliability of the system of Fig. 12.12.

operation. For example, the world's first passenger jet aircraft, the Comet, was designed using data known at that time. Unfortunately, the theory of metal fatigue was not well understood and cracks developed and spread from the aircraft's square windows, leading to disintegration of the fuselage and the consequent loss of the aircraft.

The second assumption is that the overall reliability can be calculated using the techniques for Figs. 12.9 and 12.10 (serial and parallel networks). The reliability calculations are valid for simple systems, but less so for very large systems—an aircraft or a nuclear reactor. When such a large system is analyzed, the analysis itself is made by an engineer operating under certain assumptions. Some of these may involve human behavior. For example, the reliability of a system may depend strongly on its maintenance. If, because of economic pressures, the maintenance is not carried out according to the manufacturer's specifications, the reliability of the system will not match its reliability on paper.

We now look at a different aspect of the computer—the analog interface.

12.3 The analog interface

All the systems and interfaces we've described so far have been *digital*. We now look at *analog* systems and their interface to the digital computer. In an analog world, measurable quantities are not restricted to the binary values 0 and 1. Almost everything that can be measured may take one of an infinite number of values within a given range; for example, the temperature of a room changes from one value to another by going through an infinite number of increments on its way. Similarly, air pressure, speed, sound intensity, weight, and time are all analog quantities. As long as computers are used to process text or to access databases, we don't have to worry much about the analog world. Once computers start to control their environment, or generate speech or music, or process images, we have to understand the relationship between the analog and digital worlds.

In this section we are interested in the characteristics of analog signals and how they are captured and processed by a digital computer. The final part of this section examines the hardware that converts analog signals into digital form, and digital values into analog signals.

Once we have described the way in which analog signals are *sampled periodically* and converted into digital form, we can look at some of the applications of digital computers in *signal processing* in the next section. Digital signal processing

is used in both the audio and the visual worlds. You only have to listen to almost any modern music to appreciate the meaning of audio signal processing. Many musical instruments are electronic—they generate sounds by performing operations on digital values and then convert these values into analog form before sending them to loudspeakers. Most of the special effects we take for granted in TV programs and movies rely on signal processing. However, signal processing is not used only for entertainment purposes—digital signal processing is used by sophisticated control systems, from an aircraft's automatic landing system to spacecraft and satellite navigation.

A full appreciation of the relationship between analog and digital signals and the transformation between them requires a knowledge of electronics—this is particularly true when we examine analog-to-digital and digital-to-analog converters. Readers without an elementary knowledge of electronics may wish to skip these sections. However, we cover these topics in such a way that the reader with little or no knowledge of electronics will be able to appreciate the overall principles involved.

12.3.1 Analog signals

We introduced the notion of analog and digital signals in Chapter 2. Here we will just remind you of the fundamental difference between analog and digital systems. A signal is said to be *analog* if it falls between two arbitrary levels, V_x and V_y, and can assume any one of an infinite number of values between V_x and V_y. If the analog signal, $V(t)$, is time-dependent, it is a continuous function of time, so that its *slope*, dV/dt, is never infinite, which would imply an instantaneous change of value. Figure 12.14 illustrates how both an analog voltage and a digital voltage vary with time.

Analog signals are processed by analog circuits. The principal feature of an analog circuit is its ability to process an analog signal faithfully, without distorting it—hence the expression *high fidelity*. A typical analog signal is produced at the output terminals of a microphone as someone speaks into it. The voltage varies continuously over some finite range, depending only on the loudness of the speech and on the physical characteristics of the microphone. An amplifier may be used to increase the amplitude of this time-varying signal to a level suitable for driving a loudspeaker. If the voltage gain of the amplifier is A, and the voltage from the microphone $V(t)$, the output of the amplifier is equal to $A \cdot V(t)$. The output signal from the amplifier, like the input, has an infinite range of values, but within a range A times that of the signal from the microphone.

Because digital signals in computers fall into two ranges (e.g. 0–0.4 V for logical 0 and 2.4–5.0 V for logical 1 levels

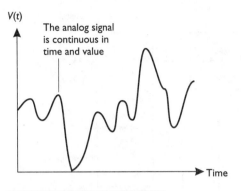

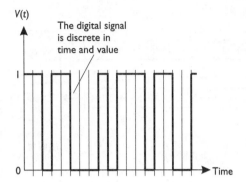

Fig. 12.14 Analog and digital signals.

in LS TTL logic systems), small amounts of *noise* and *cross-talk* have no effect on digital signals as long as the noise is less than about 0.4 V. Unfortunately, life is much more difficult for the analog systems designer. Even small amounts of noise in the millivolt (or even microvolt) region can seriously effect the accuracy of analog signals. In particular, the analog designer has to worry about power-line noise and digital noise picked up by analog circuits from adjacent digital circuits. We are now going to look at how a computer can read an analog value and then process it digitally.

12.3.2 **Signal acquisition**

At first sight it might appear that the analog and digital worlds are mutually incompatible. Fortunately a gateway exists between the analog and digital worlds called *quantization*. The fact that an analog quantity can have an infinite range of values is irrelevant. If somebody says they will arrive at 9.00 a.m., they are not being literal—9.00 a.m. exists for an infinitesimally short period. Of course, what they really mean is that they will arrive at *approximately* 9.00 a.m. In other words, if we measure an analog quantity and specify it to a precision sufficient for our purposes (i.e. quantization), the error between the actual analog value and its measured value is unimportant. Once the analog value has been measured, it exists in a *numeric* form that can be processed by a computer.

The conversion of an analog quantity into a digital value requires two separate operations; the extraction of a sample value of the signal to be processed and the actual conversion of that sample value into a binary form. Figure 12.15 gives the block diagram of an analog signal acquisition module. As the analog-to-digital converter (ADC) at the heart of this module may be rather expensive, it is not unusual to provide a number of different analog *channels*, all using the same ADC.

Each analog channel in Fig. 12.15 begins with a *transducer* that converts an analog quantity into an electrical value (we introduced transducers and devices that measure physical quantities in Chapter 8). Transducers are almost invariably separate from the signal acquisition module proper. A transducer exploits some physical property of matter to perform the conversion process. For example, the *thermistor* is a transducer composed of a substance whose electrical resistance varies with temperature. By passing a constant current through the thermistor, the voltage across it varies with temperature. Another transducer is the *strain gauge*, which measures displacement. A strain gauge uses an electrical conductor that changes its resistance when it is deformed (i.e. stretched or compressed). If you put a strain gauge on, say, a strip of metal, you can use the change in resistivity to measure how much the strip flexes (i.e. bends). Since the amount by which the strip bends depends on the force applied to it, you can use a strain gauge to measure force.

Sometimes the transducer is a *linear* device, so that a change in the physical input produces a proportional change in the electrical output. All too often, the transducer is highly *non-linear* and the relationship between the physical input and the voltage from the transducer is very complex; for example, the output of a transducer that measures temperature might be $V = V_0 e^{t/kT}$. In such cases it is usual to perform the linearization of the input in the digital computer after the signal has been digitized. It is possible, but not normal, to perform the linearization within the signal acquisition module by means of purely analog techniques.

The electrical signal from the transducer is frequently very tiny (sometimes only a few microvolts) and must be *amplified* before further processing in order to bring it to a level well above the noise voltages present in later circuits. Amplification is performed by an analog circuit called an

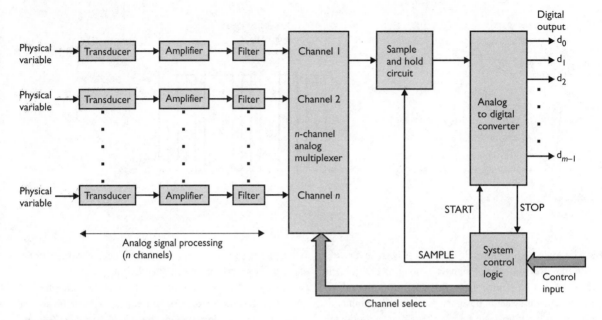

Fig. 12.15 An analog signal acquisition module.

op-amp (operational amplifier). Some transducers have an internal amplifier.

After amplification comes *filtering*, a process designed to restrict the passage of certain signals through the circuit. Filtering blocks signals with a frequency above or below a cut-off point; for example, if the signal from the transducer contains useful frequency components only in the range 0 to 20 Hz (as one might expect from, say, an electrocardiogram), it is beneficial to filter out all signals of a higher frequency. These *out of band* signals represent unwanted noise and have no useful effect on the interpretation of the electrocardiogram. Moreover, it is necessary for the filter to cut out all frequencies above one half the rate at which the analog signal is sampled. The reasons for this are explained later.

The outputs of the filters are fed to an electronic switch called a multiplexer that selects one of the analog input channels for processing. The multiplexer is controlled by the digital system to which the signal acquisition module is connected. The only purpose of the multiplexer is to allow one analog-to-digital converter to be connected to several inputs.

The analog output of the multiplexer is applied to the input of the last analog circuit in the acquisition module, the *sample and hold* (S/H) circuit. The sample and hold circuit takes an almost *instantaneous* sample of the incoming analog signal and holds it constant while the *analog-to-digital converter*, ADC, is busy determining the digital value of the signal. If

the input signal is changing rapidly, the output of an ADC (which takes an appreciable time to perform its conversion) would be meaningless without an S/H circuit to staticize the input.

The *analog-to-digital converter* (ADC) transforms the voltage at its input into an m-bit digital value, where m varies from typically 4 to 16 or more. Several types of analog-to-digital converter are discussed at the end of this section. We now look at the relationship between the analog signal and the analog-to-digital conversion process.

Signal quantization

Two fundamental questions have to be asked when considering any analog-to-digital converter. Into how many levels or values should the input signal be divided and how often should the conversion process be carried out? The precise answer to both these questions is exceedingly complex and requires much mathematics. Fortunately, they both have relatively simple conceptual answers and in many real situations a rule-of-thumb can easily be applied. We look at how analog signals are quantized in value and then how they are quantized or *sampled* in time.

When asked how much sugar you want in a cup of coffee, you might reply: none, half a spoon, one spoon, one and a half spoons, etc. Although a measure of sugar can be quantized right down to the size of a single grain, the practical unit chosen by those who add sugar to coffee is the half-spoon. This unit is both easy to measure out and offers reasonable discrimination between the quanta (i.e. half-spoons). Most drinkers could not discriminate between, say, 6/9 and 7/9 of a spoon of sugar. As it is with sugar, so it is with signals. The level of quantization is chosen to be the minimum interval between successive values that carries meaningful information. You may ask, 'Why doesn't everyone use an ADC with the greatest possible resolution?' The answer is perfectly simple. The cost of an ADC rises exponentially with resolution. A 16-bit ADC is very much more expensive than an 8-bit ADC (assuming all other parameters to be equal). Therefore, engineers select the ADC with a resolution compatible with the requirements of the job for which it is intended.

Let's look at an *ideal* 3-bit analog-to-digital converter that converts a voltage into a binary code. As the analog input to this ADC varies in the range 0–7.5 V, its digital output varies from 000 to 111. Figure 12.16 provides a *transfer function* for this ADC.

Consider the application of a linear voltage *ramp* input from 0.0 to 7.5 V to this ADC (a ramp is a signal that increases at a constant rate). Initially the analog input is 0.0 V and the digital output 000. As the input voltage rises, the output remains at 000 until the input passes 0.5 V, at which point the output code *jumps* from 000 to 001. The output code remains at 001 until the input rises above 1.5 V. Clearly, for each 1.0 V change in the input, the output code changes by

one unit. Figure 12.16 shows that the input can change in value by up to 1 V without any change taking place in the output code.

The *resolution* of an ADC, Q, is the largest change in its input required to guarantee a change in the output code, and is 1.0 V in this example. The resolution of an ADC is expressed indirectly by the number of bits in its output code, where resolution = $V_{maximum}/2^n - 1$. For example, an 8-bit ADC with an input in the range 0 V to +8.0 V has a resolution of 8.0 V/255 = 0.031 37 V = 31.37 mV. Table 12.3 gives the basic characteristics of ADCs with digital outputs ranging from 4 to 16 bits. The figures in Table 12.3 represent the optimum values for perfect ADCs. In practice, real ADCs suffer from imperfections such as non-linearity, drift, offset error, and missing codes that are described later. Some ADCs are *unipolar* and handle a voltage in the range 0 to V, and some are *bipolar* and handle a voltage in the range $-V/2$ to $+V/2$.

The column labeled '*Value of Q for 10 V FS*' in Table 12.3 indicates the size of the step (i.e. Q) if the maximum output of the ADC is 10 V. The abbreviation 'FS' means '*full-scale*'.

Figure 12.17 provides a graph of the difference or *error* between the analog input of a 3-bit ADC and its digital output. Suppose that the analog input is 5.63 V. The corresponding digital output is 110, which represents 6.0 V; that is, the digital output corresponds to the *quantized* input, rather than the *actual* input. The difference between the actual

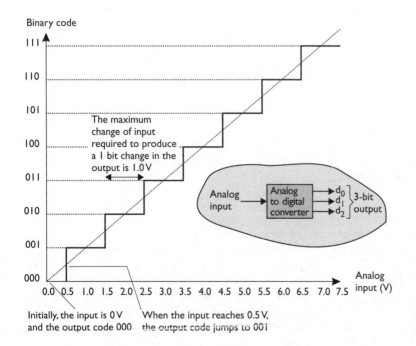

Initially, the input is 0 V and the output code 000   When the input reaches 0.5 V, the output code jumps to 001

Fig. 12.16 The transfer function of an ideal 3-bit A/D converter.

Resolution (bits)	Discrete states	Binary weight	Value of Q for 10V FS	SNR in dB	Dynamic range in dB
4	16	0.0625	0.625 V	34.9	24.1
6	64	0.0156	0.156 V	46.9	36.1
8	256	0.00391	39.1 mV	58.1	48.2
10	1024	0.000977	9.76 mV	71.0	60.2
12	4096	0.000244	2.44 mV	83.0	72.2
14	16384	0.0000610	610 µV	95.1	84.3
16	65536	0.0000153	153 µV	107.1	96.3

Table 12.3 The performance of ideal analog-to-digital converters.

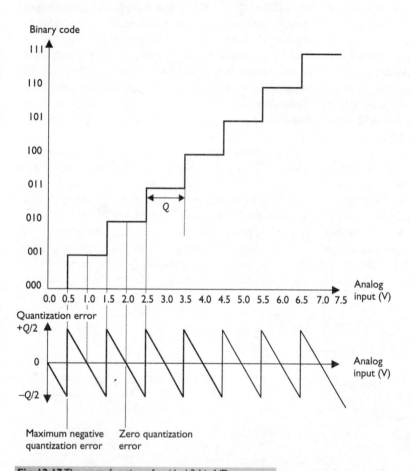

Fig. 12.17 The error function of an ideal 3-bit A/D converter.

input and the 'idealized' input corresponds to an error of 0.37 V. Figure 12.17 shows that the maximum error between the input and output is equal to $Q/2$. This error is called the *quantization error*.

The output from a real ADC can be represented by the output from a perfect ADC whose input is equal to the applied signal plus a noise component. The difference between the input and the quantized output (expressed as an analog value) is a time-varying signal between $+Q/2$ and $-Q/2$ and is called the *quantization noise* of the ADC.

Because the quantization noise is a *random* value, engineers characterize it by its r.m.s. (*root mean square*)—the r.m.s. value expresses the *power* of the signal. The r.m.s. value of a signal is obtained by squaring it, taking the average, and then taking the square root of the average. The r.m.s. of the quantization noise of an analog-to-digital converter is equal to $Q/\sqrt{12}$. Increasing the resolution of the converter reduces the amplitude of the quantization noise as Table 12.3 demonstrates.

A figure-of-merit of any analog system is its *signal-to-noise ratio*, which measures the ratio of the wanted signal to the unwanted signal (i.e. *noise*). The signal-to-noise ratio, SNR, of a system is expressed in units called *decibels*, named after Graham Bell, the inventor of the telephone. The SNR ratio of two signals is defined as $20\log(V_{signal}/V_{noise})$. The signal-to-noise ratio of an ideal n-bit ADC is given by

$$\text{SNR (in dB)} = 20\log(2^n Q)/(Q/\sqrt{12}) = 20\log(2^n) + 20\log(12)$$
$$= 6.02n + 10.8$$

This expression demonstrates that the signal-to-noise ratio of the ADC increases by 6.02 dB for each additional bit of precision. Table 12.3 gives the signal-to-noise ratio of ADCs from 4 to 16 bits. An 8-bit ADC has a signal-to-noise ratio similar to that of some low-quality audio equipment, whereas a 10-bit ADC approaches the SNR of high-fidelity equipment.

Another figure-of-merit of an analog system is its *dynamic range*. The dynamic range of an ADC is given by the ratio of its full-scale range (FSR) to its resolution, Q, and is expressed in decibels as $20\log(2^n) = 20n\log 2 = 6.02n$. Table 12.3 also gives the dynamic range of the various ADCs. Once again you can see that a 10–12-bit ADC is suitable for moderately high-quality audio signal processing. Because of other impairments in the system and the actual behavior of a real ADC, high-quality audio signal processing is normally done with a 16-bit ADC.

Sampling a time-varying signal

We have discussed the need to divide a signal into an adequate number of discrete values, and the requirement that the signal be effectively constant while it is being sampled. What remains to be considered is the *rate* at which a signal should be sampled to produce a fair and accurate digital representation of it. We need to know the minimum rate at which a signal must be sampled, because we want to use the slowest (i.e. cheapest) ADC. Moreover, it is technically difficult to sample signals at extremely high rates.

Intuitively, we would expect the rate at which a signal must be sampled to be closely related to the rate at which it is changing. For example, a computer controlling the temperature of a swimming pool might need to sample the temperature of the water no more than once every 10 minutes. The thermal inertia of such a large body of water doesn't permit sudden changes in temperature. Similarly, if a microcomputer

is employed to analyze human speech with an upper frequency limit of 3000 Hz, it is reasonable to expect that the input from a microphone must be sampled at a much greater rate than 3000 times a second, simply because in the space of 1/3000 second the signal can execute a complete sine wave.

Fortunately for the designer of signal acquisition systems, a simple relationship exists between the rate at which a signal changes and the rate at which it must be sampled if it is to be reconstituted from the samples without any loss of information content. The so called *Sampling Theorem* states: 'If a continuous signal containing no frequency components higher than f_c is sampled at a rate of at least $2f_c$ then the original signal can be completely recovered from the sampled value without distortion'. This minimum sampling rate is called the *Nyquist* rate.

There are two important points to note about this theorem. The highest frequency component in the signal means just that, and includes any noise or unwanted signals present together with the desired signal. For example, if a signal contains speech in the range 300 to 3000 Hz and noise in the range 300 to 5000 Hz, it must be sampled at least 10 000 times a second. One of the purposes of filtering a signal before sampling it is to remove components whose frequencies are higher than the signals of interest, but whose presence would nevertheless determine the lower limit of the sampling rate.

If a signal whose maximum frequency component is f_c is sampled at less than $2f_c$ times a second, some of the high-frequency components in it are *folded back* into the spectrum of the wanted signal. In other words, sampling a speech signal in the range 300 to 3000 Hz containing noise components up to 5000 Hz at only 6000 times a second would result in some of this noise appearing within the speech band. This effect is called *frequency folding* and, once it has occurred, there is no way in which the original, wanted, signal can be recovered.

Figures 12.18 and 12.19 illustrate the effect of sampling an analog signal both below and above the Nyquist rate. In Fig. 12.18 the input signal consists of a band of frequencies from zero to f_c sampled at a rate equal to f_s times a second, where f_s is greater than $2f_c$. The *spectrum* of the sampled signal contains components in the frequency range $f_s - f_c$ to $f_s + f_c$ that do not fall within the range of the input signal. Consequently, you can recover the original signal from the sampled signal.

In Fig. 12.19 the input signal has a maximum frequency component of f_c and is sampled at f_s where $f_s < 2f_c$. Some energy in the region $f_s - f_c$ to f_c falls in the range of the input frequency and is represented by the shaded region in Fig. 12.19. This situation results in *frequency folding* and a

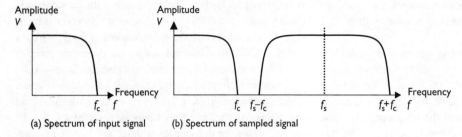

(a) Spectrum of input signal   (b) Spectrum of sampled signal

Fig. 12.18 Sampling a signal at more than the Nyquist rate.

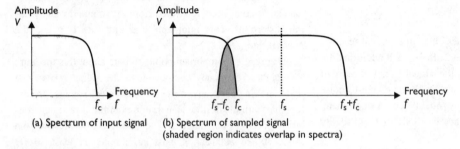

(a) Spectrum of input signal   (b) Spectrum of sampled signal
(shaded region indicates overlap in spectra)

Fig. 12.19 Sampling a signal at slightly more than the Nyquist rate.

loss of information; that is, you cannot recover the original information from the sampled signal.

The classic example of sampling at too low a rate is the *wagon wheel effect* that you sometimes see in movies. A cine film runs at 24 frames/s and each frame samples the image. If the spokes of a rotating wheel are sampled at too low a rate, the wheel appears to move backward. Why? Suppose a wheel rotates 10° clockwise between each frame. The eye perceives this as a clockwise rotation. Now suppose the wagon is moving rapidly and the wheel rotates 350° between each frame. The eye perceives this as a 10° *anticlockwise* rotation.

It is difficult to appreciate the full implications of the sampling theorem without an understanding of the mathematics of sampling and modulation. However, all we need say here is that the overlap in spectra caused by sampling at too low a frequency results in unwanted noise in the sampled signal.

Another way of looking at the relationship between a signal and its sampling rate is illustrated by Figs. 12.20 and 12.21. Figure 12.20(a) gives the continuous input waveform of an analog signal and Fig. 12.20(b) its sampled form. These sampled amplitudes are, of course, stored in a digital computer numerically. Figure 12.20(c) shows the output of a circuit, called a *filter*, fed from the digital inputs of Fig. 12.20(b). The simplest way of describing this circuit is to say that it 'joins up the dots' of the sampled signal to produce a

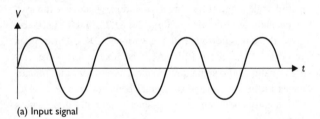

(a) Input signal

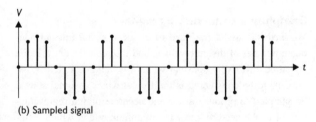

(b) Sampled signal

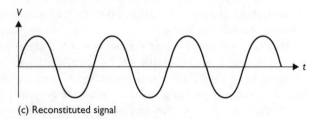

(c) Reconstituted signal

Fig. 12.20 The aliasing effect ($f_s > 2f_c$).

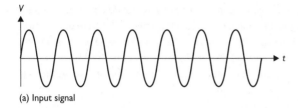

(a) Input signal

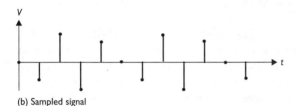

(b) Sampled signal

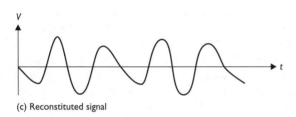

(c) Reconstituted signal

Fig. 12.21 The aliasing effect ($f_s < 2f_c$).

smooth output. As you can see, the reconstituted analog signal is virtually a copy of the original analog signal.

Figure 12.21 is similar to Fig. 12.20, except that the input signal is sampled at less than $2f_c$. A glance at the sampled values of Fig. 12.21(b) is enough to show that much of the detail in the input waveform has been lost. When this sampled signal is reconstituted into a continuous signal (Fig. 12.21(c)) its frequency is not the same as the input signal. The erroneous signal of Fig. 12.21(c) is called an *alias*. Once more, it must be stressed that if frequencies greater than $\frac{1}{2}f_s$ appear in the input signal they can play havoc with the results of sampling.

Most signal acquisition modules have low-pass filters with a sharp cut-off frequency to attenuate signals and noise outside the band of interest. As it is impossible to construct a perfect filter that passes frequencies in the range 0 to f_c and which attenuates all frequencies above f_c infinitely, it is usual to sample a signal at a much greater rate than $2f_c$ in order to reduce the effects of aliasing to an acceptable level. Typically, a signal may be sampled at up to five times the rate of its maximum frequency component.

Aperture time

In addition to the above consideration of the sampling frequency, we also have to think about the time taken by the

sampling process itself. It is very unlikely that a real signal acquisition module would have to deal with an entirely static input. Signals of interest are time-dependent. One question we should ask is, 'What happens if a signal changes while it is being measured (i.e. digitized)?' Figure 12.22 illustrates the problem of trying to measure a dynamic quantity. Suppose the quantization process takes t_a seconds, which is called the *aperture time*. The term 'aperture time' suggests an analogy with the camera—the image is captured when the camera's aperture (i.e. shutter) is open. During this time, the input voltage being measured changes by δV, where δV is given by

$$t_a \cdot \frac{\mathrm{d}V}{\mathrm{d}t}$$

The value of $\mathrm{d}V/\mathrm{d}t$ is the slope of the graph. The change in the input, δV, is called the *amplitude uncertainty*. A perfect, instantaneous digitizer has a zero aperture time and $\delta V = 0$, resulting in a spot sample of the input.

Suppose we apply a linearly rising ramp voltage to the input of an analog-to-digital converter that has a full-scale range of 5 V. Let's imagine that the input changes by 5 V in 100 ms which corresponds to a rate of change of 5 V per 100 ms = 50 V/s. If the analog-to-digital converter takes 1 ms to perform a conversion, we can write

$$\delta V = t_a \cdot \mathrm{d}V(t)/\mathrm{d}t = 1\,\mathrm{ms} \times 50\,\mathrm{V/s} = 1 \times 10^{-3} \times 50\,\mathrm{V/s} = 0.05\,\mathrm{V}$$

That is, the input changes by 0.05 V during the period that the A/D conversion is taking place. Consequently, there is little point in using an ADC with a resolution of more that 0.05 V. This resolution corresponds to 0.05 in 5, or 1 in 100, and a 7-bit ADC would be suitable for this application.

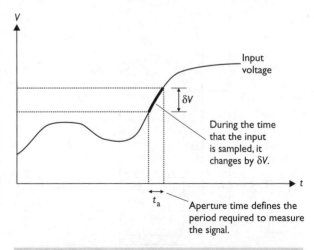

Fig. 12.22 The effect of a finite measurement time on the A/D conversion process.

In order to get a feeling for the importance of aperture time, let's consider a data acquisition system in processing human speech. Suppose a system has an 8-bit analog-to-digital converter and is required to digitize an input with an upper frequency limit of 4000 Hz. We need to know the maximum aperture time necessary to yield an accuracy of one least significant bit in the digitized output. Assuming a *sinusoidal* input (i.e. $V(t) = V \sin \omega t$), the amplitude uncertainty is given by

$$\delta V = t_a \cdot d(V \sin \omega t)/dt = t_a \cdot \omega \cdot V \cdot \cos \omega t$$

The differential of $\sin \omega t$ is $\omega \cdot \cos \omega t$, where ω is defined as $2\pi f$. The maximum rate of change of $V(t)$ occurs at the *zero-crossing* of the waveform when $t = 0$ (i.e. the maximum value of $\cos \omega t$ is 1). Therefore,

$$\delta V = t_a \cdot V \cdot \omega$$
and
$$\delta V/V = t_a \cdot \omega = t_a \cdot 2\pi \cdot f$$

We can substitute 1/256 for $\delta V/V$ and 4000 Hz for f in the above equation to calculate the desired aperture time as follows:

$$\delta V/V = 1/256 = t_a 2\pi f = t_a \times 2 \times 3.142 \times 4000$$

$$t_a = 1/(256 \times 2 \times 3.142 \times 4000) \, s = 0.146 \, \mu s$$

An aperture time of 0.146 µs (i.e. 146 ns) is very small, although not too small to be achieved by the some ADCs.

Fortunately, we can use a *sample and hold* circuit to capture a sample of the input and hold it constant while a relatively slow and cheap ADC performs the conversion. Of course, even a sample and hold circuit is itself subject to the effects of aperture uncertainty. Although an aperture time of 1 µs is relatively small for an analog-to-digital converter, a sample and hold circuit can achieve an aperture time of 50 ns with little effort. We look at the sample and hold circuit in more detail later.

12.3.3 Digital-to-analog conversion

A section on digital-to-analog converters, DACs, at this point may seem a little out of place. It is more logical to discuss analog-to-digital conversion first and then deal with the inverse process. There are two reasons for disregarding this natural sequence. The first is that the DAC is very much less complex than the corresponding ADC, and the second is that some analog-to-digital converters, paradoxically, have a digital-to-analog converter at their heart.

Conceptually, the DAC is a very simple device. If a binary value is to be converted into analog form, all we have to do is to generate an analog value proportional to each bit of the digital word and then add these values to give a composite analog sum. Figure 12.23 illustrates this process. An *m*-bit digital signal is latched by *m* D flip-flops and held constant until the next value is ready for conversion. The flip-flops constitute a digital *sample and hold circuit*. Each of the *m* bits operates an electronic switch that passes either zero or V_i volts to an

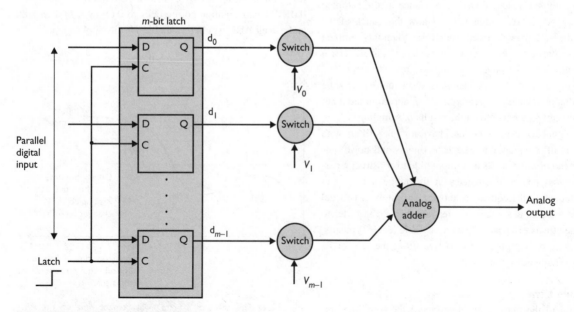

Fig. 12.23 The digital-to-analog converter.

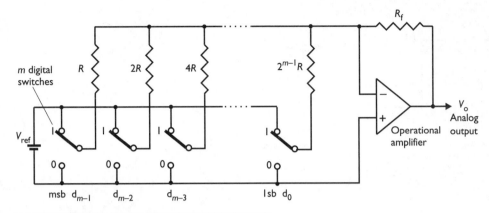

Fig. 12.24 A possible implementation of the A/D converter.

analog adder, where V_i is the output of the ith switch. The output of this adder is

$$V = d_0 V_0 + d_1 V_1 + \ldots + d_{m-1} V_{m-1}$$

Note that the $m\{d_i\}$ in this equation represent binary values 0 or 1, and the $\{V_i\}$ represent binary powers of the form $(1, 1/2, 1/4, 1/8, \ldots)$.

A possible implementation of a digital-to-analog converter is given in Fig. 12.24. The total current flowing into the inverting terminal of the *operational amplifier* is equal to the linear sum of the currents flowing through the individual resistors (the panel describes how the operational amplifier works). As each of the resistors in Fig. 12.24 can be connected to ground or to a precisely maintained reference voltage, V_{ref}, the current flowing through each resistor is either zero or $V_{ref}/2^i R$, where $i = 0, 1, 2, \ldots, m-1$. The total current flowing into the operational amplifier is given by

$$\frac{V_{ref}}{R} = \sum_{i=0}^{m-1} \frac{d_{m-i-1}}{2^i}$$

where d_i represents the state of the ith switch. The voltage at the output terminal of the operational amplifier is given by

$$V_o = -2V_{ref} \times R_f/R \times [d_{m-1} \times 2^{-1} + d_{m-2} \times 2^{-2} + \ldots + d_0 \times 2^{-m}]$$

In a real digital-to-analog converter, the m switches of Fig. 12.24 are, typically, implemented by *field effect transistors* (a field effect transistor behaves as a fast electronic switch—the voltage at its gate terminal determines whether the path between the other two terminals is open or closed). By switching the control gate of these transistors between two logic levels, the resistance between their source and drain terminals is likewise switched between a very high value (the off or open state) and a very low value (the on or closed state). A perfect field effect transistor switch has off and on values of infinity and zero, respectively. Practical transistor switches have small but finite on-resistances that degrade the accuracy of the DAC.

Although the circuit of Fig. 12.24 is perfectly reasonable for values of m below about six, larger values create manufacturing difficulties associated with the resistor chain. Suppose a 10-bit DAC is required. The ratio between the largest and smallest resistor is $2^{10}:1$ or 1024:1. If the device is to be accurate to one LSB, the precision of the largest resistor must be at least one half part in 1024, or approximately 0.05 percent. Manufacturing resistors to this absolute level of precision is difficult and costly with thin-film technology, and virtually impossible with integrated circuit technology.

The operational amplifier

The *operational amplifier* is a simple but remarkable circuit that is widely used in many applications. In the figure below, an amplifier has two input terminals, one called the *inverting input* marked by '−' and one called the *non-inverting* input marked by '+'. The output of the amplifier is $-AV_i$, where V is the voltage difference between the two input terminals.

To analyze the operational amplifier, all you need know is Ohm's law, which states 'the current i flowing through a resistor R is given by V/R, where V is the voltage across the ends of the resistor'.

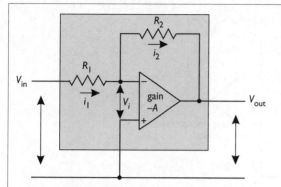

From the diagram we can immediately write down

$i_1 = (V_{in} - V_i)/R_1$
$i_2 = (V_i - V_{out})/R_2$

and

$V_{out} = -AV_i$

If we assume that the current flowing into the inverting terminal of the amplifier is zero (approximately true in practice), we have $i_1 = i_2$. That is,

$(V_{in} - V_i)/R_1 = (V_i - V_{out})/R_2$

We can substitute for $V_i = -V_{out}/A$ in this equation to get:

$(V_{in} + V_{out}/A)/R_1 = (-V_{out}/A - V_{out})/R_2$

Rearranging this equation gives

$V_{out}/V_{in} = -R_2/R_1(1 + (1 + R_2/R_1)/A)$

In a practical operational amplifier, the gain of the amplifier, $-A$, approaches infinity and $(1 + R_2/R_1)/A$ approaches zero. Therefore we can write the gain of the operational amplifier as:

$V_{out}/V_i = -R_2/R_1$

This remarkable result shows that the gain is dependent only on the value of the components R_1 and R_2 and not on the amplifier itself (as long as the value of A is very large).

The R–2R ladder

An alternative form of digital-to-analog converter is given in Fig. 12.25, where the DAC relies on the R–2R ladder (pronounced 'R two R'). This DAC is so called because all resistors in the ladder have either the value R or 2R. Although it's difficult to produce highly accurate resistors over a wide range of values, it is much easier to produce *pairs* of resistors with a precise 2 : 1 ratio in resistance.

As the current from the reference source, V_{ref}, flows down the ladder (from left to right in Fig. 12.25), it is divided at each junction (i.e. the node between the left R, right R, and 2R resistors) into two equal parts, one flowing along the ladder to the right and one flowing down the 2R shunt resistor. The network forms a linear circuit and we can apply the *Superposition Theorem*. This theorem states that, in a linear system, the effect is the sum of all the causes. Consequently, the total current flowing into the inverting terminal of the operational amplifier is equal to the sum of all the currents from the shunt (i.e. 2R) resistors, weighted by the appropriate binary value.

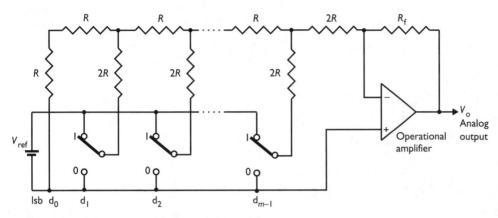

Fig. 12.25 The R–2R ladder D/A converter.

A digital-to-analog converter based on the R–$2R$ ladder has three advantages over the type described in Fig. 12.24:

1. All resistors have a value of either R or $2R$, making it easy to match resistors and to provide a good measure of temperature tracking between resistors. Furthermore, the residual on-resistance of the transistor switches can readily be compensated for.

2. By selecting relatively low values for R in the range 2.5 kΩ to 10 kΩ, it is easy both to manufacture the DAC and to achieve a good response time because of the low impedance of the network.

3. Due to the nature of the R–$2R$ ladder, the operational amplifier always sees a constant impedance at its input, regardless of the state of the switches in the ladder, which improves the accuracy of the operational amplifier circuit.

The R–$2R$ ladder forms the basis of many, if not the majority, of commercially available DACs. Real circuits are arranged slightly differently to that of Fig. 12.25 to reduce still further the practical problems associated with a DAC.

DACs based on the potentiometric network

Another form of digital-to-analog converter is called the *potentiometric* or *tree network*. Figure 12.26 describes a 3-bit arrangement of such a network where a chain of n resistors is placed in series between the reference supply and ground. The value of n is given by 2^m, where m is the resolution of the DAC. In the example of Fig. 12.26, $m=3$ and $n=8$. An 8-bit DAC requires 256 resistors in series. The voltage between

ground and the lower end of the ith resistor is given by

$$V = V_{\text{ref}}\, iR/nR = V_{\text{ref}}\, i/n \quad \text{for } i=0 \text{ to } n-1$$

The value of the resistors, R, does not appear in this equation. All that matters is that the resistors are of equal value. Because the flow of current through the resistors is constant, the effects of resistor heating found in some forms of R–2R ladder are eliminated.

The switch tree serves only to connect the input terminal of the operational amplifier to the appropriate tap (i.e. node) in the resistor network. In fact, this switching network is nothing but an n:1 demultiplexer. Moreover, because the switches do not switch a current (as in the case of the R–$2R$ network), the values of their on and off resistances are rather less critical.

A DAC based on a switch tree is also inherently *monotonic*. That is, as the digital input increases from 00...0 to 11...1, the analog output always increases for each increment in the input.

Before we look at analog-to digital conversion, we need to say something about errors in digital-to-analog converters.

Errors in DACs

The characteristics of real DACs differ from the ideal DACs we've just described. Differences between input code and output voltages represent errors that originate, of course, in the analog circuits of the DAC. Figures 12.27–12.31 provide five examples of errors in DACs. We have drawn the outputs of Figs. 12.27–12.31 as straight lines for convenience—in practice they are composed of steps because the input is a binary code.

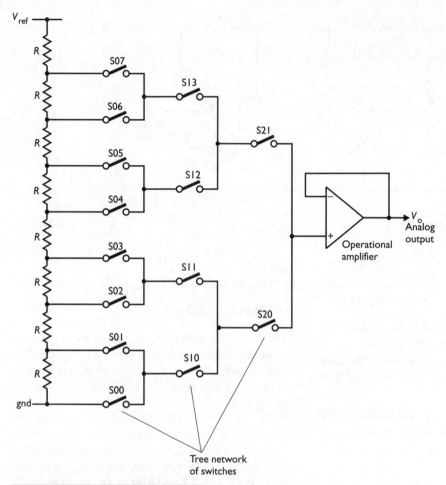

Fig. 12.26 The tree-network D/A converter.

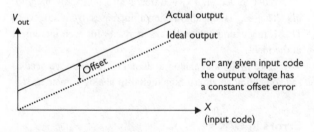

Fig. 12.27 The constant offset error.

In Fig. 12.27, the DAC's output voltage differs from its ideal value by a constant *offset*. If the input is a binary value X, the output is equivalent to that of a *perfect* DAC plus a constant error signal e; that is, $V_{out} = KX + e$. A constant error is easy to deal with because it can be *trimmed out* by adding a

compensating voltage of equal magnitude but of opposite sign to the error.

Figure 12.28 illustrates a *gain error* in which the difference between the output of the DAC and its ideal value is a linear function of the digital input. In this case, if the ideal output is $V_{out} = KX$, the actual output is given by $V_{out} = k \cdot KX$, where k is the gain error (ideally $k = 1$). The gain error can be corrected by passing the DAC's output through an amplifier with a gain factor of $1/k$.

Real DACs suffer from both offset and gain errors as illustrated in Fig. 12.29. The combined offset and gain errors can both be removed separately by injecting a negative offset and passing the output of the DAC through a compensating amplifier as we've just described.

A more serious error is the *non-linear response* illustrated in Fig. 12.30 where the change in the output, Q, for each step

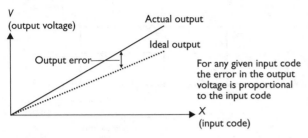

Fig. 12.28 The gain error.

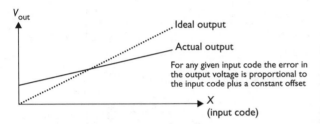

Fig. 12.29 The combined effect of offset gain errors.

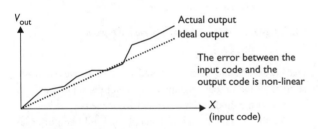

Fig. 12.30 The non-linear error.

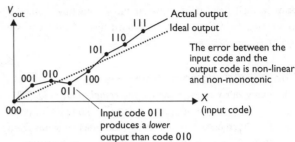

Fig. 12.31 Non-monotonicity.

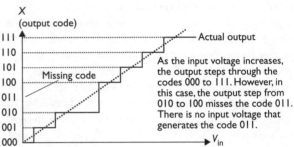

Fig. 12.32 The missing code.

in the input code is not constant. The error between the input code and the output voltage is a random value. Non-linear errors cannot easily be corrected by simple external circuitry. Many DACs are guaranteed to have a maximum non-linearity less than one half Q, the quantization error; that is, the DAC's output error is always less than $Q/2$ for any input.

Figure 12.31 illustrates another form of non-linearity called a *non-monotonic* response. Non-monotonic means that the output voltage does not always increase with increasing input code. Figure 12.31 demonstrates that the analog output for an input code 011 is less than that for an input code of 010. Non-monotonic errors can be dangerous in systems using feedback. For example, if an increasing input produces a decreasing output, the computer controlling the DAC may move the input in the wrong direction.

Analog-to-digital converters suffer from similar errors to DACs—only the axes of the graphs in Figs. 12.27–12.31 are changed. An interesting form of an ADC error is called the *missing code*, where the ADC steps from code X to code $X+2$ *without* going through code $X+1$. Code $X+1$ is said to be a missing code because there is no input voltage that will generate this code. Figure 12.32 demonstrates the transfer function of an ADC with a missing code. As the input voltage to the ADC is linearly increased, the output steps through its codes one by one in sequence. In Fig. 12.32 the output jumps from 010 to 100 without passing through 011.

12.3.4 Analog-to-digital conversion

Although converting a digital value into an analog signal is relatively easy, converting an analog quantity into a digital value is rather more difficult. In fact, apart from one special type of A/D converter, analog-to-digital conversion is performed in a roundabout way. In this section, we describe three types of A/D converter: the *parallel* converter (the only direct A/D converter), the *feedback* converter, and the *integrating* converter.

Before we describe ADCs in detail, we look at the *sample and hold* circuit used to freeze time-varying analog signals prior to their conversion. This circuit is sometimes called a *follow and hold* circuit. We mentioned this circuit when we discussed *aperture time*.

The sample and hold circuit

Like many other analog circuits, the *sample and hold* (S/H) circuit is very simple in principle and very complex in practice. The divergence between theory and practice stems from the effect of second- or even third-order non-linearities of analog circuits. Such problems don't affect digital circuits.

Figure 12.33 gives the circuit of a sample and hold amplifier. Readers without a background in electronics may skip the details of this circuit's operation—all it does is to charge a capacitor to the same level as the input signal, and then connect the capacitor to its output terminals. For a short time, the voltage on the capacitor remains constant, allowing the ADC to perform a conversion with a relatively constant input.

If we forget the *diode bridge* and regard the input resistor, R, as being directly connected to the inverting terminal of the operational amplifier, we have a simple inverting buffer with unity gain (see Fig. 12.34(a)). That is, $V_{out} = -V_{in}$. Assume also that the capacitor C has negligible effect on the circuit.

The diode bridge in Fig. 12.33 acts as an on/off switch that either connects the analog input to the inverting terminal of the op-amp via R or isolates the inverting terminal from the input. When the switch is in the closed position, the S/H circuit operates in its sample mode and $V_{out} = -V_{in}$ (Fig. 12.34(b)); that is, the output *follows* the input. At the same time, the capacitor, C, is charged up to the output voltage because its other terminal is at ground potential (the inverting terminal of the op-amp is a virtual ground).

When the diode bridge switch is opened, the output of the op-amp is held constant by the charge on the capacitor (Fig. 12.34(c)). The charge stored in the capacitor will eventually

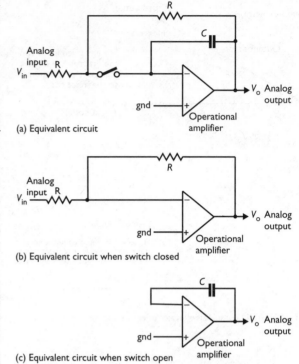

(a) Equivalent circuit

(b) Equivalent circuit when switch closed

(c) Equivalent circuit when switch open

Fig. 12.34 Operation of the sample and hold circuit.

leak away and the output will fall to zero. However, in the short term the output remains at the level the input was in at the instant the diode bridge switch was opened.

The timing parameters of a sample and hold amplifier are illustrated in Fig. 12.35. At the moment the diode switch is closed and the circuit goes into its *sample mode*, the capacitor begins to charge up to the level of the input. The period in which the capacitor is charged is called the *acquisition time*

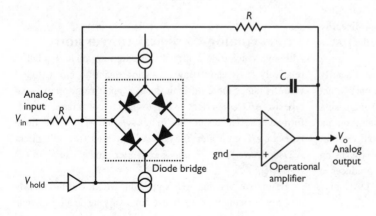

Fig. 12.33 The sample and hold circuit.

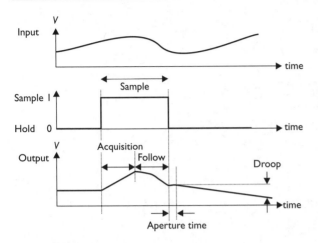

Fig. 12.35 Timing details of the sample and hold circuit.

interrelated and optimizing one parameter may degrade the values of other parameters.

Sample and hold circuits are vital when analog-to-digital converters with appreciable conversion times are to be connected to time-varying inputs. It is less apparent that sample and hold circuits must sometimes be used with digital-to analog-converters. A sample and hold circuit can be fed from a DAC and used to turn the sequence of analog values from the DAC into a continuous analog signal. In this mode the S/H circuit is called a *zero-order hold filter* and its output consists of steps between the analog values, see Fig. 12.36. Another advantage of the S/H circuit is that it deglitches the DAC and removes any glitches (spikes) in its output.

Now that we have described how an analog signal can be captured, the next step is to show how it can be converted into a digital value.

and is in the range 3 μs to 10 μs for a low-cost S/H circuit. The output now tracks the input up to the maximum *slew rate* of the S/H circuit. 'Slew rate' defines the fastest rate at which the output of a circuit can change.

When the S/H circuit is switched into its *hold mode* and the diode switch turned off, there is a finite delay during which the capacitor is disconnected from the input. This delay is the *aperture uncertainty time* of the S/H circuit. We've already met this parameter, which defines the period during which the input must not change by more than, say, a least-significant bit. Aperture times vary from about 50 ns to 50 ps, or less. One picosecond, ps, is 10^{-12} seconds.

In the hold mode, the capacitor discharges and the output begins to *droop*. Droop rates vary, typically, between 5 μV/μs and 0.01 μV/μs. The parameters of the S/H circuit are often

The parallel analog-to-digital converter

The parallel A/D converter is also called the *flash* converter because of its great speed of conversion when compared with the two indirect techniques described later. It works by simultaneously comparing the analog input with $2^m - 1$ equally spaced reference voltages. Figure 12.37 illustrates a 3-bit flash A/D converter (real flash ADCs are typically 6- to 8-bit devices). A chain of equal-valued resistors forms a *tapped potentiometer* between two reference voltages. The voltage between consecutive taps in the chain of resistors differs by $1/2^m$ of the full-scale analog input. Each of the $2^m - 1$ taps is connected to the inverting input of a high-speed differential comparator, whose output depends on the sign of the voltage difference between its two inputs. The non-inverting inputs of the comparators are all wired together and connected to the

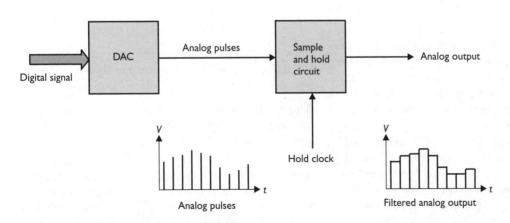

Fig. 12.36 The sample and hold circuit as a filter.

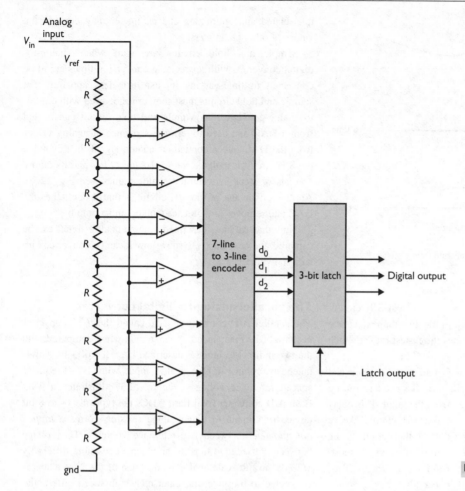

Fig. 12.37 The flash AD converter.

analog input of the ADC. Thus, the output of the ith comparator in Fig. 12.37 is given by

$$\text{sign}(V_{\text{in}} - V_{\text{ref}} i/8)$$

For any given analog input voltage, the outputs of the comparators, whose reference input is below that of the analog input to be converted into digital form, are at a logical 1 level. All other outputs are at a logical 0. The 7 outputs are fed to a *priority encoder* that generates a 3-bit output corresponding to the number of logical 1s in the input.

The parallel A/D converter is very fast and can digitize analog signals at over 30 million samples per second. High conversion rates are required in real-time signal processing in applications such as radar data processing and image processing. As an illustration of the speeds involved, consider digitizing a television picture. The total number of samples required to digitize a TV signal with 500 pixels/line in real-time is

$$\begin{aligned}
\text{samples} &= \text{pixels per line} \times \text{lines per field} \times \text{fields per second} \\
&= 500 \times 312\tfrac{1}{2} \times 50 \\
&= 7\,812\,500 \text{ samples per second (UK)} \\
&= 500 \times 256\tfrac{1}{2} \times 60 \\
&= 7\,875\,500 \text{ samples per second (USA)}
\end{aligned}$$

Because the flash converter requires so many comparators, it is difficult to produce with greater than about 8 bits' precision. Even 6-bit flash ADCs are relatively expensive.

The feedback analog-to-digital converter

The *feedback* analog-to-digital converter, paradoxically, uses a digital-to-analog converter to perform the required conversion. Figure 12.38 illustrates the basic principle behind this class of converter. A local digital-to-analog converter transforms an m-bit digital value, $D = d_0, d_1, \ldots, d_{m-1}$, into an analog voltage, V_{out}. The value of the m-bit digital word D is determined by the block labeled *control logic* in one of the ways to be described later.

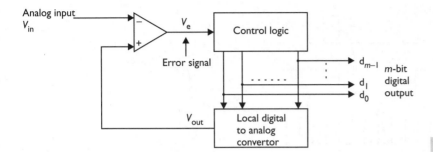

Fig. 12.38 The feedback ADC.

V_{out} from the DAC is applied to the inverting input of an operational amplifier and the analog input to be converted is applied to its non-inverting input. The output of the operational amplifier corresponds to an error signal, V_e, and is equal to A times $(V_{out} - V_{in})$, where A is the gain of the amplifier. This error signal is used by the control logic network to modify the digital data, D, to minimize the error signal $A(V_{out} - V_{in})$. When the difference between V_{in} and V_{out} is less than that between two quantized signal levels (i.e. Q), the conversion process is complete.

In plain English, the digital signal is varied by trial and error until the locally generated analog voltage is as close to the analog input as it is possible to achieve. The next step is to examine ways of implementing this *trial and error* process.

The ramp converter

The simplest feedback A/D converter is the *ramp converter* (see Fig. 12.39), which uses a binary counter to generate the digital output, D. At the start of a conversion, the binary counter is cleared to 0. A new conversion process starts with

the resetting of the RS flip-flop. When $\overline{Q}$ goes high following a reset, the AND gate is enabled and clock pulses are fed to the m-bit binary up-counter. These pulses cause the output of the counter, D, to increase monotonically from zero (i.e. 0, 1, 2, ..., 2^{m-1}).

The output from the counter is applied to both an m-bit output latch and a D/A converter. As the counter is clocked, the output of the local D/A converter ramps upwards in the manner shown in the timing diagram of Fig. 12.40. The locally generated analog signal is compared with the input to be converted in a digital comparator, whose output is the sign of the local analog voltage minus the input; that is, $\text{sign}(V_{out} - V_{in})$. When this value goes positive, the flip-flop is set. At the same time, its Q output goes low, cutting off the stream of clock pulses to the counter, and its Q output goes high, providing an `End_of_conversion` (EOC) output and latching the contents of the binary counter into the output latches.

The ramp feedback A/D converter has a variable conversion time. If the analog input is close to the maximum

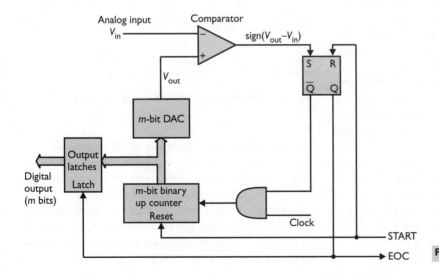

Fig. 12.39 The ramp feedback ADC.

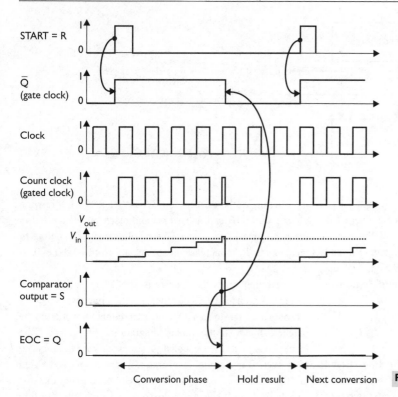

START = R

$\bar{Q}$
(gate clock)

Clock

Count clock
(gated clock)

V_{out}

V_{in}

Comparator
output = S

EOC = Q

Conversion phase   Hold result   Next conversion

Fig. 12.40 Timing diagram of a ramp feedback ADC.

(i.e. full-scale) value, approximately 2^m clock pulses are required before the locally generated analog signal reaches the unknown input. The maximum conversion time of an 8-bit ADC is 256 times the DAC's settling time plus associated delays in the comparator and counter. The ramp feedback converter produces a *biased* error in its output, because the counter stops only when the local DAC output is higher than the input to be converted. This local analog value is not necessarily closest to the true digital equivalent of the analog input. The advantage of the ramp A/D converter is its great simplicity and low hardware cost.

The *tracking converter* is a ramp converter with the addition of a *bidirectional* (i.e. up/down) counter and slightly more complex control logic. At the start of each new conversion process, the comparator determines whether the analog input is above or below the feedback voltage from the local DAC. If the analog input is greater, the counter is clocked up, and if it is lower the counter is clocked down. Thus, the counter ramps upwards or downwards until the output of the comparator changes state, at which point the analog input is said to be acquired by the converter. Figure 12.41 demonstrates the operation of this type of converter by showing how three successive conversions are performed.

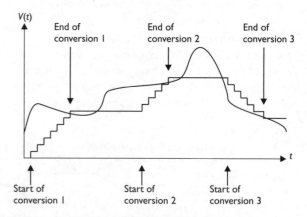

Fig. 12.41 The ramp converter using an up/down counter.

If the analog input is constant, the conversion time of the counter is effectively zero once the input has been initially acquired. As long as the input changes slowly with respect to the rate at which the output of the local DAC can ramp upward or downward, the tracking counter faithfully converts the analog input into the appropriate digital output. If the analog input changes rapidly, the local analog voltage may not be able to track the input and acquisition is lost.

The tracking A/D converter is most useful when the input is changing slowly and is highly autocorrelated. Human speech represents such a signal. If the converter is subject to essentially random inputs (e.g. it is fed from a multiplexer), it offers little or no advantage over a ramp converter.

The successive approximation converter

Intuitively, it would seem reasonable to take very large steps in increasing the analog signal from the local DAC early in the conversion process, and then to reduce the step size as the conversion proceeds and the local analog voltage approaches the analog input. Such an A/D converter is known as a *successive approximation* A/D converter and uses a binary search algorithm to guarantee an m-bit conversion in no more than m iterations (i.e. clock cycles).

The structure of a successive approximation D/A converter is adequately illustrated by the generic feedback converter of Fig. 12.39. Only the strategy used to generate successive steps makes the successive approximation converter different to a ramp converter. At the start of a new conversion process, the digital logic sets the most-significant bit, MSB, of the input of the local D/A converter to a logical 1 level and all other bits to 0 (i.e. $D = 1000\ldots0$). In other words, the first guess is equal to one half the full-scale output of the converter.

If the analog input is greater than half the full-scale output from the local D/A converter, the MSB is retained at a logical 1 level, otherwise it is cleared. On the second iteration, the next most significant bit (i.e. d_{m-2} in an m-bit word) is set to a logical 1 and retained at 1 if the output of the D/A converter is less than the analog input, or cleared if it is not. This process is repeated m times until the LSB of the D/A converter has been set and then retained or cleared. After the LSB has been dealt with in this way, the process is at an end and the final digital output may be read by the host microprocessor.

Figure 12.42 illustrates the operation of a 4-bit successive approximation A/D converter whose full-scale input is nominally 1.000 V. The analog input to be converted into digital form is 0.6400 V. As you can see, a conversion is complete after four cycles.

Figure 12.43 provides another way of looking at the successive approximation process described in Fig. 12.42. Figure 12.43 takes the form of a *decision tree* that shows every possible sequence of events that can take place when an analog signal is converted into a 4-bit digital value. The path taken through the decision tree when 0.6400 V is converted into digital form is shown by a heavy line.

Figure 12.44 illustrates the structure of a 68000-controlled successive approximation A/D converter. The microprocessor is connected to a memory-mapped D/A converter which responds only to a write access to the lower byte of the base address chosen by the address decoder. The analog output of the converter is compared with the unknown analog input in a

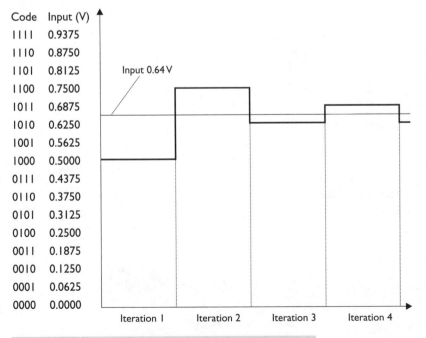

Fig. 12.42 The operation of a successive approximation A/D converter.

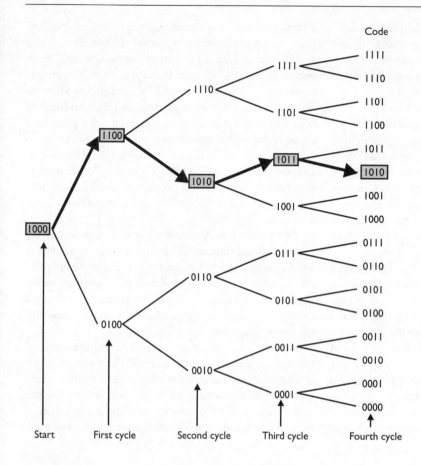

Code

Bit set and tested	1	2	3	4
DAC output (V)	0.5000	0.7500	0.6250	0.6875
Analog I/P – DAC O/P	+0.1400	−0.1100	+0.0150	−0.0475
Bit pattern at start of current cycle	1000	1100	1010	1011
Bit retained	Yes	No	Yes	No
DAC output after iteration	1000	1000	1010	1010

Fig. 12.43 The decision tree for a successive approximation ADC.

comparator, whose output is gated onto data line D_{15}, whenever
a read access is made to the upper byte of the base address. The
software to operate the A/D converter of Fig. 12.44 is

```
Successive_approximation
 DAC_output := 0
  Increment := ½ full-scale output {100...00}
 FOR I=1 TO Number_of_bits
     DAC_output := DAC_output+Increment
     Error_sign := sign(V_in−DAC_output)
```

```
        IF Error_sign negative THEN
                           DAC_output := DAC_output − Increment
        ENDIF
        Increment := Increment/2
    ENDFOR
End successive_approximation

*                  D0 contains the increment
*                  D1 is the DAC output
*                  D2 is the cycle counter
*
          ORG      $00F000      Base address of comparator
DAC_IN    DS.B     1            Reserve byte for sign input from comparator
DAC_OT    DS.B     1            Reserve byte for output to DAC
          ORG      $001000      Program origin
CONV      MOVE.B   #$80,D0      Set the half-scale increment
          MOVE.B   D0,D1        Setup initial value for the output
          MOVE.W   #7,D2        We are going to do 8 cycles
AGAIN     MOVE.B   D1,DAC_OT    Transmit output to DAC
          BTST     #7,DAC_IN    Examine output from comparator
          BPL      NEXT         IF positive THEN add next increment
          SUB.B    D0,D1        ELSE remove the increment
NEXT      LSR.B    #1,D0        Increment := increment/2
          ADD.B    D0,D1        Add increment to output
          DBRA     D2,AGAIN     Repeat for 8 cycles END
          RTS                   End of conversion
```

The integrating analog-to-digital converter

The *integrating*, or more specifically, the *dual-ramp integrating analog-to-digital converter* transforms the problem of measuring an analog voltage into the much more tractable problem of measuring another analog quantity—*time*. An integrating operational amplifier circuit converts the analog input into a charge stored on a capacitor, and then evaluates the charge by measuring the time it takes to discharge the capacitor. The block diagram of a dual-slope integrating A/D converter is given in Fig. 12.45 and its timing diagram in Fig. 12.46.

A typical integrating converter operates in three distinct phases: auto-zero, integrate the unknown analog signal, and integrate the reference voltage. The first phase, auto-zero, is a feature of many commercial dual-slope converters that reduces any offset error in the system. As it isn't a basic feature of the dual-slope process, we won't deal with it here. During the second phase of the conversion, the unknown analog input linearly charges the integrating capacitor C. In this phase, the input of the electronic switch connects the integrator to the voltage to be converted, V_{in}.

Figure 12.46 shows how the output from the integrator, V_{out}, ramps upward linearly during phase 2 of the conversion process. At the start of phase 2, a counter is triggered that counts upwards from 0 to its maximum value $2^n - 1$. After a fixed period $T_1 = 2^n/f_c$ where f_c is the frequency of the converter's clock, the counter overflows (i.e. passes its maximum count). The electronic switch connected to the integrator then connects the integrator's input to $-V_{ref}$, the negative reference supply. The output of the integrator now ramps downwards to 0, while the counter runs up from 0. Eventually, the output of the integrator reaches zero and the conversion process stops—we'll assume that the counter contains M at the end of this phase.

Readers without a knowledge of basic electronics may skip the following analysis of the dual slope integrating ADC. At the end of phase 2 the capacitor is charged up to a level

$$\frac{1}{CR} \int V_{in} dt$$

The voltage rise during the second phase is equal to the fall in the third phase because the output of the integrator

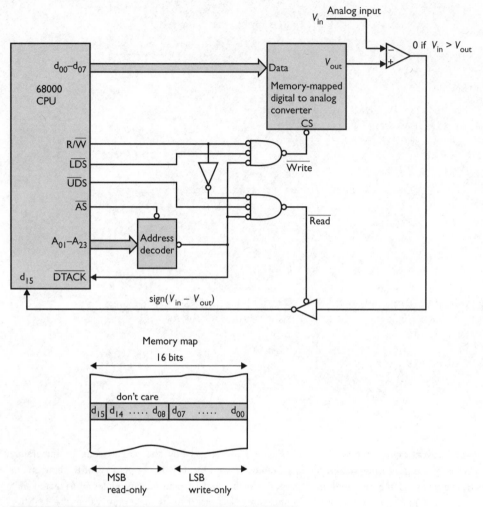

Fig. 12.44 The circuit of a successive approximation A/D converter.

begins at zero volts and ends up at zero volts. Therefore, the following equation holds:

$$\frac{1}{CR} \int_{t_1}^{t_2} V_{in}\, dt = \frac{1}{CR} \int_{t_2}^{t_3} V_{ref}\, dt$$

Assuming that $t_1 = 0$, $t_2 = 2^n/f_c$, $t_3 = t_2 + M/f_c$, we can write

$$\frac{1}{CR}\left[V_{in}t\right]_0^{2^n/f_c} = \frac{1}{CR}\left[V_{ref}t\right]_{2^n/f_c}^{2^n/f_c + M/f_c}$$

or $\quad V_{in}2^n/f_c = V_{ref}M/f_c$

$$V_{in} = \frac{V_{ref}M}{2^n}$$

This remarkable result is dependent only on the reference voltage and two integers, 2^n and M. The values of C and R and the clock frequency, f_c, do not appear in the equation. Implicit in the equation is the condition that f_c is constant throughout the conversion process. Fortunately, this is a reasonable assumption even for the simplest of clock generators.

The dual-slope integrating A/D converter is popular because of its very low cost and inherent simplicity. Moreover, it is exceedingly accurate and can provide 12 or more bits of precision at a cost below that of 8-bit ADCs. Because this converter requires no absolute reference other than V_{ref}, it is easy to fabricate the entire device in a single integrated circuit.

The conversion time is variable and takes $2^n + M$ clock periods in total. A 12-bit converter with a $1\,\mu s$ clock has

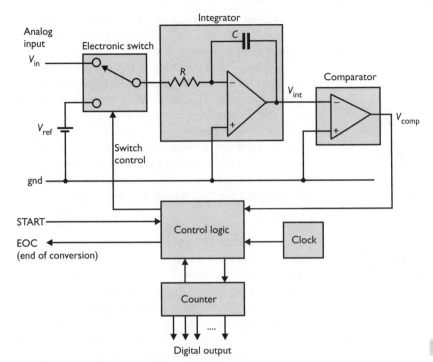

Fig. 12.45 The integrating A/D converter.

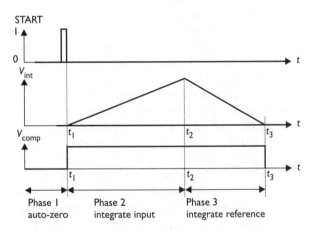

Fig. 12.46 Timing diagram of an integrating A/D converter.

a maximum conversion time of $2 \times 2^n/f_c$ seconds, since the maximum value of N is 2^n. Using these figures, the maximum conversion time is equal to $2 \times 4096 \times 1\,\mu s$, or $8.192\,ms$, which is very much slower than most forms of feedback A/D converter.

Because the analog input is integrated over a period of $2^n/f_c$ seconds, noise on the input is attenuated. Sinusoidal input signals, whose periods are submultiples of the integration period, do not affect the output of the integrator and

hence the measured value of the input. Many high-precision converters exploit this property to remove any noise at the power line frequency. Integrating converters are largely used in instrumentation such as digital voltmeters.

Now that we've described how analog signals can be captured by a computer, processed, and then used to generate an analog output, we are going to provide an insight into some of the things a computer can do with analog signals.

12.4 Introduction to digital signal processing

Digital signal processing, DSP, forms an entire branch of electronics (it covers electronic circuits, mathematics, and computer science). All we can do here is to explain why DSP is so important by looking at just two areas: *control systems* and *audio signal processing*. We set the scene by describing an early *mechanical* analog control system before looking at the principles of digital control systems. The final part of this section describes DSP that is used in control systems and sound and video processing systems.

Control systems have been used for a very long time. The most important example of a mechanical control system is the *governor* used to keep the speed of steam engines constant

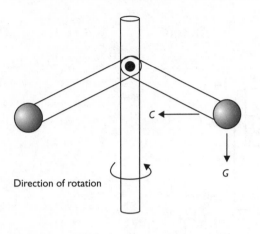

Direction of rotation

C = centripetal force required to pull the counterweight inward

G = force of gravity pulling the counterweight down

Fig. 12.47 The mechanical governor.

during the 19th century. In Fig. 12.47 the shaft of the steam engine drives a vertical spindle. Two arms are connected to the spindle by pivots and two metal balls called counterweights are placed at the ends of these arms. The arms are pivoted and are free to swing outward as the spindle rotates.

As the spindle rotates, the counterweights move outward. In everyday life people use the term *'centrifugal force'* to describe the tendency of a body following a curved path to fly outward. Centrifugal force doesn't exist. Any moving body tends to continue in a straight line. In order to force a body to follow a curved path (e.g. an orbit), a force is necessary to pull it toward the center. This force is called *centripetal* force.

In Fig. 12.47 the force of gravity on the counterweights provides the centripetal force that pulls the counterweights inward. This situation is exactly analogous to the camber in a road bend—tilting the car inward provides the centripetal force required to pull the car round the bend without skidding.

The position of the counterweights in Fig. 12.47 depends on the speed at which the spindle rotates. As the arms connected to the counterweights move in and out, they control a valve that regulates the flow of steam to the engine. Below a certain speed, the valve is open and more steam is fed to the engine to cause it to speed up. As the spindle rotates faster, the counterweights fly further out until the valve begins to close and the flow of steam is reduced. Eventually equilibrium is reached and the spindle rotates at a constant speed.

This control mechanism employs *negative feedback*, because an *increase* in the speed is used to *decrease* the flow

of steam and hence the engine's speed. Similar mechanisms were used to provide aircraft with autopilots long before the age of the microprocessor. Today, the digital computer has replaced the governor. The speed of a spindle can be read with great precision and fed to a computer. The computer processes the speed according to a suitable algorithm and generates the control signals that determine the spindle's speed.

Modern digital control systems are everywhere; for example, an automobile measures the external air pressure, the manifold pressure, the external air temperature, the speed of the engine, and the position of the gas pedal to determine the optimum amount of fuel to inject into each cylinder.

12.4.1 Control systems

Analog-to-digital and digital-to-analog conversion techniques are found in process control applications. Consider the automatic pilot of an aircraft. At any instant the position (location and altitude) of an aircraft is measured, together with its performance (heading, speed, rate of climb, rate of turn, and engine power). All these values are converted into digital form and fed into a digital computer that determines the best position for the controls (throttle, elevator, aileron, and rudder). The digital output from the computer is applied to digital-to-analog converters, whose analog outputs operate actuators that directly move the appropriate control surfaces.

Figure 12.48 describes a primitive control system. The input is an analog value that is digitized and processed by the computer. Real control systems are often much more sophisticated than that of Fig. 12.48—consider the problem of *overshoot*. Suppose you apply a new demand input to a system such as banking an aircraft's wings. The aircraft rolls into the bank and attempts to attain the angle requested. However, the mechanical inertia of the aircraft might cause it to roll past the point it was aiming for (i.e. it overshoots). A practical control system should also be able to take account of rapidly changing conditions.

Let's look at how control systems have evolved from the simplest possible mechanisms to very sophisticated controllers. The crudest control mechanism is found in central

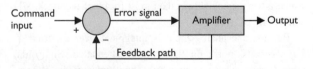

Fig. 12.48 The control system.

heating systems where the desired temperature or *setpoint* is obtained from a control unit on the wall. The demand input is compared with the actual temperature measured by a sensor. If it is colder than the setpoint, the heater is turned on. Otherwise the heater is turned off.

Figure 12.49 demonstrates the operation of such a system. The temperature of the room rises and eventually the heater is turned off. Because of the heater's thermal inertia, the temperature will continue to rise after the current has been cut off. Eventually, the room begins to cool and the heater is turned on and the temperature starts rising again.

This type of on/off control system is also called a *bang–bang* control system to indicate its crude approach—*bang* the system goes on and *bang* it goes off. There is no intermediate point between on and off, and the room is never at the correct temperature because it's either slightly too hot or too cold.

A better method of controlling the temperature of a room is to measure the difference between the desired temperature and the actual temperature and use this value to determine how much power is to be fed to the heater. The colder the room, the more power sent to the heater. If the room is close to its desired temperature, less power is fed to the heater. This is an example of a *proportional control system*. As the room temperature approaches its desired setpoint value, the power fed to the heater is progressively reduced; that is, the current supplied to the heater is $K(t_{setpoint} - t_{room})$.

The proportional control system can be improved further by taking into account *changes* in the variable you are trying to control. Suppose you're designing a camera with an automatic focusing mechanism for use at sporting events. The camera measures the distance of the subject from the camera and uses the difference between the current point-of-focus and the desired point-of-focus to drive the motor that performs the focusing.

Suppose the subject suddenly changes direction, speeds up, or slows down. A proportional control system can't deal with this situation well.

If the subject is in focus and then begins accelerating away, a proportional control signal can't apply a correction until the target is actually out of focus. What we need is a control signal that doesn't depend on the magnitude of the error but on the *rate* at which the error is changing.

A *differential* control system uses the *rate of change* of the error as a control signal; for example, a camera with auto-focusing can use any rapid change in the subject's position to control the focusing motor—even if the subject is approximately in focus and there's no 'proportional error'. A differential control system *must* also incorporate proportional control (if the subject were out of focus but not moving there would be no differential feedback signal).

If we call the error between the setpoint in a control system and its output e, the control input in a proportional plus derivative (i.e. differential) control system is given by

$$y = K_1 e + K_2 de/dt$$

where K_1 and K_2 are the proportional and derivative control coefficients, respectively.

Even this control algorithm isn't perfect. Suppose you design a radar-controlled docking system for spacecraft. One craft can track the other by using both proportional control and derivative control to minimize the difference between their trajectories. However, once their trajectories are closely (but not exactly) matched, there is neither a proportional error signal nor a derivative error signal to force exact tracking. What we need is a mechanism that takes account of a persistent small error.

An *integral* control signal adds up the error signal over a period of time. Even the smallest error eventually generates a control signal to further reduce the error. Integral control ensures that any drift over time is corrected.

A high-performance controller might combine proportional control, rate-of-change control, and integral control, as Fig. 12.50 demonstrates. This system is called a PID (proportional, integral, and derivative) controller. In Fig. 12.50 the box marked *differentiator* calculates the rate-of-change of the system output being controlled.

The equation for a PID can be expressed in the form

$$y = K_1 e + K_2 de/dt + K_3 \int e dt$$

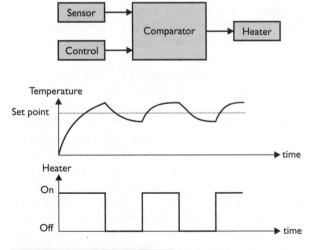

Fig. 12.49 The on/off control system.

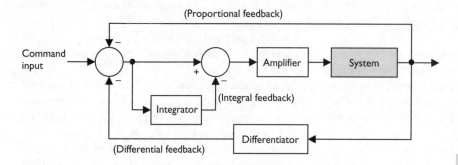

Fig. 12.50 The derivatives and integral control system.

The control signal y now depends on the *size* of the error between the desired and actual outputs from the controller, the *rate* at which the error is changing, and the *accumulated* error over a period.

We can't go into control theory here but we should mention several important points. Designing a PID system is not easy. You have to choose the amounts of proportional, derivative, and integral feedback as well as the time constant of the integrator. If the system is not correctly designed it can become unstable and oscillate.

In the final part of this section we look at how digital signals are processed by the computer.

12.4.2 Digital signal processing

Let's begin with a simple example of signal processing. Suppose music from a microphone is quantized, converted into a sequence of digital values by an ADC, fed into a computer, and stored in an array, M. We can read these consecutive digital values from the array and use a DAC to convert them into an analog signal that is fed to a loudspeaker. Consider the following algorithm.

```
FOR i=1 TO k DO
    Output=M_i
ENDFOR
```

The digitally stored music is reconverted into analog form by sending it to the output port connected to a DAC. This algorithm does nothing other than to retrieve the stored music. In the next example, the samples from the array are amplified by a scalar factor A. By changing the value of A, the amplitude (i.e. the loudness) of the music can be altered. Now we have a

digital volume control with no moving parts that can be programmed to change the sound level at any desired rate.

```
FOR i=1 TO k DO
    Output=A * M_i
ENDFOR
```

We can average a number of consecutive samples to calculate the current average loudness of the signal, and use it to choose a value for A. The following expression shows how we might average the loudness over a period of k samples.

$$\text{Loudness} = \frac{1}{k} \sqrt{\sum_{i=0}^{k-1} m_i^2}$$

Suppose we choose the scale factor A to make the average power of the signal approximately constant. When the music is soft the volume is increased, and when it is loud the volume is decreased. This process is called *compressing* the music, and is particularly useful for listeners with impaired hearing who cannot hear soft passages without turning the volume up so far that loud passages are distorted.

In the next example, the signal fed to the loudspeaker is composed of two parts. M_i represents the *current* value, and $B \cdot M_{i-j}$ represents the value of the signal j samples earlier, scaled by a factor B. Normally the factor B is less than unity. Where do we get a signal plus a delayed, attenuated value? These features are found in an *echo* and are of interest to the makers of electronic music. By very simple processing, we are able to generate echoes entirely by digital techniques. Analog signal processing requires complex and inflexible techniques—consider synthesizing an echo by analog techniques. The analog signal is first converted into sound by a small loudspeaker called a transducer. A spring is connected to the transducer and the acoustic signal travels down it to a microphone at the other end. The output of the microphone represents a delayed version of the original signal—the echo. The length of the delay is increased by using a longer spring. In the digital version, simply modifying the value of j changes the delay.

```
FOR  i=j+1 TO  k DO
     Output=M_i+B  *  M_i-j
ENDFOR
```

The final example of signal processing represents the *linear transversal equalizer* that implements a general-purpose *digital filter*. In audio terms, a digital filter acts as *tone controls* or an *equalizer*. We are going to look at this topic in a little more detail next.

```
FOR  i=1 TO  k DO
     a=K4  *  M_i-4
     b=K3  *  M_i-3
     c=K2  *  M_i-2
     d=K1  *  M_i-1
     e=K0  *  M_i
     Output=a+b+c+d+e
ENDFOR
```

The output is a fraction of the current sample plus weighted fractions of the previous four samples. Let's look at this operation in a little more detail.

Digital filters

An important application of digital signal processing is the *digital filter*. A digital filter behaves like an analog filter—it can pass or stop signals whose frequencies fall within certain ranges. Consider an analog signal, X, that has been digitized; its successive values are

$$x_0, x_1, x_2, x_3, \ldots, x_{i-1}, x_i, x_{i+1}, \ldots$$

Now suppose we generate a new sequence of digital values, Y, whose values are $y_0, y_1, y_2, \ldots$, where

$$y_i = C_0 \cdot x_i + C_1 \cdot x_{i-1}$$

An element in the output series, y_i, is given by a fraction of the *current* element from the input series (i.e. $C_0 \cdot x_i$) plus a fraction of the *previous* element (i.e. $C_1 \cdot x_{i-1}$) of the input series. Figure 12.51 illustrates this operation. The symbol Z^{-1} is used in digital signal processing literature to indicate a 1-unit delay (i.e. the time between two successive samples of a signal).

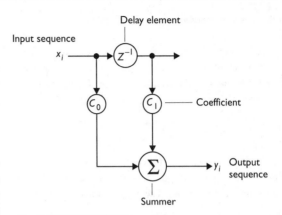

Fig. 12.51 The digital filter.

In other words the operation $x_i Z^{-1}$ is equivalent to delaying signal x_i by one time unit—similarly Z^{-2} delays x_i by two time units. This notation belongs to a branch of mathematics called *Z transforms*.

Let's see what happens when we give the filter coefficients C_0 the value 0.6 and C_1 the value 0.4, and make the input series $X = 0, 0, 1, 1, 1, 1, \ldots, 1$ which corresponds to a simple *step function*. The output sequence is given by

$$y_0 = 0.6 \cdot x_0 + 0.4 \cdot x_{-1} = 0.6 \cdot 0 + 0.4 \cdot 0.0 = 0.0$$
$$y_1 = 0.6 \cdot x_1 + 0.4 \cdot x_0 = 0.6 \cdot 0 + 0.4 \cdot 0.0 = 0.0$$
$$y_2 = 0.6 \cdot x_2 + 0.4 \cdot x_1 = 0.6 \cdot 1 + 0.4 \cdot 0.0 = 0.6$$
$$y_3 = 0.6 \cdot x_3 + 0.4 \cdot x_2 = 0.6 \cdot 1 + 0.4 \cdot 1.0 = 1.0$$
$$y_4 = 0.6 \cdot x_4 + 0.4 \cdot x_3 = 0.6 \cdot 1 + 0.4 \cdot 1.0 = 1.0$$

The output sequence is a rounded or smoothed step function (i.e. when the input goes from 0 to 1 in one step, the output goes 0.0, 0.6, 1.0). This type of circuit is called a *low-pass filter* because sudden changes in the input sequence are diminished by averaging consecutive values. Real digital filters have many more delays and coefficients. Consider the output of a filter with 4 delay units given by

$$y_i = C_0 \cdot x_i + C_1 \cdot x_{i-1} + C_2 \cdot x_{i-2} + C_3 \cdot x_{i-3} + C_4 \cdot x_{i-4}$$

If we use this filter with coefficients 0.4, 0.3, 0.2, 0.1 and subject it to a step input, we get

$$y_0 = 0.4 \cdot x_0 + 0.3 \cdot x_{-1} + 0.2 \cdot x_{-2} + 0.1 \cdot x_{-3} = 0.4 \cdot 0 + 0.3 \cdot 0 + 0.2 \cdot 0 + 0.1 \cdot 0 = 0.0$$
$$y_1 = 0.4 \cdot x_1 + 0.3 \cdot x_0 + 0.2 \cdot x_{-1} + 0.1 \cdot x_{-2} = 0.4 \cdot 1 + 0.3 \cdot 0 + 0.2 \cdot 0 + 0.1 \cdot 0 = 0.4$$
$$y_2 = 0.4 \cdot x_2 + 0.3 \cdot x_1 + 0.2 \cdot x_0 + 0.1 \cdot x_{-1} = 0.4 \cdot 1 + 0.3 \cdot 1 + 0.2 \cdot 0 + 0.1 \cdot 0 = 0.7$$
$$y_3 = 0.4 \cdot x_3 + 0.3 \cdot x_2 + 0.2 \cdot x_1 + 0.1 \cdot x_0 = 0.4 \cdot 1 + 0.3 \cdot 1 + 0.2 \cdot 1 + 0.1 \cdot 0 = 0.9$$
$$y_3 = 0.4 \cdot x_4 + 0.3 \cdot x_3 + 0.2 \cdot x_2 + 0.1 \cdot x_1 = 0.4 \cdot 1 + 0.3 \cdot 1 + 0.2 \cdot 1 + 0.1 \cdot 1 = 1.0$$

In this case, the output is even more rounded (i.e. 0.0, 0.4, 0.7, 0.9, 1.0).

A more interesting type of filter is called a *recursive filter* because the output is expressed as a fraction of the current input and a fraction of the previous output. In this case, the output sequence for a recursive filter with a single delay unit is given by

$$y_i = C_0 \cdot x_i + C_1 \cdot y_{i-1}$$

Figure 12.52 shows the structure of a recursive filter. Suppose we apply the same step function to this filter that we used in the previous examples. The output sequence is given by

$$
\begin{aligned}
y_0 &= 0.6 \cdot x_0 + 0.4 \cdot y_{-1} & y_0 &= 0.6 \cdot 0 + 0.4 \cdot 0 = 0.0 \\
y_1 &= 0.6 \cdot x_1 + 0.4 \cdot y_0 & y_1 &= 0.6 \cdot 0 + 0.4 \cdot 0 = 0.0 \\
y_2 &= 0.6 \cdot x_2 + 0.4 \cdot y_1 & y_2 &= 0.6 \cdot 1 + 0.4 \cdot 0 = 0.6 \\
y_3 &= 0.6 \cdot x_3 + 0.4 \cdot y_2 & y_3 &= 0.6 \cdot 1 + 0.4 \cdot 0.6 = 0.84 \\
y_4 &= 0.6 \cdot x_4 + 0.4 \cdot y_3 & y_4 &= 0.6 \cdot 1 + 0.4 \cdot 0.84 = 0.936 \\
y_5 &= 0.6 \cdot x_5 + 0.4 \cdot y_4 & y_5 &= 0.6 \cdot 1 + 0.4 \cdot 0.936 = 0.9744 \\
y_6 &= 0.6 \cdot x_6 + 0.4 \cdot y_5 & y_6 &= 0.6 \cdot 1 + 0.4 \cdot 0.9744 = 0.98976 \\
y_7 &= 0.6 \cdot x_7 + 0.4 \cdot y_6 & y_7 &= 0.6 \cdot 1 + 0.4 \cdot 0.98976 = 0.995904
\end{aligned}
$$

Figure 12.53 plots the input and output series for the recursive filter of Fig. 12.52. As you can see, the output series (i.e. the y_i) rises exponentially to 1. The effect of the operation $C_0 \cdot x_i + C_1 \cdot y_{i-1}$ on a digital sequence is the same as that of a *low-pass* analog filter on a step signal. You can see that the recursive digital filter is more powerful than a linear digital filter. By changing the constants in the digital equation we can change the characteristics of the digital filter. Digital filters are used to process analog signals and to remove noise.

The opposite of a low-pass filter is a *high-pass filter*, which passes rapid changes in the input sequence and rejects slow changes (or a constant level). Consider the recursive digital filter defined by

$$y_i = C_0 \cdot x_i - C_1 \cdot y_{i-1}$$

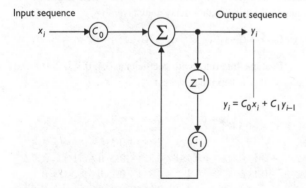

Fig. 12.52 The recursive digital filter.

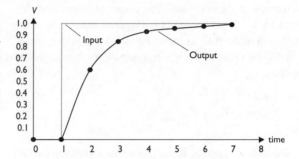

Fig. 12.53 Response of the filter of Fig. 12.52 to a step input.

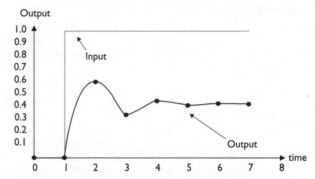

Fig. 12.54 Response of a high pass filter to a step input.

All we have done is change the sign of the constant C_1 and subtracted a fraction of the old output from a fraction of the new input. In this case, a constant or slowly changing signal is subtracted from the output. Consider the previous example with a step input and coefficients $C_0 = 0.6$ and $C_1 = 0.4$:

$$
\begin{aligned}
y_0 &= 0.6 \cdot x_0 - 0.4 \cdot y_{-1} & y_0 &= 0.6 \cdot 0 - 0.4 \cdot 0 = 0.0 \\
y_1 &= 0.6 \cdot x_1 - 0.4 \cdot y_0 & y_1 &= 0.6 \cdot 0 - 0.4 \cdot 0 = 0.0 \\
y_2 &= 0.6 \cdot x_2 - 0.4 \cdot y_1 & y_2 &= 0.6 \cdot 1 - 0.4 \cdot 0 = 0.60 \\
y_3 &= 0.6 \cdot x_3 - 0.4 \cdot y_2 & y_3 &= 0.6 \cdot 1 - 0.4 \cdot 0.6 = 0.36 \\
y_4 &= 0.6 \cdot x_4 - 0.4 \cdot y_3 & y_4 &= 0.6 \cdot 1 - 0.4 \cdot 0.36 = 0.456 \\
y_5 &= 0.6 \cdot x_5 - 0.4 \cdot y_4 & y_5 &= 0.6 \cdot 1 - 0.4 \cdot 0.456 = 0.4176 \\
y_6 &= 0.6 \cdot x_6 - 0.4 \cdot y_5 & y_6 &= 0.6 \cdot 1 - 0.4 \cdot 0.4176 = 0.43296 \\
y_7 &= 0.6 \cdot x_7 - 0.4 \cdot y_6 & y_7 &= 0.6 \cdot 1 - 0.4 \cdot 0.43296 = 0.426816
\end{aligned}
$$

In this case the step function dies away, as Fig. 12.54 demonstrates.

The Kalman filter

The so-called Kalman filter that was introduced in the early 1960s provides a spectacular application of digital filtering. This filter was proposed by Rudolf Emil Kalman who was born in Budapest but emigrated to the USA from Hungary during the Second World War. A Kalman filter can take a time-varying signal that is corrupted by noise and predict the future value of the signal; that is, it can eliminate some of the effects of noise. Kalman filters have been applied to a wide range of systems from space vehicles to medical systems.

The mathematics of Kalman filters belongs in advanced courses in control theory. All we can do here is mention some of the underlying notions. A dynamic system that varies with time can be described by state variables. For example, you can write $x_{i+1} = ax_i$, where x_{i+1} represents the state of the system at time $i + 1$, x_i represents the system at time i, and a characterizes the behavior of the system. In practice, the state equation is given by $x_{i+1} = ax_i + w_i$, where w_i represents a random noise component.

The Kalman filter lets you predict (i.e. make a best guess) the next state of the system when the system is affected by random noise and the measurements themselves are also affected by noise. Suppose you design an aircraft's autopilot to enable it to follow the ground from a very low level. The height of the aircraft above the ground is measured by radar techniques. However, the successive readings from the radar altimeter are corrupted by random noise, which means that any particular reading can't be relied on. Furthermore, successive altimeter readings can't just be averaged because the terrain itself is undulating.

If the ith estimate of the aircraft's height is h_i, the Kalman filter evaluates

$$\underline{h}_i = a_i \underline{h}_{i-1} + (1 - a_i)x_i$$

The underscore under $\underline{h}_i$ and $\underline{h}_{i-1}$ indicates that these are *estimated* values. The current value of h is obtained from the previous estimate, $\underline{h}_{i-1}$, plus the new data, x_i. The coefficient of the filter, a_i, is a function of i; that is, the coefficient varies with time. The recursive nature of the Kalman filter means that trends in the input are taken into account.

Correlation

One of the most important applications of digital signal processing is the recovery of very weak signals that have been corrupted by noise. Signals received from satellites and deep space vehicles are often so weak that there is considerably more noise than signal—anyone listening to such a signal on a

loudspeaker would hear nothing more than the hiss of white noise. Modern signal processing techniques enable you to extract signals from noise when the signal level is thousands of times weaker than the noise.

The technique used to recover signals from noise is called *correlation*. We met correlation earlier when we discussed the waveforms used to record data on disks—the more unalike that the waveforms used to record 1s and 0s are, the better. Correlation is a measure of how similar two waveforms (or binary sequences) are. Correlation varies from -1 to 0 to $+1$. If the correlation is $+1$, the signals are identical. If the correlation is 0, the two signals are unrelated. If the correlation is -1, one signal is the inverse of the other.

Two signals can be correlated by taking successive samples from each of the series, multiplying the pairs of samples, and then averaging the sum of the product. Consider now the correlation function of two series $X = x_0, x_1, x_2, x_3, x_4$ and $Y = y_0, y_1, y_2, y_3, y_4$.

The correlation between X and Y is given by $1/5(x_0 \cdot y_0 + x_1 \cdot y_1 + x_2 \cdot y_2 + x_3 \cdot y_3 + x_4 \cdot y_4)$.

An example of the use of correlation is the effect of rainfall in the mountains on crop growth in the plain. Simply correlating the sequence of rainfall measurements with crop growth doesn't help because there's a delay between rainfall and plant growth. We can generate several correlation functions by correlating one sequence with a delayed version of the other sequence. Now we have a sequence of correlation functions that depend on the delay between the sequences, and we can express the kth correlation value as

$$C_k = \sum x_i y_{i+k}$$

Suppose that $X = 1, 2, 3, -1, 4, 2, 0, 1$ and $Y = 0, 0, 1, -1, 0, 1, 1, 0, 0, 0$:

$C_0 = 1 \times 0 + 2 \times 0 + 3 \times 1 + -1 \times -1 + 4 \times 0 + 2 \times 1 + 0 \times 1 + 1 \times 0 = 6$
$C_1 = 1 \times 0 + 2 \times 1 + 3 \times -1 + -1 \times 0 + 4 \times 1 + 2 \times 1 + 0 \times 0 + 1 \times 0 = 5$
$C_2 = 1 \times 1 + 2 \times -1 + 3 \times 0 - 1 \times 1 + 4 \times 1 + 2 \times 0 + 0 \times 0 + 1 \times 0 = 2$

These results don't seem very interesting until we apply this technique to a real situation. Suppose a transmitter uses the sequence 0.25, -0.5, 1.0, -0.5, 0.25 to represent a logical 1; that is, a 1 is transmitted as the sequence of values 0.25, -0.5, 1.0, -0.5, 0.25. Suppose we receive this signal without noise and correlate it with the sequence representing a 1. That is,

$C_0 = 0.25 \times 0.25 + -0.5 \times -0.50 + 1 \times 1.0 + -0.5 \times -0.5 + 0.25 \times 0.25 = 1.625$
$C_1 = 0.25 \times 0.00 + -0.5 \times 0.25 + 1 \times -0.5 + -0.5 \times 1.0 + 0.25 \times -0.5 + 0.0 \times 0.25 = -1.25$
$C_2 = 0.25 \times 0.00 + -0.5 \times 0.00 + 1 \times 0.25 + -0.5 \times -0.5 + 0.25 \times 1.0 + 0.0 \times -0.5 + 0.0 \times 0.25 = 0.75$

As you can see, the greatest correlation factor occurs when the sequence is correlated with itself. If the sequence is corrupted by samples of random noise, the noise is not correlated with the sequence and the correlation function is low. Noisy data from, say, a satellite is correlated with the same sequence used to generate the data. This operation is performed by correlating the incoming data with the appropriate sequence and varying the delay k. A sequence of correlation values are recorded and compared with a threshold value. If the correlation is above the threshold, it is assumed that the sequence is present in the received signal.

Here we have done little more than mention a few examples of digital signal processing. The techniques we have described can be used in both the audio and visual domains. Processing the signals that represent images allows us to, for example, sharpen blurred images or to remove noise from them, or to emphasize their edges.

Tutorial example

A sine wave has a minimum amplitude of 0 V, a maximum amplitude of 1 V, and a period of 200 ms. This signal is applied to an analog-to-digital converter with a full-scale input span of $0 - 1$ V. For this signal calculate:

(a) The number of bits required to convert the signal into digital form to an accuracy of 0.01 percent.

(b) The minimum rate at which the signal must be sampled.

(c) The maximum permitted aperture time if the error due to aperture time is to be less than $\frac{1}{4}$ least-significant bit. To simplify your calculation, you may assume that a sine wave can be approximated by a triangular waveform with the same peak amplitude.

Solution
The number of bits required to convert the signal into digital form to an accuracy of 0.01 percent is given by: accuracy is 1 part in 10 000. The nearest power of 2 is $2^{14} = 16K$. Therefore a 14-bit device is required.

The minimum rate at which the signal must be sampled is twice the highest frequency component. A period of $200 \, ms = 5 \, Hz$, and the minimum sampling rate is 10 Hz.

During the aperture time, the signal must not change by more than $\frac{1}{4}$ LSB. This is given by $1 \, V/2^{16} = 1.53 \times 10^{-5} = 15 \, \mu V$. The signal changes linearly by 1 V in 100 ms. The time to change by $15 \, \mu V$ is $15 \times 10^{-1}/10^{-6} = 15 \times 10^{-7} \, s$.

Problems

1. A highly reliable computer has five CPU modules each with a probability of failure of 0.01 percent per 1000 hours. If the system gives an acceptable level of performance with at least three CPUs operational, what is the reliability of the system?

2. A computer has an MTBF of 5000 hours. If a given system uses one of these computers, what is the probability of failure due to a failure of the CPU over a period of 100 hours?

3. What are the most important constraints on the designer who is working on:
   (a) A washing machine controller?
   (b) The on-board navigation computer of a space probe?
   (c) A controller in a pace-maker for surgical implantation?

4. Describe how a successive approximation analog-to-digital converter operates (you may assume the existence of a digital-to-analog converter).

5. With the aid of a block schematic diagram explain the principles of operation of a ramp and counter ADC.

6. Analog-to-digital converters suffer from three errors: *offset* errors, *gain* errors, and *non-linearity* errors. Briefly explain how these errors affect the performance of the ADC and to what extent their effects can be overcome.

7. What is the difference between the concepts of *accuracy* and *resolution* as used to describe the operation of an ADC?

8. What is meant by the term *quantization error*?

9. Calculate the quantization error for a 12-bit ADC with an input span of 5 volts.

10. An 8-bit ADC with a $10 \, \mu s$ conversion time and an input span of 10 V is to be used to digitize a voltage ramp signal with a slew rate of 178 volts/second. Show by calculation whether or not the full resolution of the ADC can be utilized.

11. A time-varying analog voltage has a voltage swing which matches the input span of a 16-bit ADC. If the ADC has an aperture time of 4 ms determine the maximum frequency of the analog signal that will not cause loss of resolution during conversion.

12. A triangular wave has a peak-to-peak amplitude of 16 V and a period of 1000 ms. For this signal:
    (a) Calculate the number of bits required to convert the signal into digital form to an accuracy of 0.001 percent.

(b) The maximum permitted aperture time if the error due to aperture time is to be less than 1 least-significant bit.

13. What is a *sample and hold circuit* and how is it used in ADC systems?

14. How do the *aperture time*, the *droop rate*, and the *acquisition time* of a sample and hold circuit affect the ability of a sampling system to satisfactorily digitize an analog signal?

15. The output of a digital filter, y_k, is related to its input x_i by the relationship

$$y_k = C_1 \cdot x_k + C_2 \cdot x_{k-1}$$

Assume that a step input with an amplitude of 1 V is applied to this filter at time $t=0$. If the value of coefficient C_1 is 0.5 and the value of C_2 is 0.5, draw a plot of the output of the filter as a function of time.

16. Perform the same calculation for a filter defined by:

$$y_k = C_1 \cdot x_k + C_2 \cdot x_{k-1} + C_3 \cdot x_{k-2}$$

Assume that $C_1 = 0.5$, $C_2 = 0.3$, and $C_3 = 0.2$.

Appendix: The 68000 instruction set

This appendix provides details of the 68000's most important instructions (we have omitted some of the instructions that are not relevant to this book).

In each case, we have given the definition and assembly language format of the instruction. We have also provided its size (byte, word, or longword) and the addressing modes it takes for both source and destination operands.

Finally, we have included the effect of the instruction on the 68000's condition code register. Each instruction either sets/clears a flag bit, leaves it unchanged, or has an 'undefined' effect, which is indicated by the symbols *, -, and U, respectively. A 0 in the CCR indicates that the corresponding bit is always cleared.

ADD	**Add binary**
Operation:	[destination]←[source] + [destination]
Syntax:	ADD <ea>,Dn
	ADD Dn, <ea>
Attributes:	Size = byte, word, longword
Description:	Add the source operand to the destination operand and store the result in the destination location.
Condition codes:	X N Z V C
	* * * * *

Source operand addressing modes

Dn	An	(An)	(An)+	–(An)	(d,An)	(d,An,Xi)	ABS.W	ABS.L	(d,PC)	(d,PC,Xn)	imm
✔	✔	✔	✔	✔	✔	✔	✔	✔	✔	✔	✔

Destination operand addressing modes

Dn	An	(An)	(An)+	–(An)	(d,An)	(d,An,Xi)	ABS.W	ABS.L	(d,PC)	(d,PC,Xn)	imm
✔		✔	✔	✔	✔	✔	✔	✔			

ADDA	**Add address**
Operation:	[destination]←[source] + [destination]
Syntax:	ADDA <ea>,An
Attributes:	Size = word, longword
Description:	Add the source operand to the destination address register and store the result in the destination address register. The source is sign-extended before it is added to the destination; e.g. if we execute ADDA.W D3,A4 where A4 = 00000100₁₆ and D3.W = 8002₁₆, the contents of D3 are first

sign-extended to $FFFF8002_{16}$ and added to 00000100_{16} to give $FFFF8102_{16}$, which is stored in A4.

Application: To add to the contents of an address register and without updating the CCR. Note that `ADDA.W D0,A0` is the same as `LEA (A0,D0.W),A0`.

Condition codes:

```
X  N  Z  V  C
-  -  -  -  -
```

An `ADDA` operation does not affect the state of the CCR.

Source operand addressing modes

Dn	An	(An)	(An)+	–(An)	(d,An)	(d,An,Xi)	ABS.W	ABS.L	(d,PC)	(d,PC,Xn)	imm
✔	✔	✔	✔	✔	✔	✔	✔	✔	✔	✔	✔

ADDI — Add immediate

Operation: `[destination]←<literal>+[destination]`

Syntax: `ADDI #<data>,<ea>`

Attributes: Size = byte, word, longword

Description: Add immediate data to the destination operand. Store the result in the destination operand. `ADDI` can be used to add a literal directly to a memory location. For example, `ADDI.W #$1234,$2000` has the effect $[M(2000_{16})] \leftarrow [M(2000_{16})] + 1234_{16}$.

Condition codes:

```
X  N  Z  V  C
*  *  *  *  *
```

Destination operand addressing modes

Dn	An	(An)	(An)+	–(An)	(d,An)	(d,An,Xi)	ABS.W	ABS.L	(d,PC)	(d,PC,Xn)	imm
✔		✔	✔	✔	✔	✔	✔	✔			

ADDQ — Add quick

Operation: `[destination]←<literal>+[destination]`

Syntax: `ADDQ #<data>,<ea>`

Sample syntax: `ADDQ #6,D3`

Attributes: Size = byte, word, longword

Description: Add the immediate data to the contents of the destination operand. The immediate data must be in the range 1 to 8. Word and longword operations on address registers do not affect condition codes and a word operation on an address register affects all bits of the register.

Application: `ADDQ` is used to add a small constant to the operand at the effective address. Some assemblers permit you to write `ADD` and then choose `ADDQ` **automatically** if the constant is in the range 1 to 8.

Condition codes:

```
X  N  Z  V  C
*  *  *  *  *
```

The CCR is not updated if the destination operand is an address register.

Destination operand addressing modes

Dn	An	(An)	(An)+	–(An)	(d,An)	(d,An,Xi)	ABS.W	ABS.L	(d,PC)	(d,PC,Xn)	imm
✔	✔	✔	✔	✔	✔	✔	✔	✔			

ADDX   Add extended

Operation: [destination]←[source] + [destination] + [X]

Syntax: ADDX Dy,Dx

       ADDX −(Ay),−(Ax)

Attributes: Size = byte, word, longword

Description: Add the source operand to the destination operand along with the extend bit, and store the result in the destination location. The only legal addressing modes are data register direct and memory to memory with address register indirect using predecrementing.

Application: The ADDX instruction is used in chain arithmetic to add together strings of bytes (words or long-words). Consider the addition of two 128-bit numbers, each of which is stored as four consecutive longwords.

```
         LEA     Number1,A0   A0 points at the first number
         LEA     Number2,A1   A1 points at the second number
         MOVE    #3,DO        Four longwords to add
         MOVE    #$00,CCR     Clear the X-bit and Z-bit of the CCR
LOOP     ADDX    −(A0),−(A1)  Add a pair of numbers
         DBRA    DO,LOOP      Repeat until all added
```

Condition codes: X N Z V C

       * * * * *

The Z-bit is cleared if the result is non-zero, and left unchanged otherwise. The Z-bit can be used to test for zero after a chain of multiple precision operations.

AND   AND logical

Operation: [destination]←[source] · [destination]

Syntax: AND <ea>,Dn

       AND Dn,<ea>

Attributes: Size = byte, word, longword

Description: AND the source operand to the destination operand and store the result in the destination location.

Application: AND is used to mask bits. If you wish to clear bits 3 to 6 of data register D7, you can execute AND #%10000111,D7. Unfortunately, the AND operation cannot be used with an address register as either a source or a destination operand. If you wish to perform a logical operation on an address register, you have to copy the address to a data register and then perform the operation there.

Condition codes: X N Z V C

       - * * 0 0

Source operand addressing modes

Dn	An	(An)	(An)+	−(An)	(d,An)	(d,An,Xi)	ABS.W	ABS.L	(d,PC)	(d,PC,Xn)	imm
✔		✔	✔	✔	✔	✔	✔	✔	✔	✔	✔

Destination operand addressing modes

Dn	An	(An)	(An)+	−(An)	(d,An)	(d,An,Xi)	ABS.W	ABS.L	(d,PC)	(d,PC,Xn)	imm
✔		✔	✔	✔	✔	✔	✔	✔			

ANDI — AND immediate

Operation: [destination]←<literal>·[destination]

Syntax: ANDI #<data>,<ea>

Attributes: Size=byte, word, longword

Description: AND the immediate data to the destination operand. The ANDI instruction permits a literal operand to be ANDed with a destination other than a data register. For example, ANDI #$FE00,$1234 or ANDI.B #$F0,(A2)+.

Condition codes:

```
X N Z V C
- * * 0 0
```

Destination operand addressing modes

Dn	An	(An)	(An)+	-(An)	(d,An)	(d,An,Xi)	ABS.W	ABS.L	(d,PC)	(d,PC,Xn)	imm
✔		✔	✔	✔	✔	✔	✔	✔			

ANDI to CCR — AND immediate to CCR

Operation: [CCR]←<data>·[CCR]

Syntax: ANDI #<data>,CCR

Attributes: Size=byte

Description: AND the immediate data to the condition code register (i.e. the least-significant byte of the status register).

Application: ANDI is used to clear selected bits of the CCR. For example, ANDI #$FA,CCR clears the Z- and C-bits, i.e. XNZVC=X N 0 V 0.

Condition codes:

```
X N Z V C
* * * * *
```

X: cleared if bit 4 of data is zero
N: cleared if bit 3 of data is zero
Z: cleared if bit 2 of data is zero
V: cleared if bit 1 of data is zero
C: cleared if bit 0 of data is zero

ANDI to SR — AND immediate to status register

Operation:
```
IF [S]=1
    THEN
        [SR]←<literal>·[SR]
    ELSE TRAP
```

Syntax: ANDI #<data>,SR

Attributes: Size=word

Description: AND the immediate data to the status register and store the result in the status register. All bits of the SR are affected.

Application: This instruction is used to clear the interrupt mask, the S-bit, and the T-bit of the SR. ANDI #<data>,SR affects both the status byte of the SR and the CCR. For example, ANDI #$7FFF,SR clears the trace bit of the status register, whereas ANDI #$7FFE,SR clears the trace bit and also clears the carry bit of the CCR.

Condition codes:

```
X N Z V C
* * * * *
```

ASL, ASR	**Arithmetic shift left/right**
Operation:	[destination]←[destination] shifted by <count>
Syntax:	ASL Dx,Dy
	ASR Dx,Dy
	ASL #<data>,Dy
	ASR #<data>,Dy
	ASL <ea>
	ASR <ea>
Attributes:	Size=byte, word, longword
Description:	Arithmetically shift the bits of the operand in the specified direction (i.e. left or right). The shift count may be specified in one of three ways. The count may be a literal, the contents of a data register, or the value 1. An immediate (i.e. literal) count permits a shift of 1 to 8 places. If the count is in a register, the value is modulo 64 (i.e. 0 to 63). If no count is specified, one shift is made (i.e. ASL <ea> shifts the contents of the **word** at the effective address one place left).

An arithmetic shift left shifts a zero into the least-significant bit position and shifts the most-significant bit out into both the X- and the C-bits of the CCR. The overflow bit of the CCR is set if a sign change occurs during shifting (i.e. if the most-significant bit changes value during shifting).

The effect of an arithmetic shift right is to shift the least-significant bit into both the X- and C-bits of the CCR. The most-significant bit (i.e. the sign bit) is **replicated** to preserve the sign of the number.

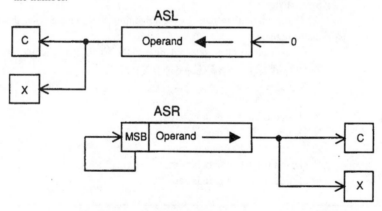

Application:	ASL multiplies a two's complement number by 2. ASL is almost identical to the corresponding logical shift, LSR. The only difference between ASL and LSL is that ASL sets the V-bit of the CCR if overflow occurs, whereas LSL clears the V-bit to zero. An ASR divides a two's complement number by 2. When applied to the contents of a memory location, all 68000 shift operations operate on a word.
Condition codes:	X N Z V C
	* * * * *

The X-bit and the C-bit are set according to the last bit shifted out of the operand. If the shift count is zero, the C-bit is cleared. The V-bit is set if the most-significant bit is changed at any time during the shift operation and cleared otherwise.

Destination operand addressing modes

Dn	An	(An)	(An)+	−(An)	(d,An)	(d,An,Xi)	ABS.W	ABS.L	(d,PC)	(d,PC,Xn)	imm
✔		✔	✔	✔	✔	✔	✔	✔			

Bcc	**Branch on condition cc**
Operation:	If cc=1 THEN [PC]←[PC]+d
Syntax:	Bcc <label>
Sample syntax:	BEQ Loop_4
	BVC *+8
Attributes:	BEQ takes an 8-bit or a 16-bit offset (i.e. displacement).
Description:	

If the specified logical condition is met, program execution continues at location [PC]+displacement, d. The displacement is a two's complement value. The value in the PC corresponds to the current location plus two. The range of the branch is -126 to $+128$ bytes with an 8-bit offset, and -32 kbyte to $+32$ kbyte with a 16-bit offset. A short branch to the next instruction is impossible, since the branch code 0 indicates a long branch with a 16-bit offset.

BCC	branch on carry clear	$\overline{C}$
BCS	branch on carry set	C
BEQ	branch on equal	Z
BGE	branch on greater than or equal	$N \cdot V + \overline{N} \cdot \overline{V}$
BGT	branch on greater than	$N \cdot V \cdot \overline{Z} + \overline{N} \cdot \overline{V} \cdot \overline{Z}$
BHI	branch on higher than	$\overline{C} \cdot \overline{Z}$
BLE	branch on less than or equal	$Z + N \cdot \overline{V} + \overline{N} \cdot V$
BLS	branch on lower than or same	$C + Z$
BLT	branch on less than	$N \cdot \overline{V} + \overline{N} \cdot V$
BMI	branch on minus (i.e. negative)	N
BNE	branch on not equal	$\overline{Z}$
BPL	branch on plus (i.e. positive)	$\overline{N}$
BVC	branch on overflow clear	$\overline{V}$
BVS	branch on overflow set	V

There are two types of conditional branch instruction: those that branch on an unsigned condition and those that branch on a signed condition; e.g. $FF is greater than $10 when the numbers are unsigned (i.e. 255 is greater than 16). However, if the numbers are signed, $FF is less than $10 (i.e. -1 is less than 16).

The signed comparisons are:

BGE	branch on greater than or equal
BGT	branch on greater than
BLE	branch on lower than or equal
BLT	branch on less than

The unsigned comparisons are:

BHS	BCC	branch on higher than or same
BHI		branch on higher than
BLS		branch on lower than or same
BLO	BCS	branch on less than

The official mnemonics BCC (branch on carry clear) and BCS (branch on carry set) can be renamed as BHS (branch on higher than or same) and BLO (branch on less than), respectively. Many 68000 assemblers support these alternative mnemonics.

Condition codes:	X N Z V C
	- - - - -

BCLR — Test a bit and clear

Operation:

$[Z] \leftarrow \overline{<\text{bit number}> \text{ OF } [\text{destination}]}$

$<\text{bit number}> \text{ OF } [\text{destination}] \leftarrow 0$

Syntax: BCLR Dn,\<ea\>

BCLR #\<data\>,\<ea\>

Attributes: Size = byte, longword

Description: A bit in the destination operand is tested and the state of the specified bit is reflected in the condition of the Z-bit in the condition code. After the test, the state of the specified bit is cleared in the destination. If a data register is the destination, the bit numbering is modulo 32, allowing bit manipulation of all bits in a data register. If a memory location is the destination, a byte is read from that location, the bit operation performed using the bit number modulo 8, and the byte written back to the location. Bit zero refers to the least-significant bit. The bit number for this operation may be specified either by an immediate value or dynamically by the contents of a data register.

Application: Suppose that the contents of memory location $1234 are 11111010_2, and the operation BCLR #4,$1234 is carried out. This instruction tests bit 4. It is a 1 and therefore the Z-bit of the CCR is set to 0. Bit 4 of the destination operand is cleared and the new contents of $1234 are: 11101010_2.

Condition codes:

```
X N Z V C
- - * - -
```

Z: set if the bit tested is zero, cleared otherwise.

Destination operand addressing modes

Dn	An	(An)	(An)+	−(An)	(d,An)	(d,An,Xi)	ABS.W	ABS.L	(d,PC)	(d,PC,Xn)	imm
✔		✔	✔	✔	✔	✔	✔	✔			

Data register direct addressing, Dn, uses a longword operand. Other modes use a byte operand.

BRA — Branch always

Operation: $[PC] \leftarrow [PC] + d$

Syntax: BRA \<label\>

BRA \<literal\>

Attributes: Size = byte, word

Description: Program execution continues at location $[PC] + d$. The displacement, d, is a two's complement value (8 bits for a short branch and 16 bits for a long branch). The value in the PC corresponds to the current location plus two. A short branch to the next instruction is impossible, since the branch code 0 is used to indicate a long branch with a 16-bit offset.

Application: A BRA is an unconditional relative jump (or goto). You use a BRA instruction to write position independent code, because the destination address (**branch target address**) is specified with respect to the current value of the PC. A JMP instruction does not produce position-independent code.

Condition codes:

```
X N Z V C
- - - - -
```

BSET	**Test a bit and set**
Operation:	[Z]←<bit number> OF [destination]
	<bit number> OF [destination]←0
Syntax:	BSET Dn,<ea>
	BSET #<data>,<ea>
Attributes:	Size=byte, longword
Description:	A bit in the destination operand is tested and the state of the specified bit is reflected in the condition of the Z-bit of the condition code. After the test, the specified bit is set in the destination. If a data register is the destination then the bit numbering is modulo 32, allowing bit manipulation of all bits in a data register. If a memory location is the destination, a byte is read from that location, the bit operation performed using bit number modulo 8, and the byte written back to the location. Bit zero refers to the least-significant bit. The bit number for this operation may be specified either by an immediate value or dynamically by the contents of a data register.
Condition codes:	X N Z V C
	- - * - -
	Z: set if the bit tested is zero, cleared otherwise.

Destination operand addressing mode for BSET Dn,<ea> form

Dn	An	(An)	(An)+	−(An)	(d,An)	(d,An,Xi)	ABS.W	ABS.L	(d,PC)	(d,PC,Xn)	imm
✔		✔	✔	✔	✔	✔	✔	✔			

BSR	**Branch to subroutine**
Operation:	[SP]←[SP]−4; [M([SP])]←[PC]; [PC]←[PC]+d
Syntax:	BSR <label>
	BSR <literal>
Attributes:	Size=byte, word
Description:	The longword address of the instruction immediately following the BSR instruction is pushed on to the system stack pointed at by A7. Program execution then continues at location [PC]+ displacement, d. The displacement is an 8-bit two's complement value for a short branch, or a 16-bit two's complement value for a long branch. The value in the PC corresponds to the current location plus two. Note that a short branch to the next instruction is impossible, since the branch code 0 is used to indicate a long branch with a 16-bit offset.
Applicaton:	BSR is used to call a procedure or a subroutine. It provides relative addressing (and therefore position-independent code) and its use is preferable to JSR.
Condition codes:	X N Z V C
	- - - - -

BTST	**Test a bit**
Operation:	[Z]←<bit number> OF [destination]
Syntax:	BTST Dn,<ea>
	BTST #<data>,<ea>
Attributes:	Size=byte, longword
Description:	A bit in the destination operand is tested and the state of the specified bit is reflected in the condition of the Z-bit in the CCR. The destination is not modified by a BTST instruction. If a data register is the destination, then the bit numbering is modulo 32, allowing bit manipulation of all

bits in a data register. If a memory location is the destination, a byte is read from that location and the bit operation performed. Bit 0 refers to the least-significant bit. The bit number for this operation may be specified either statically by an immediate value or dynamically by the contents of a data register.

Condition codes:
```
X N Z V C
- - * - -
```
Z: set if the bit tested is zero, cleared otherwise.

Destination operand addressing modes for `BTST Dn,<ea>` form

Dn	An	(An)	(An)+	–(An)	(d,An)	(d,An,Xi)	ABS.W	ABS.L	(d,PC)	(d,PC,Xn)	imm
✔		✔	✔	✔	✔	✔	✔	✔			

CLR — Clear an operand

Operation: `[destination]←0`

Syntax: `CLR <ea>`

Sample syntax: `CLR (A4)+`

Attributes: Size = byte, word, longword

Description: The destination is cleared by loading with all zeros. The `CLR` instruction can't be used to clear an address register. You can use `SUBA.L A0,A0` to clear A0.

Condition codes:
```
X N Z V C
- 0 1 0 0
```

Source operand addressing modes

Dn	An	(An)	(An)+	–(An)	(d,An)	(d,An,Xi)	ABS.W	ABS.L	(d,PC)	(d,PC,Xn)	imm
✔		✔	✔	✔	✔	✔	✔	✔			

CMP — Compare

Operation: `[destination]-[source]`

Syntax: `CMP <ea>,Dn`

Sample syntax: `CMP (Test,A6,D3.W),D2`

Attributes: Size = byte, word, longword

Description: Subtract the source operand from the destination operand and set the condition codes accordingly. The destination must be a data register. The destination is not modified by this instruction.

Condition codes:
```
X N Z V C
- * * * *
```

Source operand addressing modes

Dn	An	(An)	(An)+	–(An)	(d,An)	(d,An,Xi)	ABS.W	ABS.L	(d,PC)	(d,PC,Xn)	imm
✔	✔	✔	✔	✔	✔	✔	✔	✔	✔	✔	✔

CMPA

Compare address

Operation:	`[destination]-[source]`
Syntax:	`CMPA    <ea>,An`
Sample syntax:	`CMPA.L  #$1000,A4`
	`CMPA.W  (A2)+,A6`
	`CMPA.L  D5,A2`
Attributes:	Size = word, longword
Description:	Subtract the source operand from the destination address register and set the condition codes accordingly. The address register is not modified. The size of the operation may be specified as word or longword. Word length operands are sign-extended to 32 bits before the comparison is carried out.
Condition codes:	X N Z V C
	- * * * *

Source operand addressing modes

Dn	An	(An)	(An)+	–(An)	(d,An)	(d,An,Xi)	ABS.W	ABS.L	(d,PC)	(d,PC,Xn)	imm
✔	✔	✔	✔	✔	✔	✔	✔	✔	✔	✔	✔

CMPI

Compare immediate

Operation:	`[destination]-<immediate data>`
Syntax:	`CMPI #<data>,<ea>`
Attributes:	Size = byte, word, longword
Description:	Subtract the immediate data from the destination operand and set the condition codes accordingly—the destination is not modified. `CMPI` permits the comparison of a literal with memory.
Condition codes:	X N Z V C
	- * * * *

Destination operand addressing modes

Dn	An	(An)	(An)+	–(An)	(d,An)	(d,An,Xi)	ABS.W	ABS.L	(d,PC)	(d,PC,Xn)	imm
✔		✔	✔	✔	✔	✔	✔	✔			

CMPM

Compare memory with memory

Operation:	`[destination]-[source]`
Syntax:	`CMPM (Ay)+,(Ax)+`
Attributes:	Size = byte, word, longword
Sample syntax:	`CMPM.B (A3)+,(A4)+`
Description:	Subtract the source operand from the destination operand and set the condition codes accordingly. The destination is not modified by this instruction. The only permitted addressing mode is address register indirect with postincrementing for both source and destination operands.

Application:

Used to compare the contents of two blocks of memory. For example:

```
*           Compare two blocks of memory for equality

            LEA     Source,A0        A0 points to source block
            LEA     Destination,A1   A1 points to destination block
            MOVE.W  #Count-1,D0      Compare Count words
        RPT CMPM.W  (A0)+,(A1)+      Compare pair of words
            DBNE    D0,RPT           Repeat until all done
            .
            .
```

Condition codes:

```
X N Z V C
_ * * * *
```

DBcc   Test condition, decrement, and branch

Operation:
```
IF(condition false)
    THEN [Dn]←[Dn]-1 {decrement loop counter}
        IF [Dn]=-1 THEN [PC] ←[PC]+2 {fall through to next
            instruction}
        ELSE [PC] ←[PC]+d {take branch}
    ELSE [PC]←[PC]+2 {fall through to next instruction}
```

Syntax: DBcc Dn,<label>

Attributes: Size = word

Description:

The DBcc instruction provides an automatic looping facility. The DBcc instruction requires three parameters: a branch condition (specified by 'cc'), a data register that serves as the loop down-counter, and a label that indicates the start of the loop. The DBcc first tests the condition 'cc', and if 'cc' is true the loop is terminated and the branch back to <label> not taken. The 14 branch conditions supported by Bcc are also supported by DBcc, as well as DBF and DBT (F=false, and T=true). Many assemblers permit the mnemonic DBF to be expressed as DBRA (i.e. decrement and branch back).

The condition tested by the DBcc instruction works in the **opposite** sense to a Bcc. For example, BCC means branch on carry clear, whereas DBcc means continue (i.e. exit the loop) on carry clear. That is, the DBcc condition is a loop terminator. If the termination condition is not true, the low-order 16 bits of the specified data register are decremented. If the result is -1, the loop is not taken and the next instruction is executed. If the result is not -1, a branch is made to 'label'. The label is a 16-bit signed value, permitting a branch range of -32 to $+32$ kbyte. The loop may be executed up to 64K times.

We can use the instruction DBEQ, decrement and branch on zero, to mechanize the high-level language construct REPEAT...UNTIL.

```
LOOP ...                    REPEAT
     ...
     ...                        [D0]:=[D0]-1
     ...
     DBEQ   D0,REPEAT       UNTIL [DO]=-1 OR [Z]=1
```

Application:

Suppose we wish to input a block of 512 bytes of data (the data is returned in register D1). If the input routine returns a value zero in D1, an error has occurred and the loop must be exited.

```
                    LEA       Dest,A0      Set up a pointer to the data destination
                    MOVE.W    #511,D0      512 bytes to be input
            AGAIN   BSR       INPUT        Get a data value in D1
                    MOVE.B    D1,(A0)+     Store it
                    DBEQ      D0,AGAIN     REPEAT until D1=0 OR 512 times
```

Condition codes: X N Z V C

                  - - - - -

Not affected.

DIVS, DIVU   Signed divide, unsigned divide

Operation: `[destination]←[destination]/[source]`

Syntax: `DIVS <ea>,Dn`

                 `DIVU <ea>,Dn`

Attributes: Size = a longword is divided by a word to give a longword result quotient and remainder.

Description: Divide the destination operand by the source operand and store the result in the destination. The destination is a longword and the source is a 16-bit value. The result (i.e. destination register) is a 32-bit value arranged so that the quotient is the lower-order word and the remainder is the upper-order word. DIVU performs division on unsigned values and DIVS performs division on two's complement values. An attempt to divide by zero causes an exception. For DIVS, the sign of the remainder is always the same as the sign of the dividend (unless the remainder is zero).

Attempting to divide a number by zero results in a divide-by-zero exception. If overflow is detected during division, the operands are unaffected. Overflow is checked for at the start of the operation and occurs if the quotient is larger than a 16-bit signed integer. If the upper word of the dividend is greater than or equal to the divisor, the V-bit is set and the instruction terminated.

Application: The division of D0 by D1 is carried out by DIVU D1,D0 and results in:

`[D0(0:15)]←[D0(0:31)]/[D1(0:15)]`

`[D0(16:31)]←remainder`

Condition codes: X N Z V C

                  - * * * 0

The X-bit is not affected by a division. The N-bit is set if the quotient is negative. The Z-bit is set if the quotient is zero. The V-bit is set if division overflow occurs (in which case the Z- and N-bits are undefined). The C-bit is always cleared.

Source operand addressing modes

Dn	An	(An)	(An)+	–(An)	(d,An)	(d,An,Xi)	ABS.W	ABS.L	(d,PC)	(d,PC,Xn)	imm
✔		✔	✔	✔	✔	✔	✔	✔	✔	✔	✔

EOR   Exclusive OR logical

Operation: `[destination]←[source]⊕[destination]`

Syntax: `EOR Dn,<ea>`

Sample syntax: `EOR D3,−(A3)`

Attributes: Size = byte, word, longword

Description: EOR (exclusive or) the source operand with the destination operand and store the result in the destination location. The source operand must be a data register and the operation EOR <ea>, Dn is not permitted.

Application: The EOR instruction is used to **toggle** (i.e. change the state of) selected bits in the operand. For example, if [D0] = 00001111, and [D1] = 10101010, the operation EOR.B D0, D1 toggles bits 0 to 3 of D1 and results in [D1] = 10100101.

Condition codes:
```
X N Z V C
- * * 0 0
```

Destination operand addressing modes

Dn	An	(An)	(An)+	-(An)	(d,An)	(d,An,Xi)	ABS.W	ABS.L	(d,PC)	(d,PC,Xn)	imm
✔		✔	✔	✔	✔	✔	✔	✔			

EORI **EOR immediate**

Operation: [destination] ← <literal> ⊕ [destination]

Syntax: EORI #<data>, <ea>

Attributes: Size = byte, word, longword

Description: EOR the immediate data with the contents of the destination operand. Store the result in the destination operand.

Condition codes:
```
X N Z V C
- * * 0 0
```

Destination operand addressing modes

Dn	An	(An)	(An)+	-(An)	(d,An)	(d,An,Xi)	ABS.W	ABS.L	(d,PC)	(d,PC,Xn)	imm
✔		✔	✔	✔	✔	✔	✔	✔			

EXG **Exchange registers**

Operation: [Rx] ← [Ry]; [Ry] ← [Rx]

Syntax: EXG Rx, Ry

Sample syntax:
```
EXG D3, D4
EXG D2, A0
EXG A7, D5
```

Attributes: Size = longword

Description: Exchange the contents of two registers. This is a longword operation because the entire 32-bit contents of two registers are exchanged. The instruction permits the exchange of address registers, data registers, and address and data registers.

Application: One application of EXG is to load an address into a data register and then process it using instructions that act on data registers. Then the reverse operation can be used to return the result to the address register. Using EXG preserves the original contents of the data register.

Condition codes:
```
X N Z V C
- - - - -
```

EXT	**Sign-extend a data register**
Operation:	[destination] ← sign-extended[destination]
Syntax:	EXT.W Dn
	EXT.L Dn
Attributes:	Size = word, longword
Description:	Extend the least-significant byte in a data register to a word, or extend the least-significant word in a data register to a longword. If the operation is word sized, bit 7 of the designated data register is copied to bits (8:15). If the operation is longword sized, bit 15 is copied to bits (16:31).
Application:	If [D0] = \$12345678, EXT.W D0 results in 12340078_{16}.
	If [D0] = \$12345678, EXT.L D0 results in 00005678_{16}.
Condition codes:	X N Z V C
	- * * 0 0

ILLEGAL	**Illegal instruction**
Operation:	[SSP] ← [SSP] − 4; [M([SSP])] ← [PC];
	[SSP] ← [SSP] − 2; [M([SSP])] ← [SR];
	[PC] ← Illegal instruction vector
Syntax:	ILLEGAL
Attributes:	None
Description:	The bit pattern of the illegal instruction, $4AFC_{16}$, causes the illegal instruction trap to be taken. As in all exceptions, the contents of the program counter and the processor status word are pushed on to the supervisor stack at the start of exception processing.
Application:	Any **unknown** pattern of bits read by the 68000 during an instruction read phase would cause an illegal instruction trap. The ILLEGAL instruction can be thought of as an **official** illegal instruction. It can be used to test the illegal instruction trap and will always be an illegal instruction in any future enhancement of the 68000.
Condition codes:	X N Z V C
	- - - - -

JMP	**Jump (unconditionally)**
Operation:	[PC] ← destination
Syntax:	JMP ⟨ea⟩
Attributes:	Unsized
Description:	Program execution continues at the effective address specified by the instruction.
Application:	Apart from a simple unconditional jump to an address fixed at compile time (i.e. JMP label), the JMP instruction is useful for the calculation of **dynamic** or **computed** jumps. For example, the instruction JMP (A0,D0.L) jumps to the location pointed at by the contents of address register A0, offset by the contents of data register D0. Note that JMP provides several addressing modes, while BRA provides a single addressing mode (i.e. PC relative).
Condition codes:	X N Z V C
	- - - - -

Source operand addressing modes

Dn	An	(An)	(An)+	−(An)	(d,An)	(d,An,Xi)	ABS.W	ABS.L	(d,PC)	(d,PC,Xn)	imm
		✔			✔	✔	✔	✔	✔	✔	

JSR

Jump to subroutine

Operation:	`[SP] ← [SP]−4; [M([SP])]←[PC]`
	`[PC]←destination`
Syntax:	`JSR <ea>`
Attributes:	Unsized
Description:	JSR pushes the longword address of the instruction immediately following the JSR onto the system stack. Program execution then continues at the address specified in the instruction.
Application:	JSR (Ai) calls the procedure pointed at by address register Ai. The instruction JSR (Ai,Dj) calls the procedure at the location [Ai]+[Dj], which permits dynamically computed addresses.
Condition codes:	X N Z V C
	- - - - -

Source operand addressing modes

Dn	An	(An)	(An)+	−(An)	(d,An)	(d,An,Xi)	ABS.W	ABS.L	(d,PC)	(d,PC,Xn)	imm
		✔			✔	✔	✔	✔	✔	✔	

LEA

Load effective address

Operation:	`[An] ← <ea>`
Syntax:	`LEA <ea>,An`
Sample syntax:	`LEA  Table,A0`
	`LEA  (Table,PC),A0`
	`LEA  (−6,A0,D0.L),A6`
	`LEA  (Table,PC,D0),A6`
Attributes:	Size = longword
Description:	The effective address is computed and loaded into an address register. LEA (−6,A0,D0.W),A1 calculates the sum of address register A0 plus data register D0.W sign-extended to 32 bits minus 6, and deposits this result in address register A1. The difference between the LEA and PEA instructions is that LEA calculates an effective address and puts it in an address register, whereas PEA calculates an effective address in the same way but pushes it on the stack.
Application:	LEA is a very powerful instruction used to calculate an effective address. In particular, the use of LEA facilitates the writing of **position-independent code**. For example, LEA (TABLE,PC),A0 calculates the effective address of 'TABLE' with respect to the PC and deposits it in A0.

```
          LEA   (Table,PC),A0  Compute address of Table with respect to the pc
          MOVE  (A0),D1         Pick up the first item in the table
          .                     Do something with this item
          MOVE  D1,(A0)         Put it back in the table
          .
          .
    Table DS.W  100
```

Condition codes:	X N Z V C
	- - - - -

Source operand addressing modes

Dn	An	(An)	(An)+	−(An)	(d,An)	(d,An,Xi)	ABS.W	ABS.L	(d,PC)	(d,PC,Xn)	imm
		✔			✔	✔	✔	✔	✔	✔	

LINK

Link and allocate

Operation:	`[SP] ← [SP] − 4; [M([SP])] ← [An];` `[An] ← [SP]; [SP] ← [SP] + d`
Syntax:	`LINK An, #<displacement>`
Sample syntax:	`LINK A6, #−12`
Attributes:	Size = word
Description:	The contents of the specified address register are first pushed onto the stack. Then, this address register is loaded with the updated stack pointer. Finally, the 16-bit sign-extended displacement, d, is added to the stack pointer. The contents of the address register occupy two words on the stack. A **negative displacement** must be used to allocate stack area to a procedure. At the end of a `LINK` instruction, the old value of address register An has been pushed on the stack and the new An is pointing at the base of the stack frame. The stack pointer itself has been moved up by d bytes and is pointing at the top of the stack frame. Address register An is called the **frame pointer** because it is used to reference data on the stack frame. By convention, programmers often use A6 as a frame pointer.
Application:	The `LINK` and `UNLK` instructions are used to create local workspace on the top of a procedure's stack. Consider the code:

```
Subrtn  LINK A6,#−12    Create a 12-byte workspace
        .
        MOVE D3,(−8,A6) Access the stack frame via A6
        .
        UNLK A6         Collapse the workspace
        RTS             Return from subroutine
```

Condition codes:	X N Z V C
	- - - - - The `LINK` instruction does not affect the CCR.

LSL, LSR

Logical shift left/right

Operation:	`[destination] ← [destination] shifted by <count>`

Syntax:	`LSL Dx,Dy`
	`LSR Dx,Dy`
	`LSL #<data>, Dy`
	`LSR #<data>, Dy`
	`LSL <ea>`
	`LSR <ea>`

Attributes:	Size = byte, word, longword
Description:	Logically shift the bits of the operand in the specified direction (i.e. left or right). A zero is shifted into the input position and the bit shifted out is copied into both the C- and the X-bits of the CCR. The shift count may be specified in one of three ways. The count may be a literal, the contents of a data register, or the value 1. An immediate count permits a shift of 1 to 8 places. If the count is in a register, the value is modulo 64—from 0 to 63. If no count is specified, one shift is made (e.g. `LSL <ea>` shifts the **word** at the effective address one position left).

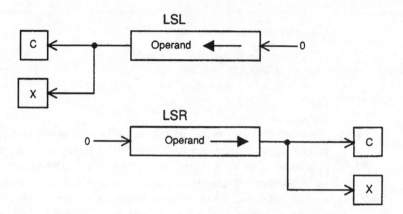

Application: If $[D3.W] = 1100110010101110_2$, LSL.W #5,D3 produces the result 1001010111000000_2. After the shift, the X-and C-bits of the CCR are set to 1 (since the last bit shifted out was a 1).

Condition codes:
```
X N Z V C
* * * 0 *
```
The X-bit is set to the last bit shifted out of the operand and is equal to the C-bit. However, a zero shift count leaves the X-bit unaffected and the C-bit cleared.

Destination operand addressing modes

Dn	An	(An)	(An)+	-(An)	(d,An)	(d,An,Xi)	ABS.W	ABS.L	(d,PC)	(d,PC,Xn)	imm
✔		✔	✔	✔	✔	✔	✔	✔			

MOVE

Copy data from source to destination

Operation: `[destination] ← [source]`

Syntax: `MOVE <ea>,<ea>`

Sample syntax:
```
MOVE  (A5),-(A2)
MOVE  -(A5),(A2)+
MOVE  #$123,(A6)+
MOVE  Temp1,Temp2
```

Attributes: Size = byte, word, longword

Description: Move the contents of the source to the destination location. The data is examined as it is moved and the condition codes set accordingly. Note that this is actually a **copy** command because the source is not affected by the move. The move instruction has the widest range of addressing modes of all the 68000's instructions.

Condition codes:
```
X N Z V C
- * * 0 0
```

Source operand addressing modes

Dn	An	(An)	(An)+	-(An)	(d,An)	(d,An,Xi)	ABS.W	ABS.L	(d,PC)	(d,PC,Xn)	imm
✔	✔	✔	✔	✔	✔	✔	✔	✔	✔	✔	✔

Destination operand addressing modes

Dn	An	(An)	(An)+	-(An)	(d,An)	(d,An,Xi)	ABS.W	ABS.L	(d,PC)	(d,PC,Xn)	imm
✔		✔	✔	✔	✔	✔	✔	✔			

MOVEA — Move address

Operation:	[An] ← [source]
Syntax:	MOVEA <ea>,An
Attributes:	Size = word, longword
Description:	Move the contents of the source to the destination location, which is an address register. The source must be a word or longword. If it is a word, it is sign-extended to a longword. The condition codes are not affected.
Application:	The MOVEA instruction is used to load an address register (some assemblers simply employ the MOVE mnemonic for both MOVE and MOVEA). The instruction LEA can often be used to perform the same operation (e.g. MOVEA.L #$1234,A0 is the same as LEA $1234,A0). Take care because the MOVEA.W #$8000,A0 instruction sign-extends the source operand to $FFFF8000 before loading it into A0, whereas LEA $8000,A0 loads A0 with $00008000. You should appreciate that the MOVEA and LEA instructions are not interchangeable. The operation MOVEA (Ai),An cannot be implemented by an LEA instruction, since MOVEA (Ai),An performs a memory access to obtain the source operand, as the following RTL demonstrates.

```
LEA    (Ai),An   = [An] ← [Ai]
MOVEA  (Ai),An   = [An] ← [M([Ai])]
```

Condition codes:	X N Z V C
	- - - - -

Source operand addressing modes

Dn	An	(An)	(An)+	-(An)	(d,An)	(d,An,Xi)	ABS.W	ABS.L	(d,PC)	(d,PC,Xn)	imm
✔	✔	✔	✔	✔	✔	✔	✔	✔	✔	✔	✔

MOVE to CCR — Copy data to CCR from source

Operation:	[CCR] ← [source]
Syntax:	MOVE <ea>,CCR
Attributes:	Size = word
Description:	Move the contents of the source operand to the condition code register. The source operand is a word, but only the low-order **byte** contains the condition codes. The upper byte is neglected. Note that MOVE <ea>,CCR is a word operation, but ANDI, ORI and EORI to CCR are all byte operations.
Application:	The move to CCR instruction permits the programmer to preset the CCR. For example, MOVE #0,CCR clears all the CCR's bits.
Condition codes:	X N Z V C
	- - - - -

Source operand addressing modes

Dn	An	(An)	(An)+	-(An)	(d,An)	(d,An,Xi)	ABS.W	ABS.L	(d,PC)	(d,PC,Xn)	imm
✔		✔	✔	✔	✔	✔	✔	✔	✔	✔	✔

MOVE from SR	**Copy data from SR to destination**
Operation:	[destination] ← [SR]
Syntax:	MOVE SR, <ea>
Attributes:	Size = word
Description:	Move the contents of the status register to the destination location. The source operand, the status register, is a word. This instruction is not privileged in the 68000, but is privileged in the 68010, 68020, and 68030. Executing a MOVE SR, <ea> while in the user mode on these processors results in a privilege violation trap.
Condition codes:	X N Z V C - - - - -

Destination operand addressing modes

Dn	An	(An)	(An)+	–(An)	(d,An)	(d,An,Xi)	ABS.W	ABS.L	(d,PC)	(d,PC,Xn)	imm
✔		✔	✔	✔	✔	✔	✔	✔			

MOVE to SR	**Copy data to SR from source**
Operation:	IF [S] = 1 THEN [SR] ← [source] ELSE TRAP
Syntax:	MOVE <ea>, SR
Attributes:	Size = word
Description:	Move the contents of the source operand to the status register. The source operand is a word and all bits of the status register are affected.
Application:	The MOVE to SR instruction allows the programmer to preset the contents of the status register. This instruction permits the trace mode, interrupt mask, and status bits to be modified. For example, MOVE #$2700, SR moves 00100111 00000000 to the status register, which clears all bits of the CCR, sets the S-bit, clears the T-bit, and sets the interrupt mask level to 7.
Condition codes:	X N Z V C * * * * *

Source operand addressing modes

Dn	An	(An)	(An)+	–(An)	(d,An)	(d,An,Xi)	ABS.W	ABS.L	(d,PC)	(d,PC,Xn)	imm
✔		✔	✔	✔	✔	✔	✔	✔	✔	✔	✔

MOVE USP	**Copy data to or from USP**
Operation 1:	IF [S] = 1 {MOVE USP, An form} THEN [USP] ← [An] ELSE TRAP
Operation 2:	IF [S] = 1 {MOVE An, USP form} THEN [An] ← [USP] ELSE TRAP

Syntax 1:	Move USP,An
Syntax 2:	Move An,USP
Attributes:	Size = longword
Description:	Move the contents of the user stack pointer to an address register or vice versa. This is a privileged instruction and allows the operating system running in the supervisor state either to read the contents of the user stack pointer or to set up the user stack pointer.
Condition codes:	X N Z V C
	- - - - -

MOVEM   Move multiple registers

Operation 1:	REPEAT [destination_register] ← [source] UNTIL all registers in list moved
Operation 2:	REPEAT [destination] ← [source_register] UNTIL all registers in list moved
Syntax 1:	MOVEM <ea>,<register list>
Syntax 2:	MOVEM <register list>,<ea>
Sample syntax:	MOVEM.L D0-D7/A0-A6,$1234
	MOVEM.L (A5),D0-D2/D5-D7/A0-A3/A6
	MOVEM.W (A7)+,D0-D5/D7/A0-A6
	MOVEM.W D0-D5/D7/A0-A6,-(A7)
Attributes:	Size = word, longword
Description:	The group of registers specified by <register list> is copied to or from consecutive memory locations. The starting location is provided by the effective address. Any combination of the 68000's sixteen address and data registers can be copied by a single MOVEM instruction. Note that either a word or a longword can be moved, and that a word is sign-extended to a longword when it is moved (even if the destination is a data register).

When a group of registers is transferred to or from memory (using an addressing mode other than predecrementing or postincrementing), the registers are transferred starting at the specified address and up through higher addresses. The order of transfer of registers is data register D0 to D7, followed by address register A0 to A7.

MOVEM.L D0-D2/D4/A5/A6,$1234 copies registers D0,D1,D2,D4,A5,A6 to memory, starting at location $1234 (where D0 is stored) and moving to locations $1238, $123C,.... The address counter is incremented by 2 or 4 after each move according to whether the operation is moving words or longwords, respectively.

If the effective address is in the predecrement mode (i.e. -(An)), only a register to memory operation is permitted. The registers are stored starting at the specified address minus two (or four for longword operands) and down through lower addresses. The order of storing is from address register A7 to address register A0, then from data register D7 to data register D0. The decremented address register is updated to contain the address of the last word stored.

If the effective address is in the postincrement mode (i.e. (An)+), only a memory to register transfer is permitted. The registers are loaded starting at the specified address and up through higher addresses. The order of loading is the inverse of that used by the predecrement mode and is D0 to D7 followed by A0 to A7. The incremented address register is updated to contain the address of the last word plus two (or four for longword operands). |

Note that the MOVEM instruction has a side effect. An extra bus cycle occurs for memory operands, and an operand at one address higher than the last register in the list is accessed. This extra access is an 'overshoot' and has no effect as far as the programmer is concerned. However, it could cause a problem if the overshoot extended beyond the bounds of physical memory. Once again, remember that MOVEM.W sign-extends words when they are moved to data registers.

Application: This instruction is used to save working registers on entry to a subroutine and to restore them at the end of a subroutine.

```
          BSR       Example
          .
          .
          .
Example   MOVEM.L  D0-D5/A0-A3,-(SP)  Save registers
          .
          .
          Body of subroutine
          .
          .
          MOVEM.L  (SP)+,D0-D5/A0-A3  Restore registers
          RTS                         Return
```

Condition codes:
```
X N Z V C
- - - - -
```

Source operand addressing modes (memory to register)

Dn	An	(An)	(An)+	-(An)	(d,An)	(d,An,Xi)	ABS.W	ABS.L	(d,PC)	(d,PC,Xn)	imm
		✔	✔		✔	✔	✔	✔	✔	✔	

Destinaton operand addressing modes (register to memory)

Dn	An	(An)	(An)+	-(An)	(d,An)	(d,An,Xi)	ABS.W	ABS.L	(d,PC)	(d,PC,Xn)	imm
		✔		✔	✔	✔	✔	✔			

MOVEQ

Move quick (copy a small literal to a destination)

Operation: [destination] ←<literal>

Syntax: MOVEQ #<data>,Dn

Attributes: Size = longword

Description: Move the specified literal to a data register. The literal is an eight-bit field within the MOVEQ op-code and specifies a signed value in the range -128 to $+127$. When the source operand is transferred, it is sign-extended to 32 bits. Consequently, although only 8 bits are moved, the MOVEQ instruction is a **longword** operation.

Application: MOVEQ is used to load small integers into a data register. Beware of its sign-extension. The two operations MOVE.B #12,D0 and MOVEQ #12,D0 are not equivalent. The former has the effect $[D0(0:7)] \leftarrow 12$, whereas the latter has the effect $[D0(0:31)] \leftarrow 12$ (with sign-extension).

Condition codes:
```
X N Z V C
- * * 0 0
```

MULS, MULU — Signed multiply, unsigned multiply

Operation: [destination] ← [destination] * [source]

Syntax: MULS <ea>,Dn
MULU <ea>,Dn

Attributes: Size = word (the product is a longword)

Description: Multiply the 16-bit destination operand by the 16-bit source operand and store the result in the destination. Both the source and destination are 16-bit word values and the destination result is a 32-bit longword. The product is therefore a correct 32-bit product and is not truncated. MULU performs multiplication with unsigned values and MULS performs multiplication with two's-complement values.

Application: MULU D1,D2 multiplies the low-order words of data registers D1 and D2 and puts the 32-bit result in D2. MULU #$1234,D3 multiplies the low-order word of D3 by the 16-bit literal $1234 and puts the 32-bit result in D3.

Condition codes:

X N Z V C
- * * 0 0

Source operand addressing modes

Dn	An	(An)	(An)+	–(An)	(d,An)	(d,An,Xi)	ABS.W	ABS.L	(d,PC)	(d,PC,Xn)	imm
✔		✔	✔	✔	✔	✔	✔	✔	✔	✔	✔

NEG — Negate

Operation: [destination] ← 0 − [destination]

Syntax: NEG <ea>

Attributes: Size = byte, word, longword

Description: Subtract the destination operand from 0 and store the result in the destination location. The difference between NOT and NEG is that NOT performs a bit-by-bit logical complementation, whereas NEG performs a 2's complement arithmetic subtraction. All bits of the condition code register are modified by a NEG operation; e.g. if D3.B = 11100111_2, the logical operation NEG.B D3 results in D3 = 00011001 (XNZVC = 10001) and NOT·B D3 results in D3 = 00011000_2 (XNZVC = −0000).

Condition codes:

X N Z V C
* * * * * Note that the X-bit is set to the value of the C-bit.

Destination operand addressing modes

Dn	An	(An)	(An)+	–(An)	(d,An)	(d,An,Xi)	ABS.W	ABS.L	(d,PC)	(d,PC,Xn)	imm
✔		✔	✔	✔	✔	✔	✔	✔			

NEGX — Negate with extend

Operation: [destination] ← 0 − [destination] − [X]

Syntax: NEGX <ea>

Attributes: Size = byte, word, longword

Description: The operand addressed as the destination and the extend bit are subtracted from zero. NEGX is the same as NEG except that the X-bit is also subtracted from zero.

Condition codes: X N Z V C
                    * * * * *

The Z-bit is cleared if the result is non-zero and is unchanged otherwise. The X-bit is set to the same value as the C-bit.

Destination operand addressing modes

Dn	An	(An)	(An)+	–(An)	(d,An)	(d,An,Xi)	ABS.W	ABS.L	(d,PC)	(d,PC,Xn)	imm
✔		✔	✔	✔	✔	✔	✔	✔			

NOP   No operation

Operation: None
Syntax: NOP
Attributes: Unsized
Description: The no operation instruction NOP performs no **computation**. Execution continues with the instruction following the NOP instruction. The processor's state is not modified by an NOP.
Application: NOPs can be used to introduce a **delay** in code. Some programmers use them to provide space for **patches**—two or more NOPs can later be replaced by branch or jump instructions to fix a bug. This use of the NOP is seriously frowned upon, as errors should be corrected by reassembling the code rather than by patching it.

Condition codes: X N Z V C
                    - - - - -

NOT   Logical complement

Operation: [destination] ← [$\overline{\text{destination}}$]
Syntax: NOT <ea>
Attributes: Size = byte, word, longword
Description: Calculate the logical complement of the destination and store the result in the destination. The difference between NOT and NEG is that NOT performs a bit-by-bit logical complementation, whereas a NEG performs a two's complement arithmetic subtraction. Moreover, NEG updates all bits of the CCR, while NOT clears the V- and C-bits, updates the N- and Z-bits, and doesn't affect the X-bit.

Condition codes: X N Z V C
                    - * * 0 0

Source operand addressing modes

Dn	An	(An)	(An)+	–(An)	(d,An)	(d,An,Xi)	ABS.W	ABS.L	(d,PC)	(d,PC,Xn)	imm
✔		✔	✔	✔	✔	✔	✔	✔			

OR   OR logical

Operation:	[destination] ← [source] + [destination]
Syntax:	OR <ea>,Dn
	OR Dn,<ea>
Attributes:	Size = byte, word, longword
Description:	OR the source operand to the destination operand and store the result in the destination location.
Application:	The OR instruction is used to set selected bits of the operand. For example, we can set the four most-significant bits of a longword operand in D0 by executing:
	OR.L #$F0000000,D0
Condition codes:	X N Z V C
	- * * 0 0

Source operand addressing modes

Dn	An	(An)	(An)+	–(An)	(d,An)	(d,An,Xi)	ABS.W	ABS.L	(d,PC)	(d,PC,Xn)	imm
✔		✔	✔	✔	✔	✔	✔	✔	✔	✔	✔

Destination operand addressing modes

Dn	An	(An)	(An)+	–(An)	(d,An)	(d,An,Xi)	ABS.W	ABS.L	(d,PC)	(d,PC,Xn)	imm
✔		✔	✔	✔	✔	✔	✔	✔			

ORI   OR immediate

Operation:	[destination] ←<literal>+[destination]
Syntax:	ORI #<data>,<ea>
Attributes:	Size=byte, word, longword
Description:	OR the immediate data with the destination operand. Store the result in the destination operand.
Condition codes:	X N Z V C
	- * * 0 0
Application:	ORI forms the logical OR of the immediate source with the effective address, which may be a memory location. For example,
	ORI.B #%00000011,(A0)+

Destination operand addressing modes

Dn	An	(An)	(An)+	–(An)	(d,An)	(d,An,Xi)	ABS.W	ABS.L	(d,PC)	(d,PC,Xn)	imm
✔		✔	✔	✔	✔	✔	✔	✔			

ORI to CCR   Inclusive OR immediate to CCR

Operation:	[CCR] ←<literal>+[CCR]
Syntax:	ORI #<data> ,CCR
Attributes:	Size=byte

Description:	OR the immediate data with the condition code register (i.e. the least-significant byte of the status register). The Z flag of the CCR can be set by ORI #$04,CCR.
Condition codes:	X N Z V C
	* * * * *

X is set if bit 4 of data = 1; unchanged otherwise
N is set if bit 3 of data = 1; unchanged otherwise
Z is set if bit 2 of data = 1; unchanged otherwise
V is set if bit 1 of data = 1; unchanged otherwise
C is set if bit 0 of data = 1; unchanged otherwise

ORI to SR — Inclusive OR immediate to status register

Operation:	IF [S]=1
	THEN
	[SR]←<literal>+[SR]
	ELSE TRAP
Syntax:	ORI #<data>,SR
Attributes:	Size=word
Description:	OR the immediate data to the status register and store the result in the status register. All bits of the status register are affected.
Application:	Used to set bits in the SR (i.e. the S, T, and interrupt mask bits). For example, ORI #$8000,SR sets bit 15 of the SR (i.e. the trace bit).
Condition codes:	X N Z V C
	* * * * *

X is set if bit 4 of data = 1; unchanged otherwise
N is set if bit 3 of data = 1; unchanged otherwise
Z is set if bit 2 of data = 1; unchanged otherwise
V is set if bit 1 of data = 1; unchanged otherwise
C is set if bit 0 of data = 1; unchanged otherwise

PEA — Push effective address

Operation:	[SP]←[SP]−4; [M([SP])]←<ea>
Syntax:	PEA <ea>
Attributes:	Size = longword
Description:	The longword effective address specified by the instruction is computed and pushed onto the stack. For example, PEA XYZ would push the address of 'XYZ' on to the stack. The difference between PEA and LEA is that LEA calculates an effective address and puts it in an address register, whereas PEA calculates an effective address in the same way but pushes it on the stack.
Application:	PEA calculates an effective address to be used later in address register indirect addressing. In particular, it facilitates the writing of position-independent code. For example, PEA (TABLE,PC) calculates the address of TABLE with respect to the PC and pushes it on the stack. This address can be read by a procedure and then used to access the data to which it points. Consider the example:

```
PEA    Wednesday    Push the parameter address on the stack
BSR    Subroutine   Call the procedure
LEA    (4,SP),SP    Remove space occupied by the parameter
```

Subroutine: `MOVEA.L (4,SP),A0` A0 points to parameter under return address
                      `MOVE.W  (A0),D2`   Access the actual parameter - Wednesday
                      `.`
                      `RTS`

Condition codes: X N Z V C
                    - - - - -

Source operand addressing modes

Dn	An	(An)	(An)+	–(An)	(d,An)	(d,An,Xi)	ABS.W	ABS.L	(d,PC)	(d,PC,Xn)	imm
		✔			✔	✔	✔	✔	✔	✔	

ROL, ROR

Rotate left/right (without extend)

Operation: [destination] ← [destination] rotated by <count>

Syntax: ROL Dx,Dy
               ROR Dx,Dy
               ROL #<data>,Dy
               ROR #<data>,Dy
               ROL <ea>
               ROR <ea>

Attributes: Size = byte, word, longword

Description: Rotate the bits of the operand in the direction indicated. The extend bit, X, is not included in the operation. A rotate operation is circular in the sense that the bit shifted out at one end is shifted into the other end. That is, no bit is lost or destroyed by a rotate operation. The bit shifted out is also copied into the C-bit of the CCR, but not into the X-bit. The shift count may be specified in one of three ways: the count may be a literal, the contents of a data register, or the value 1. An immediate count permits a shift of 1 to 8 places. If the count is in a register, the value is modulo 64, allowing a range of 0 to 63. If no count is specified, the **word** at the effective address is rotated by one place (e.g. ROL <ea>).

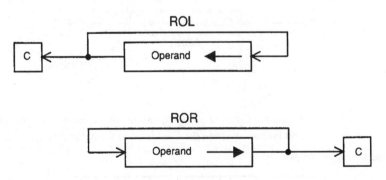

Condition codes: X N Z V C
                      - * * 0 *

The X-bit is not affected and the C-bit is set to the last bit rotated out of the operand (C is set to zero if the shift count is 0).

Destination operand addressing modes

Dn	An	(An)	(An)+	–(An)	(d,An)	(d,An,Xi)	ABS.W	ABS.L	(d,PC)	(d,PC,Xn)	imm
✔		✔	✔	✔	✔	✔	✔	✔			

ROXL, ROXR

Rotate left/right with extend

Operation: [destination] ← [destination] rotated by <count>

Syntax: ROXL   Dx,Dy
ROXR   Dx,Dy
ROXL   #<data>,Dy
ROXR   #<data>,Dy
ROXL   <ea>
ROXR   <ea>

Attributes: Size = byte, word, longword

Description: Rotate the bits of the operand in the direction indicated. The extend bit of the CCR is included in the rotation. A rotate operation is circular in the sense that the bit shifted out at one end is shifted into the other end. That is, no bit is lost or destroyed by a rotate operation. Since the X-bit is included in the rotate, the rotation is performed over 9 bits (.B), 17 bits (.W), or 33 bits (.L). The bit shifted out is also copied into the C-bit of the CCR as well as the X-bit. The shift count may be specified in one of three ways: the count may be a literal, the contents of a data register, or the value 1. An immediate count permits a shift of 1 to 8 places. If the count is in a register, the value is modulo 64 and the range is from 0 to 63. If no count is specified, the word at the specified effective address is rotated by one place (i.e. ROXL <ea>).

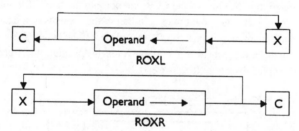

Condition codes:

```
X N Z V C
* * * 0 *
```

The X- and the C-bit are set to the last bit rotated out of the operand. If the rotate count is zero, the X-bit is unaffected and the C-bit is set to the X-bit.

Destination operand addressing modes

Dn	An	(An)	(An)+	–(An)	(d,An)	(d,An,Xi)	ABS.W	ABS.L	(d,PC)	(d,PC,Xn)	imm
✔		✔	✔	✔	✔	✔	✔	✔			

RTE

Return from exception

Operation:
```
IF [S] =1 THEN
        [SR] ← [M([SP])]; [SP] ← [SP]+2
        [PC] ← [M([SP])]; [SP] ←[SP]+4
            ELSE TRAP
```

Syntax: RTE

Attributes: Unsized

Description: The status register and program counter are pulled from the stack. The previous values of the SR and PC are lost. The RTE is used to terminate an exception handler. Note that the behavior of the RTE instruction depends on the nature of both the exception and processor type. The 68010 and later models push more information on the stack following an exception than the 68000. The processor determines how much to remove from the stack.

Condition codes:
```
X N Z V C
* * * * *
```
The CCR is restored to its pre-exception state.

RTS

Return from subroutine

Operation: `[PC] ← [M([SP])]; [SP] ← [SP]+4`

Syntax: RTS

Attributes: Unsized

Description: The program counter is pulled from the stack and the previous value of the PC is lost. RTS is used to terminate a subroutine.

Condition codes:
```
X N Z V C
- - - - -
```

STOP

Load status register and stop

Operation:
```
IF [S] =1 THEN
            [SR] ←<data>
            STOP
        ELSE TRAP
```

Syntax: STOP #<data>

Sample syntax: STOP #$2700

STOP #SetUp

Attributes: Unsized

Description: The immediate operand is copied into the entire status register (i.e. both status byte and CCR are modified), and the program counter advanced to point to the next instruction to be executed. The processor then suspends all further processing and halts. That is, the privileged STOP instruction stops the 68000.

The execution of instructions resumes when a trace, an interrupt, or a reset exception occurs. A trace exception will occur if the trace bit is set when the STOP instruction is encountered. If an interrupt request arrives whose priority is higher than the current processor priority, an interrupt exception occurs, otherwise the interrupt request has no effect. If the bit of the immediate data corresponding to the S-bit is clear (i.e. user mode selected), execution of the STOP instruction will cause a privilege violation. An external reset will always initiate reset exception processing.

Condition codes:
```
X N Z V C
* * * * *
```
Set according to the literal.

SUB

Subtract binary

Operation:	[destination] ← [destination] − [source]
Syntax:	SUB <ea>,Dn
	SUB Dn,<ea>
Attributes:	Size = byte, word, longword
Description:	Subtract the source operand from the destination operand and store the result in the destination location.
Condition codes:	X N Z V C
	* * * * *

Source operand addressing modes

Dn	An	(An)	(An)+	−(An)	(d,An)	(d,An,Xi)	ABS.W	ABS.L	(d,PC)	(d,PC,Xn)	imm
✔	✔	✔	✔	✔	✔	✔	✔	✔	✔	✔	✔

Destination operand addressing modes

Dn	An	(An)	(An)+	−(An)	(d,An)	(d,An,Xi)	ABS.W	ABS.L	(d,PC)	(d,PC,Xn)	imm
✔		✔	✔	✔	✔	✔	✔	✔			

SUBA

Subtract address

Operation:	[destination] ← [destination] − [source]
Syntax:	SUBA <ea>,An
Attributes:	Size = word, longword
Description:	Subtract the source operand from the destination operand and store the result in the destination address register. Word operations are sign-extended to 32 bits prior to subtraction.
Condition codes:	X N Z V C
	- - - - -

Source operand addressing modes

Dn	An	(An)	(An)+	−(An)	(d,An)	(d,An,Xi)	ABS.W	ABS.L	(d,PC)	(d,PC,Xn)	imm
✔	✔	✔	✔	✔	✔	✔	✔	✔	✔	✔	✔

SUBI

Subtract immediate

Operation:	[destination] ← [destination] − [source]
Syntax:	SUBI #<data>,<ea>
Attributes:	Size = byte, word, longword
Description:	Subtract the immediate data from the destination operand. Store the result in the destination operand.

Condition codes:

```
X  N  Z  V  C
*  *  *  *  *
```

Destination operand addressing modes

Dn	An	(An)	(An)+	−(An)	(d,An)	(d,An,Xi)	ABS.W	ABS.L	(d,PC)	(d,PC,Xn)	imm
✔		✔	✔	✔	✔	✔	✔	✔			

SUBQ

Subtract quick

Operation:	[destination] ← [destination] − [source]
Syntax:	SUBQ #<data>,<ea>
Attributes:	Size = byte, word, longword
Description:	Subtract the immediate data from the destination operand. The immediate data must be in the range 1 to 8. Word and longword operations on address registers do not affect condition codes. A word operation on an address register affects the entire 32-bit address.
Condition codes:	

```
X  N  Z  V  C
*  *  *  *  *
```

Destination operand addressing modes

Dn	An	(An)	(An)+	−(An)	(d,An)	(d,An,Xi)	ABS.W	ABS.L	(d,PC)	(d,PC,Xn)	imm
✔	✔	✔	✔	✔	✔	✔	✔	✔			

SUBX

Subtract extended

Operation:	[destination] ← [destination] − [source] − [x]
Syntax:	SUBX Dx,Dy
	SUBX −(Ax),−(Ay)
Attributes:	Size = byte, word, longword
Description:	Subtract the source operand from the destination operand along with the extend bit, and store the result in the destination location. The only legal addressing modes are data register direct and memory to memory with address register indirect using auto-decrementing.
Condition codes:	

```
X  N  Z  V  C
*  *  *  *  *
```

Z: Cleared if the result is non-zero, unchanged otherwise. The Z-bit can be used to test for zero after a chain of multiple precision operations.

SWAP

Swap register halves

Operation:	[Register(16:31)] ← [Register(0:15)];
	[Register(0:15)] ← [Register(16:31)]
Syntax:	SWAP Dn
Attributes:	Size = word
Description:	Exchange the upper and lower 16-bit words of a data register.
Application:	The SWAP Dn instruction enables the higher-order word in a register to take part in word operations by moving it into the lower-order position. SWAP Dn is effectively equivalent to

ROR.L Di,Dn, where [Di]=16. However, SWAP clears the C-bit of the CCR, whereas ROR sets it according to the last bit to be shifted into the carry bit.

Condition codes:

```
X N Z V C
- * * 0 0
```

The N-bit is set if most-significant bit of the 32-bit result is set and cleared otherwise. The Z-bit is set if 32-bit result is zero and cleared otherwise.

TRAP

Trap

Operation:

```
s ← 1;
[SSP] ← [SSP] −4; [M([SSP])] ← [PC];
[SSP] ← [SSP] −2; [M([SSP])] ← [SR];
[PC]  ← vector
```

Syntax: Trap #<vector>

Attributes: Unsized

Description: This instruction forces the processor to initiate exception processing. The vector number used by the TRAP instruction is in the range 0 to 15 and, therefore, supports 16 traps (i.e. TRAP #0 to TRAP #15).

Application: The TRAP instruction is used to perform operating system calls and is system independent. That is, the effect of the call depends on the particular operating environment. For example, the University of Teesside 68000 simulator uses TRAP #15 to perform I/O. The ASCII character in D1.B is displayed by the following sequence.

```
MOVE.B #6,DO  Set up to display a character parameter in D0
TRAP   #15    Now call the operating system
```

Condition codes:

```
X N Z V C
- - - - -
```

TST

Test an operand

Operation:

```
[CCR] ← tested ([operand])
i.e. [operand] −0; update CCR
```

Syntax: TST <ea>

Attributes: Size = byte, word, longword

Description: The operand is compared with zero. No results is saved, but the contents of the CCR are set according to the results. The effect of TST <ea> is the same as CMPI #0, <ea> except that the CMPI instruction also sets/clears the V- and C-bits of the CCR.

Condition codes:

```
X N Z V C
- * * 0 0
```

Source operand addressing modes

Dn	An	(An)	(An)+	−(An)	(d,An)	(d,An,Xi)	ABS.W	ABS.L	(d,PC)	(d,PC,Xn)	imm
✔		✔	✔	✔	✔	✔	✔	✔	✔	✔	

UNLK	**Unlink**
Operation:	$[SP] \leftarrow [An]$; $[An] \leftarrow [M([SP])]$; $[SP] \leftarrow [SP] + 4$
Syntax:	UNLK An
Attributes:	Unsized
Description:	The stack pointer is loaded from the specified address register and the old contents of the pointer are lost (this has the effect of collapsing the stack frame). The address register is then loaded with the longword pulled off the stack.
Application:	The UNLK instruction is used in conjuction with the LINK instruction. The LINK creates a stack frame at the start of a procedure, and the UNLK collapses the stack frame prior to a return from the procedure.
Condition codes:	X N Z V C
	- - - - -

Bibliography

Logic, computers architecture, computer organization

Clements, Alan (1997). *Microprocessor Systems Design (3rd edition)*. International Thomson Publishing.

Dowd, Kevin (1993). *High Performance Computing*. O'Reilly & Associates Inc., Sebastopol, CA.

Furber, Steve (1996). *ARM System Architecture*. Addison-Wesley, Harlow.

Hamacher, Carl V., Vranesic, Zvonko G. and Zaky, Safwat G. (1996). *Computer Organization (4th edition)*. McGraw-Hill.

Hayes, John P. (1998). *Computer Architecture and Organization (3rd edition)*. McGraw-Hill.

Karp Alan H. and Flatt, Horace P. (1990). *Measuring Parallel Processor Performance*. Communications of the ACM, Vol. 33, No. 1, May 1990, pp. 539–543.

Patterson, David A. and Hennessy, John L. (1998). *Computer Organization & Design (2nd edition)*. Morgan Kaufmann Publishers, San Francisco.

Roth, Charles H. (1992). *Fundamentals of Logic Design (4th edition)*. West Publishing Company.

Sima, Dezso, Fountain Terence and Kacsuk, Peter (1997). *Advanced Computer Architectures—A Design Space approach*. Addison-Wesley.

Skahill, Kevin (1996). *VHDL for Programmable Logic*. Addison-Wesley.

Tanenbaum, Andrew S. (1999). *Structured Computer Organization*. Prentice-Hall International.

Wakerly, John F. (2000). *Digital Design (3rd edition)*. Prentice Hall International Inc.

Warford, Stanley J. (1999). *Computer Systems*. Jones and Bartlett Publishers, Sudbury, MA.

Wilkinson, Barry (1996). *Computer Architecture (2nd edition)*. Prentice Hall Europe.

Yarbrough, John M. (1997). *Digital Logic Applications and Design*. West Publishing Company.

Operating systems

Cooling, Jim E. (1997). *Real-time Software Systems*. International Thomson Publishing.

Flynn, Ida M. and McIver McHoes, Ann (1997). *Understanding Operating Systems (2nd edition)*. International Thomson Publishing.

Stallings, William (1998). *Operating Systems—Internals and Design Principles (3rd edition)*. Prentice-Hall International.

Memory systems

Burger, Doug and Goodman James R. (1997). *Billion-Transistor Architectures*. Computer, September 1997, pp. 46–48.

Gemmell, James D. *et al.* (1994). *Delay-Sensitive Multimedia on Disks*. IEEE Multimedia, Fall, 1994, pp. 56–66.

Hewlett-Packard (1997). *Digital Modulation in Communications Systems—an Introduction*. Application Note 1298, Hewlett-Packard Company.

Hill, Mark D. (1988). *A Case for Direct-Mapped Caches*. Computer, December 1988, pp. 25–39.

Pohlmann, Ken C. (1992). *The Compact Disc Handbook*. Oxford University Press, Cambridge.

Prince, Betty (1999). *High Performance Memories (Revised edition)*. John Wiley & Sons Ltd., Chichester.

Smith, Alan Jay (1983). *Cache Memories*. Computing Surveys, Vol. 14, No. 3, September 1982, pp. 473–530.

Williams, E. W. (1996). *The CD-ROM and Optical Disc Recording Systems*. Oxford University Press, Oxford.

Lubell, Peter D. (1995). *The Gathering Storm in High-Density Compact Disks*. IEEE Spectrum, August 1995, pp. 32–37.

Bell, Alan E. (1996). *Next-Generation Compact Discs*. Scientific American, July 1996, pp. 28–37.

I/O techniques, peripherals

Marven, Craig and Ewers, Gillian (1996). *A Simple Approach to Digital Signal Processing*. John Wiley & Sons Ltd., Chichester.

Morrison, T. P. (1997). *The Art of Computerized Measurement*. Oxford University Press, Oxford.

Schultz Jerome S. (1991). *Biosensors*. Scientific American, August 1991, pp. 64–69.

Johnson, Barry W. (1987). *A Course on the Design of Reliable Digital Systems*. IEEE Transactions on Education, Vol. E-30, No. 1, February 1987, pp. 27–36.

Communications

Halsall, Fred (1995). *Data Communications, Computer Networks and Open Systems (4th edition)*. Addison-Wesley.

Shay, William A. (1995). *Understanding Data Communications Systems*. International Thomson Publishing.

Index

CD-ROM conditions of use and copyrights

Please read these terms before proceeding with the CD installation. By installing the CD you agree to be bound by these terms, including the terms applicable to the software described below.

The enclosed CD contains four major items of software, all of which run on IBM PCs and their clones. One item runs only under DOS.

· A 68000 cross-assembler and simulator
· A digital logic simulator
· A simulator the ARM microprocessor
· Documentation for the 68000 family

These items are in separate directories and have appropriate "readme" files. You also need Adobe Acrobat Reader to view some of the information such as Motorola and ARM's user manuals. The CD also contains a copy of the Adobe Acrobat Reader that you can install if you do not already have it.

The materials contained on this CD-ROM have been supplied by the author of the book. Whilst every effort has been made to check the software routines and the text, there is always the possibility of error and users are advised to confirm the information in this product through independent sources.

Alan Clements and/or his licensors grant you a non-exclusive licence to use this CD to search, view and display the contents of this CD on a single computer at a single location and to print off multiple screens from the CD for your own private use or study. All rights not expressly granted to you are reserved to Alan Clements and/or his licensors, and you shall not adapt, modify, translate, reverse engineer, decompile or disassemble any part of the software on this CD, except to the extent permitted by law.

These terms shall be subject to English laws and the English courts shall have jurisdiction.

THIS CD-ROM IS PROVIDED 'AS IS' WITHOUT WARRANTY OF ANY KIND, EXPRESS OR IMPLIED, INCLUDING BUT NOT LIMITED TO IMPLIED WARRANTIES OF SATISFACTORY QUALITY OR FITNESS FOR A PARTICULAR PURPOSE. IN NO EVENT SHALL ANYONE ASSOCIATED WITH THIS PRODUCT BE LIABLE FOR ANY DIRECT, INDIRECT, SPECIAL, CONSEQUENTIAL, OR INCIDENTAL DAMAGES RESULTING FROM ITS USE.

THIS SOFTWARE IS SUBJECT TO THE INDIVIDUAL CONDITIONS STATED BY THE APPROPRIATE COPYRIGHT HOLDERS WHICH ARE GIVEN BELOW AND ON THE CD WALLET COVER.

THE SOFTWARE IS NOT SUPPORTED.

ONE ITEM OF SOFTWARE ON THE CD, WINZIP, IS SUPPLIED AS A DEMONSTRATION COPY AND MAY NOT BE USED FOR MORE THAN 21 DAYS WITHOUT PAYMENT. This software is required only if you cannot unzip the ARM development software.

DIGITAL WORKS 95 VERSION 2.04 is © John Barker 2000. TERMS OF USE: Digital Works 95 version 2.04 (The Product) shall only be used by the individual who purchased this book. The Product may not be used for profit or commercial gain. The Product shall only be installed on a single machine at any one time. No part of the Product shall be made available over a Wide Area Network or the internet. The title and copyright in all parts of the Product remain the property of David John Baker. The Product and elements of the Product may not be reverse engineered, sold, lent, displayed, hired out or copied. It shall only be installed on a single machine at any one time.

M6800PM/AD – MOTOROLA M68000 FAMILY PROGRAMMERS REFERENCE MANUAL Copyright of Motorola. Used by permission.

Using the CD-ROM

The CD holds a number software packages in separate folders within the main folder (OUPCD_28OCT99).

The folder 68KSIM has copies of the DOS-based cross-assembler X68K and the emulator/simulator E68K, together with a number of demonstration data-files and several useful documents. The main document covering the 68000 micro-processor is held in a separate folder - 68KDOCS - as a large *.PDF file.

The folder DIGITAL holds a single program, DW20_95, which you must run to install the Windows-based DIGITAL WORKS software. There is no separate manual for DIGITAL WORKS but there is comprehensive on-line Help

The ARMSIM folder holds a compressed (zipped) file, 202U_W32_V1, which must be de-compressed (un-zipped) to generate the APM program, several example data-files and the supporting documents from ARM. A copy of WINZIP70 is provided within the ARMSIM folder.

The OUPCD_28OCT99 folder also contains:

1. Two versions of installation programs for ADOBE ACROBAT READER 4.0 - which you will need to view the documents and manuals that are stored in *.PDF format
2. a README text file which repeats much of what has been said in this overview
3. a TestingSchedule file, in Word 7 format, which may help you get the software up-and-running.

Installing the software

X68K cross-assembler and E68K emulator/simulator

In order to use the cross-assembler and the emulator/simulator, you must copy the entire contents of the 68KSIM folder to your hard disk. This will require at least 620kb of free disk space.

To copy the files to your hard disk:

1. Start Windows.
2. Put the CD into your CD-ROM drive.
3. Double-click on the MY COMPUTER icon on your desktop screen. This will open a window displaying details of all your available drives.
4. Double-click on the CD-ROM drive icon and on the icon for the destination drive to which you want to copy the files. This will open a window for each of these drives.
5. In the CD-ROM drive window, double-click on the OUPCD_28.. folder icon to reveal its contents - which include the 68KSIM folder.
6. Drag-and-drop the 68KSIM folder from the CD-ROM drive window to the destination drive window. If you are not sure how to use the mouse to drag-and-drop items, refer to the destination drive window. If you are not sure how to use the mouse to drag-and-drop items, refer to your Windows manual or to the Windows on-line Help facility which you can access by selecting START > HELP and then typing the letters 'dra'.

The DIGITAL WORKS software

The DIGITAL folder on the CD contains a single program, DW20_95, which you must run in order to install the DIGITAL WORKS software on your hard disk. DIGITAL WORKS will require at least 2.5Mb of free disk space.

To copy the DIGITAL folder to your hard disk:

1. Start Windows - if it is not already running.
2. Put the CD into your CD-ROM drive - if it is not already in.
3. Double-click on the MY COMPUTER icon on your desktop screen. This will open a window displaying details of all your available drives.
4. Double-click on the CD-ROM drive icon and on the icon for the destination drive to which you want to copy the folder. This will open a window for each of these drives.
5. In the CD-ROM drive window, double-click on the OUPCD_28.. icon to reveal its contents, which include the DIGITAL folder.
6. Drag-and-drop the DIGITAL folder from the CD-ROM drive window to the destination drive window. If you are not sure how to use the mouse to drag-and-drop items, refer to your Windows manual or to the Windows on-line Help facility which you can access by selecting START > HELP and then typing the letters 'dra'.

To install the DIGITAL WORKS software on your hard drive:

1. Open the DIGITAL folder on your hard disk by double-clicking on its icon.
2. Double-click on the DW20_95 icon and follow the on-screen instructions that appear, choosing a destination drive and a destination folder name.

Remember, there is no separate manual for the DIGITAL WORKS software, but there is comprehensive on-line Help.

The ARM software

The ARM software is supplied as a compressed (zipped) file which must be unzipped using WINZIP.

1. Start Windows - if it is not already running.
2. Put the CD into your CD-ROM drive - if it is not already in.
3. Double-click on the MY COMPUTER icon on your desktop screen. This will open a window displaying details of all your available drives.
4. In the CD-ROM drive window, double-click on the OUPCD28.. icon to reveal its contents, which include the ARCSIM folder.

If you do not have a copy of WINZIP on your hard disk then, to install one:

1. Open the ARMSIM folder on the CD by double-clicking on its icon.
2. Double-click on the WINZIP70 icon and follow the on-screen instructions that appear, choosing a destination drive and a destination folder name.

Now that you have a copy of WINZIP installed on your hard disk you can install the ARM software.

1. Start Windows - if it is not already running.
2. Put the CD into your CD-ROM drive - it is not already in.
3. Double-click on the MY COMPUTER icon on your desktop screen. This will open a window displaying details of all your available drives.
4. In the CD-ROM drive window, double-click on the OUPCD_28.. folder icon to reveal its contents - which include the ARCSIM folder.
5. Double-click on the 202U_w32_V1 icon. WINZIP will automatically open a window that shows the contents of the compressed file.
6. If you are happy to have ALL the files, including the large *.PDF files, transferred to your hard disk, simply click on the EXTRACT icon on the toolbar at the top of the WINZIP window.
7. An EXTRACT dialog box will appear. Select a destination drive (your hard disk) from the FOLDERS/DRIVES: window, then click on the EXTRACT button. The extracted files will be placed in a folder called ARM202U on your chosen destination drive.

If you choose to extract all the files, you will need slightly more than 13Mb of free disk space. If you choose to exclude the large *.PDF files, which you will be able to access directly from the CD, you will need only 7.8Mb of free disk space.

Accessing the *.PDF manuals

If you do not have a version of ADOBE ACROBAT READER installed on your computer already, then, if you want to view, or print, these manuals, you should install a copy from the CD.

You will need a computer with at least 8Mb of RAM and 10Mb of available hard-disk space to install the Reader.

To install the Reader:

1. Start Windows
2. Put the CD into your CD-ROM drive
3. Double-click on the MY COMPUTER icon on your desktop screen. This will open a window displaying details of all your available drives.
4. Double-click on the CD-ROM drive icon.
5. In the CD-ROM drive window, double-click on the OUPCD_28.. icon to reveal its contents - which include two installation programs for the ACROBAT READER. AR40ENG is the version for Windows 95. RS40ENG is for Windows 98.
6. Double-click on the icon for the operating system that your computer uses, then follow the on-screen instructions, selecting a destination drive that you know will have enough space available and a suitable (memorable) destination folder name.

Once the Reader is installed you can double-click on the ACROBAT READER icon that will appear on your Desk-top and then access any of the *.PDF files on the CD.

The following manuals are available in sub-folders of the main OUPCD_28OCT99 folder on the CD:

In the 68kdocs folder there is:-

the *MOTOROLA M68000 FAMILY Programmer's Reference Manual*   644 pages

In the 68KSIM folder there are:-

1. A three-page document which gives a brief account of the X68K cross-assembler and the E68K emulator/simulator software packages.
2. A 31-page document giving detailed instructions for the use of X68K and E68K.

In the ARMSIM\ARM202U\PDF folder there are four manuals:-

1.	ARM Programming Techniques Manual	258 pages
2.	ARM Quick Reference Card	3 pages
3.	ARM Reference Manual	470 pages
4.	ARM Windows Toolkit Guide	106 pages

You will also find a number of README.TXT files, which are intended to be helpful, scattered around the CD.

There is a RELNNOTES.TXT file in the 68KSIM folder which details changes that have been made to overcome failings of earlier versions of X68K and E68K.

All these *.TXT files can be accessed using Windows NOTEPAD, which you will find in the ACCESSORIES group

Using the software

X68K AND E68K

X68K and E68K are DOS-based and should be used in a real DOS session rather than in a DOS window from Windows.

To start a real DOS session, select :

START > SHUT DOWN > Restart the computer in MS_DOS mode

To run X68K and E68K, follow the instructions in the manuals and other (README) documents.

DIGITAL WORKS

The DIGITAL WORKS software is Windows-based and you can run it by selecting:

START > PROGRAMS > DIGITAL > DIGITAL WORKS

ARM software, APM

The ARM software is Windows-based and you can run it by selecting:

START > RUN

and then 'browsing' until you reach ARM202U\BIN\ at which point you can double-click on the APM icon.

Or you could create a 'short-cut' to APM which could sit on your desktop.

One of the first things that you should do when running the ARM software APM is to select the OPTION > DIRECTORIES menu-item and to ensure that the paths specified there correspond to those on your computer. If you have followed the instructions here, these should be:

PROJECT MANAGER   <DRIVE>:\ARM202U\BIN

LIBRARIES   <DRIVE>:\ARM202U\LIB

TOOLS   <DRIVE>:\ARM202U\BIN

where <DRIVE> represents the letter specifying the drive onto which you loaded the software.

If you have not followed the instructions your paths will be different and you are on your own!